POVERTY LAW, POLICY, AND PRACTICE

ASPEN CASEBOOK SERIES

POVERTY LAW, POLICY, AND PRACTICE

Juliet M. Brodie

Mills Professor of Law & Associate Dean for Clinical Education
Stanford Law School

Clare Pastore

Professor of the Practice of Law
University of Southern California Gould School of Law

Ezra Rosser

Professor of Law
American University Washington College of Law

Jeffrey Selbin

Clinical Professor of Law
University of California, Berkeley, School of Law

Wolters Kluwer
Law & Business

Published by Wolters Kluwer Law & Business in New York.

Wolters Kluwer Law & Business serves customers worldwide with CCH, Aspen Publishers, and Kluwer Law International products. (www.wolterskluwerlb.com)

To contact Customer Service, e-mail customer.service@wolterskluwer.com, call 1-800-234-1660, fax 1-800-901-9075, or mail correspondence to:

Wolters Kluwer Law & Business
Attn: Order Department
PO Box 990
Frederick, MD 21705

Printed in the United States of America.

1 2 3 4 5 6 7 8 9 0

ISBN 978-1-4548-1254-8

Library of Congress Cataloging-in-Publication Data

Brodie, Juliet M., 1963- author.
Poverty law, policy, and practice / Juliet M. Brodie, Mills Professor of Law & Associate Dean for Clinical Education, Stanford Law School; Clare Pastore, Professor of the Practice of Law, University of Southern California Gould School of Law; Ezra Rosser, Professor of Law, American University Washington College of Law; Jeffrey Selbin, Clinical Professor of Law, University of California, Berkeley, School of Law.
    pages cm. — (Aspen casebook series)
Includes bibliographical references and index.
ISBN 978-1-4548-1254-8 (alk. paper)
1. Public welfare—Law and legislation—United States. 2. Poor—Legal status, laws, etc.—United States. I. Pastore, Clare, author. II. Rosser, Ezra, author. III. Selbin, Jeffrey, author. IV. Title.

KF390.5.P6B76 2014
344.7303'25—dc23

2013046756

About Wolters Kluwer Law & Business

Wolters Kluwer Law & Business is a leading global provider of intelligent information and digital solutions for legal and business professionals in key specialty areas, and respected educational resources for professors and law students. Wolters Kluwer Law & Business connects legal and business professionals as well as those in the education market with timely, specialized authoritative content and information-enabled solutions to support success through productivity, accuracy and mobility.

Serving customers worldwide, Wolters Kluwer Law & Business products include those under the Aspen Publishers, CCH, Kluwer Law International, Loislaw, ftwilliam.com and MediRegs family of products.

CCH products have been a trusted resource since 1913, and are highly regarded resources for legal, securities, antitrust and trade regulation, government contracting, banking, pension, payroll, employment and labor, and healthcare reimbursement and compliance professionals.

Aspen Publishers products provide essential information to attorneys, business professionals and law students. Written by preeminent authorities, the product line offers analytical and practical information in a range of specialty practice areas from securities law and intellectual property to mergers and acquisitions and pension/benefits. Aspen's trusted legal education resources provide professors and students with high-quality, up-to-date and effective resources for successful instruction and study in all areas of the law.

Kluwer Law International products provide the global business community with reliable international legal information in English. Legal practitioners, corporate counsel and business executives around the world rely on Kluwer Law journals, looseleafs, books, and electronic products for comprehensive information in many areas of international legal practice.

Loislaw is a comprehensive online legal research product providing legal content to law firm practitioners of various specializations. Loislaw provides attorneys with the ability to quickly and efficiently find the necessary legal information they need, when and where they need it, by facilitating access to primary law as well as state-specific law, records, forms and treatises.

ftwilliam.com offers employee benefits professionals the highest quality plan documents (retirement, welfare and non-qualified) and government forms (5500/PBGC, 1099 and IRS) software at highly competitive prices.

MediRegs products provide integrated health care compliance content and software solutions for professionals in healthcare, higher education and life sciences, including professionals in accounting, law and consulting.

Wolters Kluwer Law & Business, a division of Wolters Kluwer, is headquartered in New York. Wolters Kluwer is a market-leading global information services company focused on professionals.

To my father, Michael Brodie, who taught me which side we're on. Yours for the OBU.
—J.B.

To Kurt, Michael, Jessi, Maggie, and Libby.
—C.P.

To Mario Castro Tablas (1950-2013). Buem.
—E.R.

To my parents, Marion and Joel Selbin, who taught me everything I know about justice.
—J.S.

SUMMARY OF CONTENTS

CONTENTS

CHAPTER 2:

SOCIAL WELFARE POLICY   **59**

CHAPTER 6:

HOUSING   333

CHAPTER 7:

HEALTH   **395**

CHAPTER 8:

CHAPTER 9:

CRIMINALIZATION   521

CHAPTER 10:

ACCESS TO JUSTICE   587

CHAPTER 12:

HUMAN RIGHTS   711

Preface

Poverty law as a distinct field of study and practice did not exist 50 years ago. By the late 1960s, however, lawyers were active participants in a robust and multi-faceted war on poverty. With inspiration, example, and tools from their civil rights forebears—and support from the Ford Foundation—they flooded federal courts with lawsuits designed to establish constitutional protections and substantive rights for the poor. They achieved a string of high-profile victories, perhaps best exemplified by the U.S. Supreme Court's recognition of a due process right to welfare pre-termination hearings in Goldberg v. Kelly (1970). But almost as quickly as it arose, the era of constitutional antipoverty lawyering receded as the Court refused to extend *Goldberg*'s procedural logic to recognize positive rights to social goods like welfare, housing, and education.

Law school curricula and casebooks during the time reflected the new antipoverty activism. As the tumult of the 1960s swirled outside their gates, law students demanded relevant courses and training. The first poverty law casebook was published in 1969, by which time law schools across the country were opening antipoverty clinics and offering more than 200 poverty-related courses. Responding to growing demand in this emerging area of law and practice, four more poverty law casebooks and a hornbook were published by 1976. But like the antipoverty litigation agenda, the poverty law movement in legal education began to wane almost as soon as it had begun. It would be more than 20 years before the next—and last—poverty law casebook was published, this time in the immediate shadow of welfare reform.

So, why a poverty law textbook in 2014?

First, although the Supreme Court has largely foreclosed an affirmative antipoverty avenue in the federal courts—and federal funding for legal services peaked in 1980—lawyers remain actively engaged in a wide range of antipoverty activities and initiatives. As they have for decades, lawyers for the poor continue to enforce and expand statutory rights, fight bureaucratic disentitlement, and challenge unjust policies in courts, legislatures, administrative agencies, and other settings. Relatively meager federal funding for legal services has helped to drive a more diverse and decentralized delivery system of experimentation and innovation at the state and local levels. Poverty lawyers have responded to the evolving needs of low-income clients and communities by promoting economic development, combatting the impacts of criminalization, and partnering with other professionals in multidisciplinary practices.

Second, in the wake of the Great Recession, wealth disparities in the United States are at their highest levels since the 1920s. Living wages, affordable housing, and other basic needs are increasingly out of reach for tens of millions of Americans, including many working families and an eroding middle class. Government retrenchment and disinvestment from decades-old commitments to the poor, elderly, and disabled coincide with a global movement of labor and capital that reverberates throughout the domestic landscape. These developments raise important and troubling legal and policy questions, including the role of law, lawyers, and legal institutions in efforts to address the impact of persistent and deepening economic inequality.

Given the proliferation of substantive and methodological approaches in poverty law, this book is designed for a survey course. The first three chapters introduce foundational concepts about poverty, social welfare policy, and constitutional issues. With these tools in hand, the next seven chapters — which can be taught in any order — explore major antipoverty programs and sites of activity, including welfare, work, housing, health, education, criminalization, and access to justice. Each substantive chapter brings together a mix of data, doctrine, theory, policy, and practice issues. The final two chapters describe innovations and current debates, including market-driven and human rights–based approaches to poverty reduction.

The book includes a mix of case law, social science, and popular press readings from across the ideological spectrum. We hope it will provide students with a solid introduction to the evolving field of poverty law. More importantly, we hope it will encourage them to participate in ongoing efforts to combat the causes and conditions of poverty.

ACKNOWLEDGMENTS

This textbook would not have been possible without the assistance and support of many friends, colleagues, students, and family members. We thank the editors at Aspen, particularly Lynn Churchill and Peter Skagestad, who decided that a poverty law textbook was worthy of publication and guided us through the process of actually producing one. We also want to extend our appreciation to the many colleagues who reviewed one or more chapters of the book, including Martha Davis, Constance De La Vega, Russell Engler, Catherine Fisk, Laurel Fletcher, Debra Gardner, Michael T. (Tim) Iglesias, Catherine Lhamon, John Pollock, Karen Tani, and the anonymous readers contacted by the publisher.

Students at our institutions have done everything from finding sources and checking citations to suggesting improvements and gathering permissions. Specifically, we thank our research assistants: Nick Crovo, Destiny Fullwood, and Michael Gropper at American; Caitlin Bedsworth, John Bliss, Ryan Fraser, Tetyana Gaponenko, Gregory Holtz, Ziwei Hu, Judah Lakin, Nicholas Lampros, Kelsey Mayo, Ruth Merisier, Emily Puhl, Robert Stahl, and Quynh Vu at Berkeley; Sabrina Adler, Elizabeth Dooley, Nayna Gupta, and Matthew Owens at Stanford; and Tracy Chan, Lawrence Cisneros, Kimberley David, Allison Fisher, Joel Gordon, Megan Hopkins, Allen Haiyang Li, Amy Russell, and Rachel Zolensky at the University of Southern California. We particularly thank Stanford law student Matt Owens for providing outstanding and extensive copy editing to get our manuscript ready for submission. More generally, we thank the students who have taken our poverty law courses. Though too numerous to name individually, these students have furthered our thinking and helped inspire this textbook. This book has been improved immeasurably by the lessons they have taught us.

This book has also benefitted from considerable institutional support from our schools. We are grateful to the deans who supported this project over the years: Claudio Grossman at American; Christopher Edley, Jr., at Berkeley; Larry Kramer and M. Elizabeth Magill at Stanford; and Robert K. Rasmussen at the University of Southern California. And we could not have completed the book without the help of our wonderful administrative assistants: Rosemarie Pal and Minh-Tuan Nguyen at American, Olivia Layug at Berkeley, Adelina Arroyo at Stanford, and Shirly Kennedy at the University of Southern California.

Writing a textbook involves a considerable amount of time and energy, and it would not have been possible without the love and forgiveness of our family members. Thank you Jane Schacter and Gabe and Zoe Schacter-Brodie; Kurt, Maggie, and Libby Eggert; Elvia Castro and Mateo Rosser Castro; and Laurel Fletcher and Micah and Aiden Muhr.

* * *

We gratefully acknowledge the following authors and publishers for granting permission to reprint excerpts from copyrighted material:

Excerpt from *The New Jim Crow*. Copyright © 2010 by Michelle Alexander. Reprinted by permission of The New Press. www.thenewpress.com.

Philip Alston, *Putting Economic, Social and Cultural Rights Back on the Agenda of the United States*, in *The Future of Human Rights: U.S. Policy for a New Era* (ed. William F. Schulz). © 2008, pages 120-124. Reprinted with permission of the University of Pennsylvania Press.

Anne L. Alstott, *Why the EITC Doesn't Make Work Pay*, 73 Law & Contemp. Probs. 285 (Winter 2010). Reprinted with permission of Law and Contemporary Problems and the author.

Deborah N. Archer, *Challenging the School-to-Prison Pipeline*, 54 N.Y. L. Sch. L. Rev. 867 (2009/2010). Reprinted with permission of the New York Law School Law Review and the author.

Benjamin Barton, *Against Civil* Gideon *(and for Pro Se Court Reform)*, 62 Fla. L. Rev. 1227 (2010). Reprinted with permission of the University of Florida Law Review and the author.

Annette Bernhardt, Heather Boushey, Laura Dresser & Chris Tilly, *An Introduction to the "Gloves-Off" Economy*, in *The Gloves-Off Economy: Workplace Standards at the Bottom of America's Labor Market* (2008). Reprinted with permission of the Labor and Employment Relations Center via the Copyright Clearance Center.

Jared Bernstein, *Economic Mobility in the United States: How Much Is There and Why Does It Matter?*, in *Ending Poverty in America: How to Restore the American Dream* (John Edwards et al. eds., 2007). Reprinted with permission of The New Press.

Barbara Bezdek, *Silence in the Courts*, 20 Hofstra L. Rev. 533 (1992). Reprinted with permission of the Hofstra Law Review Association and the author.

Kenneth F. Boehm, *The Legal Services Program: Unaccountable, Political, Anti-Poor, Beyond Reform, and Unnecessary*, 17 St. Louis U. Pub. L. Rev. 321 (1998). Reprinted with permission of the St. Louis University Public Law Review and the author.

Rachel Bratt, *Rebuilding a Low-Income Housing Policy*, Copyright Temple University Press (1989). Reprinted with permission of Temple University Press and the author.

Raymond H. Brescia, *Part of the Disease or Part of the Cure: The Financial Crisis and the Community Reinvestment Act*, 60 S.C. L. Rev. 617 (2009). Reprinted with permission of the author.

Juliet Brodie, *Post-Welfare Lawyering: Clinical Legal Education and A New Poverty Law Agenda*, 20 Wash. U. J.L. & Pol'y 201 (2006).

Business & Professional People for the Public Interest, *What Is* Gautreaux? Reprinted with permission of Alex Polikoff, Director, Business & Professional People for the Public Interest.

Timothy Casey, *The Sanction Epidemic in the TANF Program*, Legal Momentum: The Women's Legal Defense & Education Fund (August 2012). Reprinted with permission of Legal Momentum and the author.

Center on Budget and Policy Priorities, *EITC Policy Basics* (2013). Reprinted with permission of the Center on Budget and Policy Priorities.

Jennifer M. Chacón, *Managing Migration Through Crime*, 109 Colum. L. Rev. Sidebar 135 (2009). Reprinted with permission of Columbia Law Review.

Gabriel J. Chin, *The New Civil Death: Rethinking Punishment in the Era of Mass Conviction*, 160 U. Pa. L. Rev. 1789 (2012). Permission conveyed through Copyright Clearance Center, Inc.

John D. Colombo, *The Role of Redistribution to the Poor in Federal Tax Exemption for Charities*, National Center on Philanthropy and the Law (2009), http://www1.law.nyu.edu/ncpl/resources/documents/Conf2009JColomboPaper.pdf. Reprinted with permission of the author.

Committee on Health Insurance Status and Its Consequences, Institute of Medicine of the National Academies, *America's Uninsured Crisis: Consequences for Health and Health Care* (2009). Reprinted with permission of Rightslink.

Scott L. Cummings, *Community Economic Development as Progressive Politics: Toward a Grassroots Movement for Economic Justice*, 54 Stan. L. Rev. 399 (2001). Reprinted with permission of the author.

Karen Syma Czapanskiy, *Unemployment Insurance Reforms for Moms*, 44 Santa Clara L. Rev. 1093 (2004). Reprinted with permission of the Santa Clara Law Review and the author.

Martha Davis, *Public Rights, Global Perspectives, and Common Law*, 36 Fordham Urb. L.J. 653 (2008). Reprinted with permission of the publisher, Fordham Urban Law Journal.

Jason DeParle, *Welfare Limits Left Poor Adrift as Recession Hits*, New York Times, April 8 2012, at A1, including graphic. Reprinted with permission of the New York Times.

Jason DeParle, *Getting Opal Caples to Work*, New York Times Magazine, August 24, 1997. Reprinted with permission of the New York Times.

Janet L. Dolgin & Katherine R. Dieterich, *Social and Legal Debate About the Affordable Care Act*, 80 UMKC L. Rev. 45 (2011). Reprinted with permission of the authors and the University of Missouri–Kansas City Law Review.

Mark L. Earley & Kathryn Wiley, *The New Frontier of Public Safety*, 22 Stan. L. & Pol'y Rev. 343 (2011). Permission conveyed through Copyright Clearance Center, Inc.

Economic Policy Institute Charts, Economic Indicators, The State of Working America, stateofworkingamerica.org.

Peter Edelman, *Toward a Comprehensive Antipoverty Strategy: Getting Beyond the Silver Bullet*, 81 Geo. L.J. 1697 (1993). Reprinted with permission of the publisher, Georgetown Law Journal © 1992-1993.

Kathryn Edin & Maria Kefalas, *Promises I Can Keep: Why Poor Women Put Motherhood Before Marriage*, Copyright University of California Press. (2005). Permission conveyed through Copyright Clearance Center, Inc.

Barbara Ehrenreich, *How America Turned Poverty into a Crime* (August 9, 2011). This article first appeared in Salon.com, at http://www.Salon.com. An online version remains in the Salon archives. Reprinted with permission.

Barbara Ehrenreich, *Nickel and Dimed* (2001). Copyright Barbara Ehrenreich. Reprinted with permission of the author.

Laura Ernde, *Fee Waivers Denied For the Poor* (Los Angeles Daily Journal, Sept. 14, 2011). Reprinted with permission of the Los Angeles Daily Journal.

Janice Fine, *Worker Centers: Organizing Communities at the Edge of the Dream*, 50 N.Y.L. Sch. L. Rev. 417 (2005-06). Reprinted with permission of the New York Law School Law Review and the author.

Martha Fineman, Gwendolyn Mink & Anna Marie Smith, *No Promotion of Marriage in TANF!: Executive Summary*, 30 Social Justice No. 4 (2003). Reprinted with permission of Social Justice.

Debra Gardner & John Pollock, *Civil Right to Counsel's Relationship to Antipoverty Advocacy: Further Reflections*, 45 Clearinghouse Review 150 (July-August 2011). Reprinted with permission of the authors.

Anna Gorman, *Red Tape Hampers Care for Patients Who Are Poor and Disabled*, Los Angeles Times, Nov. 30, 2011. Reprinted with permission of the Los Angeles Times.

Marie Gottschalk, *Prison Overcrowding and Brown v. Plata*, published in The New Republic (June 8, 2011). Reprinted with permission.

Alan Grayson, *My Thanksgiving: A Turkey Sandwich at Wal-Mart*, Huffington Post, Nov. 24, 2012. Reprinted with permission of the author.

Kaaryn Gustafson, *The Criminalization of Poverty*, 99 J. Crim. L. & Criminology 643 (2009). Reprinted by special permission of the Northwestern School of Law, The Journal of Criminal Law and Criminology.

Joel F. Handler, *"Constructing the Political Spectacle": The Interpretation of Entitlements, Legalization, and Obligations in Social Welfare History*, 56 Brook. L. Rev. 899 (1990). Reprinted with permission of Brooklyn Law Review.

Joel F. Handler & Yeheskel Hasenfeld, *Blame Welfare, Ignore Poverty and Inequality* (2007). Copyright © 2007 Joel F. Handler and Yeheskel Hasenfeld. Reprinted with permission of Cambridge University Press.

Joel F. Handler & Yeheskel Hasenfeld, *The Moral Construction of Poverty: Welfare Reform in America* (1991). Reprinted with permission of the Copyright Clearance Center.

Heidi Hartmann & Ashley English, *Women and Men's Employment and Unemployment in the Great Recession* (IWPR Publication C373, January 2010). Reprinted with permission of Heidi Hartmann.

Michael Heise, *The Unintended Legal and Policy Consequences of the No Child Left Behind Act*, 86 Neb. L. Rev. 119 (2007). Reprinted with permission of the Nebraska Law Review and the author.

Louis Henkin, *The Age of Rights*. Copyright © 1990 Columbia University Press. Reprinted with permission of the publisher.

Helen Hershkoff, *"Just Words": Common Law and the Enforcement of State Constitutional Social and Economic Rights*, 62 Stan. L. Rev. 1521 (2010). Permission conveyed through Copyright Clearance Center, Inc.

Nan Hunter, *Health Insurance Reform and Intimations of Citizenship*, 159 U. Pa. L. Rev. 1955 (2011). Permission conveyed through Copyright Clearance Center, Inc.

Earl Johnson, Jr., *Justice for America's Poor in the Year 2020: Some Possibilities Based on Experiences Here and Abroad*, 58 DePaul L. Rev. 393 (2009). Reprinted with permission of the DePaul Law Review and the author.

Joint Center for Housing Studies of Harvard University, State of the Nation's Housing (2011). Reprinted with permission of the Joint Center for Housing Studies of Harvard University.

Joint Center for Housing Studies of Harvard University, State of the Nation's Housing (2012). Reprinted with permission of the Joint Center for Housing Studies of Harvard University.

Barbara Jones, *SNAP Basics*, Clearinghouse Review (Oct. 2012). Reprinted with permission of the Clearinghouse Review and the author.

Richard D. Kahlenberg, *Fixing No Child Left Behind* (Century Foundation 2008). Reprinted with permission of the author.

Kaiser Commission on Medicaid and the Uninsured, *The Medicaid Program at a Glance* (2012). Reprinted with permission of the Kaiser Family Foundation.

Risa E. Kaufman & JoAnn Kamuf Ward, *Using Human Rights Mechanisms*, 45 Clearinghouse Review: Journal of Poverty Law and Policy 259 (2011). © Sargent Shriver National Center on Poverty Law (2011). Reproduced with permission of the Sargent Shriver National Center on Poverty Law and the authors.

Micere Keels et al., *Fifteen Years Later: Can Residential Mobility Programs Provide a Long-Term Escape from Neighborhood Segregation, Crime, and Poverty?*, 42 Demography 51 (2005). Reprinted with permission of Stephen Dudley, Executive Director, Population Association of America.

Jeni Klugman, United Nations Development Programme, *Human Development Report 2010: The Real Wealth of Nations: Pathways to Human Development*, 2010, Palgrave Macmillan. Reproduced with permission of Palgrave Macmillan.

William S. Koski, *Courthouses v. Statehouses?*, 109 Mich. L. Rev. 923 (2011). Reprinted with permission of the Michigan Law Review and the author.

Paul R. Krugman, *The Conscience of a Liberal* (2007). Copyright W.W. Norton & Company, Inc. Reprinted with permission of W.W. Norton & Company.

T. William Lester, David Madland & Nick Bunker, *The Facts on Raising the Minimum Wage When Unemployment Is High*, Center for American Progress Action Fund 2013. Reprinted with permission of Center for American Progress Action Fund and the authors.

Goodwin Liu, *Rethinking Constitutional Welfare Rights*, 61 Stan. L. Rev. 203 (2008). Permission conveyed through Copyright Clearance Center, Inc.

David Luban, *Taking Out the Adversary: The Assault on Progressive Public-Interest Lawyers*, 91 Cal. L. Rev. 209 (2003). Reprinted with permission of the California Law Review and the author.

Alfred Lubrano, *Census Figures Show Record Numbers of Americans in Poverty*, Philadelphia Inquirer, Sep. 14, 2011. Used with permission of Philadelphia Inquirer. Copyright © 2013.

Jonathan R. Macey & Geoffrey P. Miller, *The Community Reinvestment Act: An Economic Analysis*, 79 Va. L. Rev. 291 (1993). Reprinted with permission of the authors.

Steven Malanga, *The Myth of the Working Poor*, City Journal (Autumn 2004). Copyright The Manhattan Institute. Reprinted with permission of the Manhattan Institute and the author.

Richard D. Marsico, *Democratizing Capital: The History, Law, and Reform of the Community Reinvestment Act*, 49 N.Y. L. Sch. L. Rev. 217 (2004). Reprinted with permission of the author.

Bhashkar Mazumder, *Upward Intergenerational Economic Mobility in the United States* (Economic Mobility Project, 2008). Reprinted with permission of The Pew Charitable Trusts.

Reprinted and edited with the permission of Simon & Schuster Publishing Group from the Free Press edition of *BEYOND ENTITLEMENT: The Social Obligation of Citizenship* by Lawrence M. Mead. Copyright © 1986 by Lawrence M. Mead. All rights reserved.

Suzanne Mettler, *Social Security Act of 1935*, in *Poverty in the United States: An Encyclopedia of History, Politics, and Poverty*, Mink and O'Connor eds. Copyright (2004). Reprinted with permission of ABC-CLIO. Permission conveyed through Copyright Clearance Center, Inc.

Lawrence Mischel, *The Wedges Between Productivity and Median Compensation Growth*, in Economic Policy Institute Issue Brief #330 (April 2012). Reprinted with permission of the Economic Policy Institute and the author.

Robert A. Moffitt & Peter T. Gottschalk, *Ethnic and Racial Differences in Welfare Receipt in the United States*, in *America Becoming: Racial Trends and Their Consequences* (Neil J. Smelser et al., eds. (2001). Permission conveyed through Copyright Clearance Center, Inc.

Copyright © 1998 Charles Murray, *Losing Ground: American Social Policy, 1950-1980* (1984). Reprinted by permission of Basic Books, a member of the Perseus Books Group.

David Nasaw, *We Can't Rely on the Kindness of Billionaires*, Washington Post, Sept. 23, 2007. Reprinted with permission of the author.

National Academy of Sciences' Panel on Poverty and Family Assistance, *Measuring Poverty: A New Approach* (C. Citro & R. Michaels eds. 1995). Reprinted with permission of the Copyright Clearance Center.

National Law Center on Homelessness & Poverty, *Criminalizing Crisis: The Criminalization of Homelessness in U.S. Cities* (2011). Reprinted with permission of National Law Center on Homelessness & Poverty.

David Neumark & William Wascher, *Minimum Wages and Low-Wage Workers: How Well Does Reality Match the Rhetoric?*, 92 Minn. L. Rev. 1296 (2008). Reprinted with permission of the Minnesota Law Review and the authors.

Julie Nice, *No Scrutiny Whatsoever: Deconstitutionalization of Poverty Law, Dual Rules of Law, and Dialogic Default*, 35 Fordham Urb. L.J. 629 (2008). Reprinted with permission of the Fordham Urban Law Journal.

Jeannie Oakes, John Rogers, Gary Blasi & Martin Lipton, *Grassroots Organizing, Social Movements, and the Right to High-Quality Education*, 4 Stan. J. C.R. & C.L. 339 (2008). Reprinted with permission of the Stanford Journal of Civil Rights and Civil Liberties via the Copyright Clearance Center.

Priscilla Ocen, *The New Racially Restrictive Covenant: Race, Welfare, and the Policing of Black Women in Subsidized Housing*, 59 UCLA L. Rev. 1540 (2012). Originally published in 59 UCLA L. Rev. 1540 (2012). Reprinted with permission from UCLA Law Review and the author.

Erik J. Olson, *No Room at the Inn: A Snapshot of an American Emergency Room*, 46 Stan. L. Rev. 449 (1994). Reprinted with permission of the author.

Opportunity Agenda, *Human Rights in State Courts*, 45 Clearinghouse Review: Journal of Poverty Law and Policy 233 (2011). © Sargent Shriver National Center on Poverty Law (2011). Reproduced with permission of the Sargent Shriver National Center on Poverty Law and Opportunity Agenda.

Michael Paris, *School Finance Reform and Educational Ideology: A Guide to Law, Politics, and Policy*, in *Framing Equal Opportunity: Law and the Politics of School Finance Reform* (2010). Copyright 2010 by the Board of Trustees of the Leland Stanford Junior University. Reprinted with permission of the Stanford University Press and the author.

Wendy E. Parmet, Lauren A. Smith & Meredith A. Benedict, *Social Determinants, Health Disparities and the Role of Law*, in *Poverty, Health and Law: Readings and Cases for Medical-Legal Partnership* (Elizabeth Tobin Tyler et al. eds. 2011). Reprinted with permission of Carolina Academic Press.

Clare Pastore, *A Civil Right to Counsel: Closer to Reality?*, 42 Loy. L.A. Law Rev. 1065 (2009). Reprinted with permission of the author.

Alex Polikoff, Philip Tegeler, et al., eds., *A Vision for the Future: Bringing Gautreaux to Scale*, in *Keeping the Promise: Preserving and Enhancing Housing Mobility in the Section 8 Housing Choice Voucher Program* (2005). Reprinted with permission of the Poverty and Race Research Action Council.

Republished with permission of Stanford Law and Policy Review, from *Backwards into the Future: How Welfare Changes in the Millennium Resemble English Poor Law of the Middle Ages*, William P. Quigley, 9 Stan. L. & Pol'y Rev. 101 (1998). Permission conveyed through Copyright Clearance Center, Inc.

William P. Quigley, *Full-Time Workers Should Not Be Poor: The Living Wage Movement*, 70 Miss. L.J. 889 (2001). Reprinted with permission of the Mississippi Law Journal and the author.

William C. Rava, *State Constitutional Protections for the Poor*, 71 Temp. L. Rev. 543 (1998). Reprinted with permission of the Temple Law Review.

Michael A. Rebell, *The Right to Comprehensive Educational Opportunity*, 47 Harv. C.R.-C.L. L. Rev. 47 (2012). Reprinted with permission of the Harvard Civil Rights-Civil Liberties Law Review and the author.

Robert Rector & Patrick F. Fagan, *The Continuing Good News About Welfare Reform*, Heritage Found. Backgrounder No. 1620, June 12, 2003. Reprinted with permission of The Heritage Foundation.

Robert Rector & Jennifer A. Marshall, *The Unfinished Work of Welfare Reform*, The Heritage Foundation (2013). Reprinted with permission of The Heritage Foundation.

Robert Rector & Rachel Sheffield, *Air Conditioning, Cable TV, and an Xbox: What Is Poverty in the United States Today?*, Heritage Foundation Backgrounder No. 2575, July 18, 2011. Reprinted with permission of The Heritage Foundation.

Allen Redlich, *Who Will Litigate Constitutional Issues for the Poor?*, 19 Hastings Const. L.Q. 745 (1992). Reprinted with permission of Tom McCarthy, Director, O'Brien Center for Scholarly Publications and Student Information Center, University of California Hastings College of Law.

Robert B. Reich, *Is Harvard Really A Charity?*, Los Angeles Times, Oct. 1, 2007. Reprinted with permission of the author.

Deborah L. Rhode, *Access to Justice* (2004). Copyright Deborah L. Rhode. Reprinted with permission of the author.

Dorothy E. Roberts, *The Value of Black Mothers' Work*, 26 Conn. L. Rev. 871 (1994). Reprinted with permission of the Connecticut Law Review.

Caterina Gouvis Roman & Jeremy Travis, *Taking Stock: Housing, Homelessness, and Prisoner Reentry, Final Report*, The Urban Institute (2004). Reprinted with permission of The Urban Institute.

Catherine K. Ruckelshaus, *Labor's Wage War*, 35 Fordham Urb. L.J. 373 (2008). Reprinted with permission of the Fordham Urban Law Journal and the author.

Russell W. Rumberger, *Parsing the Data on Student Achievement in High-Poverty Schools*, 85 N.C. L. Rev. 1293 (2007). Reprinted with permission of the North Carolina Law Review, and the author.

James E. Ryan, *Charter Schools and Public Education*, 4 Stan. J. C.R. & C.L. 393 (2008). Reprinted with permission of the Stanford Journal of Civil Rights and Civil Liberties via the Copyright Clearance Center, and the author.

Jeffrey D. Sachs, *Twentieth Century Political Economy: A Brief History of Global Capitalism*, Oxford Review of Economic Policy, Vol. 15, No. 4 (1999). Reprinted with permission of Rightslink.

Douglas W. Salvesen, *The Mandatory Pro Bono Service Dilemma: A Way Out of the Thicket*, 82 Mass. L. Rev. 197 (1997). Reprinted with permission of the Massachusetts Bar Association and the author.

Austin Sarat, *". . . The Law Is All Over": Power, Resistance, and the Legal Consciousness of the Welfare Poor*, 2 Yale J.L. & Human. 343 (1990). Reprinted with permission of the author and by *The Yale Journal of Law & the Humanities*, Vol. 2, pp. 343-379.

Liz Schott, *Policy Basics: An Introduction to TANF*, Center on Budget & Policy Priorities (2012). Reprinted with permission of the Center on Budget & Policy Priorities.

Amartya Sen, *Poor, Relatively Speaking*, Oxford Economic Papers, Vol. 35, No. 2 (1983). Reprinted with permission of Rightslink.

Thomas Shapiro et al., Inst. on Assets & Soc. Pol'y, *The Roots of the Widening Racial Wealth Gap: Explaining the Black-White Economic Divide* (2013). Reprinted with permission of the author.

David K. Shipler, *The Working Poor* (2004). Copyright Random House (2004). Reprinted with permission of Random House and the author.

Excerpted from the article that appeared as Harry Simon, *Towns Without Pity: A Constitutional and Historical Analysis of Official Efforts to Drive Homeless Persons from American Cities*, originally published in 66 Tul. L. Rev. 631 (1992). Reprinted with permission of the Tulane Law Review Association, which holds the copyright.

William H. Simon, *The Community Economic Development Movement*, 2002 Wisc. L. Rev. 377. Reprinted with permission of the author.

Russell Skiba, Suzanne E. Eckes & Kevin Brown, *African American Disproportionality in School Discipline: The Divide Between Best Evidence and Legal Remedy*, 54 N.Y.L. Sch. L. Rev. 1070 (2009/2010). Reprinted with permission of the New York Law School Law Review and the authors.

Anna Marie Smith, *The Sexual Regulation Dimension of Contemporary Welfare Law: A Fifty State Overview*, 8 Mich. J. Gender & L. 121 (2002). Reprinted with permission of the Michigan Journal of Gender and Law and the author.

Gary F. Smith, *Poverty Warriors: An Historical Perspective on the Mission of Legal Services*, 45 Clearinghouse Review 34 (May-June 2011). Reprinted with permission of the author.

Amy Sullivan, *Faith Without Works: After Four Years, the President's Faith-Based Policies Have Proven to Be Neither Compassionate Nor Conservative*, Washington Monthly, Oct. 2004. Reprinted with permission of the Washington Monthly.

R. Mona Tawatao & Colin Bailey, *Toward a Human Rights Framework*, 45 Clearinghouse Review: Journal of Poverty Law and Policy 169 (2011). © Sargent Shriver National Center on Poverty Law (2011). Reproduced with permission of the Sargent Shriver National Center on Poverty Law and the authors.

Peter Townsend, *Poverty in the United Kingdom* (1979). Reprinted with permission of the Copyright Clearance Center.

Reprinted and edited with the permission of Simon & Schuster Publishing Group from the Free Press edition of *FROM POOR LAW TO WELFARE STATE: A History of Social Welfare in America* by Walter I. Trattner. Copyright © 1974, 1979, 1984, 1989 by the Free Press. Copyright © by Walter I. Trattner. All rights reserved.

Julie Turkewitz & Juliet Linderman, *The Disability Trap*, New York Times, October 21, 2012, at SR5. Reprinted with permission of the New York Times.

Office of the United Nations High Commissioner for Human Rights, *Human Rights Treaty Bodies: Glossary of Treaty Body Terminology* (2012). Reprinted with permission of United Nations Publications.

Office of the United Nations High Commissioner for Human Rights, International Covenant on Economic, Social, and Cultural Rights, Dec. 16, 1966, 993 U.N.T.S. 3 (entered into force 1976). Reprinted with permission of United Nations Publications.

United Nations, Universal Declaration of Human Rights, GA Res. 217A (III), UN Doc A/810 at 71 (1948). Reprinted with permission of United Nations Publications.

Paul Valentine, *A Lay Word for a Legal Term: How the Popular Definition of Charity Has Muddled the Perception of the Charitable Deduction*, 89 Neb. L. Rev. 997 (2011). Reprinted with permission of the author.

Zahir Virani, *American Microfinance: Opportunities and Challenges*, 27 Rev. Banking & Fin. L. 370 (2008). Reprinted with permission of the author.

Olivia L. Walker, *The Future of Microlending in the United States: A Shift from Charity to Profits?*, 6 Entrepreneurial Bus. L.J. 383 (2011). Reprinted with permission of the author.

Washington Legal Foundation, *Court Permits Eviction of Drug Dealers from Public Housing (HUD v. Rucker, No. 00-1770)*, March 26, 2002. Reprinted with permission of Washington Legal Foundation.

Amy L. Wax, *Musical Chairs and Tall Buildings: Teaching Poverty Law in the 21st Century*, 34 Fordham Urban L.J. 1363 (2007). Reprinted with permission of the author.

Amy L. Wax, *Rethinking Welfare Rights: Reciprocity Norms, Reactive Attitudes, and the Political Economy of Welfare Reform*, 63 Law & Contemp. Probs. 257 (2000). Reprinted with permission of Law & Contemporary Problems and the author.

Bruce Western & Becky Pettit, *Incarceration & Social Inequality*, Daedalus, 139:3 (Summer 2010). © 2010 by the American Academy of Arts and Sciences. Reprinted with permission of MIT Press Journals.

William Julius Wilson, *The Great Disparity*, in The Nation, July 30/August 6, 2012. Reprinted with permission of The Nation and the author.

William Julius Wilson, *The Truly Disadvantaged: The Inner City, the Underclass, and Public Policy* (1987). © 1987 by The University of Chicago. All rights reserved. Reprinted with permission of The University of Chicago.

Peter Witte, et al., *The State of Homelessness in America: 2012*, National Alliance to End Homelessness & Homelessness Research Institute (2012). Reprinted with permission of the National Alliance to End Homelessness.

Muhammad Yunus, *How Legal Steps Can Help to Pave the Way to Ending Poverty*, ABA Human Rights Vol. 35 (Winter 2008). Reprinted with permission of the American Bar Association.

Muhammad Yunus, Nobel Lecture, Oslo, December 10, 2006. © The Nobel Foundation 2006. Source: http://nobelprize.org. Reprinted with permission of The Nobel Foundation.

Richard Zorza, *Self-Represented Litigants and the Access to Justice Revolution in the State Courts: Cross-Pollinating Perspectives Toward a Dialogue for Innovation in the Courts and the Administrative Law System*, 29 J. Nat'l Ass'n Admin. L. Judiciary 63 (2009). Reprinted with permission of the National Association of Administrative Law Judiciary and the author.

POVERTY LAW, POLICY, AND PRACTICE

CHAPTER
1

Introduction to Poverty

INTRODUCTION

Poverty as a concept and as a set of experiences—or limitations on experience—is difficult to understand and invites both personal and analytical responses. The same can be said of poverty law, where the task of defining what is and what is not covered by such a label, "poverty law," is itself dynamic and subject to debate. We invite you to consider the topic of this textbook, poverty law, intellectually, practically, and emotionally, that is, as a topic that involves your head, hands, and heart. The readings and cases that follow range from discussions of first principles and definitions of poverty to presentations of empirical understandings of the determinants of poverty to interview-based accounts of how the poor encounter the legal system.

The first three chapters of this textbook focus on the big questions: How is poverty defined and measured? What antipoverty policies have been tried? How has our approach to poverty changed over time? What constitutional protections have been extended to the poor? The middle of the book, Chapters 4-10, tackles poverty law on an issue-by-issue basis, covering Income and Food, Work, Housing, Health Care, Education, Criminalization, and Access to Justice. This structure reflects both the issue-specific nature of many of the policy responses to poverty and the expansive scope of poverty law, but it is important to look for and keep in mind the themes that are introduced in the first three chapters. Some recurring themes include: Who qualifies for public assistance? How is assistance structured or limited? What are the impacts on particular subgroups of the poor (racial minorities, women, children)? Should the law favor flexibility or formal rights? Often these themes relate to whether the people receiving assistance are considered deserving or undeserving of such assistance. The final two chapters, Markets and International Human Rights, address more broadly ways that an antipoverty agenda can be advanced, moving from a chapter on market responses to the concluding chapter on the lessons and possibilities offered by international human rights law.

Poverty is an ever-present yet often-neglected aspect of the study of law. Law school courses frequently discuss the problems of poor people—not just in criminal law, but also in torts, constitutional law, and even property. Yet the fact of their poverty is treated as secondary. Looking at the law from a poverty-centric perspective involves drawing out the concerns, struggles, and lives of poor people; the nature of the programs that serve poor communities; and the legal, economic, and political structures that contribute to and define poverty. One of the fundamental precepts of American law, inscribed over the entrance to the Supreme Court, is "Equal Justice Under Law." Poverty is a challenge to this commitment and forces us to consider whether substantive and procedural rights are going to be extended to the poor and the extent to which we as a society are *not* committed to meeting the needs of the poor. Another challenge for those who study poverty law is sorting out the many reasons given for limiting the assistance provided the poor or for not accepting a broad understanding of their rights. The seemingly intractable nature of poverty, the question of whether people are responsible for their own poverty, and the limited institutional role of the judiciary are just a few of the explanations given for the partial nature of America's legal and societal responses to poverty. Considering these and other explanations with an open mind while not losing sight of the hardships felt by those living in poverty is crucial to the study and understanding of poverty law, regardless of one's political inclination.

We hope you leave this book with a better understanding of the legal structures aiding and confronting poor people and with the determination to keep asking the questions, about the law and about society, raised by the study of poverty law. Our goal in writing this book is to help develop in a new generation of students the cognitive, practical, and analytical tools needed to advocate for the poor. And our real hope is that after studying this material, you will be better equipped and inspired to think, feel, *and* do something about poverty.

* * *

This is a *poverty law* textbook, but before we turn to the history of poverty law and the programs that serve poor people, we must first explore how poverty is defined and measured. Subsequent chapters are largely dedicated to how the law regarding poor people has changed over time and to some of the more important federal and state antipoverty programs. But the focus of this chapter is understanding *poverty*. Mollie Orshansky, the creator of the U.S. poverty line, observed:

> Poverty, like beauty, lies in the eye of the beholder. Poverty is a value judgment; it is not something one can verify or demonstrate, except by inference and suggestion, even with a measure of error. To say who is poor is to use all sorts of value judgements. The concept has to be limited by the purpose which is to be served by the definition. There is no particular reason to count the poor unless you are going to do something about them. . . . [W]hen it comes to defining poverty you can only be more subjective or less so. You cannot be nonsubjective.

Mollie Orshansky, *How Poverty Is Measured*, 92 Monthly Lab. Rev. 37 (1969).

The excerpts in this chapter tackle the question of what poverty is from different perspectives and make different value judgments regarding what makes someone poor. Although some of the discussion is couched in technical terms, the differing value judgments are never far from the surface.

A. WHAT IS POVERTY?

Some of the challenges when considering poverty and poverty law are definitional. What is poverty? What makes someone poor? The answers to these questions will help frame how poverty is understood and the extent to which government policy should focus on poverty. If, for example, poverty is given a very restrictive definition that a very small percentage of the population meets, then the problem of poverty will appear minor. On the other hand, an over-broad definition of poverty threatens to be overinclusive, diluting the significance of poverty and the connection between the definition employed and the underlying concerns that animate antipoverty efforts.

1. Competing Ways to Measure Poverty

Poverty is generally understood in either absolute or relative terms. Absolute understandings of poverty rely upon a basic needs framework: how much food does it take to survive or work, is it possible to obtain minimally adequate shelter, and so on. Changing what is considered essential can, of course, change how many people are defined as being poor, but the underlying rationale is one of individual need, not the individual's place in his or her society. Relative understandings of poverty, in contrast, emphasize a person's relative position in his or her society. Defining a person making 50 percent of a country's median income as poor is an example of a relative understanding of poverty in that it does not matter what can or cannot be purchased with such an income.

A recurring challenge for those seeking to understand and measure poverty is whether to adopt an absolute or a relative measure of poverty. A 2010 World Bank article explains:

> An important distinction is between absolute and relative lines. Absolute lines aim to measure the cost of certain "basic needs," which are often interpreted as physiological minima for human survival; nutritional requirements for good health and normal activity levels are widely used to anchor absolute lines. The monetary lines are intended to have constant "real value" (after deflating by a price index). By contrast, relative lines do not claim to represent physiological minima and are instead (typically) set at a constant proportion of current mean income or consumption. Absolute lines are common in developing countries while relative lines tend to dominate in developed countries.
>
> The strengths and weaknesses of the absolute versus relative approaches to setting poverty lines have been much debated. The position one takes in that debate carries weight for how one thinks about economic development. Absolute poverty can probably be eliminated with sufficient economic growth, which is a key element of the World Bank's strategy for attaining its "dream of a world free of poverty." Outcomes for relative poverty depend more on how income distribution changes; indeed, it is sometimes argued that relative poverty will always be with us. . . .

Martin Ravallion, *Poverty Lines Across the World* (World Bank, Working Paper No. 5284, 2010). The differences between absolute and relative poverty mirror in some respects the differences between poverty and inequality. Relative poverty measures are quite explicitly designed to take into account the relative wealth of others in the community of interest and set the poverty line at some level below the average income in that community. Absolute poverty measures, at least in theory, are based instead on the bare minimum required for a person or family to meet basic needs, independent of the relative wealth of the surrounding community. But a certain degree of category blending is built into nearly any measure that claims to be defined in solely relative or solely absolute terms. After all, the choice regarding where the relative income cut-off should be set below which people are considered poor is often going to be based on what level of consumption is available at that cut-off point. Similarly, societal understandings of what constitute basic needs change as societies develop over time. What follows is a selection written by an early, influential proponent of a relative definition of poverty.

PETER TOWNSEND, *POVERTY IN THE UNITED KINGDOM* (1979)

CONCEPTIONS OF RELATIVITY

The idea of 'the relativity' of poverty requires some explanation. The frame of reference in adopting this approach can be regional, national or international, although until formal ties between nation states are stronger, or global corporations even more strongly entrenched, the international perspective is unlikely to be given enough emphasis. The question is how far peoples are bound by the same economic, trading, institutional and cultural systems, how far they have similar activities and customs and therefore have similar needs. Needs arise by virtue of the kind of society to which individuals belong. Society imposes expectations, through its occupational, educational, economic and other systems, and it also creates wants, through its organization and customs.

This is easy enough to demonstrate for certain commodities. Tea is nutritionally worthless, but in some countries is generally accepted as a 'necessity of life.' For many people in these countries drinking tea has been a life-long custom and is psychologically essential. And the fact that friends and neighbours expect to be offered a cup of tea (or the equivalent) when they visit helps to make it socially necessary as well: a small contribution is made towards maintaining the threads of social relationships. Other goods that are consumed are also psychologically and socially 'necessary' in the same sense, though to varying degrees. The degree of necessity is not uniform for all members of society, because certain goods and services are necessary for some communities or families and other goods and services for others. Repeated advertising and imitation by friends and neighbours can gradually establish a new product or a new version of an old product as essential in a community. Minority wants are converted into majority needs. People may buy first of all out of curiosity or a sense of display, but later make purchases in a routine way. The customs which these purchases and their consumption develop become socially and psychologically ingrained.

Clothing is another good example. Climate may determine whether or not any soft forms of protection are placed over the body, and how thick they are, but social convention, itself partly dependent on resources available, determines the type and style. Who would lay down a scale of necessities for the 1970s for young women in Britain consisting of one pair of boots, two aprons, one second-hand dress, one skirt made from an old dress, a third of the cost of a new hat, a third of the cost of a shawl and a jacket, two pairs of stockings, a few unspecified underclothes, one pair of stays and one pair of old boots worn as slippers, as Rowntree did in 1899?

But convention is much more than ephemeral fashion. It is a style of living also governed by state laws and regulations. Industry conditions the population not only to want certain products and services, but to put up with certain disservices. . . .

DEFINITION OF POVERTY

Perceptions of poverty are one source of underestimation of its extent and severity. Individuals in any population hold different specific or general ideas of its nature. . . . [S]ome people think of poverty as a condition in which families go hungry or starve, and others as a condition relative to standards enjoyed on average or by most people in society. But the majority take the view that poverty is a condition under which people are unable to obtain subsistence, or the basic necessities of life, or is a condition which applies to particular low-income minorities, such as pensioners or the unemployed.

. . . Nevertheless, one country's definition is certainly not the only, and is unlikely to be an objective, definition of poverty. There are variations between societies which have to be accounted for. There are also variations within any single society in history. . . .

The state's (and the public's) conception of subsistence poverty is different from, and more generous than, starvation poverty. Yet it is none the less a severely limited conception of need, fostered by motives of condescension and self-interest as well as duty by the rich. Ideas of 'need' are socially conditioned, and scientific substantiation of such ideas may be non-existent or insufficient. This is independent of the fact that objective needs are socially determined. . . . [T]he traditional conceptions of 'subsistence' poverty restrict people's understanding of modern social conditions as well as their willingness to act generously. On the one hand, they are encouraged to believe that 'subsistence' represents the limit of basic human needs, and this tends to restrict their assessment of what individual rights or entitlements could be introduced and guaranteed. A limited definition of need leads to a limited appreciation of rights. On the other hand, needs other than those included in the conception of 'subsistence' are denied full acknowledgement. There are goods, amenities and services which men and women are impelled to seek and do seek, and which by the tests of both subjective choice and behaviour are therefore social necessities, that have traditionally been excluded from consideration in devising poverty standards. People do not live by bread alone, and sometimes they are prepared to forego bread to meet a more pressing social need.

I have suggested that an alternative, and more objective, conception might be founded on 'relative deprivation' — by which I mean the absence or inadequacy of those diets, amenities, standards, services and activities which are common or customary in society. People are deprived of the conditions of life which ordinarily define membership of society. If they lack or are denied resources to obtain access to these conditions of life and so fulfil membership of society, they are in poverty. Deprivation can arise in any or all of the major spheres of life — at work, where the means largely determining one's position in other spheres are earned; at home, in neighbourhood and family; in travel; and in a range of social and individual activities outside work and home or neighbourhood. In principle, there could be extreme divergencies in the experience of different kinds of deprivation. In practice, there is a systematic relationship between deprivation and level of resources. The 'subsistence' approach ignores major spheres of life in which deprivation can arise. A physically efficient diet is regarded as the basis of subsistence or a national minimum, which then provides the rationale for Britain's income maintenance system. It could be argued that this preoccupation with nutritional deprivation as the centrally evident problem of meeting need in society has, first, to be extended logically to dietary deprivation, thereby putting stress on the kind of food and drink which people actually consume (and the distribution of the budgets from which they purchase it), as well as the amount and quality of nutrients which they absorb, so acknowledging the social definition of dietary need. Secondly, membership of society involves the satisfaction . . . of other needs which are socially defined. The necessities of life are not fixed. They are continuously being adapted and augmented as changes take place in a society and its products. Increasing stratification and a developing division of labour, as well as the growth of powerful new organizations, create, as well as reconstitute, 'need'. In particular, the rich set fashions of consumption which gradually become diffused.

NOTES AND QUESTIONS

1. Just how relative a concept is poverty? Is a law student who does not own a laptop computer poor in any meaningful way? What about someone who makes $5 per day in a community where most people make $2 per day? A relative understanding of poverty might suggest that that person is not poor even if he or she cannot afford items we consider essentials (such as running water).
2. What do you think should be included in the social "need" category referred to by Townsend in the United States today? Is cable television a need? What about a computer and/or Internet access? How about a cell phone? What items of clothing are "needed"? Do people "need" a car not to be poor?
3. Should poverty be defined in income terms, wealth terms, or some combination of income and wealth? Suppose someone who had made well above the poverty line and owned her house suddenly lost her job. Assuming she was unable to find another job, at what point should she be considered poor? When she can no longer go to the movies, when she can no longer afford gas for her car, when she has to sell her house, or when she cannot buy groceries?

2.   *U.S. Poverty Line*

In the United States, defining poverty is laden with politics. Whether the definition of who is considered poor should be adjusted to take into account changing circumstances, such as the relative increase in the cost of housing as a share of income, is not merely of academic interest but can lead to political battles. Even though there is general agreement that the poverty measure being used is out-of-date and a recalibration is necessary, the design of any such measure requires making assumptions and drawing lines that are likely to be debatable and inherently imperfect, both overinclusive and underinclusive. If anything—given American beliefs regarding the culpability of the poor for their poverty and the political toll associated with changing poverty measures such that more

2013 Poverty Guidelines

Persons in family/ household	Poverty guideline for 48 contiguous states and the District of Columbia	Poverty guideline for Alaska	Poverty guideline for Hawaii
1	$11,490	$14,350	$13,230
2	15,510	19,380	17,850
3	19,530	24,410	22,470
4	23,550	29,440	27,090
5	27,570	34,470	31,710
6	32,590	39,500	36,330
7	35,610	44,530	40,950
8	39,630	49,560	45,570
More than 8 persons per household	For families/ households with more than 8 persons, add $4,020 for each additional person.	For families/households with more than 8 persons, add $5,030 for each additional person.	For families/households with more than 8 persons, add $4,620 for each additional person.

Source: U.S. Dep't of Health & Human Servs., *2013 Poverty Guidelines, available at* http://aspe.hhs.gov/poverty/13poverty.cfm.

people are labeled "poor" — the poverty line is likely to be underinclusive and fail to account for the hardships faced by the near poor. This section begins with the poverty guidelines used by the Department of Health and Human Services. It then turns to a history of the U.S. poverty line with arguments for and against changing the current method of defining what poverty means in the United States.

The U.S. Department of Health and Human Services (HHS) issues annual poverty guidelines that are used to determine eligibility for numerous federal and state programs. Based on family or household size, those whose pretax income falls below these figures are considered poor according to the 2013 poverty guidelines.

The HHS poverty guidelines are based on, but not identical to, the U.S. Census Bureau's annual poverty thresholds. In part this difference can be traced to the different purposes they serve. The census bureau's poverty thresholds, which include 48 different classifications, are used for statistical purposes and are retrospective. That is, poverty thresholds for each year are finalized *after* the year for which they are associated. Poverty guidelines, in contrast, are prospective; the guidelines to be used for each year are issued in January of that year. The HHS poverty guidelines are a simplified version of the census bureau's poverty thresholds from the previous year, updated to account for inflation. The poverty guidelines "standardize the differences between family sizes" and, unlike the poverty thresholds, include a limited acknowledgment of geographical difference. For more on the differences between these measures, see HHS's *Frequently Asked Questions Related to the Poverty Guidelines and Poverty*, at http://aspe.hhs.gov/poverty/faq.shtml#differences.

The poverty guidelines are used to determine eligibility for programs administered by HHS as well as programs in the Departments of Agriculture, Energy,

Labor, and Treasury. Such programs include everything from Head Start and Medicare to weatherization assistance and taxpayer clinics. Arguably in recognition of the needs felt by those above the poverty line, eligibility is often based on some multiple of the poverty guidelines. For example, the Supplemental Nutrition Assistance Program (SNAP), formerly called food stamps, sets income eligibility based on 130 percent of the poverty guideline amounts for gross income and 100 percent for net income. *See* U.S. Dep't of Agric., *SNAP Eligibility*, http://www.fns.usda.gov/snap/applicant_recipients/eligibility.htm. Additionally, many state programs piggyback on the federal poverty guidelines and use the guidelines or multiples of guideline amounts to determine eligibility for state programs. Even eligibility to receive legal aid through offices supported by the Legal Services Corporation is limited to people with incomes below 125 percent of the poverty guideline amounts.

NOTES AND QUESTIONS

1. The poverty thresholds for the current and past years can be found on the census bureau's website at http://www.census.gov/hhes/www/poverty/data/threshld/index.html.
2. Are the poverty guidelines higher or lower than you expected? Should they be higher or lower? To better understand the poverty guideline amounts, it may help to think about these figures on a per month basis. For example, for a household of four in the continental United States, the monthly amount was $1962.50 in 2013. What would be the advantages and disadvantages of setting the poverty guidelines higher? What about setting them lower?
3. The poverty guidelines promulgated by HHS seem to recognize a higher cost of living in Hawaii and Alaska, but lump all other states and the District of Columbia into a single average. Doing so fails to take into account how purchasing power — such as for housing and food — can vary dramatically by location. Should the federal government promulgate different poverty guidelines for every state?
4. Advocacy groups have created a number of alternative measures of poverty or adequacy. For example, the Center for Women's Welfare promotes use of its Self-Sufficiency Standard, which is defined as the amount needed to meet basic needs without public assistance or informal aid. *See* Ctr. for Women's Welfare, *The Self-Sufficiency Standard*, http://www.selfsufficiencystandard.org (last visited Sept. 10, 2013). As will be discussed in Chapter 6 (Housing), the National Low Income Housing Coalition has a Housing Wage Calculator, which is the amount of income, based on geographic location, a person must earn to spend at most only 30 percent of her income on housing in that location. *See* Nat'l Low Income Hous. Coal., *Housing Wage Calculator*, http://nlihc.org/library/wagecalc (last visited Sept. 10, 2013). Another similar tool is the Economic Policy Institute's Family Budget Calculator, which "measures the income a family needs in order to attain a secure yet modest living standard" for given locations and family types. *See* Econ. Policy Inst., *Family Budget Calculator*, http://www.epi.org/resources/budget/.

* * *

The excerpt that follows presents the history of the U.S. poverty line. Although originally by Mollie Orshansky for a much more narrow purpose, Orshansky's poverty line became the official U.S. poverty line as part of the Johnson Administration's War on Poverty.

GORDON M. FISHER, *THE DEVELOPMENT AND HISTORY OF THE POVERTY THRESHOLDS*

Social Security Bulletin, Vol. 55, No. 4 (1992)

The poverty thresholds are the primary version of the Federal poverty measure — the other version being the poverty guidelines. The thresholds are currently issued by the Bureau of the Census and are generally used for statistical purposes for example, estimating the number of persons in poverty and tabulating them by type of residence, race, and other social, economic, and demographic characteristics. The poverty guidelines, on the other hand, are issued by the Department of Health and Human Services and are used for administrative purposes for instance, for determining whether a person or family is financially eligible for assistance or services under certain Federal programs.

THE DEVELOPMENT OF THE POVERTY THRESHOLDS

The poverty thresholds were developed in 1963-64 by Mollie Orshansky, an economist working for the Social Security Administration. As Orshansky later indicated, her original purpose was not to introduce a new general measure of poverty, but to develop a measure to assess the relative risks of low economic status (or, more broadly, the differentials in opportunity) among different demographic groups of families with children. She actually developed two sets of poverty thresholds one derived from the Agriculture Department's economy food plan and one derived from its somewhat less stringent low cost food plan. . . .

The Johnson Administration announced its War on Poverty in January 1964, not long after the publication of Orshansky's initial poverty article. The 1964 Report of the Council of Economic Advisers (CEA) contained a chapter on poverty in America. The chapter set a poverty line of $3,000 (in 1962 dollars) for families of all sizes; for unrelated individuals, the chapter implicitly set a poverty line of $1,500 (a selection that was shortly made explicit). The $3,000 figure was specified as being on the basis of before tax annual money income. There was a brief discussion of the theoretical desirability of using estimates of "total" incomes including nonmoney elements such as the rental value of owner occupied dwellings and food raised and consumed on farms but it was not possible to obtain such estimates. The CEA chapter pointed out that the total of money plus nonmoney income that would correspond to the cash-income only poverty line of $3,000 would be somewhat higher than $3,000.

The CEA chapter referred to Orshansky's July 1963 article and its $3,165 "economy plan" poverty line for a nonfarm family of four. . . . Orshansky was concerned by the CEA report's failure to adjust its poverty line for family size, which resulted in understating the number of children in poverty relative to aged persons. This prompted her to begin the work that resulted in her January 1965 *Social Security Bulletin* article, extending the two sets of poverty thresholds at the "economy level" and at the "low cost level" to the whole population. This article appeared just as the Office of Economic Opportunity (OEO) was being established. The OEO adopted the lower ("economy level") of Orshansky's two sets of poverty thresholds as a working or quasi official definition of poverty in May 1965. As noted below, the thresholds were designated as the Federal Government's official statistical definition of poverty in August 1969.

Orshansky did not develop the poverty thresholds as a standard budget that is, a list of goods and services that a family of a specified size and composition would need to live at a designated level of well being, together with their estimated monthly or annual costs. If generally accepted standards of minimum need had been available for all or most of the major essential consumption items of living (for example, housing, medical care, clothing, and transportation), the standard budget approach could have been used by costing out the standards and adding up the costs. However, except for the area of food, no definitive and accepted standards of minimum need for major consumption items existed either then or today.

The "generally accepted" standards of adequacy for food that Orshansky used in developing the thresholds were the food plans prepared by the Department of Agriculture. At the time there were four of these food plans, at the following cost levels: liberal, moderate, low cost, and economy. The first three plans had been introduced in 1933, and the economy food plan was developed and introduced in 1961. Data underlying the latter plan came from the Agriculture Department's 1955 Household Food Consumption Survey. In developing her two sets of poverty thresholds, Orshansky used the low cost and economy food plans.

. . . The three steps Orshansky followed in moving from the cost of food for a family to minimum costs for all family requirements were (1) to define the family size and composition prototypes for which food costs would be computed, (2) to decide on the amount of additional income to allow for items other than food, and (3) to relate the cash needs of farm families to those of comparable nonfarm families.

Because of a special interest in the economic status of families with children and because income requirements are related to the number of persons in the family, Orshansky estimated food costs separately for nonfarm families varying in size from two members to seven or more. Families were further classified by sex of head and the number of members who were related children under age 18. Among three person families, for instance, there were separate subcategories with the following compositions: three adults; two adults, one child; and one adult, two children. . . .

To get from food plan costs to estimates of minimum necessary expenditures for all items, Orshansky made use of the economic principle known as Engel's Law, which states that the proportion of income allocated to "necessaries," and in particular to food, is an indicator of economic well being. Orshansky made use of this law by assuming that equivalent levels of well-being were reached by families (of three or more persons) only when the proportion of income they required to purchase an adequate diet was the same.

To determine the proportion of total income that should be assumed to be spent for food, Orshansky used the Agriculture Department's Household Food Consumption Survey, a survey conducted at approximately 10 year intervals. The 1955 survey the most recent one then available had found that for families of three or more persons, the average expenditure for all food used both inside and outside of the home during a week accounted for about one third of their average money income after taxes. (Note that this finding relates to families at all income levels, not just those at lower income levels; one of the most common errors made about the thresholds is to claim they are based on a finding that "poor people spend a third of their income on food.")

Besides considering the Agriculture Department's 1955 Household Food Consumption Survey, Orshansky also reviewed the 1960-61 Consumer Expenditure Survey of the Bureau of Labor Statistics (BLS), which also provided an estimate of the proportion of total after tax income going for food. To use the BLS survey to derive a poverty measure would have resulted in a "multiplier" of just over four, rather than three. However, the questions used by BLS to get data on annual food outlays had usually yielded lower average expenditures than the more detailed item by item checklist of foods consumed in a week used in the Agriculture Department survey. Orshansky finally decided to use the Agriculture Department survey, with its one to three ratio of food expenditures to after tax money income, in developing the poverty thresholds.

Orshansky started her food costs-to-total expenditures procedure by considering a hypothetical average (middle income) family, spending one-third of its income on food, which was faced with a need to cut back on its expenditures. She made the assumption that the family would be able to cut back its food expenditures and its nonfood expenditures by the same proportion. This assumption was, of course, a simplifying assumption or first approximation. Under this assumption, one third of the family's expenditures would be for food no matter how far it had cut back on its total expenditures.

When the hypothetical family cut back its food expenditures to the point where they equaled the cost of the economy food plan (or the low cost food plan) for a family of that size, the family would have reached the point at which its food expenditures were minimal but adequate, assuming that "the housewife will be a careful shopper, a skillful cook, and a good manager who will prepare all the family's meals at home." Orshansky made the assumption that, at that point, the family's nonfood expenditures would also be minimal but adequate, and established that level of total expenditures as the poverty threshold for a family of that size. Since the family's food expenditures would still be one third of its total expenditures, this meant that (for families of three or more persons) the poverty threshold for a family of a particular size and composition was set at three times the cost of the economy food plan (or the low cost food plan) for such a family. The factor of three by which the food plan cost was multiplied became known as the "multiplier."

It is important to note that Orshansky's "multiplier" methodology for deriving the thresholds was normative, not empirical that is, it was based on a normative assumption involving consumption patterns of the population as a whole, and not on the empirical consumption behavior of lower income groups. . . .

Having calculated poverty thresholds from each food plan for 58 categories of nonfarm families and 4 categories of nonfarm unrelated individuals, Orshansky had 62 detailed poverty thresholds (from each food plan) for nonfarm family units. . . . Because farm families purchased for cash only about 60 percent of the food they consumed, and because of the issue of classifying farm housing expenses as part of the farm business operation, Orshansky decided to set farm poverty thresholds at 60 percent of the corresponding nonfarm thresholds. . . .

It is important to note that Orshansky's farm/nonfarm distinction was *not* the same as a rural/urban (or nonmetropolitan/metropolitan) distinction. . . . The nonfarm poverty thresholds were applied to the rural nonfarm population as well as to the urban population. It should also be noted that the reason for the farm/nonfarm distinction was *not* a generalized "living costs are cheaper in farm or rural areas" argument.

. . . The poverty thresholds were presented as a measure of income inadequacy "if it is not possible to state unequivocally 'how much is enough,' it should be possible to assert with confidence how much, on an average, is too little."

NOTES AND QUESTIONS

1. For a more general, less technical, introduction to the U.S. poverty line, see John Cassidy, *Relatively Deprived: How Poor Is Poor?*, The New Yorker (Apr. 3, 2006).
2. Is the U.S. poverty line developed by Orshansky an absolute or a relative measure of poverty?
3. Orshansky's poverty line not only became the official poverty line for the United States (and has remained so ever since), but also became a tool for determining individual eligibility for programs and services even though it was not originally designed for that purpose.

* * *

The excerpt that follows, taken from a government report, highlights the challenge of defining poverty in a developed country and argues that poverty in the United States can only be understood in relative terms.

U.S. DEPARTMENT OF HEALTH, EDUCATION, AND WELFARE, *A MEASURE OF POVERTY: A REPORT TO CONGRESS AS MANDATED BY THE EDUCATION AMENDMENTS OF 1974* (1976)

Poor persons living in the United States . . . are rich in contrast to their counterparts in other times and places. They are not poor if by poor is meant the subsistence levels of living common in some other countries. Nor are most poor like their counterparts in this country fifty or one hundred years ago. This being so, why worry about poverty and its measure? This country is concerned about poverty, its causes and correlates. It is willing to relieve the poverty of some of the poor and it wants to measure the effectiveness of its efforts to do so. . . .

The dictionary assigns to the word poverty a limited if imprecise meaning: lack of money or personal possessions. However, even a cursory review of the literature on poverty reveals that for many people the word has connotations broader or more narrow than the dictionary definition. For example, the dictionary does not limit poverty to a condition arrived at or remained in involuntarily. A family is none the less poor for having arrived at that state of its own accord. Similarly, the fact that an individual could with modest and reasonable effort escape from poverty has nothing to do with whether he is currently poor.

. . . To say that someone is poor merely because he occupies a place lower on the scale than someone else . . . is not a sufficient definition. To say that someone is poor, then, must be to say that he lacks the money or possessions necessary to obtain some state or condition. A poverty threshold is the point on the scale of poverty below which people are deemed incapable of achieving this defined state; it has no intrinsic meaning apart from the state or condition it is meant to delimit.

Most people have an intuitive notion that there is a subgroup of the population that is poor; the term "the poor" can be used repeatedly without definition. But the criteria by which people distinguish the poor from the rest are almost inevitably circular in reasoning: the poor are people who behave like poor people. This circular reasoning is hard to avoid. In general we all take "the poor" to be persons on the lower end of the measure of poverty. But how do we decide how far down? What is the poverty threshold? What is the state of being poor?

The further down the scale of poverty, that is, the closer one approaches mere physical subsistence, or the more limited the degree of consumer choice assumed, the more likely it is that there will be agreement that people there and below are "poor." This is so because there are several, perhaps many, possible senses of the word poor and persons on the lower end of the measure are more likely to fit one of these senses than persons further up. Because of this, it is tempting to think that there is a consensus poverty threshold, a point on the scale of poverty below which people would be considered poor by almost everyone. Nonetheless, it is unlikely that a measure of poverty can be developed which will serve equally well for all purposes. . . .

Poverty definitions serve two quite different functions for public policy purposes: first, they allow program administrators to identify individuals or families that require and are eligible for help. Second, they are essential to policy makers in the design and evaluation of programs to help the poor. . . .

Economic definitions of poverty can be formulated in two rather different ways. In one, poverty is defined specifically in terms of what the overall population has. These are usually called relative definitions. A purely relative measure defines a fixed percent of the population as poor. A quasi-relative measure defines the poor as those whose income is below a fixed percent of the median income. A commonly proposed quasi-relative definition of poverty would set the threshold at 50 percent of median income.

In the second type of definition, poverty is defined in terms of a family's ability to purchase a specified market basket of goods and services. These are usually called absolute definitions because the cost of the market basket is determined objectively and serves as threshold. However, the composition of the market is subjective and represents a judgment about some minimally acceptable level of living. Since this judgment varies with the general standard of living, absolute definitions of poverty are meaningful only with reference to a given period and place.

3. Recommendations to Change the U.S. Poverty Line

The official poverty line is controversial, in part because the nature of the measure has remained the same, except for inflation adjustments, even as spending patterns have changed. The poverty line invites political debate because changing how poverty is calculated would change the number of people defined as poor and could increase or decrease political will to combat poverty. Moreover,

many conservatives and progressives argue that the line itself is flawed and
outdated. The most significant new methodology for measuring poverty was
proposed in a 1995 report released by the National Academy of Sciences.

NAT'L ACAD. OF SCIS., PANEL ON POVERTY & FAMILY ASSISTANCE, *MEASURING POVERTY: A NEW APPROACH* (CONSTANCE F. CITRO & ROBERT T. MICHAELS EDS., 1995)

[W]e recommend a new official poverty measure for the United States. Our
recommendation is to retain the basic notion of poverty as material deprivation,
but to use a revised concept for setting a threshold and a revised definition of the
resources to be compared with the threshold to determine if a family or individual is or is not in poverty. Equally importantly, we recommend procedures for
devising an equivalent poverty threshold for families of different sizes and for
families in different geographic locations and for updating the poverty threshold over time.

The current poverty measure has weaknesses both in the implementation of
the threshold concept and in the definition of family resources. Changing social
and economic conditions over the last three decades have made these weaknesses more obvious and more consequential. As a result, the current measure
does not accurately reflect differences in poverty across population groups and
across time. We conclude that it would be inadvisable to retain the current
measure for the future.

In deciding on a new measure to recommend, we used scientific evidence
to the extent possible. However, the determination of a particular type of
poverty measure and, even more, the determination of a particular poverty
threshold are ultimately subjective decisions. "Expertise" can only carry one
so far. To help us choose among alternatives, we developed a set of criteria,
namely, that the poverty measure should be understandable and broadly
acceptable to the public, statistically defensible (e.g., internally consistent),
and operationally feasible. Finally, for the most judgemental aspect of a poverty measure, namely, setting the level of the threshold, we recommend a
specific procedure to follow—but we do not recommend a precise number.
We suggest a range that we believe provides reasonable limits for the initial
poverty threshold, but we leave the ultimate choice of a specific value to the
policy arena.

. . . From the beginning, the poverty measure had weaknesses, and they have
become more apparent and consequential because of far-reaching changes in
the U.S. society and economy and in government policies.

- First, because of the increased labor force participation of mothers, there
  are more working families who must pay for child care, but the current
  measure does not distinguish between the needs of families in which the
  parents do or do not work outside the home. More generally, the current
  measure does not distinguish between the needs of workers and
  nonworkers.
- Second, because of differences in health status and insurance coverage,
  different population groups face significant variations in medical care
  costs, but the current measure does not take account of them.

- Third, the thresholds are the same across the nation, although significant price variations across geographic areas exist for such needs as housing.
- Fourth, the family size adjustments in the thresholds are anomalous in many respects, and changing demographic and family characteristics (such as the reduction in average family size) underscore the need to reassess the adjustments.
- Fifth, more broadly, changes in the standard of living call into question the merits of continuing to use the values of the original thresholds updated only for inflation. Historical evidence suggests that poverty thresholds — including those developed according to "expert" notions of minimum needs — follow trends in overall consumption levels. Because of rising living standards in the United States, most approaches for developing poverty thresholds (including the original one) would produce higher thresholds today than the current ones.
- Finally, because the current measure defines family resources as gross money income, it does not reflect the effects of important government policy initiatives that have significantly altered families' disposable income and, hence, their poverty status. Examples are the increase in the Social Security payroll tax, which reduces disposable income for workers, and the growth in the Food Stamp Program, which raises disposable income for beneficiaries. Moreover, the current poverty measure cannot reflect the effects of future policy initiatives that may have consequences for disposable income, such as changes in the financing of health care, further changes in tax policy, and efforts to move welfare recipients into the work force.

The Panel on Poverty and Family Assistance concludes that the poverty measure should be revised to reflect more accurately the trends in poverty over time and the differences in poverty across population groups. Without revision, and in the face of continuing socioeconomic change as well as changes in government policies, the measure will become increasingly unable to inform the public or support research and policy making.

It is not easy to specify an alternative measure. There are several poverty concepts, each with merits and limitations, and there is no scientific basis by which one concept can be indisputably preferred to another. Ultimately, to recommend a particular concept requires judgement as well as science.

Our recommended changes are based on the best scientific evidence available, our best judgement, and three additional criteria. First, a poverty measure should be acceptable and understandable to the public. Second, a poverty measure should be statistically defensible. In this regard, the concepts underlying the thresholds and the definition of resources should be consistent. Third, a poverty measure should be feasible to implement with data that are available or can fairly readily be obtained. . . .

Recommendation 1.1. The official U.S. measure of poverty should be revised to reflect more nearly the circumstances of the nation's families and changes in them over time. The revised measure should comprise a set of poverty thresholds and a definition of family resources — for comparison with the thresholds to determine who is in or out of poverty — that are consistent with each other and otherwise statistically defensible. The concepts underlying both the thresholds and the definition of family resources should be broadly acceptable and understandable and operationally feasible.

Recommendation 1.2. On the basis of the criteria in Recommendation 1.1, the poverty measure should have the following characteristics:

- The poverty thresholds should represent a budget for food, clothing, shelter (including utilities), and a small additional amount to allow for other needs (e.g., household supplies, personal care, non-work-related transportation).
- A threshold for a reference family type should be developed using actual consumer expenditure data and updated annually to reflect changes in expenditures on food, clothing, and shelter over the previous 3 years.
- The reference family threshold should be adjusted to reflect the needs of different family types and to reflect geographic differences in housing costs.
- Family resources should be defined—consistent with the threshold concept—as the sum of money income from all sources together with the value of near-money benefits (e.g., food stamps) that are available to buy goods and services in the budget, minus expenses that cannot be used to buy these goods and services. Such expenses include income and payroll taxes, child care and other work-related expenses, child support payments to another household, and out-of-pocket medical care costs, including health insurance premiums. . . .

Recommendation 4.2. The definition of family resources for comparison with the appropriate poverty threshold should be disposable money and near-money income. Specifically, resources should be calculated as follows:

- estimate gross money income from all public and private sources for a family or unrelated individual (which is income as defined in the current measure);
- add the value of near-money nonmedical in-kind benefits, such as food stamps, subsidized housing, school lunches, and home energy assistance;
- deduct out-of-pocket medical care expenditures, including health insurance premiums;
- deduct income taxes and Social Security payroll taxes;
- for families in which there is no nonworking parent, deduct actual child care costs, per week worked, not to exceed the earnings of the parent with the lower earnings or a cap that is adjusted annually for inflation;
- for each working adult, deduct a flat amount per week worked (adjusted annually for inflation and not to exceed earnings) to account for work-related transportation and miscellaneous expenses; and
- deduct child support payments from the income of the payer. . . .

WHAT IS POVERTY?

We define poverty as economic deprivation. A way of expressing this concept is that it pertains to people's lack of economic resources (e.g., money or near-money income) for consumption of economic goods and services (e.g., food, housing, clothing, transportation). Thus, a poverty standard is based on a level of family resources (or, alternatively, of families' actual consumption) deemed necessary to obtain a minimally adequate standard of living, defined appropriately for the United States today. . . .

Yet general agreement about basic needs does not mean that everyone agrees about the level of consumption that distinguishes a state of poverty from a state of adequacy. Thus, there is a question about how much food, shelter, and clothing distinguish a person in poverty from one who is not in poverty. This question cannot be answered in the abstract. No concept of economic poverty, whether ours or another, will of itself determine a level for a poverty threshold. That determination necessarily involves judgement. Moreover, . . . no matter what the particular concept, the determination of a poverty threshold invariably considers people's actual spending patterns and hence, inevitably, has a relative aspect.

Under our threshold concept, we propose that the values for food, shelter, and clothing — the basic bundle — and for a small amount of other needed spending — the multiplier — be developed by direct reference to spending patterns of American families below the median expenditure level. More important, we propose that real changes in spending on food, clothing, and shelter be used to update the poverty thresholds each year. By so doing, the thresholds will maintain a relationship to real changes in living standards, but only to the extent that these changes affect consumption of basic goods and services that pertain to a concept of poverty, not all goods and services. In this sense, our concept is quasi-relative in nature.

NOTES AND QUESTIONS

1. Though the recommendations of the National Academy of Sciences (NAS) report have not yet been followed, most proposed or experimental poverty measures developed since 1995 rely heavily upon the NAS recommendations. The U.S. Census Bureau, for example, began releasing two sets of poverty data in 1999, one using the official poverty measure and the other using an experimental method based upon the NAS report. In 2009, the census bureau developed a second experimental method, the supplemental poverty measure (SPM), that again relied upon insights from the NAS report, but differs slightly from the experimental NAS-based measure the Bureau had already been using. *See* Kathleen Short, U.S. Census Bureau, *The Research Supplemental Poverty Measure: 2010* (2011). The census bureau is careful to note that the SPM "will not replace the official poverty measure and will not be used to determine eligibility for government programs." For more on the NAS-based experimental poverty estimates and the SPM measure, see U.S. Census Bureau, *Poverty — Experimental Measures*, http://www.census.gov/hhes/povmeas/.

2. The NAS recommendations would change how poverty is measured and, accordingly, would change the percentage of people who are considered poor along a number of different demographic lines. The following table shows differences between the official poverty rate and the NAS-based measure for 2010 according to select demographic characteristics.

3. Use of the NAS-based poverty measure would change the percentage of the population reported as living in poverty annually. But complications would still remain. For example, should annual changes to poverty thresholds produced according to NAS standards be based on changes in the Consumer Price Index (CPI) or on Consumer Expenditure (CE) surveys? The CPI measures overall changes in prices, while CE surveys look at the subset of goods being purchased by the population being considered. For 2010, use of the CPI would make the poverty rate according to the NAS-based poverty

Characteristic	Official poverty measure	NAS based poverty measure
All people	15.1	15.5
People in families	13.2	13.1
People in married-couple families	7.6	8.1
People in families with a female householder, no husband present	34.2	30.8
People in families with a male householder, no wife present	17.3	20.1
Age		
Under 18 years	22.0	17.3
18 to 64 years	13.5	14.5
65 years and over	9.0	16.5
Race and Hispanic origin		
White alone	13.0	13.9
Non-Hispanic White alone	9.9	10.6
Black alone	27.4	24.2
Non-Hispanic Black alone	27.3	23.9
Asian alone	12.1	15.7
Hispanic (of any race)	26.6	27.9
Region		
Northeast	12.8	15.4
Midwest	13.9	12.1
South	16.9	15.6
West	15.3	18.5

Source: U.S. Census Bureau, *Current Population Survey, 2010 Annual Social and Economic Supplement.* Data available at http://www.census.gov/hhes/povmeas/data/nas/tables/2010/index.html.

measure fall below the official poverty measure, while use of CE would make the poverty rate according to the NAS-based poverty measure more similar to, albeit a bit higher than, the official poverty measure. One thing such differences tell us is that NAS-based measures are not inevitably higher or lower than the official measure. Second, these differences tell us that the choice of index plays a large role in how the poverty rate changes from year to year.

4. Despite the recognized shortcomings of the official poverty measure, it has not been replaced. One explanation for its resilience is the political importance of poverty counts, as is explained in a 2008 report from the Brookings Institution:

> For many years, both Democratic and Republican administrations have chosen not to deal with the potential political issues of changing the poverty measure. Virtually any change would mean that the number of people in poverty would go up or down, and that relative poverty rates would change among age, race, and ethnic groups, and between states. Thus, there are political costs to making any changes that might change the poverty count. It has been easier simply not to make changes.

Rebecca M. Blank & Mark H. Greenberg, The Brookings Inst., *Improving the Measurement of Poverty* 7 (2008). Besides political calculations, are there other reasons to retain the existing measure?

4. Capability Approach

The capability approach, developed principally by Nobel Laureate Amartya Sen, is increasingly the way that international organizations think about poverty and development. Blending absolute and relative approaches to understanding poverty, Sen's contributions have been supported by the work of many scholars, most notably Martha Nussbaum. Based on the extent to which it has been embraced as a metric for understanding poverty within and across nations, the capability approach is likely to shape how poverty is understood going forward.

What follows are two selections by Sen and two from the United Nations Development Program on the challenge of measuring poverty and the goals of such work. Together these four excerpts introduce the capability approach and show how thinking about poverty has evolved in recent decades in the international sphere.

AMARTYA SEN, *POOR, RELATIVELY SPEAKING*
35 Oxford Econ. Papers 153 (1983)

When on the 6th January 1941, amidst the roar of the guns of the second world war, President Roosevelt announced that "in the future days . . . we look forward to a world founded upon four essential freedoms", including "freedom from want", he was voicing what was soon to become one of the major themes of the post-war era. While the elimination of poverty all over the world has become a much-discussed international issue, it is in the richer countries that an immediate eradication seemed possible. That battle was joined soon enough after the war in those affluent countries, and the ending of poverty has been a major issue in their policy discussions. . . .

. . . There is, I would argue, an irreducible absolutist core in the idea of poverty. One element of that absolutist core is obvious enough, though the modern literature on the subject often does its best to ignore it. If there is starvation and hunger, then no matter what the relative picture looks like there clearly is poverty. In this sense the relative picture—if relevant—has to take a back seat behind the possibly dominating absolutist consideration. While it might be thought that this type of poverty—involving malnutrition or hunger—is simply irrelevant to the richer countries, that is empirically far from clear, even though the frequency of this type of deprivation is certainly much less in these countries.

Even when we shift our attention from hunger and look at other aspects of living standard, the absolutist aspect of poverty does not disappear. The fact that some people have a lower standard of living than others is certainly proof of inequality, but by itself it cannot be a proof of poverty unless we know something more about the standard of living that these people do in fact enjoy. It would be absurd to call someone poor just because he had the means to buy only one Cadillac a day when others in that community could buy two of these cars each day. The absolute considerations cannot be inconsequential for conceptualising poverty.

The temptation to think of poverty as being altogether relative arises partly from the fact that the absolute satisfaction of some of the needs might depend on a person's relative position vis-à-vis others. . . .

At the risk of oversimplification, I would like to say that poverty is an absolute notion in the space of capabilities but very often it will take a relative form in the space of commodities or characteristics.

. . . In the commodity space, therefore, escape from poverty in the form of avoiding shame requires a varying collection of commodities — and it is this collection and the resources needed for it that happen to be relative vis-à-vis the situations of others. But on the space of the capabilities themselves — the direct constituent of the standard of living — escape from poverty has an absolute requirement, to wit, avoidance of this type of shame. Not so much having equal shame as others, but just not being ashamed, absolutely.

If we view the problem of conceptualising poverty in this light, then there is no conflict between the irreducible absolutist element in the notion of poverty (related to capabilities and the standard of living) and the "thoroughgoing relativity" to which Peter Townsend refers, if the latter is interpreted as applying to commodities and resources. . . .

In a poor community the resources or commodities needed to participate in the standard activities of the community might be very little indeed. In such a community the perception of poverty is primarily concerned with the commodity requirements of fulfilling nutritional needs and perhaps some needs of being clothed, sheltered and free from disease. This is the world of Charles Booth or Seebohm Rowntree in nineteenth century or early twentieth century London or York, and that of poverty estimation today, say, in India. The more physical needs tend to dominate over the needs of communal participation, on which Townsend focuses, at this less affluent stage both because the nutritional and other physical needs would tend to have a more prominent place in the standard-of-living estimation and also because the requirements of participation are rather easily fulfilled. For a richer community, however, the nutritional and other physical requirements (such as clothing as protection from climatic conditions) are typically already met, and the needs of communal participation — while absolutely no different in the space of capabilities — will have a much higher demand in the space of commodities and that of resources. Relative deprivation, in this case, is nothing other than a relative failure in the commodity space — or resource space — having the effect of an absolute deprivation in the capability space. . . .

Similarly, in a society in which most families own cars, public transport services might be poor, so that a carless family in such a society might be absolutely poor in a way it might not have been in a poorer society. To take another example, widespread ownership of refrigerators and freezers in a community might affect the structure of food retailing, thereby making it more difficult in such a society to make do without having these facilities oneself.

It is, of course, not my point that there is no difference in the standards of living of rich and poor countries. There are enormous differences in the fulfilment of some of the most basic capabilities, e.g., to meet nutritional requirements, to escape avoidable disease, to be sheltered, to be clothed, to be able to travel, and to be educated. But whereas the commodity requirements of these capability fulfilments are not tremendously variable between one community and another, such variability is enormous in the case of other capabilities. The capability to live without shame emphasized by Adam Smith, that of being able to participate in the activities of the community discussed by Peter Townsend, that of having self-respect discussed by John Rawls, are examples of capabilities with extremely variable resource requirements. And as it happens the resource requirements typically go up in these cases with the average prosperity of the nation, so that the relativist view acquires plausibility despite the absolutist basis of the concept of poverty in terms of capabilities and deprivation.

NOTES AND QUESTIONS

1. Amartya Sen later would expand upon the capability approach found in the above excerpt by giving four examples of the "various types of contingencies which result in variations in the conversion of income into the kinds of lives that people can lead." Amartya Sen, *The Idea of Justice* (2009). Sen's examples are:

    (1) *Personal heterogeneities:* People have disparate physical characteristics in relation to age, gender, disability, proneness to illness and so on, making their needs extremely diverse; for example, a disabled or an ill person may need more income to do the same elementary things that a less afflicted person can do with a given level of income. . . .
    (2) *Diversities in the physical environment:* How far a given income will go will depend also on environmental conditions, including climatic circumstances, such as temperature ranges, or flooding. The environmental conditions need not be unalterable — they could be improved with communal efforts, or worsened by pollution or depletion. But an isolated individual may have to take much of the environmental conditions as given in converting incomes and personal resources into functionings and quality of life.
    (3) *Variations in social climate:* The conversion of personal resources into functionings is influenced also by social conditions, including public health-care and epidemiology, public educational arrangements and the prevalence or absence of crime and violence in the particular location. Aside from public facilities, the nature of community relationships can be very important, as the recent literature on 'social capital' has tended to emphasize.
    (4) *Differences in relational perspectives:* Established patterns of behaviour in a community may also substantially vary the need for income to achieve the same elementary functionings; for example, to be able to "appear in public without shame" may require higher standards of clothing and other visible consumption in a richer society than in a poorer one (as Adam Smith noted more than two centuries ago in the *Wealth of Nations*). The same applies to the personal resources needed for taking part in the life of the community, and in many contexts, even to fulfill the elementary requirements of self-respect.

    Id.

2. Sen won the Nobel Prize in 1998 for his work in economics and is now a professor at Harvard University. His major works that explore the capability approach, among other things, include: *Inequality Reexamined* (1992), *Development as Freedom* (1999), and *The Idea of Justice* (2009). In *Creating*

Capabilities: The Human Development Approach (2011), Martha Nussbaum covers similar ground from the perspective of a law professor and philosopher.

3. The capability approach offers a more nuanced understanding of both what makes someone poor and why we are concerned about poverty, but at what cost? An advantage of simple metrics, such as the poverty line, is that they are relatively simple. They are easy to understand and can more easily be used to generate headcounts of those who should be classified as poor. A capability approach, in contrast, by seeming to require greater attention to the particularities of individual people, may be harder to administer on a large scale.

4. Is Sen right that not having the goods needed to avoid feeling ashamed in public can amount to a capability deprivation? Adam Smith's observations regarding customary, expected goods in England are frequently cited for this idea, yet if the customary good is more of a status symbol than a necessity, should it be included in how poverty is understood?

* * *

How might the capability approach inform how global poverty is understood and tackled? The two selections from the United Nations Development Program (UNDP) below address both questions of measurement and of the policy relevance of such questions.

UNITED NATIONS DEV. PROGRAMME, *HUMAN DEVELOPMENT REPORT 2003: MILLENNIUM DEVELOPMENT GOALS: A COMPACT AMONG NATIONS TO END HUMAN POVERTY* (SAKIKO FUKUDA-PARR ED., 2003)

MEASURING INCOME POVERTY: WHERE TO DRAW THE LINE?

The animated debate on whether the Millennium Development Goal of halving poverty will be achieved is largely driven by the lack of agreement on the best way to measure poverty. [Ed. note: The Millennium Development Goals (MDGs) are a set of goals for reducing poverty and deprivation that came out of a United Nations resolution in 2000, with the target date for meeting the goals set as 2015. For more on the MDGs and the progress that has been made towards meeting the goals, see the United Nations Development Programme's MDGs webpage, http://www.undp.org/content/undp/en/home/librarypage/mdg/.] . . .

Absolute poverty is the main indicator used to assess progress towards the Goal. This indicator measures the proportion of a population surviving on less than a specific amount of income per day. This specific amount is the poverty line — arguably the most contentious issue in the debate. Shifting the international poverty line by just a few cents can alter world poverty estimates immensely, "moving" millions of individuals in or out of poverty.

Poverty rates based on national poverty lines can capture the dynamics of poverty over time in a single country. . . . Because the costs of the consumption bundles used to estimate poverty lines vary across countries, poverty lines vary as well. The concepts and criteria used to define poverty lines also differ across countries, making national poverty lines problematic when the analytical purpose is to make international poverty comparisons — as with the monitoring of regional and global progress towards the Millennium Development Goal for poverty.

AN INTERNATIONAL POVERTY LINE — MESSY BUT NECESSARY

To compare poverty rates across countries, poverty data based on an internationally defined poverty line would be more suitable, at least in theory. To that end the World Bank uses an extreme poverty line of about $1 a day (measured in purchasing power parity terms). [Ed. note: Purchasing Power Parity (PPP) is a price index that allows for cross-country comparisons, similar to exchange rates but based on the price of goods, rather than on international capital flows. In one famous example, scholars now study the relative price of a Big Mac from McDonald's in order to understand the purchasing power of the local currency in the country being studied.] Behind this approach is the assumption — based on national poverty lines from a sample of developing countries — that, after adjusting for cost of living differences, $1 a day is the average minimum consumption required for subsistence in the developing world. . . .

UNITED NATIONS DEV. PROGRAMME, *HUMAN DEVELOPMENT REPORT 2010: THE REAL WEALTH OF NATIONS: PATHWAYS TO HUMAN DEVELOPMENT* (2010)

MEASURING POVERTY — THE MULTIDIMENSIONAL POVERTY INDEX

A focus on deprivation is fundamental to human development. The dimensions of poverty go far beyond inadequate income — to poor health and nutrition, low education and skills, inadequate livelihoods, bad housing conditions, social exclusion and lack of participation. Experienced by people around the world . . . poverty is multifaceted and thus multidimensional.

Money-based measures are obviously important, but deprivations in other dimensions and their overlap also need to be considered, especially because households facing multiple deprivations are likely to be in worse situations than income poverty measures suggest.

The MPI is grounded in the capability approach. It includes an array of dimensions for participatory exercises among poor communities and an emerging international consensus. . . .

The MPI, simple and policy relevant, complements monetary-bases methods by taking a broader approach. . . .

This new measure replaces the Human Poverty Index (HPI), published since 1997. Pioneering in its day, the HPI used country averages to reflect aggregate deprivations in health, education and standard of living. It could not identify specific individuals, households or larger groups of people as jointly deprived. The MPI addresses this shortcoming by capturing how many people experience overlapping deprivations and how many deprivations they face on average. It can be broken down by dimension to show how the composition of multidimensional poverty changes in incidence and intensity for different regions, ethnic groups and so on — with useful implications for policy. . . .

OVERALL PATTERNS OF MULTIDIMENSIONAL POVERTY

In sum, we estimate that about a third of the population in 104 countries, or almost 1.75 billion people, experience multidimensional poverty. For example, they might live in a household that has a member who is undernourished, that has experienced a child death or that has no member with five years of education and no school-age children who are enrolled in school. Or they might live in a household deprived of cooking fuel, sanitation facilities, water, electricity, floor and assets.

Today, the most widely used measure of poverty is income poverty, using either a national poverty line or an international standard. Preliminary analysis suggests that the MPI captures overlapping but still distinct aspects of poverty. Plotting the national headcounts of those who are income poor (using the $1.25 a day poverty line) against those who are multidimensionally poor shows that in most countries—including Ethiopia, Guatemala and Morocco—the number of people who are multidimensionally poor is higher. . . .

Our aggregate estimate of 1.75 billion multidimensionally poor people exceeds the 1.44 billion people estimated to be living on less than $1.25 a day in the same countries, but it is below the 2.6 billion people estimated to be living on less than $2 a day.

NOTES AND QUESTIONS

1. These UNDP readings highlight the importance of converting survey data regarding the nominal income of populations into the purchasing power associated with that income. Arguably such a conversion was the goal of Mollie Orshansky's original poverty line, which similarly was based on the market value of a basket of goods. One of the reasons purchasing price parity (PPP) is used is because of the differential purchasing power of currencies in different countries. Currency exchange rates are an imperfect gauge of PPP as it relates to poor people because the basket of goods that drive fluctuations in exchange rates are not the same set of basic goods linked to poverty measures.

2. The global poverty lines used by the United Nations and the Bretton Woods institutions—the World Bank and the International Monetary Fund—attempt to flatten out differences across countries so that international comparisons and poverty counts are possible. Should poverty be understood as being capable of international comparison, or is the experience of being poor so intrinsically local that such efforts obscure as much as they enlighten? Arguably, the same is true of the U.S. poverty line, which is used across the United States despite dramatic cost-of-living and other differences between, for example, New York City and rural parts of Oklahoma. Professor Lisa Pruitt, for example, has argued in a series of articles on rural poverty that poverty approaches tend to be based on urban issues and fail to take account of the unique challenges facing the rural poor. *See, e.g.,* Lisa R. Pruitt, *Missing the Mark: Welfare Reform and Rural Poverty*, 10 J. Gender, Race & Just. 439 (2007). Similarly, an alternative poverty measure for poverty was proposed in 2008 by New York City because the extraordinary housing costs made the national poverty line inappropriate. For more on New York City's different antipoverty efforts, see Wendy A. Bach, *Governance, Accountability and the New Poverty Agenda,* 2010 Wis. L. Rev. 239 (2010).

B. POVERTY IN THE UNITED STATES

According to the U.S. Census Bureau, more than one in seven people living in the United States in 2010, 46.2 million people, were below the official poverty rate. Carmen DeNavas-Walt et al., *U.S. Census Bureau, Income, Poverty, and Health Insurance Coverage in the United States: 2010* (2011). The poverty rate for children was 22 percent, or more than one in five children. Additionally, almost 50 million people did not have health insurance. Poverty, however, is not distributed evenly across demographic characteristics or racial groups. More than one-third of female-headed households live in poverty. And racial minorities are much more likely to live in poverty than Whites living in the United States. The poverty rate in 2010 for non-Hispanic Whites was 9.9 percent, but it was 27.4 percent for Blacks, 12.1 percent for Asians, and 26.6 percent for Hispanics. Using a different measure, the international relative standard of 50 percent of median income, the poverty rate before taxes and transfers in the late 2000s was 27 percent. As Figure 1.1 highlights, taxes and transfers — government programs that provide cash or benefits — manage to reduce the poverty rate by 10 percent, but the poverty rate in the United States post taxes and transfers remains higher than that in similarly wealthy countries. Indeed, of the countries presented in Figure 1.1, only Luxembourg and Denmark had a higher GDP per capita than the United States. This means that, with the exception of Israel, all these peer nations managed to use taxes and transfers to lower their poverty rate more than the United States, despite having a lower GDP per capita.

Although some of these countries had higher initial levels of poverty than the United States, they all succeeded in lifting a larger percentage of their populations above the relative international standard of poverty through a more robust use of taxes and transfers. Moreover, Figure 1.1 suggests that poverty is tolerated by Americans, or by American politics at least, to a greater extent than is true in many other developed countries. The standard measure of inequality is the Gini coefficient, which ranges from 0 (complete equality) to 1 (complete inequality) — the larger the number, the greater the inequality. As measured by the Gini coefficient, the United States also has a higher level of economic inequality than all similarly wealthy countries. Figure 1.2 shows the relatively high level of U.S. inequality compared to its peer group as defined by membership in the Organization for Economic Cooperation and Development (OECD) and a GDP per capita income of greater than $25,000 for 2008.

Inequality and poverty are not synonymous. A country could have high inequality, for example, and low poverty rates if those in the bottom of the income distribution still made enough to not be considered poor. Or, alternatively, a country where everyone was making near-starvation wages would have the entire population living in poverty, but would have little inequality. But in practice poverty and inequality are often linked: Societies that permit great inequality often have high poverty rates. The challenges presented by the often overlooked problem of poverty in a developed economy are presented vividly in the selection that follows, taken from one of the most influential works on poverty of the twentieth century.

Figure 1.1
Effect of Taxes and Transfers on Poverty Rate in Wealthy Countries

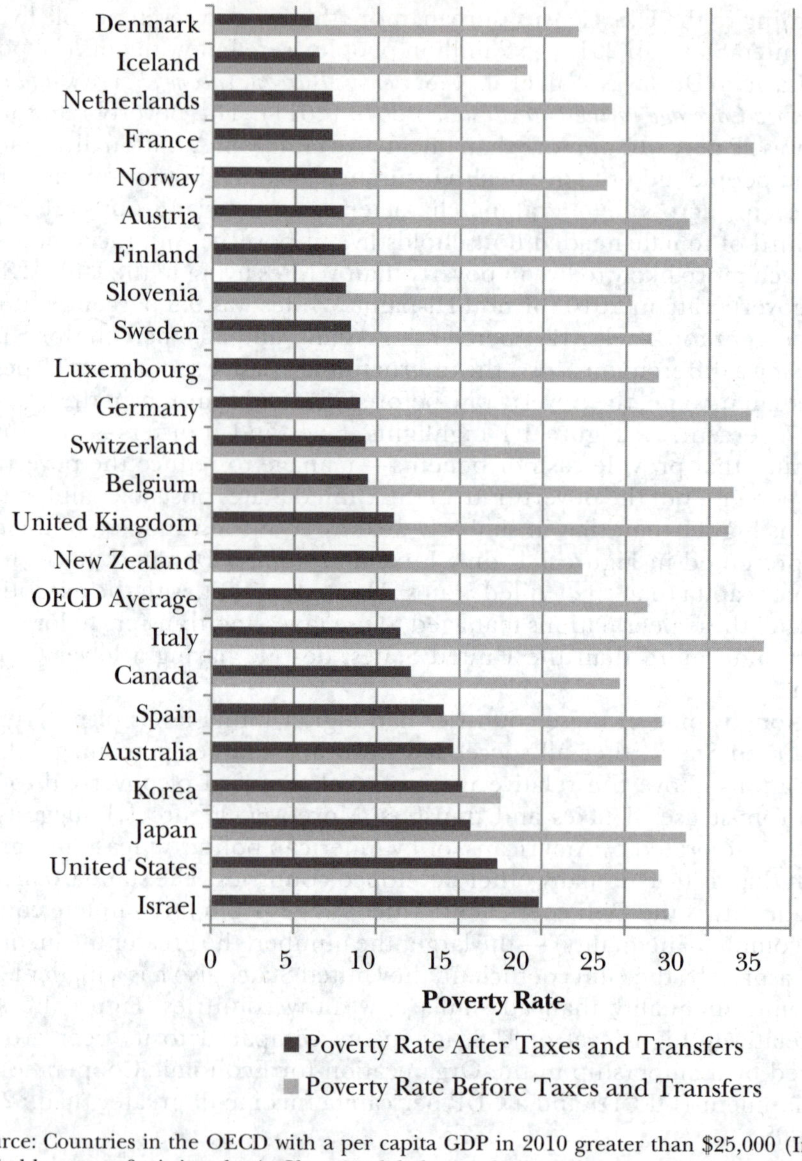

Poverty Rate

■ Poverty Rate After Taxes and Transfers

■ Poverty Rate Before Taxes and Transfers

Source: Countries in the OECD with a per capita GDP in 2010 greater than $25,000 (Ireland excluded because of missing data). Chart modeled on a similar one created by Jared Bernstein, *available at* http://jaredbernsteinblog.com/wp-content/uploads/2011/12/indi_pov.jpg. Data taken from OECD StatExtracts, *available at* http://stats.oecd.org/index.aspx?queryid = 559 (data for period of the "late 2000s").

MICHAEL HARRINGTON, *THE OTHER AMERICA: POVERTY IN THE UNITED STATES* (1962)

There is a familiar America. It is celebrated in speeches and advertisements on television and in the magazines. It has the highest mass standard of living the world has ever known. . . .

Figure 1.2
Gini Coefficient for Inequality in Wealthy Countries

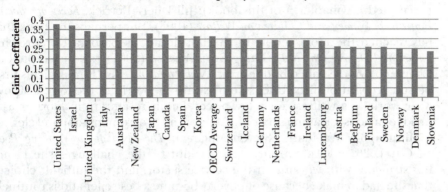

Source: Countries in the OECD with a per capita GDP in 2010 greater than $25,000 (Ireland excluded because it was previously excluded in prior chart because of missing data). Data taken from OECD StatExtracts, *available at* http://stats.oecd.org/index.aspx?queryid=559.

[T]he other America is not impoverished in the same sense as those poor nations where millions cling to hunger as a defense against starvation. This country has escaped such extremes. That does not change the fact that tens of millions of Americans are, at this very moment, maimed in body and spirit, existing at levels beneath those necessary for human decency. . . .

. . . To have one bowl of rice in a society where all other people have half a bowl may well be a sign of achievement and intelligence; it may spur a person to act and to fulfill his human potential. To have five bowls of rice in a society where the majority have a decent balanced diet is a tragedy. . . .

Poverty should be defined in terms of those who are denied the minimal levels of health, housing, food, and education that our present stage of scientific knowledge specifies as necessary for life as it is now lived in the United States.

Poverty should be defined psychologically in terms of those whose place in society is such that they are internal exiles who, almost inevitably, develop attitudes of defeat and pessimism and who are therefore excluded from taking advantage of new opportunities.

Poverty should be defined absolutely, in terms of what man and society could be. As long as America is less than its potential, the nation as a whole is impoverished by that fact. As long as there is the other America, we are, all of us, poorer because of it. . . .

NOTES AND QUESTIONS

1. One of the most significant pieces of writing on American poverty, *The Other America*, was written by Michael Harrington and published in 1964. Six years earlier, John Kenneth Galbraith had published *The Affluent Society*, which focused on the effect of widely shared wealth on American society. Harrington's book served as a reminder of the existence and hardships of the American poor and helped fuel President Johnson's War on Poverty.

2. Has the "familiar America . . . celebrated in speeches and advertisements on television and in the magazines" changed?

3. There have been numerous books portraying the poor since *The Other America. See, e.g.,* David Shipler, *The Working Poor: Invisible in America* (2005) (excerpted in Chapter 5 of this book); Jill Duerr Berrick, *Faces of Poverty: Portraits of Women and Children on Welfare* (1995). But perhaps the book that has reached the most people in the last decade is Barbara Ehrenreich's *Nickel and Dimed: On (Not) Getting By in America* (2001) (also excerpted in Chapter 5). As described by one critic, *Nickel and Dimed* is "Ehrenreich's first-person account of three brief sojourns into the world of the lowest of low-wage work: as a waitress for a low-priced family restaurant in Florida; as a maid for a housecleaning service in Maine; and as a women's-apparel clerk at a Minneapolis Wal-Mart." Steven Malanga, *The Myth of the Working Poor*, 14 City J. 26 (2004). Ehrenreich's account of the challenges she faced, her struggles with working in the service sector, and the difficult choices that she had to make because of poverty became a bestseller and is routinely assigned to undergraduate students across the country.

1. Historical Overview of Poverty and Economic Growth in the United States

There has also been poverty in the United States, but the extent, severity, and nature of poverty in the United States has not been constant. Professor William Quigley writes of the colonial period:

> The poor people in early America were much like the impoverished of today. The indigent included mothers who had been abandoned or widowed, the sick, disabled, elderly, and mentally ill. They were also those considered lazy and criminal. Of those who came voluntarily to America, most were of modest means, if not destitute.

William P. Quigley, *Work or Starve: Regulation of the Poor in Colonial America*, 31 U.S.F. L. Rev. 35, 39 (1996). Unfortunately, data on the prevalence of poverty in America before World War II is limited, in part because there was no official poverty measure until the adoption of Orshansky's measure. That qualifier aside, poverty rates are linked to the overall strength of the economy, which means that in general poverty rates increase as economic output decreases.

Before discussing the post–World War II period, it is worth emphasizing that the subordination of minority groups has been and, arguably, continues to be an integral part of the country's social and economic policy. Chattel slavery, which represented a particularly oppressive form of subordination common in the Americas from before independence until the end of the Civil War, deserves to be distinguished from "ordinary" poverty. For slaves, and later for Blacks living under Jim Crow segregation, paths out of poverty were almost nonexistent, and their secondary status was formally and informally institutionalized across the country. Although the nature and mechanisms of oppression have been different for other racial minorities, the past and present economic hardships faced by many Native Americans, Latin Americans, and Asian Americans also reflect to a considerable degree race-based discrimination in the United States. Subsequent chapters will address some of the particular ways that, historically and presently, race and poverty are linked.

Figure 1.3

The Benefits of Increased Productivity over the Last 35 Years Have Not Gone to the Middle Class (Productivity and Real Median Family Income Growth, 1947-2010)

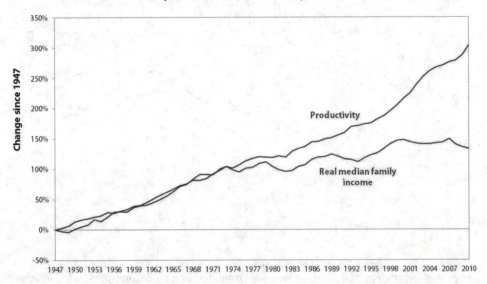

Source: Econ. Policy Inst., *State of Working America*, http://stateofworkingamerica.org/.

Besides slavery and the conquest of the continent from Native Americans, perhaps the most significant event in the economic history of the United States is the Great Depression. Although such an account obscures some internal fluctuations, the Great Depression is ordinarily seen as starting with Black Tuesday, October 29, 1929, and lasting until the buildup associated with the Second World War. By 1933, unemployment in the United States had reached 25 percent.

With poverty and economic hardship affecting such a broad swath of the American public, the politics of the period called for the government to take a larger role in the market. President Franklin D. Roosevelt responded with a smorgasbord of new programs as part of "The New Deal," including numerous social safety net programs that continue to aid the poor today. But, ultimately, it was not until the military buildup and debt spending associated with World War II that the country was able to escape the economic hardships of the 1930s. For those interested in reading more about the politics and economics of the Great Depression, an excellent overview can be found in the first half of David Kennedy's Pulitzer Prize-winning work *Freedom from Fear: The American People in Depression and War, 1929-1945* (1999).

After the war, aided by a lack of international competition as Europe and Asia engaged in a lengthy rebuilding period, America's economy grew steadily. Even with the pressures, at home and abroad, of the wars in Korea and later Vietnam, productivity and median family income grew together. The synchronized growth of productivity and median family income, however, began to fall apart in the 1970s, roughly corresponding to the two oil shocks of that decade. Figure 1.3, from the Economic Policy Institute's State of Working America, shows that this divergence between productivity growth and median family income has continued to the present, with productivity enjoying a much steeper growth over that period than median family income.

Figure 1.4
Income Growth for Families at the 20th, 50th, and 95th Percentiles, 1947-2011

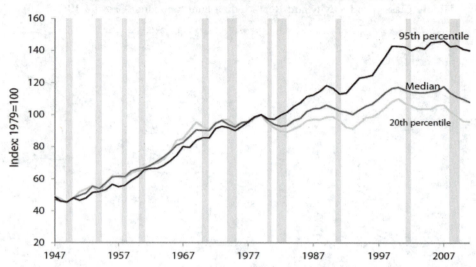

Source: Econ. Policy Inst., *Low-, Middle-, and High-Income Growth, 1947-2011*, http://
stateofworkingamerica.org/charts/real-income-growth-for-different-income-percentiles-diverged-
in-the-1970s-with-real-incomes-flattening-in-the-20th-percentile-and-the-median-and-increasing-
in-the-95th-percentile/.

The benefit from the continued rise in productivity largely flowed to the
wealthiest Americans. As captured in Figure 1.4, while the top 5 percent of
the population saw continued income growth, those in the bottom quartile
did not see similar growth. In fact, their income, adjusted for inflation, was
the same in 2010 as it was in 1973.

Subsequent chapters, particularly Chapters 2-4, will explore in more depth
some of the social and political changes surrounding poverty in the period from
1973 to the present, but it is worth highlighting a few other changes and broader
trends. The rise in median family incomes following World War II reflects, in
part, changes in the demographics of work. Women, long treated as second-class
citizens, both socially and legally, began to enter the workforce in large numbers
in the postwar period. For two-parent households, work outside the home meant
that such households were being supported by two incomes. Data on median
family income by itself masks the shift from one wage earner to families with two
wage earners. The increase in median household income that is seen since 1973
therefore is not a reflection of across-the-board wage increases. During this
period those with more education experienced wage improvements that were
not shared by those whose education ended at high school. Even among college
graduates, general productivity growth outstripped wage growth. But as households moved from single earner to two wage earners, largely through the increasing entrance of women into the formal workforce, the increase in median
household income that switch made possible helped hide the flattening out
of wages.

As can be seen in Figure 1.5, during economic growth years of the Clinton
Administration, from 1992 to 2000, Black and Hispanic populations experienced sharper poverty-rate reductions than Whites. But since then, the gap

Figure 1.5
U.S. Poverty Rates by Race or Ethnicity, 1959-2010

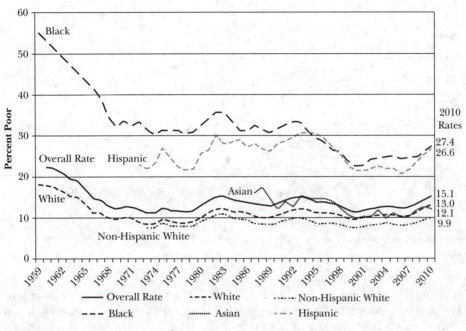

Source: Univ. of Wisconsin Institute for Research on Poverty website, FAQs page, *Who is Poor?*, http://www.irp.wisc.edu/faqs/faq3.htm (based on census data issued Sept. 2011).

has increased, such that more than one-quarter of Blacks and Hispanics lived below the poverty line in 2010.

Poverty is also gendered. As Figure 1.6 shows, poverty rates in families headed by single mothers are significantly higher than those in families with two parents present.

But even Figure 1.6 tells only part of the story because of the ways in which race and gender can combine to create special categories of disadvantage. Pioneering work by scholars, including Kimberlé Crenshaw, Angela Harris, and Dorothy Roberts, emphasizes the importance of looking at "intersectionality," in other words, looking not just at racial or gender comparisons, but race *and* gender categories such as Black woman, Hispanic man, and so on. Figure 1.7 shows how the poverty rates of female-headed households differ by race.

Overall, according to the U.S. Census Bureau, 15.1 percent of the population, or 46.2 million people, lived below the poverty line in 2010. See Figure 1.8.

The figures for 2010 reflect, in part, the impact of the so-called "Great Recession," that began in 2008 and has continued for almost half a decade as of the publication of this textbook. A housing bubble that built up throughout the early part of the new millennium burst in 2008 as defaults and foreclosures spiked following a wave of subprime lending, speculative home buying, and equity stripping by homeowners. Although President Bush and, later, President Obama reacted by injecting billions of dollars into the financial markets to shore up banks at risk of failure, the other stimulus packages passed so far have been unable to lift the economy out of its current stagnation or right the housing market. The poor and the young (including college graduates unable to find work) have been the most impacted by the recession. Anger over the recession

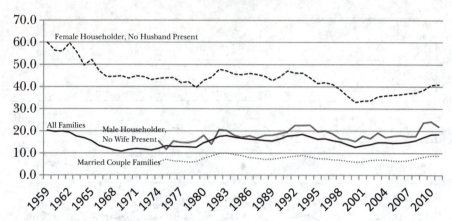

Figure 1.6
Poverty Rates for Families with Children Under 18

Source: U.S. Census Bureau, *Historical Poverty Tables—Families*, *Table 4*, http://www.census
.gov/hhes/www/poverty/data/historical/families.html.

and inequality reached a head in 2011 with the birth of the Occupy Movement.
The newspaper article that follows provides a good window into poverty in the
United States in the midst of the Great Recession.

ALFRED LUBRANO, *CENSUS FIGURES SHOW RECORD NUMBERS OF AMERICANS IN POVERTY*

Philadelphia Inquirer (Sept. 14, 2011)

Stymied by a relentlessly dismal economy, more Americans were in poverty in
2010 than at any other time since poverty levels were first published 52 years ago,
new government figures show.

Overall, 46.2 million Americans lived in poverty in 2010, up from 43.6 million
in 2009. The poverty standard for a family of four is an annual income of $22,113.

The poverty rate last year was 15.1 percent, compared with 14.3 percent in
2009. It was the highest rate in 17 years, according to U.S. Census figures
released Tuesday.

In addition, the report showed, median household income fell 2.3 percent
between 2009 and 2010, from $50,599 to $49,445, adjusted to 2010 dollars.

At the same time, the number of people without health insurance increased
from 49 million to 49.9 million, which the census deemed a statistically insignificant change.

Worse, 6.7 percent of Americans (20.5 million people) were living in deep
poverty in 2010, defined as half the poverty rate or less. That is up from 6.3
percent (19 million people) in 2009.

"That's an all-time high" since records of deep poverty were first calculated in
1975, said Elise Gould, director of health and policy research for the Economic
Policy Institute, a nonprofit, nonpartisan think tank in Washington that studies
low-income people. She spoke Tuesday at a news conference on the census
findings.

Figure 1.7
Poverty Rates of Female-Headed Households by Racial Groups

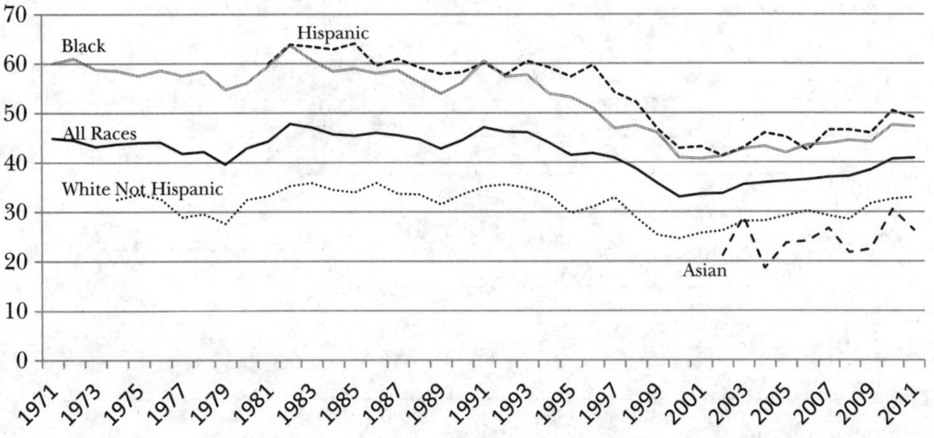

Source: U.S. Census Bureau, *Historical Poverty Tables — Families, Table 4*, http://www.census
.gov/hhes/www/poverty/data/historical/families.html.

"I think it's astonishing to have so many Americans below $11,000 a year," she said.

Even more dire is the increase in the proportion of families living below 125 percent of the poverty line: from 18.7 percent (56.8 million) in 2009 to 19.8 percent (60.4 million) in 2010.

Women fared particularly poorly. Poverty climbed to 14.5 percent for women in 2010 from 13.9 percent in 2009, the highest rate in 17 years. Men's poverty was lower, increasing from 10.5 percent to 11.2 percent.

Census figures that showed that U.S. poverty would have been worse without antipoverty programs such as food stamps, federal earned-income tax credits, and unemployment insurance.

This safety net faces potential cuts and is fodder in presidential-year debates on how much help the government should offer Americans.

The census estimates that tax credits to the poor lifted 5.4 million families out of poverty.

In addition, census figures show that 3.2 million people were kept out of poverty by unemployment insurance.

And, without food stamps, an additional 3.9 million people would be in poverty, 1.7 million of them children, according to Robert Greenstein, president of the Center on Budget and Policy Priorities, a nonprofit, nonpartisan group that studies policies affecting the poor.

These programs are "vital to the social and economic fabric of our country," said Mariana Chilton, professor at Drexel University's School of Public Health and a national expert on hunger. She said that last week's U.S. Department of Agriculture's hunger report showed that hunger levels in 2010 were around the same as 2009, proof that food stamps are helping.

"Ultimately, we need policies that invest in Americans rather than depleting it of jobs, and education, and resources," said Carey Morgan, executive director of the Greater Philadelphia Coalition Against Hunger.

What makes Tuesday's report even more grim is the expectation that no relief is in sight, EPI economist Heidi Shierholz said at the news conference.

Figure 1.8
Number in Poverty and Poverty Rate, 1959-2010

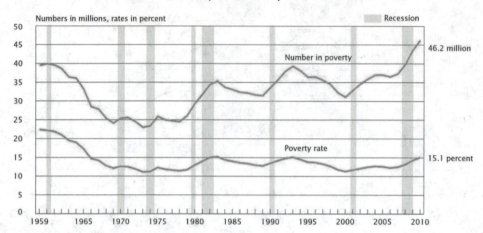

Source: Carmen DeNavas-Walt et al., *U.S. Census Bureau, Income, Poverty, and Health Insurance Coverage in the United States: 2010* (2011), *available at* http://www.census.gov/hhes/www/poverty/data/incpovhlth/2010/figure4.pdf.

"This is just another reminder of the huge impact of the Great Recession on the families of this country," she said. "I'm not surprised to see the deterioration. And unemployment is expected to stay very high for years to come."

That is especially bad news for people like Jennifer Markee, a 29-year-old single woman who lives with her boyfriend and five children in Frankford. She is part of the 9.9 percent of white people in poverty in 2010, up from 9.4 percent in 2009. (Black poverty went from 25.8 to 27.4 percent, while Hispanic poverty increased from 25.3 percent to 26.6 percent.)

Afflicted with epilepsy since birth, Markee's boyfriend cannot keep a job.

Meanwhile, Markee had to put her goal of becoming a dental hygienist on hold to care for a year-old son with severe asthma and a 10-year-son [*sic*] who is autistic.

The family receives welfare, food stamps, and Supplemental Security Income for various disabilities but is still left below the $33,270 poverty line for a family of seven.

"I know people would say, 'Why does she have five kids?'" Markee said. "Well, I don't believe in abortion, and I wasn't planning on having to not work to care for my sick kids. Walk a day in my shoes. Then you'd understand."

NOTES AND QUESTIONS

1. What should the federal and state governments do about the increase in poverty that accompanies recessions? Should the focus be on shoring up the general economy or on providing relief to individuals?
2. Updated statistics and reports on poverty, unemployment, and income can be easily found on a number of different websites, including:
   a. The U.S. Census Bureau's Poverty page, http://www.census.gov/hhes/www/poverty/
   b. The Economic Policy Institute's State of Working America website, http://stateofworkingamerica.org

    c.   The Center on Budget and Policy Priorities' Poverty and Income page, http://www.cbpp.org/research/?fa = topic&id = 36

    d.   The National Center for Children in Poverty, http://www.nccp.org/

    e.   The National Poverty Center, http://www.npc.umich.edu/

3. Poverty does not affect all groups equally. Although it is beyond the scope of this book to fully explore the details of every particular group, not surprisingly poverty tracks economic and social subordination. This point can perhaps best be made by revisiting the data on poverty and select demographic characteristics that have been presented already in this chapter. Unemployment rates in 2010 were fairly similar: 8.7 percent for Whites, 25.6 percent for Blacks, 7.5 percent for Asians, and 12.5 percent for Hispanics. The poverty rate for families with children varies from a low of 6.2 percent for married couples to a rate of 15.8 percent for male-headed households with no wife present to double that, 31.6 percent, for female-headed households with no husband present. (The census bureau reporting does not include information on same-sex couples.) Finally, the poverty rate of those born in the United States was 14.4 percent; the poverty rate of naturalized citizens was lower, 11.3 percent; and the rate for noncitizens was 26.7 percent. Subsequent chapters of this book examine aspects of the history underlying these statistics and the social structure of work and family that contribute to the differences across groups. For now, we want to emphasize the important connection between race, gender, immigration status, and poverty.

2. Are the Poor in the United States Really Poor?

The Heritage Foundation, a conservative think tank, has a different perspective on U.S. poverty. The Heritage Foundation regularly publishes a report emphasizing the relative affluence of the poor in the United States. The 2011 version of that report is below.

ROBERT RECTOR & RACHEL SHEFFIELD, *AIR CONDITIONING, CABLE TV, AND AN XBOX: WHAT IS POVERTY IN THE UNITED STATES TODAY?* (HERITAGE FOUND. BACKGROUNDER NO. 2575, 2011)

Each year for the past two decades, the U.S. Census Bureau has reported that over 30 million Americans were living in "poverty." In recent years, the Census has reported that one in seven Americans are poor. But what does it mean to be "poor" in America? How poor are America's poor?

For most Americans, the word "poverty" suggests destitution: an inability to provide a family with nutritious food, clothing, and reasonable shelter. For example, the Poverty Pulse poll taken by the Catholic Campaign for Human Development asked the general public: "How would you describe being poor in the U.S.?" The overwhelming majority of responses focused on homelessness, hunger or not being able to eat properly, and not being able to meet basic needs. That perception is bolstered by news stories about poverty that routinely feature homelessness and hunger.

Yet if poverty means lacking nutritious food, adequate warm housing, and clothing for a family, relatively few of the more than 30 million people identified as being "in poverty" by the Census Bureau could be characterized as poor. While material hardship definitely exists in the United States, it is restricted in scope and severity. The average poor person, as defined by the government, has a living standard far higher than the public imagines.

As scholar James Q. Wilson has stated, "The poorest Americans today live a better life than all but the richest persons a hundred years ago." In 2005, the typical household defined as poor by the government had a car and air conditioning. For entertainment, the household had two color televisions, cable or satellite TV, a DVD player, and a VCR. If there were children, especially boys, in the home, the family had a game system, such as an Xbox or a PlayStation. In the kitchen, the household had a refrigerator, an oven and stove, and a microwave. Other household conveniences included a clothes washer, clothes dryer, ceiling fans, a cordless phone, and a coffee maker.

The home of the typical poor family was not overcrowded and was in good repair. In fact, the typical poor American had more living space than the average European. The typical poor American family was also able to obtain medical care when needed. By its own report, the typical family was not hungry and had sufficient funds during the past year to meet all essential needs.

Poor families certainly struggle to make ends meet, but in most cases, they are struggling to pay for air conditioning and the cable TV bill as well as to put food on the table. Their living standards are far different from the images of dire deprivation promoted by activists and the mainstream media.

Regrettably, annual Census reports not only exaggerate current poverty, but also suggest that the number of poor persons and their living conditions have remained virtually unchanged for four decades or more. In reality, the living conditions of poor Americans have shown significant improvement over time.

Consumer items that were luxuries or significant purchases for the middle class a few decades ago have become commonplace in poor households. In part, this is caused by a normal downward trend in price following the introduction of a new product. Initially, new products tend to be expensive and available only to the affluent. Over time, prices fall sharply, and the product saturates the entire population, including poor households.

As a rule of thumb, poor households tend to obtain modern conveniences about a dozen years after the middle class. Today, most poor families have conveniences that were unaffordable to the middle class not too long ago.

POVERTY: A RANGE OF LIVING CONDITIONS

However, there is a range of living conditions within the poverty population. The average poor family does not represent every poor family. Although most poor families are well housed, a small minority are homeless.

Fortunately, the number of homeless Americans has not increased during the current recession. Although most poor families are well fed and have a fairly stable food supply, a sizeable minority experiences temporary restraints in food supply at various times during the year. The number of families experiencing such temporary food shortages has increased somewhat during the current economic downturn.

Of course, to the families experiencing these problems, their comparative infrequency is irrelevant. To a family that has lost its home and is living in a homeless shelter, the fact that only 0.5 percent of families shared this experience in 2009 is no comfort. The distress and fear for the future that the family experiences are real and devastating. Public policy must deal with that distress. However, accurate information about the extent and severity of social problems is imperative for the development of effective public policy.

In discussions about poverty, however, misunderstanding and exaggeration are commonplace. Over the long term, exaggeration has the potential to promote a substantial misallocation of limited resources for a government that is facing massive future deficits. In addition, exaggeration and misinformation obscure the nature, extent, and causes of real material deprivation, thereby hampering the development of well-targeted, effective programs to reduce the problem. Poverty is an issue of serious social concern, and accurate information about that problem is always essential in crafting public policy.

Living Conditions of the Poor

Each year, the U.S. Census Bureau releases its annual report on income and poverty. This report, though widely publicized by the press, provides only a bare count of the number of Americans who are allegedly poor. It provides no data on or description of their actual living conditions.

This does not mean that such information is not available. The federal government conducts several other surveys that provide detailed information on the living conditions of the poor. These surveys provide a very different sense of American poverty. They reveal that the actual standard of living among America's poor is far higher than the public imagines and that, in fact, most of the persons whom the government defines as "in poverty" are not poor in any ordinary sense of the term. Regrettably, these detailed surveys are almost never reported in the mainstream press.

One of the most interesting surveys that measures actual living conditions is the Residential Energy Consumption Survey (RECS), which the Department of Energy has conducted regularly since 1980. The RECS survey measures energy consumption and ownership of various conveniences by U.S. households. It also provides information on households at different income levels, including poor households.

Availability of Amenities in Poor Households

This section uses RECS data from 2005, the most recent year for which data are available, to analyze the amenities typically found in poor households. The 2005 RECS data represent the living conditions of the poor before the current recession. Conditions are likely quite similar today.

Because the current recession has increased the number of poor persons in the U.S. since 2005, it might seem likely that poor households would have fewer amenities and conveniences today than in 2005. However, the increase in poverty during the recession is, to a considerable degree, the result of working-class families losing employment. One would not expect these families to dispose of their normal household conveniences in those circumstances. Thus, paradoxically, the increase in the number of working- and middle-class families who have become temporarily poor is likely to increase slightly the share of poor households that own various items. When the present recession ends, the living conditions of the poor are likely to continue to improve as they have in the past.

[Ed. note: The chart below, a combination of two charts in the original version of this report, shows the percentage of all U.S. households and the percentage of poor households that owned or had available various household amenities and conveniences in 2005.] For example, it shows that 84 percent of all U.S. households had air conditioning, 79 percent had cable or satellite television, and 68 percent had a personal computer.

. . . While poor households were slightly less likely to have conveniences than the general population, most poor households had a wide range of amenities. As [the chart] shows, 78 percent of poor households had air conditioning, 64 percent had cable or satellite TV, and 38 percent had a personal computer. . . .

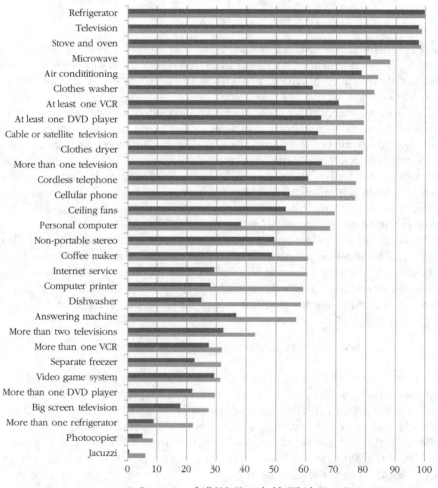

Percentage of Households with Various Household Amenities

■ Percentage of All U.S. Households Which Have Various Amenities
■ Percentage of Poor U.S. Households Which Have Various Amenities

Source: Combination of Charts 1 and 2 in this Rector and Sheffield excerpt.

Improvement in Poor Households over Time. Because the RECS has reported on the living conditions of the poor for several decades, it is a useful tool for charting the improvement in living conditions among the poor over time. . . . Although poor households were less likely to have air conditioning in any given year, the share of households with air conditioning increased steadily for both groups over the 25-year period. By 2005, the two rates converged as air conditioning became nearly universal in U.S. society. . . .

[Similarly, personal] computers were rare in 1990 but spread widely through society over the next 15 years. Computer ownership among the poor increased substantially during the period. In 1990, only 5 percent of poor households had a computer. By 2005, the number had risen to almost 40 percent.

. . . The share of poor households that have a given amenity tends to equal the share of all U.S. households that had the same amenity 10 to 15 years earlier. There seems to be a general lag effect in which poor households acquire a given amenity roughly a dozen years after the general population acquires it.

HOUSING AND POVERTY

Of course, the typical poor family could have a host of modern conveniences and still live in dilapidated, overcrowded housing. However, data from other government surveys show that this is not the case. Poor Americans are well housed and rarely overcrowded. In fact, the houses and apartments of America's poor are quite spacious by international standards. The typical poor American has considerably more living space than does the average European.

Forty-three percent of all poor households own their own homes. The average home owned by persons classified as poor by the Census Bureau is a three-bedroom house with one-and-a-half baths, a garage, and a porch or patio.

Nearly all of the houses and apartments of the poor are in good condition. According to the government's data, only one in 10 has moderate physical problems. Only 2 percent of poor domiciles have "severe" physical problems, the most common of which is sharing a bathroom with another household living in the building.

FOOD SHORTAGES, NUTRITION, AND POVERTY

It is possible that most poor households could be well housed and have many modern conveniences but still face chronic food shortages and undernutrition. Poor families might have microwaves but a limited and sporadic supply of food to put in the microwave. Government surveys show that this is not the case for the overwhelming majority of poor families.

On average, the poor are well nourished. The average consumption of protein, vitamins, and minerals is virtually the same for poor and middle-class children. In most cases, it is well above recommended norms. Poor children actually consume more meat than higher-income children consume, and their protein intake averages 100 percent above recommended levels. In fact, most poor children are super-nourished and grow up to be, on average, one inch taller and 10 pounds heavier than the GIs who stormed the beaches of Normandy in World War II.

However, even though the poor, in general, have an ample food supply, some do suffer from temporary food shortages. For example, a poor household with an adequate long-term food supply might need temporarily to cut back meals, eat cheap food, or go without if cash and food stamps run out at the end of the month.

Still, government data show that most poor households do not suffer even from temporary food shortages. . . . 92.5 percent of poor households assert that they always had "enough food to eat" during the previous four months, although 26 percent of these did not always have the foods that they would have preferred. Some 6 percent of poor households state that they "sometimes" did not have enough food, and 1.5 percent say they "often" did not have enough food.

The bottom line is that, although a small portion of poor households report temporary food shortages, the overwhelming majority of poor households report that they consistently have enough food to eat.

Temporary food shortages have increased during the current recession but still remain atypical among poor households. During 2009, less than one poor household in five experienced even a single instance of "reduced food intake and disrupted eating patterns" due to a lack of financial resources. Strikingly, only 4 percent of poor children experienced even a single instance of "reduced food intake and disrupted eating patterns" due to a lack of financial resources.

FOOD BANKS AND SOUP KITCHENS

TV news stories that inform audiences that one in seven Americans are poor routinely depict "the poor" collecting free groceries at a food pantry or eating meals at a free food kitchen. The audience is led to conclude that gathering free food from a charity pantry or eating free meals at a soup kitchen is the norm for those in poverty.

In fact, while the use of food pantries and emergency kitchens has increased during the current recession, poor families generally did not use charity food pantries or soup kitchens. The U.S. Department of Agriculture (USDA) reports that only one poor family in five took food from a food pantry even once during all of 2009. Far fewer ate at a food kitchen.

In the whole U.S. population, 5.6 million households (4.8 percent of all households) used a food pantry at any point during 2009. Far fewer ate meals at a soup kitchen. Only 625,000 of all U.S. households (0.5 percent) had a member who ate a meal in a free-food kitchen at any time in 2009.

POVERTY AND HOMELESSNESS

The mainstream press and activist groups also frequently conflate poverty with homelessness. News stories about poverty often feature homeless families living "on the street." This depiction is seriously misleading because only a small portion of persons "living in poverty" will become homeless over the course of a year. The overwhelming majority of the poor reside throughout the year in non-crowded housing that is in good repair.

The 2009 *Annual Homeless Assessment Report* published by the U.S. Department of Housing and Urban Development (HUD) states that on a given night in 2009, some 643,000 persons in the U.S. were homeless (without permanent domicile). This means that at any given time, one out of 470 persons in the general population or one out of 70 persons with incomes below the poverty level was homeless.

Moreover, two-thirds of these 643,000 homeless persons were residing in emergency shelters or transitional housing. Only 240,000 were without shelter. These "unsheltered" individuals were "on the street," meaning that they were living in cars, abandoned buildings, alleyways, or parks. At any point in 2009, roughly one person out of 1,250 in the general population or one out of 180 poor persons was homeless in the literal sense of being on the street and without shelter.

Homelessness is usually a transitional condition. Individuals typically lose housing, reside in an emergency shelter for a few weeks or months, and then reenter permanent housing. The transitional nature of homelessness means that many more people become temporarily homeless over the course of a year than are homeless at any single point in time.

Thus, HUD reports that 1.56 million persons resided in an emergency shelter or transitional housing at least one night during 2009. The year-round total of individuals who ever stayed in a shelter or transitional housing was nearly four times larger than the 403,000 who resided in such facilities on an average night.

Based on the year-round data on shelter use, roughly one person in 195 in the general population resided in an emergency shelter or transitional housing for at least one night during a full 12-month period. Roughly one in 25 poor persons (4 percent of all poor persons) resided in an emergency shelter or transitional housing for at least one night during the full year.

Despite news stories that assert that the current recession has caused a great increase in homelessness, homeless shelter use, in general, has not increased during the current economic downturn. In addition, shelters are not overcrowded. On a typical night, shelters have an average vacancy rate of 10 percent. . . .

Although news stories often suggest that poverty and homelessness are similar, this is inaccurate. In reality, the gap between the living conditions of a homeless person and the typical poor household is proportionately as great as the gap between the poor household and a middle-class family in the suburbs.

ESSENTIAL NEEDS

Although the public equates poverty with physical deprivation, the overwhelming majority of poor households do not experience any form of physical deprivation. Some 70 percent of poor households report that during the course of the past year, they were able to meet "all essential expenses," including mortgage, rent, utility bills, and important medical care.

It is widely supposed that the poor are unable to obtain medical care, but in reality, only 13 percent of poor households report that a family member needed to go to a doctor or hospital at some point in the prior year but was unable because the family could not afford the cost.

PUBLIC UNDERSTANDING OF POVERTY

In 2005, the typical poor household, as defined by the government, had air conditioning and a car. For entertainment, the household had two color televisions, cable or satellite TV, a DVD player, and a VCR. In the kitchen, it had a refrigerator, an oven and stove, and a microwave. Other household conveniences included a clothes washer, clothes dryer, ceiling fans, a cordless phone, and a coffee maker. The family was able to obtain medical care when needed. Their home was not overcrowded and was in good repair. By its own report, the family was not hungry and had sufficient funds during the past year to meet all essential needs.

The overwhelming majority of the public do not regard a family living in these conditions as poor. For example, a poll conducted in June 2009 asked a nationally representative sample of the public whether they agreed or disagreed with the following statement: "A family in the U.S. that has a decent, un-crowded house or apartment to live in, ample food to eat, access to medical care, a car, cable television, air conditioning and a microwave at home should not be considered poor."

A full 80 percent of Republicans and 77 percent of Democrats agreed that a family living in those living conditions should not be considered poor.

NOTES AND QUESTIONS

1. What aspects of this report did you most agree with and why? Do you think Rector and Sheffield overstate their case? Where? Did you find this report or aspects of this report convincing? Does government data support or conflict with this report?
2. Is possession of consumer goods or household amenities a good proxy for poverty or wealth?
3. Do you think progressive policy institutions do a better or worse job advocating their positions than the Heritage Foundation? What explains any differences in effectiveness and messaging?
4. For more on the role of conservative think tanks in shaping national policy, see Jean Stefancic & Richard Delgado, *No Mercy: How Conservative Think Tanks and Foundations Changed America's Social Agenda* 82-95 (1996).

C. ECONOMIC MOBILITY

Just as poverty and inequality are related but not equivalent, the same is true of poverty and economic mobility. In the selection that follows, Professor Amy Wax presents some of the central debates in poverty law: Do the poor deserve their poverty? Is poverty mainly the result of individual decisions or structural causes? Wax argues that rather than focusing on the poverty rate at a given moment in time, the focus should include the degree of economic mobility in a society and the way in which society rewards some traits but not others.

AMY L. WAX, *MUSICAL CHAIRS AND TALL BUILDINGS: TEACHING POVERTY LAW IN THE 21ST CENTURY*

34 Fordham Urb. L.J. 1363 (2007)

. . . Poverty law is about economic disadvantage. But, as fifty years of academic research and practical politics have revealed, it is difficult to cabin that subject. The problem is a lot more complicated than we thought, and an inquiry into poverty cannot avoid confronting social disadvantage and difference in all its aspects. It is difficult to do justice to that subject without discussing economic and social disparities in general. Indeed, one could argue that the proper subject of a social welfare law and policy course is inequality. . . .

James Galbraith's *Created Unequal* . . . draws a contrast between the shape of the economy as a whole (analogous to a skyscraper or tall building with a set number of floors of fixed size) and the position, or level, occupied by specific individuals within the building (analogous to the floor on which each person resides). Galbraith analogizes the building to the economy as a whole, with particular emphasis on the structure of labor markets. He writes, "the wage structure, that is, the shape of the building and the number of spaces available on each floor, is a built structure." Galbraith also advances a particular theory of the origins of this structure. In his view, "it is a product of history, built up by the rules, institutions, and political forces that influence how the economy works." But he acknowledges that not all embrace this account. Some neoclassical economists believe that labor markets are largely independent of politics and institutional priorities. Rather, competitive free market forces dominate. Supply and demand for goods and services, levels of technological development, and the availability of wealth for investment determine the quality and quantity of jobs on offer and fix the levels of compensation. From this perspective, these factors are fairly autonomous within competitive economies and subject to only limited effective manipulation.

Leaving aside the question of whether the structure of the system is politically "constructed" or chiefly the product of difficult-to-manipulate free-market forces, the main point is that, for particular persons living within the system, the overall shape of the building, in Galbraith's metaphor, is a given. It is independent of the positions particular individuals come to occupy. In Galbraith's example, residents cannot directly control this structure or the number and position of places it provides. Rather, they take the building as they find it. Where individuals end up within the structure, however, is another matter. . . . [I]t is largely a function of how they perform within the constraints established by space limits and the rules for shuttling between floors. In other words, "the demographic composition of the distribution of people across the floors . . . is a matter of [people's] individual characteristics and of how those characteristics are treated."

Exploring the relationship between external forces and performance . . . gives rise to a host of difficult questions. What is the nature of the characteristics that lead to victory . . . or high placement (in Galbraith's metaphor) and how do people acquire them? . . . [F]inal outcomes rest on performance. But what determines performance? . . .

. . . Galbraith's tall building can be regarded as a meritocracy of sorts. His metaphor gives rise to a similar set of questions. How much of a person's placement is due to her own choices and how much to forces over which she exerts little or no control? What is the role of endowments like talent, ability, temperament, or upbringing? Can the crucial choices be viewed as closely conditioned or constrained by these givens, or do people retain a meaningful amount of freedom and discretion to determine their own fate? Finally—and perhaps most importantly—why does the system assign people who possess certain attributes or display certain behaviors a position on particular floors, whether high or low? What gives rise to the rules for transfer between floors? Why does society elevate some and demote others?

These types of questions — and the distinctions that help elucidate them — are crucial to understanding poverty and economic inequality in the United States and deciding what to do about it. One persistent fault line in discussions of disadvantage in America is the distinction between the deserving and the undeserving poor. As Martin Gilens has documented, voter surveys, focus groups, and data collected by social psychologists reveal that these categories are firmly entrenched in political discourse and strongly influence citizens' views on welfare policy and economic redistribution. The differential treatment of the deserving and undeserving in turn implicates the distinction between impersonal social forces and performance. Is deprivation due to chance — that is, factors or events beyond people's control? Or is it due to choice — that is, a person's own decisions and behavior? These questions have powerful resonance. Most people stand ready to assist the disadvantaged through centralized public welfare programs only if the recipients are needy through no fault of their own. In judging whether people meet this standard, voters apply the expectation that able-bodied persons will make reasonable good faith efforts to achieve economic self-sufficiency. Persons who fall short of this expectation are not generally regarded as entitled to public assistance.

. . . [Returning to Galbraith's tall-building metaphor, is] the structure of our building really fixed, or is there some elasticity? Can we reconfigure the building — perhaps by providing more space at higher levels? . . . The practical aspect of these inquiries cannot be separated from normative questions about why the current structure exists. Once again, much depends on whether, as Galbraith suggests, the building's configuration is a product of historic accident, political interests, and institutional choices, or whether it is the outgrowth of impersonal market forces. But whether it is open to us to radically transform the status quo does not end the inquiry. We can ask, for example, why our system rewards particular attributes — such as talent — and what the consequences might be if the reward structure were altered. Thus even assuming we know how to change the structure, the question is whether we should and what price will be paid if we do. For example, if talent and hard work are rewarded because they create wealth and lead to the efficient satisfaction of human wants, then muting those rewards might undermine some of these goods. But if talent is rewarded because it serves the powers that be, revising the rules of compensation might prove less costly for overall well-being. More generally, any proposal for change begs the question of whether the proposed transformation will generate unintended and undesirable consequences. The question comes down to what works: assuming we want to do so, can government action improve the economic structure and/or the fate of individuals within it?

* * *

In the selection that follows, Jared Bernstein explores intragenerational and intergenerational economic mobility. Bernstein questions the American belief that hard work is a guaranteed route from poverty to the American dream.

JARED BERNSTEIN, *ECONOMIC MOBILITY IN THE UNITED STATES: HOW MUCH IS THERE AND WHY DOES IT MATTER?*, IN *ENDING POVERTY IN AMERICA: HOW TO RESTORE THE AMERICAN DREAM* (JOHN EDWARDS ET AL. EDS., 2007)

The historically high degree of income or wealth concentration in America in recent years has been amply documented. The Congressional Budget Office (CBO) produces especially comprehensive household data by income class, including the value of capital gains, an important dimension of inequality omitted from census analysis. These data . . . show that between the business-cycle peaks of 1979 and 2000, the real income of the bottom fifth of households grew 6 percent, that of the middle fifth grew 12 percent, and that of the top fifth grew 70 percent. The household income of the top 1 percent grew 184 percent over these years.

Such data compare two snapshots of the income distribution at two points in time. These kinds of comparisons inform us of the changes in real income levels for different income classes of households. They tell us, for example, how low-income households have fared relative to middle- and higher-income households; they reveal how economic growth was distributed among different income groups. They do not, however, compare the income trajectories of the same people or families over time.

To take another common example, living-standard analysts often examine the inflation-adjusted level of the median income at two points in time and discuss these results in terms of how "middle-income families" are faring. These are clearly not, however, the same families. That is, the family in the middle of the income scale today may be at the 70th percentile 10 years later. . . .

STUDYING INCOME MOBILITY

Why is the distinction between snapshots and longitudinal analysis important? One principal reason has to do with how the rate of mobility has changed over time. Here the critical question is: has the rate of economic mobility increased enough to offset the increase in inequality? The answer is "no," but before I examine the evidence, it will be helpful to "unpack" this pointed, if seemingly obscure, question.

Imagine a hotel whose 10 floors improve in quality as you go up the elevator. The poor reside on the bottom floor, the wealthy in the penthouse. The same families live in this hotel, and over time some move up, others move down, and others stay put.

Now imagine that over the years the hotel changes in the following manner. There are still 10 floors, but the quality of life in the penthouse has soared, while that of the bottom floors is largely unchanged. The distance between the floors, in terms of living standards, has greatly expanded. Compared with earlier years, those in the middle and lower floors are much further behind top-floor residents than used to be the case.

Comparing the two snapshots of the old more equal hotel and the newer one would reveal this increase in inequality. . . . But suppose that the likelihood of moving up the floors had increased. That is, suppose that a family from the bottom floor now had a much better chance of making it into the penthouse. This change would represent an increase in mobility, and if it were large enough, it could potentially offset the increase in inequality. True, the floors are further apart in terms of living standards, and we might bemoan this increase in inequality, but if the rate of mobility accelerated enough to give folks a better chance of climbing the ladder, that might mitigate our concern.

As noted, the research on this question has been quite clear on this point: the rate of mobility had not increased. A number of studies suggest that the rate has decreased, though others maintain that it remains essentially unchanged. In other words, people are much further from each other across the economic spectrum and are no more likely to span the increased distances.

Thus far, my discussion has focused on intragenerational mobility: the economic mobility of families as they age. If families move between the floors of the hotels a lot over the span of their lifetimes, this would imply a high level of intragenerational mobility. Conversely, if families tend to stay on or near the floor on which they started, this implies less such mobility.

A related part of the analysis examines the extent to which children's fortunes differ from that of their parents. This refers to the role of intergenerational mobility: the degree to which a child's position in the economy is determined by that of his or her parents. Surely, if class barriers are such that children's economic fates are largely determined by their family's position in the income scale, then the likelihood that, for example, a poor child will be a middle-class adult is diminished.

In fact, there are significant positive correlations between parents and their children, implying that income mobility is at least somewhat restricted because one generation's position in the income scale is partially dependent on its parents' position. One recent study finds the correlation between parents and children to be 0.6. One way to view the significance of this finding is to note that it implies that it would take a poor family of four with two children approximately 9 to 10 generations — over 200 years — to achieve the income of the middle-income four-person family. Were that correlation only half that size, meaning that income differences were half as persistent across generations, it would take 4 to 5 generations for the poor family to catch up.

These two concepts — intra- and intergenerational mobility — both shed light on the fluidity, or lack thereof, of class in America. The evidence presented here shows some degree of mobility: families do change hotel floors, and the correlation between parents and children is far from one. Yet two important points emerge. First, there is not as much mobility as American mythology might lead one to expect. Most families end up at or near the same relative income position in which they start, and, as noted, when it come to parent/child income correlations, the apple does not fall very far from the tree. Second, the rate of mobility has not increased and may have fallen. The United States is a more unequal society, yet Americans have not become more mobile.

INTRAGENERATIONAL FAMILY INCOME MOBILITY

[The table below] presents three "transition matrices" for three time periods, essentially the 1970s, 1980s, and 1990s. Across the columns for each row in the

Family Income Mobility over Three Decades

Quintile in 1969	Quintile in 1979				
	First	Second	Third	Fourth	Fifth
First	**49.4**	24.5	13.8	9.1	3.3
Second	23.2	**27.8**	25.2	16.2	7.7
Third	10.2	23.4	**24.8**	23	18.7
Fourth	9.9	15	24.1	**27.4**	23.7
Fifth	5	9	13.2	23.7	**49.1**

Quintile in 1979	Quintile in 1989				
	First	Second	Third	Fourth	Fifth
First	**50.4**	24.1	15	7.4	3.2
Second	21.3	**31.5**	23.8	15.8	7.6
Third	12.1	23.3	**25**	24.6	15
Fourth	6.8	16.1	24.3	**27.6**	25.3
Fifth	4.2	5.4	13.4	26.1	**50.9**

Quintile in 1989	Quintile in 1998				
	First	Second	Third	Fourth	Fifth
First	**53.3**	23.6	12.4	6.4	4.3
Second	25.7	**36.3**	22.6	11	4.3
Third	10.9	20.7	**28.3**	27.5	12.6
Fourth	6.5	12.9	23.7	**31.1**	25.8
Fifth	3	5.7	14.9	23.2	**53.2**

Source: Katherine Bradbury & Jane Katz, "Women's Labor Market Involvement and Family Income Mobility When Marriages End," *Federal Reserve Bank of Boston New England Economic Review* Q4 (2002).

table, the numbers reveal the percentage of persons who either stayed in the same fifth or moved to a higher or lower one. For example, the first entry in the top panel shows that just under half—49.4 percent—of families in the bottom fifth in 1969 were also in the bottom fifth in 1979. The family income data are adjusted for family size. (Size adjustments divide family income by the poverty threshold for families of the relevant size, and then these values are ranked by the bottom fifth.) About the same share—49.1 percent—started and ended the 1970s in the richest fifth. The percentages of "stayers" (those who did not move out of the fifth they started in) are shown in bold.

Note that large transitions are uncommon. In each of the periods covered, the share of families moving from the poorest to the richest fifth never exceeds 4.3 percent. Conversely, the share moving from the top fifth to the bottom fifth never exceeds 5 percent. Those transitions that do occur are most likely to be a move up or down to the neighboring fifth. For example, in both the 1970s and the 1980s about 25 percent began and remained in the middle fifth. But close to 50 percent of those who started in the middle ended up in either the second or fourth quintile (for example, summing the relevant percentages in the 1980s table gives 47.9 percent—23.3 percent plus 24.6 percent).

Comparing mobility rates across the decades answers the question of how these rates have changed over time. In the 1990s the entries on the diagonal, that is, the "stayers," are larger than in either of the other two decades. For example, 36.3 percent started and ended in the second fifth in the 1990s, compared with 27.8 percent in the 1970s and 31.5 percent in the 1980s. In terms of upward mobility, whereas 12.4 percent move from the poorest fifth to the fourth or fifth highest in the 1970s, in the 1980s and 1990s that share was 10.6 percent and 10.7 percent. Finally, the share of families staying in the top fifth grew consistently over the decade, implying diminished mobility over time.

Combining all family types masks important differences in mobility by race. Economist Tom Hertz analyzes the extent of upward and downward mobility by white and African American families. The data . . . reveal far less upward mobility—and more downward mobility—among black families relative to whites. The data give the percentage of families by race who moved between the bottom and top 25 percent of the income scale between 1968 and 1998 (income data are again adjusted for family size). The share of upwardly mobile families—those moving from the bottom quartile to the top—was 7.3 percent, slightly lower than the share moving the other direction (9.2 percent). But this overall measure is quite different by race. For white families, 10.2 percent were upwardly mobile, compared with 4.2 percent for black families, a statistically significant difference. Note also that far more black families than whites were likely to fall from the top 25 percent to the bottom quartile, 18.5 percent compared with 9 percent (though given the small sample size of black families in the top 25 percent, the difference does not reach statistical significance). . . .

These mobility studies show that while some degree of family income mobility certainly exists in America, it has not accelerated in such a way as to offset the increase in income inequality. . . . In addition what mobility does exist varies significantly by race, as white families are more than twice as likely to be upwardly mobile.

INTERGENERATIONAL MOBILITY

This section looks at just how far the apple falls from the tree by tracking the correlations between parents' economic status and that of their children. If one's position in the earnings, income, or wealth distribution is largely a function of birth, this implies a more rigid society where even those with prodigious talents will be held back by entrenched class barriers. Conversely, a society with a high level of intergenerational mobility, implying little correlation between parents' position and that of their children, is one with more fluidity between classes. There is solid evidence of considerable persistence, and some evidence that these correlations have grown larger over time.

What drives these correlations? Certainly unequal educational opportunities and historical discrimination play a role. In fact, the transmission of these variables across generations appears to be correlated as well, such that opportunities for advancement are limited for those with fewer economic resources. For example, children from wealthy families have much greater access to top-tier universities than children from low-income families, even once we control for innate skills. Though the data on the persistence of wealth across generations are less rich, such data also suggest that this is an important channel that restricts the mobility of the "have-nots."

Economists measure the extent of intergenerational mobility by a statistic called the intergenerational elasticity (which is similar to a correlation) in income, earnings, or wealth between parents and children. For example, one recent study finds the correlation between the incomes of parents and those of their sons and daughters to be 0.49 and 0.46, respectively. That is, a 1 percent increase in parents' income translates into a .5 percent increase in the child's income.

Is this a high, medium, or low level of income persistence? Certainly a correlation of about half belies any notion of a totally fluid society with no class barriers. Yet without various benchmarks against which to judge these correlations, it is difficult to know what to make of their magnitude. . . .

. . . Sons of low-earning [10th percentile] fathers have slightly less than a 60 percent chance of reaching about the 20th percentile by adulthood, about a 20 percent chance of surpassing the median, and a very slight chance — 4.5 percent — of ending up above the 80th percentile. A son whose father earns about $16,000 a year has only a 5 percent chance of earning over $55,000 per year.

How stable are these values over time? Has the degree of mobility between generations increased or fallen in recent years?

One long-term analysis that tracked the extent of intergenerational mobility since 1940 found that, in fact, the rate of mobility has declined significantly in recent decades. . . . [T]he correlation between the earnings of sons and the income of their families was flat or falling from 1950 to 1980 and then climbed through 2000. This implies a trend toward diminished mobility (the relationship between mobility and the intergenerational correlation is inverse — higher correlations mean greater income persistence across generations and thus less mobility). Note that this trend occurred over the very post-1970s period when cross-sectional inequality was increasing. Thus, instead of faster mobility that might have offset the rise in inequality, the opposite trend occurred. . . .

INTERGENERATIONAL MOBILITY FROM AN INTERNATIONAL PERSPECTIVE

A deeply embedded piece of U.S. social mythology is the Horatio Alger story: the notion that anyone who is willing and able can "pull themselves up by their bootstraps" and can achieve significant upward mobility. What is more, conventional wisdom holds that there are many more Algers in the United States than in Europe or Scandinavia. The idea behind such thinking is that there is a trade-off between unregulated markets and mobility. Since our economic model hews much more closely to the fundamentals of market capitalism — lower tax base, fewer regulations, less union coverage, no universal health care, and a much less comprehensive social contract — there should be greater mobility here.

However, as shown in [the chart below], this is not the case, because the correlations between fathers' and sons' earnings are lower in all the comparison countries except the United Kingdom. . . .

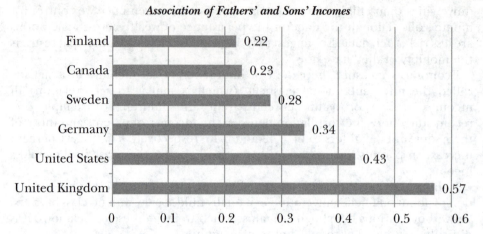

Association of Fathers' and Sons' Incomes

Source: Gary Solon, *Cross-Country Differences in Intergenerational Earnings Mobility*, 16(3) J. Econ. Perspectives 59 (2002). Reprinted with permission of the author and the American Economic Association.

CONCLUSION

It is widely acknowledged that income inequality has increased sharply over time, because income growth at the top of the income scale has far surpassed that of middle- and low-income families. That analysis, however, depended on snapshots of the U.S. income distribution in different periods. These developments have legitimately prompted concern among those of us concerned about diminished equity in the U.S. economy. Yet a counterargument maintains that while the United States may be more unequal "in the cross section," Americans are more likely to vault across the income distribution, offsetting this increased inequality.

The data presented [here] belie this claim. Some of the findings . . . show that Americans have become less mobile over time; others suggest little change. None shows greater mobility.

* * *

Founded and supported by a coalition of conservative and progressive think tanks—The American Enterprise Institute, The Brookings Institution, The Heritage Foundation, The New America Foundation, and The Urban Institute—the Economic Mobility Project exemplifies the possibility that work targeting issues of mobility might be more politically feasible than efforts billed as antipoverty work. Below is a report from the Project on the lack of economic mobility in the United States.

BHASHKAR MAZUMDER, THE PEW CHARITABLE TRUSTS, ECON. MOBILITY PROJECT, *UPWARD INTERGENERATIONAL ECONOMIC MOBILITY IN THE UNITED STATES* (2008)

In an era of rising income inequality, understanding the extent of economic mobility from one generation to the next in America has never been more important. Only if there is considerable opportunity for children from disadvantaged backgrounds to move beyond their parents' place in the income distribution may economic inequality be viewed as tolerable. . . . [Findings:]

The vast majority of individuals, 71 percent, whose parents were in the bottom half of the income distribution actually improved their rankings relative to their parents. However, the amount of their movement was not large.

- Only about 45 percent of those who started in the bottom half moved up the income distribution by more than 20 percentiles relative to their parents' ranking.
- Many of those who did manage to exceed their parents' income started near the very bottom, where exceeding one's parents is not a very steep hurdle. As a result, only 38 percent of individuals who started in the bottom half of the income distribution moved to the top half of the distribution as adults.

Men experience sharply higher rates of upward economic mobility than women.

- While 41 percent of women who start in the bottom income quintile remain there, just 27 percent of men do.
- Only 38 percent of women who start in the bottom half of the income distribution surpass their parents by at least 20 percentiles, compared to 51 percent of men.
- Further, women born to parents in all 5 quintiles are significantly more likely to fall down to the bottom quintile than men. For example, women born to parents in the fourth and top quintiles are more than twice as likely as men to fall to the bottom quintile.

Blacks experience dramatically less upward economic mobility than whites.

- Forty-four percent of blacks will remain in the bottom income quintile in adulthood compared with just 25 percent of whites.
- Although the vast majority of blacks in the bottom half of the income distribution will exceed their parents' place in the distribution, the extent of their movement is markedly lower than that of whites.
- Only about 35 percent of blacks who start in the bottom half of the income distribution will increase their relative position by 20 percentiles compared to nearly 50 percent of whites.

Rates of upward economic mobility are highest for white men, followed by white women, black men and, finally, black women.

- The economic mobility gender gap is more pronounced among whites and the economic mobility racial gap is more pronounced among men.

Measures of human capital during adolescence, particularly test scores, could explain the entire black-white upward economic mobility gap.

- Individuals, both black and white, with higher academic test scores are more likely to move up and out of the bottom quintile. Both black and white children born in the bottom quintile with median academic test scores are twice as likely to move up and out of the bottom quintile than if they had scores in the lowest percentile of the test score distribution.

- Some other factors, such as self-esteem and health, also appear to be important in determining upward economic mobility, but they account for little of the racial gap in economic mobility.
- The racial gap in economic mobility out of the bottom quintile remains even when controlling for single- or two-parent families. . . .

One of the fundamental ways to evaluate the fairness of a society is by measuring the degree to which there is equality of opportunity. Do children who are born into poorer families have the same chances to achieve economic success as those from more advantaged backgrounds? One useful way to answer this question is by measuring the rate at which families change their *relative* standing in the income distribution over successive generations. A large and growing body of research has developed measures of relative intergenerational economic mobility and used these measures to characterize the degree of equality of opportunity. In recent years, these studies have begun to receive considerable attention from the media as well as the policy-making community. A consensus view has emerged suggesting that the United States exhibits much less intergenerational economic mobility than previously thought and appears to be less economically mobile than are many other industrialized countries.

NOTES AND QUESTIONS

1. Is it surprising to you to read that economic mobility is lower in the United States than in many other developed countries? Why or why not?
2. Does work on economic mobility offer more possibilities for conservatives and progressives to come to political agreement than antipoverty efforts? Why or why not?

D. LIVING WITH POVERTY AND LAW

So far, we have been focusing on what poverty is and how it is measured. We end this chapter by turning to poverty law, or more specifically, law as it is experienced by the poor. In the excerpt that follows, Professor Austin Sarat describes the pervasiveness of law in the lives of poor people.

AUSTIN SARAT, ". . . THE LAW IS ALL OVER": POWER, RESISTANCE AND THE LEGAL CONSCIOUSNESS OF THE WELFARE POOR
2 Yale J.L. & Human. 343 (1990)

"For me the law is all over. I am caught, you know; there is always some rule that I'm supposed to follow, some rule I don't even know about that they say. It's just different and you can't really understand." These words were spoken by Spencer, a thirty-five-year-old man on public assistance, whom I first encountered in the waiting room of a legal services office. I introduced myself and told him that I was interested in talking to him about law and finding out why he was using legal services; I asked if he would be willing to talk with me and allow me to be present when he met with his lawyer. While he seemed, at first, both puzzled and amused that I had, as he put it, "nothing more important to do," he agreed to both of my requests.

As my research unfolded, what Spencer said in our first conversation, ". . . the law is all over," served as a reference point for understanding the meaning and significance of law in the lives of the welfare poor. His words helped me interpret how people on welfare think about law and use legal ideas as well as how they respond to problems with the welfare bureaucracy. . . . I present that interpretation and describe what I call the legal consciousness of power and domination, in which the keynote is enclosure and dependency, and a consciousness of resistance, in which welfare recipients assert themselves and demand recognition of their personal identities and their human needs.

The legal consciousness of the welfare poor is . . . substantially different from other groups in society for whom law is a less immediate and visible presence. Law is, for people on welfare, repeatedly encountered in the most ordinary transactions and events of their lives. Legal rules and practices are implicated in determining whether and how welfare recipients will be able to meet some of their most pressing needs. Law is immediate and powerful because being on welfare means having a significant part of one's life organized by a regime of legal rules invoked by officials to claim jurisdiction over choices and decisions which those not on welfare would regard as personal and private. Thus, Spencer's sense that ". . . the law is all over" is an introduction to the pervasiveness and obtrusiveness of legal rules and practices in the lives of people on welfare.

For Spencer and other welfare recipients law is not a distant abstraction; it is a web-like enclosure in which they are "caught." It is a space which is not their own and which allows them only a "tactical" presence. It is both a metaphorical trap and a material force. Like the man from the country in Franz Kafka's parable "Before the Law," law is, for Spencer and others on welfare, an irresistible and inescapable presence. For them, however, it is an already entered space, an enclosure seen from the inside, an enclosure whose imperative power, whose "supposed to(s)," is clothed in the categories and abstractions of rules.

The rules Spencer confronts are a series of "they say(s)." The rules speak, but what Spencer hears is the embodied voice of law's bureaucratic guardians. For him, as for Kafka's character, the power of legal rules and practices is derived, at least in part, from the incomplete, yet authoritative, representation of law's categories and abstractions by officials authorized to say what the law is. Legal rules and practices are all around, immediately and visibly present; yet the law itself remains a shadowy presence.

The law that the welfare poor confront is neither a law of reason and justification nor of sacred texts and shared normative commitments. Spencer and others like him are not invited to participate in the interpretation of those texts, and they are included in neither the official explication of welfare law nor the construction of meaningful accounts of the legal practices they regularly encounter. They are "caught" inside law's rules, but are, at the same time, excluded from its interpretive community. In all of their dealings with welfare they act on "a terrain imposed . . . and organized by the law of foreign power." Their law is a law of power and of compulsion, and their experience of being inside, but yet excluded, is one indication of the way that power is exercised over the welfare poor.

While the welfare poor are surrounded and entrapped by legal rules as well as by officials and institutions which claim authority to say what the law is and what the rules mean, they are not, like the man from the country, transfixed or paralyzed. . . . [T]he welfare poor subscribe to neither an allegedly hegemonic "myth of rights" nor to a picture of law as autonomous, apolitical, objective, neutral and disinterested. They are not the passive recipients of an ideology encoded in doctrine which is allegedly taken seriously among legal elites. Power and domination are thus only part of the story of the legal consciousness of the welfare poor. Because welfare recipients are trapped or "caught," because they are involved in an ongoing series of transactions with officials visibly engaged in the interpretation and use of rules, the welfare poor have access to inside knowledge not generally available to those whose contacts with law are more episodic or for whom law is less visible. This inside knowledge means, as we will see, that they have few illusions about what law is or what it can do. They are, as a result, able, when the need arises, to respond strategically, to maneuver and to resist the "they say(s)" and "supposed to(s)" of the welfare bureaucracy.

Resistance exists side-by-side with power and domination. Thus, when people like Spencer seek legal assistance or go to legal services they fight the welfare bureaucracy and its "legal order" even as they submit themselves to another of law's domains. They use legal ideas to interpret and make sense of their relationship to the welfare bureaucracy even as they refine those ideas by making claims the meaning and moral content of which are often at variance with dominant understandings. They resist those understandings by "vigilantly making use of the cracks that particular conjunctions open in . . . proprietary powers. . . ." Yet their use of legal services and legal ideas further inscribes them in the world of state law and helps to reproduce official understandings of law and justice. It is, however, always an incomplete inscription.

Spencer and others like him stand in a contradictory, paradoxical and ambivalent relationship to legal authority, mobilizing one set of legal officials against another, moving from one arena of rules to another, seeking recognition and help while being very dubious about the treatment they receive and seeking to establish spaces for, or moments of, resistance. While they seek legal redress for wrongs done in the name of law, they contest what are sometimes said to be key symbols of law and legal authority, in particular the association of law with neutrality, disinterestedness, rule determinacy and rights.

The dynamic of power and resistance that I observed is, of course, played out on the "foreign" terrain of the lawyer's office, and the welfare poor seem very conscious of the fact that neither here nor in their dealings with the welfare bureaucracy are they able to find a "place that can be delineated as . . . [their] own and serves as a base from which relations of exteriority . . . can be managed." The recognition that ". . . the law is all over" expresses, in spatial terms, the experience of power and domination; resistance involves spaces of personal identity and integrity.

Power and domination are, however, represented in the legal consciousness of the welfare poor in temporal as well as spatial terms; thus, the people I studied often spoke of an interminable waiting that they said marks the welfare experience. In that waiting they are frozen in time as if time itself were frozen; power defines whose time is valued and whose time is valueless. For the welfare poor resistance involves a use of time against space, an insistence on the immediacy of their material needs, an attempt to substitute human for bureaucratic time. Thus metaphors of space and time become important signs of the way the welfare poor understand power and resistance as well as a currency for tactical maneuvers within a "world bewitched by the . . . powers of the Other."

To this point I have talked about the welfare poor as if they were a homogeneous group whose legal consciousness and relationship to power and resistance were uniform. There is, however, considerably more fragmentation and division among people on welfare than might be suggested by my repeated references to the welfare poor. As Spencer put it, "[A]ll welfare recipients aren't the same." He reminded me that the welfare poor are not a natural social group. They neither share a distinctive background nor common ties of sentiment; they vary greatly in their life situations, their ability to survive without public assistance and their disposition to do so.

Spencer insisted that many welfare recipients have lives not unlike my own only without the material comfort which a regular job would provide, that many have stable ties to their community and its major social institutions. They are often regular churchgoers, who maintain close relationships with their extended families. They invest heavily in the effort to attain symbols of respectability even as they confront conditions of material deprivation. Others lack such stable social ties and aspirations. They are cut off from their families or do not know the identities of parents and relatives; some are involved in serious drug use and have criminal records.

Spencer helped me see that there are, if you will, at least two ways of life concealed by the singular label — the welfare poor — and that serious antagonisms sometimes occur between people whose lives on welfare are very different. One group defines itself, in part, by differentiating itself from what Spencer referred to as the "welfare crowd." In contrast, as I later came to appreciate, many members of that so-called "crowd" take pleasure in mocking efforts by people like Spencer to maintain "respectability" in the midst of misery. These differences suggest that legal consciousness among people on welfare may be as internally divided and plural as it is different from the legal consciousness of other social groups.

NOTES AND QUESTIONS

1. Isn't the "law all over" for everyone, not just the poor? After all, the law tells people where they can build shelter, it structures the return they can expect on labor and investments, and it even can specify the gender of people they can marry. Is the law really that different for poor people?
2. Although those receiving public assistance are described above as having simultaneously limited agency within the rules of the system and the capacity to use those same rules as a tool for resistance, is Sarat right that such resistance "helps to reproduce official understandings of law and justice"? How might welfare recipients, together with their advocates, use existing rules to question the status quo or to create space for new understandings of the relationship between the state and poor people?

* * *

Besides establishing a set of rules that those dependent on government assistance must follow, poverty law also plays an important expressive function. Poverty law rules arguably are directed at multiple audiences, not just the poor. Rules tell both welfare recipients and nonrecipients how members of society are expected to structure their lives. For those receiving government assistance, rules structure everything from the bureaucratic hurdles they encounter in accessing government benefits to the larger question of whether they will be able to meet their basic needs. For those not receiving welfare, welfare rules serve as an implicit validation of their relatively higher place in society and as a warning about deviating from work expectations. In the short passage that follows, Professors Joel Handler and Yeheskel Hasenfeld highlight the connection between welfare rules and societal values.

JOEL F. HANDLER & YEHESKEL HASENFELD, *THE MORAL CONSTRUCTION OF POVERTY: WELFARE REFORM IN AMERICA* (1991)

WHAT IS WELFARE POLICY?

Who the poor are and what to do about their poverty form the basis of welfare policy. For most of human history, such questions were never asked; the poor were considered part of the natural order. Why then, do the poor emerge as a social problem? Why do particular categories of the poor become social problems? These are moral questions. The construction of the nature, causes, and remedies for poverty reflect fundamental values as to how society should be organized, how people should act, how to assign blame, and when to relieve misery.

Responses to poverty are designed to perform a number of social purposes. We tend to focus on the practical, social control, regulatory interests of the state — maintain labor discipline, relieve misery, or, when necessary, quell disorder. But welfare programs perform other functions as well. They define values and confirm status; they are expressive and symbolic. Poverty is a social problem. Conditions become social problems, enter political language, not because they suddenly materialize or change in character; usually they have always been present. Rather, conditions become social problems for ideological purposes. Social problems are constructed. They serve the interests of those who define them. The distinction between the "deserving" poor and the "undeserving" poor is a moral issue; it affirms the values of the dominant society by stigmatizing the outcasts. The meaning ascribed to events is thus reciprocal; observers construct themselves by constructing others. The definition of problems creates authority and status; it allocates resources and rewards. Explanations rationalize particular actions and justify authority in people who claim competence in dealing with particular causes; explanations will endure if they comport with dominant ideologies. We construct problems and symbols to further our interests; interests, in turn, may be both symbolic and tangible.

Welfare policy is part of the larger normative order of society — in our society, the capitalist market economy. The normative order justifies itself by providing for the well-being of its citizens in exchange for work. The state offers protection, comfort, and material rewards for those who participate in the productive system. For those who cannot participate, because of conditions beyond their control, the state provides relief. This is the moral contract of citizenship: rewards for those who are productive, care for those who are unable to work. The persistence of poor people inevitably calls into question the economic order; after all, how can the state command allegiance if so many of its citizens are not being provided for? The relief of those who cannot work legitimates the state.

NOTES AND QUESTIONS

1. In pointing out the expressive and symbolic functions of poverty law, are Handler and Hasenfeld overly deterministic about the structural role welfare plays in American society?
2. There are many possible goals of poverty law programs, from what Handler and Hasenfeld call "labor discipline" to relieving misery. What do you think the goals should be? Chapters 2 and 4 discuss these issues in more detail.

CHAPTER
2

Social Welfare Policy

INTRODUCTION

Social welfare policy in the United States has often been characterized by its exceptionalism. Though rooted in English Poor Laws, the United States has a less comprehensive and less generous national welfare scheme than most developed democracies. As a result, we have greater inequality than peer nations and lag behind in a number of important indicators of societal health. As in other countries, U.S. social welfare policy embodies shifting views of human organization and obligation, evolving in ways highly contingent on time, place, and people. This chapter introduces some of the events, forces, and ideas that have shaped domestic antipoverty efforts.

Modern social welfare policy is often described in a grand arc with government intervention or retrenchment at the center of the story. The 1930s New Deal ushered in a period of increased federal attention and resources devoted to relieving suffering caused by the Depression. The New Frontier and Great Society of the 1960s — and particularly the War on Poverty — were designed to reduce persistent inequities, especially those concentrated in urban areas. 1990s welfare reform was the culmination of two decades of conservative critique of federal action. As President Ronald Reagan famously said in 1981 during his first inaugural address, "... government is not the solution to our problem; government *is* the problem."

While these historical moments are helpful for understanding broad developments in social welfare policy, the sources and expressions of the animating debates predate the American Revolution and involve other important sites of activity like the states, the courts, and protest movements. As described in this chapter, laws governing poverty relief in the early American colonies were based on English statutes from the Middle Ages, which for centuries distinguished between the deserving and undeserving poor. Given the distrust of central authority that characterized our nation's founding, poor relief through the nineteenth century largely took place at the state and local levels. Even major shifts at the national level, such as the New Deal and welfare reform, reflected developments in the states that preceded federal action.

Although the nature of social obligation is at the core of social welfare policy — what is owed to and expected from our fellow community members — a number of common themes have run throughout its evolution. As noted above, social welfare policy has often made *moral* distinctions between the worthy and unworthy poor. Such distinctions often turn on our understanding of the causes of poverty, for example, whether we think people are poor due to individual failings or as a result of larger structural forces. U.S. antipoverty policy reflects vacillation between these understandings of the causes of poverty and thereby society's obligation to the poor.

Our moral views, in turn, shape and are influenced by *economic* arguments, especially concerns about dependency and liberty. How much aid should government give to help the poor attain a level of independence sufficient to meet basic needs and participate in a democratic society? How much aid is too much, such that recipients become dependent and nonproductive? Even if we can agree on what level of aid is appropriate, why should the nonpoor pay to care for others through taxes, payroll deductions, health care mandates, or other transfers? These moral and economic arguments — with the value of work often at the center of the debate — have fueled the development of two basic kinds of government aid: (1) insurance programs, like Social Security, which are contributory and therefore considered "earned"; and (2) welfare programs, like Temporary Assistance to Needy Families, which are noncontributory, means-tested, and "unearned."

In addition to moral and economic questions, *institutional competence* and *democratic legitimacy* arguments have featured prominently in policy debates, especially with respect to the role of the courts. As described in Chapter 3, the judicial branch has often deferred to the political branches on matters of social welfare design and implementation. This deference echoes debates internationally, as we will see in Chapter 12, about the justiciability and enforcement of social and economic rights. In general, U.S. courts have been very reluctant to recognize substantive rights to any other form of government assistance designed to reduce poverty or economic inequality.

Section A of this chapter traces the pre-twentieth-century origins of U.S. social welfare policy. Section B explores the 1930s New Deal (Roosevelt) and the emergence of the modern welfare state. Section C describes the 1960s New Frontier (Kennedy) and Great Society (Johnson), with a focus on the War on Poverty and the associated expansion of federal programs. Section D considers the 1990s welfare reform as the culmination of a sustained and racialized backlash against public assistance. Section E introduces recent developments in health care reform as the latest site of activity and contest in social welfare policy.

A.   THE ORIGINS OF POVERTY RELIEF IN THE UNITED STATES

While the emergence of welfare states is a relatively modern phenomenon, the contours of poverty relief in the United States can be traced directly to the English Poor Laws originating in the 1300s. Such laws, which might appear harsh to our eyes, drew early distinctions between the deserving and undeserving poor. This section describes the origins of poverty relief in the United States prior to the New Deal.

1. The English Poor Laws

WILLIAM P. QUIGLEY, *BACKWARDS INTO THE FUTURE: HOW WELFARE CHANGES IN THE MILLENNIUM RESEMBLE ENGLISH POOR LAW OF THE MIDDLE AGES*

9 Stan. L. & Pol'y Rev. 101 (1998)

English Poor Laws are the single most influential legal source in the historical development of the poor laws of the United States. It should not come as a surprise that the English Poor Laws were so influential since American colonial law and the subsequent development of the poor laws of the original thirteen states grew out of the English legal tradition. . . .

The Statutes of Labourers of 1349-1350 are generally considered the first poor laws. They came about in response to two factors: the large number of poor people who were roaming England begging and looking for better paying work as feudalism broke down; and the Black Plague and the famine of 1348-1349 that together caused the loss of nearly one third of the population. These factors led to instability in the locally-available labor supply, and a general overall shortage of workers.

The Statutes of Labourers sought to force the non-working poor to labor and to hold down the wages of those who were already working. The Statute of Labourers required anyone not already working to work at a legally-mandated low maximum wage for any employer who needed that person as a worker under pain of imprisonment. . . .

Begging by the poor and even giving alms to the able-bodied poor were outlawed. The law ultimately forced the non-working poor to become the working poor: all were compelled to go to work, to stay at work, and to work for low wages, and they were subject to prison if they disobeyed.

Nearly two hundred years after the enactment of the Statute of Labourers the number of beggars and vagrants in England began to cause concern again since the destitute poor were reported to represent as much as twenty percent of the population[, and] . . . Parliament responded with reforms to the Poor Laws by creating the first comprehensive English system of poor relief.

The 1530 statute was titled "An act directing how aged, poor, and impotent persons, compelled to live by alms, shall be ordered, and how vagabonds and beggars shall be punished." The law divided the poor into two categories: (1) the aged and the impotent poor who were worthy of help, and (2) the able-bodied poor, the vagabonds and beggars, who were unworthy of help and who were punished if they refused to work. This law had several mandates: only those poor unable to work were assisted; responsibility for the poor was placed squarely on local authorities who determined eligibility for assistance; criminal penalties upon the non-working poor were increased; and local authorities were allowed to expel non-working able-bodied poor, i.e., people who had not lived and worked in the area for at least three years.

The 1535 statute amended the law of 1530 with the following provisions: it precluded assistance to the poor who were not able to work unless they met the three-year residency requirement; it ordered forced work for the non-working able-bodied poor, including children over five years of age; it prohibited giving alms to the able-bodied poor; and yet again it increased the criminal penalties imposed on the non-working able-bodied poor.

In 1562, Parliament enacted the Statute of Artificers. Although its primary purpose was, like the Statute of Labourers of two hundred years before, the regulation of the hiring, firing, wages, and employment conditions of workers, the Statute of Artificers also provided for the poor, primarily by insisting that all of the poor work. It required the skilled unemployed poor who were under thirty or unmarried to work for whoever needed their services. The unskilled unemployed poor between the ages of twelve and sixty were required to perform agricultural work, a year at a time, and unmarried women between the ages of twelve and forty were required to work for whoever needed them. Refusal to work was punishable by jail and/or sentence to indentured service. Even impoverished little children as young as one year old and as old as twenty, could be apprenticed out as workers for seven years at a time.

Reforms of the laws regulating the poor continued and in 1601, Parliament passed An Act for the Relief of the Poor. This act ordered local authorities called overseers of the poor to administer and enforce the poor laws. These overseers forced to work "all such persons, married or unmarried, having no means to maintain them." The poor who would not work were jailed. The 1601 Act authorized overseers to bind out or apprentice the children of the poor who were not "thought able to keep and maintain their children." Only the "impotent poor" were to be cared for and housed. The 1601 Act also obligated private families to accept three generational responsibility for their poor relatives before the public assumed any responsibility: "the father and grandfather, and the mother and grandmother, and the children of every poor, old, blind, lame and impotent person, or other poor person not able to work . . . [were to] relieve and maintain" their relatives. Finally, local justices of the peace were charged with ensuring compliance with the 1601 Act upon pain of fines.

These first English Poor Laws from 1349 to 1601 regulated both the working poor and the non-working poor by forcing every possible person to labor upon pain of imprisonment. Poverty was perceived not as a social or economic problem but as an individual problem. Lack of adequate compensation or employment or someone to provide child care was not a recognized reason not to work. The law was simple: poor people worked or they went to jail. The responsibility for making sure people worked was placed upon the local authorities, as was the responsibility for assisting those poor who could not work and who were legal residents.

2.   The Pre- and Post-Revolutionary Periods

Many American colonies adopted the English Poor Laws, providing "outdoor relief" — meaning aid outside of institutional settings — to eligible residents. In the face of rising destitution and dislocation in the late 1700s, outdoor relief gave way to the poorhouse or "indoor relief." As described next, indoor relief was both socially punitive to deter the able-bodied from seeking assistance and morally corrective to signal the individual failings of the poor.

JOEL F. HANDLER & YEHESKEL HASENFELD, *BLAME WELFARE, IGNORE POVERTY AND INEQUALITY* (2007)

. . . Contrary to the American myth, as well as the stories told by many historians, from the earliest days of the colonies, there was significant poverty. In addition to slaves, many whites arrived as and remained indentured servants. There were large numbers of single-mother families. Husbands were often absent as sailors, were killed in the wars, were looking for work, or had left the family. There were accidents, disease, fires, and calamities that impoverished individuals and families.

Initially, aid was outdoor relief in the community and was reserved for settled residents — strangers (including those looking for work) were "warned out," or expelled. At least as far as men were concerned, poverty was a moral fault; the individual was to blame rather than accidents, disease, wars, and depressions. Local officials determined who was worthy, how much aid to extend, and the circumstances of aid. Men were expected to find work and support themselves and their families. Single mothers were viewed more favorably, but this too was a moral judgment. They were widows, deserted, or never married. The distinction reflected the patriarchal norms — women were not expected to take care of themselves when they were without a husband; they were inherently dependent. Most often children and mothers were bound out to families who would provide shelter and assistance (carefully specified by the town officials) in return for indenture. Aid was usually brief, to help a family over a bad patch.

Although mothers in general were more likely to receive some form of relief from the earliest days, single mothers of color (African American, Indian) and their children were treated differently. . . .

Town officials closely monitored women of color but seldom gave them relief. More often, they were warned out — expelled from the town to fend for themselves and their children. More women were warned out than men in the towns of eighteenth-century Rhode Island, but these women were disproportionately of color. "Between 1750 and 1800, about one-fifth (22%) of those warned out were identified as 'Indian,' 'mustee,' 'mulatto,' 'Negro,' 'black' and 'of color.'" In Providence, in 1800, half of all those warned out were women of color even though "Negroes" were only 5 percent of the population. When black or Indian women were mentioned on the relief rolls, they were usually very old. Typically, they received a small amount for a final illness or burial. . . .

In the latter part of the eighteenth century, there were two wars, depressions, and changes in demography. Destitution and disorder increased. There was an increase in "needy strangers." Towns, already paying high taxes, first sought to cut relief expenses. Relief was seen as encouraging idleness, so the use of work-houses caught on, where all the poor in the town could be boarded together and engage in some useful occupation. The basic idea was to get poor men back to work. Rehabilitating men and putting them back to work was viewed as the solution to women's poverty. In Philadelphia, the Pennsylvania Hospital for the Sick Poor was opened in 1752, followed by the Bettering House in 1768. Although strongly opposed by the overseers of the poor, outdoor relief was abolished. Women, along with their children, were more likely to be sent to the Bettering House, but women were also sent to the almshouse, whereas men were sent to the workhouse. . . . [A]ttitudes toward poverty did not change.

What did change was the promotion of male independence as the major poverty policy.

Between 1790 and 1820, county poorhouses replaced outdoor relief. Several reasons were advanced: to control the costs of outdoor relief and to avoid the "pampering" by private households, a more careful division of "worthy" and "unworthy" was needed to effectively relieve the misery of the former and to reform the latter. There was to be rigid schedules of work, very little social intercourse (and no sexual intercourse), and teaching the "'habits of industry' necessary for success in an increasingly commercial economy." Increasingly, the poor were blamed for their condition. Idleness and intemperance were particularly condemned. "Almshouse rules and regulations . . . strongly suggest a punitive intent on the part of legislators and relief officials, that is, an effort to make institutional life so unpleasant that most poor folk would take pains to avoid it." Poorhouse inmates were criticized as lazy drunkards who used the poorhouse when the weather was too cold. Of course, there were those who had no choice but to enter the poorhouse — the old, the sick, the infirm. Thus, . . . those who had to enter the poorhouse were held "hostage" to deter those who might think that welfare was preferable to work. . . . There often was a commercial and social relationship between the poorhouse and the local community, which administrators regarded inmates as residents of the community sometimes referred to as "family."

In most towns, poorhouses did not work, and the towns turned to "auctioning off" the poor; that is, interested households would bid for the opportunity to board "certain 'lots' of poor people." For a while, auctioning off, especially children, became the preferred method of relief for those not warned out. Rates of warned out fluctuated (reached its peak in the mid-1780s), depending on economic conditions and increases in population. The Revolutionary War was particularly hard on the poor. Before the war, . . . poor relief was the most significant budget item for towns in Rhode Island. Then, the war taxes came, along with the severe dislocations of husbands leaving for the army, others looking for work, and large numbers of needy strangers. Poor relief was cut drastically. Eventually, . . . taxpayers grew weary of caring for the poor on an individual basis within the community. In early nineteenth century, the poor would be segregated in farms, orphanages, and other institutions.

During the Colonial period, several themes are noted that will endure throughout welfare history. Despite significant adverse structural conditions — wars, depression, accidents, disease, sickness — the poor were judged as morally blameworthy. This was universally true of men — outdoor relief was usually denied or they were sent to the workhouses. Single mothers were also individually judged, but white mothers were viewed as "naturally" dependent. They constituted most of the outdoor relief rolls. The moral evaluation was different for women of color. They were not deserving of relief; it was denied or they were expelled from the community. Children (of white single mothers) were treated differently. Whereas relief for the mothers was usually brief and carefully itemized, children were more likely to be boarded out or indentured for long periods. They were supported in the indentured families, who were expected to provide them with education and work experience.

The creation, administration, and ultimate demise of the poorhouses illustrate several continuing themes. There was the disjuncture (at least in many cases) between legislation, rules, and regulations and actual administration. Public statements were harsh, full of blame, and called for severe conditions.

Yet, on the ground, administration was different. Ground-level administrators exercised discretion and made their own moral judgments about recipients. The creation of the poorhouses was an exercise in symbolic politics, of myth and ceremony. The legislature loudly proclaimed to majoritarian society that the poor were idle, shiftless, and abused the system and that confining them to the poorhouse would not only correct their behavior but also serve as an example to others similarly inclined. . . .

We shall find these themes as welfare history unfolds in the next two centuries — moral blame, race and gender discrimination, and symbolic politics.

NOTES AND QUESTIONS

1. While the English Poor Laws and their progeny in the American colonies and states distinguished between the deserving and undeserving poor, they implicitly recognized that unemployment was at times involuntary or unavoidable and therefore not an individual moral failing. They also established, under prescribed circumstances, the obligation of the state to provide — and the right of eligible individuals to receive — public assistance. How would you frame current arguments about who deserves and does not deserve government assistance?

2. Scholars have noted the tension between religious commitments to serving the poor on one hand with Calvinist precepts about the virtue of hard work on the other. Influential New England Puritan Cotton Mather put the latter view this way: "[A]s for those that Indulge themselves in Idleness, the Express Command of God unto us, is, That we Should Let them Starve." Cotton Mather, *Durable Riches* 20 (1695). Is this tension between charity and hard work reconcilable as a matter of social welfare policy?

3. After the revolution, responsibility for poverty relief gradually shifted from localities to the states, and poor laws were extended to new states as the country grew. Congress passed the Revolutionary War Pension Act of 1818, which provided lifetime benefits to needy veterans. At the same time, since the "general welfare" clause of the U.S. Constitution, Article I, Section 8, was broad and not specific, states retained considerable latitude with respect to poor relief. What does our system of federalism, in which authority is shared between the national and state governments, mean for social welfare policy, especially relative to Europe, where such policy generally has been developed and implemented through more centralized planning and authority?

4. After the Civil War, the Freedmen's Bureau provided various forms of federal assistance to former slaves from 1865 to 1872, including employment assistance, legal assistance, educational opportunities, and basic necessities such as shelter, health care, and food rations. The federal government also established and expanded veterans' pensions, which represented one-quarter of the federal budget in the decades following the war. By 1910, more than a quarter of White men aged 65 and older were receiving federal benefits, though African Americans, Southerners, and immigrants were excluded. As we will see later in the chapter, debates about the New Deal in the 1930s took place in the wake of concerns about the expansive and expensive Civil War pension system, including considerable corruption and patronage.

3.   The Progressive Era

With rapid industrialization, urbanization, and immigration at the turn of the twentieth century, the "Progressive Era" ushered in renewed attention to social ills and poverty relief. While much of Europe was establishing contributory (insurance) and noncontributory (public assistance) social welfare schemes to support and protect male workers and their dependents (women and children), the United States focused relief almost exclusively on needy (fatherless) children and vulnerable (widowed) women.

Over a 25-year span beginning in 1911, 46 states enacted laws providing aid to widows with children who were "fit" parents in "suitable homes." These "mothers' pensions" maintained the connection between public aid and moral worthiness and laid the groundwork for key elements of the New Deal's Social Security Act. By 1920, more than 40 states had also enacted workers' compensation schemes — though not unemployment insurance — to help injured workers and to shield employers from job-related liability.

WALTER I. TRATTNER, FROM POOR LAW TO WELFARE STATE: A HISTORY OF SOCIAL WELFARE IN AMERICA (6TH ED. 1998)*

By the late nineteenth century, welfare work had become more of a private or voluntary matter than a public one; save for placing the destitute elderly and the permanently disabled in public institutions, public assistance had been substantially curtailed or in many cases even abolished.

In the early years of the twentieth century, however, as the complex of problems associated with rapid industrialization, a market economy, urbanization, and immigration intensified — especially economic insecurity and deprivation — a growing number of reformers saw the need for more public assistance. . . .

For many, widows' pensions, or public aid to women with dependent children, was the answer. . . . Proponents of the idea argued that changes in the family and in the economic system required greater government or public intervention on a "regular" basis. The family's survival was contingent upon uninterrupted earnings, yet because of a variety of impersonal matters — forced unemployment, illness, death of the family breadwinner, and so on — that was not always possible. There was a need, then, for a new, impersonal mechanism that would assure income flow in the event of a decline in an individual's or a family's earnings. Furthermore, mothers' pensions were based on the idea that married women who stayed home (where they "belonged") and raised their children were performing an ongoing service to society, and they should be rewarded for such service. Clearly, then, widows' pensions were gender-specific; they explicitly rejected equal treatment of the sexes in favor of special policies for women. Whether or not they were designed to keep women out of the workplace or to remove those already in it, *in order to benefit male wage earners*, or to subsidize low wages for females who continued to work, *and thus profit employers*, or merely were *innocent products of the prevailing maternalism of the day*, are matters of data.

In either case, . . . they led to a "gendered" welfare state in the 1930s, with high-status contributory benefits (old age pensions and unemployment compensation) going mostly to white men and low-status (means-tested) welfare going largely to women and minorities. . . .

In April 1911, Missouri enacted America's first widows' pension law, a permissive statute allowing the counties to provide cash assistance to "full-time" mothers with dependent children (although evidence suggests that many women who received such aid, in Missouri and elsewhere, also worked for wages). Two months later, Illinois followed suit, and so rapidly did the idea spread that within two years seventeen other states did the same. By 1919, similar statutes had been enacted in thirty-nine states, and by 1935, all but two — South Carolina and Georgia — were extending aid to widows with children.

While the specific provisions of the statutes differed, they were similar in that they were compromise measures. Patterned on the nineteenth-century concept of relief, they were based upon behavioral considerations as well as economic need. All the statutes contained "suitable home" provisions; that is, they applied to needy widows who, in the opinion of the authorities, were "fit" or worthy parents, exposing them, of course, to administrative discretion and possible abuses — and thus were not as impersonal as some would have liked. . . .

Widows' pension laws marked a definite turning point in the welfare policies of many states. In theory at least, they removed the stigma of charity for a large number of welfare recipients. They also broke down the nineteenth-century tradition against public home relief. Their enactment constituted public recognition of the facts that poverty did not necessarily reflect moral weakness, that long-time care must be provided for children whose fathers were dead or incapacitated or who had deserted them, that security at home was an essential part of such care, and that such security could be gained only through public aid. . . .

The drive for widows' pensions was part of a broader movement, during and after the so-called Progressive era, designed to increase the social and economic security of all citizens living in a modern industrial society. That movement also included efforts to enact workmen's compensation legislation, health and unemployment insurance schemes, and old-age pensions. . . .

In any event, optimism pervaded the social insurance forces as a result of the rapidity with which states passed both mothers' pensions and workmen's compensation laws, which automatically paid injured workers according to a uniform scale of benefits on the assumption that "industrial accidents are not accidents at all, but normal results of modern industry." Between 1909 and 1920, forty-three states enacted workmen's compensation, mainly, however, the record indicates, because such measures had a good deal of appeal for employers, who thus pushed for their enactment. Compensation programs (which avoided the large payments the courts occasionally awarded in injury cases) made it easier for businessmen to insure against losses resulting from industrial accidents, the cost of which easily could be added to the price of production and passed on to the consumer. Further, most compensation statutes omitted many workers, did not include occupational diseases, provided fairly low benefits to disabled laborers, and in other ways were quite weak.

Still, these statutes were important. Whatever their limitations, they at least established the principle that workers injured on the job had a right to compensation. Thus, like widows' pensions, they represented a small but irreversible step from charity toward entitlement. . . .

The drive for unemployment compensation moved even more slowly. Although bills were introduced in a number of states between 1916 and 1931, none was enacted during that time.

B.   THE NEW DEAL

The stock market crash of 1929 heralded the nation's greatest economic crisis, with many millions of Americans losing their jobs, farms, housing, and savings in a period of months. With the exception of widows' pensions and workers' compensation in most states, many local systems for public relief had been dismantled in favor of private charitable relief in the decades before the Depression, and remaining public relief programs collapsed under the weight of need. When one-third of private relief agencies were forced to close their doors during the Depression, rising suffering went largely unattended. The absence of a public safety net and the inadequacy of private relief efforts eventually motivated calls—from an unemployed workers' movement to progressive politicians—for a national government response. Following an administration that opposed almost all efforts to marshal meaningful federal intervention, newly elected President Franklin Roosevelt pursued the most aggressive and comprehensive social welfare policy in U.S. history, known as the New Deal.

The following excerpt describes some of the central social welfare features of Roosevelt's legislative agenda, including the establishment of federal entitlement to benefits and the delineation of categories of the poor that distinguish programs to this day. The enduring piece of legislation was the Social Security Act of 1935. As with other parts of the New Deal, it was not obvious that core elements of the Act would pass constitutional muster before a divided Supreme Court. In a series of cases decided at the height of a power struggle among the three branches of government, including one case excerpted below, the Act survived and created much of the infrastructure of the American welfare state.

JOEL F. HANDLER, *"CONSTRUCTING THE POLITICAL SPECTACLE": THE INTERPRETATION OF ENTITLEMENTS, LEGALIZATION, AND OBLIGATIONS IN SOCIAL WELFARE HISTORY*
56 Brook. L. Rev. 899 (1990)

The New Deal consisted of four parts: (1) work relief; (2) unemployment insurance; (3) Social Security for the retired; and (4) the grant-in-aid programs for aid to dependent children, old-age assistance, and aid to the blind. Together, these parts show continuity with the past by the strengthening of the categories.

The first and most immediate crisis facing the new administration was massive unemployment. There was significant local disorder and serious concern about threats to social order at all levels of government. The initial New Deal reforms were constructed during this state of crisis and widespread poverty. The Roosevelt administration quickly put together an extensive system of public employment. While these programs turned out to be temporary, their brief history tells us much about the future course of the American welfare state.

Within a year, more than 4,500,000 families and single people were receiving some sort of relief. Even though administration was through grants-in-aid to the states, the federal government insisted on separate administrative agencies (to distinguish these programs from welfare), the prohibition of racial, religious, and political discrimination, and uniform benefits. Between 1.4 and 2.4 million people per month worked at wages higher than both direct relief and market wages. Nevertheless, despite the apparent success of the work programs, they were instantly and bitterly attacked, and ultimately seriously crippled by the business community on the grounds that the federal programs did not follow traditional welfare requirements and compromised industrial discipline. Under extreme pressure, Congress rescinded the minimum wage, imposed a means test, and shortly, despite their national popularity, scaled back the programs drastically. . . .

Race politics also became more overtly important at this time. Prior to the New Deal, African-Americans were simply excluded from welfare. They were the most undeserving of the undeserving poor. The Roosevelt administration tried to open up the new programs, which incurred the wrath of the South. The South, at this time, was largely a plantation economy, with African-American tenant farming taking the place of slavery. The great majority of African-Americans lived in the South and on the land. As a one-party region, with a large part of its citizenry disenfranchised, the South exercised a virtual veto power in Congress. Southern politicians refused to tolerate any federal intervention in their labor and race relations. Southern race and labor politics would prove to be very important in the other New Deal programs as well.

President Roosevelt himself was opposed to the work relief programs. He feared the creation of a large, permanent, entrenched bureaucracy and worried about the effects of relief on work incentives. His Committee on Economic Security unsuccessfully floated a guaranteed public employment program. However, the position of business was that all relief programs should be returned to the states, work relief should be abolished, and direct relief payments should be reduced. The resulting program produced a small number of public jobs only for those not employable in the private sector.

This was the context in which the Social Security Act was debated. Despite the massive unemployment and the impressive accomplishments of the work programs, traditional attitudes towards relief and labor discipline prevailed. Even though the Depression poor were in no sense the stereotypical malingerer, regulating employment was more a matter of industrial discipline and preventing dependency than meeting need. Moreover, the federal government was not to be trusted. Social control was best left to the states and local governments, which were more sensitive to local labor markets. It was this dominant ideology towards work and relief that explains the outcome of the first major task of the Social Security reformers: unemployment insurance.

Here, an important influence was the experience of the Civil War pensions system. Initially tied to service-connected injuries or death, this program, under political pressure, expanded into a vast social welfare program blanketing all veterans and their families. In practice, ninety days of service and old age (sixty-two) became the test. Most northern white males or their widows were covered; excluded were African-Americans, southerners, and immigrants. By the turn of the century, the program was infected with political patronage and corruption, and this strongly affected the Progressive-era social reformers who were arguing for professionally administered social insurance systems in the European tradition. Their fears of corruption-prone, public-spending programs were fueled by the post-World War I experience in Europe, especially in Britain, where the unemployment insurance system yielded to an open-ended system of relief for the unemployed.

The experience of the Civil War pension system, the specter of Europe, and the work relief experience helped determine the fate of unemployment insurance. Roosevelt insisted that unemployment insurance be separate from relief, and be actuarially "sound" — that is, financed by contributions and taxes. There would be maximum state control. This was of central importance; in fact, the dispute over the administrative form of unemployment insurance was *the* dominant political issue in 1934. Why were state interests so important? It was in local labor markets that the interests of capitalists and labor were fought out. "Sensitivity" or "control over local labor markets" was the code for the social control of marginal workers; the capitalists insisted that the price and availability of local labor not be disturbed. The South was able to make sure that all the provisions of the Social Security Act, including unemployment insurance, left undisturbed its economy and race relations.

In the end, state unemployment insurance laws reflected these positions; programs were state and local and they failed to reach those most in need, the "less deserving" workers such as employees of small firms, agricultural workers, women, African-Americans, and migrants. State benefits varied widely, but the most common was sixteen weeks at half pay, with a maximum of fifteen dollars per week. Significantly, the maximum was about the average federal work relief (WPA) rate. Once benefits were exhausted, there was no other relief available except WPA, which was difficult to obtain. In sum, unemployment insurance was more in the nature of temporary emergency relief. Moreover, it was for the deserving workers — those who worked in steady, reliable, covered employment. Benefits were calibrated to length of employment and rates of pay. There were waiting periods. Workers were excluded if they quit voluntarily, were discharged for cause or a labor dispute, or failed to register at a public employment office and be available for suitable alternative work. All attempts to impose significant, substantive national standards on the states were defeated.

The centerpiece of the Social Security Act was the establishment of a contributory, national pension for the aged — old age insurance (OAI) [Ed. note: what most people currently call "Social Security"]. As we have seen, prior to the New Deal, aid to the dependent aged was controversial, and the South considered such pensions as family grants which would weaken control over African-American farm tenants. By 1935, however, the political climate outside the South had changed. The elderly, along with the working population, were politically active and various radical redistribution plans were being proposed.

Nevertheless, Roosevelt was strongly committed to an actuarially sound contributory insurance system and adamantly opposed to anything resembling the dole. He believed that the program would only attain solid legitimacy if it was "earned," if it was financed by contribution, if it had no means test, if it clearly defined the risks, and if it had a fixed retirement age. Benefits would reflect wages, thus strengthening incentives rather than redistribution. Only in this way would recipients avoid the stigma of welfare. The program was (and is) sold on its insurance features. This was a dignified program paying individually earned benefits as of right rather than relief for people who had to demonstrate need.

There was now a strong desire to get older workers out of the labor market. Families had changed, and young people did not want their parents moving back in. In contrast to unemployment insurance, there were strong arguments in favor of a uniform, national scheme. It was in the interests of big business to avoid different state taxes, and the fact that there was a general relationship between wages and benefits (and not much redistribution), meant that wage structures and regional variations would not be disturbed. The South was opposed, and insisted on the exclusion of agricultural and domestic workers, insuring that planter control over African-Americans would not be disturbed. The exclusion of these workers, plus the elimination of national standards from state old-age assistance, meant that the vast majority of elderly African-Americans were almost completely excluded.

Why was OAI national while Unemployment Insurance (UI) was not? The arguments in favor of a national OAI applied as well to UI — namely, the mobility of labor and uniform taxes. The reason lies in the differential effects on labor markets. OAI wanted its beneficiaries *out* of the labor market; UI wanted to make sure that its beneficiaries stayed in. And in the United States, the regulation of work tests are invariably at the local level. Local businesses want to keep close control over economic issues (and avoid taxes), and the local community wants to keep control over moral behavior. OAI, as originally conceived, touched on these issues in the South, but the exclusion of agricultural and domestic workers left race relations undisturbed. Once a consensus was reached on this "deserving" category, the program could be nationalized.

The last piece of the Social Security Act were the grants-in-aid to the states to rescue their old age, aid to the blind, and aid to dependent children programs. At this time, the separation of OAI and old age assistance was not a foregone conclusion. There was strong support for a universal, national, flat pension for the aged. By now, the aged were excused from work. Again, the influence of the South was crucial. As the price of southern support, important national standards, which would have allowed federal funds to go directly to African-Americans, were stripped from old age assistance. The states could set their own eligibility requirements and enjoy an independent administration. Southern intentions were carried out. They were the slowest to enact old age assistance programs; eligibility was more stringent; administration was at the local level under broad discretion; there were strict residency requirements and removal powers — characteristics of traditional poor law. In the South, the African-American aged agricultural tenant farmer was still considered part of the labor force since the South considered an old age grant to be a family subsidy. Benefits to African-Americans were substantially lower than to whites and carefully monitored. Elsewhere, old age assistance was popular, especially since substantial numbers of insurance retirees were not scheduled to receive OAI benefits until 1942. Programs spread rapidly; benefits and federal contributions were higher than they were with aid to dependent children (ADC).

Of course, the plight of poor single mothers worsened during the Depression. Divorce and desertion increased, as did joblessness and homelessness. Nevertheless, despite the lobbying efforts of the Federal Children's Bureau, there was little interest in ADC on the part of either the administration or Congress. The basic thinking was that as OAI took hold, more and more of the elderly and widows would be covered and that public assistance as well as ADC would wither. The old problems continued to dog this category of the poor — the stigma of poor single mothers, labor discipline, and race. "No one in 1935 imagined throwing millions of dollars into broken homes." Some important federal requirements, however, were imposed — for example, programs had to be implemented statewide, eligibility standards were broadened, benefits had to be paid in cash, and there had to be fair hearings.

However, while access to ADC was increased formally, in practice the programs stayed the same. In contrast to Old Age Assistance (OAA), most states lagged in buying into grant-in-aid and did little to encourage enrollments. Congress did not encourage the states to either adopt grant-in-aid or enroll poor single mothers. Despite the different federal subsidies and benefits between OAA and ADC (the latter were lower than the former), which were noticed during the Social Security Act deliberations, there was little interest expressed by either Congress or the administration in harmonizing the programs. This pattern of treating the adult programs (OAA and Aid to the Blind) more generously than ADC was not a mere oversight. In fact, higher appropriations, matching formulae and benefit levels for the former continue to the present.

At the local level, social control of the poor single mother continued. Through the use of "suitable home" and "employable mother" policies, states were able to exclude the unworthy, maintain labor markets, and reduce costs. Even under the Social Security Act, ADC remained small and primarily for white widows.

In the meantime, what was happening to the general mass of poor? During the 1920s, there had been a rapid growth of public relief programs at the local level. These were, of course, overwhelmed by the Depression, and there was little change during the New Deal period. Public relief for the undifferentiated poor (which included the great bulk of single mothers and their children who were excluded from ADC) was always miserly. In the Depression, there was simply no money left for the noncategorical poor.

NOTES AND QUESTIONS

1. Handler describes the "continuity of the past with the strengthening of the categories." Social Security was designed to move older workers out of the labor market by providing a modest, contributory (earned) safety net. Unemployment Insurance, through time-limited benefits to those recently employed, was designed to support younger workers while keeping them closely tied to the workforce. Grants-in-aid (welfare) remained reserved almost exclusively for White widows. What do the categories of the Social Security Act tell us about the relative power of political interest groups — such as employers, farmers, Southerners, and others — and national conceptions of the deserving and undeserving poor?

2. Helvering v. Davis, excerpted next, was one of three challenges to the Social Security Act decided by the U.S. Supreme Court in 1937 (the two others involved the unemployment compensation provisions). The decision should be read in the context of larger battles underway at the time. Since the Court had already invalidated several New Deal programs by 5-4 majorities, including the analogous Railroad Retirement Act, President Roosevelt and his allies in Congress had proposed what became known as his court-packing plan (a bill to permit him to appoint an additional Justice for every sitting Justice aged 70 and older, which would have increased the Court to 15 members). In the months before the Social Security Act cases were decided, swing Justice Owen Roberts — in the "switch in time that saved nine" — joined the liberal justices in upholding a state minimum wage law, preserving the New Deal, and ending Roosevelt's court reform efforts.

HELVERING v. DAVIS
301 U.S. 619 (1937)

Mr. Justice CARDOZO delivered the opinion of the Court.

The Social Security Act [of 1935] . . . is challenged once again.

In Steward Machine Co. v. Davis [301 U.S. 548 (1937)], decided this day, . . . we have upheld the validity of Title IX of the act, imposing an excise upon employers of eight or more. In this case, Titles VIII and II are the subject of attack. Title VIII lays another excise upon employers in addition to the one imposed by Title IX (though with different exemptions). It lays a special income tax upon employees to be deducted from their wages and paid by the employers. Title II provides for the payment of Old Age Benefits, and supplies the motive and occasion, in the view of the assailants of the statute, for the levy of the taxes imposed by Title VIII. . . .

We were asked to determine: (1) "whether the tax imposed upon employers by §804 of the Social Security Act is within the power of Congress under the Constitution," and (2) whether the validity of the tax imposed upon employees by §801 of the Social Security Act is properly in issue in this case, and if it is, whether that tax is within the power of Congress under the Constitution. . . .

Congress may spend money in aid of the "general welfare." There have been great statesmen in our history who have stood for other views. We will not resurrect the contest. It is now settled by decision. . . . Yet difficulties are left when the power is conceded. The line must still be drawn between one welfare and another, between particular and general. Where this shall be placed cannot be known through a formula in advance of the event. There is a middle ground, or certainly a penumbra, in which discretion is at large. The discretion, however, is not confided to the courts. The discretion belongs to Congress, unless the choice is clearly wrong, a display of arbitrary power, not an exercise of judgment. This is now familiar law. "When such a contention comes here we naturally require a showing that by no reasonable possibility can the challenged legislation fall within the wide range of discretion permitted to the Congress." Nor is the concept of the general welfare static. Needs that were narrow or parochial a century ago may be interwoven in our day with the wellbeing of the nation. What is critical or urgent changes with the times.

The purge of nation-wide calamity that began in 1929 has taught us many lessons. Not the least is the solidarity of interests that may once have seemed to be divided. Unemployment spreads from State to State, the hinterland now settled that in pioneer days gave an avenue of escape. Spreading from State to State, unemployment is an ill not particular but general, which may be checked, if Congress so determines, by the resources of the nation. If this can have been doubtful until now, our ruling today in the case of the Steward Machine Co., *supra*, has set the doubt at rest. But the ill is all one or at least not greatly different whether men are thrown out of work because there is no longer work to do or because the disabilities of age make them incapable of doing it. Rescue becomes necessary irrespective of the cause. The hope behind this statute is to save men and women from the rigors of the poor house as well as from the haunting fear that such a lot awaits them when journey's end is near.

Congress did not improvise a judgment when it found that the award of old age benefits would be conducive to the general welfare. The President's Committee on Economic Security made an investigation and report, aided by a research staff of Government officers and employees, and by an Advisory Council and seven other advisory groups. Extensive hearings followed before the House Committee on Ways and Means, and the Senate Committee on Finance. A great mass of evidence was brought together supporting the policy which finds expression in the act. Among the relevant facts are these: The number of persons in the United States 65 years of age or over is increasing proportionately as well as absolutely. What is even more important, the number of such persons unable to take care of themselves is growing at a threatening pace. More and more our population is becoming urban and industrial instead of rural and agricultural. The evidence is impressive that, among industrial workers, the younger men and women are preferred over the older. In times of retrenchment, the older are commonly the first to go, and even if retained, their wages are likely to be lowered. The plight of men and women at so low an age as 40 is hard, almost hopeless, when they are driven to seek for reemployment. Statistics are in the brief. A few illustrations will be chosen from many there collected. In 1930, out of 224 American factories investigated, 71, or almost one third, had fixed maximum hiring age limits; in 4 plants the limit was under 40; in 41 it was under 46. In the other 153 plants there were no fixed limits, but in practice few were hired if they were over 50 years of age. With the loss of savings inevitable in periods of idleness, the fate of workers over 65, when thrown out of work, is little less than desperate. A recent study of the Social Security Board informs us that "one-fifth of the aged in the United States were receiving old-age assistance, emergency relief, institutional care, employment under the works program, or some other form of aid from public or private funds; two-fifths to one-half were dependent on friends and relatives, one-eighth had some income from earnings; and possibly one-sixth had some savings or property. Approximately three out of four persons 65 or over were probably dependent wholly or partially on others for support." We summarize in the margin the results of other studies by state and national commissions. They point the same way.

The problem is plainly national in area and dimensions. Moreover, laws of the separate states cannot deal with it effectively. Congress, at least, had a basis for that belief. States and local governments are often lacking in the resources that are necessary to finance an adequate program of security for the aged. This is brought out with a wealth of illustration in recent studies of the problem. Apart from the failure of resources, states and local governments are at times reluctant to increase so heavily the burden of taxation to be borne by their residents for fear of placing themselves in a position of economic disadvantage as compared with neighbors or competitors. We have seen this in our study of the problem of unemployment compensation. A system of old age pensions has special dangers of its own, if put in force in one state and rejected in another. The existence of such a system is a bait to the needy and dependent elsewhere, encouraging them to migrate and seek a haven of repose. Only a power that is national can serve the interests of all.

Whether wisdom or unwisdom resides in the scheme of benefits set forth in Title II it is not for us to say. The answer to such inquiries must come from Congress, not the courts. Our concern here, as often, is with power, not with wisdom. Counsel for respondent has recalled to us the virtues of self-reliance and frugality. There is a possibility, he says, that aid from a paternal government may sap those sturdy virtues and breed a race of weaklings. If Massachusetts so believes and shapes her laws in that conviction, must her breed of sons be changed, he asks, because some other philosophy of government finds favor in the halls of Congress? But the answer is not doubtful. One might ask with equal reason whether the system of protective tariffs is to be set aside at will in one state or another whenever local policy prefers the rule of *laissez faire*. The issue is a closed one. It was fought out long ago. When money is spent to promote the general welfare, the concept of welfare or the opposite is shaped by Congress, not the states. So the concept be not arbitrary, the locality must yield.

NOTES AND QUESTIONS

1. As a leading social welfare scholar has observed, the Social Security Act of
    1935 "was rooted in state-level laws or legislative proposals under active
    debate in the 1930s." Theda Skocpol, *Social Policy in the United States: Future
    Possibilities in Historical Perspective* (1995). Indeed, the Act marked the first
    major federal intervention into a policy arena that previously had been the
    purview of the states. The Supreme Court in *Helvering* expressed deference
    to Congress through its spending authority while disavowing any institu-
    tional role in shaping the substance of the policy: "Whether wisdom or
    unwisdom resides in the scheme of benefits set forth in Title II it is not
    for us to say." At the same time, the Court articulated its own understanding
    of the nature and extent of unemployment, suggesting it was a general
    problem, not a particular one, and required a national response. We do
    not have the benefit of a dissenting opinion — two Justices dissented without
    comment — but do you agree with the Court's policy reasoning for permit-
    ting federalization of social welfare policies? What are arguments against the
    Court's description of the problem and Congress's solution?

C.   THE NEW FRONTIER, GREAT SOCIETY, AND A WAR ON POVERTY

Economic gains in the 1940s and 1950s were not shared by all. As Handler noted
above, the Social Security Act of 1935 maintained deference to the states on
almost all matters beyond contributory social insurance (Social Security), leaving behind large numbers of the "undifferentiated" or "non-categorical poor,"
including non-White mothers, elderly African Americans, and younger workers
of all races who were not disabled or blind but could not find work. New Deal
employment relief programs like the Works Progress Administration and the
Civilian Conservation Corps employed millions of workers. But they were short-
lived, due in part to opposition to government intervention in the labor market
and in part to U.S. entry into World War II with the resulting demands on labor.
Even the generous G.I. Bill — often credited with creating the (White) middle
class — did not reach many urban and rural poor.

   As noted earlier in this chapter, to appease southern Democrats, many New
Deal programs excluded African Americans from their reach. But as the South
continued to enforce racial discrimination and labor market discipline, African
Americans embarked on a "Great Migration" to the North and West, drawn to
industrial jobs in major urban areas. In two waves beginning in 1910 and 1940,
6 million African Americans left the Jim Crow South to seek a better life. While
African Americans made important gains on the employment front, continued
discrimination in the private and public sectors helped to fuel both the civil
rights and welfare rights movements.

   An influential book by Michael Harrington, excerpted in Chapter 1, exposed
some of the unfinished business with respect to the "other America" — those
left behind in the New Deal. As Harrington noted,

   Even more explosive is the possibility that people who participated in the gains of
   the thirties and the forties will be pulled back down into poverty. Today the mass-
   production industries where unionization made such a difference are contracting.

Jobs are being destroyed. In the process, workers who had achieved a certain level of wages, who had won working conditions in the shop, are suddenly confronted with impoverishment. This is particularly true for anyone over forty years of age and for members of minority groups. Once their job is abolished, their chances of ever getting similar work are very slim.

It is too early to say whether or not this phenomenon is temporary, or whether it represents a massive retrogression that will swell the numbers of the poor. To a large extent, the answer to this question will be determined by the political response of the United States in the sixties.

Michael Harrington, *The Other America: Poverty in the United States* (1962).

Harrington argued that one-quarter of the country was living in poverty, and Democratic Presidents John Kennedy and Lyndon Johnson responded to this persistent inequality through the New Frontier, Great Society, and a "War on Poverty." Though heralded (and criticized) as a New Deal–like expansion of the welfare state, most of the legislative initiatives were designed to bring low-income urban and rural communities into the mainstream through increased economic opportunities. As we will see in Chapter 3, for a brief period in the 1960s courts joined the chorus by recognizing or enforcing procedural rights — both statutory and constitutional — to public assistance. At the same time, the public perception of welfare recipients and the subsequent expansion of benefits sparked a backlash against government programs.

WALTER I. TRATTNER, *FROM POOR LAW TO WELFARE STATE: A HISTORY OF SOCIAL WELFARE IN AMERICA* (6TH ED. 1998)*

Despite [social welfare advances in the 1940s and 1950s], many Americans continued to suffer throughout this period, especially those who were marginally employed or who were not in the labor force at all — the old, the sick, the disabled, women with children whose husbands had deserted them or who had no husbands, and so on. For the most part, they were ignored; most Americans knew little and cared less about them and the other needy. The prevailing belief was that prosperity and economic growth had conquered or soon would conquer the remaining poverty problem, that it would "wither away," to use James Patterson's words, or that it was "more nearly an afterthought," to use Galbraith's.

Before long, however, the situation would change. Indeed, by the early 1960s, when some of the optimism of the postwar years had begun to fade, a change was already evident. . . .

The running debate in the 1950s on American foreign policy, especially the question of foreign aid, may have had some effect; no doubt it awakened many Americans to the discrepancies between the affluent and poorer nations of the world and this, in turn, may have awakened some citizens to the existence of similar discrepancies at home. Also, poverty was an embarrassment that gave the Soviet Union ammunition to use against the United States in the Cold War.

More important was the coming into office of President John F. Kennedy, who not only made poverty, unemployment, and hunger major themes in the bid for

---

his party's nomination, but also was elected to the presidency after a campaign that was highly critical of the 1950s, one that conveyed a sense of vitality and urgency in the approach to social problems neglected by his predecessor. Setting the tone in his inaugural address of 1961, Kennedy asked the nation to "bear the burden of a long twilight struggle against the common enemies of man: tyranny, poverty, disease, and war. . . ." "The hand of hope," he said, "must be extended to the poor and the depressed." Such statements aroused many citizens, especially the nation's young people, and helped to revive faith in purposeful social action.

Even more important was the staggering relief explosion that accompanied the mass migration to the nation's cities of people who belonged to groups for whom poverty was endemic but who, for the most part, had been left out of the mainstream of American life: displaced and unemployed southern blacks and mountain whites, Mexican Americans and American Indians leaving their hovels and reservations in the West and Southwest, and Puerto Ricans moving to the mainland in search of a better life. While this massive urban movement by members of these "fringe" groups resulted from a variety of factors, the major cause was the agricultural revolution that occurred between the 1940s and 1960s, especially modernization and mechanization, which lessened the need for farm labor. Thus, a Presidential Commission on Rural Poverty found that between 1950 and 1965 new machines and new agricultural methods increased farm output in the United States by 45 percent, and at the same time reduced farm employment by the same percentage. Between 1940 and 1970, well over twenty million people (a great many of whom were black) were forced off the land, especially in the South, where these forces had their greatest impact.

This tremendous upheaval caused a good deal of suffering, especially since, as these displaced citizens migrated to the nation's cities, mainly in the North and West, the need for unskilled labor was declining. They were unable to secure adequate employment (or employment at all) and were forced to live in wretched, crowded ghettos, swelling the relief rolls. The number of persons receiving public assistance more than doubled from 1960 to 1970, from approximately six to twelve million as did the amount of money distributed to them, which increased from about $3.1 billion to well over $6 billion. . . .

The civil rights movement, which centered attention on the desperate economic conditions of millions of black citizens, also played a prominent role in the changes that occurred during the decade. Again, Americans who had regarded poverty as somehow an exception in an otherwise affluent nation were confronted with a militant reform movement that arose precisely because that was not the case. It was demonstrated that social and legal discrimination against African-Americans — the last to be hired, the first to be fired, the lowest paid, and so on — had induced and prolonged their poverty. . . .

The literature on poverty grew large as it was demonstrated that, beneath the layers of American affluence, there were strata of deprivation, and that the deprived were not merely those who lived in Harlem or other black ghettos, or even those who lived in the depressed areas of the rural South. Rather, the poor were ubiquitous; they could be found in all sections of the country, in all parts of the population, in all age groups. . . .

As Harrington and others demonstrated, poverty was one of the nation's gravest social problems, one that was not disappearing but growing worse, a way of life that had become permanent for some forty to fifty million Americans.

As if to bear out what these writers were saying, America's cities exploded in the mid-sixties. Riots erupted not only in the slums of New York, Los Angeles, Detroit, and Newark, but also in hundreds of other African-American communities around the nation. And while the various outbreaks differed in their origin and development, all resulted from long-festering wounds— unemployment, poverty, poor housing, crowded living conditions, economic exploitation, widespread desperation, frustration, hopelessness, and a profound disillusionment with urban conditions; clearly, the city was not the promised land full of economic opportunity and free of institutionalized oppression, as many Americans had been led to believe. . . .

Following the 1967 riots, President Lyndon B. Johnson created a National Advisory Commission on Civil Disorders, the so-called Kerner Commission, to determine the cause of disturbances and to recommend ways to prevent their future occurrence. After intensive study, the commission placed most of the blame for the riots on "white racism." Its report stated that the civil rights gains of the previous fifteen years had done very little to improve the quality of life in the black ghetto, where millions of citizens continued to be denied an equal chance in American society. In fact, "our nation is moving toward two societies, one black, one white—separate and unequal," the commission concluded, and then went on to make a series of modest proposals for social change, including the creation, or re-creation, of a federal jobs program for the poor unemployed, few of which were implemented; the principal response to the riots was greater expenditures for police and weaponry.

Still, the urban violence and wide variety of other developments, throughout the decade—social, political, economic, and demographic—which clearly shattered the prevailing belief that America was a classless and relatively homogeneous society, led to a new look at poverty and new attempts to prevent, or at least alleviate, its effects. Those attempts began early in the Kennedy administration, long before the eruptions in the nation's ghettos. Among the more important of the early measures was the extension, in 1961, of A.F.D.C. to needy two-parent families whose heads of households were both out of work and had exhausted their unemployment benefits. Not only would such a change help families in need but it also would keep them together by discouraging desertion by unemployed fathers in order to get wives and children off general relief and onto the more generous federally aided categorical assistance programs, for which they were ineligible with a "man" present in the home. Although the change was not made mandatory and many states, especially poorer rural ones, refused to participate in it, Aid to Families with Dependent Children-Unemployed Parent (A.F.D.C.-U.P.) was an important step forward.

The Kennedy administration also turned to the areas of juvenile delinquency and mental health. Shortly after taking office in the spring of 1961, Kennedy created the President's Committee on Juvenile Delinquency and Youth Crime, which led to the passage, that same year, of the Juvenile Delinquency and Youth Offenses Control Act, a measure that, among other things, helped fund and operate projects for the prevention and treatment of delinquency in inner-city neighborhoods, including Mobilization for Youth. Two years later, after receiving a message from the President on the subject, Congress enacted the Mental Retardation Facilities and Community Mental Health Centers Act, which provided federal funds for research, training, and the construction and staffing of community mental health centers throughout the United States.

The most widely heralded of the Kennedy administration's responses to the growing welfare crisis, however, were the 1962 Public Welfare Amendments to the Social Security Act, signed into law by the President on July 25, 1962. These measures, more familiarly known as the Social Service Amendments, greatly increased federal support (from 50 to 75 percent of the cost) to the states for the provision by local welfare departments of casework, job training, job placement, and other "soft" services to public assistance recipients. The amendments grew out of lengthy study and extensive advice from social workers and other experts who promised the President, the Congress, and the nation that their new approach would rehabilitate and bring financial independence to the needy and, hence, a reduction in the relief rolls and in public welfare expenditures.

Actually, the amendments were the product of several forces, including the fact that "social services" were added to the A.F.D.C. program in 1956 but, for various reasons, went unfunded. Basically they reflected social workers' renewed concern with casework — the belief that the poor needed not just, or even primarily, financial aid, but rather psychological assistance and other forms of counseling; they had to "adjust" to being single parents or to life in the city; they needed instruction on how to keep house and manage their meager resources in order to make ends meet; they needed to learn how to make friendships and develop self-esteem; above all, of course, they had to be taught how to secure and retain jobs. In reality, then, the new approach was an old one: attributing the needy's problems to personal shortcomings and providing "counseling," or advice, in order to promote participation in the labor force.

Nevertheless, by putting the power of the White House and the federal bureaucracy behind the drive for welfare reform — or at least the notion that the federal government had the responsibility to help poor Americans to help themselves — Kennedy shattered the relative complacency that characterized the previous decade, and his successor, Lyndon B. Johnson, followed suit. Under their administrations, dubbed the New Frontier and the Great Society, respectively, the poor obviously were moved from a state of benign neglect to a prominent place on the public agenda. Most of the measures enacted at the time, however, failed to deal with the social, economic, and demographic forces that were responsible for the increase in the welfare rolls. Instead, they were based on the idea that the economic well-being of the period could lead to the abolition of poverty if only the poor would take advantage of the opportunities before them; hence they were designed to do the same things as the Social Service Amendments — to reinforce commitment to the work ethic by those who were economically marginal, a clear shift away from many cash and public works programs of the New Deal. . . . [A]bove all, there was the so-called War on Poverty, conceived by Kennedy before his death — or more accurately, by Walter Heller, his chief economic adviser — but carried out by his successor.

In his State of the Union Message in January 1964 — a time when the President's Council on Economic Advisors concluded that about one-fifth of the American people, including nearly half of the nation's blacks, were poor — Lyndon Johnson, a Roosevelt protégé who wanted to start his own New Deal, called upon Congress to enact a thirteen-point program that would declare "unconditional war on poverty [in America.]" . . . Seven months later, the Economic Opportunity Act (E.O.A.), or the antipoverty bill, was passed, establishing the Office of Economic Opportunity (O.E.O.), an independent federal agency headed by a director (Sargent Shriver) responsible to the President. The measure also called for the creation of Volunteers in Service to America or

V.I.S.T.A., a domestic peace corps; a Job Corps for school dropouts; an Upward Bound program to encourage bright slum children to go to college; a Neighborhood Youth Corps for jobless teenagers; Operation Head Start, a project to give preschool training to children; special programs of grants and loans to low-income rural families and migrant workers; a very controversial and never fully agreed upon comprehensive Community Action Program designed, in theory, to empower the poor by securing their "maximum feasible participation" in the creation and operation of community action agencies (or CAAs) to combat poverty in their communities; and a number of other programs designed to "pursue victory over the most ancient of mankind's enemies." . . .

Congress in 1964 [passed] the Food Stamp Act, a considerable improvement over an existing food distribution program. At the time the nation had a commodity scheme that was designed primarily to promote the interests of commercial farmers rather than those of poor consumers; economic, rather than social welfare, policy determined its operation. Under its provisions, which were embodied in the Agriculture Act of 1949, the Secretary of Agriculture, in order to reduce surpluses and prevent waste, was directed to distribute commodities acquired through federal price supports to low-income families. The level of program activity, then, as well as the type of items provided, depended entirely on the availability of surplus foods rather than on the nutritional needs or desires of those participating in the program.

The Food Stamp Program was aimed at overcoming these deficiencies, largely by expanding the purchasing power of the needy and by separating operation of the program from the concerns of agricultural producers and the conditions of their markets. Certified low-income families could purchase stamps at substantial savings — a family of four with a monthly income of $100, for example, could buy $78 worth of stamps for $44 — which in effect replaced cash in food stores, allowing their users the freedom to purchase what they wished and needed. And while the scheme was by no means perfect — it was optional rather than mandatory, and many communities chose not to participate in it; each state set its own eligibility requirements and hence there was a good deal of variation within the program; the cost of the stamps was too high for some, who could not take advantage of the arrangement and, in fact, when the program began the number of participants dropped considerably from those who had been receiving federal "commodities," especially in the South — it was an important welfare-oriented program that served the needs of many low-income families, one that would grow and be improved later. . . .

An advance for the nation's aged — considered by most to be both especially needy and deserving — was also scored at that time with the adoption of Title XVIII, or the "Medicare" amendments to the Social Security Act, approved by President Johnson on July 30, 1965. The measure represented the nation's first major stride toward some sort of national health insurance scheme, at least for more than twenty million of its older citizens. . . .

In brief, Medicare provided hospital and medical insurance (as well as coverage for some post-hospital care) for virtually all Americans on reaching age sixty-five. The hospital insurance was compulsory and financed by an increase in Social Security taxes, while enrollment in the medical plan was voluntary and paid for by a monthly premium of three dollars (and general tax revenues). While this measure also had its shortcomings — it, too, covered only the aged, it was relatively costly, it did not cover all medical and hospital expenses, it was curative rather than preventive, and so on — the fact is that a large number of older people received medical and hospital care that previously they could not have obtained, or that otherwise would have exhausted their savings—and did so "free" from the stigma of relief.

A mixed blessing, too, were the "Medicaid" amendments to the Social Security Act, usually referred to as Title XIX, signed into law by President Johnson on July 30, 1965. Under their provisions, the federal government provided grants to the states to assist them in helping needy citizens receive improved medical and hospital services. While the plan was established primarily for recipients of federally aided public assistance programs, if funds were available, coverage would be extended to citizens who were not on welfare but who otherwise could not afford medical treatment (the "medically indigent," in other words). The program was designed to end "charity medical care" by giving the needy the money and, presumably, access to the entire health care system: whereas previously most of the poor were forced to depend on overcrowded and sometimes distant public hospitals and clinics, where they frequently received inadequate care, Medicaid recipients could now visit any doctor or hospital willing to treat them. . . .

Meanwhile, the welfare crisis continued. Neither the Public Welfare Amendments of 1962 nor the Economic Opportunity Act of 1964—or the spate of other measures enacted during the Kennedy-Johnson administration, including a rent supplement program (1965), the Elementary and Secondary Education Act of 1965, the Higher Education Act of the same year, and the 1966 Demonstration (Model) Cities and Metropolitan Development Act—succeeded in getting people off the relief rolls and onto the tax rolls, as had been hoped—and promised. Indeed, the number of recipients and total expenditures continued to climb: despite the fact that between 1963 and 1966 federal grants to the states for social services more than doubled, approximately one million new public assistance cases were added to the welfare rolls, especially in the A.F.D.C. programs—and another 3.3 million would be added before the end of the decade. . . .

NOTES AND QUESTIONS

1. As Trattner notes, welfare caseloads continued to climb in the face of increased spending on economic development and social services designed to reduce dependency and costs, and policymakers were looking for explanations. In 1965, the government released a report entitled "The Negro Family: The Case for National Action." The "Moynihan Report," named after its principal author and then Assistant Secretary of Labor Daniel Patrick Moynihan, was a highly controversial assessment of the state of poverty in the African-American community. Drafted as an internal agency memo to bolster the case for the War on Poverty, many critics assailed the report for pathologizing the African-American family—especially female-headed households—while others thought it justified scaling back the AFDC program. In fact, Moynihan concluded a chapter on the family by stating that "[t]he steady expansion of this welfare program [AFDC], as of public assistance programs in general, can be taken as a measure of the steady disintegration of the Negro family structure over the past generation in the United States." Do you think that Moynihan was suggesting that welfare causes family disintegration or reflects it?

2. Sociologist William Julius Wilson has lamented the lack of sustained inquiry that resulted from the controversy surrounding the Moynihan Report as well as the challenge of using research to inform public policy: "When figures on black crime, teenage pregnancy, female-headed families, and welfare dependency are released to the public without sufficient explanation, racial stereotypes are reinforced." Williams Julius Wilson, *The Truly Disadvantaged: The Inner City, the Underclass, and Public Policy* 21 (1987). While noting that "the social problems of urban life in the United States are, in large measure, the problems of racial inequality" (*id.* at 20), Wilson went on to describe both individual *and* societal causes for widespread poverty among African Americans in urban areas. He argued for more nuanced policy prescriptions than the traditional all-or-none role for government that characterizes much of the social welfare debate. An excerpt from his important work is included later in this chapter.

3. The War on Poverty was launched during a period of significant national job losses in the farming and manufacturing sectors. To the extent that social welfare policy is related to labor policy, what impact do you think these structural changes had on the success or failure of the War on Poverty? How do we know if increased social spending made things better or worse for workers and others?

4. The War on Poverty coincided with a robust welfare rights movement, which increased demands for public relief. For more on the welfare rights movement, see Francis Fox Piven & Richard A. Cloward, *Poor People's Movements: Why They Succeed, How They Fail* (1977). As described in more detail in Chapters 3 and 10, welfare rights lawyers also pursued active litigation in the federal courts attempting to establish substantive benefit entitlements and to defeat state-legislated morality or other restrictions on aid. King v. Smith, excerpted next, is one of a series of cases brought by advocates in an aggressive effort to defend and extend welfare rights.

KING v. SMITH
392 U.S. 309 (1968)

Chief Justice WARREN delivered the opinion of the Court.

Alabama, together with every other State, Puerto Rico, the Virgin Islands, the District of Columbia, and Guam, participates in the Federal Government's Aid to Families With Dependent Children (AFDC) program, which was established by the Social Security Act of 1935. This appeal presents the question whether a regulation of the Alabama Department of Pensions and Security, employed in that Department's administration of the State's federally funded AFDC program, is consistent with Subchapter IV of the Social Security Act, 42 U.S.C. §§601-609, and with the Equal Protection Clause of the Fourteenth Amendment. At issue is the validity of Alabama's so-called "substitute father" regulation, which denies AFDC payments to the children of a mother who "cohabits" in or outside her home with any single or married able-bodied man.

The AFDC program is one of three major categorical public assistance programs established by the Social Security Act of 1935. The category singled out for welfare assistance by AFDC is the "dependent child," who is defined in the Act, as an age-qualified "needy child . . . who has been deprived of parental support or care by reason of the death, continued absence from the home or physical or mental incapacity of a parent, and who is living with" any one of several listed relatives. Under this provision, and, insofar as relevant here, aid can be granted only if "a parent" of the needy child is continually absent from the home. Alabama considers a man who qualifies as a "substitute father" under its regulation to be a nonabsent parent within the federal statute. The State therefore denies aid to an otherwise eligible needy child on the basis that his substitute parent is not absent from the home.

Under the Alabama regulation, an "able-bodied man, married or single, is considered a substitute father of *all the children of the applicant . . .* mother" in three different situations: (1) if "he lives in the home with the child's natural or adoptive mother for the purpose of cohabitation"; or (2) if "he visits (the home) frequently for the purpose of cohabiting with the child's natural or adoptive mother"; or (3) if "he does not frequent the home but cohabits with the child's natural or adoptive mother elsewhere." Whether the substitute father is actually the father of the children is irrelevant. It is also irrelevant whether he is legally obligated to support the children, and whether he does, in fact, contribute to their support. What is determinative is simply whether he "cohabits" with the mother.

The testimony below by officials responsible for the administration of Alabama's AFDC program establishes that "cohabitation," as used in the regulation, means essentially that the man and woman have "frequent" or "continuing" sexual relations. With regard to how frequent or continual these relations must be, the testimony is conflicting. One state official testified that the regulation applied only if the parties had sex at least once a week; another thought once every three months would suffice, and still another believed once every six months sufficient. The regulation itself provides that pregnancy or a baby under six months of age is *prima facie* evidence of a substitute father.

Between June, 1964, when Alabama's substitute father regulation became effective, and January, 1967, the total number of AFDC recipients in the State declined by about 20,000 persons, and the number of children recipients by about 16,000, or 22%. As applied in this case, the regulation has caused the termination of all AFDC payments to the appellees, Mrs. Sylvester Smith and her four minor children.

Mrs. Smith and her four children, ages 14, 12, 11, and 9, reside in Dallas County, Alabama. For several years prior to October 1, 1966, they had received aid under the AFDC program. By notice dated October 11, 1966, they were removed from the list of persons eligible to receive such aid. This action was taken by the Dallas County welfare authorities pursuant to the substitute father regulation, on the ground that a Mr. Williams came to her home on weekends and had sexual relations with her.

Three of Mrs. Smith's children have not received parental support or care from a father since their natural father's death in 1955. The fourth child's father left home in 1963, and the child has not received the support or care of his father since then. All the children live in the home of their mother, and, except for the substitute father regulation, are eligible for aid. The family is not receiving any other type of public assistance, and has been living, since the termination of AFDC payments, on Mrs. Smith's salary of between $16 and $20 per week which she earns working from 3:30 a.m. to 12 noon as a cook and waitress.

Mr. Williams, the alleged "substitute father" of Mrs. Smith's children, has nine children of his own and lives with his wife and family, all of whom are dependent upon him for support. Mr. Williams is not the father of any of Mrs. Smith's children. He is not legally obligated, under Alabama law, to support any of Mrs. Smith's children. Further, he is not willing or able to support the Smith children, and does not, in fact, support them. His wife is required to work to help support the Williams household.

The AFDC program is based on a scheme of cooperative federalism. It is financed largely by the Federal Government, on a matching fund basis, and is administered by the States. States are not required to participate in the program, but those which desire to take advantage of the substantial federal funds available for distribution to needy children are required to submit an AFDC plan for the approval of the Secretary of Health, Education, and Welfare (HEW). The plan must conform with several requirements of the Social Security Act and with rules and regulations promulgated by HEW.

One of the statutory requirements is that "aid to families with dependent children . . . shall be furnished with reasonable promptness to all eligible individuals. . . ." As noted above, the Act defines a "dependent child" as one who has been deprived of "parental" support or care by reason of the death, continued absence, or incapacity of a "parent." In combination, these two provisions of the Act clearly require participating States to furnish aid to families with children who have a parent absent from the home, if such families are in other respects eligible.

The State argues that its substitute father regulation simply defines who is a nonabsent "parent" under the Social Security Act. The State submits that the regulation is a legitimate way of allocating its limited resources available for AFDC assistance, in that it reduces the caseload of its social workers and provides increased benefits to those still eligible for assistance. Two state interests are asserted in support of the allocation of AFDC assistance achieved by the regulation: first, it discourages illicit sexual relationships and illegitimate births; second, it puts families in which there is an informal "marital" relationship on a par with those in which there is an ordinary marital relationship, because families of the latter sort are not eligible for AFDC assistance.

We think it well to note at the outset what is *not* involved in this case. There is no question that States have considerable latitude in allocating their AFDC resources, since each State is free to set its own standard of need and to determine the level of benefits by the amount of funds it devotes to the program. Further, there is no question that regular and actual contributions to a needy child, including contributions from the kind of person Alabama calls a substitute father, can be taken into account in determining whether the child is needy. In other words, if by reason of such a man's contribution, the child is not in financial need, the child would be ineligible for AFDC assistance without regard to the substitute father rule. The appellees here, however, meet Alabama's need requirements; their alleged substitute father makes no contribution to their support; and they have been denied assistance solely on the basis of the substitute father regulation. Further, the regulation itself is unrelated to need, because the actual financial situation of the family is irrelevant in determining the existence of a substitute father.

Also not involved in this case is the question of Alabama's general power to deal with conduct it regards as immoral and with the problem of illegitimacy. This appeal raises only the question whether the State may deal with these problems in the manner that it has here — by flatly denying AFDC assistance to otherwise eligible dependent children.

Alabama's argument based on its interests in discouraging immorality and illegitimacy would have been quite relevant at one time in the history of the AFDC program. However, subsequent developments clearly establish that these state interests are not presently legitimate justifications for AFDC disqualification. Insofar as this or any similar regulation is based on the State's asserted interest in discouraging illicit sexual behavior and illegitimacy, it plainly conflicts with federal law and policy.

A significant characteristic of public welfare programs during the last half of the 19th century in this country was their preference for the "worthy" poor. Some poor persons were thought worthy of public assistance, and others were thought unworthy because of their supposed incapacity for "moral regeneration." This worthy-person concept characterized the mothers' pension welfare programs, which were the precursors of AFDC. Benefits under the mothers' pension programs, accordingly, were customarily restricted to widows who were considered morally fit.

In this social context it is not surprising that both the House and Senate Committee Reports on the Social Security Act of 1935 indicate that States participating in AFDC were free to impose eligibility requirements relating to the "moral character" of applicants. During the following years, many state AFDC plans included provisions making ineligible for assistance dependent children not living in "suitable homes." As applied, these suitable home provisions frequently disqualified children on the basis of the alleged immoral behavior of their mothers.

In the 1940's, suitable home provisions came under increasing attack. Critics argued, for example, that such disqualification provisions undermined a mother's confidence and authority, thereby promoting continued dependency; that they forced destitute mothers into increased immorality as a means of earning money; that they were habitually used to disguise systematic racial discrimination, and that they senselessly punished impoverished children on the basis of their mothers' behavior, while inconsistently permitting them to remain in the allegedly unsuitable homes. In 1945, the predecessor of HEW produced a state letter arguing against suitable home provisions and recommending their abolition. Although 15 States abolished their provisions during the following decade, numerous other States retained them.

In the 1950's, matters became further complicated by pressures in numerous States to disqualify illegitimate children from AFDC assistance. Attempts were made in at least 18 States to enact laws excluding children on the basis of their own or their siblings' birth status. All but three attempts failed to pass the state legislatures, and two of the three successful bills were vetoed by the governors of the States involved. In 1960, the federal agency strongly disapproved of illegitimacy disqualifications.

Nonetheless, in 1960, Louisiana enacted legislation requiring, as a condition precedent for AFDC eligibility, that the home of a dependent child be "suitable," and specifying that any home in which an illegitimate child had been born subsequent to the receipt of public assistance would be considered unsuitable. In the summer of 1960, approximately 23,000 children were dropped from Louisiana's AFDC rolls. In disapproving this legislation, then Secretary of Health, Education, and Welfare Flemming issued what is now known as the Flemming Ruling, stating that, as of July 1, 1961,

> A State plan . . . may not impose an eligibility condition that would deny assistance with respect to a needy child on the basis that the home conditions in which the child lives are

unsuitable, while the child continues to reside in the home. Assistance will therefore be continued during the time efforts are being made either to improve the home conditions or to make arrangements for the child elsewhere.

Congress quickly approved the Flemming Ruling, while extending until September 1, 1962, the time for state compliance. At the same time, Congress acted to implement the ruling by providing, on a temporary basis, that dependent children could receive AFDC assistance if they were placed in foster homes after a court determination that their former homes were, as the Senate Report stated, "unsuitable because of the immoral or negligent behavior of the parent."

In 1962, Congress made permanent the provision for AFDC assistance to children placed in foster homes and intended such coverage to include children placed in child-care institutions. At the same time, Congress modified the Flemming Ruling by amending the Act. As amended, the statute permits States to disqualify from AFDC aid children who live in unsuitable homes, provided they are granted other "adequate care and assistance."

Thus, under the 1961 and 1962 amendments to the Social Security Act, the States are permitted to remove a child from a home that is judicially determined to be so unsuitable as to "be contrary to the welfare of such child." The States are also permitted to terminate AFDC assistance to a child living in an unsuitable home if they provide other adequate care and assistance for the child under a general welfare program. The statutory approval of the Flemming Ruling, however, precludes the States from otherwise denying AFDC assistance to dependent children on the basis of their mothers' alleged immorality or to discourage illegitimate births.

The most recent congressional amendments to the Social Security Act further corroborate that federal public welfare policy now rests on a basis considerably more sophisticated and enlightened than the "worthy person" concept of earlier times. State plans are now required to provide for a rehabilitative program of improving and correcting unsuitable homes; to provide voluntary family planning services for the purpose of reducing illegitimate births; and to provide a program for establishing the paternity of illegitimate children and securing support for them.

In sum, Congress has determined that immorality and illegitimacy should be dealt with through rehabilitative measures rather than measures that punish dependent children, and that protection of such children is the paramount goal of AFDC. In light of the Flemming Ruling and the 1961, 1962, and 1968 amendments to the Social Security Act, it is simply inconceivable, as HEW has recognized, that Alabama is free to discourage immorality and illegitimacy by the device of absolute disqualification of needy children. Alabama may deal with these problems by several different methods under the Social Security Act. But the method it has chosen plainly conflicts with the Act. . . .

Alabama's substitute father regulation, as written and as applied in this case, requires the disqualification of otherwise eligible dependent children if their mother "cohabits" with a man who is not obligated by Alabama law to support the children. The regulation is therefore invalid because it defines "parent" in a manner that is inconsistent with the Social Security Act. In denying AFDC assistance to appellees on the basis of this invalid regulation, Alabama has breached its federally imposed obligation to furnish "aid to families with dependent children . . . with reasonable promptness to all eligible individuals. . . ."

Our conclusion makes unnecessary consideration of appellees' equal protection claim, upon which we intimate no views.

We think it well, in concluding, to emphasize that no legitimate interest of the State of Alabama is defeated by the decision we announce today. The State's interest in discouraging illicit sexual behavior and illegitimacy may be protected by other means, subject to constitutional limitations, including state participation in AFDC rehabilitative programs. Its interest in economically allocating its limited AFDC resources may be protected by its undisputed power to set the level of benefits and the standard of need, and by its taking into account in determining whether a child is needy all actual and regular contributions to his support.

All responsible governmental agencies in the Nation today recognize the enormity and pervasiveness of social ills caused by poverty. The causes of and cures for poverty are currently the subject of much debate. We hold today only that Congress has made at least this one determination: that destitute children who are legally fatherless cannot be flatly denied federally funded assistance on the transparent fiction that they have a substitute father.

Mr. Justice DOUGLAS, concurring.

The Court follows the statutory route in reaching the result that I reach on constitutional grounds. It is, of course, traditional that our disposition of cases should, if possible, be on statutory, rather than constitutional, grounds, unless problems of statutory construction are insurmountable. We do have, however, in this case, a longstanding administrative construction that approves state AFDC plans containing a "man in the house" provision. Certainly that early administrative construction, which, so far as I can ascertain, has been a consistent one, is entitled to great weight.

The Department of Health, Education, and Welfare balked at the Alabama provision only because it reached all nonmarital sexual relations of the mother, not just nonmarital relations on a regular basis in the mother's house. Since I cannot distinguish between the two categories, I reach the constitutional question.

The Alabama regulation describes three situations in which needy children, otherwise eligible for relief, are to be denied financial assistance. In none of these is the child to blame. The disqualification of the family, and hence the needy child, turns upon the "sin" of the mother.

First, if a man not married to the mother and not the father of the children lives in her home for purposes of cohabiting with her, the children are cast into the outer darkness.

Second, if a man who is not married to the mother and is not the father of the children visits her home for the purpose of cohabiting with her, the needy children meet the same fate.

Third, if a man not married to the mother and not the father of the children cohabits with her outside the home, then the needy children are likewise denied relief. In each of these three situations, the needy family is wholly cut off from AFDC assistance without considering whether the mother's paramour is, in fact, aiding the family, is financially able to do so, or is legally required to do so. Since there is "sin," the paramour's wealth or indigency is irrelevant.

In other words, the Alabama regulation is aimed at punishing mothers who have nonmarital sexual relations. The economic need of the children, their age, their other means of support, are all irrelevant. The standard is the so-called immorality of the mother.

. . . [W]e [have] held that the Equal Protection Clause of the Fourteenth Amendment barred discrimination against illegitimate children. We held that they cannot be denied a cause of action because they were conceived in "sin," that the making of such a disqualification was an invidious discrimination. I would think precisely the same result should be reached here. I would say that the immorality of the mother has no rational connection with the need of her children under any welfare program. . . .

NOTES AND QUESTIONS

1. A unanimous Court in *King* struck down the Alabama statute for conflicting with amendments to the Social Security Act that proscribed "suitable home" provisions in the AFDC program. In rejecting an Alabama rule that was designed both to legislate morality (discouraging "illicit sexual relationships and illegitimate births") and to enforce labor-market discipline (making sure families on welfare were not economically better off than those in "an ordinary marital relationship"), the Court said that "federal public welfare policy now rests on a basis considerably more sophisticated and enlightened than the 'worthy-person' concept of earlier times." This appears to signal an important rhetorical shift, but is that how you read the opinion? Do the majority and concurring opinions suggest that moral arguments about the deserving and undeserving poor are no longer in play here?

2. Chapters 3 and 4 discuss the constitutional welfare cases in more detail, but in the term following *King*, the Court struck down Connecticut's one-year residency requirement for AFDC as violating a fundamental constitutional right to travel. Shapiro v. Thompson, 394 U.S. 619 (1969). In Goldberg v. Kelly, 397 U.S. 254 (1970), the Court subsequently held that AFDC benefits are a form of property entitling recipients to constitutional due process protections before they can be terminated. These cases limited traditional state discretion in legislating morality, eligibility, and procedures, and contributed in part to the significant expansion in welfare rolls described above. As scholars have noted, cases like *King* and expanded caseloads helped to fuel a public backlash against welfare. *See* Amy L. Wax, *Norm Change or Judicial Decree—The Courts, the Public, and Welfare Reform*, 32 Harv. J.L. & Pub. Pol'y 45 (2009).

3. In 1969, President Richard Nixon proposed the Family Assistance Plan (FAP) as a major overhaul of the welfare system. The principal architect of the FAP was Assistant for Urban Affairs Daniel Patrick Moynihan — author of the controversial report described earlier — and it would have replaced AFDC with a guaranteed annual income of $1,600 for a family of four (more than $10,000 in 2013), along with $800 in food stamps. Two-parent working and non-working poor families would have qualified, and states could have supplemented the grant, partly with additional federal funding. The FAP would have had the greatest impact in the impoverished South, where the proposed income would have exceeded meager AFDC payments and extended benefits to many not covered by the existing program.

The FAP passed the House of Representatives in 1970 but died in the Senate, where conservatives and liberals opposed it for being at once too generous and too stingy. Moynihan himself placed most of the blame on liberals, who also had concerns about the FAP's work requirements. Daniel P. Moynihan, *The Politics of a Guaranteed Income: The Nixon Administration and the Family Assistance Plan* (1973). Nevertheless, elements of the proposal, including work requirements and work incentives, would find their way into later amendments and programs.

4. In *Regulating the Poor: The Functions of Public Welfare* (1971), sociologists Francis Fox Piven and Richard A. Cloward argue that:

> [E]xpansive relief policies are designed to mute civil disorder, and restrictive ones to reinforce work norms. In other words, relief policies are cyclical — liberal or restrictive depending on the problems of regulation in the larger society with which government must contend[, which] . . . clearly belies the popular supposition that government social policies, including relief policies, are becoming progressively more responsible, humane and generous. . . .

Does their analysis sound right to you given the period in which they were writing? Consider their thesis in the following section on welfare reform.

D. CRITIQUE, RETRENCHMENT, AND WELFARE REFORM

> She has eighty names, thirty addresses, twelve Social Security cards and is collecting veterans' benefits on four non-existing deceased husbands. And she's collecting Social Security on her cards. She's got Medicaid, getting food stamps and she is collecting welfare under each of her names. Her tax-free cash income is over $150,000.
> —Ronald Reagan's 1976 stump speech describing the "welfare queen"

If welfare recipients achieved a modest measure of procedural protection in the courts, they were not immune from political attacks. California Governor Ronald Reagan introduced the "welfare queen" into public discourse during his 1976 primary campaign for the Republican nomination for President. While his caricature about a woman from Chicago's South Side did not mention race, Reagan's gendered and barely coded racial critique resonated strongly with a White middle class fearful of losing further economic ground during the 1970s "stagflation" — a period of slow economic growth and high unemployment and inflation. In fact, such attacks helped to fuel a grassroots antitax movement opposed to "big government" generally and social welfare spending in particular. Reagan himself rode this antitax sentiment — beginning with the 1978 passage of Proposition 13 in California — to the White House in 1980.

1. Social Welfare Policy Critics

During the 1980s, critics challenged existing social welfare policies on moral and philosophical grounds. Charles Murray led the moral critique against so-called "transfers" — from the rich to the poor and between the poor — while Lawrence

Mead argued that public assistance should come with reciprocal responsibility (what he called the social obligations of citizenship). In response to Murray's and Mead's individualistic accounts of social obligation, William Julius Wilson offered a structural account that took seriously historical and contemporary discrimination and labor market experiences in the African-American community, without absolving individuals of responsibility for their own actions.

CHARLES MURRAY, *LOSING GROUND: AMERICAN SOCIAL POLICY, 1950-1980* (1984)

"WHY GIVE ANYTHING AT ALL?"

If social policy may be construed, as I suggested at the beginning of the book, as transfers from the haves to the have-nots, the proper first question is, "What is the justification for any transfers at all?" Why should one person give *anything* to a stranger whose only claim to his help is a common citizenship?

Suppose that I am not opposed to the notion of government transfers, but neither do I think that equality of outcome is always a good in itself. I attach considerable value to the principle that people get what they deserve. In other words, "I" am a fairly typical citizen with a middle-of-the-road, pragmatic political philosophy.

I am asked to consider the case of a man who has worked steadily for many years and, in his fifties, is thrown out of his job because the factory closes. Why should I transfer money to him — provide him with unemployment checks, and perhaps, permanent welfare support? The answer is not difficult. I may rationalize it any number of ways, but at bottom I consent to transfer money to him because I want to. The worker has plugged along as best he could, contributed his bit to the community, and now faces a personal disaster. He is one of my fellows in a very meaningful way — "There but for the grace of God . . ." — and I am happy to see a portion of my income used to help him out.

A second man, healthy and in the prime of life, refuses to work. I offer him a job, and he still refuses to work. I am called upon to answer the question again: Why would I transfer money to him? Why should I not let him starve, considering it a form of suicide?

It is a question to ponder without escape hatches. I may not assume that the man can be made to change his ways with the right therapeutic intervention. I may not assume that he has some mental or environmental handicap that relieves him of responsibility. He is a man of ordinary capacities who wishes to live off my work rather than work for himself. Why should I consent?

Suppose that I decide not to let him starve in the streets, for reasons having to do with the sanctity of life (I would prevent a suicide as well). The decision does not take me very far in setting up an ideal policy. At once, I run into choices when I compare his situation (we will call him the drone) with that of the laid-off worker.

Suppose that I have only enough resources either (a) to keep both alive at a bare subsistence level or (b) to support the laid-off worker at a decent standard of living and the drone at a near-starvation level. What would be the just policy? Would it be right, would it be fair, to make the worker live more miserably so that I might be more generous to the drone?

We may put the question more provocatively: Suppose that scarce resources were not a problem — that we could afford to support both at a decent standard of living. Should we do so? Is it morally appropriate to give the same level of support to the two men? Would it be right to offer the same respect to the two men? The same discretionary choice in how to use the help that was provided?

These are not rhetorical questions nor are they questions about expedient policy. They ask about the justice and humanity of the alternatives. I submit that it is not humane to the laid-off worker to treat him the same as the drone. It is not just to accord the drone the respect that the laid-off worker has earned.

The point is that, in principle, most of us provide some kinds of assistance gladly, for intuitively obvious reasons. We provide other kinds of assistance for reasons that, when it comes down to it, are extremely hard to defend on either moral or practical grounds. An ethically ideal social policy — an intuitively satisfying one — would discriminate among recipients. It would attach a pat on the back to some transfers and give others begrudgingly.

We have yet to tackle the question of whether the point has anything to do with recipients in the workaday world. Who is to say that the drone has no justification for refusing work (he was trained as a cook and we offer him a job sweeping floors)? Who is to say whether the laid-off worker is blameless for the loss of his job (his sloppy workmanship contributed to the factory's loss of business to the Japanese)? Who is to say that the income of the taxpaying donor is commensurate with his value to society — that he "deserves" his income any more than the drone deserves the gift of a part of it? But such questions define the operational barriers to establishing a social policy that discriminates among recipients according to their deserts. They do not touch on the legitimacy of the principle.

ROBBING PETER TO PAY PAUL: TRANSFERS FROM POOR TO POOR

When we think of transfers, we usually think in terms of economic transfers from richer to poorer. In reality, social policy can obligate one citizen to turn over a variety of "goods" as a donation on behalf of some other person; access to parking spaces reserved for the handicapped is a simple example.

Sometimes these noneconomic transfers, like the economic ones, are arranged so that the better-off give up something to the worse-off, and the argument about whether the transfer is appropriate follows the lines of the issues I have just raised. But in a surprising number of instances, the transfers are mandated by the better-off, while the price must be paid by donors who are just as poor as the recipient.

Now suppose that the same hypothetical "I" considers the case of two students in an inner-city high school. Both come from poor families. Both have suffered equal deprivations and social injustices. They have the same intelligence and human potential. For whatever reasons — let us assume pure accident — the two students behave differently in school. One student (the good student) studies hard and pays attention in class. The other student (the mischievous student) does not study and instead creates disturbances, albeit good-natured disturbances in the classroom.

I observe a situation in which the teacher expels the mischievous student from the classroom more or less at will. The result is that he becomes further alienated from school, drops out, and eventually ends up on welfare or worse. I know that the cause of this sequence of events (his behavior in class) was no worse than the behavior of millions of middle-class students who suffer nothing like the same penalty. They too are kicked out of class when they act up, but for a variety of reasons they stay in school and eventually do well. Further yet, I know that the behavior of the teacher toward the student is biased and unfairly harsh because the student is an inner-city black and the teacher is a suburban white who neither understands nor sympathizes with such students.

On all counts, then, I observe that the mischievous student expelled from the classroom is a victim who deserves a system that does not unfairly penalize him. I therefore protect him against the bias and arbitrariness of the teacher. The teacher cannot expel the student from class unless the student's behavior meets certain criteria far beyond the ordinary talking and laughing out of turn that used to get him in trouble.

The result, let us say, is that the student continues to act as before, but remains in the classroom. Other students also respond to the reality of the greater latitude they now have. The amount of teaching is reduced, and so is the ability of students to concentrate on their work even if they want to.

I know, however, that some benefits are obtained. The mischievous student who formerly dropped out of school does not. He obtains his diploma, and with it some advantages in the form of greater education (he learned something, although not much, while he stayed in school) and a credential to use when applying for a job.

This benefit has been obtained at a price. The price is not money — let us say it costs no more to run the school under the new policy than under the old. No transfers have been exacted from the middle class. The transfer instead is wholly from the good student to the mischievous one. For I find that the quality of education obtained by the good student deteriorated badly, both because the teacher had less time and energy for teaching and because the classroom environment was no longer suitable for studying. One poor and disadvantaged student has been compelled (he had no choice in the matter) to give up part of his education so that the other student could stay in the classroom.

What is my rationale for enforcing this transfer? In what sense did the good student have an excess of educational opportunity that he could legitimately be asked to sacrifice?

The example has deliberately been construed so that neither student was intrinsically more deserving than the other. The only difference between the two was behavioral, with one student behaving in a more desirable way than the other student. Even under these unrealistically neutral conditions, it is hard to avoid the conclusion that the transfer was unjustifiable. Now, let us make the example more realistic.

A student who reaches adolescence in an inner-city school with high motivation to study and learn does not do so by accident. The motivation is likely to reflect merit — on the student's part, on the parents' part, or on a combination of the two. In the good student's behavior I am observing not just a "desirable" response, but a praiseworthy one.

Further, if we make the example realistic, the good student does not transfer simply an abstract deterioration in the quality of education, from a potentially fine education to a merely adequate one. The more likely loss is a much greater one, from an adequate education that might have prepared the good student to take advantage of opportunities for higher education to an inadequate education that leaves the good student, no matter how well motivated, without essential tools to pursue basic routes to advancement.

Once again, let me consider my rationale without giving myself an easy way out. I may not assume that classroom instruction is not really affected by disruption; it is. I may not assume that counselors will be able shortly to change the behavior of the mischievous student. I may not assume that the school will provide separate tracks for the attentive student; the same philosophy that led to greater student rights also led to restrictions and even prohibitions on separate tracks for the better students. Most of all, I may not assume that the good student is superhuman. He may be admirable, but he is not necessarily able to get himself a good education no matter how many obstacles I put in his way.

Such transfers from poor to poor are at the heart of the inequities of social policy. Saying that we meant well does not quite cover our transgressions. Even during the period of the most active reform we could not help being aware, if only at the back of our minds, of certain moral problems. When poor delinquents arrested for felonies were left on probation, as the elite wisdom prescribed they should be, the person put most at risk were poor people who lived in their neighborhoods. They, not the elite, gave up the greater part of the good called "safety" so that the disadvantaged delinquent youth should not experience the injustice of punishment. When job-training programs were set up to function at the level of the least competent, it was the most competent trainees who had to sacrifice their opportunities to reach their potentials. When social policy reinforced the ethic that certain jobs are too demeaning to ask people to do, it was those who preferred such jobs to welfare whose basis for self-respect was stripped from them.

More generally, social policy after the mid-1960s demanded an extraordinary range of transfers from the most capable poor to the least capable, from the most law-abiding to the least law-abiding, and from the most responsible to the least responsible. In return, we gave little to these most deserving persons except easier access to welfare for themselves — the one thing they found hardest to put to "good use."

We blinked at these realities at the time. The homogenizing process helped us to blink; the poor were all poor, all more or less in the same situation, we said. All *would* be deserving, we preferred to assume, if they had not been so exploited by society, by the system. But at bottom it is difficult to imagine under what logic we thought these transfers appropriate.

The peculiarity of a transfer, as opposed to the other uses of tax monies, is that the direct benefit goes only to the recipient. If I pay for garbage collection, I, the payer, get a benefit. My garbage disappears. I may argue about whether the garbage collection service is efficiently operated and whether I am getting value for the money, but I do not argue about whether, somehow, my garbage must be made to disappear, and so must my neighbor's garbage. If I pay for Food Stamps with my tax dollars, the government is making quite a different request of me and undertaking a much different responsibility. The government judges that my income is large enough that a portion of it should be given to someone whose income, the government has decided, is too small. And when, for example, the Food Stamps are buying milk for a malnourished child, I am pleased that they should do so. But I may legitimately ask two things of the government that exercises such authority. First, I may ask that the government be *right* — right in deciding that, in some cosmic scheme of things, my resources are "large enough" and the recipient's are "too small." Second, I may ask that the transfer be successful, and therein lies a problem.

If the transfer is successful, I, the donor, can be satisfied on either of two grounds: general humanitarianism ("I am doing good") or more self-interested calculations that make transfers not so very different from police service or garbage collection. For the sake of my own quality of life, I do not want to live in a Calcutta with people sleeping in the streets in front of my house. If it is true that putting delinquents in jail only makes them into worse criminals later on, then putting the neighbors at just a little more risk by leaving delinquents at large is worth it *to them*, because eventually it will reduce their risk. The short-term injustices are rescued by a long-term greater good for everyone.

Whether I choose humanitarianism or long-term self-interest as the basis for approving the transfer, I must confront the "net happiness" challenge. If the first question of social policy asks why we approve of transfers at all, the next questions ask how we know whether our expectations are being justified. How, in an ideal world, would we measure "success" in assessing a transfer?

The social scientists who measure the effects of transfers look for success at two levels and, of necessity, ignore a third. The first level is, "Did the transfer reach the people it was intended to reach in the intended form?" (Do Food Stamps reach people who need extra food money?) The second level is, "Did the transfer have the intended direct effect on the behavior or condition of the recipients?" (Do Food Stamps improve nutrition?) The third, unattainable level is, "Did the transfer, in the long run, add to net happiness in the world?"

We may presume that better housing, nutrition, and medical care contribute to less misery and more happiness; so also do good parents, a loving spouse, safe streets, personal freedom, and respect of one's neighbors. We know how to measure some of these aspects of the quality of life; others we cannot measure at all; and, most certainly, we are unable to compare their relative worth or to add up a net total. We have no "misery" or "happiness" indexes worthy of the name. But the concept of reducing misery and increasing happiness is indispensable to deciding whether a social policy is working or failing.

With that in mind, let us consider yet another hypothetical example. In this case, I am deciding upon my stance in support or opposition of a policy that automatically provides an adequate living allowance for all single women with children. I am informed that one consequence of this policy is that large numbers of the children get better nutrition and medical care than they would otherwise obtain. Using this known fact and no others, I support the program.

Now let us assume two more known facts, that the program induces births by women who otherwise would have had fewer children (or had them under different circumstances), and that the child abuse and neglect among these children runs at twice the national average. Does this alter my judgment about whether the allowance is a net good—that it is better to have it than not have it? I must now balance the better health of some children against the pain suffered by others who would not have suffered the pain if the program had not existed. I decide—although I wish I could avoid the question altogether—that, all in all, I still support the program.

What if the incidence of abuse and neglect is three times as high? Five times? Ten times? A hundred times?

The crossover point will be different for different people. But a crossover will occur. At some point, I will say that the benefits of better nutrition and medical care are outweighed by the suffering of the abused and neglected children. What then is the humane policy? Once more I must avoid false escape hatches. I may continue to search for a strategy that does not have the overbalancing side-effects. But what is my position toward the existing program in the meantime?

All these examples — the worker versus the drone, the good student versus the bad student, the children helped versus the children hurt — are intended to emphasize a reality we tend to skirt. Devising a system of transfers that is just, fair, and compassionate involves extraordinarily difficult moral choices in which the issue is not how much good we can afford to do (as the choice is usually put), but how to do good at all. In the debate over social policy, the angels are not arrayed against the accountants.

The examples do not force one set of principles over all others. A socialist may use them in support of an internally consistent rationale for sweeping redistributive measures. At the other end of the spectrum, a libertarian may use them to support the eradication of transfers altogether. For those who fall somewhere in the middle, two more modest conclusions about what constitutes a just and humane social policy are warranted.

The first conclusion is that transfers are inherently treacherous. They can be useful; they can be needed; they can be justified. But we should approach them as a good physician uses a dangerous drug — not at all if possible, and no more than absolutely necessary otherwise.

The second conclusion is that, as a general rule, compulsory transfers from one poor person to another are uncomfortably like robbery. When we require money transfers from the obviously rich to the obviously poor, we at least have some room for error. Mistaken policies may offend our sense of right and wrong, but no great harm has been done to the donor. The same is not true of the noneconomic transfers from poor to poor. We have no margin for error at all. If we are even a little bit wrong about the consequences of the transfer, we are likely to do great injustices to people who least deserve to bear the burden.

And that, finally, is what makes the question of social policy not one of polite philosophical dispute but one of urgent importance. For the examples in this chapter are not really hypothetical. They are drawn directly from the data we reviewed. It is impossible to examine the statistics on a topic such as single teenaged mothers without admitting that we are witnessing a tragedy. *If* it had been inevitable, *if* there had been nothing we could have done to avoid it, then we could retain the same policies, trying to do more of the same and hoping for improvement. But once we must entertain the possibility that we are bringing it on ourselves, as I am arguing that both logic and evidence compel us to do, then it is time to reconsider a social policy that salves our consciences ("Look how compassionate I am") at the expense of those whom we wished to help.

LAWRENCE M. MEAD, *BEYOND ENTITLEMENT: THE SOCIAL OBLIGATIONS OF CITIZENSHIP* (1986)*

My question is why federal programs since 1960 have coped so poorly with the various social problems that have come to afflict American society. These twenty-five years have seen a succession of new programs for the needy, disadvantaged, and unemployed pour forth from Washington. But during the same period welfare dependency and unemployment have grown, standards have fallen in

*Reprinted and edited with the permission of Simon & Schuster Publishing Group from the Free Press edition of *BEYOND ENTITLEMENT: The Social Obligation of Citizenship* by Lawrence M. Mead. Copyright © 1986 by Lawrence M. Mead. All rights reserved.

the schools, and rising crime has made some areas of American cities almost uninhabitable. In all these respects, there has been a sharp decline in the habits of competence and restraint that are essential to humane society. The public never wished for this state of affairs, but government has seemed powerless to affect it.

Part of the explanation, I propose, is that the federal programs that support the disadvantaged and unemployed have become permissive in character, not authoritative. That is, they have given benefits to their recipients, but have set few requirements for how they ought to function in return. In particular, the programs have as yet no serious requirements that employable recipients work in return for support. There is good reason to think that recipients subject to such requirements would function better. . . .

The "welfare state" is more than a metaphor. By what they do and do not expect, social programs directly govern their recipients. The fatal weakness of federal programs is that they award their benefits essentially as entitlements, expecting next to nothing from the beneficiaries in return. The world the recipients live in is economically depressed, yet privileged in one sense, that it emphasizes their claims and needs almost to the exclusion of obligations. . . .

This history reflects the fact that American politics has largely been about the *extent* and not the *nature* of government. The main questions have been where to divide public authority from individual rights, and government regulation from the unfettered market. Those are the issues that chiefly divide Republicans and Democrats, and have done so since the New Deal. Firmly in that tradition, most prescriptions for American social policy say that Washington is doing either *too much* or *too little* for the poor.

There is substantial agreement about the nature of the social problem. A class of Americans, heavily poor and nonwhite, exists apart from the social mainstream. That is, it has very little contact with other Americans in the public aspects of American life, especially in schools, the workplace, and politics. This *social* separation is more worrisome to most Americans than the material deprivations that go along with disadvantage. . . . There is also substantial agreement that the solution for the disadvantaged must mean integration, that is, an end to the separation so that the disadvantaged can publicly interact with others and be accepted by them as equals. . . .

The disagreement is over the role of government in that solution, and specifically over the *scale* of government. Conservatives, for example, George Gilder or Charles Murray, say that an overblown welfare state has undermined the vitality of the private economy and deterred the needy from getting ahead on their own. Liberals say that the "war on poverty" achieved much, and would have achieved more if spending had not been cut by Republican Administrations since 1969. Those further left, for example Michael Harrington, deny the "war" ever amounted to much at all.

These criticisms have weight, but mainly in ways their makers do not intend. Washington does give too much to the poor — in the sense of benefits given as entitlements. It also gives too little — in the sense of meaningful obligations to go along with the benefits. What undermines the economy is not so much the burden on the private sector, as the message government programs have given that hard work in available jobs is no longer required of Americans. The main problem with the welfare state is not its size but its permissiveness, a characteristic that *both* liberals and conservatives seem to take for granted. The challenge to welfare statesmanship is not so much to change the extent of benefits as to couple them with serious work and other obligations that would encourage functioning and thus promote the integration of recipients. The goal must be to create for recipients *inside* the welfare state the same balance of support and expectation that other Americans face *outside* of it, as they work to support themselves and meet the other demands of society. . . .

Once we face these realities, the welfare problem emerges as one of authority rather than freedom. The best hope for solving it is, not mainly to shift the boundary between society and government, but to require recipients to function where they already are, as dependents. Even more than income and opportunity, they need to face the requirements, such as work, that true acceptance in American society requires. To create those obligations, they must be made *less* free in certain senses rather than more. . . .

As Hobbes said, government's essential, if not only, purpose is to maintain public order. "Order" here means more than just "law and order" in the narrow, police sense. It encompasses all of the social and economic conditions people depend on for satisfying lives, but which are the government's responsibility rather than their own. It includes, in other words, all of the *public* conditions for the *private* assurances of what Jefferson called "life, liberty, and the pursuit of happiness." Which conditions are a public responsibility is, of course, for politics to decide. . . .

Even the most liberal government, however, could never assure the conditions for order by itself. . . . It depends on the concurrence of people with government, and with each other. . . . Government is really a mechanism by which people force themselves to search and obey *each other* in necessary ways.

"Compliance," further, is too passive a term for what order requires, particularly in complex modern societies. People must not only refrain from offenses against others, but fulfill the expectations others have of them in public roles, as workers on the job, as neighbors, or simply as passers-by on the streets of our cities. Order requires not only self-discipline, but *activity* and *competence*. It is achieved when a population displays those habits of mutual forbearance and reliability which we call civility. . . .

The conditions for order also extend across the border between the public and private sectors in the usual meanings of those words. Obligation usually connotes governmental duties such as paying taxes, obeying the law, or serving in the military (if there is a draft). But order also requires that people function well in areas of life that are not directly regulated. They must be educated in minimal ways, able to maintain themselves, able also to cooperate with others for common ends, whether political or economic — what Samuel Huntington has called the "art of associating together." The capacities to learn, work, support one's family, and respect the rights of others amount to a set of *social* obligations alongside the political ones. A civil society might also be defined as one in which people are competent in all senses, as citizens and as workers. . . .

Social policy should be seen as one of government's means of achieving order. Social programs define much of what society expects of people in the social realm, just as other laws and the Constitution do in the political realm. By the benefits they give to and withhold from different groups, the programs declare which needs government will help people manage, and which they must manage for themselves. The structure of benefits and requirements in the programs, then, constitutes an *operational definition of citizenship*. One of the things a government must do to improve social order is to use these programs to require better functioning of recipients who have difficulty coping. The tragedy of federal social programs is that they have only begun to do this. . . .

To speak of obligating the poor may sound like abandonment of the goal of equality in the sense of mainstream income and status for the poor, the traditional aim of social policy. In reality, the lack of standards in programs has probably increased inequality in this sense by undercutting the competences the disadvantaged need to achieve status. But more importantly, equality to Americans tends not to mean middle-class income or status at all, but rather the enjoyment of equal citizenship, meaning the same rights *and* obligations as others. While we usually think of citizenship as something political, specifying rights like free speech and duties such as obedience to the law, it has a social dimension too. Benefit programs define a set of social rights for vulnerable groups, while Americans tend to regard minimal social competences like work or getting through school as obligatory even if they are not legally enforced. These *social* obligations may not be governmental, but they are public in that they fall within the collective expectation that structures an orderly society. Both political and social duties are included in what I call the common obligations of citizenship.

WILLIAM JULIUS WILSON, *THE TRULY DISADVANTAGED: THE INNER CITY, THE UNDERCLASS, AND PUBLIC POLICY* (1987)

I.   CYCLES OF DEPRIVATION AND THE GHETTO UNDERCLASS DEBATE

In the mid-1960s, urban analysts began to speak of a new dimension to the urban crisis in the form of a large subpopulation of low-income families and individuals whose behavior contrasted sharply with the behavior of the general population. Despite a high rate of poverty in ghetto neighborhoods throughout the first half of the twentieth century, rates of inner-city joblessness, teenage pregnancy, out-of-wedlock births, female-headed families, welfare dependency, and serious crime were significantly lower than in later years and did not reach catastrophic proportions until the mid-1970s.

These increasing rates of social dislocation signified changes in social organization of inner-city areas. . . . The liberal perspective on the ghetto underclass has become less persuasive and convincing in public discourse principally because many of those who represent liberal views on social issues have been reluctant to discuss openly or, in some instances, even to acknowledge the sharp increase in social pathologies in ghetto communities. . . .

By 1980, however, the problems of inner-city social dislocations had reached such catastrophic proportions that liberals were forced to readdress the question of the ghetto underclass, but this time their reactions were confused and defensive. The extraordinary rise in inner-city social dislocations following the passage of the most sweeping antidiscrimination and antipoverty legislation in the nation's history could not be explained by the 1960 explanations of ghetto-specific behavior. Moreover, because liberals had ignored these problems throughout most of the 1970s, they had no alternative explanations to advance and were therefore ill prepared to confront a new and forceful challenge from conservative thinkers.

The new conservative challenge does not represent a change in the basic premise of the interplay among cultural tradition, family biography, and individual
character; rather, it builds on this premise with the argument that the growth
of liberal social policies has exacerbated, not alleviated, ghetto-specific cultural
tendencies and problems of inner-city social dislocation. . . . Thus, unlike their
liberal counterparts, conservatives have attempted to explain the sharp rise in the
rates of dislocation among the ghetto underclass, and their arguments, which
strike many as new and refreshing, have dominated public discourse on this
subject for the last several years. . . . Probably no work has done more to promote
the view that federal programs are harmful to the poor [than Charles Murray's
Losing Ground]. . . .

II. SOCIAL CHANGE AND SOCIAL DISLOCATIONS IN THE INNER CITY

The social problems of urban life in the United States are, in large measure, the
problems of racial inequality. . . . There is no single explanation for the racial or
ethnic variations in the rates of social dislocation. . . . But I should like to suggest
several interrelated explanations that represent a comprehensive set of
variables — including societal, demographic, and neighborhood variables.
In the process, I hope to show that the sources of current problems in the
inner city are exceedingly complex and that their amelioration calls for imag-
inative and comprehensive programs of economic and social reform that are in
sharp contrast to the current approaches to social policy in America, which are
based on short-term political considerations.

THE EFFECTS OF HISTORIC AND CONTEMPORARY DISCRIMINATION

Discrimination is the most frequently invoked explanation of social
dislocations in the urban ghetto. However, proponents of the discrimination thesis often fail to make a distinction between the effects of historic
discrimination, that is, discrimination before the middle of the twentieth
century, and the effects of discrimination following that time. They therefore find it difficult to explain why the economic position of poor urban
blacks actually deteriorated during the very period in which the most
sweeping antidiscrimination legislation and programs were enacted and
implemented. Their emphasis on discrimination becomes even more
problematic in view of the economic progress of the black middle class
during the same period.

There is no doubt that contemporary discrimination has contributed to or
aggravated the social and economic conditions of the ghetto underclass. But is
discrimination really greater today than it was in 1948, when . . . black unemployment was less than half of what it is now, and the black-white unemployment
ratio was [much lower]? . . . My view is that historic discrimination is far more
important than contemporary discrimination in explaining the plight of the
ghetto underclass, but that a full appreciation of the effects of historic discrimination is impossible without taking into account other historical and
contemporary forces that have also shaped the experiences and behavior of
impoverished urban communities.

THE IMPORTANCE OF THE FLOW OF MIGRANTS

If different population sizes accounted for a good deal of the difference in the economic success of blacks and Asians, they also helped determine the dissimilar rates of progress of urban blacks and the new European arrivals. The dynamic factor behind these differences, and perhaps the most important single contributor to the varying rates of urban racial and ethnic progress in the twentieth-century United States, is the flow of migrants. After the changes in immigration policy that halted Asian immigration to America came drastic restrictions on new European immigration. However, black migration to the urban North continued in substantial numbers for several decades. The sizable and continuous migration of blacks from the South to the North, coupled with the curtailment of immigration from eastern, central and southern Europe, created a situation in which other whites muffled their negative disposition toward the new Europeans and directed their antagonism against blacks. . . .

THE RELEVANCE OF CHANGES IN THE AGE STRUCTURE

The flow of migrants also affects the average age of an ethnic group. For example, the black migration to urban centers — the continual replenishment of urban black populations by poor newcomers — predictably skewed the age profile of the urban black community and kept it relatively young. The higher the median age of a group, the greater its representation in higher income categories and professional positions. . . . Youth [is also associated with higher rates of crime], out-of-wedlock births, female-headed homes, and [welfare] dependency. . . . In short, much of what has gone awry in the inner city is due in part to the sheer increase in the number of young people, especially young minorities.

THE IMPACT OF BASIC ECONOMIC CHANGES

The population explosion among minority youths occurred at a time when changes in the economy posed serious problems for unskilled individuals, both in and out of the labor force. Urban minorities have been particularly vulnerable to structural economic changes, such as the shift from goods-producing to service-producing industries, the increasing polarization of the labor market into low-wage and high-wage sectors, technological innovation, and the relocation of manufacturing industries out of the central cities. These economic shifts point out the fact that nearly all of the large and densely populated metropolises experienced their most rapid development during an earlier industrial and transportation era. . . .

This has created "a serious mismatch between the current education distribution of minority residents in large northern cities and the changing education requirements of their rapidly transforming industries bases. This mismatch is one major reason why both unemployment rates and labor-force dropout rates among central-city blacks are much higher than those of central-city residents, and why black unemployment rates have not responded well to the economic recovery in many northern cities." . . . Heavily concentrated in central cities, blacks have experienced a deterioration in their economic position on nearly all labor-market indicators. . . .

CONCENTRATION EFFECTS: THE SIGNIFICANCE OF THE SOCIAL TRANSFORMATION
OF THE INNER CITY

. . . It is the growth of the high- and extreme-poverty areas that epitomizes the social transformation of the inner-city, a transformation that represents a change in the class structure in many inner city neighborhoods as the non-poor black middle and working classes tend no longer to reside in these neighborhoods, thereby increasing the proportion of truly disadvantaged individuals and families. What are the effects of this growing concentration of poverty on individuals and families in the inner city? . . . The problem is much more complex [than the ascendancy of a ghetto culture of poverty].

More specifically, I believe that the exodus of middle- and working-class families from many ghetto neighborhoods removes an important "social buffer" that could deflect the full impact of the kind of prolonged and increasing joblessness that plagued inner-city neighborhoods in the 1970s and early 1980s, joblessness created by uneven economic growth and periodic recessions. . . . [T]he very presence of these families during such periods provides mainstream role models that help keep alive the perception that education is meaningful, that steady employment is a viable alternative to welfare, and that family stability is the norm, not the exception. . . .

If I had to use one term to capture the differences in the experiences of low-income families who live in inner-city areas from the experience of those who live in other areas of the central city today, that term would be *concentration effects*. The social transformation of the inner-city has resulted in a disproportionate concentration of the most disadvantaged segments of the urban black population, creating a social milieu significantly different from the environment that existed in these communities several decades ago. . . .

What is significant to emphasize, however, is that inner-city communities are not only "ecologically and economically" very different from areas in which poor urban whites tend to reside, they are also very different from their own ecological and economic makeup of several decades ago. . . . The net result is that the degree of social isolation — defined in this context as the lack of contact or of sustained interaction with individuals and institutions that represent mainstream society — in these highly concentrated poverty areas has become far greater than we had previously assumed. . . . Inner-city isolation makes it much more difficult for those who are looking for jobs to be tied into the job network[,] . . . [and] also generates behavior not conducive to good work histories. . . .

The key theoretical concept, therefore, is not *culture of poverty* but *social isolation*. Culture of poverty implies that basic values and attitudes of the ghetto subculture have been internalized and thereby influence behavior. Accordingly, efforts to enhance the life chances of groups such as the ghetto underclass require, from this perspective, social policies (e.g., programs of training and education as embodied in mandatory workfare) aimed at directly changing these subcultural traits. Social isolation, on the other hand, not only implies that contact between groups of different class and/or racial background is either lacking or has become increasingly intermittent but that the nature of this contact enhances the effects of living in a highly concentrated poverty area [such as] access to jobs and job networks, availability of marriageable partners, involvement in quality schools, and exposure to conventional role models. . . . From a public policy perspective, this would mean shifting the focus from changing sub-cultural traits (as suggested by the "culture of poverty" thesis) to changing the structure of constraints and opportunities.

NOTES AND QUESTIONS

1. Murray, Mead, and Wilson were influential in the debates about social welfare policy in the 1980s and 1990s. How do their views—moral, economic, and structural—comport with your own understanding of the causes of poverty and the design of social welfare programs? That is, what sounds more right to you, that social welfare transfers are treacherous and perhaps especially damaging to the poor (Murray); that such transfers constitute an operational definition of citizenship and should come with reciprocal obligations (Mead); or that social problems are substantially the result of structural forces and therefore require responses that are not predicated on the moral worthiness or reciprocity of those in need (Wilson)?

2. All three scholars have continued to write actively on these issues. With psychologist Richard Herrnstein, Murray published a controversial book about the relationship between intelligence and socioeconomic outcomes, including highly contested data on racial and genetic differences in intelligence. *The Bell Curve: Intelligence and Class Structure in American Life* (1994). In 2012, he published a book on the growing economic and social stratification of White America. *Coming Apart: The State of White America, 1960-2010.* Mead has authored several additional books on social welfare policy with a continued focus on reciprocal obligation. *The New Politics of Poverty: The Nonworking Poor in America* (1993); *Government Matters: Welfare Reform in Wisconsin* (2004). Wilson published important works both before and after *The Truly Disadvantaged,* attempting to identify the complex and varied causes of disadvantage among the urban poor. *The Declining Significance of Race: Blacks and Changing American Institutions* (1978); *When Work Disappears: The World of the New Urban Poor* (1996).

2. The Personal Responsibility and Work Opportunity Reconciliation Act of 1996

Although Republican Ronald Reagan helped to usher in the anti-welfare era, it was Democratic candidate Bill Clinton who pledged to "end welfare as we know it" during the 1992 presidential campaign. In midterm elections after he became President, an emboldened Republican Congress twice passed welfare reform bills that Clinton vetoed as too draconian. At the same time, the Clinton administration granted waivers to more than 40 states allowing them to experiment with policies otherwise prohibited by federal law. When Congress passed welfare reform a third time in the midst of his re-election campaign, President Clinton signed the Personal Responsibility and Work Opportunity Reconciliation Act of 1996 (PRWORA).

PRWORA eliminated AFDC and ended the six-decade-long federal entitlement to benefits established by the Social Security Act of 1935. In its place, the Act created Temporary Assistance to Needy Families (TANF) through a block grant program to the states. Under TANF, benefits were time limited—not open ended like under AFDC—with a maximum lifetime grant of no more than 60 months (states were permitted to set a lower limit). Consistent with a return to animating themes of deservingness—including labor market concerns and morality—the Act also imposed stringent work requirements on most recipients and gave the states wide latitude to establish provisions "reasonably calculated to accomplish the purposes of TANF," including reducing dependency, preventing out-of-wedlock pregnancies, and encouraging two-parent families.

WILLIAM J. CLINTON, *PRESIDENT'S STATEMENT ON SIGNING THE PERSONAL RESPONSIBILITY AND WORK OPPORTUNITY RECONCILIATION ACT OF 1996*

Pub. Papers 1328 (Aug. 22, 1996)

Today, I have signed into law H.R. 3734, the "Personal Responsibility and Work Opportunity Reconciliation Act of 1996." While far from perfect, this legislation provides an historic opportunity to end welfare as we know it and transform our broken welfare system by promoting the fundamental values of work, responsibility, and family.

This Act honors my basic principles of real welfare reform. It requires work of welfare recipients, limits the time they can stay on welfare, and provides child care and health care to help them make the move from welfare to work. It demands personal responsibility, and puts in place tough child support enforcement measures. It promotes family and protects children.

This bipartisan legislation is significantly better than the bills that I vetoed. The Congress has removed many of the worst provisions of the vetoed bills and has included many of the improvements that I sought. I am especially pleased that the Congress has preserved the guarantee of health care for the poor, the elderly, and the disabled.

Most important, this Act is tough on work. Not only does it include firm but fair work requirements, it provides $4 billion more in child care than the vetoed bills—so that parents can end their dependency on welfare and go to work—and maintains health and safety standards for day care providers. The bill also gives States positive incentives to move people into jobs and holds them accountable for maintaining spending on welfare reform. In addition, it gives States the ability to create subsidized jobs and to provide employers with incentives to hire people off welfare.

The Act also does much more to protect children than the vetoed bills. It cuts spending on childhood disability programs less deeply and does not unwisely change the child protection programs. It maintains the national nutritional safety net, by eliminating the Food Stamp annual spending cap and the Food Stamp and School Lunch block grants that the vetoed bills contained. In addition, it preserves the Federal guarantee of health care for individuals who are currently eligible for Medicaid through the AFDC program or are in transition from welfare to work.

Furthermore, this Act includes the tough personal responsibility and child support enforcement measures that I proposed 2 years ago. It requires minor mothers to live at home and stay in school as a condition of assistance. It cracks down on parents who fail to pay child support by garnishing their wages, suspending their driver's licenses, tracking them across State lines, and, if necessary, making them work off what they owe.

For these reasons, I am proud to have signed this legislation. The current welfare system is fundamentally broken, and this may be our last best chance to set it straight. I am doing so, however, with strong objections to certain provisions, which I am determined to correct.

First, while the Act preserves the national nutritional safety net, its cuts to the Food Stamp program are too deep. Among other things, the Act reinstates a maximum on the amount that can be deducted for shelter costs when determining a household's eligibility for Food Stamps. This provision will disproportionately affect low-income families with children and high housing costs.

Second, I am deeply disappointed that this legislation would deny Federal assistance to legal immigrants and their children, and give States the option of doing the same. My Administration supports holding sponsors who bring immigrants into this country more responsible for their well-being. Legal immigrants and their children, however, should not be penalized if they become disabled and require medical assistance through no fault of their own. Neither should they be deprived of food stamp assistance without proper procedures or due regard for individual circumstances. Therefore, I will direct the Immigration and Naturalization Service to accelerate its unprecedented progress in removing all bureaucratic obstacles that stand in the way of citizenship for legal immigrants who are eligible. In addition, I will take any possible executive actions to avoid inaccurate or inequitable decisions to cut off food stamp benefits—for example, to a legal immigrant who has performed military service for this country or to one who has applied for and satisfied all the requirements of citizenship, but is awaiting governmental approval of his or her application.

In addition to placing an undue hardship on affected individuals, denial of Federal assistance to legal immigrants will shift costs to States, localities, hospitals, and medical clinics that serve large immigrant populations. Furthermore, States electing to deny these individuals assistance could be faced with serious constitutional challenges and protracted legal battles.

I have concerns about other provisions of this legislation as well. It fails to provide sufficient contingency funding for States that experience a serious economic downturn, and it fails to provide Food Stamp support to childless adults who want to work, but cannot find a job or are not given the opportunity to participate in a work program. In addition, we must work to ensure that States provide in-kind vouchers to children whose parents reach the 5-year Federal time limit without finding work.

This Act gives States the responsibility that they have sought to reform the welfare system. This is a profound responsibility, and States must face it squarely. We will hold them accountable, insisting that they fulfill their duty to move people from welfare to work and to do right by our most vulnerable citizens, including children and battered women. I challenge each State to take advantage of its new flexibility to use money formerly available for welfare checks to encourage the private sector to provide jobs.

The best antipoverty program is still a job. Combined with the newly increased minimum wage and the Earned Income Tax Credit—which this legislation maintains—H.R. 3734 will make work pay for more Americans.

I am determined to work with the Congress in a bipartisan effort to correct the provisions of this legislation that go too far and have nothing to do with welfare reform. But, on balance, this bill is a real step forward for our country, for our values, and for people on welfare. It should represent not simply the ending of a system that too often hurts those it is supposed to help, but the beginning of a new era in which welfare will become what it was meant to be: a second chance, not a way of life. It is now up to all of us — States and cities, the Federal Government, businesses and ordinary citizens — to work together to make the promise of this new day real.

NOTES AND QUESTIONS

1. In *Toward a Comprehensive Antipoverty Strategy: Getting Beyond the Silver Bullet*, 81 Geo. L.J. 1697 (1993), Professor Peter Edelman contrasted the "opportunity-creating" strategy of the 1960s with the "maintenance-oriented" programs of the 1990s:

    > The Great Society did, in fact, reflect a strategy — an opportunity strategy. . . . Head Start, federal aid for the education of poor children, Upward Bound, job training, and a number of other programs were all geared to prepare people to participate fully in the economy. The civil rights laws were enacted to break down barriers of discrimination and legal services for the poor were designed to create access for the poor to protection by way of the courts. Access to health care for the poor was geared towards creating a healthy work force. Because it was an opportunity strategy, the Great Society guaranteed no outcomes, whether in the form of a guaranteed job or a guaranteed income. . . . The economic theory of the Great Society was that macroeconomic policy would create the jobs; the purposes of government programs and policies were to get people ready for the jobs and break down barriers of discrimination. . . .
    >
    > Our current antipoverty policy is essentially maintenance-oriented. Yet we blame the recipients for continuing on welfare when that is all we offer in an economy that is not producing enough jobs at decent wages, or, indeed, enough jobs at all. . . . From prenatal care to early childhood development to elementary and secondary education to job training to a variety of family support services that might make a difference, we are suffering huge gaps in the quantity and quality of needed offerings. We are, consequently, not producing young adults who are ready and able to perform on the job (even as we fail to produce enough jobs to employ them if large numbers should suddenly be prepared for jobs). From housing to community economic development to law enforcement, we have similar gaps. We are, consequently, producing neither an increase in economic opportunity close to home, or community environments that can nurture people with an ethos of success that accords with the values of larger society. The consequence of all of this is that the major antipoverty program we have for adults is called welfare: cash and food assistance that keeps people dependent, but at least enables them to survive — barely.

2. Welfare caseloads dropped quickly and significantly after the enactment of PRWORA. To supporters, this meant that welfare reform was a resounding success. To people like Edelman — one of several Department of Health and Human Services officials to resign in protest over President Clinton's signing of PRWORA — welfare reform was an abdication of government's responsibility to the poor. What, if anything, do the declining caseloads tell us about the living conditions and life chances of people no longer eligible

for or receiving assistance? Are reduced welfare rolls the same thing as increased independence?

3. As noted above, more than 40 states received federal waivers to implement pilot or experimental welfare policy projects *prior* to the enactment of PRWORA. This allowed states to waive out of the rules and regulations governing AFDC, and many of these state reforms were later incorporated into PRWORA. Was welfare reform, like the New Deal, perhaps less a momentous change emanating from the federal government and more a reflection of policy judgments already being made at the state and local levels? If so, what are the strategic implications for advocates about the most effective locus for advancing social welfare policy?

E. THE NATURE OF TWENTY-FIRST-CENTURY SOCIAL OBLIGATION

As the 1990s welfare debate has slowly receded, successive administrations have tried to address spiraling health care costs. President Clinton himself undertook a major reform initiative that was ultimately unsuccessful. In a significant extension of Medicare—though not aimed at low-income people in particular—President George W. Bush signed into law the Medicare Prescription Drug Improvement and Modernization Act (MMA) of 2003. The MMA added prescription drug coverage to Medicare, which now substantially subsidizes medication costs for the elderly and disabled.

In 2010, President Barack Obama signed into law the Patient Protection and Affordable Care Act (PPACA). In 2012, the U.S. Supreme Court upheld the law in a landmark and bitterly divided 5-4 decision. *See* Nat'l Fed'n of Indep. Bus. v. Sebelius, 132 S. Ct. 2566 (2012). The PPACA is by far the most important health care reform since Medicare and Medicaid were established in 1965. It includes a number of provisions that go into effect over time, but the overall aim is to reduce the number of uninsured Americans and to bring down system-wide costs. While details of the Act and the 2011 Supreme Court case will be covered in Chapter 7, the following excerpt explores how health care reform raises questions about the nature of social obligation, including many of the arguments we have seen throughout the development of U.S. social welfare policy.

NAN HUNTER, *HEALTH INSURANCE REFORM AND INTIMATIONS OF CITIZENSHIP*
159 U. Pa. L. Rev. 1955 (2011)

[T]he political debate that preceded the enactment of the Patient Protection and Affordable Care Act (PPACA), as well as the legal debate that now swirls around the question of its constitutionality, mask a foundational question about national identity. PPACA, of course, does not literally constitute or reconstitute citizenship (although it does require legal residence as the price of admission). But it creates the potential for broad public conversation—as has never before occurred in the United States — regarding the question of what the relationship should be between membership in the American community and meaningful access to health care.

At face value, PPACA primarily seeks to make the individual and small-group health insurance markets rational and workable, to fill the enormous gap that has existed in coverage, and to create insurance exchanges to regulate quality and police access. Upon full implementation, it will achieve nearly universal, but also probably quite uneven, coverage and will perpetuate a deeply fragmented model of social insurance. If one imagines the health care system as a political domain, with the various institutions and subsystems as components, PPACA is less like our Constitution and more like a reinvention of the Articles of Confederation. Under PPACA, health insurance in the United States will remain a federated collection of risk pools, located in workplaces, public systems, and the new exchanges.

The dominant American tradition of liberal rights has long existed in a dialectical relationship with a tradition of communitarian relationships and obligations. The concept of citizenship as a reciprocal relationship dates from the liberal tradition that fueled the American Revolution. In the same vein, Kenneth Karst's work on the equal-dignity understanding of citizenship presupposes "two related and overlapping values: participation and responsibility. . . . To be a citizen is not merely to be a consumer of rights, but to be responsible to other members of the community." Despite the conventional pairing of rights and duties, there has been significantly less elaboration of the responsibility branch than of the rights branch, either in political theory or in constitutional law or scholarship. A robust debate about obligations of citizenship has emerged, however, in the legal challenges to PPACA. . . .

Of greatest importance to this emerging discourse is the individual mandate portion of PPACA. Under the Act's "minimum essential coverage" provision, all but a small number of Americans must either purchase health insurance or pay a penalty. The individual mandate requires most U.S. residents to obtain health insurance for themselves and their dependents no later than 2014; those who do not comply will be subject to a tax penalty. Enrollment in most private sector health plans will satisfy the mandate; acceptable plans include employer-sponsored policies, policies sold on the individual market, existing health plans grandfathered into the new regulations, or any other plan or policy providing "minimum essential coverage" as defined by the Secretary of Health and Human Services. Those who enroll in public plans such as Medicaid or Medicare will also be in compliance. . . .

My focus in this article is not the doctrinal analysis of the debate that will be before the Supreme Court but on the underlying social messages and meanings that are implicated in that debate. In cultural terms, the Court will have to decide whether PPACA is about preserving a fiscally and otherwise healthy collectivity — the nation — or about preserving an individually defined bundle of rights. Perhaps subconsciously, the Justices must frame the relationship between government and individual access to the health care system as primarily either about collective governance or about fostering individual self-governance. Fundamentally, the legitimacy of the individual mandate turns on whether the Court will accept that a sacrifice of individual economic liberty is justified by an obligation to contribute to the common good that accompanies membership in the American political community.

The centrality of economic liberty claims to the individual mandate debate is evident from the current litigation, in which individual plaintiffs have described the harm they suffer from the allegedly unconstitutional exercise of power in economic terms. In Florida ex rel. McCollum v. United States Department of Health and Human Services, for example, one plaintiff asserted that he had no health insurance nor any intention of purchasing any, and that, further, "he is, and expects to remain, financially able to pay for his own healthcare services if and as needed." In Thomas More Law Center v. Obama, the District Court found that the individual plaintiffs had standing because of the present injury of

> being compelled to "reorganize their [financial] affairs." . . . Plaintiffs' decision to forego certain spending today, so that they will have the funds to pay for health insurance when the Individual Mandate takes effect in 2014, are injuries fairly traceable to the Act for the purposes of conferring standing. There is nothing improbable about the contention that the Individual Mandate is causing plaintiffs to feel economic pressure today.

These assertions recall two cases decided by the Supreme Court slightly more than a century ago, which also concerned the legitimacy of a health-related mandate grounded in social welfare policy. In Jacobson v. Massachusetts, the Court upheld a requirement that every resident of Cambridge, Massachusetts, be vaccinated for smallpox, rejecting the argument that it violated bodily liberty. Less than two months later, in Lochner v. New York, the Court upheld the primacy of economic liberty and the right of contract by invalidating a law that set a maximum daily number for hours worked, a law that looked like a present-day occupational health and safety regulation.

The contemporary controversy over the legitimacy of the individual mandate in PPACA resonates with these two constitutional landmarks, not at the level of doctrine or precedent but in the realm of social meaning. At bottom, both Jacobson and Lochner concerned how much sacrifice of liberty could be demanded of the individual by the state in the interest of furthering the social compact, specifically in the context of health. In each case, the Court had to determine how direct or necessary the sacrifice of a right was to achieving the common good. In Jacobson, the Court framed the justification for coerced vaccination as necessary, literally, for community survival, a linkage that made sense in the context of an epidemic of infectious disease at the turn of the last century: "Upon the principle of self-defense, of paramount necessity, a community has the right to protect itself against an epidemic of disease which threatens the safety of its members." The Court also described the individual's duty as part of a social compact with the state:

> There are manifold restraints to which every person is necessarily subject for the common good. . . . This court has more than once recognized it as a fundamental principle that "persons and property are subjected to all kinds of restraints and burdens in order to secure the general comfort, health, and prosperity of the State; of the perfect right of the legislature to do which no question ever was, or upon acknowledged general principles ever can be made, so far as natural persons are concerned."

By contrast, the same Court in Lochner viewed the maximum hours law as an illegitimate ruse used to curtail the dynamics of the labor market:

> The act is not, within any fair meaning of the term, a health law, but is an illegal interference with the rights of individuals, both employers and employés [*sic*], to make contracts regarding labor upon such terms as they may think best, or which they may agree upon with the other parties to such contracts.

The Court's reasoning in both cases, together with the citizenship cases and *Helvering*, demonstrates that as context and historical circumstance shift, so do the formulations of a citizen's duty. . . .

At the level of social meaning, however, PPACA challenges are not about federalism, the Commerce Clause, or taxation. Just as today I would doubt that a person quarantined after arriving on a flight from New York to Los Angeles would much care whether federal or state health authorities ordered the quarantine, I doubt that the final ruling on the constitutionality of the individual mandate will be understood as resolving the question of which level of government has the power to force an individual into a community-rating insurance system. Rather, the popular understanding likely will center on the issue of whether persons can be compelled by any level of government to participate in a social insurance compact for the common good, or whether, when the rational economic choice of particular individuals would be to go it alone, a requirement to obtain health insurance would amount to what the Lochner court called "meddlesome interference[] with the rights of the individual." . . .

If the individual mandate is found to be within the scope of Article I powers, it will trump any and all conflicting state laws by virtue of the Supremacy Clause. The value of the "health insurance freedom" campaign to its proponents lies in the very process of enactment—in the opportunity created by the legislative debates and electoral campaigns to build public participation in the discourse of individual liberty as superior to collective obligation.

NOTES AND QUESTIONS

1. According to Professor Hunter, political and judicial debate over the PPACA is but the latest iteration of a long-running social discourse about the proper balance between individual liberty and the common good. Does the enactment of the PPACA reflect a post-welfare reform swing of the pendulum back toward a greater sense of collective obligation?

2. Though the PPACA Court did not cite to *Helvering*, consider these passages from the majority opinions in each case:

   > Helvering (1937): "Whether wisdom or unwisdom resides in the scheme of benefits set forth in Title II [of the Social Security Act of 1935] it is not for us to say. The answer to such inquiries must come from Congress, not the courts. Our concern here, as often, is with power, not with wisdom."

   > National Federation of Independent Business (2012): "We do not consider whether the [Patient Protection and Affordable Care] Act embodies sound policies. That judgment is entrusted to the Nation's elected leaders. We ask

only whether Congress has the power under the Constitution to enact the challenged provisions."

Why does the Court defer to Congress in some areas of social welfare policy but limit congressional authority in others? What do you think explains the Court's almost verbatim deference to the elected branches in these two cases some 75 years apart? As you move to Chapter 3 on constitutional doctrine, consider how this same judicial deference sometimes frustrates efforts of those who would like to see a more interventionist judiciary on some matters of economic and social rights.

CHAPTER
3

Poverty and the Constitution

INTRODUCTION

The practice of "poverty lawyers" is very diverse, and includes litigation, economic development, legislative advocacy, community organizing, and a range of other strategic advocacy tools to fight poverty in the United States and globally. Within the realm of litigation, the work of poverty lawyers has historically and to this day included both "service" cases, where a lawyer represents an individual poor person in a particular case with the purpose of assisting that one person (or persons) with a specific problem, and "impact" cases, whose purpose is to use an individual piece of litigation to make a significant change in the law for others facing the same asserted injustice. (Note that the line between "service" and "impact" cases is a blurry one; many impact cases start as individual cases, and every impact case has to have at least one individual with a true personal stake in the case to go forward.) This chapter focuses on the impact cases—mostly brought before the U.S. Supreme Court—that have sought justice for poor people through impact litigation under the federal Constitution.

Unsurprisingly, most of the cases presented in this chapter were brought during the War on Poverty, which was addressed in the previous chapter. The earliest case in this chapter was decided by the Court in 1956 (Griffin v. Illinois), and most were decided in the late 1960s and early 1970s. The social unrest in the United States during this era—including the civil rights movement, the anti-(Vietnam) war movement, and the burgeoning women's rights movement—is palpable in the decisions. You will read the Court's oblique reference to our "Nation's . . . present troubles" and should consider throughout the chapter how, if at all, that social context affected the Court's reasoning in the various poverty cases it faced.

These cases all arise under the Fourteenth Amendment to the U.S. Constitution. Section 1 of the Amendment reads:

> All persons born or naturalized in the United States, and subject to the jurisdiction thereof, are citizens of the United States and of the State wherein they reside. No State shall make or enforce any law which shall abridge the privileges or immunities of citizens of the United States; *nor shall any State deprive any person of life, liberty, or property, without due process of law; nor deny to any person within its jurisdiction the equal protection of the laws.*

U.S. Const. amend. XIV (emphasis added). The italicized language is the source of the claim in most of the cases you are about to read, with the question being some version of: Does the challenged governmental action deprive the party(ies) of either due process of law or equal protection of the law?

Central to many of these cases is the coming together of poverty and race. The Fourteenth Amendment was adopted in 1868 as one of the post–Civil War Reconstruction amendments. Claims of racial discrimination, or of deprivations based on race, have therefore been the most self-evident and powerful applications of the Amendment. The poverty law cases ask whether the poor should also enjoy the Amendment's protection. This question can be understood in two distinct ways. First, are poor people *qua* poor people "like" racial minorities for purposes of the Constitution, such that government action that burdens them should be closely scrutinized? If that question is answered in the negative, as it has been, we turn to the more complex question of how the racial make-up of the poor affects the analysis. As an empirical matter, low-income people in the United States are disproportionately people of color, including the African Americans whose legal rights the Amendment was originally drafted to protect. Several of the cases presented here either address or allude to the question of whether the racial composition of the class, even if not strictly a component of its definition, is relevant. That is, a distinction is drawn between intentional disparate treatment of a group on the one hand and disparate impact of an otherwise neutral law on a particular group on the other. This question is an important one across equal protection law, and nowhere more than in the poverty cases.

This chapter proceeds in two parts, mirroring the two important clauses of the Fourteenth Amendment: Due Process and Equal Protection. We begin with the "procedural due process" cases, the first of which, Goldberg v. Kelly, 397 U.S. 254 (1970), has had far-reaching significance for the so-called "administrative state" beyond the welfare benefits that it directly addressed. We then turn to *Goldberg*'s progeny, including a 2001 case that addresses the question of *Goldberg*'s application to cash assistance benefits after 1996 welfare reform.

We then turn to the Equal Protection Clause, coverage of which is itself separated into two distinct, but related, lines of reasoning: the fundamental rights cases and the classifications cases. You will see that certain "goods" or features of citizenship have been ruled "fundamental," such that they cannot be burdened economically absent a very compelling rationale. The clearest example of this is the Court's striking down of a $1.50 poll tax in Harper v. Va. State Bd. of Elections, 383 U.S. 663 (1966), based on a holding that the vote is fundamental and constitutive of other rights. The right to travel has also been recognized in the context of poverty as fundamental. Importantly, designation as "fundamental" has not been extended into housing, education, or minimum economic welfare, and you will be asked to consider why not.

The study of the classifications branch of the equal protection law of poverty proceeds chronologically. This line of cases is generally thought to establish the black letter law that, unlike race, "wealth is not a suspect class." You will be asked whether you agree that the Court has so held, or whether, as some scholars argue, the question is still somewhat open. As in other classification cases, the first question should be: What two classes does the challenged law create? Does the law draw a distinction between the poor and the non-poor, between subclasses of the poor, or between other categories? You will also see that the analytic boundaries provided here — between the Due Process and Equal Protection Clauses, and between the fundamental rights and classification branches of equal protection — are hardly impermeable. Many of the cases discuss both due process and equal protection. For example, does charging a fee for a criminal trial transcript violate a defendant's due process right to a fair appeal, or does it draw a classification between defendants who can pay the fee and defendants who cannot? You will see that in the criminal law realm, the due process argument has gone further than it has in the civil law.

We end the chapter with a brief overview of state constitutions, many of which have affirmative rights to welfare, shelter, and relief that are not present in the federal Constitution. In the decades since the War on Poverty, advocates have looked to state courts as much if not more than to the federal courts for justice for the poor.

* * *

During the War on Poverty in the 1960s and 1970s, issues affecting the poor were brought to the Supreme Court of the United States at a pace never matched before or after. Some of these cases were brought by federally funded lawyers in the years before their practice was restricted in various ways precluding such cases. See Chapter 10. There were some dramatic victories, and some long-lasting defeats. The following article provides an overview of that era, and introduces many of the cases you will read in this chapter.

ALLEN REDLICH, *WHO WILL LITIGATE CONSTITUTIONAL ISSUES FOR THE POOR?*

19 Hastings Const. L.Q. 745 (1992)

Until the creation of the Legal Services Program in 1965 [Ed. note: see Chapter 10], the poor had very few lawyers and none with the resources to engage in the appellate process where constitutional doctrine is fashioned. As a result, among the unfulfilled legal needs of the poor were several issues of constitutional dimension, such as the existing right to due process, the right to privacy, and the necessity of establishing rights to subsistence, to adequate housing, and to an education. These issues were brought before the Supreme Court during the first "war against poverty" by legal services lawyers who at first achieved substantial successes, but soon thereafter suffered bruising defeats. . . .

THE CONSTITUTIONAL LITIGATIONS

The literature discussing the major constitutional litigations instituted by legal services lawyers generally discusses only the leading cases, Shapiro v. Thompson [*infra*, p. 140], Goldberg v. Kelly [*infra*, p. 116], Lindsey v. Normet [*infra*, p. 381], Dandridge v. Williams [*infra*, p. 157], San Antonio Independent School District v. Rodriguez [*infra*, p. 169], and Wyman v. James [*infra*, p. 549]. . . .

In the area of due process, Justice Brennan held in Goldberg v. Kelly that welfare benefits could not be terminated unless the recipient first was offered a hearing satisfactory to the essential elements of due process. He reasoned that without a continuation of benefits, the recipient would not survive, survival was necessary for a meaningful hearing, and due process thus mandated that the hearing precede the termination. The Court also invoked due process on other occasions. Fuentes v. Shevin invalidated a state prejudgment replevin statute. Goss v. Lopez gave a modicum of process to public school students threatened with suspension. O'Connor v. Donaldson upheld the due process rights of persons improperly committed to state mental institutions. Stanley v. Illinois upheld the due process rights of natural fathers threatened with loss of custody of their children. The Court also invalidated a number of state statutes that conflicted with federal law, asserting that the state laws were preempted, sometimes relying on the Supremacy Clause.

The Court also acted in the area of access to justice. In Boddie v. Connecticut, the Court held a destitute woman need not pay publication costs as a prerequisite to divorcing her missing spouse. But the Court refused to go farther, holding in United States v. Kras that bankruptcy filing fees must be paid, even by the indigent; and in Ortwein v. Schwab, the Court held an appeal from a welfare department decision could be conditioned on payment of the court's filing fee.

The Court refused to use equal protection in many instances. More precisely, the Court applied the rational or reasonable basis test to state actions or inactions. In Dandridge v. Williams, the Court held states could "cap" welfare grants, which in effect meant each child in a large family would receive less than a child in a smaller family. The Court accepted the state's argument that the cap provided a work incentive, because welfare allotments higher than one could earn working at the minimum wage were a disincentive to work. The Court announced, in the best tradition of Pontius Pilate, that allocation of state resources in the area of public assistance was not a matter of judicial concern. The Court also threw up its hands at the thought of involvement in school financing, stating there was no constitutional right to a public school education. In Lindsey v. Normet, the Court declined future involvement with housing.

Dandridge shattered the hopes of those who thought social change could quickly be achieved in the courts. In the spring of 1969, the State of New York had enacted a statute that sharply reduced welfare benefits. Rosado v. Wyman, a major, complex challenge to the state plan, was quickly commenced. Months later, Rothstein v. Wyman was instituted, as an afterthought, when Rosado floundered. While *Rosado*, the carefully planned litigation, sat on a Supreme Court docket, a three-judge district court in *Rothstein* held that the state's disparate treatment of residents of New York's suburbs violated the Equal Protection Clause of the Fourteenth Amendment. Rejecting the state's assertion that the "higher social cost of living" in New York City justified the differential, the Court stated:

> Receipt of welfare benefits may not at the present time constitute the exercise of a constitutional right. But among our Constitution's expressed purposes was the desire to "insure domestic tranquility" and "promote the general Welfare." Implicit in those phrases are certain basic concepts of humanity and decency. One of these, voiced as a goal in recent years by most responsible governmental leaders, both federal and state, is the desire to insure that indigent, unemployable citizens will at least have the bare minimums required for existence, without which our expressed fundamental constitutional rights and liberties frequently cannot be exercised and therefore become meaningless. . . . It can hardly be doubted that

the subsistence level of our indigent and unemployable aged, blind and disabled involves a more crucial aspect of life and liberty than the right to operate a business on Sunday or to extract gas from subsoil. We believe that with the stakes so high in terms of human misery the equal protection standard to be applied should be stricter than that used upon review of commercial legislation and more nearly approximate that applied to laws affecting fundamental constitutional rights.

[Advocates'] strategy had envisioned attacks on substantive and procedural flaws in state welfare programs, followed by challenges to the adequacy of statewide benefit levels, implicitly based on a constitutional right to subsistence. Finally having achieved those goals, the poor would demand a national welfare system or, at the very least, a national standard of benefits. State welfare systems had already been battered by thousands of cases. The constitutional challenge to the level of benefits provided by particular states had arrived swiftly, but just as swiftly was resolved by the Court in *Dandridge*; the battle, but not the war, was over.

NOTES AND QUESTIONS

1. Professor Redlich provides a guide to the "wins" and "losses" of the constitutional litigation conducted during the War on Poverty, most of which are contained in this chapter. As wins he cites:

   • Shapiro v. Thompson, 394 U.S. 618 (1969) (holding unconstitutional certain statutes that conditioned eligibility for welfare benefits on one year's residence within the jurisdiction);
   • Goldberg v. Kelly, 397 U.S. 254 (1970) (holding that procedural due process required that welfare benefits could not be terminated prior to the holding of a hearing);
   • Thorpe v. Housing Auth. of Durham, 386 U.S. 670 (1967) (holding that tenants in public housing projects could not be evicted without notice of the reasons thereof and an opportunity to respond); and
   • Boddie v. Connecticut, 401 U.S. 371 (1971) (holding that access to the courts could not be denied to indigent women who sought dissolution of their marriages and lacked funds to pay certain costs).

   He cites as losses:

   • Dandridge v. Williams, 397 U.S. 471 (1970) (holding allocation of welfare resources a matter of state concern and refusing to apply a heightened level of scrutiny to state actions challenged as denying equal protection to welfare recipients);
   • Lindsey v. Normet, 405 U.S. 56 (1972) (upholding expedited state eviction procedures against due process attacks); and
   • San Antonio Independent School District v. Rodriguez, 411 U.S. 1 (1973) (declining to hold school financing scheme that resulted in disparate educational opportunities violative of the Equal Protection Clause).

This chapter includes other decisions understood as victories for low-income people, Harper v. Virginia State Board of Elections, 383 U.S. 663 (1966) and Saenz v. Roe, 526 U.S. 489 (1999), as well as other losses, including Jefferson v. Hackney, 406 U.S. 535 (1972).

A. NEW PROPERTY AND PROCEDURAL DUE PROCESS

In general, poor people's claims to procedural rights have fared better than their claims to substantive rights. As previewed above, one of the Court's best-known discussions of the constitutional rights of poor people is from the 1970 case Goldberg v. Kelly, which remains good law, and which involved procedural rights. The core question of the case was whether welfare benefits, under the now-defunct Aid to Families with Dependent Children program, were "property" under the Due Process Clause of the U.S. Constitution. If construed as "property," such benefits could not be terminated or removed without due process. The intellectual lynchpin of the Court's holding that the benefits were, in fact, property was a 1964 law review article by Professor Charles Reich giving birth to the concept of "the New Property." The article argued that the modern world demanded that the social conception of "property" be updated to include certain entitlements from the government. *See* Charles Reich, *The New Property*, 73 Yale L.J. 733 (1964).

GOLDBERG v. KELLY
397 U.S. 254 (1970)

Mr. Justice BRENNAN delivered the opinion of the Court.

The question for decision is whether a State that terminates public assistance payments to a particular recipient without affording him the opportunity for an evidentiary hearing prior to termination denies the recipient procedural due process in violation of the Due Process Clause of the Fourteenth Amendment.

The constitutional issue to be decided . . . is the narrow one whether the Due Process Clause requires that the recipient be afforded an evidentiary hearing *before* the termination of benefits. . . .

[The government] does not contend that procedural due process is not applicable to the termination of welfare benefits. Such benefits are a matter of statutory entitlement for persons qualified to receive them. Their termination involves state action that adjudicates important rights. The constitutional challenge cannot be answered by an argument that public assistance benefits are "a 'privilege' and not a 'right.'" Relevant constitutional restraints apply as much to the withdrawal of public assistance benefits as to disqualification for unemployment compensation, or to denial of a tax exemption, or to discharge from public employment. The extent to which procedural due process must be afforded the recipient is influenced by the extent to which he may be "condemned to suffer grievous loss," and depends upon whether the recipient's interest in avoiding that loss outweighs the governmental interest in summary adjudication. . . .

It is true, of course, that some governmental benefits may be administratively terminated without affording the recipient a pre-termination evidentiary hearing. But we agree with the District Court that when welfare is discontinued, only a pre-termination evidentiary hearing provides the recipient with procedural due process. For qualified recipients, welfare provides the means to obtain essential food, clothing, housing, and medical care. Thus the crucial factor in this context—a factor not present in the case of the blacklisted government contractor, the discharged government employee, the taxpayer denied a tax exemption, or virtually anyone else whose governmental entitlements are ended — is that termination of aid pending resolution of a controversy over eligibility may deprive an *eligible* recipient of the very means by which to live while he waits. Since he lacks independent resources, his situation becomes immediately desperate. His need to concentrate upon finding the means for daily subsistence, in turn, adversely affects his ability to seek redress from the welfare bureaucracy.

Moreover, important governmental interests are promoted by affording recipients a pre-termination evidentiary hearing. From its founding the Nation's basic commitment has been to foster the dignity and well-being of all persons within its borders. We have come to recognize that forces not within the control of the poor contribute to their poverty. This perception, against the background of our traditions, has significantly influenced the development of the contemporary public assistance system. Welfare, by meeting the basic demands of subsistence, can help bring within the reach of the poor the same opportunities that are available to others to participate meaningfully in the life of the community. At the same time, welfare guards against the societal malaise that may flow from a widespread sense of unjustified frustration and insecurity. Public assistance, then, is not mere charity, but a means to "promote the general Welfare, and secure the Blessings of Liberty to ourselves and our Posterity." The same governmental interests that counsel the provision of welfare, counsel as well its uninterrupted provision to those eligible to receive it; pre-termination evidentiary hearings are indispensable to that end.

Appellant does not challenge the force of these considerations but argues that they are outweighed by countervailing governmental interests in conserving fiscal and administrative resources. . . . These interests, the argument goes, justify the delay of any evidentiary hearing until after discontinuance of the grants. Summary adjudication protects the public fisc by stopping payments promptly upon discovery of reason to believe that a recipient is no longer eligible. Since most terminations are accepted without challenge, summary adjudication also conserves both the fisc and administrative time and energy by reducing the number of evidentiary hearings actually held.

We agree with the District Court, however, that these governmental interests are not overriding in the welfare context. The requirement of a prior hearing doubtless involves some greater expense, and the benefits paid to ineligible recipients pending decision at the hearing probably cannot be recouped, since these recipients are likely to be judgment-proof. But the State is not without weapons to minimize these increased costs. Much of the drain on fiscal and administrative resources can be reduced by developing procedures for prompt pre-termination hearings and by skillful use of personnel and facilities. . . .

We also agree with the District Court, however, that the pre-termination hearing need not take the form of a judicial or quasi-judicial trial. We bear in mind that the statutory "fair hearing" will provide the recipient with a full administrative review. Accordingly, the pre-termination hearing has one function only: to produce an initial determination of the validity of the welfare department's grounds for discontinuance of payments in order to protect a recipient against an erroneous termination of his benefits. . . .

"The fundamental requisite of due process of law is the opportunity to be heard." The hearing must be "at a meaningful time and in a meaningful manner." In the present context these principles require that a recipient have timely and adequate notice detailing the reasons for a proposed termination, and an effective opportunity to defend by confronting any adverse witnesses and by presenting his own arguments and evidence orally. . . .

The opportunity to be heard must be tailored to the capacities and circumstances of those who are to be heard. It is not enough that a welfare recipient may present his position to the decisionmaker in writing or secondhand through his caseworker. Written submissions are an unrealistic option for most recipients, who lack the educational attainment necessary to write effectively and who cannot obtain professional assistance. Moreover, written submissions do not afford the flexibility of oral presentations; they do not permit the recipient to mold his argument to the issues the decisionmaker appears to regard as important. Particularly where credibility and veracity are at issue, as they must be in many termination proceedings, written submissions are a wholly unsatisfactory basis for decision. The secondhand presentation to the decisionmaker by the caseworker has its own deficiencies; since the caseworker usually gathers the facts upon which the charge of ineligibility rests, the presentation of the recipient's side of the controversy cannot safely be left to him. Therefore a recipient must be allowed to state his position orally. Informal procedures will suffice; in this context due process does not require a particular order of proof or mode of offering evidence.

In almost every setting where important decisions turn on questions of fact, due process requires an opportunity to confront and cross-examine adverse witnesses. What we said in Greene v. McElroy, 360 U.S. 474, 496-497 (1959), is particularly pertinent here:

> Certain principles have remained relatively immutable in our jurisprudence. One of these is that where governmental action seriously injures an individual, and the reasonableness of the action depends on fact findings, the evidence used to prove the Government's case must be disclosed to the individual so that he has an opportunity to show that it is untrue. While this is important in the case of documentary evidence, it is even more important where the evidence consists of the testimony of individuals whose memory might be faulty or who, in fact, might be perjurers or persons motivated by malice, vindictiveness, intolerance, prejudice, or jealousy. . . .

Welfare recipients must therefore be given an opportunity to confront and cross-examine the witnesses relied on by the department.

The right to be heard would be, in many cases, of little avail if it did not comprehend the right to be heard by counsel. We do not say that counsel must be provided at the pre-termination hearing, but only that the recipient must be allowed to retain an attorney if he so desires. Counsel can help delineate the issues, present the factual contentions in an orderly manner, conduct cross-examination, and generally safeguard the interests of the recipient. We do not anticipate that this assistance will unduly prolong or otherwise encumber the hearing. . . .

Finally, the decisionmaker's conclusion as to a recipient's eligibility must rest solely on the legal rules and evidence adduced at the hearing. To demonstrate compliance with this elementary requirement, the decisionmaker should state the reasons for his determination and indicate the evidence he relied on, though his statement need not amount to a full opinion or even formal findings of fact and conclusions of law. And, of course, an impartial decisionmaker is essential. We agree with the District Court that prior involvement in some aspects of a case will not necessarily bar a welfare official from acting as a decisionmaker. He should not, however, have participated in making the determination under review.

Mr. Justice BLACK, dissenting.

In the last half century the United States, along with many, perhaps most, other nations of the world, has moved far toward becoming a welfare state, that is, a nation that for one reason or another taxes its most affluent people to help support, feed, clothe, and shelter its less fortunate citizens. The result is that today more than nine million men, women, and children in the United States receive some kind of state or federally financed public assistance in the form of allowances or gratuities, generally paid them periodically, usually by the week, month, or quarter. Since these gratuities are paid on the basis of need, the list of recipients is not static, and some people go off the lists and others are added from time to time. These ever-changing lists put a constant administrative burden on government and it certainly could not have reasonably anticipated that this burden would include the additional procedural expense imposed by the Court today. . . .

Representatives of the people of the Thirteen Original Colonies spent long, hot months in the summer of 1787 in Philadelphia, Pennsylvania, creating a government of limited powers. They divided it into three departments — Legislative, Judicial, and Executive. The Judicial Department was to have no part whatever in making any laws. In fact proposals looking to vesting some power in the Judiciary to take part in the legislative process and veto laws were offered, considered, and rejected by the Constitutional Convention. In my judgment there is not one word, phrase, or sentence from the beginning to the end of the Constitution from which it can be inferred that judges were granted any such legislative power. True, Marbury v. Madison, 1 Cranch 137 (1803), held, and properly, I think, that courts must be the final interpreters of the Constitution, and I recognize that the holding can provide an opportunity to slide imperceptibly into constitutional amendment and law making. But when federal judges use this judicial power for legislative purposes, I think they wander out of their field of vested powers and transgress into the area constitutionally assigned to the Congress and the people. That is precisely what I believe the Court is doing in this case. Hence my dissent.

The more than a million names on the relief rolls in New York, and the more than nine million names on the rolls of all the 50 States were not put there at random. The names are there because state welfare officials believed that those people were eligible for assistance. Probably in the officials' haste to make out the lists many names were put there erroneously in order to alleviate immediate suffering, and undoubtedly some people are drawing relief who are not entitled under the law to do so. Doubtless some draw relief checks from time to time who know they are not eligible, either because they are not actually in need or for some other reason. Many of those who thus draw undeserved gratuities are without sufficient property to enable the government to collect back from them any money they wrongfully receive. But the Court today holds that it would violate the Due Process Clause of the Fourteenth Amendment to stop paying those people weekly or monthly allowances unless the government first affords them a full "evidentiary hearing" even though welfare officials are persuaded that the recipients are not rightfully entitled to receive a penny under the law. In other words, although some recipients might be on the lists for payment wholly because of deliberate fraud on their part, the Court holds that the government is helpless and must continue, until after an evidentiary hearing, to pay money that it does not owe, never has owed, and never could owe. I do not believe there is any provision in our Constitution that should thus paralyze the government's efforts to protect itself against making payments to people who are not entitled to them.

Particularly do I not think that the Fourteenth Amendment should be given such an unnecessarily broad construction. That Amendment came into being primarily to protect Negroes from discrimination, and while some of its language can and does protect others, all know that the chief purpose behind it was to protect ex-slaves. The Court, however, relies upon the Fourteenth Amendment and in effect says that failure of the government to pay a promised charitable installment to an individual deprives that individual of *his own property*, in violation of the Due Process Clause of the Fourteenth Amendment. It somewhat strains credulity to say that the government's promise of charity to an individual is property belonging to that individual when the government denies that the individual is honestly entitled to receive such a payment.

I would have little, if any, objection to the majority's decision in this case if it were written as the report of the House Committee on Education and Labor, but as an opinion ostensibly resting on the language of the Constitution I find it woefully deficient. Once the verbiage is pared away it is obvious that this Court today adopts the views of the District Court "that to cut off a welfare recipient in the face of . . . 'brutal need' without a prior hearing of some sort is unconscionable," and therefore, says the Court, unconstitutional. The majority reaches this result by a process of weighing "the recipient's interest in avoiding" the termination of welfare benefits against "the governmental interest in summary adjudication." Today's balancing act requires a "pre-termination evidentiary hearing," yet there is nothing that indicates what tomorrow's balance will be. Although the majority attempts to bolster its decision with limited quotations from prior cases, it is obvious that today's result does not depend on the language of the Constitution itself or the principles of other decisions, but solely on the collective judgment of the majority as to what would be a fair and humane procedure in this case.

This decision is thus only another variant of the view often expressed by some members of this Court that the Due Process Clause forbids any conduct that a majority of the Court believes "unfair," "indecent," or "shocking to their consciences." Neither these words nor any like them appear anywhere in the Due Process Clause. If they did, they would leave the majority of Justices free to hold any conduct unconstitutional that they should conclude on their own to be unfair or shocking to them. . . .

The procedure required today as a matter of constitutional law finds no precedent in our legal system. Reduced to its simplest terms, the problem in this case is similar to that frequently encountered when two parties have an ongoing legal relationship that requires one party to make periodic payments to the other. Often the situation arises where the party "owing" the money stops paying it and justifies his conduct by arguing that the recipient is not legally entitled to payment. The recipient can, of course, disagree and go to court to compel payment. But I know of no situation in our legal system in which the person alleged to owe money to another is required by law to continue making payments to a judgment-proof claimant without the benefit of any security or bond to insure that these payments can be recovered if he wins his legal argument. Yet today's decision in no way obligates the welfare recipient to pay back any benefits wrongfully received during the pre-termination evidentiary hearings or post any bond, and in all "fairness" it could not do so. These recipients are by definition too poor to post a bond or to repay the benefits that, as the majority assumes, must be spent as received to insure survival.

The Court apparently feels that this decision will benefit the poor and needy. In my judgment the eventual result will be just the opposite. While today's decision requires only an administrative, evidentiary hearing, the inevitable logic of the approach taken will lead to constitutionally imposed, time-consuming delays of a full adversary process of administrative and judicial review. In the next case the welfare recipients are bound to argue that cutting off benefits before judicial review of the agency's decision is also a denial of due process. Since, by hypothesis, termination of aid at that point may still "deprive an *eligible* recipient of the very means by which to live while he waits," . . . I would be surprised if the weighing process did not compel the conclusion that termination without full judicial review would be unconscionable. After all, at each step, as the majority seems to feel, the issue is only one of weighing the government's pocketbook against the actual survival of the recipient, and surely that balance must always tip in favor of the individual. Similarly today's decision requires only the opportunity to have the benefit of counsel at the administrative hearing, but it is difficult to believe that the same reasoning process would not require the appointment of counsel, for otherwise the right to counsel is a meaningless one since these people are too poor to hire their own advocates. Cf. Gideon v. Wainwright, 372 U.S. 335, 344 (1963). Thus the end result of today's decision may well be that the government, once it decides to give welfare benefits, cannot reverse that decision until the recipient has had the benefits of full administrative and judicial review, including, of course, the opportunity to present his case to this Court. Since this process will usually entail a delay of several years, the inevitable result of such a constitutionally imposed burden will be that the government will not put a claimant on the rolls initially until it has made an exhaustive investigation to determine his eligibility. While this Court will perhaps have insured that no needy person will be taken off the rolls without a full "due process" proceeding, it will also have insured that many will never get on the rolls, or at least that they will remain destitute during the lengthy proceedings followed to determine initial eligibility.

NOTES AND QUESTIONS

1. The Court's decision in *Goldberg* referred to Reich's article, *The New Property*, as well as the following quotation from his subsequent piece, *Individual Rights and Social Welfare*:

> It may be realistic today to regard welfare entitlements as more like "property" than a "gratuity." Much of the existing wealth in this country takes the form of rights that do not fall within traditional common-law concepts of property. It has been aptly noted that "society today is built around entitlement. The automobile dealer has his franchise, the doctor and lawyer their professional licenses, the worker his union membership, contract, and pension rights, the

executive his contract and stock options; all are devices to aid security and independence. Many of the most important of these entitlements now flow from government: subsidies to farmers and businessmen, routes for airlines and channels for television stations; long term contracts for defense, space, and education; social security pensions for individuals. Such sources of security, whether private or public, are no longer regarded as luxuries or gratuities; to the recipients they are essentials, fully deserved, and in no sense a form of charity. It is only the poor whose entitlements, although recognized by public policy, have not been effectively enforced.

Goldberg, 397 U.S. at 262 n.8 (quoting Charles A. Reich, *Individual Rights and Social Welfare: The Emerging Legal Issues,* 74 Yale L.J. 1245, 1255 (1965)).

Do you agree with the analogies Professor Reich draws? Are welfare benefits and a law license comparable? An executive's stock options? An airline's routes?

2. Justice Brennan uses language to describe the purposes and nature of welfare and the people who receive welfare benefits that are rarely heard in contemporary times. Note his comments that "[w]e have come to recognize that forces not within the control of their poor contribute to their poverty" and that welfare enables the indigent to "participate meaningfully in the life of the community" and "guards against . . . social malaise." What social conditions made these observations possible? Compare these characterizations to those that animated the Personal Responsibility and Work Opportunity Reconciliation Act in 1996, discussed in Chapters 2 and 4.

3. In his dissent, Justice Black suggests that the majority has built a slippery slope to so-called "civil *Gideon,*" arguing that "it is difficult to believe that the same reasoning process would not require the appointment of counsel, for otherwise the right to counsel is a meaningless one since these people are too poor to hire their own advocates." Do you agree? Are there ways to limit the *Goldberg* holding such that it doesn't require the appointment of counsel?

4. When speaking about the "shock the conscience" test, Justice Black also comments about judges' ability to separate their own personal views from their jurisprudential conclusions:

> I am aware that some feel that the process employed in reaching today's decision is not dependent on the individual views of the Justices involved, but is a mere objective search for the "collective conscience of mankind," but in my view that description is only a euphemism for an individual's judgment. Judges are as human as anyone and as likely as others to see the world through their own eyes and find the "collective conscience" remarkably similar to their own.

Goldberg, 397 U.S. at 276 n.6. Do you agree or disagree?

* * *

Often considered a companion case to *Goldberg,* six years later Mathews v. Eldridge limited the reach of a recipient's entitlement to a pre-termination hearing. Because it arose under the federal Social Security Act, rather than a state AFDC program, *Mathews* was decided under the Fifth Amendment's Due Process Clause, rather than that of the Fourteenth Amendment. The "*Mathews* factors" remain good law not only in the public benefits context but across administrative law.

The program at issue in *Mathews* is the wholly federal "Social Security disability payment" program administered by the Social Security Administration. The program provides cash benefits to workers who are completely disabled, as defined by the statute and regulations, and unable to engage in any "substantial gainful activity." Recipients are subject to periodic review to establish their continued disability. If the worker is found to be no longer disabled, benefits will terminate. The process invoked to review those terminations was the issue in the case.

MATHEWS v. ELDRIDGE
424 U.S. 319 (1976)

Mr. Justice POWELL delivered the opinion of the Court.

The issue in this case is whether the Due Process Clause of the Fifth Amendment requires that prior to the termination of Social Security disability benefit payments the recipient be afforded an opportunity for an evidentiary hearing. . . .

Procedural due process imposes constraints on governmental decisions which deprive individuals of "liberty" or "property" interests within the meaning of the Due Process Clause of the Fifth or Fourteenth Amendment. The Secretary does not contend that procedural due process is inapplicable to terminations of Social Security disability benefits. He recognizes, as has been implicit in our prior decisions, that the interest of an individual in continued receipt of these benefits is a statutorily created "property" interest protected by the Fifth Amendment. Rather, the Secretary contends that the existing administrative procedures, detailed below, provide all the process that is constitutionally due before a recipient can be deprived of that interest.

This Court consistently has held that some form of hearing is required before an individual is finally deprived of a property interest. The "right to be heard before being condemned to suffer grievous loss of any kind, even though it may not involve the stigma and hardships of a criminal conviction, is a principle basic to our society." The fundamental requirement of due process is the opportunity to be heard "at a meaningful time and in a meaningful manner." Eldridge agrees that the review procedures available to a claimant before the initial determination of ineligibility becomes final would be adequate if disability benefits were not terminated until after the evidentiary hearing stage of the administrative process. The dispute centers upon what process is due prior to the initial termination of benefits, pending review. . . .

[Our] decisions underscore the truism that "'[d]ue process,' unlike some legal rules, is not a technical conception with a fixed content unrelated to time, place and circumstances." "[D]ue process is flexible and calls for such procedural protections as the particular situation demands." Accordingly, resolution of the issue whether the administrative procedures provided here are constitutionally sufficient requires analysis of the governmental and private interests that are affected. More precisely, our prior decisions indicate that identification of the specific dictates of due process generally requires consideration of three distinct factors: First, the private interest that will be affected by the official action; second, the risk of an erroneous deprivation of such interest through the procedures used, and the probable value, if any, of additional or substitute procedural safeguards; and finally, the Government's interest, including the function involved and the fiscal and administrative burdens that the additional or substitute procedural requirement would entail. . . .

[Ed. note: The opinion here describes the procedures in place for evaluating a recipient's continuing eligibility for the program, which require periodic communication between the disabled worker, his medical providers, and the agency. If the agency determines that the worker is no longer disabled, the worker is notified of the evidence on which that conclusion is based and given an opportunity to review that evidence. Once that determination is final, the worker is notified in writing, given the reasons, and informed of the opportunity to seek *de novo* reconsideration by the agency. Benefits are terminated effective two months after the "medical recovery" is determined to have occurred. The worker can then request an evidentiary hearing before an administrative law judge. The government acknowledged that the time between a request for hearing and a decision was between 10 and 11 months.]

Despite the elaborate character of the administrative procedures provided by the Secretary, the courts below held them to be constitutionally inadequate, concluding that due process requires an evidentiary hearing prior to termination. In light of the private and governmental interests at stake here and the nature of the existing procedures, we think this was error.

Since a recipient whose benefits are terminated is awarded full retroactive relief if he ultimately prevails, his sole interest is in the uninterrupted receipt of this source of income pending final administrative decision on his claim. His potential injury is thus similar in nature to that of the welfare recipient in *Goldberg*.

Only in *Goldberg* has the Court held that due process requires an evidentiary hearing prior to a temporary deprivation. It was emphasized there that welfare assistance is given to persons on the very margin of subsistence:

> The crucial factor in this context — a factor not present in the case of . . . virtually anyone else whose governmental entitlements are ended — is that termination of aid pending resolution of a controversy over eligibility may deprive an *eligible* recipient of the very means by which to live while he waits.

Eligibility for disability benefits, in contrast, is not based upon financial need. Indeed, it is wholly unrelated to the worker's income or support from many other sources, such as earnings of other family members, workmen's compensation awards, tort claims awards, savings, private insurance, public or private pensions, veterans' benefits, food stamps, public assistance, or the "many other important programs, both public and private, which contain provisions for disability payments affecting a substantial portion of the work force. . . ."

As *Goldberg* illustrates, the degree of potential deprivation that may be created by a particular decision is a factor to be considered in assessing the validity of any administrative decisionmaking process. The potential deprivation here is generally likely to be less than in *Goldberg*, although the degree of difference can be overstated. . . .

In view of the torpidity of this administrative review process, and the typically modest resources of the family unit of the physically disabled worker, the hardship imposed upon the erroneously terminated disability recipient may be significant. Still, the disabled worker's need is likely to be less than that of a welfare recipient. In addition to the possibility of access to private resources, other forms of government assistance will become available where the termination of disability benefits places a worker or his family below the subsistence level. In view of these potential sources of temporary income, there is less reason here than in *Goldberg* to depart from the ordinary principle, established by our decisions, that something less than an evidentiary hearing is sufficient prior to adverse administrative action.

An additional factor to be considered here is the fairness and reliability of the existing pretermination procedures, and the probable value, if any, of additional procedural safeguards. Central to the evaluation of any administrative process is the nature of the relevant inquiry. In order to remain eligible for benefits the disabled worker must demonstrate by means of "medically acceptable clinical and laboratory diagnostic techniques," that he is unable "to engage in any substantial gainful activity by reason of any medically determinable physical or mental impairment. . . ." In short, a medical assessment of the worker's physical or mental condition is required. This is a more sharply focused and easily documented decision than the typical determination of welfare entitlement. In the latter case, a wide variety of information may be deemed relevant, and issues of witness credibility and veracity often are critical to the decision-making process. *Goldberg* noted that in such circumstances "written submissions are a wholly unsatisfactory basis for decision."

By contrast, the decision whether to discontinue disability benefits will turn, in most cases, upon "routine, standard, and unbiased medical reports by physician specialists," concerning a subject whom they have personally examined. . . . The potential value of an evidentiary hearing, or even oral presentation to the decisionmaker, is substantially less in this context than in *Goldberg*.

The decision in *Goldberg* also was based on the Court's conclusion that written submissions were an inadequate substitute for oral presentation because they did not provide an effective means for the recipient to communicate his case to the decisionmaker. Written submissions were viewed as an unrealistic option, for most recipients lacked the "educational attainment necessary to write effectively" and could not afford professional assistance. In addition, such submissions would not provide the "flexibility of oral presentations" or "permit the recipient to mold his argument to the issues the decision maker appears to regard as important." In the context of the disability-benefits-entitlement assessment the administrative procedures under review here fully answer these objections. . . .

In striking the appropriate due process balance the final factor to be assessed is the public interest. This includes the administrative burden and other societal costs that would be associated with requiring, as a matter of constitutional right, an evidentiary hearing upon demand in all cases prior to the termination of disability benefits. The most visible burden would be the incremental cost resulting from the increased number of hearings and the expense of providing benefits to ineligible recipients pending decision. . . .

Financial cost alone is not a controlling weight in determining whether due process requires a particular procedural safeguard prior to some administrative decision. But the Government's interest, and hence that of the public, in conserving scarce fiscal and administrative resources is a factor that must be weighed. At some point the benefit of an additional safeguard to the individual affected by the administrative action and to society in terms of increased assurance that the action is just, may be outweighed by the cost. Significantly, the cost of protecting those whom the preliminary administrative process has identified as likely to be found undeserving may in the end come out of the pockets of the deserving since resources available for any particular program of social welfare are not unlimited.

But more is implicated in cases of this type than ad hoc weighing of fiscal and administrative burdens against the interests of a particular category of claimants. The ultimate balance involves a determination as to when, under our constitutional system, judicial-type procedures must be imposed upon administrative action to assure fairness. We reiterate the wise admonishment of Mr. Justice Frankfurter that differences in the origin and function of administrative agencies "preclude wholesale transplantation of the rules of procedure, trial and review which have evolved from the history and experience of courts." The judicial model of an evidentiary hearing is neither a required, nor even the most effective, method of decisionmaking in all circumstances. The essence of due process is the requirement that "a person in jeopardy of serious loss [be given] notice of the case against him and opportunity to meet it." All that is necessary is that the procedures be tailored, in light of the decision to be made, to "the capacities and circumstances of those who are to be heard," Goldberg v. Kelly, to insure that they are given a meaningful opportunity to present their case. In assessing what process is due in this case, substantial weight must be given to the good-faith judgments of the individuals charged by Congress with the administration of social welfare programs that the procedures they have provided assure fair consideration of the entitlement claims of individuals. This is especially so where, as here, the prescribed procedures not only provide the claimant with an effective process for asserting his claim prior to any administrative action, but also assure a right to an evidentiary hearing, as well as to subsequent judicial review, before the denial of his claim becomes final.

We conclude that an evidentiary hearing is not required prior to the termination of disability benefits and that the present administrative procedures fully comport with due process.

Mr. Justice BRENNAN, with whom Mr. Justice MARSHALL concurs, dissenting.

. . . I agree with the District Court and the Court of Appeals that, prior to termination of benefits, Eldridge must be afforded an evidentiary hearing of the type required for welfare beneficiaries under Title IV of the Social Security Act. I would add that the Court's consideration that a discontinuance of disability benefits may cause the recipient to suffer only a limited deprivation is no argument. It is speculative. Moreover, the very legislative determination to provide disability benefits, without any prerequisite determination of need in fact, presumes a need by the recipient which is not this Court's function to denigrate. Indeed, in the present case, it is indicated that because disability benefits were terminated there was a foreclosure upon the Eldridge home and the family's furniture was repossessed, forcing Eldridge, his wife, and their children to sleep in one bed. Finally, it is also no argument that a worker, who has been placed in the untenable position of having been denied disability benefits, may still seek other forms of public assistance.

NOTES AND QUESTIONS

1. Note that the Court drew two distinctions between Social Security disability benefits and the welfare benefits at issue in *Goldberg*. First, the Court noted

that Social Security is an insurance program rather than a means-tested welfare program ("unlike eligibility for welfare benefits, [disability eligibility] is not based on financial need"). Second, the difference in the types of facts involved in the Social Security determinations and AFDC determinations were important to the Court's holding in *Mathews* ("issues of credibility and veracity do not play a significant role in the disability entitlement decision, which turns primarily on medical evidence"). Are these distinctions persuasive to you? Recalling the other examples of entitlements to which the Court analogized in *Goldberg* (professional licenses, broadcasting rights, etc.), how would you envision termination hearings in those other contexts faring under the *Mathews* test?

2. There are two federal programs that provide cash assistance to people whose disabilities preclude them from working. The one discussed in *Mathews*, Social Security Disability, or "SSD," is a *social insurance* program, in that a recipient's eligibility and benefit level are based on payments into the system while in the labor force. The other program is Supplemental Security Income, or "SSI," which is not tied to a person's participation in the labor market, and is therefore understood as a *social welfare* program. More information about these and other cash assistance programs can be found in Chapter 4.

* * *

As we know from Chapter 2, in 1996 Congress ended AFDC — the program under which *Goldberg* was decided — and replaced it with Temporary Assistance to Needy Families (TANF). Among the signature features of TANF was its inclusion of an express congressional statement that the benefits it conferred were not "entitlements." In the 2001 case below, the Colorado Court of Appeals rejected the government's argument that this statutory change vitiated *Goldberg*'s holding. This case is a good example of poverty lawyers' creative use of courts other than the U.S. Supreme Court to advance their clients' interest. Plaintiffs sued under the state's Administrative Procedures Act as well as under federal law (42 U.S.C. § 1983), claiming that Colorado's procedures for handling sanction notices were inadequate.

WESTON v. CASSATA
37 P.3d 469 (Colo. App. 2001)

Participants in the TANF program are required to enter into an Individual Responsibility Contract (IRC), which outlines the program requirements. Individual counties will sanction participants who fail to comply with TANF IRC requirements, and that sanction is in the form of a reduction of their cash assistance. Before a participant is sanctioned, however, the participant must receive a sanction notice stating the basis for the county's decision or action, detailing the participant's rights to a county conference under the dispute resolution process and to a state-level appeal, and describing the process of such an appeal.

All members of the plaintiff class are or were recipients of welfare benefits in Adams County under the revised welfare system administered by defendants; all were sent sanction notices by the Adams County Department of Social Services. . . .

Plaintiffs brought this class action to determine whether the sanction notices were insufficient. . . . Defendants' primary argument is that plaintiffs were not deprived of due process under the notice scheme. . . . Defendants first assert that plaintiffs have no property interest in welfare benefits. We disagree.

Prior to the enactment of the 1996 federal legislative changes in the welfare system, welfare recipients had a statutory entitlement to welfare benefits under the AFDC — in essence, a property right subject to due process protections. *See* Goldberg v. Kelly, 397 U.S. 254, (1970) (describing welfare benefits as "property"). However, with the enactment of [the Personal Responsibility and Work Opportunity Reconciliation Act,] PRWORA, Congress stated that there no longer would be any individual entitlement to welfare benefits. In doing so, Congress intended to eliminate the "entitlement mentality" behind the existing welfare system by removing individual entitlement to cash benefits and making welfare benefits temporary and conditional.

PRWORA states, in pertinent part: "No individual entitlement. This part . . . shall not be interpreted to entitle any individual or family to assistance under any State program funded under this part. . . ." Similarly, CWPA, the Colorado statute implementing the federal statute, states: "Nothing in this part 7 or in any rules promulgated pursuant to this part 7 shall be interpreted to create a legal entitlement in any participant to assistance provided pursuant to the works program."

Its "no entitlement" language notwithstanding, the state statutory scheme nevertheless contains mandatory language concerning the payment of available funding to eligible participants ("Except as provided in this part 7 and subject to available appropriations, a participant *shall* receive a basic assistance grant . . ."); ("participant *shall* continue to receive the basic cash assistance grant" during pendency of an appeal), and the issuance of sanction notices.

To have a property interest in a government benefit, a person must have more than a unilateral expectation — he or she must have a "legitimate claim of entitlement to it." Entitlements derive from "an independent source such as state law — rules or understandings that secure certain benefits and that support claims of entitlement to those benefits." . . .

[After identifying a "spectrum" of property rights from "absolute" entitlement to "no entitlement at all," the court went on to say:] When the federal government enacted the 1996 welfare reform laws, its purposeful inclusion of "no entitlement" in the plain language of the statute indicated an intent to dispose of an individual's absolute entitlement to welfare benefits. However, because we must interpret a statute in its entirety, we may not, as defendants urge, end our analysis with that single phrase. Despite the forcefulness and apparent specificity of the "no entitlement" language, the construction of the remainder of the welfare statutory scheme illustrates that the federal government did not, and constitutionally could not, eliminate all forms of entitlement to welfare benefits. . . .

. . . [W]e conclude that, once welfare recipients have complied with statutory standards and have begun receiving welfare benefits, the right to welfare benefits is a property right that cannot be compromised without procedural due process protections. If money has been allocated by the federal government to the state, and if a participant meets the criteria set forth by statute, defendants have no discretion to determine whether that participant should receive welfare benefits. *See* Board of Regents v. Roth, *supra*. Despite the state officials' active role in distributing welfare monies, that role has no discretionary component beyond the authority to withhold or distribute benefits according to statute.

Thus, the due process right under the new scheme is not "the guarantee of getting the benefit," but rather the guarantee that, if and when the benefit is granted, the "government will employ a decisionmaking protocol reasonably likely to yield correct application of the legally relevant substantive criteria to the individual case." Although the government has unambiguously expressed an intent to do away with the absolute entitlement to welfare benefits previously available under the AFDC program, it did not intend to eliminate welfare benefits altogether, but merely to create a more conditional property right in the receipt of federal benefits and to make the requirements of attaining a property right in those benefits more rigorous.

. . . [T]he General Assembly may not constitutionally authorize the deprivation of a property interest, once conferred, without appropriate procedural safeguards. Consistent with that principle, federal regulations still require that hearings at the state agency level "shall meet the due process standards set forth in the U.S. Supreme Court decision in Goldberg v. Kelly."

Accordingly, we conclude that because plaintiffs had a property right, albeit not an unlimited one, in continued receipt of welfare benefits, plaintiffs were constitutionally entitled to procedural due process.

NOTES AND QUESTIONS

1. Do you agree with the court's test for determining whether something is an "entitlement" or not?
2. In deciding *Mathews*, the Court explained that the requirements of due process should shift with changing circumstances. Specifically, the balance between the private interest at stake, the risk of erroneous deprivation, and the government's interest in adding additional procedural safeguards presumably should shift as social conditions change. For example, as one scholar has noted, *Goldberg* and *Mathews* were both decided in an era of paper checks, which have now been widely replaced by electronic transfers. The import of this digitalization of deposits has been litigated in the context of collections and the seizure of bank accounts containing public benefits deposits in New York. Under New York state law, no hearing was required before a creditor was able to seize a debtor's bank account. A series of cases spanning two decades made the case that, where these bank accounts contained exclusively public benefits money that is exempt from seizure, the absence of a hearing (to establish the susceptibility of the accounts to seizure) violates due process and the *Mathews* test. In the early cases, the existing procedure was upheld as sufficient. In 2003, the New York courts revisited the issue and, still applying the *Mathews* test, held that these prehearing seizures were unconstitutional in light of technological advances that reduce the burden on a creditor for determining before seizure whether an account held exclusively exempt funds. This and

other aspects of the contemporary application of *Mathews* and *Goldberg* are the subject of Jason Perkins, *Adaptable Due Process*, 160 U. Pa. L. Rev. 1309 (2012).

B. EQUAL PROTECTION: OVERVIEW

The application of the Equal Protection Clause of the Fourteenth Amendment in the arena of poverty and poor people's rights is complex. Students of constitutional law understand the basic equal protection rubric that governmental actions are presumptively subjected to a mere "rational basis" test, whereby legislation will be upheld if it is rationally related to a legitimate government purpose. (Scholars have also identified "rational basis plus" or "rational basis with bite" as a standard of review to which some government action is subjected. This phraseology is used to describe cases where a court applies the "rational basis" test, but strikes down a law that would likely have been upheld under a "pure," highly deferential, rational basis standard. Common examples of this "biting" rational basis standard are the Court's decisions in Romer v. Evans, 517 U.S. 620 (1996) and City of Cleburne v. Cleburne Living Center, Inc., 473 U.S. 432 (1985).) If, however, a law, regulation, or official action operates to classify people on a basis considered "suspect," a reviewing court will take a closer look, and subject the law to so-called "elevated scrutiny," the most stringent version of which is known as "strict scrutiny." If subjected to strict scrutiny, a law will be upheld only if it is narrowly tailored to meet a "compelling state interest." Classifications based on race are the paradigm of a suspect classification, and thus will be upheld only upon the government's satisfaction of this highest test. Other classifications have been held to be intrinsically suspect as well: religion, national origin, and alienage. Some bases for classification, including gender, are subjected to so-called "intermediate scrutiny," something higher than rationality but not as high as compelling state interest.

Where does poverty fit into this classification taxonomy? That is the question to which we now turn. It is often said that "wealth is not a suspect class," but, as you will soon see, that statement may be too facile to account for the complex and often inconsistent approaches that the Court has taken to claims by poor people. Are poor people a "suspect class"? Do they fit within what the Court in one case described as the "traditional indicia of suspectness": having been "subjected to such a history of purposeful unequal treatment, or relegated to such a position of political powerlessness as to command extraordinary protection from the majoritarian political process"? San Antonio Indep. Sch. Dist. v. Rodriguez, 411 U.S. 1, 28 (1973). Consider also the classic "*Carolene Products* footnote four" designation of a suspect class as a "discrete and insular minority." *See* United States v. Carolene Prods. Co., 304 U.S. 144, 152 (1938). Does this rubric offer hope for poor people?

In addition to the classifications scheme, another aspect of equal protection jurisprudence has been used by poverty lawyers seeking justice for their clients. Suspect (or quasi-suspect) classifications give rise to elevated scrutiny, but so do government actions that burden so-called "fundamental rights." Where the government has erected a barrier to something considered "fundamental," the action will only be sustained if the government can justify the barrier by a compelling state interest. Poverty lawyers have sought to leverage this "fundamental rights" doctrine into protection for the poor by arguing that a variety of goods or services are "fundamental," and thus may not be restricted to those who can pay for them absent a compelling rationale. Indeed, there was at one time a robust intellectual and lawyering movement to establish a fundamental right to some level of minimum welfare or subsistence. This movement did not meet great success. The fundamental rights argument has succeeded only in a limited set of circumstances, mostly related to the democratic process, such as the vote, and has not been extended to substantive fundamental rights, such as housing or education.

The classifications branch and the fundamental rights branch are not wholly independent. Rather, the intellectual history of equal protection for poor people is a complex hybrid of these concepts. Should the Constitution be read to preclude differentiation between poor and non-poor people? How could it, in light of capitalism and private pricing for goods? Does every "price" exacted by the government, be it a driver's license fee or a poll tax, violate a poor person's right to equal protection of the law? In an echo to the distinction between relative and absolute poverty introduced in Chapter 1, the poverty equal protection cases invoke the questions: Does it violate equal protection for one group to have a lot more than another group? Does it violate equal protection (or due process) for one group to be excluded altogether from a good or service? Consider these questions as you explore the Equal Protection Clause and poverty.

As a prelude to the cases themselves, the following law review article, by former law professor, now California Supreme Court Justice, Goodwin Liu, introduces some of the important jurisprudential themes.

GOODWIN LIU, *RETHINKING CONSTITUTIONAL WELFARE RIGHTS*

61 Stan. L. Rev. 203 (2008)

Once a subject of intense interest in the courts and legal academy, the idea that our Constitution guarantees affirmative rights to social and economic welfare has for some time been out of fashion. In 2001, William Forbath observed that "like Banquo's ghost, the idea of constitutional welfare rights will not die down, but it is not exactly alive, either. No fresh or even sustained arguments on its behalf have appeared for over a decade; only nods, and glancing acknowledgments." As a doctrinal matter, the prevailing view is that issues of poverty and distributive justice should be resolved through legislative policymaking rather than constitutional adjudication. Some commentators (myself included) have argued that such policymaking may yet have constitutional significance if the existence and binding force of constitutional welfare rights are distinguished from the question of judicial enforcement. But it remains a fact of our legal culture that what counts as a constitutional right is deeply shaped by the courts, and for a generation, our courts have steered clear of social or economic rights even as severe deprivation and inequality continue to pose serious challenges to our commitment to human dignity and equal citizenship.

Things were not always so. During the 1960s and 1970s, welfare rights held a prominent place on the public agenda not only in the legislative process but also in mainstream constitutional discourse. In the Supreme Court, the subject percolated long enough in equal protection and due process doctrine for us to see justiciable welfare rights as more than an idle aspiration, and the resulting precedents remain on the books. . . .

My point of departure is Professor Michelman's justly famous 1969 Foreword to the Harvard Law Review, titled *On Protecting the Poor Through the Fourteenth Amendment.* In that article, Michelman sought to rationalize an emerging line of equal protection decisions by the Supreme Court under a theory of minimum welfare rights. His key insight was that, in attacking the ills of poverty, claims nominally styled as wealth "discrimination" are better understood as claims of material "deprivation" — that is, as claims of inadequate rather than unequal provision of certain basic goods. This characterization, he argued, provides not only a better descriptive account of judicial decisions on welfare rights but also a better tactical approach for engaging the courts in this area within the limitations of the judicial role. . . .

. . . Even as Michelman sought to bring coherence to welfare rights jurisprudence, he worried a great deal about the democratic legitimacy of grounding constitutional adjudication in moral theory. The normative thesis I shall advance begins with the contention that his worries were well justified. However alluring it may be to posit that our Constitution embodies substantive moral principles reflecting the terms of a rational if hypothetical consensus, judicial reasoning in this vein faces serious obstacles to gaining broad public acceptance. As Michelman acknowledged, the derivation of welfare rights through philosophical argument from first principles seems unlikely to capture the ways in which our nonideal society actually develops and understands its moral commitments. Our basic commitments to mutual provision are bound to reflect collective judgments that are more contingent, eclectic, and historically and culturally particular than the neat entailments of a comprehensive moral theory. My central claim is that the legitimacy of judicial recognition of welfare rights depends on socially situated modes of reasoning that appeal not to abstract moral principle but to our society's own understandings of our fundamental values.

I. ON PROTECTING THE POOR

Written in the wake of the Civil Rights Movement and War on Poverty, *On Protecting the Poor* sought to bring intellectual coherence to an emerging line of equal protection decisions loosely united by an anti-poverty thrust. Michelman's central insight was that the Supreme Court's jurisprudence, while conventionally understood as an attack on "wealth discrimination," more accurately reflected an overriding if inexplicit concern that all persons are entitled to a minimum, not necessarily equal, level of provision with respect to certain important goods. As he put it, "the judicial 'equality' explosion of recent times has largely been ignited by reawakened sensitivity, not to equality, but to a quite different sort of value or claim which might better be called 'minimum welfare.'"

In elaborating this view, Michelman drew a distinction between "discrimination," the harm that lies in the stigmatic or dignitary offense caused by governmental classification, and "deprivation," the harm that lies in the nonsatisfaction of certain needs as and when they occur. Although discrimination and deprivation often go together, the two concepts differ in important ways. First, the remedy for deprivation "need not entail or suggest any 'equalization' of treatment or circumstances" of the sort typically sought as relief for discrimination. Relieving deprivation may result in greater equality, but the core remedial principle is adequate provision rather than equalization. Second, unlike discrimination, deprivation is "determined largely without reference to whether the complainant's predicament is somehow visibly related to past or current governmental activity." A duty to remedy deprivation is less susceptible to limitation by a requirement of state action. Third, whereas claims of "discrimination against the poor" tend to draw into question the free-market premises of our social order, attacking poverty-related hardships as unjust "deprivation" is less radical. On the minimum welfare view, "a state's duty to the poor . . . is not to avoid unequal treatment at all, but rather to provide assurances against certain hazards associated with impecuniousness which even a society strongly committed to competition and incentives would have to find unjust."

In articulating the minimum welfare thesis, Michelman sought to describe the underlying if unstated logic of judicial behavior in a set of equal protection cases purporting to target wealth discrimination. The leading example is Shapiro v. Thompson, which struck down a one-year state residence requirement for receipt of welfare benefits. Although the Court rested its holding on the ground that the requirement deterred or penalized poor people in their right to interstate travel, the validity of this rationale "depends upon the prior existence, in the state of former residence, of a public-assistance program to which the migrant had access." Yet nothing in the opinion hints that the plaintiffs did receive or could have received welfare benefits in their original states of residence. And the Court never considered whether the residence requirement in fact deterred or penalized any person's decision to migrate.

The weakness of the travel rationale suggests that the heart of *Shapiro* lies elsewhere, and the Court left little doubt about its ultimate concern. The waiting period, according to the Court, denies impoverished migrants "welfare aid upon which may depend the ability of the families to obtain the very means to subsist — food, shelter, and other necessities of life." In rejecting the state's interest in fencing out poor migrants who seek higher welfare benefits, the Court saw no reason "why a mother who is seeking to make a new life for herself and her children should be regarded as less deserving because she considers, among others factors, the level of a State's public assistance." The result in Shapiro turns more intelligibly on the judicial intuition that need, not desert, is the only constitutionally valid basis for distributing welfare benefits, which is an indirect way of recognizing that welfare provision has constitutional significance.

Indeed, the travel rationale cannot explain why the Court, after *Shapiro*, upheld residence requirements for access to in-state tuition or divorce proceedings in state court while striking down such requirements for access to state-funded medical care. The answer, as the Court acknowledged in Memorial Hospital v. Maricopa County, is that "governmental privileges or benefits necessary to basic sustenance have . . . greater constitutional significance than less essential forms of governmental entitlements." There the Court recognized medical care to be "as much 'a basic necessity of life' to an indigent as welfare assistance," adding that

> [i]t would be odd, indeed, to find that the State . . . was required to afford [the plaintiff] welfare assistance to keep him from discomfort of inadequate housing or the pangs of hunger but could deny him the medical care necessary to relieve him from the wheezing and gasping for breath that attend his illness.

. . . Michelman's prescient articulation of welfare rights sounding in minimum entitlement, not unjust discrimination, stands as the enduring insight of *On Protecting the Poor.*

Beyond rationalizing the case law, however, Michelman's article had a normative ambition. His exposition of the minimum welfare view was laced with concern that focusing on "wealth discrimination" not only clouds understanding of judicial behavior but also introduces a host of conceptual and tactical problems. Conceptually, Michelman believed it was too narrow to frame the ills of poverty as wealth discrimination because "[a] severe . . . absolute deprivation may beget no response unless a 'discrimination' suggestive of prevalent, institutionalized, relative deprivation is also present." At the same time, a doctrine against wealth discrimination would be too broad in at least two respects. First, because it "responds to relative deprivation, even [where] the presence of . . . severe absolute deprivation is doubtful," the doctrine would have difficulty distinguishing the needs of the poor from the claims of the nonpoor who plausibly suffer wealth discrimination when compared to the rich. Second, the doctrine logically leads to "a kind of disparagement of pricing practices" instead of targeting "nonsatisfaction of a particular want." Given the ubiquity of pricing practices, actionable wealth discrimination would seem to infect a limitless range of goods from the essential to the trivial. A rule that "appl[ies] non-selectively to the pricing practice and refer[s] not at all to any exceptional attributes in the excepted commodities" cannot answer the question "why education and not golf?"

Tactically, for judges, advocates, and scholars sympathetic to the plight of the poor, the latter concern is what worried Michelman the most. Wealth discrimination, he observed,

> is usually nothing more or less than the making of a market . . . or the failure to relieve someone of the vicissitudes of market pricing. . . . But the risk of exposure to markets and their "decisions" is not normally deemed objectionable, to say the least, in our society. . . . We usually regard it as both the fairest and most efficient arrangement to require each consumer to pay the full market price of what he consumes, limiting his consumption to what his income permits.

Michelman warned the Court that, unless it planned to radically alter our market system, judicial opinions with loose language condemning "discrimination against the poor" would generate only false hopes and "mistakenly heard promises." Moreover, he saved his firmest admonition for welfare advocates and scholars eager to make the Court into an "instrument of income equalization" through claims of "discrimination against the poor." Such an approach was "tactically ill-advised," he said, in light of "the possibility that judges specially sensitive to the overbreadth of that formulation will be deterred by its recital from recognizing claims which might have been acceptable if presented without invoking it."

CONCLUSION

. . . In explaining the legitimacy of judicial review in our constitutional democracy, Archibald Cox once wrote:

> Constitutional adjudication depends, I think, upon a delicate, symbiotic relation. The Court must know us better than we know ourselves. Its opinions may . . . sometimes be the voice of the spirit, reminding us of our better selves. In such cases the Court . . . provides a stimulus and quickens moral education. But while the opinions of the Court can help to shape our national understanding of ourselves, the roots of its decisions must be already in the nation. The aspirations voiced by the Court must be those the community is willing not only to avow but in the end to live by. For the power of the great constitutional decisions rests upon the accuracy of the Court's perception of this kind of common will and upon the Court's ability, by expressing its perception, ultimately to command a consensus.

The quotation is appealing not least because it manages to capture the "delicate" function of the Court with a somewhat heroic flourish. But Professor Cox's central insight—that "the roots of [the Court's] decisions must be already in the nation"—envelops many layers of complexity in the exercise of judicial review.

By giving voice to our shared understandings, the Court may ultimately command a consensus. But the task cannot be done in one fell swoop, and because the Court unavoidably "labors under the obligation to succeed," it must approach the task not with an eye toward heroism but with cautious judgment and respectful attention to the evolving understandings of our public culture. Some day yet, the Court may be presented with an opportunity to recognize a fundamental right to education or housing or medical care. But the recognition, if it comes, will not come as a moral or philosophical epiphany but as an interpretation and consolidation of the values we have gradually internalized as a society. As Alexander Bickel explained:

> [T]he moment of ultimate judgment need not come either suddenly or haphazardly. Its timing and circumstances can be controlled. . . . Over time, as a problem is lived with, the Court does not work in isolation to divine the answer that is right. It has the means to elicit partial answers and reactions from the other institutions, and to try tentative answers itself.

Should the Court ever reach a "moment of ultimate judgment," its decision will win acceptance only if "in the course of a continuing colloquy with the political institutions and with society at large, the Court has shaped and reduced the question, and perhaps because it has rendered the answer familiar if not obvious."

In the quest for constitutional welfare rights, our political commitments in many areas currently provide too little grist for the judicial mill to render enduring solutions to distributive injustice either familiar or obvious. There is no substitute for the hard work of constructing, contesting, and enacting the distributive commitments in our public culture, and it is there that any effort to engage the courts in adjudicating welfare rights must begin.

C.   EQUAL PROTECTION: FUNDAMENTAL RIGHTS

Professor (now Justice) Liu above described a moment in constitutional history where arguments were made in support of a constitutional right to minimum economic welfare. One might ground an argument for such a right in the idea of "fundamental rights," a branch of equal protection doctrine. The fundamental rights doctrine has not, so far, been extended into substantive social goods such as housing, income, or health care. Rather, such rights are found in more process-oriented realms. This section presents cases in two realms where the government, in the context of poverty, has burdened some right that the Court deems democratically "fundamental" — voting and travel (the *Shapiro* case discussed by Justice Liu). Once so deemed, the Court applies elevated scrutiny to strike down the burden.

In the case that follows, a poor person's right to vote was considered fundamental, and a $1.50 poll tax burdening it was held unconstitutional. Note that while this case is understood as a fundamental rights case, it can also be seen as a classification case, where the classification between those who can and cannot pay the tax is struck down on equal protection grounds. Indeed, the Court's rhetoric focuses as much on the "invidious discrimination" exacted by the poll tax as on the fundamental and constitutive nature of the vote. This duality — this puzzle between discrimination and minimum access — persists in many of the equal protection cases.

HARPER v. VA. STATE BD. OF ELECTIONS
383 U.S. 663 (1966)

Mr. Justice DOUGLAS delivered the opinion of the Court.

These are suits by Virginia residents to have declared unconstitutional Virginia's poll tax. . . . While the right to vote in federal elections is conferred by Art. I, §2, of the Constitution, the right to vote in state elections is nowhere expressly mentioned. It is argued that the right to vote in state elections is implicit, particularly by reason of the First Amendment and that it may not constitutionally be conditioned upon the payment of a tax or fee. We do not stop to canvass the relation between voting and political expression. For it is enough to say that once the franchise is granted to the electorate, lines may not be drawn which are inconsistent with the Equal Protection Clause of the Fourteenth Amendment. That is to say, the right of suffrage "is subject to the imposition of state standards which are not discriminatory and which do not contravene any restriction that Congress, acting pursuant to its constitutional powers, has imposed." We were speaking there of a state literacy test which we sustained, warning that the result would be different if a literacy test, fair on its face, were used to discriminate against a class.[3] But [that case] does not govern

---

3. We recently held in Louisiana v. United States, 380 U.S. 145 (1965), that a literacy test which gave voting registrars "a virtually uncontrolled discretion as to who should vote and who should not" had been used to deter Negroes from voting and accordingly we struck it down. While the "Virginia poll tax was born of a desire to disenfranchise the Negro" (Harman v. Forssenius, 380 U.S. 528, 543 [1965]), we do not stop to determine whether on this record the Virginia tax in its modern setting serves the same end.

the result here, because, unlike a poll tax, the "ability to read and write . . . has some relation to standards designed to promote intelligent use of the ballot."

We conclude that a State violates the Equal Protection Clause of the Fourteenth Amendment whenever it makes the affluence of the voter or payment of any fee an electoral standard. Voter qualifications have no relation to wealth nor to paying or not paying this or any other tax. Our cases demonstrate that the Equal Protection Clause of the Fourteenth Amendment restrains the States from fixing voter qualifications which invidiously discriminate. Thus without questioning the power of a State to impose reasonable residence restrictions on the availability of the ballot, we [have] held that a State may not deny the opportunity to vote to a bona fide resident merely because he is a member of the armed services. . . . Previously we had said that neither homesite nor occupation "affords a permissible basis for distinguishing between qualified voters within the State." We think the same must be true of requirements of wealth or affluence or payment of a fee.

. . . [I]n Yick Wo v. Hopkins, the Court referred to "the political franchise of voting" as a "fundamental political right, because preservative of all rights." Recently in Reynolds v. Sims, we said, "Undoubtedly, the right of suffrage is a fundamental matter in a free and democratic society. Especially since the right to exercise the franchise in a free and unimpaired manner is preservative of other basic civil and political rights, any alleged infringement of the right of citizens to vote must be carefully and meticulously scrutinized." . . . [In *Sims*, we] concluded:

> A citizen, a qualified voter, is no more nor no less so because he lives in the city or on the farm. This is the clear and strong command of our Constitution's Equal Protection Clause. This is an essential part of the concept of a government of laws and not men. This is at the heart of Lincoln's vision of "government of the people, by the people, [and] for the people." The Equal Protection Clause demands no less than substantially equal state legislative representation for all citizens, of all places as well as of all races.

We say the same whether the citizen, otherwise qualified to vote, has $1.50 in his pocket or nothing at all, pays the fee or fails to pay it. The principle that denies the State the right to dilute a citizen's vote on account of his economic status or other such factors by analogy bars a system which excludes those unable to pay a fee to vote or who fail to pay.

It is argued that a State may exact fees from citizens for many different kinds of licenses; that if it can demand from all an equal fee for a driver's license, it can demand from all an equal poll tax for voting. But we must remember that the interest of the State, when it comes to voting, is limited to the power to fix qualifications. Wealth, like race, creed, or color, is not germane to one's ability to participate intelligently in the electoral process. Lines drawn on the basis of wealth or property, like those of race, are traditionally disfavored. To introduce wealth or payment of a fee as a measure of a voter's qualifications is to introduce a capricious or irrelevant factor. The degree of the discrimination is irrelevant. In this context — that is, as a condition of obtaining a ballot — the requirement of fee paying causes an "invidious" discrimination that runs afoul of the Equal Protection Clause. . . .

[T]he Equal Protection Clause is not shackled to the political theory of a particular era. In determining what lines are unconstitutionally discriminatory, we have never been confined to historic notions of equality, any more than we have restricted due process to a fixed catalogue of what was at a given time deemed to be the limits of fundamental rights. Notions of what constitutes equal treatment for purposes of the Equal Protection Clause *do* change. This Court in 1896 held that laws providing for separate public facilities for white and Negro citizens did not deprive the latter of the equal protection and treatment that the Fourteenth Amendment commands. Plessy v. Ferguson, 163 U.S. 537. Seven of the eight Justices then sitting subscribed to the Court's opinion, thus joining in expressions of what constituted unequal and discriminatory treatment that sound strange to a contemporary ear. When, in 1954 — more than a half-century later — we repudiated the "separate-but-equal" doctrine of *Plessy* as respects public education we stated: "In approaching this problem, we cannot turn the clock back to 1868 when the Amendment was adopted, or even to 1896 when Plessy v. Ferguson was written." Brown v. Board of Education, 347 U.S. 483, 492.

. . . We have long been mindful that where fundamental rights and liberties are asserted under the Equal Protection Clause, classifications which might invade or restrain them must be closely scrutinized and carefully confined. Those principles apply here. For to repeat, wealth or fee paying has, in our view, no relation to voting qualifications; the right to vote is too precious, too fundamental to be so burdened or conditioned.

Mr. Justice HARLAN, whom Mr. Justice STEWART joins, dissenting.

. . . The Equal Protection Clause prevents States from arbitrarily treating people differently under their laws. Whether any such differing treatment is to be deemed arbitrary depends on whether or not it reflects an appropriate differentiating classification among those affected; the clause has never been thought to require equal treatment of all persons despite differing circumstances. The test evolved by this Court for determining whether an asserted justifying classification exists is whether such a classification can be deemed to be founded on some rational and otherwise constitutionally permissible state policy. This standard reduces to a minimum the likelihood that the federal judiciary will judge state policies in terms of the individual notions and predilections of its own members, and until recently it has been followed in all kinds of "equal protection" cases.

In substance the Court's analysis of the equal protection issue goes no further than to say that the electoral franchise is "precious" and "fundamental," and to conclude that "to introduce wealth or payment of a fee as a measure of a voter's qualifications is to introduce a capricious or irrelevant factor." These are of course captivating phrases, but they are wholly inadequate to satisfy the standard governing adjudication of the equal protection issue: Is there a rational basis for Virginia's poll tax as a voting qualification? I think the answer to that question is undoubtedly "yes."[4]

Property qualifications and poll taxes have been a traditional part of our political structure. In the Colonies the franchise was generally a restricted one. Over the years these and other restrictions were gradually lifted, primarily because popular theories of political representation had changed. . . .

4. I have no doubt that poll taxes that deny the right to vote on the basis of race or color violate the Fifteenth Amendment and can be struck down by this Court. . . . The Virginia poll tax is on its face applicable to all citizens, and there was no allegation that it was discriminatorily enforced. . . .

Similarly with property qualifications, it is only by fiat that it can be said, especially in the context of American history, that there can be no rational debate as to their advisability. Most of the early Colonies had them; many of the States have had them during much of their histories; and, whether one agrees or not, arguments have been and still can be made in favor of them. For example, it is certainly a rational argument that payment of some minimal poll tax promotes civic responsibility, weeding out those who do not care enough about public affairs to pay $1.50 or thereabouts a year for the exercise of the franchise. It is also arguable, indeed it was probably accepted as sound political theory by a large percentage of Americans through most of our history, that people with some property have a deeper stake in community affairs, and are consequently more responsible, more educated, more knowledgeable, more worthy of confidence, than those without means, and that the community and Nation would be better managed if the franchise were restricted to such citizens. . . .

These viewpoints, to be sure, ring hollow on most contemporary ears. Their lack of acceptance today is evidenced by the fact that nearly all of the States, left to their own devices, have eliminated property or poll-tax qualifications. . . . Property and poll-tax qualifications, very simply, are not in accord with current egalitarian notions of how a modern democracy should be organized. It is of course entirely fitting that legislatures should modify the law to reflect such changes in popular attitudes. However, it is all wrong, in my view, for the Court to adopt the political doctrines popularly accepted at a particular moment of our history and to declare all others to be irrational and invidious, barring them from the range of choice by reasonably minded people acting through the political process. It was not too long ago that Mr. Justice Holmes felt impelled to remind the Court that the Due Process Clause of the Fourteenth Amendment does not enact the *laissez-faire* theory of society, Lochner v. New York, 198 U.S. 45, 75-76. The times have changed, and perhaps it is appropriate to observe that neither does the Equal Protection Clause of that Amendment rigidly impose upon America an ideology of unrestrained egalitarianism.

NOTES AND QUESTIONS

1. At the time *Harper* was decided, four other states still had a poll tax (though their terms varied): Alabama, Texas, Mississippi, and Virginia.
2. The footnotes in the *Harper* opinion underscore that racial classifications are the paradigm of the suspect, disfavored classification. Justice Douglas's footnote reminds readers that the Court struck down a Louisiana literacy test that had the effect of deterring African Americans from voting, and asserts that the Virginia poll tax at issue in *Harper* was originally motivated, when passed in 1902, by a desire to "disenfranchise the Negro." (The sponsor of the measure at the Constitutional Convention said, "Discrimination! Why, that is precisely what we propose; that, exactly, is what this Convention was elected for—to discriminate to the very extremity of permissible action under the limitations of the Federal Constitution, with a view to the elimination of every negro voter who can be gotten rid of, legally, without materially impairing the numerical strength of the white electorate!" *See* Harman v. Forssenius, 380 U.S. 538, 543 (1965)). However, Douglas notes that in striking down the poll tax the court does "not stop to

determine" the question of any disparate impact of the tax on African-American voters.

3. In striking down Virginia's poll tax as unconstitutional, the Court did not use the now-canonical rhetoric of "strict scrutiny" and "compelling state interest." The Court speaks instead of the lack of a basis for the "invidious discrimination" between voters. When speaking about the scrutiny that should be applied, the Court used the terminology that a statute that burdens a "fundamental right or liberty" must be "closely scrutinized and carefully confined."

4. Another "democratic process" right that has been held to be fundamental such that a person cannot be excluded from it on the basis of inability to pay is the right to be a candidate on a ballot. Bullock v. Carter, 405 U.S. 134 (1972) (invalidating Texas scheme under which candidates for local office had to pay fees as high as $8,900 to get on the ballot).

5. The fundamental rights doctrine, under both the Equal Protection and Due Process Clauses of the Fourteenth Amendment, is far from clear. Indeed, one must ask, "which interests are deemed 'fundamental,' and on what basis?" One scholar notes that "fundamental rights" rhetoric first appeared in the famous 1942 case Skinner v. Oklahoma, which struck down the forced sterilization of certain convicted criminals. 316 U.S. 535 (1942). The basis for that decision was the unavoidable link between sterilization and "the very existence and survival of the race." *Id.* at 541. In a 2007 article, Professor Robert Farrell notes that "the simplicity of this test has the effect of proving too much. If a right is fundamental for constitutional purposes because of its importance to the survival of the human race, then basic claims to food, clothing, and shelter would also seem to be fundamental as well. And what about education, which the Supreme Court called 'the most important function of state and local governments?'" *See* Robert C. Farrell, *An Excess of Methods: Identifying Implied Fundamental Rights in the Supreme Court*, 26 St. Louis U. Pub. L. Rev. 203 (2007).

6. In 2008, the Supreme Court reviewed an Indiana statute that required voters to present photo identification at the polls. Crawford v. Marion Cnty. Election Bd., 553 U.S. 181 (2008). The statute had an exemption for indigent people, as well as some others, who were permitted to cast provisional ballots but required to provide an affidavit at the court clerk's office within ten days. The Court acknowledged the right to vote, but balanced the statute's burdens on that right with the government's interest in preventing fraud, and upheld the law on a 6-3 vote. The dissent, authored by Justice Souter, concluded that the burden on low-income voters, among others, rendered the law unconstitutional. He noted both that the facilities where the identification cards were issued were not as well distributed across the state as were voting precincts, but also that provisional and absentee ballots were not treated identically to in-person ballots.

SHAPIRO v. THOMPSON
394 U.S. 618 (1969)

Mr. Justice BRENNAN delivered the opinion of the Court.

[Each of these three consolidated cases] is an appeal from a decision of a three-judge District Court holding unconstitutional a . . . statutory provision which denies welfare assistance to residents of the State or District who have not resided within their jurisdictions for at least one year immediately preceding their applications for such assistance.

. . . There is no dispute that the effect of the waiting-period requirement in each case is to create two classes of needy resident families indistinguishable from each other except that one is composed of residents who have resided a year or more, and the second of residents who have resided less than a year, in the jurisdiction. On the basis of this sole difference the first class is granted and the second class is denied welfare aid upon which may depend the ability of the families to obtain the very means to subsist — food, shelter, and other necessities of life.

. . . Primarily, appellants justify the waiting-period requirement as a protective device to preserve the fiscal integrity of state public assistance programs. It is asserted that people who require welfare assistance during their first year of residence in a State are likely to become continuing burdens on state welfare programs. Therefore, the argument runs, if such people can be deterred from entering the jurisdiction by denying them welfare benefits during the first year, state programs to assist long-time residents will not be impaired by a substantial influx of indigent newcomers.

There is weighty evidence that exclusion from the jurisdiction of the poor who need or may need relief was the specific objective of these provisions. In the Congress, sponsors of federal legislation to eliminate all residence requirements have been consistently opposed by representatives of state and local welfare agencies who have stressed the fears of the States that elimination of the requirements would result in a heavy influx of individuals into States providing the most generous benefits. . . . We do not doubt that the one-year waiting-period device is well suited to discourage the influx of poor families in need of assistance. An indigent who desires to migrate, resettle, find a new job, and start a new life will doubtless hesitate if he knows that he must risk making the move without the possibility of falling back on state welfare assistance during his first year of residence, when his need may be most acute. But the purpose of inhibiting migration by needy persons into the State is constitutionally impermissible.

This Court long ago recognized that the nature of our Federal Union and our constitutional concepts of personal liberty unite to require that all citizens be free to travel throughout the length and breadth of our land uninhibited by statutes, rules, or regulations which unreasonably burden or restrict this movement. That proposition was early stated by Chief Justice Taney in the Passenger Cases, 7 How. 283, 492 (1849):

> For all the great purposes for which the Federal government was formed, we are one people, with one common country. We are all citizens of the United States; and, as members of the same community, must have the right to pass and repass through every part of it without interruption, as freely as in our own States.

We have no occasion to ascribe the source of this right to travel interstate to a particular constitutional provision. It suffices that, as Mr. Justice Stewart said for the Court in United States v. Guest, 383 U.S. 745, 757-758 (1966):

> The constitutional right to travel from one State to another . . . occupies a position fundamental to the concept of our Federal Union. It is a right that has been firmly established and repeatedly recognized.

... The right finds no explicit mention in the Constitution. The reason, it has been suggested, is that a right so elementary was conceived from the beginning to be a necessary concomitant of the stronger Union the Constitution created. In any event, freedom to travel throughout the United States has long been recognized as a basic right under the Constitution.

Thus, the purpose of deterring the in-migration of indigents cannot serve as justification for the classification created by the one-year waiting period, since that purpose is constitutionally impermissible. If a law has "no other purpose . . . than to chill the assertion of constitutional rights by penalizing those who choose to exercise them, then it [is] patently unconstitutional."

Alternatively, appellants argue that even if it is impermissible for a State to attempt to deter the entry of all indigents, the challenged classification may be justified as a permissible state attempt to discourage those indigents who would enter the State solely to obtain larger benefits. . . . [A] State may no more try to fence out those indigents who seek higher welfare benefits than it may try to fence out indigents generally. Implicit in any such distinction is the notion that indigents who enter a State with the hope of securing higher welfare benefits are somehow less deserving than indigents who do not take this consideration into account. But we do not perceive why a mother who is seeking to make a new life for herself and her children should be regarded as less deserving because she considers, among others factors, the level of a State's public assistance. Surely such a mother is no less deserving than a mother who moves into a particular State in order to take advantage of its better educational facilities. . . .

We recognize that a State has a valid interest in preserving the fiscal integrity of its programs. It may legitimately attempt to limit its expenditures, whether for public assistance, public education, or any other program. But a State may not accomplish such a purpose by invidious distinctions between classes of its citizens. It could not, for example, reduce expenditures for education by barring indigent children from its schools. Similarly, in the cases before us, appellants must do more than show that denying welfare benefits to new residents saves money. The saving of welfare costs cannot justify an otherwise invidious classification. . . .

Appellants next advance as justification certain administrative and related governmental objectives allegedly served by the waiting-period requirement. They argue that the requirement (1) facilitates the planning of the welfare budget; (2) provides an objective test of residency; (3) minimizes the opportunity for recipients fraudulently to receive payments from more than one jurisdiction; and (4) encourages early entry of new residents into the labor force.

At the outset, we reject appellants' argument that a mere showing of a rational relationship between the waiting period and these four admittedly permissible state objectives will suffice to justify the classification. The waiting-period provision denies welfare benefits to otherwise eligible applicants solely because they have recently moved into the jurisdiction. But in moving from State to State or to the District of Columbia appellees were exercising a constitutional right, and any classification which serves to penalize the exercise of that right, unless shown to be necessary to promote a *compelling* governmental interest, is unconstitutional. . . .

We conclude therefore that appellants in these cases do not use and have no need to use the one-year requirement for the governmental purposes suggested. Thus, even under traditional equal protection tests a classification of welfare applicants according to whether they have lived in the State for one year would seem irrational and unconstitutional. But, of course, the traditional criteria do not apply in these cases. Since the classification here touches on the fundamental right of interstate movement, its constitutionality must be judged by the stricter standard of whether it promotes a *compelling* state interest. Under this standard, the waiting-period requirement clearly violates the Equal Protection Clause.

Mr. Justice HARLAN, dissenting.

. . . [T]he welfare residence requirements are alleged to be unconstitutional on two grounds: *first,* because they impose an undue burden upon the constitutional right of welfare applicants to travel interstate; *second,* because they deny to persons who have recently moved interstate and would otherwise be eligible for welfare assistance the equal protection of the laws assured by the Fourteenth Amendment (in the state cases) or the analogous protection afforded by the Fifth Amendment (in the District of Columbia case). Since the Court basically relies upon the equal protection ground, I shall discuss it first.

In upholding the equal protection argument, the Court has applied an equal protection doctrine of relatively recent vintage: the rule that statutory classifications which either are based upon certain "suspect" criteria or affect "fundamental rights" will be held to deny equal protection unless justified by a "compelling" governmental interest.

The "compelling interest" doctrine, which today is articulated more explicitly than ever before, constitutes an increasingly significant exception to the long-established rule that a statute does not deny equal protection if it is rationally related to a legitimate governmental objective. The "compelling interest" doctrine has two branches. The branch which requires that classifications based upon "suspect" criteria be supported by a compelling interest apparently had its genesis in cases involving racial classifications, which have, at least since Korematsu v. United States, 323 U.S. 214, 216 (1944), been regarded as inherently "suspect." The criterion of "wealth" apparently was added to the list of "suspects" as an alternative justification for the rationale in Harper v. Virginia Bd. of Elections, 383 U.S. 663, 668 (1966), in which Virginia's poll tax was struck down. The criterion of political allegiance may have been added in Williams v. Rhodes, 393 U.S. 23 (1968). Today the list apparently has been further enlarged to include classifications based upon recent interstate movement, and perhaps those based upon the exercise of *any* constitutional right, for the Court states, *ante,* at 634:

> The waiting-period provision denies welfare benefits to otherwise eligible applicants solely because they have recently moved into the jurisdiction. But in moving . . . appellees were exercising a constitutional right, and any classification which serves to penalize the exercise of that right, unless shown to be necessary to promote a *compelling* governmental interest, is unconstitutional.

I think that this branch of the "compelling interest" doctrine is sound when applied to racial classifications, for historically the Equal Protection Clause was largely a product of the desire to eradicate legal distinctions founded upon race. However, I believe that the more recent extensions have been unwise. For the reasons stated in my dissenting opinion in Harper v. Virginia Bd. of Elections, I do not consider wealth a "suspect" statutory criterion. . . .

The second branch of the "compelling interest" principle is even more troublesome. For it has been held that a statutory classification is subject to the "compelling interest" test if the result of the classification may be to affect a "fundamental right," regardless of the basis of the classification. This rule was foreshadowed in Skinner v. Oklahoma, 316 U.S. 535, 541 (1942), in which an Oklahoma statute providing for compulsory sterilization of "habitual criminals" was held subject to "strict scrutiny" mainly because it affected "one of the basic civil rights." After a long hiatus, the principle re-emerged in Reynolds v. Sims, 377 U.S. 533, 561-562 (1964), in which state apportionment statutes were subjected to an unusually stringent test because "any alleged infringement of the right of citizens to vote must be carefully and meticulously scrutinized." *Id.*, at 562. The rule appeared again in Carrington v. Rash, 380 U.S. 89, 96 (1965), in which, as I now see that case, the Court applied an abnormally severe equal protection standard to a Texas statute denying certain servicemen the right to vote, without indicating that the statutory distinction between servicemen and civilians was generally "suspect." This branch of the doctrine was also an alternate ground in Harper v. Virginia Bd. of Elections, *supra, see* 383 U.S., at 670, and apparently was a basis of the holding in Williams v. Rhodes, *supra.* It has reappeared today in the Court's cryptic suggestion that the "compelling interest" test is applicable merely because the result of the classification may be to deny the appellees "food, shelter, and other necessities of life," as well as in the Court's statement that "since the classification here touches on the fundamental right of interstate movement, its constitutionality must be judged by the stricter standard of whether it promotes a *compelling* state interest."

I think this branch of the "compelling interest" doctrine particularly unfortunate and unnecessary. It is unfortunate because it creates an exception which threatens to swallow the standard equal protection rule. Virtually every state statute affects important rights. This Court has repeatedly held, for example, that the traditional equal protection standard is applicable to statutory classifications affecting such fundamental matters as the right to pursue a particular occupation, the right to receive greater or smaller wages or to work more or less hours, and the right to inherit property. Rights such as these are in principle indistinguishable from those involved here, and to extend the "compelling interest" rule to all cases in which such rights are affected would go far toward making this Court a "super-legislature." This branch of the doctrine is also unnecessary. When the right affected is one assured by the Federal Constitution, any infringement can be dealt with under the Due Process Clause. But when a statute affects only matters not mentioned in the Federal Constitution and is not arbitrary or irrational, I must reiterate that I know of nothing which entitles this Court to pick out particular human activities, characterize them as "fundamental," and give them added protection under an unusually stringent equal protection test. . . .

Today's decision, it seems to me, reflects to an unusual degree the current notion that this Court possesses a peculiar wisdom all its own whose capacity to lead this Nation out of its present troubles is contained only by the limits of judicial ingenuity in contriving new constitutional principles to meet each problem as it arises. For anyone who, like myself, believes that it is an essential function of this Court to maintain the constitutional divisions between state and federal authority and among the three branches of the Federal

Government, today's decision is a step in the wrong direction. This resurgence of the expansive view of "equal protection" carries the seeds of more judicial interference with the state and federal legislative process, much more indeed than does the judicial application of "due process" according to traditional concepts about which some members of this Court have expressed fears as to its potentialities for setting us judges "at large." I consider it particularly unfortunate that this judicial roadblock to the powers of Congress in this field should occur at the very threshold of the current discussions regarding the "federalizing" of these aspects of welfare relief.

NOTES AND QUESTIONS

1. Note Justice Harlan's reference to the Nation's "present troubles" in his dissent. To what do you assume he was referring?
2. The majority opinion in *Shapiro* notes that the waiting period for welfare benefits has its "antecedents" in the Poor Laws imported from England to the colonies. Recall the description of those laws from Chapter 2. Do you agree that they are antecedents to contemporary welfare waiting periods?
3. The Chief Justice's dissenting opinion warns that the majority's view of the right to travel "reveals only the top of the iceberg. Lurking beneath are the multitude of situations in which States have imposed residence requirements including eligibility to vote, to engage in certain professions or occupations or to attend a state-supported university." This is of course correct. Under the majority's reasoning, can durational residency requirements for in-state tuition or hunting licenses be distinguished? Do these not unconstitutionally burden the right to travel? Are there compelling government interests in those situations that do not apply to welfare benefits?
4. Note the stories and circumstances of the plaintiffs in *Shapiro* and its companion cases as summarized by Justice Brennan below. What do they tell you about the lawyers' strategy in bringing the *Shapiro* case?

> Appellee Minnie Harrell, now deceased, had moved with her three children from New York to Washington in September 1966. She suffered from cancer and moved to be near members of her family who lived in Washington.
>
> Appellee Barley, a former resident of the District of Columbia, returned to the District in March 1941 and was committed a month later to St. Elizabeths Hospital as mentally ill. She has remained in that hospital ever since. She was deemed eligible for release in 1965, and a plan was made to transfer her from the hospital to a foster home. The plan depended, however, upon Mrs. Barley's obtaining welfare assistance for her support. Her application for assistance under the program for Aid to the Permanently and Totally Disabled was denied because her time spent in the hospital did not count in determining compliance with the one-year [residency] requirement.
>
> Appellee Brown lived with her mother and two of her three children in Fort Smith, Arkansas. Her third child was living with appellee Brown's father in the District of Columbia. When her mother moved from Fort Smith to Oklahoma, appellee Brown, in February 1966, returned to the District of Columbia where she had lived as a child. Her application for AFDC assistance was approved insofar as it sought assistance for the child who had lived in the District with her father but was denied to the extent it sought assistance for the two other children.

Appellee Smith and her five minor children moved in December 1966 from Delaware to Philadelphia, Pennsylvania, where her father lived. Her father supported her and her children for several months until he lost his job. Appellee then applied for AFDC assistance and had received two checks when the aid was terminated. Appellee Foster, after living in Pennsylvania from 1953 to 1965, had moved with her four children to South Carolina to care for her grandfather and invalid grandmother and had returned to Pennsylvania in 1967.

5. In Edwards v. California, 314 U.S. 160 (1941), the Court struck down a state statute making it a crime to transport an indigent into the state:

> There remains to be noticed only the contention that the limitation upon State power to interfere with the interstate transportation of persons is subject to an exception in the case of "paupers." It is true that support for this contention may be found in early decisions of this Court. In City of New York v. Miln (1837) . . . it was said that it is "as competent and as necessary for a state to provide precautionary measures against the moral pestilence of paupers, vagabonds, and possibly convicts; as it is to guard against the physical pestilence, which may arise from unsound and infectious articles imported." . . . [W]e do not think that it will now be seriously contended that because a person is without employment and without funds he constitutes a "moral pestilence." Poverty and immorality are not synonymous.

6. Two years after *Shapiro*, the Court considered other durational residency and citizenship requirements in Graham v. Richardson, 403 U.S. 365 (1971). The Court struck down an Arizona statute that limited welfare (in that case, benefits for people with disabilities) to citizens and lawful residents who had been in the state at least 15 years, and a Pennsylvania statute that similarly restricted benefits to citizens and those who had filed a declaration of intent to become a citizen. The court noted that while *Shapiro* had turned on the fundamental nature of the right at stake (travel), here the equal protection issue was one of classifications — between "aliens" and "citizens." Citing the famous *Carolene Products* reference to "discrete and insular" minority groups, the Court held that "aliens" are entitled to heightened judicial scrutiny, and concluded that the states' "desire to preserve limited welfare benefits for its own citizens is inadequate to justify . . . making noncitizens ineligible for public assistance, [or] . . . restricting benefits to citizens and longtime resident aliens." Notably, the *Graham* decision considered whether *states* have the power to discriminate against "aliens" in that manner, but left open the question whether Congress could do so.

* * *

At the time *Shapiro* was decided, over 40 states had residency requirements for welfare benefits. Despite the invalidation of these measures by *Shapiro*, the 1996 welfare reform act expressly authorized states to "apply to a family the rules (including benefits amounts) of the [TANF] program . . . of another State if the family has moved to the State from the other State and has resided in the State for less than 12 months." 42 U.S.C. § 604(c) (2012). As of 2000, at least six states had some form of residency duration requirement for welfare benefits, and approximately 12 others restricted newcomers' benefits in some way. *See* Nan S. Ellis & Cheryl M. Miller, *Welfare Waiting Periods: A Public Policy Analysis of*

Saenz v. Roe, 11 Stan. L. & Pol'y Rev. 343 (2000). In 1999, the Court reviewed California's post–welfare reform newcomer scheme and found that it, like the one in *Shapiro*, was unconstitutional.

SAENZ v. ROE
526 U.S. 489 (1999)

Justice STEVENS delivered the opinion of the Court.

In 1992, California enacted a statute limiting the maximum welfare benefits available to newly arrived residents. The scheme limits the amount payable to a family that has resided in the State for less than 12 months to the amount payable by the State of the family's prior residence. The questions presented by this case are whether the 1992 statute was constitutional when it was enacted and, if not, whether an amendment to the Social Security Act enacted by Congress in 1996 affects that determination.

California is not only one of the largest, most populated, and most beautiful States in the Nation; it is also one of the most generous. Like all other States, California has participated in several welfare programs authorized by the Social Security Act and partially funded by the Federal Government. Its programs, however, provide a higher level of benefits and serve more needy citizens than those of most other States. In one year the most expensive of those programs, Aid to Families with Dependent Children (AFDC), which was replaced in 1996 with Temporary Assistance to Needy Families (TANF), provided benefits for an average of 2,645,814 persons per month at an annual cost to the State of $2.9 billion. In California the cash benefit for a family of two—a mother and one child—is $456 a month, but in the neighboring State of Arizona, for example, it is only $275.

In 1992, in order to make a relatively modest reduction in its vast welfare budget, the California Legislature enacted § 11450.03 of the state Welfare & Institutions Code. That section sought to change the California AFDC program by limiting new residents, for the first year they live in California, to the benefits they would have received in the State of their prior residence. . . .

On December 21, 1992, three California residents who were eligible for AFDC benefits filed an action in the Eastern District of California challenging the constitutionality of the durational residency requirement in § 11450.03. Each plaintiff alleged that she had recently moved to California to live with relatives in order to escape abusive family circumstances. . . . Each alleged that her monthly AFDC grant for the ensuing 12 months would be substantially lower under § 11450.03 than if the statute were not in effect. . . .

The word "travel" is not found in the text of the Constitution. Yet the "constitutional right to travel from one State to another" is firmly embedded in our jurisprudence. Indeed, as Justice Stewart reminded us in Shapiro v. Thompson, 394 U.S. 618 (1969), the right is so important that it is "assertable against private interference as well as governmental action . . . a virtually unconditional personal right, guaranteed by the Constitution to us all." . . .

In this case California argues that § 11450.03 was not enacted for the impermissible purpose of inhibiting migration by needy persons and that, unlike the legislation reviewed in *Shapiro*, it does not penalize the right to travel because new arrivals are not ineligible for benefits during their first year of residence.

California submits that, instead of being subjected to the strictest scrutiny, the statute should be upheld if it is supported by a rational basis and that the State's legitimate interest in saving over $10 million a year satisfies that test. . . . The debate about the appropriate standard of review, together with the potential relevance of the federal statute, persuades us that it will be useful to focus on the source of the constitutional right on which respondents rely.

The "right to travel" discussed in our cases embraces at least three different components. It protects the right of a citizen of one State to enter and to leave another State, the right to be treated as a welcome visitor rather than an unfriendly alien when temporarily present in the second State, and, for those travelers who elect to become permanent residents, the right to be treated like other citizens of that State. . . .

What is at issue in this case, then, is the third aspect of the right to travel: the right of the newly arrived citizen to the same privileges and immunities enjoyed by other citizens of the same State. That right is protected not only by the new arrival's status as a state citizen, but also by her status as a citizen of the United States. That additional source of protection is plainly identified in the opening words of the Fourteenth Amendment:

> All persons born or naturalized in the United States, and subject to the jurisdiction thereof, are citizens of the United States and of the State wherein they reside. No State shall make or enforce any law which shall abridge the privileges or immunities of citizens of the United States. . . .

. . . Writing for the majority in the *Slaughter-House Cases*, Justice Miller explained that one of the privileges conferred by this Clause "is that a citizen of the United States can, of his own volition, become a citizen of any State of the Union by a *bona fide* residence therein, with the same rights as other citizens of that State." . . .

That newly arrived citizens "have two political capacities, one state and one federal," adds special force to their claim that they have the same rights as others who share their citizenship. Neither mere rationality nor some intermediate standard of review should be used to judge the constitutionality of a state rule that discriminates against some of its citizens because they have been domiciled in the State for less than a year. The appropriate standard may be more categorical than that articulated in *Shapiro*, but it is surely no less strict.

Because this case involves discrimination against citizens who have completed their interstate travel, the State's argument that its welfare scheme affects the right to travel only "incidentally" is beside the point. Were we concerned solely with actual deterrence to migration, we might be persuaded that a partial withholding of benefits constitutes a lesser incursion on the right to travel than an outright denial of all benefits. But since the right to travel embraces the citizen's right to be treated equally in her new State of residence, the discriminatory classification is itself a penalty.

It is undisputed that respondents and the members of the class that they represent are citizens of California and that their need for welfare benefits is unrelated to the length of time that they have resided in California. We thus have no occasion to consider what weight might be given to a citizen's length of residence if the bona fides of her claim to state citizenship were questioned. Moreover, because whatever benefits they receive will be consumed while they remain in California, there is no danger that recognition of their claim will encourage citizens of other States to establish residency for just long enough to acquire some readily portable benefit, such as a divorce or a college education, that will be enjoyed after they return to their original domicile. . . .

These classifications may not be justified by a purpose to deter welfare applicants from migrating to California for three reasons. First, although it is reasonable to assume that some persons may be motivated to move for the purpose of obtaining higher benefits, the empirical evidence reviewed by the District Judge, which takes into account the high cost of living in California, indicates that the number of such persons is quite small — surely not large enough to justify a burden on those who had no such motive. Second, California has represented to the Court that the legislation was not enacted for any such reason. Third, even if it were, as we squarely held in Shapiro v. Thompson, such a purpose would be unequivocally impermissible.

Disavowing any desire to fence out the indigent, California has instead advanced an entirely fiscal justification for its multitiered scheme. The enforcement of § 11450.03 will save the State approximately $10.9 million a year. The question is not whether such saving is a legitimate purpose but whether the State may accomplish that end by the discriminatory means it has chosen. An evenhanded, across-the-board reduction of about 72 cents per month for every beneficiary would produce the same result. But our negative answer to the question does not rest on the weakness of the State's purported fiscal justification. It rests on the fact that the Citizenship Clause of the Fourteenth Amendment expressly equates citizenship with residence: "That Clause does not provide for, and does not allow for, degrees of citizenship based on length of residence." . . .

The question that remains is whether congressional approval of durational residency requirements in the 1996 amendment to the Social Security Act somehow resuscitates the constitutionality of § 11450.03. That question is readily answered, for we have consistently held that Congress may not authorize the States to violate the Fourteenth Amendment. Moreover, the protection afforded to the citizen by the Citizenship Clause of that Amendment is a limitation on the powers of the National Government as well as the States. . . .

Citizens of the United States, whether rich or poor, have the right to choose to be citizens "of the State wherein they reside." U.S. Const., Amdt. 14, § 1. The States, however, do not have any right to select their citizens. The Fourteenth Amendment, like the Constitution itself, was, as Justice Cardozo put it, "framed upon the theory that the peoples of the several states must sink or swim together, and that in the long run prosperity and salvation are in union and not division."

Chief Justice REHNQUIST, with whom Justice THOMAS joins, dissenting.

The Court today breathes new life into the previously dormant Privileges or Immunities Clause of the Fourteenth Amendment. . . .

In unearthing from its tomb the right to become a state citizen and to be treated equally in the new State of residence, however, the Court ignores a State's need to assure that only persons who establish a bona fide residence receive the benefits provided to current residents of the State. The *Slaughter-House* dicta at the core of the Court's analysis specifically condition a United States citizen's right to "become a citizen of any state of the Union" and to enjoy the "same rights as other citizens of that State" on the establishment of a "*bona fide residence therein.*" Even when redefining the right to travel in *Shapiro* and its progeny, the Court has "always carefully distinguished between bona fide residence requirements, which seek to differentiate between residents and non-residents, and residence requirements, such as durational, fixed date, and fixed point residence requirements, which treat established residents differently based on the time they migrated into the State."

... While the physical presence element of a bona fide residence is easy to police, the subjective intent element is not. It is simply unworkable and futile to require States to inquire into each new resident's subjective intent to remain. Hence, States employ objective criteria such as durational residence requirements to test a new resident's resolve to remain before these new citizens can enjoy certain in-state benefits. Recognizing the practical appeal of such criteria, this Court has repeatedly sanctioned the State's use of durational residence requirements before new residents receive in-state tuition rates at state universities. ... The Court has done the same in upholding a 1-year residence requirement for eligibility to obtain a divorce in state courts, and in upholding political party registration restrictions that amounted to a durational residency requirement for voting in primary elections.

If States can require individuals to reside in-state for a year before exercising the right to educational benefits, the right to terminate a marriage, or the right to vote in primary elections that all other state citizens enjoy, then States may surely do the same for welfare benefits. Indeed, there is no material difference between a 1-year residence requirement applied to the level of welfare benefits given out by a State, and the same requirement applied to the level of tuition subsidies at a state university. The welfare payment here and in-state tuition rates are cash subsidies provided to a limited class of people, and California's standard of living and higher education system make both subsidies quite attractive. ...

... [T]he durational residence requirement challenged here is a permissible exercise of the State's power to "assur[e] that services provided for its residents are enjoyed only by residents." The 1-year period ... does not deprive welfare recipients of all benefits; indeed, the limitation has no effect whatsoever on a recipient's ability to enjoy the full 5-year period of welfare eligibility; to enjoy the full range of employment, training, and accompanying supportive services; or to take full advantage of health care benefits under Medicaid. This waiting period does not preclude new residents from all cash payments, but merely limits them to what they received in their prior State of residence. Moreover, as the Court recognizes, any pinch resulting from this limitation during the 1-year period is mitigated by other programs such as homeless assistance and an increase in food stamp allowance. The 1-year period thus permissibly balances the new resident's needs for subsistence with the State's need to ensure the bona fides of their claim to residence.

D. EQUAL PROTECTION: THE PROBLEM OF CLASSIFICATIONS

Our analysis of the equal protection classification cases begins with two criminal law cases that provide an important analytical backdrop against which the welfare cases in the late 1960s and early 1970s were decided. At the time the welfare cases were brought, the Court had recently taken up questions about criminal defendants' rights to procedural protections for which there was ordinarily a fee. In the two cases presented here, challenges were brought under both the Due Process and Equal Protection Clauses. Griffin v. Illinois concerned whether a criminal defendant who had been convicted at trial must be provided a certified copy of the record, necessary to lodge an appeal, without cost. In Douglas v. California, the Court considered a defendant's right to a lawyer in an appeal as of right.

GRIFFIN v. ILLINOIS
351 U.S. 12 (1956)

Mr. Justice BLACK announced the judgment of the Court:

The petitioners Griffin and Crenshaw were tried together and convicted of armed robbery in the Criminal Court of Cook County, Illinois, Immediately after their conviction they filed a motion in the trial court asking that a certified copy of the entire record, including a stenographic transcript of the proceedings, be furnished them without cost. They alleged that they were "poor persons with no means of paying the necessary fees to acquire the Transcript and Court Records needed to prosecute an appeal. . . ." These allegations were not denied. Under Illinois law in order to get full direct appellate review of alleged errors by a writ of error it is necessary for the defendant to furnish the appellate court with a bill of exceptions or report of proceedings at the trial certified by the trial judge. As Illinois concedes, it is sometimes impossible to prepare such bills of exceptions or reports without a stenographic transcript of the trial proceedings. Indigent defendants sentenced to death are provided with a free transcript at the expense of the county where convicted. In all other criminal cases defendants needing a transcript, whether indigent or not, must themselves buy it. The petitioners contended in their motion before the trial court that failure to provide them with the needed transcript would violate the Due Process and Equal Protection Clauses of the Fourteenth Amendment. The trial court denied the motion without a hearing.

. . . Providing equal justice for poor and rich, weak and powerful alike is an age-old problem. People have never ceased to hope and strive to move closer to that goal. This hope, at least in part, brought about in 1215 the royal concessions of Magna Charta: "To no one will we sell, to no one will we refuse, or delay, right or justice. . . . No free man shall be taken or imprisoned, or disseised, or out-lawed, or exiled, or anywise destroyed; nor shall we go upon him nor send upon him, but by the lawful judgment of his peers or by the law of the land." These pledges were unquestionably steps toward a fairer and more nearly equal application of criminal justice. In this tradition, our own constitutional guaranties of due process and equal protection both call for procedures in criminal trials which allow no invidious discriminations between persons and different groups of persons. Both equal protection and due process emphasize the central aim of our entire judicial system — all people charged with crime must, so far as the law is concerned, "stand on an equality before the bar of justice in every American court."

Surely no one would contend that either a State or the Federal Government could constitutionally provide that defendants unable to pay court costs in advance should be denied the right to plead not guilty or to defend themselves in court. Such a law would make the constitutional promise of a fair trial a worthless thing. Notice, the right to be heard, and the right to counsel would under such circumstances be meaningless promises to the poor. In criminal trials a State can no more discriminate on account of poverty than on account of religion, race, or color. Plainly the ability to pay costs in advance bears no rational relationship to a defendant's guilt or innocence and could not be used as an excuse to deprive a defendant of a fair trial. Indeed, a provision in the Constitution of Illinois of 1818 provided that every person in Illinois "ought to obtain right and justice freely, and without being obliged to purchase it, completely and without denial, promptly and without delay, conformably to the laws."

There is no meaningful distinction between a rule which would deny the poor the right to defend themselves in a trial court and one which effectively denies the poor an adequate appellate review accorded to all who have money enough to pay the costs in advance. It is true that a State is not required by the Federal Constitution to provide appellate courts or a right to appellate review at all. But that is not to say that a State that does grant appellate review can do so in a way that discriminates against some convicted defendants on account of their poverty.

Mr. Justice HARLAN, dissenting:

The Court thus holds that, at least in this area of criminal appeals, the Equal Protection Clause imposes on the States an affirmative duty to lift the handicaps flowing from differences in economic circumstances. That holding produces the anomalous result that a constitutional admonition to the States to treat all persons equally means in this instance that Illinois must give to some what it requires others to pay for. Granting that such a classification would be reasonable, it does not follow that a State's failure to make it can be regarded as discrimination. It may as accurately be said that the real issue in this case is not whether Illinois has discriminated but whether it has a duty to discriminate.

I do not understand the Court to dispute either the necessity for a bill of exceptions or the reasonableness of the general requirement that the trial transcript, if used in its preparation, be paid for by the appealing party. The Court finds in the operation of these requirements, however, an invidious classification between the "rich" and the "poor." But no economic burden attendant upon the exercise of a privilege bears equally upon all, and in other circumstances the resulting differentiation is not treated as an invidious classification by the State, even though discrimination against "indigents" by name would be unconstitutional. Thus, while the exclusion of "indigents" from a free state university would deny them equal protection, requiring the payment of tuition fees surely would not, despite the resulting exclusion of those who could not afford to pay the fees. And if imposing a condition of payment is not the equivalent of a classification by the State in one case, I fail to see why it should be so regarded in another. Thus if requiring defendants in felony cases to pay for a transcript constitutes a discriminatory denial to indigents of the right of appeal available to others, why is it not a similar denial in misdemeanor cases or, for that matter, civil cases?

It is no answer to say that equal protection is not an absolute, and that in other than criminal cases the differentiation is "reasonable." The resulting classification would be invidious in all cases, and an invidious classification offends equal protection regardless of the seriousness of the consequences. Hence it must be that the differences are "reasonable" in other cases not because the "classification" is reasonable but simply because it is not unreasonable in those cases for the State to fail to relieve indigents of the economic burden. That is, the issue here is not the typical equal protection question of the reasonableness of a "classification" on the basis of which the State has imposed legal disabilities, but rather the reasonableness of the State's failure to remove natural disabilities. The Court holds that the failure of the State to do so is constitutionally unreasonable in this case although it might not be in others. I submit that the basis for that holding is simply an unarticulated conclusion that it violates "fundamental fairness" for a State which provides for appellate review, and thus apparently considers such review necessary to assure justice, not to see to it that such appeals are in fact available to those it would imprison for serious crimes. That of course is the traditional language of due process, see Betts v. Brady, 316 U.S. 455, and I see no reason to import new substance into the concept of equal protection to dispose of the case, especially when to do so gives rise to the all-too-easy opportunity to ignore the real issue and solve the problem simply by labeling the Illinois practice as invidious "discrimination."

DOUGLAS v. CALIFORNIA
372 U.S. 353 (1963)

Mr. Justice DOUGLAS delivered the opinion of the Court:

Petitioners, Bennie Will Meyes and William Douglas, were jointly tried and convicted in a California court on an information charging them with 13 felonies. A single public defender was appointed to represent them. At the commencement of the trial, the defender moved for a continuance, stating that the case was very complicated, that he was not as prepared as he felt he should be because he was handling a different defense every day, and that there was a conflict of interest between the petitioners requiring the appointment of separate counsel for each of them. This motion was denied. Thereafter, petitioners dismissed the defender, claiming he was unprepared, and again renewed motions for separate counsel and for a continuance. These motions also were denied, and petitioners were ultimately convicted by a jury of all 13 felonies, which included robbery, assault with a deadly weapon, and assault with intent to commit murder. Both were given prison terms. Both appealed as of right to the California District Court of Appeal. That court affirmed their convictions. Both Meyes and Douglas then petitioned for further discretionary review in the California Supreme Court, but their petitions were denied without a hearing. . . .

Although several questions are presented in the petition for certiorari, we address ourselves to only one of them. The record shows that petitioners requested, and were denied, the assistance of counsel on appeal, even though it plainly appeared they were indigents. In denying petitioners' requests, the California District Court of Appeal stated that it had "gone through" the record and had come to the conclusion that "no good whatever could be served by appointment of counsel." The District Court of Appeal was acting in accordance with a California rule of criminal procedure which provides that state appellate courts, upon the request of an indigent for counsel, may make "an independent investigation of the record and determine whether it would be of advantage to the defendant or helpful to the appellate court to have counsel appointed. . . . After such investigation, appellate courts should appoint counsel if in their opinion it would be helpful to the defendant or the court, and should deny the appointment of counsel only if in their judgment such appointment would be of no value to either the defendant or the court."

We agree, however, with Justice Traynor of the California Supreme Court, who said that the "[d]enial of counsel on appeal [to an indigent] would seem to be a discrimination at least as invidious as that condemned in Griffin v. People of State of Illinois." . . . [In *Griffin,*] we held that a State may not grant appellate review in such a way as to discriminate against some convicted defendants on account of their poverty. There . . . the right to a free transcript on appeal was in issue. Here the issue is whether or not an indigent shall be denied the assistance of counsel on appeal. In either case the evil is the same: discrimination against the indigent. For there can be no equal justice where the kind of an appeal a man enjoys "depends on the amount of money he has." . . .

In spite of California's forward treatment of indigents, under its present practice the type of an appeal a person is afforded in the District Court of Appeal hinges upon whether or not he can pay for the assistance of counsel. If he can the appellate court passes on the merits of his case only after having the full benefit of written briefs and oral argument by counsel. If he cannot the appellate court is forced to prejudge the merits before it can even determine whether counsel should be provided. At this stage in the proceedings only the barren record speaks for the indigent, and, unless the printed pages show that an injustice has been committed, he is forced to go without a champion on appeal. Any real chance he may have had of showing that his appeal has hidden merit is deprived him when the court decides on an ex parte examination of the record that the assistance of counsel is not required.

We are not here concerned with problems that might arise from the denial of counsel for the preparation of a petition for discretionary or mandatory review beyond the stage in the appellate process at which the claims have once been presented by a lawyer and passed upon by an appellate court. We are dealing only with the first appeal, granted as a matter of right to rich and poor alike, from a criminal conviction. . . . But it is appropriate to observe that a State can, consistently with the Fourteenth Amendment, provide for differences so long as the result does not amount to a denial of due process or an "invidious discrimination." . . . Absolute equality is not required; lines can be and are drawn and we often sustain them. . . . But where the merits of the one and only appeal an indigent has as of right are decided without benefit of counsel, we think an unconstitutional line has been drawn between rich and poor.

Mr. Justice CLARK, dissenting.

We all know that the overwhelming percentage of in forma pauperis appeals are frivolous. Statistics of this Court show that over 96% of the petitions filed here are of this variety. California, in the light of a like experience, has provided that upon the filing of an application for the appointment of counsel the District Court of Appeal shall make "an independent investigation of the record and determine whether it would be of advantage to the defendant or helpful to the appellate court to have counsel appointed." California's courts did that here and after examining the record certified that such an appointment would be neither advantageous to the petitioners nor helpful to the court. It, therefore, refused to go through the useless gesture of appointing an attorney. In my view neither the Equal Protection Clause nor the Due Process Clause requires more. I cannot understand why the Court says that this procedure afforded petitioners "a meaningless ritual." To appoint an attorney would not only have been utter extravagance and a waste of the State's funds but as surely "meaningless" to petitioners.

With this new fetish for indigency the Court piles an intolerable burden on the State's judicial machinery. Indeed, if the Court is correct it may be that we should first clean up our own house. We have afforded indigent litigants much less protection than has California. Last Term we received over 1,200 in forma pauperis applications in none of which had we appointed attorneys or required a record.

Mr. Justice HARLAN, whom Mr. Justice STEWART joins, dissenting.

In holding that an indigent has an absolute right to appointed counsel on appeal of a state criminal conviction, the Court appears to rely both on the Equal Protection Clause and on the guarantees of fair procedure inherent in the Due Process Clause of the Fourteenth Amendment, with obvious emphasis on "equal protection." In my view the Equal Protection Clause is not apposite, and its application to cases like the present one can lead only to mischievous results. This case should be judged solely under the Due Process Clause, and I do not believe that the California procedure violates that provision.

EQUAL PROTECTION

To approach the present problem in terms of the Equal Protection Clause is, I submit, but to substitute resounding phrases for analysis. . . . The States, of course, are prohibited by the Equal Protection Clause from discriminating between "rich" and "poor" as such in the formulation and application of their laws. But it is a far different thing to suggest that this provision prevents the State from adopting a law of general applicability that may affect the poor more harshly than it does the rich, or, on the other hand, from making some effort to redress economic imbalances while not eliminating them entirely.

Every financial exaction which the State imposes on a uniform basis is more easily satisfied by the well-to-do than by the indigent. Yet I take it that no one would dispute the constitutional power of the State to levy a uniform sales tax, to charge tuition at a state university, to fix rates for the purchase of water from a municipal corporation, to impose a standard fine for criminal violations, or to establish minimum bail for various categories of offenses. Nor could it be contended that the State may not classify as crimes acts which the poor are more likely to commit than are the rich. And surely, there would be no basis for attacking a state law which provided benefits for the needy simply because those benefits fell short of the goods or services that others could purchase for themselves.

Laws such as these do not deny equal protection to the less fortunate for one essential reason: the Equal Protection Clause does not impose on the States "an affirmative duty to lift the handicaps flowing from differences in economic circumstances." To so construe it would be to read into the Constitution a philosophy of leveling that would be foreign to many of our basic concepts of the proper relations between government and society. The State may have a moral obligation to eliminate the evils of poverty, but it is not required by the Equal Protection Clause to give to some whatever others can afford.

NOTES AND QUESTIONS

1. Justice Douglas dramatically states that "there can be no equal justice where the kind of an appeal a man enjoys 'depends on the amount of money he has.'" Should this argument extend to things other than "justice"? Why or why not?

2. *Douglas* was issued on March 18, 1963, the same day as Gideon v. Wainwright, 372 U.S. 335 (1963). *Gideon*'s holding, that indigent felony defendants facing threat of incarceration must be provided counsel, was based on the Due Process Clause. Justice Harlan's dissent in *Douglas* is based, in part, on his conclusion that *Douglas*, like *Gideon*, should have turned exclusively on the Due Process Clause. In other words, he did not join the Court's view that the Equal Protection Clause applied at all; he did not share the view that the state's failure to provide appellate counsel to criminal defendants operated as "invidious discrimination" against the poor.

3. Chapter 10 discusses claims that state filing fees and other costs pose unconstitutional barriers to indigents' access to the courts. However, it is worth noting here that there is another context besides criminal cases in which courts have been relatively hospitable to such claims: family law matters. In Boddie v. Connecticut, 401 U.S. 371 (1971), the Court held that a person could not be denied access to the courts for purposes of seeking a divorce because she could not afford the filing fees and other court costs. Such a barrier was held to violate the Due Process Clause. Twenty-five years later, in M.L.B. v. S.L.J., 519 U.S. 102 (1996), the Court similarly held that record preparation fees could not be required before an indigent mother could appeal the judicial termination of her parental rights. Relying on *Griffin* and *Douglas*, as well as *Boddie*, the Court in *M.L.B.* noted that the fee waiver cases "reflect both equal protection and due process concerns. As we [have said, in these cases], '[d]ue process and equal protection principles converge.' The equal protection concern relates to the legitimacy of fencing out would-be appellants based solely on their inability to pay core [*sic*] costs. The due process concern homes in on the essential fairness of the state-ordered proceedings anterior to adverse state action." Summarizing the status of the law in equal protection in this context and citing *Griffin*, Justice Ginsburg wrote,

   > States are not forced by the Constitution to adjust all tolls to account for "disparity in material circumstances." But our cases solidly establish two exceptions to that general rule. The basic right to participate in political processes as voters and candidates cannot be limited to those who can pay for a license. Nor may access to judicial processes in cases criminal or "quasi criminal in nature.

4. Recall Professor Michelman's distinction between claims of discrimination (against the poor) versus claims of a right to some minimum subsistence or minimum value. Do you see that distinction operating in the Court's equal protection and due process jurisprudence?

* * *

Three important, noncriminal, equal protection poverty law cases are presented next. These cases, brought in 1970-1973, sought to extend some of the constitutional protections for indigent criminal defendants into the civil realm, in the context of two vitally important domains where states interact with poor people: welfare benefits and public education. These cases also involved the crucial intersection between race and poverty; poverty lawyers sought to leverage the suspect class status of racial classifications into elevated scrutiny for poor people, who disproportionately were also racial minorities. Recalling the overview of the constitutional law of poverty, as you read each case, ask yourself: What classification has the government drawn here? Is it between the poor and the non-poor? Between subclasses of the poor? How, if at all, does the racial composition of the affected class(es) affect the arguments or the Court's analysis?

The first case, Dandridge v. Williams, is considered by many poverty lawyers and scholars the deathknell of the quest for equal protection for the poor. The case arose from Maryland's operation of its AFDC program. Maryland promulgated a "maximum grant regulation," which calculated AFDC grants according to number of children in a household, providing money in decreasing increments as the size of the household increased and placing an ultimate cap of a certain total dollar amount. Maryland families with more than four or five (depending on the county) children, asserted two claims against the regulation. First, they argued that it violated the Social Security Act's requirement that all eligible children be aided, a statutory argument the Court rejected. Second, appellants argued that the maximum grant regulation violated the Equal Protection Clause of the Fourteenth Amendment. Because we are concerned in this chapter with the constitutional treatment of poverty, the excerpt below includes only the equal protection argument.

DANDRIDGE v. WILLIAMS
397 U.S. 471 (1970)

Mr. Justice STEWART delivered the opinion of the Court.

Like every other State in the Union, Maryland participates in the Federal Aid to Families With Dependent Children (AFDC) program, which originated with the Social Security Act of 1935. Under this jointly financed program, a State computes the so-called "standard of need" of each eligible family unit within its borders. . . .

[Maryland's AFDC program] computes the standard of need for each eligible family based on the number of children in the family and the circumstances under which the family lives. In general, the standard of need increases with each additional person in the household, but the increments become proportionately smaller. The regulation here in issue imposes upon the grant that any single family may receive an upper limit of $250 per month in certain counties and Baltimore City, and of $240 per month elsewhere in the State. The appellees all have large families, so that their standards of need as computed by the State substantially exceed the maximum grants that they actually receive under the regulation. The appellees urged in the District Court that the maximum grant limitation operates to discriminate against them merely because of the size of their families, in violation of the Equal Protection Clause of the Fourteenth Amendment. . . .

Although a State may adopt a maximum grant system in allocating its funds available for AFDC payments without violating the Act, it may not, of course,

impose a regime of invidious discrimination in violation of the Equal Protection
Clause of the Fourteenth Amendment. Maryland says that its maximum grant
regulation is wholly free of any invidiously discriminatory purpose or effect, and
that the regulation is rationally supportable on at least four entirely valid
grounds. The regulation can be clearly justified, Maryland argues, in terms of
legitimate state interests in encouraging gainful employment, in maintaining an
equitable balance in economic status as between welfare families and those
supported by a wage-earner, in providing incentives for family planning, and
in allocating available public funds in such a way as fully to meet the needs of the
largest possible number of families. . . .

   In the area of economics and social welfare, a State does not violate the Equal
Protection Clause merely because the classifications made by its laws are
imperfect. If the classification has some reasonable basis, it does not offend
the Constitution simply because the classification is not made with mathematical
nicety or because in practice it results in some inequality. The problems of
government are practical ones and may justify, if they do not require, rough
accommodations — illogical, it may be, and unscientific. A statutory discrimination will not be set aside if any state of facts reasonably may be conceived to
justify it.

   To be sure, the cases cited, and many others enunciating this fundamental
standard under the Equal Protection Clause, have in the main involved state
regulation of business or industry. The administration of public welfare assistance, by contrast, involves the most basic economic needs of impoverished
human beings. We recognize the dramatically real factual difference between
the cited cases and this one, but we can find no basis for applying a different
constitutional standard.[17] It is a standard that has consistently been applied to
state legislation restricting the availability of employment opportunities. And it
is a standard that is true to the principle that the Fourteenth Amendment gives
the federal courts no power to impose upon the States their views of what constitutes wise economic or social policy.

   Under this long-established meaning of the Equal Protection Clause, it is clear
that the Maryland maximum grant regulation is constitutionally valid. We need
not explore all the reasons that the State advances in justification of the
regulation. It is enough that a solid foundation for the regulation can be
found in the State's legitimate interest in encouraging employment and in
avoiding discrimination between welfare families and the families of the working
poor. By combining a limit on the recipient's grant with permission to retain
money earned, without reduction in the amount of the grant, Maryland provides
an incentive to seek gainful employment. And by keying the maximum family
AFDC grants to the minimum wage a steadily employed head of a household
receives, the State maintains some semblance of an equitable balance between
families on welfare and those supported by an employed breadwinner.

   It is true that in some AFDC families there may be no person who is
employable. It is also true that with respect to AFDC families whose determined
standard of need is below the regulatory maximum, and who therefore receive
grants equal to the determined standard, the employment incentive is absent.
But the Equal Protection Clause does not require that a State must choose
between attacking every aspect of a problem or not attacking the problem at

_____

   17. It is important to note that there is no contention that the Maryland regulation is infected
with a racially discriminatory purpose or effect such as to make it inherently suspect.

all. It is enough that the State's action be rationally based and free from invidious discrimination. The regulation before us meets that test.

We do not decide today that the Maryland regulation is wise, that it best fulfills the relevant social and economic objectives that Maryland might ideally espouse, or that a more just and humane system could not be devised. Conflicting claims of morality and intelligence are raised by opponents and proponents of almost every measure, certainly including the one before us. But the intractable economic, social, and even philosophical problems presented by public welfare assistance programs are not the business of this Court. The Constitution may impose certain procedural safeguards upon systems of welfare administration, Goldberg v. Kelly. But the Constitution does not empower this Court to second-guess state officials charged with the difficult responsibility of allocating limited public welfare funds among the myriad of potential recipients. *The judgment is reversed.*

Mr. Justice MARSHALL, whom Mr. Justice BRENNAN joins, dissenting.

More important in the long run than [the majority's] misreading of a federal statute . . . is the Court's emasculation of the Equal Protection Clause as a constitutional principle applicable to the area of social welfare administration. The Court holds today that regardless of the arbitrariness of a classification it must be sustained if any state goal can be imagined that is arguably furthered by its effects. This is so even though the classification's underinclusiveness or over-inclusiveness clearly demonstrates that its actual basis is something other than that asserted by the State, and even though the relationship between the classification and the state interests which it purports to serve is so tenuous that it could not seriously be maintained that the classification tends to accomplish the ascribed goals.

The Court recognizes, as it must, that this case involves "the most basic economic needs of impoverished human beings," and that there is therefore a "dramatically real factual difference" between the instant case and those decisions upon which the Court relies. The acknowledgment that these dramatic differences exist is a candid recognition that the Court's decision today is wholly without precedent. I cannot subscribe to the Court's sweeping refusal to accord the Equal Protection Clause any role in this entire area of the law, and I therefore dissent. . . .

. . . The Maryland AFDC program in its basic structure operates uniformly with regard to all needy children by taking into account the basic subsistence needs of all eligible individuals in the formulation of the standards of need for families of various sizes. However, superimposed upon this uniform system is the maximum grant regulation, the operative effect of which is to create two classes of needy children and two classes of eligible families: those small families and their members who receive payments to cover their subsistence needs and those large families who do not.[11]

---

11. In theory, no payments are made with respect to needy dependent children in excess of four or five as the case may be. In practice, of course, the excess children share in the benefits that are paid with respect to the other members of the family. The result is that support for the entire family is reduced below minimum subsistence levels. However, for purposes of equal protection analysis, it makes no difference whether the class against which the maximum grant regulation discriminates is defined as eligible dependent children in excess of the fourth or fifth, or, alternatively, as individuals in large families generally, that is, those with more than six members.

This classification process effected by the maximum grant regulation produces a basic denial of equal treatment. Persons who are concededly similarly situated (dependent children and their families), are not afforded equal, or even approximately equal, treatment under the maximum grant regulation. Subsistence benefits are paid with respect to some needy dependent children; nothing is paid with respect to others. Some needy families receive full subsistence assistance as calculated by the State; the assistance paid to other families is grossly below their similarly calculated needs.

Yet, as a general principle, individuals should not be afforded different treatment by the State unless there is a relevant distinction between them, and "a statutory discrimination must be based on differences that are reasonably related to the purposes of the Act in which it is found." . . .

In the instant case, the only distinction between those children with respect to whom assistance is granted and those children who are denied such assistance is the size of the family into which the child permits himself to be born. The class of individuals with respect to whom payments are actually made (the first four or five eligible dependent children in a family), is grossly underinclusive in terms of the class that the AFDC program was designed to assist, namely, *all* needy dependent children. Such underinclusiveness manifests "a prima facie violation of the equal protection requirement of reasonable classification," compelling the State to come forward with a persuasive justification for the classification.

The Court never undertakes to inquire for such a justification; rather it avoids the task by focusing upon the abstract dichotomy between two different approaches to equal protection problems that have been utilized by this Court.

Under the so-called "traditional test," a classification is said to be permissible under the *Equal Protection Clause* unless it is "without any reasonable basis." On the other hand, if the classification affects a "fundamental right," then the state interest in perpetuating the classification must be "compelling" in order to be sustained.

This case simply defies easy characterization in terms of one or the other of these "tests." The cases relied on by the Court, in which a "mere rationality" test was actually used are most accurately described as involving the application of equal protection reasoning to the regulation of business interests. The extremes to which the Court has gone in dreaming up rational bases for state regulation in that area may in many instances be ascribed to a healthy revulsion from the Court's earlier excesses in using the Constitution to protect interests that have more than enough power to protect themselves in the legislative halls. This case, involving the literally vital interests of a powerless minority—poor families without breadwinners—is far removed from the area of business regulation, as the Court concedes. Why then is the standard used in those cases imposed here? We are told no more than that this case falls in "the area of economics and social welfare," with the implication that from there the answer is obvious.

In my view, equal protection analysis of this case is not appreciably advanced by the *a priori* definition of a "right," fundamental or otherwise. Rather, concentration must be placed upon the character of the classification in question, the relative importance to individuals in the class discriminated against of the governmental benefits that they do not receive, and the asserted state interests in support of the classification. As we said only recently, "In determining whether or not a state law violates the Equal Protection Clause, we must consider the facts and circumstances behind the law, the interests which the State claims to be protecting, and the interests of those who are disadvantaged by the classification."

It is the individual interests here at stake that, as the Court concedes, most clearly distinguish this case from the "business regulation" equal protection cases. AFDC support to needy dependent children provides the stuff that sustains those children's lives: food, clothing, shelter. And this Court has already recognized several times that when a benefit, even a "gratuitous" benefit, is necessary to sustain life, stricter constitutional standards, both procedural and substantive, are applied to the deprivation of that benefit.

Nor is the distinction upon which the deprivation is here based — the distinction between large and small families — one that readily commends itself as a basis for determining which children are to have support approximating subsistence and which are not. Indeed, governmental discrimination between children on the basis of a factor over which they have no control — the number of their brothers and sisters — bears some resemblance to the classification between legitimate and illegitimate children which we condemned as a violation of the Equal Protection Clause in Levy v. Louisiana, 391 U.S. 68 (1968).

. . . [T]here have now appeared several different rationales for the maximum grant regulation, prominent among them being those relied upon by the majority — the notions that imposition of the maximum serves as an incentive to welfare recipients to find and maintain employment and provides a semblance of equality with persons earning a minimum wage.

With regard to the latter, Maryland has urged that the maximum grant regulation serves to maintain a rough equality between wage earning families and AFDC families, thereby increasing the political support for — or perhaps reducing the opposition to — the AFDC program. . . . Vital to the employment-incentive basis found by the Court to sustain the regulation is, of course, the supposition that an appreciable number of AFDC recipients are in fact employable. For it is perfectly obvious that limitations upon assistance cannot reasonably operate as a work incentive with regard to those who cannot work or who cannot be expected to work. In this connection, Maryland candidly notes that "only a very small percentage of the total universe of welfare recipients are employable." The State, however, urges us to ignore the "total universe" and to concentrate attention instead upon the heads of AFDC families. Yet the very purpose of the AFDC program since its inception has been to provide assistance for dependent *children*. The State's position is thus that the State may deprive certain needy children of assistance to which they would otherwise be entitled in order to provide an arguable work incentive for their parents. But the State may not wield its economic whip in this fashion when the effect is to cause a deprivation to needy dependent children in order to correct an arguable fault of their parents.

Even if the invitation of the State to focus upon the heads of AFDC families is accepted, the minimum rationality of the maximum grant regulation is hard to discern. The District Court found that of Maryland's more than 32,000 AFDC families, only about 116 could be classified as having employable members, and, of these, the number to which the maximum grant regulation was applicable is not disclosed by the record. The State objects that this figure includes only families in which the father is unemployed and fails to take account of families in which an employable mother is the head of the household. At the same time, however, the State itself has recognized that the vast proportion of these mothers are in fact unemployable because they are mentally or physically incapacitated, because they have no marketable skills, or, most prominently, because the best interests of the children dictate that the mother remain in the home. . . . In short, not only has the State failed to establish that there is a substantial or even a significant proportion of AFDC heads of households as to whom the maximum grant regulation arguably serves as a viable and logical work incentive, but it is also indisputable that the regulation at best is drastically *overinclusive* since it applies with equal vigor to a very substantial number of persons who like appellees are completely disabled from working.

Finally, it should be noted that, to the extent there is a legitimate state interest in encouraging heads of AFDC households to find employment, application of the maximum grant regulation is also grossly *underinclusive* because it singles out and affects only large families. No reason is suggested why this particular group should be carved out for the purpose of having unusually harsh "work incentives" imposed upon them. Not only has the State selected for special treatment a small group from among similarly situated families, but it has done so on a basis — family size — that bears no relation to the evil that the State claims the regulation was designed to correct. There is simply no indication whatever that heads of large families, as opposed to heads of small families, are particularly prone to refuse to seek or to maintain employment. . . .

In the final analysis, Maryland has set up an AFDC program structured to calculate and pay the minimum standard of need to dependent children. Having set up that program, however, the State denies some of those needy children the minimum subsistence standard of living, and it does so on the wholly arbitrary basis that they happen to be members of large families. One need not speculate too far on the actual reason for the regulation, for in the early stages of this litigation the State virtually conceded that it set out to limit the total cost of the program along the path of least resistance. Now, however, we are told that other rationales can be manufactured to support the regulation and to sustain it against a fundamental constitutional challenge.

However, these asserted state interests, which are not insignificant in themselves, are advanced either not at all or by complete accident by the maximum grant regulation. Clearly they could be served by measures far less destructive of the individual interests at stake. Moreover, the device assertedly chosen to further them is at one and the same time both grossly underinclusive — because it does not apply at all to a much larger class in an equal position — and grossly overinclusive — because it applies so strongly against a substantial class as to which it can rationally serve no end. Were this a case of pure business regulation, these defects would place it beyond what has heretofore seemed a borderline case, and I do not believe that the regulation can be sustained even under the Court's "reasonableness" test.

In any event, it cannot suffice merely to invoke the spectre of the past and to recite from Lindsley v. Natural Carbonic Gas Co. and Williamson v. Lee Optical Co. to decide the case. Appellees are not a gas company or an optical dispenser; they are needy dependent children and families who are discriminated against by the State. The basis of that discrimination — the classification of individuals into large and small families — is too arbitrary and too unconnected to the asserted rationale, the impact on those discriminated against — the denial of even a subsistence existence — too great, and the supposed interests served too contrived and attenuated to meet the requirements of the Constitution. In my view Maryland's maximum grant regulation is invalid under the Equal Protection Clause of the Fourteenth Amendment.

NOTES AND QUESTIONS

1. In *Dandridge*, the majority held that welfare regulation is subject to mere rationality review. What test did Justice Marshall propose in his dissent? If that view had been adopted, how might the case have been decided?

2. Justice Marshall's dissent includes a note referring to the fundamental rights branch of Equal Protection doctrine:

> At the same time the Court's insistence that equal protection analysis turns on the basis of a closed category of "fundamental rights" involves a curious value judgment. It is certainly difficult to believe that a person whose very survival is at stake would be comforted by the knowledge that his "fundamental" rights are preserved intact.

Justice Marshall then cited several law review articles on the subject of rights to minimum subsistence, and Article 25 of the Universal Declaration of Human Rights, which provides:

> Everyone has the right to a standard of living adequate for the health and well-being of himself and of his family, including food, clothing, housing and medical care and necessary social services, and the right to security in the event of unemployment, sickness, disability, widowhood, old age or other lack of livelihood in circumstances beyond his control.

Other than a human right to some standard of living, are there "fundamental rights" the plaintiffs might have argued are burdened by the Maryland regulation? In Chapter 12, we will study various international human rights instruments and norms and consider how they might advance antipoverty claims in the United States.

3. The majority notes in note 17 of the opinion that there was no claim that the Maryland regulation had a disparate impact on any racial classification of people. Do you suspect such a claim could have been mounted? On what bases? Could a facially neutral regulation like Maryland's operate to discriminate against groups other than racial groups?

4. Appellants' statutory argument is worth noting, particularly as it relates to the overhaul of welfare in 1996. The relevant subsection of the Social Security Act, section 402(a)(10), required that a state's plan "provide . . . that all individuals wishing to make application for [AFDC] shall have opportunity to do so, and that [AFDC] shall be furnished with reasonable promptness to all eligible individuals." The families argued that Maryland's program operated to deny aid entirely to younger children in a large family and thus violated the statutory language that entitled "*all* eligible individuals" to aid. The majority rejected this argument, reasoning that the regulation merely caps the amount of aid that the family unit would receive, but that it is wrong to characterize that as no aid to the younger children. Rather, all the children in the family receive aid, as commanded by the statute. In dissent, Justice Douglas noted that

> the fact that parents may take portions of the payments intended for certain children to give to other children who are not given payments under the State's AFDC plan, does not alter the fact that aid is not being given by the

> State to the latter children. And it is payments by the State, not by the parents, to which the command of section 402(a)(10) is directed.

Dandridge, 397 U.S. at 503.

* * *

In the case that follows, AFDC recipients challenged the Texas program's practice of providing different percentage funding levels for four distinct public benefits programs: Aid to Families with Dependent Children (AFDC), Old Age Assistance (OAA), Aid to the Blind (AB), and Aid to the Permanently and Totally Disabled (APTD). For all of the programs, a "standard of need" was calculated for recipients, but the programs varied with respect to what percentage of that standard was funded: OAA recipients received 100 percent of their standard; AB and APTD recipients received 95 percent; and AFDC recipients received 50 percent and later 75 percent. AFDC recipients challenged the funding scheme as a violation of their rights to equal protection. Basing their attack on the fact that the AFDC rolls were constituted with minority recipients at a higher rate than the rolls of other programs, they argued that this disparate impact should trigger the elevated scrutiny demanded by racial classification cases. Decided four years before *Washington v. Davis*, 426 U.S. 229 (1976), which stands for the proposition that discriminatory effect alone is insufficient to establish an equal protection violation, *Jefferson* previews its holding.

JEFFERSON v. HACKNEY
406 U.S. 535 (1972)

Mr. Justice Rehnquist delivered the opinion of the Court.

[AFDC recipients] challenge the constitutionality of applying a lower percentage reduction factor to AFDC than to the other categorical assistance programs. They claim a violation of equal protection because the proportion of AFDC recipients who are black or Mexican-American is higher than the proportion of the aged, blind, or disabled welfare recipients who fall within these minority groups. Appellants claim that the distinction between the programs is not rationally related to the purposes of the Social Security Act, and violates the Fourteenth Amendment for that reason as well. . . .

We turn . . . to appellants' claim that the Texas system of percentage reductions violates the Fourteenth Amendment. Appellants believe that once the State has computed a standard of need for each recipient, it is arbitrary and discriminatory to provide only 75% of that standard to AFDC recipients, while paying 100% of recognized need to the aged, and 95% to the disabled and the blind. They argue that if the State adopts a percentage-reduction system, it must apply the same percentage to each of its welfare programs.

This claim was properly rejected by the court below. It is clear from the statutory framework that, although the four categories of public assistance found in the Social Security Act have certain common elements, the States were intended by Congress to keep their AFDC plans separate from plans under the other titles of the Act. A State is free to participate in one, several, or all of the categorical assistance programs, as it chooses. It is true that each of the programs is intended to assist the needy, but it does not follow that there is only one constitutionally permissible way for the State to approach this important goal.

This Court emphasized only recently, in Dandridge v. Williams, that in "the area of economics and social welfare, a State does not violate the Equal Protection Clause merely because the classifications made by its laws are imperfect." A legislature may address a problem "one step at a time," or even "select one phase of one field and apply a remedy there, neglecting the others." So long as its judgments are rational, and not invidious, the legislature's efforts to tackle the problems of the poor and the needy are not subject to a constitutional straitjacket. The very complexity of the problems suggests that there will be more than one constitutionally permissible method of solving them.

The standard of judicial review is not altered because of appellants' unproved allegations of racial discrimination. . . . There has never been a reduction in the amount of money appropriated by the legislature to the AFDC program, and between 1943 and the date of the opinion below there had been five increases in the amount of money appropriated by the legislature for the program, two of them having occurred since 1959. The overall percentage increase in appropriation for the programs between 1943 and the time of the District Court's hearing in this case was 410% for AFDC, as opposed to 211% for OAA and 200% for AB. The court further concluded:

> The depositions of Welfare officials conclusively establish that the defendants did not know the racial make-up of the various welfare assistance categories prior to or at the time when the orders here under attack were issued.

. . . Appellants are thus left with their naked statistical argument: that there is a larger percentage of Negroes and Mexican-Americans in AFDC than in the other programs,[17] and that the AFDC is funded at 75% whereas the other programs are funded at 95% and 100% of recognized need. As the statistics cited in the footnote demonstrate, the number of minority members in all categories is substantial. The basic outlines of eligibility for the various categorical grants are established by Congress, not by the States; given the heterogeneity of the Nation's population, it would be only an infrequent coincidence that the racial composition of each grant class was identical to that of the others. The acceptance of appellants' constitutional theory would render suspect each difference in treatment among the grant classes, however lacking in racial motivation and however otherwise rational the treatment might be. Few legislative efforts to deal with the difficult problems posed by current welfare programs could survive such scrutiny, and we do not find it required by the Fourteenth Amendment.

Applying the traditional standard of review under that amendment, we cannot say that Texas' decision to provide somewhat lower welfare benefits for AFDC recipients is invidious or irrational. Since budgetary constraints do not allow the payment of the full standard of need for all welfare recipients, the State

17.

Program	Year	Percentage of Negroes and Mexican-Americans	Percentage of White-Anglos	Number of Recipients
OAA	1969	39.8	60.2	230,000
	1968	38.7	61.3	
	1967	37.0	63.0	
APTD	1969	46.9	53.1	4,213
	1968	45.6	54.4	
	1967	46.2	53.8	
AB	1969	55.7	44.3	14,043
	1968	54.9	45.1	
AFDC	1969	87.0	13.0	136,000
	1968	84.9	15.1	
	1967	86.0	14.0	

may have concluded that the aged and infirm are the least able of the categorical grant recipients to bear the hardships of an inadequate standard of living. While different policy judgments are of course possible, it is not irrational for the State to believe that the young are more adaptable than the sick and elderly, especially because the latter have less hope of improving their situation in the years remaining to them. Whether or not one agrees with this state determination, there is nothing in the Constitution that forbids it.

In conclusion, we re-emphasize what the Court said in Dandridge v. Williams:

> We do not decide today that the [state law] is wise, that it best fulfills the relevant social and economic objectives that [the State] might ideally espouse, or that a more just and humane system could not be devised. Conflicting claims of morality and intelligence are raised by opponents and proponents of almost every measure, certainly including the one before us. But the intractable economic, social, and even philosophical problems presented by public welfare assistance programs are not the business of this Court. . . . The Constitution does not empower this Court to second-guess state officials charged with the difficult responsibility of allocating limited public welfare funds among the myriad of potential recipients.

Affirmed.

Mr. Justice MARSHALL, with whom Mr. Justice BRENNAN joins, and with whom Mr. Justice STEWART joins as to Part I only, dissenting.

It is agreed that Texas has established an identical standard of need for the four social welfare programs that it administers — Old Age Assistance (OAA), Aid to the Blind (AB), Aid for the Permanently and Totally Disabled (APTD), and AFDC. But Texas provides 100% of recognized need to the aged and 95% to the disabled and the blind, while it provides only 75% to AFDC recipients. It is this disparity to which appellants also object.

Appellants base their primary attack on the Fourteenth Amendment; they argue that the percentage distinctions between the other welfare programs and AFDC reflect a racially discriminatory motive on the part of Texas officials. Thus, they argue that there is a violation of the Equal Protection Clause. I believe that it is unnecessary to reach the constitutional issue that appellants raise, and, therefore, I offer no opinion on its ultimate merits. I do wish to make it clear, however, that I do not subscribe in any way to the manner in which the Court treats the issue.

If I were to face this question, I would certainly have more difficulty with it than either the District Court had or than this Court seems to have. The record contains numerous statements by state officials to the effect that AFDC is funded at a lower level than the other programs because it is not a politically popular program. There is also evidence of a stigma that seemingly attaches to AFDC recipients and no others. This Court noted in King v. Smith, 392 U.S., at 322, that AFDC recipients were often frowned upon by the community. The evidence also shows that 87% of the AFDC recipients in Texas are either Negro or Mexican-American. Yet, both the District Court and this Court have little difficulty in concluding that the fact that AFDC is politically unpopular and the fact that AFDC recipients are disfavored by the State and its citizens, have nothing whatsoever to do with the racial makeup of the program. This conclusion is neither so apparent, nor so correct in my view.

Moreover, because I find that each one of the State's reasons for treating AFDC differently from the other programs dissolves under close scrutiny, as is demonstrated, *infra*, I am not at all certain who should bear the burden of proof on the question of racial discrimination. Nor am I sure that the "traditional" standard of review would govern the case as the Court holds. In Dandridge v. Williams, *supra*, on which the Court relies for the proposition that strict scrutiny of the State's action is not required, the Court never faced a question of possible racial discrimination. Percentages themselves are certainly not conclusive, but at some point a showing that state action has a devastating impact on the lives of minority racial groups must be relevant.

The Court reasons backwards to conclude that because appellants have not proved racial discrimination, a less strict standard of review is necessarily tolerated. In my view, the first question that must be asked is what is the standard of review and the second question is whether racial discrimination has been proved under the standard. It seems almost too plain for argument that the standard of review determines in large measure whether or not something has been proved.

These are all complex problems, and I do not propose to resolve any of them here. It is sufficient for me to note that I believe that the constitutional issue raised by appellants need not be reached, and that in choosing to reach it, the Court has so greatly oversimplified the issue as to distort it. . . .

* * *

Dandridge and *Jefferson* raise the important question of the disparate impact on racial minorities of facially neutral welfare policies. This is an enduring question in poverty law overall, and arises in virtually every substantive policy area, not just welfare. You will see in Chapter 6, for example, how the issue emerges in the context of federal housing policy. The Supreme Court's holdings regarding so-called "disparate impact" cases under the Equal Protection Clause are therefore important.

In Washington v. Davis, 426 U.S. 229 (1976), the Court considered a case brought by African-American applicants for employment with the Washington, D.C., police department. The applicants claimed that "Test 21," a passing score on which was a requirement for employment, was unconstitutional because it bore no relationship to job performance and had a discriminatory effect on minority applicants. The Court rejected the claim, citing, among other authorities, its holding in *Jefferson*:

> The central purpose of the Equal Protection Clause of the Fourteenth Amendment is the prevention of official conduct discriminating on the basis of race. It is also true that the Due Process Clause of the Fifth Amendment contains an equal protection component prohibiting the United States from invidiously discriminating between individuals or groups. But our cases have not embraced the proposition that a law or other official act, without regard to whether it reflects a racially discriminatory purpose, is unconstitutional *solely* because it has a racially disproportionate impact. . . .
>
> The school desegregation cases have also adhered to the basic equal protection principle that the invidious quality of a law claimed to be racially discriminatory must ultimately be traced to a racially discriminatory purpose. That there are both predominantly black and predominantly white schools in a community is not, alone, violative of the Equal Protection Clause. The essential element of *de jure* segregation is "a current condition of segregation resulting from intentional state

action." The differentiating factor between *de jure* segregation and so-called *de facto* segregation . . . is *purpose* or *intent* to segregate. . . .

This is not to say that the necessary discriminatory racial purpose must be express or appear on the face of the statute, or that a law's disproportionate impact is irrelevant in cases involving Constitution-based claims of racial discrimination. A statute, otherwise neutral on its face, must not be applied so as invidiously to discriminate on the basis of race. . . .

Nor, on the facts of the case before us, would the disproportionate impact of Test 21 warrant the conclusion that it is a purposeful device to discriminate against Negroes, and hence an infringement of the constitutional rights of respondents, as well as other black applicants. As we have said, the test is neutral on its face, and rationally may be said to serve a purpose the Government is constitutionally empowered to pursue.

The Court refined its approach to constitutional disparate impact claims in the following year, in Village of Arlington Heights v. Metropolitan Housing Development Corp., 429 U.S. 252 (1977), which concerned a zoning board's refusal to change a zoning rule precluding multifamily housing. A housing developer sued, claiming that the denial violated the Equal Protection Clause. Staying the *Washington* course, the Court held that a violation would only be found if a provision embodied discriminatory intent. However, in *Arlington Heights*, the Court articulated a set of factors that should be considered in ascertaining such intent:

Determining whether invidious discriminatory purpose was a motivating factor demands a sensitive inquiry into such circumstantial and direct evidence of intent as may be available. The impact of the official action whether it 'bears more heavily on one race than another' may provide an important starting point. Sometimes a clear pattern, unexplainable on grounds other than race, emerges from the effect of the state action even when the governing legislation appears neutral on its face.

The Court articulated factors in addition to that impact: (1) the historical background of the official action, (2) the sequence of events, both procedural and substantive, that led to the action, and (3) the legislative or administrative history of the action.

NOTES AND QUESTIONS

1. Justice Marshall's dissent in *Jefferson* notes that a state can elect not to participate in any one of the four Social Security Act programs but argues that, if it does participate, it must provide equal percentage funding for each of the categorical assistance programs. The majority dubs this an "all-or-nothing policy judgment." What do you think of this argument?

2. The Court's requirement that discrimination must be *intentional* to be actionable under the Constitution is complicated by social science scholarship about so-called "implicit bias." The implications of this research have been explored in the legal context. *See, e.g.*, Ralph Richard Banks & Richard Thompson Ford, *(How) Does Unconscious Bias Matter?: Law, Politics, and Racial Inequality*, 58 Emory L.J. 1053 (2009).

3. The question of a characteristic's immutability has some salience in the Supreme Court's equal protection jurisprudence. The fact that race — and,

to a somewhat lesser extent, gender — is an immutable characteristic is a basis for subjecting racial classifications to strictest scrutiny. *See, e.g.,* Frontiero v. Richardson, 411 U.S. 677, 686 (1973) (comparing the immutability of race and gender). Is poverty "immutable"? This question is considered by Professors Mario Barnes and Erwin Chemerinsky in their article *The Disparate Treatment of Race and Class in Constitutional Jurisprudence,* 79 Law & Contemp. Probs. 109 (2009).

* * *

One of the Court's most important decisions affecting poor people and their rights is the well-known case of San Antonio v. Rodriguez. This case was decided in 1973, after the rash of welfare and other poverty cases discussed in this chapter, but before *Washington.* Because the case arises in the context of educational equity, its discussion of the plaintiffs' argument that education is a fundamental right is principally addressed in Chapter 8. However, because it includes an analysis of the Court's equal protection jurisprudence after *Dandridge, Jefferson,* and *Harper* as well as some of the important criminal access cases, the classification portion of the opinion is presented here.

The San Antonio case involved a challenge to Texas's system of financing its public schools, which allocated dollars to each school district based on that district's "relative taxpaying ability." While the details of the financing formula are complex, for our purposes the important fact is that it resulted in extraordinary divergence in per-pupil funding levels by district. The plaintiffs resided in the Edgewood School district, where 96 percent of the students were of color when the suit was filed (90 percent Mexican American and 6 percent African American). The Edgewood average assessed property value per pupil was just under $6,000 at the time of filing. This district was compared with the Alamo Heights district, which was 80 percent White, and where the comparable average was $49,000 per student. When taking federal contributions into account, the Edgewood district spent $356 per year per student, where the Alamo Heights district spent $594. The Court addressed the plaintiffs' two theories of equal protection: one classification based, and the other arising from an asserted fundamental right to education. Both theories were rejected, and the funding scheme was upheld. Note that the rejection of the classification theory comes in the form of an argument that the class cannot be identified, a point that is addressed, among others, by the scholarly analysis that follows the case and summarizes the state of equal protection law for poor people.

SAN ANTONIO INDEP. SCH. DIST. v. RODRIGUEZ
411 U.S. 1 (1973)

Mr. Justice POWELL delivered the opinion of the Court:

We must decide, first, whether the Texas system of financing public education operates to the disadvantage of some suspect class or impinges upon a fundamental right explicitly or implicitly protected by the Constitution, thereby requiring strict judicial scrutiny. If so, the judgment of the District Court should be affirmed. If not, the Texas scheme must still be examined to determine whether it rationally furthers some legitimate, articulated state purpose and therefore does not constitute an invidious discrimination in violation of the Equal Protection Clause of the Fourteenth Amendment.

The District Court's opinion does not reflect the novelty and complexity of the constitutional questions posed by appellees' challenge to Texas' system of school financing. In concluding that strict judicial scrutiny was required, that court relied on decisions dealing with the rights of indigents to equal treatment in the criminal trial and appellate processes, and on cases disapproving wealth restrictions on the right to vote. Those cases, the District Court concluded, established wealth as a suspect classification. Finding that the local property tax system discriminated on the basis of wealth, it regarded those precedents as controlling. It then reasoned, based on decisions of this Court affirming the undeniable importance of education, that there is a fundamental right to education and that, absent some compelling state justification, the Texas system could not stand.

We are unable to agree that this case, which in significant aspects is *sui generis*, may be so neatly fitted into the conventional mosaic of constitutional analysis under the Equal Protection Clause. Indeed, for the several reasons that follow, we find neither the suspect-classification nor the fundamental-interest analysis persuasive.

The wealth discrimination discovered by the District Court in this case, and by several other courts that have recently struck down school-financing laws in other States, is quite unlike any of the forms of wealth discrimination heretofore reviewed by this Court. Rather than focusing on the unique features of the alleged discrimination, the courts in these cases have virtually assumed their findings of a suspect classification through a simplistic process of analysis: since, under the traditional systems of financing public schools, some poorer people receive less expensive educations than other more affluent people, these systems discriminate on the basis of wealth. This approach largely ignores the hard threshold questions, including whether it makes a difference for purposes of consideration under the Constitution that the class of disadvantaged "poor" cannot be identified or defined in customary equal protection terms, and whether the relative — rather than absolute — nature of the asserted deprivation is of significant consequence. Before a State's laws and the justifications for the classifications they create are subjected to strict judicial scrutiny, we think these threshold considerations must be analyzed more closely than they were in the court below.

The case comes to us with no definitive description of the classifying facts or delineation of the disfavored class. . . . [We can discern] at least three ways in which the discrimination claimed here might be described. The Texas system of school financing might be regarded as discriminating (1) against "poor" persons whose incomes fall below some identifiable level of poverty or who might be characterized as functionally "indigent," or (2) against those who are relatively poorer than others, or (3) against all those who, irrespective of their personal incomes, happen to reside in relatively poorer school districts. Our task must be to ascertain whether, in fact, the Texas system has been shown to discriminate on any of these possible bases and, if so, whether the resulting classification may be regarded as suspect.

The precedents of this Court provide the proper starting point. The individuals, or groups of individuals, who constituted the class discriminated against in our prior cases shared two distinguishing characteristics: because of their impecunity they were completely unable to pay for some desired benefit, and as a consequence, they sustained an absolute deprivation of a meaningful opportunity to enjoy that benefit. In Griffin v. Illinois (1956), and its progeny, the Court invalidated state laws that prevented an indigent criminal defendant from acquiring a transcript, or an adequate substitute for a transcript, for use at several stages of the trial and appeal process. . . .

Likewise, in Douglas v. California (1963), a decision establishing an indigent defendant's right to court-appointed counsel on direct appeal, the Court dealt only with defendants who could not pay for counsel from their own resources and who had no other way of gaining representation. . . .

[I]n support of their charge that the system discriminates against the "poor," appellees have made no effort to demonstrate that it operates to the peculiar disadvantage of any class fairly definable as indigent, or as composed of persons whose incomes are beneath any designated poverty level. Indeed, there is reason to believe that the poorest families are not necessarily clustered in the poorest property districts. . . .

Second, neither appellees nor the District Court addressed the fact that, unlike each of the foregoing cases, lack of personal resources has not occasioned an absolute deprivation of the desired benefit. The argument here is not that the children in districts having relatively low assessable property values are receiving no public education; rather, it is that they are receiving a poorer quality education than that available to children in districts having more assessable wealth. Apart from the unsettled and disputed question whether the quality of education may be determined by the amount of money expended for it, a sufficient answer to appellees' argument is that, at least where wealth is involved, the Equal Protection Clause does not require absolute equality or precisely equal advantages. Nor indeed, in view of the infinite variables affecting the educational process, can any system assure equal quality of education except in the most relative sense. . . .

For these two reasons — the absence of any evidence that the financing system discriminates against any definable category of "poor" people or that it results in the absolute deprivation of education — the disadvantaged class is not susceptible of identification in traditional terms.

As suggested above, appellees and the District Court may have embraced a second or third approach, the second of which might be characterized as a theory of relative or comparative discrimination based on family income. Appellees sought to prove that a direct correlation exists between the wealth of families within each district and the expenditures therein for education. That is, along a continuum, the poorer the family the lower the dollar amount of education received by the family's children. . . .

This brings us, then, to the third way in which the classification scheme might be defined — *district* wealth discrimination. Since the only correlation indicated by the evidence is between district property wealth and expenditures, it may be argued that discrimination might be found without regard to the individual income characteristics of district residents. Assuming a perfect correlation between district property wealth and expenditures from top to bottom, the disadvantaged class might be viewed as encompassing every child in every district except the district that has the most assessable wealth and spends the most on education. Alternatively, as suggested in Mr. Justice Marshall's dissenting opinion, the class might be defined more restrictively to include children in districts with assessable property which falls below the statewide average, or median, or below some other artificially defined level.

However described, it is clear that appellees' suit asks this Court to extend its most exacting scrutiny to review a system that allegedly discriminates against a large, diverse, and amorphous class, unified only by the common factor of residence in districts that happen to have less taxable wealth than other districts. The system of alleged discrimination and the class it defines have none of the traditional indicia of suspectness: the class is not saddled with such disabilities, or subjected to such a history of purposeful unequal treatment, or relegated to such a position of political powerlessness as to command extraordinary protection from the majoritarian political process.

We thus conclude that the Texas system does not operate to the peculiar disadvantage of any suspect class.

JULIE NICE, *NO SCRUTINY WHATSOEVER: DECONSTITUTIONALIZATION OF POVERTY LAW, DUAL RULES OF LAW, AND DIALOGIC DEFAULT*

35 Fordham Urb. L.J. 629 (2008)

Poverty Law in the United States subsists within a constitutional framework that constructs a separate and unequal rule of law for poor people. Across constitutional doctrines, poor people suffer diminished protection, with their claims for liberty and equality formally receiving the least judicial consideration and functionally being routinely denied. As Justice Marshall succinctly put it [in James v. Valtierra, 402 U.S. 137 (1971)], poor people receive "no scrutiny whatsoever."

First, the Supreme Court normally considers claims of discrimination according to an established doctrinal analysis for determining which level of judicial scrutiny should apply. When those affected are poor, however, the Court instead has created a unique categorical immunization from judicial scrutiny for "social or economic legislation."

Second, the Supreme Court normally considers whether heightened judicial scrutiny might be necessary because either the affected group is a "suspect class" or the trait defining the affected group is a "suspect classification." When those affected are poor, however, the Court has circumvented these questions, never directly or adequately determining whether poor people meet the criteria for a suspect class or whether poverty meets the criteria for a suspect classification.

Third, when cases reveal evidence of invidious governmental discrimination against other groups, the Supreme Court normally has been willing to invalidate such governmental action by applying its rationality review "with bite." When those affected are poor the Supreme Court instead has applied its rationality review without bite, that is, in a reflexive manner designed to uphold governmental regulation.

Fourth, when other groups or individuals claim infringements of various established fundamental rights, the Supreme Court normally applies some version of heightened judicial scrutiny. When those affected by the fundamental rights infringements are poor, the Court instead has reversed its normal level of scrutiny, ratcheting down from heightened scrutiny to rationality review and applying it in a reflexive manner to uphold the governmental regulation.

Over time, these forces of deconstitutionalization have constructed dual rules of constitutional law based on economic means. On one hand is the rule of law that respects the dignity of the haves and protects rights that benefit them, thereby perpetuating their advantages. On the other hand is the rule of law that refuses to protect rights in a manner that might protect or benefit the have-nots. This second-class rule of law adds insult to injury by constantly monitoring and invading the lives of the have-nots — comprehensively scrutinizing and regulating both their work and family lives — while simultaneously denying them the protection of legal rights to defend themselves within this regulatory regime.

Both deconstitutionalization and the resulting dual rules of constitutional law operate comprehensively to deny equal constitutional protection to poor people. The reason the Supreme Court has given for reflexively upholding governmental action is that judicial scrutiny is unnecessary precisely because the Justices presume any problems will be remedied within the political process. Here is where the poverty paradox comes in. Not only may poor people not expect equal constitutional protection from the judiciary, they also lack the types of resources typically required for effective political mobilization to pursue protection from the political branches of government. While many impoverished individuals have put up a valiant fight not only for economic survival but also for greater political inclusion and protection, rarely have their extraordinary efforts proven sustainable, as exemplified by the defeat of the short-lived War on Poverty and its welfare rights movement.

. . . As for the possibility of scholarly progress toward framing rights claims for poor people, several dominant views have led most research away from constitutional rights. The first view is the "hollow hope" critique of rights, that is, the assessment that "U.S. courts can almost never be effective producers of significant social reform." The second view is the belief that a claim for constitutional protection for poor people is either futile or unintelligible within the logic of Supreme Court precedents. The third view is acquiescence to the notion that the Supreme Court has held that poor people are not a suspect class or that poverty is not a suspect classification, presumably as a means to explain the patently clear pattern of constitutional losses experienced by poor people. Moreover, although other rights movements on the ground have resisted these critiques by continuing to pursue constitutional litigation, no comparable movement for constitutional rights persists for poor people. . . .

I. Deconstitutionalization of Poverty Law

A. Categorical Immunization of "Social or Economic Legislation"

The first method of deconstitutionalization is the Court's categorical immunization of social or economic legislation. The primary instrument of this deconstitutionalization is Dandridge v. Williams, in which the Supreme Court broadly declared that only the most deferential form of rationality review would be applied to review governmental actions regarding the category of economics and social welfare.

Dandridge represents a significant departure from the Supreme Court's normal doctrinal analysis designed to assess the constitutionality of any governmental reliance on a classification that treats similarly situated people differently. Regardless of the type of regulation at issue, the Supreme Court normally reviews challenges to governmental discrimination by considering whether either the disadvantage of the affected class or the irrelevance of the trait makes the class or classification "suspect." Dandridge mandated instead that allegations of discrimination regarding one particular type of regulatory field — economics and social welfare — would be treated differently than allegations of discrimination regarding other types of regulatory fields. By limiting judicial review of this category to its most deferential rationality review, the Court uniquely and categorically immunized the government's social or economic regulation from heightened scrutiny and its greater likelihood of judicial invalidation. . . .

Regardless of some outlier exceptions, the gravity of Dandridge was simply enormous. It extinguished the hope that poor people would receive meaningful constitutional protection. Its force continues to this day. As a doctrinal matter, Dandridge set the precedent that immunizes the government's economic and welfare policies from heightened scrutiny or any real threat of invalidation. As a dialogic matter, it stifles the prospect of meaningful dialogue about any proper scope of the so-called welfare state. As a practical matter, it leaves those most economically vulnerable outside the Constitution's protection.

B. CIRCUMVENTION OF NORMAL SUSPECT CLASS OR CLASSIFICATION ANALYSIS

For other disadvantaged groups claiming a violation of the Equal Protection Clause, the Supreme Court generally has considered whether the group meets the criteria for a "suspect class," meaning that the group has suffered historical discrimination, is unable to protect itself in the political process, and is defined by a trait that is immutable or very difficult to change. The Court also has considered whether the trait defining the group is relevant to an individual's ability to perform or contribute to society, and, if not, treats any stereotypical reliance on such trait as a "suspect classification."

Because of the categorical immunization of "social or economic legislation," the Supreme Court arguably has never needed to reach and decide the question of whether a classification distinguishing on its face between poor people and non-poor people was sufficiently "suspect" to trigger heightened judicial scrutiny. Moreover, the major Poverty Law cases the Court has considered have not directly presented discrimination between poor and non-poor people, but instead mostly have involved discrimination among subgroups of poor people. With regard to various classifications not facially discriminating on poverty but nonetheless alleged to have a disproportionate impact on poor claimants, the Supreme Court has repeatedly asserted that it has never held that poverty is a suspect classification. Various feedback loops have repeated this dictum — that poverty has never been held to be a suspect classification — to such an extent that they have made it seem as if the direct question had been reached and decided. Legal scholars as well as courts have acquiesced in treating this dictum as a holding.

Tracking the original source of the Supreme Court's supposed holding that poverty is not a suspect classification leads back to frequently-quoted dicta from a canon of cases. Not long after the Court directly suggested it would generally apply heightened scrutiny to wealth or poverty classifications, the Court quickly backpedaled. In three subsequent cases the Court examined government classifications that discriminated among types of poor families but did not present comparisons between poor and non-poor families. As we have seen, the Supreme Court in Dandridge v. Williams famously upheld Maryland's maximum welfare grant that disproportionately burdened larger poor families as compared to smaller poor families. The Court declared that "social and economic legislation" would be subjected only to the most deferential form of rationality review. Similarly, a pair of abortion funding decisions compared poor women who sought funding for abortion with other poor women who received funding for childbirth. In Maher v. Roe, the Court accurately stated that it had "never held that financial need alone identifies a suspect class for equal protection analysis." Three years later in Harris v. McRae, the Supreme Court asserted, more problematically, that it had "held repeatedly that poverty, standing alone, is not a suspect classification." In support of this statement, the Court cited only to James v. Valtierra. But *James* also did not involve a classification distinguishing between poor and non-poor persons. . . .

Similarly, another case sometimes cited for the proposition that poverty is not a suspect classification is San Antonio Independent School District v. Rodriguez. But *Rodriguez* also did not involve a comparison between poor and non-poor persons. In *Rodriguez*, the Court considered the constitutionality of public school funding in Texas that arguably advantaged students in school districts with more taxable wealth and disadvantaged students in school districts with less taxable wealth. The Supreme Court refused to assume that the poorest students were concentrated in the poorest school districts and emphasized "the absence of any evidence that the financing system discriminates against any definable category of 'poor' people." As a result, the Court defined the class at issue as "unified only by the common factor of residence in districts that happen to have less taxable wealth than other districts." Nonetheless, the Court speculated, in a dictum, that lawyers for plaintiffs probably had not relied on a wealth discrimination theory "in recognition of the fact that this Court has never heretofore held that wealth discrimination alone provides an adequate basis for invoking strict scrutiny."

The critical distinction is between the accurate statement—that the Court has not held poor people to be a suspect class or poverty to be a suspect classification—and the inaccurate assertion that the Court has reached and decided that poverty is not a suspect classification or that poor people are not a suspect class. Instead, the Court effectively has avoided reaching the question at least in part because the facts of these cases did not require it to do so. These cases involved discrimination based on family size (between larger and smaller families in *Dandridge*), reproductive choice (between funding childbirth and abortion in *Maher* and *Harris*), advocacy of low-income housing (between those for and against it in *James*), and taxable school district wealth (*Rodriguez*), none of which directly raised the question of the constitutionality of discriminating based on poverty or between poor and non-poor persons. Although *Rodriguez* came the closest because it directly compares the poverty of one school district with the wealth of another, the Court there painstakingly explained why it refused to treat the case as presenting a wealth-based classification.

This level of doctrinal nitpicking matters because the Supreme Court simply has never grappled with whether poor people meet the indicia of a suspect class, nor with whether poverty is irrelevant to ability or merit such that it should be treated as a suspect classification. . . . The Court has not given actual consideration to whether poor people meet the suspect class criteria or whether they need judicial protection because they have suffered historical discrimination, are unable to protect themselves in the political process, and find it difficult or sometimes impossible to reduce their poverty—especially given recent data demonstrating the difficulty of an impoverished child escaping poverty as an adult. . . .

C. APPLICATION OF RATIONALITY REVIEW IN A REFLEXIVE MANNER

Until the Supreme Court extends heightened scrutiny to poor people, might rationality review that is extremely deferential to the government nonetheless afford sufficient constitutional protection for poor people? This depends on how the Court applies it. For some "discrete and insular minorities," such as hippies, disabled people, and gay people, the Supreme Court has applied its rationality review with bite, and has invalidated governmental actions burdening these groups. Such meaningful review has not been afforded to poor people. Instead, and again presumably because of its categorical exception for "social or economic legislation," the Supreme Court has emphasized that regulations affecting poor people should receive only minimal rationality review, meaning extreme deference to the government, which will rarely result in invalidation. As a result, poor people are left with no judicial scrutiny to smoke out and protect them from invidious discrimination. In other words, when applying rationality review to poor people, the Supreme Court has applied it reflexively, that is mechanically, and routinely has upheld governmental actions that burden those living in poverty. . . .

D. REVERSAL OF NORMAL HEIGHTENED SCRUTINY FOR FUNDAMENTAL RIGHTS

. . . Might poor people nonetheless receive protection of established rights guaranteed by other constitutional provisions? The Supreme Court normally applies some version of heightened judicial scrutiny to enforce established constitutional rights, regardless of the nature of the class asserting an infringement. But, again, the Court has departed from its normal use of heightened scrutiny for alleged infringements of established constitutional rights when those affected are poor. . . .

[S]ome dormant potential remains for using even the existing unequal constitutional framework to benefit poor people. First, the Supreme Court has formally conceded that constitutional limitations do apply to regulation of poverty. Of course, the challenge remains to get the courts actually to conduct at least meaningful rationality review, rather than engage in categorical exclusion and reflexive rationality review that repeats the most deferential mantras followed in quick succession by the conclusion that the regulation must be presumed to be rational and therefore, must be upheld.

Second, perhaps because poverty has not been treated as a suspect classification, the government has made little to no effort to hide its intent to target poor people for differential treatment, thus leaving poverty classifications rather plainly apparent in many social or economic regulations. In other words, the singling out of poor people frequently happens on the face of the law. When the singling out of a group is facial, there is no need for plaintiffs to prove that the regulation has any disparate impact or for the courts to check for a discriminatory intent behind the regulation.

Third, because the courts have subjected classifications relating to poverty only to rationality review, any classification designed to benefit people based on their poverty would receive rationality review as well. In other words, affirmative action based on class would be upheld much more easily than affirmative action based on race (which is subjected to strict scrutiny) or based on sex (which is subjected to intermediate scrutiny).

Finally, another possibility is to use state constitutions to build gradual momentum that the Supreme Court will notice and consider when interpreting the United States Constitution. Some scholars have argued that state constitutions include language that is directly, or at least indirectly, protective of social welfare. The Supreme Court has taken notice of the success of other social movements in accomplishing a changed interpretation of state constitutions and then relied on such "emerging awareness" in changing its interpretation of the United States Constitution. The school finance movement, for example, appears to be following this approach on behalf of poor people with some success at the state level.

E.   SPECIAL TOPIC: STATE CONSTITUTIONS AS A SOURCE OF RIGHTS AND PROTECTIONS

WILLIAM C. RAVA, *STATE CONSTITUTIONAL PROTECTIONS FOR THE POOR*

71 Temp. L. Rev. 543 (1998)

State constitutions are, of course, different than the Federal Constitution. They are concerned more with the details of governance and include many provisions that the Framers of the Federal Constitution would certainly have considered legislative by nature, not of constitutional import. These structural differences, of course, do not render state constitutional guarantees any less important than their federal counterparts. Indeed, state constitutional protections for individual rights, because they can go beyond the floor established by Supreme Court interpretations of the Federal Constitution, might be more important guarantors. Many state constitutions also expressly protect specific rights not provided for in the Federal Constitution. Some state constitutions, for example, include explicit guarantees for the needy. . . .

III.   STATE CONSTITUTIONAL WELFARE PROVISIONS

One reason that Congress and the federal courts have passed on poverty is the lack of explicit constitutional support for the national government to care for the needy. The federal government is, after all, one of "limited and enumerated powers." Nowhere does the Federal Constitution expressly direct the government to assist the indigent. The Preamble aims high — "to . . . promote the general Welfare, and secure the blessings of Liberty" — but does not specifically empower any governmental actor to provide assistance for the needy. Article I, section 8 vests specific powers in Congress, none of which includes the explicit power to provide assistance for those in need. The executive and judicial branches also are not explicitly empowered to take action with regards to welfare. If anything, on its face, the Federal Constitution, through the Tenth Amendment, leaves the care of the needy to the states.

Some state constitutions include protections for the needy — express welfare provisions. This Part identifies and groups these state constitutional provisions. It defines four categories of state constitutional provisions based upon the degree to which those provisions command the state to care for the needy. It then examines several states' jurisprudence interpreting those provisions.

A. AN OBLIGATION TO CARE? — FOUR CATEGORIES OF WELFARE PROVISIONS

Twenty-three state constitutions recognize that someone or something in the individual states will provide for those in need. No two constitutional provisions are exactly the same. The duty of providing welfare — or mere recognition of the need for it — is unique in each state. This Subpart identifies and categorizes these various state constitutional welfare clauses. . . .

. . . Four categories of state constitutional welfare provisions were identified. The first group includes those states whose constitutions impose an affirmative duty on the state to care for indigent residents. These constitutional welfare provisions are typified by mandatory language and explicit identification of the poor as the beneficiaries of state action. The second group includes state constitutions that include a permissive grant of power to care for the needy. These provisions use less obligatory language, but also identify the poor as the recipients of state assistance. The third category includes state constitutions that contain broad grants of legislative authority to provide public welfare. These provisions are more specific than the general grants of plenary power often found in state constitutions, but they do not command the state to do anything in particular for the indigent. The fourth category of state constitutional welfare provisions consists of those state constitutions that include an implied grant of state authority to care for the needy. These provisions often direct the state to establish and support institutions or agencies that might be used to aid the needy. . . .

1. *Affirmative Duty*

Four state constitutions direct the state to provide care for the needy. In Alabama, Kansas, New York, and Oklahoma, the constitution can be interpreted to impose an affirmative duty on the state to provide assistance based on need and state citizens have a positive right to welfare benefits. These provisions vary in their exact textual details, but they nonetheless have several common elements. Each provision sets forth in general terms what governmental entity must provide the assistance, what assistance must be provided, and who is entitled to that assistance. . . .

All of these clauses also use some explicit mandatory language. The Alabama Constitution, for example, states that it "shall be the duty of the legislature." This is the only state constitution to use an unqualified mandatory verb. The constitutions of Kansas, New York, and Oklahoma also use a directive construction — the state shall provide — in the first instance. These states' welfare provisions later qualify this affirmative obligation with permissive clauses. The Kansas and Oklahoma sections both limit the state's duty with the phrase "as may be prescribed by law." The New York Constitution uses similar qualifying language: "in such manner and by such means, as the legislature may from time to time determine." So, although the constitutional texts in Kansas, New York, and Oklahoma mandate that the state care for the needy, the constitutional provisions only unequivocally require implementation of those programs designated by the legislatures; there is no express requirement that the legislatures pass any laws in the first instance. . . .

2. *Permissive Grants*

Four constitutional welfare provisions permit the state to care for the needy. The constitutions of Montana, New Mexico, Pennsylvania, and Texas all contain such permissive grants of power. . . .

Similar to the affirmative duty provisions, the constitutionally permissible state action varies widely from state to state. In Montana, the legislature is allowed to "provide such economic assistance and social and rehabilitative services" as it deems appropriate. In New Mexico, any state authority can provide "care and maintenance." The Pennsylvania Constitution allows "appropriations . . . for pensions or gratuities" and the Texas legislature may provide "medical care, rehabilitation, and other similar services."

These permissive grants also limit the potential beneficiaries of this state action. In Montana, the legislature may only assist "those who, by reasons of age, infirmities, or misfortune are determined by the legislature to be in need." The New Mexico Constitution allows assistance for the "sick and indigent" and Texas permits care for "needy persons." The Pennsylvania Constitution defines more narrowly those whom the state may aid.

3. Broad Grants

Four state constitutions grant the state the generalized power to care for the needy. The constitutions of Alaska, California, Hawaii, and Louisiana each contain such broad grant welfare provisions although the clauses are markedly different from each other. The Alaska Constitution directs the legislature to provide for public welfare, without defining either what assistance is necessary to meet this command or who should get the assistance. Something, however, is required. The Louisiana provision is similar to Alaska's, but it uses permissive language and specifies the sorts of services (economic and social) that the state may provide. The California Constitution, by contrast, is less obligatory but more specific. It simply permits the legislature to take action, but delineates what action may be taken, allowing the state or counties to provide for "relief of hardship and destitution." Hawaii's Constitution expressly grants the legislature the power to define who is eligible for state assistance on account of need. It provides the state with broad powers — financial, medical, and social — to meet those needs. Although this Hawaii provision does not mandate state action, it does little to limit state options in caring for indigents.

These grants are distinct from the plenary grants of legislative power often found in state constitutions. For example, the Michigan Constitution declares that, "[t]he public health and general welfare of the people" are "matters of primary concern" and requires the legislature to "pass suitable laws for the protection and promotion of the public health." Unlike the grants contained in the Alaska, California, and Hawaii Constitutions, the Michigan Constitution does not specifically allow or direct a "provision for" welfare. Furthermore, the Michigan clause, like other plenary grants and as distinct from broad welfare grants, addresses the "general" welfare of the people rather than the "public" welfare, removing the onus from the government. It lacks the specificity of the California, Hawaii, and Louisiana clauses. These broad grants of welfare power, then, constitute a textual source of a state duty to care for the needy that is stronger and more specific than the plenary grant of legislative authority.

4. Implied Grants

Eleven state constitutions implicitly grant the state the power to service the needs of the indigent. The constitutions of Arizona, Colorado, Idaho, Indiana, Mississippi, Missouri, Nevada, North Carolina, Washington, West Virginia, and Wyoming all contain implied grants of constitutional authority. Like the affirmative duty provisions, these constitutional sections generally describe who must take action, what action must or can be taken, and who is entitled to benefit from this action.

All implied welfare rights provisions require some state actor to do something. The constitution of North Carolina, for example, specifically directs the legislature to take action. Indiana and West Virginia place the burden on the counties. All of the other state constitutions simply mandate that the "state" take action.

Seven of these implied grant provisions then require the state actor to establish a state institution. Most of these provisions use a combination of mandatory and permissive constructions. According to their constitutions, Arizona, Colorado, Idaho, and Wyoming "shall establish and support" some institution "as may be prescribed by law." In Nevada and Washington, such institutions shall be "fostered and supported" by the state, again qualified by an "as may be prescribed by law" clause. The constitution of West Virginia uses stronger language—an unqualified mandatory directive that the state establish institutions. The Indiana Constitution is unique in that it only permits the counties to establish benevolent institutions. . . .

In some respects, these constitutional provisions might be a more secure guarantee than the affirmative provisions described above; they are, in many cases, more specific and directed. At the very least, these implied welfare clauses are more pragmatic; they create a mechanism with a mission. In other respects, these provisions are a weaker guarantee. Unlike the four state constitutions in the first category, the required legislative action—the substance of the mandate—is the creation of an institution rather than direct provision for the needy. The constitutional command for the care of the needy, then, is less direct in this grouping.

B. STATE WELFARE RIGHTS JURISPRUDENCE

There is, then, textual support in twenty-three state constitutions for the claim that the state has an obligation to care for its indigent residents. None of these constitutional clauses, however, is perfectly clear. In almost all twenty-three states, the state legislatures must take some action to provide state assistance for the needy. Exactly what the legislature must provide and for whom it must be provided is largely unspecified. Many of the provisions use a combination of mandatory and permissive language, making the scope of the command unclear. The provisions also use numerous undefined terms, such as "poor," "needy," "care," and "provide." The courts must interpret these vague and ambiguous clauses. On the one hand, state courts could subject welfare statutes to searching scrutiny, closely supervising the substantive policy decisions reached by the legislature. Under such a regime, state courts could play an active role in guaranteeing welfare rights. On the other hand, state courts could employ a minimally rigorous standard of review, allowing the legislature wide discretion to meet its constitutional mandate. There are also innumerable options in between these poles. The courts themselves must ultimately decide whether they will closely police the definitional decisions reached by the legislature, but only rarely have they been called upon to interpret their constitutions' welfare rights provisions. . . .

New York's state welfare jurisprudence is both instructive and illustrative. In *Tucker v. Toia* [1977], the New York Court of Appeals was faced with the question of whether the state legislature could "deny all aid to certain individuals who are admittedly needy, solely on the basis of criteria having nothing to do with need." The legislature had passed a statute making state-provided home relief for residents under age twenty-one only where parents were adjudge unfit under the federally-subsidized AFDC program. Under this law, some needy residents who would qualify for home relief would have to pursue disposition hearings against their relatives, delaying receipt of any benefits for weeks or even months. The court acknowledged that the law served legitimate state interests — requiring responsible adults to care for their dependent minors and preventing unnecessary welfare expenditures — but found that the consequential delays in aid violated the New York Constitution's express welfare provision which appears in Article 17, section 1. This section, the court stated, imposed "upon the State an affirmative duty to aid the needy." Quoting extensively from the 1938 Constitutional Convention, which adopted the welfare provision, and citing the mandatory language of the provision, the court concluded that although the constitution granted the legislature discretion to define eligibility and set benefit levels, "it unequivocally prevents the Legislature from simply refusing to aid those whom it has classified as needy. Such a definite constitutional mandate cannot be ignored or easily evaded in either its letter or its spirit." Because the delays in benefits for the eligible needy amounted to a refusal to aid, the court held the statute unconstitutional.

Only weeks later, the same New York court considered another constitutional challenge to a welfare statute, this claim based on the sufficiency of, rather than the eligibility for, state assistance. In *Bernstein v. Toia* [1977], a state regulation fixed a cap on shelter allowances, precluding consideration of "special circumstances in individual cases." Recipients sued, alleging that the statute violated their due process and equal protection rights, as well as New York's constitutional welfare provision. The trial court found the regulation unconstitutional based on the state constitutional guarantee of care for the needy, and the court of appeals reversed. The court first examined the Federal Constitutional issues, concluding that the grant regulation passed muster. The court then moved on to the state constitutional analysis, rejecting that claim with strong language:

> We do not read [the welfare provision] as a mandate that public assistance must be granted on an individual basis in every instance, thus precluding recourse to the flat grant concept, or indeed as commanding that, in carrying out the constitutional duty to provide aid, care and support of the needy, the State must always meet in full measure all the legitimate needs of each recipient. When, as here, the over-all consequence of the method of distribution of aid to the needy adopted initially by the Legislature, and subsequently by the department charged with executing the social services program, is reasonably expected to be in furtherance of the optimum utilization of public assistance funds, there has been no violation of the constitutional command.

This case was distinguishable from *Tucker v. Toia*, the court stated, because the Legislature has more discretion in determining levels of benefits than eligibility for benefits; that is, the court would play a less active supervisory role in welfare cases involving benefit issues than in those involving eligibility issues. . . .

Other state courts have attempted to play a more active policing role with regards to welfare rights. Montana is illustrative. Between 1973 and 1988, the Montana Constitution contained a welfare clause imposing an affirmative duty on the state. Article XII, section 3(3) then required that the "legislature shall provide such economic assistance and social and rehabilitative services as may be necessary for those inhabitants who, by reason of age, infirmities, or misfortune may have need for the aid of society." The Montana Supreme Court overturned two welfare statutes in the space of two years, finding that both violated this express mandate.

In *Butte I* [1987], the court considered a constitutional challenge to a regulation which would have limited or denied state assistance to needy, able-bodied residents under the age of thirty-five who had no minor dependents. The trial court had held that public assistance was a fundamental right and accordingly had subjected the law to a strict scrutiny equal protection analysis. The Montana Supreme Court rejected both the classification of the right and the application of the test. First, the court held that, because there is no welfare right in the state constitution's Declaration of Rights, welfare could not be deemed fundamental. Strict scrutiny therefore did not apply. The court did not limit itself, however, to federal equal protection jurisprudence; instead, it adopted its own middle-tier equal protection test applicable to constitutional but not fundamental rights. To survive constitutional scrutiny, the classification had to be reasonable and the state's interest in that classification had to outweigh the citizen's interest. Applying this two-part test, the court found that the age cut-off was arbitrary and that the state's asserted interest in saving money did not outweigh the indigents' interests in receiving benefits. The regulation was therefore unconstitutional.

Following *Butte I*, the Montana legislature passed a revised welfare reform measure which provided that "able-bodied persons without dependent minor children were eligible for no more than two months of nonmedical general relief assistance within a 12 month period." The court in *Butte II* [1987] considered the constitutionality of this new law under the welfare clause. This clause, the court stated initially, "embraced a bold concept," was "visionary and idealistic," and "[c]learly and grammatically . . . imposes upon the legislature a duty to provide necessary economic assistance to inhabitants who need societal aid by reason of three disparate conditions over which they have no control, age, infirmity, or misfortune." The court found the new statute faulty because it "eliminated from economic assistance misfortunate able-bodied persons who may have need for the aid of society." The constitution does not distinguish between able-bodied persons with dependents and those with none, and therefore the court held that the legislature could not "escape its constitutional duty by defining out the persons to whom the constitutional protection attaches." The court next applied the two-factor middle-tier equal protection analysis defined in *Butte I*: to justify the classification, the state must show both that it was reasonable and that the state's interest in the classification outweighed residents' interest in public assistance. The court, citing factual findings by the trial court, found the classification to be arbitrary and unreasonable, and therefore unconstitutional. In closing, the court clarified the breadth of its holding, "[w]e do not hereby declare that inhabitants have a constitutional right to public assistance. We do declare that the legislature, in performing its duty under Art. XII, §3(3), must not act arbitrarily between classes of entitled persons."

Following these two cases, the Montana Legislature considered its options for reforming state public assistance programs, paying particularly close attention to the court's explication of the legislature's constitutional duty in *Butte I* and *II*. The legislative possibilities increased dramatically when, in 1988, the citizens of Montana amended their constitution, replacing the mandatory "shall" of the welfare clause with a permissive "may" and adding a final qualifying clause expressly granting the legislature the task of defining who qualifies for state assistance. The practical effect of these alterations is to remove legislative welfare choices from substantive judicial review. . . .

CHAPTER
4

Welfare

INTRODUCTION

The foregoing three chapters have introduced the American welfare system indirectly. In Chapter 3, for example, various features of the AFDC system were discussed in the context of setting up the constitutional questions about the Fourteenth Amendment rights of the poor. This chapter turns *directly* to welfare, to its history, its culturally important terms, and its significant reform in 1996. By *welfare*, we refer to cash assistance programs that are based on categorical (or status-based) eligibility alone, differentiating them from programs that are based on a recipient's having paid into a system as a condition of eligibility. This chapter covers the three largest such federal welfare programs: Temporary Assistance for Needy Families (TANF, introduced in Chapter 2, and created by the Personal Responsibility and Work Opportunity Act, or PRWORA), Supplemental Security Income (SSI), and the Supplemental Nutrition Assistance Program (SNAP).[1]

As the three foregoing chapters have shown, welfare is the most consistent terrain on which large sociopolitical questions—about labor discipline, the deserving versus the undeserving poor, the proper role of women (specifically single mothers of young children) in the economy, the role of government in ameliorating economic inequalities, and so on—are debated. While only a very small number of people in the United States receive cash welfare, it remains the programmatic and political home for profoundly contested ideological disagreements about poverty, work, race, procreation, and the family.

Contributory, insurance-style programs, in which benefits are based on a participant's prior contributions to the system, are not covered in this chapter. In these insurance-style programs, recipients are eligible for payments based on the contributions they have made into the system while in the workforce, prior to drawing benefits. These income insurance programs are thus tied to formal wage employment. The amount of monthly benefit payment depends on how long the worker was in covered employment and how much the worker earned while in the wage labor force. The most significant of these is the federal Social Security system, known formally as Old-Age, Survivors, and Disability Insurance (OASDI). Other contributory cash assistance programs include Unemployment Insurance (UI) and Social Security Disability Insurance

---

1. The Earned Income Tax Credit, characterized by some by the biggest income support program currently operating in the United States, is covered in Chapter 5.

(SSDI), both of which provide cash payments to workers under certain circumstances and are based on their contributions to the system.

The distinction between insurance and welfare is important for poverty lawyers to observe and understand. The arguments for and against policy changes in these various cash assistance programs tend to track this distinction, which itself tracks notions of the "deserving" versus the "undeserving" poor. Recipients of insurance-type benefits tend to be characterized as *deserving*, because they are understood to be withdrawing money from an account into which they have made deposits. Welfare recipients, by contrast, are typically seen as *undeserving* because their eligibility for a given cash assistance program is not connected to any personal financial contribution.

The persistent policy concern about welfare is that it disincentivizes work: Why work if you can stay home and get welfare? As discussed in Chapter 2, welfare programs are designed to provide income only to narrowly drawn categories of people who are understood to be somehow exempt from work. Policy debates about welfare can be viewed as policy debates about who should be so exempted. For example, people with disabilities that prevent them from working are exempt, and thus eligible for cash assistance — provided they meet the government's standard for "disabled." Elderly people, even those who did not work when younger, are similarly exempt from the work requirement and thus categorically eligible for aid.

This framework is useful in understanding the history of the public, often racialized debate about single mothers: Should single mothers of young children be exempt from the social expectation of wage labor and, if so, for how long and on what conditions? The overwhelming majority of AFDC/TANF recipients are single mothers, and a disproportionate number of them are women of color. Debates about welfare must also be understood, then, as debates about women's role with respect to work and children, and specifically in the context of poor women and women of color.

After a snapshot of current, post-recessionary, welfare, and food stamp usage, this chapter proceeds in four parts. Part A presents the Social Security Act of 1935 as the statutory origin of contemporary cash assistance programs, and the still vital distinction between "welfare" and "insurance," as well as the social hierarchies embedded in federal policy on the bases of race and gender. Part B goes into depth on TANF, with materials providing some detail on its most important policy features and the decisions that they embody, specifically in the areas of block granting, time limits, work requirements, and marriage promotion. Part C addresses SSI and reviews the categories of eligibility and the 1996 changes to that program that eliminated substance abuse as a disability. Finally, Part D presents information on food assistance, focused on SNAP but also introducing the National School Lunch and other nutrition assistance programs.

In addition to considering the policy preferences that are expressed through these requirements, reflect as you read on the balance of power and responsibility between the federal and state governments with respect to cash and food assistance. Which programs — or specific features of programs — have been standardized across the nation, and which remain within the purview of a state or local entity? Questions of federal standardization versus state experimentation (and states' rights) have been important throughout the history of U.S. welfare law and policy, which you should consider as you review these programs.

* * *

New York Times reporter Jason DeParle is one of the nation's most prolific commentators on welfare, and specifically the welfare reform of 1996. In 2012, DeParle wrote a piece about cash assistance in the context of the recession that followed the global economic crisis of 2007-2008. DeParle used Arizona as an example to examine the impact of welfare reform in the recession, and to explore the rise in food stamp usage that came about in the first significant economic downturn following the passage of welfare reform.

JASON DEPARLE, *WELFARE LIMITS LEFT POOR ADRIFT AS RECESSION HIT*

N.Y. Times (Apr. 8, 2012), at A1

Perhaps no law in the past generation has drawn more praise than the drive to "end welfare as we know it," which joined the late-'90s economic boom to send caseloads plunging, employment rates rising and officials of both parties hailing the virtues of tough love.

But the distress of the last four years has added a cautionary postscript: much as overlooked critics of the restrictions once warned, a program that built its reputation when times were good offered little help when jobs disappeared. Despite the worst economy in decades, the cash welfare rolls have barely budged.

Faced with flat federal financing and rising need, Arizona is one of 16 states that have cut their welfare caseloads further since the start of the recession — in its case, by half. Even as it turned away the needy, Arizona spent most of its federal welfare dollars on other programs, using permissive rules to plug state budget gaps.

The poor people who were dropped from cash assistance here, mostly single mothers, talk with surprising openness about the desperate, and sometimes illegal, ways they make ends meet. They have sold food stamps, sold blood, skipped meals, shoplifted, doubled up with friends, scavenged trash bins for bottles and cans and returned to relationships with violent partners — all with children in tow.

Esmeralda Murillo, a 21-year-old mother of two, lost her welfare check, landed in a shelter and then returned to a boyfriend whose violent temper had driven her away. "You don't know who to turn to," she said.

Maria Thomas, 29, with four daughters, helps friends sell piles of brand-name clothes, taking pains not to ask if they are stolen. "I don't know where they come from," she said. "I'm just helping get rid of them."

To keep her lights on, Rosa Pena, 24, sold the groceries she bought with food stamps and then kept her children fed with school lunches and help from neighbors. Her post-welfare credo is widely shared: "I'll do what I have to do."

Critics of the stringent system say stories like these vindicate warnings they made in 1996 when President Bill Clinton fulfilled his pledge to "end welfare as we know it": the revamped law encourages states to withhold aid, especially when the economy turns bad.

The old program, Aid to Families with Dependent Children, dates from the New Deal; it gave states unlimited matching funds and offered poor families extensive rights, with few requirements and no time limits. The new program, Temporary Assistance for Needy Families, created time limits and work rules, capped federal spending and allowed states to turn poor families away.

"My take on it was the states would push people off and not let them back on, and that's just what they did," said Peter B. Edelman, a law professor at Georgetown University who resigned from the Clinton administration to protest the law. "It's been even worse than I thought it would be." . . .

No Money, No Job

While data on the very poor is limited and subject to challenge, recent studies have found that as many as one in every four low-income single mothers is jobless and without cash aid — roughly four million women and children. Many of the mothers have problems like addiction or depression, which can make assisting them politically unpopular, and they have received little attention in a downturn that has produced an outpouring of concern for the middle class.

Poor families can turn to other programs, like food stamps or Medicaid, or rely on family and charity. But the absence of a steady source of cash, however modest, can bring new instability to troubled lives.

One prominent supporter of the tough welfare law is worried that it may have increased destitution among the most disadvantaged families. "This is the biggest problem with welfare reform, and we ought to be paying attention to it," said Ron Haskins of the Brookings Institution, who helped draft the 1996 law as an aide to House Republicans and argues that it has worked well for most recipients.

"The issue here is, can you create a strong work program, as we did, without creating a big problem at the bottom?" Mr. Haskins said. "And we have what appears to be a big problem at the bottom."

He added, "This is what really bothers me: the people who supported welfare reform, they're ignoring the problem."

The welfare program was born amid apocalyptic warnings and was instantly proclaimed a success, at times with a measure of "I told you so" glee from its supporters. Liberal critics had warned that its mix of time limits and work rules would create mass destitution — "children sleeping on the grates," in the words of Senator Daniel Patrick Moynihan, a New York Democrat who died in 2003.

But the economy boomed, employment soared, poverty fell and caseloads plunged. Thirty-two states reduced their caseloads by two-thirds or more, as officials issued press releases and jostled for bragging rights. The tough law played a large role, but so did expansions of child care and tax credits that raised take-home pay.

In a twist on poverty politics, poor single mothers, previously chided as "welfare queens," were celebrated as working-class heroes, with their stories of leaving the welfare rolls cast as uplifting tales of pluck. Flush with federal money, states experimented with programs that offered counseling, clothes and used cars.

But if the rise in employment was larger than predicted, it was also less transformative than it may have seemed. Researchers found that most families that escaped poverty remained "near poor."

And despite widespread hopes that working mothers might serve as role models, studies found few social or educational benefits for their children. (They measured things like children's aspirations, self-esteem, grades, drug use and arrests.) Nonmarital births continued to rise.

But the image of success formed early and stayed frozen in time.

"The debate is over," President Clinton said a year after signing the law, which he often cites in casting himself as a centrist. "Welfare reform works."

The recession that began in 2007 posed a new test to that claim. Even with $5 billion in new federal funds, caseloads rose just 15 percent from the lowest level in two generations. Compared with the 1990s peak, the national welfare rolls are still down by 68 percent. Just one in five poor children now receives cash aid, the lowest level in nearly 50 years. . . .

Since the states get fixed federal grants, any caseload growth comes at their own expense. By contrast, the federal government pays the entire food stamp bill no matter how many people enroll; states encourage applications, and the rolls have reached record highs. . . .

TRYING TO MAKE DO

Asked how they survived without cash aid, virtually all of the women interviewed here said they had sold food stamps, getting 50 cents for every dollar of groceries they let others buy with their benefit cards. Many turned to food banks and churches. Nationally, roughly a quarter have subsidized housing, with rents as low as $50 a month.

Several women said the loss of aid had left them more dependent on troubled boyfriends. One woman said she sold her child's Social Security number so a relative could collect a tax credit worth $3,000.

"I tried to sell blood, but they told me I was anemic," she said.

Several women acknowledged that they had resorted to shoplifting, including one who took orders for brand-name clothes and sold them for half-price. Asked how she got cash, one woman said flatly, "We rob wetbacks" — illegal immigrants, who tend to carry cash and avoid the police. At least nine times, she said, she has flirted with men and led them toward her home, where accomplices robbed them.

"I felt bad afterwards," she said. But she added, "There were times when we didn't have nothing to eat."

One family ruled out crime and rummaged through trash cans instead. The mother, an illegal immigrant from Mexico, could not get aid for herself but received $164 a month for her four American-born children until their time limit expired. Distraught at losing her only steady source of cash, she asked the children if they would be ashamed to help her collect discarded cans.

"I told her I would be embarrassed to steal from someone — not to pick up cans," her teenage daughter said.

Weekly park patrols ensued, and recycling money replaced about half of the welfare check.

Despite having a father in prison and a mother who could be deported, the children exude earnest cheer. A daughter in the fifth grade won a contest at school for reading the most books. A son in the eighth grade is a student leader praised by his principal for tutoring younger students, using supplies he pays for himself.

"That's just the kind of character he has," the principal said.

After losing cash aid, the mother found a cleaning job but lost it when her boss discovered that she was in the United States illegally. The family still gets subsidized housing and $650 a month in food stamps.

The boy worries about homelessness, but his younger sisters, 9 and 10, see an upside in scavenging.

"It's kind of fun because you get to look through the trash," one of the girls said.

"And you get to play in the park a little while before you go home," her sister agreed.

* * *

The article above was accompanied by the following chart showing TANF and food stamp trends since 1990.

Fewer Receiving Welfare, but Food Stamps Soaring (the number of Americans receiving cash welfare has fallen since the 1990s, while the number receiving food stamps has risen sharply)

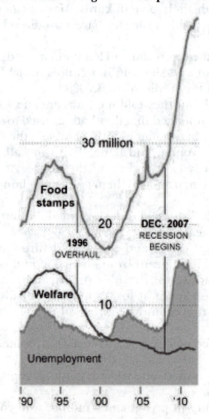

Source: N.Y. Times, based on data from U.S. Dept. of Health and Human Services (welfare); U.S. Dept. of Agriculture (food stamps); Bureau of Labor Statistics.

NOTES AND QUESTIONS

1. For more general information on cash assistance in the United States, see Nat'l Bureau of Econ. Research, *Means-Tested Transfer Programs in the United States* (Robert A. Moffitt ed., 2003), *available at* http://papers.nber .org/books/moff03-1.

2. The piece above refers to Peter Edelman's resignation from the Clinton administration in protest over the President's signing of PRWORA. Mary Jo Bane, at the time Assistant Secretary for Children & Families at the U.S. Department of Health & Human Services resigned on the same day as Peter Edelman. The month before, Deputy Assistant Secretary for Policy & Evaluation Wendell Primus also announced his resignation because of welfare reform. In a March 1997 piece in the Atlantic Monthly, *The Worst Thing Bill Clinton Has Done*, Edelman articulates his critiques of specific provisions of the bill — its time limits, elimination of entitlements, and anti-immigrant rules — as well as what he viewed as its abdication of a mission to reduce or end *poverty*. The article is available at http://www.theatlantic.com/past/ docs/issues/97mar/edelman/edelman.htm.

3. At various points in U.S. history there have been movements for a so-called "guaranteed minimum income," or "guaranteed annual income," but none has succeeded as policy. Proposed models have ranged from Thomas Paine's 1795 proposal for "capital grants provided at the age of majority," to the provision in then President Richard Nixon's 1967 Family Assistance Plan that called for a guaranteed stipend to all poor families with children. *See* Daniel P. Moynihan, *The Politics of A Guaranteed Income: The Nixon Administration and the Family Assistance Plan* (1973). As chronicled by Professor Richard K. Caputo in his 2011 book *U.S. Social Welfare Reform: Policy Transitions from 1981 to the Present*, "some 1300 economists at approximately 150 institutions signed a petition to Congress in 1968 urging adoption of a 'national system of income guarantees and supplements petitioned Congress in favor of a national "system of income guarantees and supplements.'" Martin Luther King, Jr., called for a guaranteed income in his 1967 book *Where Do We Go from Here: Chaos or Community?* Antipoverty advocates have also argued at times in U.S. history for a "negative income tax" that would use the tax code to provide for payments to those whose incomes fall below a certain level. Liberal economist Milton Friedman is the most well-known intellectual associated with the negative income tax. *See* Milton Friedman, *Capitalism and Freedom* (1962).

   What are the arguments for and against a guaranteed minimum income? Does it matter whether any conditions (work requirements?) are paired with it? Does a positive (welfare) versus negative (income tax) instrumentality make a difference?

4. Recall from Chapter 1 that over 46 million people live below the poverty line in the United States, and compare annual income figures for the poverty line, for TANF grants, and for full-time work at the federal minimum wage. In 2013, the poverty line for a family of three was $19,530 annually, or $1,627.50 per month. The federal minimum wage only guarantees $15,080 annually for a person working a full 40-hour workweek. Cash assistance provided by welfare programs also falls well below the poverty line. In Mississippi, for example, a family of three on TANF receives $2,040

annually, or less than 11 percent of the poverty line. Although Mississippi's TANF grant is the lowest of any state, other states are comparable. Alaska's TANF grant—the most generous of any state—is $11,076 annually, or 57 percent of the poverty line. Notably, in 2012 only 1.8 million families (4.1 million individuals) received TANF assistance nationwide.

5. Not all Americans live in the urban contexts traditionally conjured when one thinks of "welfare." Indeed, Professor Lisa Pruitt has argued that American welfare policy systematically fails to address the unique issues of the rural poor, who are geographically isolated from educational, employment, and other opportunities. Her work also debunks certain myths about rural poverty and its alleviation, including the ideas that the informal economy eases the burdens of rural poverty and that the smaller scale of some rural communities enables enhanced and more personalized social services. *See, e.g.,* Lisa R. Pruitt. "Missing the Mark: Welfare Reform and Rural Poverty," *Journal of Gender, Race & Justice* 10.3 (2007): 439-479

6. In 2009 and 2010, DeParle wrote a series of articles for the New York Times that "examine[d] how the safety net is holding up under the worst economic crisis in decades." *See The Safety Net,* N.Y. Times, http://topics.nytimes.com/ top/news/us/series/the_safety_net; *see also* Jason DeParle, *Contesting Jobless Claims Becomes a Boom Industry,* N.Y. Times (Apr. 4, 2010), at A1; Jason DeParle & Robert Gebeloff, *Once Stigmatized, Food Stamps Find Acceptance,* N.Y. Times (Feb. 11, 2010), at A11; Jason DeParle & Robert Gebeloff, *Living on Nothing but Food Stamps,* N.Y. Times (Jan. 3, 2010), at A1; Jason DeParle & Robert Gebeloff, *Food Stamp Use Soars, and Stigma Fades,* N.Y. Times (Nov. 29, 2009), at A1; Jason DeParle, *Jobless Checks for Millions Delayed as States Struggle,* N.Y. Times (July 24, 2009), at A1; Jason DeParle, *Slumping Economy Tests Aid System Tied to Jobs,* N.Y. Times (June 1, 2009), at A10; Jason DeParle, *For Victims of Recession, Patchwork State Aid,* N.Y. Times (May 10, 2009), at A1.

A. THE BIRTH OF MODERN CASH ASSISTANCE PROGRAMS: THE SOCIAL SECURITY ACT OF 1935

The Social Security Act of 1935 is the statutory foundation for much of the safety net that still exists in the United States. A linchpin of the New Deal, the Act created the Social Security retirement system (on which millions of U.S. workers and their families still rely) as well as the precursors to numerous other programs that still provide cash payments based on statutorily defined eligibility.

The Act was the signature response of the federal government to the Great Depression (see Chapter 2 for more information on the history of the Act). It represented the consolidation and federalization of numerous state programs that preceded it, and signaled a federal policy of providing some guarantees of ongoing income to some Americans. In his signing statement of August 14, 1935, President Roosevelt explained that the purpose of the Act was to provide some economic security in inevitable periods of need:

We can never insure one-hundred percent of the population against one-hundred percent of the hazards and vicissitudes of life. But we have tried to frame a law which will give some measure of protection to the average citizen and to his family against the loss of a job and against poverty-ridden old age.

The original Act created programs in four categories, each of which persists in some form in the modern federal social welfare system: (1) Old-Age Insurance (OAI), (2) Unemployment Insurance (UI), (3) Old-Age Assistance (OAA), and (4) Aid to Dependent Children (ADC). The first two are insurance-style programs, based on and financed by the recipients having paid into the system; the second two are not contribution based, but are instead so-called "categorical" eligibility programs (referring to the "category" of persons eligible), paid for out of general funds.

The first of the above-listed programs, OAI, was the precursor to what we today call "Social Security." Social Security provides retirement benefits to those workers who reach retirement age (age 62 for partial benefit, with full retirement at ages 65-67 depending on personal circumstances) and have contributed to the Social Security system via payroll deductions. Soon after its enactment, the Act was amended to reflect new policy preferences. In 1939 the Act was amended to add coverage to surviving spouses after the death of a covered worker, and to their dependents. Twenty years later, in 1956, coverage was added for contributing workers who leave the workforce because of disability prior to reaching retirement age (this program is known currently as Social Security Disability Insurance). The other insurance program created by the Act in 1935, UI, also persists to this day. Again, it is based on worker contributions, and provides some income to workers who are laid off from work because of no fault of their own.

The two *assistance* programs (OAA and ADC) created by the Social Security Act of 1935 were targeted to people in phases of the life cycle where one was not expected to be in the wage force. Importantly, both of these programs were based on pre-existing state programs; the new federal programs enabled states to maintain significant autonomy in these areas, provided they complied with some basic federal requirements. The original Act included some additional funding for state programs that provided cash assistance to needy blind and disabled people, without regard to workforce participation. In 1972, these latter two programs were consolidated and federalized with the creation of the Supplemental Security Income (SSI) program. The modern Social Security Administration thus administers both "insurance programs" (for retired workers, disabled workers, and their survivors) and "assistance" or "welfare" programs (for the blind, elderly, and disabled, regardless of workforce participation).

The contours of the Social Security Act, and how they live on in today's safety net programs, are outlined in the Handler article excerpted in Chapter 2, p. 63, which is worth reviewing again here. The article below supplements that history and explains the bitter regional and other conflicts in Congress regarding categorical exclusions of certain categories of workers from the Act in order to preserve dominant racial and gender hierarchies.

SUZANNE METTLER, *SOCIAL SECURITY ACT OF 1935*, IN *POVERTY IN THE UNITED STATES: AN ENCYCLOPEDIA OF HISTORY, POLITICS AND POLICY* (GWENDOLYN MINK & ALICE O'CONNOR EDS., 2004)

Unlike programs and rules established in earlier eras that clearly distinguished between citizens on the basis of sex or race, such as protective labor laws for women or Jim Crow segregation laws, the Social Security Act was free of discriminatory language. The fact that eligibility for some programs depended on work status while others did not guaranteed a gendered division in program coverage. Public officials in the Roosevelt administration did not intend, however, to establish a higher and lower tier of social provision. In the context of the 1930s, the programs geared to white men appeared least likely to succeed: Both OAI and UI lacked precedents in the United States and relied on unconventional financing arrangements, but OAA and ADC built on preexisting programs and adhered to the established grant-in-aid model.

In the course of implementation, however, the program coverage became stratified in a manner that was gendered and racialized, functioning as income-maintenance programs especially for white males and their families while doing little to keep people of color or single or divorced white women out of poverty. These outcomes were attributable in part to financing distinctions between the programs: OAI and UI were "contributory" programs, funded through automatic payroll taxes, while OAA and ADC depended on repeated appropriations of funds from general government revenues, controversial processes in which the question of whether recipients were "deserving" was constantly revisited. The different administrative arrangements for the programs, national versus primarily state-level authority, also proved deeply divisive. . . .

. . . . Because only 25.4 percent of women in the late 1930s participated in the paid labor force at any given time, compared to 79 percent of men, and because women workers tended to have intermittent employment histories or to work part-time due to their domestic roles, they were much less likely than were men to qualify for the work-related programs.

. . . Policy officials also aimed to build upon mothers' pensions, state-level programs aimed at assisting mothers and children who had lost their male breadwinner. Such programs enjoyed a positive reputation, and officials believed that their inclusion within the Social Security Act would help gain political support for the more unfamiliar features of the package. Aid to Dependent Children (ADC) was planned in the Children's Bureau of the Department of Labor. . . . [The Bureau] designed a federal grant-in-aid program that would enhance and extend mothers' pensions by offering federal funds to assist those states that planned statewide programs in keeping with federal rules. At the same time, states would retain considerable authority for administering their programs. [Drafters] hoped that such arrangements would promote the development and professionalization of state-level welfare departments generally. They also believed that the educational component of the program, through which social workers would instruct poor women in child rearing and in domestic skills, was essential and would be handled best by local officials.

In Congress, the administration's bill was considered by the House Ways and Means Committee and the Senate Finance Committee, both dominated by southern Democrats. Throughout the New Deal years, southern congress members offered strong support for federal spending but opposed measures that might threaten the prevailing racial hierarchy. Arguing for states' rights, they consistently sought to limit the extent of national programs within the Social Security Act and to undermine [the Committee's] efforts to impose national standards on the states. Following warnings from [Treasury] Secretary Morgenthau about the potential administrative difficulties involved in providing social insurance to agricultural, domestic, and temporary workers, the House committee dropped such workers from coverage in OAI. Given patterns of occupational segregation, these exclusions disproportionately withheld old-age insurance from African Americans, Latinos, and Asian Americans. Women of all races similarly were deprived of coverage when religious and nonprofit organizations successfully argued that they could not survive if they had to cover their employees, who were predominantly women who worked as teachers, nurses, and social workers. All such exclusions under OAI were applied to UI as well, and in addition, workers employed twenty weeks or fewer per year were dropped from coverage.

. . . Although including married women in the contributory program on a noncontributory basis, the council also proposed to disqualify those same women from receiving benefits based on their own participation in the paid workforce. The system would be organized so that a married woman would be eligible for either a wife's allowance or a benefit based on her own previous earnings, whichever would be larger. Given the differential in average wage between men and women, women's earned benefits would typically be smaller than 50 percent of their husbands'. In opting for the wives' allowance, however, they would gain nothing from the payroll taxes they themselves had paid into the system. No provisions were made for spousal or survivors' benefits for husbands, denying working women the opportunity to provide for their husbands in retirement or death. . . .

Although Old Age Assistance had originally been understood as an honorable program aimed to reward elderly people for their earlier service to society, over time, coverage became increasingly stigmatizing. Owing to its grassroots support, OAA benefits remained higher on average than benefits under the contributory old-age program until 1950, by which time national administrative officials had pushed successfully to enhance the latter program. The 1939 amendments made the OAA's procedural rules more demanding by giving states authority to use means testing to determine program benefit levels. Eligibility standards and benefits varied substantially from one state to another, and decisions about coverage were made by social workers who exercised a high degree of discretion. Over time, the differences in coverage and delivery between old-age and survivors' insurance, on the one hand, and old-age assistance, on the other, stratified the fates of women, depending largely on their race and marital status, and of men, depending on their race and occupational status. . . .

ADC became, in the course of implementation, the program least able to extend rights of social citizenship to its beneficiaries. It was the most decentralized of all of the major programs in the Social Security Act, providing states with the least incentive and assistance to develop programs and to raise standards. Though the policy design of OAA was not very different from that of ADC, OAA benefited at least initially from strong grassroots support on the part of . . . groups struggling to improve conditions for the elderly. Lacking such support, ADC benefits grew little, and the administration of the program came to take on the worst features of the mothers' pensions program. In determining client eligibility, for example, "suitable home" rules were used to scrutinize the lives of potential beneficiaries, evaluating their child-rearing and housekeeping abilities and the school and church attendance of their children. In addition, some states and localities used "man in the house" rules to withdraw aid from women suspected of or found to have "male callers." Such investigations were often conducted through "midnight raids" by local officials.

. . . Throughout the mid-twentieth century, coverage within the state-run public assistance programs became increasingly inferior to coverage under

OASI and to higher wage earners' experience of UI. As a result, the women and minority men still disproportionately relegated to such programs were governed differently as social citizens than were those who had gained access to nationalized social benefits. Even today, African American women are less likely than white women to qualify for spouse and widow benefits, and when they do qualify, the racial wage gap means that their benefits are significantly lower than those of white women. In addition, middle and upper class women are far more likely than lower-class women to receive spousal or widows' benefits; in effect, the benefits heighten class inequality. The framework of the American welfare state, as established by the Social Security Act, has perpetuated poverty among some social groups even as it has lifted or kept others out of poverty.

NOTES AND QUESTIONS

1. Legal historian Michele Landis Dauber has argued that the New Deal should be understood in a U.S. legal tradition of disaster relief, with the Great Depression and its ensuing catastrophic unemployment and poverty levels a disaster akin to natural disasters such as Hurricane Katrina. Such a construction interrupts conventional notions about who among the poor is "deserving." *See* Michele Landis Dauber, *The Sympathetic State: Disaster Relief and the Origins of the American Welfare State* (2013).

2. For more on the creation of the disability insurance program within the Social Security Act, see John R. Kearney, *Social Security and the "D" in OASDI: The History of a Federal Program Insuring Earners Against Disability,* 66 Soc. Security Bull. 1 (2006), *available at* http://www.ssa.gov/policy/docs/ssb/v66n3/v66n3p1.pdf.

* * *

The formal name for the modern Social Security program is Old-Age, Survivors, and Disability Insurance (OASDI), a title that captures all three of the categories of eligible recipients: (1) elderly retired workers whose own contributions form the basis of their benefits, (2) their survivors, and (3) those workers who have become disabled prior to retirement age and who are able to draw on their benefits upon proof of disability. As explained above, all three categories are based on the social insurance model of coverage, and the programs are not means tested. Even the very wealthy are eligible to receive their Social Security upon retirement. Thus, while these programs provide income to people who are out of the workforce, they are not ordinarily considered part of the "safety net" for poor people. There is no doubt, however, that these programs operate to *prevent* the poverty that would await many workers once they retired from the labor force. According to the AARP (formerly known as the "American Association of Retired Persons"), "More than 19 million older Americans [half of all the elderly] relied on Social Security for 50 percent or more of their family income and almost half of them [23 percent of the elderly], about 9 million, relied on Social Security for 90 percent or more of their family income. Social Security is such a vital source of income for older Americans that it kept 36 percent, or almost 14 million, of older Americans out of poverty in 2009." *See* AARP, *Social Security Is a Critical Income Source for Older Americans: State-Level Estimates, 2007-2009* (2011), *available at* http://assets.aarp.org/rgcenter/ppi/econ-sec/fs236.pdf.

In October 2012, over 56 million people were receiving some form of OASDI benefits. Of those, over 46 million were retired workers, along with their spouses and children, and another 10 million were disabled workers and their beneficiaries. The amount of monthly benefits depends entirely on wages during employment. The Social Security Administration reports that the *average* monthly benefit for a retired worker is just over $1,200 per month; that of a disabled worker is closer to $1,100 per month. Benefits provided to survivors are comparable. Family members of current beneficiaries are entitled to some benefits, but at significantly lower amounts.

Unlike the social welfare programs, and most significantly TANF, Social Security is an *entitlement* program: If a person contributed and is otherwise eligible for the program, that person will receive benefits. There is no appropriated cap that, once spent, is exhausted. The sufficiency of funding for Social Security is the perennial subject of congressional debate and presidential politics. Indeed, proposals for Social Security reform, such as raising the retirement age, are near-constant topics in the federal budgeting process.

B.   TANF: PRECURSORS, VALUES, AND POLICY CHOICES

The word "welfare" typically conjures up the image of a single mother of children receiving cash assistance from the government. In the United States today, the program that provides that child-based cash assistance is Temporary Assistance for Needy Families (TANF).[2] As was presented in Chapter 2, the debate surrounding the creation of TANF and its implementation reflects an ongoing public conversation about the enduring questions in U.S. welfare policy: Who should get aid? Should single mothers be supported to stay home or incentivized into the workforce? Should immigrants be covered? Is poverty relief the goal? How do we view welfare recipients — as victims or survivors of social and economic "disasters" beyond their control, or as shirkers, reliant on a public system that has inadvertently enabled their long-term dependency? The welfare reform bill of 1996 provided some answers, at least for the purposes of federal policymaking, to these questions.

Under PRWORA, each state receives a block grant (a lump sum of money) to use in any way "reasonably calculated" to achieve the following four statutory goals:

(1) provide assistance to needy families so that children may be cared for in their own homes or in the homes of relatives; (2) end the dependence of needy parents on government benefits by promoting job preparation, work, and marriage; (3) prevent and reduce the incidence of out-of-wedlock pregnancies and establish annual numerical goals for preventing and reducing the incidence of these pregnancies; and (4) encourage the formation and maintenance of two-parent families.

42 U.S.C. § 601(a) (2012). The next section starts with overview information about TANF's funding and caseload, as well as a review of the significant structural changes to cash assistance under PRWORA, specifically the imposition of mandatory lifetime time limits, the elimination of an entitlement to assistance,

---

2. Only families with a minor child or children are eligible for TANF-funded aid. 42 U.S.C. § 608(a)(1) (2012).

and the conversion of a once-federalized program into state block grants. We then turn to two areas of the statute's most express normative features: work requirements, and continued and revitalized regulation of the sexual and private lives of recipients.

1. Programmatic and Structural Overview: Block Grants and Time Limits

The Congressional Research Service (CRS) described the operation of the TANF program in the following 2010 report, which also provides important caseload data.

GENE FALK, CONG. RESEARCH SERV., R40946, *THE TEMPORARY ASSISTANCE FOR NEEDY FAMILIES BLOCK GRANT: AN INTRODUCTION* (2010)

TANF is not synonymous with cash welfare. In [fiscal year] 2009, only 28 percent of federal and state TANF dollars were for cash welfare. TANF also funds child care; programs that address child abuse and neglect; various early childhood initiatives, including prekindergarten programs; earnings supplements for workers in low-income families; emergency and short-term aid; pregnancy prevention programs; responsible fatherhood programs; and initiatives to encourage healthy marriages.

The bulk of federal TANF funding is in a fixed block grant, which has been set at $16.5 billion since FY1997. The basic block grant is not adjusted for inflation, or for changes in the circumstances of a state such as its cash welfare caseload, population, or number of children in poverty. States are also required to spend a specified minimum of $10.4 billion in state funds on TANF-related activities and populations. This amount also has not changed since FY1997.

TANF cash welfare programs today reflect a long history (going back to the early 1900s) and much controversy. States set their own cash welfare benefit levels. In 2009, cash benefits in all states represented a fraction of poverty-level income. In New York, the state with the highest benefit among the 48 contiguous states, the maximum TANF cash benefit for a family of three was $721, which translates to 47% of poverty-level income. Families with adult recipients (and certain nonrecipient parents) come under work participation rules. Federally funded aid is also time-limited for such families.

The cash welfare caseload has declined dramatically from its pre-welfare-reform high of 5.1 million families in 1994 to 1.7 million families in July 2008. The cash welfare caseload increased during the recession, standing at 1.9 million families in December 2010. The cash welfare caseload has traditionally consisted of families headed by a nonworking parent, usually a single mother. However, in FY2008, less than half of the TANF cash caseload fit this description. The TANF cash caseload is very diverse, with more than half the caseload having different characteristics than the historical traditional cash welfare family.

TANF is not a program per se, but a flexible funding stream used to provide a wide range of benefits and services that address the effects of, and the root causes of, disadvantage among families with children. . . .

Benefit Amounts

There are no federal rules on how much a state pays needy families in its TANF cash welfare program. TANF cash welfare benefits in all states represent only a fraction of poverty-level income. In 2009, the maximum benefit for a family of three was $923 per month in Alaska or 48% of poverty-level income. New York had the highest benefits in the lower 48 contiguous states and the District of Columbia, paying $721 per month (47% of poverty-level income). . . .

The Welfare Caseload

In June 2010, the cash welfare caseload stood at 1.9 million families—about 13% higher than the 1.7 million families on the rolls in July 2008 when the caseload reached its lowest levels since 1969. The caseload is down dramatically from its pre-welfare-reform level, reduced by about two-thirds from the historic peak of 5.1 million families in March 1994.

[The graph below] shows the trend in the monthly number of families receiving cash welfare. It shows the sharp rise in the caseload in the 1960s and early 1970s, a period of relative stability from 1975 through 1987, the rise in the caseload to its historic peak from 1988 to 1994, and its decline after 1994. The period of rapid decline ended in 2001, coincident with a recession in that year. The caseload declined more slowly thereafter through July 2008. The uptick in the caseload began in August 2008 and continued through December 2009.

Figure 2
Monthly Number of Families Receiving Cash Welfare: 1959-2010
Cash welfare from Aid to Dependent Children (ADC), Aid to Families
with Dependent Children (AFDC), or Temporary Assistance
for Needy Families (TANF)

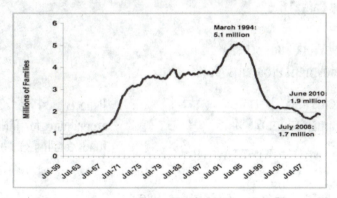

Source: Prepared by the Congressional Research Service (CRS) with data from the U.S. Department of Health and Human Services (HHS).

Note: TANF caseload for October 1999 to June 2010 includes families receiving aid in Separate State Programs (SSPs) that have expenditures countable toward the TANF maintenance of effort requirement.

The post-1994 period saw not only a decline in the cash welfare caseload, but a change in its composition. The cash welfare population is composed both of families that have been the focus of the traditional concern about welfare dependency — those in which a parent or parents are not working but are receiving welfare — and other types of families. These other types represent families in several different types of situations: families with working adults, families where nonparent relatives (e.g., grandparents, aunts, uncles) are caring for children for whom they have no legal financial responsibility, families headed by a disabled parent receiving Supplemental Security Income, and families with ineligible noncitizen adults who have eligible (usually citizen) children. All but the first categories of these families come under the umbrella of "child-only" TANF cases, with the family receiving benefits on behalf of the children but not the adults. These families generally are not subject to work participation requirements or time limits.

* * *

The Congressional Research Service is eager to point out that TANF is not a "program," but a "funding stream," and that only 28% of TANF dollars are spent on cash assistance. In December 2012, the nonpartisan advocacy group Center on Budget and Policy Priorities (CBPP) reported that the total $33 billion expended in federal and state dollars were allocated as follows:

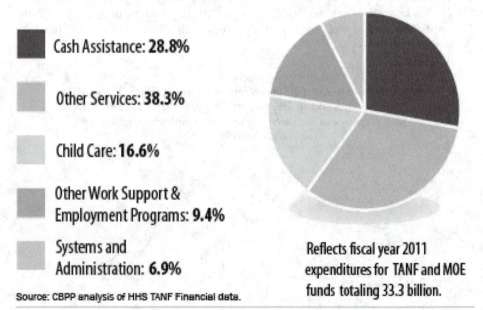

How TANF Dollars Are Spent

Cash Assistance: **28.8%**

Other Services: **38.3%**

Child Care: **16.6%**

Other Work Support & Employment Programs: **9.4%**

Systems and Administration: **6.9%**

Source: CBPP analysis of HHS TANF Financial data.

Reflects fiscal year 2011 expenditures for TANF and MOE funds totaling 33.3 billion.

Center on Budget and Policy Priorities | cbpp.org

http://www.cbpp.org/cms/?fa=view&id=936.

NOTES AND QUESTIONS

1. Review the four statutory goals of TANF. Are they what you would have expected? Are they goals you share? Are they the goals you would have expected for the nation's welfare program?

2. TANF's block grant structure minimizes federal programmatic control and maximizes state flexibility and experimentation. Block grants also eliminate the federal government's ability to compel a consistent national response to economic conditions. What are the policy advantages and disadvantages of this approach? Are there regional forces that might affect how a state designs its TANF program? Some might say that the Civil Rights Act of 1964 and other federal civil rights statutes were designed to rein in state "experimentation" in the area of race relations in favor of some federal policy values. Is this a useful analogy in the welfare context?

3. The passage of PRWORA was a crucial moment for immigrant eligibility for public benefits. Indeed, the actual date of passage, August 22, 1996, is a statutorily salient date for coverage. PRWORA eliminated TANF and Medicaid eligibility for even most "qualified immigrants" for five years after enactment of the statute (states can decide their own eligibility rules for those immigrants who arrived prior to that date).

    Immigrants' eligibility for cash assistance, including but not limited to TANF, is a complex subject. Note first that only certain categories of "legal" immigrants are eligible for any government programs; undocumented immigrants are categorically ineligible. For lawful immigrants, eligibility rules differ based on the welfare program, the classification of immigrant, and how recently the immigrant entered the United States. Additionally, states are able to design their own coverage programs for immigrants, so long as they do not run afoul of federal rules. Advocates working with immigrant populations must therefore master both the federal and the governing state regime for welfare program eligibility.

    The federal government's summary of immigrant eligibility (as of 2009) can be found at http://aspe.hhs.gov/hsp/immigration/restrictions-sum.shtml.

    Qualified aliens who entered the United States on or after August 22, 1996, are also ineligible for SSI until they become U.S. citizens, which generally requires at least five years of residency. "Qualified immigrants" include those with lawful permanent residence status, asylees, refugees, battered alien spouses, and victims of human trafficking. Qualified immigrants who were already receiving SSI when the statute passed retain their benefits, including the Medicaid coverage that accompanies it. Legal permanent residents who have worked 40 qualifying quarters are eligible for SSI, but after December 31, 1996, no quarter can be considered a "qualifying quarter" if the individual received a "federal means-tested public benefit" during the quarter. Similarly, qualified immigrants are not eligible for the SNAP (formerly the Food Stamp Program) for five years after their entry into the United States (children under 18 years of age are excepted).

* * *

Under AFDC, any person who was categorically eligible (that is, who was under income requirements and caring for a dependent child) would receive benefits. The statute placed a mandate on states: "[A]id to families with dependent children *shall* be furnished with reasonable promptness to all eligible individuals." Act of Aug. 28, 1950, ch. 809, Pub. L. No. 81-734, 64 Stat. 550 (1950), emphasis added. There was no cap on AFDC appropriations; by its own terms, the program was designed to expand to meet need. This design permitted the significant expansion of welfare participation in the 1960s-1980s. With one simple sentence, PRWORA eliminated, at least formally, this entitlement to benefits. After setting forth the four purposes of the Act, the statute states:

NO INDIVIDUAL ENTITLEMENT

This part shall not be interpreted to entitle any individual or family to assistance under any State program funded under this part.

42 U.S.C § 601(b) (2012).

Nor is eligibility based simply on the application of categorical tests, such as being under a certain income/asset level or having dependent children under a certain age who are deprived of the support of a parent. Meeting those categorical definitions is necessary but not sufficient to receive aid. States can, and do, impose their own priorities and requirements for assistance and will not receive federal financial support above the allotted block grant. Moreover, as explained by the Center on Budget and Policy Priorities in a 2012 report, PRWORA gave states the "flexibility . . . to redirect" funds saved from caseload reductions in the early years of TANF to other uses:

Some of the freed-up funds were channeled to child care and welfare-to-work programs to further welfare reform efforts, particularly in TANF's early years. But over time, states redirected a substantial portion of their TANF and [state welfare] funds to other purposes, with some funds being used to substitute for (or "supplant") existing state spending and thereby help plug holes in state budgets or free up funds for purposes unrelated to low-income families or children. When the recent recession hit in late 2007, many states were unable — for fiscal or political reasons — to reclaim those dollars to address the substantial increases in need for cash assistance among the growing numbers of poor families; instead, facing budget shortfalls, many states cut already-low TANF benefit amounts further, shortened TANF time limits, or took other actions to shrink caseloads or keep them from rising much in the face of mounting need.

Liz Schott et al., Ctr. on Budget & Pol'y Priorities, *How States Have Spent Federal and State Funds Under the TANF Block Grant* (2012), *available at* http://www .cbpp.org/cms/?fa=view&id=3808_ftn5.

TANF's mandatory time limits are another programmatic expression of the end of entitlements. PRWORA conditions a state's block grant on its operating a program that imposes specific time limits on recipients. To receive its federal grant, a state program must not permit any recipient to receive TANF assistance for more than 24 consecutive months; additionally, each recipient is limited to 60 months of assistance over her lifetime (unless subject to a sanctioned state programmatic exemption). States are free to craft programs that are more restrictive (as of 2005, 16 states had lifetime limits of fewer than 60 months), but they may not be more generous, at least not with federal monies. States may use their own monies for benefits outside of federal mandates, including for cash benefits to people who have "timed out" of TANF. *See* Liz Schott, Ctr. on Budget & Pol'y Priorities, *Policy Basics: An Introduction to TANF* (2012), *available at* http://www.centeronbudget.org/cms/index.cfm?fa =view&id=936.

2.   *Work Requirements*

A signature feature of PRWORA was the imposition of mandatory work requirements on TANF recipients. While work requirements had long been a focus of
various reform proposals and pre-TANF state experiments, the 1996 bill
changed the very nature of the federal welfare program overnight. States are
only eligible for their federal block grants if their programs conform to the work
requirement regulations set forth at 45 C.F.R. § 261.

LIZ SCHOTT, CTR. ON BUDGET & POL'Y PRIORITIES,
POLICY BASICS: AN INTRODUCTION TO TANF (2012)

States must require recipients to engage in work activities and must impose
sanctions (by reducing or terminating benefits) [Ed. note: sanctions are discussed later in this chapter.] if an individual refuses to participate. States can
set their own sanction policies, and nearly all states have chosen to use "full-
family" sanctions that terminate benefits to the entire family if a parent fails to
meet the work requirements.

   States can set their own policies on who must participate in work activities and
what an individual must do. Their decisions, however, are heavily influenced by
the federal TANF Work Participation Rates, which are measured in accordance
with detailed provisions of federal law; states that do not meet the work rates face
a fiscal penalty. While a state may choose to allow a family to participate in
activities that do not count toward the federal work rates and can spend federal
(or state) TANF funds to support activities that do not count toward the rates,
states will be less likely to do so if it may prevent them from meeting the federal
work rates.

   For a state to meet the federal work rates, half of the families receiving TANF
assistance must be engaged in a work activity for at least 30 hours a week
(20 hours a week for single parents with young children). States also must
have 90 percent of *two-parent* families engaged in work, generally for 35 hours
per week. States can get credit against the 50 percent or 90 percent rates for
recent declines in their assistance caseload; this is known as the "caseload reduction credit." Changes in the Deficit Reduction Act of 2005 (DRA) and
subsequent federal regulations effectively increased states' work requirements
and made it more difficult for states to meet the federal work rates.

   The 1996 law sets forth 12 categories of work activities that can count toward
the work rates; the parameters for each activity are shaped by definitions set by
post-DRA federal rules. Nine of these 12 categories are core categories that can
count toward any hours of participation; participation in the three non-core
categories can only count if the individual also participates in core activities
for at least 20 hours per week (30 hours for two-parent families).

   The nine core activities are:

- Unsubsidized employment;
- Subsidized private-sector employment;
- Subsidized public-sector employment;
- Work experience;
- On-the-job training;

- Job search and job readiness assistance;
- Community service programs;
- Vocational educational training (for up to 12 months); and
- Providing child care services to an individual who is participating in a community service program.

The three non-core activities are:

- Job skills training directly related to employment;
- Education directly related to employment;
- Satisfactory attendance at secondary school or in a course of study leading to a GED.

Federal law includes additional rules on when certain activities can count toward the federal work rate. For example, an individual's participation in job search or job readiness activities can only count for six weeks in a year (12 weeks in hard economic times) and for four consecutive weeks. In addition, no more than 30 percent of the families that a state counts toward its federal work rates may do so through participation in vocational educational training or, for parents under age 20, school attendance or education directly related to employment. (Under a special rule, secondary or GED-related school attendance or education directly related to employment can count as participation for parents under age 20 even if it would otherwise be a non-core activity that can only count after 20 hours per week of core participation.)

* * *

Long before TANF, poor women with young children and without breadwinning partners had been the subject of social welfare policy debate. Recall the early Aid to Dependent Children program within the original Social Security Act, and the "mothers' pensions" that preceded it. The foundational idea for ADC and its precursors was the gendered ideal that mothers of young children should be at home, rather than in the labor force, and that absent a breadwinner the government should provide the economic support necessary to effectuate that ideal. Consider how overall economic conditions, and attempts to regulate the supply and demand of labor, interact with other forces to create welfare policy.

SUSAN W. BLANK & BARBARA B. BLUM, *A BRIEF HISTORY OF WORK EXPECTATIONS FOR WELFARE MOTHERS*

7 The Future of Children (A Publication of the David and Lucile Packard Foundation from 1991 to 2004, Spring 1997)

A modest initiative under the new Social Security Act, ADC provided a subsidy to families with fathers who were deceased, absent, or unable to work. While the law was not limited to families headed by widows, it was viewed as a means of extending help to these families, who had had the misfortune to lose a breadwinner and who, it was widely believed, should not be forced to rely on the paid work of a mother, who belonged at home. ADC was to give children "assistance at least great enough to provide, when added to the income of the family, a reasonable subsistence compatible with decency and health." . . .

The 1935 Social Security Act, however, was not the first government income support provided to poor children in the United States. In most cases, ADC added federal aid to state mothers' pension programs, which were already assisting "deserving" poor lone mothers. Several features of the new ADC program kept states from abandoning their efforts following the passage of the Social Security Act. Federal ADC aid was contingent on state contributions, and states were given considerable discretion to determine ADC eligibility and grant levels. For example, a state could continue to require that only children living in so-called "suitable homes" could receive assistance. Until they were struck down in 1960, these requirements were used to exclude "undesirable" families from aid, particularly children of never-married or African-American mothers. . . .

Although the ADC subsidy was originally intended to allow mothers to stay at home to care for their children, a series of cultural, demographic, and policy shifts related to marriage, poverty, and women's employment began to undermine public support for that goal. Concerns about whether the ADC subsidy inadvertently encouraged unwed motherhood arose early on in some states. From a federal perspective, these concerns were short-circuited by the perception that ADC was a program for families headed by widows. In 1939, however, Survivors Benefits were added to the mainstream Social Security program that separately aided widows — the most "deserving" of mothers — and left the ADC program to serve a caseload of apparently less deserving single mothers.

The impact of this policy shift on the image of the ADC program was reinforced by changes in the nation's marriage patterns, as rates of divorce and unwed childbearing began to rise. As early as 1942, the proportion of ADC families in which the mother was divorced, separated, or not married was roughly equal to that headed by widows. To limit the program's support of this politically unpopular group, at least 19 states moved in the 1950s to exclude children from the program on the basis of their birth status, typically denying eligibility to any child born to an unwed mother after she began receiving the subsidy.

Another demographic change focused attention on the dilemma concerning mothers' work and child care that has also attracted recent attention. Large numbers of U.S. mothers began to enter the paid workforce during World War II, and many placed their children in child care programs. As this trend escalated through the 1950s and 1960s, it began to alter public assumptions about women's work, child care, and the merits of helping poor mothers stay home with their children.

In the 1960s simmering concerns about ADC began to boil over into national public policy debates. Intensified criticisms of the program coincided with a sharp increase in its size: Between 1960 and 1970, its caseload almost doubled. This growth partly stemmed from the effects of a 20-year migration from the rural South to northern cities that brought millions of Americans (especially African Americans) to cities to seek work just as the urban need for unskilled labor began to decline. These migrants and others were helped to gain access to ADC benefits by the court-ordered cessation of discriminatory state regulations like the "suitable homes" rules, by the influence of a growing welfare rights movement, and by welfare officials and social workers who encouraged the poor to take advantage of public assistance. Together with the changes in divorce and out-of-wedlock child-bearing, these factors expanded the size of the welfare population.

In response to these growing caseloads and cultural and demographic changes, the ADC program was modified in the 1960s. Partly reflecting concern that the program's benefits and eligibility rules discouraged marriage, the program was renamed AFDC — Aid to Families with Dependent Children — in 1962. By 1967, federal law required state efforts to establish paternity for AFDC children and allowed aid to go to unemployed male parents with a work history. Although small, these changes were the first in a series of federal realignments of the program aimed at better resolution of the dilemma of assisting children while stressing parental responsibility. Nevertheless, until the late 1960s, mothers were not expected to work outside the home in order to "deserve" benefits. . . .

THE WORK INCENTIVE PROGRAM (WIN)

Propelled by the demographic and cultural changes discussed above, Congress moved away from the principle of providing support to enable mothers to stay at home, toward the theory that adults who received welfare benefits should make good-faith efforts to become economically self-sufficient. The Work Incentive Program (WIN), created in 1967, for the first time required states to establish employment and training programs for welfare recipients. These programs provided a mix of services, including job training, education, and structured job search — in which recipients carry out and report back on efforts to find work. Some WIN programs also used so-called work experience components, putting participants to work at public service agencies.

Originally WIN was voluntary, but in 1971 the federal government mandated participation for welfare recipients with no special responsibilities at home or no preschool-age children (this latter provision meant that mothers were allowed to remain at home until their children entered elementary school). However, as would often be the case for federal welfare-to-work programs, limited resources permitted only partial translation of the mandate into practice. . . . Operating the WIN employment and training programs cost welfare agencies more than issuing monthly benefit checks, so WIN became little more than a registration requirement for many recipients. . . .

THE FAMILY SUPPORT ACT

By 1987, Congress was ready to take up the issue of welfare reform, passing in the next year the Family Support Act (FSA). The law called upon states to operate programs that would be successors to WIN. These were generically known as Job Opportunities and Basic Skills (JOBS) Training Programs and were to provide education and training services and at least two of four additional activities — job search, on-the-job training, work supplementation, and community work experience. If services (including child care) could be made available to them, all AFDC recipients who were not specifically exempted were obliged to participate in welfare-to-work activities or face financial sanctions. In practice, however, states have lacked the resources to offer services to all who are eligible for them. . . .

The FSA legislation reflected both an impulse to engage more mothers in welfare-to-work programs and an interest in expanding support services to facilitate their participation. States were to require participation for a recipient when her youngest child turned three (or earlier, at state option). To help defray child care costs, Congress for the first time agreed to match state contributions for child care, substantially increasing the availability of child care subsidies. FSA also allowed most participants to continue to receive child care and Medicaid subsidies for a year following a transition from welfare to work. . . .

When enacted in 1988, FSA was hailed by many as landmark legislation. Proponents of the new law cited its emphasis on engaging mothers of preschoolers in JOBS, its targeting of teen parents, its requirements that states provide education and training in their mix of services, and its provisions for transitional child care and Medicaid benefits. Even at the time, however, some were less enthusiastic. Policy analyst Robert Reischauer wrote in 1989 that, while the changes wrought by FSA "represented important shifts of policy and direction," they were modest in relation to the nation's problems of poverty and dependency. According to Reischauer, "Future administrations and Congresses will thus be compelled to revisit the same policy battleground."

* * *

Jason DeParle's 2004 book about welfare reform, *American Dream: Three Women, Ten Kids, and a Nation's Drive to End Welfare*, describes the implementation of the new TANF program in Milwaukee, Wisconsin, the largest city in a state that had made its own name as a welfare innovator in the decade leading up to PRWORA. The following piece, featuring one of the women whose stories were told in the book, appeared in the *New York Times Magazine* soon after passage of the statute and focuses on the work requirements of Wisconsin's TANF program, known as "Wisconsin Works," or "W-2." When this article appeared in 1997—and when the book appeared in 2004—economic conditions were still favorable. The tone in this piece matched the tone of the times: Will it work, and, if so, what if economic conditions change? Recall DeParle's 2012 article about cash assistance during the recession that started this chapter.

JASON DEPARLE, *GETTING OPAL CAPLES TO WORK*

N.Y. Times Magazine (Aug. 24, 1997)

"Ooooh, I was mad!" Opal Caples says, recalling the notice from the welfare office. "They said we had to start working for our welfare check! I said, 'How could they do this to us?' I didn't feel it was right, to take our money—that's for our children." And as a black woman living in Milwaukee's sprawling black ghetto, Caples detected a hidden agenda. No one talked about work rules in the 1930's, when "welfare was made for middle-class white women," she says. "They're really just targeting the black women."

A bright, animated, street-smart woman who punctuates her speech with knowing glances—you know what I'm talking about, her look insists—Caples is telling her story on the No. 12 bus one July afternoon as it shakes and wheezes down Teutonia Avenue, past the check-cashing counters, liquor stores and lounges. She has dropped her three young daughters with her cousin, Jewel (actually with Jewel's 13-year-old nephew, Little Chuck, since Jewel wasn't around), and before long she'll be toting trash and swabbing toilets in the gastrointestinal lab of a downtown hospital. It's second-shift work and she's unhappy that her girls are asleep by the time the No. 12 shakes home. "They don't even see me at night," she complains.

As the hours wear on, Caples never surrenders her contention that with the strict new work rules pushing people from the rolls, something dangerous and unfair is under way—crime, drugs and prostitution will rise, since "women gonna do what they gotta do." Yet it turns out she enjoys her work. "I like this job," she says that evening, mopping the lab with the radio loud. "Every job I had, you always had somebody gawking over you. This job ain't like that." She also likes the money, which is "more than welfare was giving you anyway." At times she even sounds as if she's campaigning for the work rules she distrusts. "You ain't dealing with the system," she says. "You ain't waiting on no man. You're doing for yourself." Then just as she seems half-convinced, Caples mocks herself with a laugh. "Now if I could take a break and come back in a month!"

[Welfare reform] leaves Caples, like 40,000 other Wisconsin recipients, crossing uncertain ground. Falling somewhere between easy cases and the hardest ones, she seems to operate with a kind of dual citizenship, fluent in the language of the streets and of the working world above. She is a high-school graduate of obvious intelligence whom employers like to hire. "I have a personality that attracts people to me—I do," she says accurately. But she loses jobs as fast as she finds them, and a few months after joining the hospital, she has supervisors fretting over her absences. That is to say she's the kind of woman—with untapped talents and unpredictable troubles—that the state, the nation, is seeking to transform. . . .

It doesn't take a crystal ball to picture all that could still go wrong. With her attendance problems, Caples has shown she can get a job—not that she can keep one. There are few opportunities for education and training. There may not be enough jobs to go around, and the jobs women find may not offer a route from poverty. Work may well be its own reward, but will it prove a broader elixir? It's possible that putting women to work will do nothing to shore up the prospects of men, and the absence of fathers may be the more corrosive force in the ghetto. To the extent the new system leads women to work, it also leads them away from their kids, who will be left in arrangements of varying quality. The effect on children is anyone's guess. . . .

. . . On the one hand, [Caples] seems to like the job. At $7.69 an hour, it pays more than she has ever made. It offers benefits—medical, dental and life insurance. And it also offers the chance to train for other hospital jobs, which could pay up to $10 an hour. Though it involves emptying trash and cleaning toilets, she seems to feel it offers a certain status. She talks with delight about being invited to a company picnic and having doctors know her name. On the other hand, she hates working second shift, and like many inner-city women, she distrusts center-based child care, worrying about the reports of molestation that travel the ghetto grapevine. She remains convinced that W-2 is racially biased, and she even quotes Malcolm X, to warn what women without welfare may do. "Any means necessary to take care of your kids," she says. "If I don't have a job, who's to say I wouldn't prostitute myself? I pray to God it don't happen, but to some people it will."

It wasn't a complete surprise to discover, earlier this month, that Caples was missing from work. She hadn't called in for three days, and under hospital policy that probably meant she was fired. She doesn't have a phone, so I left a message with her boyfriend's mother, and the next day she placed a collect call back. The verve in her voice was gone. She and her boyfriend had had a fight, and he had moved out. She said she was too distraught the night of the breakup to bother calling work. Then figuring she was fired anyway, she simply didn't go back. Plus she now had day-care problems: Jewel had found a job, and Caples, suddenly single, had no place for her girls. "I don't know what I'm going to do," she said.

But her boss had asked me to pass on a message, and Caples sounded surprised that he wanted to see her. She summoned the courage to give him a call, and a few hours later she was in his office, describing her hapless week. When it comes to supervisors, Caples couldn't have drawn better luck. Having served on the board of a homeless shelter, Charles Lee wasn't looking to see another family on the streets. And it couldn't have hurt that he was taking a master's-degree course called Social Influences on Business Management—and that he had written his term paper on W-2. "I know how tough it can be," he said. "I'm going to do everything I can."

Sitting in his office that afternoon, Caples wrote out a three-page plea for mercy that impressed Lee with its eloquence. She explained what had happened. She pledged to do better. She said she had arranged for child care. Lee passed it on to the hospital vice president. The appeal is pending.

It's a disappointing moment, but the architects of W-2 would call it progress. Caples may still save her job, or she may quickly find another. . . . If things really fall apart, she could find herself doubled up with Jewel — or suddenly out on the streets. The one route no longer open to her is to simply return to the rolls. She's striking off, on shaky legs, into an uncharted, post-welfare world.

* * *

As we read in Chapter 2, from when the Moynihan Report was issued in 1965 to Ronald Reagan's speech about the "welfare queen" in 1976, the use of welfare programs by African-American women, children, and families has been fraught with controversy and misinformation. It is undisputed that African Americans receive welfare at a higher rate than do other families. While disproportionate usage by African Americans may be an empirical fact, the explanation and social meaning of that fact are extremely contested and controversial. In 2001, Professors Robert A. Moffitt and Peter T. Gottschalk reported on a study of welfare receipt in the United States in *America Becoming: Racial Trends and Their Consequences.* The report noted that in the period of 1994-1996, 14 percent of African-American families used welfare, while only 2.7 percent of non-Hispanic White households did so. Moffitt and Gottschalk find, however, that this higher usage is attributable to measurable risk factors, such as nonwelfare income, rather than to nonmeasurable factors, such as "cultural and social norms."

DOROTHY E. ROBERTS, *THE VALUE OF BLACK MOTHERS' WORK*
26 Conn. L. Rev. 871 (1994)

The common ground of contemporary welfare reform discourse is the belief that single mothers' dependence on government support is irresponsible and should be remedied by requiring these mothers to get jobs. "Workfare" is a refrain of the general theme that blames the poor, because of their dependence mentality, deviant family structure, and other cultural depravities, for their poverty. Martha Minow reveals workfare's injustice by asking the unspoken question, "why should single mothers responsible for young children be expected to work outside the home?" Why does society focus on welfare mothers' dependence on public assistance rather than on their children's dependence on them for care?

Minow correctly points out that the focus on welfare mothers' dependence rather than their valuable care reflects a radical departure from the original welfare policy towards mothers. During the late nineteenth century, women successfully lobbied for public relief for widowed mothers. In her recent book, *Protecting Soldiers and Mothers: The Political Origins of Social Policy in the United States,* Theda Skocpol demonstrates how women's organizations and their allies exploited the ideology of motherhood to attain mothers' pensions and other "maternalist" legislation. The logic that propelled maternalist welfare policy was precisely the opposite of that backing workfare: widowed mothers needed government aid so that they would not have to relinquish their maternal duties in the home in order to join the work force. This maternalist rhetoric was powerful enough to mobilize disenfranchised women, defeat conservative opponents, and convince American legislatures to embark on social welfare programs far ahead of those of most European countries.

The current workfare proposals, then, reflect an unprecedented depreciation of welfare mothers' contribution to society. The rhetoric of motherhood has lost all of the persuasive force it wielded during the Progressive Era. The modern welfare state has increasingly degraded the work all mothers perform. It has abandoned the moral mother ideology and diminished the control of mothers over child care. As increasing numbers of women join the work force, society decreasingly rewards mothers' socially productive labor in the home. An individual's entitlement to welfare benefits now depends on his or her relationship to the market. Former workers are entitled to compensation by social insurance programs for their prior participation in the wage labor force. As unpaid caregivers with no connection to a male breadwinner, single mothers are considered undeserving clients of the welfare system.

This universal devaluation of mothers' work, however, does not explain entirely the revolution in welfare reform. When welfare reformers devise remedies for maternal irresponsibility, they have Black single mothers in mind. Although marital status does not determine economic well-being, there is a strong association between Black single motherhood and family poverty. The image of the lazy Black welfare queen who breeds children to fatten her allowance shapes public attitudes about welfare policy. Part of the reason that maternalist rhetoric can no longer justify public financial support is that the public views this support as benefitting primarily Black mothers. Society particularly devalues Black mothers' work in the home because it sees these mothers as inherently unfit and their children as inherently useless.

The Value of Black Mothering

Maternalist rhetoric has no appeal in the case of Black welfare mothers because society sees no value in supporting their domestic service. The public views these mothers as less fit, less caring, and less hurt by separation from their children. First, workfare advocates fail to see the benefit in poor Black mothers' care for their young children. To the contrary, contemporary poverty rhetoric blames Black single mothers for perpetuating poverty by transmitting a deviant lifestyle to their children. Far from helping children, payments to Black single mothers merely encourage this transgenerational pathology. Dominant images have long depicted Black mothers as unfit. The ideal Black mother figure, Mammy, self-lessly nurtured white children (under her mistress's supervision). In contrast, whites portrayed Black slave mothers as careless and unable to care properly for their own children. Modern social pundits from Daniel Patrick Moynihan to Charles Murray have held Black single mothers responsible for the disintegration of the Black family and the Black community's consequent despair.

Second, workfare advocates fail to see the injury in requiring Black mothers to leave their young children. Welfare reform discourse gives little attention to the relationship between poor Black mothers and their children. The forced separation of Black mothers from their children began during slavery, when Black family members faced being auctioned off to different masters. Slave mothers knew the regular pain of seeing their loved ones "rented out, loaned out, bought up, brought back, stored up, mortgaged, won, stolen or seized." The disproportionate state disruption of Black families through the child welfare system reflects a continuing depreciation of the bond between Black mothers and their children.

Finally, workfare advocates are not hindered by any disharmony in the idea of a Black working mother. The conception of motherhood confined to the home and opposed to wage labor never applied to Black women. Slave women's hard labor in the field defied the Victorian norm of female domesticity. Even after Emancipation, political and economic conditions forced many Black mothers to earn a living outside the home. Americans expected Black mothers to look like Aunt Jemima, working in somebody else's kitchen: "(o)utfitted in an unflatter-ing dress, apron, and scarf (a 'headrag'), she is always ready for work and never ready for bed." American culture reveres no Black madonna; it upholds no popular image of a Black mother nurturing her child. Given this history, it is not surprising that policymakers do not think twice about requiring welfare mothers to leave their young children in order to go to work.

THE VALUE OF BLACK CHILDREN

. . . Underlying the consensus that welfare mothers should work is often the conviction that their children are socially worthless, lacking any potential to contribute to society. Welfare reform rhetoric assumes that these children will grow up to be poor and, consequently, burdens to society. The proposals dismiss any possible reason to nurture, inspire, or love these children. Minow asks at the end of her essay, "why not consider paying mothers of especially young children to care for their children?" In addition to the historic resistance to compensat-ing mothers' work, society's response is, "because these children are not worth it."

The reason for society's bleak assessment is not only the belief that Black mothers are likely to corrupt their children, but that Black children are predis-posed to corruption. Blaming single mothers for "nurturing a next generation of pathology" stigmatizes not only mothers, but their children as well. The powerful Western image of childhood innocence does not seem to benefit Black children. Black children are born guilty. They are potential menaces — criminals, crackheads, and welfare mothers waiting to happen. Newspaper stories about "crack babies" warn of a horde of Black children, irreparably damaged by their mothers' prenatal drug use, who are about to descend on inner-city kindergartens. These stories present drugs, poverty, and race as fungible marks that inevitably doom Black children to a worthless future. As one reporter wrote, "(c)all them 'welfare babies,' 'crack babies,' 'at-risk babies,' or 'deficit babies' — by whatever term, they constitute a new 'bio-underclass' of infants who are disadvantaged almost from the moment of conception." The authors' primary concern typically seems to be the huge costs "crack babies" impose on society, rather than the children's welfare. . . .

Serious talk about alternatives to current welfare reform proposals must center on society's dismissal of poor Black families' relationships and futures. Perhaps recognizing workfare's particular devaluation of Black mothers' work will lead some to reject these proposals and to search for ways of supporting poor single mothers' struggle to raise their children against terrifying odds. Perhaps recognizing the sheer dissonance of the hope that majority America will treasure poor Black children will lead others to work more strenuously toward "an economic game plan for poor black communities."

AMY L. WAX, *RETHINKING WELFARE RIGHTS: RECIPROCITY NORMS, REACTIVE ATTITUDES, AND THE POLITICAL ECONOMY OF WELFARE REFORM*

63 Law & Contemp. Probs. 257 (2000)

The AFDC program, which has been the mainstay of federal relief for the poor since the New Deal, initially embodied expectations consistent with strong reciprocity, but only in light of customs, understandings, and social practices prevailing at the time of enactment. Because the program was confined to single parents with children, it denied benefits to most able-bodied men. The expectation that able-bodied women would work was not part of the program's design at its inception. On the contrary, the program implemented the understanding that single mothers should personally care for their children, which required them to depend on public support. Twenty-five years after the enactment of the AFDC legislation, however, the consensus that single mothers should depend on the government began to fade as more mothers started to work and the number of out-of-wedlock births exploded. . . .

Popular acceptance of basic norms of reciprocity can also help explain the apparent paradox of widespread support for work requirements for single mothers on welfare, coupled with the general approval (or at least lack of disapproval) of married mothers' staying home to care for their own children. It is sometimes claimed that public condemnation of single mothers' "dependency" on the government is inconsistent with applauding married mothers' "dependency" on breadwinner husbands. Our analysis suggests, however, why the public might view these two forms of dependency very differently. What offends the norm of reciprocity is not the dependency (or interdependency) of individuals on one another as such, but rather attempts by private individuals or entities to call upon collective resources willfully or without necessity.

Indeed, within the mutual aid context, the "dependency" of individual family members on one another is of no practical concern to the broader collective overall, so long as the family arrangement is consensual and mutually agreeable and the smaller social unit "pays its way." But most families consisting of mothers with employed spouses do indeed pay their own way. Considered as a unit, breadwinner-homemaker families, and two-parent families generally, are almost always self-supporting and able to live decently without public subsidy. Most contribute to common assets through taxes and may also generate other forms of social value. Because these types of families almost always function as donors rather than recipients for purposes of public subsidies, they are generally regarded as living up to expectations. Most do not break with the demands of strong reciprocity because they rarely need to draw from the common pot at all, let alone for impermissible reasons.

What of traditional breadwinner-homemaker families that cannot manage to support themselves? Although unusual, such "working poor" families do exist. Some of these families, which include but are not confined to breadwinner-homemaker units, pay little or no taxes or actually receive a net subsidy within our system through programs such as the Earned Income Tax Credit. These subsidies are not necessarily inconsistent with an adherence to strong reciprocity within the mutual aid paradigm, however. Families in which one or more members work reasonably hard in the paid labor market thereby demonstrate their willingness to help themselves. They make a good faith effort to function as a net contributor to collective resources maintained for mutual security, which is all that strong reciprocity requires. If economic reality is such that this effort does not suffice to achieve self-support for the unit or to generate a surplus for the group, the family does not thereby show itself to be "undeserving." On the contrary, the inability to achieve donor status within the game despite best efforts is precisely the situation that establishes desert and permits players to accede to the status of recipients of group resources. Players in the mutual aid game are entitled to draw on collective help only if they are in need for reasons beyond their control. Many of the working poor arguably meet this description.

Single mothers' dependency on government aid presents a different story. The parallel between married mothers' dependency on their husbands' earnings and single mothers' dependency on government programs is often put forward to justify public assistance for the latter without any requirement that they engage in paid work at all. The contention is, in effect, that single mothers, by virtue of their mothering function, should have an unconditional right to full public support. By definition, then, these mothers function as recipients rather than as donors in the mutual aid game. Under strong reciprocity, this would immediately trigger an inquiry into whether they could do more to help themselves. For many single mothers, the answer would appear to be yes: They could go to work and earn something, even if not quite enough to live on. Their earnings would at least offset some of the draw on public funds.

As already suggested, however, matters are not quite so simple. The case of single mothers with children is considerably complicated by cultural norms regarding what mothers can reasonably be expected to do, whether mothers belong at home, and whether having children out-of-wedlock is immoral or deviant. Fairness-based critiques of public aid for single mothers must also confront the claim that although single mothers on welfare may not have market earnings, they perform the valuable work of raising children and thereby making a substantial (and adequate) contribution to social welfare. In the currency of the mutual aid game, this suggests that rearing children ought to count as a reasonably sufficient contribution or noncash "donation" to the common pot, which triggers a quid-pro-quo entitlement to public help. Put another way, the contention is that mothers, simply by functioning as mothers, have done "enough" to satisfy fairness and reciprocity requirements.

Should it matter for purposes of satisfying the requirement of strong reciprocity that raising children is, in some sense, "work"? Childrearing certainly requires an expenditure of effort. It also generates benefits of various kinds, including, perhaps, "public goods" or positive externalities from the production of good citizens. These are benefits in which the wider public can potentially share. Yet the creation of these forms of value, and the expenditure of effort that produces them, does not in itself establish entitlement to full public support if strong reciprocity norms are taken seriously. Even if a single mother can be said to "donate" some resources to the collective, most of her efforts go toward her own (and the father's) "consumption value" in having and rearing the child, or toward conferring an altruistic gift of care on the child itself. These are purely private benefits, for which the collective is being asked to pay. Whether the private gains that mothers and children enjoy at public expense exceed any public benefit, such that the balance of costs and benefits is negative for the collective, is difficult to determine. However, because private "consumption" and investment value would appear to loom large for each individual mother and child compared with any externalized benefits to others, it seems unlikely that the collective would come out ahead overall from underwriting the support for all single women with children who choose to avail themselves of help. The impression of net cost is exacerbated by certain negative externalities attributed to single motherhood as a social practice. There is some evidence that single mothers, especially among the poor and poorly educated, produce a disproportionate number of dysfunctional children. This fosters the view that support for single mothers comes at society's expense. The analysis suggests that a belief that unconditional public assistance for single mothers violates norms of reciprocity begins with a perception that welfare mothers and their families give back to society less than they receive.

But the perception that single parent families are a net drain on collective resources is not the end of the story. As we have seen, an imbalance between individual contribution and public support does not pose a problem for strong reciprocity if the individual who calls upon group support is unable to improve upon the situation or to reduce her need for public funds. If the net balance is beyond her control or not her own fault, public subsidies will not elicit resentment and will generally be forthcoming. But whether the neediness of many poor single mothers is in some sense "involuntary" is a hotly contested question that, for many voters, yields a negative answer. In considering whether single mothers "deserve" public support, the public is asked to determine whether each step on the road that so often leads to public dependency — lack of educational success, drug use, failure to marry, unprotected sexual intercourse, pregnancy, giving birth and keeping the child, failure to seek or retain employment — can be regarded as within an individual's meaningful control and thus one for which the would-be recipient can properly be held responsible. How should these decisions be situated on the continuum from choice to luck, and how should they count in establishing a person's status as "defector" or "cooperator" in the game? The answers to these questions necessarily depend on empirical facts as well as normative judgments. To add to the complication, neediness among single mothers often results from past decisions with present irrevocable consequences. Whereas someone could have avoided their current dilemma, there may now be little they can do to improve the situation or engage in meaningful self-help. One question that consistently arises in the application of the strong reciprocity norm is whether persons will be held strictly accountable for past imprudence, or will be viewed as "deserving" because future efforts are bound to prove largely unavailing. . . .

NOTES AND QUESTIONS

1. In a 2003 article, Professor Wax takes her argument even further. Responding to what she describes as feminist critics who seek to "broaden the category of persons who are regarded as deserving of society's approbation and material support" to include poor mothers, she says:

> [T]he crux of the debate over how the welfare system should treat "caretaking units" — usually single mothers and their children — centers on what should count as work. The oft-heard claim is that caretaking performed without pay is no less socially useful than work performed for wages and should be rewarded. Society should offer collective support to those who care for others. The principal problem with the assertion that society should support caretakers and their dependents is that it threatens to prove too much. Any recommendation that resources be reserved for these individuals begs the question of why other persons who volunteer to generate a variety of goods and services that either appear to create value or require effortful exertion cannot also lay claim to social support. Consider the example of the third rate artist, dedicated to his craft, who labors strenuously at his sculptural creations in his basement studio. What exactly is he doing down there? Can we deny that he "works hard"? We know that he enjoys his work — that is, that he gets "consumption value" from the performance — because he chooses to sculpt rather than to do something more lucrative. But neither consumption value nor choice distinguish his case from that of many others in the paid economy, including law professors. Yet we harbor the intuition that we owe him nothing. But why treat a second-rate single mother differently than a third-rate visual artist? That no one wants to buy the artist's creations is important to us. It counts as good evidence that they are of little value to anyone but the artist himself. That no one wants to pay the mother to raise the child may indicate something similar, however callous that sounds.

Amy L. Wax, *Something for Nothing: Liberal Justice and Welfare Work Requirements,* 52 Emory L.J. 1 (2003).

2. For a comprehensive discussion of the social meaning of the "racialization" of welfare, see Martin Gilens, *Why Americans Hate Welfare: Race, Media, and the Politics of Antipoverty Policy* (1999). In that book, Gilens presents public opinion data and analysis of media content and argues that "racial stereotypes play a central role in generating opposition to welfare in America. In particular, the centuries-old stereotype of blacks as lazy remains credible for large numbers of white Americans. . . . In a culture in which economic failure is often attributed to lack of effort, blacks' economic problems themselves reinforce the stereotype of laziness."

3. In his bestselling book, *Losing Ground* (see Chapter 2, p. 90), Charles Murray posits a hypothetical young heterosexual couple, Harold and Phyllis, facing

choices about pregnancy, marriage, work, and welfare in 1960 and then again in 1970. Murray argues that the intervening decade witnessed increases in benefits levels and changes to the "man in the house" and other AFDC rules that removed incentives for people like Harold and Phyllis to work and marry. Claiming that the race, intelligence, and "culture" of his "dramatic personae" were irrelevant, Murray argues that, assuming that Phyllis and Harold were rational economic actors, by 1970 they would elect nonmarriage and welfare over other options:

> In 1960, the logic of their world led them to behave in traditional working-class ways. Ten years later, the logic of their world had changed and, lo and behold, they behaved indistinguishably from "welfare types." What if we had hypothesized a more typical example — or at least one that fits the stereotype? What if we had posited the lower-class and black cultural influences that are said to foster high illegitimacy rates and welfare dependency? The answer is that the same general logic would apply, but with even more power. When economic incentives are buttressed by social norms, the effects on behavior are multiplied. But the main point is that the social factors are not necessary to explain behavior. There is no "breakdown of the work ethic" in this account of rational choices among alternatives. There is no shiftless irresponsibility. It makes no difference whether Harold is white or black. There is no need to invoke the spectres of cultural pathologies or inferior upbringing. The choices may be seen much more simply, much more naturally, as the behavior of people responding to the reality of the world around them and making the decisions — the legal, approved, and even encouraged decisions — that maximize their quality of life.

Murray's description of the effect of welfare rule changes on behavior has been the subject of numerous critiques that question the assumptions Murray makes as well as the conclusions he reaches. *See, e.g.*, Lucie White, *No Exit: Rethinking "Welfare Dependency" from a Different Ground*, 81 Geo. L.J. 1961 (1993).

4. In the 1960s and 1970s welfare recipients organized to resist and protest government control over their lives, and the National Welfare Rights Organization (NWRO) was formed in 1967 as a mostly African-American political coalition of state and local affiliates. At its peak, membership was about 25,000 people. By 1971, over 500 local organizations nationwide were members of the NWRO. In 1967, the NWRO sent delegates to Washington, D.C., to sit in at Senate committee hearings on proposed amendments to the Social Security Act, and in 1968, Martin Luther King, Jr., acknowledged the group as an important political force, embracing its role in the Poor People's Campaign. In the same era, Frances Fox Piven and Richard Cloward, two Columbia University social work professors, advanced as an antipoverty campaign the idea that welfare organizing would lead to increased enrollment in AFDC, which would lead to fiscal and bureaucratic crisis, which in turn would create political support for a guaranteed minimum income. Cloward and Piven are best known as coauthors of the 1971 book *Regulating the Poor: The Functions of Public Welfare* and the 1978 book *Poor People's Movements: Why They Succeed, How They Fail.* For more information on the NWRO, see Felicia Kornbluh, *The Battle for Welfare Rights: Politics and Poverty in Modern America* (2007).

5. There is no contemporary analog to the welfare rights movement of the 1960s and 1970s. What factors do you think contribute to the development

of such a movement? Is there an analogous political movement of poor people in the United States today? If not, why not? What is the role of lawyers in developing or supporting such a movement?

* * *

Welfare rolls plummeted in the years immediately following passage of PRWORA, and remain lower than the high years of AFDC usage. As you will see ("Did It Work?" below), the cause for these reductions is the subject of academic and empirical debate. While studies are ongoing, some data indicate that the imposition of sanctions (which can include being cut from the program) is a statistically significant factor contributing to the decline in welfare caseloads. In other words, people are not only "choosing" not to be on welfare or timing out of TANF, but are also being thrown off because of rule violations.

TIMOTHY CASEY, LEGAL MOMENTUM: THE WOMEN'S LEGAL DEF. & EDUC. FUND, *THE SANCTION EPIDEMIC IN THE TANF PROGRAM* (2012)

The federal TANF statute specifies the minimum circumstances in which sanctions must be imposed, the minimum sanction amounts, and the minimum duration of a sanction. Most states go far beyond the minimum.

Federal TANF rules require parents to seek work, accept work, and/or train for work. Federal rules also require parents to cooperate with state efforts to collect child support as a means of reimbursing the state for the family's TANF benefits.

Federal rules require sanctions for violations of work or of child support cooperation requirements. Sanctions are also permitted for violations of any other requirements that a state opts to prescribe. Most states do impose additional sanctionable requirements. For example, 33 states impose sanctions for violations of state requirements related to a child's school attendance or grades.

Federal rules require at least a pro rata grant reduction for a work requirement violation and a grant reduction of at least 25% for a violation of a child support cooperation requirement. States may impose harsher penalties, including a full family sanction, for violations of these requirements and for violations of any additional state-prescribed requirement.

At least 32 states impose full family sanctions for work requirement violations by applicant parents, denying the application if an applicant parent fails to comply with application process work requirements such as "job search," meaning the requirement to contact employers to seek work. Forty-five states impose full family sanctions for work requirement violations by recipient parents, about half immediately for an initial violation, and about half beginning with a partial sanction that escalates to a full family sanction if the violation continues beyond a specified period or if there is a subsequent violation.

States continue a sanction at least until a parent demonstrates that she is willing to comply and may continue the sanction for a longer period. A majority of states impose minimum sanction periods generally ranging from 1 to 3 months for a first work requirement violation. Most states impose longer minimums generally ranging from 3 to 12 months for any subsequent work requirement violation. Four states [Idaho, Mississippi, Pennsylvania, and Wisconsin] authorize lifetime full family sanctions for repeated violations. . . .

The percentage of eligible families receiving benefits fell from 84% in the last full year of the AFDC program in 1995, to 40% of eligible families receiving TANF benefits in 2005, the most recent year for which HHS has reported estimates of the number of TANF-eligible families. The eligible family participation rate has likely fallen significantly below 40% since 2005. Although the average monthly unemployment rate was almost twice as high in 2009 (9.3%) as in 2005 (5.1%), fewer families received TANF in 2009 (1.84 million a month) than in 2005 (2.06 million a month).

Based on the available data, it is impossible to know exactly how much of the TANF participation decline is due to sanctions. HHS recently acknowledged that full family sanctions were a contributing factor, stating that it is difficult to isolate the effect of any one factor, and expressing the hope that "additional work may help refine understanding of the sharp drop in participation among eligible families."

Texas and Georgia case studies provide strong evidence that full family sanctions can lead to a sharp drop in TANF participation. In 2003, Texas shifted from partial to full family sanctions for work requirement violations by recipient parents. Over the next three years the state's TANF caseload declined by almost half, from 118,927 to 61,333 families, with about 10% of families a month suffering a full family sanction. An HHS-funded study by the social research organization Mathematica Policy Research, Inc. concluded that "[w]hile the advent of full-family sanctions may not account for Texas's entire caseload decline, it likely accounts for a substantial portion of it."

In 2004, Georgia significantly expanded the applicant work requirements, the violation of which results in an application denial in that state. Georgia's application approval rate, which [was] 51% in 2003, declined to 22% in 2006, and its caseload fell from 57,663 families in June 2003 to 29,237 families in June 2006. A Mathematica analysis found that "[i]ncreasingly, Georgia is denying TANF applications because applicants either cannot or do not want to comply with work requirements during the eligibility process."

The conclusion that full family sanctions have contributed significantly to the fall in TANF participation is also supported by the "TANF leaver" studies (studies of families leaving or exiting the TANF program), and by the change over time in the events associated with case closings. In the late 1990's HHS funded fifteen state studies of families whose TANF cases had been closed. All fifteen studies found that many parent TANF leavers were unemployed, with the percent unemployed in the quarter after exit ranging from 32% to 53%. Nationally, the percentage of AFDC/TANF case closings associated with increased maternal earnings decreased from 55% in the period 1993-1995 to 34% in the period 2001-2003.

Predictably, the sharp decline in TANF participation has led to a sharp increase in the number of single-mother families living in the most extreme poverty. One recent study found that in 2004 over 1.7 million single-mother families each had a combined annual income from welfare and work of less than $3,000, a 56% increase since 1995 in this measure of extreme poverty.

NOTES AND QUESTIONS

1. In a 2011 book, Professor Kaaryn Gustafson reports the results of her qualitative study of welfare recipients in a Northern California county and

specifically their knowledge of governing welfare rules. Her emphasis is on welfare fraud and the criminalization of the poor (see Chapter 9, p. 543), but her findings also bear on the prevalence of sanctions. Do the women on TANF know the rules? Are their violations intentional? Gustafson divides her interview subjects into three categories: the Informed, the Misinformed, and the Preoccupied/Disengaged. In her concluding chapter, Professor Gustafson writes:

> This study has revealed that welfare recipients possess little knowledge of the welfare system and that their ignorance often comes at a high cost. Both the general public and policy makers have ignored the realities of the daily lives of welfare recipients and their difficulties negotiating their way through, and out of, the welfare system.

Kaaryn S. Gustafson, *Cheating Welfare: Public Assistance and the Criminalization of Poverty* (2011).

2. Assuming some form of sanctions are appropriate for violating TANF rules, what considerations are relevant to designing an effective and humane sanction system? What measure should be used to assess the effectiveness of a sanction program?

3. Sexual Regulation and Marriage Promotion

While work requirements are the most publicly debated aspect of TANF, the congressional findings underlying PRWORA concern marriage and procreation more than the labor market or employability. Review the four goals of the statute, *supra,* p. 197. Those goals flow from the findings in the Act itself:

> The Congress makes the following findings:
> (1) Marriage is the foundation of a successful society.
> (2) Marriage is an essential institution of a successful society which promotes the interests of children.
> (3) Promotion of responsible fatherhood and motherhood is integral to successful child rearing and the well-being of children. . . .
> (5) The number of individuals receiving aid to families with dependent children (in this section referred to as "AFDC") has more than tripled since 1965. More than two-thirds of these recipients are children. Eighty-nine percent of children receiving AFDC benefits now live in homes in which no father is present. . . .
> (6) The increase of out-of-wedlock pregnancies and births is well documented. . . .
> (8) The negative consequences of an out-of-wedlock birth on the mother, the child, the family, and society are well documented. . . .
> (9) Currently 35 percent of children in single-parent homes were born out-of-wedlock, nearly the same percentage as that of children in single-parent homes whose parents are divorced (37 percent).
> While many parents find themselves, through divorce or tragic circumstances beyond their control, facing the difficult task of raising children alone, nevertheless, the negative consequences of raising children in single-parent homes are well documented as follows:
> (A) Only 9 percent of married-couple families with children under 18 years of age have income below the national poverty level. In contrast, 46 percent of female-headed households with children under 18 years of age are below the national poverty level.

(10) Therefore, in light of this demonstration of the crisis in our Nation, it is the sense of the Congress that prevention of out-of-wedlock pregnancy and reduction in out-of-wedlock birth are very important Government interests. . . .

Concern about welfare recipients' private lives — rationalized by public financial support — has been a feature of welfare since the Poor Laws and the early-twentieth-century "suitable home" requirements. The regulation of the sexual lives of welfare recipients was the explicit subject of King v. Smith (see Chapter 2, p. 82), which struck down an Alabama law that terminated AFDC benefits upon evidence that the single mother head of household had a sexual relationship with a man not the father of her children. So was procreation at least the subtext of the Court's decision in Dandridge v. Williams (see Chapter 3, p. 157), upholding Maryland's "maximum grant" system that capped a family's benefits once a family reached a certain size.

TANF continues the long history of regulating the sexual and family lives of the women who participate in the program. Professor Anna Marie Smith's article reviews these features of welfare policy.

ANNA MARIE SMITH, *THE SEXUAL REGULATION DIMENSION OF CONTEMPORARY WELFARE LAW: A FIFTY STATE OVERVIEW*

8 Mich. J. Gender & L. 121 (2002)

. . . [T]he once-controversial "family cap" has become a common feature of welfare programs. It is widely believed in American public policy circles that poor women approach reproductive sex in a purely entrepreneurial manner. It is alleged that they engage in unprotected heterosexual intercourse in the hope that should they become pregnant and bear a newborn child, they would profit handsomely in the form of either public assistance eligibility or — where they are already participating in a welfare program — increased cash payments and relief from the mandatory work requirements. The fact that the additional payments are often miniscule, and that no reasonable woman would believe that pregnancy, childbirth, and caring for a newborn amount to a carefree vacation, is disregarded.

TANF/AFDC BENEFIT LIMITS AS REPRODUCTIVE "DISINCENTIVES"

TANF benefits usually reflect household size; when a household increases in number, benefits increase accordingly by a small amount. Under the "family cap" laws and regulations that many states have adopted, however, no additional benefits are paid due solely to the birth of a child if he/she was conceived during a period in which the family was eligible for public assistance. Where the states had to seek special waivers from the federal government for the "family cap" before 1996, the PRWORA's block grant system allows them to impose this benefit limit without federal approval. . . .

The average number of children in welfare families is roughly equivalent to the national average: in 1999, the average number of persons in TANF households was 2.8; the approximate average number of children receiving benefits in these households was two; two in five TANF families had only one child; and only one in ten of the TANF families had more than three children, while the average number of children under the age of eighteen in each American family was 1.85 in 1998. . . . The empirical evidence also suggests that the availability of welfare benefits does not cause poor women to have more children. . . .

The social science research findings also suggest that the availability of welfare benefits does not cause illegitimate births, female-headed families, and teenage pregnancies.

. . . [M]oral conservatives argue that poverty ought to be addressed primarily by promoting marriage and sexual abstinence for unmarried teenagers. The PRWORA contributes to the institutionalization of their position. It states that the purpose of the TANF program is not only to provide assistance to impoverished families, but also to "end the dependence of needy parents on government benefits by promoting job preparation, work and marriage; [to] prevent and [to] reduce the incidence of out-of-wedlock pregnancies and [to] establish numerical goals for preventing and reducing the incidence of these pregnancies; and [to] encourage the formation and maintenance of two-parent families." None of the previous laws that defined the purpose of ADC or AFDC referred to a governmental interest in the promotion of marriage, the reduction of out-of-wedlock births, and the encouragement of two-parent families. The PRWORA's purpose is so broad that programs designed to reduce out-of-wedlock births and to promote two-parent families may be funded under this law even if they are aimed at both needy and non-needy persons. . . .

In addition to these broadly-aimed measures, the PRWORA imposes strict rules on teen parent TANF recipients themselves. In order to receive benefits, they must attend high school and, if they are not married, they must reside with their parents or legal guardians.

However, the PRWORA also reaches far beyond the relatively small numbers of teen parents on welfare. Under the PRWORA, federal funds are provided to the states in a matching grant system for the purposes of conducting abstinence education programs. These programs are explicitly defined in the PRWORA. They must have, as their sole purpose, the promotion of abstinence: "[T]he term 'abstinence education' means an educational or motivational program which has as its exclusive purpose, teaching the social, psychological, and health gains to be realized by abstaining from sexual activity." They must teach that sex outside of marriage is psychologically "harmful"; that abstaining from sex outside of marriage is "the only certain way to avoid out-of-wedlock pregnancy, sexually transmitted diseases, and other associated health problems"; and that "a mutually faithful monogamous relationship in the context of marriage is the expected standard of human sexual activity." The abstinence education programs are also supposed to be operated "with a focus on those groups which are most likely to bear children out-of-wedlock." Researchers have found that abstinence education programs have had no impact whatsoever on students' sexual behavior. Forty-nine states have nevertheless accepted PRWORA funds for the operation of teenage pregnancy prevention programs and sexual abstinence education programs. . . .

The laws and regulations governing the TANF program's child support enforcement measures, "family cap" provisions, and family planning promotions and the encouragement of relinquishing nonabused poor children for adoption have greatly intensified and expanded the already flourishing sexual regulation dimension of welfare policies. In the early twentieth century, the recipients of mothers' pensions were subjected to intrusive home inspections and moralistic policing; later, single mothers in the ADC and AFDC programs had the "substitute father," "man-in-the-house," and illegitimate children rules imposed upon them. Today's poor single mothers on welfare face even more intense intrusions: they are required to submit to interrogations about their sexual histories, to undergo genetic tests to establish paternity, and to assist the state in collecting support payments from the absent fathers of their children even if they do not want to be dependent upon them and, in many cases, even if they are fleeing from the absent fathers' violent conduct. The social science research suggests that poverty assistance programs can play a key role for domestic violence victims when they engage in the difficult work of leaving a controlling and abusive relationship. Welfare benefits might make all the difference — they might even save the lives of the women and children at risk — and yet the domestic violence dimension of the states' TANF programs has been either insufficiently developed or neglected altogether.

Further, in twenty-three states, TANF households do not receive any additional benefits when a child is born. Sixteen states make provisions for the systematic initiation of family planning promotion for all adult TANF recipients. Three states encourage recipients to relinquish their children for adoption even though the families in question have not necessarily been investigated for child abuse or neglect. The moralistic dimension of these policies clearly has its roots in the bi-partisan consensus which holds that there is a causal relation between irresponsible sexual conduct, out-of-wedlock births, teenage pregnancies, and the decline of the traditional nuclear family on the one hand and [the increase in] poverty on the other.

NOTES AND QUESTIONS

1. During the PRWORA debate, some members of Congress and others argued for a so-called "child exclusion" policy, which is another term for "family cap." Under such a rule, implemented in Wisconsin before the 1996 reform, any children born after a family's benefit level was set were "excluded" from any future benefit calculation. In other words, the birth of a new child would not result in an increase in the benefit level of the family. A requirement of a child exclusion rule did not make it into the federal law, but several states included a version of such a rule in their post-PRWORA state programs. *See* Martha Davis, *The Child Exclusion in a Global Context*, 60 Case W. Res. L. Rev. 4 (2010).

2. Family cap policies have been the subject of litigation around the country. In 1995, a case was brought challenging the family cap provision of New Jersey's AFDC regime. The Third Circuit denied the plaintiffs' claim that the cap violated the Social Security Act itself, the Administrative Procedure Act, and various provisions of the federal Constitution, including due process and equal protection. Citing many of the cases found in Chapter 3, including Dandridge v. Williams and Jefferson v. Hackney, the court held that the state's welfare policy was subject to rational basis review, and that the government had met that test. C.K. v. N.J. Dep't of Health & Human Servs., 92 F.3d 171 (3d Cir. 1996). State constitutional challenges have not been more successful. In Sojourner A. v. New Jersey Department of Human Services, the plaintiff class argued that the state's family cap policy violated the right to privacy and equal protection guarantees in the state constitution. 828 A.2d 306 (N.J. 2003). The Court rejected these claims, holding that "the

State is not required to provide additional cash assistance when a woman chooses to bear a child more than ten months after her family has received welfare benefits." *Id.* at 337.

One of the arguments advanced in support of family cap rules — both in legislatures and as a rational basis for those rules — is that they parallel the economic realities of the working poor, whose wages do not increase with the birth of a new child. What do you think of this argument?

3. TANF and other cash assistance programs are not the only sites of regulation of the private lives of participants in public programs. Chapter 6 presents materials about the Housing Choice Voucher Program ("Section 8"), one of the housing subsidy programs operated by the U.S. Department of Housing and Urban Development (HUD). A participant's voucher can be terminated if she is determined to have violated one of the "family obligations" set forth in the governing federal regulations, found at 24 C.F.R. §962. One of the family obligations is to report any changes to household composition. In what can be considered a modern version of the "man in the house" rule, this obligation can be used to terminate a family based on an "unauthorized occupant" of the household. Some housing authorities (the local agencies that administer HUD programs in a given community) employ investigators to examine allegations of unauthorized occupants. The rationale for these terminations is not to police the private lives of recipients, but instead to monitor the income and assets of a participant family so that the amount of the subsidy can properly reflect its situation. What do you make of this rule and its rationale?

4. According to scholar Rebekah J. Smith, "The racial implications of caps has not gone unnoticed by policymakers; one TANF reauthorization bill included a finding that 'states in which African Americans make up a higher proportion of recipients are statistically more likely to adopt family cap policies.'" *Family Caps in Welfare Reform: Their Coercive Effects and Damaging Consequences,* 29 Harv. J.L. & Gender 151, 179 (2006).

5. States may provide TANF assistance only to those teen parents who comply with additional, specific requirements. Parents under the age of 18 are required to "engage in educational activities directed toward the attainment of a high school diploma or its equivalent; or an alternative educational or training program that has been approved by the State." 42 U.S.C. §608(a)(4)-(5) (2012). This requirement kicks in when the baby turns 12 weeks of age.

* * *

Proponents of welfare reform and, indeed, Congress itself, identified increased rates of marriage among poor men and women as chief among the bill's antidependency tools. States were encouraged to use TANF monies for so-called "marriage promotion" initiatives. A 2002 report on state marriage promotion activities revealed that every state had undertaken some kind of marriage promotion activity, ranging from issuing a proclamation to providing specific financial incentives to TANF recipients to marry. Karen N. Gardiner et al., with The Lewin Group., Inc., *State Policies to Promote Marriage* (2002). Marriage promotion initiatives have been the subject of scathing feminist critique. For example, three leading feminist legal scholars, including Anna Marie Smith whose work is featured *infra*, issued a position paper called "No

Promotion of Marriage in TANF!" that leads off with the following statement of principles:

MARTHA FINEMAN, GWENDOLYN MINK & ANNA MARIE SMITH, *NO PROMOTION OF MARRIAGE IN TANF!: EXECUTIVE SUMMARY*
30 Soc. Just. 126 (2003)

We oppose the welfare marriage promotion initiative because it violates women's rights to shape their own intimate lives, diverts valuable resources, and does nothing to address poverty. The TANF marriage promotion initiative:

1. Puts governmental pressure on women's intimate decisions;
2. Fails to support women's family choices and caregiving work;
3. Discriminates against same-sex couples, single parents, and parents who choose not to marry their partners; and increases the chance that TANF recipients will be exposed to religious proselytizing;
4. Perpetuates the myth that single mothers, especially African-American and Latina women, are to blame for poverty in the United States;
5. Shifts needed resources away from women's economic empowerment and codifies the specious claim that marriage itself can solve poverty;
6. Exacerbates the risks and problems of domestic violence;
7. Wastes taxpayers' money on conservative anti-feminist, anti-choice, and anti-lesbian-and-gay organizations that promote marriage.

Poor single mothers should not be subjected to moralistic propaganda in exchange for their benefits.

We oppose this measure in solidarity with the poor, in support of poor single mothers, and in a feminist, anti-racist and pro-lesbian-and-gay rights spirit.

* * *

While poor people's lower rates of marriage have been "explained" by some policymakers as the result of irresponsibility or promiscuity, social science poverty researchers Kathryn Edin and Joanna M. Reed published an analysis of poor people's low rates of marriage in 2005 that states:

> Social barriers to marriage include marital attitudes, childbearing attitudes, norms about the standard of living required for marriage, relationship quality, an aversion to divorce, and the tendency of both men and women to bring children from previous partners to the new relationship. The economic barriers that, at least in theory, affect the marriage rates of the poor include low earnings and employment among unskilled men, increasing employment among unskilled women, and the welfare state, which imposes a significant "tax" on marriage for low-income populations.

Kathryn Edin & Joanna M. Reed, *Why Don't They Just Get Married? Barriers to Marriage Among the Disadvantaged*, 15 Future of Child. 117 (2005). In their book *Promises I Can Keep*, Kathryn Edin and Maria Kefalas report on detailed interviews with poor women about marriage. Their findings indicate that some poor women eschew or delay marriage out of a reverence for the institution and a belief that they cannot uphold its values.

KATHRYN EDIN & MARIA KEFALAS, *PROMISES I CAN KEEP: WHY POOR WOMEN PUT MOTHERHOOD BEFORE MARRIAGE* (2005)

We tell the story of Deena Vallas, who has had one nonmarital birth and is about to have another. She's in a stable relationship with the unborn child's father, a steady worker in a legitimate job who's off drugs, doesn't beat her or cheat on her, and eagerly plays daddy to her son, a child from a prior relationship. Yet there's no marriage. Is that a sign that marriage has no meaning in poor neighborhoods like hers? No. Her story doesn't indicate a disinterest in marriage; to the contrary, she believes her reluctance shows her deep reverence for marriage. So why does she feel she must avoid marriage for now?

Stories like Deena's show that the retreat from marriage among the poor flows out of a radical redefinition of what marriage means. In the 1950s childrearing was the primary function of marriage, but, as we show, these days the poor see its function very differently. A steady job and the ability to pay the rent on an apartment no longer automatically render a man marriageable. We investigate exactly what does.

Poor women often say they don't want to marry until they are "set" economically and established in a career. A young mother often fears marriage will mean a loss of control—she believes that saying "I do" will suddenly transform her man into an authoritarian head of the house who insists on making all the decisions, who thinks that he "owns" her. Having her own earnings and assets buys her some "say-so" power and some freedom from a man's attempts to control her behavior. After all, she insists, a woman with money of her own can credibly threaten to leave and take the children with her if he gets too far out of line. But this insistence on economic independence also reflects a much deeper fear: no matter how strong the relationship, somehow the marriage will go bad. Women who rely on a man's earnings, these mothers warn, are setting themselves up to be left with nothing if the relationship ends.

So does marriage merely represent a list of financial achievements? Not at all. The poor women we talked to insist it means lifelong commitment. In a surprising reversal of the middle-class norm, they believe it is better to have children outside of marriage than to marry unwisely only to get divorced later. One might dismiss these poor mothers' marriage aspirations as deep cynicism, candy-coated for social science researchers, yet demographers project that more than seven in ten will marry someone eventually. What moral code underlies the statement of one mother who said, "I don't believe in divorce—that's why none of the women in my family are married"? And what does it take to convince a young mother that her relationship is safe enough from the threat of divorce to risk marriage?

Dominique Watkins' story illustrates why poor young mothers seldom view an out-of-wedlock birth as a mark of personal failure, but instead see it as an act of valor. [Our research] reveals our mothers' remarkable confidence in their ability to parent their children well and describes the standards they hold themselves to. As we explain, it is possible for a poor woman to judge her mothering a success even when her child fails in school, gets pregnant as a teen, becomes addicted to drugs, or ends up in juvenile detention. The women whose stories we share believe the central tenet of good mothering can be summed up in two words — being there. This unique definition of good parenting allows mothers to take great pride in having enough Pampers to diaper an infant, in potty training a two-year-old and teaching her to eat with a spoon, in getting a grade-schooler to and from school safely, in satisfying the ravenous appetite of a growing teenager, and in keeping the light on to welcome a prodigal adolescent back home.

. . . [We also tell the story of] Millie Acevedo, who, like many of her friends and neighbors, believes that having children young is a normal part of life, though she admits she and Carlos got started a year or two earlier than they should have. Millie's story helps to resolve a troubling contradiction raised in our earlier account: If the poor hold marriage to such a high standard, why don't they do the same for childbearing? Shouldn't they audition their male partners even more carefully for the father role than they do for the husband role? Millie's experiences show why the standards for prospective fathers appear to be so low. The answer is tangled up in these young women's initial high hopes regarding the men in their lives, and the supreme confidence they have in their ability to rise to the challenge of motherhood. The key to the mystery lies not only in what mothers believe they can do for their children, but in what they hope their children will do for them.

Through the tales of mothers like Millie we paint a portrait of the lives of these young women before pregnancy, a portrait that details the extreme loneliness, the struggles with parents and peers, the wild behavior, the depression and despair, the school failure, the drugs, and the general sense that life has spun completely out of control. Into this void comes a pregnancy and then a baby, bringing the purpose, the validation, the companionship, and the order that young women feel have been so sorely lacking. In some profound sense, these young women believe, a baby has the power to solve everything.

The redemptive stories our mothers tell speak to the primacy of the mothering role, how it can become virtually the only source of identity and meaning in a young woman's life. There is an odd logic to the statements mothers made when we asked them to imagine life without children: "I'd be dead or in jail," "I'd still be out partying," "I'd be messed up on drugs," or "I'd be nowhere at all." These mothers, we discovered, almost never see children as bringing them hardship; instead, they manage to credit virtually every bit of good in their lives to the fact they have children — they believe motherhood has "saved" them.

* * *

Sexual abstinence is another policy preference expressed in PRWORA, which provided $50 million per year for the federal Abstinence Education Program. These funds are available for programs that teach very specific messages about sexuality and family. The statute, codified at 42 U.S.C. § 710 (2012), provides funding for a state to create an "abstinence education" program that:

(A) has as its exclusive purpose, teaching the social, psychological, and health gains to be realized by abstaining from sexual activity;
(B) teaches abstinence from sexual activity outside marriage as the expected standard for all school age children;
(C) teaches that abstinence from sexual activity is the only certain way to avoid out-of-wedlock pregnancy, sexually transmitted diseases, and other associated health problems;

(D) teaches that a mutually faithful monogamous relationship in context of marriage is the expected standard of human sexual activity;

(E) teaches that sexual activity outside of the context of marriage is likely to have harmful psychological and physical effects;

(F) teaches that bearing children out-of-wedlock is likely to have harmful consequences for the child, the child's parents, and society;

(G) teaches young people how to reject sexual advances and how alcohol and drug use increases vulnerability to sexual advances; and

(H) teaches the importance of attaining self-sufficiency before engaging in sexual activity.

* * *

Welfare reform embodies the mainstream value that people should support themselves and their dependents with the fruits of wage labor. A companion value, perhaps even less controversial, is that parents should support their children financially; public support should be the last resort. TANF thus also directs attention to noncustodial parents who *should* be supporting those children, and to child support enforcement. The statute requires state TANF programs to sanction participants who fail to "cooperate" with state child support enforcement mechanisms:

If the agency responsible for administering the State plan . . . determines that an individual is not cooperating with the State in establishing paternity or in establishing, modifying, or enforcing a support order with respect to a child of the individual, and the individual does not qualify for any good cause or other exception . . . then the State

(A) shall deduct from the assistance that would otherwise be provided to the family of the individual under the State program funded under this part an amount equal to not less than 25 percent of the amount of such assistance; and

(B) may deny the family any assistance under the State program.

42 U.S.C. § 608(a)(2) (2012).

ANNA MARIE SMITH, *THE SEXUAL REGULATION DIMENSION OF CONTEMPORARY WELFARE LAW: A FIFTY STATE OVERVIEW*
8 Mich. J. Gender & L. 121 (2002)

Many policy experts — feminists and non-feminists alike — would agree with the following abstract principle: where a custodial parent and his/her children have become poor because they have been abandoned by a relatively prosperous second parent who had voluntarily agreed to share child rearing costs, the absent parent should make a good faith effort to support the children in question until they reach the age of majority. The actual implementation of concrete child support enforcement policies in the context of welfare programs, however, raises serious difficulties. What measures should the state be able to take to identify the absent biological father when he has not already acknowledged paternity and when the mother does not want to cooperate in paternity identification and child support enforcement measures? Should the state be able to pressure a poor single mother to cooperate by making her cooperation a condition of eligibility for a public good that she desperately needs, such as a poverty assistance benefit? . . .

Contemporary welfare laws and regulations dictate that any man who is the biological father of a child in the AFDC/TANF program is obliged to pay support for that child, regardless of the custodial mother's views on the matter, the nature of the father's relationship with the child and the custodial mother, his income, and his employment status. Where poverty assistance might be treated as a responsibility that ought to be borne collectively by society as a whole, it is now regarded as a private familial obligation that is imposed—by virtue of mere biological ties—upon absent fathers. Further, the dominant bipartisan approach to welfare policy treats child support payments not as one small element within a comprehensive ensemble of anti-poverty policies that would bring about structural economic transformation, job creation, and the redistribution of wealth, but as a "silver bullet." Paternity identification and child support enforcement measures are widely regarded in the United States today as the single most important initiative that we can take to address poverty. . . .

Under the current system, the custodial parent must also assign his/her right to the support payments to the state. Because the support payments are assigned to the states, and typically allow the custodial parents to receive no part of the payments themselves or only a small portion—often as little as fifty dollars—the state enjoys the greatest benefit from the successful collection of child support as it recoups welfare expenditures. The child support enforcement system is therefore using the private funds of absent parents to replace public expenditures in poverty programs; it is, in short, diminishing public responsibility and expanding private responsibilities that are assessed according to traditional patriarchal norms. . . .

The PRWORA orders the states to make maternal cooperation a condition of welfare eligibility, to assess each single mother's cooperation, to punish those women who do not appear to be doing all that they can to identify the absent fathers, and to assist in the collection of support from them by reducing or eliminating their benefits. It also combines incentives—bonuses are offered to the states that have good records of welfare case-related child support payment collection—with sanctions. Any state that fails to enforce the paternity identification and child support enforcement cooperation requirement will lose up to five percent of its total block grant.

. . . The vast majority of TANF families that are affected by its invasive procedures do not subsequently enjoy any improvement in their standard of living, and the regime absolutely fails to address the underlying causes of poverty among the custodial and absent parents alike. . . .

NOTES AND QUESTIONS

1. Consider the impact on TANF's child support enforcement mechanisms of disproportionate rates of incarceration among low-income men and men of color. According to a recent survey, the number of children of incarcerated parents in 2007 was 1.7 million, and represented an 80 percent increase between 1991 and 2007. An additional 7.5 million children have a parent on probation or parole, which affects his or her employability. How, if at all, should incarceration affect child support obligations? Should arrears continue to accrue during a period of incarceration? For citations to these statistics and a discussion of states' policy approaches to this question, see

Ann Cammett, *Deadbeats, Deadbrokes, and Prisoners*, 18 Geo. J. Poverty L. & Pol'y 127 (2011). For more information and discussion on the relationship between poverty and the criminal justice system, see Chapter 9.

2. One scholar has noted that the legislative rationale for child support enforcement statutes does not reflect the economic realities of low-income parents who fail to make payments:

> Congress' assumptions in designing the child support enforcement statutes were based on studies indicating that most unwed fathers could pay some financial support for their children, and that their incomes tend to "rise relatively rapidly" within the few years after paternity is established. However, this model does not reflect the large number of noncustodial parents — particularly in families receiving welfare benefits — who are as poor as the custodial parents and have the same problems getting and keeping jobs. . . . In a 2002 report, HHS's Office of the Inspector General concluded that the delinquency of 60 percent of low-income non-payors is attributable to income levels, employment history, education levels, and rate of institutionalization rather than unwillingness to pay.

Elizabeth G. Patterson, *Civil Contempt and the Indigent Child Support Obligor: The Silent Return of Debtor's Prison*, 18 Cornell J.L. & Pub. Pol'y 95 (2008).

3. In addition to being subject to wage garnishment and other civil remedies to satisfy child support obligations, noncustodial parents can be found in contempt — and jailed — for arrears owed to custodial parents or the state. As we will see in Chapter 10, the Supreme Court has held that "[t]he Fourteenth Amendment's Due Process Clause does not *automatically* require the State to provide counsel at civil contempt proceedings to an indigent noncustodial parent who is subject to a child support order, even if that individual faces incarceration." Turner v. Rogers, 131 S. Ct. 2507, 2510 (2011).

Professor Tonya Brito has argued that civil incarceration of low-income parents who fail to meet child support obligations is at odds with the broader goals of the child support system:

> Few would imagine that the child support system views as consistent with its mission the practice of repeated civil incarcerations of fathers like Michael Turner [the plaintiff in *Turner v. Rogers*], whose indigence prevents them from paying their crushing child support debts. Indeed, Turner's jail terms undoubtedly do far more to hinder his efforts to find stable employment than they do to provide economic security to his children. However, across the United States, destitute noncustodial parents are incarcerated for failing to meet child support obligations they have no means to pay. The end result is that indigent child support debtors fill jails across the country.

Tonya L. Brito, *Fathers Behind Bars: Rethinking Child Support Policy Toward Low-Income Noncustodial Fathers and Their Families*, 15 J. Gender Race & Just. 617, 618-619 (2012).

* * *

Welfare policy has generally included some special considerations for domestic violence survivors, typically in the form of waivers of some of requirements (e.g., work participation and/or custodial parent notification). These waivers survived, but were narrowed, under TANF. First, PRWORA gave states the choice of whether or not to include domestic violence waivers in their TANF programs. Second, if elected, the waiver programs can only be applied where there has been a "determination of good cause" and the program requirements will make it "more difficult for individuals receiving [TANF] assistance . . . to escape domestic violence or unfairly penalize such individuals who are or have been victimized by such violence, or individuals who are at risk of further domestic violence." 42 U.S.C. §602(a)(7) (2012). In 2010, the National Resource Center on Domestic Violence and Legal Momentum released a national survey they conducted of 600 domestic violence survivors in the TANF program. Among the findings was that "the requirement to 'prove' the violence" is a "significant barrier."

> Respondents describe TANF staff requiring particular types of documentation, such as hospital records, even if the victim reports she's not been to a hospital. Victims are also asked to produce paperwork that they left behind when escaping violence. Some TANF workers determine that a domestic violence shelter is not a "proper address," thereby making it more difficult for victims to access benefits after they've sought the safety of a shelter. Requests for documentation may also come with an attitude of skepticism and ignorance — for example, one respondent wrote that workers often assume a victim in shelter does not need family violence protections because she's "safe" and those who've yet to leave are endangering themselves and therefore not in need of a waiver or other family violence specific response. . . .
>
> [Additionally,] the pressures on victims to cooperate with enforcement of child support can be great. One respondent reported that, "workers constantly harass victims to establish support, even when it will expose them and their children to mortal danger." Another respondent wrote that she has "women in tears, BEG-GING that they not be forced to ask for child support and told that there is no choice." And another wrote "in our area we have had a worker require a woman to give the name of her rapist to pursue child support."

Timothy Casey et al., Legal Momentum & Nat'l Res. Ctr. on Domestic Violence, *Not Enough: What TANF Offers Family Violence Victims* 7, 14-15 (2010).

For more information about TANF's family violence provisions, see Joan Meier, *Domestic Violence, Character, and Social Change in the Welfare Reform Debate,* 19 Law & Pol'y 205 (1997).

* * *

Domestic violence crosses socioeconomic lines, of course, but low-income women are more likely to be abused. *See, e.g.,* Callie Marie Rennison & Sarah Welchans, Dep't of Justice, NCJ 178247, *Intimate Partner Violence* (2000). As a 2011 law review article explains, "Domestic violence exacerbates variables of poverty. It often forces a choice of staying in an abusive relationship or risking homelessness. Women are often coerced to return to their abusers as a result of economic reality. . . ." Rachel J. Gallagher, *Welfare Reform's Inadequate Implementation of the Family Violence Option: Exploring the Dual Oppression of Poor Domestic Violence Victims,* 19 J. Gender, Soc. Pol'y & L. 987 (2011). Not surprisingly perhaps, this means that professional women are more likely to leave, and leave sooner, a violent relationship than less well-off women. Poverty can operate as both a cause and a consequence. Poverty can cause women to stay with violent men. It can also be a consequence of domestic violence: "[M]any women become impoverished precisely because they had to leave an abusive partner, and then turn to poverty assistance programs such as TANF for economic support." Anna Marie Smith, *The Sexual Regulation Dimension of Contemporary Welfare Law: A Fifty State Overview, supra,* p. 220.

Sexuality and living arrangements are not the only arenas in which welfare recipients are subject to government scrutiny. The provision of public money has been the rationale for intrusion into many areas of private life, and into recipients' actual physical homes as well. These subjects are covered in some detail in Chapter 9, which includes Wyman v. James, a 1971 case in which the U.S. Supreme Court upheld a mandatory home visit by a case worker as a condition of AFDC receipt against a Fourth Amendment challenge, and Lebron v. Wilkins, a 2011 Florida case striking down a Florida TANF drug testing regime against a Fourth Amendment challenge. In January 2013, the Kansas legislature undertook debate on a proposal to submit TANF participants and UI recipients to drug testing. Under the proposal, a positive test would result in a loss of benefits pending completion of drug treatment and job-training programs. Subsequent positive tests would result in increasingly long suspensions. Proponents of the measure say its purposes are to prevent taxpayer money from being spent on illegal drugs, and to get more people into drug treatment and job readiness programs. A representative from Independence, Kansas, told the media, "This is not meant to be punitive in any way. . . . This is to identify people with substance abuse problems and get them the help and job skills they need to get out and be productive in the job market." *See* Brett D. Wistrom, *Kansas Legislature to Debate Drug Testing Recipients of Welfare, Unemployment Benefits,* The Wichita Eagle (Jan. 19, 2013), http://www.kansas.com/2013/01/19/v-print/2643029/kansas-legislature-to-debate-drug.html. Notably, Kansas is one of the states that shortened the federal lifetime limit of 60 months of TANF receipt to 48 months. The average Kansas TANF benefit is $280 per month. According to the National Conference of State Legislatures (NCSL), seven states have passed some form of drug test requirement for public benefits recipients. As of 2012, new proposals brought the number of states considering such measures to 28. Some proposals reach from TANF into Medicaid and/or SNAP. A comprehensive list of the laws and proposals can be found at the NCSL website, http://www.ncsl.org/issues-research/human-services/drug-testing-and-public-assistance.aspx.

Other proposals intrude on less important, but nevertheless extant, autonomous choices of welfare recipients. Legislators in North Carolina are considering a ban on welfare recipients (and those who are in bankruptcy) from buying lottery tickets; the proposal would also prohibit vendors from knowingly selling tickets to those consumers.

NOTES AND QUESTIONS

1. What behavioral or other restrictions do you think should be placed on welfare recipients? What analogous restrictions are placed on users/recipients of other government programs?

4. Did It Work?

From the moment Congress passed and President Clinton signed PRWORA, it and TANF have been the subject of extensive social scientific study. The statute itself required the Secretary of Health and Human Services to "conduct research" on the costs and benefits of TANF, and on the effects of various state TANF programs on "welfare dependency, illegitimacy, teen pregnancy, employment rates, child well-being, and any other area the Secretary deems appropriate." 42 U.S.C. § 613(a) (2012). Three universities have received grants from the federal government to be designated official "poverty research centers": the University of Wisconsin–Madison, the University of California–Davis, and Stanford University. Each of these institutions sponsors research on poverty and inequality in the United States, including about the effects of welfare reform and other important policy developments. Study of welfare policy reform has blossomed at many other university and research institutions in the wake of the 1996 statute.

One of the most important subjects that these and other researchers investigate is where the women formerly on welfare are now. It is relatively easy to quantify the numbers of people receiving welfare, and that number has plainly plummeted. It is somewhat harder to speak with confidence about the employment and/or economic well-being of those who left. Harder still is the task of isolating variables that account for those numbers. As the next materials show, a question of intense—and often ideological—debate exists about whether some of the catastrophic predictions that liberals made about PRWORA failed to come true because of the Act's soundness or because of contemporaneous strong economic conditions. This debate has changed, but become no less intense, as the economic boom of the late 1990s and early 2000s morphed into economic recession and the global economic crisis of the late 2000s. A comprehensive summary of those debates is beyond the scope of this book—and is more the subject of social science than of law. The academic study is relevant to lawyers, however, as lawmakers are subjected to data and reports from all sides as they are urged to maintain or modify some of PRWORA's features.

We start with a 2003 white paper from the conservative Heritage Foundation. Written before the economic crisis of 2007-2008, this paper heralds the "success" of welfare reform.

ROBERT RECTOR & PATRICK F. FAGAN, *THE CONTINUING GOOD NEWS ABOUT WELFARE REFORM* (HERITAGE FOUND. BACKGROUNDER NO. 1620, 2003)

Poverty has dropped substantially. Although liberals predicted that welfare reform would push an additional 2.6 million persons into poverty, 3.5 million fewer people live in poverty today than in 1995, according to Census Bureau figures.

Some 2.9 million fewer children live in poverty today than in 1995.

Decreases in poverty have been greatest among black children. In fact, the poverty rate for black children has fallen to the lowest point in U.S. history. There are 1.2 million fewer black children in poverty today than there were in the mid-1990s.

The poverty rate of children living with single mothers is at the lowest point in U.S. history, having fallen substantially since the onset of welfare reform.

The poverty rate of black children and children in single mother families has continued to fall even during the current recession. Historically, poverty among these groups has risen sharply during recessions; the continuing decline of child poverty among black and single-mother families is an unprecedented departure from past poverty trends.

Hunger among children has been cut roughly in half. According to the U.S. Department of Agriculture, in 1995, before welfare reform was enacted, 1.3 percent of children experienced hunger; by 2001, the number had fallen to 0.6 percent.

The AFDC/TANF caseload has been more than cut in half. The decreases in welfare have been greatest among disadvantaged groups with the greatest propensity for long-term intergenerational dependence: for example, younger never-married mothers with young children.

Employment of single mothers has increased greatly. The largest increases in employment have been among the most disadvantaged mothers with the greatest barriers to obtaining work. Employment of young single mothers (ages 18 to 24) has nearly doubled. Employment of single mothers who are high-school dropouts has risen by two-thirds.

The explosive growth of out-of-wedlock childbearing has come to a virtual halt. Since the beginning of the War on Poverty, the share of births that are outside marriage had increased relentlessly at nearly one percentage point per year. Overall, the percentage of births that were out-of-wedlock rose from 7.7 in 1965 to an astonishing 32.6 percent in 1994. However, since welfare reform, the growth in illegitimacy has slowed to a near halt. The out-of-wedlock birth rate has remained almost flat for the past five years, and among blacks it has actually dropped.

Marriage has been strengthened. The share of children living in single-mother families has fallen, and the share living in married-couple families has increased, especially among black families. Some incorrectly attribute these positive trends to the strong economy in the late 1990s. Although a strong economy contributed to some of these trends, most of the positive changes greatly exceed shifts that occurred during prior economic expansions. The difference is due to welfare reform. A recent analysis by former Congressional Budget Office Director June O'Neill finds that welfare reform has been responsible for three-quarters of the increase in employment of single mothers and three-quarters of the drop in welfare caseload. By contrast, good economic conditions were responsible for only one-quarter of the changes in these variables. The increase in employment of single mothers, in turn, is a major factor behind the drop in child poverty.

* * *

By contrast, in 2012, the liberal Center on Budget and Policy Priorities reported that TANF was failing the poor during the recession.

LIZ SCHOTT, CTR. ON BUDGET & POL'Y PRIORITIES, *POLICY BASICS: AN INTRODUCTION TO TANF* (2012)

TANF's early years witnessed unprecedented declines in the number of families receiving cash assistance — and unprecedented *increases* in the share of single mothers working, especially those with less than a high school education. But since then, as the economy has weakened, nearly all of the employment gains have disappeared, and TANF caseloads have responded only modestly to increased need during the deep economic downturn that started in 2007.

The national TANF caseload has declined by 60 percent over the last 16 years, even as poverty and deep poverty (i.e., income below half the poverty line) have worsened. The poverty rate among families fell in the late 1990s, when the economy was booming and unemployment was extremely low, but started rising in 2000 and now exceeds its 1996 level. The increase in deep poverty has been especially large: the number of families in deep poverty rose by 13 percent between 1996 and 2009, from 2.7 million to 3 million.

Because TANF reaches so many fewer families than AFDC did, it provides substantially less protection against poverty and deep poverty. In 1996, 68 families received TANF for every 100 families in poverty; in 2011, only 27 families received TANF for every 100 families in poverty.

While employment rates improved significantly among single mothers in TANF's early years, they started declining more than a decade ago. The share of never-married mothers with a high school education or less who were employed jumped from 51 percent in 1992 to a high of 76 percent in 2000, but by 2011, it had fallen back to 54 percent, the same level as in 1997. And, although the sharp improvement in employment among single mothers in the 1990s is often attributed to welfare reform, research has shown that other factors — especially a very strong labor market (with unemployment as low as 4 percent) and the Earned Income Tax Credit (EITC) — were far more important.

In addition, while some of the families that left the TANF rolls went to work, many others left because they were terminated due to time limits or sanctions for failing to comply with program requirements. Research has shown that these families often have barriers to employment that can impede their ability to meet the state's expectations, such as: mental and physical impairments; substance abuse; domestic violence; low literacy or skill levels; learning disabilities; having a child with a disability; and problems with housing, child care, or transportation. TANF has, for the most part, failed this group of families — many of whom have become disconnected from both work and welfare — by providing them with neither a reliable safety net nor employment assistance that adequately addresses their employment barriers.

TANF's response to the recession demonstrated just how weak a safety net it has become. Caseloads rose by just 16 percent before peaking in December 2010, while the number of unemployed grew by 88 percent during the same time period. TANF caseloads then fell by 5 percent over the course of 2011 even though unemployment remained at or above 8.5 percent.

* * *

In a 2012 book, Peter Edelman argues that any "success" attributed to welfare reform in fact should be chalked up to strong economic growth, and that the alarming growth in food stamp usage and economic hardship during the recession proves that economic conditions, not PRWORA, deserve credit for declining poverty in the late 1990s. *See* Peter Edelman, *So Rich, So Poor: Why It's So Hard to End Poverty in America* (2012). Even in 2013, the Heritage Foundation was encouraging the expansion of the reform spirit that had created PRWORA into other (all) features of the safety net.

ROBERT RECTOR & JENNIFER A. MARSHALL, THE HERITAGE FOUND., *THE UNFINISHED WORK OF WELFARE REFORM* (2013)

Among the public-policy achievements of the past two decades, welfare reform may simultaneously be the best known and least understood. It is now remembered as a bipartisan triumph that ended "welfare as we know it," to use President Clinton's phrase, transforming the character of federal anti-poverty policy. The true history, however, is less august: The struggle to enact welfare reform was in fact bitter and arduous, and the policy changes that finally became law were but a first step toward a real transformation of the system.

The lip service that welfare reform today receives from all sides of our politics obscures how sharply the issue divided the left and right. New York Democratic senator Daniel Patrick Moynihan called the 1996 reform law a "brutal act of social policy" and a "disgrace" that would dog proponents "to their graves." Marian Wright Edelman, president of the Children's Defense Fund (a liberal advocacy group), said welfare reform would "leave a moral blot on [Bill Clinton's] presidency and on our nation that will never be forgotten." Her husband, poverty-law specialist Peter Edelman, resigned his post as an assistant secretary at the Department of Health and Human Services in protest of the law.

Conservatives heralded the change with an equal and opposite fervor. They believed that the reform would help restrain welfare spending, but they also felt the law served a crucial social purpose — that its work requirement offered a hand up rather than a handout to people in need, and thus held the key to reducing welfare-state dependency.

The immediate results clearly vindicated the conservative hypothesis about "workfare," as droves of former (and potential future) welfare dependents became productive employees in the private economy. So successful was the policy overhaul, in fact, that many conservatives concluded that their work on welfare was finished. But the reactions of both sides were overwrought: Liberals' dire predictions that millions more Americans would fall into poverty and that social dysfunction would increase proved mistaken; conservative workfare, meanwhile, has become the victim of its own success.

Because the reform law was a breakthrough, many saw it as a terminus rather than as the mere beginning of a long-term effort to transform the welfare state. And a massive, decades-long overhaul is what the welfare state desperately needs. For all the hype about the 1996 law, it dramatically reformed only one of nearly 80 federal means-tested programs providing aid to the poor. The reform replaced the largest cash-welfare program, Aid to Families with Dependent Children (AFDC), with a new program, Temporary Assistance for Needy Families (TANF), which included work requirements and a time limit on aid — all funded through block grants to states. But to put that achievement in perspective, in fiscal year 2011, federal spending on TANF was $17.1 billion — a mere 2.4% of the $717 billion the federal government spent on all means-tested welfare programs.

And while conservatives believed the '96 law would bring welfare spending under control, it in fact barely paused the overall growth of that spending. TANF spending has remained relatively flat since 1996, but overall means-tested spending has nearly doubled. By 2008, such means-tested welfare spending had risen to 5% of gross domestic product, up from an average of 4.4% in the 1990s when TANF was created. Since the beginning of the War on Poverty in the mid-1960s, means-tested spending as a share of GDP has increased, on average, between one-half a percentage point and a full percentage point per decade. All evidence indicates that this trend will continue, with welfare spending as a share of GDP hovering around 6% in the decade ahead. These numbers demonstrate that the 1996 reform was far too narrow to slow the overall growth of the welfare system. . . .

BUILDING ON WELFARE REFORM

Of the nearly 80 federal means-tested aid programs, only AFDC was significantly reformed in the '90s; none has been touched since. And, as noted above, even the reform that replaced AFDC with TANF was weaker and more limited than is generally understood. Half of able-bodied TANF recipients are typically idle on the rolls, collecting a check without performing any work activity. And the leniency and limited scope of the 1996 welfare reform has meant that total means-tested spending and overall dependence on government have continued to rise steadily in the post-reform period. Even worse, marriage in low-income communities has continued to erode, boosting dependence, poverty, and other social ills. Welfare reform should thus be extended by pursuing three goals: extending workfare, controlling welfare spending, and strengthening marriage.

First and foremost, work requirements should be established throughout the welfare system. There is no reason why only TANF should have a work requirement while other major welfare programs are treated like old-style entitlements. The food-stamp program and federal housing programs, for instance, could easily be reformed along the same lines by setting work as a condition of receiving benefits.

Workfare is particularly needed in the food-stamp program, the second most costly means-tested aid program. Food-stamp spending has exploded in recent years, from $19.8 billion in 2000 to $84.6 billion in 2011. Part of that growth was caused by the recession, but there is no evidence that spending discipline will return as the economy recovers: Under President Obama's most recent budget proposal, food-stamp spending will remain well above historic norms for the foreseeable future. The food-stamp program today discourages work, rewards idleness, and promotes long-term dependency in the way that AFDC once did; able-bodied food-stamp recipients should thus be required to work, prepare for work, or at least look for a job as a condition of receiving taxpayer aid. These work-activation requirements should be phased in gradually as the economy improves.

Second, the future growth of means-tested welfare spending should be limited. In fiscal year 2011, total federal and state spending on the roughly 80 means-tested federal welfare programs reached $927 billion. More than 100 million people, or a third of the U.S. population, received aid from at least one of these programs (Social Security and Medicare are not included in these figures). Average benefits amounted to roughly $9,000 per recipient. If converted to cash, means-tested welfare spending would be more than sufficient to bring the income of every American in the least affluent third of the population up to 200% of the federal poverty level—roughly $44,000 per year for a family of four. . . .

To get control of this runaway spending, Congress should establish a cap on future aggregate welfare expenditures. It is critical that Americans understand the full price tag of the welfare state, and that policymakers treat some 80 means-tested programs as one system in need of massive reform. Liberals dominate the debate over welfare spending when each program is discussed in isolation without reference to the entire welfare state's size and scope — a trick that allows for vast understatement of the broader problem. . . .

Finally, welfare reformers must seek ways to strengthen marriage among lower-income Americans. This is the most difficult of the goals that must guide the continuing work of welfare reform, but it is also the most important. Married parents are easily the most effective insurance against child poverty, but increasing the rates of married childbearing has never seriously been considered as a tactic in the War on Poverty.

The connection between unwed childbearing on one hand and poverty and welfare dependence on the other is dramatic. A child born and raised outside of marriage is six times more likely to experience poverty than one who is born and raised by married parents in an intact family. Roughly three-quarters of welfare assistance to low-income families with children goes to single-parent families. The medical expenses associated with most non-marital births are currently paid for by taxpayers through the Medicaid system, and a wide variety of welfare assistance will continue to be given to both the mother and the child for the first two decades of the child's life. . . .

To combat poverty and dependence, it is vital to strengthen marriage. There is no easy public-policy path toward this goal, only modest steps to make a modest difference. But one plausible proposal would be to reduce the penalties against marriage in the welfare system. Currently, because benefits are reduced as a family's income rises, our welfare programs create disincentives to marriage. A mother will receive far more from welfare if she is single than if she has an employed husband in the home. For many low-income couples, marriage means a reduction in government assistance and an overall decline in the couple's joint income. The welfare system should be overhauled to reduce such counterproductive incentives.

A public-information campaign about the benefits of marriage could also help. To strengthen marriage, it is vital that at-risk populations gain a clear, factual understanding of the advantages marriage confers and the costs and consequences of non-marital childbearing. To develop this understanding, government and key institutions of civil society should establish a broad education campaign in low-income areas. This campaign should be similar to current efforts to convince young Americans of the importance of staying in school or to inform the public about the health risks of smoking. While the costs of such an effort would be small, its impact could be considerable. . . .

NOTES AND QUESTIONS

1. How would you measure the success or failure of welfare reform? What data would you seek and what barriers to its collection would you anticipate? How would you revise PRWORA? Would your proposals depend on accurate data, or are there other bases for public policy in this area? What are they?
2. Poverty lawyers and other advocates have continued the fight for economic justice and sound antipoverty policy in the courts and elsewhere. States' implementation of TANF has been the subject of considerable litigation

around the nation. One well-known example is the New York class action case Reynolds v. Giuliani, which attacked so-called "diversion" tactics of New York's welfare agencies. No. 98 Civ. 8877(WHP), 2005 WL 3428213 (S.D.N.Y. Dec. 14, 2005). The plaintiff class, composed of "all New York City residents who have sought, are seeking or will seek to apply for food stamps, Medicaid or cash assistance [i.e. TANF] at the City's job centers," argued that the agencies' policies and practices had wrongfully denied eligible people access to these benefits. Reynolds v. Giuliani, 506 F.3d 183, 186 (2d Cir. 2007). A final judgment for plaintiffs was entered in 2005, which included a permanent injunction requiring that the City:

> (a) Provide expedited food stamp service to class members eligible for expedited processing of their food stamp application within seven (7) days after the date of the application . . .
> (e) Provide class members with adequate and timely notice of decisions on eligibility for cash assistance (including immediate needs cash grants), food stamps (including expedited food stamps), and Medicaid applications by correctly completing the applicable forms . . .
> (f) Provide class members with accurate information concerning eligibility for cash assistance, food stamps or Medicaid in relation to a withdrawal from the cash assistance, food stamp or Medicaid programs;
> (g) Provide expedited food stamp service to class members eligible for expedited processing of their food stamp applications within five (5) days of the date of application . . . and
> (h) Provide immediate needs grants on the same day of application to eligible class members.

Reynolds, 2005 WL 3428213, at *1.[3] The Legal Aid Society of New York estimates the number of persons affected by this injunction to be approximately 188,000 people annually — that is, the number of people who file applications for Family Assistance and Safety Net Assistance in New York City. See Right to Receive Expedited Food Stamps and Emergency Cash Assistance, Legal Aid Soc'y, http://www.legal-aid.org/en/lawreform/lawreform/civillawreformunit/activecases/publicbenefits/reynoldsvgiuliani.aspx?vm=r. Statistics on public assistance programs in New York City suggest that this estimate may be conservative. See N.Y. State Office of Temp. and Disability Assistance, 2012 Statistical Report on the Operations of New York State Public Assistance Programs 12 (2012), available at http://otda.ny.gov/resources/legislative-report/2012-Legislative-Report.pdf (reporting that a combined total of 260,088 Family Assistance and Safety Net Assistance applications were approved from June 2011 to June 2012).

Information about this landmark case and other post-PRWORA welfare rights litigation can be found on the National Center for Law & Economic Justice's website, www.nclej.org. Another good source for information and resources about nationwide antipoverty advocacy efforts, both in the form of litigation and nonlitigation, is the Sargent Shriver National Center on Poverty Law's website, www.povertylaw.org.

---

3. On appeal, the Second Circuit reversed the injunction against the state defendants. Reynolds, 506 F.3d at 199. However, because the City withdrew its appeal, the portion of the injunction quoted here was left undisturbed. Id. at 186-187.

C. SUPPLEMENTAL SECURITY INCOME — "WELFARE" FOR THE ELDERLY, BLIND, AND DISABLED

TANF is the best-known cash assistance program, but another of the "welfare" (as opposed to insurance) programs originating with the Social Security Act in 1935 remains a vitally important part of the safety net for America's poor: Supplemental Security Income (SSI). SSI is a means-tested program for low-income people in three categories: elderly (over age 65), blind, or disabled. SSI is the current incarnation of what began as Title I of the original Social Security Act. Known then as Old-Age Assistance (OAA), at its origin this program provided cash assistance to low-income *seniors* regardless of labor force participation.

Like the other welfare program in the original Social Security Act, OAA was a federal "grant-in-aid" program that provided federal dollars to states to operate programs that conformed to certain basic federal requirements. Because the insurance program for retired workers was funded by contributions, the reserve of those funds would take time to build up (while the Act was passed in 1935, the first check was not cut until 1940). One of the functions of OAA was to provide some income stability for seniors who would not build up enough contributions in time for their retirement. Providing this relief to the elderly was not controversial at the time, even though it was not contributory.

While the insurance program for the retired was entirely federalized, the welfare program for the aged remained a state-by-state program with federal subsidization. At the time OAA was created, many states had their own form of cash assistance for the elderly. The Social Security Act federalized the program, but permitted states to maintain many features of their own programs, provided that they met certain federal requirements, such as statewide coverage, eligibility established at an age no higher than 65, and an appeals process for people who felt they had been wrongly denied benefits. At the program's inception, the federal government provided states with 50 percent of the amount of benefits they paid out, up to a cap of $30.00 per month per recipient.

As you read in the history of the Social Security Act, the reach of SSI was expanded to people with disabilities in 1974. All three categories of SSI (aged, blind, or disabled) are targeted to the poor. Recall that of the 8.1 million people on SSI in 2011, almost 7 million were disabled, while just over 1 million were eligible due to age and the remainder due to blindness.

Because it is a safety net program that provides income to people who would likely otherwise have no income whatsoever, many legal aid offices and other nonprofit organizations provide representation to people who are seeking SSI benefits on the basis of disability (categorical eligibility on the basis of age or blindness is less difficult to prove, for obvious reasons). There are also private attorneys who take on these cases, typically for a contingency fee, a portion of any lump sum "backpay" award that might be made based on the onset date of a condition found to be disabling. To receive SSI based on disability, the applicant must prove that he or she is disabled under the government's codified five-step sequential evaluation process. The process requires that the Social Security Administration determine:

(1) whether the claimant is presently engaging in substantial gainful activity;
(2) whether the claimant has a severe impairment;

(3) whether the impairment is listed, or equivalent to an impairment listed, in . . . the regulations;

(4) whether the impairment prevents the claimant from doing past relevant work; and

(5) whether the impairment prevents the claimant from performing any other substantial gainful activity.

20 C.F.R. § 404.1520(a)(4).

Reflecting legislators' concern that some people were receiving disability payments based on impairments that were attributable to drug or alcohol abuse, as part of the Contract with America Advancement Act (CAAA), Congress amended the Social Security Act in 1996 specifically to preclude a finding of disability if drug or alcohol abuse is "a contributing factor material to the [Social Security] Commissioner's determination that the individual is disabled." 42 U.S.C. § 423(d)(2)(C) (2012). The claimant bears the burden of proof that such abuse is not material to the alleged disability. *See, e.g.*, Parra v. Astrue, 481 F.3d 742 (9th Cir. 2007), *cert. denied*, 552 U.S. 1141 (2008). In another case, the Ninth Circuit upheld the constitutionality of this portion of the CAAA against an equal protection challenge, holding that classifications that burden alcoholics are not entitled to elevated scrutiny and that the provision was rationally related to a legitimate government purpose: "to discourage alcohol and drug abuse, or at least not to encourage it with a permanent government subsidy." Ball v. Massanari, 254 F.3d 817, 824 (9th Cir. 2001); *see also* H.R. Rep. No. 104-379, at 17 (1995) (explaining that the amendment eliminates "a perverse incentive that affronts working taxpayers and fails to serve the interests of addicts and alcoholics, many of whom use their disability checks to purchase drugs and alcohol, thereby maintaining their addictions").

Regulations effectuating the CAAA indicate that in deciding whether drug or alcohol abuse is a material contributing factor, "[t]he key factor we will examine in determining whether drug addiction or alcoholism is a contributing factor material to the determination of disability is whether we would still find you disabled if you stopped using drugs or alcohol." 20 C.F.R. § 404.1535 (1999).

NOTES AND QUESTIONS

1. What value judgments are embedded in sequential evaluation processes? Does this definition track notions of the deserving versus the undeserving poor?

2. Consider the role of an attorney in contesting a denial of benefits, and recall from Chapter 3 that in Mathews v. Eldridge the Court refused to extend Goldberg v. Kelly's requirement of a pre-termination hearing to the disability context, in part because, it reasoned, SSI determinations tend to turn on medical evidence, which it held was suitable to a mere paper review. If you were an attorney representing a client seeking to be found disabled under the regulations, what types of investigative and advocacy tasks would you undertake?

3. Do you think the statutory reform regarding drug and/or alcohol abuse in the SSI program is a good one? If you were a member of Congress, would you

have voted for this provision of the CAAA? Can you fashion a response to the argument that opposition to the amendment "encourages" substance abuse?

* * *

Income limits for SSI eligibility vary by state, and many states simply mandate that an applicant is ineligible for SSI if she has income exceeding what the state's SSI grant would be. For example, in Massachusetts, a disabled SSI recipient living alone would typically receive a total grant of approximately $850 per month, made up of about $700 in SSI and a $150-per-month state supplement; an applicant whose income exceeds that amount would be denied benefits. Nor may an applicant have more than $2,000 in total assets (subject to a few exclusions, such as a car). The 2012 profile of an SSI recipient below explained that the program's design classifies people as either disabled (and thus eligible) or nondisabled (and thus ineligible). This all-or-nothing classification system has the perhaps unintended consequence of disincentivizing SSI recipients from engaging in part-time work.

JULIE TURKEWITZ & JULIET LINDERMAN, *THE DISABILITY TRAP*
N.Y. Times (Oct. 21, 2012), at SR5

Brad Crelia was rushing around the vast media room at an international AIDS conference last summer in Washington, interviewing people for a series of articles on Hivster.com, a Web magazine he founded for people who are H.I.V. positive. The ease with which he moved through the crowd made it clear he'd done this kind of political networking before: he'd worked first as a field organizer for Hillary Rodham Clinton and later as a regional field organizer for President Obama.

But Mr. Crelia, 27, nearly didn't make it home from the AIDS conference; without the $17 necessary to buy a bus ticket, he'd had to beg a stranger for a ride back to New York. It was the end of the month, he said. He'd simply run out of money.

He is one of more than 8.7 million disabled Americans who rely on cash assistance from the government through a program called Supplemental Security Income. The program was created in 1974 to help blind, aged and disabled people meet basic needs for food, clothing and shelter. By 2035, the federal government expects to spend $60.9 billion in payments to 9.9 million people.

Discussion of Medicare, Medicaid and Social Security programs has been at the forefront of election-year debate. But there has been no discussion of S.S.I. The fact is that expenditures for the S.S.I. program are rising while the economic status of disabled people is on the decline.

The very program that is supposed to be their safety net is actually the source of the problem, experts say. S.S.I. traps many disabled people by limiting their income to levels just above the poverty line, and taking away their cash benefits if they achieve any level of security.

At 16, Mr. Crelia was given a diagnosis of porphyria, an incurable hereditary blood disorder. His symptoms — seizures, paralysis, blackouts, nausea and extreme pain — became more and more severe, preventing him from finishing college and landing him in the hospital for days or weeks at a time. In addition, in 2009, he learned he had H.I.V. That has not affected his ability to work. But his porphyria has made maintaining a traditional full-time job nearly impossible.

So he and others like him need a flexible financial safety net for the periods during which they cannot work. But no such program exists. The only way for Mr. Crelia to qualify for cash assistance was to sign up for S.S.I. — and demonstrate that he was unable to "engage in substantial gainful activity" because of his physical impairment.

He now receives a monthly check for $506 through the S.S.I. program, and he is allowed to earn $85 more. (He also receives some assistance toward his rent and food expenses.) Once he surpasses the $85, his benefit check will be reduced by $1 for every $2 he earns. And if his income reaches $1,097 a month, he will no longer be eligible for any cash S.S.I. benefits at all. So he must be poor or he must give up all government support. Mr. Crelia is never permitted to have more than $2,000 in the bank, a restriction that places the trappings of a middle-class life — a car, a modest home, a family — far out of reach.

"I've been kept financially sort of in this cage," Mr. Crelia said. "Just basic things that people rely upon, having a normal life, aren't things that are really accessible. And won't be."

People like Mr. Crelia — ill, but ambitious, motivated and able to work the majority of the time — don't fit into a rigid system set up primarily to provide support for those who will never be able to enter the workplace in any capacity. Instead of accounting for a spectrum of ability and administering a benefits package accordingly, the system offers a one-size-fits-all plan: you can either work and not qualify for financial assistance, or you're sick, and barred from earning any substantial income.

"Instead of helping people achieve their full potential," David Stapleton, who directs the Mathematica Center for Studying Disability Policy, testified before Congress last month, "the current disability support system has created a poverty trap." The employment rate for people with disabilities, he said, is just 21 percent of the rate for people without disabilities, down from 32 percent in 1981. The problems stem from the Social Security Administration's failure in 1974 to structure a program that motivates work. It is relatively easy to accept cash benefits but very hard to get into the workplace. Mr. Stapleton said that Congress had the power to push to change the structure of the program, but that it had not done so.

Today, 70 percent of people with disabilities live in poverty. The Affordable Care Act may eventually ease the burden for some individuals with disabilities, namely those who rely on Medicaid through the S.S.I. program, by eliminating exclusions based on pre-existing conditions and annual or lifetime benefits caps. But the impact on the disabled is not yet clear, and experts are calling for additional targeted reforms.

Richard Burkhauser, a professor at Cornell, and Mary Daly, a government economist, have studied the welfare of people with disabilities for more than three decades, and offer some solutions. They suggest a work-first approach that would help people get job training or employment before they go through the red-tape-ridden path of getting on S.S.I. Now people must go through the lengthy process of proving that they cannot work before they are given access to job training and other programs.

Instead of enrolling Mr. Crelia in S.S.I., the Social Security Administration could have helped him apply for a loan to finish his bachelor's degree, increasing his chances of finding a flexible, high-paying job with health insurance.

Mr. Burkhauser and Ms. Daly borrow another idea from the lessons learned from the 1996 welfare overhaul. Welfare moved from a federal program that did not encourage single mothers to work to a state-run program that offered the incentive of an earned-income tax credit for working mothers. They say S.S.I. should copy this model by allowing people like Mr. Crelia to hold a paying job as often as possible — whether for 20, 25 or 30 hours a week — and having the federal or state government chip in with tax credits to round out his income.

For now, Mr. Crelia is doing his best to stay busy. He clocks far more than 40 hours most weeks, mostly in unpaid writing. "When I work, I thrive both physically and emotionally," Mr. Crelia said. "When I am not sick and can control my disease with medication — like now — I want to be able to contribute to society, have a family, grow my business. But not as a volunteer; I want to be paid like everyone else."

NOTES AND QUESTIONS

1. The "cliff" problem described above, where a participant in a program's having or earning of a dollar too much results in his or her being thrown "off the cliff" of eligibility, is endemic to means-tested programs. Are such cliffs inevitable in means-tested programs? As shown by Mr. Crelia's story above, some programs reduce benefits because of earnings based on a formula (reduce benefits by $1 for each $2 earned). Does this seem like a sensible way to handle this? Are there programs for middle-class people that have the same design feature?
2. Earnings are not the only "cliff" associated with SSI. The $2,000 asset limit also disincentivizes some behavior thought socially valuable. Advocates report, for example, stories of SSI applicants somehow saving up some money during the years their applications are in process only to find when their benefits are finally granted those savings render them ineligible. One California SSI lawyer tells the story of a recipient who spent down his small nest egg on peanut butter and other nonperishable food that would last him but not count as a disqualifying asset.
3. SSI was in the news in December 2012 when *New York Times* columnist Nicholas Kristof published an op-ed claiming that poor parents were preventing their children from advancing in school because poor academic performance was a positive indicator of a disability that formed the basis for a child's eligibility for SSI benefits. The piece began:

> This is what poverty sometimes looks like in America: parents here in Appalachian hill country pulling their children out of literacy classes. Moms and dads fear that if kids learn to read, they are less likely to qualify for a monthly check for having an intellectual disability. Many people in hillside mobile homes here are poor and desperate, and a $698 monthly check per child from the Supplemental Security Income program goes a long way — and those checks continue until the child turns 18.

Noting changes in SSI eligibility policy, Kristof went on:

About four decades ago, most of the children [SSI] covered had severe physical handicaps or mental retardation that made it difficult for parents to hold jobs—about 1 percent of all poor children. But now 55 percent of the disabilities it covers are fuzzier intellectual disabilities short of mental retardation, where the diagnosis is less clear-cut. More than 1.2 million children across America—a full 8 percent of all low-income children—are now enrolled in S.S.I. as disabled, at an annual cost of more than $9 billion.

That is a burden on taxpayers, of course, but it can be even worse for children whose families have a huge stake in their failing in school. Those kids may never recover: a 2009 study found that nearly two-thirds of these children make the transition at age 18 into S.S.I. for the adult disabled. They may never hold a job in their entire lives and are condemned to a life of poverty on the dole—and that's the outcome of a program intended to fight poverty.

Nicholas Kristof, *Profiting from a Child's Illiteracy*, N.Y. Times (Dec. 9, 2012), at SR1.

Two legal services attorneys from Philadelphia's Community Legal Services program authored a rebuttal to Kristof, including critiques of his data and sources, which he posted on his blog along with a rejoinder. The exchange is available at http://kristof.blogs.nytimes.com/2013/01/23/chipping-away-at-poverty-an-exchange/.

4. PRWORA eliminated SSI eligibility for "fleeing felons," even if they are otherwise eligible for the program. A fleeing felon is defined as anyone who:

(1) flees to avoid prosecution for a crime, or attempt to commit a crime, which is a felony in the jurisdiction fled from; or
(2) flees to avoid custody or confinement after conviction for a crime, or attempt to commit a crime, that is a felony in the jurisdiction fled from; or
(3) violates a condition of state or federal probation or parole.

24 C.F.R. § 416.1339(a). A 2001 report by the Office of the Inspector General noted that the vast majority (89 percent) of the over 45,000 people who were terminated from SSI under the program were never arrested or convicted for the felony that prompted the termination. *See* Kathryn J. Lewis, *Income Injustice: The Impact of Welfare Reform's Fleeing Felon Regulations on SSI Recipients* (2002), *available at* http://blogs.law.columbia.edu/4cs/files/2008/11/fleeingfeloncjcj.pdf. In 2009, President Obama signed the No Social Security Benefits for Prisoners Act of 2009, which prohibits the payment of any Social Security benefits to recipients for a time during which they were in prison or in violation of terms of probation or parole.

5. While there is no federal program for poor adults *without* dependents, states do operate their own programs for these individuals; the programs tend to be called "General Assistance" or "General Relief." Thirty out of the 50 states operate such programs, with varying requirements for and conditions of eligibility. The chart on the page that follows illustrates the various state programs. Some of the policy themes with which you are already familiar—work requirements, concerns about the undeserving poor—play themselves out in the "GA" context as they do elsewhere. For a review of states' GA programs and the policy issues they raise, see Liz Schott & Clare Cho, Ctr. on Budget & Policy Priorities, *General Assistance Programs: Safety Net Weakening Despite Increased Need* (2011).

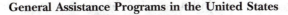

General Assistance Programs in the United States

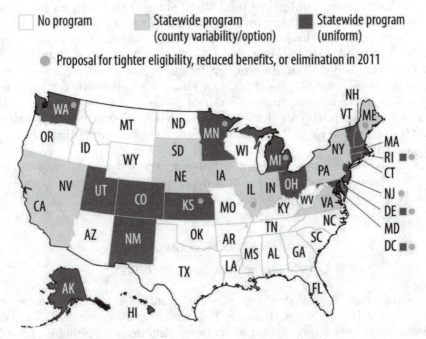

D. FOOD AND NUTRITION SUPPORT

As of this writing, almost 47 million Americans receive Supplemental Nutrition Assistance Program (SNAP) benefits, formerly known as "food stamps." This number vastly eclipses TANF usage, which hovers around 4.5 million. The 2012 average household monthly SNAP benefit, excluding the outliers of Hawai'i, Guam, and Alaska, is approximately $260.

While they have a "new" (as of 2008) name, "food stamps" remain a high-profile public assistance program. The first precursor to the current federal program was, unsurprisingly, a part of the New Deal. The first Food Stamp Program operated from 1939 to 1943. From its origin, the program was motivated by the desire to prop up the U.S. agriculture industry as well as to feed its needy people. According to the U.S. Department of Agriculture, the program's first administrator, Milo Perkins, is credited with having said, "We got a picture of a gorge, with farm surpluses on one cliff and under-nourished city folks with outstretched hands on the other. We set out to find a practical way to build a bridge across that chasm." The program was dramatically extended with the Food Stamp Act of 1964, which launched a pilot program in 40 counties and three cities. Participation soared from about a half million in 1965 to 15 million in 1974, largely because of expanded geographical reach of the program. The program began operation nationwide in 1974. Important amendments were made in 1977, designed to streamline the program, curb abuse, and reach the neediest potential participants.

In the early 1980s, program expansion and expense gave rise to political attention. Congress passed important reforms in this era, including changing financial eligibility standards, and requiring job search activities of applicants as well as participants. The exclusion for strikers, the subject of the *Lyng* case, *infra,* was the result of a 1981 amendment. The pendulum swung back the other way later in that decade as hunger in the United States rose. Categorical eligibility was restored, and benefits were increased by the introduction of a new formula.

The welfare reform initiative of 1996 affected food stamps, as it did every benefits program. The Food Stamp Act was reauthorized at that time, but PRWORA changed important program features, and in ways consistent with the larger 1996 overhaul. Specifically, it eliminated eligibility for most legal immigrants, placed a time limit of 3 out of 36 months for able-bodied adults without dependents who are not working or participating in a work program at least 20 hours per week, and retooled the formula once again, bringing benefits levels back down.

The article below summarizes important features of the SNAP program as of 2012. As you read about food support programs, recall the dual purposes of reducing hunger and supporting U.S. agriculture.

BARBARA JONES, *SNAP BASICS*
46 Clearinghouse Rev. 236 (2012)

The global financial crisis that began in 2007 resulted in a palpable increase in hunger in the United States. The U.S. Department of Agriculture (USDA) categorizes hunger into levels of food insecurity in American households [Ed. note: the categories are "very low," "low," and "marginal," and can be found on the USDA's website at http://www.ers.usda.gov/topics/food-nutrition-assistance/food-security-in-the-us/definitions-of-food-security.aspx]. Food insecurity remains at a crisis level. Inadequate access to sufficient food, or food insecurity, occurs in more than 10 percent of households in the United States and can be as high as 80 percent among high-risk populations. Food insecurity is a complex problem that has become what some researchers call a "silent epidemic." Frequent sufferers are elderly adults or children who do not seek help because they are either too embarrassed to ask or misinformed about the benefits for which they qualify. . . .

Clients seeking assistance on legal problems such as foreclosure or divorce seldom mention that they do not have enough to eat. Such clients are sometimes not even aware of what nutrition or other benefits they qualify for, or such clients may be too embarrassed to mention that they do not have enough food. . . . Households with children are at a high risk of food insecurity. One-in-five or more American children in forty states and the District of Columbia lived in food-insecure households in 2009. Older people are particularly at risk of not having enough to eat. About three-quarters of households receiving SNAP benefits included a child, a person age 60 or older, or a disabled person.

Note that, while related, poverty and food insecurity are not the same thing. Some reports say that unemployment can be a stronger predictor of food insecurity than poverty. Recent data further reflect that food insecurity is not limited to the people who fall under the federal poverty guidelines. One-in-four people who are at or above 185 percent of the poverty guidelines are food-insecure. Several studies link food insecurity to ethnicity, low education, individual health problems, and lack of medical coverage as well as housing and utility costs. Some parts of the country have higher incidences of food insecurity than other parts. People who live in central cities of metropolitan areas or in the South have higher incidence of food insecurity, although people in rural areas also suffer from food insecurity. The rates of black (25.1 percent) and Hispanic

(26.2 percent) households having food insecurity are far higher than the national average. Several academic studies show that low-income women who have increased body mass indexes (i.e., who are overweight or obese) frequently suffer from food insecurity. . . .

The Food and Nutrition Service administers SNAP and other domestic food assistance programs authorized in the Farm Bill as well as the Special Supplemental Nutrition Program for Women, Infants, and Children (WIC) and child nutrition programs. SNAP benefits can be a significant supplement to income for many poor households: "On average, SNAP benefits boosted gross monthly income by 39 percent for all participating households and by 45 percent for households with children." SNAP provides food benefits to low-income eligible households on an EBT (electronic benefit transfer) card which can be used like a debit card to receive food at authorized retailers. Eligible applicants are entitled to SNAP benefits within thirty days after applying. Expedited SNAP benefits must be provided to eligible households no later than seven days following the date of application. Some states provide shorter time frames. . . .

Federal and State Rules. Federal law provides two basic pathways to qualify for SNAP benefits. Applicants can either qualify by meeting federal financial eligibility requirements or qualify automatically (or "categorically") by receiving benefits from Supplemental Security Income (SSI), Temporary Assistance for Needy Families (TANF), or state-run General Assistance programs. Migrant and seasonal farm workers have additional rights under federal law. States have the option to expand categorical eligibility under certain specified state policy options. USDA's State Options Report details twenty-seven different options and the state and federal rules regarding these options.

A few state policy options actually curtail eligibility for the program. For example, states may choose whether to ban people from receiving SNAP benefits permanently if they have been convicted of a state or federal felony offense involving the possession, use, or distribution of a controlled substance. . . .

Categorical Eligibility. Some states have raised the gross-income test as high as 200 percent for categorically eligible recipients. Households in which all members are authorized to receive means tested cash assistance from TANF or General Assistance funds are categorically eligible for SNAP benefits. SSI recipients in all states, except California, are categorically eligible for SNAP benefits. Since 1996, states have been able to expand categorical eligibility if an applicant receives a TANF "benefit," not just TANF cash welfare. A household with an income too high to qualify for TANF cash assistance may typically still obtain TANF benefits other than cash assistance. . . .

Resources and Assets. In most states, categorically eligible families are not subject to asset test for SNAP eligibility. Generally households that are not categorically eligible may have no more than $2,000 in countable resources (such as bank account) or $3,250 in countable resources if at least one person is 60 or older or disabled. However, certain resources are not counted — a home and lot, most retirement or pension plans, and the resources of people who receive SSI and TANF benefits. In all states, except California, the resources of people who get SSI and TANF are not counted at all. In California SSI applicants whose applications are pending and have not yet begun receiving benefits may receive SNAP benefits while their application is pending. . . .

Immigrant Eligibility. Immigrant eligibility for SNAP benefits has changed throughout the years. There was a sharp decline in immigrant enrollment in SNAP after passage of [PRWORA], including a decline in the enrollment of U.S.

citizen children with immigrant parents. Some lawful immigrants and U.S. citizen children have been deterred from applying for benefits because of concerns that the state agency that processes SNAP benefits may report other family members to immigration services. To ensure that eligible people receive benefits, USDA and the U.S. Department of Health and Human Services have issued policy guidance noting that applicants need not disclose their non-applicant relatives' immigration status or social security numbers.

The 2002 Farm Bill restored SNAP eligibility to legal immigrant children. Legal immigrants of any age who receive disability-related assistance or benefits regardless of entry date now qualify for SNAP. Legal immigrants who have lived in the country for five years also qualify for SNAP benefits. Certain noncitizens who gained entry for humanitarian reasons are also eligible. "Undocumented noncitizens" do not qualify for SNAP. Noncitizens who are in the United States temporarily—such as students or tourists—are not eligible for SNAP benefits. More detailed information on noncitizen eligibility is available on the USDA website.

People Ineligible for SNAP. Some categories of people—such as strikers—are not eligible for SNAP regardless of how low their income and assets may be. College students who are enrolled at least half-time do not qualify for SNAP benefits unless they meet one of the exceptions provided by federal law. As a rule, "able-bodied" childless adults between 18 and 49 who do not work at least twenty hours per week in approved work activities may receive SNAP benefits for only three months out of every three years. Adults over 50 are exempt from the work requirements. There are exceptions to the work requirement for people under 50 who live in areas with high unemployment. Adults receiving temporary or permanent disability benefits or are determined "mentally or physically unfit for employment" are exempted from the work requirement.

NOTES AND QUESTIONS

1. The average number of individuals receiving food stamps per month has risen every year since 2008, and stood at almost 47 million in 2012. Monthly averages by year (in millions) are as follows:

FY '08	*FY '09*	*FY '10*	*FY '11*	*FY '12*
28.2	33.5	40.3	44.7	46.9

Noting the significant rise in food stamp usage during the first term of President Barack Obama, in January 2012, presidential candidate Newt Gingrich called Obama "the best food stamp president in American history." Note that, according to the Clearinghouse Review piece above, at least a third of people eligible for SNAP did not even apply in 2011.

2. Why do you think there are no categorical eligibility requirements for SNAP? An able-bodied man living without children is eligible for SNAP, provided he meets the income and asset tests and is not an undocumented or otherwise excluded immigrant. Even if he is not engaged in 20 hours of work activity, he is eligible for three out of 36 months. What other differences do you observe between the reach of SNAP and TANF or SSI? Do these differences make sense?

3. Technological advances have enabled issuance of SNAP benefits on an "Electronic Benefit Card," rather than the paper currency–style "food stamps" from earlier eras. This reform was designed in part to minimize the stigma that some users experienced from using a form of payment so different from "regular" consumers. Other visible indicia of cash or food assistance include a separate line in the cafeteria. Do you think such indicia should be eliminated or minimized? Why or why not?

4. From the inception of the food stamp program, there have been restrictions on the items one may purchase with stamps. SNAP benefits can be used only to buy food, and cannot include food that will be consumed in the store. Nonfood items (such as toiletries, cleaning products, or vitamins) cannot be purchased with food stamps; nor can alcoholic beverages. The USDA's list of eligible and ineligible items can be found at http:// www.fns.usda.gov/snap/retailers/eligible.htm. Do you think that food stamps should be limited to certain items? If so, what do you think of the specific restrictions?

5. The federal government operates other nutritional support programs. The Special Supplemental Nutrition Program for Women, Infants, and Children, known as "WIC," provides food, health care referrals, and nutrition education to poor pregnant women and mothers of children up to five years of age. Approximately 25 percent of young children in the United States receive these benefits. Low-income seniors are eligible for assistance from the USDA's "Farmers' Market Nutrition Program," which provides coupons that can be used at farmers' markets and other community agriculture programs. Native Americans over age 55 can participate in a separate nutrition program targeted to that at-risk group. The Older Americans Act also provides meals to seniors who are homebound and to senior centers.

* * *

While there are no categorical eligibility requirements (age, deprived of the support of a parent, disability, etc.), there are certain program requirements and exclusions which, like those in other public assistance programs, have been the subject of policy debate and litigation. The case below was among those that, like many in Chapter 3, were litigated in the 1960s and 1970s as participation rates increased and the War on Poverty animated legal aid and other lawyers to push for protections of their clients' constitutional rights.

U.S. DEP'T OF AGRIC. v. MORENO

413 U.S. 528 (1973)

Mr. Justice BRENNAN delivered the opinion of the Court.

This case requires us to consider the constitutionality of §3(e) of the Food Stamp Act of 1964, 7 U. S. C. §2012(e), as amended in 1971 which, with certain exceptions, excludes from participation in the food stamp program any household containing an individual who is unrelated to any other member of the household. In practical effect, §3(e) creates two classes of persons for food stamp purposes: one class is composed of those individuals who live in households all of whose members are related to one another, and the other class consists of those individuals who live in households containing one or more members who are unrelated to the rest. The latter class of persons is denied federal food assistance. . . .

The federal food stamp program was established in 1964 in an effort to alleviate hunger and malnutrition among the more needy segments of our society. Eligibility for participation in the program is determined on a household rather than an individual basis. An eligible household purchases sufficient food stamps to provide that household with a nutritionally adequate diet. The household pays for the stamps at a reduced rate based upon its size and cumulative income. The food stamps are then used to purchase food at retail stores, and the Government redeems the stamps at face value, thereby paying the difference between the actual cost of the food and the amount paid by the household for the stamps.

As initially enacted, § 3(e) defined a "household" as "a group of *related or non-related* individuals, who are not residents of an institution or boarding house, but are living as one economic unit sharing common cooking facilities and for whom food is customarily purchased in common." In January 1971, however, Congress redefined the term "household" so as to include only groups of *related* individuals. Pursuant to this amendment, the Secretary of Agriculture promulgated regulations rendering ineligible for participation in the program any "household" whose members are not "all related to each other."

Appellees in this case consist of several groups of individuals who allege that, although they satisfy the income eligibility requirements for federal food assistance, they have nevertheless been excluded from the program solely because the persons in each group are not "all related to each other." Appellee Jacinta Moreno, for example, is a 56-year-old diabetic who lives with Ermina Sanchez and the latter's three children. They share common living expenses, and Mrs. Sanchez helps to care for appellee. . . . Despite her poverty, appellee has been denied federal food assistance solely because she is unrelated to the other members of her household. Moreover, although Mrs. Sanchez and her three children were permitted to purchase $108 worth of food stamps per month for $18, their participation in the program will be terminated if appellee Moreno continues to live with them.

Appellee Sheilah Hejny is married and has three children. Although the Hejnys are indigent, they took in a 20-year-old girl, who is unrelated to them, because "we felt she had emotional problems." The Hejnys receive $144 worth of food stamps each month for $14. If they allow the 20-year-old girl to continue to live with them, they will be denied food stamps by reason of § 3(e).

Appellee Victoria Keppler has a daughter with an acute hearing deficiency. The daughter requires special instruction in a school for the deaf. The school is located in an area in which appellee could not ordinarily afford to live. Thus, in order to make the most of her limited resources, appellee agreed to share an apartment near the school with a woman who, like appellee, is on public assistance. Since appellee is not related to the woman, appellee's food stamps have been, and will continue to be, cut off if they continue to live together.

. . . In essence, appellees contend, and the District Court held, that the "unrelated person" provision of § 3(e) creates an irrational classification in violation of the equal protection component of the Due Process Clause of the Fifth Amendment.[5] We agree.

Under traditional equal protection analysis, a legislative classification must be sustained if the classification itself is rationally related to a legitimate governmental interest. The purposes of the Food Stamp Act were expressly set forth in the congressional "declaration of policy":

> It is hereby declared to be the policy of Congress . . . to safeguard the health and well-being of the Nation's population and raise levels of nutrition among low-income households. The Congress hereby finds that the limited food purchasing power of low-income households contributes to hunger and malnutrition among members of such households. The Congress further finds that increased utilization of food in establishing and maintaining adequate national levels of nutrition will promote the distribution in a beneficial manner of our agricultural abundances and will strengthen our agricultural economy, as well as result in more orderly marketing and distribution of food. To alleviate such hunger and malnutrition, a food stamp program is herein authorized which will permit low-income households to purchase a nutritionally adequate diet through normal channels of trade.

The challenged statutory classification (households of related persons versus households containing one or more unrelated persons) is clearly irrelevant to the stated purposes of the Act. As the District Court recognized, "the relationships among persons constituting one economic unit and sharing cooking facilities have nothing to do with their abilities to stimulate the agricultural economy by purchasing farm surpluses, or with their personal nutritional requirements."

Thus, if it is to be sustained, the challenged classification must rationally further some legitimate governmental interest other than those specifically stated in the congressional "declaration of policy." Regrettably, there is little legislative history to illuminate the purposes of the 1971 amendment of § 3(e). The legislative history that does exist, however, indicates that that amendment was intended to prevent so-called "hippies" and "hippie communes" from participating in the food stamp program. The challenged classification clearly cannot be sustained by reference to this congressional purpose. For if the constitutional conception of "equal protection of the laws" means anything, it must at the very least mean that a bare congressional desire to harm a politically unpopular group cannot constitute a *legitimate* governmental interest. As a result, "[a] purpose to discriminate against hippies cannot, in and of itself and without reference to [some independent] considerations in the public interest, justify the 1971 amendment."

Although apparently conceding this point, the Government maintains that the challenged classification should nevertheless be upheld as rationally related to the clearly legitimate governmental interest in minimizing fraud in the administration of the food stamp program.[7] In essence, the Government

5. "While the Fifth Amendment contains no equal protection clause, it does forbid discrimination that is 'so unjustifiable as to be violative of due process.'" Schneider v. Rusk, 377 U.S. 163, 168 (1964); *see* Frontiero v. Richardson, 411 U.S. 677, 680 n. 5 (1973); Shapiro v. Thompson, 394 U.S. 618, 641-642 (1969); Bolling v. Sharpe, 347 U.S. 497 (1954).

7. The Government initially argued to the District Court that the challenged classification might be justified as a means to foster "morality." In rejecting that contention, the District Court noted that "interpreting the amendment as an attempt to regulate morality would raise serious constitutional questions." Indeed, citing this Court's decisions in Griswold v. Connecticut, 381 U.S. 479 (1965), Stanley v. Georgia, 394 U.S. 557 (1969), and Eisenstadt v. Baird, 405 U.S. 438 (1972), the District Court observed that it was doubtful, at best, whether Congress, "in the name of morality,"

contends that, in adopting the 1971 amendment, Congress might rationally have thought (1) that households with one or more unrelated members are more likely than "fully related" households to contain individuals who abuse the program by fraudulently failing to report sources of income or by voluntarily remaining poor; and (2) that such households are "relatively unstable," thereby increasing the difficulty of detecting such abuses. But even if we were to accept as rational the Government's wholly unsubstantiated assumptions concerning the differences between "related" and "unrelated" households, we still could not agree with the Government's conclusion that the denial of essential federal food assistance to *all* otherwise eligible households containing unrelated members constitutes a rational effort to deal with these concerns.

At the outset, it is important to note that the Food Stamp Act itself contains provisions, wholly independent of § 3(e), aimed specifically at the problems of fraud and of the voluntarily poor. For example, with certain exceptions, [the Act] renders ineligible for assistance any household containing "an able-bodied adult person between the ages of eighteen and sixty-five" who fails to register for, and accept, offered employment. Similarly, [the Act] specifically impose[s] strict criminal penalties upon any individual who obtains or uses food stamps fraudulently. The existence of these provisions necessarily casts considerable doubt upon the proposition that the 1971 amendment could rationally have been intended to prevent those very same abuses.

Moreover, in practical effect, the challenged classification simply does not operate so as rationally to further the prevention of fraud. As previously noted, § 3(e) defines an eligible "household" as "a group of related individuals . . . [1] living as one economic unit [2] sharing common cooking facilities [and 3] for whom food is customarily purchased in common." Thus, two *unrelated* persons living together and meeting all three of these conditions would constitute a single household ineligible for assistance. If financially feasible, however, these same two individuals can legally avoid the "unrelated person" exclusion simply by altering their living arrangements so as to eliminate any one of the three conditions. By so doing, they effectively create two separate "households," both of which are eligible for assistance. Indeed, as the California Director of Social Welfare has explained:

"The 'related household' limitations will eliminate many households from eligibility in the Food Stamp Program. It is my understanding that the Congressional intent of the new regulations are specifically aimed at the 'hippies' and 'hippie communes.' Most people in this category can and will alter their living arrangements in order to remain eligible for food stamps. However, the AFDC mothers who try to raise their standard of living by sharing housing will be affected. They will not be able to utilize the altered living patterns in order to continue to be eligible without giving up their advantage of shared housing costs."

Thus, in practical operation, the 1971 amendment excludes from participation in the food stamp program, *not* those persons who are "likely to abuse the program" but, rather, *only* those persons who are so desperately in need of aid that they cannot even afford to alter their living arrangements so as to retain their eligibility. Traditional equal protection analysis does not require that every

---

could "infringe the rights to privacy and freedom of association *in the home*." (Emphasis in original.) Moreover, the court also pointed out that the classification established in § 3 (e) was not rationally related "to prevailing notions of morality, since it in terms disqualifies all households of unrelated individuals, without reference to whether a particular group contains both sexes." The Government itself has now abandoned the "morality" argument.

classification be drawn with precise "'mathematical nicety.'" Dandridge v. Williams, 397 U.S., at 485. But the classification here in issue is not only "imprecise," it is wholly without any rational basis. The judgment of the District Court holding the "unrelated person" provision invalid under the Due Process Clause of the Fifth Amendment is therefore *affirmed*.

Mr. Justice DOUGLAS, concurring.

... This case involves desperately poor people with acute problems who, though unrelated, come together for mutual help and assistance. The choice of one's associates for social, political, race, or religious purposes is basic in our constitutional scheme. It extends to "the associational rights of the members" of a trade union.

I suppose no one would doubt that an association of people working in the poverty field would be entitled to the same constitutional protection as those working in the racial, banking, or agricultural field. I suppose poor people holding a meeting or convention would be under the same constitutional umbrella as others. The dimensions of the "unrelated" person problem under the Food Stamp Act are in that category. As the facts of this case show, the poor are congregating in households where they can better meet the adversities of poverty. This banding together is an expression of the right of freedom of association that is very deep in our traditions.

Other like rights have been recognized that are only peripheral First Amendment rights — the right to send one's child to a religious school, the right to study the German language in a private school, the protection of the entire spectrum of learning, teaching, and communicating ideas, the marital right of privacy.

As the examples indicate, these peripheral constitutional rights are exercised not necessarily in assemblies that congregate in halls or auditoriums but in discrete individual actions such as parents placing a child in the school of their choice. Taking a person into one's home because he is poor or needs help or brings happiness to the household is of the same dignity. ...

The "unrelated" person provision of the present Act has an impact on the rights of people to associate for lawful purposes with whom they choose. When state action "may have the effect of curtailing the freedom to associate" it "is subject to the closest scrutiny." The "right of the people peaceably to assemble" guaranteed by the First Amendment covers a wide spectrum of human interests — including "political, economic, religious, or cultural matters." Banding together to combat the common foe of hunger is in that category. The case therefore falls within the zone represented by Shapiro v. Thompson, *supra,* which held that a waiting period on welfare imposed by a State on the "immigration of indigents" penalizing the constitutional right to travel could not be sustained absent a "*compelling* governmental interest."

Mr. Justice REHNQUIST, with whom THE CHIEF JUSTICE concurs, dissenting.

... The Court's opinion would make a very persuasive congressional committee report arguing against the adoption of the limitation in question. Undoubtedly, Congress attacked the problem with a rather blunt instrument and, just as undoubtedly, persuasive arguments may be made that what we conceive to be its purpose will not be significantly advanced by the enactment of the limitation. But questions such as this are for Congress, rather than for this Court; our role is limited to the determination of whether there is any rational basis on which

Congress could decide that public funds made available under the food stamp program should not go to a household containing an individual who is unrelated to any other member of the household.

I do not believe that asserted congressional concern with the fraudulent use of food stamps is, when interpreted in the light most favorable to sustaining the limitation, quite as irrational as the Court seems to believe. A basic unit which Congress has chosen for determination of availability for food stamps is the "household," a determination which is not criticized by the Court. By the limitation here challenged, it has singled out households which contain unrelated persons and made such households ineligible. I do not think it is unreasonable for Congress to conclude that the basic unit which it was willing to support with federal funding through food stamps is some variation on the family as we know it—a household consisting of related individuals. This unit provides a guarantee which is not provided by households containing unrelated individuals that the household exists for some purpose other than to collect federal food stamps.

Admittedly, as the Court points out, the limitation will make ineligible many households which have not been formed for the purpose of collecting federal food stamps, and will at the same time not wholly deny food stamps to those households which may have been formed in large part to take advantage of the program. But, as the Court concedes, "traditional equal protection analysis does not require that every classification be drawn with precise 'mathematical nicety[.]'" . . .

The limitation which Congress enacted could, in the judgment of reasonable men, conceivably deny food stamps to members of households which have been formed solely for the purpose of taking advantage of the food stamp program. Since the food stamp program is not intended to be a subsidy for every individual who desires low-cost food, this was a permissible congressional decision quite consistent with the underlying policy of the Act. The fact that the limitation will have unfortunate and perhaps unintended consequences beyond this does not make it unconstitutional.

NOTES AND QUESTIONS

1. How would you describe the specific client stories that the lawyers told in the *Moreno* case? What do they tell you about the lawyers' litigation strategy in this case, and about poverty lawyers' impact litigation strategies generally?
2. In light of *Moreno*, how might you have argued *Dandridge* differently? Can you make a First Amendment argument against Maryland's maximum grant regulation?
3. *Moreno* is an important case overall in equal protection law, standing as it does for the proposition that animus against an unpopular group is not sufficient as a rational basis to uphold a government classification. In her concurrence in the 2003 case striking down Texas's sodomy laws, Justice O'Connor cited *Moreno* as follows:

   We have consistently held, however, that some objectives, such as "a bare . . . desire to harm a politically unpopular group," are not legitimate state interests. Dep't of Agriculture v. Moreno, 413 U.S. at 534; When a law exhibits such a desire to harm a politically unpopular group, we have applied a more

searching form of rational basis review to strike down such laws under the
Equal Protection Clause.

4. Food stamps are often in the news in two contexts. The eligibility for food
   stamps of working people (see discussion of "the working poor" in Chapter 5) is a subject of popular media, in particular, usage by employees of
   major mainstream employers, such as Wal-Mart and McDonald's. On the
   other hand, the popular media also often report on food stamp fraud and
   other misuse of food stamps, as well as the lack of available information
   about the kinds of goods actually purchased with the benefits. *See, e.g.,*
   Food Stamps Exchanged for Drugs, Weapons, Contraband, Judicial Watch
   (Mar. 9, 2013), http://www.judicialwatch.org/blog/2012/03/food-stamps-
   exchanged-for-drugs-weapons-contraband/.

* * *

Food stamp eligibility is one site where labor policy and social welfare policy
come in direct contact. Unlike the other programs (TANF, SSI, etc.), many
people with solid attachments to the labor force are eligible for food stamps.
This gave rise to the following case upholding the restriction on food stamps for
strikers.

LYNG v. AUTO. WORKERS
485 U.S. 360 (1988)

Justice WHITE delivered the opinion of the Court.

A 1981 amendment to the Food Stamp Act states that no household shall
become eligible to participate in the food stamp program during the time
that any member of the household is on strike or shall increase the allotment
of food stamps that it was receiving already because the income of the striking
member has decreased. [Ed. note: The amendment provided: "Notwithstanding any other provision of law, a household shall not participate in the food
stamp program at any time that any member of the household [is on strike] . . . .
Provided, That a household shall not lose its eligibility to participate in the food
stamp program as a result of one of its members going on strike if the household
was eligible for food stamps immediately prior to such strike, however, such
household shall not receive an increased allotment as the result of a decrease
in the income of the striking member or members of the household."] We
must decide whether this provision is valid under the First and the Fifth
Amendments. . . .

We deal first with the District Court's holding that § 109 violates the associational and expressive rights of appellees under the First Amendment. These
claimed constitutional infringements are also pressed as a basis for finding
that appellees' rights of "fundamental importance" have been burdened,
thus requiring this Court to examine appellees' equal protection claims
under a heightened standard of review. Since we conclude that the statute
does not infringe either the associational or expressive rights of appellees, we
must reject both parts of this analysis.

The challenge to the statute based on the associational rights asserted by
appellees is foreclosed by the reasoning this Court adopted in Lyng v. Castillo
(1986). There we considered a constitutional challenge to the definition of

"household" in the Food Stamp Act which treats parents, siblings, and children who live together, but not more distant relatives or unrelated persons who do so, as a single household for purposes of defining eligibility for food stamps. Although the challenge in that case was brought solely on equal protection grounds, and not under the First Amendment, the Court was obliged to decide whether the statutory classification should be reviewed under a stricter standard than mere rational-basis review because it "'directly and substantially' interfere[s] with family living arrangements and thereby burden[s] a fundamental right." The Court held that it did not, explaining that the definition of "household" does not "order or prevent any group of persons from dining together. Indeed, in the overwhelming majority of cases it probably has no effect at all. It is exceedingly unlikely that close relatives would choose to live apart simply to increase their allotment of food stamps, for the costs of separate housing would almost certainly exceed the incremental value of the additional stamps."

The same rationale applies in this case. As was true of the provision at issue in *Castillo*, it is "exceedingly unlikely" that § 109 will "prevent any group of persons from dining together." Even if isolated instances can be found in which a striking individual may have left the other members of the household in order to increase their allotment of food stamps, "in the overwhelming majority of cases [the statute] probably has no effect at all." The statute certainly does not "order" any individuals not to dine together nor does it in any other way "'directly and substantially' interfere with family living arrangements."

The statute also does not infringe the associational rights of appellee individuals and their unions. We have recognized that "one of the foundations of our society is the right of individuals to combine with other persons in pursuit of a common goal by lawful means," and our recognition of this right encompasses the combination of individual workers together in order better to assert their lawful rights. But in this case, the statute at issue does not "'directly and substantially' interfere" with appellees' ability to associate for this purpose. It does not "order" appellees not to associate together for the purpose of conducting a strike, or for any other purpose, and it does not "prevent" them from associating together or burden their ability to do so in any significant manner. As we have just stated with respect to the effect of this statute on an individual's decision to remain in or to leave his or her household, it seems "exceedingly unlikely" that this statute will prevent individuals from continuing to associate together in unions to promote their lawful objectives. . . .

Any impact on associational rights in this case results from the Government's refusal to extend food stamp benefits to those on strike, who are now without their wage income. Denying such benefits makes it harder for strikers to maintain themselves and their families during the strike and exerts pressure on them to abandon their union. Strikers and their union would be much better off if food stamps were available, but the strikers' right of association does not require the Government to furnish funds to maximize the exercise of that right. "We have held in several contexts [including the First Amendment] that a legislature's decision not to subsidize the exercise of a fundamental right does not infringe the right." Exercising the right to strike inevitably risks economic hardship, but we are not inclined to hold that the right of association requires the

Government to minimize that result by qualifying the striker for food stamps. . . .

Because the statute challenged here has no substantial impact on any fundamental interest and does not "affect with particularity any protected class,"[8] we confine our consideration to whether the statutory classification "is rationally related to a legitimate governmental interest." We have stressed that this standard of review is typically quite deferential; legislative classifications are "presumed to be valid," largely for the reason that "the drawing of lines that create distinctions is peculiarly a legislative task and an unavoidable one."

Appellant submits that this statute serves three objectives. Most obvious, given its source in OBRA, is to cut federal expenditures. Second, the limited funds available were to be used when the need was likely to be greatest, an approach which Congress thought did not justify food stamps for strikers. Third was the concern that the food stamp program was being used to provide one-sided support for labor strikes; the Senate Report indicated that the amendment was intended to remove the basis for that perception and criticism.

We have little trouble in concluding that § 109 is rationally related to the legitimate governmental objective of avoiding undue favoritism to one side or the other in private labor disputes. . . . It was no part of the purposes of the Food Stamp Act to establish a program that would serve as a weapon in labor disputes; the Act was passed to alleviate hunger and malnutrition and to strengthen the agricultural economy. The Senate Report stated that "allowing strikers to be eligible for food stamps has damaged the program's public integrity" and thus endangers these other goals served by the program. Congress acted in response to these problems.

It would be difficult to deny that this statute works at least some discrimination against strikers and their households. For the duration of the strike, those households cannot increase their allotment of food stamps even though the loss of income occasioned by the strike may well be enough to qualify them for food stamps or to increase their allotment if the fact of the strike itself were ignored. Yet Congress was in a difficult position when it sought to address the problems it had identified. Because a striking individual faces an immediate and often total drop in income during a strike, a single controversy pitting an employer against its employees can lead to a large number of claims for food stamps for as long as the controversy endures. It is the disbursement of food stamps in response to such a controversy that constitutes the source of the concern, and of the dangers to the program, that Congress believed it was important to remedy. We are not free in this instance to reject Congress' views about "what constitutes wise economic or social policy." *Dandridge, supra,* 397 U.S. at 486, 90 S. Ct., at 1162.

---

8. We reject the proposition that strikers as a class are entitled to special treatment under the Equal Protection Clause. Department of Agriculture v. Moreno, 413 U.S. 528, 93 S.Ct. 2821, 37 L.Ed.2d 782 (1973), does not counsel otherwise. There we upheld an equal protection challenge to a provision of the Food Stamp Act and concluded that "a bare congressional desire to harm a politically unpopular group cannot constitute a *legitimate* governmental interest." This statement is merely an application of the usual rational-basis test: if a statute is not rationally related to any legitimate governmental objective, it cannot be saved from constitutional challenge by a defense that relates it to an *illegitimate* governmental interest. Accordingly, in *Moreno* itself we examined the challenged provision under the rational-basis standard of review.

It is true that in terms of the scope and extent of their ineligibility for food stamps, §109 is harder on strikers than on "voluntary quitters."[9] But the concern about neutrality in labor disputes does not arise with respect to those who, for one reason or another, simply quit their jobs. As we have stated in a related context, even if the statute "provides only 'rough justice,' its treatment . . . is far from irrational." . . .

Appellees contend and the District Court held that the legislative classification is irrational because of the "critical" fact that it "impermissibly strikes at the striker through his family." This, however, is nothing more than a description of how the food stamp program operates as a general matter, a fact that was acknowledged by the District Court. Whenever an individual takes any action that hampers his or her ability to meet the program's eligibility requirements, such as quitting a job or failing to comply with the work-registration requirements, the entire household suffers accordingly. We have never questioned the constitutionality of the entire Act on this basis, and we just recently upheld the validity of the Act's definition of "household" even though that definition embodies the basic fact that the Act determines benefits "on a 'household' rather than an individual basis." That aspect of the program does not violate the Constitution any more so today.

Justice MARSHALL, with whom Justice BRENNAN and Justice BLACKMUN join, dissenting.

. . . The thrust of appellees' equal protection challenge is that the striker amendment to the Food Stamp Act singles them out for special punitive treatment without reasonable justification. As the Court observes, this Fifth Amendment challenge to an allegedly arbitrary legislative classification implicates our least intrusive standard of review — the so-called "rational basis" test, which requires that legislative classifications be "'rationally related to a legitimate governmental interest.'" The Court fails to note, however, that this standard of review, although deferential, "'is not a toothless one.'" . . .

The Secretary's argument that the striker amendment will save money proves far too much. According to the Secretary's reasoning, the exclusion of any unpopular group from a public benefit program would survive rational-basis scrutiny, because exclusion always would result in a decrease in governmental expenditures. . . .

Perhaps recognizing this necessity, the Secretary defends the singling out of strikers and their households as rationally related to the goal of channeling resources to those persons most "genuinely in need." As a threshold matter, however, households denied food stamps because of the presence of a striker are as "needy" in terms of financial resources as households that qualify for food stamps: the former are denied food stamps *despite* the fact that they meet the financial eligibility requirements of [the Act], even after strike-fund payments are counted as household income. This point has particular poignancy for the infants and children of a striking worker. Their need for nourishment is in no logical way diminished by the striker's action. The denial to these children of what is often the only buffer between them and

---

9. For example, one who voluntarily quits a job is disqualified for food stamps for 90 days. Thereafter, he is eligible as long as he registers for work and cannot find a job. The striker, unless he quits his job, is disqualified for as long as he is on strike.

malnourishment and disease cannot be justified as a targeting of the most needy: they *are* the most needy.

The Secretary argues, however, that the striker amendment is related to need at least in the sense of willingness to work, if not in the strict sense of financial eligibility. Because the Food Stamp Act generally excludes persons unwilling to work — and their households — the Secretary argues that it is consistent to exclude strikers and their households as well, on the ground that strikers remain "unwilling to work," at least at the struck business, for the duration of the strike. In the Secretary's eyes, a striker is akin to an unemployed worker who day after day refuses to accept available work. One flaw in this argument is its false factual premise. It is simply not true, as the Secretary argues, that a striker always has a job that "remains available to him." Many strikes result in the complete cessation of a business' operations, so that the decision of an individual striker to return to work would be unavailing. Moreover, many of the businesses that continue to operate during a strike hire permanent replacements for the striking workers. In this situation as well, a striker no longer has the option of returning to work. In fact, the record in this case reveals that a number of appellees were denied food stamps even though they had been permanently replaced by their employers.

But even if it were true that strikers always can return to their jobs, the Secretary's "willingness to work" rationale falls apart in light of the glaring disparity between the treatment of strikers and the treatment of those who are unwilling to work for other reasons. People who voluntarily quit their jobs are not disqualified from receiving food stamps if, after notice and a hearing, they can demonstrate that they quit with "good cause." Moreover, even if the state agency determines that the quit was without good cause, the voluntary quitter is disqualified only for a period of 90 days, and the quitter's household is disqualified only if the quitter was the "head of household." In contrast, a striker is given no opportunity to demonstrate that the strike was for "good cause," even though strikers frequently allege that unfair labor practices by their employer precipitated the strike. In addition, strikers and their entire households, no matter how minimal the striker's contribution to the household's income may have been, are disqualified for the duration of the strike, even if the striker is permanently replaced or business operations temporarily cease. . . .

Unable to explain completely the striker amendment by the "willingness to work" rationale, the Secretary relies most heavily on yet a third rationale: the promotion of governmental neutrality in labor disputes. Indeed, the Court relies solely on this explanation in rejecting appellees' equal protection challenge to the amendment. According to the Secretary and the Court, this last goal rationalizes the discrepancies in the treatment of strikers and voluntary quitters, and of strikers and nonstrikers unwilling to cross a picket line. As the Court explains it, excluding strikers from participation in the food stamp program avoids "undue favoritism to one side or the other in private labor disputes" by preventing governmental " 'subsidization' " of strikes. . . .

[T]he "neutrality" argument on its merits is both deceptive and deeply flawed. Even on the most superficial level, the striker amendment does not treat the parties to a labor dispute evenhandedly: forepersons and other management employees who may become temporarily unemployed when a business ceases to operate during a strike remain eligible for food stamps. Management's burden during the course of the dispute is thus lessened by the receipt of public funds, whereas labor must struggle unaided. This disparity cannot be justified by the argument that the strike is labor's "fault," because strikes are often a direct response to illegal practices by management, such as failure to abide by the terms of a collective-bargaining agreement or refusal to bargain in good faith.

On a deeper level, the "neutrality" argument reflects a profoundly inaccurate view of the relationship of the modern Federal Government to the various parties to a labor dispute. Both individuals and businesses are connected to the Government by a complex web of supports and incentives. On the one hand, individuals may be eligible to receive a wide variety of health, education, and welfare-related benefits. On the other hand, businesses may be eligible to receive a myriad of tax subsidies through deductions, depreciation, and credits, or direct subsidies in the form of Government loans through the Small Business Administration (SBA). Businesses also may receive lucrative Government contracts and invoke the protections of the Bankruptcy Act against their creditors. None of these governmental subsidies to businesses is made contingent on the businesses' abstention from labor disputes, even if a labor dispute is the direct cause of the claim to a subsidy. . . . When viewed against the network of governmental support of both labor and management, the withdrawal of the single support of food stamps—a support critical to the continued life and health of an individual worker and his or her family—cannot be seen as a "neutral" act. Altering the backdrop of governmental support in this one-sided and devastating way amounts to a penalty on strikers, not neutrality.

. . . [S]upporters of the striker amendment likened strikers to "hippies" and "commune residents"—groups whose exclusion from the food stamp program this Court struck down 15 years ago in Department of Agriculture v. Moreno, 413 U.S. 528. The exhortation by the sponsor of the 1971 version of the striker amendment to his colleagues to "say to strikers what we have said . . . to hippies," strongly suggests that the same sort of hostility informed the two amendments, although the striker amendment was not enacted into law until 1981. Our warning in *Moreno* that "a bare congressional desire to harm a politically unpopular group cannot constitute a *legitimate* governmental interest" would seem directly applicable to the instant case. I find the Court's refusal to heed that warning both inexplicable and ill considered.

I agree with the Court that "[i]t was no part of the purposes of the Food Stamp Act to establish a program that would serve as a weapon in labor disputes." The striker amendment under consideration today, however, seems to have precisely that purpose—one admittedly irreconcilable with the legitimate goals of the food stamp program. No other purpose can adequately explain the especially harsh treatment reserved for strikers and their families by the 1981 enactment. Because I conclude that the striker amendment cannot survive even rational-basis scrutiny, I would affirm the District Court's invalidation of the amendment. I dissent.

* * *

In 1946, Congress approved the National School Lunch Act, to provide permanent status and funding to a program that had, for the previous ten years, been an ad hoc program of support to schools based largely on agricultural surpluses in a particular year. Section 2 of the 1946 Act defined its purpose:

> It is hereby declared to be the policy of Congress, as a measure of national security, to safeguard the health and well-being of the Nation's children and to encourage

the domestic consumption of nutritious agricultural commodities and other food, by assisting the States, through grants-in aid and other means, in providing an adequate supply of food and other facilities for the establishment, maintenance, operation and expansion of nonprofit school lunch programs.

The Act set up a system for calculating appropriations to states and required that lunches served by participating schools meet minimum nutritional requirements.

Congress amended the National School Lunch Act in 1962 to address the problems of inequities in the apportionment of funds among the states. Instead of apportioning based on a per capita income and number of school children formula, the 1962 amendments required that funding be more closely tied to the "participation rate," or number of school lunches actually served by schools participating in the program. This more accurately aligned the distribution of funds to states to the need in those states. The Act is codified at 42 U.S.C. § 1751 (2012).

In addition to the National School Lunch Program, two other programs serve children free or reduced-cost meals in schools: the School Breakfast Program, 42 U.S.C. § 1773 (2012), and the Summer Food Service Program, 42 U.S.C. § 1761 (2012). According to the Congressional Research Service, of the three programs, the National School Lunch Program serves the most children and schools. It provides federal assistance to elementary and secondary schools that provide lunch to school children. The total amount of assistance is based on the number of free, reduced-price, and paid lunches served. To receive free lunch, a child's household income must be at or below 130 percent of the federal poverty guidelines for children. For families with household income between 130 percent and 185 percent of the federal poverty guidelines, children can receive a reduced price meal. Moreover, families enrolled in SNAP, TANF, or the Food Distribution Program on Indian Reservations automatically qualify for free lunch. In the fiscal year of 2010, an average of 31.7 million students participated daily. Of those, 17.6 million received a free lunch, 3 million received a reduced price lunch, and 11.1 million received a paid lunch. *See* Randy Alison Aussenberg & Kirsten J. Colello, Cong. Research Serv., R42353, *Domestic Food Assistance: Summary of Programs* (2012). Importantly, the percentage of lunches that are free or reduced rate (even the "full-price" NSLP lunches are subsidized) has risen significantly in the years since the 2007 financial crisis.

In addition to free meals provided to students in schools and at sites during the summer, the federal government also provides support and free meals to eligible elderly individuals and young children through the Child and Adult Care Food Program. 42 U.S.C. § 1766(o) (2012). This program provides cash subsidies to participating family day care homes, nonresidential adult-care centers, child care centers, and after-school programs. The program serves children, chronically disabled individuals, and the elderly.

Eligibility for free and reduced price meals for the elderly, disabled, and children is based on the same criteria as eligibility for school lunches. In FY 2010, the average daily participation of children and adults in this program was 3.4 million, 3.2 million of whom were children.

NOTES AND QUESTIONS

1. As you will see in Chapter 12, international human rights instruments recognize rights to a variety of economic, civil, and social rights, among them

the right to subsistence. Additionally, some nations have recognized subsistence rights as a matter of positive law. For example, in November 2001, the Supreme Court of India issued the following order:

> We direct the State Governments/Union Territories to implement the Mid-Day Meal Scheme by providing every child in every Government and Government assisted Primary Schools with a prepared mid day meal with a minimum content of 300 calories and 8-12 grams of protein each day of school for a minimum of 200 days.

The source of law for this order was a provision of the Indian constitution protecting a "right to life." For information about the November 2001 order and about India's Right to Food Campaign of which it was a vital part, see http://www.righttofoodindia.org/mdm/mdm_scorders.html.

2. Do you support a positive right-to-subsistence income in the United States? Do you think the arguments are different for a right to income versus a right to food? As you proceed through the forthcoming chapters on other social goods and services (work, education, health care, housing, legal aid), consider whether you rank them on a hierarchy of needs. Are there some more suitable to "rights" litigation than others? Why? What do you see as the role of lawyers in advancing or advocating for these rights? What other social actors are relevant to a campaign for such rights?

CHAPTER
5

Work

INTRODUCTION

The connection between work and poverty often seems obvious. Is not the cure for poverty for the poor to work, or work more? Indeed, as discussed in earlier chapters of this book, the economic and moral value of work as a solution to poverty is ever present in both the history of antipoverty policy in the United States and in changes to our welfare programs in recent decades. In particular, promoting work was explicitly established as a goal of the federal welfare program (formerly AFDC, now TANF) in 1996 and celebrated as both an intrinsic virtue and an economic engine. "Nonwork" among the poor has often been identified as a cause not only of poverty, but also of moral failure. As discussed in this chapter, the nation's largest antipoverty program is now the Earned Income Tax Credit (EITC), which provides an income supplement to low-income workers, but nothing to those who do not or cannot work.

Despite the embrace of work as the solution to poverty, however, in America many workers are poor. Indeed, we have a recognized term, "the working poor," to describe those who are not outside the norms of labor and yet who still live in poverty. According to the U.S. Department of Labor, there were 10.5 million "working poor" people in America in 2010, comprising 7.2 percent of the workforce.

Many legal services programs and law school clinics now handle issues related to low-wage work. Where poverty and employment law were once viewed as separate and mutually exclusive fields of law, with distinct clients, lawyers for poor people today increasingly work on both work and non-work-related issues, in much the same way as clients often cycle between welfare and work, rather than inhabiting exclusively one sphere or the other.

This chapter explores the relationship between work and poverty, with particular attention to whether work is indeed the solution to poverty, or if not, why not. Throughout, we consider the relative importance of macroeconomic conditions and personal choices to the poverty of low-wage workers. We begin Section A with narrative and statistical information about the working poor, followed by an examination (Section B) of macroeconomic trends that have altered the distribution of income and the likelihood of increased wages for those at the bottom of the income ladder. Section C examines the problem of wage theft and the "underground economy," which is that sector of the American economy where employers flout labor laws and where workers —

often immigrants, women, and workers of color—earn low wages and are easy prey for wage theft, health and safety violations, and other exploitation. In this context, we explore some of the reasons why violations of law are so widespread in this sector, including the inadequacy of current enforcement resources, the vulnerability of many low-wage workers (because of immigration status, lack of education, or other factors), and gain a glimpse of the day-to-day work of lawyering for the working poor, including assessments of the effectiveness of legal tools.

In Section D, we explore government responses to the problems of the working poor, including the minimum wage, the unemployment insurance system and its gaps, and the EITC. After examining these established institutional responses, we conclude in Section E with measures and tools not yet in widespread use, but often urged by lawyers and other advocates, such as living wages, worker centers, and community benefits agreements. Throughout the chapter, the question of what role lawyers (as litigators, advocates, or policymakers) can play in addressing the problems of low-wage workers is raised.

A. THE WORKING POOR

DAVID K. SHIPLER, *THE WORKING POOR: INVISIBLE IN AMERICA* (2004)

The man who washes cars does not own one. The clerk who files cancelled checks at the bank has $2.02 in her own account. The woman who copy-edits medical textbooks has not been to a dentist in a decade.

This is the forgotten America. At the bottom of its working world, millions live in the shadow of prosperity, in the twilight between poverty and well-being. Whether you're rich, poor, or middle-class, you encounter them every day. They serve you Big Macs and help you find merchandise at Wal-Mart. They harvest your food, clean your offices, and sew your clothes. In a California factory, they package lights for your kids' bikes. In a New Hampshire plant, they assemble books of wallpaper samples to help you redecorate.

They are shaped by their invisible hardships. Some are climbing out of welfare, drug addiction, or homelessness. Others have been trapped for life in a perilous zone of low-wage work. Some of their children are malnourished. Some have been sexually abused. Some live in crumbling housing that contributes to their children's asthma, which means days absent from school. Some of their youngsters do not even have the eyeglasses they need to see the chalkboard clearly.

. . . While the United States has enjoyed unprecedented affluence, low-wage employees have been testing the American doctrine that hard work cures poverty. Some have found that work works. Others have learned that it doesn't. Moving in and out of jobs that demand much and pay little, many people tread just above the official poverty line, dangerously close to the edge of destitution. An inconvenience to an affluent family—minor car trouble, a brief illness, disrupted child care—is a crisis to them, for it can threaten their ability to stay employed. They spend everything and save nothing. They are always behind on their bills. They have minuscule bank accounts or none at all, and so pay more fees and higher interest rates than more secure Americans. Even when the economy is robust, many wander through a borderland of struggle, never getting very far from where they started. When the economy weakens, they slip back toward the precipice. . . .

Breaking away and moving a comfortable distance from poverty seems to require a perfect lineup of favorable conditions. A set of skills, a good starting wage, and a job with the likelihood of promotion are prerequisites. But so are clarity of purpose, courageous self-esteem, a lack of substantial debt, the freedom from illness or addiction, a functional family, a network of upstanding friends, and the right help from private or governmental agencies. Any gap in that array is an entry point for trouble, because being poor means being unprotected. You might as well try playing quarterback with no helmet, no padding, no training, and no experience, behind a line of hundred-pound weaklings. With no cushion of money, no training in the ways of the wider world, and too little defense against the threats and temptations of decaying communities, a poor man or woman gets sacked again and again — buffeted and bruised and defeated. When an exception breaks this cycle of failure, it is called the fulfillment of the American Dream.

As a culture, the United States is not quite sure about the causes of poverty, and is therefore uncertain about the solutions. The American Myth still supposes that any individual from the humblest origins can climb to well-being. We wish that to be true, and we delight in examples that make it seem so, whether fictional or real. . . .

But the American Myth also provides a means of laying blame. In the Puritan legacy, hard work is not merely practical but also moral; its absence suggests an ethical lapse. A harsh logic dictates a hard judgment: If a person's diligent work leads to prosperity, if work is a moral virtue, and if anyone in the society can attain prosperity through work, then the failure to do so is a fall from righteousness. The marketplace is the fair and final judge; a low wage is somehow the worker's fault, for it simply reflects the low value of his labor. In the American atmosphere, poverty has always carried a whiff of sinfulness. . . .

There is an opposite extreme, the American Anti-Myth, which holds the society largely responsible for the individual's poverty. The hierarchy of racial discrimination and economic power creates a syndrome of impoverished communities with bad schools and closed options. The children of the poor are funneled into delinquency, drugs, or jobs with meager pay and little future. The individual is a victim of great forces beyond his control, including profit-hungry corporations that exploit his labor. . . .

. . . Forty years [after Michael Harrington's influential 1962 book *The Other America*], after all our economic achievements, the gap between rich and poor has only widened, with a median net worth of $833,600 among the top 10 percent and just $7,900 for the bottom 20 percent. Life expectancy in the United States is lower, and infant mortality higher, than in Japan, Hong Kong, Israel, Canada, and all the major nations of Western Europe. Yet after all that has been written, discussed, and left unresolved, it is harder to surprise and shock and outrage. So it is harder to generate action.

In reality, people do not fit easily into myths or anti-myths, of course. . . . [W]orking individuals . . . are neither helpless nor omnipotent, but stand on various points along the spectrum between the polar opposites of personal and societal responsibility. Each person's life is the mixed product of bad choices and bad fortune, of roads not taken and roads cut off by the accident of birth or circumstance. It is difficult to find someone whose poverty is not somehow related to his or her unwise behavior — to drop out of school, to have a baby out of wedlock, to do drugs, to be chronically late to work. And it is difficult to find behavior that is not somehow related to the inherited conditions of being poorly parented, poorly educated, poorly housed in neighborhoods from which no distant horizon of possibility can be seen. . . .

BUREAU OF LABOR STATISTICS, U.S. DEP'T OF LABOR, REPORT NO. 1035, *A PROFILE OF THE WORKING POOR, 2010* (2012)

In 2010, according to the Census Bureau, about 46.2 million people, or 15.1 percent of the nation's population, lived below the official poverty level. Although the poor were primarily children and adults who had not participated in the labor force during the year, 10.5 million individuals were among the "working poor" in 2010; this measure was little changed from 2009. The working poor are persons who spent at least 27 weeks in the labor force (that is, working or looking for work) but whose incomes still fell below the official poverty level. In 2010, the working-poor rate — the ratio of the working poor to all individuals in the labor force for at least 27 weeks — was 7.2 percent, also little different from the previous year's figure (7.0 percent).

Following are additional highlights from the 2010 data:

- Full-time workers were less likely to be among the working poor than were part-time workers. Among persons in the labor force for 27 weeks or more, 4.2 percent of those usually employed full time were classified as working poor, compared with 15.1 percent of part-time workers.
- Blacks and Hispanics continued to be much more likely than Whites and Asians to be among the working poor.
- The likelihood of being classified as working poor greatly diminishes as workers attain higher levels of education. Among college graduates, 2.1 percent of those who were in the labor force for at least 27 weeks were classified as working poor, compared with 21.4 percent of those with less than a high school diploma.
- The likelihood of being among the working poor was lower for individuals employed in management, professional, and related occupations than for those employed in service jobs.
- Among families with at least one member in the labor force for 27 weeks or more, those families with children under 18 years old were about 4 times more likely than those without children to live in poverty.
- Women who maintain families were more likely than their male counterparts to be among the working poor. . . .

The specific income thresholds used to determine people's poverty status vary, depending on whether the individuals are living with family members or are living alone or with nonrelatives. For family members, the poverty threshold is determined by their family's total income; for individuals not living in families, their personal income is used as the determinant. Data were collected in the 2011 Annual Social and Economic Supplement to the Current Population Survey. . . .

DEMOGRAPHIC CHARACTERISTICS

Among those who were in the labor force for 27 weeks or more in 2010, about the same number of men (5.3 million) and women (5.2 million) were classified as working poor. The working-poor rate, however, continued to be higher for women (7.6 percent) than for men (6.7 percent). The working-poor rates for both men and women were essentially unchanged from a year earlier. Hispanics and Blacks continued to be much more likely than Whites and Asians to be among the working poor. In 2010, 14.1 percent of Hispanics and 12.6 percent of Blacks were among the working poor, compared with 6.5 percent of Whites and 4.8 percent of Asians.

Table A
Poverty Status of Persons and Primary Families in the Labor Force for 27 Weeks or More, 2007-2010 (numbers in thousands)

Characteristic	2007	2008	2009	2010
Total persons[1]	146,567	147,838	147,902	146,859
In poverty	7,521	8,883	10,391	10,512
Working-poor rate	5.1	6.0	7.0	7.2
Unrelated individuals	33,226	32,785	33,798	34,099
In poverty	2,558	3,275	3,947	3,947
Working-poor rate	7.7	10.0	11.7	11.6
Primary families[2]	65,158	65,907	65,467	64,931
In poverty	4,169	4,538	5,193	5,269
Working-poor rate	6.4	6.9	7.9	8.1

[1]Includes persons in families, not shown separately.
[2]Primary families with at least one member in the labor force for more than half the year.

Working-Poor Rate of Persons in the Labor Force for 27 or More Weeks, 1987-2010

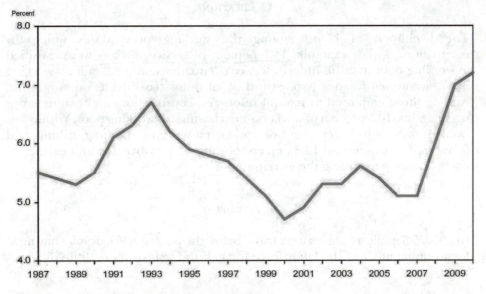

Source: U.S. Bureau of Labor Statistics, Current Population Survey (CPS), Annual Social and Economic Supplement.

White men and women who spent at least 27 weeks or more in the labor force were about equally likely in 2010 to be poor (6.4 percent and 6.6 percent, respectively). Among Hispanics, the rates for men (14.4 percent) and women (13.8 percent) also were about the same. In contrast, the working-poor rate for Black men (10.4 percent) was lower than the rate for Black women (14.5 percent).

Young workers are more vulnerable to poverty than are older age groups, in part because earnings are lower for young workers, and their unemployment rate is higher. In 2010, among youths who were in the labor force for 27 weeks or more, 14.4 percent of 16- to 19-year-olds and 15.5 percent of 20- to 24-year-olds were in poverty, about double the rate for workers age 35 to 44 (7.3 percent). Workers age 45 to 54 (4.9 percent), 55 to 64 (3.4 percent), and 65 and older (2.0 percent) had lower working-poor rates than did other age groups in 2010.

EDUCATIONAL ATTAINMENT

Achieving higher levels of education greatly reduces the incidence of living in poverty. Individuals who complete more years of education have greater access to higher paying jobs—such as management, professional, and related occupations—than those with fewer years of education. Of all the people in the labor force for 27 weeks or more in 2010, those with less than a high school diploma had a higher working-poor rate (21.4 percent) than did high school graduates with no college (9.2 percent). Workers with an associate's degree and those with a bachelor's degree or higher had the lowest working-poor rates: 4.5 percent and 2.1 percent, respectively. At nearly all levels of educational attainment, Blacks and Hispanics were more likely to be among the working poor, in 2010, than were Whites and Asians. . . .

OCCUPATION

The likelihood of being among the working poor varies widely by occupation. . . . For example, 13.1 percent of service workers were classified as working poor in 2010. Indeed, service occupations, with 3.2 million working poor, accounted for nearly one-third of all those classified as working poor. Among those employed in natural resources, construction, and maintenance occupations, 10.5 percent of workers were classified as working poor. Within this occupation group, 19.5 percent of workers employed in farming, fishing, and forestry occupations and 12.8 percent of those in construction and extraction occupations were among the working poor.

FAMILIES

In 2010, 5.3 million families were living below the poverty level, despite having at least one member in the labor force for half the year or more, little different than the 2009 figure. Among families with only one member in the labor force for at least 27 weeks in 2010, married-couple families had a lower likelihood of living below the poverty level (10.1 percent) than did families maintained by women (26.3 percent) or by men (15.6 percent)—a pattern that held, regardless of which member of the married-couple family was in the labor force.

Families with children with at least one member in the labor force for half the year had greater odds of living below the poverty level than did those without children. The proportion of families with children age 18 years and younger that lived in poverty was 12.7 percent, in contrast to 2.8 percent for families without children. About 28.2 percent of families maintained by a woman with children under the age of 18 were in poverty. For such families maintained by men, the proportion in poverty also was relatively high, at 18.0 percent. Married-couple families with children had a working-poor rate of 7.3 percent in 2010. . . .

LABOR MARKET PROBLEMS

As noted earlier, workers who usually work full time are less likely to live in poverty than are others who do not work full time, yet there remains a sizable group of full-time workers who live below the poverty threshold. Among those who participated in the labor force for 27 weeks or more and usually worked in full-time wage and salary jobs, 4.1 million, or 3.8 percent, were classified as working poor in 2010, essentially unchanged from 2009.

There are three major labor market problems that can hinder a worker's ability to earn an income above the poverty threshold: low earnings, periods of unemployment, and involuntary part-time employment. . . .

In 2010, 84 percent of the working poor who usually worked full time experienced at least one of the major labor market problems.

NOTES AND QUESTIONS

1. What does the *Profile of the Working Poor* report above suggest about the causes of low-wage work? Is the existence of low-wage work a legal problem? What do you think are the principal roles for lawyers in addressing the problems of low-wage workers?
2. The ranks of the working poor today include a group not historically strongly represented among workers in large numbers. That group is mothers of young children. As Chapter 4 discussed in detail, the 1996 federal welfare reform imposed stringent work requirements on welfare recipients, and welfare caseloads dropped dramatically during the 1990s. In the following excerpt, Professor Juliet Brodie describes the connection between former welfare recipients and today's working poor, and the cultural significance of the shift toward viewing these mothers as workers rather than welfare recipients.

JULIET M. BRODIE, *POST-WELFARE LAWYERING: CLINICAL LEGAL EDUCATION AND A NEW POVERTY LAW AGENDA*

20 Wash. U. J.L. & Pol'y 201 (2006)

. . . Because it frames the current cultural potency of the phrase "the working poor," the rhetoric surrounding welfare reform and its effects should be briefly reviewed. While welfare reform changed the daily economic lives of millions of former AFDC recipients, it also represented the triumph of a new view of poor people, work, and dependency. The official goal of the nation's "welfare" policy became connecting welfare recipients to work. TANF, the cash assistance program that replaced AFDC, has two cornerstones: first, recipients must engage in "work activity" to remain eligible; second, there is a sixty-month lifetime limit on aid. The rhetoric of welfare reform in the 1990s sounded in work; the problem to be solved was not "poverty," but, rather, the "nonwork" of welfare recipients. Indeed, while ending "dependence" on welfare is among the legislative goals of PRWORA, decreasing poverty is not. . . .

For purposes of AFDC and TANF, the most salient "non-working poor person" was the single mother, whose prevalence on the AFDC rolls was the problem to be solved. Welfare reform embodies the view that a single mother without other means of economic support (husband or other responsible adult) is not, without other factors, exempt from the social expectation of work. Reform proponents, indeed, prevailed with the argument that it was the availability of welfare itself that kept these women and their children in poverty by creating a dependency on public support that squelched their abilities to become self-supporting through work (or supported by a husband, through marriage). With welfare reform, work was officially anointed as the national "welfare" (really, "non-welfare") policy. . . .

. . . While [welfare leavers] may be employed in large numbers, that employment has not necessarily led to an improved economic position. Focusing on the economic well-being of women who left welfare, the Institute for Research on Poverty at the University of Wisconsin found that, in the first year after leaving welfare, families' incomes dropped twenty percent. Even after three years, only forty percent of leavers had annual incomes higher than they had while on welfare. Other analysts also concluded that the real income of low-income mothers declined after welfare reform and that the remaining safety net failed to make up the difference. One of the early studies of the economic impact of welfare reform's implementation concluded, not surprisingly, that in many situations, former welfare recipients' economic situation worsened in part because they had higher expenses in the work force than they had had on welfare. . . . With these sobering labor market statistics as background, I turn to one potential "bright side" of welfare reform for low-income people: the rise of the terminology and rhetoric of "the working poor," with its elevated, somewhat noble, social status and its potential to increase political power for the post-welfare poor.

Social scientists' interest in the welfare leavers, and in the success or failure generally of a piece of legislation as dramatic as welfare reform, has a partner on the popular culture side. Several journalists followed the progress of welfare reform, telling new stories to the American public about low-income people, and giving new familiarity to the term "the working poor." Where American popular rhetoric about poverty was once dominated by the figure of the "welfare queen" enjoying a leisurely life of AFDC entitlements, a new figure emerged with welfare reform: the hard-working, barely-making-ends-meet member of a new social class, the working poor. . . .

While in the AFDC era poor people were dismissed as non-workers, lazy, and outside of dominant American culture, in the post-welfare era, poverty and work are no longer plausibly opposed. As a social category, "the working poor" takes the wind out of the sails of the traditional dichotomy between the "deserving" and the "undeserving" poor, which associated the former with work and the latter with sloth. Former Labor Secretary Robert Reich expressed it thus:

> The one clearly positive consequence of welfare reform has been to move several million people from being considered "undeserving poor" because they don't work to being viewed as "deserving" poor because they do. Most former welfare recipients are as poor as they were before, but the fact that they now work for their meager living has altered the politics surrounding the question of what to do about their poverty.

Robert B. Reich, *Introduction*, in *Making Work Pay: America After Welfare* (Robert Kuttner ed., 2002).

New York Times reporter and author Jason DeParle also notes the new moral status of the post-welfare working poor: "Trading welfare checks for pay stubs, [the working poor] staked a moral claim to a greater share of the nation's prosperity." (Jason DeParle, *American Dream: Three Women, Ten Kids, and a Nation's Drive to End Welfare* (2004) (excerpted in Chapter 4)).

* * *

Professor Brodie's article goes on to discuss changing trends in the caseload of many legal services clinics and organizations, which have begun handling such matters as the wage theft cases discussed in Section C of this chapter, and to urge poverty lawyers to adopt a "consolidated workers' agenda" that draws on the rise of workers' centers (discussed in Section E.2) and explicitly addresses the needs of low-wage workers, whether connected to the welfare system or not. In a similar vein, Professor Karl Klare observed in 1995 that "poverty law" and "employment law" were traditionally viewed as separate and mostly mutually exclusive fields, reflecting in part the "social distance" between workers and welfare recipients, even though "organized labor itself was once a 'poor people's movement.'" He called for advocates in both fields to work and strategize collectively on the problems of poor people, workers and welfare recipients alike. Karl E. Klare, *Toward New Strategies for Low-Wage Workers*, 4 B.U. Pub. Int. L.J. 245 (1995). To a great degree, the inclusion of this chapter on work in a poverty law textbook reflects the acceptance of these ideas and strategies.

Two popular books from the first decade of the new millennium set out to humanize America's low-wage workers. In *The Working Poor* (excerpted at the beginning of this chapter), David K. Shipler profiles a number of low-wage workers in various occupations, attempting to connect the macro and micro forces that lead individuals to such jobs and often trap them there. In the best-selling *Nickel and Dimed: On (Not) Getting By in America*, columnist and social critic Barbara Ehrenreich narrates the three months she spent working as a waitress, hotel maid, house cleaner, nursing home aide, and Wal-Mart clerk, using her own and her coworkers' experiences to illustrate vividly the difficulty of affording rent, food, transportation, and other necessities on minimum wage and near-minimum-wage salaries. Both books, and the criticism of them that follows, also raise the question of how much responsibility workers themselves bear for their poverty.

DAVID K. SHIPLER, *THE WORKING POOR: INVISIBLE IN AMERICA* (2004)

Work didn't work for Debra Hall. . . . Like many welfare mothers forced off the rolls into the labor force, she found almost everything in her life changed except her material standard of living. She had to buy a car to get to work, wake up before dawn, struggle to learn new skills, and weave her way among racial tensions on the job. Her budget had more complexity but no surplus. Her major gain was emotional — she felt better about herself — and so, on balance, she was tentatively glad to be working.

Debra was fortunate enough to live downstairs in a two-family house owned by her mother, in a Cleveland neighborhood of faded comfort. With her meager wage on the open market, she would have been confined to a dreadful flat. Here, the houses needed paint and their roofs needed shingles, but the rooms were spacious and the streets were not so hard. . . .

Inside, the living room was dark at the height of the afternoon. She had been sleeping on the couch since returning from her 3:30-11:30 a.m. shift in a bakery, and she still wore her white uniform shirt with "Debra" on a label stitched above the right-hand pocket. Her black hair was straightened, and a perpetual smile illuminated her broad face, touched by a flicker of sadness now and then as she managed to laugh pungently through the tales she told of hardship.

The television set was on, and an upright vacuum cleaner stood in the middle of the living room floor. Decorating an end table were pictures of her two children: a younger son who was handicapped by Down syndrome, and an older daughter who was progressing modestly at the lower levels of a banking career. "Thank God she didn't get on welfare," Debra declared in her deep voice.

It was the birth of her daughter, when Debra was eighteen, that launched a twenty-one-year career of welfare checks and "under-the-table-type jobs," as she put it, including positions as a housekeeper and bar hostess that paid her in unrecorded cash. The widespread practice of holding undeclared jobs while getting welfare meant that "welfare-to-work" should have been called "work only," for it slashed people's actual incomes. "I got used to that, having the extra money," Debra explained. "I could make like, per week, probably like $120 'cause they would pay you like $30 a night, plus tips. . . . So I got used to that and got stuck on it and forgot about the outside world."

The letter reminding her of the real world came from her caseworker. At age thirty-nine, Debra had no skills to speak of. She had dropped out of community college — "I wasn't puttin' anything into it," she confessed. She judged herself "lazy" and had never tried to learn a trade. She had lived off her welfare check, her illicit earnings, and her Supplementary Security Income (SSI) payments from Social Security for her son, a teenager who was in special schooling. Welfare reform was now catching up with her. The 1996 act allowing states to impose time limits and work requirements gave Ohio the right to demand that Debra get a job or do job training.

She found her way to the Cleveland Center for Employment Training, whose board members were executives of local industries that needed machinists, welders, and other laborers, and because she liked wearing jeans and sneakers instead of dress-up clothes, she chose warehouse work — "shipping and receiving," in the trade vernacular. As part of its real-life training, the center dispatched UPS packages for companies in a small industrial park, so Debra learned how to type, how to operate the computerized UPS system, how to keep an inventory, how to run a forklift. The course "settled me down and made me want to learn and want to do something as far as getting into the workforce," she said. It was the first time in her life that she felt motivated, and it made her think that welfare-to-work wasn't a bad idea. "People will want more," she predicted, "and be able to teach their kids that's growing up to want more. . . . And if they put us into these training centers and show us that we can do it, we can show our kids."

That's how it looked when Debra was still a trainee. It didn't look as bright once she got into a job. First, the car she had to buy to avoid a long bus ride to work was not cheap and not reliable. Then, UPS had no openings, so she took her forklift certification, her carefully prepared résumé, and her newly acquired interviewing skills to Orlando Bakery. Poised to answer all questions brilliantly, she never got to speak. A man guided her quickly around the plant, and then asked, "Can you start at seven?"

She was stunned. "All this rehearsing I did to talk and everything like that, and he just asks me can I start at seven." She gave a sour laugh. "I thought I was being hired as a forklift operator," she continued. "I was wanting to run a forklift 'cause they have forklifts. They have them in shipping and receiving, the dock area where the trucks pick up. You have to load the trucks up and everything. But it's all men!" she yelped. When she arrived at work the first day, she was put on an assembly line. "Excuse me, heh," she told a supervisor. "You just hired a woman that can drive a forklift.'"

"'Oh, we don't have any openings for a forklift operator.'"

On-the-job training could be summed up in a single command: copy the worker next to you. Debra watched closely and began by flipping bread on the dreaded garlic line, a conveyer that required employees to start at 7 a.m. and stay until the entire day's production was packaged, usually about 5 p.m. and sometimes as late as 6. "Everybody there can't stand it," she said. "The garlic loaves, the sticks, garlic sticks, garlic rolls — and every chance they got they was coming over with a different type of bread to see if they could make it garlic." . . .

The workers were unionized, but the conditions were unworthy of a union contract. The pay was $7 an hour, including a paid lunch hour and a fifteen-minute break after nine hours of work. Benefits didn't kick in until an employee had been on the job for six months. It wasn't hard labor, but it challenged Debra's mental and physical agility. "The first day I worked there, I'm like, I'm not gonna get this. It was terrible." She was laughing again. "I'm like, oh, God, my whole body was sore. And just lookin' at the conveyors 'cause the stuff is steady movin', you know, and it's movin' fast 'cause it's comin' past you. . . . I was crying almost. I was like, I can't do this."

After a while she was offered a welcome chance to move off the garlic line, and even though it meant getting out of bed at 2 a.m. for her shift, she would be doing less stressful work: packing bread into bags and cartons. The respite from tension was short-lived, however. No sooner had Debra learned the packing task than she was yanked again into panic when a supervisor abruptly assigned her to a machine that she was untrained to operate. "I didn't even know the name of the machine," she said. "I just happened to hear them say, 'You be Number Two.' I was like, 'What you all be talking about?'" Number Two was, indeed, the name of the machine, a huge piece of equipment that needed somebody to "flip switches," Debra explained. "You have to feed the bags in, make sure the zip locks that close the breads is on. You have to set the machine a certain way — different kinds of bread, hamburger buns, hotdog buns. You know, different parts of the line you have to set the slicer to slice the bread. You have to know how deep.''

She was having nightmares. "I'm still disoriented because I can't think. All I keep doing is feel like I'm floating, because of this machine. . . . I done had dreams where my supervisor was fussin' because this didn't go right. You know what I'm saying? The job came home with me. . . . This doesn't make sense for this little seven dollars.'' A few months later her wage went to $7.90.

. . . Debra had no confidence that she could move up in position and pay. Whenever she asked supervisors about the salary at their level, they'd answer vaguely, "It varies.'' She couldn't get specific figures, so she had no sense of what her goal might be. She seemed doomed to repeat her family's inability to emerge from low wages. She barely knew her father and couldn't remember what work he did. Her mother had cleaned houses and had drawn a welfare check. Two of her brothers had been shot dead, one in a bar fight, the other in his car. A third was in prison for burglaries, a fourth worked as a truck driver, and a fifth did maintenance at a retirement center. One sister worked in a factory, another in a bar, and a third took care of her grandchildren. Debra's daughter had taken the modest step from bank teller to a promotional sales job, but Debra was mostly delighted that she had avoided pregnancy. "I was lucky. I just did a lot of preaching to her,'' Debra said. "I did escape being a grandma early.''

Debra's cash flow was so anemic, compared with her expenses, that she barely had a bank balance. Her wages from the bakery were deposited directly, but they were gone as soon as they hit the ledger. "I have maybe $8 in the account every week,'' she said. "You can't get less than ten from the money machine, so if I have five, I can't get five.'' If she went to a teller, the bank levied a $3 charge. She was so low on January that she had to pay a $15 fee for a two-week $100 advance from a storefront payday load operation.

Her fellow workers in the bakery were trapped in gloom. Nothing there encouraged her. As she began the job, one employee after another cautioned her: "You don't want to work here.'' She heard the warning even from an assistant supervisor who had been her high school classmate.

"Debra, I know you don't want to work here,'' she remembered her classmate saying.

"How long you been here?'' Debra asked.

"I've been here twelve years,'' her friend replied.

"And I didn't have anything to say,'' Debra remarked to me, "but my mind was saying, 'What the hell you doing here so long?'''

BARBARA EHRENREICH, *NICKEL AND DIMED: ON (NOT) GETTING BY IN AMERICA* (2001)

Mostly out of laziness, I decide to start my low-wage life in the town nearest to where I actually live, Key West, Florida, which with a population of about 25,000 is elbowing its way up to the status of a genuine city. . . .

My first task is to find a place to live. I figure that if I can earn $7 an hour— which, from the want ads, seems doable—I can afford to spend $500 on rent or maybe, with severe economies, $600 and still have $400 or $500 left over for food and gas. In the Key West area, this pretty much confines me to flophouses and trailer homes—like the one, a pleasing fifteen-minute drive from town, that has no air-conditioning, no screens, no fans, no television, and, by way of diversion, only the challenge of evading the landlord's Doberman pinscher. The big problem with this place, though, is the rent, which at $675 a month is well beyond my reach. All right, Key West is expensive. But so is New York City, or the Bay Area, or Jackson, Wyoming, or Telluride, or Boston, or any other place where tourists and the wealthy compete for living space with the people who clean their toilets and fry their hash browns. Still, it is a shock to realize that "trailer trash" has become, for me, a demographic category to aspire to.

So I decide to make the common trade-off between affordability and convenience and go for a $500-a-month "efficiency" thirty miles up a two-lane highway from the employment opportunities of Key West, meaning forty-five minutes if there's no road construction and I don't get caught behind some sundazed Canadian tourists. . . .

. . . Best Western, Econo Lodge, and HoJo's all let me fill out application forms, and these are, to my relief, mostly interested in whether I am a legal resident of the United States and have committed any felonies. My next stop is Winn-Dixie, the supermarket, which turns out to have a particularly onerous application process, featuring a twenty-minute "interview" by computer since, apparently, no human on the premises is deemed capable of representing the corporate point of view. I am conducted to a large room decorated with posters illustrating how to look "professional" (it helps to be white and, if female, permed) and warning of the slick promises that union organizers might try to tempt me with. The interview is multiple-choice: Do I have anything, such as child care problems, that might make it hard for me to get to work on time? Do I think safety on the job is the responsibility of management? Then, popping up cunningly out of the blue: How many dollars' worth of stolen goods have I purchased in the last year? Would I turn in a fellow employee if I caught him stealing? Finally, "Are you an honest person?"

Apparently I ace the interview, because I am told that all I have to do is show up in some doctor's office tomorrow for a urine test. This seems to be a fairly general rule: if you want to stack Cheerios boxes or vacuum hotel rooms in chemically fascist America, you have to be willing to squat down and pee in front of a health worker (who has no doubt had to do the same thing herself). The wages Winn-Dixie is offering — $6 and a couple of dimes to start with — are not enough, I decide, to compensate for this indignity. . . .

Three days go by like this and, to my chagrin, no one from the approximately twenty places at which I've applied calls me for an interview. I had been vain enough to worry about coming across as too educated for the jobs I sought, but no one even seems interested in finding out how overqualified I am. Only later will I realize that the want ads are not a reliable measure of the actual jobs available at any particular time. They are . . . the employers' insurance policy against the relentless turnover of the low-wage workforce. Most of the big hotels run ads almost continually, if only to build a supply of applicants to replace the current workers as they drift away or are fired, so finding a job is just a matter of being in the right place at the right time and flexible enough to take whatever is being offered that day. This finally happens to me at one of the big discount chain hotels where I go, as usual, for housekeeping and am sent instead to try out as a waitress at the attached "family restaurant," a dismal spot looking out on a parking garage. . . .

So begins my career at the Hearthside, where for two weeks I work from 2:00 'till 10:00 p.m. for $2.43 an hour plus tips. . . .

. . . You might imagine, from a comfortable distance, that people who live, year in and year out, on $6 to $10 an hour have discovered some survival stratagems unknown to the middle class. But no. It's not hard to get my coworkers talking about their living situations, because housing, in almost every case, is the principal source of disruption in their lives, the first thing they fill you in on when they arrive for their shifts. After a week, I have compiled the following survey:

> Gail is sharing a room in a well-known downtown flophouse for $250 a week. Her roommate, a male friend, has begun hitting on her, driving her nuts, but the rent would be impossible alone.
>
> Claude, the Haitian cook, is desperate to get out of the two-room apartment he shares with his girlfriend and two other, unrelated people. As far as I can determine, the other Haitian men live in similarly crowded situations.
>
> Annette, a twenty-year-old server who is six months pregnant and abandoned by her boyfriend, lives with her mother, a postal clerk.
>
> Marianne, who is a breakfast server, and her boyfriend are paying $170 a week for a one-person trailer. . . .
>
> Tina, another server, and her husband are paying $60 a night for a room in the Days Inn. This is because they have no car and the Days Inn is in walking distance of the Hearthside. When Marianne is tossed out of her trailer for subletting (which is against trailer park rules), she leaves her boyfriend and moves in with Tina and her husband.
>
> Joan, who had fooled me with her numerous and tasteful outfits (hostesses wear their own clothes), lives in a van parked behind a shopping center at night and showers in Tina's motel room. The clothes are from thrift shops.

It strikes me, in my middle-class solipsism, that there is gross improvidence in some of these arrangements. When Gail and I are wrapping silverware in napkins—the only task for which we are permitted to sit—she tells me she is thinking of escaping from her roommate by moving into the Days Inn herself. I am astounded: how she can even think of paying $40 to $60 a day? But if I was afraid of sounding like a social worker, I have come out just sounding like a fool. She squints at me in disbelief: "And where am I supposed to get a month's rent and a month's deposit for an apartment?" I'd been feeling pretty smug about my $500 efficiency, but of course it was made possible only by the $1,300 I had allotted myself for start-up costs when I began my low-wage life: $1,000 for the first month's rent and deposit, $100 for initial groceries and cash in my pocket, $200 stuffed away for emergencies. In poverty, as in certain propositions in physics, starting conditions are everything.

There are no secret economies that nourish the poor; on the contrary, there are a host of special costs. If you can't put up the two months' rent you need to secure an apartment, you end up paying through the nose for a room by the week. If you have only a room, with a hot plate at best, you can't save by cooking up huge lentil stews that can be frozen for the week ahead. You eat fast food or the hot dogs and Styrofoam cups of soup that can be microwaved in a convenience store. If you have no money for health insurance—and the Hearthside's [paltry] plan kicks in only after three months—you go without routine care or prescription drugs and end up paying the price. Gail, for example, was doing fine, healthwise anyway, until she ran out of money for estrogen pills. She is supposed to be on the company health plan by now, but they claim to have lost her application form and to be beginning the paperwork all over again. So she spends $9 a pop for pills to control the migraines she wouldn't have, she insists, if her estrogen supplements were covered. Similarly, Marianne's boyfriend lost his job as a roofer because he missed so much time after getting a cut on his foot for which he couldn't afford the prescribed antibiotic.

My own situation, when I sit down to assess it after two weeks of work, would not be much better if this were my actual life. The seductive thing about wait-ressing is that you don't have to wait for payday to feel a few bills in your pocket, and my tips usually cover meals and gas, plus something left over to stuff into the kitchen drawer I use as a bank. But as the tourist business slows in the summer heat, I sometimes leave work with only $20 in tips (the gross is higher, but servers share about 15 percent of their tips with the busboys and bartenders). With wages included, this amounts to about the minimum wage of $5.15 an hour. The sum in the drawer is piling up but at the present rate of accumulation will be more than $100 short of my rent when the end of the month comes around. Nor can I see any expenses to cut. True, I haven't gone the lentil stew route yet, but that's because I don't have a large cooking pot, potholders, or a ladle to stir with (which would cost a total of about $30 at Kmart, somewhat less at a thrift store), not to mention onions, carrots, and the indispensible bay leaf. I do make my lunch almost every day — usually some slow-burning, high-protein combo like frozen chicken patties with melted cheese on top and canned pinto beans on the side. Dinner is at the Hearthside, which offers its employees a choice of BLT, fish sandwich, or hamburger for only $2. The burger lasts longest, especially if it's heaped with gutpuckering jalapeños, but by midnight my stomach is growling again.

So unless I want to start using my car as a residence, I have to find a second or an alternative job. . . .

In Key West, I earned $1,039 in one month and spent $517 on food, gas, toiletries, laundry, phone, and utilities. Rent was the deal breaker. If I had remained in my $500 efficiency, I would have been able to pay the rent and have $22 left over (which is still $78 less than the cash I had in my pocket at the start of the month). This in itself would have been a dicey situation if I had attempted to continue for a few more months, because sooner or later I would have had to spend something on medical and dental care or drugs other than ibuprofen. But my move to the trailer park — for the purpose, you will recall, of taking a second job — made me responsible for $625 a month in rent alone, utilities not included. Here I might have economized by giving up the car and buying a used bike (for about $50) or walking to work. Still, two jobs, or at least a job and a half, would be a necessity, and I had learned that I could not do two physically demanding jobs in the same day, at least not at any acceptable standard of performance.

In Portland, Maine, I came closest to achieving a decent fit between income and expenses, but only because I worked seven days a week. Between my two jobs, I was earning approximately $300 a week after taxes and paying $480 a month in rent, or a manageable 40 percent of my earnings. It helped, too, that gas and electricity were included in my rent and that I got two or three free meals each weekend at the nursing home. But I was there at the beginning of the off-season. If I had stayed until June 2000 I would have faced the Blue Haven's summer rent of $390 a week, which would of course have been out of the question. So to survive year-round, I would have had to save enough, in the months between August 1999 and May 2000, to accumulate the first month's rent and deposit on an actual apartment. I think I could have done this — saved

$800 to $1,000 — at least if no car trouble or illness interfered with my budget. I am not sure, however, that I could have maintained the seven-day-a-week regimen month after month or eluded the kinds of injuries that afflicted my fellow workers in the housecleaning business. . . .

I was baffled, initially, by what seemed like a certain lack of get-up-and-go on the part of my fellow workers. Why didn't they just leave for a better-paying job, as I did when I moved from the Hearthside to Jerry's? Part of the answer is that actual humans experience a little more "friction" than marbles do, and the poorer they are, the more constrained their mobility usually is. Low-wage people who don't have cars are often dependent on a relative who is willing to drop them off and pick them up again each day, sometimes on a route that includes the babysitter's house or the child care center. Change your place of work and you may be confronted with an impossible topographical problem to solve, or at least a reluctant driver to persuade. Some of my coworkers, in Minneapolis as well as Key West, rode bikes to work, and this clearly limited their geographical range. For those who do possess cars, there is still the problem of gas prices, not to mention the general hassle, which is of course far more onerous for the carless, of getting around to fill out applications, to be interviewed, to take drug tests. I have mentioned, too, the general reluctance to exchange the devil you know for one that you don't know, even when the latter is tempting you with a better wage-benefit package. At each new job, you have to start all over, clueless and friendless.

There is another way that low-income workers differ from "economic man." For the laws of economics to work, the "players" need to be well informed about their options. The ideal case — and I've read that the technology for this is just around the corner — would be the consumer whose Palm Pilot displays the menu and prices for every restaurant or store he or she passes. Even without such technological assistance, affluent job hunters expect to study the salary-benefit packages offered by their potential employers, watch the financial news to find out if these packages are in line with those being offered in other regions or fields, and probably do a little bargaining before taking the job.

But there are no Palm Pilots, cable channels, or Web sites to advise the low-wage job seeker. She has only the help-wanted signs and the want ads to go on, and most of these coyly refrain from mentioning numbers. So information about who earns what and where has to travel by word of mouth, and for inexplicable cultural reasons, this is a very slow and unreliable route. . . .

* * *

While Shipler's and especially Ehrenreich's books became hugely popular, with Ehrenreich's becoming a staple of high school and college assignments, they are not without their critics. The excerpt below captures some of the criticism.

STEVEN MALANGA, *THE MYTH OF THE WORKING POOR*
14 City J. 26 (2004)

Forty years ago a young, radical journalist helped ignite the War on Poverty with his pioneering book *The Other America*. In its pages, Michael Harrington warned that the recently proclaimed age of affluence was a mirage, that beneath the surface of U.S. prosperity lay tens of millions of people stuck in hopeless poverty that only massive government intervention could help.

Today, a new generation of journalists is straining to duplicate Harrington's feat — to convince contemporary America that its economic system doesn't work for millions and that only government can lift them out of poverty. These new journalists face a tougher task than Harrington's, though, because all levels of government have spent about $10 trillion on poverty programs since his book appeared, with disappointing, even counterproductive, results. And over the last four decades, millions of poor people, immigrants and native-born alike, have risen from poverty, without recourse to the government programs that Harrington inspired.

But brushing aside the War on Poverty's failure and the success of so many in climbing America's economic ladder, this generation of authors dusts off the old argument for a new era. Books like Barbara Ehrenreich's *Nickel and Dimed* and David Shipler's *The Working Poor* tell us that the poor are doing exactly what America expects of them — finding jobs, rising early to get to work every day, chasing the American dream — but that our system of "carnivorous capitalism" is so heavily arrayed against them that they can't rise out of poverty or live a decent life. These new anthems of despair paint their subjects as forced off welfare by uncompassionate conservatives and trapped in low-wage jobs that lead nowhere. They claim, too, that the good life that the country's expanding middle class enjoys rests on the backs of these working poor and their inexpensive labor, so that prosperous Americans owe them more tax-funded help.

Though these books resolutely ignore four decades' worth of lessons about poverty, they have found a big audience. The commentariat loves them. Leftish professors have made them required course reading. And Democratic candidates have made their themes central to the 2004 elections. So it's worth looking closely at what these tomes contend, and at the economic realities that they distort.

To begin with, they follow Harrington's 1962 classic by seeing the poor as victims of forces over which they have no control. From the hills of Appalachia to the streets of Harlem, Harrington had found a generation of impoverished former sharecroppers whose jobs had been replaced by mechanization. For them, the advances that enriched everyone else spelled disaster: "progress is misery" and "hopelessness is the message." Unprepared for life off the farm, many could never find productive work, Harrington argued, and would need perpetual government aid. . . .

Ehrenreich's anger propelled her to write *Nickel and Dimed.* Beginning life as a piece of "undercover journalism" for Harper's, the 2001 book purports to reveal the truth about poverty in post-welfare reform America. "In particular," Ehrenreich asks in the introduction, how were "the roughly four million women about to be booted into the labor market by welfare reform . . . going to make it on $6 or $7 an hour?"

Nickel and Dimed doesn't fuss much with public-policy agendas, messy economic theories, or basic job numbers. Instead, it gives us Ehrenreich's first-person account of three brief sojourns into the world of the lowest of low-wage work: as a waitress for a low-priced family restaurant in Florida; as a maid for a housecleaning service in Maine; and as a women's-apparel clerk at a Minneapolis Wal-Mart. In her journeys, she meets a lively and sympathetic assortment of co-workers: Haitian busboys, a Czech dishwasher, a cook with a gambling problem, and assorted single working mothers. But the focus is mostly on Ehrenreich, not her colleagues.

The point that *Nickel and Dimed* wants to prove is that in today's economy, a woman coming off welfare into a low-wage job can't earn enough to pay for basic living expenses. Rent is a burden, Ehrenreich discovers. In Florida, she lands a $500-a-month efficiency apartment; in Maine, she spends $120 a week for a shared apartment in an old motel (she turns down a less expensive room elsewhere because it's on a noisy commercial street); in Minneapolis, she pays $255 a week for a moldy hotel room. These seem like reasonable enough rents, except perhaps for Minneapolis, judging from her description of the place. But with her entry-level wages — roughly the minimum wage (when tips are included) as a waitress, about $6 an hour as a maid, and $7 an hour to start at Wal-Mart — Ehrenreich quickly finds that she'll need a second job to support herself. This seems to startle her, as if holding down two jobs is something new to America. "In the new version of supply and demand," she writes, "jobs are so cheap — as measured by the pay — that a worker is encouraged to take on as many as she possibly can."

What's utterly misleading about Ehrenreich's exposé, though, is how she fixes the parameters of her experiment so that she inevitably gets the outcome that she wants — "proof" that the working poor can't make it. Ehrenreich complains that America's supposedly tight labor market doesn't produce entry-level jobs at $10 an hour. For people with no skills, that's probably true in most parts of the country; but everywhere, the U.S. economy provides ample opportunity to move up quickly. Yet Ehrenreich spends only a few weeks with each of her employers, and so never gives herself the chance for promotion or to find better work (or better places to live).

In fact, few working in low-wage jobs stay in them long. And most workers don't just move on quickly — they also move on to better jobs. The Sphere Institute, a California public-policy think tank founded by Stanford University professors, charted the economic path of workers in the state from 1988 to 2000 and found extraordinary mobility across industries and up the economic ladder. Over 40 percent of the lowest income group worked in retail in 1988; by 2000, more than half of that group had switched to other industries. Their average inflation-adjusted income gain after moving on: 83 percent, to over $32,000 a year.

The workers who stayed in retail, moreover, were usually the higher earners, making about $10,000 more a year than the leavers. They had already started improving their lots back in 1988, in other words, and probably elected to stay because they rightly saw further opportunity in retailing, though the study doesn't say what happened to them. The same dynamic occurs in other industries where low-wage jobs are concentrated, the study found: those who do well stay and watch earnings go up; those who feel stuck often depart and see earnings rise, too, as they find more promising jobs. In total, over 12 years, 88 percent of those in California's lowest economic category moved up, their incomes rising as they gained experience on the job and time in the workforce, two things that the marketplace rewards.

Such results are only the latest to confirm the enormous mobility that the U.S. economy offers. As a review of academic, peer-reviewed mobility studies by two Urban Institute researchers put it: "It is clear that there is substantial mobility — both short-term and long-term — over an average life-cycle in the United States." Perhaps most astonishingly, mobility often occurs within months. The Urban

Institute report points out that several mobility studies based on the University of Michigan's Panel Study of Income Dynamics, which has traced thousands of American families since 1968, show that about 20 percent of those in the lowest economic quintile rise at least one economic class within a year. If Ehrenreich had given herself 12 months in her low-wage stints, instead of a week or two, she might have worked her way into the lower middle class by the end of her experiment.

This mobility explains why poverty rates didn't soar in the 1990s, even though some 13 million people, most of them dirt-poor, immigrated here legally. In fact, the country's poverty rate actually fell slightly during the nineties — which could only happen because millions already here rose out of the lowest income category. . . .

Given that such data subvert Ehrenreich's case against the U.S. economic system, she unsurprisingly puts statistics aside in *Nickel and Dimed* and instead seeks to paint the low-wage workplace as oppressive and humiliating to workers forced by reformers to enter it. But given the author's self-absorption, what the reader really gets is a self-portrait of Ehrenreich as a longtime rebel with an anti-authoritarian streak a mile wide, who can't stomach the basic boundaries that most people easily accept in the workplace.

At Wal-Mart, for instance, she's "oppressed by the mandatory gentility" that the company requires of her, as if being nice to customers and co-workers were part of the tyranny of capitalism. (I suspect that most customers, if they encountered a snarling Ehrenreich as a clerk while shopping, would flee for the exit.) . . .

In Ehrenreich's looking-glass world, opportunity becomes oppression. Hired by Wal-Mart shortly after applying, she weirdly protests that "there is no intermediate point [between applying and beginning orientation] . . . in which you confront the employer as a free agent, entitled to cut her own deal." Though she admits that in such a tight labor market, "I would probably have been welcome to apply at any commercial establishment I entered," she still feels "like a supplicant with her hand stretched out."

Unable to understand why her fellow workers don't share her outrage, this longtime socialist and radical feminist turns on the very people with whom she's trying to sympathize, imagining that they can only accept their terrible exploitation because they've become psychologically incapable of resisting. Why are the maids so loyal to the owner of the cleaning service? she asks. They're so emotionally "needy" that they can't break free, she speculates. Why do Wal-Mart workers accept their place in "Mr. Sam's family" instead of rising in a tide of unionization against the company? The Waltons have hoodwinked them, she surmises, misunderstanding completely the appeal to employees of Wal-Mart's opportunity culture, where two-thirds of management has come up from hourly-employee store ranks and where workers own a good chunk of company stock. . . .

Not everybody is taking this force-feeding of leftist propaganda sitting down. Conservative students at the University of North Carolina at Chapel Hill protested the freshman-orientation reading committee's choice of *Nickel and Dimed*, bringing in local conservative groups and state legislators to try to force greater ideological balance on the school's reading program. What students objected to, explains Michael McKnight, a UNC grad who helped lead the protest, was the book's biased and misleading depiction of the American workplace, along with UNC's failure to provide any counterweight, such as critical reviews of the book.

Says McKnight, "The freshman-orientation package of resources on the book included nothing but glowing reviews of it and lists of Ehrenreich's awards."

There's other evidence that students aren't buying Ehrenreich's pessimistic line on the U.S. economy. Professor Larry Schweikart, who teaches U.S. economic history at the University of Dayton, assigns his students *Nickel and Dimed* along with other books that paint a brighter picture of the American economy. Schweikart says that many students quickly grasp what's wrong with Ehrenreich's book. "Many of these kids have worked in the low-wage marketplace, so they are more familiar with it than their professors or media reviewers. They tell me that there are better jobs out there than the ones Ehrenreich stuck herself with, that those jobs aren't long-term, and that they understand that she didn't give herself any time to find better work or advance."

If the holes in Ehrenreich's argument are clear even to some college kids, the logical gaps gape even wider in the 2004 book that hopes to succeed *Nickel and Dimed* as the definitive left statement on the oppressiveness of low-wage work: *The Working Poor,* by former *New York Times* reporter David Shipler. To his credit, Shipler, unlike Ehrenreich, cares enough about the workers who are his subjects to try to give a comprehensive account of their struggles to make it, delving into their lives and addressing important economic and cultural issues head-on. Following Ehrenreich, however, Shipler wants to blame an unjust U.S. economy for the plight of the poor. Yet his own evidence proves a very different, and crucial, point: it's often dysfunctional behavior and bad choices, not a broken economy, that prevent people from escaping poverty.

Consider some of the former welfare recipients Shipler profiles in his chapter called "Work Doesn't Work." Christie, a day-care worker, describes herself as "lazy" for never finishing college (her brother, who did, is an accountant, and her sister is a loan officer). She has had several children out of wedlock with various men, and now lives with one of them — Kevin, an ex-con — in public housing. Christie can't make ends meet, but that's partly because, having never learned to cook, she blows her $138-a-month food-stamp allocation on "an abundance of high-priced, well-advertised snacks, junk food, and prepared meals."

Then there's Debra, who had her first illegitimate child at 18. Forced to work by welfare reform, Debra actually lands a job in a unionized factory — the holy grail of low-wage work to the Left. Unfortunately, she can't adjust to work in the shop, has nightmares about the assembly line, and imagines that the bosses prefer the Hispanic workers to her, since she's black. Shipler understands that with such attitudes, she is unlikely to move up. . . .

How has the U.S. economy let these workers down? In each of these cases, bad choices have kept someone from getting ahead. . . .

. . . Shipler . . . has reversed cause and effect. [He] sees social dysfunction . . . and blames it on poverty. But it typically is personal failure and social dysfunction that create poverty. To stay out of poverty in America, it's necessary to do three simple things, social scientists have found: finish high school, don't have kids until you marry, and wait until you are at least 20 to marry. Do those three things, and the odds against your becoming impoverished are less than one in ten. Nearly 80 percent of everyone who fails to do those three things winds up poor.

That's a crucial truth that left-wing social thinkers have tried to deny from the earliest days of the welfare-rights movement. And as these books show, even after the conclusive failure of the War on Poverty and the resounding success of welfare reform, they are still at it.

NOTES AND QUESTIONS

1. Shipler to a limited extent, and Malanga to a much greater extent, discuss the role of poor personal decision making, which leads many people to a lifetime, or at least a long period, of low-wage jobs. What are some of these decisions? Are they independent of or connected to social forces or conditions? Do you believe society, individuals, or both are responsible for the persistence of low-wage work and the difficulty so many workers have at exiting this sector?

2. Why are the particular workers profiled by Shipler and Ehrenreich poor? Are there legal tools that could improve their economic situation?

3. What do you make of Ehrenreich's outrage at Winn-Dixie's drug testing policy? Is the lack of dignity on the job a valid reason for a worker to quit or reject a job? Section D.2 in this chapter explains the unemployment benefits system and the importance of the reason for which a worker is unemployed. How much should society's (and the law's) response to poverty depend on the reason a person is poor?

B.   HOW HAVE MACROECONOMIC TRENDS AFFECTED THE WORKING POOR?

Income inequality in America is a topic of increasing attention in both the popular press and the academy. In the excerpts that follow, economists Lawrence Mischel and Paul Krugman explain and discuss trends in wages and productivity in recent decades, particularly the growing income inequality in America, and their effect on the economic well-being of workers.

LAWRENCE MISCHEL, *THE WEDGES BETWEEN PRODUCTIVITY AND MEDIAN COMPENSATION GROWTH* (ECON. POLICY INST., ISSUE BRIEF NO. 330, APR. 26, 2012)

Income inequality has grown over the last 30 years or more driven by three dynamics: rising inequality of labor income (wages and compensation), rising inequality of capital income, and an increasing share of income going to capital income rather than labor income. As a consequence, examining market-based incomes one finds that "the top 1 percent of households have secured a very large share of all of the gains in income — 59.9 percent of the gains from 1979-2007, while the top 0.1 percent seized an even more disproportionate share: 36 percent. In comparison, only 8.6 percent of income gains have gone to the bottom 90 percent."

A key to understanding this growth of income inequality — and the disappointing increases in workers' wages and compensation and middle-class incomes — is understanding the divergence of pay and productivity. Productivity growth has risen substantially over the last few decades but the hourly compensation of the typical worker has seen much more modest growth, especially in the last 10 years or so. The gap between productivity and the compensation growth for the typical worker has been larger in the "lost decade" since the early 2000s than at any point in the post–World War II period. In contrast, productivity and the compensation of the typical worker grew in tandem over the early postwar period until the 1970s.

Productivity growth, which is the growth of the output of goods and services per hour worked, provides the basis for the growth of living standards. However, the experience of the vast majority of workers in recent decades has been that productivity growth actually provides only the potential for rising living standards: Recent history, especially since 2000, has shown that wages and compensation for the typical worker and income growth for the typical family have lagged tremendously behind the nation's fast productivity growth. . . .

The hourly compensation of a typical worker grew in tandem with productivity from 1948-1973. . . . After 1973, productivity grew strongly, especially after 1995, while the typical worker's compensation was relatively stagnant. This divergence of pay and productivity has meant that many workers were not benefitting from productivity growth — the economy could afford higher pay but it was not providing it.

[During the period between 1973 and 2010], there were three important "wedges" between [economic] growth and the experience of American workers.

First, average hourly compensation — which includes the pay of CEOs and day laborers alike — grew just 39.2 percent from 1973 to 2011, far lagging productivity growth. In short, workers, on average, have not seen their pay keep up with productivity. This partly reflects the first wedge: an overall shift in how much of the income in the economy is received in wages by workers and how much is received by owners of capital. The share going to workers decreased.

Second, . . . the hourly compensation of the median worker grew just 10.7 percent. Most of the growth in median hourly compensation occurred in the period of strong recovery in the mid- to late-1990s: Excluding 1995-2000, median hourly compensation grew just 4.9 percent between 1973 and 2011. There was a particularly large divergence between productivity and median hourly compensation growth from 2000 to 2011. In sum, the median worker (whether male or female) has not enjoyed growth in compensation as fast as that of higher-wage workers, especially the very highest paid. This reflects the wedge of growing wage and compensation inequality.

A third "wedge" important to examine . . . is the "terms of trade" wedge, which concerns the faster price growth of things workers buy relative to what they produce. This wedge is due to the fact that the output measure used to compute productivity is converted to real, or constant (inflation-adjusted), dollars, based on the components of national output (GDP). On the other hand, average hourly compensation and the measures of median hourly compensation are converted to real, or constant, dollars based on measures of price change in what consumers purchase. Prices for national output have grown more slowly than prices for consumer purchases. Therefore, the same growth in nominal, or current dollar, wages and output yields faster growth in real (inflation-adjusted) output (which is adjusted for changes in the prices of investment goods, exports, and consumer purchases) than in real wages (which is adjusted for changes in consumer purchases only). That is, workers have suffered worsening terms of trade, in which the prices of things they buy (i.e., consumer goods and services) have risen faster than the items they produce (consumer goods but also capital goods). Thus, if workers consumed microprocessors and machine tools as well as groceries, their real wage growth would have been better and more in line with productivity growth.

PAUL KRUGMAN, *THE CONSCIENCE OF A LIBERAL* (2007)

Medieval theologians debated how many angels could fit on the head of a pin. Modern economists debate whether American median income has risen or fallen since the early 1970s. What's really telling is the fact that we're even having this debate. America is a far more productive and hence far richer county than it was a generation ago. The value of the output an average worker produces in an hour, even after you adjust for inflation, has risen almost 50 percent since 1973. Yet the growing concentration of income in the hands of a small minority has proceeded so rapidly that we're not sure whether the typical American has gained *anything* from rising productivity. . . .

   . . . [A]*verage* income — the total income of the nation, divided by the number of people — has gone up substantially since 1973, the last year of the great boom. . . .

   Average income, however, doesn't necessarily tell you how most people are doing. If Bill Gates walks into a bar, the average wealth of the bar's clientele soars, but the men already there when he walked in are no wealthier than before. That's why economists trying to describe the fortunes of the typical member of a group, not the few people doing extremely well or extremely badly, usually talk not about *average* income but about *median* income — the income of a person richer than half the population but poorer than the other half. The median income in the bar, unlike the average income, doesn't soar when Bill Gates walks in.

   As it turns out, Bill Gates walking into a bar is a pretty good metaphor for what has actually happened in the United States over the past generation: Average income has risen substantially, but that's mainly because a few people have gotten much, much richer. Median income, depending on which definition you use, has either risen modestly or actually declined. . . .

   . . . [M]edian household income, adjusted for inflation, grew modestly from 1973 to 2005, the most recent year for which we have data: The total gain was about 16 percent.

   Even this modest gain may, however, overstate how well American families were doing, because it was achieved in part through longer working hours. In 1973 many wives still didn't work outside the home, and many who did worked only part-time. I don't mean to imply that there's something wrong with more women working, but a gain in family income that occurs because a spouse goes to work isn't the same thing as a wage increase. . . .

   We get a considerably more pessimistic take on the data if we ask how easy it is for American families today to live the way many of them did a generation ago, with a single male breadwinner. According to the available data, it has gotten harder: The median inflation-adjusted earnings of men working full-time in 2005 were slightly lower than they had been in 1973. And even that statistic is deceptively favorable. Thanks to the maturing of the baby boomers today's work force is older and more experienced than the work force of 1973 — and more experienced workers should, other things being equal, command higher wages. If we look at the earnings of men aged thirty-five to forty-four — men who would, a generation ago, often have been supporting stay-at-home wives — we find that inflation-adjusted wages were 12 percent *higher* in 1973 than they are now. . . .

If gains in productivity had been evenly shared across the workforce, the typical worker's income would be about 35 percent higher now than it was in the early seventies. But the upward redistribution of income meant that the typical worker saw a far smaller gain. Indeed, everyone below roughly the 90th percentile of the wage distribution — the bottom of the top 10 percent — saw his or her income grow more slowly than average, while only those above the 90th percentile saw above-average gains. . . .

Only the top 1 percent has done better since the 1970s than it did in the generation after World War II. Once you get way up the scale, however, the gains have been spectacular — the top tenth of a percent saw its income rise fivefold, and the top .01 percent of Americans is seven times richer than they were in 1973.

* * *

In the next excerpt, noted poverty scholar William Julius Wilson, the Lewis P. and Linda L. Geyser University Professor at Harvard University, reviews a book by journalist Timothy Noah, *The Great Divergence* (2012). Noah took his book title from a chapter of Paul Krugman's 2007 book, *The Conscience of a Liberal*, excerpted above. Wilson's review succinctly summarizes and synthesizes Noah's arguments regarding the causes of wage stagnation and increasing income inequality.

WILLIAM JULIUS WILSON, *THE GREAT DISPARITY*
The Nation (July 10, 2012)

Between 1947 and 1970, every income group in America experienced economic advancement. As James K. Galbraith reminds us in *Created Unequal*, the 1950s and '60s were unique because government policies — social as well as economic — provided a firm foundation for the gains experienced by families across the board. Lower-wage workers benefited from a wide range of protections, including steady increases in the minimum wage, and the government made full employment a high priority. There was also a strong union movement that ensured higher wages and more nonwage benefits for ordinary workers.

But by the '80s, the trends for lower-wage workers had been reversed. Families in the higher income groups — the top 20 percent — continued to enjoy steady income gains, adjusted for inflation, while families in the lower income brackets experienced stagnating or declining incomes. The labor movement began its downward spiral; macroeconomic policy was no longer geared to tight labor markets; and monetary policy, focused on lowering inflation above all else, became dominant. As part of the "Reagan experiment," the tax structure became more regressive and Social Security taxes increased; also, when George W. Bush took office, tax cuts were passed that distinctly favored the wealthy at the expense of ordinary families. Finally, Congressional resistance to raising the minimum wage further threatened the economic security of disadvantaged families.

The growing American disparity became a hotly debated issue in academic circles, and concerns about rising inequality generated numerous research studies. Economists focused mainly on the causes of income inequality, while many sociologists and political scientists examined the related factors of social inequality, such as the increasingly limited access to affluent neighborhoods and elite colleges and universities. Before the emergence of Occupy Wall Street last year, Americans remained largely ignorant of these trends. But OWS, which morphed into Occupy as the protests spread to other cities across the country, had one important effect: [I]t raised public awareness of the growing economic inequality in the United States. As a result, research by social scientists on the subject, which had been largely ignored in public debates, has figured prominently in op-eds and news articles about the recession.

Giving this public attention, the publication of Timothy Noah's *The Great Divergence* and Charles Murray's *Coming Apart* could not be more timely. . . .

Although scholars of inequality will find little that's new in *The Great Divergence*, it is nonetheless a very impressive and important book. Fully aware of the public's belated — but growing — interest in the rising inequality, Noah thinks the problem has to be fully understood before it can be adequately addressed. Accordingly, he has attempted "to synthesize the best [social science research] for nonexperts who would like to know, at long last, what's been happening to the economy, especially in the United States."

Noah documents the drastic changes between the Great Compression (the period of growing income equality between 1932 and 1979) and the Great Divergence (the period of increasing income inequality after 1979). He shows that the level of inequality in the United States is not only more extreme than in other advanced industrialized democracies, but has also increased at a much faster rate. This trend, he points out, is not linked to the usual factors, such as black/white income disparity, the unequal treatment of women[,] or the influx of immigrants. Although African-Americans have certainly felt the adverse effects of the Great Divergence, black/white income disparity hasn't been a factor in its emergence, as both the black middle class and the white middle class have fallen behind. Nor has the unequal treatment of women been a factor, since the male/female wage gap has actually shrunk by nearly half during the past several decades. As for immigration, the most dramatic difference between the Great Compression and the Great Divergence is the pronounced and widening income gap between the rich and the middle class, not between the rich and the poor. And immigration's impact on the income of middle-class Americans — as distinct from its impact on the income of high school dropouts — has been minimal.

So what have been the significant factors underlying the Great Divergence? Noah identifies four: the increasing importance of a college degree due to the shortage of better-educated workers; trade between the United States and low-wage nations; changes in government policy in labor and finance; and the decline of the labor movement. He also considers the extreme changes in the wage structure of corporations and the financial industry, in which American CEOs typically receive three times the salaries earned by their European counterparts.

Noah cites a widely discussed study by the Harvard economists Claudia Goldin and Lawrence Katz, *The Race Between Education and Technology*, which estimates, in Noah's words, that the increase in the economic returns to "people with college diplomas or advanced degrees, whose limited supply bid up their salaries," accounts for roughly 60 percent of the growth in wage inequality between 1973 and 2005. The American education system has not been able to supply a sufficient number of better-educated workers to meet demand during the Great Divergence, which he calls "terrible news for everyone else."

The research Noah draws on reveals that trade with low-wage nations, "which was negligible until the twenty-first century," is responsible for around 12 to 13 percent of the Great Divergence. Why? The increasing trade in manufactured goods with developing countries has resulted in a larger number of trading partners whose workers earn considerably less than their counterparts in the United States. "As recently as 1975," states Noah,

> America's top ten trading partners had included Italy, the Netherlands, and Belgium, all high-wage nations. China didn't make the cut. By 1990, China made the top ten, but just barely; it ranked tenth. By 2005, the three European nations had all been displaced by Asian nations, of which the biggest player by far was China.

As of 2005, China paid workers 3 percent of what workers in the United States received. This recent dramatic shift in international trade, Noah argues, drove up the wage gap between skilled and low-skilled workers in this country, as the latter found themselves in greater competition with workers producing the same goods for lower wages in developing nations. We replaced high-wage nations with low-wage nations as our main trading partners, and this lowered average wages in the United States.

The evidence on how government policy — particularly under Republican presidents — and a resurgent business lobby altered income distribution tends to be less comprehensive and more impressionistic, but, according to Noah, "the impact of government action (and inaction) in three particular areas — labor, finance, and corporate compensation — is relatively clear and well documented." As for the fortunes of the labor movement during the Great Divergence, Noah cites a 2007 study by the Harvard economist Richard Freeman, which estimates that the decline of union membership accounts for about 20 percent of the Great Divergence among all workers. And a 2011 study by the sociologists Bruce Western and Jake Rosenfeld concludes that the demise of unions has contributed as much to men's wage inequality as the relative increase in salaries for college graduates. Western and Rosenfeld associate the demise of organized labor with changes in the economy and intensified political opposition. In particular, employment growth outside the traditional union stronghold of manufacturing created a newly competitive economic environment and prompted employers in unionized industries to intensify their opposition to organized labor's demands. Employer resistance unfolded in an increasingly adverse political environment for unions, especially corporate donations to anti-union policy-makers and the rightward shift of the National Labor Relations Board under Republican administrations, which made union organizing more difficult. "Draw one line on a graph charting the decline of union membership," Noah writes, "then superimpose a second line charting the decline in middle-class income share (with 'middle class' defined broadly as the middle 60 percent), and you will find that the two lines are nearly identical."

Finally, one cause of the spectacular rise in top income gains in the United States during the Great Divergence has been the shift in the principal activity and structure of investment banks — from banking to trading, and from partnership structures to publicly traded corporations — as well as the government deregulation of Wall Street. While top income gains have increased in many developed countries, nowhere are they growing as fast as in the United States.

For example, the top 1 percent's increase in the share of income during the Great Divergence (through 2005) was 17 percent in the United States, in comparison with an increase of 2 percent or less in France and Germany. . . .

NOTES AND QUESTIONS

1. Are these macroeconomic explanations for the persistence of low-wage work persuasive? Are there ways that law or lawyers can respond to these trends? Can lawsuits or legislation address any of them? Is there a role for lawyers and legal institutions in setting, evaluating, or challenging macroeconomic policy? For provocative discussion of some of these questions, see Mark Kelman, *Could Lawyers Stop Recessions? Speculations on Law and Macroeconomics*, 45 Stan. L. Rev. 1215 (1993).

2. Wilson's review and Noah's book both point to the decline in unions as a factor in the stagnation of wages for the working poor and middle class. While a history of American unionism is beyond the scope of this book, it is worth noting that union membership in the United States is at its lowest level in nearly a century. The Bureau of Labor Statistics reported in 2013 that even though total employment increased by 2.4 million jobs, the number of union members decreased by 400,000, bringing the rate of unionization down to 11.3 percent, its lowest level since 1916. In the private sector, only 6.6 percent of workers were unionized in 2013, compared to 6.9 percent in 2011. (By comparison, in the 1950s, approximately 35 percent of non-governmental workers were unionized.) Legislative and political attacks on unions succeeded in great numbers in 2012 and 2013, with measures in important industrial states such as Wisconsin and Indiana stripping rights from union members. The changes, along with theories as to causes, and data about union participation in various states, are explored in Steven Greenhouse, *Share of the Workforce in a Union Falls to a 97-Year Low, 11.3%*, N.Y. Times (Jan. 23, 2013), at B1. Official data regarding union participation is found in U.S. Dep't of Labor, Bureau of Labor Statistics, *Economic News Release: Union Members Summary* (2013), *available at* http://www.bls.gov/news.release/union2.nr0.htm.

C. WAGE THEFT, THE UNDERGROUND ECONOMY, AND LAWYERING FOR THE WORKING POOR

"Wage theft" is a term often credited to Kim Bobo, founder and executive director of the advocacy organization Interfaith Worker Justice. The phrase refers to a variety of illegal means by which employers fail or refuse to pay workers wages they have lawfully earned, including failure to pay minimum wage or overtime, requiring "off the clock" or other uncompensated work, misclassification of hourly employees subject to federal minimum wage laws as exempt employees not covered, and other such practices. It has become a familiar term among advocates and even appears in statutes such as New York's and California's "Wage Theft Prevention Acts" and the labor laws of Tennessee and Illinois. The National Employment Law Project found in 2009 that over 25 percent of the responding low-wage workers in New York, Los Angeles, and Chicago were paid less than minimum wage, more than three-quarters were illegally denied overtime pay, and over two-thirds did not receive pay for all work performed. Overall, the study estimated that wage theft victims are robbed of approximately 15 percent of their income through wage theft. Annette Bernhardt et al., Nat'l Emp't Law Project, *Broken Laws, Unprotected Workers: Violations of Employment and Labor Laws in America's Cities* (2009), *available at* http://nelp.3cdn.net/ 1797b93dd1ccdf9e7d_sdm6bc50n.pdf. The UCLA Institute for Research on Labor and Employment estimated in 2010 that in Los Angeles alone, workers were deprived of over $26.2 million per week in earned but unpaid income. In July 2013, the National Employment Law Project released a report that catalogs the growing body of research on wage theft across geographical regions and industries, and by category of worker. *See* Nat'l Emp't Law Project, *Winning Wage Justice: A Summary of Research on Wage and Hour Violations in the United States* (2013), *available at* http://nelp.3cdn.net/6eb6a53686715c5463_2wm6bno4u.pdf.

The related but distinct term "underground economy" refers to the sectors of the nation's economy that operate outside the reach of traditional labor, licensing, regulatory, and health and safety laws. Many underground economy businesses vigorously resist unionization, chronically fail to pay their employees all wages due (often by undercounting hours, ignoring overtime and break requirements, or simply refusing to pay at all), and employ vulnerable workers, such as undocumented or non-English-speaking immigrants. Studies suggest that women are overrepresented in the underground economy.

The size of the underground economy is difficult to determine with precision, but the International Monetary Fund has estimated that the nation's underground economy represented 9 percent of the GDP in 2000, and the National Center for Policy Analysis estimates that up to 25 million Americans earn a large part of their income from activities in the underground economy.

Although "underground economy" is a familiar term, an important new book uses the term "gloves-off economy" instead, reflecting the authors' belief that

> discussions of the informal sector and the underground or undeclared economy place primary emphasis on microenterprises and self-employment, whereas we focus on employment relationships in the formal sector, extending even to the very largest employers (including the largest private employer in the world, Wal-Mart, currently facing a spate of overtime violation lawsuits).

Annette Bernhardt et al., *An Introduction to the "Gloves-Off" Economy,* in *The Gloves-Off Economy: Workplace Standards at the Bottom of America's Labor Market* (Annette Bernhardt et al. eds., 2008). Whatever title is used, it is important to understand the existence and extent of the combination of wage theft, exploitation, labor and health law violations, and other deplorable conditions that characterize some of the nation's lowest-paid jobs.

ANNETTE BERNHARDT ET AL., *AN INTRODUCTION TO THE "GLOVES-OFF" ECONOMY,* IN *THE GLOVES-OFF ECONOMY: WORKPLACE STANDARDS AT THE BOTTOM OF AMERICA'S LABOR MARKET* (ANNETTE BERNHARDT ET AL. EDS., 2008)

At 6:00 a.m. in New York City, a domestic worker wakes up her employer's children and starts to cook breakfast for them, in a work week in which she will earn a flat $400 for as many hours as her employer needs. In Chicago, men are picked up at a homeless shelter at 8:00 a.m. and bussed by a temp agency to a wholesale distribution center to spend the next 10 hours packing toys into boxes, for the minimum wage without overtime. In Atlanta, workers at a poultry processing plant break for lunch, hands raw from handling chemicals without protective gear. At 3:00 p.m. in Dallas, a new shift of nursing home workers start their day, severely understaffed and underpaid. During the evening rush hour in Minneapolis, gas station workers fill up tanks, working only for tips. In New Orleans, a dishwasher stays late into the night finishing the evening's cleaning, off the clock and unpaid. And at midnight, a janitor in Los Angeles begins buffing the floor of a major retailer, working for a contract cleaning company that pays $8 an hour with no benefits.

These workers — and millions more — share more than the fact that they are paid low wages. The central thesis of this volume is that they are part of the "gloves-off" economy, in which some employers are increasingly breaking, bending, or evading long-established laws and standards designed to protect workers. Such practices are sending fault lines into every corner of the low-wage labor market, stunting wages and working conditions for an expanding set of jobs. In the process, employers who play by the rules are under growing pressure to follow suit, intensifying the search for low-cost business strategies across a wide range of industries and eventually ratcheting up into higher wage parts of the labor market.

When we talk about the "gloves-off economy," we are identifying a set of employer strategies and practices that either evade or outright violate the core laws and standards that govern job quality in the U.S. While such strategies have long been present in certain sectors, such as sweatshops and marginal small businesses, we argue that they are spreading. This trend, driven by competitive pressures, has been shaped by an environment where other major economic actors — government, unions, and civil society — have either promoted deregulation or have been unable to contain gloves-off business strategies. The result, at the start of the 21st century, is the reality that a major segment of the U.S. labor market increasingly diverges from the legal and normative bounds put into place decades ago.

The workplace laws in question are a familiar list of regulations at the federal, state, and local level. They include laws that regulate wages and hours worked, setting minimum standards for the wage floor, for overtime pay, and in some states, for rest and meal breaks. They also comprise laws governing health and safety conditions in the workplace, setting detailed requirements for particular industries and occupations. Others on the list include antidiscrimination laws, right-to-organize laws, and laws mandating employers' contribution to social welfare benefits such as Social Security, unemployment insurance, and workers' compensation.

By contrast, the standards we have in mind are set not by laws, but rather by norms that have enough weight (and organizing force behind them) to shape employers' decisions about wages and working conditions. At least until the past few decades, such normative standards typically included predictability of schedules, vacation and/or sick leave, annual raises, full-time hours, and, in some industries, living wages and employer-provided health insurance and pensions. Though it may seem utopian to focus on standards at a time when even legally guaranteed rights are frequently abrogated, we argue that both are being eroded for similar reasons as employers seek to reduce labor costs. Further, we argue that the existence of strategies to subvert or ignore laws by some employers pulls down labor norms further up in the labor market.

We do not suggest that all U.S. employers have shed the gloves of workplace protection, or that every strategy to cut labor costs is inherently "gloves off." Millions of employers comply with current regulations and do their best to uphold strong labor standards. However, we contend that gloves-off strategies have reached such prevalence that they are leaving their imprint on the broader labor market, creating significant challenges for responsible employers, government, and labor unions and other representatives of civil society. Responsible employers are undercut when unscrupulous employers gain unfair advantage by violating labor laws and standards. Government's mandate to enforce worker protections is stressed by widespread and constantly shifting forms of violation and evasion. Unions and other worker advocates face an uneven playing field. When the floor of labor standards is driven down or dismantled altogether, all of us are affected, not just those at the very bottom. . . .

Our focus on what has happened to both legal and normative standards governing the workplace is intentional. In the U.S., employment and labor laws largely set a "floor" of minimum standards (e.g., the minimum wage), while, historically at least, norms have built additional workplace standards on top of that floor (e.g., annual raises, voluntary employer provided health insurance). Moreover, laws are particularly important in regulating the labor practices of smaller and economically marginal businesses, whereas labor norms are particularly relevant in larger, more profitable enterprises. But laws and norms are inextricably linked. For example, as a growing share of the construction industry moves toward cash payment and labor brokers that facilitate violation of wage and hour laws and misclassification of employees as independent contractors, the more established and higher-wage contractors face increasingly difficult competition, in some cases driving them to dilute or abandon long-established norms. In other industries, subcontracting by large businesses in order to delink some jobs from their core workforce norms may shift employment to subcontractors who compete by skirting or violating the law. Erosions of both legal and normative labor market standards thus move in mutually reinforcing ways.

Finally, a word about the legislative exclusion of a number of occupations from coverage by employment and labor laws (as is the case for certain domestic workers, home care workers, and agricultural workers). These exclusions are widely regarded as historical legacies of the more narrow (and, frankly, racist) legal frameworks for worker protections that existed in the first half of the last century. In fact, these workers are clearly in an employment relationship, and in what follows, we consider their jobs as squarely within the realm of our analysis.

VIOLATION AND EVASION OF WORKPLACE LAWS

Research on workplace violations is still very much an underdeveloped field, and there are currently few comprehensive estimates of the prevalence of violations. However, the evidence available points to a significant level of violations in some industries. The best evidence we have to date stems from a series of rigorous "employer compliance surveys" conducted by the U.S. Department of Labor in the late 1990s, focusing on minimum wage and overtime violations. For example, the department found that in 1999, only 35% of apparel plants in New York City were in compliance with wage and hour laws; in Chicago, only 42% of restaurants were in compliance; in Los Angeles, only 43% of grocery stores were in compliance; and nationally, only 43% of residential care establishments were in compliance. Confirming this, Weil (2005), in an independent analysis of Department of Labor administrative compliance data, found that 46% of garment contractors in Los Angeles were in compliance with the minimum wage in 2000. Unfortunately, however, these surveys were largely limited to only a handful of industries and/or regions, and most are no longer being conducted.

As a result, academics and applied researchers have recently begun to generate their own studies of workplace violations, especially of minimum wage and overtime laws. One of the most carefully constructed is a national survey of a random sample of day labor hiring sites across the country; the authors found that 49% of day laborers reported at least one instance of nonpayment of wages and 48% reported at least one instance of underpayment of wages in the preceding two months. More common are studies relying on convenience samples of workers; while not representative, these often yield suggestive evidence of minimum wage and overtime violations in key industries including restaurants, building services, domestic work, and retail. For example, in a survey of New York City restaurant employees, researchers found that 13% earned less than the minimum wage, 59% suffered overtime law violations, 57% had worked more than four hours without a paid break, and workers reported a plethora of occupational safety and health violations. Shifting to other workplace violations, we have recently seen a spate of studies that make innovative use of state administrative data to suggest that 10% or more of employers misclassify their workers as independent contractors. Breaches of the right to organize unions, guaranteed by the National Labor Relations Act, have become common. A study by the Fiscal Policy Institute (2007) estimated that between half a million and one million eligible New Yorkers are not receiving workers' compensation coverage from their employers, as they are legally due. And while data are rarely available on health and safety violations in the workplace, a study of Los Angeles garment factories in the late 1990s is suggestive, finding that 54% had serious Occupational Safety and Health Administration (OSHA) violations. As an indirect measure of workers at risk, the Department of Labor has documented that workplace fatalities are disproportionately concentrated in the private construction industry and especially among Latino men.

The most extreme form of workplace violations is forced labor and trafficking, where the worker is totally controlled by the "employer" and prevented from leaving the situation. Though such practices are very difficult to document, experts estimate that between ten and twenty thousand workers are trafficked into the country every year and that the average amount of time spent in forced labor as a result of trafficking is between two and five years. One of the most extreme examples is a slave labor operation discovered in 1995 in El Monte, California, where 72 Thai garment workers were forced to work 18 hours a day in a small apartment building enclosed by barbed wire, patrolled by armed guards without pay. .

Employer strategies to bend, twist, sidestep, and otherwise evade the laws governing the U.S. workplace are even harder to measure than outright violations, because such strategies are not illegal and so are not monitored by regulatory agencies. Academic researchers have for several decades tracked changes in how employers are reorganizing work and production, but they have often been stymied by the inherent challenges in measuring workplace practices and business strategies. As a result, the best documentation comes largely from in-depth studies focused on particular industries, offering a rich, qualitative understanding of why employers use particular strategies and of the impact they have on workers and job quality; comprehensive quantitative data generally are not available.

Probably the most important evasion strategy is to subcontract certain jobs or functions to outside companies. The workers performing those jobs may still be located on-site (as with subcontracted janitorial workers) or be moved off-site (as with industrial laundry workers cleaning linens for hotels and hospitals). Of course, greater use of subcontracting in and of itself does not necessarily imply an attempt to evade workplace laws — but it certainly can facilitate such evasion. . . . [S]ubcontracting can help employers evade responsibility for compliance with employment and labor laws, creating greater legal distance in cases where, for example, a fly-by-night cleaning subcontractor pays less than the minimum wage.

Similarly with the growing use of temp, leased, and contract workers, for some employers the motivation for using these strategies is to lessen legal liability for working conditions and social welfare contributions. The deliberate misclassification of employees as independent contractors is perhaps the most extreme version of this strategy, since independent contractors are not covered by most employment and labor laws. . . .

A few direct measures indicate increases in outright violations of labor law. Françoise Carré and Randall Wilson (2004) reported that the percentage of Massachusetts employers misclassifying workers climbed from 8% to 13% in 1995 to 1997 to 13% to 19% in 2001 to 2003 and that the percentage of employees misclassified by offending employers likewise increased over this period. Researchers have also documented a marked weakening in compliance with the National Labor Relations Act over the past several decades, with a particularly steep rise in the 2000s relative to the last half of the 1990s in illegal firings of pro-union workers. For example, recent research has found that almost one in five union organizers or activists can expect to be fired as a result of their activities in a union election campaign, up sharply from the end of the 1990s.

There is also evidence of growing evasion or erosion of labor standards. Employment in temporary help services increased twentyfold between the early 1960s and mid-1990s, an evasion strategy of both normative standards and, potentially, legal liability for working conditions. Hard numbers also document recent shifts in health and pension coverage. Whereas in the 1970s employers typically paid the full cost of health insurance premiums, by 2005, fully 76% of employees were contributing to their individual coverage premiums. Similarly, defined-benefit pension plans (which specify the amount of the pension, unlike a 401k) tumbled from covering 84% of full-time workers holding pensions in 1980 to 33% in 2003. So while on paper both health and pension benefits are still offered, in reality their cost has become prohibitive for some, with very low take-up rates for low-wage workers in particular.

Significant numbers of employers have crossed the line from erosion to abandonment of standards. For example, the percentage of workers covered by any employer-provided health plan declined from 69% in 1979 to 56% in 2004. At the same time, the proportion of U.S. workers covered by any retirement plan dropped, from 91% of full-time employees in 1985 to 65% in 2003. Another instance of standards abandonment is the permanent conversion of full-time jobs to part-time, a practice widespread in retail, where large food stores now typically employ 60% to 80% part-timers. More generally, companies that dismantle internal labor markets are walking away from historical job standards.

Beyond direct measures of changing employer practices, there is considerable indirect evidence that points to likely increases in gloves-off practices. In particular, to the extent that subcontracting has become more common, we would infer that there is a strong likelihood that evasions or violations of workplace laws and standards have increased as well. Again, while subcontracting in and of itself does not necessarily constitute a gloves-off practice, there is ample evidence that the competitive pressures pushing firms toward subcontracting often encourage the erosion of labor standards. While some industries (e.g., construction and apparel) have incorporated subcontracting for over a century, research on other industries suggests that the practice has spread throughout the U.S. economy. Both the case study literature and aggregate industry and occupational statistics show an increase in contracting and outsourcing. In some cases, subcontracting has become so prevalent that entire new industries have been created or dramatically expanded, as with security services, food services, janitorial services, call centers, and dry cleaning and laundry (serving institutions such as hospitals).

Similarly, to the extent that union density has declined, we would infer a likely increase in gloves-off workplace practices, through two mechanisms. First, in industries that had high density, loss of union membership typically results in an industry-wide lowering of wage standards and working conditions. Employers compete on the basis of labor costs instead of quality services and products, lowering the wage floor toward the minimum and increasing the likelihood that some employers will go below that floor (or adopt other erosive strategies such as subcontracting or adopting two-tiered wage systems). Second, unions have historically been, and continue to be, key agents in enforcing employment and labor laws, actively monitoring their workplaces for adherence to wage and hour, health and safety, right to organize, and other laws. The decades-long decline in union density in the U.S., therefore, does not bode well: In 1948, almost one in three workers were in a union; by 2005, the fraction had fallen to just one in eight.

Finally, federal capacity to enforce labor standards has waned. The Brennan Center for Justice reports that "between 1975 and 2004, the number of [federal] workplace investigators declined by 14 percent and the number of compliance actions completed declined by 36 percent — while the number of covered workers grew by 55 percent, and the number of covered establishments grew by 112 percent." In similar fashion, the Occupational Safety and Health Administration's budget has been cut by $14.5 million since 2001, and at the same time the agency has shifted resources away from enforcement and deterrence toward "compliance assistance." At its current staffing and inspection levels, it would take federal OSHA 133 years to inspect each workplace under its jurisdiction just once. . . .

1. Current Labor Laws and the Low-Wage Workforce

In the article below, longtime workers' advocate Catherine Ruckelshaus of the National Employment Law Project identifies specific unlawful practices that increasing numbers of employers of low-wage workers adopt, and examines the reason that legal action to stop these practices is so difficult.

CATHERINE K. RUCKELSHAUS, *LABOR'S WAGE WAR*
35 Fordham Urb. L.J. 373 (2008)

As we lose manufacturing jobs to overseas markets, the jobs left behind — health care, child care, retail, building services, construction, and hospitality — are not good jobs. In addition to providing paltry benefits, if any, employers in these sectors routinely violate bedrock employment rights like the right to be paid fully for work and the right to a safe workplace. Employers in these industries maneuver to cut costs at any price: they hide behind subcontractors, call their workers "independent contractors" not covered by workplace laws, and hire immigrant workers who are vulnerable to exploitation. As if that were not enough, workers face barriers to enforcing their basic job rights, including antiquated rules for bringing class actions in private litigation, and fear of reprisals that go unchecked when workers complain.

A. The United States Department of Labor ("DOL") Is Not Enforcing Its Laws, and Interprets Its Role Narrowly

Public enforcement of the Fair Labor Standards Act ("FLSA") and other baseline workplace standards is down, with some notable exceptions; federal and state agencies charged with enforcing baseline wage and hour laws are not having an impact. Employers know that there is little to fear from public enforcement of workplace violations, and so do not change their practices. In addition, the DOL has interpreted laws to exempt large classes of low-wage workers from basic wage and hour protections, including professional home health-care companions. In general, despite the persistence of sub-par jobs, the DOL has not made it a priority to stem these abuses. . . .

While public agencies are by their nature underfunded and understaffed, the DOL has been particularly undersubsidized in recent years. In addition, it has failed to use its resources strategically to have the broadest impact, as it has in the past with, for instance, targeted audits and affirmative task forces aimed at priority industries.

From 1975 to 2004, the budget for DOL WHD [Wage and Hour Division] investigators decreased by 14% (to a total of only 788 individuals nationwide), and enforcement actions decreased by 36%, while the number of businesses covered by the wage and hour law increased from 7.8 million to 8.3 million. The DOL's overall budget to enforce wage and hour laws is now 6.1% less than before President George W. Bush took office.

DOL legal resources have also suffered, impacting its ability to enforce the laws. In fiscal year 1992, the Solicitor's Office, responsible for enforcing all laws under the DOL's jurisdiction, had 786 employees, an increase of 59% since fiscal year 1966. But, since fiscal year 1992, despite the fact that two additional laws have been added to the responsibilities of the Solicitor's Office, the Family and Medical Leave Act of 1993 and substantial amendments to the Mine Safety and Health Act in 2006, the number of employees of the Solicitor's Office has declined markedly; in January 2007, it was down to 590 employees nationwide. . . .

Because it has not emphasized its ability to conduct audits or investigations generated internally, the DOL conducts its current wage and hour law enforcement based almost wholly on worker complaints. This is a problem for low-wage and immigrant workers in particular, who face serious barriers to complaining to the DOL.

In 2001, the WHD conducted as many as 55% of its investigations by fax or phone, and it is five times more likely to find violations of recordkeeping requirements when it visits a workplace. When the risk of enforcement is small, systemic violations of wage and hour laws become the norm in these sectors. When the DOL does enforce its workplace laws, it makes a difference in the wage levels of workers in workplaces beyond those it chooses to bring enforcements actions against.

In addition, in the context of fewer enforcement resources overall, the DOL has taken the unusual step of intervening in ongoing litigation on the side of employers. In one instance, the DOL supported the employer's argument in an opinion letter sought by a trade association during the pendency of litigation, and in another, wrote an internal memorandum purporting to clarify the intent of its previously-enacted regulations regarding coverage of home health-care workers under minimum wage and overtime law, supporting the employer's argument while the case was pending before the U.S. Supreme Court. . . .

B. Employers Are Maneuvering in This Climate of Non-Accountability

With increasing frequency, employers misclassify employees as "independent contractors," either by giving their employees an IRS Form 1099 instead of a Form W-2, or by paying them off-the-books and not reporting or paying taxes. Businesses also insert subcontractors who are often undercapitalized, including temporary help firms and labor brokers, between them and their workers. This creates another layer of potentially-responsible entities and creates confusion among workers as to who is actually their employer. While there are true independent business people not covered by labor and employment protections as "employees," and while there is nothing inherently wrong with firms subcontracting-out labor, these mechanisms create barriers to enforcing the baseline work rules such as minimum wage and overtime and cost the government billions of dollars in lost tax and insurance revenues.

1. SUBCONTRACTING

Outsourcing employees to labor intermediaries such as temporary or leasing firms or labor brokers allows companies to argue that the intermediate entity is the sole employer responsible for pay rules, and allows them to dodge responsibility. Often, the subcontractor lacks the resources to pay legally-mandated wages. Walmart and leading restaurant chains such as Outback Steakhouses have recently come under fire for hiring cleaning services through fly-by-night labor brokers who underpay janitors. Microsoft shifted handling of computer software programmers' pay checks to a leasing company and then argued the programmers were not entitled to Microsoft's benefits because they were not "employees" of Microsoft.

Many companies seek to shift all employment-related responsibility to labor contractors. When workers are fired unjustly or fail to receive the pay they are owed, companies often claim that they do not employ the workers and that the labor contractor is solely responsible. . . .

2. MISCLASSIFYING WORKERS AS INDEPENDENT CONTRACTORS

In independent contractor schemes, firms argue they are off-the-hook for any violations of rules protecting "employees." This deprives workers of essential rights, including: minimum wage and overtime premium pay, a healthy and safe workplace, family and medical leave, equal opportunity, and the right to join a union and engage in collective bargaining. Workers also lose out on safety-net benefits including unemployment insurance, workers' compensation, Social Security, and Medicare. For example, FedEx calls its drivers "independent contractors," while UPS treats its drivers as employees. By misclassifying its employees, employers stand to save upwards of 30% of their payroll costs, including employer-side FICA and FUTA tax obligations, workers' compensation and state unemployment, and disability taxes paid for "employees." Businesses that "1099" and pay off-the-books can undercut competitors in labor-intensive sectors like construction and building services, which creates an unfair marketplace. . . .

C. WORKERS FACE SIGNIFICANT BARRIERS TO PRIVATE ENFORCEMENT OF WAGE AND HOUR STANDARDS

Employees with wage and hour complaints face significant barriers to seeking redress for those violations. Because employment in the United States is at-will, most workers fear employer reprisals for complaining about wage and hour violations, including losing their jobs. In addition, as illustrated above, public agency enforcement at the DOL has largely abandoned audit- and investigation-based enforcement, to become primarily reliant on worker complaints. In the face of government non-involvement, private lawsuits have become more popular, but employees bringing private lawsuits cannot bring class actions because of a unique federal law limitation in the federal FLSA requiring each individual worker to affirmatively opt-in to a lawsuit by filing a written consent to sue with the court [29 U.S.C. § 216(b)]. This mechanism, not found in almost all other labor and employment laws, hampers the workers' ability to stand up for their rights as a group. Immigrant workers face an additional barrier to enforcing their rights if the employer threatens to or does in fact call in the Bureau of Immigration and Customs Enforcement ("ICE"), which has the power to detain and, in some cases, deport workers without work authorization.

1. DECLINE OF UNIONS

Unions are an important protective buffer for workers seeking to improve their jobs, and a lack of union presence in the workplace causes workplace standards to decline. Ninety percent of workers in this country are not represented by a union, even though most workers (57%) would vote for a union if an election were held at their worksite. Without the security a union offers, individual workers are much less likely to come forward to complain about or enforce their rights.

Additionally, without a union, employment is "at-will." This means an employer may terminate its employee when it wishes, "for good cause, for no cause, or even for a reason that is morally wrong, without being legally wrong." Thus, the vast majority of workers may risk losing their jobs if they complain.

2. FEAR OF REPRISALS

Workers fear retaliation (including termination) by their employers if they complain, which may cause them to quietly accept substandard conditions. The United States General Accounting Office ("GAO") observed in a report on day labor in the United States that government agencies are unable to do their job with respect to day laborers because they do not find out about violations.

Undocumented workers are particularly vulnerable to workplace abuse, discrimination, and exploitation, as well as the fear of being turned over to ICE. Recent ICE raids on workplaces with pending workplace violation investigations create confusion and fear among workers, and send a message that the U.S. government will enforce immigration laws against workers, but not labor standards laws against employers. . . .

3. PRIVATE ENFORCEMENT PROBLEMS

In recent years, in part due to the DOL's quiescence, workers have turned to the courts to enforce their fair pay rights in increasing numbers. These lawsuits have brought important back wage remedies to large numbers of workers and, in some cases, lasting changes in firms' pay practices. Even if massive DOL enforcement reform is achieved, private wage and hour enforcement by workers will continue to be an important supplement to ensure compliance.

The primary obstacle workers face is the requirement that each complaining worker affirmatively consents or "opts-in" to a lawsuit. This condition blocks many workers from pursuing their claims privately, because workers fear reprisals, including job loss, often putting them in a job-or-pay situation. In addition, individual workers' claims for unpaid wages often do not amount to enough to make expensive litigation economically feasible, and thus, workers lose access to the courts. The opt-in structure also means other worker representatives may not bring a lawsuit on behalf of a group of co-workers, as is the case in almost every other federal labor and employment law. . . .

. . . FLSA's opt-in rule thus results in smaller numbers of employees participating in a lawsuit and substantially less exposure to liability for employers, who then have less to fear and less incentive to change their pay practices when caught. The opt-in regime undermines wage and hour enforcement. . . .

For an individual employee to hire a private attorney to press a claim in court for unpaid overtime or minimum wages against an employer, a worker would likely have to spend a good part of his or her annual salary to retain the attorney. If the worker could convince the private attorney to represent him, the attorney would require periodic fee payments. While the FLSA permits recovery of attorneys' fees for successful plaintiffs, the actual amounts recovered in low-wage cases are often insufficient to tempt private attorneys to undertake the case. As the fight in court against the employer progressed, the individual worker would have to continue to make periodic fee payments, pay for discovery, preliminary discovery motions, and any substantive legal motions filed by either side. For a relatively small amount of damages, this is not economically feasible for the vast majority of workers.

* * *

Ruckelshaus goes on to identify four promising models for enforcing labor standards: union- and management-funded projects to police wage and hour violations, worker centers, the wage and hour project of the Service Employees International Union (which aids in enforcing wage rights in three specific occupations), and the New York Civic Participation Project, "a union-community collaboration that promotes worker justice and civil empowerment for new immigrants." Catherine K. Ruckelshaus, *Labor's Wage War*, 35 Fordham Urb. L.J. 373 (2008).

NOTES AND QUESTIONS

1. What do you make of Ruckelshaus's analysis of the reasons wage theft and exploitation persists? What is the most useful role that lawyers can play in addressing these issues? Are the problems most amenable to litigation, administrative enforcement, policy initiatives, legislation, or some combination?
2. Some legal aid offices and an increasing number of law school clinics now include wage theft and other employment law problems of low-wage workers on their dockets. One veteran legal services attorney listed the following as typical employment problems experienced by working poor clients: "criminal records as a barrier to employment, records of child abuse or neglect created by child welfare agencies, problems with occupational licenses, employment discrimination, illness of the worker or his/her family member, requiring time away from the job, and requiring assistance in being able to keep the job and in obtaining income while out of work, and payment of wages due to the worker." Sharon M. Dietrich, *When Working Isn't Enough: Low-Wage Workers Struggle to Survive*, 6 U. Pa. J. Lab. & Emp. L. 613 (2004).

2. Immigrant Workers

As noted above, undocumented immigrant workers are heavily represented in the underground or "gloves-off" economy. They also work in companies and sectors that are not "underground" in the conventional sense of flouting regulatory or wage requirements. Even in these settings, undocumented immigrants' lack of legal status leaves them vulnerable to unlawful practices and creates remedial conundrums when employers break the law. While a full examination of all issues raised by the immigrant labor force is beyond the scope of this book, the following landmark case raises several questions that still vex scholars, judges, and advocates today.

HOFFMAN PLASTIC COMPOUNDS, INC. v. NLRB
535 U.S. 137 (2002)

Chief Justice REHNQUIST delivered the opinion of the Court.

The National Labor Relations Board (Board) awarded backpay to an undocumented alien who has never been legally authorized to work in the United States. We hold that such relief is foreclosed by federal immigration policy, as expressed by Congress in the Immigration Reform and Control Act of 1986 (IRCA).

Petitioner Hoffman Plastic Compounds, Inc. custom-formulates chemical compounds for businesses that manufacture pharmaceutical, construction, and household products. In May 1988, petitioner hired Jose Castro to operate various blending machines that "mix and cook" the particular formulas per customer order. Before being hired for this position, Castro presented documents that appeared to verify his authorization to work in the United States. In December 1988, the United Rubber, Cork, Linoleum, and Plastic Workers of America, AFL-CIO, began a union-organizing campaign at petitioner's production plant. Castro and several other employees supported the organizing campaign and distributed authorization cards to co-workers. In January 1989, Hoffman laid off Castro and other employees engaged in these organizing activities.

Three years later, in January 1992, respondent Board found that Hoffman unlawfully selected four employees, including Castro, for layoff "in order to rid itself of known union supporters" in violation of § 8(a)(3) of the National Labor Relations Act (NLRA).[1] To remedy this violation, the Board ordered that Hoffman (1) cease and desist from further violations of the NLRA, (2) post a detailed notice to its employees regarding the remedial order, and (3) offer reinstatement and backpay to the four affected employees. Hoffman entered into a stipulation with the Board's General Counsel and agreed to abide by the Board's order.

In June 1993, the parties proceeded to a compliance hearing before an Administrative Law Judge (ALJ) to determine the amount of backpay owed to each discriminatee. On the final day of the hearing, Castro testified that he was born in Mexico and that he had never been legally admitted to, or authorized to work in, the United States. He admitted gaining employment with Hoffman only after tendering a birth certificate belonging to a friend who was born in Texas. He also admitted that he used this birth certificate to fraudulently obtain a California driver's license and a Social Security card, and to fraudulently obtain employment following his layoff by Hoffman. Neither Castro nor the Board's General Counsel offered any evidence that Castro had applied or intended to apply for legal authorization to work in the United States. Based on this testimony, the ALJ found the Board precluded from awarding Castro backpay or reinstatement as such relief would be contrary to *Sure-Tan, Inc. v. NLRB*, 467 U.S.

---

1. Section 8(a)(3) of the NLRA prohibits discrimination "in regard to hire or tenure of employment or any term or condition of employment to encourage or discourage membership in any labor organization."

883 (1984), and in conflict with [IRCA], which makes it unlawful for employers knowingly to hire undocumented workers or for employees to use fraudulent documents to establish employment eligibility.

In September 1998, four years after the ALJ's decision, and nine years after Castro was fired, the Board reversed with respect to backpay. Citing [an earlier Board decision], the Board determined that "the most effective way to accommodate and further the immigration policies embodied in [IRCA] is to provide the protections and remedies of the [NLRA] to undocumented workers in the same manner as to other employees." The Board thus found that Castro was entitled to $66,951 of backpay, plus interest. It calculated this backpay award from the date of Castro's termination to the date Hoffman first learned of Castro's undocumented status, a period of 4 1/2 years. A dissenting Board member would have affirmed the ALJ and denied Castro all backpay.

Hoffman filed a petition for review of the Board's order in the Court of Appeals. A panel of the Court of Appeals denied the petition for review. After rehearing the case en banc, the court again denied the petition for review and enforced the Board's order. We granted certiorari, and now reverse.[2]

This case exemplifies the principle that the Board's discretion to select and fashion remedies for violations of the NLRA, though generally broad, is not unlimited. Since the Board's inception, we have consistently set aside awards of reinstatement or backpay to employees found guilty of serious illegal conduct in connection with their employment. In [*NLRB v.*] *Fansteel*, [306 U.S. 240 (1939)], the Board awarded reinstatement with backpay to employees who engaged in a "sit down strike" that led to confrontation with local law enforcement officials. We set aside the award, saying:

> We are unable to conclude that Congress intended to compel employers to retain persons in their employ regardless of their unlawful conduct,—to invest those who go on strike with an immunity from discharge for acts of trespass or violence against the employer's property, which they would not have enjoyed had they remained at work.

Though we found that the employer had committed serious violations of the NLRA, the Board had no discretion to remedy those violations by awarding reinstatement with backpay to employees who themselves had committed serious criminal acts. Two years later, . . . the Board awarded reinstatement with backpay to five employees whose strike on shipboard had amounted to a mutiny in violation of federal law. We set aside the award, saying:

> It is sufficient for this case to observe that the Board has not been commissioned to effectuate the policies of the Labor Relations Act so single-mindedly that it may wholly ignore other and equally important [c]ongressional objectives.

Although the Board had argued that the employees' conduct did not in fact violate the federal mutiny statute, we rejected this view, finding the Board's interpretation of a statute so far removed from its expertise merited no deference from this Court. Since [then], we have accordingly never deferred to the Board's remedial preferences where such preferences potentially trench upon federal statutes and policies unrelated to the NLRA. Thus, we have precluded

---

2. The Courts of Appeals have divided on the question whether the Board may award backpay to undocumented workers. . . .

the Board from enforcing orders found in conflict with the Bankruptcy Code, rejected claims that federal antitrust policy should defer to the NLRA, and precluded the Board from selecting remedies pursuant to its own interpretation of the Interstate Commerce Act.

Our decision in *Sure-Tan* followed this line of cases and set aside an award closely analogous to the award challenged here. There we confronted for the first time a potential conflict between the NLRA and federal immigration policy, as then expressed in the Immigration and Nationality Act (INA). Two companies had unlawfully reported alien-employees to the Immigration and Naturalization Service (INS) in retaliation for union activity. Rather than face INS sanction, the employees voluntarily departed to Mexico. The Board investigated and found the companies acted in violation of §§ 8(a)(1) and (3) of the NLRA. The Board's ensuing order directed the companies to reinstate the affected workers and pay them six months' backpay.

We affirmed the Board's determination that the NLRA applied to undocumented workers, reasoning that the immigration laws "as presently written" expressed only a "peripheral concern" with the employment of illegal aliens. "For whatever reason," Congress had not "made it a separate criminal offense" for employers to hire an illegal alien, or for an illegal alien "to accept employment after entering this country illegally." Therefore, we found "no reason to conclude that application of the NLRA to employment practices affecting such aliens would necessarily conflict with the terms of the INA." With respect to the Board's selection of remedies, however, we found its authority limited by federal immigration policy. For example, the Board was prohibited from effectively rewarding a violation of the immigration laws by reinstating workers not authorized to reenter the United States. Thus, to avoid "a potential conflict with the INA," the Board's reinstatement order had to be conditioned upon proof of "the employees' legal reentry." "Similarly," with respect to backpay, we stated: "[T]he employees must be deemed 'unavailable' for work (and the accrual of backpay therefore tolled) during any period when they were not lawfully entitled to be present and employed in the United States." "[I]n light of the practical workings of the immigration laws," such remedial limitations were appropriate even if they led to "[t]he probable unavailability of the [NLRA's] more effective remedies." . . .

[Prior] cases established that where the Board's chosen remedy trenches upon a federal statute or policy outside the Board's competence to administer, the Board's remedy may be required to yield. Whether or not this was the situation at the time of *Sure-Tan*, it is precisely the situation today. In 1986, two years after *Sure-Tan*, Congress enacted IRCA, a comprehensive scheme prohibiting the employment of illegal aliens in the United States. 8 U.S.C. § 1324a. As we have previously noted, IRCA "forcefully" made combating the employment of illegal aliens central to "[t]he policy of immigration law." *INS v. Nat'l Ctr. for Immigrants' Rights, Inc.*, 502 U.S. 183, 194 (1991). It did so by establishing an extensive "employment verification system," § 1324a(a)(1), designed to deny employment to aliens who (a) are not lawfully present in the United States, or (b) are not lawfully authorized to work in the United States, § 1324a(h)(3). This verification system is critical to the IRCA regime. To enforce it, IRCA mandates that employers verify the identity and eligibility of all new hires by examining specified documents before they begin work. § 1324a(b). If an alien applicant is unable to present the required documentation, the unauthorized alien cannot be hired. § 1324a(a)(1).

Similarly, if an employer unknowingly hires an unauthorized alien, or if the alien becomes unauthorized while employed, the employer is compelled to discharge the worker upon discovery of the worker's undocumented status. § 1324a(a)(2). Employers who violate IRCA are punished by civil fines, § 1324a(e)(4)(A), and may be subject to criminal prosecution, § 1324a(f)(1). IRCA also makes it a crime for an unauthorized alien to subvert the employer verification system by tendering fraudulent documents. § 1324c(a). . . . There is no dispute that Castro's use of false documents to obtain employment with Hoffman violated these provisions.

Under the IRCA regime, it is impossible for an undocumented alien to obtain employment in the United States without some party directly contravening explicit congressional policies. Either the undocumented alien tenders fraudulent identification, which subverts the cornerstone of IRCA's enforcement mechanism, or the employer knowingly hires the undocumented alien in direct contradiction of its IRCA obligations. The Board asks that we overlook this fact and allow it to award backpay to an illegal alien for years of work not performed, for wages that could not lawfully have been earned, and for a job obtained in the first instance by a criminal fraud. We find, however, that awarding backpay to illegal aliens runs counter to policies underlying IRCA, policies the Board has no authority to enforce or administer. Therefore, as we have consistently held in like circumstances, the award lies beyond the bounds of the Board's remedial discretion.

The Board contends that awarding limited backpay to Castro "reasonably accommodates" IRCA, because, in the Board's view, such an award is not "inconsistent" with IRCA. The Board argues that because the backpay period was closed as of the date Hoffman learned of Castro's illegal status, Hoffman could have employed Castro during the backpay period without violating IRCA. The Board further argues that while IRCA criminalized the misuse of documents, "it did not make violators ineligible for back pay awards or other compensation flowing from employment secured by the misuse of such documents." . . . What matters here, and what sinks both of the Board's claims, is that Congress has expressly made it criminally punishable for an alien to obtain employment with false documents. There is no reason to think that Congress nonetheless intended to permit backpay where but for an employer's unfair labor practices, an alien-employee would have remained in the United States illegally, and continued to work illegally, all the while successfully evading apprehension by immigration authorities. Far from "accommodating" IRCA, the Board's position, recognizing employer misconduct but discounting the misconduct of illegal alien employees, subverts it.

Indeed, awarding backpay in a case like this not only trivializes the immigration laws, it also condones and encourages future violations. The Board admits that had the INS detained Castro, or had Castro obeyed the law and departed to Mexico, Castro would have lost his right to backpay. *See* Brief for Respondent 7-8 ("[U]ndocumented aliens taken into custody are not entitled to work") (construing 8 CFR § 103.6(a)(1991)). Castro thus qualifies for the Board's award only by remaining inside the United States illegally. . . .

We therefore conclude that allowing the Board to award backpay to illegal aliens would unduly trench upon explicit statutory prohibitions critical to federal immigration policy, as expressed in IRCA. It would encourage the successful evasion of apprehension by immigration authorities, condone prior violations of the immigration laws, and encourage future violations. However broad the Board's discretion to fashion remedies when dealing only with the NLRA, it is not so unbounded as to authorize this sort of an award.

Lack of authority to award backpay does not mean that the employer gets off scot-free. The Board here has already imposed other significant sanctions against Hoffman—sanctions Hoffman does not challenge. These include orders that Hoffman cease and desist its violations of the NLRA, and that it conspicuously post a notice to employees setting forth their rights under the NLRA and detailing its prior unfair practices. Hoffman will be subject to contempt proceedings should it fail to comply with these orders. We have deemed such "traditional remedies" sufficient to effectuate national labor policy regardless of whether the "spur and catalyst" of backpay accompanies them. ("This threat of contempt sanctions . . . provides a significant deterrent against future violations of the [NLRA]"). As we concluded in *Sure-Tan*, "in light of the practical workings of the immigration laws," any "perceived deficienc[y] in the NLRA's existing remedial arsenal" must be "addressed by congressional action," not the courts. In light of IRCA, this statement is even truer today.

The judgment of the Court of Appeals is reversed.

It is so ordered.

Justice BREYER, with whom Justice STEVENS, Justice SOUTER, and Justice GINSBURG join, dissenting.

I cannot agree that the backpay award before us "runs counter to," or "trenches upon," national immigration policy. As *all* the relevant agencies (including the Department of Justice) have told us, the National Labor Relations Board's limited backpay order will *not* interfere with the implementation of immigration policy. Rather, it reasonably helps to deter unlawful activity that *both* labor laws *and* immigration laws seek to prevent. Consequently, the order is lawful. *See ante*, at 1280 (recognizing "broad" scope of Board's remedial authority). . . .

The Court does not deny that the employer in this case dismissed an employee for trying to organize a union—a crude and obvious violation of the labor laws. And it cannot deny that the Board has especially broad discretion in choosing an appropriate remedy for addressing such violations. Nor can it deny that in such circumstances backpay awards serve critically important remedial purposes. Those purposes involve more than victim compensation; they also include deterrence, i.e., discouraging employers from violating the Nation's labor laws.

Without the possibility of the deterrence that backpay provides, the Board can impose only future-oriented obligations upon law-violating employers—for it has no other weapons in its remedial arsenal. And in the absence of the backpay weapon, employers could conclude that they can violate the labor laws at least once with impunity. . . . Hence the backpay remedy is necessary; it helps make labor law enforcement credible; it makes clear that violating the labor laws will not pay.

Where in the immigration laws can the Court find a "policy" that might warrant taking from the Board this critically important remedial power? Certainly not in any statutory language. The immigration statutes say that an employer may not knowingly employ an illegal alien, that an alien may not submit false documents, and that the employer must verify documentation. They provide specific penalties, including criminal penalties, for violations. But the statutes' language itself does not explicitly state how a violation is to effect the enforcement of other laws, such as the labor laws. What is to happen, for example, when an employer hires, or an alien works, in violation of these provisions? Must the alien forfeit all pay earned? May the employer ignore the labor laws? More to the point, may the employer violate those laws with impunity, at least once — secure in the knowledge that the Board cannot assess a monetary penalty? The immigration statutes' language simply does not say.

Nor can the Court comfortably rest its conclusion upon the immigration laws' purposes. For one thing, the general purpose of the immigration statute's employment prohibition is to diminish the attractive force of employment, which like a "magnet" pulls illegal immigrants toward the United States. H.R. Rep. No. 99-682, pt. 1, p. 45 (1986). To permit the Board to award backpay could not significantly increase the strength of this magnetic force, for so speculative a future possibility could not realistically influence an individual's decision to migrate illegally.

To *deny* the Board the power to award backpay, however, might very well increase the strength of this magnetic force. That denial lowers the cost to the employer of an initial labor law violation (provided, of course, that the only victims are illegal aliens). It thereby increases the employer's incentive to find and to hire illegal-alien employees. . . . The Court has recognized these considerations in stating that the labor laws must apply to illegal aliens in order to ensure that "there will be no advantage under the NLRA in preferring illegal aliens" and therefore there will be "fewer incentives for aliens themselves to enter." *SureTan, supra,* at 893-894. The Court today accomplishes the precise opposite.

The immigration law's specific labor-law-related purposes also favor preservation, not elimination, of the Board's backpay powers. And a policy of *applying* the labor laws must encompass a policy of *enforcing* the labor laws effectively. Otherwise, as Justice Kennedy once put the matter, "we would leave helpless the very persons who most need protection from exploitative employer practices." That presumably is why those in Congress who wrote the immigration statute stated explicitly and unequivocally that the immigration statute does *not* take from the Board *any* of its remedial authority (IRCA does not "undermine or diminish in any way labor protections in existing law, or . . . limit the powers of federal or state labor relations boards . . . to remedy unfair practices committed against undocumented employees"). . . .

Of course, the Court believes it is necessary to do so in order to vindicate what it sees as conflicting immigration law policies. I have explained why I believe the latter policies do not conflict. But even were I wrong, the law requires the Court to respect the Board's conclusion, rather than to substitute its own independent view of the matter for that of the Board. The Board reached its conclusion after carefully considering both labor law and immigration law. In doing so the Board has acted "with a discriminating awareness of the consequences of its action" on the immigration laws. The Attorney General, charged with immigration law enforcement, has told us that the Board is right. And the Board's position is, at the least, a reasonable one. Consequently, it is lawful. *Chevron U.S.A. Inc. v. Natural Resources Defense Council, Inc.,* 467 U.S. 837 (1984) (requiring courts to uphold reasonable agency position).

For these reasons, I respectfully dissent.

U.S. DEP'T OF LABOR, WAGE & HOUR DIV., FACT SHEET NO. 48, *APPLICATION OF U.S. LABOR LAWS TO IMMIGRANT WORKERS: EFFECT OF* HOFFMAN PLASTICS *DECISION ON LAWS ENFORCED BY THE WAGE AND HOUR DIVISION* (2008)

On March 27, 2002, the U.S. Supreme Court ruled in *Hoffman Plastic Compounds, Inc. v. NLRB*, that the National Labor Relations Board (NLRB) lacked authority to order back pay to an undocumented worker who was laid off from his job because of union activities.

In *Hoffman Plastics*, the Supreme Court decided that providing back pay to the undocumented worker would conflict with policies under U.S. immigration laws. Those laws require employees to present documents establishing their identity and authorization to work at the time they are hired. An employer must check those documents and cannot knowingly hire someone who is not authorized to work. In *Hoffman Plastics*, the employee presented false documentation when he was hired. He was later laid off for trying to organize a union, in violation of the National Labor Relations Act (NLRA). The NLRB sought back pay for a period of time after the layoff. The Supreme Court concluded that back pay should not be awarded "for years of work not performed, for wages that could not lawfully have been earned, and for a job obtained in the first instance by a criminal fraud."

The Supreme Court's decision does not mean that undocumented workers do not have rights under other U.S. labor laws. In *Hoffman Plastics*, the Supreme Court interpreted only one law, the NLRA. The Department of Labor does not enforce that law. The Supreme Court did not address laws the Department of Labor enforces, such as the Fair Labor Standards Act (FLSA) and the Migrant and Seasonal Agricultural Worker Protection Act (MSPA), that provide core labor protections for vulnerable workers. The FLSA requires employers to pay covered employees a minimum wage and, in general, time and a half an employee's regular rate of pay for overtime hours. The MSPA requires employers and farm labor contractors to pay the wages owed to migrant or seasonal agricultural workers when the payments are due.

The Department's Wage and Hour Division will continue to enforce the FLSA and MSPA without regard to whether an employee is documented or undocumented. Enforcement of these laws is distinguishable from ordering back pay under the NLRA. In *Hoffman Plastics*, the NLRB sought back pay for time an employee would have worked if he had not been illegally discharged, under a law that permitted but did not require back pay as a remedy. Under the FLSA or MSPA, the Department (or an employee) seeks back pay for hours an employee has actually worked, under laws that require payment for such work. The Supreme Court's concern with awarding back pay "for years of work not performed, for wages that could not lawfully have been earned," does not apply to work actually performed. Two federal courts already have adopted this approach. See *Flores v. Albertson's, Inc.*, 2002 WL 1163623 (C.D. Cal. 2002); *Liu v. Donna Karan International, Inc.*, 207 F. Supp. 2d 191 (S.D.N.Y. 2002).

The Department of Labor is still considering the effect of *Hoffman Plastics* on other labor laws it enforces, including those laws prohibiting retaliation for engaging in protected conduct.

NOTES AND QUESTIONS

1. Do you believe *Hoffman Plastics* is correctly decided? Should it apply to workers' compensation as well? To remedies for racial discrimination? Should workers in the country illegally have any recourse to the law? Why or why not?

2. Poverty lawyers have a long history of employment practice in the agricultural arena, where workers are especially vulnerable and undocumented immigrants are numerous. The California Rural Legal Assistance Program, for example, has litigated dozens of landmark cases in its nearly 50-year history, including cases protecting farmworkers from use of the crippling short-handled hoe, Carmona v. Div. Indus. Safety, 13 Cal. 3d 303 (1975), and enforcing minimum-wage and other labor rights, Cuadra v. Millan, 17 Cal. 4th 855 (1998) (calculation of back pay in unpaid wage cases).

3. A practical problem with representation of undocumented workers in litigation to enforce labor or other rights is their vulnerability to deportation or other immigration consequences if defendants are allowed discovery into immigration status. Whether such discovery is permissible is often hotly contested. *See, e.g.*, Raquel E. Aldana, *The Subordination and Anti-Subordination Story of the U.S. Immigrant Experience in the 21st Century*, 7 Nev. L.J. 713, 721 (2007) ("Despite its narrower holding, employers took the *Hoffman* decision as a green light to contend that undocumented workers lack state and federal workplace rights. In doing so, employers have resorted to intimidating discovery practices during litigation to compel courts to release the plaintiffs' immigration status, which, even when unsuccessful, deter plaintiffs from coming forward."). Is a worker's immigration status ever relevant in an employment law case? In a 2012 article, Professor Ruben J. Garcia gathered cases from a variety of jurisdictions holding that *Hoffman* barred remedies that could be classified as "pay for work not performed." Ruben J. Garcia, *Ten Years After* Hoffman Plastic Compounds, Inc. v. NLRB: *The Power of a Labor Law Symbol*, 21 Cornell J.L. & Pub. Pol'y 659, 661 n.13 (2012).

D. GOVERNMENT RESPONSES TO THE PROBLEMS OF LOW-WAGE WORKERS

1. Minimum Wage

For many people, raising the minimum wage seems like an obvious method of improving the economic lot of low-wage workers. The first federal minimum wage was enacted in 1938 (and set at $0.38 per hour). The current federal minimum wage for most workers has been $7.25 since July 2009. The federal minimum wage for tipped workers is $2.13. The federal minimum wage is not indexed to inflation and has been increased only sporadically by Congress. (Eighteen states and the District of Columbia have state minimum wages higher than the federal level, and ten of them have indexed their minimum wages.) Despite three raises in the first decade of the new millennium (taking the federal minimum wage from its decade-long $5.15 to $5.85, $6.55, and then $7.25), its value has diminished significantly in recent decades. In 1968, for example, the federal minimum wage was $1.60 per hour, which translates to approximately $10.27 in 2011 dollars. In the late 1960s, the federal minimum wage was approximately 50 percent of average wage, shrinking to approximately 40 percent in the early 1990s. In 2011, the minimum wage represented only about 37 percent of what the nation's average worker earned per hour.

Debate about whether the minimum wage actually helps low-income workers has been ongoing since the first days of the measure's enactment. While proponents tout the importance of increasing the incomes of the nation's poorest workers, opponents caution that raising the cost of labor may reduce employment and/or harm the least skilled workers. The excerpt below by Professors Neumark and Wascher summarizes some history of the minimum wage, surveys dozens of studies of its effects, and reports their conclusion that minimum wage does have negative employment effects. The Lester, Madland, and Bunker piece that follows reaches the opposite conclusion based on the experience of state minimum wage increases.

DAVID NEUMARK & WILLIAM WASCHER, *MINIMUM WAGES AND LOW-WAGE WORKERS: HOW WELL DOES REALITY MATCH THE RHETORIC?*

92 Minn. L. Rev. 1296 (2008)

The minimum wage has long been a fixture of U.S. labor market policy. The federal minimum, which was introduced in 1938 as part of the Fair Labor Standards Act (FLSA), is currently set at . . . $7.25 per hour [since] 2009. According to the U.S. Department of Labor, the FLSA covers more than 130 million U.S. workers, although most are paid above the federal minimum wage. In addition, most states have their own minimum wage laws, which sometimes specify a minimum wage and typically extend coverage to workers exempt from the federal law.

Despite their widespread application, minimum wages remain controversial among economists and policymakers. Many supporters point to the potential benefits of minimum wages; for example, they claim that minimum wages increase the incomes of the poor and ensure a fair and decent wage to low-skilled workers who have insufficient bargaining power to attain such a wage on their own. In contrast, minimum wage opponents emphasize the potential adverse effects of minimum wages on labor market opportunities for low-skilled workers, and some argue that minimum wages may harm the aggregate economy. . . .

The first legislation establishing a minimum wage in the United States was enacted in Massachusetts in 1912. Other states soon followed, and by 1923, minimum wage laws were on the books in fifteen states, the District of Columbia, and Puerto Rico. . . . [M]inimum wage advocates were concerned about poor working conditions and low wages in a variety of manufacturing industries that employed low-skilled workers. Chief among their concerns was a belief that many workers were receiving a wage below what was necessary to provide them with an adequate standard of living.

In this context, advocates for minimum wages frequently argued that individuals had a moral right to a "living" wage, and that minimum wages were necessary to aid individuals who were worthy of such a wage, but who were unable to bargain with their employers to obtain it. Opponents of minimum wages did not necessarily disagree with that rationale, but argued that laws requiring that workers be paid a wage higher than their productivity warranted would lead employers to reduce their staffing levels. Interestingly, some (although certainly not all) advocates of minimum wages acknowledged that wage floors would likely cause some of the lowest-skilled workers to lose their jobs. But some of these advocates also believed that society as a whole would benefit when the lowest-skilled workers, willing to accept very low wages, were replaced by higher-productivity workers to whom employers would turn in response to the minimum wage. Other proponents argued that a minimum wage would provide an incentive for low-skilled workers to increase their effort or would "shock" businesses into reducing inefficiencies in other areas of their operations. Thus, businesses could absorb the higher labor costs associated with the minimum wage without reducing the size of their workforce. In effect, these proponents viewed higher productivity as a secondary benefit of a minimum wage.

Because the balance of bargaining power between workers and employers was an important rationale for minimum wages in the early 1900s, the original minimum wage laws applied only to women and minors. The industries most identified with poor working conditions, such as clothing, candy-making, and box-making industries, tended to employ disproportionate numbers of women and youth, who were generally viewed at the time as more likely than men to be subject to unfair labor practices. In contrast, many in society believed that men should be able to bargain on equal terms with employers concerning the conditions of their employment, and thus that it would be "repugnant" for the government to regulate wages for men. Even so, courts often overturned minimum wage laws for women and minors on the grounds that they interfered with the rights of workers and employers to engage in voluntary contracts. . . .

A different set of motivations initially stimulated the legislation that established the federal minimum wage. . . . [M]inimum wages were proposed as a way of combating the extraordinarily high levels of unemployment during the Great Depression. In particular, many proponents argued that a minimum wage would raise household income levels and thus stimulate aggregate demand. . . . Many economists would now dismiss this line of argument as wishful thinking and point out that conventional economic theory suggests that higher real wages will tend to reduce aggregate output. But the "high-wage doctrine," as it came to be known, was clearly quite popular among economists and politicians in the 1920s and 1930s. . . . Support for the minimum wage as a means of raising purchasing power continued into the early years of the FLSA. For example, the Truman administration viewed a higher minimum wage as an insurance policy against another economic depression. Over time, however, the chief rationale for a higher minimum wage — as well as expansion of its coverage — shifted toward its effects on the distribution of income, in particular the potential to provide additional income to low-wage workers and poor families. In 1960, according to

Jerold Nordlund, "Senator [Hubert H.] Humphrey and many others argued the poverty reduction aspect of increases in coverage and in the minimum wage." Similarly, extending coverage of the minimum wage was one element of President Lyndon B. Johnson's War on Poverty. However, many other politicians remained concerned about the effects of minimum wages on jobs and inflation.

Continuing this shift in the rhetoric, few advocates or opponents of minimum wages now base their arguments on the potential effects of minimum wages on the macroeconomy. Instead, the debate over the minimum wage during the past two decades has shifted almost entirely to its potential effects on the economic well-being of low-skilled individuals and low-income families. In particular, proponents of a higher minimum wage typically cite the need for the minimum wage to be a living wage for the "working poor"; Senator Edward Kennedy has referred to it as "one of the best . . . anti-poverty programs we have." In contrast, opponents of minimum wages emphasize the potential for a higher minimum wage to cause job losses among young or low-skilled workers. These opponents also emphasize that many minimum wage workers are not from poor families but rather secondary workers (such as teenagers) in higher-income families; as a result, they argue that minimum wages are unlikely to help the poor and may harm them. . . .

The traditional textbook model used to describe the effects of minimum wages on labor and product markets is neoclassical in nature, and the predictions from this model are relatively straightforward: In an economy with competitive labor and product markets and homogenous workers, a broad-based increase in the minimum wage to a level higher than the market wage leads to a decline in employment and, because of the higher cost of labor, an increase in prices. However, the magnitude of job loss depends importantly on the nature of the production process—in particular, the extent to which employers can substitute capital for labor in response to the higher minimum wage—and on the sensitivity of product demand to the higher price. As a result, the number of workers who will lose their jobs in response to an increase in the minimum wage will depend on the elasticity of demand for labor.

Moreover, this representation of the labor market is surely too simplistic, and relaxing some of the assumptions that underlie the textbook model considerably complicates the deductions that can be drawn from it. To give one particularly relevant example, we can extend the model to allow for the possibility that each firm employs workers with a range of skill levels. In this case, a higher minimum wage causes employers to substitute away from the lowest-skilled workers not only toward capital, but also toward workers with greater skills. As a result, the magnitude of the effect of a minimum wage increase on aggregate employment is smaller than in the simple model (although overall employment almost surely falls). Perhaps more importantly, the distributional effects are noticeably different. In particular, in this version of the model, higher-skilled workers benefit from the higher minimum wage because it increases the demand for their services. In contrast, employment opportunities for the lowest-skilled workers are even more adversely affected. . . .

Finally, and perhaps most importantly given the current rhetoric, none of the theoretical models in the literature provide a clear prediction about the effects of the minimum wage on the incomes of the poor—the main societal goal of minimum wages. From the standpoint of the competitive model, Richard Freeman notes that "[m]inimum wages do not increase the pay of workers by magic . . . but rather take money from some citizens and pay it to others."

Because individuals potentially affected by the minimum wage may range from teenagers in well-off families to heads of poor families, the distributional question becomes: who are the winners and who are the losers from an increase in the minimum wage? . . . Because of the wide range of results in studies conducted over the past two decades, we recently undertook a careful and exhaustive review of this research. Despite numerous claims that the recent research fails to support the traditional view that the minimum wage reduces employment, our survey indicates that the bulk of the research conducted in the past two decades finds negative employment effects for low-skilled workers. In particular, about two-thirds of the studies in our survey, and more than eighty percent of the studies we view as most credible, give a consistent indication of negative employment effects. In contrast, only eight studies consistently find a positive effect of the minimum wage on employment, and most of these were case studies of the effects of a specific minimum wage increase on employment in a narrowly defined industry.

Moreover, the evidence for negative employment effects is especially strong for the least-skilled groups of workers across all industries and in studies that allow for minimum wages to affect employment with a lag. Thus, when researchers focus on broad groups of individuals most likely to be affected by the minimum wage and allow sufficient time for policy changes to affect the labor market, the evidence for disemployment effects seems overwhelming.

T. WILLIAM LESTER ET AL., *THE FACTS ON RAISING THE MINIMUM WAGE WHEN UNEMPLOYMENT IS HIGH*, CTR. FOR AM. PROGRESS ACTION FUND (JUNE 20, 2012)

Raising the minimum wage would be good for our economy. A higher minimum wage not only boosts workers' incomes — something that is sorely needed to boost demand and get the economy going — but it also reduces turnover and shifts businesses toward a high-road, high-human-capital model.

Still, some policymakers may be nervous about increasing the minimum wage while unemployment is so high. Yet, both the federal and states governments have raised the minimum wage numerous times during periods of high unemployment and the evidence indicates that employment has been unaffected.

A significant body of academic research has found that raising the minimum wage does not result in job losses even during hard economic times. There are at least five different academic studies focusing on increases to the minimum wage made during periods of high unemployment — with unemployment rates ranging from 7 percent to 12.3 percent — that find an increase in the minimum wage has no significant effect on employment levels. The results are likely because the boost in demand and reduction in turnover provided by a minimum wage counteracts the higher wage costs.

Similarly, a simple analysis of increases to the minimum wage on the state level, even during periods of state unemployment rates above 8 percent, shows that the minimum wage does not kill jobs. Indeed the states in our simple analysis had job growth slightly above the national average.

In our analysis we reference five academic studies of the minimum wage that include periods of high unemployment, cover different geographical areas and different time periods, and use a range of methodologies — from small case

studies to large econometric analysis—lending great credibility to their findings. The most recent studies are considered significant improvements over all
previous studies because of the methodology employed. One recent study, for
example, used the same methodology as earlier studies finding a small disemployment effect on teenagers, but the newer study controlled for the condition
of the regional economy, something previous studies had failed to do. Additionally, other recent studies have examined U.S. counties that border one another
but had different minimum wages (because they are in different states). All the
studies came to the same conclusion—that raising the minimum wage had no
effect on employment. Moreover, all of the studies included cases where the
minimum wage was raised during a period of high unemployment. These studies should go a long way in assuaging policymakers' fears and boost their willingness to raise the minimum wage. . . .

We examined every state minimum wage increase from 1990 through 2011
where the state unemployment rate was above 8 percent. We then compared the
rate of job creation over the next 12 months following the minimum wage
increase in these states to the national average.

Of the 35 cases where a state minimum wage was increased during a period of
high unemployment, 21 saw job increases over the next year at a rate faster than
the national average, while 14 witnessed job growth at a rate below the national
average. The average rate of job creation for a state after a minimum wage
increase during a period of high unemployment was 0.48 percentage points
above the national average. The median employment growth was also slightly
above the national average.

A few states, including Alabama and Tennessee in 2009, saw 12-month
job increases well above the national average. Some states, however, including
Michigan in 2008 and Arizona in 2011, had significantly worse employment
outcomes than the national average. But the average state that increased its
minimum wage had 12-month job growth that mirrored the national average,
with most states doing slightly better than the national average.

Likewise, separate analysis of minimum wage increases that occurred as a
result of federal action versus increases coming from state action yields nearly
identical results—national and state employment growth virtually matched.

While this simple analysis does not have the rigorous controls required of full-
blown academic research, these results provide additional evidence demonstrating increases in the minimum wage are unlikely to have harmful effects on
employment. When combined with the academic studies, these more anecdotal
findings provide a compelling picture of the employment effects of the
minimum wage.

NOTES AND QUESTIONS

1. The economic effects of the minimum wage remain hotly contested. For
   example, the Economic Policy Institute, a strong supporter of raising and
   indexing the minimum wage, released a study in August 2012 analyzing a
   legislative proposal to raise the federal minimum wage from $7.25 (where it
   has been since 2009) to $9.80 in three steps and index it to inflation. The
   study concluded that the proposal would raise the wages of 28 million workers by nearly $40 billion, increase GDP by approximately $25 billion, and
   create 100,000 new jobs over the three-year phase-in period. Doug Hall &
   David Cooper, Econ. Policy Inst., *Report: How Raising the Federal Minimum*

Wage Would Help Working Families and Give the Economy a Boost (2012). The conservative Heritage Foundation and American Enterprise Institute, opponents of minimum wage increases, have issued a series of briefing papers and reports arguing that minimum wage increases reduce employment, especially among youth, discourage investment in new businesses, and reduce opportunities for on-the-job training for low-skilled workers. *See, e.g.,* James Sherk, *Minimum Wage, Maximum Trouble,* Heritage Found. (July 27, 2009), *available at* http://www.heritage.org/research/commentary/2009/07/minimum-wage-maximum-trouble; Nick Schulz, *Raising Minimum Wage Is Maximum Stupidity,* Boston Herald (Apr. 11, 2012), *available at* http://www.aei.org/article/economics/fiscal-policy/labor/raising-minimum-wage-is-maximum-stupidity/. In his January 2013 State of the Union Address, President Obama called for an increase in the minimum wage to $9 per hour, and for the wage to be indexed to account for inflation. Should legislators raise the minimum wage? If you were a legislator, what data would help you decide whether to support an increase in the minimum wage?

2. The Neumark and Wascher excerpt above speculates as to why the minimum wage remains popular despite economic data they characterize as demonstrating that its success as an antipoverty tool is mixed at best. Law professor Noah Zatz has suggested in a provocative article that minimum wage laws should be regarded not primarily as economic tools but as tools of antidiscrimination law. He notes that "for many . . . , wage disparities can offend a commitment to human equality," and that "often the lowest paid workers hail from groups central to antidiscrimination [law]." Accordingly, he proposes that we should regard wage laws through a prism of fairness or justice rather than economic efficiency, comparing them to laws barring employment discrimination based on race, gender, disability, and national origin. Discussing these types of discrimination, Zatz notes that:

> The wrongfulness of such conduct is not a function of the economic condition in which it leaves the worker or her household. This point is reflected in the fact that antidiscrimination law applies without regard to workers' wage levels, incomes, and household structures. The point is not to redistribute income to the poor but to protect workers' civil rights to be treated as equals. Employers who act with animus or contempt treat workers wrongfully. The law prohibits them from doing so and, when employers act otherwise, the law demands a remedy in the spirit of corrective justice. The worker's economic situation is beside the point. So, too, with cases of wage theft.

Noah D. Zatz, *The Minimum Wage as a Civil Rights Protection: An Alternative to Antipoverty Arguments?,* 1 U. Chi. Legal F. 1 (2009). Is this persuasive? Should analysis of the benefits of the minimum wage take into account noneconomic effects or values? Is it appropriate for law to embrace dignitary values such as "a commitment to human equality"?

3. Despite the centrality of the minimum wage to the ideological debate, as well as to many attempts to combat wage theft, it is important to realize that many workers are not covered by the federal minimum wage requirements. Independent contractors (who are not considered "employees" under the FLSA), farmworkers, some in-home caregivers, and non-hourly professional workers are all excluded from coverage. Litigation over whether workers are properly classified as exempt from minimum wage is

frequent, with many recent cases focusing on whether employers who contract with intermediaries for workers should nonetheless be responsible for labor law compliance. *See, e.g.*, Brishen Rogers, *Toward Third-Party Liability for Wage Theft*, 31 Berk. J. Emp. & Lab. L. 1 (2010).

4. Despite the limits on minimum wage coverage, the Economic Policy Institute estimates that approximately 2.9 million workers, 64 percent of them women, receive minimum wage, and that minority workers disproportionately receive it. Kai Filion, Econ. Policy Inst., *Minimum Wage Issue Guide* (July 2009), *available at* http://www.epi.org/files/page/-/mwig/epi_minimum _wage_issue_guide.pdf.

2. Unemployment Insurance

U.S. DEP'T OF LABOR, OFFICE OF UNEMPLOYMENT INS., *UNEMPLOYMENT COMPENSATION: FEDERAL-STATE PARTNERSHIP* (2012)

INTRODUCTION

The federal-state unemployment compensation (UC) program, created by the Social Security Act (SSA) of 1935, offers the first economic line of defense against the ripple effects of unemployment. Through payments made directly to eligible, unemployed workers, it ensures that at least a significant proportion of the necessities of life, most notably food, shelter, and clothing, can be met on a week-to-week basis while a search for work takes place. As temporary, partial wage replacement to the unemployed, UC is of vital importance in maintaining purchasing power and in stabilizing the economy.

Unemployment compensation is a social insurance program. It is designed to provide benefits to most individuals out of work, generally through no fault of their own, for periods between jobs. In order to be eligible for benefits, jobless workers must demonstrate workforce attachment, usually measured by amount of wages and/or weeks of work, and must be able and available for work.

The UC program is a federal-state partnership based upon federal law, but administered by state employees under state law. Because of this structure, the program is unique among the country's social insurance programs. The UC program is also unique in that it is almost totally funded by employer taxes, either federal or state — only three states collect taxes from employees. Federal law defines certain requirements for the program. The SSA and the Federal Unemployment Tax Act (FUTA) set forth broad coverage provisions, some benefit provisions, the federal tax base and rate, and administrative requirements. The major functions of the federal government are to:

- ensure conformity and substantial compliance of state law, regulations, rules, and operations with federal law;
- determine administrative fund requirements and provide money to states for proper and efficient administration;
- set broad overall policy for administration of the program, monitor state performance, and provide technical assistance as necessary; and

- hold and invest all money in the unemployment trust fund until drawn down by states for the payment of compensation.

Each state designs its own UC program within the framework of the federal requirements. The state statute sets forth the benefit structure (e.g., eligibility/disqualification provisions, benefit amount) and the state tax structure (e.g., state taxable wage base and tax rates). The primary functions of the state are to:

- determine operation methods and directly administer the program;
- take claims from individuals, determine eligibility, and insure timely payment of benefits to workers; and
- determine employer liability, and assess and collect contributions.

Originally, most states paid benefits for a maximum duration of 13 to 16 weeks. Most states currently pay a maximum of 26 weeks, although Massachusetts and under certain conditions Washington pay 30 weeks. In periods of very high and rising unemployment in individual states, benefits are payable for up to 13 additional weeks (20 in some cases), up to a maximum of 39 weeks (or 46). These "extended benefits" are funded on a shared basis — approximately half from state funds and half from federal sources. The federal government [paid] for 100 percent of most EB costs (where EB costs are typically shared with the federal government) for weeks of unemployment beginning after February 9, 2009, through December 31, 2012.

In periods of national recession, when all states are impacted by high and sustained unemployment, federally-funded programs of supplemental benefits have been adopted occasionally. There were two such programs during the 1970s, one during the early 1980s, one during the 1990s, and one during the early 2000s. Currently, the Emergency Unemployment Compensation program of 2008 (EUC08) is effective from July 2008, through January 2, 2013. . . . [Ed. note: The American Taxpayer Relief Act of 2012 (Pub. L. No. 112-240) extended the EUC program until January 1, 2014.]

THE BASIC SYSTEM

Almost all wage and salary workers are now covered by the federal-state UC program. Railroad workers are covered by a separate federal program. Ex-service members with recent service in the Armed Forces and civilian federal employees are covered by a federal program, with the states paying benefits from federal funds as agents of the federal government. . . .

FINANCING THE PROGRAM

Pursuant to the provisions of the FUTA, a federal tax is levied on covered employers at a current rate of 6.0 percent on wages up to $7,000 a year paid to an employee. [Because of tax credits, however, most] employers pay an effective federal tax rate of 0.6 percent, or a maximum $42 per covered employee, per year. . . .

Coverage

As indicated previously, FUTA applies to employers who employ one or more employees in covered employment in at least 20 weeks in the current or preceding calendar year or who pay wages of $1,500 or more during any calendar quarter of the current or preceding calendar year. Also included are large employers of agricultural labor and some employment in domestic service.... [Except for federally-mandated coverage of employees of nonprofits, providers of service to Indian tribes, and state and local government employees], each state is ... free to determine the employers who are liable for contributions and the workers who accrue rights under the laws.

Benefit Rights

There are no federal standards for benefits in terms of qualifying requirements, benefit amounts, or duration of regular benefits. Hence, there is no common pattern of benefit provisions comparable to that in coverage and financing. The states have developed diverse and complex formulas for determining workers' benefit rights.

Under all state UC laws, a worker's benefit rights depend on his/her experience in covered employment in a past period of time, called the base period. The time period during which the weekly rate and the duration of benefits determined for a given worker apply to such worker is called the benefit year.

The qualifying wage or employment provisions attempt to measure the worker's attachment to the labor force. An insured worker must also be free from disqualification for causes which vary among the states. All but a few states require a claimant to serve a waiting period before his/her unemployment may be compensable.

All states determine an amount payable for a week of total unemployment as defined in the state law. Usually a week of total unemployment is a week in which the claimant performs no work and receives no pay. In most states a worker is partially unemployed in a week of less than full-time work when he/she earns less than his/her weekly benefit amount....

Qualifying Wages and Employment

All states require that a claimant must have earned a specified amount of wages or must have worked a certain number of weeks or calendar quarters in covered employment, or must have met some combination of the wage and employment requirements within his/her base period, to qualify for benefits. The purpose of such qualifying requirements is to restrict benefits to covered workers who are genuinely attached to the labor force.

Benefit Eligibility and Disqualification

All state laws provide that, to receive benefits, a claimant must be able to work and available for work, and actively seeking work. Also, he/she must be free from disqualification for such acts as voluntary leaving without good cause, discharge for misconduct connected with the work, and refusal of suitable work. The purpose of these provisions is to limit payments to workers unemployed primarily as a result of economic causes.

In all states, claimants who are held ineligible for benefits because of inability to work, unavailability for work, refusal of suitable work, or any other disqualification are entitled to a notice of determination and an appeal of the determination.

* * *

As the excerpt above notes, federal law does not mandate the provision of any set benefit level. The Center on Budget and Policy Priorities reported, based on federal data, that the average unemployment benefit was about $300 per week in 2010, 2011, and 2012. Moreover,

> State laws typically aim to replace about half of a worker's previous earnings up to a maximum benefit level. The maximum state-provided benefit in 2012 ranged from $133 in Puerto Rico and $235 in Mississippi (the lowest for a state) to $653 ($979 with dependents) in Massachusetts. Because the benefit is capped, UI benefits replace a smaller share of previous earnings for higher-wage workers than lower-wage workers. In 2011, the most recent year for which data are available, the average UI recipient nationwide got a benefit that replaced 46.0 percent of his or her earnings, but that "replacement rate" ranged from 32.9 percent in Alaska to 57.1 percent in Hawaii.

Chad Stone & William Chen, *Introduction to Unemployment Insurance*, Ctr. on Budget & Policy Priorities (2013).

In addition to low benefit levels, the UI system has often been criticized for not reflecting the realities of today's economy, especially for "contingent workers," a term used to describe temporary, part-time, seasonal, and leased workers, as well as independent contractors, all of whom generally earn lower wages than traditional employees. Notably, the U.S. Government Accountability Office reported in 2000 that "low-wage workers were twice as likely to be out of work as higher-wage workers but only half as likely to receive UI benefits." U.S. Gov't Accountability Office, GAO-01-181, *Unemployment Insurance: Role as Safety Net for Low-Wage Workers Is Limited* (2000).

The requirement that an employee have worked a certain requisite number of quarters in the system and at a certain level of wages leads to a disproportionate disqualifying effect on female and low-wage workers. The Institute for Women's Policy Research issued a Briefing Paper in 2010 that explained:

> There are three major reasons women are less likely than men to collect unemployment benefits. First, women tend to earn less and work more intermittently, moving in and out of jobs more, whereas many states use benefit calculation formulas that penalize those with low earnings, less continuous employment, and no periods of high earnings. Second, women's greater responsibilities for family care often force them to leave employment for reasons that disqualify them from benefit receipt, since caring for family members is often not a covered reason for not being at work. Third, in many states, workers who seek part-time employment are ineligible for insurance even if they had a work history that included part-time employment.

Heidi Hartmann & Ashley English, Inst. for Women's Policy Research, *Women and Men's Employment and Unemployment in the Great Recession*, IWPR Publication

C373 (Jan. 2010). Law professor Deborah Maranville has also written extensively about the gaps in the current unemployment insurance compensation system, especially as applied to women. *See, e.g.*, Deborah Maranville, *Changing Economy, Changing Lives: Unemployment Insurance and the Contingent Workforce*, 4 B.U. Pub. Int. L.J. 291, 323 (1995); Deborah Maranville, *Feminist Theory and Legal Practice: A Case Study on Unemployment Compensation Benefits and the Male Norm*, 43 Hastings L.J. 1081, 1092 (1992).

   In the following excerpt, Professor Karen Syma Czapanskiy summarizes many of the critiques of the unemployment insurance system, especially as to its inadequate coverage of women and other marginalized workers.

KAREN SYMA CZAPANSKIY, *UNEMPLOYMENT INSURANCE REFORMS FOR MOMS*
44 Santa Clara L. Rev. 1093 (2004)

[W]omen are fifteen percent less likely than men to collect unemployment insurance benefits. Women who recently left welfare are nearly one-third less likely than other women to qualify for UI.

   The unemployment insurance system was designed with the "ideal worker" in mind, that is, the man who could focus on work and call on others, such as a wife, to provide household and child care labor. Changes in UI in recent decades have made it more difficult for caregivers to qualify. To make unemployment insurance more available to low-income women with children, eligibility rules need to be changed to take into account the larger degree of responsibility that women take for family care. Five changes are widely advocated:

a. good cause for leaving work needs to include fulfilling family caregiving responsibilities, such as caring for a sick child or other relative, moving to accompany a relocating family member, remedying disruptions in child care, or attending to a child's school problems;
b. good cause also needs to give women with serious family problems such as domestic violence opportunities to seek safety;
c. the requirement that a worker be available for work needs to include part-time as well as full-time work;
d. minimum earnings requirements, used by states to ensure that unemployment insurance is available only to people who are committed to the labor force, need to be changed to minimum hours of work requirements; and
e. hours of work performed in recent quarters (alternative base period) need to be counted so that people with intermittent work histories, such as caregivers, qualify for unemployment insurance.

   None of these changes is cost-free. Cost estimates are not perfect, but one respected analyst has suggested that the range is approximately $100 million in 1996 dollars, a 0.5% increase in costs over the 1998 costs.

NOTES AND QUESTIONS

1. As explained above, a worker is ineligible for unemployment insurance if she was terminated for "misconduct," or if she quit employment without

"good cause." (A worker who is not available for or refuses "suitable work" is similarly ineligible.) These statutory terms provide the terrain on which many UI cases are litigated, most often in the administrative tribunals created by the state agencies that run the state UI programs. A 1941 Wisconsin Supreme Court decision is still frequently cited today for its explanation that "misconduct" which blocks a worker's eligibility for UI does not generally include mere poor performance. That court held that if mere negligence, such as "mistakes, errors in judgment or in the exercise of discretion, minor and but casual or unintentional carelessness or negligence, and similar minor peccadilloes" were held to be misconduct disqualifying workers from unemployment benefits, then

> there will be defeated, as to many of the great mass of less capable industrial workers, who are in the lower income brackets and for whose benefit the act was largely designed, the principal purpose and object under the act of alleviating the evils of unemployment by cushioning the shock of a lay-off, which is apt to be most serious to such workers.

Boynton Cab Co. v. Neubeck, 296 N.W. 636 (Wis. 1941).

Should only "willful or wanton disregard of an employer's interests" trigger exclusion from UI coverage? What are some arguments for and against a more expansive interpretation of "misconduct"?

2. Do you agree with Professor Czapanskiy that unemployment insurance should be extended to more part-time and short-term workers, and made more widely available when caretaking responsibilities cause job loss? Why or why not?

3. In addition to many caretakers (often women), the unemployment system also leaves out most part-time workers, denies benefits to those whose hours are reduced but not eliminated, and in many states excludes the most recent three to five months of employment when determining whether a worker has enough base period earnings to qualify. These and other disqualifying rules result in fewer than half of all unemployed workers actually receiving benefits. *See* Ctr. on Budget and Policy Priorities, *Unemployment Insurance Reforms Should Be Part of Economic Recovery Package* (2009), *available at* http://www.cbpp.org/cms/index.cfm?fa=view&id=2221.

4. An increasing number of law school clinics are taking on unemployment cases (generally appeals from the denial of benefits). Attorney and clinic supervisor Colleen Shanahan has written about the legal issues, as well as the benefits, to clients and students of this type of practice. *See* Colleen Shanahan, *Cultivating Justice for the Working Poor: Clinical Representation of Unemployment Claimants*, 18 Geo. J. on Poverty L. & Pol'y 401 (2011).

5. Criticism of the UI system is not limited to those who believe it is insufficiently generous. The libertarian Cato Institute has criticized the system for, *inter alia*, encouraging unemployment, distorting the marketplace by subsidizing certain industries, suppressing personal savings, and both subsidizing and penalizing workers. *See* Chris Edwards & George Leef, Cato Inst., *Failures of the Unemployment Insurance System* (2011), *available at* http://www.downsizinggovernment.org/labor/failures-of-unemployment-insurance#5.

3.   The Earned Income Tax Credit

The Earned Income Tax Credit, or EITC, has become the nation's largest income transfer and wage subsidy program. It is only available to working adults and is administered through the tax system, not the Department of Health and Human Services. The following excerpt from the nonpartisan Center on Budget and Policy Priorities explains the program.

CTR. ON BUDGET AND POLICY PRIORITIES, POLICY BASICS: THE EARNED INCOME TAX CREDIT (2013)

The Earned Income Tax Credit (EITC) is a federal tax credit for low- and moderate-income working people. It encourages and rewards work as well as offsetting federal payroll and income taxes. Twenty-five states, including the District of Columbia, have established their own EITCs to supplement the federal credit.

WHO IS ELIGIBLE, AND FOR HOW MUCH?

In the 2012 tax year, working families with children that have annual incomes below about $36,900 to $50,300 (depending on marital status and the number of dependent children) may be eligible for the federal EITC. Also, working-poor people without children that have incomes below about $13,900 ($19,200 for a married couple) can receive a very small EITC. In the 2010 tax year, the most recent year for which the data are available, some 27 million working families and individuals received the EITC.

The amount of EITC depends on a recipient's income, marital status, and number of children. . . . [W]orkers receive the credit beginning with their first dollar of earned income; the amount of the credit rises with earned income until it reaches a maximum level and then begins to phase out at higher income levels. The EITC is "refundable," which means that if it exceeds a low-wage worker's income tax liability, the IRS will refund the balance. During the 2010 tax year, the average EITC was $2,805 for a family with children and $262 for a family without children.

Research indicates that families mostly use the EITC to pay for necessities, repair homes, maintain vehicles that are needed to commute to work, and in some cases, obtain additional education or training to boost their employability and earning power.

ENCOURAGING AND REWARDING WORK

The EITC is designed to encourage and reward work. As noted, a worker's EITC grows with each additional dollar of earnings until reaching the maximum value. This creates an incentive for people to leave welfare for work and for low-wage workers to increase their work hours.

This incentive feature has made the EITC highly successful. Studies show that the EITC encourages large numbers of single parents to leave welfare for work, especially when the labor market is strong.

Specifically, EITC expansions are the most important reason why employment rose among single mothers with children during the 1990s—the EITC was more effective in encouraging work than either welfare reform or the strong economy. The Committee for Economic Development, an organization of 250 corporate executives and university presidents, concluded in 2000 that "[t]he EITC has become a powerful force in dramatically raising the employment of low-income women in recent years."

The EITC reduces poverty directly by supplementing the earnings of low-wage workers. There has been broad bipartisan agreement that a two-parent family with two children with a full-time, minimum-wage worker should not have to raise its children in poverty. At the federal minimum wage's current level, such a family can move above the poverty line only if it receives the EITC as well as SNAP (food stamp) benefits. . . .

STRENGTHENING THE EITC

The 2009 Recovery Act temporarily expanded the EITC in two ways. First, it added a "third tier" of the EITC for families with three or more children. These larger families can now receive up to $655 more than they would have without this improvement. This addition recognizes that larger families face a higher cost of living and that families with three or more children are more than twice as likely as smaller families to be poor.

Second, the Recovery Act expanded marriage penalty relief in the EITC, reducing the financial penalty some couples receive when they marry by allowing married couples to receive larger benefits at modestly higher income levels.

In 2011, these two expansions together lifted an estimated 500,000 people out of poverty and reduced the severity of poverty for approximately 10 million poor people. Under the American Taxpayer Relief Act, enacted in January 2013, Congress extended these improvements through 2017.

In contrast to the EITC for working families with children, the EITC for workers without children remains extremely small—too small even to fully offset federal taxes for workers at the poverty line. Under current law, a childless adult or noncustodial parent working full-time at the minimum wage is ineligible to receive any EITC benefits. (Such an individual would receive the maximum EITC if he or she had children.) As a result, low-wage workers not raising minor children are the only Americans whom the federal income tax taxes into poverty.

* * *

While the EITC has enjoyed broad bipartisan support and its success at lifting families out of poverty is often touted, not all observers are so sanguine. The following excerpt by Professor Anne Alstott calls into question whether the EITC is really the best option for low-income Americans.

ANNE L. ALSTOTT, *WHY THE EITC DOESN'T MAKE WORK PAY*
73 Law & Contemp. Probs. 285 (2010)

Since 1975, the earned income tax credit (EITC) has transformed from a small, obscure provision of the federal tax code into one of the largest programs in the

U.S. social-welfare system. Today, the EITC stands as the largest cash-transfer program for low-income workers with children, providing $47 billion in benefits each year to 24 million families.

Politicians, advocates, and scholars have praised the EITC. President Bill Clinton famously called the EITC "a cornerstone of our effort to reform the welfare system and make work pay." Steve Holt of the Brookings Institution (among others) argues that the EITC "has proved remarkably successful in reducing poverty . . . , [lifting] more children out of poverty than any other social program or category of programs." And, as often noted, support for the EITC spans the political spectrum.

Among its other attributes, the EITC is a political winner, as well: Congress has legislated major increases in funding while spending on other cash transfers has remained flat. . . . [T]he EITC as a percentage of GDP [has grown] since 1975, alongside declines in federal spending on unemployment insurance and Temporary Assistance for Needy Families (TANF).

. . . The EITC arose from the ashes of the negative income tax in the mid-1970s. From its earliest days, the EITC prospered politically because it appeared to promote and reward paid work — helping answer the charge that a negative income tax would support the idle. Still, remaining supporters of the negative income tax sounded a cautionary note: they worried that the EITC did too little to address poverty, unemployment, and eroding wages.

. . . [I challenge] two assumptions that underlie conventional praise for the EITC. First, analysts often adopt the official poverty line as the metric for success in "making work pay," despite its inadequacy as a measure of economic distress and social exclusion. Adopting a more realistic version of the poverty line reveals how little the EITC accomplishes — or, put another way, how ambitious a program would have to be to make work pay.

Second, discussions of the EITC typically focus on the situation of workers while they hold jobs, ignoring the frequent spells of job disruption due to unemployment, disability, and family needs that are common among low-wage workers. This limited perspective may be appropriate for technocratic discussions of EITC program design, because the EITC, like any wage or earnings subsidy, is designed only to assist the employed. It is, thus, a shortcoming of wage subsidies in general, and not the EITC in particular, that gaps in the social safety net leave low-income workers vulnerable to involuntary work disruption. But the contours of complementary programs should inform claims about the success of the EITC in "making work pay" — that is, in assuring a decent standard of living to those willing to work, even if (like many low-income workers) they do not succeed in working full-time, year-round. . . .

Progressive praise for the EITC may reflect the political assumption that a modest wage subsidy is the best that U.S. politics can produce for low-wage workers. The ongoing debate over health-care reform stands as a reminder of how difficult it can be for U.S. political institutions to enact redistributive measures. But it seems to me important to make political assumptions explicit in our discussions and to understand that the EITC is part and parcel of the harsh and meager U.S. welfare state. It pays a wage subsidy that is too small to lift workers to a decent living standard, and it conditions payments on continuous employment — an aspiration that is unrealistic for many in the low-wage workforce. Despite political rhetoric, the EITC does not — and, given its legal context, cannot — "make work pay" in a meaningful sense. . . .

Among the EITC's accomplishments, advocates say, are major reductions in poverty: according to the Center on Budget and Policy Priorities, for example, "the EITC lifts more children out of poverty than any other single program or category of programs." But such statements typically adopt the official U.S. poverty level as their benchmark, even though its shortcomings as a measure of social inclusion and economic wellbeing are well known. According to more appealing and realistic measures of poverty, the EITC has a small effect. . . .

To be sure, the EITC alters the official poverty status of nearly a million families and about three-and-one-half million people. Still, this is a strikingly modest achievement for a program that, advocates say, "lifts more children out of poverty than any other single program or category of programs."

Measured by a more realistic benchmark (200% of the official line), poverty is only 2% higher without the EITC than with it. . . . This effect may be deliberate. Analysts note that the EITC concentrates assistance near the official poverty line, and it hardly seems accidental that the program's parameters produce the largest political bang for the buck: the program maximizes the perception of helping the poor, without helping many families achieve a level of wellbeing that ensures social participation. Clearly, then, the EITC does not reduce poverty significantly, despite advocates' claims.

* * *

While Professor Alstott criticizes the EITC for its inadequacy in actually improving the lot of low-wage workers relative to a sensible measure of poverty, Professor Karen Czapanskiy, in another part of the article excerpted above, argues that better unemployment coverage is superior as a policy tool to an increased EITC. She points out that while EITC costs are borne by the taxpayers, UI is funded by employers, and argues that liberalizing the UI rules would both increase wages and prompt employers to adopt more realistic policies regarding part-time work, sick days, and the needs of workers.

KAREN SYMA CZAPANSKIY, *UNEMPLOYMENT INSURANCE REFORMS FOR MOMS*

44 Santa Clara L. Rev. 1093 (2004)

. . . [M]illions of young women with young children have . . . entered the paid labor force since 1990. Employers have not, however, paid the price for their expanded workforce. Instead, the principal incentives have come from changes in federal public benefit and tax expenditure policies. Some of the incentives have been in the form of "pulls," such as increases in the Earned Income Tax Credit (EITC) and the refundable child tax credit. Others have been in the form of "pushes," such as the work participation requirements and sanction policies of welfare reform and similar changes in other public benefit programs. None of these changes has solved the basic problem, however, which is that employment practices remain heavily incompatible with parental responsibilities. Employers have had to make few of the necessary changes to accommodate workers who are parents. When federal public benefit and tax expenditure policies helped to expand the work force and increase family dependency on earnings, the pressure was taken off of employers. The failure of employers to change their practices remains an issue, however, because mothers and fathers lose their jobs when they try to meet family responsibilities while working for pay. One consequence is that, when they do lose their jobs, most states deny them the partial wage replacement benefit called unemployment insurance (UI). . . .

My argument is that the recent changes in federal public benefits and tax expenditure policies have, in effect, insulated employers from doing what would have happened in my fantasy scenario. The increased costs that employers should be paying to lure young women with young children into the paid labor force and to keep them there is instead being paid by the families and by federal and state taxpayers. Employers have not had to increase pay or benefits or modify employment practices to reduce work-family conflicts. As a result, parents with caretaking responsibilities lose their jobs or are forced into the part-time job market. Given the benefits enjoyed by employers in getting young mothers into the workforce without paying the full cost, employers should not be able to avoid the relatively low cost of increasing unemployment insurance coverage for these workers.

The public benefit programs at issue are Temporary Assistance to Needy Families (TANF), Food Stamps, State Child Health Insurance Program (SCHIP), child care subsidies, and public housing. The principal tax expenditure policy is the Earned Income Tax Credit (EITC). All of these programs have a work requirement applicable to some or all participants, or they provide subsidies to people with earnings. All of the programs are targeted at low-income parents. All of them can have an impact on increasing the labor pool and on enhancing the value of the wage that the worker receives. All of them demand worker discipline because losing a job means losing eligibility for vital aid as well as earnings. As the result of the combined effect of programs such as these, employers have a larger pool of workers from whom to choose and employers can resist pressure to increase wages and benefits. Employees, on the other hand, have more incentive to remain employed and to make few demands on their employers because the costs of leaving work are greater than continuing in an unfavorable employment situation.

Unemployment insurance is paid for by taxes on employers. Expanding UI eligibility to respond to employment issues related to work/family conflicts, therefore, would result in higher costs to employers. In the current system, almost all of the costs of work/family conflict are placed elsewhere. Families pay when a caregiver loses employment and no temporary wage or income replacement is available, whether through unemployment insurance or welfare. Taxpayers generally pay to the extent that unemployed caregivers qualify for partial income replacement in the form of public benefits such as welfare, food stamps, or housing assistance. Employees could pay through a payroll tax to fund, for example, temporary disability insurance available to parents after the birth or adoption of a child. Employees who are parents could be made to pay through a payroll tax applicable only to them. The question is whether changes in public benefits and tax expenditure policies justify shifting some of the costs of work/family conflicts to employers through expanding UI eligibility.

NOTES AND QUESTIONS

1. Is EITC, an increased minimum wage, liberalized unemployment insurance, or some other tool entirely, the best method for increasing wages of the working poor? Who should pay for higher wages, and who pays under each of the proposed tools?

2. Professor Czapanskiy's call for employers to shoulder more of the costs of employing low-wage workers is echoed in the debate over the wage policies of Wal-Mart, America's largest employer. Wal-Mart has come under scrutiny and criticism for the large percentage of its workforce drawing taxpayer-funded benefits such as EITC, Medicaid, and food stamps. *See, e.g.,* Annette Bernhardt et al., Brennan Ctr. for Justice, What Do We Know About Wal-Mart? (2005), *available at* http://nelp.3cdn.net/c2b825db82518d6e25_tam6bnxs1.pdf.

In November 2012, U.S. Congressman-elect Alan Grayson penned an op-ed on the costs to the public and the workers of Wal-Mart's wage policies, and urged the employees to unionize:

> I did not spend Thanksgiving evening with my wife and my five children. I spent it, instead, handing out turkey sandwiches to workers in Walmart. And showing my support for one brave soul who walked off the job in protest against exploitation.
>
> Walmart "associates" make an average of just more than $10 an hour. That means that if they manage to get a full 40 hours a week — and many don't — they get paid $1,700 a month, before taxes. Somehow, that is supposed to pay for their food, shelter, clothing[,] and medical care, and that of their children. Quite a trick.
>
> In state after state, the largest group of Medicaid recipients is Walmart employees. I'm sure that the same thing is true of food stamp recipients. Each Walmart "associate" costs the taxpayers an average of more than $1,000 in public assistance.
>
> How underpaid are Walmart employees? This underpaid: if every one of them got a 30 percent raise, Walmart would still be profitable. . . .
>
> And so it begins. Walmart accounts for more than 10 percent of all of the retail sales in the United States. It is the largest private employer in the world, with more than two million employees. And even though those employees comprise barely 10 percent of its cost of doing business, Walmart exploits them mercilessly. Now Walmart employees are starting to organize, starting to fight back.

Alan Grayson, *My Thanksgiving: A Turkey Sandwich at Walmart*, Huffington Post (Nov. 24, 2012), http://www.huffingtonpost.com/rep-alan-grayson/walmart-black-friday-_b_2185675.html.

E. ADVOCACY RESPONSES TO THE PROBLEMS OF LOW-WAGE WORKERS

1. *The Living Wage Movement*

WILLIAM QUIGLEY, *FULL-TIME WORKERS SHOULD NOT BE POOR: THE LIVING WAGE MOVEMENT*

70 Miss. L.J. (2001)

Los Angeles' prototypical poor person is no longer a scruffy panhandler on the freeway offramp, or a skid row derelict camped beneath a blue tarp. Today's poverty icon is a working mother, toiling eight hours or more a day at a job that does not pay enough to cover the rent, clothe the baby or provide a life of even minimal comfort.

If a person works full-time, she should not have to raise her family in poverty. Advocacy for enactment of a living wage is summed up in that simple statement. . . .

The current living wage movement is trying, primarily through local legislation, to bring justice to low wage workers by requiring that businesses which have public contracts pay their workers wages sufficient to support their families. The living wage movement is made up of a fabric of local coalitions of community groups, labor organizations and interfaith religious denominations. The main argument of living wage supporters is, as the Wall Street Journal aptly summarized: "Businesses which benefit from public largesse should pay their workers at least enough money to keep them out of poverty."

The living wage movement is built on a recognition that the current federal minimum wage does not provide enough income for an individual to live on, much less an individual with a family. The current minimum wage is several dollars an hour short of a living wage and even several dollars short of matching its own value of thirty years ago. Living wage supporters seek to supersede the low federal minimum wage with a local requirement for a true living wage. Local living wage ordinances seek to implement living wages by one or more of a series of actions: requiring private contractors with local government contracts to pay all their employees a living wage; restricting local public aid to private corporations which pay their employees a living wage; or requiring all employers within the jurisdiction to pay a living wage.

Advocacy for living wages is not a new concept, but one that has been discussed for well over 100 years. What is new is the growing energy in the living wage movement because of a series of local victories which resulted in the enactment of a number of living wage ordinances. By early 2001 more than fifty jurisdictions had enacted living wage ordinances and another seventy-five were engaged in ongoing living wage campaigns.

The first victory achieved by the current living wage movement came in the mid 1990s in Baltimore and emerged from action taken by a coalition of churches and labor organizations. A coalition of fifty churches approached the American Federation of State, County and Municipal Employees (AFSCME) to join in creating an organization of churches, labor union members and low-wage service workers. The churches were seeing an increase in the use of soup kitchens and pantries by workers and concluded that minimum wage jobs with no benefits were not helping people escape poverty. AFSCME members were concerned about the privatization of formerly government jobs in areas like janitorial and food services which replaced good public jobs with low wage private jobs. Together they concluded that private companies were paying low wages in order to win low-bid government contracts. Low-wage workers were often turning to food stamps, publicly financed health care and private assistance from churches to make up the difference from their low-wage work. The coalition viewed this as municipal subsidization of poverty. In response, the coalition created a local campaign for a law that would require businesses which had contracts with the city to pay their workers at least a living wage. Both the churches and labor unions contributed people and funds to create a working coalition to educate the public about the problem of low wages and to lobby for the living wage bill. The city ultimately enacted the local living wage law and it went into effect in July of 1996. The law required city contractors to pay a minimum of $6.10 an hour in 1996, rising in annual increments to $7.70 an hour in 1999. The goal of the law is to place the wage at a level sufficient to lift a family of four over the poverty level. The law was estimated to apply to between 2000 and 3000 workers.

The success of the Baltimore effort inspired the development of other living wage coalitions made up of labor, community, and religious organizations.

Labor organizations have been pushing living wage ordinances in order to show their commitment to low-wage workers. They have also followed the lead of labor leaders in Baltimore by working to prevent privatization efforts from replacing well-paying city jobs with low-paying private jobs. Labor organizations have also re-invigorated their efforts to work in coalitions with religious and community groups.

Community groups organize around living wage campaigns because of a combination of energies from national and local groups and a continuing national resource effort by the organizations of the AFL-CIO, ACORN and the New Party.

Religious organizations and groups have become active in this movement because their faith compels them to speak up about issues of justice and poverty. Religious advocacy for just wages and living wages have been articulated by religious groups for more than 100 years. . . .

The living wage movement is also buoyed by broad public support. An April, 2000 survey found that 94% of the one thousand adults questioned agreed with the statement that "as a country, we should make sure that people who work full-time should be able to earn enough to keep their families out of poverty." There also has been consistent public backing for raising the minimum wage. Other polls continue to show overwhelming support for modest raises in the minimum wage. Conservative Pat Buchanan received wide support for his call for "a standard of living that rises each year, and a 'family wage' that enables a single parent to feed, clothe, house, and educate a large family in decency." Students and faculty in universities are now advocating for their institutions to pay all their workers at least living wages. . . .

Not everyone supports the living wage movement. As in all efforts to legislate reform, there are countervailing forces. Most of the opposition to the living wage movement comes from the same sources that oppose raising, or sometimes even the existence of, the minimum wage. These people often seek to put a legislative maximum on the minimum wage that local communities can set.

Opponents of living wages argue that these ordinances could potentially increase the local poverty rate and cost too much. A survey of over 300 economists conducted in 2000 for the Employment Policies Institute, a non-profit research organization generally opposed to raises in both the minimum wage and the enactment of living wage ordinances, found that nearly eight in ten of the labor economists surveyed thought living wage ordinances would result in employers hiring higher skilled workers, and over 70% said the laws could potentially reduce the number of entry-level jobs and thus increase the local poverty rate. The opposition also suggests that living wage ordinances increase the cost of governmental contracts. Pasadena, California, estimated their living wage ordinance cost to be about $200,000 for the year 2000; Cambridge, Massachusetts, estimated its cost at $300,000; Madison, Wisconsin, estimated its cost at $47,000. While there is certainly some cost associated with living wages, this article will not join in the aforementioned melee of economists. Others disagree.

THE ECONOMIC IMPACT OF THE LIVING WAGE

A brief word about the economic impact of living wages. Ever since government was first involved in the setting of minimum wages, there have been controversies about the economic impact of setting wage floors. It is no different for living wages. The economic impact of the living wage ordinances varies significantly depending on the wage rate and scope of coverage of the ordinance. . . . Living wage proponents point to data that suggests the actual financial impact on covered businesses is very small, less than 1% of the overall spending of these concerns. Opponents disagree, arguing that living wages put too big a burden on business and actually harm the cause of the working poor by making entry-level employment less available. These economic issues will continue to be debated as long as there are opportunities to do so.

NOTES AND QUESTIONS

1. Are the arguments for a living wage persuasive? How much of a decrease in employment should be tolerable as the price for a living wage? Should living wage obligations be limited to employers contracting with government agencies?

2. Living wage ordinances have been challenged in a variety of ways, including passage of state measures preempting localities' ability to enact living wages, lawsuits alleging that the ordinances violate state minimum wage laws or impede state police powers, and municipalities' refusal to enforce living wage ordinances where enacted. Some of these legal challenges are described in Rachel Harvey, *Labor Law: Challenges to the Living Wage Movement: Obstacles in a Path to Economic Justice*, 14 U. Fla. J.L. & Pub. Pol'y 229 (2003). One of the few cases to reach a state supreme court was New Orleans Campaign for a Living Wage v. City of New Orleans, 825 So. 2d 1098 (La. 2002), in which the state Supreme Court held, over a dissent, that a state statute prohibiting local minimum wage laws for private employers was a valid exercise of the state's police power and that the city's minimum wage law was therefore unconstitutional.

3. Despite their mixed success in court, living wage campaigns remain ongoing in many states and localities, and statutes or ordinances are in effect in Maryland, San Francisco, Santa Fe, and dozens of other jurisdictions. However, their effects are limited, as they typically cover only employees of firms that contract with governments. The *New York Times Magazine* published a lengthy article discussing the living wage movement in 2006. Jon Gertner, *What Is a Living Wage?*, N.Y. Times Mag. (Jan. 15, 2006).

2. Worker Centers

Another advocacy strategy in increasing use is the development of worker self-help centers. Professor Janice Fine explains:

> Worker centers are community-based and community-led organizations that engage in a combination of service, advocacy, and organizing to provide support to low-wage workers. The vast majority of worker centers have grown to serve predominantly, or exclusively, immigrant populations; however, there are a few

centers that serve the African-American community or bring immigrants together with African-Americans. As work is the primary focus of life for many newly arriving immigrants, it is also the locus of many of the problems they experience. This is why, although they actually pursue a broad agenda that includes many aspects of immigrant life in America, most of the organizations call themselves "worker centers."

Difficult to categorize, worker centers have some features that are reminiscent of earlier U.S. civic institutions, including settlement houses, fraternal organizations, local civil rights organizations, and unions. They identify with social movement traditions and draw upon community organizing strategies. Other features, especially cooperatives and popular education approaches, are suggestive of the civic traditions of the home countries from which many of these immigrants came. Some are based in a specific industry while others are non-industry based; however, many are a mixture of both — they have specific industry projects as well as other geographic and issue-based activities.

Centers pursue their mission through a combination of approaches: 1) Service delivery, including legal representation to recover unpaid wages, English classes, worker rights education, and access to health clinics, bank accounts, and loans; 2) Advocacy, including researching and releasing exposés about conditions in low-wage industries, lobbying for new laws and changes in existing ones, working with government agencies to improve monitoring and grievance processes, and bringing suits against employers; and 3) Organizing, including building ongoing organizations and engaging in leadership development against workers to take action on their own behalf for economic and political change.

Worker centers vary in terms of their organizational models, how they think about their mission, and how they carry out their work. Nonetheless, in the combination of services, advocacy, and organizing they undertake, worker centers are playing a unique role in helping low-wage immigrants navigate the world of work in the United States. They provide low-wage immigrant workers with a range of opportunities for expressing their "collective voice" as well as for taking collective action. The number of worker centers in the United States has increased significantly over the past decade, paralleling the decline of labor unions and the increased flow of specific immigrant groups in large numbers to the United States. In 1992, there were fewer than five centers nationwide. This number increased dramatically in the early- to mid-1990s, growing at a rate of ten to twenty new centers each year for several years. As of 2005, there are at least 139 worker centers in over eighty U.S. cities, towns, and rural areas.

Janice Fine, *Worker Centers: Organizing Communities at the Edge of the Dream*, 50 N.Y.L. Sch. L. Rev. 417 (2006).

One of the first and still most influential discussions of worker centers is found in Jennifer Gordon, *We Make the Road by Walking: Immigrant Workers, the Workplace Project, and the Struggle for Social Change*, 30 Harv. C.R.-C.L. L. Rev. 407 (1995). Gordon's article highlighted in particular the non-law-focused advocacy of the worker center she profiled, and the occasional tension created by the center's decision to require worker participation in exchange for advocacy assistance. In the years since, scholars have begun analyzing the sometimes uneasy relationship between worker centers and unions. *See, e.g.*, David Rosenfeld, *Worker Centers: Emerging Labor Organizations — Until They Confront the National Labor Relations Act*, 27 Berkeley J. of Emp. & Lab. L. 469 (2006).

3. *Community Benefits Agreements*

Another advocacy strategy gaining currency in many cities is Community Benefits Agreements. In a foreword to a 2008 journal symposium devoted to CBAs, Professor Scott Cummings explains:

> [C]ommunity benefits agreements (CBAs) . . . have emerged over the past several years as a new tool for low-income communities to secure gains from city-supported development projects. Although . . . CBAs come in many forms and there are significant disagreements about "what counts" as a CBA, we may generally think of the CBA as a negotiated agreement between community groups and developers (or sometimes city agencies) that requires the delivery of specific benefits to communities affected by the development project. Examples of benefits include affordable housing, living wage jobs, first-source hiring, card-check neutrality, and parks and open space. What benefits are provided and at what level are the subject of intense negotiations, usually undertaken by a coalition that includes representatives from different community organizations. The question of who is "in" the coalition and who is "out" is an important one that implicates questions about accountability and legitimacy. For instance, as the CBA becomes a more common feature of urban planning, some have questioned whether it has been co-opted in certain instances by developers and city officials who are able to gain approval for projects by negotiating agreements with preferred groups that may not reflect the full range of community concerns.

Scott L. Cummings, *The Emergence of Community Benefits Agreements*, 17 J. Affordable Hous. & Community Dev. L. 5 (2008).

Attorney and author Julian Gross, the director of the Community Benefits Law Center in Oakland, California, is one of the most active advocates of CBAs. His article *Community Benefits Agreements: Definitions, Values, and Legal Enforceability*, 17 J. Affordable Hous. & Community Dev. L. 35 (2008), provides a comprehensive overview of the field and urges adherence to inclusiveness in negotiating CBAs and accountability in measuring their outcomes.

CHAPTER
6

Housing

INTRODUCTION

Housing is a basic human need and most families' largest single expenditure, and is thus central to an understanding of poverty law and policy in the United States. The inadequate supply of affordable housing, and its inevitable consequence of housing insecurity for moderate- and low-income Americans, are major features of the U.S. poverty law and policy picture. Because of the vital nature of housing and the susceptibility of poor people to eviction, it is likely no surprise that virtually every legal aid office in the country includes housing work on its docket.

This chapter begins with foundational information about law, poverty, and housing in the United States. It then turns to the crux of the matter for low-income people: affordability and access. As in other chapters, the major federal programs in this policy area are presented. Starting with the Housing Act of 1934, Congress has established a variety of programs designed to produce affordable housing, to provide rental assistance, and/or to incentivize the private real estate market to create housing within reach of low- and moderate-income people. The results have been a typical, evolving "alphabet soup" of federal programs ranging from public housing units to portable "vouchers" to be used in the private rental market, to tax breaks for developers. State and local complements to these federal programs are also introduced.

In this context, the now-familiar theme of the intersection between poverty and race arises again, as does the complex policy response to that intersection. As we saw in the cash assistance context, support for housing subsidies evaporated as historical and economic factors increased the proportion of people of color among their beneficiaries. This chapter reveals again the twentieth-century historical arc: programs were created during the New Deal, expanded during the War on Poverty, and then slashed under President Reagan and welfare reform of the 1990s. While many federal programs still exist, they are subject to frequent debate and are often cut during lean government budget times.

Poor people's access to decent housing is not restricted only by affordability concerns. If by "housing," one means decent, affordable, safe units located with access to schools, health care, basic commerce, and employment opportunities, the price of rent is but one barrier. Housing issues for the poor also include decrepit conditions, discrimination, and poor location and ancillary services. All of these issues involve and have been the subject of complex public policy attention; lawyers representing poor people or seeking to use law to advance their housing rights must appreciate this network of issues.

With respect to poor conditions, much of poverty law and policy attention to housing issues, for example, concerns the deteriorating and aging stock of affordable housing in the United States. The federal government's HOPE VI program, see *infra*, p. 363, is designed to provide federal funding to renovate or replace aging public housing stock. On the private market, the implied warranty of habitability, a mechanism to enforce basic living standards (see *infra*, p. 380), is understood as a vital affirmative defense to eviction; it can also be used as a tool to enforce tenants' rights to decent housing as a basis for an affirmative lawsuit for damages.

Discrimination works another significant barrier to low-income tenants' ability to find affordable, decent housing. The history of residential segregation in the United States, including the legal and policy regimes that permitted and in fact promoted it, is itself a vast subject, well beyond the scope of this chapter. Poor people live and poverty lawyers work, however, every day in neighborhoods and cities that remain shaped by Jim Crow, the Great Migration, redlining, restrictive covenants, and other macrohistorical trends — often enforced by violence — ensuring de facto if not de jure housing segregation by race and class. According to a 2012 study by the Pew Research Center, residential segregation by income has gone up in the past three decades in 27 of the country's 30 largest metropolitan areas. The Pew Center reports that racial segregation between African Americans and Whites has been declining in the same period, but is still more pervasive than even the growing income segregation. *See* Richard Fry & Paul Taylor, Pew Research Ctr., *The Rise of Residential Segregation by Income* (2012), *available at* http://www.pewsocialtrends.org/files/2012/08/Rise-of-Residential-Income-Segregation-2012.2.pdf. For information on racial segregation in the United States, and specifically the explicit and violently enforced exclusion of African Americans (as well as Chinese Americans, Jews, and other racial and ethnic minorities) from numerous U.S. cities and towns, see James W. Loewen, *Sundown Towns: A Hidden Dimension of American Racism* (2005).

As a formal legal matter, the federal Fair Housing Act, originally passed as part of the Civil Rights Act of 1968, now prohibits discrimination on the bases of race, color, sex religion, disability, family status, and national origin in rental or purchase of homes, mortgage lending, homeowners insurance, and other features of the housing market. *See* Fair Housing Act, Pub. L. No. 90-284, 82 Stat. 81 (1968) (codified as amended at 42 U.S.C. 3601-3619, 3631 (2012)); *see also* Act of Sept. 13, 1988, Pub. L. No. 100-430, 102 Stat. 1619. States also have their own analogous fair housing statutes, some of which include other bases — notably sexual orientation, which is not included in the federal law — upon which it is unlawful to discriminate in housing. The federal statute is enforced by the U.S. Department of Housing and Urban Development (HUD) through its Fair Housing and Equal Opportunity (FHEO) office. The FHEO provides grants to private agencies throughout the country for investigative and enforcement activities.[1] The U.S. Department of Justice also has jurisdiction to bring fair

---

1. Although the Fair Housing Act does not prohibit discrimination on the basis of sexual orientation, HUD issued a final rule in 2012 to "ensure that its core programs are open to all eligible individuals and families regardless of sexual orientation, gender identity, or marital status." Equal Access to Housing in HUD Programs Regardless of Sexual Orientation or Gender Identity, 77 Fed. Reg. 5,622, 5,676 (Feb. 3, 2012) (codified at 24 C.F.R. pts. 5, 200, 203, 236, 400, 570, 574, 882, 891 & 982).

housing lawsuits in federal court when there is evidence of a pattern or practice of discrimination.

Note that "source of income" is not a protected category under the federal fair housing statute. Thus, there is no federal law prohibiting a landlord, for example, from refusing to accept a Section 8 voucher as partial payment of rent for a unit or refusing to rent to a family on welfare even if the amount of the family's income meets the landlord's requirements. Some states and cities have passed their own "source of income" nondiscrimination provisions. It is not clear, however, whether a Section 8 voucher is "income" for purposes of non-discrimination. A California appellate court, for example, analyzed how the voucher program operates and concluded that the voucher was not "income," and that a landlord was therefore free to refuse to participate in the program without running afoul of the state's "source of income" provision. *See* Sabi v. Sterling, 183 Cal. App. 4th 916 (Ct. App. 2010).

The above statutory rights, however, are made real only by meaningful access to lawyers and courts to enforce them. Public enforcement of fair housing rules is formally available, but underresourced federal and state agencies are not able to represent every individual with a housing discrimination claim. See Chapter 10 for a discussion of poor people's access to legal representation in housing and other realms.

Securing affordable housing is a poor family's first challenge. Keeping it is another. This chapter ends where most poverty lawyers' housing practices begin: with landlord-tenant law, specifically, an overview of the development of the law of eviction and its defenses. This section starts with the constitutionality of "summary process," the accelerated litigation afforded to landlords seeking to evict tenants, and then turns to the key victory that poverty lawyers secured for renters in the 1970s—the judicial recognition of breach of the implied warranty of habitability as a defense to eviction based on nonpayment of rent. We also review eviction law in the special context of public and subsidized housing, and preview the discussion in Chapter 10 about the lack of attorneys for low-income tenants in civil cases generally, including eviction cases.

A. HOUSING AS A POVERTY ISSUE: FOUNDATIONAL CONSIDERATIONS

1. Housing Matters

Housing is arguably essential to human survival. It is also, from an empirical perspective, a proxy for numerous other measures of well-being. In December 2000, Congress established a bipartisan commission to study housing issues. Called the Millennial Housing Commission (MHC), the group, made up of scholars and providers from both the public and private sectors, was charged to:

conduct a study that examines, analyzes, and explores:

(1) the importance of housing, particularly affordable housing which includes housing for the elderly, to the infrastructure of the United States;
(2) the various possible methods for increasing the role of the private sector in providing affordable housing in the United States, including the effectiveness and efficiency of such methods; and

(3) whether the existing programs of the Department of Housing and Urban Development work in conjunction with one another to provide better housing opportunities for families, neighborhoods, and communities, and how such programs can be improved with respect to such purpose.

Act of Oct. 20, 1999, Pub. L. No. 106-74, § 206(b), 113 Stat. 1070.

The Commission's 2002 report provides a useful framework for considering the importance of housing to family well-being and to the U.S. economy. Written before the housing market's crash in 2007 and the ensuing global economic crisis, you will note the report's anachronistic references to housing as the "engine of the national economy" and essential to its strength. This section of the report underscores the significance of the housing crash to the entire U.S. economic outlook.

THE MILLENNIAL HOUS. COMM'N, *MEETING OUR NATION'S HOUSING CHALLENGES* (2002)

Securing access to decent, affordable housing is fundamental to the American Dream. All Americans want to live in good-quality homes they can afford without sacrificing other basic needs. All Americans want to live in safe communities with ready access to job opportunities, good schools, and amenities. All parents want their children to grow up with positive role models and peer influences nearby. And the overwhelming majority of Americans want to purchase a home as a way to build wealth.

The importance of helping more Americans satisfy these objectives cannot be overstated. Decent, affordable, and accessible housing fosters self-sufficiency, brings stability to families and new vitality to distressed communities, and supports overall economic growth. Very particularly, it improves life outcomes for children. In the process, it reduces a host of costly social and economic problems that place enormous strains on the nation's education, public health, social service, law enforcement, criminal justice, and welfare systems. . . .

Decent, affordable, and stable housing promotes family stability and creates a positive environment for raising children. Families lacking the means to pay for good-quality housing may have to make frequent moves in search of appropriate accommodations. Two studies have found that disruptive moves during childhood and adolescence have a strong negative impact on school performance. In addition, struggles to provide for daily needs also interfere with both school and job performance.

Although only a handful of studies have examined the impact of rental housing assistance on the transition from welfare to work, the available research suggests the effect is positive. Two studies point to a positive employment impact even in the absence of work supports such as childcare. . . .

Other research suggests the stability that homeownership brings can have especially positive effects on school success and social behavior. All else equal, children of parents who own their homes and live in neighborhoods with low turnover have a higher probability of completing high school. Teenaged daughters of homeowners are also less likely to become pregnant. Even after controlling for parents' age, income, and other influences, homeowners' children have significantly higher math and reading scores as well as significantly fewer behavioral problems and a better quality home environment than renters' children.

The physical condition of housing makes a difference for families as well. Better-quality housing is related to lower levels of psychological distress, which in turn reduce health care costs and improve productivity. In contrast, housing that exposes families to hazards such as lead paint can limit lifelong educational and economic achievement. The presence of dust, molds, and roach allergens in the home increases the incidence of asthma and allergies, while electrical problems, poor lighting, and other system deficiencies increase the risk of illness, injuries, and even death. . . .

The vast majority of Americans live in communities with good-quality schools and ready access to jobs. But for millions of households, particularly those living in high-poverty urban or rural areas, such opportunities are severely limited. Unemployment, crime, high-school dropout, and teen-pregnancy rates are all significantly higher in these locations. The incidence of post-traumatic stress disorder, depression, and anxiety among inner-city youth is also higher. These problems make it especially difficult for local residents to find decent paying jobs and to improve their lives by saving enough to invest in homeownership, higher education, and other wealth-enhancing measures.

As a result, neighborhood quality plays an important role in positive outcomes for families. Stable housing in an unstable neighborhood does not necessarily allow for positive employment and child education outcomes. Federal demonstration programs enabling the poor to move from distressed city neighborhoods to lower-poverty communities underscore the potent impact of neighborhood quality on family stability. Research from the Gautreaux and Moving to Opportunity demonstrations indicates that relocating families to better neighborhoods can improve educational, mental health, and behavioral outcomes. Evidence of the impact of these programs on employment, however, is mixed.

While relocating lower-income families is one way to support economic independence and individual advancement, so too is the revitalization of distressed neighborhoods. Without strengthening schools, providing access to services, and connecting residents to jobs, housing development by itself cannot provide a platform for opportunity.

Both theory and empirical evidence suggest that when several owners fail to maintain their properties, others nearby follow suit because their neighbors' inaction undermines property values. Rundown and abandoned properties can have a contagious effect that accelerates neighborhood decline. Replacing or upgrading distressed properties is therefore a precondition for neighborhood revitalization. Indeed, public investment in housing often triggers private investment that ultimately lifts property values. Although larger economic and social forces can undermine such efforts, recent comprehensive community development projects suggest that concentrated public investment in mixed-income housing can initiate neighborhood reclamation.

Homeownership not only insulates families from rising rents and home prices, but it also enables them to build financial resources that can be tapped for other purposes. In 1998, 50 percent of the average homeowner's net worth was in home equity.

By refinancing their mortgages, owners can reduce their monthly payments and/or take out equity—freeing up cash for other spending and investment. In 2001, families saved $10 billion in mortgage interest payments by refinancing their existing mortgage debt, for an average monthly savings of $100 over the life of the loan. In addition, homeowners cashed out more than $100 billion in equity through refinancing, using the proceeds for debt consolidation, home improvements, consumer purchases, investment, and other purposes that helped to stimulate the economy. . . .

Contribution to Economic Growth and Stability. Beyond its benefits to families and communities, housing is an engine of the national economy and crucial to its strength. The residential housing stock itself represents more than one-third of the nation's tangible assets. Just as important, the housing sector—including residential investment, housing consumption, and related spending— consistently generates more than 20 percent of the nation's gross domestic product. . . .

Housing production stimulates employment growth. In 2001, new residential construction was associated with roughly 3.5 million jobs nationally and $166 billion in local income. The National Association of Home Builders estimates that the construction of 100 single-family homes supports about 250 full-time equivalent jobs and $11.6 million in wages. The families occupying these new homes then bring an estimated $2.8 million in income and 65 jobs to the local economy.

Home building activity also adds significantly to federal, state, and local revenues. In 2001, home building was the source of about $65 billion in combined taxes and fees. Once constructed, housing continues to contribute to local government coffers through the property taxes—as well as the income, sales, and excise taxes—that homeowners pay. Such taxes amount to nearly $500,000 annually per 100 single-family units constructed.

In the last 20 years, the nation's housing finance system has become a mainstay of the economy. Once subject to frequent credit crunches, the system today serves as a critical stabilizing force, relying on global capital markets rather than volatile local savings deposits. The system now manages risk better, provides expanded access to mortgage credit, and ensures that financing is continuously available even in the midst of international credit swings. As a result, U.S. citizens are some of the best-housed people in the world.

Not only does the nation's housing finance system provide unparalleled access to mortgage credit, but by doing so it also strengthens the overall economy. Without continuous access to mortgage credit on favorable terms, the nation's nearly $12 trillion investment in household real estate would be vulnerable to depreciation—with cascading effects on home equity, consumer confidence, and the overall financial system. Uninterrupted access to development and construction finance also helps to prevent disruptive swings in building activity.

For consumers, today's narrower spreads between interest rates on mortgages and Treasury securities have provided great savings. The introduction of automated underwriting has also led to lower origination and servicing costs. These benefits largely derive from the evolution of strong secondary markets. The federal government has developed a variety of mechanisms to ensure that Americans have continuous access to affordable credit, including the creation of Fannie Mae and Freddie Mac, mission-driven secondary-market companies dedicated to providing liquidity to mortgage markets and contributing to meeting affordable housing needs. . . .

To reiterate, housing does matter—in every aspect of society. For this reason, the Millennial Housing Commission is convinced that investment in housing production, preservation, and assistance will prove to be a cost-effective and life-enhancing investment in the future — and particularly for those millions of households who are otherwise unable to obtain decent, affordable, and stable housing.

2. Housing Is Not a Legal Right

While it might be intuitively foundational to a family's thriving, housing is not a "fundamental" right under law in the United States. With the exception of limited subsidized housing programs — none of which create an entitlement to assistance — the government neither provides housing, nor ensures that the private economy does so. Housing is a *market* in which people participate as owners, renters, and borrowers. The U.S. Constitution neither explicitly creates a right to shelter, nor has one been implied from general constitutional principles (as has, for example, a right of privacy). Moreover, no right to housing has been created legislatively at the federal level, although some members of Congress have made attempts in that direction.

Congress and various presidents have expressed the general policy goal of suitable housing for all Americans (e.g., as discussed below, the Housing Act of 1949 stated as one of its goals "a decent home and suitable living arrangement for every American family"), but such a goal has never been transformed into a justiciable right or realized as a practical matter. The most recent federal nod toward a "right" to housing was in the 2003 Bringing America Home Act, which, if passed, would have "acknowledge[d] that housing has been recognized as a basic human right by many and varied — (1) religious and faith organizations; (2) States, cities, and counties; (3) national and local organizations; (4) international organizations, including the United Nations through its Declaration of Human Rights." Bringing America Home Act, H.R. 2897, 108th Cong. § 101(1)(2003). While studiously avoiding the creation of a right to housing, the language of the bill did state that:

> (1) the Constitution of the United States of America guarantees every American the right to life, liberty, and the pursuit of Happiness; (2) the exercise of such rights is contingent upon the fulfillment of basic needs crucial for the proper development of human life: food, clothing, shelter, medical care, work, and rest; and (3) it is a National goal to act in concord with the aforementioned rights and fulfill the basic human need of shelter by ending homelessness in the United States and to provide the security of a home to people in cases of sickness, inability to work, old age, unemployment, and in any other case in which one is deprived of the means of subsistence.

Id. § 102.

Poverty lawyers sought recognition of a *right* to housing as part of the robust constitutional litigation campaign of the 1960s and 1970s that was the subject of Chapter 3. In Lindsey v. Normet, 405 U.S. 56 (1972), a case challenging Oregon's eviction statute, the lawyers argued that housing should be recognized as a fundamental right, and that any legislative burden on it should be subjected to elevated scrutiny. In language that is still oft-cited, that argument was rejected:

> [Appellants] contend that the "need for decent shelter" and the "right to retain peaceful possession of one's home" are fundamental interests which are

particularly important to the poor and which may be trenched upon only after the State demonstrates some superior interest. . . .

We do not denigrate the importance of decent, safe, and sanitary housing. But the Constitution does not provide judicial remedies for every social and economic ill. We are unable to perceive in that document any constitutional guarantee of access to dwellings of a particular quality, or any recognition of the right of a tenant to occupy the real property of his landlord beyond the term of his lease without the payment of rent or otherwise contrary to the terms of the relevant agreement. Absent constitutional mandate, the assurance of adequate housing and the definition of landlord-tenant relationships are legislative, not judicial, functions.

Approximately half of the *states'* constitutions contain affirmative provisions mandating some kind of assistance for the poor, sometimes including express references to shelter. These provisions vary significantly from mere statements of principle to the creation of an actual duty of the state to care for its poor people. In 1979, a group of homeless men brought suit under article XVII, section 1 of the New York Constitution, which states that "[t]he aid, care and support of the needy are public concerns and shall be provided by the state . . . in such manner and by such means as the legislature may from time to time determine." The trial court recognized the plaintiffs' claim, and the case resulted in a settlement "guaranteeing a right to shelter for all homeless men in the city and establishing minimum health and safety standards for homeless shelters," which was later modified to include homeless women and families as well. Callahan v. Carey, N.Y.L.J. No. 79-42582 (N.Y. Sup. Ct. Dec. 15, 1979) (ruling on the motion for a preliminary injunction). For more on the case, see Coal. for the Homeless, *The Callahan Legacy: Callahan v. Carey and the Legal Right to Shelter Coalition for the Homeless* (2012), *available at* http://www.coalitionforthe homeless.org/pages/the-callahan-legacy-callahan-v.-carey-and-the-legal-right-to-shelter.

NOTES AND QUESTIONS

1. How would you make a case for a "fundamental right" to housing? Which of the cases from Chapter 3 would you cite and what doctrinal and policy arguments would you make in support of such a claim? How would you defend against those arguments? How would the judicial establishment of a right to housing be effectuated?
2. As discussed in more detail in Chapter 12, international human rights instruments recognize a right to housing. Article 25 of the Universal Declaration of Human Rights, adopted by the General Assembly of the United Nations in 1948, proclaims that:

> Everyone has the right to a standard of living adequate for the health and well-being of himself and of his family, including food, clothing, housing and medical care and necessary social services, and the right to security in the event of unemployment, sickness, disability, widowhood, old age or other lack of livelihood in circumstances beyond his control.

Article 11 of the International Covenant on Economic, Social, and Cultural Rights, signed but never ratified by the United States, also proclaimed a human right "to an adequate standard of living for himself and his family, including adequate food, clothing and housing. . . ."

3. The Bill of Rights embedded in South Africa's constitution of 1996 includes a right to housing. Chapter 26 provides:

1. Everyone has the right to have access to adequate housing.
2. The state must take reasonable legislative and other measures, within its available resources, to achieve the progressive realisation [*sic*] of this right.
3. No one may be evicted from their home, or have their home demolished, without an order of court made after considering all the relevant circumstances. No legislation may permit arbitrary evictions.

S. Afr. Const. 1996, ch. II (Bill of Rights), § 26.

The Legal Resources Center (LRC), a public interest law organization in South Africa, works on effectuating the right to housing, as well as other affirmative rights enshrined in the nation's constitution. The constitution also recognizes a right to property, and therefore the protections from eviction are controversial and the subject of litigation. The LRC's website can be found at http://www.lrc.org.za/, and Geoff Budlender, director of LRC's constitutional litigation unit, has summarized South African legislative and litigation efforts to effectuate the right to housing in a 2003 book about Housing Rights. *See* Geoff Budlender, *Justiciability of the Right to Housing— The South African Experience,* in *National Perspectives on Housing Rights* 207(Scott Leckie ed., 2003).

B.   ACCESS TO AFFORDABLE HOUSING

Housing is not a right, but poor people and their lawyers and allies have been working for decades to increase access to decent, affordable housing. The report that follows presents national data on housing from the perspective of affordability, in both the rental and homeownership contexts, and reveals a deepening crisis, in no small part as a result of the Great Recession, as more Americans than ever before expend a sizable portion of their income on housing.

JOINT CTR. FOR HOUS. STUDIES OF HARVARD UNIV., *STATE OF THE NATION'S HOUSING 2011* (2011)

The Great Recession exacerbated the affordability challenges that had been building for a half-century. At last measure in 2009, 19.4 million households paid more than half their incomes for housing, including 9.3 million owners and

10.1 million renters. While low-income households are most likely to have such severe burdens, cost pressures have moved up the income scale. Households earning between $45,000 and $60,000 saw the biggest increase in the share paying more than 30 percent of their incomes for housing, up 7.9 percentage points since 2001. Among those earning less than $15,000, the share rose by only 2.9 percentage points — primarily because nearly 80 percent of these households were already housing-cost burdened in 2001.

In addition to longstanding and worsening affordability challenges, the housing crash and ensuing economic downturn drained household wealth, ruined the credit standing of many borrowers, and devastated communities with widespread foreclosures. The collapse of house prices has left nearly 15 percent of homeowners with properties worth less than their mortgages and eroded the equity of most others. Overall, the amount of real home equity fell from $14.9 trillion at its peak in the first quarter of 2006 to $6.3 trillion at the end of 2010 — well below the $10.1 trillion in outstanding mortgage debt. This has reduced the amount that owners can cash out if they sell, as well as the amount they can borrow to finance spending and investment.

Meanwhile, the foreclosure crisis continues. As of March 2011, Lender Processing Services reports that about 2.0 million home loans were at least 90 days delinquent. Another 2.2 million properties were still in the foreclosure pipeline, with 67 percent of owners having made no payments in more than a year, and 31 percent having made no payments in two years. The crisis is especially acute in pockets across the country. Indeed, just 5 percent of census tracts accounted for more than a third of all homes lost to foreclosure since 2008. It will take years for these neighborhoods — which are disproportionately minority — to recover from this calamity.

* * *

The 2012 version of the above-quoted report carries the data forward, noting that:

> Between 2007 and 2010 the number of U.S. households paying more than half of their incomes for housing rose by an astounding 2.3 million. While renters accounted for the vast majority of the increase, the number of severely cost-burdened owners also rose by more than 350,000 as many households locked into expensive mortgages were unable to refinance. . . . For households paying large shares of income for housing, making ends meet is a daily challenge. Among families with children in the bottom expenditure quartile, those with severe housing cost burdens spend about three-fifths as much on food, half as much on clothes, and two-fifths as much on healthcare as those living in affordable housing. In addition, affordable housing makes it more feasible for low-income households to set aside some savings as a cushion against emergencies or as an investment in education, business, or other advancement opportunities.

Joint Ctr. for Hous. Studies of Harvard Univ., *State of the Nation's Housing 2012* 5 (2012), *available at* http://www.jchs.harvard.edu/sites/jchs.harvard.edu/files/son2012.pdf.

1. Rental Affordability

Most low-income Americans are renters. In its annual report *Out of Reach*, the National Low Income Housing Coalition (NLIHC) provides comprehensive national and state data about the affordability of rental housing. The report is based on NLIHC's concept of a "housing wage," the amount a renter would have to earn in each state to pay the recommended 30 percent of total income for rent. NLIHC bases its findings on HUD data on average fair market rent (FMR) for apartments in various localities (HUD's FMR data is based on the fortieth percentile of gross rents for typical, nonsubstandard rental units, and includes rent and utilities). The excerpt below from the 2012 report states that, based on the national average FMR for a two-bedroom apartment of $949 per month, the national housing wage is $18.75 per hour. It starts by noting the effect of the overall economic recession of the late 2000s on the cost of housing in the United States.

ELINA BRAAVE ET AL., NAT'L LOW INCOME HOUS. COAL., *OUT OF REACH 2012: AMERICA'S FORGOTTEN HOUSING CRISIS* (2012)

Although the recession may have temporarily stalled the rising cost of housing in the United States, it did not result in increased access to affordable rental housing for households that need it most: extremely low income families facing the greatest housing cost burden. As demand flooded the rental market over the past year, indicated by the vacancy rate dropping to the lowest level since 2001, rental costs have begun to inch up, impacting those households already most vulnerable to price fluctuations. The rental market is expected to continue to heat up, with more moderate income households choosing to rent, making even fewer housing options available to low income renters.

By the fourth quarter of 2011, the homeownership rate dropped to 66%, the lowest since 1998, reflecting caution among prospective homeowners. Over the past four years, renter household growth has consistently surpassed owner household growth. It is estimated that the number of renter households rose by nearly 4 million between 2005 and 2010. Over the next decade, the number of renters may increase by upwards of 470,000 annually, further straining the rental market and disproportionately affecting extremely low income households.

Among renter households, the number of extremely low income renters, those earning 30% or less of the Area Median Income (AMI), jumped by nearly 900,000 in the years between 2007 and 2010. Extremely low income (ELI) renters, competing with an ever-growing number of households in search of decent, safe and affordable rental units, face a tightening market with fewer and fewer options. With the recent surge in demand, the need for affordable rental units has never been greater. . . .

The Housing Wage is an estimate of the full-time hourly wage a household must earn in order to afford a decent apartment at the HUD estimated Fair Market Rent (FMR) while spending no more than 30% of income on housing costs. Nationally, the average two-bedroom FMR for 2012 is $949. Accordingly, the

2012 Housing Wage is $18.25, significantly surpassing the $14.15 hourly wage actually earned by renters, on average, nationally. The gap between the Housing Wage and the average renter wage is an indicator of the magnitude of need for more affordable rental units. In 2012, in 86% of counties studied nationwide, the housing wage exceeds the average hourly wage earned by renters. . . .

EXTREMELY LOW-INCOME HOUSEHOLDS FACE THE GREATEST HOUSING NEED

By 2010, the number of ELI renter households rose to 9.8 million, accounting for one out of every four renter households. ELI renter households face a tough rental market: for every 100 such households seeking an apartment, only 30 units both affordable and available can be found. In sum, 6.8 million additional units are required to address the need for affordable housing among ELI households.

Despite the immense need, the supply of low-cost rental units is actually shrinking, as more units are converted to serve higher income tenants or fall into disrepair. According to recent [American Community Survey (ACS)] data [Ed. note: The ACS is an ongoing survey conducted by the U.S. Census Bureau], the number of units renting for $500 or less fell by one million from 2007 to 2010, and during that same time period, the number of units renting at $1,250 or more grew by two million units.

This year's edition of *Out of Reach* underscores the great need for additional affordable housing among ELI households. In 2012, the average ELI household will earn roughly $20,210 and can afford to spend no more than $505 on rent. Yet, this year, the national two-bedroom FMR is $949, and the one-bedroom FMR is $797, both far more than the rent ELI households are able to pay. . . .

AFFORDABILITY IS A NATIONAL CONCERN

Housing costs vary across the nation, but uniformly, low income households are likely to face a grueling search for affordable housing with few decent options available to them. Nationally, the Housing Wage is highest in Hawaii, where costs of land development and building materials drive up the cost of housing. California and the highly urbanized Northeast corridor between Boston and Washington, D.C. also are home to communities with extremely high housing wages.

Yet, the lack of affordable housing is not an issue constrained to high-cost, urbanized regions. In fact, according to *Out of Reach* calculations, a worker earning the renter wage is unable to afford a two-bedroom unit in nearly every state, unless they pick up extra hours by cobbling together several jobs. In 28 states, the one-bedroom FMR exceeds the rent affordable to the average renter. And, in all but one state (WY), the two-bedroom FMR exceeds the rent affordable to the average renter.

For each state, *Out of Reach* combines data for counties outside metropolitan areas and calculates the Housing Wage for these rural communities. Our findings this year demonstrate that while housing costs are lower in rural areas, these areas also generally have lower wages than metropolitan areas.

Low income renters continue to struggle to overcome poverty and limited economic opportunities, while facing rents that are likely to rise in the coming years as demand grows. In both rural and urbanized America, more renters are not making ends meet: over half of all renters (53%) are cost burdened, paying over 30% of their income for housing. Only 25% of renters faced such a burden in 1960. And, of course, this issue affects the lowest income families more severely than others. Seventy-six percent of ELI renter households spend more than 50% of their income on housing costs, or have a severe housing cost burden.

CONCLUSIONS

This year, as in years past, *Out of Reach* speaks to a fundamental truth: a mismatch exists between the cost of living, the availability of rental assistance and the wages people earn day to day across the country. With the number of low income renters on the rise, the argument for sustaining affordable housing assistance is timely.

- In 2012, a household must earn the equivalent of $37,960 in annual income to afford the national average two-bedroom FMR of $949 per month.
- Assuming full-time, year-round employment, this translates into a national Housing Wage of $18.25 in 2012.
- This year the housing wage exceeds the average renter wage, $14.15, by over four dollars and is nearly three times the minimum wage.

Despite the great need for affordable housing units, subsidies for critical affordable housing programs continue to face the threat of cuts, as do many social safety net programs. For FY12, HUD suffered cuts of $3.7 billion dollars, 9% below FY11 funding levels. Although HUD estimates that its public housing capital needs are in excess of $25 billion, the Public Housing Capital Fund received 8% lower funding for FY12. The HOME program, key to the production of many new affordable units at the local level, suffered a cut of 38% between FY11 and FY12, a cut that is estimated to result in 31,000 fewer affordable rental homes. Meanwhile, the National Housing Trust Fund (NHTF), which Congress authorized in 2008, remains unfunded. The NHTF would fund the production and preservation of homes affordable to the lowest income households. [Ed. note: The programs referred to in this paragraph are among those discussed *infra* where federal housing programs are described.]

NOTES AND QUESTIONS

1. Wages are the other side of the "housing wage" equation. Materials in Chapter 5 address low-wage work and the struggles of working poor families to make ends meet. Should the affordability crisis be conceived as a wage crisis rather than a housing crisis? Is raising the minimum wage a sensible *housing* policy?
2. According to the NLIHC 2012 report, the five states with the highest housing wages (for two-bedroom apartments) are: Hawaii ($31.65), California ($26.02), New Jersey ($25.04), Maryland ($24.83), and New York ($24.68). Even the lowest housing wage — Puerto Rico's at $9.88 — exceeds the federal minimum wage of $8 per hour.

* * *

The 30 percent standard used by the NLIHC in its *Out of Reach* report conforms to the prevailing wisdom that a family should spend 30 percent of its after-tax income on housing costs; spending more means the family will likely have to forego other important expenditures. This "30 percent standard," which was codified in the 1960s as the percentage of income that public housing residents were asked to pay for their subsidized units, does not function rationally for very low income families, who must spend a higher percentage on housing. Indeed, it is increasingly illusory across income brackets, as housing costs have grown faster over the past 20 years than both wages and the costs of other goods. By 2010, over 20 million U.S. households paid *more than half* their incomes for housing (up from the 19.4 million in 2009 referenced below).

The Joint Center for Housing Studies of Harvard University has also concluded that the United States faces a housing affordability crisis. Tackling the data from a different perspective than does the NLIHC, the Center's 2011 report notes that the affordability problem is not limited to low-income Americans. The study found that the cost burden of rent on an increasing number of U.S. families was forcing some to choose between the most basic necessities in life — food, medical care, and shelter. Severely cost-burdened households (those spending more than 50 percent of their income on housing) spent on average 40 percent less on food than did other families.

2. *Affordability in Homeownership: Wealth and Foreclosure*

Homeownership is one of the most important indicia of financial security in the United States, and one from which not only poor people but even moderate-income Americans are typically excluded. Importantly, too, homeownership is the leading predictor of family wealth. While rising *income* equality in the twenty-first century has been the subject of much commentary (see Chapter 1), the *wealth* gap between African Americans and other people of color and Whites has also been growing. The following research concludes that gaps in rates of home-ownership do more than any other factor to explain lagging wealth rates among American families of color.

THOMAS SHAPIRO ET AL., INST. ON ASSETS & SOC. POLICY,
THE ROOTS OF THE WIDENING RACIAL WEALTH GAP:
EXPLAINING THE BLACK-WHITE ECONOMIC DIVIDE (2013)

Growing concerns about wealth inequality and the expanding racial wealth gap have in recent years become central to the debate over whether our nation is on a sustainable economic path. . . .

. . . In the U.S. today, the richest 1 percent of households owns 37 percent of all wealth. This toxic inequality has historical underpinnings but is perpetuated by policies and tax preferences that continue to favor the affluent. Most strikingly, it has resulted in an enormous wealth gap between white households and households of color. In 2009, a representative survey of American households revealed that the median wealth of white families was $113,149 compared with $6,325 for Latino families and $5,677 for black families.

Looking at the *same set of families* over a 25-year period (1984-2009), our research offers key insight into how policy and the real, lived-experience of families in schools, communities, and at work affect wealth accumulation. Tracing the same households during that period, the total wealth gap between white and African-American families nearly triples, increasing from $85,000 in 1984 to $236,500 in 2009. To discover the major drivers behind this dramatic $152,000 increase, we tested a wide range of possible explanations, including family, labor market, and wealth characteristics. This allowed us, for the first time, to identify the primary forces behind the racial wealth gap. Our analysis found little evidence to support common perceptions about what underlies the ability to build wealth, including the notion that personal attributes and behavioral choices are key pieces of the equation. Instead, the evidence points to policy and the configuration of both opportunities and barriers in workplaces, schools, and communities that reinforce deeply entrenched racial dynamics in how wealth is accumulated and that continue to permeate the most important spheres of everyday life.

Data for this analysis derived from the Panel Study of Income Dynamics (PSID), a nationally representative longitudinal study that began in 1968. We followed nearly 1,700 working-age households from 1984 through 2009 . . . and we have determined how different factors affect the widening racial wealth gap over a generation. The compelling evidence-based story is that policy shaping opportunities and rewards where we live, where we learn, and where we work propels the large majority of the widening racial wealth gap. . . .

HOMEOWNERSHIP

The number of years families owned their homes was the largest predictor of the gap in wealth growth by race. Residential segregation by government design has a long legacy in this country and underpins many of the challenges African-American families face in buying homes and increasing equity. There are several reasons why home equity rises so much more for whites than African-Americans:

- Because residential segregation artificially lowers demand, placing a forced ceiling on home equity for African-Americans who own homes in non-white neighborhoods;
- Because whites are far more able to give inheritances or family assistance for down payments due to historical wealth accumulation, white families buy homes and start acquiring equity an average eight years earlier than black families;
- Because whites are far more able to give family financial assistance, larger up-front payments by white homeowners lower interest rates and lending costs; and
- Due to historic differences in access to credit, typically lower incomes, and factors such as residential segregation, the homeownership rate for white families is 28.4 percent higher than the homeownership rate for black families.

Homes are the largest investment that most American families make and by far the biggest item in their wealth portfolio. Homeownership is an even greater part of wealth composition for black families, amounting to 53 percent of wealth for blacks and 39 percent for whites. Yet, for many years, redlining, discriminatory mortgage-lending practices, lack of access to credit, and lower incomes have blocked the homeownership path for African-Americans while creating and reinforcing communities segregated by race. African-Americans, therefore, are more recent homeowners and more likely to have high-risk mortgages, hence they are more vulnerable to foreclosure and volatile housing prices. . . .

Unfortunately the end to this story has yet to be written. Since 2007, 10.9 million homes went into foreclosure. While the majority of the affected families are white, borrowers of color are more than twice as likely to lose their homes. These higher foreclosure rates reflect a disturbing reality: borrowers of color were consistently more likely to receive high-interest risky loan products, even after accounting for income and credit scores. Foreclosures not only have a direct impact on families, they also result in severe collateral damage to surrounding neighborhoods. One report estimates that this collateral destruction led to nearly $2 trillion in lost property wealth for communities across the country. More than half of this loss is associated with communities of color, reflecting concentrations of high-risk loans, subsequent higher foreclosure rates, and volatile housing prices.

While homeownership has played a critical role in the development of wealth for communities of color in this country, the return on investment is far greater for white households, significantly contributing to the expanding racial wealth gap. The paradox is that even as homeownership has been the main avenue to building wealth for African-Americans, it has also increased the wealth disparity between whites and blacks.

* * *

While increasing homeownership might help close the racial wealth gap, and otherwise be a laudable goal, recent history teaches that pursuing such an increase has its own perils. Before leaving the general subject of affordability, it is important to make at least brief mention of its effects in the context of homeownership, and in particular the 2007 foreclosure crisis that rocked the United States, with ripple effects across global financial markets. Many scholars, analysts, and commentators note that an important cause of the foreclosure crisis was the aggressive marketing of "subprime" mortgage instruments to first-time homeowners in minority and low-income communities. Sometimes with a rationale based on Community Reinvestment Act obligations (see Chapter 11), banks marketed loans to people who hadn't before been eligible, but based on extremely dubious, and ultimately catastrophic, assessments of loan-worthiness.

Subprime loans are generally defined as those with an average percentage rate at least three percentage points above other analogous U.S. securities. While subprime loans made up less than 5 percent of the lending market in 1994, by 2006, such loans comprised at least 23 percent of the total mortgage market. Many of the loans, too, were at terms that borrowers did not understand, including so-called "balloon clauses," that provided for a regular monthly payment for a small number of years, with the balance of the loan becoming due in full upon their expiration, upon pain of refinancing at much less favorable rates. These types of loans came to be known collectively as "predatory lending" because they effectively preyed on often unsophisticated borrowers, who were at exceptionally high risk for default, foreclosure, and economic catastrophe. The lenders, meanwhile, insulated themselves from the risk of these inevitable defaults by "bundling" the loans into securities and selling them to investors.

The rate of mortgage foreclosures exploded in 2007. While there were nationally just under 850,000 foreclosures in 2005, that number climbed to 2.4 million by 2009. The national first-lien loan foreclosure rate grew a full 62 percent in the single year between 2007 and 2008. The loss of equity in these properties has fallen particularly hard on communities of color. In a 2008 report, the organization United for a Fair Economy stated that "subprime borrowers of color will lose between $164 billion and $213 billion for loans taken during the past eight years," and noted that this represents "the greatest loss of wealth for people of color in modern US history." Robert G. Schwemm & Jeffrey L. Taren, *Discretionary Pricing, Mortgage Discrimination, and the Fair Housing Act*, 45 Harv. C.R.-C.L. L. Rev. 375, 382 (2010) (citing Amaad Rivera et al., *Foreclosed: State of the Dream* vii (2008), *available at* http://www.faireconomy.org/files/pdf/StateOfDream_01_16_08_Web.pdf).

Promoting homeownership has been an explicit policy goal of every president since the Great Depression. If measured by financial commitment, the federal government vastly prefers homeownership to renting. According to the Congressional Budget Office, in 2009 the federal government spent about $60 billion on programs designed to promote rental affordability, while devoting almost four times that amount, $230 billion, to homeownership initiatives. The most valuable "expenditure" by the federal government on homeownership is the mortgage interest deduction in the Internal Revenue Code. In 2011, the lost tax revenue attributable to that deduction was an estimated $78 billion. Some scholars and economists have proposed elimination of the mortgage interest deduction, arguing that it does not empirically promote homeownership among those who would not otherwise own, and that it disproportionately benefits high-income people, who itemize deductions on their tax returns. *See, e.g.*, Eric Toder et al., Tax Policy Ctr., *Reforming the Mortgage Interest Deduction* (2010). Some explicitly propose using those newly "captured" dollars for housing assistance and/or other antipoverty programs.

NOTES AND QUESTIONS

1. Should closing the wealth gap be a priority for poverty lawyers? Assuming yes, what is the role for lawyers in such a social agenda? How should legal rules be shaped to advance that goal while addressing the kind of market behavior that led to subprime lending and the foreclosure crisis? For more on the wealth gap, see Thomas M. Shapiro, *The Hidden Cost of Being African American* (2004).
2. What arguments can you formulate for and against elimination or reform of the mortgage interest tax deduction?
3. Low- and moderate-income homeowners were obviously hit very hard by the foreclosure crisis. Also affected, however, were the tenants who rented homes (apartments, condominiums, or single-family houses) that were foreclosed upon by lenders. Recognizing these effects, in May 2009, President Barack Obama signed the Protecting Tenants in Foreclosure Act (PTFA). As discussed below, eviction law is generally governed by state law. The PTFA, however, supplements each state's law with some baseline protections for tenants in foreclosed properties facing eviction. Specifically, the lease of any "bona fide tenant" must be respected by an owner or entity acquiring the property after foreclosure (subject to a few exceptions), and such a tenant is entitled to at least 90 days notice before her tenancy is terminated.

3. The Problem of (Rising) Homelessness

An examination of poverty and housing would not be complete without some reference to homelessness. There have always been homeless people in the United States, known in earlier eras as "vagabonds" or "hobos," with predictable spikes in times of national crisis, such as Reconstruction, the Great Depression, and, now, the Great Recession. While there are many causes of modern homelessness, so-called "deinstitutionalization" of people with mental illness in the 1970s was an important historical development. In 1963, President Kennedy signed the Community Mental Health Act, which led to the release of patients from public mental health institutions in favor of community-based treatment. Such treatment was not readily available, however, which resulted in an increase in people with mental illness living on the streets.

The public regulation of homeless people — in the form of so-called "sit/lie ordinances" that prohibit, in various forms and with various consequences, sitting or lying down on a public street — is addressed in more detail in Chapter 9. By one count, over 200 cities in the United States have some form of sit/lie ordinance. Basic data about the "unhoused," however, is relevant to the consideration of poverty law in the housing realm.

PETER WITTE ET AL., NAT'L ALLIANCE TO END HOMELESSNESS & HOMELESSNESS RESEARCH INST., *THE STATE OF HOMELESSNESS IN AMERICA: 2012* (2012)

Each January, communities across the country conduct a comprehensive census of their homeless populations. Known as the "point-in-time counts," this process consists of a census of the mostly electronic administrative bed counts of people sleeping in emergency shelters and in transitional housing units on a given night. It also includes a street census, conducted by outreach workers and volunteers, of people sleeping on the streets, in cars, in abandoned properties, or in other places not meant for human habitation. This process results in the most comprehensive annual population estimate available of people experiencing homelessness in the United States.

The most recently available national data are from the January 2011 point-in-time count. The 2011 count data show that an estimated 636,017 people experienced homelessness in the United States on a given night. This translates to an incidence, or rate, of 21 homeless people per 10,000 people in the general population.

Analysis of the 2011 point-in-time count conducted for this report provides a more detailed portrait of the population of people who experience homelessness in the nation. Figure 1.1 [below] shows a breakdown of the 2011 homeless populations. . . . A majority of the homeless population is composed of individuals (63 percent or 399,836 people). The number of people in families with children makes up 37 percent of the overall population, a total of 236,181 people in 77,186 family households. Of the individuals, about one quarter of the population is chronically homeless (107,148 people).

A majority of homeless people lives in shelters or transitional housing units (392,316 people), but 38 percent of the homeless population lives on the streets or in other places not meant for human habitation. Veterans comprise 11 percent of the homeless population (67,495 people). Data on unaccompanied homeless youth are not included in the main text of this report, as a reliable national youth population count has not yet been completed.

Figure 1.1
Homeless Population and Subpopulations, 2011

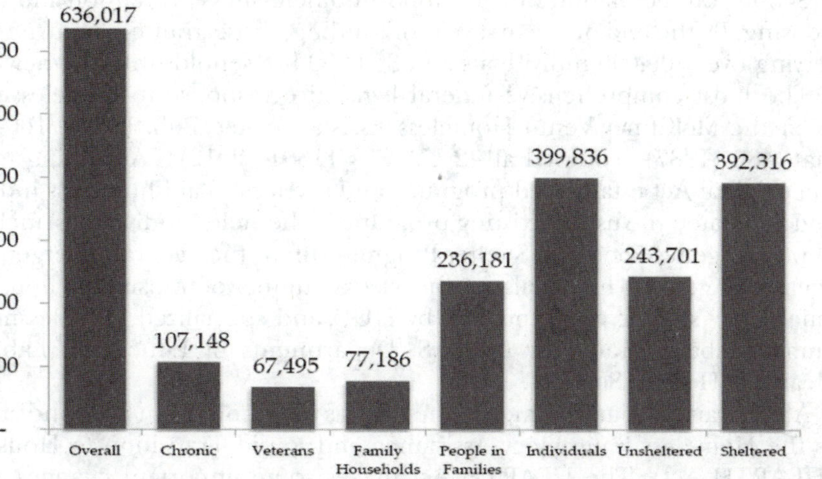

Note: Subpopulation data do not equal the overall homeless population number. This is because people could be counted as part of more than one subpopulation (e.g., a person could be an unsheltered, chronic, veteran individual). Further, family households are a separate measure as a household is comprised of numerous people (e.g., at least one adult and at least one child).

* * *

The risk of homelessness is not evenly distributed. Nationally, over the entire population, the risk of being homeless in any given year is 1 in 194. However, for the group with the highest risk, veterans, that risk rises to an astounding 1 in 10. Other groups at elevated risk are people being discharged from prison or jail, teens aging out of foster care, and anyone who is currently "doubled up," or living with friends and family as a result of economic need. The number of people doubled up, and thus at higher risk for homelessness, rose 53 percent between 2005 and 2010, from 4.3 million to 6.8 million. Nor are all states the same with respect to homelessness. The National Alliance report excerpted above notes that Iowa is the state with the largest 2009-2010 rise in the number of doubled-up people (a 74 percent increase), while some states saw a decrease in that rate (e.g., Montana's rate decreased 30 percent in that time period). The states with the highest rates of homelessness are Oregon and Hawaii; both have a rate of 45 per 10,000.

Unsurprisingly, homelessness rose during the recession. The U.S. Conference of Mayors reported in 2009 that 19 cities saw an increase in family homelessness between October 2008 and September 2009, in its view attributable to the recession and a lack of affordable housing. Interestingly, in the same period, 16 cities reported a decrease in individual homelessness, which the Conference attributed to successful outreach and other programs targeted to that population. According to Reuters, in the year following the foreclosure crisis, local homeless groups reported a 61 percent rise in homelessness. The economic stimulus package passed by Congress in response to the financial crisis, the American Recovery and Reinvestment Act of 2009, included $1.5 billion for a new, three-year program called the Homelessness Prevention and Rapid Re-Housing Program (HPRP). HUD reports that in its first year, HPRP provided funds to over 500 grantees nationwide to support homelessness prevention and rapid re-housing. By the end of the first year of funding, those grantees in turn reported serving over 700,000 individuals and 300,000 households with the new money.

The most comprehensive federal legislative response to homelessness has been the McKinney-Vento Homeless Assistance Act. Pub. L. No. 100-77, 101 Stat. 482 (1987) (codified at 42 U.S.C. §11301 (2012)). According to HUD, the original Act established programs and services to aid homeless individuals and facilitated the use of existing programs by homeless individuals, including a new Emergency Food and Shelter Program run by the Federal Emergency Management Agency. The Act also authorized a number of transitional housing and emergency shelter programs run by HUD and specialized homelessness programs to be operated by the U.S. Departments of Education, Labor, and Health & Human Services.

After a variety of amendments, the Act was reauthorized in 2009 and amended as the Homeless Emergency Assistance and Rapid Transition to Housing Act (HEARTH Act). The HEARTH Act makes some important changes, such as creating a Rural Housing Stability Program, an increase in prevention resources, an increase in emphasis on performance, and a consolidation of HUD's competitive grant programs. This meant, among other things, that a larger percentage of federal grant funding was to be allocated to the emergency shelter grant program (20 percent up from 10 percent). The reauthorized Act also changes HUD's definition of homelessness and chronic homelessness in several specific ways, including allowing people to be considered homeless if they will be displaced from their current shelter within 14 days (the prior time period was 7 days). This change and others primarily serve to allow more individuals to be included under a definition of homelessness.

Because at the time of passage, it was reported that up to 50 percent of homeless children were not regularly attending school, the original Act included the Education of Homeless Children and Youth Program (EHCY). (This program has since been recodified as a piece of the federal No Child Left Behind Act.) This program has garnered significant attention from legal and policy scholars. Under EHCY, each state must appoint a state homeless education coordinator to facilitate disbursement of EHCY grants and to identify the education needs of homeless children and youth. In addition, EHCY requires that the state and local educational agencies (LEAs) provide transportation to and from the child's school of origin. It also contains an explicit provision that homeless youth may not be segregated from other students, and it requires each LEA, even those not receiving a McKinney-Vento subgrant, to designate a local liaison, who serves as the primary contact between the school and homeless families or youth.

The National Alliance to End Homelessness publicizes successful efforts by state and city governments to combat homelessness. Highlighted local solutions include the provision of transitional housing, targeted prevention and mental health services, and interagency collaboration designed to rapidly re-house any individuals and families who become or are at risk of homelessness. For example, in Wichita, Kansas, in 2006 a joint city and Sedgwick County task force was formed to combat the homelessness in the community, which, at the time, far outpaced the state's rate. The Sedgwick County point-in-time data identified over 700 homeless people, 25 percent of whom were chronically homeless, although the state rate was 6.6 percent in 2005. (HUD defines as chronically homeless "an individual with a disabling condition who has either been continuously homeless for a year or more or has had at least four episodes of homelessness in the past three years.") Targeting the chronically homeless, the task force worked with private charities to provide additional units of supported housing, with staff from the city and county. After placing people in these new units, the program focus turned to supportive services for the residents and to prevention and community-based services, such as mental health case management and job training. The rate of chronic homelessness was reduced 61% over four years through these efforts.

* * *

Having reviewed various barriers to safe, stable, and affordable housing for America's poor, we turn next to the federal government's involvement in the rental market. As in the arenas of cash assistance, health care, and legal services, the federal government has taken steps to provide *some* help to *some* people. The reach of those programs and the challenges to their effectiveness, are reviewed in the next section.

C.   FEDERAL HOUSING ASSISTANCE

1.   The "Alphabet Soup" of HUD Programs

A patchwork of below-market, regulated, subsidized housing operates alongside and within the private rental housing market. Units in this diverse "portfolio" include federal public housing, federally subsidized private housing, state and local "affordable" housing, and private housing that is subject to a rent control ordinance. The availability of such affordable housing, however, is extremely limited. According to a 2012 report by the Joint Center for Housing Studies of Harvard University, only one-quarter of all families classified as "very low income" (up to half of area median income) benefited at the time from any federal housing assistance.

The production of subsidized housing has always been the subject of policy debate. Private housing industry interests have historically objected to government involvement in the market that could drive prices down. At the same time, government has sought to provide some assistance to families priced out of private housing. In this section, we review the history of the major federal housing programs and state and local initiatives to help families access affordable housing.

Readers may be familiar with some of the federal government's housing programs, such as public housing, Section 8 vouchers, and perhaps even the Low Income Housing Tax Credit (LIHTC) program. Largely administered by HUD, these are but a few of the programs existing today, all of which are the progeny of nearly 100 years of federal policymaking in the area of rental support. According to housing policy scholar Rachel Bratt, the four principal ways by which governments, including the U.S. government, have attempted to produce or incentivize the production of housing are "by providing supports to financial institutions, through tax incentives, by regulating the private market, and through direct subsidies for production." Rachel G. Bratt, *Rebuilding a Low-Income Housing Policy* (1989). In the 2011 report below, the Congressional Research Service provides a history of major federal housing programs that serves as an overview.

MAGGIE McCARTY ET AL., CONG. RESEARCH SERV. RL34591, *OVERVIEW OF FEDERAL HOUSING ASSISTANCE PROGRAMS AND POLICY* (2008)

The federal government has been involved in providing housing assistance to lower-income households since the 1930s. In the beginning, the federal government was involved in supporting the mortgage market (through establishment of the Federal Housing Administration (FHA) and the government-sponsored enterprises) and in promoting construction of low-rent public housing for lower-income families through local public housing authorities (PHAs). Over time, the role of the federal government has shifted away from providing construction-based subsidies to providing rental subsidies; private developers and property owners now play a larger role; and more federal funding has been provided to states and localities.

Today's federal housing assistance programs fall into three main categories: rental housing assistance, assistance to state and local governments, and assistance for homeowners. Most of these programs are administered by the Department of Housing and Urban Development (HUD). Current housing assistance programs include Section 8 vouchers and project-based rental assistance, public housing, housing for the elderly, housing for persons with disabilities, rural rental assistance, Community Development Block Grants (CDBG), HOME Investment Partnerships Block Grants, Low-Income Housing Tax Credits (LIHTC), homeless assistance programs, FHA and Veterans' Administration mortgage insurance, and the mortgage interest deduction in the tax code.

Most of the federal housing assistance programs are aimed at making housing affordable for low-income families. Housing affordability—housing that costs no more than 30% of family income—is considered the largest housing problem today. Rental assistance programs, which are the largest source of direct housing assistance for low-income families, all allow families to pay affordable, income-based rents; however, different forms of assistance target different types of households, including the elderly, persons with disabilities, and families with children. Several trends in federal housing policy have emerged in recent decades. As the focus of federal housing assistance has shifted away from construction-based subsidies to rental assistance, block grants, and LIHTC, state and local governments have had greater access to federal resources to fund local housing and community development priorities. This shift in federal funding has also led affordable housing developers to pursue mixed financing: the use of multiple streams of federal funding, state, and local funding, or private financing. . . .

History and Evolution of Federal Housing Assistance Policy

The federal government's first major housing policy was formulated in response to trouble in the mortgage market resulting from the Great Depression. Until the early 1930s, most mortgages were written for terms of three to five years and required borrowers to make payments only on an annual basis. At the end of the three- or five-year terms, the remaining loan balance had to be repaid or the mortgage had to be renegotiated. . . . During the Great Depression, however, lenders were unable or unwilling to refinance many of the loans that became due. When borrowers could not pay the loan balances, lenders foreclosed on the loans and took possession of the properties.

It was against this background that the Housing Act of 1934 was enacted. The broad objectives of the act were to (1) encourage lenders to invest in housing construction, and (2) to stimulate employment in the building industry. The act created the Federal Housing Administration (FHA), [which] . . . institutionalized a revolutionary idea: 20-year mortgages on which a loan would be completely repaid at the end of its term. If borrowers defaulted, FHA insured that the lender would be fully repaid. Eventually, lenders began to make long-term mortgages without FHA insurance as long as borrowers made significant down payments. Over time, 25- and 30-year mortgages have become standard mortgage products.

As in the case of the mortgage finance market, the federal government initially became involved in the provision of rental housing assistance in response to the Great Depression. In the early 1930s, a housing division was added to President Franklin D. Roosevelt's Works Progress Administration as a part of the effort to create jobs and spur economic growth. The Housing Division acquired land and built multifamily housing projects for occupancy by lower income families across the country. However, the Housing Division's activities proved controversial with local government officials who thought that they were not consulted in the process.

Against this backdrop, the U.S. Housing Act of 1937 was enacted. . . . The act declared that it was the policy of the United States:

> . . . to promote the general welfare of the nation by employing its funds and credit, as provided in this Act, to assist the several states and their political subdivisions to alleviate present and recurring unemployment and to remedy the unsafe and unsanitary housing conditions and the acute shortage of decent, safe, and sanitary dwellings for families of low-income, in rural or urban communities, that are injurious to the health, safety, and morals of the citizens of the nation.

Housing was a major issue in the presidential and congressional races during 1948. President Harry S. Truman's pledge to address the postwar housing shortage and the problem of urban slums played a key role in his margin of victory. In his State of the Union Address in 1949 unveiling the "Fair Deal," President Truman observed that "[f]ive million families are still living in slums and firetraps. Three million families share their homes with others." He further stated:

> The housing shortage continues to be acute. As an immediate step, the Congress should enact the provisions for low-rent public housing, slum clearance, farm housing, and housing research which I have repeatedly recommended.

The number of low-rent public housing units provided for in the legislation should
be increased to 1 million units in the next 7 years. Even this number of units will
not begin to meet our need for new housing.

The Housing Act of 1949 declared the goal of "a decent home and a suitable
living environment for every American family." The act: (1) established a federal
urban redevelopment and slum clearance program, authorizing federal loans of
$1 billion over a five-year period to help local redevelopment agencies acquire
slum properties and assemble sites for redevelopment; (2) reactivated the public
housing program for low-income families (which had been on hold during
World War II), authorizing subsidies to local housing authorities sufficient to
build 810,000 units over six years; (3) expanded the FHA's mortgage insurance
program to promote home building and homeownership; (4) created within the
U.S. Department of Agriculture a program of financial assistance and subsidies
to improve housing conditions on farms and in rural areas; and (5) authorized
federal grants for research, primarily to improve the productivity of the housing
industry.

GOVERNMENT SUBSIDIZATION OF PRIVATE DEVELOPMENT

Through the 1950s, the federal government's role in housing assistance focused
largely on public housing, which served a mostly poor population. Congress
recognized that a gap existed in the market — few options existed for moderate
income families whose incomes were too high to qualify for public housing, but
too low to afford adequate market rate housing. Proposals in Congress had been
made to address the shortage of housing for moderate income households
during the 1950s; however, no legislation had been enacted, in part due to
the cost to the government of creating and funding a new program. In order
to avoid creating another large housing program with high expenditures, while
at the same time finding a way to serve this segment of the population, Congress
approved legislation at the end of the 1950s and throughout the 1960s that
engaged the private sector in the development of affordable housing.

The Housing Act of 1959 was the first significant instance where government
incentives were used to persuade private developers to build housing that would
be affordable to low- and moderate-income households. . . . As part of [the Act],
Congress created [the Section 202 Housing for the Elderly program, through
which] the federal government extended low-interest loans to private non-profit
organizations for the development of affordable housing for moderate-income
residents age 62 and older. The low interest rates were meant to ensure that
units would be affordable, with non-profit developers able to charge lower rents
and still have adequate revenue to pay back the government loans.

[The Housing Acts of 1961 and 1965] further expanded the role of the private
sector in providing housing to low- and moderate-income households. [The
1961 act created a program like Section 202, but targeting multifamily housing,
and the 1965 act created the precursor to today's Section 8 Housing Choice
Voucher Program, which] authorized payments to landlords who rented units to
low-income tenants. Tenants paid one quarter of their income toward rent in
these private units, and the federal subsidies made up the difference between
the tenant payments and rent for the units. . . .

Under the public housing program, tenants generally paid rent in an amount equal to the costs of operating the assisted housing in which they lived. Over time, as operating costs rose, there was a concern that the below-market rents being charged to families were too high to be affordable to the poorest families. The Brooke Amendment, which was included as part of the Housing and Urban Development Act of 1969, limited tenant contributions toward rent in all rent assisted units (including public housing and all project-based rental assistance units) to an amount equal to 25% of tenant income (this was later raised to 30%). The Brooke Amendment is considered responsible for codifying an income-based rent structure in federal housing programs.

By the end of the 1960s, subsidies to private developers had resulted in the creation of hundreds of thousands of housing units. . . . Despite the growth in the role of private developers, public housing was still the largest housing subsidy program, with roughly a million units built and subsidized by the early 1970s.

RETHINKING THE STRATEGY: FROM CONSTRUCTION SUBSIDIES TO RENT SUBSIDIES

By the early 1970s, concern was growing about the cost, efficacy, and equity of the construction-based housing subsidy programs. . . . Then-President Richard M. Nixon criticized the existing programs as not equitably serving families in the same circumstances, providing poor quality housing, being too costly, and placing some families in homes they could not afford. Out of these concerns, President Nixon declared a moratorium on all new activity under the major housing subsidy programs. [This moratorium held until after Nixon's resignation, when in 1974 Congress created the Section 8 program, which was not a voucher-based system until 1983.] Through [the original] Section 8, the federal government provided private property owners monthly assistance payments for new or substantially rehabilitated rental units. In exchange for monthly rental payments, property owners would agree to rent to eligible low income families (defined as families with incomes at or below 80% of local area median income) who would pay an income-based rent. It also provided PHAs with the authority to enter into rental assistance contracts for existing, private market units. . . .

INCREASING ROLE OF STATE AND LOCAL GOVERNMENTS

By the mid-1980s, federal housing programs had gone through a number of iterations. Some programs had been scrapped as inefficient, subject to fraud and abuse, or too expensive. Shifting federal priorities — toward reducing taxes and increasing military spending in response to the Cold War — reduced funding available for social programs, including housing assistance. Creation of assisted housing with federal funds was on the decline, with production between 1982 and 1988 slowing significantly. In addition, existing affordable rental units were being lost as use restrictions between private owners and HUD expired or owners chose to prepay their low interest mortgages and begin charging market-rate rent.

As a result of reduced federal support for housing, state and local governments and private for- or non-profit organizations began to take the initiative in developing innovative ways of providing housing in their communities.

Policymakers acknowledged that, in some cases, local communities had better knowledge about how to provide housing than the federal government, and might be able to provide housing more efficiently than HUD. From the late 1980s through the 1990s, Congress acknowledged the value of local control and gave more decision-making authority over housing policy to state and local governments through the creation of block grants and tax credits.

In 1986, the Low Income Housing Tax Credit (LIHTC) program was created as part of the Tax Reform Act of 1986. . . . The LIHTC program, intentionally or not, was one of the first major programs to give a good deal of control over housing policy to states and localities. Tax credits are allocated to states based on population. States then have discretion in setting priorities as to how the credits will be used. While states must prioritize projects that serve the lowest income tenants for the longest period of time, they may choose to allocate credits based on criteria such as the tenant populations served — those with special needs, families with children, or those on public housing waitlists. . . .

REFORMING RENTAL ASSISTANCE

Throughout the 1990s, concern about the state of public housing grew. The public perceived public housing as mismanaged, of poor quality, and dangerous. At the same time, interest was growing in reforming social programs by devolving control to the states and increasing their focus on promoting work and self sufficiency. Concern over the state of public housing — and the influence of the 1996 welfare reform debate and legislation — led to proposals for major public and assisted housing reforms. Several years of debate in Congress culminated with the enactment of the Quality Housing and Work Opportunity Reconciliation Act of 1998.

The purposes of QHWRA, as defined in the act, were to deregulate PHAs; provide more flexible use of federal assistance to PHAs; facilitate mixed income communities; decrease concentrations of poverty in public housing; increase accountability and reward effective management of PHAs; create incentives and economic opportunities for residents assisted by PHAs to work and become self-sufficient; consolidate the Section 8 voucher and certificate programs into a single market driven program; remedy the problems of troubled PHAs; and replace or revitalize severely distressed public housing projects. . . .

NOTES AND QUESTIONS

1. The congressional history above is comprehensive as to programs introduced, but virtually silent as to any of the social or political forces that drove the history. How do you see any of the policy debates regarding welfare, gender, family composition, race, and poverty generally affecting the development of federal housing policy?
2. The "Brooke Amendment" of 1969, discussed above, placed a limit on subsidized tenant contributions to 25 percent of their income (raised later to 30 percent). This standard is the origin of the persistent 30 percent affordability standard for housing expenditures. The Republican senator for whom the amendment was named, Edward Brooke (R-MA), was the first African American popularly elected to the U.S. Senate. In 1968 he

coauthored, with Walter Mondale (D-MN), the Fair Housing Act, which prohibited discrimination in housing and created a division within HUD for its enforcement. His legislative achievements also include, during the Nixon administration, successfully opposing elimination of the Office of Economic Opportunity and Jobs Corps and the weakening of the Equal Employment Opportunity Commission. In 1974, he led the fight to retain Title IX, protecting educational funding for women and girls.

3. In addition to the programs referenced above, the Servicemen's Readjustment Act of 1944, known as the "G.I. Bill," included mortgage support for military personnel returning from World War II. The program provided low-interest and zero down payment loans, and is credited with enabling millions of families to move out of apartments in urban areas and into suburban homes. The "VA loan program" is still in effect, and is administered by the U.S. Department of Veterans Affairs.

* * *

The Congressional Research Service (CRS) report above refers to the "Nixon moratorium." Most poverty lawyers also identify the 1980s — the Reagan years — as a significant turning point in the history of the federal commitment to housing for low-income people. According to Rachel Bratt, "During the Reagan administration, between 1981 and 1988, the total new budget authority for low-income housing programs fell from $32 billion to less than $8 billion." Professor Bratt has provided an important thematic history of federal support for housing that puts some of the CRS information into historical context and introduces important and resonant themes, such as the drive for "urban renewal" in the late 1940s and early 1950s, the increasing percentage of subsidized tenants who were people of color and persistently poor, and the balance between federal funding and local control.

RACHEL G. BRATT, *REBUILDING A LOW-INCOME HOUSING POLICY* (1989)

The country's first major subsidized housing program was not enacted until the need for better housing could be coupled with another national objective: the need to reduce unemployment resulting from the Great Depression. Section 1 of the Housing Act of 1937 made clear the dual objectives of the legislation: "to alleviate present and recurring unemployment and to remedy the unsafe and insanitary housing conditions and the acute shortage of decent, safe, and sanitary dwellings for families of low income." Although the need to stimulate the economy was key to creation of the program, other forces determined its shape.

Probably the major factor that contributed to the form of the public housing program was the extent of the opposition to it. Although the 1937 Housing Act held out the promise of jobs and apartments for the "deserving poor," there were still many dissenters. President Roosevelt himself had to be coaxed; a large-scale public housing program had not been part of the first phase of the New Deal. Organized opposition came from several interest groups, such as the U.S. Chamber of Commerce and the U.S. Savings and Loan League. Also in the forefront of the opposition was the National Association of Real Estate Boards, whose president summarized the views of the private homebuilding industry as follows:

> Housing should remain a matter of private enterprise and private ownership. It is contrary to the genius of the American people and the ideals they have established that government become landlord to its citizens. . . . There is sound logic in the continuance of the practice under which those who have initiative and the will to save acquire better living facilities and yield their former quarters at modest rents to the group below.

Within Congress, conservative members labeled public housing a socialist program and opposed it on the grounds that it would put the government in competition with private property.

Largely as a concession to the private housing industry, the public housing legislation included an "equivalent elimination" provision requiring local housing authorities to eliminate a substandard or unsafe dwelling unit for each new unit of public housing built. Public housing could replace inadequate units, but it was not to increase the overall supply of housing, since doing so could drive down rents in the private market.

The argument that public housing should not interfere with the private market logically led to the view that public housing should be clearly differentiated. This had important implications, for example, for its physical design. Public housing, with its austere appearance, is usually easily distinguished from the overall housing stock.

The early public housing program was short-lived. World War II interrupted all non-war-related programs, and public housing construction fell victim to defense needs. Because thousands of units were in the "pipeline" before the war, however, it was not until 1944 that production virtually stopped. Before the program was reactivated by the 1949 Housing Act, the real estate lobby launched an all-out attack on public housing. The familiar cry of socialism and the warning that public housing would destroy the private building industry were heard again. President Truman, a supporter of the program, responded with this pointed counterattack:

> I have been shocked in recent days at the extraordinary propaganda campaign that has been unleashed against this bill [Housing Act of 1949] by the real estate lobby. I do not recall ever having witnessed a more deliberate campaign of misrepresentation and distortion against legislation of such crucial importance to the public welfare. The propaganda of the real estate lobby consistently misrepresents what will be the actual effect of the bill, and consistently distorts the facts of the housing situation in the country.

Ultimately, proponents of public housing prevailed, but the legislative intent was clear: Public housing was to serve only those people who could not compete for housing on the private market. Private interest groups were willing to tolerate public housing as long as it was explicitly serving a different consumer.

But not all low-income people were eligible for a public housing unit. From the program's inception, it was aimed at providing housing only for the deserving, temporarily poor — the "submerged middle class." The program therefore targeted those who could not find decent, affordable housing on the private market, but not the so-called unworthy poor and those with no means to pay rent.

The expectation that tenants should pay their own way expressed itself in the formula the federal government devised for financing public housing. Tenant rents were to cover all operating expenses, exclusive of debt service. Only the principal and interest on bonds, which were floated by the local authorities to construct the buildings, were paid by the federal government, through annual contribution contracts. Thus the federal government covered the long-term debt financing, while ownership and management were vested in local public agencies. This arrangement worked well during the early years of the program.

After World War II, however, the country's demographic picture began to shift, and so did the population served by public housing. As Federal Housing Administration and Veterans Administration mortgage insurance and guarantee programs became available to vast numbers of new home buyers, and as the interstate highway system took form, most of the submerged middle-class residents of public housing surfaced, to assume full-fledged suburban middleclass status. As a further concession to the private construction industry, the 1949 Housing Act limited public housing to very-low-income people by requiring that the highest rents be 20 percent lower than the lowest prevailing rents for decent housing in the private market, and by authorizing the eviction of above-income families. Publicly provided housing thus was now to be available only to the very poor. Once public housing was reactivated and could no longer claim to be a depression-stimulated support for the temporarily poor, it became clearly defined as permanent housing for people who were more or less separated from society's mainstream.

As a result of these postwar changes, vacated units were quickly occupied by a new group of tenants, many of whom had very low incomes and multiple problems. The large housing authorities of the Midwest and Northeast also began to accommodate black migrants from the South. In addition, displacees from urban renewal and highway programs, the majority of whom were members of minorities, were given priority for public housing units. By 1978, over 60 percent of the residents of public housing were minority-group members, whereas from 1944 to 1951 nonwhite families represented between 26 and 39 percent of all public housing tenants. . . .

During the 1970s, the overall problems facing public housing worsened. Inflation continued to boost operating expenses, and many buildings that were, by then, twenty or more years old, began to show signs of aging and a need for major repairs. At the same time, rental revenues were either declining or, at best, not keeping up with expenses. . . .

The highly polarized nature of the debate surrounding the 1937 Housing Act also helped shape the administrative structure of the public housing program. Administration was to be decentralized, and participation by localities was to be voluntary. According to Lawrence Friedman, "For legal and political reasons and to disarm conservative opposition, a decentralized program was desirable. Local initiative would govern as much as possible; states and communities would be allowed to opt out if they wished."

This meant that decisions about public housing—whether to build it and where to locate it—would be made by local officials, who would be under significant pressure from their constituents. The decentralized structure also eliminated the potential for the federal government either to enforce more progressive policies or override local decisions.

The right of local communities not to participate in the public housing program guaranteed that within metropolitan areas, public housing would be most prevalent in large cities. As a result, low income people, already lacking housing options, were to be restricted still further; the choice to move to the suburbs usually was not available to them. Local control over the program meant that little or no public housing was built in more affluent areas.

As the program evolved, accommodating increasing numbers of blacks and other minorities, local control over public housing contributed to patterns of racial segregation with white areas effectively keeping out blacks. Large cities, with large minority populations, also served a high percentage of minorities in their public housing developments. As of 1976, 83 percent of public housing tenants in twenty large cities were members of minorities, compared to 61 percent for the overall public housing population.

Thus, opposition by the private homebuilding industry, maintenance and operating fund shortfalls, and class and racial segregation have continuously plagued the public housing program. As early as the 1950s, some of public housing's most ardent supporters began to lose heart. Catherine Bauer Wurster, one of the key proponents from the 1930s, bemoaned "The Dreary Deadlock of Public Housing" and commented that "after more than two decades, [public housing] still drags along in a kind of a limbo, continuously controversial, not dead but never more than half alive." . . .

* * *

The "alphabet soup" of federal housing programs is vast, although as noted above, the percentage of low-income Americans who receive any rental assistance from the federal government is small. Overall, the reach of federal rental assistance programs today is relatively narrow compared to the need. Indeed the 2012 JCHS report notes that "only one in four families with very low incomes (up to half of area median, adjusted for family size), the typical target of many government programs, benefit from federal rental assistance." The Harvard Joint Center for Housing Studies' 2012 report includes basic inventory data for the major programs:

> In fiscal 2011, HUD's principal rental housing programs provided assistance to an estimated 4.8 million low-income families, a 1.5 percent increase (73,000 households) over the previous two years. At the same time, however, the number of severely housing cost-burdened renter households with incomes under $15,000 soared 6.5 percent (430,000 households).

In addition to the more publically familiar Section 8 voucher program and public housing, students of federal housing law should also be aware of special programs to create or incentivize housing for people with disabilities, the elderly, and rural low-income populations. HUD's website provides a portal to all the programs as well as links to the local public housing authorities (PHAs) that administer them: http://portal.hud.gov/hudportal/HUD.

The primary form of support for today's low-income renters comes through rental assistance including Section 8, Section 202 (elderly), and Section 811 (people with disabilities). In 2009, these three programs accounted for over 3.5 million units of federally assisted housing. Public housing accounted for just over 1.1 million units. To put these numbers in perspective, recall that in 2012 the U.S. Census Bureau reported that 46.5 million Americans lived below the official poverty line.

Section 8 is the largest of the rental assistance programs and falls into two discrete categories — project-based Section 8 and voucher-based Section 8. Under project-based Section 8, HUD enters into contracts with private property owners in which owners agree to rent their housing units to eligible low-income tenants for an income-based rent, and HUD agrees to pay the difference between tenants' contributions and a rent set by the landlord (subject to HUD limits). No new project-based Section 8 grants have been made since the mid-1980s, although existing contracts can be renewed upon their expiration. By contrast, Section 8 vouchers allow an eligible family to live in the housing of their choice in the private market. The voucher pays the difference between the family's contribution (typically 30 percent of its adjusted income) toward rent and the actual rent for the unit. Another distinguishing feature of Section 8 vouchers is that they are nationally portable, which enables a family with a voucher to move to any other area of the country that has a Section 8 voucher program.

The second-largest source of assistance to low-income renters is public housing, constituting approximately 1.1 million units. Public housing differs from other rental programs because these units are owned and operated by local public housing authorities,, which are subsidized and regulated by the federal government. As they do in the Section 8 voucher program, families living in public housing pay 30 percent of their adjusted income toward rent.

The federal government also provides funding for localities under Community Development Block Grants and HOME Block Grants. Both of these grants are designed to help communities create additional affordable, decent housing through a variety of eligible activities, including rehabilitation of owner-occupied housing, removal of blighted properties, and services for low- and moderate-income individuals including crime prevention, childcare, and others.

Finally, as mentioned above, the federal government incentivizes low-income housing through the use of the LIHTC. This tax credit is allocated to designated state agencies by the Internal Revenue Service. The agencies in turn award the projects to developers who design programs that comply with requirements. To comply, programs must meet one of two types of affordability packages (either 20 percent of the supported units must be rented to families with incomes less than 50 percent of area median, or 40 percent of the units must go to families below 60 percent of the median income), and must maintain that affordability for a minimum of 15 years (or 30 years if commenced after 1990, pursuant to an amendment to the law passed by Congress in 1989). From its inception in 1986 through 2007, the LIHTC helped to develop 1.7 million units of affordable rental housing. With fairly consistent additions of 100,000 units per year, by 2009, 1.9 million LIHTC units were in use.

Preserving and renovating those units already developed is also a policy priority for advocates for low-income tenants. According to the National Low Income Housing Coalition, "[s]ince 1995, about 360,000 project-based Section 8 units have been lost to conversion to market rate housing. Annually, another 10,000 to 15,000 units leave this federally subsidized, affordable housing inventory. Of the nation's 1.4 million units of multifamily assisted housing stock, 450,000 units are at risk of leaving the affordable inventory because of owners opting out of the program, maturation of the assisted mortgages, or failure of the property under HUD's standards." *Project-Based Housing,* Nat'l Low Income Hous. Coal., http://nlihc.org/issues/project-based. Additionally, the original 15-year LIHTC use restrictions started to expire in 2001, requiring original owners to either sell or re-up their commitments for another 15 years.

In response to a report issued by the National Commission on Severely Distressed Public Housing, in 1992 Congress created the HOPE VI program, designed to respond to the Commission's recommendations for improvements in dilapidated and poorly managed public housing complexes. HOPE VI makes funds available to public housing authorities for the renovation and demolition of old public housing, the construction of new public housing, and social services for residents.

NOTES AND QUESTIONS

1. What are the arguments for and against federal involvement in the housing market? As a policy matter, what are some of the advantages and disadvantages of "pure" public housing versus housing provided through a public-private collaboration, such as the LIHTC?
2. There are voluminous data about HUD programs, much of it easily identifiable on the HUD website and sites of national, regional, and local housing advocacy organizations, such as the National Housing Law Project (http://www.nhlp.org), the National Low Income Housing Coalition (http://www.nlihc.org), and the Sargent Shriver National Center on Poverty Law (http://www.povertylaw.org).
3. As you read in the next section about the *Gautreaux* case and the siting of public housing, consider siting issues in public-private partnerships like the LIHTC and project-based Section 8 housing. If residential desegregation is a goal, what type of government programs do you think would be most likely to achieve it?
4. What themes, if any, from the historical arc of policy debates on antipoverty programming generally are echoed in the historical debate about housing assistance?

2. Race, "Renewal," and Gautreaux

Both the CRS report and Professor Bratt's book mention the "urban renewal" program and its displacees. The CRS report stated that the Housing Act of 1949 "established a federal urban redevelopment and slum clearance program, authorizing federal loans of $1 billion over a five-year period to help local redevelopment agencies acquire slum properties and assemble sites for redevelopment." This funding spurred the controversial "urban renewal" program, through which dilapidated housing was razed, and communities and businesses relocated. The legacy of urban renewal is with us to this day. A 1986 publication issued by the Bureau of National Affairs claims that the federal urban renewal program:

> remade the face of many American cities — and generated more controversy than perhaps any other federal housing and development program in history. Thousands of acres of city land were cleared, buildings were demolished, and residents and businesses were forced to move. In many communities, urban renewal programs replaced slums and rundown areas with new housing and productive commercial areas that brought much-needed tax revenues to city treasuries. In other cities, however, the money ran out and redevelopment plans fell through after the land was cleared, leaving large tracts of vacant land as a visible reminder of the program's problems.

Barry G. Jacobs et al., *Guide to Federal Housing Programs* 12 (2d ed. 1986).

The eradication of "blight" predictably resulted in the displacement of a disproportionate number of African-American families. Interviewed on PBS in 1963, prominent African-American novelist and social commentator James Baldwin called the program "Negro removal": "San Francisco is engaging — as most Northern cities now are engaged — in something called urban renewal, which means moving the Negroes out. It means Negro removal, that is what it means. The federal government is an accomplice to this fact."

Urban renewal was based upon the ability of government entities to use the powers of eminent domain to condemn property. The U.S. Supreme Court expressly upheld the federal government's use of its eminent domain power pursuant to the urban renewal program in Berman v. Parker, 348 U.S. 26 (1954). The plaintiff, owner of a commercial parcel in Washington, D.C., that was to be appropriated and placed into the publicly controlled redevelopment project, claimed that the appropriation amounted to a "taking" in violation of the takings clause in the Fifth Amendment. That claim was rejected. For more about the history and contemporary consequences of urban renewal, see George Lefcoe, *Redevelopment Takings After* Kelo: *What's Blight Got to Do with It?*, 17 S. Cal. Rev. L. & Soc. Just. 803 (2008).

Materials about a 1993 federal program called "The Empowerment Zone and Enterprise Cities Demonstration Program" are presented in Chapter 11. This program, understood as a form of community economic development, targets funds to distressed areas of inner cities. According to one scholar, the program:

> promises a definitive counter to all rules of inner city existence and targets federal financial resources to those distressed areas as a signal that the inner city should no longer be shunned by business and neglected by government. Rather, inner city communities are now to be reunderstood (i.e., reconfigured in our understanding) in terms of their underestimated or overlooked potential, assets, and resources.

Audrey McFarlane, *Race, Space, and Place: The Geography of Economic Development*, 36 San Diego L. Rev. 295 (1999). Some might call this an "anti-urban renewal" program. Do you think there are strengths in this model?

* * *

"Urban renewal" was hardly the only federal housing program with at least implicit racial overtones. In fact, the concentration of African-American poverty in certain neighborhoods, and the role of the federal government in creating and/or remediating that concentration, has pervaded public discourse about housing policy since the 1950s. Changing eligibility standards for public housing resulted in a dramatic increase in the proportion of people of color residing there (recall that by 1978, over 60 percent of the residents of public housing were minority-group members, whereas from 1944 to 1951 non-White families represented between 26 and 39 percent of all public housing tenants), which in turn generated ill will toward the program. The Great Migration of African Americans from the South, and particularly its second wave from 1940 to 1970, also resulted in increased Black populations in many northern U.S. cities, many of whom became eligible for the expanding stock of subsidized units.

The concentration of poor Blacks in subsidized housing, and in blighted neighborhoods generally, has had far-reaching policy consequences in the housing policy context as it has in other (e.g., cash assistance) contexts.

The "debate" arises in many contexts, none more volatile than the question of where low-income housing should be located. That subject is addressed in the case below, James v. Valtierra, and more generally in the materials about the landmark *Gautreaux* litigation that follows it. With themes reminiscent of our exploration of the constitutional cases in the 1960s and 1970s, the U.S. Supreme Court in *Valtierra* addressed a California state constitutional provision mandating that no proposed "low-rent housing project" could be constructed unless a majority of the local community had voted in favor of it. The Court rejected the low-income prospective tenants' claim that the provision violated the Equal Protection Clause of the U.S. Constitution. As you read the case, recall the discussion of Washington v. Davis, 426 U.S. 229 (1976), and Village of Arlington Heights v. Metropolitan Housing Development Corp., 429 U.S. 252 (1977), from Chapter 3 and note the Court's distinguishing of an analogous provision of an Akron, Ohio, city charter. That provision, also arising in the context of housing, referred explicitly to race, and was thus subjected to elevated scrutiny and struck down.

JAMES v. VALTIERRA
402 U.S. 137 (1971)

Mr. Justice BLACK delivered the opinion of the Court.

[This case] grows out of the United States Housing Act of 1937, 42 U. S. C. § 1401 et seq., which established a federal housing agency authorized to make loans and grants to state agencies for slum clearance and low-rent housing projects. In response, the California Legislature created in each county and city a public housing authority to take advantage of the financing made available by the federal Housing Act. . . . [In 1950], the California voters adopted Article XXXIV of the state constitution to bring public housing decisions under the State's referendum policy. The Article provided that no low-rent housing project should be developed, constructed, or acquired in any manner by a state public body until the project was approved by a majority of those voting at a community election.[2]

The present suits were brought by citizens of San Jose, California, and San Mateo County, localities where housing authorities could not apply for federal funds because low-cost housing proposals had been defeated in referendums. The plaintiffs, who are eligible for low-cost public housing, sought a declaration that Article XXXIV was unconstitutional because its referendum requirement

---

2. "Section 1. No low rent housing project shall hereafter be developed, constructed, or acquired in any manner by any state public body until, a majority of the qualified electors of the city, town or county, as the case may be, in which it is proposed to develop, construct, or acquire the same, voting upon such issue, approve such project by voting in favor thereof at an election to be held for that purpose, or at any general or special election."

"For the purposes of this article the term 'low rent housing project' shall mean any development composed of urban or rural dwellings, apartments or other living accommodations for persons of low income, financed in whole or in part by the Federal Government or a state public body or to which the Federal Government or a state public body extends assistance by supplying all or part of the labor, by guaranteeing the payment of liens, or otherwise. . . .

"For the purposes of this article only 'persons of low income' shall mean persons or families who lack the amount of income which is necessary (as determined by the state public body developing, constructing, or acquiring the housing project) to enable them, without financial assistance, to live in decent, safe and sanitary dwellings, without overcrowding."

violated: (1) the Supremacy Clause of the United States Constitution; (2) the Privileges and Immunities Clause; and (3) the Equal Protection Clause. A three-judge court held that Article XXXIV denied the plaintiffs equal protection of the laws and it enjoined its enforcement. . . . For the reasons that follow, we reverse.

The three-judge court found the Supremacy Clause argument unpersuasive, and we agree. By the Housing Act of 1937 the Federal Government has offered aid to state and local governments for the creation of low-rent public housing. However, the federal legislation does not purport to require that local governments accept this or to outlaw local referendums on whether the aid should be accepted. We also find the privileges and immunities argument without merit.

While the District Court cited several cases of this Court, its chief reliance plainly rested on Hunter v. Erickson, 393 U.S. 385 (1969). The first paragraph in the District Court's decision stated simply: "We hold Article XXXIV to be unconstitutional. *See* Hunter v. Erickson. . . ." The court below erred in relying on *Hunter* to invalidate Article XXXIV. Unlike the case before us, *Hunter* rested on the conclusion that Akron's referendum law denied equal protection by placing "special burdens on racial minorities within the governmental process." In *Hunter* the citizens of Akron had amended the city charter to require that any ordinance regulating real estate on the basis of race, color, religion, or national origin could not take effect without approval by a majority of those voting in a city election. The Court held that the amendment created a classification based upon race because it required that laws dealing with racial housing matters could take effect only if they survived a mandatory referendum while other housing ordinances took effect without any such special election. The opinion noted:

> Because the core of the Fourteenth Amendment is the prevention of meaningful and unjustified official distinctions based on race, [citing a group of racial discrimination cases] racial classifications are "constitutionally suspect" . . . and subject to the "most rigid scrutiny." . . . They "bear a far heavier burden of justification" than other classifications.

The Court concluded that Akron had advanced no sufficient reasons to justify this racial classification and hence that it was unconstitutional under the Fourteenth Amendment.

Unlike the Akron referendum provision, it cannot be said that California's Article XXXIV rests on "distinctions based on race." The Article requires referendum approval for any low-rent public housing project, not only for projects which will be occupied by a racial minority. And the record here would not support any claim that a law seemingly neutral on its face is in fact aimed at a racial minority. The present case could be affirmed only by extending *Hunter*, and this we decline to do.

California's entire history demonstrates the repeated use of referendums to give citizens a voice on questions of public policy. A referendum provision was included in the first state constitution, Cal. Const. of 1849, Art. VIII, and referendums have been a commonplace occurrence in the State's active political life. Provisions for referendums demonstrate devotion to democracy, not to bias, discrimination, or prejudice. Nonetheless, appellees contend that Article XXXIV denies them equal protection because it demands a mandatory referendum while many other referendums only take place upon citizen initiative.

They suggest that the mandatory nature of the Article XXXIV referendum constitutes unconstitutional discrimination because it hampers persons desiring public housing from achieving their objective when no such roadblock faces other groups seeking to influence other public decisions to their advantage. But of course a lawmaking procedure that "disadvantages" a particular group does not always deny equal protection. Under any such holding, presumably a State would not be able to require referendums on any subject unless referendums were required on all, because they would always disadvantage some group. And this Court would be required to analyze governmental structures to determine whether a gubernatorial veto provision or a filibuster rule is likely to "disadvantage" any of the diverse and shifting groups that make up the American people.

. . . The people of California have also decided by their own vote to require referendum approval of low-rent public housing projects. This procedure ensures that all the people of a community will have a voice in a decision which may lead to large expenditures of local governmental funds for increased public services and to lower tax revenues. It gives them a voice in decisions that will affect the future development of their own community. This procedure for democratic decisionmaking does not violate the constitutional command that no State shall deny to any person "the equal protection of the laws."

Mr. Justice MARSHALL, whom Mr. Justice BRENNAN and Mr. Justice BLACKMUN join, dissenting.

Article XXXIV explicitly singles out low-income persons to bear its burden. Publicly assisted housing developments designed to accommodate the aged, veterans, state employees, persons of moderate income, or any class of citizens other than the poor, need not be approved by prior referenda.

In my view, Art. XXXIV on its face constitutes invidious discrimination which the Equal Protection Clause of the Fourteenth Amendment plainly prohibits. "The States, of course, are prohibited by the Equal Protection Clause from discriminating between 'rich' and 'poor' as such in the formulation and application of their laws." Douglas v. California, 372 U.S. 353, 361 (1963) (HARLAN, J., dissenting). Article XXXIV is neither "a law of general applicability that may affect the poor more harshly than it does the rich," nor an "effort to redress economic imbalances." It is rather an explicit classification on the basis of poverty—a suspect classification which demands exacting judicial scrutiny, see McDonald v. Board of Election, 394 U.S. 802, 807 (1969) [holding that Illinois did not violate the Equal Protection Clause by allowing some individuals, including those who are physically incapacitated, to vote by absentee ballot, but making no equivalent arrangements for those unable to come to the polls because of pre-trial incarceration]; Harper v. Virginia Board of Elections, 383 U.S. 663 (1966); Douglas v. California, *supra*.

The Court, however, chooses to subject the article to no scrutiny whatsoever and treats the provision as if it contained a totally benign, technical economic classification. . . . It is far too late in the day to contend that the Fourteenth Amendment prohibits only racial discrimination; and to me, singling out the poor to bear a burden not placed on any other class of citizens tramples the values that the Fourteenth Amendment was designed to protect.

I respectfully dissent.

* * *

One important site for discussion and study of the enduring questions regarding poverty, public housing, and racial segregation has been the "*Gautreaux* litigation," the first major public housing desegregation case filed in the United States. In 1966, six African Americans brought suit against the Chicago Housing Authority (CHA) and HUD, alleging that, by citing substantially all of its public housing in "the Negro Ghetto," the agency and federal government violated federal statutes and the Fourteenth Amendment. The plaintiffs prevailed, and the suit led to a consent decree lasting decades that imposed specific requirements on CHA's siting policy and gave rise to new models of subsidized housing, essentially dismantling decades of race-based public housing siting and segregation. *See* Gautreaux v. Chi. Hous. Auth., 296 F. Supp. 907 (1969). The litigation also spawned considerable social science interest as the "*Gautreaux* leavers" were relocated to low-poverty neighborhoods. The lead lawyer in the *Gautreaux* litigation was Alex Polikoff, who, along with his colleagues at Business & Professional People for the Public Interest (BPI), has dedicated his career to issues of public housing and racial justice in Chicago and in the nation. The BPI website hosts the following (undated) basic summary of *Gautreaux*.

BUS. & PROF'L PEOPLE FOR THE PUB. INTEREST, *WHAT IS* GAUTREAUX? (MAY 1, 1991)

In 1969, a federal judge issued a judgment order prohibiting [the Chicago Housing Authority ("CHA")] from constructing any new public housing in areas of the city that were predominantly African-American unless CHA also built public housing elsewhere. The 1969 order also placed other restrictions on CHA—most notably that the housing authority could no longer build high-rise public housing for families and could not build dense concentrations of public housing in any neighborhood. These restrictions continue to govern where and how public housing can be built in Chicago today.

In 1971, the U.S. Court of Appeals ruled that because HUD had funded CHA even though it was well aware of the Authority's discriminatory practices, HUD was also liable for CHA's illegal actions, and in 1976, the U.S. Supreme Court ruled unanimously that HUD could be required to work throughout the Chicago metropolitan area to remedy its past discriminatory behavior in Chicago. That Supreme Court decision paved the way for the remedial program that is most often associated with the case—the *Gautreaux* Assisted Housing Program—the nation's first major housing mobility program. Families who were part of the *Gautreaux* plaintiff class could receive special Section 8 rent certificates for private apartments in neighborhoods in which no more than 30 percent of the residents were African-American. Participants received assistance from the Leadership Council for Metropolitan Open Communities in finding housing in diverse city neighborhoods or in the suburbs. Between 1976 and 1998, when it ended, the *Gautreaux* Assisted Housing Program helped more than 25,000 voluntary participants move to more than 100 communities throughout the metropolitan area, roughly half to integrated suburbs and half to integrated neighborhoods in the city.

The *Gautreaux* decision also led to the creation of the "scattered site" public housing program, under which public housing was built not in enormous, isolated communities, but rather on a small scale, dispersed in neighborhoods throughout the city, indistinguishable from surrounding buildings. The program had a long and difficult birth, and after nearly two decades of CHA intransigence, the court eventually concluded that a receiver should be appointed to carry out the program and do what CHA would not. Since 1987 when it was appointed, the Receiver has constructed or rehabilitated nearly 2,000 scattered site public housing units in more than 57 Chicago communities.

Now, in the third remedial phase of the case, *Gautreaux* requirements are helping to ensure that CHA's Plan for Transformation creates well-working, mixed income communities in what were once public housing-dominated neighborhoods. Although the *Gautreaux* court orders generally restrict construction of public housing in segregated neighborhoods, the court has permitted some exceptions when a neighborhood is "revitalizing" — that is, enough development activity is underway or planned that economic integration is likely in the short run, and racial integration might follow in the long run. As a result, hundreds of new public housing units have been built and hundreds more are planned.

* * *

The most controversial piece of the *Gautreaux* litigation was its remedial scheme, which permitted CHA to look beyond the limits of the City of Chicago, and into the surrounding White suburbs, for sites for new subsidized housing. This remedial scheme reached the U.S. Supreme Court, which upheld the broad scope of the remedy. Hills v. Gautreaux, 425 U.S. 284 (1976). In so holding, the Court distinguished its decision in Milliken v. Bradley, 418 U.S. 717 (1974), striking down a school desegregation remedial scheme that extended beyond the City of Detroit and into surrounding (nonminority) suburbs. The basis for the distinction was that because schools are operated by local public entities, federal orders implicating non-party jurisdictions in desegregation decrees exceeded the equitable power of the federal courts. Basing its reasoning on the HUD's statutory discretion to site public housing and statutorily mandated roles for local governments in that process, the Court held:

> In contrast to the [school] desegregation order in [*Milliken*], a metropolitan area relief order directed to HUD would not consolidate or in any way restructure local governmental units. The remedial decree would neither force suburban governments to submit public housing proposals to HUD nor displace the rights and powers accorded local government entities under federal or state housing statutes or existing land-use laws. The order would have the same effect on the suburban governments as a discretionary decision by HUD to use its statutory powers to provide the respondents with alternatives to the racially segregated Chicago public housing system created by CHA and HUD.

425 U.S. 284, 306 (1976).

* * *

In the provocative piece that follows, Alex Polikoff argued in 2005 that racial segregation and the maintenance of segregated Black ghettoes continued to be a national emergency, demanding a bold and creative response. Recalling Alexis de Tocqueville's nineteenth-century description of racial inequality as "the most formidable evil threatening the future of the United States," Polikoff proposed "taking *Gautreaux* to scale" — a national program of vouchers dedicated to families living in segregated African-American areas to enable them to move out of those neighborhoods. As you read the following, which sets out anticipated arguments against the proposal, consider your own views. Are there arguments for or against a national *Gautreaux*-style program that Polikoff does not include? What do you make of his characterization of twenty-first-century race relations?

ALEX POLIKOFF, *A VISION FOR THE FUTURE: BRINGING GAUTREAUX TO SCALE, IN KEEPING THE PROMISE: PRESERVING AND ENHANCING HOUSING MOBILITY IN THE SECTION 8 HOUSING CHOICE VOUCHER PROGRAM* (PHILIP TEGELER ET AL. EDS., 2005)

Reading [*New York Times* reporter Jason DeParle's 2004 book about welfare reform in Milwaukee, *American Dream*], one is struck (for the thousandth time?) by the unremitting, intergenerational persistence of ghetto poverty. From W.E.B. DuBois through James Baldwin and Kenneth Clark, in compelling reportage by Nicholas Lemann, Alex Kotlowitz, and DeParle, in statistical analyses, ethnographic studies, and academic research papers without number, the point is made over and over again: the concentrated poverty of urban ghettos condemns generation after generation of black Americans to what Clark called lives of impotence and despair.

Yet, some may object, only 2.8 million black Americans live in concentrated urban poverty—metropolitan census tracts with poor populations of 40 percent or more. That's only one percent of Americans. Sad to be sure, but not a big enough deal in terrorism times to get worked up about unless you're some bleeding liberal. The country has more pressing matters to attend to.... How could 1 percent of Americans, confined to ghettos, be a nation-threatening matter? Bear with me, and I'll try to explain.

First, take small comfort from small numbers. In an earlier New York Times piece, DeParle makes this point about the small ghetto population:

> The poverty and disorder of the inner cities lacerate a larger civic fabric, drawing people from shared institutions like subways, buses, parks, schools and even cities themselves.... Perhaps most damaging of all is the effect that urban poverty has on race relations. It is like a poison in the national groundwater that is producing a thousand deformed fruits....

Sixty years ago Gunnar Myrdal wrote, "White prejudice and discrimination keep the Negro low in standards of living, health, education, manners and morals. This, in its turn, gives support to white prejudice." Decades later sociologist Elijah Anderson's studies of a ghetto and an adjacent nonghetto neighborhood led him to conclude:

> The public awareness is color-coded. White skin denotes civility, law-abidingness, and trustworthiness, while black skin is strongly associated with poverty, crime, incivility, and distrust.

In American society at large most whites act like the ones Anderson studied—their public awareness is also color-coded and they therefore steer clear of poor blacks and keep them in their ghettos. Predictable ghetto behavior then intensifies whites' sense of danger, validates their color-coding, and drives their conduct.

Urban economist George Galster describes a self-reinforcing "ghettoizing cycle." First, ghettoization induces "behavioral adaptations" by ghetto dwellers. Widely reported by the media, ghetto behavior is then seen as validating and legitimizing whites' prejudicial attitudes toward blacks. The prejudices translate into withdrawal from blacks, and into discriminatory conduct in housing, zoning, employment, and institutional arrangements of all sorts, which in turn lead to more ghettoization. . . .

So what can we do about it? One answer is a *Gautreaux*-type housing mobility program writ large (high quality pre- and post-move counseling, coupled with housing search assistance and identification of homes and apartments, to enable inner-city families to move with housing vouchers into middle-class neighborhoods far from the ghetto). . . .

Suppose 50,000 housing choice vouchers were made available annually, were earmarked for use by black families living in urban ghettos, and could be used only in nonghetto locations — say, census tracts with less than 10 percent poverty and not minority impacted. Suppose that the vouchers were allocated to our 125 largest metropolitan areas. Suppose, that to avoid "threatening" any community, no more than a specified number of families (an arbitrary number — say, 10, or a small fraction of occupied housing units) could move into any city, town, or village in a year.

If an average of 40 municipalities in each metropolitan area served as "receiving communities," the result would be — using 10 as the hypothetical annual move-in ceiling — that 50,000 families each year, or 500,000 in a decade, would move in "*Gautreaux* fashion." Notably, the 500,000 moves would equal almost half the black families living in metropolitan ghetto tracts. We cannot, of course, assume that half of all black families in metropolitan ghettos would choose to participate (though they might). But neither would it require the departure of every other black household to change radically the black ghetto as we know it.

With enough participants, radical change would be inevitable. Whatever the time frame, we would at last be treating a disease that has festered untreated in the body politic for over a century. . . . 100,000 new vouchers per year is not a fanciful figure; Congress authorized more than that number as recently as the year 2000.

. . . The cost of assisting mobility moves must of course be included in the calculus. But at an average of $4,000 per family — a reasonable, even generous, figure based on the *Gautreaux* experience — we are talking about $200 million a year, $2 billion over 10 years (excluding inflation). To put that figure in perspective and address the question of whether we could "afford" it, consider [recent U.S. military budgets of approximately $400 billion per year]. It is true that almost any program can be viewed as affordable by comparison with our military budget. But we aren't talking about "any" program. We are talking about a program to end the successor to slavery and Jim Crow that is perpetuating a caste structure in the United States and threatening incalculable harm to American society. Achieving that, for a negligible fraction — 0.0005 — of our military budget, would be our best bargain since the Louisiana Purchase. . . .

Would enough families volunteer to participate? We will not know until we try, but the *Gautreaux* experience suggests that they may. An average of 400 families moving each year in each participating metropolitan area would be required to reach the hypothetical goal (a smaller average number if more metropolitan areas were used). The 400-per-year number was surpassed more than once by the *Gautreaux* program even though the number of entering families was artificially limited, not by market factors but by the funding and staff that could be extracted from HUD in the *Gautreaux* consent decree bargaining process.

Finally, could 50,000 homes and apartments be found each year? The *Gautreaux* program placed families in over 100 cities, towns and villages in the Chicago area, while the hypothetical assumes an average of only 40. The Census Bureau counts 331 metropolitan areas in the country, while the hypothetical assumes that the mobility program would operate in only 125. Each assumption is conservative with respect to unit supply. . . .

A different kind of question is prompted by the notion of setting aside 50,000 vouchers each year for black families. How can one justify denying poor whites, poor Latinos, and poor Asians, many also living in high-poverty neighborhoods, an opportunity to participate in the mobility program? Would it even be legal?

A dual justification can be offered. The first is that the proposal is designed to help the nation confront its "most formidable evil," an evil that results in significant degree from fears and conduct generated by confining black Americans, not others, to ghettos. The second is that the country is responsible for the confinement of blacks to ghettos in a manner and degree that is not the case with other groups. This is obviously so as to poor whites, who already live mostly among the non-poor. Latinos and Asians do not have slavery or Jim Crow in their histories. Nor have they been confined among their own to a comparable degree. . . .

Even if a national *Gautreaux*-type program were doable and legal, objections remain to be addressed. One is that the program would be harmful to the moving families, severing them from family, friends, and institutional support systems, and subjecting them to hostility and racial discrimination. One answer is to ask who are "we" to withhold a purely voluntary, escape-the-ghetto opportunity from "them" on the ground that we know better than they what is in their interest. . . .

Moreover, studies of the *Gautreaux* program show that "evacuation" works well for many participating families. A variation on the bad-for-them argument is that dismantling the ghetto will undermine black institutions, political power, and ghetto communities that have values deserving preservation. As for black institutional and political strength, Italians, Irish, Jews and others have survived far more mobility than black Americans are likely to experience; it is absurd to contend that the strong, resilient black American culture has anything to fear from a *Gautreaux*-type program. As for values in ghetto communities, even apart from the butchery [in the ghetto streets] of which [*New York Times* writer Brent] Staples writes it is plain to any objective observer that the bad far outweighs the good.

A further variation on the bad-for-them argument is that non-movers will be worse off once some of the ablest and most motivated among ghetto residents leave. Even if true, this is not a sufficient reason to reject the approach. Should we not have passed the Fair Housing Act because the departure of better-off ghetto residents may have left those who remained worse off? . . .

A final objection is that my entire proposal looks like an indulgent fantasy. Don't we clearly lack the political stomach for allowing large numbers of black families to move from inner-city ghettos to white neighborhoods? What on earth makes me think that a nation that has treated blacks the way America has through most of its history—the way it still treats the black poor—would give a moment's consideration to the course I am proposing? This very black ghetto issue was instrumental in shifting the political alignment of the entire country just a few decades ago, changing American character in the bargain. We remain today the uncaring nation we then became.... A *Gautreaux*-type program would certainly be portrayed as liberal social engineering. Should it ever be seriously considered, wouldn't some modern-day George Wallace whip up the country's hardly dormant Negrophobia, perhaps especially easy to do at a time when working and even middle-class Americans are having a hard time?

Maybe. Still, history is full of close calls and surprises. England might have succumbed to the Nazis if Roosevelt had not dreamed up lend-lease and persuaded a reluctant, America First Congress to go along. In 1941, selective service survived by a 203 to 202 vote in the House of Representatives. Truman beat Dewey. Nixon went to China. The Soviet Union collapsed. In one decade the Civil Rights Movement ended generations of seemingly impregnable Jim Crow. In a single fair housing enactment Congress stripped historically sacred private property rights from American landowners. Even with respect to black Americans, history tells us that we can sometimes manage forward steps....

America confronts two courses. The first is to continue to coexist with black ghettos. The second is to dismantle and transform them. The prospect along the first course, as Tocqueville prophesied, is that the evil of racial inequality will not be solved. Integration of some middle-class and affluent blacks will not change the prospect. Until the vast proportion of black Americans is securely middle-class, says the noted sociologist Herbert J. Gans, so long will whites continue to treat middle-class blacks as surrogates for the poor who might move in behind them. So long as black ghettos exist, threatening inundation should there be a break in any neighborhood's dike, most white Americans will fear the entry of blacks, any blacks, into their communities. And so long as that is the case, America's "most formidable evil" will continue to afflict the nation. The other part of Tocqueville's prophecy—result in disaster—is less certain. Yet so long as we continue to tolerate the black ghetto, the prospect is for continuation of the two unequal societies described by the Kerner Report, and continued fear of blacks by white Americans. As long as that fear persists, whites will continue to treat black Americans as the feared Other. They are likely to continue to act fearfully and repressively, possibly to incarcerate still more black Americans in still more prisons. In that event, the Tocqueville prophecy of disaster may indeed become the American reality.

The alternative is to dismantle our black ghettos and replace them wherever possible with mixed-income communities, thereby to lessen the fear and the fearful conduct they generate. Nothing can bring that about overnight, and any approach will be fraught with difficulty and uncertainty. But a national *Gautreaux* mobility program is a sensible way to begin a task that we postpone at our peril.

NOTES AND QUESTIONS

1. What do you think of Polikoff's proposal for 50,000 new vouchers dedicated to "ghetto" families? Can you envision a political organizing campaign for such a strategy? How would you approach it?
2. Polikoff's description of race relations and racial attitudes in the United States, from "butchery" in the streets to "predictable ghetto behavior," is quite blunt as well as bleak. Does it comport with your experience? Does he use language you would feel comfortable using as a lawyer or advocate? Why or why not?
3. Polikoff refers to the "Kerner Report." In 1967, in the face of race riots in U.S. cities, President Johnson appointed the National Advisory Commission on Civil Disorders, named the "Kerner Commission" for its chair, Illinois Governor Otto Kerner. The Commission's report, issued in February 1968, included the famous line: "Our nation is moving toward two societies, one black, one white — separate and unequal." The report identified failed federal policies in education, housing, and social services, as well as White racism as among the causes for the segregation that was threatening the fabric of the nation. It made several specific recommendations, including the elimination of concentrated slum housing and the creation of scattered-site subsidized housing. Rioting continued into 1968 and on April 4 of that year, Martin Luther King, Jr., was assassinated.

* * *

The *Gautreaux* approach of giving poor families the opportunity to relocate out of high-poverty neighborhoods has been broadened, and is now known generally as "housing mobility." Once the defendant in *Gautreaux*, HUD itself now operates its own housing mobility program known as "MTO," Moving to Opportunity. MTO is a "research program," participation in which was made available to the 21 largest housing authorities in the country. Five were selected to participate: Baltimore, Boston, Chicago, Los Angeles, and New York City. Families chosen for the experimental MTO group receive Section 8 vouchers, which can only be used in neighborhoods with less than 10 percent poverty, and are provided with counseling to help them find such housing. Two control groups are included to test the effects of the program: one group already receiving Section 8 assistance and another just coming into the Section 8 program. Notably, unlike the *Gautreaux* remedy, which expressly required that the vouchers be used in nonmajority African-American communities, the MTO demonstration projects are silent on racial composition of the "new" residential locations.

Northwestern University's Institute for Policy Research has been studying the *Gautreaux* and MTO families for more than 20 years. Writing in 2005, researchers reported that 15 years after relocating with a *Gautreaux* voucher, "[f]amilies who were placed in higher-income, mostly white neighborhoods were currently living in the most-affluent neighborhoods. Families who were placed in lower-crime and suburban locations were most likely to reside in low-crime neighborhoods. . . ." Micere Keels et al., *Fifteen Years Later: Can Residential Mobility Programs Provide a Long-Term Escape from Neighborhood Segregation, Crime, and Poverty?*, 42 Demography 51 (2005).

Noting that families faced considerable barriers to stability in the original new neighborhoods to which they moved — such as neighbor hostility, turnover of their new housing to a landlord no longer willing to participate in the program, and children moving to schools with higher expectations than those from which they came — researchers examined the characteristics of the neighborhoods in which families were living 15 years after their initial move:

> Our evidence suggests that the *Gautreaux* program produced long-term gains in neighborhood resources and reductions in racial segregation of the poor urban minority families who volunteered for it. All but a handful of participants were able to escape long term from their inner-city origin neighborhoods, and two thirds of those who initially moved to the suburbs continued to live in the suburbs some 6 to 22 years after their initial moves.
>
> *Gautreaux*'s success in moving low-income black families into higher [socioeconomic status] and lower crime neighborhoods is particularly striking. Compared with conditions in their origin neighborhoods, the participating families enjoyed large and persistent improvements in neighborhood quality. There has been surprisingly little regression to the mean in the 15 years after the families were placed in the program. Current neighborhoods average household incomes of $63,754, a 16% poverty rate, 75% of households with wage income, 25% of adults with college degrees, and 20 violent and 65 property crimes per 1,000 per month. We found no support for the argument that the current clustering of minority Section 8 recipients in racially and economically isolated inner-city neighborhoods is due to their preferences for these neighborhoods, since almost no *Gautreaux* families returned to communities similar to those that they left.

Id. at 69-70.

Studying educational attainment of the children in MTO households, scholars from several nonpartisan research organizations and universities at the National Bureau of Economic Research (NBER), a nonpartisan research organization with a group dedicated to studying MTO, have found less sanguine results. Noting that about half of the families to whom a voucher was offered took up the opportunity, researchers used a randomized methodology to compare MTO students to a control group. They found that:

> families offered housing vouchers in the MTO demonstration moved on average to residential neighborhoods that were substantially less impoverished, and sent their children to schools that were of modestly-higher quality. We did not find evidence of improvements in reading scores, math scores, behavior or school problems, or school engagement, overall or for any age group. . . . The lack of impacts was particularly surprising in the case of young children in the MTO sample, most of whom were preschoolers at the time that their families moved.

Lisa Sanbonmatsu et al., *Neighborhoods and Academic Achievement: Results from the Moving to Opportunity Experiment*, 41 J. Hum. Resources 649 (2006). Several hypotheses were offered for the lack of educational improvement in the MTO children, including that while they had originally relocated to neighborhoods substantially better than their original neighborhoods, later relocations removed some of that improvement, as they moved to more communities with midrange poverty rates compared with the original new homes. Researchers also noted that, unlike *Gautreaux*, the MTO project did not include any race consciousness in its placements and that, in fact, 60 percent of the MTO-moving families still lived in neighborhoods that were comprised of at least 80 percent racial minorities:

It appears that it may take a program like *Gautreaux*, which defined target neigh-borhoods in terms of both poverty and race, to induce permanent moves to neigh-borhoods that are both more affluent and more integrated. Since *Gautreaux* lacked a compelling control group, we cannot say whether or not its "treatment" produced larger academic gains for children in participating families. The lack of integration may have been slightly more pronounced for MTO children's new schools relative to their new neighborhoods due to the number of white non-Hispanic children in some urban areas who attend private schools.

Id.

NBER has published other studies, however, that show improvements in physical and mental health of the MTO movers. In some important realms, outcomes became more muted at the 10-15 year mark than they had been at an interim point, after four to seven years. The interim data showed "large declines" in violent crime arrest for both male and female youth, which did not hold at the longer-term measurement. Nor did the differential between boys and girls hold up; at the interim mark, girls generally benefited, while moves actually had some adverse effects for boys.

The portal to the IPR's research in this area can be found at http://www.ipr.northwestern.edu/publications/Gautreaux.html. NBER studies of the MTO program are located at http://www.nber.org/mtopublic. HUD's website also includes empirical and narrative materials about *Gautreaux* and MTO.

3. *State and Local Housing Policy*

Thus far, we have focused exclusively on federal housing assistance programs (including those that partner with states or localities). As in other subject areas, including cash assistance, health care, and education, the federal government is but one source of public policymaking and expenditures. States, counties, and cities all have their own housing assistance programs, and poverty lawyers and advocates must be versed in these as well. As a complement to scarce federal dollars, many states, counties, and cities have developed their own programs and policies to create and protect their stock of affordable housing. These include direct subsidies, state tax credits for the production of affordable housing, the creation of housing "trust funds," the use of zoning rules to incentivize or require affordable housing, and local eviction and rent control protections.

The American Planning Association identifies three major regional strategies to create and protect affordable housing: "fair share" programs, housing trust funds, and accelerated permitting processes for affordable housing projects. Stuart Meck et al., Am. Planning Ass'n, *Regional Approaches to Affordable Housing* (2003), *available at* http://www.huduser.org/Publications/PDF/regional_app_aff_hsg.pdf. "Fair share" programs are designed to ensure that each region in the state provides its "fair share" of affordable housing. In the case of New Jersey, this approach came about as a result of two well-known state supreme court decisions: Mount Laurel I, 336 A.2d 713 (N.J. 1975), and Mount Laurel II, 456 A.2d 390 (N.J. 1983). *Mount Laurel I* held that developing municipalities are constitutionally required to provide a realistic opportunity for low- and moder-ate-income housing to be built. In *Mount Laurel II*, the court pushed the *Mount Laurel I* decision further to say that under the New Jersey state constitution, all municipalities must supply realistic opportunities to provide their fair share of the region's housing needs. In response to the litigation, the New Jersey legislature passed the state's Fair Housing Act, which established a Council on Affordable Housing and charged it with determining housing regions and establishing a fair share of affordable housing for each of these regions. The state has determined that regions must accommodate affordable housing based on growth share, whereby "one unit among every five housing units created in a municipality must be affordable; one affordable housing unit must be provided for every 16 jobs created in a municipality, measured by new commercial development." New Jersey reports that more than 60,000 units of affordable housing have been created that are attributable to the program.

Other jurisdictions with a "fair share" approach to affordable housing include California, New Hampshire, and the city of Portland, Oregon. Unlike New Jersey's approach to fair share housing, California's legislative action was not spurred by court decisions. In 1980, California enacted the California State Housing Element Law, in response to a drought of affordable housing. Building upon the preexisting obligation that each municipality's "General Plan" include a "Housing Element," the statute requires that the housing element take into account the housing needs of the region, including local needs for affordable housing, as determined by a Regional Housing Needs Assessment. Therefore, local governments are provided their share of affordable housing only if their comprehensive plans allow for such housing to be built. While there are clearly benefits to identifying local accountability for affordable housing, the housing element "program" has been criticized as lacking teeth in the form of any substantial enforcement mechanism.

The second regional or local strategy identified for promoting affordable housing is the use of housing "trust funds." As part of the Housing and Economic Recovery Act of 2008, Congress created the National Housing Trust Fund. As of this writing, full funding for the national trust fund remains a top priority for affordable housing advocates. Proposals to fund the trust fund include reform to the mortgage interest tax deduction. Advocates' goal is to raise sufficient monies such that the trust fund has an annual distribution of $30 billion over ten years to produce 3.5 million affordable homes. Other units of government have also created trust funds. Over 700 jurisdictions, including 47 states and numerous cities, counties, and towns in the United States, have established some form of housing trust fund, and collectively they generate over $1 billion per year for affordable housing. One of the goals of the trust fund model is to protect these funds from ordinary budget debates.

The third way some states support affordable housing is through the creation of a streamlined process for affordable housing projects. For example, Rhode Island and Massachusetts have established such streamlined systems, whereby affordable housing projects may receive one permit from a special board as opposed to going through the regular multistep permitting process. In addition, Connecticut has established a single appeals board to handle appeals from applicants whose affordable housing application is denied by a municipality.

Fourth, many municipalities engage in efforts to create, support, and protect affordable housing. In addition to rent control, discussed *infra*, over 300 jurisdictions — cities, counties, and towns — in the United States have passed so-called "inclusionary zoning" ordinances. These laws generally require that any new residential development in the city include some proportion (usually 10-30 percent) of units defined as "affordable" (typically defined in terms of some relation between rent and area median income). (Ordinances vary considerably in their specific terms.) Some permit a developer to buy out of the requirement, some allow the affordable units to be built on a different site than the principal development, and some apply only to developments over a certain size. Like many housing assistance programs, inclusionary zoning has been the subject of intense political and academic debate. Proponents argue that these schemes increase the availability of affordable housing, while opponents claim that the opposite is true: they chill development.

Finally, some municipalities seek to protect affordable housing by passing rent control ordinances. Such ordinances, generally passed by a city or a county, can take many forms, but in general they regulate the pace and extent to which landlords can raise rents in governed units. Many *rent* control ordinances also contain *eviction* control provisions, requiring that a landlord prove good cause to terminate a tenancy, which otherwise would be terminable at will by the landlord.

Many contemporary rent control measures arise from federal rent regulation imposed after World War II under the Emergency Price Control Act of 1942 (EPCA). New York, however, experimented with rent control in the 1920s. The first laws allowing tenants to challenge increases in rent, giving discretion to judges to determine the reasonableness of rent increases, and placing the burden on landlords to show the reasonableness of the rent increases were enacted in September 1920. These regulations lost some of their usefulness when a construction boom increased the supply of housing in New York and rents, in turn, fell naturally. Rent control reemerged as a serious issue during World War II, with the federal government passing the EPCA to prevent wartime profiteering in many sectors, including defense-area housing. As it had following World War I, when the post–World War II housing shortage lessened, the federal government allowed its rent control regulations to lapse, and by 1961, New York City was the only locality that had opted to retain federal government rent controls. As of 2012 over 100 cities nationwide have some kind of rent control in place. For one history of rent control, focused on New York as a pioneer in this area, see Guy McPherson, *It's the End of the World as We Know It (and I Feel Fine): Rent Regulation in New York City and the Unanswered Questions of Market and Society*, 72 Fordham L. Rev. 1125 (2004).

Economists and policymakers disagree about the value of rent control as a strategy to preserve affordable housing. Many economists, including Nobel Prize winner Paul Krugman, argue that a ceiling on rents reduces the quality and quantity of housing. In short, Krugman asserts that fear from landlords about potential rent control ordinances quashes new construction, leaving a supply of housing that is below the demand, driving prices up in non-rent-controlled properties. On the other side of the debate are those who claim that rent control is essential because it creates social good. Proponents of rent control claim that it stabilizes communities, ensures that vulnerable populations (such as elderly or disabled long-term tenants) are not pushed out, and prevents landlords from engaging in illegal behavior (such as raising rents to constructively evict a tenant who requests legally required repairs).

Landlords are often the strongest opponents of rent control and have challenged, unsuccessfully, rent control in courts for many years under a Takings Clause theory. *See, e.g.*, Yee v. City of Escondido, 503 U.S. 519 (1992); Rent Stabilization Ass'n of New York City, Inc. v. Higgins, 83 N.Y.2d 156 (1993). The Second Circuit in 2011 affirmed the constitutionality of rent control, ruling against landlords challenging New York's Rent Stabilization Laws in Harmon v. Markus, 412 F. App'x 420, 423 (2d Cir. 2011), *cert. denied*, 132 S. Ct. 1991 (2012). The court held that "where, as here, 'a property owner offers property for rental housing, the Supreme Court has held that governmental regulation of the rental relationship does not constitute a physical taking.'"

NOTES AND QUESTIONS

1. Is housing policy better made at the federal, state, or local level?
2. Which of the strategies introduced above do you think is most likely to succeed? If you were on your local city council, which would you promote, and why?
3. The legal and policy issues involved in the development of affordable housing form their own rich and complex subject. Timely information, scholarly analysis, and discussion of advocacy strategies are available in the *Journal of Affordable Housing and Community Development*, a quarterly publication of ABA Forum on Affordable Housing and Community Development. *See also* Alan Mallach, *A Decent Home: Planning, Building, and Preserving Affordable Housing* (2009); James A. Kushner et al., *Housing and Community Development: Cases and Materials* (4th ed. 2011); *The Legal Guide to Affordable Housing Development* (Tim Iglesias & Rochelle E. Lento eds., 2d ed. 2011).

D. EVICTION DEFENSE

The affordability crisis renders poor people vulnerable to eviction for nonpayment of rent. Eviction defense has long been a mainstay of legal services lawyers' practices, and virtually every legal services provider makes some form of eviction defense a priority. This section explains "summary process," the accelerated civil trial calendar that every state in the country has created in its statutes for the disposition of eviction cases, and includes an excerpt from the U.S. Supreme Court case in which Oregon's version of that process was upheld against a constitutional challenge, again during the historical period when poverty lawyers were frequently at the Court arguing for poor people's rights. While that case, Lindsey v. Normet, was lost, important victories were secured in another area of tenants' rights: habitability. While not in the U.S. Supreme Court, numerous state supreme courts recognized a landlord's breach of the warranty of habitability as a defense to nonpayment of rent. The much-cited 1970 holding to this effect by Judge Skelley Wright of the D.C. Circuit Court, excerpted later in this chapter, sets out the rationale for this change in landlord-tenant contract law. *See* Javins v. First Nat'l Realty Corp., 428 F.2d 1071 (D.C. Cir. 1970). This "mutuality of covenants" is now recognized in every state in the country, both through judicial decision and subsequent codification by state legislatures.

We conclude by examining eviction in the specific context of the public and subsidized programs created by HUD, as described above. In that context, tenants enjoy certain protections, unavailable to other renters — most notably that even after expiration of a lease term their tenancies can only be terminated for "cause." By contrast, they come under special scrutiny, as is evidenced in the so-called "innocent renter" doctrine established in the *Rucker* case, below.

1.   *Constitutionality of "Summary Process"*

Lindsey v. Normet is still cited frequently for the proposition with which we started this chapter: that there is no fundamental right to housing under the U.S. Constitution. Poverty lawyers sought recognition of such a right in the context of attacking Oregon's summary process statute, claiming that the fundamental nature of the interest at stake should elevate the level of scrutiny of any statutory scheme that burdened it. As you read above (see *supra*, p. 339), that argument was rejected, as were most of the lawyers' attacks on the statute. The vital portion of the opinion regarding the "fundamental right" to housing is not included below. What follows is the Court's discussion of several procedural features of Oregon's summary process regime for eviction. While each state's specific procedure differs, summary process in eviction is still the law today.

LINDSEY v. NORMET
405 U.S. 56 (1972)

Mr. Justice WHITE delivered the opinion of the Court.

This case presents the question of whether Oregon's judicial procedure for eviction of tenants after nonpayment of rent violates either the Equal Protection Clause or the Due Process Clause of the Fourteenth Amendment.

Appellants were the month-to-month tenants of appellee Normet and paid $100 a month for the use of a single-family residence in Portland, Oregon. On November 10, 1969, the City Bureau of Buildings declared the dwelling unfit for habitation due to substandard conditions on the premises. Appellants requested appellee to make certain repairs which, with one minor exception, appellee refused to do. Appellants, who had paid the November rent, refused to pay the December rent until the requested improvements had been made.... Before the statutory eviction procedures were begun in the Oregon courts, appellants filed suit in federal district court under 42 U.S.C. § 1983, seeking a declaratory judgment that the Oregon Forcible Entry and Wrongful Detainer (FED) Statute was unconstitutional on its face, and an injunction against its continued enforcement.... The District Court [] granted appellee's motion to dismiss the complaint after concluding that the statute was not unconstitutional under either the Due Process Clause or the Equal Protection Clause of the Fourteenth Amendment.... Appellants promptly appealed, and we noted probable jurisdiction.

I.

[The Oregon eviction statute] establishes a procedure intended to insure that any entry upon real property "shall be made in a peaceable manner and without force." A landlord may bring an action for possession whenever the tenant has failed to pay rent within 10 days of its due date, when the tenant is holding contrary to some other covenant in a lease, and whenever the landlord has terminated the rental arrangement by proper notice and the tenant remains in possession after the expiration date specified in the notice. Service of the complaint on the tenant must be not less than two nor more than four days before the trial date; a tenant may obtain a two-day continuance, but grant of a longer continuance is conditioned on a tenant's posting security for the payment of any rent that may accrue, if the plaintiff ultimately prevails, during the period of the continuance. The suit may be tried to either a judge or a jury, and the only issue is whether the allegations of the complaint are true. The only award that a plaintiff may recover is restitution of possession. A defendant who loses such a suit may appeal only if he obtains two sureties who will provide security for the payment to the plaintiff, if the defendant ultimately loses on appeal, of twice the rental value of the property from the time of commencement of the action to final judgment.

Appellants' principal attacks are leveled at three characteristics of the Oregon FED Statute: the requirement of a trial no later than six days after service of the complaint unless security for accruing rent is provided; the provisions which, either on their face or as construed, are said to limit the triable issues in an FED suit to the tenant's default and to preclude consideration of defenses based on the landlord's breach of a duty to maintain the premises; and the requirement of posting bond on appeal from an adverse decision in twice the amount of the rent expected to accrue pending appellate decision. These provisions are asserted to violate both the Equal Protection and Due Process Clauses of the Fourteenth Amendment. Except for the appeal bond requirement, we reject these claims.

We are unable to conclude that either the early-trial provision or the limitation on litigable issues is invalid on its face under the Due Process Clause of the Fourteenth Amendment. In those recurring cases where the tenant fails to pay rent or holds over after expiration of his tenancy and the issue in the ensuing litigation is simply whether he has paid or held over, we cannot declare that the Oregon statute allows an unduly short time for trial preparation. Tenants would appear to have as much access to relevant facts as their landlord, and they can be expected to know the terms of their lease, whether they have paid their rent, whether they are in possession of the premises, and whether they have received a proper notice to quit, if one is necessary. Particularly where, as here, rent has admittedly been deliberately withheld and demand for payment made, claims of prejudice from an early trial date are unpersuasive. The provision for continuance of the action if the tenant posts security for accruing rent means that in cases where tenant defendants, unlike appellants, deny nonpayment of rent and may require more time to prepare for litigation, they will not be forced to trial if they provide for rent payments in the interim. A requirement that the tenant pay or provide for the payment of rent during the continuance of the action is hardly irrational or oppressive. It is customary to pay rent in advance, and the simplicity of the issues in the typical FED action will usually not require extended trial preparation and litigation, thus making the posting of a large security deposit unnecessary. Of course, it is possible for this provision to be applied so as to deprive a tenant of a proper hearing in specific situations, but there is no such showing made here, and possible infirmity in other situations does not render it invalid on its face.

Nor does Oregon deny due process of law by restricting the issues in FED actions to whether the tenant has paid rent and honored the covenants he has assumed, issues that may be fairly and fully litigated under the Oregon procedure. The tenant is barred from raising claims in the FED action that the landlord has failed to maintain the premises, but the landlord is also barred from claiming back rent or asserting other claims against the tenant. The tenant is not foreclosed from instituting his own action against the landlord and litigating his right to damages or other relief in that action.

"Due process requires that there be an opportunity to present every available defense." Appellants do not deny, however, that there are available procedures to litigate any claims against the landlord cognizable in Oregon. Their claim is that they are denied due process of law because the rental payments are not suspended while the alleged wrongdoings of the landlord are litigated. We see no constitutional barrier to Oregon's insistence that the tenant provide for accruing rent pending judicial settlement of his disputes with the lessor. [Ed. note: At oral argument, appellants conceded that if a tenant remained in possession without paying rent, a landlord might be deprived of property without due process of law.]

Underlying appellants' claim is the assumption that they are denied due process of law unless Oregon recognizes the failure of the landlord to maintain the premises as an operative defense to the possessory FED action and as an adequate excuse for nonpayment of rent. The Constitution has not federalized the substantive law of landlord-tenant relations, however, and we see nothing to forbid Oregon from treating the undertakings of the tenant and those of the landlord as independent rather than dependent covenants. Likewise, the Constitution does not authorize us to require that the term of an otherwise expired tenancy be extended while the tenant's damage claims against the landlord are litigated. The substantive law of landlord-tenant relations differs widely in the various States. In some jurisdictions, a tenant may argue as a defense to eviction for nonpayment of rent such claims as unrepaired building code violations, breach of an implied warranty of habitability, or the fact that the landlord is evicting him for reporting building code violations or for exercising constitutional rights. Some States have enacted statutes authorizing rent withholding in certain situations. In other jurisdictions, these claims, if cognizable at all, must be litigated in separate tort, contract, or civil rights suits. There is no showing that Oregon excludes any defenses it recognizes as "available" on the three questions (physical possession, forcible withholding, legal right to possession) at issue in an FED suit.

We also cannot agree that the FED Statute is invalid on its face under the Equal Protection Clause. It is true that Oregon FED suits differ substantially from other litigation, where the time between complaint and trial is substantially longer, and where a broader range of issues may be considered. But it does not follow that the Oregon statute invidiously discriminates against defendants in FED actions.

The statute potentially applies to all tenants, rich and poor, commercial and noncommercial; it cannot be faulted for over-exclusiveness or under-exclusiveness. And classifying tenants of real property differently from other tenants for purposes of possessory actions will offend the equal protection safeguard "only if the classification rests on grounds wholly irrelevant to the achievement of the State's objective," or if the objective itself is beyond the State's power to achieve. It is readily apparent that prompt as well as peaceful resolution of disputes over the right to possession of real property is the end sought by the Oregon statute. It is also clear that the provisions for early trial and simplification of issues are closely related to that purpose. The equal protection claim with respect to these provisions thus depends on whether the State may validly single out possessory disputes between landlord and tenant for especially prompt judicial settlement. In making such an inquiry a State is "presumed to have acted within (its) constitutional power despite the fact that, in practice, (its) laws result in some inequality."

At common law, one with the right to possession could bring an action for ejectment, a "relatively slow, fairly complex, and substantially expensive procedure." But, as Oregon cases have recognized, the common law also permitted the landlord to "enter and expel the tenant by force, without being liable to an action of tort for damages, either for his entry upon the premises, or for an assault in expelling the tenant, provided he uses no more force than is necessary, and do(es) no wanton damage." The landlord-tenant relationship was one of the few areas where the right to self-help was recognized by the common law of most States, and the implementation of this right has been fraught with "violence and quarrels and bloodshed." An alternative legal remedy to prevent such breaches of the peace has appeared to be an overriding necessity to many legislators and judges. Hence, the Oregon statute was enacted in 1866 to alter the common law and obviate resort to self-help and violence. The statute, intended to protect tenants as well as landlords, provided a speedy, judicially supervised proceeding to settle the possessory issue in a peaceful manner. . . .

There are unique factual and legal characteristics of the landlord-tenant relationship that justify special statutory treatment inapplicable to other litigants. The tenant is, by definition, in possession of the property of the landlord; unless a judicially supervised mechanism is provided for what would otherwise be swift repossession by the landlord himself, the tenant would be able to deny the landlord the rights of income incident to ownership by refusing to pay rent and by preventing sale or rental to someone else. . . .

We agree with appellants, however, that the double-bond prerequisite for appealing an FED action violates their right to the equal protection of the laws. To appeal a civil case in Oregon, the ordinary litigant must file an undertaking, with one or more sureties, covering "all damages, costs and disbursements which may be awarded against him on the appeal." . . . In an FED action, however, a defendant who loses in the district court and who wishes to appeal must give "in addition to the undertaking now required by law upon appeal," an undertaking with two sureties for the payment of twice the rental value of the premises "from the commencement of the action in which the judgment was rendered until final judgment in the action." In the event the judgment is affirmed, the landlord is automatically entitled to twice the rents accruing during the appeal without proof of actual damage in that amount.

We have earlier said that Oregon may validly make special provision for the peaceful and expeditious settlement of disputes over possession between landlord and tenant and that the early-trial and continuance bond provisions of the FED statute rationally implement that purpose because the tenant's right to possession beyond the initial six-day period is conditioned on securing the landlord against the loss of accruing rent. Similar conditions on the tenant's right to appeal . . . would also raise no serious constitutional questions at least on the face of such a statute. [The double-bond provision], however, imposes additional requirements that in our judgment bear no reasonable relationship to any valid state objective and that arbitrarily discriminate against tenants appealing from adverse decisions in FED actions.

This Court has recognized that if a full and fair trial on the merits is provided, the Due Process Clause of the Fourteenth Amendment does not require a State to provide appellate review, and the continuing validity of these cases is not at issue here. When an appeal is afforded, however, it cannot be granted to some litigants and capriciously or arbitrarily denied to others without violating the Equal Protection Clause.

2. Warranty of Habitability and the Mutuality of Covenants

Justice Douglas dissented in *Lindsey*, relying in part on his conclusion that tenants should be able to assert alleged breaches of the implied warranty of habitability as a defense in an eviction case based on nonpayment of rent. Other judges, relying on state contract law, agreed with this analysis, including Judge Skelly Wright of the D.C. Circuit Court, who wrote one of the most influential decisions establishing that defense in the following case, Javins v. First National Realty Corp. The warranty of habitability is a central tool in an eviction lawyer's toolbox. Because poor tenants frequently live in conditions of serious disrepair, the establishment of this defense has given them some leverage in defending themselves against eviction, and negotiating for the correction of conditions that make their homes legally "uninhabitable."

JAVINS v. FIRST NAT'L REALTY CORP.
428 F.2d 1071(D.C. Cir. 1970)

J. Skelly WRIGHT, Circuit Judge:

These cases present the question whether housing code violations which arise during the term of a lease have any effect upon the tenant's obligation to pay rent. The Landlord and Tenant Branch of the District of Columbia Court of General Sessions ruled proof of such violations inadmissible when proffered as a defense to an eviction action for nonpayment of rent. . . . [We hold] that a warranty of habitability, measured by the standards set out in the Housing Regulations for the District of Columbia, is implied by operation of law into leases of urban dwelling units covered by those Regulations and that breach of this warranty gives rise to the usual remedies for breach of contract.

I.

The facts revealed by the record are simple. By separate written leases, each of the appellants rented an apartment in a three-building apartment complex in Northwest Washington known as Clifton Terrace. The landlord, First National Realty Corporation, filed separate actions in the Landlord and Tenant Branch of the Court of General Sessions on April 8, 1966, seeking possession on the ground that each of the appellants had defaulted in the payment of rent due for the month of April. The tenants, appellants here, admitted that they had not paid the landlord any rent for April. However, they alleged numerous violations of the Housing Regulations as "an equitable defense or (a) claim by way of recoupment or set-off in an amount equal to the rent claim," as provided in the rules of the Court of General Sessions. They offered to prove "that there are approximately 1500 violations of the Housing Regulations of the District of Columbia in the building at Clifton Terrace, where Defendant resides some affecting the premises of this Defendant directly, others indirectly, and all tending to establish a course of conduct of violation of the Housing Regulations to the damage of Defendants. . . ."

Since, in traditional analysis, a lease was the conveyance of an interest in land, courts have usually utilized the special rules governing real property transactions to resolve controversies involving leases. However, as the Supreme Court has noted in another context, "the body of private property law . . . , more than almost any other branch of law, has been shaped by distinctions whose validity is largely historical." Courts have a duty to reappraise old doctrines in the light of the facts and values of contemporary life — particularly old common law doctrines which the courts themselves created and developed. As we have said before, "The continued vitality of the common law . . . depends upon its ability to reflect contemporary community values and ethics."

. . . When American city dwellers, both rich and poor, seek "shelter" today, they seek a well known package of goods and services — a package which includes not merely walls and ceilings, but also adequate heat, light and ventilation, serviceable plumbing facilities, secure windows and doors, proper sanitation, and proper maintenance. . . . In our judgment the trend toward treating leases as contracts is wise and well considered. Our holding in this case reflects a belief that leases of urban dwelling units should be interpreted and construed like any other contract.

Modern contract law has recognized that the buyer of goods and services in an industrialized society must rely upon the skill and honesty of the supplier to assure that goods and services purchased are of adequate quality. In interpreting most contracts, courts have sought to protect the legitimate expectations of the buyer and have steadily widened the seller's responsibility for the quality of goods and services through implied warranties of fitness and merchantability. . . .

The rigid doctrines of real property law have tended to inhibit the application of implied warranties to transactions involving real estate. Now, however, courts have begun to hold sellers and developers of real property responsible for the quality of their product. . . .

Despite this trend in the sale of real estate, many courts have been unwilling to imply warranties of quality, specifically a warranty of habitability, into leases of apartments. Recent decisions have offered no convincing explanation for their refusal; rather they have relied without discussion upon the old common law rule that the lessor is not obligated to repair unless he covenants to do so in the written lease contract. . . . In our judgment, the old no-repair rule cannot coexist with the obligations imposed on the landlord by a typical modern housing code, and must be abandoned in favor of an implied warranty of habitability.

In our judgment the common law itself must recognize the landlord's obligation to keep his premises in a habitable condition. This conclusion is compelled by three separate considerations. First, we believe that the old rule was based on certain factual assumptions which are no longer true; on its own terms, it can no longer be justified. Second, we believe that the consumer protection cases discussed above require that the old rule be abandoned in order to bring residential landlord-tenant law into harmony with the principles on which those cases rest. Third, we think that the nature of today's urban housing market also dictates abandonment of the old rule.

The common law rule absolving the lessor of all obligation to repair originated in the early Middle Ages. Such a rule was perhaps well suited to an agrarian economy; the land was more important than whatever small living structure was included in the leasehold, and the tenant farmer was fully capable of making repairs himself. . . .

It is overdue for courts to admit that these assumptions are no longer true with regard to all urban housing. Today's urban tenants, the vast majority of whom live in multiple dwelling houses, are interested, not in the land, but solely in "a house suitable for occupation." Furthermore, today's city dweller usually has a single, specialized skill unrelated to maintenance work; he is unable to make repairs like the "jack-of-all-trades" farmer who was the common law's model of the lessee. Further, unlike his agrarian predecessor who often remained on one piece of land for his entire life, urban tenants today are more mobile than ever before. A tenant's tenure in a specific apartment will often not be sufficient to justify efforts at repairs. In addition, the increasing complexity of today's dwellings renders them much more difficult to repair than the structures of earlier times. In a multiple dwelling repair may require access to equipment and areas in the control of the landlord. Low and middle income tenants, even if they were interested in making repairs, would be unable to obtain any financing for major repairs since they have no long-term interest in the property.

. . . [T]he relationship of landlord and tenant suggests further compelling reasons for the law's protection of the tenants' legitimate expectations of quality. The inequality in bargaining power between landlord and tenant has been well documented. Tenants have very little leverage to enforce demands for better housing. Various impediments to competition in the rental housing market, such as racial and class discrimination and standardized form leases, mean that landlords place tenants in a take it or leave it situation. The increasingly severe shortage of adequate housing further increases the landlord's bargaining power and escalates the need for maintaining and improving existing stock. Finally, the findings by various studies of the social impact of bad housing has led to the realization that poor housing is detrimental to the whole society, not merely to the unlucky ones who must suffer the daily indignity of living in a slum.

We believe, in any event, that the District's housing code requires that a warranty of habitability be implied in the leases of all housing that it covers. . . . As Judge Cardozo wrote [in another case]:

> We may be sure that the framers of this statute, when regulating tenement life, had uppermost in thought the care of those who are unable to care for themselves. The Legislature must have known that unless repairs in the rooms of the poor were made by the landlord, they would not be made by any one. The duty imposed became commensurate with the need. The right to seek redress is not limited to the city or its officers. The right extends to all whom there was a purpose to protect.

This principle of implied warranty is well established. . . . In view of these circumstances, we think the conclusion reached by the Supreme Court of Wisconsin as to the effect of a housing code on the old common law rule cannot be avoided:

> The legislature has made a policy judgment—that it is socially (and politically) desirable to impose these duties on a property owner—which has rendered the old common law rule obsolete. To follow the old rule of no implied warranty of

habitability in leases would, in our opinion, be inconsistent with the current legislative policy concerning housing standards.

We therefore hold that the Housing Regulations imply a warranty of habitability, measured by the standards which they set out, into leases of all housing that they cover.

In the present cases, the landlord sued for possession for nonpayment of rent. Under contract principles, however, the tenant's obligation to pay rent is dependent upon the landlord's performance of his obligations, including his warranty to maintain the premises in habitable condition. In order to determine whether any rent is owed to the landlord, the tenants must be given an opportunity to prove the housing code violations alleged as breach of the landlord's warranty.

At trial, the finder of fact must make two findings: (1) whether the alleged violations existed during the period for which past due rent is claimed, and (2) what portion, if any or all, of the tenant's obligation to pay rent was suspended by the landlord's breach.

* * *

The doctrinal recognition of a defense to eviction is one thing; successfully asserting such a defense is another. As we will see in Chapter 10, poor people have no right to a lawyer in most civil contexts, and certainly not in eviction cases. While most legal services offices practice in the area of housing law, it is unusual for that practice to include full trial representation of individual tenants in individual eviction cases. The lack of representation in housing courts, as well as the crushing, bureaucratic nature of the summary process in urban courts, has been the subject of numerous articles. Among the most cited is Professor Barbara Bezdek's *Silence in the Courts*, 20 Hofstra L. Rev. 533(1992), which includes a riveting description of Baltimore's housing court:

Inside, the six courtrooms on the main level are used primarily for criminal cases, which explains the number of police officers throughout the first floor. Rent court is in the basement past the offices of the Public Defender and the Constables who execute evictions. If one arrives before the morning session begins at 9 a.m., one sees the blankness of the wide, bright linoleum corridor, leading past closed doors that read, "Rent Court Clerk," "Eviction Prevention Office," and "Legal Aid." Around the corner, two sets of double doors are marked simply, "Silence — Court in Session."

Come an hour or so later, particularly in the busy middle of the month, and one sees an ever-replenished line of people who are mostly women, mostly black, and mostly with little kids. These tenants are waiting in turn to be called into the Eviction Prevention Office, where they will be quizzed about whether they are facing a "housing emergency" sufficient to entitle them to emergency assistance from the Department of Social Services ("DSS"). The tenants in line have already waited in the courtroom for their cases to be called. Each has received a "DSS slip" in exchange for which a judgment was entered against her for possession on the ground of nonpayment. Now they wait to be screened, and the lucky ones will be directed to their local DSS office to apply for an emergency assistance ("EA") grant. If the tenant has no other funds with which to satisfy the judgment and retain her housing, and if the tenant has not had two prior grants in the year, then she will likely receive an EA grant. But in no event will this grant ever exceed $250, and if there are no children in the household, or a prior grant has been made, it will in fact be less. Yet in 75% of the cases, the monthly rent sued for in rent court exceeds $250. Plainly, even the EA grant does not "prevent" the tenant's eviction.

As one heads for the double-doors to enter Courtroom 7, one may notice off to the right a tilted counter — the docket board. Stapled to it are the cases on the docket for the day, listed by address and case number alone — neither landlord's nor tenant's name appears. No explanation is posted. One might assume, as some tenants do, that the list indicates the order in which cases will be called. This is not so, since cases are called by the courtroom clerk so as to facilitate rapid disposition. Thus, periodically throughout the morning session, the clerk will call from the bench, "All those tenants paying rent to or renting from AB Management Company, come forward and bring your rent notice." Landlord agents (non-attorneys appearing on behalf of client landlords) prefer to have all of their cases heard in sequence, so that they can either come later in the docket or leave before its end. This wish is accommodated by court personnel as a matter of course.

Tenants, on the other hand, are extended no similar control over their schedule or expectation. They are given no idea when their case will be called, and throughout the long session they are at their peril should they leave the room to find the lavatory or to quiet the baby. In a few instances where the landlord appears on his or her own behalf rather than through an agent (no more than about 15% of the cases) the landlord and tenant may in fact know or recognize each other and realize that the momentarily missing party is in the court house. In the rare instances when this happens and it is brought to the judge's attention, the court may recall the case a few minutes later. Our court observation however, documented this only when the missing party was the landlord, never the tenant. But if a tenant's case is called and she does not move *directly* to the bench, the court will observe, "Landlord claims $330 rent due, tenant has failed to appear, judgment is entered for landlord for possession." It all takes less than a minute.

NOTES AND QUESTIONS

1. To prevail on a warranty of habitability defense to nonpayment, a tenant must establish, generally, that (1) the breach was substantial and affected the health and safety of the unit (under some state statutes, a report from an official building inspector can create a presumption of breach), (2) the condition constituting the breach was not the fault of the tenant, and (3) the landlord had reasonable notice about the condition(s) and a reasonable opportunity to repair. As a lawyer defending an eviction case, what kind of evidence would you rely upon to meet this burden? How would you go about building your case? How would an unrepresented tenant build such a case?

2. For more on the development of the warranty of habitability as part of a tenants' rights movement analogous to that for welfare rights, see David A. Super, *The Rise and Fall of the Implied Warranty of Habitability*, 99 Cal. L. Rev. 389 (2011).

3. Nonpayment of rent is only one basis for a landlord's filing an eviction case against a residential tenant. Other common bases include breach of the lease, committing a nuisance or disturbance on the premises, or simply a tenant holding over after the expiration of a lease term. Of course, landlord-tenant law does not draw formal distinctions based on the wealth status of the tenants, but how might these fundamental landlord-tenant concepts play out differently in a poor neighborhood than in a non-poor neighborhood?

4. Consider your own experience as a tenant (or as a landlord), if you have had any. Have you signed a written lease? How well did you understand its terms? Did you have legal advice when signing?

3. Eviction in Public Housing Context

Tenants in subsidized housing enjoy some protections that tenants in strictly private tenancies do not. Federal regulations governing many subsidy programs require that leases created pursuant to those programs include "good cause" provisions and longer termination periods than private tenants enjoy. *See, e.g.,* 24 CFR 966.4(l)(2) for lawful bases for eviction from public housing. On the other hand, residents of public housing are also subject to federal regulations importing the "war on drugs" into their tenancies.

DEP'T OF HOUS. AND URBAN DEV. v. RUCKER
535 U.S. 125 (2002)

Chief Justice Rehnquist delivered the opinion of the Court.

With drug dealers "increasingly imposing a reign of terror on public and other federally assisted low-income housing tenants," Congress passed the Anti-Drug Abuse Act of 1988. The Act, as later amended, provides that each "public housing agency shall utilize leases which . . . provide that any criminal activity that threatens the health, safety, or right to peaceful enjoyment of the premises by other tenants or any drug-related criminal activity on or off such premises, engaged in by a public housing tenant, any member of the tenant's household, or any guest or other person under the tenant's control, shall be cause for termination of tenancy." 42 U.S.C. § 1437d(l)(6). Petitioners say that this statute requires lease terms that allow a local public housing authority to evict a tenant when a member of the tenant's household or a guest engages in drug-related criminal activity, regardless of whether the tenant knew, or had reason to know, of that activity. Respondents say it does not. We agree with petitioners.

Respondents are four public housing tenants of the Oakland Housing Authority (OHA). Paragraph 9(m) of respondents' leases, tracking the language of § 1437d(l)(6), obligates the tenants to "assure that the tenant, any member of the household, a guest, or another person under the tenant's control, shall not engage in . . . [a]ny drug-related criminal activity on or near the premise[s]." Respondents also signed an agreement stating that the tenant "understand[s] that if I or any member of my household or guests should violate this lease provision, my tenancy may be terminated and I may be evicted."

In late 1997 and early 1998, OHA instituted eviction proceedings in state court against respondents, alleging violations of this lease provision. The complaint alleged: (1) that the respective grandsons of respondents William Lee and Barbara Hill, both of whom were listed as residents on the leases, were caught in the apartment complex parking lot smoking marijuana; (2) that the daughter of respondent Pearlie Rucker, who resides with her and is listed on the lease as a resident, was found with cocaine and a crack cocaine pipe three blocks from Rucker's apartment; and (3) that on three instances within a 2-month period, respondent Herman Walker's caregiver and two others were found with cocaine in Walker's apartment. OHA had issued Walker notices of a lease violation on the first two occasions, before initiating the eviction action after the third violation.

United States Department of Housing and Urban Development (HUD) regulations administering § 1437d(l)(6) require lease terms authorizing evictions in these circumstances. The HUD regulations closely track the statutory language, and provide that "[i]n deciding to evict for criminal activity, the [public housing authority] shall have discretion to consider all of the circumstances of the case. . . ." 24 CFR § 966.4(l) (5)(i) (2001). The agency made clear that local public housing authorities' discretion to evict for drug-related activity includes those situations in which "[the] tenant did not know, could not foresee, or could not control behavior by other occupants of the unit."

After OHA initiated the eviction proceedings in state court, respondents . . . challenged HUD's interpretation of the statute under the Administrative Procedure Act, arguing that 42 U.S.C. § 1437d(l)(6) does not require lease terms authorizing the eviction of so-called "innocent" tenants, and, in the alternative, that if it does, then the statute is unconstitutional. The District Court issued a preliminary injunction, enjoining OHA from "terminating the leases of tenants pursuant to paragraph 9(m) of the 'Tenant Lease' for drug-related criminal activity that does not occur within the tenant's apartment unit when the tenant did not know of and had no reason to know of, the drug-related criminal activity."

A panel of the Court of Appeals reversed, holding that § 1437d(l)(6) unambiguously permits the eviction of tenants who violate the lease provision, regardless of whether the tenant was personally aware of the drug activity, and that the statute is constitutional. An en banc panel of the Court of Appeals reversed and affirmed the District Court's grant of the preliminary injunction. That court held that HUD's interpretation permitting the eviction of so-called "innocent" tenants "is inconsistent with Congressional intent and must be rejected" under the first step of Chevron U.S.A. Inc. v. Natural Resources Defense Council, Inc., 467 U.S. 837, 842-843 (1984).

We granted certiorari and now reverse, holding that 42 U.S.C. § 1437d(l)(6) unambiguously requires lease terms that vest local public housing authorities with the discretion to evict tenants for the drug-related activity of household members and guests whether or not the tenant knew, or should have known, about the activity.

That this is so seems evident from the plain language of the statute. It provides that "[e]ach public housing agency shall utilize leases which . . . provide that . . . any drug-related criminal activity on or off such premises, engaged in by a public housing tenant, any member of the tenant's household, or any guest or other person under the tenant's control, shall be cause for termination of tenancy." The en banc Court of Appeals thought the statute did not address "the level of personal knowledge or fault that is required for eviction." Yet Congress' decision not to impose any qualification in the statute, combined with its use of the term "any" to modify "drug-related criminal activity," precludes any knowledge requirement. As we have explained, "the word 'any' has an expansive meaning, that is, 'one or some indiscriminately of whatever kind.'" Thus, *any* drug-related activity engaged in by the specified persons is grounds for termination, not just drug-related activity that the tenant knew, or should have known, about.

The en banc Court of Appeals also thought it possible that "under the tenant's control" modifies not just "other person," but also "member of the tenant's household" and "guest." The court ultimately adopted this reading, concluding that the statute prohibits eviction where the tenant, "for a lack of knowledge or other reason, could not realistically exercise control over the conduct of a household member or guest." But this interpretation runs counter to basic rules of grammar. The disjunctive "or" means that the qualification applies only to "other person." Indeed, the view that "under the tenant's control" modifies everything coming before it in the sentence would result in the nonsensical reading that the statute applies to "a public housing tenant . . . under the tenant's control." HUD offers a convincing explanation for the grammatical imperative that "under the tenant's control" modifies only "other person": "by 'control,' the statute means control in the sense that the tenant has permitted access to the premises." Implicit in the terms "household member" or "guest" is that access to the premises has been granted by the tenant. Thus, the plain language of § 1437d(l)(6) requires leases that grant public housing authorities the discretion to terminate tenancy without regard to the tenant's knowledge of the drug-related criminal activity.

Comparing § 1437d(l)(6) to a related statutory provision reinforces the unambiguous text. The civil forfeiture statute that makes all leasehold interests subject to forfeiture when used to commit drug-related criminal activities expressly exempts tenants who had no knowledge of the activity: "[N]o property shall be forfeited under this paragraph . . . by reason of any act or omission established by that owner to have been committed or omitted without the knowledge or consent of that owner." Because this forfeiture provision was amended in the same Anti-Drug Abuse Act of 1988 that created 42 U.S.C. § 1437d(l)(6), the en banc Court of Appeals thought Congress "meant them to be read consistently" so that the knowledge requirement should be read into the eviction provision. But the two sections deal with distinctly different matters. The "innocent owner" defense for drug forfeiture cases was already in existence prior to 1988 as part of 21 U.S.C. § 881(a)(7). All that Congress did in the 1988 Act was to add leasehold interests to the property interests that might be forfeited under the drug statute. And if such a forfeiture action were to be brought against a leasehold interest, it would be subject to the pre-existing "innocent owner" defense. But 42 U.S.C. § 1437(d)(l)(6), with which we deal here, is a quite different measure. It is entirely reasonable to think that the Government, when seeking to transfer private property to itself in a forfeiture proceeding, should be subject to an "innocent owner defense," while it should not be when acting as a landlord in a public housing project. The forfeiture provision shows that Congress knew exactly how to provide an "innocent owner" defense. It did not provide one in § 1437d(l)(6).

The en banc Court of Appeals next resorted to legislative history. The Court of Appeals correctly recognized that reference to legislative history is inappropriate when the text of the statute is unambiguous. Given that the en banc Court of Appeals' finding of textual ambiguity is wrong, there is no need to consult legislative history.

Nor was the en banc Court of Appeals correct in concluding that this plain reading of the statute leads to absurd results. The statute does not *require* the eviction of any tenant who violated the lease provision. Instead, it entrusts that decision to the local public housing authorities, who are in the best position to take account of, among other things, the degree to which the housing project suffers from "rampant drug-related or violent crime," "the seriousness of the offending action," and "the extent to which the leaseholder has . . . taken all reasonable steps to prevent or mitigate the offending action." It is not "absurd" that a local housing authority may sometimes evict a tenant who had no knowledge of the drug-related activity. Such "no-fault" eviction is a common "incident of tenant responsibility under normal landlord-tenant law and practice." Strict liability maximizes deterrence and eases enforcement difficulties.

And, of course, there is an obvious reason why Congress would have permitted local public housing authorities to conduct no-fault evictions: Regardless of knowledge, a tenant who "cannot control drug crime, or other criminal activities by a household member which threaten health or safety of other residents, is a threat to other residents and the project." With drugs leading to "murders, muggings, and other forms of violence against tenants," and to the "deterioration of the physical environment that requires substantial government expenditures," it was reasonable for Congress to permit no-fault evictions in order to "provide public and other federally assisted low-income housing that is decent, safe, and free from illegal drugs."

In another effort to avoid the plain meaning of the statute, the en banc Court of Appeals invoked the canon of constitutional avoidance. But that canon "has no application in the absence of statutory ambiguity." "Any other conclusion, while purporting to be an exercise in judicial restraint, would trench upon the legislative powers vested in Congress by Art. I, § 1, of the Constitution." There are, moreover, no "serious constitutional doubts" about Congress' affording local public housing authorities the discretion to conduct no-fault evictions for drug-related crime.

The en banc Court of Appeals held that HUD's interpretation "raise[s] serious questions under the Due Process Clause of the Fourteenth Amendment," because it permits "tenants to be deprived of their property interest without any relationship to individual wrongdoing." But both of [the cited] cases deal with the acts of government as sovereign. In *Scales*, the United States criminally charged the defendant with knowing membership in an organization that advocated the overthrow of the United States Government. In *Danaher*, an Arkansas statute forbade discrimination among customers of a telephone company. The situation in the present cases is entirely different. The government is not attempting to criminally punish or civilly regulate respondents as members of the general populace. It is instead acting as a landlord of property that it owns, invoking a clause in a lease to which respondents have agreed and which Congress has expressly required. *Scales* and *Danaher* cast no constitutional doubt on such actions.

The Court of Appeals sought to bolster its discussion of constitutional doubt by pointing to the fact that respondents have a property interest in their leasehold interest, citing Greene v. Lindsey, 456 U.S. 444 (1982). This is undoubtedly true, and *Greene* held that an effort to deprive a tenant of such a right without proper notice violated the Due Process Clause of the Fourteenth Amendment. But, in the present cases, such deprivation will occur in the state court where OHA brought the unlawful detainer action against respondents. There is no indication that notice has not been given by OHA in the past, or that it will not be given in the future. Any individual factual disputes about whether the lease provision was actually violated can, of course, be resolved in these proceedings.

We hold that "Congress has directly spoken to the precise question at issue." Chevron U.S.A. Inc. v. Natural Resources Defense Council, Inc., 467 U.S., at 842. Section 1437d(*l*)(6) requires lease terms that give local public housing authorities the discretion to terminate the lease of a tenant when a member of the household or a guest engages in drug-related activity, regardless of whether the tenant knew, or should have known, of the drug-related activity.

NOTES AND QUESTIONS

1. Do you agree with the Court that the statutory language is clear? If the subject of the statute had been something other than public housing (e.g., the loss of the mortgage interest deduction if a household member or guest were convicted of securities, drug, or other criminal activity), might the case have come out differently? Are there legitimate reasons for a distinction?
2. Some legal services offices have a policy of not representing tenants in eviction cases where the allegations involve the use, possession, or distribution of illegal drugs. What would you imagine are the rationales for such a policy? Would you support such a policy? Why or why not? Does it matter to you whether the office is publicly or privately funded?
3. In addition to controlling rent levels, most rent control ordinances also include "eviction control" provisions, requiring that a landlord have good cause before terminating a tenancy and evicting a tenant. Should tenants generally be entitled to "good cause" protections, or should landlords be able to evict tenants for no cause? What legal arguments are persuasive on each side?

CHAPTER
7

Health

INTRODUCTION

This textbook is being written during exciting times when it comes to health care and poverty. President Obama's signature legislative victory of his first term, the Affordable Care Act (ACA), will dramatically increase health care coverage for low-income Americans when it is fully adopted. Though his Republican challenger in the 2012 election cycle, Mitt Romney, who helped develop the state-level health care plan in Massachusetts that served as the precursor to the ACA, vowed to repeal "Obamacare" if elected, Obama's reelection ensured that the ACA would be implemented in 2014. In part because this is a period of transition and in part because of the importance of understanding the programs as they existed prior to the enactment of the ACA, this chapter includes an in-depth presentation of Medicaid eligibility and program characteristics.

As the passage of the ACA underscores, antipoverty advocacy can take the form of health care advocacy. Not only do the poor have worse health outcomes and suffer more health problems compared to the non-poor, but the health care system in the United States also has significant coverage gaps relative to the more universal forms of coverage common in other developed countries. Upon full implementation of the ACA, some of these gaps will close, particularly those affecting poor working-age adults, but despite the controversy surrounding it, the ACA falls short of creating a *right* to health care. This chapter focuses on programs that provide access to health care, but it is important that this focus not obscure the overwhelming importance of environmental conditions affecting the health of poor people. "[T]he conditions in which people are born, grow, live, work, and age play a greater role in health disparities than access to health insurance and health care, which are important pathways to reducing health disparities but do not address the root causes of illness." Wendy E. Parmet et al., *Social Determinants, Health Disparities and the Role of Law*, in *Poverty, Health, and Law: Readings and Cases for Medical-Legal Partnership* (Elizabeth Tobin Tyler et al. eds., 2011).

This chapter begins, in Part A, by presenting some of the disparities related to race and poverty that plague U.S. health care. But in light of the role of environmental conditions, this chapter is best understood as being closely connected to the other chapters describing the ways in which poor people live and work. Poor housing conditions lead to greater susceptibility to illness, even decreased nutritional status relative to households receiving housing subsidies. Low-wage work is often physically demanding and dangerous, increased education is associated with better health outcomes, the earned income tax credit is linked to improved health of pregnant mothers and of newborns, and so on. A recent comprehensive report published by the National Academy of Sciences notes that health determinants reflect both public- and private-sector policies: "Decisions made by government officials, business leaders, voters, and other stakeholders affect access to health care, the location of supermarkets, school lunch menus, crime rates, public transportation, toxic waste sites, employment opportunities, and the quality of schools." Nat'l Research Council & Inst. of Med., *U.S. Health in International Perspective: Shorter Lives, Poorer Health* (2013). A comprehensive approach to health-related antipoverty advocacy consequently is multifaceted and involves working to improve both environmental conditions and access to health care. Indeed, because of society's relatively high level of attention to health, framing arguments in terms of health outcomes may be a way to garner support for improvements in other areas that struggle for public support.

As this chapter will show, the United States is an outlier relative to the rest of the developed world, both in how much of its health care system costs and in the partial nature of the health care coverage for the poor. Part B situates U.S. spending on health care in a global context, discusses the role insurance plays in the market for health care, and draws out the relationship between insurance coverage and health. Part C is the bulk of chapter. Proceeding chronologically through government health programs, it starts with Medicaid and the State Children's Health Insurance Program (SCHIP), and, to a lesser extent, Medicare, and ends with the ACA. But before moving to programs that help provide the poor access to the U.S. health care system, the chapter begins with an overview of the relationship between social conditions and health.

A. HEALTH DISPARITIES

In a 1993 article, Amartya Sen highlighted the work of Colin McCord and Harold P. Freeman, who showed "that black men in Harlem are less likely to reach the age of 65 than are men in Bangladesh. In fact, Harlem men fall behind Bangladeshi men in terms of survival rates by the age of 40." Amartya Sen, *The Economics of Life and Death*, Scientific American (May 1993). Though the McCord-Freeman study was based on data from 1980, a subsequent study based on 1990 data concluded that the mortality outcomes for Black youths in high-poverty urban areas were even worse. Arline Geronimus et al., *Excess Black Mortality in the United States and in Selected Black and White High-Poverty Areas, 1980-2000*, 101 Am. J. Pub. Health 720 (2011). The most recent study, published in 2011, found that declines in the homicide-related deaths from 1990 to 2000 did lower the mortality rate for urban Black men to levels below those found for 1980. *Id.* Less positively, the ratio of Black to White mortality rates remained roughly the same as it was in 1980 because, despite the reduction in homicide, improvements in health among White men and women outpaced mortality improvements among Blacks for the same period. *Id.*

Health disparities are not limited to mortality rates and cannot be explained simply in terms of individual risk factors. As reported in Wendy E. Parmet et al., *supra*, health disparities seem to reflect relative social position:

> A growing body of research in the latter half of the twentieth and early twenty-first century has provided a "more precise definition of both the physical dimensions of the environment that are toxic to health as well as conditions in the social environment, such as social exclusion, racism, educational achievement and opportunities to advance in the workplace, that shape behavior and access to resources that promote health." Seminal work in the field includes the Whitehall studies, launched in Britain in 1967, which revealed differences in the disease prevalence and mortality rates of British civil servants according to their grade levels. Such studies uncovered "social gradients" in health and revealed that "the overall structure of hierarchy somehow has a significant effect on health, over and above the general issue of whether people are suffering from material deprivation."
>
> For example, Whitehall I (1967-77) showed that the coronary heart disease (CHD) mortality of men in the lowest civil service grade was 3.6 times higher than men in the highest grade; adjusting for health and lifestyle factors did not obviate the strong "inverse association between grade of employment and CHD mortality," leading researchers to conclude that established risk factors only partly explain the higher mortality of working-class men in the study and in national statistics.

Health disparities, according to this line of research, cannot be limited simply to behavioral differences that make poor people different. Very much in line with the Whitehall studies, a 2013 NAS report on U.S. health outcomes noted the importance of social factors, including relative position in society:

> Extensive evidence documents the association between income and mortality. Unhealthy behaviors, such as smoking, tend to be more prevalent among low-income groups. Income or wealth enables one to afford a nutritious diet, to buy or rent healthy housing in a healthy neighborhood, and to engage in regular exercise (e.g., through gym membership or living where it is safe and pleasant to exercise outdoors). However, careful analysis of longitudinal data has revealed that the association between adverse economic conditions and mortality persists even after adjusting for unhealthy behaviors, suggesting that economic stresses may also affect health through other pathways.

Nat'l Research Council & Inst. of Med., *U.S. Health in International Perspective: Shorter Lives, Poorer Health* (2013).

The mechanisms by which low socioeconomic status (SES) translates into poor health vary according to the health outcome being considered. For example, when it comes to cancer, "[t]obacco use, suboptimal diet, and physical inactivity, all of which increase cancer risk, are more prevalent among low SES individuals. Low income neighborhoods are often characterized by less access to fresh fruits and vegetables, fewer opportunities for exercise compared to high income neighborhoods and heavy tobacco marketing. . . ." Howard K. Koh et al., *Poverty, Socioeconomic Position, and Cancer Disparities: Global Challenges and Opportunities*, 15 Geo. J. on Poverty L. & Pol'y 663 (2008). Poverty not only increases cancer risk, it also makes cancer more deadly; one study reported that "high-income counties had a ten percentage point higher survival rate than low-income counties." *Id.*

Though the association between poverty and poor health outcomes in the United States and globally is known, "the specific mechanisms by which low socioeconomic status . . . of individuals — or . . . [a] greater degree of income inequality within a society — exerts its harmful effects" is not fully known. Chris Feudtner & Kathleen G. Noonan, *Poorer Health: The Persistent and Protean Connections Between Poverty, Social Inequality, and Child Well-Being*, 163 Archives of Pediatrics & Adolescent Med. 668 (2009). Feudtner and Noonan go on to highlight what is known about this association and the overriding significance of environmental factors:

> Broadly speaking . . . , poverty can wreak havoc on one's health either by the poor material conditions in which one lives (such as having inadequate nutrition or unsafe housing) or by diminishing one's degree of social engagement and control over one's life. These two primary mechanisms can have direct effects on health: one can cite as examples how the poor material conditions of poverty increase exposure to lead and subsequently harm children's cognitive function or how the diminished levels of social engagement and control that result from poverty exacerbate maternal depression and thereby influence behavioral outcomes in young children. The two mechanisms can also combine and have more indirect effects on health through biological mechanisms (such as poverty begetting chronic stress, in turn affecting basal cortisol levels or diminishing working memory) or a complex process of socialization, whereby people in certain similar social and economic circumstances tend to shape their behavior and expectations in similar ways, including their health-related behaviors (such as cigarette smoking or sedentary lifestyle), their degree of psychological vulnerability or resilience, the skills they learn to facilitate social participation and support, and whether they incline to a future time perspective (which places value on future goals, considers long-term consequences, and has implications for the types of health-relevant choices people make). . . .
>
> We as health care providers likely also have to come to grips with the facts that health care is not the most important determinant of health and that improving access to health care, while an important undertaking for reasons of social equity and a necessary prerequisite for ethical efforts to constrain health care expenditures, may do little to reduce the SES-health gradient. Universal access will not by itself translate into universal health; instead, social support programs may be far more important.

* * *

Though it is beyond the scope of this chapter to present the full details of the nature of the relationship between poverty and health, the excerpt that follows presents additional information on this relationship and on the ways in which poverty affects health.

WENDY E. PARMET ET AL., *SOCIAL DETERMINANTS, HEALTH DISPARITIES AND THE ROLE OF LAW*, IN *POVERTY, HEALTH AND LAW: READINGS AND CASES FOR MEDICAL-LEGAL PARTNERSHIP* (ELIZABETH TOBIN TYLER ET AL. EDS., 2011)

RACIAL AND ETHNIC HEALTH DISPARITIES

As discussed earlier, studies confirm a social gradient in health outcomes — people with higher socioeconomic status . . . have better health outcomes than people with lower SES. The relationship among SES, race or ethnicity and health status are [*sic*] not easy for researchers and policy makers to untangle. Some disparities that were once thought to be race-based today have been shown to be better understood as SES-based. As Paula Braveman and colleagues note:

> Without adequate socioeconomic information, racial or ethnic differences in health may be interpreted, implicitly if not explicitly, as reflecting genetic or entrenched "cultural" differences that are unlikely to be influenced by policy. In fact, modifiable social factors shaped by income, education, wealth, and childhood and neighborhood socioeconomic conditions, which vary systematically by race or ethnic group, are likely to be more important in explaining health differences by race or ethnicity.

In recent years, careful attention has been paid by the research community to these issues; although certain disparities that once were deemed to be race-based are now more correctly understood as SES-based, racial and ethnic disparities in health persist. . . .

The reasons for persistent racial and ethnic health disparities are not well understood. Some posit that they may be due to the "adverse health effects of more concentrated disadvantage . . . or a range of experiences related to racial bias that are not captured in [routine SES studies]." Some of the social factors that may contribute to racial and ethnic health disparities are discussed shortly.

RESIDENTIAL RACIAL SEGREGATION

The concentration of racial groups in specific neighborhoods as a result of residential segregation means that the social conditions in those communities impact racial differences in health. Thus, "race is a marker for differential exposure to multiple disease-producing social factors," with racially unequal patterns in exposure to societal risks and resources forming a critical component of racial disparities in health.

Area-based differences in SES "are likely an important contributor to the residual effects of race after adjustment for individual and household level indicators of SES. These differences in neighborhood quality are driven by residential segregation by race — a neglected but enduring legacy of institutional racism in the United States." Health and development impacts arising from this legacy are irrefutable. One study found that 76 percent of black children and 69 percent of Latino children live under worse conditions than the worst-off white children in one hundred U.S. metropolitan areas. An assessment of the 171 largest cities "reported that there was not even one city where blacks lived under similar ecological conditions to those of whites in terms of concentrated poverty and female headed households."

Pathways Through Which Concentrated Poverty Arising from Segregation Adversely Affects Health

1. Limiting socioeconomic mobility by limiting access to high-quality education and employment
2. Creating conditions in which practicing healthy behaviors is more challenging[:] limited availability of affordable, healthy foods and opportunities for exercise, greater exposure to tobacco and alcohol advertising
3. Heightening exposure to economic hardship and other stressors, including neighborhood disorder, crime, community violence and incarceration, that affect individuals, communities, and neighborhoods
4. Adversely affecting interpersonal relationships and trust among neighbors due to weakened community and neighborhood infrastructure
5. Increasing exposure to environmental toxins, poor-quality housing, and criminal victimization due to institutional neglect and disinvestment
6. Limiting access to medical care and the quality of health services received

GENERATIONAL EXPOSURE AND DISCRIMINATION

Additionally, the early onset of disease for minorities measured across SES, and the accumulation of exposures over the life course and across generations affect current health status. As noted earlier, evidence increasingly suggests that "psychological, social, and economic adversity in childhood can have long-term consequences for health" for all races. However, given that more blacks and other minorities live in poorer quality environments than do whites, these groups suffer in a greater proportion from these risks. Studies are beginning to document the multigenerational impact of environmental contaminants and stressors. For example, prenatal exposure to pollutants has been linked to neurodevelopmental impacts well into childhood. . . .

Additionally, studies have begun to measure the impact of racism and discrimination on health. Nancy Krieger and colleagues have documented associations between self-reported experiences of racial discrimination and poor health outcomes; for example, associations between self-reported experiences of racial discrimination and preterm and low-birth-weight deliveries among black women. It is possible that discrimination (or perceptions thereof) play an influential role in disparities measured among minorities who have achieved middle-class SES. . . .

How the Social Becomes Biologic

SOCIAL ENVIRONMENT AND STRESS

In the past few years researchers have developed a better understanding of the effect of social environment in producing stress and, in turn, the effect of this stress on longterm health outcomes. "Stress responses" are specific physiological expressions that impact brain circuitry and other health factors. The scientific community is increasingly uncovering evidence of specific changes to brain structure — including in areas that help us respond to stress — as a result of chronic stress and documenting stress effects on child development and subsequent adult health.

The Effects of Toxic Stress on Brain Development in Early Childhood

The ability to manage stress is controlled by brain circuits and hormone systems that are activated early in life. When a child feels threatened, hormones are released and circulate throughout the body. Prolonged exposure to stress hormones can impact the brain and impair functioning in a variety of ways.

- Toxic stress can impair the connection of brain circuits and, in the extreme, result in the development of a smaller brain.
- Brain circuits are especially vulnerable as they are developing during early childhood. Toxic stress can disrupt the development of these circuits. This can cause an individual to develop a low threshold for stress, [and to] thereby becom[e] overly reactive to adverse experiences throughout life.
- High levels of stress hormones, including cortisol, can suppress the body's immune response. This can leave an individual vulnerable to a variety of infections and chronic health problems.
- Sustained high levels of cortisol can damage the hippocampus, an area of the brain responsible for learning and memory. These cognitive deficits can continue into adulthood.

The "physiological expression of the stress response system" occurring in the context of stable, protective relationships can be a normal[] and necessary part of healthy development (positive stress) or have no lasting impact (tolerable stress). But children who have stress response from "frequent or sustained adverse experiences such as extreme poverty, physical or emotional abuse, chronic neglect, maternal depression, parental substance abuse, and exposure to violence, without the buffer of adult support" experience harm (toxic stress).

The Adverse Childhood Experiences (ACE) study by the CDC and Kaiser Permanente found among 17,000 adults that "exposure to ACE showed a strong, graded relationship with conditions and outcomes including ischemic heart disease, cancer, chronic lung disease, depression, alcoholism, illicit drug use, sexually transmitted diseases, suicide attempts, smoking, and premature death." Children of lower SES have greater likelihood of experiencing toxic stress, and research examining underlying physiological responses (salivary cortisol levels, for example) show children of lower SES have higher levels of this stress indicator on a daily basis than children of higher SES.

Stress in adulthood has a negative health effect. Research shows that the experience of environmental conditions, work stressors, discrimination, and chronic poverty can impact adult health. Higher stress reactivity—a predictor of adult mood and anxiety disorders—is associated with lower SES childhood environments with high conflict and adversity. . . .

ACCESS TO AN ADEQUATE SUPPLY OF AFFORDABLE, HEALTHY FOOD

Good nutrition promotes the healthy development of a child's body and mind and impacts the health status of adults. A family's ability to afford and purchase healthy foods has multiple effects on a child's health, growth and development even before conception. Examination of families' levels of food insecurity, defined as not having access at all times to enough food for an active healthy life, show that poor children are five times more likely to experience food insecurity and hunger and have significantly lower intake of calories, iron, folate, and other nutrients, compared with nonpoor children. Among food-insecure families with children, half reported that they were sometimes not able to feed their children balanced meals, and 25 percent reported that their children did not have enough to eat.

There is substantial evidence indicating that food insecurity poses a substantial threat to child health and well-being, which in turn may have lifelong implications for an individual's health and ability to work, play, and achieve. A nutritionally inadequate diet makes children susceptible to an "infection-malnutrition cycle" by impairing their immune function. An inadequate food supply prevents children from fully recovering from weight loss or interrupted growth during illness episodes, leading to poor nutritional status that puts them at risk for a subsequent illness, creating a cycle of poor growth and increased risk of illness.

Food insecurity also has a pernicious effect on the health of adults, especially those with chronic disease or advancing age. In families, a "child preference" "at lower levels of food insecurity [may cause] adult caregivers [to sacrifice] their own food consumption to maintain adequate levels for their children." People with chronic illnesses, such as hypertension and diabetes, may struggle to manage their disease; poor self-management increases their risk and rate of complications, in turn increasing morbidity and mortality. Elders who are food insecure have poor overall health status and compromised ability to resist infections, experience deteriorating mental and physical health, show a greater incidence of hospitalizations and extended hospital stays and place increasing care giving demands on their families. Some studies have found an association between very-low food security and lower cognitive performance, although causality requires further study.

Adverse Health Effects of Food Insecurity

Food-insecure children:

- Are two to three times more likely to be in fair or poor health or chronically ill
- Are 30 percent more likely to be hospitalized by age three years
- Are more likely to show poor growth
- Score lower on measures of physical and psychosocial functioning
- Have deficits in cognitive and behavioral development that affect school performance

Food-insecure adults more frequently:

- Report poorer health status
- Score significantly lower on measures of physical and mental health
- Have greater likelihood of hypoglycemia if diabetic
- Have compromised health status if elderly

In addition to the relationship between food insecurity and poor health outcomes, there is a relationship between availability of healthy food and poor health outcomes. In recent years, researchers have increasingly focused on disparities in populations' access to healthy foods. Researchers have documented the "food deserts" of many low-income communities, where affordable, healthful food is not available. One influential report, "The Grocery Gap," reports that although 31 percent of whites live in a census tract with a grocery store, only 8 percent of African Americans do. Twenty percent of rural U.S. counties are food desert counties where all residents live more than ten miles from a supermarket or supercenter.

There are well-established relationships between healthy food access and health: "residents who live near supermarkets or in areas where food markets selling fresh produce (supermarkets, grocery stores, farmers' markets, etc.) outnumber food stores that generally do not (such as corner stores) have lower rates of diet-related diseases than their counterparts in neighborhoods lacking food access." There are also substantial data documenting the increased density of fast-food restaurants, which are known to offer food that is higher in fat, sodium, and calories, in low-income and minority neighborhoods. . . .

HOUSING AFFORDABILITY AND SAFETY

Housing costs are usually the largest portion of household budgets and are usually paid first, limiting income available for other expenses such as food, clothing, health care, utilities, or transportation. Although housing is considered affordable if a family spends less than 30 percent of their income on it, half of low-income working families with children spend more than half of their income on rent. Families facing high housing costs combined with limited income experience "shelter poverty," which means they cannot adequately meet their other needs after paying for housing.

Confronted with unaffordable housing, families make budget trade-offs between housing and important basic needs. A 2005 national study of housing costs indicated that low-income families who pay more than 50 percent of their income for housing spend: 30 percent less on food, 70 percent less on health care, and 70 percent less on transportation. Trade-offs resulting in food insecurity are particularly important for children's health and well-being. "Rent or eat" is a well-documented dilemma. Children whose families are eligible for but not receiving rent subsidies are up to eight times more likely to demonstrate malnutrition and stunted growth.

Physical housing conditions have been associated with many common chronic diseases in children and adults. The most common of these are asthma, lead poisoning and unintentional injuries. The American Housing Survey conducted by the Department of Housing and Urban Development has found that rodent and cockroach infestation, lack of heat during the winter, leaks and related mold, uncovered radiators, peeling paint and lead paint, exposed wires, holes in walls, and lack of running water in [the] past three months increase the risk of asthma, injuries, lead poisoning, and infectious diseases.

The lack of affordable housing is one of multiple factors that can lead to housing instability and homelessness. Homeless families experience overcrowding, often with entire families living in one room; inadequate food preparation and storage facilities; unsanitary conditions; sleep deprivation; lack of transportation to get to school, work, and healthcare appointments; and social and geographic isolation. Both homeless families and those in unsanitary conditions have higher exposure to allergens that cause or exacerbate asthma, such as cockroach and rodent infestations, dust mites, inadequate heat, excess moisture, poor ventilation, and mold. Medical management of asthma or other health conditions may be more difficult for homeless than housed families due to inability to purchase and/or store medications as well as limited access to electricity and refrigeration. . . .

UNCOUPLING THE SOCIAL FROM THE BIOLOGIC: LOOKING FOR THE PUMP HANDLE
The primary task of uncoupling social factors from their adverse health outcomes is related to changing the social contexts in which people live, work, and play. At the population level, it can be very difficult to make healthy choices when the constraints of the environment tend to promote less healthy choices. For example, a study of cardiovascular health and diet documented racial differences in access to supermarkets—blacks had decreased access to healthy food, with only 8 percent living close to a supermarket. Even more important, the differential access to grocery stores had a dramatic effect on whether study participants met the recommended dietary guidelines, including eating more fruits and vegetables and less saturated and total fat.

Most physicians who counsel their patients on dietary interventions to manage chronic disease, such as hypertension, elevated cholesterol, coronary artery disease, or diabetes, would not consider the proximity of their patients to grocery stores. Yet without access to affordable, healthy food, patients who want to follow the sound advice offered by clinicians will not be able to do so. At the same time that low-income and minority populations experience decreased access to healthy nutrition options, they have increased exposure to unhealthy ones. Fast-food restaurant density is related to both race and income with increased density in minority and low-income neighborhoods. In a recent study, predominantly black neighborhoods had up to six times more fast food restaurants. A recently published Massachusetts report on childhood body mass index by town showed a striking correlation between a biologic condition, obesity and overweight, and a social factor, median household income. Those towns with lower median household income had significantly higher rates of childhood obesity and overweight. This suggests that income-associated differences in social context are at play, including easy access to affordable, healthy food and safe opportunities for physical activity.

Influences may be the result of restrictive policies, lack of services or facilities, or collective decision making that limits individual choices, but may also arise from contextual cues within an environment, such as fast-food and tobacco advertising or the opinions of peers. Such cues and influences exist in all social strata but with different messages and pressures—differences that may partially explain behavior variations among groups.

Although healthcare has a critical role in avoiding or mitigating adverse health outcomes once individuals have already experienced social health risks, public health advocacy can prevent exposure to those risks in the first place. There is a strong tradition in public health for primary prevention from exposure to or experience of risk. An often cited example is that of John Snow, who during a cholera outbreak in London in 1854 removed a pump handle from a water supply he suspected was the source of the illness.

By preventing access to the contaminated water, he averted subsequent deaths. Snow's elegantly simple intervention illustrates the power of changing the social context to promote health. . . .

A focus on primary prevention and influencing the social context is also at work in the Health Impact Pyramid introduced in 2010 by Thomas R. Frieden after he assumed leadership of the CDC. He makes the case for the importance of working on issues that will change the context of individual decision making so that healthier choices become easier, sometimes "default" choices. This approach does not eliminate individual responsibility for behavior, but it recognizes that people develop preferences and make choices in contexts that can be more or less supportive of healthier choices. Changing contexts may be more cost-effective and yield more sustainable population-level changes than efforts focusing on individual behavioral change through counseling and education or clinical intervention alone. . . .

NOTES AND QUESTIONS

1. Although life expectancy has risen in the developed countries, a 2012 study notes that "beneath the surface of national vital statistics is an alarming persistent divide among subgroups within the United States." S. Jay Olshansky et al., *Differences in Life Expectancy Due to Race and Educational Differences Are Widening, and Many May Not Catch Up*, 31 Health Aff. 1803 (2012). The authors conclude that given the significant differences in life expectancy along race and class lines, there are "two Americas" in terms of health. *Id.* For more on the federal government's increasing attention to racial and gendered health disparities, see Lisa C. Ikemoto, *In the Shadow of Race: Women of Color in Health Disparities Policy*, 39 U.C. Davis L. Rev. 1023 (2006).

B. HEALTH INSURANCE

The place of individual poor people and families in the U.S. health care system depends on eligibility standards for government-based insurance programs and on the availability of health professionals who are willing to participate in such programs. The overall health care market is designed around private, often employment-based, insurance coverage, and government medical support for poor people generally piggybacks on this structure. A central characteristic of health insurance coverage is the creation of risk pools. As in other forms of insurance, the cost of being insured is directly related to the nature and size of the pool. It would be very expensive to insure a group of people who have all been diagnosed with cancer. On the other hand, it is much less risky to insure a pool of young adults because they would tend to have lower health expenses. The private insurance market attempts to mitigate the problem of adverse selection and the danger that individuals with unusually high health care expenses will swamp insurer resources by creating large pools and grouping those pools according to nonmedical characteristics, such as place of employment.

Generally, the categories of poor people covered by federal health insurance have reflected evolving understandings of need and of government's reach. But by attempting to ensure that all, or at least most, Americans have health coverage, the ACA breaks from the distinctions—familiar from earlier chapters of this book—between deserving and undeserving poor when it comes to coverage. The challenge presented by a guarantee that individuals can rely on the government as the insurer of last resort is that it incentivizes people to not pay for or concern themselves with insurance until it is needed, in other words, when they get sick. Such an insurance scheme would not benefit from the cross-subsidization that occurs when people with lower health risks participate in pools that also insure those more likely to need care. As will be discussed later in the chapter, the solution to this problem in the ACA is an individual mandate that everyone purchase health insurance, that is, that everyone join an insurance pool.

But before turning to government health programs it is worth situating the U.S. health care system in a global context. The United States is an outlier among developed nations when it comes to health care spending. According to the World Health Organization, the United States spends more on health care as a percentage of the GDP, 18 percent, than any other Organization for Economic Co-operation and Development (OECD) country. That corresponds with $2.584 trillion in overall spending. Indeed, in 2010, no other OECD country had a total health expenditure relative to GDP above 12 percent. U.S. spending on health care per capita, at more than $8,300 (using a purchasing power parity calculation), exceeded all other nations in the world in 2010. Despite such relatively high spending on health care, U.S. life expectancy at birth in 2009 left the United States in a six-way tie—with Chile, Costa Rica, Denmark, Portugal, and Slovenia—for twenty-ninth place. First-place finisher Japan had a four-year advantage over the United States. The United States also has the highest prevalence of both obesity and diabetes according to a 2013 report. Nat'l Research Council & Inst. of Med., *U.S. Health in International Perspective: Shorter Lives, Poorer Health* (2013). Perhaps not surprisingly then, the 2000 World Health Report ranked the overall performance of the United States' health system as thirty-seventh in the world. Although the World Health Organization has not come out with a similar list since 2000, other organizations report similar results. The findings of the 2011 National Scorecard on U.S. Health System Performance, produced by the Commonwealth Fund, are worth quoting at length:

> [T]he U.S. failed to keep pace with gains in health outcomes achieved by the leading countries. The U.S. ranks last out of 16 industrialized countries on a measure of mortality amenable to medical care (deaths that might have been prevented with timely and effective care), with premature death rates that are 68 percent higher than in the best-performing countries. As many as 91,000 fewer people would die prematurely if the U.S. could achieve the leading country rate.
>
> Sharply rising costs are putting both access and budgets at risk. Health care spending per person in the U.S. is double that in several other major industrialized countries, and costs in the U.S. continue to rise faster than income. We are headed toward spending $1 of every $5 of national income on health care. We should expect a better return on this investment. . . .
>
> Overall, the *National Scorecard on U.S. Health System Performance, 2011* finds that the United States is losing ground in the effort to ensure affordable access to health care. Although there are promising improvements on key indicators, quality

of care remains uneven. The Scorecard also finds broad evidence of inefficient and inequitable care. Other advanced countries are outpacing the U.S. in providing timely access to primary care, reducing premature mortality, and extending healthy life expectancy, all while spending considerably less on health care and administration. . . .

Part of the explanation for the poor performance of the U.S. health system relative to other developed countries can be found in coverage gaps in the United States. Among developed countries, universal coverage is the norm. "Canada's national health insurance program," for example, "is designed to ensure that all residents have reasonable access to medically necessary hospital and physician services, on a prepaid basis." *Canada's Health Care System (Medicare)*, Health Canada, http://www.hc-sc.gc.ca/hcs-sss/medi-assur/index-eng .php. Indeed, the "United States is the only developed country without some form of universal health care coverage." Timothy Stoltzfus Jost, *Comparative and International Health Law*, 14 Health Matrix 141, 144 (2004).

According to the U.S. Census Bureau, 15.7 percent of people in the United States did not have health insurance in 2011. Carmen DeNavas-Walt et al., *U.S. Census Bureau, Income, Poverty, and Health Insurance Coverage in the United States: 2011* (2012). In the same year, 9.4 percent of children were without coverage, a figure that rose to 13.8 percent for children in poverty and 29.2 percent for noncitizen children. Among the insured, 63.9 percent of people were covered by private health insurance and 55.1 percent of people had employment-based coverage. Further, 32.2 percent of people have some form of government insurance: 15.2 percent have Medicare coverage, 16.5 percent have Medicaid coverage, and 4.4 percent are covered by military health care. Because some people have multiple forms of coverage, there is overlap in the figures for government and private insurance, but 20.4 percent of people are insured by a government plan alone. Not surprisingly, being uninsured closely tracks household income, as Figure 7.1 from the same report illustrates.

The dual-track U.S. health care system is built upon employment-based coverage and government coverage. The federal government supports both tracks. Employment-based insurance is partly paid for by the federal government through tax expenditures, which tend to attract less attention politically than

Figure 7.1
Uninsured Rate by Real Household Income, 1999-2011

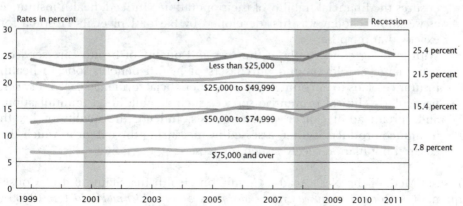

fiscal expenditures but have the same budgetary effect. Since this is the type of insurance coverage enjoyed by working professionals, the government contribution to this form of health coverage is more hidden than the directly funded programs that serve other populations. The Bipartisan Policy Center explains:

> Under current law, employer contributions to employee health benefits are tax deductible as business expenses to the employer and are excluded from an employee's taxable income. Additionally, most employees — 54 percent of workers in firms with under 200 employees and over 90 percent of workers in larger firms — are permitted to use pre-tax income to pay for their employer-sponsored health insurance (ESI) premium contributions.
>
> The employer-sponsored health insurance tax exclusion allows employers to offer generous health plan benefits at a lower net cost. For example, consider a worker earning $50,000. She pays a marginal rate of 25 percent in federal income taxes, 6.3 percent (on average) in state income taxes if she lives in a state with an income tax, and, in effect, a combined (employee and employer) payroll tax of 12.4 percent for Social Security and 2.9 percent for Medicare. If her total ESI plan premium is $10,000, the exclusion saves her $4,660, or 46.6 percent of the total cost, in taxes. Therefore, her after-tax cost of health insurance is only $5,340. This heavy subsidization of ESI can make additional health insurance benefits more valuable to many workers than additional cash compensation.
>
> Moreover, the ESI tax exclusion is regressive in the sense that it generally subsidizes individuals at higher incomes more than individuals at lower incomes. The ESI tax exclusion represents a total of about $250 billion in annual revenue loss to the U.S. Treasury.

Loren Adler et al., Bipartisan Policy Ctr., *What Is Driving U.S. Health Care Spending? America's Unsustainable Health Care Cost Growth* (2012).

Health insurance does more than just help secure access to health care; it also helps pool risk and payments. For insurance companies, of course, the profit motive is paramount. But the risk pooling and care management aspects of health insurance also arguably serve other functions as well. According to a 2009 report:

- For consumers, health insurance often serves two purposes: (1) it provides a gateway to affordable health care through preferential pricing of health care services and (2) it offers financial protection from unexpected health care costs.
- For clinicians, hospitals, and other health providers, health insurance ensures the financial stability of their operations. Indeed, health insurance as we know it today was first developed by Baylor University Hospital for exactly that purpose.
- With growing concern about the cost and quality of health care services, many large employers and purchasers of health benefits look to health insurance plans to encourage the use of beneficial, evidence-based services, particularly clinical preventive services such as childhood immunizations and certain adult cancer screening tests. Indeed, the quality of health insurance products is often assessed by measuring the extent to which the covered population receives such services.

Inst. of Med. of the Nat'l Acads., Comm. on Health Ins. Status and Its Consequences, *America's Uninsured Crisis: Consequences for Health and Health Care* (2009).

Unfortunately, the employment-based system of private health care coverage does not reach all people in the United States, especially the poor. In 2009 the National Academy of Sciences published a comprehensive study, *America's Uninsured Crisis*, exploring health insurance coverage or lack thereof. Though this excerpt describes the state of the nation's housing prior to full implementation of the ACA, it also highlights the health consequences of being uninsured.

INST. OF MED. OF THE NAT'L ACADS., COMM. ON HEALTH INS. STATUS AND ITS CONSEQUENCES, *AMERICA'S UNINSURED CRISIS: CONSEQUENCES FOR HEALTH AND HEALTH CARE* (2009)

Some issues, like the problems of the uninsured in the United States, are with us for so long that we end up adapting to them as a seemingly inevitable chronic condition of our health care system. We become inured to another annual report on the number of people without health insurance coverage, and another report on the consequences — consequences that are often obscured for many of us and easiest to ignore. And we become cynical about yet another set of recommendations, and another debate on what to do.

That cycle must be broken. The lack of health insurance coverage for tens of millions of Americans cannot be ignored and should not be a chronic underpinning of American health care — it is in fact treatable and indeed preventable. . . .

KEY FINDINGS ON TRENDS IN HEALTH INSURANCE COVERAGE

Health insurance coverage has declined over the last decade despite increases in public program coverage and will continue to decline. There is no evidence to suggest that the trends driving loss of insurance coverage will reverse without concerted action. High and rising health care costs threaten not only employer sponsored coverage, but also recent expansions in public coverage.

PRIVATE HEALTH INSURANCE

- The rising cost of health care is driving the decline in private health insurance coverage. Health care costs and insurance premiums are growing substantially faster than the economy and family incomes.
- As the costs of health care increase, the importance and value of coverage increases for individuals, while at the same time it becomes less affordable.
- Employment has shifted away from industries with traditionally high rates of coverage to jobs with historically lower rates of coverage. In some industries, employers have relied more heavily on jobs without health benefits, such as part-time and shorter-term employment and contract and temporary jobs.
- Fewer workers, particularly among those with lower wages, are being offered employer-sponsored coverage and fewer among them can afford the premiums. And, early retirees are less likely to be offered retiree health insurance benefits than in the past.

NONGROUP INSURANCE

- For many without employer-sponsored group coverage, nongroup health insurance coverage is prohibitively expensive or unavailable.
  - Access to nongroup coverage is highly dependent on individual circumstances and geographic location.
  - People with preexisting health conditions who lose employer-sponsored insurance face significant barriers to coverage, including unaffordable premiums.

PUBLIC HEALTH INSURANCE

- Long-term fiscal pressures on the federal budget threaten to undermine bedrock state and federal health care programs.
- With a severely weakened economy and rising health care costs, some states will not be able to sustain their recent expansions of public programs for low-income children and adults.
- Increases in unemployment will further fuel the decline in the number of people with employer-sponsored coverage and put additional stress on state Medicaid and SCHIP programs. . . .

Children benefit considerably from health insurance, as demonstrated by recent evaluations of enrollment in Medicaid and SCHIP programs:

- When previously uninsured children acquire insurance, their access to health care services, including ambulatory care, preventive health care (e.g., immunizations), prescription medications, and dental care improves.
- When previously uninsured children who are well or have special health needs acquire insurance, they are less likely to experience unmet health care needs. Uninsured children with special health care needs are much more likely to have an unmet health need than their counterparts with insurance.
- When previously uninsured children acquire insurance, they receive more timely diagnosis of serious health conditions, experience fewer avoidable hospitalizations, have improved asthma outcomes, and miss fewer days of school.

Adults benefit substantially from health insurance for preventive care when they are well and for early diagnosis and treatment when they are sick or injured:

- Without health insurance, men and women are less likely to receive effective clinical preventive services.
- Without health insurance, chronically ill adults are much more likely to delay or forgo needed health care and medications.
- Without health insurance, adults with cardiovascular disease or cardiac risk factors are less likely to be aware of their conditions, their conditions are less likely to be well controlled, and they experience worse health outcomes.
- Without health insurance, adults are more likely to be diagnosed with later-stage breast, colorectal, or other cancers that are detectable by screening or

symptom assessment by a clinician. As a consequence, when uninsured adults are diagnosed with such cancers, they are more likely to die or suffer poorer health outcomes.

- Without health insurance, adults with serious conditions, such as cardiovascular disease or trauma, have higher mortality.

- The benefits of health insurance have been clearly demonstrated through recent studies of the experiences of previously uninsured adults after they acquire Medicare coverage at age 65. These studies demonstrate when previously uninsured adults gain Medicare coverage:
  - Their access to physician services and hospital care, particularly for adults with cardiovascular disease or diabetes, improves.
  - Their use of effective clinical preventive services increases.
  - They experience substantially improved trends in health and functional status.
  - Their risk of death when hospitalized for serious conditions declines.

NOTES AND QUESTIONS

1. Should employers be faulted for not providing health insurance for their employees? For example, a recurring critique of Wal-Mart is that, in addition to low wages, they do not offer affordable health insurance to their employees, particularly part-time employees. Employees instead are given information about applying for Medicaid coverage. But why should Wal-Mart offer better health coverage if not required by the law to do so, given their obligation to maximize the value for shareholders? One answer comes from a Wal-Mart competitor, Costco, which pays employees substantially more and offers low-cost health insurance. According to Costco's CEO, such benefits ensure a low turnover, low rates of employee theft, and can even attract customers. *See* Steven Greenhouse, *How Costco Became the Anti-Wal-Mart*, N.Y. Times (July 17, 2012).

* * *

For those who are poor or middle class, a single illness or need for medical care can have devastating financial consequences. In a 2001 study, Senator Elizabeth Warren, when she was still Professor Warren, together with professors Melissa Jacoby and Teresa Sullivan, estimated that "nearly half of *all* bankruptcies involved a medical problem, and certain groups—particularly women heads of households and the elderly—were even more likely to report a health-related bankruptcy." Melissa B. Jacoby et al., *Rethinking the Debates over Health Care Financing: Evidence from the Bankruptcy Courts*, 76 N.Y.U. L. Rev. 375 (2001). Of debtors in bankruptcy, one-quarter identify a medical problem as the reason for being in bankruptcy, one-third owe substantial medical debt, and more than 45 percent have either substantial medical debt or identify a medical problem as the reason for being in bankruptcy. Surprisingly, Jacoby, Sullivan, and Warren also found that even middle-class families *with* insurance were in "similarly precarious positions" as those families without insurance. They explain that "having a basic health insurance plan [including a government funded plan] does not necessarily protect these families from being crushed by the financial consequences of an illness or accident." For families with significant out-of-pocket medical expenses, bankruptcy serves as the "insurer of last resort." *Id.*

C. GOVERNMENT HEALTH CARE PROGRAMS

The Hill-Burton Act of 1946 offered grants and loan assistance to modernize and expand hospitals, on the condition that those that accepted such assistance agree to provide a reasonable volume of services to poor people living in their service area. Funding for the Hill-Burton Act was discontinued in 1997 and only about 170 hospitals remain obligated to provide such services as of 2013. But at least since 1986, when Congress passed the Emergency Medical Treatment and Active Labor Act (EMTALA), all hospitals have been required to treat anyone requiring emergency medical care, regardless of immigration status or ability to pay. While arguably not exactly a government health care program, this requirement defines the bare minimum right to health care in the United States. However, through various entitlement programs, many Americans do receive state-funded health care coverage. The principal programs serving the poor are Medicaid, the closely related SCHIP program, and Medicare. Medicaid is a means-tested program covering poor people who fit into one of the program's defined paths to eligibility. A broad program with multiple paths to coverage, Medicaid covers not only poor children and some categories of poor parents, but also the blind and disabled. Recognition that many children in households with annual incomes that exceed the Medicaid cutoffs will still need government assistance to have regular access to health care led to the State Children's Health Insurance Program (SCHIP). Accordingly, SCHIP acts largely as a gap filler for children of working-class parents who cannot afford private health insurance and do not qualify for Medicaid. Medicare's coverage, though it extends to some younger disabled workers, primarily benefits those over age 65. While Medicare has a broader reach than the poor and is best classified as a social insurance, not an antipoverty, program, it plays an important role in providing health care access and coverage to the older poor. Additionally, some targeted programs, such as those serving veterans or Indian reservations, provide health care directly, rather than in the form of government insurance payments to private providers. But the nature of government health care programs is somewhat in flux as of the publication of this textbook because President Obama's signature legislative victory lies in the area of health care reform. The Affordable Care Act (ACA), although not amounting to universal health care, includes an individual mandate that all Americans be insured and significantly expands eligibility for Medicaid. The table below gives an introductory overview of these programs, the details of which are covered in more detail later in the chapter.

	Medicaid	Medicare	SCHIP	ACA
Legal Foundation	42 USCA § 1396-1 to 1396w-5. Created in 1965. Coverage for people with lower incomes, older people, people with disabilities, and some families and children.	42 USCA § 1395 to 1395kkk-1. Created in 1965. Coverage for U.S. citizens, 65 years of age and older.	42 USCA § 1397aa-mm (1997). Created in 1997. Coverage for uninsured children in families with incomes above Medicaid limits.	42 USCA § 18001 (2010) Created in 2010. Near-universal coverage through either private insurance or government-mandated insurance pools.
Eligibility	Eligibility in income based. For man eligible groups, income is calculated in relation to a percentage of the Federal Poverty Level (FPL). . . . For other groups, income standards are based on income or other nonfinancial criteria standards for other programs, such as the Supplemental Security Income (SSI) program.	Generally, [a person is] eligible for Medicare if [they] or their spouse [has] worked for at least 10 years in Medicare-covered employment and [is] 65 years or older and a citizen or permanent resident of the United States. If a person is not yet 65, [he/she] might also qualify for coverage if [they] have a disability or with end-stage renal disease.	Children, ages 19 and younger, in families with incomes of $45,000/year or less (for a family of four) are likely to be eligible for coverage. In many states, children with families with higher incomes can also qualify. Pregnant women may be eligible for CHIP, which includes lab testing and labor and delivery costs, and at least 60 days of care after delivery.	No one may be turned down for coverage because of a medical condition, and all Americans should be eligible for some form of coverage, whether through their employer, the new statewide Health Insurance Marketplaces, Medicare, or Medicaid.

As can be seen by the table above, instead of a single-payer system of government health insurance secured by a right to health care, the patchwork of programs and systems of coverage in the United States leaves many without full coverage. As a 2011 law review article notes, "[t]his potpourri of health care systems has been expensive, and it has been ineffective for millions of people." Janet L. Dolgin & Katherine R. Dietrich, *Social and Legal Debate About the Affordable Care Act*, 80 UMKC L. Rev. 45 (2011). The same article explains:

> [T]he American health care system has been and remains difficult to characterize because it offers first-rate care to some people and very little to others. The great majority of developed nations provide health coverage, and thus health care, to everyone, regardless of class, age, or status. In sharp contrast, access to health care in the United States reflects basic inequalities. American health-care professionals are well-educated; hospitals are well-equipped; and U.S. companies manufacture advanced medical technology that competes successfully with that of every other nation. Yet . . . on a measure of "avoidable mortality" (deaths from conditions that are amenable to cures), the United States is ranked at the very bottom among developed nations.

The patchwork of public and private coverage will remain in effect even after the ACA is fully phased in. As Professor Nan Hunter explains, the ACA "retains a private system of market exchange, but 'publicizes' it by importing a limited, but significant set of public-sector characteristics." Nan D. Hunter, *Health Insurance Reform and Intimations of Citizenship*, 159 U. Pa. L. Rev. 1955 (2011).

This section begins with the right to emergency treatment before covering Medicaid and Medicare, SCHIP, and the ACA.

1. Emergency Care

The excerpt that follows presents the legal history of the obligation placed on hospital emergency rooms to treat people in need of emergency care regardless of their ability to pay.

ERIK J. OLSON, *NO ROOM AT THE INN: A SNAPSHOT OF AN AMERICAN EMERGENCY ROOM*

46 Stan. L. Rev. 449 (1994)

Traditionally, emergency room operators, like all other private health care providers, had no obligation to provide care to patients. But in the middle of this century, the legal obligations of hospitals began to change as states and the federal government imposed new duties of care. During the 1960s and the 1970s, several state courts replaced the traditional no duty rule with limited duties of care. For example, in *Wilmington General Hospital v. Manlove*, Delaware fashioned a duty of care based on a patient's reliance on the hospital's custom of providing emergency room services. The elements of the cause of action included: a hospital with an emergency room, an unmistakable emergency, a well-established custom of care, and reliance on that custom of care by the patient. Although a few states later followed this approach, it did not achieve wide acceptance.

Arizona was the next intellectual leader. In *Guerrero v. Copper Queen Hospital*, the Supreme Court of Arizona concluded that all public and private hospitals had a duty to provide emergency care. The court derived this public policy from a regulation that required all hospitals to have emergency rooms. *Thompson v. Sun City Community Hospital, Inc.* extended and clarified *Guerrero*. An Arizona hospital must now provide all medically indicated emergency care, but it may transfer financially ineligible patients to another appropriate hospital when, in the judgment of the medical staff or the emergency physician, such transfer can be effected without subjecting the patient to an unreasonable risk of harm to his life or health. Other state courts have fashioned similar duties of care on the basis of broad public policy justifications derived from statutes.

In response to increased concern about the denial of emergency services to uninsured patients in the 1980s, Congress passed the Emergency Medical Treatment and Active Labor Act as a part of the Consolidated Omnibus Budget Reconciliation Act of 1986 (COBRA). The Act creates affirmative treatment obligations for emergency rooms and imposes penalties for inappropriate patient transfers.

Under the Act, the hospital must provide any individual . . . an appropriate medical screening examination within the capability of the hospital's emergency department. This examination should determine whether an emergency medical condition exists. An emergency medical condition manifests itself through acute symptoms of sufficient severity . . . such that the absence of immediate medical attention could reasonably be expected to result in (i) placing the health of the individual . . . in serious jeopardy, (ii) serious impairment to bodily functions, or (iii) serious dysfunction of any bodily organ or part. Active labor also amounts to an emergency. Although considerable ambiguity exists concerning what constitutes an appropriate medical screening examination, courts have yet to require a full treatment examination or an examination that meets the standard of the reasonable doctor. A routine triage examination probably suffices.

If a hospital finds that an incoming patient has an emergency medical condition, it may not transfer the patient. The hospital must first stabilize the patient unless she requests a transfer or the physician signs a certification that the medical benefits reasonably expected from the provision of the appropriate medical treatment at another medical facility outweigh the increased risks to the individual . . . from effecting the transfer. The hospital may transfer any stabilized patient as long as it uses certain precautions. The patient's condition is stable if no material deterioration of the condition is likely, within reasonable medical probability, to result from or occur during the transfer.

Penalties for inappropriate transfer include fines of up to $50,000 for the doctor and hospital and the potential loss of the hospital's Medicare contract. More importantly, the statute gives patients a civil right of action to recover damages for personal harm that is a direct result of a participating hospital's violation. The right to damages arises regardless of the hospital's fault.

Some state governments have also responded to the emergency care access problem with legislation. Twenty-six states impose on hospitals a statutory duty to provide emergency services. The statutory approaches vary widely in scope and procedure. . . .

NOTES AND QUESTIONS

1. Figure 7.2, produced by the Department of Health and Human Services,
    visually presents the basic EMTALA requirements that were described in the
    article above.

Figure 7.2
Basic EMTALA Requirements

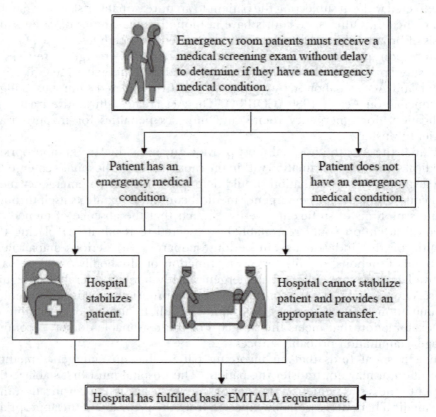

Source: Dep't of Health & Human Servs., Office of Inspector Gen., *The Emergency Medical Treatment and Labor Act: The Enforcement Process* (2001).

2. A county-based residency requirement for receiving nonemergency care
    that the county had decided to give at the county's expense was struck
    down by the U.S. Supreme Court in Memorial Hospital v. Maricopa County,
    415 U.S. 250 (1973). Drawing upon Shapiro v. Thompson, 394 U.S. 618
    (1969), which invalidated a state-residency requirement for welfare assis-
    tance, Justice Marshall, writing for the Court, explained that "medical
    care is as much 'a basic necessity of life' to an indigent as welfare assistance."
    In his dissent, Justice Rehnquist argued that there was no constitutional
    right to such treatment, that the state had a rational basis for setting up
    such eligibility requirements, and that therefore, the county-based residency
    requirement should not have been struck down.
3. Given the requirement that hospitals at least examine people in the emer-
    gency room to see if they need immediate treatment, for many poor people

without regular access to primary care, the emergency room examination serves as their only mechanism for getting treatment. Consequently, there has been a rise in "inappropriate visits," which "occur when a patient enters an emergency room to obtain primary care that the emergency room is not designed to provide." Olson, *supra*. The cost per patient visit is much higher in an emergency room compared with the cost of a scheduled office visit with a primary care doctor. As a result, some hospitals particularly burdened by inappropriate utilization of their emergency rooms by the indigent turn to community clinics, which can provide primary care at a much lower cost, to help ease the burden on their emergency rooms and on their budgets.

* * *

Being forced to treat people who are unable to pay imposes financial costs on hospitals that, not surprisingly, they often seek to avoid. Refusing to treat the indigent even when they need care is one mechanism for avoiding such expenses. Another practice, "patient dumping," occurs when a hospital transfers a patient to another hospital, often to a public hospital. Especially in cases where the patient will need long-term, inpatient care, there can be significant financial incentives to dump the patient on another hospital even where doing so is not allowed or fits in a gray area of the EMTALA. The Office of Inspector General of the U.S. Department of Health & Human Services (OIG) is tasked with enforcing the prohibition against patient dumping. Below is a selection of summaries of settlements reached in 2012 and 2013 between the OIG and hospitals that have allegedly engaged in patient dumping:

- Holmes Regional Medical Center (HRMC), Florida, agreed to pay $50,000 to resolve its liability for Civil Monetary Penalties under the patient dumping statute. The OIG alleged that HRMC failed to provide a medical screening examination and to adequately stabilize a 30-year-old pregnant woman who presented to their emergency department experiencing chest pains, in potential cardiac arrest, and became unresponsive. Both the patient and her baby died.
- Duke University Hospital, North Carolina, agreed to pay $180,000 to resolve its liability for Civil Monetary Penalties under the patient dumping statute. The OIG alleged that Duke failed to accept five appropriate transfers of individuals with unstable psychiatric emergency medical conditions.
- Northside Hospital, Florida, agreed to pay $38,000 to resolve its liability for Civil Monetary Penalties under the patient dumping statute. The OIG alleged that Northside failed to provide an appropriate medical screening examination and stabilizing treatment to a patient with a history of mitral valve replacement. Specifically, the patient presented to Northside's emergency department (ED) by ambulance with flu symptoms and a high fever. A triage nurse instructed the patient to go home and to follow his primary care physician's orders. Two days later the patient presented again to Northside's ED and was admitted to their intensive care unit. On August 8, 2009, the patient died due to influenza A (H1N1).

For these and other summaries of patient dumping settlements, see the running list on the OIG's website at https://oig.hhs.gov/fraud/enforcement/cmp/patient_dumping.asp. Given the high cost of providing EMTALA-compliant care to everyone who enters an emergency room regardless of ability to pay, the low probability of being investigated for a violation, and the expected settlement amounts for violations, notice that in some circumstances it might make economic sense—though perhaps not moral sense—for hospitals to dump patients. This is likely to be especially the case when patients present with the need for particularly costly medical treatment.

In an extreme version of patient dumping, hospitals have even leased aircraft to repatriate immigrants to their home country as a way to reduce expenses associated with treating such patients. Below is Professor Nathan Cortez's recounting of the most famous such case:

> In 2000, Luis Alberto Jiménez, a gardener from Guatemala, suffered traumatic brain damage while riding in a car struck by a drunk driver in Florida. Jiménez was treated by Martin Memorial Hospital, which spent $1.5 million caring for him over several years, only $80,000 of which was reimbursed by Medicaid. Unable to find a rehabilitation center that would accept him, the hospital intervened in his guardianship hearing and obtained a court order allowing the hospital to transfer him to a facility in Guatemala. Jiménez's guardian appealed the ruling and attempted to stay the transfer. But before the district court could rule on the stay, Martin Memorial spent $30,000 for an air ambulance and transported Jiménez to Guatemala's sole public rehabilitation hospital, which does not provide services to rehabilitate traumatic brain injuries.

Nathan Cortez, *Embracing the New Geography of Health Care: A Novel Way to Cover Those Left Out of Health Reform*, 84 S. Cal. L. Rev. 859 (2011). Such international patient dumping is not limited to immigrants: Though the effort was ultimately blocked at the airport by police, a Tucson hospital tried to fly a U.S. citizen, a child born in the United States to immigrant parents, to Mexico. Deborah Sontag, *Immigrants Facing Deportation by U.S. Hospitals*, N.Y. Times (Aug. 3, 2008), at A1.

2.   Medicare

Medicaid and Medicare are the core government health care programs, and have been for nearly half a century since they were signed into law in 1965 by the Johnson administration as part of the Great Society. A means-tested program, Medicaid covers certain classes of eligible poor people, particularly poor children and disabled adults. Medicare primarily covers Americans aged 65 and older, but because of a change made in 1972, it also covers younger Americans with disabilities and people with end-stage renal disease. In 2001 it was again amended, this time to cover people with Lou Gehrig's disease. Although other paths to eligibility exist, these two health insurance programs track closely SSI, Social Security, and TANF. As the Social Security Administration website reports, "Medicaid is linked to receipt of SSI benefits in most States. Medicare is linked to entitlement to Social Security benefits." The connection between welfare and Medicaid is a bit more complicated, as is explained in a Congressional Research Service report:

> Prior to TANF, families qualifying for cash assistance under the former Aid to Families with Dependent Children (AFDC) program were automatically eligible for, and in most states, automatically enrolled in, Medicaid. In contrast, there is no direct link between eligibility for TANF and eligibility for Medicaid. Although

TANF eligibility does not confer automatic Medicaid eligibility, Medicaid entitlement was retained for those individuals who meet the requirements of the former
AFDC program as in effect on July 16, 1996. These old state-specific AFDC-related
income standards are typically well below the federal poverty level (FPL). However,
states may modify (i.e., liberalize or further restrict) these criteria for determining
Medicaid eligibility for low-income families like those receiving TANF. Anecdotal
evidence suggests that some states have chosen to align income rules for TANF and
Medicaid, thus facilitating Medicaid coverage for some TANF recipients.

Elicia J. Herz, Cong. Research Serv., RS22035, *Coverage of the TANF Population
Under Medicaid and SCHIP* (2005). Even these categories are not exclusive,
however. So-called "dual eligibles"—younger persons with disabilities and
low-income seniors—qualify for coverage under both Medicare and Medicaid.

Because this is a poverty law textbook, we are going to focus primarily on
Medicaid, but it is worth acknowledging the significant antipoverty effects of
Medicare. Federally funded, Medicare serves as a form of social insurance, with
universal coverage and benefits that do not vary across state lines. Medicare
accounts for 12 percent of the federal budget and 20 percent of all health
care spending. In 2010, Medicare covered 47 million people: 39 million who
were 65 or more years old and 8 million with permanent disabilities who were
less than 65 years old. The poor and near poor are among those covered: one-
third of those covered by Medicare have incomes below 150 percent of the
poverty line. At the signing ceremony for Medicare on July 30, 1965, President
Johnson summarized the values embodied by Medicare:

> No longer will older Americans be denied the healing miracle of modern
> medicine. No longer will illness crush and destroy the savings they have so carefully
> put away over a lifetime so they might enjoy dignity in their later years. No longer
> will young families see their own incomes, and their own hopes, eaten away simply
> because they are carrying out their deep moral obligations.

As Johnson's statement highlights, Medicare provides a level of security for
older Americans *and* for their families. Medicare's coverage is not without limitations. "For many elderly people, Medicare thus provides essential, but incomplete, protection against medical expenses. In addition to the required
premiums and cost sharing, Medicare's benefit package does not cover the
full range of health services needed by many elderly people." Diane Rowland &
Barbara Lyons, *Medicare, Medicaid, and the Elderly Poor*, 18 Health Care Financing
Rev. 61 (1996).

Medicare coverage gaps have been and are addressed in a number of ways.
Seniors who can afford to often purchase supplemental insurance designed to
fill such gaps. And in 2003, President George W. Bush signed the Medicare
Modernization Act that created Medicare Part D, which provides prescription
drug coverage. With Part D, individuals enroll in plans administered by private
health insurance companies; drug coverage varies across plans. Income- and
asset-based tests determine if those enrolled are eligible for government support
for Part D. In 2009, 36 percent, 9.6 million, of the 27 million Medicare Part D
enrollees received low-income subsidies designed to partially or fully cover out-
of-pocket expenses associated with this drug coverage benefit.

One of the biggest coverage gaps for many older Americans is that Medicare
does not include long-term care. As described by the Congressional Budget
Office:

Long-term care is the personal assistance that enables impaired people to perform daily routines such as eating, bathing, and dressing. Such services may be provided at home by family and friends, through home and community-based services such as home health care, personal care, and adult day care; or in institutional settings, such as nursing or residential care facilities.

Cong. Budget Office, *Financing Long-Term Care for the Elderly* (2004). Not surprisingly, such constant personal assistance is costly and beyond the means of many seniors. For lower-income "dual eligible" seniors, Medicaid covers long-term care. According to the Kaiser Commission, "Dual eligibles account for a large share (39 percent) of total Medicaid spending, although they represent just 15 percent of Medicaid enrollment. In 2007, more than two-thirds (70 percent) of Medicaid expenditures for dual eligibles were for long-term care services." Kaiser Comm'n on Medicaid and the Uninsured, *Dual Eligibles: Medicaid's Role for Low-Income Medicare Beneficiaries* (2011). The excerpt that follows highlights the bureaucratic challenges facing "dual eligibles," those covered by both Medicare and Medicaid.

ANNA GORMAN, *RED TAPE HAMPERS CARE FOR PATIENTS WHO ARE POOR AND DISABLED*

L.A. Times (Nov. 30, 2011)

M.C. Kim had four heart attacks in as many years. Each time he left the hospital not knowing why his heart had failed.

When he tried to enter a cardiac rehabilitation program to learn how to reduce the odds of having more heart trouble, the Medicare office told him to call Medicaid. The Medicaid office told him to call Medicare. In the end, he said, both denied coverage.

"I was like a pingpong ball," said Kim, 51, who lives in Los Angeles. "Nobody wanted to take responsibility."

So Kim kept returning to the emergency room, racking up expensive medical bills for taxpayers.

Kim and other patients like him are among the nation's sickest and poorest residents, and their high-cost medical care places a financial burden on states and the federal government. Because he is poor and disabled, he qualifies for both the federal Medicare program and the state-federal Medicaid program.

These patients are some of the country's priciest government health care consumers. Called dual eligibles, they accounted for close to 40 percent of Medicaid spending in California in 2009, for example, nearly $10 billion, but constitute about 15 percent of enrollees.

Nationwide, the nearly 9 million dual eligibles have similarly disproportionate outlays and cost roughly $250 billion annually in Medicare and Medicaid funding.

Now, as federal officials look for ways to control health care costs, they are zeroing in on millions of patients like Kim. But change is a sensitive issue.

"It's a much more fragile population," said Casey Young, who works for AARP. "It is always concerning when the motivation is cost savings and not improving care."

The government spends so much on dual eligibles because of their illnesses: multiple sclerosis, cerebral palsy, Alzheimer's disease and other debilitating conditions. The expenditures also are high because patients bounce between the two plans and often receive unnecessary, duplicative and poorly coordinated services.

They cycle through emergency rooms, hospitals and nursing homes more than other Medicare or Medicaid enrollees, according to health researchers at the Kaiser Family Foundation.

The result, health care officials and other experts say, is not only inflated expenditures but also gaps in medical treatment for the most vulnerable patients: elderly, poor, and disabled Americans.

"When beneficiaries have to navigate two programs separately, it is no surprise that the care they receive is often inefficient and ineffective," Health and Human Services Secretary Kathleen Sebelius said in a speech in September. "We can dramatically improve health outcomes and reduce costs for dual eligibles if we do a better job coordinating their care."

Bertha Poole, who is covered by both Medicare and Medicaid, said her problems navigating the programs have been small but extremely frustrating. Poole, a quadriplegic, lives on her own in an apartment equipped with special chairs and lifts. She relies on an aide to help her bathe, eat, and dress.

When a wheel fell off her shower chair, it took nearly a year for the Long Beach resident to convince Medi-Cal, California's version of Medicaid, to fix it.

"It sounds frivolous until you need it," she said.

Dual eligibles typically qualify for Medicaid because they are poor and for Medicare because they are either elderly or disabled. Medicare pays for most doctor visits and hospital stays. Medicaid pays for what isn't covered under Medicare, including long-term care at nursing homes.

Each program has tried to shift costs to the other. A federal study last year found that leads to higher bills for taxpayers, as well as lower-quality patient care. Among the problems driving up spending, the study said, are unneeded hospitalizations.

One often-cited example of the financial tug of war involves nursing homes. If a dual eligible patient in a nursing home contracts pneumonia and is treated there, for example, Medicaid picks up the bill. But if the person is transferred to a hospital, Medicaid doesn't pay. Medicare does.

"Patients get shuttled from one bed to the next and sometimes fall on the floor in between," said Joe Baker, president of the Medicare Rights Center.

Kim, the heart patient, said better coordination might have prevented him from going to the emergency room roughly 20 times in the past six years.

"I appreciate the programs, but they are in such disarray," he said. "There is so much red tape." . . .

NOTES AND QUESTIONS

1. The Kaiser Commission's regularly updated publication, *Medicare: A Primer*, is a good starting point for learning more about Medicare. The Kaiser Family Foundation's website also includes fact sheets and analysis of Medicare and Medicaid, http://www.kff.org. Both Medicaid and Medicare are administered by the Department of Health and Human Services' Center for

Medicare and Medicaid Services, which also maintains updated eligibility and usage information for both programs on its website, http://www .cms.hhs.gov.

2. Although Medicare coverage is primarily age or disability defined, the program also covers end-stage renal disease (ESRD, permanent kidney failure requiring dialysis or a kidney transplant) and Amyotrophic Lateral Sclerosis (ALS, also known as Lou Gehrig's disease). And whereas those who qualify for Medicare because of a disability have to wait two years before coverage begins, those with either ESRD or ALS immediately qualify. Does this piecemeal preference for two particular diseases make sense? What might explain why they are singled out whereas diseases affecting other people are not similarly covered?

3. Medicaid

a. Overview of Medicaid History and Program

Created in 1965, Medicaid "is a federal and state entitlement program that pays for medical assistance for certain individuals and families with low incomes and resources." U.S. Soc. Security Admin., *Medicaid Program Description and Legislative History, Annual Statistical Supplement* (2011). For the poor, Medicaid is the biggest source of funding for medical and health-related services. *Id.* Although Medicaid began as a fee for services program, it has increasingly taken the managed care form as states and the federal government sought to control costs. John V. Jacobi, *Mission and Markets in Health Care: Protecting Essential Community Providers for the Poor*, 75 Wash. U. L.Q. 1431 (1997). The excerpt that follows presents the mechanics of the Medicaid program, the program's eligibility requirements, and what is covered by the program.

KAISER COMM'N ON MEDICAID AND THE UNINSURED, *THE MEDICAID PROGRAM AT A GLANCE* (2012)

Medicaid, the largest public health insurance program in the United States, covers over 60 million low-income individuals — roughly 1 in every 5 Americans. The program is administered by states within broad federal rules and financed jointly by states and the federal government. Medicaid beneficiaries include children and some parents, people with disabilities, and seniors. Without Medicaid, most of its beneficiaries would be uninsured or lack coverage for care they need. Medicaid coverage improves access to care for these low-income individuals and families by lowering the financial barriers they face and connecting them with health plans and providers. As a major payer of services, Medicaid also provides essential funding to safety-net providers including hospitals and health centers that provide care to underserved communities and many of the nation's uninsured. The Medicaid program is also the single largest source of coverage for nursing home and community-based long-term care. Altogether, Medicaid finances 17% of all personal health spending.

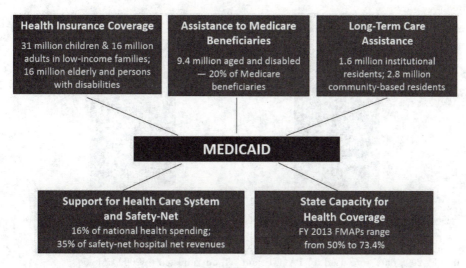

Figure 1
Medicaid's Role in Filling Coverage Gaps

Under the Affordable Care Act (ACA), Medicaid eligibility will expand in 2014 to reach millions more poor Americans — mostly, uninsured adults. This federal reform of Medicaid will establish the program as the coverage pathway for most low-income people and the foundation of the broader public-private system of health coverage created under the new law.

WHO DOES MEDICAID COVER?

Currently, to qualify for Medicaid, a person must meet financial criteria and also belong to one of Medicaid's categorically eligible groups: children; pregnant women; adults with dependent children; people with severe disabilities; and seniors. States must cover these groups up to federal minimum income thresholds and cannot cap enrollment or establish waiting lists.

Many states have expanded Medicaid beyond what federal law requires, mostly for children. Nearly half the states cover children up to at least 150% of the federal poverty level (FPL) — $34,575 for family of four in 2012 — and, in 2010, over one-third of all children were enrolled in Medicaid. Adult eligibility for Medicaid is much more restrictive. In 33 states, the income eligibility threshold for working parents is now set below 100% FPL; in 17 of these states, the threshold is lower than 50% FPL. Nondisabled adults without dependent children have long been excluded from Medicaid by federal law, and states wishing to cover them have had to use state-only dollars or obtain a federal waiver to do so. Overall, about half of all Medicaid enrollees are children, and nonelderly adults (mostly, working parents) make up another quarter. Seniors and people with disabilities account for the remaining quarter (Figure 3).

Figure 3
Medicaid Enrollees and Expenditures, FY 2009

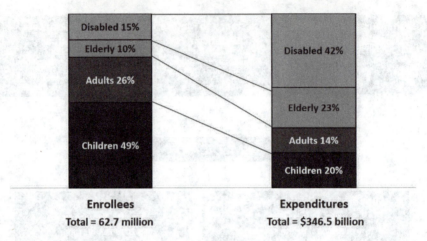

Enrollees	Expenditures
Total = 62.7 million	**Total = $346.5 billion**

Source: KCMU/Urban Institute estimates based on data from FY 2009 MSIS and CMS-64, 2012. MSIS FY 2008 data were used for PA, UT, and WI, but adjusted to 2009 CMS-64.

Note: Percentages may not add to 100 due to rounding.

In 2009, Medicaid covered:

- 31 million children;
- 16 million nonelderly adults;
- 6 million seniors; and
- 9.5 million persons with disabilities (including 4 million children).

Almost all elderly Medicaid enrollees and 39% of disabled Medicaid enrollees are also covered by Medicare. These 9.4 million "dual eligibles" are very poor and many have very high health and long-term care needs and costs. Most states provide Medicaid for the "medically needy" — categorically eligible individuals who have income exceeding Medicaid cutoffs, but very high medical expenses.

Under the ACA, beginning in 2014, states are required to determine Medicaid eligibility based solely on income (i.e., categorical criteria are eliminated), and to expand eligibility to most nonelderly individuals with income up to 138% FPL; millions of uninsured adults who were previously excluded from Medicaid will thus gain coverage. The Supreme Court upheld the expansion of Medicaid (along with the rest of the ACA), but limited the HHS Secretary's enforcement authority as it pertains to the expansion. Some states have signaled that they do not intend to comply with the requirement; it remains to be seen how states will ultimately respond. The ACA did not change the federal mandatory eligibility rules for current Medicaid eligibles, children, the elderly, or the disabled.

WHAT SERVICES DOES MEDICAID COVER?

Medicaid covers a wide spectrum of services to meet the diverse needs of the populations it serves. In addition to acute health services, Medicaid covers a broad array of long-term services that Medicare and most private insurance exclude or tightly limit. Medicaid enrollees receive their care mostly from private providers. Two-thirds receive all or most of their care in managed care arrangements, predominantly capitated managed care organizations (MCOs), and many others receive at least some services through capitated plans. Increasingly, states are enrolling beneficiaries with more complex needs, including the disabled and dual eligibles, in managed care. State Medicaid programs are required to cover:

- inpatient and outpatient hospital services;
- physician, midwife, and nurse practitioner services;
- laboratory and x-ray services;
- nursing facility and home health care for individuals [over] age 21;
- early and periodic screening, diagnosis, and treatment (EPSDT) for children under age 21;
- family planning services and supplies; and
- rural health clinic/federally qualified health center services.

Many states also offer "optional" services, including prescription drugs, dental care, durable medical equipment, and personal care services. EPSDT rules require states to cover all medically necessary Medicaid services for children, including services considered optional for adults. Dual eligibles get most of their acute care services under Medicare, but Medicaid assists them with their Medicare premiums and cost-sharing and covers key benefits that Medicare does not cover — especially, long-term care. Premiums are prohibited and out-of-pocket costs are tightly limited in Medicaid for beneficiaries below 150% FPL [Federal Poverty Level]. Less restrictive rules apply for others, but premiums and cost-sharing cannot total more than 5% of income for any Medicaid beneficiary.

Generally, the same Medicaid benefit package must be covered for all enrollees statewide. However, states can provide some groups with more limited packages modeled on one of three specified commercial "benchmark" plans, or with "Secretary-approved coverage." People with disabilities, dual eligibles, medically frail individuals, and specified other beneficiaries are exempt from mandatory enrollment in benchmark coverage. Under the ACA, all benchmark coverage will be required to include at least the "essential health benefits" (EHB) set forth in the new law, and most people who gain Medicaid due to the ACA expansion will receive benchmark coverage. CMS has indicated that states will be able to offer their traditional Medicaid benefit package as a benchmark plan under the Secretary-approved option.

How Is Access in Medicaid?

Medicaid improves access to care and reduces unmet health needs for low-income Americans. The vast majority of children and adults covered by either Medicaid or private insurance have a usual source of care, while the uninsured fare significantly less well (Figure 4). Similarly, few children and relatively few adults with either Medicaid or private coverage postpone or go without needed care due to cost, in contrast to sizeable shares of the uninsured who face these difficulties; compared to privately insured adults, adults with Medicaid are somewhat more likely to report these problems. Recently, a randomized, controlled study in Oregon provided strong evidence regarding the difference

Figure 4
Access to Care by Health Insurance Status, 2011

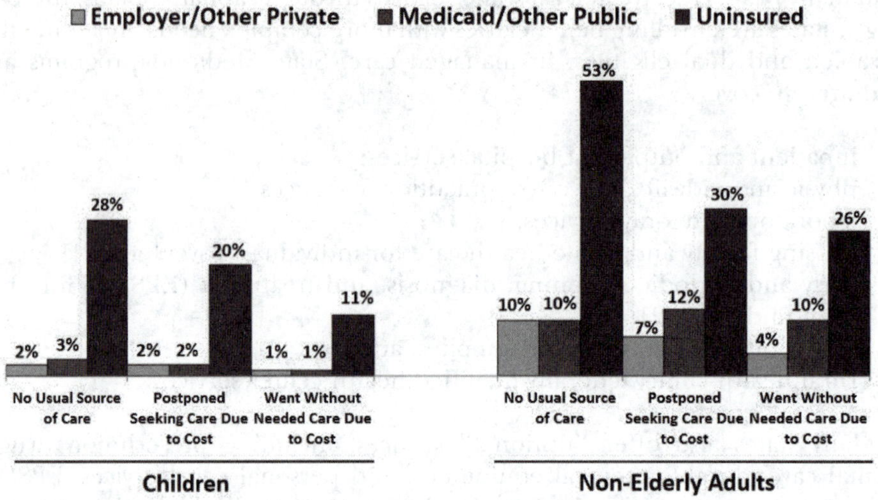

■ Employer/Other Private   ■ Medicaid/Other Public   ■ Uninsured

Source: KCMU analysis of 2001 NHIS data.

Note: In past 12 months. Respondents who said usual source of care was the emergency room were included among those with no usual source of care. All differences between the uninsured and the two insurance groups were statistically significant ($p < 0.05$).

Medicaid makes in access to care. The study found that enrollment in Medicaid by uninsured adults age 19-64 increased their use of care, including primary and preventive care, reduced their financial burdens, and improved their self-reported health and well-being, relative to the adults who remained uninsured.

HOW MUCH DOES MEDICAID COST?

In 2010, Medicaid spending for services totaled about $390 billion (Figure 5). Nearly two-thirds of spending (64%) was for acute care, while about one-third went to long-term care. Another 4.5% of spending was attributable to "DSH" — supplemental payments to hospitals that serve a disproportionate share of Medicaid and indigent patients — and payments for Medicare premiums totaled about 3%. Medicaid administrative costs (not shown) accounted for 4.5% of total program spending.

Roughly two-thirds of Medicaid spending is attributable to elderly and disabled beneficiaries although they make up just a quarter of all Medicaid enrollees. And almost 40% of Medicaid spending is attributable to dual eligibles, even though Medicare covers most of their acute care costs. The high spending on these groups is due to their high needs and intensive use of both acute and long-term care (Figure 6).

HOW IS MEDICAID FINANCED?

The federal government and the states share the cost of Medicaid through a system of federal matching payments. The federal share, known as the Federal

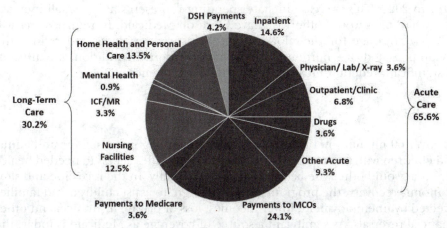

Figure 5
Medicaid Expenditures by Service, FY 2011

Total = $413.9 billion

Source: Urban Institute estimates based on FY 2011 data from CMS-64, prepared for KCMU.

Note: Includes DSH payments and payments to Medicare. Excludes administrative spending, adjustments and payments to the Territories.

Figure 6
Medicaid Payments per Enrollee by Acute and Long-Term Care, FY 2009

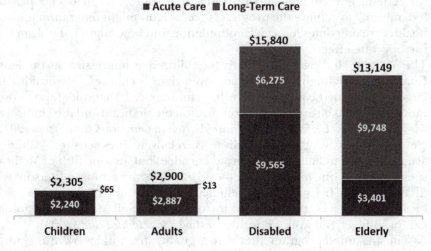

Source: KCMU and Urban Institute estimates based on FY 2009 MSIS and CMS-64 data. MSIS FY 2008 data were used for PA, UT, and WI, but adjusted to 2009 CMS-64.

Medical Assistance Percentage, or FMAP, is based on a formula in the law and is at least 50% in every state but higher in poorer states, reaching 74% in the poorest state in 2012. Currently, the federal government funds about 57% of Medicaid costs overall.

Under the ACA, during the period 2014-2016, the federal government will finance 100% of the costs for individuals newly eligible for Medicaid due to the expansion. The federal share will phase down gradually, to 90% in 2020 and thereafter. The Congressional Budget Office estimates the total federal cost of the Medicaid expansion to be $931 billion and state costs to be $73 billion from 2014 to 2022. This increase in state spending represents a very small increase over what states would otherwise have spent on Medicaid. In return, states will increase coverage for their low-income uninsured residents and reduce the uncompensated care burden on safety-net providers. In addition, the infusion of significant federal funds will bolster their economies.

LOOKING AHEAD

For over 60 million low-income Americans, including many seniors and adults and children with severe disabilities, Medicaid provides access to needed health care that would otherwise be out of reach financially. In the recession and slow economic recovery, the program grew, by design, to assist children and families affected by unemployment, lower incomes, loss of private insurance, and other financial reversals. As significant a source of coverage as Medicaid is today, the program is designed to serve as the foundation for broader coverage in the years ahead, expanding to reach millions of additional people, most of whom are uninsured. . . .

NOTES AND QUESTIONS

1. What are the advantages and disadvantages of Medicaid's reliance on both the federal government and on individual states, so-called "cooperative federalism," to achieve the program's goals? How might federalism improve health care outcomes for a given population and how might federalism have the opposite effect?

2. The reach of Medicaid, particularly for children, is impressive. As the Kaiser Commission highlights, "Medicaid covers 1 in 3 children. Medicaid is the largest source of health coverage for children. . . . Medicaid [also] covers more than 1 in 3 births." Kaiser Commission on Medicaid and the Uninsured, *Medicaid Matters: Understanding Medicaid's Role in Our Heath Care System* (2011). Nevertheless, coverage of children is relatively inexpensive: "Children account for about half of all Medicaid enrollees but just one-fifth of Medicaid spending. Only one-quarter of Medicaid enrollees are seniors or persons with disabilities, but because these beneficiaries need more (and more costly) health-care services, they account for two-thirds of all Medicaid spending." Ctr. on Budget and Policy Priorities, *Introduction to Medicaid* (2008).

3. As a means-tested program, there are arguably structural work disincentives built into Medicaid. When family earnings move from just below the particular Medicaid cutoff points to just above, families can lose Medicaid eligibility. Although Medicaid used to be tied almost exclusively to welfare receipt, the separation of Medicaid from welfare has not solved the eligibility cliff problem. According to the Cato Institute's Director of Health Policy Studies:

    > Individuals sometimes respond to means-tested government programs by failing to take steps they would otherwise take to alleviate their own poverty. Because eligibility depends on one's income and assets, many beneficiaries become or remain eligible by avoiding self-help — such as striving to earn

more or save more — that would make them ineligible. The prospect of losing Medicaid benefits can be a significant deterrent for individuals who might otherwise enter the workforce or increase their earnings.

Michael F. Cannon, Cato Inst., *Medicaid's Unseen Costs* (2005). The Cato Institute's argument raises two related questions. First, is this an accurate description of beneficiaries avoiding self-help in order to be eligible for Medicaid accurate? Second, assuming it is accurate, what should be done about this moral hazard problem? Solutions are likely to be inherently expensive. Means-testing could be abandoned in favor of universal coverage, but that would dramatically expand eligibility. As an alternative, extended phaseouts could be implemented such that families retain most of the value of increased earnings and only gradually lose coverage. This alternative seems to work in the EITC context, though phaseouts increase program costs.

4. Immigrants, especially illegal immigrants, have less right to Medicaid than U.S. citizens. Legal permanent residents ("green card" holders) are not eligible for Medicaid for the first five years of their residency in the United States, though this five-year ban does not apply to most humanitarian refugees as well as active-duty members or veterans of the Armed Forces and their families. Kaiser Comm'n on Medicaid and the Uninsured, *Medicaid and SCHIP Eligibility for Immigrants* (2006). Undocumented immigrants are generally not eligible for Medicaid but there are federal matching funds available for prenatal care for women regardless of immigration status. Additionally, state-only funded coverage is available to otherwise unqualified immigrants in 16 states and in Washington, D.C., though such coverage is often limited based on the needs and status of the recipient. U.S. Dep't of Health & Human Servs., *Overview of Immigrants' Eligibility for SNAP, TANF, Medicaid, and CHIP* (2012).

b. Medicaid Litigation

Professor Ed Sparer, one of the leading advocates of the rights of the poor in the twentieth century, wrote shortly before his death about the different health care rules and systems encountered by the poor. Sparer argued:

> There is a "dual track" in health care. The poor do move through a medical care system consisting of Medicaid mills, fragmented hospital clinics and ward systems which emphasize social distance and powerlessness. The well-to-do do not go to the mills; they do not rely upon the clinics; the social experience of a well-to-do patient, with a committed doctor in private service, is quite different from that of the ward-service patient. Those separate systems for the poor and rich do stand as separate and unequal tracks of health care, even though, as earlier emphasized, many millions of non-Medicaid-eligible citizens have care more like the poor people's track than the rich people's. Our medical system is riddled with inequalities, and the government monies flowing into it entrench some of the inequalities, e.g., by providing financing for the clinic system, as well as new unequal settings, such as the Medicaid mills.

Ed Sparer, *Gordian Knots: The Situation of Health Care Advocacy for the Poor Today*, 15 Clearinghouse Rev. 1 (1981-1982). The existence of this dual track is perhaps best seen in limits on what is covered by Medicaid. Coverage limits reflect both political choices regarding what the public should and should not be asked to pay for as well as litigation on behalf of Medicaid enrollees to challenge those limits. From the perspective of attorneys for the poor, litigation is also used to ensure that states do not use the flexibility of Medicaid's structure as an excuse for denying services to those covered by Medicaid. Stated more neutrally, litigation helps flesh out the significance of federal- and state-level Medicaid regulations and guidelines. This section presents two of the more salient examples of litigation regarding Medicaid coverage: reproductive rights; and EPSDT, early and periodic screening, diagnostic, and treatment services. The case that follows highlights the politics, and the contested nature, of publicly funded health care coverage for the poor.

1. Reproductive Rights

HARRIS v. McRAE ET AL.
448 U.S. 297 (1980)

Mr. Justice STEWART delivered the opinion of the Court.

This case presents statutory and constitutional questions concerning the public funding of abortions under Title XIX of the Social Security Act, commonly known as the "Medicaid" Act, and recent annual Appropriations Acts containing the so-called "Hyde Amendment." The statutory question is whether Title XIX requires a State that participates in the Medicaid program to fund the cost of medically necessary abortions for which federal reimbursement is unavailable under the Hyde Amendment. The constitutional question, which arises only if Title XIX imposes no such requirement, is whether the Hyde Amendment, by denying public funding for certain medically necessary abortions, contravenes the liberty or equal protection guarantees of the Due Process Clause of the Fifth Amendment, or either of the Religion Clauses of the First Amendment.

I.

The Medicaid program was created in 1965, when Congress added Title XIX to the Social Security Act, for the purpose of providing federal financial assistance to States that choose to reimburse certain costs of medical treatment for needy persons. Although participation in the Medicaid program is entirely optional, once a State elects to participate, it must comply with the requirements of Title XIX.

One such requirement is that a participating State agree to provide financial assistance to the "categorically needy"[1] with respect to five general areas of

---

1. The "categorically needy" include families with dependent children eligible for public assistance under the Aid to Families with Dependent Children program, 42 U. S. C. § 601 *et seq.*, and the aged, blind, and disabled eligible for benefits under the Supplemental Security Income program, 42 U. S. C. § 1381 *et seq. See* 42 U. S. C. § 1396a(a)(10)(A). Title XIX also permits a State to extend Medicaid benefits to other needy persons, termed "medically needy." *See* 42 U. S. C. § 1396a(a)(10)(C). If a State elects to include the medically needy in its Medicaid plan, it has the option of providing somewhat different coverage from that required for the categorically needy. *See* 42 U. S. C. § 1396a(a)(13)(C).

medical treatment: (1) inpatient hospital services, (2) outpatient hospital services, (3) other laboratory and X-ray services, (4) skilled nursing facilities services, periodic screening and diagnosis of children, and family planning services, and (5) services of physicians. Although a participating State need not "provide funding for all medical treatment falling within the five general categories, [Title XIX] does require that [a] state Medicaid [plan] establish 'reasonable standards . . . for determining . . . the extent of medical assistance under the plan which . . . are consistent with the objectives of [Title XIX].'"

Since September 1976, Congress has prohibited — either by an amendment to the annual appropriations bill for the Department of Health, Education, and Welfare[2] or by a joint resolution — the use of any federal funds to reimburse the cost of abortions under the Medicaid program except under certain specified circumstances. This funding restriction is commonly known as the "Hyde Amendment," after its original congressional sponsor, Representative Hyde. The current version of the Hyde Amendment, applicable for fiscal year 1980, provides:

> "[None] of the funds provided by this joint resolution shall be used to perform abortions except where the life of the mother would be endangered if the fetus were carried to term; or except for such medical procedures necessary for the victims of rape or incest when such rape or incest has been reported promptly to a law enforcement agency or public health service."

This version of the Hyde Amendment is broader than that applicable for fiscal year 1977, which did not include the "rape or incest" exception, but narrower than that applicable for most of fiscal year 1978, and all of fiscal year 1979, which had an additional exception for "instances where severe and long-lasting physical health damage to the mother would result if the pregnancy were carried to term when so determined by two physicians."

On September 30, 1976, the day on which Congress enacted the initial version of the Hyde Amendment, these consolidated cases were filed in the District Court for the Eastern District of New York. The plaintiffs — Cora McRae, a New York Medicaid recipient then in the first trimester of a pregnancy that she wished to terminate, the New York City Health and Hospitals Corp., a public benefit corporation that operates 16 hospitals, 12 of which provide abortion services, and others — sought to enjoin the enforcement of the funding restriction on abortions. They alleged that the Hyde Amendment violated the First, Fourth, Fifth, and Ninth Amendments of the Constitution insofar as it limited the funding of abortions to those necessary to save the life of the mother, while permitting the funding of costs associated with childbirth. . . .

III.

Having determined [in Part II of the opinion] that Title XIX does not obligate a participating State to pay for those medically necessary abortions for which Congress has withheld federal funding, we must consider the constitutional validity of the Hyde Amendment. The appellees assert that the funding

---

2. The Department of Health, Education, and Welfare was recently reorganized and divided into the Department of Health and Human Services and the Department of Education. The original designation is retained for purposes of this opinion.

restrictions of the Hyde Amendment violate several rights secured by the Constitution — (1) the right of a woman, implicit in the Due Process Clause of the Fifth Amendment, to decide whether to terminate a pregnancy, (2) the prohibition under the Establishment Clause of the First Amendment against any "law respecting an establishment of religion," and (3) the right to freedom of religion protected by the Free Exercise Clause of the First Amendment. The appellees also contend that, quite apart from substantive constitutional rights, the Hyde Amendment violates the equal protection component of the Fifth Amendment.

It is well settled that, quite apart from the guarantee of equal protection, if a law "impinges upon a fundamental right explicitly or implicitly secured by the Constitution [it] is presumptively unconstitutional." Accordingly, before turning to the equal protection issue in this case, we examine whether the Hyde Amendment violates any substantive rights secured by the Constitution.

A.

We address first the appellees' argument that the Hyde Amendment, by restricting the availability of certain medically necessary abortions under Medicaid, impinges on the "liberty" protected by the Due Process Clause as recognized in *Roe v. Wade*, 410 U.S. 113, and its progeny.

In the *Wade* case, this Court held unconstitutional a Texas statute making it a crime to procure or attempt an abortion except on medical advice for the purpose of saving the mother's life. The constitutional underpinning of *Wade* was a recognition that the "liberty" protected by the Due Process Clause of the Fourteenth Amendment includes not only the freedoms explicitly mentioned in the Bill of Rights, but also a freedom of personal choice in certain matters of marriage and family life.[13] This implicit constitutional liberty, the Court in *Wade* held, includes the freedom of a woman to decide whether to terminate a pregnancy.

But the Court in *Wade* also recognized that a State has legitimate interests during a pregnancy in both ensuring the health of the mother and protecting potential human life. These state interests, which were found to be "separate and distinct" and to "[grow] in substantiality as the woman approaches term," pose a conflict with a woman's untrammeled freedom of choice. In resolving this conflict, the Court held that before the end of the first trimester of pregnancy, neither state interest is sufficiently substantial to justify any intrusion on the woman's freedom of choice. In the second trimester, the state interest in maternal health was found to be sufficiently substantial to justify regulation reasonably related to that concern. And at viability, usually in the third trimester, the state interest in protecting the potential life of the fetus was found to justify a criminal prohibition against abortions, except where necessary for the preservation of the life or health of the mother. Thus, inasmuch as the Texas criminal statute

---

13. The Court in *Wade* observed that previous decisions of this Court had recognized that the liberty protected by the Due Process Clause "has some extension to activities relating to marriage, *Loving v. Virginia*, 388 U.S. 1, 12 (1967); procreation, *Skinner v. Oklahoma*, 316 U.S. 535, 541-542 (1942); contraception, *Eisenstadt v. Baird*, 405 U.S. [438,] 453-454; id., at 460, 463-465 (White, J., concurring in result); family relationships, *Prince v. Massachusetts*, 321 U.S. 158, 166 (1944); and child rearing and education, *Pierce v. Society of Sisters*, 268 U.S. 510, 535 (1925); *Meyer v. Nebraska*, [262 U.S. 390, 399 (1923)]." 410 U.S., at 152-153.

allowed abortions only where necessary to save the life of the mother and without regard to the stage of the pregnancy, the Court held in *Wade* that the statute violated the Due Process Clause of the Fourteenth Amendment.

In *Maher v. Roe*, 432 U.S. 464, the Court was presented with the question whether the scope of personal constitutional freedom recognized in *Roe v. Wade* included an entitlement to Medicaid payments for abortions that are not medically necessary. At issue in *Maher* was a Connecticut welfare regulation under which Medicaid recipients received payments for medical services incident to childbirth, but not for medical services incident to nontherapeutic abortions. The District Court held that the regulation violated the Equal Protection Clause of the Fourteenth Amendment because the unequal subsidization of childbirth and abortion impinged on the "fundamental right to abortion" recognized in *Wade* and its progeny.

It was the view of this Court that "the District Court misconceived the nature and scope of the fundamental right recognized in *Roe*." The doctrine of *Roe v. Wade*, the Court held in *Maher*, "protects the woman from unduly burdensome interference with her freedom to decide whether to terminate her pregnancy," such as the severe criminal sanctions at issue in *Roe v. Wade, supra*, or the absolute requirement of spousal consent for an abortion challenged in *Planned Parenthood of Central Missouri v. Danforth*, 428 U.S. 52.

But the constitutional freedom recognized in *Wade* and its progeny, the *Maher* Court explained, did not prevent Connecticut from making "a value judgment favoring childbirth over abortion, and . . . [implementing] that judgment by the allocation of public funds." As the Court elaborated:

> "The Connecticut regulation before us is different in kind from the laws invalidated in our previous abortion decisions. The Connecticut regulation places no obstacles — absolute or otherwise — in the pregnant woman's path to an abortion. An indigent woman who desires an abortion suffers no disadvantage as a consequence of Connecticut's decision to fund childbirth; she continues as before to be dependent on private sources for the service she desires. The State may have made childbirth a more attractive alternative, thereby influencing the woman's decision, but it has imposed no restriction on access to abortions that was not already there. The indigency that may make it difficult — and in some cases, perhaps, impossible — for some women to have abortions is neither created nor in any way affected by the Connecticut regulation." *Ibid.*

The Court in *Maher* noted that its description of the doctrine recognized in *Wade* and its progeny signaled "no retreat" from those decisions. In explaining why the constitutional principle recognized in *Wade* and later cases — protecting a woman's freedom of choice — did not translate into a constitutional obligation of Connecticut to subsidize abortions, the Court cited the

> "basic difference between direct state interference with a protected activity and state encouragement of an alternative activity consonant with legislative policy. Constitutional concerns are greatest when the State attempts to impose its will by force of law; the State's power to encourage actions deemed to be in the public interest is necessarily far broader."

Thus, even though the Connecticut regulation favored childbirth over abortion by means of subsidization of one and not the other, the Court in *Maher* concluded that the regulation did not impinge on the constitutional freedom recognized in *Wade* because it imposed no governmental restriction on access to abortions.

The Hyde Amendment, like the Connecticut welfare regulation at issue in *Maher*, places no governmental obstacle in the path of a woman who chooses to terminate her pregnancy, but rather, by means of unequal subsidization of abortion and other medical services, encourages alternative activity deemed in the public interest. The present case does differ factually from *Maher* insofar as that case involved a failure to fund nontherapeutic abortions, whereas the Hyde Amendment withholds funding of certain medically necessary abortions. Accordingly, the appellees argue that because the Hyde Amendment affects a significant interest not present or asserted in *Maher* — the interest of a woman in protecting her health during pregnancy — and because that interest lies at the core of the personal constitutional freedom recognized in *Wade*, the present case is constitutionally different from *Maher*. It is the appellees' view that to the extent that the Hyde Amendment withholds funding for certain medically necessary abortions, it clearly impinges on the constitutional principle recognized in *Wade*.

It is evident that a woman's interest in protecting her health was an important theme in *Wade*. In concluding that the freedom of a woman to decide whether to terminate her pregnancy falls within the personal liberty protected by the Due Process Clause, the Court in *Wade* emphasized the fact that the woman's decision carries with it significant personal health implications — both physical and psychological. In fact, although the Court in *Wade* recognized that the state interest in protecting potential life becomes sufficiently compelling in the period after fetal viability to justify an absolute criminal prohibition of nontherapeutic abortions, the Court held that even after fetal viability a State may not prohibit abortions "necessary to preserve the life or health of the mother." Because even the compelling interest of the State in protecting potential life after fetal viability was held to be insufficient to outweigh a woman's decision to protect her life or health, it could be argued that the freedom of a woman to decide whether to terminate her pregnancy for health reasons does in fact lie at the core of the constitutional liberty identified in *Wade*.

But, regardless of whether the freedom of a woman to choose to terminate her pregnancy for health reasons lies at the core or the periphery of the due process liberty recognized in *Wade*, it simply does not follow that a woman's freedom of choice carries with it a constitutional entitlement to the financial resources to avail herself of the full range of protected choices. The reason why was explained in *Maher*: although government may not place obstacles in the path of a woman's exercise of her freedom of choice, it need not remove those not of its own creation. Indigency falls in the latter category. The financial constraints that restrict an indigent woman's ability to enjoy the full range of constitutionally protected freedom of choice are the product not of governmental restrictions on access to abortions, but rather of her indigency. Although Congress has opted to subsidize medically necessary services generally, but not certain medically necessary abortions, the fact remains that the Hyde Amendment leaves an indigent woman with at least the same range of choice in deciding whether to obtain a medically necessary abortion as she would have had if Congress had chosen to subsidize no health care costs at all. We are thus not persuaded that the Hyde Amendment impinges on the constitutionally protected freedom of choice recognized in *Wade*.

Although the liberty protected by the Due Process Clause affords protection against unwarranted government interference with freedom of choice in the context of certain personal decisions, it does not confer an entitlement to such funds as may be necessary to realize all the advantages of that freedom. To hold otherwise would mark a drastic change in our understanding of the Constitution. It cannot be that because government may not prohibit the use of contraceptives, *Griswold v. Connecticut*, 381 U.S. 479, or prevent parents from sending their child to a private school, *Pierce v. Society of Sisters*, 268 U.S. 510, government, therefore, has an affirmative constitutional obligation to ensure that all persons have the financial resources to obtain contraceptives or send their children to private schools. To translate the limitation on governmental power implicit in the Due Process Clause into an affirmative funding obligation would require Congress to subsidize the medically necessary abortion of an indigent woman even if Congress had not enacted a Medicaid program to subsidize other medically necessary services. Nothing in the Due Process Clause supports such an extraordinary result. Whether freedom of choice that is constitutionally protected warrants federal subsidization is a question for Congress to answer, not a matter of constitutional entitlement. Accordingly, we conclude that the Hyde Amendment does not impinge on the due process liberty recognized in *Wade*.

B.

[The Court then rejected a challenge that the Hyde Amendment violates the Religion Clauses of the First Amendment.]

C.

It remains to be determined whether the Hyde Amendment violates the equal protection component of the Fifth Amendment. This challenge is premised on the fact that, although federal reimbursement is available under Medicaid for medically necessary services generally, the Hyde Amendment does not permit federal reimbursement of all medically necessary abortions. . . .

The guarantee of equal protection under the Fifth Amendment is not a source of substantive rights or liberties, but rather a right to be free from invidious discrimination in statutory classifications and other governmental activity. It is well settled that where a statutory classification does not itself impinge on a right or liberty protected by the Constitution, the validity of classification must be sustained unless "the classification rests on grounds wholly irrelevant to the achievement of [any legitimate governmental] objective." This presumption of constitutional validity, however, disappears if a statutory classification is predicated on criteria that are, in a constitutional sense, "suspect," the principal example of which is a classification based on race, e.g., *Brown v. Board of Education*, 347 U.S. 483.

1.

For the reasons stated above, we have already concluded that the Hyde Amendment violates no constitutionally protected substantive rights. We now conclude as well that it is not predicated on a constitutionally suspect classification. In reaching this conclusion, we again draw guidance from the Court's decision in *Maher v. Roe.* As to whether the Connecticut welfare regulation providing funds for childbirth but not for nontherapeutic abortions discriminated against a suspect class, the Court in *Maher* observed:

> "An indigent woman desiring an abortion does not come within the limited category of disadvantaged classes so recognized by our cases. Nor does the fact that the impact of the regulation falls upon those who cannot pay lead to a different conclusion. In a sense, every denial of welfare to an indigent creates a wealth classification as compared to nonindigents who are able to pay for the desired goods or services. But this Court has never held that financial need alone identifies a suspect class for purposes of equal protection analysis."

432 U.S., at 470-471, citing *San Antonio Independent School Dist. v. Rodriguez*, 411 U.S. 1, 29; *Dandridge v. Williams*, 397 U.S. 471.

Thus, the Court in *Maher* found no basis for concluding that the Connecticut regulation was predicated on a suspect classification.

It is our view that the present case is indistinguishable from *Maher* in this respect. Here, as in *Maher*, the principal impact of the Hyde Amendment falls on the indigent. But that fact does not itself render the funding restriction constitutionally invalid, for this Court has held repeatedly that poverty, standing alone, is not a suspect classification. *See, e.g., James v. Valtierra*, 402 U.S. 137. That *Maher* involved the refusal to fund nontherapeutic abortions, whereas the present case involves the refusal to fund medically necessary abortions, has no bearing on the factors that render a classification "suspect" within the meaning of the constitutional guarantee of equal protection.

2.

[The Court then found that the Hyde Amendment passed the rational basis test because "Congress has established incentives that make childbirth a more attractive alternative than abortion for persons eligible for Medicaid. These incentives bear a direct relationship to the legitimate congressional interest in protecting potential life."]

Mr. Justice BRENNAN, with whom Mr. Justice MARSHALL and Mr. Justice BLACKMUN join, dissenting.

. . . It is important to put this congressional decision in human terms. Nonpregnant women may be reimbursed for all medically necessary treatments. Pregnant women with analogous ailments, however, will be reimbursed only if the treatment involved does not happen to include an abortion. Since the refusal to fund will in some significant number of cases force the patient to forgo medical assistance, the result is to refuse treatment for some genuine maladies not because they need not be treated, cannot be treated, or are too expensive to treat, and not because they relate to a deliberate choice to abort a pregnancy, but merely because treating them would as a practical matter require termination of that pregnancy. Even were one of the view that legislative hostility to abortions could justify a decision to fund obstetrics and child delivery services while refusing to fund nontherapeutic abortions, the present statutory scheme could not be saved. For here, that hostility has gone a good deal farther. Its consequence is to leave indigent sick women without treatment simply because of the medical fortuity that their illness cannot be treated unless their pregnancy is terminated. Antipathy to abortion, in short, has been permitted not only to ride roughshod over a woman's constitutional right to terminate her pregnancy in the fashion she chooses, but also to distort our Nation's health-care programs. As a means of delivering health services, then, the Hyde Amendment is completely irrational. As a means of preventing abortions, it is concededly rational — brutally so. But this latter goal is constitutionally forbidden. . . .

[T]he Hyde Amendment is a transparent attempt by the Legislative Branch to impose the political majority's judgment of the morally acceptable and socially desirable preference on a sensitive and intimate decision that the Constitution entrusts to the individual. Worse yet, the Hyde Amendment does not foist that majoritarian viewpoint with equal measure upon everyone in our Nation, rich and poor alike; rather, it imposes that viewpoint only upon that segment of our society which, because of its position of political powerlessness, is least able to defend its privacy rights from the encroachments of state-mandated morality. The instant legislation thus calls for more exacting judicial review than in most other cases. . . .

Moreover, it is clear that the Hyde Amendment not only was designed to inhibit, but does in fact inhibit the woman's freedom to choose abortion over childbirth. "Pregnancy is unquestionably a condition requiring medical services. . . . Treatment for the condition may involve medical procedures for its termination, or medical procedures to bring the pregnancy to term, resulting in a live birth. '[Abortion] and childbirth, when stripped of the sensitive moral arguments surrounding the abortion controversy, are simply two alternative medical methods of dealing with pregnancy. . . .'" *Beal v. Doe, supra,* at 449 (BRENNAN, J., dissenting). In every pregnancy, one of these two courses of treatment is medically necessary, and the poverty-stricken woman depends on the Medicaid Act to pay for the expenses associated with that procedure. But under the Hyde Amendment, the Government will fund only those procedures incidental to childbirth. By thus injecting coercive financial incentives favoring childbirth into a decision that is constitutionally guaranteed to be free from governmental intrusion, the Hyde Amendment deprives the indigent woman of her freedom to choose abortion over maternity, thereby impinging on the due process liberty right recognized in *Roe v. Wade.*

The Court's contrary conclusion is premised on its belief that "[the] financial constraints that restrict an indigent woman's ability to enjoy the full range of constitutionally protected freedom of choice are the product not of governmental restrictions on access to abortions, but rather of her indigency." Accurate as this statement may be, it reveals only half the picture. For what the Court fails to appreciate is that it is not simply the woman's indigency that interferes with her freedom of choice, but the combination of her own poverty and the Government's unequal subsidization of abortion and childbirth.

A poor woman in the early stages of pregnancy confronts two alternatives: she may elect either to carry the fetus to term or to have an abortion. In the abstract, of course, this choice is hers alone, and the Court rightly observes that the Hyde Amendment "places no governmental obstacle in the path of a woman who chooses to terminate her pregnancy." But the reality of the situation is that the Hyde Amendment has effectively removed this choice from the indigent woman's hands. By funding all of the expenses associated with childbirth and none of the expenses incurred in terminating pregnancy, the Government literally makes an offer that the indigent woman cannot afford to refuse. It matters not that in this instance the Government has used the carrot rather than the stick. What is critical is the realization that as a practical matter, many poverty-stricken women will choose to carry their pregnancy to term simply because the Government provides funds for the associated medical services, even though these same women would have chosen to have an abortion if the Government had also paid for that option, or indeed if the Government had stayed out of the picture altogether and had defrayed the costs of neither procedure.

The fundamental flaw in the Court's due process analysis, then, is its failure to acknowledge that the discriminatory distribution of the benefits of governmental largesse can discourage the exercise of fundamental liberties just as effectively as can an outright denial of those rights through criminal and regulatory sanctions. Implicit in the Court's reasoning is the notion that as long as the Government is not obligated to provide its citizens with certain benefits or privileges, it may condition the grant of such benefits on the recipient's relinquishment of his constitutional rights.

It would belabor the obvious to expound at any great length on the illegitimacy of a state policy that interferes with the exercise of fundamental rights through the selective bestowal of governmental favors. It suffices to note that we have heretofore never hesitated to invalidate any scheme of granting or withholding financial benefits that incidentally or intentionally burdens one manner of exercising a constitutionally protected choice. . . .

Mr. Justice MARSHALL, dissenting.

. . . The Court's opinion studiously avoids recognizing the undeniable fact that for women eligible for Medicaid — poor women — denial of a Medicaid-funded abortion is equivalent to denial of legal abortion altogether. By definition, these women do not have the money to pay for an abortion themselves. If abortion is medically necessary and a funded abortion is unavailable, they must resort to back-alley butchers, attempt to induce an abortion themselves by crude and dangerous methods, or suffer the serious medical consequences of attempting to carry the fetus to term. Because legal abortion is not a realistic option for such women, the predictable result of the Hyde Amendment will be a significant increase in the number of poor women who will die or suffer significant health damage because of an inability to procure necessary medical services.

The legislation before us is the product of an effort to deny to the poor the constitutional right recognized in *Roe v. Wade*, 410 U.S. 113 (1973), even though the cost may be serious and long-lasting health damage. . . . The denial of Medicaid benefits to individuals who meet all the statutory criteria for eligibility, solely because the treatment that is medically necessary involves the exercise of the fundamental right to chose abortion, is a form of discrimination repugnant to the equal protection of the laws guaranteed by the Constitution. The Court's decision today marks a retreat from *Roe v. Wade* and represents a cruel blow to the most powerless members of our society. I dissent.

I.

In its present form, the Hyde Amendment restricts federal funding for abortion to cases in which "the life of the mother would be endangered if the fetus were carried to term" and "for such medical procedures necessary for the victims of rape or incest when such rape or incest has been reported promptly to a law enforcement agency or public health service." Federal funding is thus unavailable even when severe and long-lasting health damage to the mother is a virtual certainty. Nor are federal funds available when severe health damage, or even death, will result to the fetus if it is carried to term. . . .

The impact of the Hyde Amendment on indigent women falls into four major categories. First, the Hyde Amendment prohibits federal funding for abortions that are necessary in order to protect the health and sometimes the life of the mother. Numerous conditions — such as cancer, rheumatic fever, diabetes, malnutrition, phlebitis, sickle cell anemia, and heart disease — substantially increase the risks associated with pregnancy or are themselves aggravated by pregnancy. Such conditions may make an abortion medically necessary in the judgment of a physician, but cannot be funded under the Hyde Amendment. Further, the health risks of undergoing an abortion increase dramatically as pregnancy becomes more advanced. By the time a pregnancy has progressed to the point where a physician is able to certify that it endangers the life of the mother, it is in many cases too late to prevent her death because abortion is no longer safe. There are also instances in which a woman's life will not be immediately threatened by carrying the pregnancy to term, but aggravation of another medical condition will significantly shorten her life expectancy. These cases as well are not fundable under the Hyde Amendment.

Second, federal funding is denied in cases in which severe mental disturbances will be created by unwanted pregnancies. The result of such psychological disturbances may be suicide, attempts at self-abortion, or child abuse. The Hyde Amendment makes no provision for funding in such cases.

Third, the Hyde Amendment denies funding for the majority of women whose pregnancies have been caused by rape or incest. The prerequisite of a report within 60 days serves to exclude those who are afraid of recounting what has happened or are in fear of unsympathetic treatment by the authorities. Such a requirement is, of course, especially burdensome for the indigent, who may be least likely to be aware that a rapid report to the authorities is indispensable in order for them to be able to obtain an abortion.

Finally, federal funding is unavailable in cases in which it is known that the fetus itself will be unable to survive. In a number of situations it is possible to determine in advance that the fetus will suffer an early death if carried to term. The Hyde Amendment, purportedly designed to safeguard "the legitimate governmental objective of protecting potential life," excludes federal funding in such cases. . . .

II.

. . . As in *Maher*, the governmental benefits at issue here are "of absolutely vital importance in the lives of the recipients." An indigent woman denied governmental funding for a medically necessary abortion is confronted with two grotesque choices. First, she may seek to obtain "an illegal abortion that poses a serious threat to her health and even her life." Alternatively, she may attempt to bear the child, a course that may both significantly threaten her health and eliminate any chance she might have had "to control the direction of her own life."

The class burdened by the Hyde Amendment consists of indigent women, a substantial proportion of whom are members of minority races. As I observed in *Maher*, nonwhite women obtain abortions at nearly double the rate of whites. In my view, the fact that the burden of the Hyde Amendment falls exclusively on financially destitute women suggests "a special condition, which tends seriously to curtail the operation of those political processes ordinarily to be relied upon to protect minorities, and which may call for a correspondingly more searching judicial inquiry." For this reason, I continue to believe that "a showing that state action has a devastating impact on the lives of minority racial groups must be relevant" for purposes of equal protection analysis. . . .

III.

The consequences of today's opinion — consequences to which the Court seems oblivious — are not difficult to predict. Pregnant women denied the funding necessary to procure abortions will be restricted to two alternatives. First, they can carry the fetus to term — even though that route may result in severe injury or death to the mother, the fetus, or both. If that course appears intolerable, they can resort to self-induced abortions or attempt to obtain illegal abortions — not because bearing a child would be inconvenient, but because it is necessary in order to protect their health.[7] The result will not be to protect what the Court describes as "the legitimate governmental objective of protecting potential life," but to ensure the destruction of both fetal and maternal life. "There is another world 'out there,' the existence of which the Court . . . either chooses to ignore or fears to recognize." In my view, it is only by blinding itself to that other world that the Court can reach the result it announces today.

. . . In this case, the Federal Government has taken upon itself the burden of financing practically all medically necessary expenditures. One category of medically necessary expenditure has been singled out for exclusion, and the sole basis for the exclusion is a premise repudiated for purposes of constitutional law in *Roe v. Wade*. The consequence is a devastating impact on the lives and health of poor women. I do not believe that a Constitution committed to the equal protection of the laws can tolerate this result. I dissent.

NOTES AND QUESTIONS

1. Can a policy of not funding abortions for poor people covered by Medicaid be justified by the need to save public money? In a separate dissent, Justice Stevens argued that it could not. Stevens explained:

    Fiscal considerations may compel certain difficult choices in order to improve the protection afforded to the entire benefited class. But, ironically, the

---

7. Of course, some poor women will attempt to raise the funds necessary to obtain a lawful abortion. A court recently found that those who were fortunate enough to do so had to resort to "not paying rent or utility bills, pawning household goods, diverting food and clothing money, or journeying to another state to obtain lower rates or fraudulently use a relative's insurance policy. . . . [Some] patients were driven to theft." *Women's Health Services, Inc. v. Maher*, 482 F.Supp. 725, 731 n.9.

> exclusion of medically necessary abortions harms the entire class as well as its specific victims. For the records in both McRae and Zbaraz demonstrate that the cost of an abortion is only a small fraction of the costs associated with childbirth. Thus, the decision to tolerate harm to indigent persons who need an abortion in order to avoid "serious and long-lasting health damage" is one that is financed by draining money out of the pool that is used to fund all other necessary medical procedures. Unlike most invidious classifications, this discrimination harms not only its direct victims but also the remainder of the class of needy persons that the pool was designed to benefit.

According to Stevens, given the difference in cost of an abortion and childbirth, the Hyde Amendment *cost* the government $20 million per year at the time of the decision.

2. Based on the U.S. Constitution, *Harris* leaves open the possibility that state courts can come out differently on state constitutional grounds. Quite a few state supreme courts for example have found that abortion must be funded on an equal basis as other pregnancy and health services are funded. *See, e.g.*, N.M. Right to Choose/NARAL v. Johnson, 975 P.2d 841 (N.M. 1998); Comm. to Defend Reprod. Rights v. Myers, 625 P.2d 779 (Cal. 1981). For a state-by-state guide to low-income women's access to abortion, see http://prochoiceamerica.org/government-and-you/state-governments/.

2. *Filling In the Content of Medicaid Coverage*

Lawyers working in the Medicaid field have also dedicated themselves to filling in the content of Medicaid coverage and to challenging gaps in coverage that are not allowed for under the Medicaid scheme. One example of this form of continuing Medicaid litigation has been the EPSDT requirement. As the Sixth Circuit explained in 2002 case, the federal government requires:

> that participating states provide "early and periodic screening, diagnostic, and treatment services . . . for individuals who are eligible under the plan and are under the age of 21." The required services include periodic physical examinations, immunizations, laboratory tests, health education, eye examinations, eyeglasses, teeth maintenance, diagnosis and treatment of hearing disorders, and hearing aids.

Westside Mothers v. Haveman, 289 F.3d 852 (6th Cir. 2002). Although the EPSDT requirement seems straight forward on its face, litigation has played a leading role in defining the scope and content of the requirement. In *Westside Mothers*, the Sixth Circuit held that suits alleging that state administrators were not fulfilling their obligations under the EPSDT requirement are not barred by state sovereign immunity. The court further held that Medicaid regulations are a form of law that create enforceable rights and the program cannot treated as simply a contract between the federal and state governments.

The representative EPSDT case below showcases both the technical nature of medical litigation designed to improve access to services for low-income enrollees and the challenges of securing meaningful rights for clients in the context of a program that is designed to ensure flexibility in how states meet the federal requirements.

KATIE A. v. BONTA
481 F.3d 1150 (9th Cir. 2007)

TASHIMA, Circuit Judge:

Defendants, the Director of the California Department of Health Services ("DHS") and the Director of the California Department of Social Services ("DSS"), appeal from the district court's grant of a preliminary injunction ordering them to screen members of a statewide class of foster children and, where medically necessary, provide the children with the forms of mental health care known as wraparound services and therapeutic foster care. The district court found that "the early and periodic screening, diagnostic, and treatment services" ("EPSDT") provisions of the Medicaid Act obligate the State of California ("State") to provide wraparound services and therapeutic foster care to Medicaid-eligible children under 21, and that the State does not currently provide those forms of assistance, "as such." ...

BACKGROUND

THE KATIE A. CLASS ACTION

In July 2002, a class of children who were in Los Angeles County foster care or at risk of being placed into foster care (Katie A., et al.) filed a complaint seeking declaratory and injunctive relief against the Director of DHS and the Director of DSS, as well as Los Angeles County, the Los Angeles County Department of Children and Family Services ("DCFS"), and the Director of DCFS ("LA County Defendants"). The complaint alleged that the class was entitled to and had not received "medically necessary mental health services in a home-like setting." Separate claims were alleged under 42 U.S.C. § 1983, based on violations of the children's rights under the Medicaid Act, 42 U.S.C. § 1396 *et seq.*, and the Due Process Clause of the federal Constitution; under the Americans with Disabilities Act and the Rehabilitation Act; under the Due Process Clause of the California Constitution; and under California statutory law.

Plaintiffs then moved for a preliminary injunction to require the Director of DHS and the Director of DSS ("defendants") to provide wraparound services ("wraparound") and therapeutic foster care ("TFC") to members of the class. Plaintiffs described wraparound and TFC as highly effective "integrated community-based interventions for children with emotional, behavioral, and mental health disorders." Plaintiffs argued that the EPSDT provisions obligate the State to provide wraparound and TFC to them. In particular, they alleged that MediCal policies impeding access to wraparound services or TFC violated the Medicaid statute. They alleged that MediCal covered only some components of wraparound and TFC, and that State policies made it difficult to access either type of care. ...

THE MEDICAID FRAMEWORK AND THE EPSDT OBLIGATION

Medicaid is a cooperative federal-state program that directs federal funding to states to assist them in providing medical assistance to low-income individuals.

States choose whether to participate in Medicaid. Once a state enters the program, the state must comply with the Medicaid Act and its implementing regulations. California has chosen to participate in Medicaid.

. . . California, like all other states participating in Medicaid, is required to provide EPSDT care to eligible children under the age of 21. The EPSDT services at issue in this case, wraparound and TFC, are claimed to fall under subsection (r)(5) as "[s]uch other necessary health care, diagnostic services, treatment, and other measures described in subsection (a) of this section to correct or ameliorate defects and physical and mental illnesses and conditions discovered by the screening services, whether or not such services are covered under the State plan." . . .

The EPSDT obligation is thus extremely broad. The federal agency charged with administering the Medicaid Act, the Centers for Medicare and Medicaid Services ("CMS"), has described EPSDT as a "comprehensive child health program of prevention and treatment."

THE MEDICAID ACT

The district court's determination that the EPSDT provisions of the Medicaid Act require the State to provide wraparound and TFC was the foundation for its ruling that plaintiffs have a strong likelihood of success on the merits.

Defendants contend that the district court erred in determining that the EPSDT provisions of the Medicaid Act require the State to provide wraparound and TFC. They argue that, even assuming all the components are covered under § 1396d(a), federal law does not require the State to offer the components as a "bundle" of services. They also dispute the court's conclusion that all the component services included within wraparound and TFC fall under § 1396d(a).

We conclude that the district court applied an erroneous legal standard in concluding that the EPSDT provisions require the State to provide wraparound and TFC. The district court mistakenly assumed that if all the components of wraparound and TFC fall within categories listed in § 1396d(a), and that wraparound and TFC can be deemed health care "services" in themselves, then the package of components must be offered in the form of wraparound or TFC. This assumption was flawed, for reasons that we explain below.

In general, the EPSDT provisions require only that the individual services listed in § 1396d(a) be provided, without specifying that they be provided in any particular form.

The EPSDT Provisions Require That a Specified Set of Health Services Be Provided in an Effective Manner to Eligible Children

States also must ensure that the EPSDT services provided are reasonably effective. Thus, the *State Medicaid Manual* states at several points that EPSDT services must be sufficient "to achieve their purpose." . . .

Federal courts have scrutinized state Medicaid systems to be sure that those systems are adequately designed to provide EPSDT services. . . .

As Long as a State Provides All EPSDT Services in an Effective Manner,
the Medicaid Statute Does Not Dictate That Services Must Be "Bundled"

While the states must live up to their obligations to provide all EPSDT services, the statute and regulations afford them discretion as to how to do so. There is nothing in the EPSDT statutory provisions or regulations that indicates that the state must generally design its Medicaid system to fund "packages" of EPSDT services. The legislative history of the EPSDT provisions simply indicates a Congressional purpose to provide a broad program of health care to poor children, one that would include all the forms of care listed in § 1396d(a).

In a number of cases, courts have held that particular types of health services must be provided to Medicaid-eligible children under a state's EPSDT obligations. Those cases, however, did not require a state to fund distinct services covered under separate categories of § 1396d(a) as a single package of services. *See S.D. ex rel. Dixon*, 391 F.3d at 597 (incontinence underwear falls under § 1396d(a)(7) as "home health care services"); *Collins*, 349 F.3d at 374-76 (long-term care at psychiatric residential treatment facility falls under § 1396d(a)(16) as "inpatient psychiatric hospital services"); *Pediatric Specialty Care, Inc.*, 293 F.3d at 480-81 (early intervention day treatment services fall under § 1396d(a)(13) as "other diagnostic, screening, preventive, and rehabilitative services"); *Chisholm II*, 133 F. Supp. 2d at 897-98 (behavioral and psychological services for the autistic fall under both § 1396d(a)(6) as "any other type of remedial care recognized under State law" and § 1396d(a)(13) as "other preventive, and rehabilitative services").

The issue of whether the state must provide "bundled" EPSDT services was raised in a recent case quite similar to this one in Massachusetts, in which a class of children with serious emotional disturbances claimed a right under the EPSDT provisions to "intensive home-based services," which would have included components falling under various categories of § 1396d(a). The district court avoided ruling on the question of whether EPSDT required the state to provide "intensive home-based services" to the children. Instead it "looked behind the phrase to the array of actual clinical interventions that constitute, in the terms of the Medicaid statute, 'medically necessary' services for class members." On that basis, the court concluded that comprehensive assessment of the children's clinical needs, ongoing case management and monitoring, and adequate in-home behavioral support services were each required EPSDT services which the state had failed to provide. We believe that that analytic approach was correct, insofar as it required the State to supply the substantive EPSDT services described in § 1396d(a) without curtailing the state's administrative discretion as to how to do so.

The conclusion that as a general rule, states may fund or provide medically necessary EPSDT services as separate components is consistent with the overall structure and principles of the Medicaid program. Medicaid is a *cooperative* federal-state program. While the states must meet the substantive obligations of the Medicaid Act, they nonetheless retain the discretion to design and administer their Medicaid systems as they wish. . . .

NOTES AND QUESTIONS

1. The case above, included for illustrative purposes, reflects but a single chapter of a much longer and more successful story for the *Katie A.* plaintiffs. As the California Department of Health Care Services website reports:

> The plaintiffs filed a class action suit on July 18, 2002, alleging violations of federal Medicaid laws, the American with Disabilities Act, Section 504 of the Rehabilitation Act and California Government Code Section 11135. The suit sought to improve the provision of mental health and supportive services for children and youth in, or at imminent risk of placement in, foster care in California.
>
> . . . The settlement agreement [approved on December 2, 2011] seeks to accomplish systemic change for mental health services to children and youth within the class by promoting, adopting, and endorsing three new service array approaches for existing Medicaid covered services. The state Department of Social Services and Department of Health Care Services will work together with the federal court appointed Special Master, the plaintiffs' counsel, and other stakeholders to develop and implement a plan to accomplish the terms of the settlement agreement.

Notice the significant amount of time and effort, in this and similar cases, that is required of the plaintiffs challenging Medicaid rules or their implementation.

2. Should the treating physician or the state have the final say on what medical services a patient requires? In Moore v. Reese, 637 F.3d 1220 (11th Cir. 2011), a severely disabled 16-year-old challenged Georgia's determination that she did not need more than 84 hours of in-home assistance. Her long-term doctor calculated that she needed 94 hours of care weekly but a state medical review team reduced that amount to 84 hours per week. The court held that "the Medicaid Act does not give the treating physician unilateral discretion to define medical necessity" and that, based on criteria of medical necessity, the state retains the ability to place appropriate limits on required services.

4. Affordable Care Act

The signature piece of legislation of President Obama's first term was the Affordable Care Act (ACA). Although it faced and faces significant opposition, his reelection virtually ensures that the ACA will come into full force. As emphasized in the introduction to the 2010 Medicaid Primer, published by the Kaiser Commission, the ACA makes significant changes to the health care system of the United States:

> No major health program or issue can be considered today outside the context of the nation's new health care reform law, known as the "Affordable Care Act." The health reform law, the most significant social legislation in the U.S. since 1965, seeks to eliminate large and growing gaps in health insurance by increasing access to affordable coverage and instituting a new legal obligation on the part of individuals to obtain it. To accomplish this reform, the law creates a national framework for near-universal coverage and also outlines a comprehensive set of strategies to improve care and contain costs. Integral to the coverage framework

laid out in the reform law is a dramatic expansion of the Medicaid program; half the expected gains in coverage due to health reform will be achieved through this expansion.

Kaiser Comm'n on Medicaid & the Uninsured, *Medicaid: A Primer* (2010). Signed into law on March 23, 2010, the ACA was passed despite not having the support of even a single Republican in either the House or the Senate. There were, of course, precursors to the ACA—most significantly the effort to pass health care reform led by then First Lady Hillary Clinton in the 1990s—but the ACA most certainly represents the biggest change in U.S. health care since the passage of Medicare and Medicaid.

The ACA attempts to move the U.S. health care system a great deal closer to universal coverage, most controversially through an individual mandate that every American purchase health insurance. Under the ACA, exchanges serve as the marketplace for qualified health plans. The exchanges are either set up by and authorized by states or, should states not create such exchanges, by the federal government. States can choose if their exchanges engage in directly purchasing insurance or merely serve as an information clearinghouse. For poor people, perhaps the most important component of the ACA is its expansion of eligibility for Medicaid to include poor, working-age adults. The ACA attempts to straddle the line between supporting states in their core functions, including in this case the regulation of health, and coercing states to provide increased coverage to poor people who prior to the ACA were not considered deserving. It does this by recognizing that states are free to choose not to expand their Medicaid programs, but providing that the majority of the expansion would be covered by federal, not state, funds. But the ACA is not without controversy, as is discussed in the excerpt that follows.

JANET L. DOLGIN & KATHERINE R. DIETERICH, *SOCIAL AND LEGAL DEBATE ABOUT THE AFFORDABLE CARE ACT*

80 UMKC L. Rev. 45 (2011)

1. CONSERVATIVE OPPONENTS OF THE AFFORDABLE CARE ACT

In the year after passage of the Act, opponents of health care reform reshaped their rhetoric but not their underlying concerns. They continued to focus on a perceived lack of fairness in providing "free" health care coverage to people with incomes below—and even more, to those with incomes slightly above—the federal poverty line. That sense of injustice was buttressed by the perception that those in the intermediate strata, increasingly fearful of losing their place in the nation's class hierarchy, would not be similarly rewarded. Assumptions underlying these fears harmonized with a longstanding expectation within the United States that one's position in the nation's class hierarchy follows from a set of personal choices. Thus, Americans, especially those in the middle- and upper-classes have long believed that hard work and a good education result in socio-economic success and that their success is thus "deserved." Soon after President Obama signed the Affordable Care Act, Marcia Alesan Dawkins noted its presumed consequences in the eyes of many people anxious about slipping in socio-economic status: "By making health care available to more people, those who believe it's a privilege they've earned are now placed on the same hierarchical rung as others who they believe don't deserve or haven't earned it."

By 2010, however, the rhetoric voiced by opponents of health care reform began also to reflect the discourse of professional opponents. Posters responding to media stories about legal challenges to the Act appropriated models crafted by lawyers, politicians, and judges. Increasingly, opposition from among the public described the Act as a violation of American tradition and of the Constitution. One post, typical of many others in the week after the Act became law, began by noting that the author was "not a constitutional lawyer," and then explained:

> [I]t is the first time you are going to be required by the federal government to buy something from a private company for the act of existing. Now, as Mr. Barnett says, if this is deemed constitutional, couldn't the federal government mandate that you buy anything from a private company. . . . [W]hy can't the feds force me to buy a computer or face a fine, a car or face a fine etc.

Another post expressed amazement "at the number of people here who just don't understand the constitution." This poster then explained that allowing Congress to "tax" those who do not have health coverage would end badly for the nation:

> Make no mistake, the next phase of this, within 10 years, will be to keep costs down by limiting caloric intake of all Americans AND enforcing regimented exercise programs of all able bodie[d] citizens. The US now owns you. And you sold yourselves to them. . . . That's not slavery, that's indentured servitude, and you fell for it.

This post thus cloaks a message about freedom and choice inside a frame stressing the ACA as an abuse of federal power. . . .

Most opposition to the Act was grounded in comparatively mainstream aspects of American ideology and was peaceful. Some, however, was neither mainstream nor peaceful. The next subsection describes more extremist, even sometimes violent, opposition. That opposition suggests the intensity of anger that affected at least some of those who opposed the Affordable Care Act and the values they understood the Act to signal.

2. EXTREMIST OPPOSITION

A more hateful, desperate response to the Affordable Care Act emerged openly in the days immediately before, and in the months after, the Act's passage. In large part, these manifestations of opposition were grounded on an elaboration and magnification of claims detailed above. Angry opposition emerged in a public arena a few hours before Congress passed the Affordable Care Act. Activists opposing passage of the reform bill surrounded one of the Capitol buildings. As Barney Frank, an openly gay member of the House, and John Lewis, a 70-year-old one-time civil-rights activist, walked into the Capitol, protesters screamed "faggot" and "nigger." Others screamed "liar" and "crook" at Representative Henry Waxman (D-Cal.), a supporter of the reform bill. Democratic Whip Jim Clyburn (D-S.C.) watched a protester spit on a black member of the House. Clyburn, himself Black, exclaimed that he heard things that day that he had not heard since 1960 when he was "marching to try to get off the back of the bus."

. . . Other House Democrats reported similar angry acts directed against them. An Alabama blogger and one-time leader of the Alabama Constitutional Militia, suggested that readers throw bricks into the offices of Democratic head-quarters throughout the nation, as a message in opposition to the party's support for health care reform. In the week in which the House passed the Affordable Care Act, at least ten Democrats in the House reported death threats, harassment, or vandalism.

Angry opponents of health care reform resembled more moderate oppo-nents, in stressing the threat that health care reform presented to efforts to safeguard liberty and freedom. One vandal in Rochester, N.Y. attached a note to a brick thrown into the Democratic Committee's headquarters. It read: "Extremism in defense of liberty is no vice." And the blogger from Arizona who encouraged readers to respond with violence to those who supported health care reform referred to those who followed his call as the "modern 'Sons of Liberty.'"

* * *

In 2012, the U.S. Supreme Court considered a challenge to the ACA. In an unusual move, but one reflecting the significance of the issues involved in the challenge, the Court allowed three days for oral argument. An excerpt from the groundbreaking opinion is below.

NAT'L FED'N OF INDEP. BUS. v. SEBELIUS
132 S. Ct. 2566 (2012)

Chief Justice ROBERTS announced the judgment of the Court and delivered the opinion of the Court with respect to Parts I, II, and III-C, an opinion with respect to Part IV, in which Justice BREYER and Justice KAGAN join, and an opinion with respect to Parts III-A, III-B, and III-D.

Today we resolve constitutional challenges to two provisions of the Patient Protection and Affordable Care Act of 2010: the individual mandate, which requires individuals to purchase a health insurance policy providing a minimum level of coverage; and the Medicaid expansion, which gives funds to the States on the condition that they provide specified health care to all citizens whose income falls below a certain threshold. We do not consider whether the Act embodies sound policies. That judgment is entrusted to the Nation's elected leaders. We ask only whether Congress has the power under the Constitution to enact the challenged provisions.

I.

In 2010, Congress enacted the Patient Protection and Affordable Care Act, 124 Stat. 119. The Act aims to increase the number of Americans covered by health insurance and decrease the cost of health care. The Act's 10 titles stretch over 900 pages and contain hundreds of provisions. This case concerns constitutional challenges to two key provisions, commonly referred to as the individual mandate and the Medicaid expansion.

The individual mandate requires most Americans to maintain "minimum essential" health insurance coverage. . . . Many individuals will receive the required coverage through their employer, or from a government program such as Medicaid or Medicare. But for individuals who are not exempt and do not receive health insurance through a third party, the means of satisfying the requirement is to purchase insurance from a private company.

Beginning in 2014, those who do not comply with the mandate must make a "[s]hared responsibility payment" to the Federal Government. That payment, which the Act describes as a "penalty," is calculated as a percentage of household income, subject to a floor based on a specified dollar amount and a ceiling based on the average annual premium the individual would have to pay for qualifying private health insurance. In 2016, for example, the penalty will be 2.5 percent of an individual's household income, but no less than $695 and no more than the average yearly premium for insurance that covers 60 percent of the cost of 10 specified services (e.g., prescription drugs and hospitalization). . . .

The second provision of the Affordable Care Act directly challenged here is the Medicaid expansion. Enacted in 1965, Medicaid offers federal funding to States to assist pregnant women, children, needy families, the blind, the elderly, and the disabled in obtaining medical care. In order to receive that funding, States must comply with federal criteria governing matters such as who receives care and what services are provided at what cost. By 1982 every State had chosen to participate in Medicaid. Federal funds received through the Medicaid program have become a substantial part of state budgets, now constituting over 10 percent of most States' total revenue.

The Affordable Care Act expands the scope of the Medicaid program and increases the number of individuals the States must cover. For example, the Act requires state programs to provide Medicaid coverage to adults with incomes up to 133 percent of the federal poverty level, whereas many States now cover adults with children only if their income is considerably lower, and do not cover childless adults at all. The Act increases federal funding to cover the States' costs in expanding Medicaid coverage, although States will bear a portion of the costs on their own. If a State does not comply with the Act's new coverage requirements, it may lose not only the federal funding for those requirements, but all of its federal Medicaid funds. . . .

III.

The Government advances two theories for the proposition that Congress had constitutional authority to enact the individual mandate. First, the Government argues that Congress had the power to enact the mandate under the Commerce Clause. Under that theory, Congress may order individuals to buy health insurance because the failure to do so affects interstate commerce, and could undercut the Affordable Care Act's other reforms. Second, the Government argues that if the commerce power does not support the mandate, we should nonetheless uphold it as an exercise of Congress's power to tax. According to the Government, even if Congress lacks the power to direct individuals to buy insurance, the only effect of the individual mandate is to raise taxes on those who do not do so, and thus the law may be upheld as a tax.

A.

The Government's first argument is that the individual mandate is a valid exercise of Congress's power under the Commerce Clause and the Necessary and Proper Clause. According to the Government, the health care market is characterized by a significant cost-shifting problem. Everyone will eventually need health care at a time and to an extent they cannot predict, but if they do not have insurance, they often will not be able to pay for it. Because state and federal laws nonetheless require hospitals to provide a certain degree of care to individuals without regard to their ability to pay, hospitals end up receiving compensation for only a portion of the services they provide. To recoup the losses, hospitals pass on the cost to insurers through higher rates, and insurers, in turn, pass on the cost to policy holders in the form of higher premiums. Congress estimated that the cost of uncompensated care raises family health insurance premiums, on average, by over $1,000 per year.

In the Affordable Care Act, Congress addressed the problem of those who cannot obtain insurance coverage because of preexisting conditions or other health issues. It did so through the Act's "guaranteed-issue" and "community-rating" provisions. These provisions together prohibit insurance companies from denying coverage to those with such conditions or charging unhealthy individuals higher premiums than healthy individuals.

The guaranteed-issue and community-rating reforms do not, however, address the issue of healthy individuals who choose not to purchase insurance to cover potential health care needs. In fact, the reforms sharply exacerbate that problem, by providing an incentive for individuals to delay purchasing health insurance until they become sick, relying on the promise of guaranteed and affordable coverage. The reforms also threaten to impose massive new costs on insurers, who are required to accept unhealthy individuals but prohibited from charging them rates necessary to pay for their coverage. This will lead insurers to significantly increase premiums on everyone.

The individual mandate was Congress's solution to these problems. By requiring that individuals purchase health insurance, the mandate prevents cost-shifting by those who would otherwise go without it. In addition, the mandate forces into the insurance risk pool more healthy individuals, whose premiums on average will be higher than their health care expenses. This allows insurers to subsidize the costs of covering the unhealthy individuals the reforms require them to accept. The Government claims that Congress has power under the Commerce and Necessary and Proper Clauses to enact this solution.

[Chief Justice Roberts's opinion then rejects the argument that the ACA's individual mandate could be sustained under the Commerce Clause but goes on to sustain the individual mandate on the basis of the power to tax.]

IV.

A.

The States also contend that the Medicaid expansion exceeds Congress's authority under the Spending Clause. They claim that Congress is coercing the States to adopt the changes it wants by threatening to withhold all of a State's

Medicaid grants, unless the State accepts the new expanded funding and complies with the conditions that come with it. This, they argue, violates the basic principle that the "Federal Government may not compel the States to enact or administer a federal regulatory program."

There is no doubt that the Act dramatically increases state obligations under Medicaid. The current Medicaid program requires States to cover only certain discrete categories of needy individuals — pregnant women, children, needy families, the blind, the elderly, and the disabled. There is no mandatory coverage for most childless adults, and the States typically do not offer any such coverage. The States also enjoy considerable flexibility with respect to the coverage levels for parents of needy families. On average States cover only those unemployed parents who make less than 37 percent of the federal poverty level, and only those employed parents who make less than 63 percent of the poverty line.

The Medicaid provisions of the Affordable Care Act, in contrast, require States to expand their Medicaid programs by 2014 to cover *all* individuals under the age of 65 with incomes below 133 percent of the federal poverty line. The Act also establishes a new "[e]ssential health benefits" package, which States must provide to all new Medicaid recipients — a level sufficient to satisfy a recipient's obligations under the individual mandate. The Affordable Care Act provides that the Federal Government will pay 100 percent of the costs of covering these newly eligible individuals through 2016. In the following years, the federal payment level gradually decreases, to a minimum of 90 percent. In light of the expansion in coverage mandated by the Act, the Federal Government estimates that its Medicaid spending will increase by approximately $100 billion per year, nearly 40 percent above current levels.

. . . Congress may use its spending power to create incentives for States to act in accordance with federal policies. But when "pressure turns into compulsion," the legislation runs contrary to our system of federalism. "[T]he Constitution simply does not give Congress the authority to require the States to regulate." That is true whether Congress directly commands a State to regulate or indirectly coerces a State to adopt a federal regulatory system as its own.

. . . Congress may attach appropriate conditions to federal taxing and spending programs to preserve its control over the use of federal funds. In the typical case we look to the States to defend their prerogatives by adopting "the simple expedient of not yielding" to federal blandishments when they do not want to embrace the federal policies as their own. The States are separate and independent sovereigns. Sometimes they have to act like it.

The States, however, argue that the Medicaid expansion is far from the typical case. They object that Congress has "crossed the line distinguishing encouragement from coercion," in the way it has structured the funding: Instead of simply refusing to grant the new funds to States that will not accept the new conditions, Congress has also threatened to withhold those States' existing Medicaid funds. The States claim that this threat serves no purpose other than to force unwilling States to sign up for the dramatic expansion in health care coverage effected by the Act.

Given the nature of the threat and the programs at issue here, we must agree. . . .

In this case, the financial "inducement" Congress has chosen is much more than "relatively mild encouragement" — it is a gun to the head. Section 1396c of the Medicaid Act provides that if a State's Medicaid plan does not comply with the Act's requirements, the Secretary of Health and Human Services may declare that "further payments will not be made to the State." A State that opts out of the Affordable Care Act's expansion in health care coverage thus stands to lose not merely "a relatively small percentage" of its existing Medicaid funding, but *all* of it. . . .

The Medicaid expansion, however, accomplishes a shift in kind, not merely degree. The original program was designed to cover medical services for four particular categories of the needy: the disabled, the blind, the elderly, and needy families with dependent children. Previous amendments to Medicaid eligibility merely altered and expanded the boundaries of these categories. Under the Affordable Care Act, Medicaid is transformed into a program to meet the health care needs of the entire nonelderly population with income below 133 percent of the poverty level. It is no longer a program to care for the neediest among us, but rather an element of a comprehensive national plan to provide universal health insurance coverage. . . .

The Court in *Steward Machine* did not attempt to "fix the outermost line" where persuasion gives way to coercion. The Court found it "[e]nough for present purposes that wherever the line may be, this statute is within it." We have no need to fix a line either. It is enough for today that wherever that line may be, this statute is surely beyond it. Congress may not simply "conscript state [agencies] into the national bureaucratic army," and that is what it is attempting to do with the Medicaid expansion.

B.

Nothing in our opinion precludes Congress from offering funds under the Affordable Care Act to expand the availability of health care, and requiring that States accepting such funds comply with the conditions on their use. What Congress is not free to do is to penalize States that choose not to participate in that new program by taking away their existing Medicaid funding. Section 1396c gives the Secretary of Health and Human Services the authority to do just that. It allows her to withhold *all* "further [Medicaid] payments . . . to the State" if she determines that the State is out of compliance with any Medicaid requirement, including those contained in the expansion. In light of the Court's holding, the Secretary cannot apply § 1396c to withdraw existing Medicaid funds for failure to comply with the requirements set out in the expansion. . . .

The Affordable Care Act is constitutional in part and unconstitutional in part. The individual mandate cannot be upheld as an exercise of Congress's power under the Commerce Clause. That Clause authorizes Congress to regulate interstate commerce, not to order individuals to engage in it. In this case, however, it is reasonable to construe what Congress has done as increasing taxes on those who have a certain amount of income, but choose to go without health insurance. Such legislation is within Congress's power to tax.

As for the Medicaid expansion, that portion of the Affordable Care Act violates the Constitution by threatening existing Medicaid funding. Congress has no authority to order the States to regulate according to its instructions. Congress may offer the States grants and require the States to comply with accompanying conditions, but the States must have a genuine choice whether to accept the offer. The States are given no such choice in this case: They must either accept a basic change in the nature of Medicaid, or risk losing all Medicaid funding. The remedy for that constitutional violation is to preclude the Federal Government from imposing such a sanction. That remedy does not require striking down other portions of the Affordable Care Act.

The Framers created a Federal Government of limited powers, and assigned to this Court the duty of enforcing those limits. The Court does so today. But the Court does not express any opinion on the wisdom of the Affordable Care Act. Under the Constitution, that judgment is reserved to the people. . . .

Justice GINSBURG, with whom Justice SOTOMAYOR joins, and with whom Justice BREYER and Justice KAGAN join as to Parts I, II, III, and IV, concurring in part, concurring in the judgment in part, and dissenting in part.

I agree with The Chief Justice that the Anti-Injunction Act does not bar the Court's consideration of this case, and that the minimum coverage provision is a proper exercise of Congress' taxing power. I therefore join Parts I, II, and III-C of The Chief Justice's opinion. Unlike The Chief Justice, however, I would hold, alternatively, that the Commerce Clause authorizes Congress to enact the minimum coverage provision. I would also hold that the Spending Clause permits the Medicaid expansion exactly as Congress enacted it.

I.

The provision of health care is today a concern of national dimension, just as the provision of old-age and survivors' benefits was in the 1930's. In the Social Security Act, Congress installed a federal system to provide monthly benefits to retired wage earners and, eventually, to their survivors. Beyond question, Congress could have adopted a similar scheme for health care. Congress chose, instead, to preserve a central role for private insurers and state governments. According to The Chief Justice, the Commerce Clause does not permit that preservation. This rigid reading of the Clause makes scant sense and is stunningly retrogressive.

Since 1937, our precedent has recognized Congress' large authority to set the Nation's course in the economic and social welfare realm. The Chief Justice's crabbed reading of the Commerce Clause harks back to the era in which the Court routinely thwarted Congress' efforts to regulate the national economy in the interest of those who labor to sustain it. It is a reading that should not have staying power.

A.

In enacting the Patient Protection and Affordable Care Act (ACA), Congress comprehensively reformed the national market for healthcare products and services. By any measure, that market is immense. Collectively, Americans spent $2.5 trillion on health care in 2009, accounting for 17.6% of our Nation's economy. Within the next decade, it is anticipated, spending on health care will nearly double.

The healthcare market's size is not its only distinctive feature. Unlike the market for almost any other product or service, the market for medical care is one in which all individuals inevitably participate. Virtually every person residing in the United States, sooner or later, will visit a doctor or other health-care professional. Most people will do so repeatedly.

When individuals make those visits, they face another reality of the current market for medical care: its high cost. In 2010, on average, an individual in the United States incurred over $7,000 in health-care expenses. Over a lifetime, costs mount to hundreds of thousands of dollars. When a person requires non-routine care, the cost will generally exceed what he or she can afford to pay. A single hospital stay, for instance, typically costs upwards of $10,000. Treatments for many serious, though not uncommon, conditions similarly cost a substantial sum.

Although every U.S. domiciliary will incur significant medical expenses during his or her lifetime, the time when care will be needed is often unpredictable. An accident, a heart attack, or a cancer diagnosis commonly occurs without warning. Inescapably, we are all at peril of needing medical care without a moment's notice.

To manage the risks associated with medical care — its high cost, its unpredictability, and its inevitability — most people in the United States obtain health insurance. Many (approximately 170 million in 2009) are insured by private insurance companies. Others, including those over 65 and certain poor and disabled persons, rely on government-funded insurance programs, notably Medicare and Medicaid. Combined, private health insurers and State and Federal Governments finance almost 85% of the medical care administered to U.S. residents.

Not all U.S. residents, however, have health insurance. In 2009, approximately 50 million people were uninsured, either by choice or, more likely, because they could not afford private insurance and did not qualify for government aid. As a group, uninsured individuals annually consume more than $100 billion in health-care services, nearly 5% of the Nation's total. Over 60% of those without insurance visit a doctor's office or emergency room in a given year.

B.

The large number of individuals without health insurance, Congress found, heavily burdens the national health-care market. As just noted, the cost of emergency care or treatment for a serious illness generally exceeds what an individual can afford to pay on her own. Unlike markets for most products, however, the inability to pay for care does not mean that an uninsured individual will receive no care. Federal and state law, as well as professional obligations and embedded social norms, require hospitals and physicians to provide care when it is most needed, regardless of the patient's ability to pay.

As a consequence, medical-care providers deliver significant amounts of care to the uninsured for which the providers receive no payment. In 2008, for example, hospitals, physicians, and other health-care professionals received no compensation for $43 billion worth of the $116 billion in care they administered to those without insurance.

Health-care providers do not absorb these bad debts. Instead, they raise their prices, passing along the cost of uncompensated care to those who do pay reliably: the government and private insurance companies. In response, private insurers increase their premiums, shifting the cost of the elevated bills from providers onto those who carry insurance. The net result: Those with health insurance subsidize the medical care of those without it. As economists would describe what happens, the uninsured "free ride" on those who pay for health insurance.

The size of this subsidy is considerable. Congress found that the cost-shifting just described "increases family [insurance] premiums by on average over $1,000 a year." Higher premiums, in turn, render health insurance less afford- able, forcing more people to go without insurance and leading to further cost- shifting.

And it is hardly just the currently sick or injured among the uninsured who prompt elevation of the price of health care and health insurance. Insurance companies and health-care providers know that some percentage of healthy, uninsured people will suffer sickness or injury each year and will receive medical care despite their inability to pay. In anticipation of this uncompensated care, health-care companies raise their prices, and insurers their premiums. In other words, because any uninsured person may need medical care at any moment and because health-care companies must account for that risk, every uninsured person impacts the market price of medical care and medical insurance.

The failure of individuals to acquire insurance has other deleterious effects on the health-care market. Because those without insurance generally lack access to preventative care, they do not receive treatment for conditions — like hyperten- sion and diabetes — that can be successfully and affordably treated if diagnosed early on. When sickness finally drives the uninsured to seek care, once treatable conditions have escalated into grave health problems, requiring more costly and extensive intervention. The extra time and resources providers spend serving the uninsured lessens the providers' ability to care for those who do have insurance.

C.

States cannot resolve the problem of the uninsured on their own. Like Social Security benefits, a universal health-care system, if adopted by an individual State, would be "bait to the needy and dependent elsewhere, encouraging them to migrate and seek a haven of repose." An influx of unhealthy individuals into a State with universal health care would result in increased spending on medical services. To cover the increased costs, a State would have to raise taxes, and private health-insurance companies would have to increase premiums. Higher taxes and increased insurance costs would, in turn, encourage busi- nesses and healthy individuals to leave the State.

States that undertake health-care reforms on their own thus risk "placing themselves in a position of economic disadvantage as compared with neighbors or competitors." Facing that risk, individual States are unlikely to take the initiative in addressing the problem of the uninsured, even though solving that problem is in all States' best interests. Congress' intervention was needed to overcome this collective-action impasse.

D.

Aware that a national solution was required, Congress could have taken over the health-insurance market by establishing a tax-and-spend federal program like

Social Security. Such a program, commonly referred to as a single-payer system (where the sole payer is the Federal Government), would have left little, if any, room for private enterprise or the States. Instead of going this route, Congress enacted the ACA, a solution that retains a robust role for private insurers and state governments. To make its chosen approach work, however, Congress had to use some new tools, including a requirement that most individuals obtain private health insurance coverage. As explained below, by employing these tools, Congress was able to achieve a practical, altogether reasonable, solution.

A central aim of the ACA is to reduce the number of uninsured U.S. residents. The minimum coverage provision advances this objective by giving potential recipients of health care a financial incentive to acquire insurance. Per the minimum coverage provision, an individual must either obtain insurance or pay a toll constructed as a tax penalty. . . .

V.

Medicaid is a prototypical example of federal-state cooperation in serving the Nation's general welfare. Rather than authorizing a federal agency to administer a uniform national health-care system for the poor, Congress offered States the opportunity to tailor Medicaid grants to their particular needs, so long as they remain within bounds set by federal law. In shaping Medicaid, Congress did not endeavor to fix permanently the terms participating states must meet; instead, Congress reserved the "right to alter, amend, or repeal" any provision of the Medicaid Act. States, for their part, agreed to amend their own Medicaid plans consistent with changes from time to time made in the federal law. And from 1965 to the present, States have regularly conformed to Congress' alterations of the Medicaid Act. . . .

A.

Expansion has been characteristic of the Medicaid program. Akin to the ACA in 2010, the Medicaid Act as passed in 1965 augmented existing federal grant programs jointly administered with the States. States were not required to participate in Medicaid. But if they did, the Federal Government paid at least half the costs. To qualify for these grants, States had to offer a minimum level of health coverage to beneficiaries of four federally funded, state-administered welfare programs: Aid to Families with Dependent Children; Old Age Assistance; Aid to the Blind; and Aid to the Permanently and Totally Disabled. At their option, States could enroll additional "medically needy" individuals; these costs, too, were partially borne by the Federal Government at the same, at least 50%, rate.

Since 1965, Congress has amended the Medicaid program on more than 50 occasions, sometimes quite sizably. Most relevant here, between 1988 and 1990, Congress required participating States to include among their beneficiaries pregnant women with family incomes up to 133% of the federal poverty level, children up to age 6 at the same income levels, and children ages 6 to 18 with family incomes up to 100% of the poverty level. These amendments added millions to the Medicaid-eligible population. . . .

Compared to past alterations, the ACA is notable for the extent to which the Federal Government will pick up the tab. Medicaid's 2010 expansion is financed largely by federal outlays. In 2014, federal funds will cover 100% of the costs for newly eligible beneficiaries; that rate will gradually decrease before settling at 90% in 2020. By comparison, federal contributions toward the care of beneficiaries eligible pre-ACA range from 50% to 83%, and averaged 57% between 2005 and 2008.

Nor will the expansion exorbitantly increase state Medicaid spending. The Congressional Budget Office (CBO) projects that States will spend 0.8% more than they would have, absent the ACA. Whatever the increase in state obligations after the ACA, it will pale in comparison to the increase in federal funding.

Finally, any fair appraisal of Medicaid would require acknowledgment of the considerable autonomy States enjoy under the Act. Far from "conscript[ing] state agencies into the national bureaucratic army," Medicaid "is designed to advance cooperative federalism." . . .

Justice SCALIA, Justice KENNEDY, Justice THOMAS, and Justice ALITO, dissenting.

Congress has set out to remedy the problem that the best health care is beyond the reach of many Americans who cannot afford it. It can assuredly do that, by exercising the powers accorded to it under the Constitution. The question in this case, however, is whether the complex structures and provisions of the Patient Protection and Affordable Care Act (Affordable Care Act or ACA) go beyond those powers. We conclude that they do.

This case is in one respect difficult: it presents two questions of first impression. The first of those is whether failure to engage in economic activity (the purchase of health insurance) is subject to regulation under the Commerce Clause. Failure to act does result in an effect on commerce, and hence might be said to come under this Court's "affecting commerce" criterion of Commerce Clause jurisprudence. But in none of its decisions has this Court extended the Clause that far. The second question is whether the congressional power to tax and spend, permits the conditioning of a State's continued receipt of all funds under a massive state-administered federal welfare program upon its acceptance of an expansion to that program. Several of our opinions have suggested that the power to tax and spend cannot be used to coerce state administration of a federal program, but we have never found a law enacted under the spending power to be coercive. Those questions are difficult.

The case is easy and straightforward, however, in another respect. What is absolutely clear, affirmed by the text of the 1789 Constitution, by the Tenth Amendment ratified in 1791, and by innumerable cases of ours in the 220 years since, is that there are structural limits upon federal power — upon what it can prescribe with respect to private conduct, and upon what it can impose upon the sovereign States. Whatever may be the conceptual limits upon the Commerce Clause and upon the power to tax and spend, they cannot be such as will enable the Federal Government to regulate all private conduct and to compel the States to function as administrators of federal programs.

That clear principle carries the day here. . . .

The Act before us here exceeds federal power both in mandating the purchase of health insurance and in denying nonconsenting States all Medicaid funding. These parts of the Act are central to its design and operation, and all the Act's other provisions would not have been enacted without them. In our view it must follow that the entire statute is inoperative.

I. The Individual Mandate

... Here ... Congress has impressed into service third parties, healthy individuals who could be but are not customers of the relevant industry, to offset the undesirable consequences of the regulation. Congress' desire to force these individuals to purchase insurance is motivated by the fact that they are further removed from the market than unhealthy individuals with pre-existing conditions, because they are less likely to need extensive care in the near future. If Congress can reach out and command even those furthest removed from an interstate market to participate in the market, then the Commerce Clause becomes a font of unlimited power, or in Hamilton's words, "the hideous monster whose devouring jaws ... spare neither sex nor age, nor high nor low, nor sacred nor profane." ...

The Government was invited, at oral argument, to suggest what federal controls over private conduct (other than those explicitly prohibited by the Bill of Rights or other constitutional controls) could *not* be justified as necessary and proper for the carrying out of a general regulatory scheme. It was unable to name any. As we said at the outset, whereas the precise scope of the Commerce Clause and the Necessary and Proper Clause is uncertain, the proposition that the Federal Government cannot do everything is a fundamental precept. See *Lopez*, 514 U.S., at 564, 115 S. Ct. 1624, 131 L. Ed. 2d 626 ("[I]f we were to accept the Government's arguments, we are hard pressed to posit any activity by an individual that Congress is without power to regulate"). Section 5000A is defeated by that proposition.

B.

... It is true enough that everyone consumes "health care," if the term is taken to include the purchase of a bottle of aspirin. But the health care "market" that is the object of the Individual Mandate not only includes but principally consists of goods and services that the young people primarily affected by the Mandate *do not purchase*. They are quite simply not participants in that market, and cannot be made so (and thereby subjected to regulation) by the simple device of defining participants to include all those who will, later in their lifetime, probably purchase the goods or services covered by the mandated insurance. Such a definition of market participants is unprecedented, and were it to be a premise for the exercise of national power, it would have no principled limits.

... It is true that, at the end of the day, it is inevitable that each American will affect commerce and become a part of it, even if not by choice. But if every person comes within the Commerce Clause power of Congress to regulate by the simple reason that he will one day engage in commerce, the idea of a limited Government power is at an end ...

II. The Taxing Power

[The dissent here argues that it is inappropriate to construe the individual mandate and associated penalty as a tax, and therefore the ACA cannot be sustained under the power to tax.]

IV. The Medicaid Expansion

We now consider respondents' second challenge to the constitutionality of the ACA, namely, that the Act's dramatic expansion of the Medicaid program exceeds Congress' power to attach conditions to federal grants to the States. . . .

B.

One way in which Congress may spend to promote the general welfare is by making grants to the States. Monetary grants, so-called grants-in-aid, became more frequent during the 1930's, and by 1950 they had reached $20 billion or 11.6% of state and local government expenditures from their own sources. . . . As of 2010, federal outlays to state and local governments came to over $608 billion or 37.5% of state and local government expenditures.

When Congress makes grants to the States, it customarily attaches conditions, and this Court has long held that the Constitution generally permits Congress to do this.

C.

This practice of attaching conditions to federal funds greatly increases federal power. "[O]bjectives not thought to be within Article I's enumerated legislative fields, may nevertheless be attained through the use of the spending power and the conditional grant of federal funds."

This formidable power, if not checked in any way, would present a grave threat to the system of federalism created by our Constitution. . . .

Once it is recognized that spending-power legislation cannot coerce state participation, two questions remain: (1) What is the meaning of coercion in this context? (2) Is the ACA's expanded Medicaid coverage coercive? We now turn to those questions.

D.

1.

The answer to the first of these questions — the meaning of coercion in the present context — is straightforward. As we have explained, the legitimacy of attaching conditions to federal grants to the States depends on the voluntariness of the States' choice to accept or decline the offered package. Therefore, if States really have no choice other than to accept the package, the offer is coercive, and the conditions cannot be sustained under the spending power. . . .

2.

The Federal Government's argument in this case at best pays lip service to the anticoercion principle. The Federal Government suggests that it is sufficient if States are "free, *as a matter of law*, to turn down" federal funds. According to the Federal Government, neither the amount of the offered federal funds nor the amount of the federal taxes extracted from the taxpayers of a State to pay for the program in question is relevant in determining whether there is impermissible coercion.

This argument ignores reality. When a heavy federal tax is levied to support a federal program that offers large grants to the States, States may, as a practical matter, be unable to refuse to participate in the federal program and to substitute a state alternative. Even if a State believes that the federal program is ineffective and inefficient, withdrawal would likely force the State to impose a huge tax increase on its residents, and this new state tax would come on top of the federal taxes already paid by residents to support subsidies to participating States. . . .

E.

Whether federal spending legislation crosses the line from enticement to coercion is often difficult to determine, and courts should not conclude that legislation is unconstitutional on this ground unless the coercive nature of an offer is unmistakably clear. In this case, however, there can be no doubt. In structuring the ACA, Congress unambiguously signaled its belief that every State would have no real choice but to go along with the Medicaid Expansion. If the anticoercion rule does not apply in this case, then there is no such rule. . . .

The stated goal of the ACA is near-universal health care coverage. To achieve this goal, the ACA mandates that every person obtain a minimum level of coverage. It attempts to reach this goal in several different ways. The guaranteed issue and community-rating provisions are designed to make qualifying insurance available and affordable for persons with medical conditions that may require expensive care. Other ACA provisions seek to make such policies more affordable for people of modest means. Finally, for low-income individuals who are simply not able to obtain insurance, Congress expanded Medicaid, transforming it from a program covering only members of a limited list of vulnerable groups into a program that provides at least the requisite minimum level of coverage for the poor. This design was intended to provide at least a specified minimum level of coverage for all Americans, but the achievement of that goal obviously depends on participation by every single State. If any State — not to mention all of the 26 States that brought this suit — chose to decline the federal offer, there would be a gaping hole in the ACA's coverage.

. . . Congress never dreamed that any State would refuse to go along with the expansion of Medicaid. Congress well understood that refusal was not a practical option. . . .

For the reasons here stated, we would find the Act invalid in its entirety. We respectfully dissent.

NOTES AND QUESTIONS

1. In advance of the ruling, how the Court would come out regarding the constitutionality of the ACA was a matter of considerable public speculation. Chief Justice Roberts's decision to join Justices Ginsburg, Sotomayor, Breyer, and Kagan in upholding the individual mandate surprised many people because of the expectation that he would side with the conservative camp. In the wake of the decision, Dean Martha Minow celebrated Roberts's opinion as "a work of legal craftsmanship." Martha Minow, *Affordable*

Convergence: "Reasonable Interpretation" and the Affordable Care Act, 126 Harv. L. Rev. 117 (2012).

2. Concerns about judicial activism have been heard for more than a decade and the decision seems to reflect awareness of these critiques of the judiciary. Which side is right? Is the majority engaged in judicial activism when it reads the ACA in a way that deviates from a strict reading of the legislation in order to fit it under Congress's tax authority? Or is the dissent putting its thumb too heavily on the scale in favor of decisionmaking through the judiciary instead of decisionmaking through the political branches when it rejects the possibility of piecemeal changes to the Medicaid program, even as it acknowledges that such changes would have been allowed if the ACA simply replaced Medicaid?

3. How does the ACA change who we are as Americans? Professor Edward Rubin, for example, argues that "the Act represents a genuine revolution in the way we think about American citizenship and the nature of our political economy." Edward Rubin, *The Affordable Care Act, the Constitutional Meaning of Statutes, and the Emerging Doctrine of Positive Constitutional Rights,* 53 Wm. & Mary L. Rev. 1639 (2012).

4. We will end with a big-picture question. Having read this chapter, where should antipoverty advocates concerned about health place their attention?

CHAPTER
8

Education

INTRODUCTION

Many Americans, if asked whether education was a constitutional right in the United States, might answer in the affirmative. Indeed, many might think the Supreme Court so held in Brown v. Board of Education. In the course of determining that racial segregation in public schools violated the Equal Protection Clause of the Fourteenth Amendment, the Court issued a ringing endorsement of the importance of education in American life:

> Today, education is perhaps the most important function of state and local governments. Compulsory school attendance laws and the great expenditures for education both demonstrate our recognition of the importance of education to our democratic society. It is required in the performance of our most basic public responsibilities, even service in the armed forces. It is the very foundation of good citizenship. Today it is a principal instrument in awakening the child to cultural values, in preparing him for later professional training, and in helping him to adjust normally to his environment. In these days, it is doubtful that any child may reasonably be expected to succeed in life if he is denied the opportunity of an education. Such an opportunity, where the state has undertaken to provide it, is a right which must be made available to all on equal terms.

Brown v. Board of Education, 347 U.S. 483, 493 (1954).

As the readings in this chapter demonstrate, however, the status of education in federal law is actually far more tenuous than the stirring language of *Brown* suggested, with the result that the federal Constitution has not been the powerful tool *Brown* seemed to promise in ending segregation or improving schools for children of color. Accordingly, the chapter examines the turn toward state court advocacy and nonlitigation strategies to improve schools. Throughout, a question that appears in many chapters, particularly Chapter 3, also echoes here: whether the goal of antipoverty advocacy should be equal treatment of the poor and non-poor, or the securing for the poor of a "floor" or minimum acceptable quantum of (in this case) education. In the education arena, this theme appears as the debate between "equity" and "adequacy" goals. "Equity" litigation, popular in the late 1960s and early 1970s, sought to equalize resources between poor and wealthier schools. "Adequacy" lawsuits, currently more prevalent, are based on the idea that certain bare essentials (of resources, physical plant, qualified teachers, curriculum, etc.) are necessary to fulfill legal duties to provide education.

In addition to litigation, this chapter examines the federal policy role in education as set forth in the Elementary and Secondary Education Act, whose most recent chapter is the No Child Left Behind (NCLB) Act of 2001, now criticized by stakeholders from across the political spectrum. We examine NCLB and its critiques, as well as other alternatives to traditional public education.

Finally, the strands of race and poverty are deeply intertwined in education, perhaps even more so than they are in many of the other substantive areas covered in this book. Accordingly, many of the materials in this chapter discuss racial as well as socioeconomic differences in education and educational achievement. We also include notes regarding desegregation and resegregation and differential rates of school discipline.

Following this Introduction, we begin in Section A with a brief examination of what is known about the connection between poverty and education. Section B includes *Rodriguez* and the status of education under federal law. Section C covers the turn to state courts after *Rodriguez*, while Section D returns to the federal role in education and discusses the landmark No Child Left Behind law in detail. Section E discusses the charter school movement. The chapter concludes in Section F with an emerging topic in both racial justice and antipoverty work, the effect of "zero tolerance" discipline policies, popularly known as the "school-to-prison pipeline."

A. THE EFFECTS OF POVERTY ON COGNITIVE DEVELOPMENT AND EDUCATIONAL OUTCOME

Unsurprisingly, poverty and educational risk are heavily correlated, and lack of education correlates strongly with adult poverty. The excerpt below summarizes some of the research findings.

KRISTIN ANDERSON MOORE ET AL., *CHILDREN IN POVERTY: TRENDS, CONSEQUENCES, AND POLICY OPTIONS* (CHILD TRENDS, RESEARCH BRIEF NO. 2009-11, 2009)

A review of ten studies on the effects of poverty on children concluded that poverty has large and consistent associations with negative academic outcomes. . . .

. . . Poor children are more likely than their more affluent peers to be raised by parents who have completed fewer years of education, and to grow up in households that are less cognitively stimulating, which can negatively affect children's cognitive and academic attainment. They are also more likely to attend schools that lack the resources and rigor of schools in more prosperous neighborhoods. Moreover, emerging research is finding that socioeconomic status affects neuro-cognitive brain functioning. One recent study finds that chronic stress due to family poverty undermines children's working memory.

Poorer health and social behavior due to poverty also undermine educational achievement. . . .

. . . Studies find that those who experienced persistent poverty as children are much more likely to be poor as adults than those who were not poor during childhood. For example, adolescents who have experienced poverty are more likely to earn low wages than their peers who grew up in less dire circumstances. While upward mobility among adults who grew up poor is not uncommon, adults who experienced persistent childhood poverty are more likely to fall below the poverty line at least once later in life. However, upward mobility is not uniform across all races of children; 33 percent of African-American children who were poor during childhood remained poor at ages 25-27, compared with 7 percent of poor white children.

In the long run, childhood poverty poses economic costs to the United States through reduced productivity and output, the cost of crime, and increased health expenditures. Children who grow up in poverty are more likely to have low productivity and low earnings relative to children who did not grow up in poverty. It has been estimated that the reduced productivity lowers the gross domestic product by 1.3 percent annually. . . .

* * *

Likewise, federal Department of Education statistics confirm the link between limited education and poverty. In *The Condition of Education 2013*, the National Center for Education Statistics reported that for all age groups, those with more education had higher rates of employment. For example, those without a high school degree or its equivalent saw rates of employment ranging from 48 percent to 56 percent (depending on age), while those with a high school degree were employed at rates of 64 percent to 69 percent (see Figure 8.1).

Figure 8.1
Employment Rates by Level of Educational Attainment

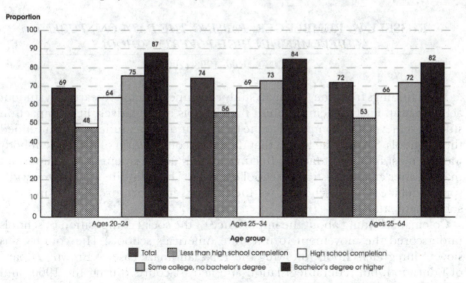

Source: U.S. Dep't of Labor, Bureau of Labor Statistics, unpublished annual average data from the Current Population Survey (CPS) (2012). *See Digest of Education Statistics 2012*, table 431.

Lack of educational achievement correlates not only with lower rates of employment, but also with higher incidence of poverty, especially for women. For example, "[i]n 2009, about 21 percent of young adults were living in poverty. . . . [But] a higher percentage of young adults without a high school diploma (31 percent) were living in poverty than were those who had completed high school (24 percent) and those who had earned a bachelor's or higher degree (14 percent)." Nat'l Ctr. for Educ. Statistics, *Youth Indicators 2011* (2011), *available at* http://nces.ed.gov/pubs2012/2012026/chapter3_31.asp. Median earnings data show that "those with a bachelor's or higher degree in 2009 had median earnings of $33,000, while those who had not completed high school had median earnings of $18,000." *Id.* at Indicator 30, *available at* http:// nces.ed.gov/pubs2012/2012026/chapter3_30.asp.

While data on the correlation between educational achievement and the likelihood of higher earnings is clear and consistent over time, the reasons that poor children generally have less educational success are less clear. The first and still the largest study on the reasons for differing student achievement in U.S. schools was conducted in 1965 by sociologist James Coleman of Johns Hopkins University. Pursuant to language in the Civil Rights Act of 1964 requiring the U.S. Office of Education (a precursor of the Department of Education) to conduct a survey and make a report to Congress and the President on "the lack of availability of equal educational opportunities for individuals by reason of race, color, religion, or national origin in public educational institutions at all levels in the United States," the study covered 570,000 children in 4,000 schools across the nation. The resulting report, formally titled "Equality of Educational Opportunity," but commonly known as the Coleman Report, sampled schools to assess their quality on a myriad of measures, such as qualifications of teachers, number of laboratories, number of books in libraries, and age and condition of school buildings. The researchers also examined the socioeconomic status of the children. The findings of the Coleman Report, highly controversial in its day, continue to influence education research today.

RUSSELL W. RUMBERGER, *PARSING THE DATA ON STUDENT ACHIEVEMENT IN HIGH-POVERTY SCHOOLS*

85 N.C. L. Rev. 1293 (2007)

. . . Two findings from the Coleman study continue to shape research on student achievement. First, Coleman found that schools had relatively little impact on student achievement compared to the background of the students who attended these schools. Second, he found that the social composition of the student body was the most important factor affecting student achievement, more important than teacher characteristics or school facilities. These findings generated widespread debate among scholars, yet the findings have been replicated in many subsequent studies.

Coleman's finding about the importance of the social composition of schools underscored the movement to integrate America's schools. The country was slow to integrate schools following the 1954 landmark case of Brown v. Board of Education, but federal legislation and activist courts during the 1960s and 1970s helped to increase racial integration, especially in Southern schools. In the last twenty years, however, these trends have been reversed, resulting in increased segregation. Nationwide, more than 70% of all black and Latino students in the United States attended predominantly minority schools in 2000, a higher percentage than thirty years earlier.

Racial and ethnic segregation is closely tied to socioeconomic segregation because blacks and Latinos have much higher poverty rates than other racial and ethnic groups. In 2004, almost one-third of all black and Latino children under the age of eighteen were living in poverty, compared to 14% of white children. Thus, not only are black and Latino children more likely to be poor, they are also more likely to attend schools with other poor children. In 2000, the average black or Latino student attended a school in which over 44% of students were poor, whereas the average white student attended a school in which 19% of the students were poor.

To the extent that both individual poverty and school poverty affect academic achievement, black and Hispanic students are doubly disadvantaged. Some recent data suggest this is indeed the case among elementary school students. Data from the fourth-grade results of the 2003 National Assessment of Educational Progress not only showed that poor students had lower math achievement than students who were not poor, but also that both poor and non-poor students had lower achievement in high-poverty schools. In fact, non-poor students attending high-poverty schools had lower achievement than poor students attending low-poverty schools. . . .

Researchers have developed a voluminous body of literature on the determinants of student achievement since the publication of the Coleman report in 1966. This research has identified a wide array of factors that contribute to educational achievement. Although many in number, these factors vary along two primary dimensions.

First, they vary with respect to whether they focus on the attributes of individual students or the attributes of the three primary settings in which these students live: families, schools, and communities. Although student achievement is clearly the result of individual attitudes, behaviors, and experiences, these individual attributes are shaped by the institutional settings in which people live. One challenge, therefore, is to determine the extent to which the attributes of individuals versus the attributes of institutional settings explain educational outcomes. . . .

In the largest study of student achievement ever undertaken, Coleman found that schools accounted for only 5% to 38% of the total variation in student test scores among different grade levels, ethnic groups, and regions of the country. Since that time, virtually every study of school effectiveness has confirmed that most of the variation in student achievement is attributable to differences among students and their families, rather than differences among schools. Yet despite the common understanding that the Coleman report and subsequent studies show that schools do not make a significant difference, research clearly demonstrates that schools can still have a powerful effect on student achievement. For example, one recent study found that students learn twice as much in the highest-performing high schools compared to the lowest-performing high schools. A more reasonable conclusion from existing research is that student achievement results both from the actions and attributes of individuals, and from the actions and attributes of their families, schools, and communities.

Second, the factors on education achievement vary with respect to the types of attributes they identify. Although a wide array of specific attributes has been identified, they primarily are of two types. The first type concerns material resources. Many researchers have argued that the major factor that explains differences in student achievement is the disparity in material resources and conditions that exists among students, their families, and their schools. For example, research has consistently found that socioeconomic status—a measure of parental education and family income, or family resources—is often the single most powerful predictor of student achievement. School resources have also been shown to affect student achievement, although there is considerable controversy over whether financial resources matter or simply human resources, such as the quality of teachers. Because racial and ethnic minority students are more likely to live in families and attend schools with fewer resources, these differences also contribute to differences in student achievement.

The second category of attributes that contribute to student achievement are attitudes and behaviors of students, families, and school personnel. Research has found that, among students, social and academic-related behaviors— sometimes referred to as social and academic engagement—are strongly related to student achievement in early elementary school. Research has also found that parental beliefs and practices—sometimes referred to as parenting style—are related to student achievement and help explain the relationship between family resources (socioeconomic status) and achievement. And research has demonstrated that within schools, teachers' beliefs and instructional practices are related to student achievement.

Differences in the relative importance of material resources versus attitudes and behaviors also have important implications for policy. If material resources are most important in affecting student achievement, then policies should be aimed at improving the material resources of students and the settings in which they live—their families, schools, and communities. If, however, attitudes and behaviors matter most, then policies should be aimed at improving the attitudes and behaviors of students, their parents, and school personnel. . . .

NOTES AND QUESTIONS

1. Is it surprising that the Coleman Report and much subsequent research has found that differences among students, rather than differences among schools, play the major part in determining student achievement? As the discussion of education equity and advocacy litigation later in this chapter illustrates, the question of whether "money matters" in improving schools and student performance has continued to divide policymakers, courts, and researchers.

2. What are the implications for public policy and for advocacy strategies of research suggesting that school readiness and environmental factors in the years before children enter school are at least as important as conditions within schools?

3. Research shows that the achievement gap between children in high- and low-income families is now nearly twice as large as the racial achievement gap between Black and White children, a stark reversal of historic trends. Professor Sean Reardon reports that "the achievement gap [measured by performance on standardized tests] between children from high- and low-income families is roughly 30 to 40 percent larger among children born in

2001 than among those born twenty-five years earlier." *See* Sean F. Reardon, *The Widening Academic Achievement Gap Between the Rich and the Poor: New Evidence and Possible Explanations, Whither Opportunity?: Rising Inequality and the Uncertain Life Chances of Low-Income Children* (Greg J. Duncan & Richard Murnane eds., 2011).

4. School desegregation has played a large role in legal and public policy debates over education since the days of *Brown*. Research includes important findings regarding the relationship of desegregation and student achievement. For example, Rucker C. Johnson examined national longitudinal data on the life trajectories of children born between 1950 and 1970 and concluded that "desegregation plans were effective in narrowing black-white gaps in per-pupil school spending and class size and decreasing school segregation." Johnson also investigated "the long-run impacts of the court-ordered desegregation plans on subsequent attainment outcomes, including educational attainment, adult earnings, income and poverty status, probability of incarceration, and adult health status" and found that

> [s]chool desegregation and the accompanied increases in school quality resulted in significant improvements in adult attainments for blacks. . . . [F]or blacks, school desegregation significantly increased educational attainment and adult earnings, reduced the probability of incarceration, and improved adult health status; desegregation had no effects on whites across each of these outcomes. The results suggest that the mechanisms through which school desegregation led to beneficial adult attainment outcomes for blacks include improvement in access to school resources reflected in reductions in class size and increases in per-pupil spending.

> Rucker C. Johnson, *Long-Run Impacts of School Desegregation & School Quality on Adult Attainments* (Nat'l Bureau of Econ. Research, Working Paper No. 16664, 2011).

5. In 2007, the U.S. Supreme Court struck down voluntary integration programs that used race as part of the criteria for assignment of pupils to magnet schools in Seattle, Washington, and Louisville, Kentucky. Parents Involved in Cmty. Sch. v. Seattle Sch. Dist., 551 U.S. 701 (2007). The effect of the decision on modern desegregation efforts has been the subject of much scholarly interest, including numerous proposals to focus efforts on socioeconomic rather than racial integration. *See, e.g.*, William J. Glenn, *Altering Grade Configurations in Virginia Schools: Reducing School Segregation Without Necessarily Considering Race in Light of the Parents Involved Ruling*, 88 N.C. L. Rev. 1091 (2010); L. Darnell Weeden, *Income Integration as a Race-Neutral Pursuit of Equality and Diversity in Education After the Parents Involved in Community Schools Decision*, 21 U. Fla. J.L. & Pub. Pol'y 365 (2010).

B.   THE STATUS OF EDUCATION IN THE LAW: IS EDUCATION A RIGHT?

As noted in the introduction to this chapter, the Supreme Court's sweeping language in *Brown* might lead readers (and the public) to believe the Court was articulating a federal right to education. As the next two excerpts make clear, this is not the case.

JEANNIE OAKES ET AL., *GRASSROOTS ORGANIZING, SOCIAL MOVEMENTS, AND THE RIGHT TO HIGH-QUALITY EDUCATION*

4 Stan. J. C.R. & C.L. 339 (2008)

THE CONTRADICTORY STATUS OF THE "RIGHT" TO EDUCATION

At our nation's founding, Thomas Jefferson argued that democracy required educated citizens who could employ reason and deliberate publicly about the competing ideas for guiding the nation. To serve this end, Jefferson claimed that government should provide every non-slave child with three years of schooling to ready them for citizenship. Jefferson advocated basic literacy—reading, writing, and mathematics—and beyond that, students might also learn the rudiments of Greek, Roman, European, and American history.

In the mid-nineteenth century, Horace Mann argued that all Americans should be educated in "common" schools that would complement what families taught their children at home. These would be equal schools—not charity schools for the poor, but free public schools for the sons and daughters of farmers, businessmen, professionals, and the rest of society. Mann intended common schools to teach the knowledge and habits, as well as the basic literacy, that citizens needed to function in a democracy. He envisioned the common school as the "great equalizer" and a creator of wealth, as a force for eliminating poverty and crime and shaping the destiny of a wise, productive country. Like other modern thinkers of the day, Mann believed that social improvement would follow from advances in knowledge and that schooling would extend individual rights and liberties to all.

Jefferson and Mann set the terms on which the U.S. would think about schooling and about schooling equality. Schooling served society, and equal schools served society best. Although both viewed education as benefitting the individual, both framed schools primarily as a social good, rather than as a fundamental right.

A.   CONSTITUTIONALLY PROTECTED RIGHTS

Writing the U.S. Bill of Rights, American revolutionaries relied on a long European rights tradition extending back to the Magna Carta and the English Bill of Rights. These rights were framed as enforceable privileges of citizenship, which if interfered with by another, give rise to an action for injury. Following the Civil War, these rights were expanded to end slavery and to extend the privileges of citizenship to all Americans. The Fourteenth Amendment promised that no state "shall make or enforce any law which shall abridge the privileges or immunities of the citizens of the United States . . . [or] deprive any person of life, liberty, or property without due process of law . . . [or] deny to any person within its jurisdiction the equal protection of the laws." This "equal protection" clause established that the government should take positive action to protect citizens from the actions of other citizens and government agencies that impinged on their rights.

In the two decades following the passage of the Fourteenth Amendment, Congress, viewing education as an entitlement necessary to make national citizenship meaningful and effective, sought to enforce the national citizenship guarantee. Legal scholar Goodwin Liu cites Congressional discussion to this effect surrounding several pieces of Reconstruction Era legislation. For example, Congressional discussion around the creation of the federal Department of Education noted the federal responsibility "to enforce education, without regard to race or color, upon the population of all such States as shall fall below a standard to be established by Congress" and to ensure that "every child . . . receives a sufficient education to qualify him to discharge all the duties that may devolve upon him as an American citizen." Similar strong Congressional statements recognizing education as central to securing full and equal national citizenship accompanied other legislative efforts between 1870 and 1890 to establish federal leadership and funding for public education.

B.   CONSTITUTIONAL RIGHTS FOLLOWING WORLD WAR II

In the decades following the enactment of the Fourteenth Amendment, the courts narrowed the concept of civil rights—a trend that continued until 1947, when President Harry Truman, frustrated that Congress failed to respond to his repeated calls for civil rights legislation, established the President's Committee on Civil Rights. The Committee's recommendations included anti-segregation laws, voting rights legislation, and creation of a civil rights unit within the Department of Justice. The report became a blueprint for Civil Rights legislation of the 1950s and 1960s, and encouraged the pivotal reconsideration of de jure segregation. However, it did not specify education as a right deserving "equal protection" by federal or state governments.

Moreover, the 1954 Brown v. Board of Education decision, capping a decades-long effort to establish that racially segregated schools were not equal, fell just short of establishing education as a fundamental civil right. . . .

Rather than asserting that all Americans have a right to education, then, the court echoed the Jefferson/Mann convictions that education is fundamental to democratic society and the life chances of American young people. The court ruled that education must be equal only "where the state has undertaken to provide it." It did not, however, compel states to provide education. In fact, in the wake of *Brown*, some states chose to close their public schools rather than integrate them, and Virginia's Prince Edward County shut down its public schools for five years. . . .

* * *

Nearly 20 years after Brown, the question of whether there was a federal constitutional right to education came before the Supreme Court. The case alleged that disparities in education funding disadvantaged a suspect class and violated a fundamental right to education. The portion of the Court's opinion rejecting the "classification" argument appears in Chapter 3 (Poverty and the Constitution). The excerpt here deals with plaintiffs' argument that education should be regarded as a fundamental right under the Constitution.

SAN ANTONIO INDEP. SCH. DIST. v. DEMETRIO P. RODRIGUEZ
411 U.S. 1 (1973)

Mr. Justice POWELL delivered the opinion of the Court.

This suit attacking the Texas system of financing public education was initiated by Mexican-American parents whose children attend the elementary and secondary schools in the Edgewood Independent School District, an urban school district in San Antonio, Texas. They brought a class action on behalf of schoolchildren throughout the State who are members of minority groups or who are poor and reside in school districts having a low property tax base. Named as defendants were the State Board of Education, the Commissioner of Education, the State Attorney General, and the Bexar County (San Antonio) Board of Trustees.

[Plaintiffs attacked the use of property taxes as the principal determinant of school funding. The evidence showed that the Edgewood school district, where plaintiffs lived, was one of the poorest in the San Antonio area. Its population was 90 percent Mexican-American and 6 percent black. The average assessed property value per pupil was $5,960 and the median family income was $4,686. In Alamo Heights, the most affluent school district in San Antonio, the population was predominately "Anglo" with 18 percent Mexican-Americans and less than 1 percent black students. The assessed property value per student was over $49,000 and the median family income was $8,001. With a tax rate of $1.05 per $100 of assessed property (the highest in the metropolitan area), the Edgewood district contributed $26 per student above the state contribution. Alamo Heights, with a tax rate of $0.85 per $100 of valuation, yielded $333 per pupil.]

The first Texas State Constitution, promulgated upon Texas' entry into the Union in 1845, provided for the establishment of a system of free schools.[6] Early in its history, Texas adopted a dual approach to the financing of its schools, relying on mutual participation by the local school districts and the State. [Texas provided funding for each school district based on the number of students in the district. The district made up the difference in operating expense with funds from local property taxes. This reliance on property taxes resulted in a large disparity in per student spending between districts with extensive or high-value taxable property and those with less or lesser value taxable property. The plaintiffs contended that this denied the children in poor districts equal protection of the laws in violation of the Fourteenth Amendment.]

. . . The District Court held that the Texas system discriminates on the basis of wealth in the manner in which education is provided for its people. Finding that wealth is a "suspect" classification and that education is a "fundamental" interest, the District Court held that the Texas system could be sustained only if the State could show that it was premised upon some compelling state interest. On this issue the court concluded that "(n)ot only are defendants unable to demonstrate compelling state interests . . . they fail even to establish a reasonable basis for these classifications." Texas virtually concedes that its historically rooted dual system of financing education could not withstanding the strict judicial scrutiny that this Court has found appropriate in reviewing legislative judgments that interfere with fundamental constitutional rights or that involve suspect classifications. . . .

[Plaintiffs] . . . assert that the State's system impermissibly interferes with the exercise of a "fundamental" right and that accordingly the prior decisions of this Court require the application of the strict standard of judicial review. It is this question — whether education is a fundamental right, in the sense that it is

---

6. Tex. Const., Art. X § 1 (1845): "A general diffusion of knowledge being essential to the preservation of the rights and liberties of the people, it shall be the duty of the legislature of this State to make suitable provision for the support and maintenance of public schools." Id., § 2: "The Legislature shall, as early as practicable, establish free schools throughout the State, and shall furnish means for their support by taxation on property. . . ."

among the rights and liberties protected by the Constitution—which has so consumed the attention of courts and commentators in recent years.

In Brown v. Board of Education, a unanimous Court recognized that "education is perhaps the most important function of state and local governments." . . . This theme, expressing an abiding respect for the vital role of education in a free society, may be found in numerous opinions of Justices of this Court writing both before and after *Brown* was decided.

Nothing this Court holds today in any way detracts from our historic dedication to public education. We are in complete agreement with the conclusion of the three-judge panel below that "the grave significance of education both to the individual and to our society" cannot be doubted. But the importance of a service performed by the State does not determine whether it must be regarded as fundamental for purposes of examination under the Equal Protection Clause. Mr. Justice Harlan, dissenting from the Court's application of strict scrutiny to a law impinging upon the right of interstate travel, admonished that "(v)irtually every state statute affects important rights." Shapiro v. Thompson [394 U.S. 618 (1969)]. In his view, if the degree of judicial scrutiny of state legislation fluctuated, depending on a majority's view of the importance of the interest affected, we would have gone "far toward making this Court a 'super-legislature.'" We would, indeed, then be assuming a legislative role and one for which the Court lacks both authority and competence. But Mr. Justice Stewart's response in *Shapiro* to Mr. Justice Harlan's concern correctly articulates the limits of the fundamental-rights rationale employed in the Court's equal protection decisions:

> The Court today does not "pick out particular human activities, characterize them as 'fundamental,' and give them added protection. . . ." To the contrary, the Court simply recognizes, as it must, an established constitutional right, and gives to that right no less protection than the Constitution itself demands.

Lindsey v. Normet, decided only last Term, firmly reiterates that social importance is not the critical determinant for subjecting state legislation to strict scrutiny. [Rejecting a challenge to expedited eviction procedures, the Court held:]

> We do not denigrate the importance of decent, safe and sanitary housing. But the Constitution does not provide judicial remedies for every social and economic ill. We are unable to perceive in that document any constitutional guarantee of access to dwellings of a particular quality or any recognition of the right of a tenant to occupy the real property of his landlord beyond the term of his lease, without the payment of rent. . . . Absent constitutional mandate, the assurance of adequate housing and the definition of landlord-tenant relationships are legislative, not judicial functions.

The lesson of these cases in addressing the question now before the Court is plain. It is not the province of this Court to create substantive constitutional rights in the name of guaranteeing equal protection of the laws. Thus, the key to discovering whether education is "fundamental" is not to be found in comparisons of the relative societal significance of education as opposed to subsistence or housing. Nor is it to be found by weighing whether education is as important as the right to travel. Rather, the answer lies in assessing whether there is a right to education explicitly or implicitly guaranteed by the Constitution.

Education, of course, is not among the rights afforded explicit protection under our Federal Constitution. Nor do we find any basis for saying it is implicitly so protected. As we have said, the undisputed importance of education will not alone cause this Court to depart from the usual standard for reviewing a State's social and economic legislation. It is appellees' contention, however, that education is distinguishable from other services and benefits provided by the State because it bears a peculiarly close relationship to other rights and liberties accorded protection under the Constitution. Specifically, they insist that education is itself a fundamental personal right because it is essential to the effective exercise of First Amendment freedoms and to intelligent utilization of the right to vote. . . .

Even if it were conceded that some identifiable quantum of education is a constitutionally protected prerequisite to the meaningful exercise of either right, we have no indication that the present levels of educational expenditures in Texas provide an education that falls short. Whatever merit appellees' argument might have if a State's financing system occasioned an absolute denial of educational opportunities to any of its children, that argument provides no basis for finding an interference with fundamental rights where only relative differences in spending levels are involved and where—as is true in the present case—no charge fairly could be made that the system fails to provide each child with an opportunity to acquire the basic minimal skills necessary for the enjoyment of the rights of speech and of full participation in the political process. . . .

It must be remembered, also, that every claim arising under the Equal Protection Clause has implications for the relationship between national and state power under our federal system. Questions of federalism are always inherent in the process of determining whether a State's laws are to be accorded the traditional presumption of constitutionality, or are to be subjected instead to rigorous judicial scrutiny. While "(t)he maintenance of the principles of federalism is a foremost consideration in interpreting any of the pertinent constitutional provisions under which this Court examines state action," it would be difficult to imagine a case having a greater potential impact on our federal system than the one now before us, in which we are urged to abrogate systems of financing public education presently in existence in virtually every State. . . .

[The Court went on to find that Texas' school financing system was rationally related to the legitimate state purpose of providing education while respecting local autonomy.]

Reversed.

Mr. Justice MARSHALL, with whom Mr. Justice DOUGLAS concurs, dissenting.

. . . [T]he majority's holding can only be seen as a retreat from our historic commitment to equality of educational opportunity and as unsupportable acquiescence in a system which deprives children in their earliest years of the chance to reach their full potential as citizens. . . . In my judgment, the right of every American to an equal start in life, so far as the provision of a state service as important as education is concerned, is far too vital to permit state discrimination on grounds as tenuous as those presented by this record. . . .

I . . . cannot accept the majority's labored efforts to demonstrate that fundamental interests, which call for strict scrutiny of the challenged classification, encompass only established rights which we are somehow bound to recognize from the text of the Constitution itself. . . .

. . . Although not all fundamental interests are constitutionally guaranteed, the determination of which interests are fundamental should be firmly rooted in the text of the Constitution. The task in every case should be to determine the extent to which constitutionally guaranteed rights are dependent on interests not mentioned in the Constitution. As the nexus between the specific constitutional guarantee and the nonconstitutional interest draws closer, the nonconstitutional interest becomes more fundamental and the degree of judicial scrutiny applied when the interest is infringed on a discriminatory basis must be adjusted accordingly. Thus, it cannot be denied that interests such as procreation, the exercise of the state franchise, and access to criminal appellate processes are not fully guaranteed to the citizen by our Constitution. But these interests have nonetheless been afforded special judicial consideration in the face of discrimination because they are, to some extent, interrelated with constitutional guarantees. Procreation is now understood to be important because of its interaction with the established constitutional right of privacy. The exercise of the state franchise is closely tied to basic civil and political rights inherent in the First Amendment. And access to criminal appellate processes enhances the integrity of the range of rights implicit in the Fourteenth Amendment guarantee of due process of law. Only if we closely protect the related interests from state discrimination do we ultimately ensure the integrity of the constitutional guarantee itself. . . .

Education directly affects the ability of a child to exercise his First Amendment rights, both as a source and as a receiver of information and ideas, whatever interests he may pursue in life. . . . The opportunity for formal education may not necessarily be the essential determinant of an individual's ability to enjoy throughout his life the rights of free speech and association guaranteed to him by the First Amendment. But such an opportunity may enhance the individual's enjoyment of those rights, not only during but also following school attendance. Thus, in the final analysis, "the pivotal position of education to success in American society and its essential role in opening up to the individual the central experiences of our culture lend it an importance that is undeniable." . . .

NOTES AND QUESTIONS

1. Was it essential to the *Rodriguez* case to determine that there was no federal constitutional right to education? Why does this question take up so much of the opinion?
2. The San Antonio Independent School District was one of seven school districts in the San Antonio metropolitan area that were originally named as defendants. After a pretrial conference, the district court issued an order dismissing the school districts from the case. Subsequently, the San Antonio Independent School District joined in the plaintiffs' challenge to the state's school finance system and filed an *amicus curiae* brief in support of that position in the Supreme Court. In other education litigation as well, school districts have sometimes joined plaintiffs in their attacks on statewide funding decisions or policies. Why would defendants do this? What does this suggest about the politics of education litigation?

3. Although the Court held unequivocally in *Rodriguez* that education is not a fundamental right under the U.S. Constitution and upheld Texas's financing scheme as rationally related to the state goal of providing education while respecting local autonomy in school decisions, it rejected a measure nine years later that would have allowed the same state to exclude undocumented immigrant children from its public schools. In Plyler v. Doe, 457 U.S. 202 (1982), a divided Court reaffirmed that education is not a federal fundamental right, and held that undocumented aliens are not a suspect class. However, the Court went on to require something more than a mere rational basis from the state for its measure:

> But more is involved in these cases than the abstract question whether § 21.031 [the Texas provision excluding undocumented children from public school] discriminates against a suspect class, or whether education is a fundamental right. Section 21.031 imposes a lifetime hardship on a discrete class of children not accountable for their disabling status. The stigma of illiteracy will mark them for the rest of their lives. By denying these children a basic education, we deny them the ability to live within the structure of our civic institutions, and foreclose any realistic possibility that they will contribute in even the smallest way to the progress of our Nation. In determining the rationality of § 21.031, we may appropriately take into account its costs to the Nation and to the innocent children who are its victims. In light of these countervailing costs, the discrimination contained in § 21.031 can hardly be considered rational unless it furthers some substantial goal of the State.

Id. at 223-224.

C.   EDUCATION ADVOCACY IN STATE COURTS

After *Rodriguez*, strategies to improve education through litigation shifted to state courts. In contrast to the federal Constitution's lack of a textual basis for a right to education, most state constitutions explicitly mandate that the state provide free public education. For example, Kentucky's constitution requires "an efficient system of common schools throughout the state," New Jersey's "a general, uniform, and thorough system" of education, Kansas's a "suitable education" for all students, and Montana's a "basic system of free quality public elementary and secondary schools." These and similar state guarantees became the basis of decades of litigation in state courts over equality and adequacy of public education, much of which continues today. The two seminal cases excerpted below, California's Serrano v. Priest and Kentucky's Rose v. Council for Better Education, exemplify two strands of state court education litigation.

SERRANO v. PRIEST
557 P.2d 929 (Cal. 1976)

SULLIVAN, J: The instant proceeding, which involves a constitutional challenge to the California public school financing system, is before us for the second time. In 1971, we reversed a judgment of dismissal and remanded the cause with directions that it proceed to trial. (*Serrano I.*) In so doing we held that the facts alleged in plaintiffs' complaint were sufficient to constitute the three causes of action there set forth, and that if such allegations were sustained at trial, the state public school financing system must be declared invalid as in violation of state and federal constitutional provisions guaranteeing the equal protection of the laws. . . .

A. The System Prior to S.B. 90 and A.B. 1267

In *Serrano I*, we described the prior financing system as follows: At the threshold we find a fundamental statistic — over 90 percent of our public school funds derive from two basic sources: (a) local district taxes on real property and (b) aid from the State School Fund.

By far the major source of school revenue is the local real property tax. Pursuant to article IX, section 6 of the California Constitution, the Legislature has authorized the governing body of each county to levy taxes on the real property within a school district at a rate necessary to meet the district's annual education budget. The amount of revenue which a district can raise in this manner thus depends largely on its tax base — i.e., the assessed valuation of real property within its borders. Tax bases very widely throughout the state; in 1969-1970, for example, the assessed valuation per unit of average daily attendance of elementary school children ranged from a low of $103 to a peak of $952,156 — a ratio of nearly 1 to 10,000.

The other factor determining local school revenue is the rate of taxation within the district. Although the Legislature has placed ceilings on permissible district tax rates, these statutory maxima may be surpassed in a "tax override" election if a majority of the district's voters approve a higher rate. Nearly all districts have voted to override the statutory limits. Thus the locally raised funds which constitute the largest portion of school revenue are primarily a function of the value of the realty within a particular school district, coupled with the willingness of the district's residents to tax themselves for education. . . .

Although [state funds] temper the disparities which result from the vast variations in real property assessed valuation, wide differentials remain in the revenue available to individual districts and, consequently, in the level of educational expenditures. For example, in Los Angeles County, where plaintiff children attend school, the Baldwin Park Unified School District expended only $577.49 to educate each of its pupils in 1968-1969; during the same year the Beverly Hills Unified School District paid out $1,231.72 per child. The source of these disparities is unmistakable: in Baldwin Park the assessed valuation per child totaled only $3,706; while in Beverly Hills, the corresponding figure was $50,885 — a ratio of 1 to 13. Thus, the state grants are inadequate to offset the inequalities inherent in a financing system based on widely varying local tax bases. . . .

B. The New System

[Ed. note: Following the *Serrano I* decision, the California Legislature passed a series of measures intended to address the constitutional deficiencies identified by the court. These measures are the "new system" discussed in this section of the opinion.]

The changes brought about by the passage of S.B. 90 and A.B. 1267, while significant, did not purport to alter the basic concept underlying the California public school financing system. That concept, which we may refer to as the "foundation approach," undertakes in general to insure a certain guaranteed dollar amount for the education of each child in each school district, and to defer to the individual school district for the provision of whatever additional funds it deems necessary to the furtherance of its particular educational goals. . . .

With this background in mind we turn to a consideration of the trial court's findings and judgment. . . . The court found in substance as follows: The California public school financing system following the adoption of S.B. 90 and A.B. 1267 continues to be based upon the foundation concept. Although there have been substantial increases in foundation levels, those increases, considered alone, do not eliminate any of the unconstitutional features which existed at the time of *Serrano I*. . . . Basic-aid districts [the wealthier districts] continue to be favored over equalization-aid districts [the poorer districts] insofar as they may reach the foundation level with a [lower tax rate]. . . .

There exist several alternative potential methods of financing the public school system of this state which would not produce wealth-related spending disparities. These alternative methods, which are "workable, practical and feasible," include:

> (1) full state funding, with the imposition of a statewide property tax; (2) consolidation of the present 1,067 school districts into about five hundred districts, with boundary realignments to equalize assessed valuations of real property among all school districts; (3) retention of the present school district boundaries but the removal of commercial and industrial property from local taxation for school purposes and taxation of such property at the state level; (4) school district power equalizing, which has as its essential ingredient the concept that school districts could choose to spend at different levels but for each level of expenditure chosen the tax effort would be the same for each school district choosing such level whether it be a high-wealth or a low-wealth district; (5) vouchers; and (6) some combination of two or more of the above.

Substantial disparities in expenditures per pupil among school districts cause and perpetuate substantial disparities in the quality and extent of availability of educational opportunities. For this reason the school financing system before the court fails to provide equality of treatment to all the pupils in the state. Although an equal expenditure level per pupil in every district is not educationally sound or desirable because of differing educational needs, equality of educational opportunity requires that all school districts possess an equal ability in terms of revenue to provide students with substantially equal opportunities for learning. The system before the court fails in this respect, for it gives high-wealth districts a substantial advantage in obtaining higher quality staff, program expansion and variety, beneficial teacher-pupil ratios and class sizes, modern equipment and materials, and high-quality buildings. . . .

C. Conclusions of Law and Judgment

... [A]ny system in which the two basic elements of this description are present—i.e., (1) the conditioning of the availability of school revenues upon district wealth, with resultant disparities in school revenue, and (2) the dependency of the quality of education upon the level of district expenditure—must be declared invalid unless it finds justification sufficient to satisfy the applicable equal protection test. . . .

In *Serrano I* this court, in its determination of whether or not the allegations of the complaint stated a cause of action, was faced at the outset with the task of choosing the proper equal protection standard to be applied. . . .

Concluding on the basis of the complaint that the case before us involved both a "suspect classification" (because the discrimination in question was made on the basis of wealth) and affected a "fundamental interest" (education), we proceeded to apply the [strict scrutiny] standard. Addressing ourselves to the state interest advanced by defendants—local decision-making power and fiscal control—we concluded that it was not incumbent upon us to decide whether that asserted interest was "compelling" or whether the existing financial system was "necessary" to its furtherance because under the facts as alleged the notion of local control was a "cruel illusion for the poor school districts" due to limitations placed upon them by the system itself. "In summary," we held,

> so long as the assessed valuation within a district's boundaries is a major determinant of how much it can spend for its schools, only a district with a large tax base will be truly able to decide how much it really cares about education. The poor district cannot freely choose to tax itself into an excellence which its tax rolls cannot provide. Far from being necessary to promote local fiscal choice, the present financing system actually deprives the less wealthy districts of that option.

During the progress of trial proceedings below, the United States Supreme Court rendered its decision in *Rodriguez*. There, addressing itself to an equal protection attack on the Texas public school financing system—which like the system here in question is based on the "foundation approach"—the high court held that that system (1) did not result in a suspect classification based upon wealth, and (2) did not affect any fundamental interest, education being less than fundamental for these purposes because it was not explicitly or implicitly guaranteed or protected by the terms of the federal Constitution. Accordingly, the court held, the so-called "strict scrutiny test" for equal protection review of state laws under the Fourteenth Amendment to the United States Constitution was inappropriate. . . .

. . . [O]ur state equal protection provisions, while "substantially the equivalent of" the guarantees contained in the Fourteenth Amendment to the United States Constitution, are possessed of an independent vitality which, in a given case, may demand an analysis different from that which would obtain if only the federal standard were applicable. We have recently stated in a related context:

> (I)n the area of fundamental civil liberties—which includes . . . all protections of the California Declaration of Rights—we sit as a court of last resort, subject only to the qualification that our interpretations may not restrict the guarantees accorded the national citizenry under the federal charter. In such constitutional

adjudication, our first referent is California law and the full panoply of rights Californians have come to expect as their due. Accordingly, decisions of the United States Supreme Court defining fundamental rights are persuasive authority to be afforded respectful consideration, but are to be followed by California courts only when they provide no less individual protection than is guaranteed by California law.

For these reasons then, we now adhere to our determinations, made in *Serrano I*, that for the reasons there stated and for purposes of assessing our state public school financing system in light of our state constitutional provisions guaranteeing equal protection of the laws (1) discrimination in educational opportunity on the basis of district wealth involves a suspect classification, and (2) education is a fundamental interest. Because the school financing system here in question has been shown by substantial and convincing evidence produced at trial to involve a suspect classification (insofar as this system, like the former one, draws distinctions on the basis of district wealth), and because that classification affects the fundamental interest of the students of this state in education, we have no difficulty in concluding today, as we concluded in *Serrano I*, that the school financing system before us must be examined under our state constitutional provisions with that strict and searching scrutiny appropriate to such a case. . . .

[The Court went on to uphold the trial court's determination that the school financing system violated the state constitution's equal protection guarantee.]

ROSE v. COUNCIL FOR BETTER EDUC.
790 S.W.2d 186 (Ky. 1989)

STEPHENS, C.J.: The issue we decide on this appeal is whether the Kentucky General Assembly has complied with its constitutional mandate to "provide an efficient system of common schools throughout the state."

In deciding that it has not, we intend no criticism of the substantial efforts made by the present General Assembly and by its predecessors, nor do we intend to substitute our judicial authority for the authority and discretion of the General Assembly. We are, rather, exercising our constitutional duty in declaring that, when we consider the evidence in the record, and when we apply the constitutional requirement of Section 183 [the state constitution's "efficient schools" provision] to that evidence, it is crystal clear that the General Assembly has fallen short of its duty to enact legislation to provide for an efficient system of common schools throughout the state. In a word, the present system of common schools in Kentucky is not an "efficient" one in our view of the clear mandate of Section 183. The common school system in Kentucky is constitutionally deficient.

In reaching this decision, we are ever mindful of the immeasurable worth of education to our state and its citizens, especially to its young people. The framers of our constitution intended that each and every child in this state should receive a proper and an adequate education, to be provided for by the General Assembly. This opinion dutifully applies the constitutional test of Section 183 to the existing system of common schools. We do no more, nor may we do any less. . . .

This declaratory judgment action was filed in the Franklin Circuit Court by multiple plaintiffs, including the Council for Better Education, Inc. a non-profit Kentucky corporation whose membership consists of sixty-six local school districts in the state. Twenty-two public school students from McCreary, Wolfe, Morgan and Elliott Counties and Harlan and Dayton Independent School districts were also named. . . .

The complaint included allegations that the system of school financing provided for by the General Assembly is inadequate; places too much emphasis on local school board resources; and results in inadequacies, inequities and inequalities throughout the state so as to result in an inefficient system of common school education in violation of Kentucky Constitution, Sections 1, 3 and 183 and the equal protection clause and the due process of law clause of the 14th Amendment to the United States Constitution. Additionally the complaint maintains the entire system is not efficient under the mandate of Section 183.

The relief sought by the plaintiffs was a declaration of rights to the effect that the system be declared unconstitutional; that the funding of schools also be determined to be unconstitutional and inadequate; that the defendant Superintendent of Public Instruction be enjoined from further implementing said school statutes; that a mandamus be issued, directing the Governor to recommend to the General Assembly the enactment of appropriate legislation which would be in compliance with the aforementioned constitutional provisions; that a mandamus be issued, directing the President Pro Tempore of the Senate and the Speaker of the House of Representatives to place before the General Assembly appropriate legislation which is constitutionally valid; and that a mandamus be issued, directing the General Assembly to provide for an "equitable and adequate funding program for all school children so as to establish an 'efficient system of common schools.'" . . .

The case was tried by the court without the intervention of a jury. Evidence was presented by deposition, along with oral testimony and much documentary evidence. The trial court . . . found Kentucky's common school finance system to be unconstitutional and discriminatory and held that the General Assembly had not produced an efficient system of common schools throughout the state.

The evidence in this case consists of numerous depositions, volumes of oral evidence heard by the trial court, and a seemingly endless amount of statistical data, reports, etc. We will not unduly lengthen this opinion with an extensive discussion of that evidence. As a matter of fact, such is really not necessary. The overall effect of appellants' evidence is a virtual concession that Kentucky's system of common schools is underfunded and inadequate; is fraught with inequalities and inequities throughout the 177 local school districts; is ranked nationally in the lower 20-25% in virtually every category that is used to evaluate educational performance; and is not uniform among the districts in educational opportunities. When one considers the evidence presented by the appellants, there is little or no evidence to even begin to negate that of the appellants.

. . . [T]here are wide variations in financial resources and dispositions thereof which result in unequal educational opportunities throughout Kentucky. The local districts have large variances in taxable property per student. Even a total elimination of all mismanagement and waste in local school districts would not correct the situation as it now exists. A substantial difference in the curricula offered in the poorer districts contrasts with that of the richer districts, particularly in the areas of foreign language, science, mathematics, music and art.

The achievement test scores in the poorer districts are lower than those in the richer districts and expert opinion clearly established that there is a correlation between those scores and the wealth of the district. Student-teacher ratios are higher in the poorer districts. Moreover, although Kentucky's per capita income is low, it makes an even lower per capita effort to support the common schools.

Students in property poor districts receive inadequate and inferior educational opportunities as compared to those offered to those students in the more affluent districts.

That Kentucky's overall effort and resulting achievement in the area of primary and secondary education are comparatively low, nationally, is not in dispute. Thirty-five percent of our adult population are high school drop-outs. Eighty percent of Kentucky's local school districts are identified as being "poor," in terms of taxable property. The other twenty percent remain under the national average. Thirty percent of our local school districts are "functionally bankrupt." . . . In the area of per pupil expenditures, Kentucky ranks 6th among the 8 [neighboring] states and ranks 40th, nationally. With respect to the average annual salary of instructional staff, Kentucky again ranks 6th among its neighbors and 37th nationally. In the area of classroom teacher compensation, Kentucky is 7th and 37th. Our classroom teacher average salary is 84.68% of the national average and our per pupil expenditure is 78.20% of the national average.

. . . If any more evidence is needed to show the inadequacy of our overall effort, consider that only 68.2% of ninth grade students eventually graduate from high school in Kentucky. That ranks us 7th among our eight adjacent sister states. . . .

Numerous well-qualified educators and school administrators testified before the trial court and all described Kentucky's educational effort as being inadequate and well below the national effort.

With this background of Kentucky's overall effort with regard to education and its comparison to other states in the area, and nationally, we proceed to examine the trial court's finding relative to inequity and lack of uniformity in the overabundance of local school districts. We will discuss the educational opportunities offered and then address the disparity in financial effort and support.

EDUCATIONAL EFFORT

The numerous witnesses that testified before the trial court are recognized experts in the field of primary and secondary education. . . . Without exception, they testified that there is great disparity in the poor and the more affluent school districts with regard to classroom teachers' pay; provision of basic educational materials; student-teacher ratio; curriculum; quality of basic management; size, adequacy and condition of school physical plants; and per year expenditure per student. Kentucky's children, simply because of their place of residence, are offered a virtual hodgepodge of educational opportunities. The quality of education in the poorer local school districts is substantially less in most, if not all, of the above categories.

Can anyone seriously argue that these disparities do not affect the basic educational opportunities of those children in the poorer districts? To ask the question is to answer it. Children in 80% of local school districts in this Commonwealth are not as well-educated as those in the other 20%.

Moreover, most of the witnesses before the trial court testified that not only were the state's educational opportunities unequal and lacking in uniformity, but that *all* were inadequate. Testimony indicated that not only do the so-called poorer districts provide inadequate education to fulfill the needs of the students but the more affluent districts' efforts are inadequate as well, as judged by accepted national standards.

Summarizing appellants' argument, and without intending to give it short shrift, it is contended that over the years the General Assembly has continually enacted [new measures]. . . . Moreover, uncontroverted evidence is adduced to show that the overall amount of money appropriated for local schools has increased by a substantial amount. The argument seems to be to the effect that "we have done our best." However, it is significant that *all* the experts were keenly aware of the legislative history, including substantive legislation and increased funding and yet, all of them stated that inequalities still exist, and indeed have been exacerbated by some of the legislation. Appellants conceded, the trial court found and we concur that in spite of legislative efforts, the total local and state effort in education in Kentucky's primary and secondary education is inadequate and is lacking in uniformity. It is discriminatory as to the children served in 80% of our local school districts.

FINANCIAL EFFORT

Uniform testimony of the expert witnesses at trial, corroborated by data, showed a definite correlation between the money spent per child on education and the quality of the education received. As we have previously stated in our discussion of the history of Kentucky's school finances, our system does not *require* a minimum local effort. . . .

The disparity in per pupil expenditure by the local school boards runs in the thousands of dollars per year. Moreover, between the extreme high allocation and the extreme low allocation lies a wide range of annual per pupil expenditures. . . .

X. What Is an "Efficient System of Common Schools"?

In a few simple but direct words, the framers of our present Constitution set forth the will of the people with regard to the importance of providing public education in the Commonwealth. "*General Assembly to provide for school system*—The General Assembly shall, by appropriate legislation, provide for an efficient system of common schools throughout the State." Ky. Const. Sec. 183.

Several conclusions readily appear from a reading of this section. First, it is the obligation, the sole obligation, of the General Assembly to provide for a system of common schools in Kentucky. The obligation to so provide is clear and unequivocal and is, in effect, a constitutional mandate. Next, the school system must be provided throughout the entire state, with no area (or its children) being omitted. The creation, implementation and maintenance of the school system must be achieved by appropriate legislation. Finally, the system must be an efficient one.

It is, of course, the last "conclusion" that gives us pause and requires study and analysis. What, indeed, is the meaning of the word "efficient" as used in Section 183? . . .

DEFINITION OF "EFFICIENT"

We now hone in on the heart of this litigation. In defining "efficient," we use all the tools that are made available to us. In spite of any protestations to the contrary, we do not engage in judicial legislating. We do not make policy. We do not substitute our judgment for that of the General Assembly. We simply take the plain directive of the Constitution, and, armed with its purpose, we decide what our General Assembly must achieve in complying with its solemn constitutional duty.

Any system of common schools must be created and maintained with the premise that education is absolutely vital to the present and to the future of our Commonwealth. As Herbert Spencer observed, "Education has for its object the formation of character." H. Spencer, *Social Studies* (1851). No tax proceeds have a more important position or purpose than those for education in the grand scheme of our government. The importance of common schools and the education they provide Kentucky's children cannot be overemphasized or overstated.

The sole responsibility for providing the system of common schools is that of our General Assembly. It is a duty — it is a constitutional mandate placed by the people on the 138 members of that body who represent those selfsame people.

The General Assembly must not only establish the system, but it must monitor it on a continuing basis so that it will always be maintained in a constitutional manner. The General Assembly must carefully supervise it, so that there is no waste, no duplication, no mismanagement, at any level.

The system of common schools must be adequately funded to achieve its goals. The system of common schools must be substantially uniform throughout the state. Each child, *every child*, in this Commonwealth must be provided with an equal opportunity to have an adequate education. Equality is the key word here. The children of the poor and the children of the rich, the children who live in the poor districts and the children who live in the rich districts must be given the same opportunity and access to an adequate education. This obligation cannot be shifted to local counties and local school districts. . . .

Having declared the system of common schools to be constitutionally deficient, we have directed the General Assembly to recreate and redesign a new system that will comply with the standards we have set out. Such system will guarantee to all children the opportunity for an adequate education, through a *state* system. To allow local citizens and taxpayers to make a supplementary effort in no way reduces or negates the minimum quality of education required in the statewide system.

We do not instruct the General Assembly to enact any specific legislation. We do not direct the members of the General Assembly to raise taxes. It is their decision how best to achieve efficiency. We only decide the nature of the constitutional mandate. We only determine the intent of the framers. Carrying-out that intent is the duty of the General Assembly.

A child's right to an adequate education is a fundamental one under our Constitution. The General Assembly must protect and advance that right.

We concur with the trial court that an efficient system of education must have as its goal to provide each and every child with at least the seven following capacities: (i) sufficient oral and written communication skills to enable students to function in a complex and rapidly changing civilization; (ii) sufficient knowledge of economic, social, and political systems to enable the student to make informed choices; (iii) sufficient understanding of governmental processes to enable the student to understand the issues that affect his or her community, state, and nation; (iv) sufficient self-knowledge and knowledge of his or her mental and physical wellness; (v) sufficient grounding in the arts to enable each student to appreciate his or her cultural and historical heritage; (vi) sufficient training or preparation for advanced training in either academic or vocational fields so as to enable each child to choose and pursue life work intelligently; and (vii) sufficient levels of academic or vocational skills to enable public school students to compete favorably with their counterparts in surrounding states, in academics or in the job market. . . .

SUMMARY/CONCLUSION

We have decided this case solely on the basis of our Kentucky Constitution, Section 183. We find it unnecessary to inject any issues raised under the United States Constitution or the United States Bill of Rights in this matter. We decline to issue any injunctions, restraining orders, writs of prohibition or writs of mandamus.

We have decided one legal issue—and one legal issue only—viz., that the General Assembly of the Commonwealth has failed to establish an efficient system of common schools throughout the Commonwealth.

Lest there be any doubt, the result of our decision is that Kentucky's *entire system* of common schools is unconstitutional. There is no allegation that only part of the common school system is invalid, and we find no such circumstance. This decision applies to the entire sweep of the system—all its parts and parcels. This decision applies to the statutes creating, implementing and financing the *system* and to all regulations, etc., pertaining thereto. This decision covers the creation of local school districts, school boards, and the Kentucky Department of Education. . . . It covers school construction and maintenance, teacher certification—the whole gamut of the common school system in Kentucky.

While individual statutes are not herein addressed specifically or considered and declared to be facially unconstitutional, the statutory system as a whole and the interrelationship of the parts therein are hereby declared to be in violation of Section 183 of the Kentucky Constitution. Just as the bricks and mortar used in the construction of a schoolhouse, while contributing to the building's facade, do not ensure the overall structural adequacy of the schoolhouse, particular statutes drafted by the legislature in crafting and designing the current school system are not unconstitutional in and of themselves. Like the crumbling schoolhouse which must be redesigned and revitalized for more efficient use, with some component parts found to be adequate, some found to be less than adequate, statutes relating to education may be reenacted as components of a constitutional system if they combine with other component statutes to form an efficient and thereby constitutional system.

Since we have, by this decision, declared the system of common schools in Kentucky to be unconstitutional, Section 183 places an absolute duty on the

General Assembly to re-create, re-establish a new system of common schools in the Commonwealth. As we have said, the premise of this opinion is that education is a basic, fundamental constitutional right that is available to all children within this Commonwealth. The General Assembly should begin with the same premise as it goes about its duty. The system, as we have said, must be efficient, and the criteria we have set out are binding on the General Assembly as it develops Kentucky's new system of common schools. . . .

NOTES AND QUESTIONS

1. What remedy did the Kentucky Supreme Court order for the constitutional deficiencies it identified? How could the legislature know if it had complied? What did the California Supreme Court require in *Serrano*?
2. Following the *Rose* decision, the governor and legislature established a task force to draft a comprehensive reform proposal, which resulted in the Kentucky Education Reform Act of 1990. Notably, most stakeholders, including the governor and many legislators, seemed to embrace the court's direction to overhaul the state's education system. In *Framing Equal Opportunity: Law and the Politics of School Finance Reform* (2010), Michael Paris describes the unusual tenor of the state's reaction to the *Rose* decision:

   > . . . Anyone situated before the materials — the newspaper articles, the minutes of some forty-six task force meetings, the statements and actions of various players — would come away with a sense that the people involved felt themselves to be caught up in something historic, something that called them to take extraordinary action and make an extraordinary efforts [*sic*]. They had reached, as the *Courier-Journal* put it, "a crossroads." . . . Newspaper coverage portrayed the Court's decision as historic. The *Louisville Courier-Journal*'s immediate editorial response trumpeted a "new beginning" in which the governor and legislators now stood "together as partners in the quest imposed by the Supreme Court in its monumental decision last week."

3. How do the plaintiffs' theories in *Serrano* and *Rose* differ? How does the California Supreme Court's analysis in *Serrano* differ from that of the U.S. Supreme Court in *Rodriguez*? What accounts for the difference? Do you agree with the California Supreme Court that "substantial disparities in expenditures per pupil among school districts cause and perpetuate substantial disparities in the quality and extent of availability of educational opportunities"? Do you agree that "an equal expenditure level per pupil in every district is not educationally sound or desirable because of differing educational needs"? Why or why not?
4. Unsurprisingly, stakeholders are divided about the effectiveness of school finance reform litigation. The excerpt from Professor William Koski later in this chapter summarizes much of the debate. There is also a voluminous literature examining the effects of particular school finance decisions. *See, e.g.*, Kirk Stark & Jonathan Zasloff, *Tiebout and Tax Revolts: Did* Serrano *Really Cause Proposition 13?*, 50 UCLA L. Rev. 801 (2003); Debra H. Dawahare, *Public School Reform: Kentucky's Solution*, 27 U. Ark. Little Rock L. Rev. 27 (2004).

* * *

Another case often cited in discussions of the earliest state-court education equity and adequacy efforts, and that amply illustrates the protracted nature of some education reform litigation, is Abbott v. Burke, a New Jersey case now nearing the end of its third decade. *Abbott* followed Robinson v. Cahill, 62 N.J. 473 (1973), an earlier New Jersey decision holding that the New Jersey constitutional guarantee of thorough and effective education could not be met where there were large discrepancies in per-pupil expenditures.

The *Abbott* litigation spans 21 New Jersey Supreme Court decisions from 1985 to the most recent *Abbott XXI* decision handed down by the New Jersey Supreme Court on May 24, 2011. In *Abbott*, public school students from New Jersey's poorest school districts alleged that the state's reliance on property taxes for the majority of school funding violated the "thorough and efficient" education clause in the state constitution. The New Jersey Supreme Court agreed in 1990, holding that:

> [U]nder the present system the evidence compels but one conclusion: the poorer the district and the greater its need, the less the money available, and the worse the education. That system is neither thorough nor efficient. We hold the [Public School Education Act] unconstitutional as applied to poorer urban school districts. Education has failed there, for both the students and the State. We hold that the Act must be amended to assure funding of education in poorer urban districts at the level of property-rich districts; that such funding cannot be allowed to depend on the ability of local school districts to tax; that such funding must be guaranteed and mandated by the State; and that the level of funding must also be adequate to provide for the special educational needs of these poorer urban districts in order to redress their extreme disadvantages.

Abbott v. Burke, 119 N.J. 287, 297 (1990).

In the subsequent *Abbott* decisions, the court grappled with the question of what type of funding scheme is sufficient to satisfy the constitutional requirements. In the *Abbott IV* decision of 1997, the court required the New Jersey legislature to match the average per-pupil expenditures of the poorest school districts with those of the wealthier districts as a form of interim remedial relief while the legislature came up with a constitutionally acceptable system of funding. Abbott v. Burke (*Abbott IV*), 149 N.J. 145, 156 (1997). Finally, in 2009, the New Jersey Supreme Court decided that a new funding law, the School Funding Reform Act of 2008 (SFRA), is constitutional and ended the parity funding mandated by previous decisions. Abbott v. Burke (*Abbott XX*), 199 N.J. 140 (2009). The latest court decision concerned the underfunding of SFRA because of the recent recession. The Court held in *Abbott XXI* that the state must make up the $500 million shortfall, but limited the decision to the plaintiffs' districts instead of all the school districts in New Jersey. Abbott v. Burke (*Abbott XXI*), 206 N.J. 332 (2011). The Education Law Center, plaintiffs' counsel in *Abbott*, maintains a website with a wealth of information about the *Abbott* litigation at http://www.edlawcenter.org/cases/abbott-v-burke.html.

* * *

The next excerpt summarizes the evolution of education reform litigation.

MICHAEL PARIS, *SCHOOL FINANCE REFORM AND EDUCATIONAL IDEOLOGY: A GUIDE TO LAW, POLITICS, AND POLICY,* IN *FRAMING EQUAL OPPORTUNITY: LAW AND THE POLITICS OF SCHOOL FINANCE REFORM* (2010)

Legal and policy observers typically divide the history of school finance litigation into three distinct "waves" or "phases." The first phase runs from the mid-1960s to the U.S. Supreme Court's decision in *San Antonio v. Rodriguez* in 1973. The second phase runs from 1973 until 1989 and the third from 1989 to date. The principles of division among these three waves involve the fluctuating fortunes of litigation efforts and, more importantly, what most observers characterize as the transition from "equity" to "adequacy" in litigation theories and policy approaches....

[In the late 1960s, law professors John Coons, William Clune, and Stephen Sugarman] urged reform advocates and courts to endorse "wealth neutrality" as a constitutional constraint on a valid state school finance system. Wealth neutrality holds that a valid system, whatever else it does, may not allow the level of spending for education to be a function of local school district wealth....

In Serrano v. Priest (1971), the California Supreme Court held that wealth neutrality was what the federal equal protection clause required. Education was a fundamental right, and wealth was a suspect classification. *Serrano* was national news. It marked the beginnings of sustained nationwide communication among reform lawyers, and it provided other courts with a model opinion endorsing wealth neutrality. Other major trial court decisions soon followed....

Reform lawyers in New Jersey filed Robinson v. Cahill in state court in 1970. The lawyer representing the named plaintiffs grounded his argument primarily in wealth neutrality. However, at the trial phase, Rutgers-Newark Law Professor Paul Tractenberg entered the case as the representative of [*amici curiae* NAACP and the ACLU]. Tractenberg ... argued that the education clause of the state constitution guaranteed each child a substantive right to access "the best possible" education. This claim invited the courts to wade into the briar patch of substantive educational reform. In 1972, a trial court endorsed wealth neutrality and struck down the New Jersey school finance system. The state appealed.

While *Robinson* was pending before the New Jersey high court, the U.S. Supreme Court handed down its decision in *Rodriguez.* Twelve days later, the New Jersey Supreme Court handed down its own landmark decision. Following Tractenberg's lead to some extent, it rejected wealth neutrality but held that the state education clause did guarantee each child the equal opportunity to receive an adequate education. It struck down the state's school finance system in light of this "standard."

With *Serrano* still pending in the California state courts, and with the New Jersey high court's decision in *Robinson*, reform-oriented lawyers and policy analysts were back in business. The first inklings of national communication and coordination that arose after *Serrano I* now took on organizational form and garnered foundation funding. A national "equity network" developed, with much support from the Ford Foundation.

After 1973, and up until 1989, reform litigation succeeded in producing state high court victories in six states, in addition to New Jersey: California, Connecticut, Washington, West Virginia, Wyoming, and Arkansas. The presence of education clauses in all state constitutions could be invoked to say that education was a "fundamental" right under state law for equal protection purposes. State courts could also find some sort of right to educational equality or adequacy in their own state constitutions' education clauses, standing on their own. However, over this period, state high courts in thirteen states rejected challenges. Even when important victories were won, as in New Jersey and California, judicial decisions produced long, drawn-out legislative processes, which in turn produced policies that reformers ultimately found disappointing. The bulk of the litigation during the second phase focused on equal protection arguments. Many state high courts simply appealed to the *Rodriguez* majority's arguments to turn back challenges.

The third phase runs from 1989 to date. It is marked by far more success in court and more innovation in court decisions and remedies. The year 1989 is singled out because it saw state high court victories in Kentucky, Montana, and Texas. Observers point to "the Kentucky landmark" in particular as the key moment in ushering in a new era of "educational adequacy litigation." One year later, the New Jersey Supreme Court handed down its central decision in Abbott v. Burke. In a new twist, the New Jersey Court held that what was "adequate" for poor, minority children had to be judged against what already advantaged children received in the state's wealthiest districts.

In response to new adequacy claims, many state high courts soon struck down school finance systems, with several explicitly modeling their opinions on the Kentucky Supreme Court's opinion in Rose v. Council for Better Education. Many observers also explain the new success of adequacy arguments as an unintended consequence of the "standards movement" in state education policy. The widespread enactment of educational content standards and statewide tests to measure performance has helped finance reformers by giving them state-endorsed norms for "adequacy" and concrete evidence of educational failure. . . .

* * *

Not surprisingly, observers and stakeholders differ strongly on virtually every normative question about education litigation as well as on whether the results of plaintiffs' victories have improved education or not. In particular, proponents and opponents vigorously dispute whether "inputs," or funds spent on education, can be used as a proxy for educational quality, whether litigation has improved conditions on the ground in the states, and whether adjudicating claims of educational inadequacy or inequity is beyond the scope of judicial competence or invites the judiciary to violate the separation of powers. In the following excerpt, law professor William Koski reviews two books by leading advocates for and against school reform litigation, using them to examine and evaluate in detail the principal objections to and defenses of education litigation.

WILLIAM S. KOSKI, *COURTHOUSES v. STATEHOUSES?*
109 Mich. L. Rev. 923 (2011)

Just over twenty years ago, the Kentucky Supreme Court declared the commonwealth's primary and secondary public-education finance system—indeed, the entire system of primary and secondary public education in Kentucky—unconstitutional under the "common schools" clause of the education article in Kentucky's constitution. That case has been widely cited as having ushered in the "adequacy" movement in school-finance litigation and reform, in which those challenging state school-funding schemes argue that the state has failed to ensure that students are provided an adequate education guaranteed by their state constitutions. Since the *Rose* decision in Kentucky, some thirty-three school-finance lawsuits have reached final decisions in thirty-one states. For plaintiffs, the campaign has been relatively successful in court, as school-funding schemes in twenty-two states have been declared unconstitutional. Recently, however, a few courts seem to be taking a more cautious approach, either declining to become embroiled in school-finance lawsuits or declaring the school-finance systems constitutional and relinquishing jurisdiction. Yet the pace of litigation appears unabated. In light of the overall success of the adequacy movement in court, the wariness with which some courts have begun to approach the matter, and the continued press for school reform through the courts, it is fair to say that the adequacy-finance-litigation movement has matured and it is time to take stock of it. Two recent books—Eric Hanushek and Al Lindseth's *Schoolhouses, Courthouses, and Statehouses* and Michael Rebell's *Courts & Kids*—do just that. And they reach very different conclusions (at least on the face of it).

If one were to stage a bout between contenders for the school-finance-reform-litigation heavyweight championship, it would be nearly impossible to find a better match than Rebell vs. Hanushek and Lindseth. In the plaintiffs' corner and fighting for an appropriate role for the courts is Michael Rebell. A professor at Columbia University's Teachers College, Rebell is a battle-tested veteran of school reform litigation, having sued the New York Public Schools in the 1980s for its failure to ensure that children with disabilities had access to an appropriate education and, more recently, having successfully challenged New York's failure to provide a sound, basic education to the children of low-income communities in the state. Outside of the courtroom, Rebell has advanced the adequacy movement by developing his theory of "public engagement" in the education-reform process, studying the role of courts in institutional (school) reform, and establishing a network of researchers, policy-thinkers, and lawyers to collaborate in advocating school-finance reform.

In *Courts & Kids*, Rebell makes the case for the authority and responsibility of the courts to protect the constitutional rights of children who have been denied a sound, basic education. Rebell believes not only that it is incumbent upon state supreme courts to recognize and enforce the educational rights of children, but also that courts in educational-finance litigations have been effective in enhancing equality of educational opportunity for all children. Looking to the future of judicial involvement in educational policy, however, Rebell proposes a nuanced model—what he calls the "successful remedies" model—of judicial engagement that establishes a "functional separation of powers" among the three branches of government, "in which the judicial, legislative, and executive branches working together can deal effectively with difficult social policy issues like providing a meaningful educational opportunity for all children."

In the defendants' (read: states') corner and fighting against court intervention in matters of school finance are Eric Hanushek and Al Lindseth. Hanushek is a senior fellow at the Hoover Institution at Stanford University and is widely regarded as a leading figure in the study of the economics of education. Perhaps more salient, Hanushek has testified on behalf of state defendants in numerous educational-finance-reform litigations. Hanushek is a leading proponent of performance-based school funding and accountability and is known for his position that "differences in either the absolute [public education] spending level or spending increases bear little or no consistent relationship to differences in student achievement." Lindseth, a partner with the Atlanta-based law firm Sutherland Asbill & Brennan, has represented states in school-finance lawsuits in various states, including New York, Florida, and North Dakota, and over the last twenty-five years has advised governors, elected officials, and state education leaders on topics related to school finance and reform. . . .

A. THE COURTS, THE LEGISLATURES, AND SCHOOL REFORM

In the wake of the so-called "third wave" of school-finance litigation and the success of the adequacy argument in state supreme courts, the once white-hot debate over "judicial activism" in educational policymaking and practice (think desegregation litigation) has rekindled. In the last four years alone at least five full volumes have been published on the subject, most of which are skeptical, if not highly critical, of court intervention. *Courts & Kids* vs. *Schoolhouses, Courthouses, and Statehouses* could serve as closing arguments in that rekindled debate. While Rebell recognizes that courts alone cannot produce meaningful educational reform, he nonetheless calls for a robust role for the courts in educational policy-making — a "functional" separation-of-powers model that recognizes and capitalizes on the relative institutional strengths of the three branches of government. Citing "the courts' principled approach to issues and their long-term staying power" as well as their "inherent constitutional responsibilities," Rebell calls for a judicial role in ensuring the development and implementation of educational reform measures. In contrast, while Hanushek and Lindseth don't completely reject any role for the courts, they argue for a bare minimalist approach: "[I]f the court abuses its power and intrudes in areas reserved to the other branches, there is no 'check' within the constitution itself to bring the courts back into the fold. . . . Therefore, the potential of judicial 'tyranny' from adequacy suits is very real. . . ." . . .

1.   THE SEPARATION-OF-POWERS OBJECTION

As the authors all note, a number of courts in the past two decades have declined to review the merits of plaintiffs' claims that their states' school funding schemes are unconstitutional under separation-of-powers principles or the political question doctrine. Hanushek and Lindseth do not discuss the extensive scholarly treatments of the countermajoritarian dilemma, opting instead to simply quote Hamilton's Federalist No. 78 for the abstract principle that the judiciary possesses neither the power of "the sword [n]or the purse." For that reason, their theoretical argument against court involvement seems thin, particularly compared to Rebell's more robust treatment of the subject. Rebell grounds his argument in favor of court intervention in a critique of the doctrinal underpinnings of the political question doctrine and, relying on John Hart Ely's famous case for judicial review, a relatively robust theoretical case for the judiciary's authority and obligation to enforce positive state constitutional rights, such as the right to a "sound basic education" and to "correct malfunctions of the political process" where minority rights are compromised at the hands of electoral majorities. To the extent that the primary objection to judicial intervention in educational policymaking is one of political theory and legal doctrine, Rebell would have the better of the matter, but that is hardly the authors' only concern about the courts.

2. THE STANDARDS OBJECTION

Rebell contends that courts, which must interpret constitutional terms such as "adequate" or "sound basic" education in their states' education articles, are capable of applying these concepts in school reform litigations. Others, like Hanushek and Lindseth, counter that such language provides courts with no clear principles or standards to guide the development of school reform policies. As Frank Michelman famously argued, such conceptual indeterminacy can stymie judicial intervention because reform proceeds without coherence or clear objectives. Indeed the quest for a unified theory of equality of educational opportunity has bedeviled scholars, judges, and lawyers since the inception of equity-finance-reform litigation through to the modern adequacy movement. In response to this "standards objection," neither book attempts a comprehensive theory of educational opportunity; rather, both look at the same guideposts for reform and draw different conclusions.

Hanushek and Lindseth argue that the complex educational research, policy, and practice questions that must be answered to come up with an operational definition of "adequacy" doom the entire judicial educational-policymaking enterprise. What are the appropriate educational outcomes? What educational resources are correlated with educational outcomes? How much of those resources is enough? None of these is answerable with any degree of certainty, they argue. Consequently, courts cannot and should not be involved in dictating a standard for adequacy. Not to worry, responds Rebell: legislatively authorized state content standards "put into focus the fundamental goals and purposes of our system of public education," and those standards provide courts with the politically recognized specific expectations and outcome measures needed to develop appropriate remedies in school reform cases. But those standards are frequently mere aspirations, are not intended to guide constitutional decision making, and cannot be reliably linked with specific educational resources to be of any remedial guidance, Hanushek and Lindseth reply.

So, this standards debate ultimately resolves itself into a debate over whether legislatively mandated standards for what all children should know and be able to do can, as a matter of judicial command, reliably guide educational-resource distribution. In Chapter Seven of their book, Hanushek and Lindseth unequivocally say "no," while Rebell argues that in the complex world of educational governance and policy, it is appropriate for courts to use those standards as guideposts for continuous improvement, even if scientific certainty is elusive. More on this in a moment.

3. THE JUDICIAL CAPACITY OBJECTION

Hanushek and Lindseth argue that, as institutions and decision-making bodies, courts have neither the expertise nor the capacity to design and implement effective remedies for educational failure. Building on their argument that there are no workable standards for judicial remedies, they forcefully argue that the courts therefore tend toward "spending remedies because they believe they will work and because they are the easiest to monitor and enforce." They go on to criticize generalist judges for their lack of educational-policy expertise, their limited access to information in a trial setting, and their reliance on distorted adversarial evidentiary presentations to develop remedies (though some of those presentations are hardly adversarial, Hanushek and Lindseth point out quite sagely; instead, they are wink-and-nod agreements to plunder the state treasury).

Rebell meets this objection head-on in two different ways. He first points out that modern courts have developed processes and organizations to both formulate and administer complex reform decrees. Courts have become adept at sifting through complex and contradictory social science evidence. Indeed, given the access to information parties enjoy during the discovery phase, two scholars have argued that judicial investigation into complex educational-finance issues may, at times, exceed the investigations of researchers. Although Rebell does not specifically mention it, I note that even after the remedial decree is handed down (whether by consent or judicial fiat), courts employ numerous administrative structures to monitor and enforce their remedial schemes. These include monitoring committees that may be composed of party representatives, magistrates, and masters, who may be charged with resolving disputes or tweaking remedial schemes; and monitors who evaluate progress toward compliance with those decrees.

Rebell's second response to the capacity objection is, to be blunt, "compared to what?" This is the heart of his case for a principled and pragmatic judicial role in educational policymaking and governance — that courts possess unique institutional attributes that make them well suited to making certain types of educational-policy decisions, particularly when compared to the legislative and executive branches. This comparative institutional analysis reveals that courts have the staying power to pursue educational reform, a notoriously long and arduous process. He further argues that the judiciary's relative political independence makes it more likely to advance equitable remedies in the face of majoritarian politics. And the courts' rational, analytic, and evidence-based decision-making methods make them well suited to guiding rational, long-range reform efforts. Of course, this process must be done in "colloquy" with the political branches, particularly legislatures, which are better suited to making the delicate tradeoffs on specific policies; and executive agencies, which are better suited to day-to-day implementation on the ground. "When disputes arise on whether specific mechanisms are, in fact, meeting constitutional requirements, judicial fact-finding mechanisms should be invoked." In other words, there is a proper judicial role in Rebell's functional separation-of-powers model of public education reform.

Modern public law litigation is far from the ham-handed command-and-control model of judicial intervention that was often justly criticized during the desegregation era. Courts have learned from that experience and have developed both the internal administrative mechanisms and a proper awareness of their institutional limitations that permit them to play a productive role in institutional reform. This is the coming-of-age of school reform litigation in which courts — fulfilling their obligation to ensure that constitutional values, not merely political and economic expediency, are considered in educational policymaking — are playing the more modest role of destabilizing the status quo, reprioritizing the legislative agenda, and providing the political branches with guidance on how to move educational policy in a more equitable direction. Courts act as catalysts and facilitators in what then becomes a political process in which the previously disempowered communities and actors find a place at the table. This experimentalist — or in Rebell's terms, "functional" — role for the courts is not the outdated and caricatured image of courts and the judicial process that many court critics deploy.

Moreover, Hanushek and Lindseth — though hardly overstating the effectiveness of legislative reform — do not fully acknowledge the failures of the legislative and executive branches in ensuring equal and meaningful educational opportunities for all children. Rather, in claiming the superiority of the legislative process in developing remedies for school failure, they state that courts "do not have staff members with educational expertise at their disposal, in contrast to legislative bodies, which through their various senate and house committees and their permanent staffs, can draw upon a wide range of experience and expertise in complex education policy and finance issues". Two responses: (1) this, as noted, fails to recognize the fact-finding capabilities of courts, and (2) it appears to stylize the actual workings of harried, sometimes part-time state legislators and their overtaxed staffers. Beyond their staffing argument, and a modest defense of the legislative school appropriations process, Hanushek and Lindseth have not made the case that legislatures and executive branches alone will ensure appropriate educational policies most of the time.

Perhaps equally important, state court judges in many school reform litigations appear to be keenly aware of their comparative institutional strengths and know when to stay the course and when to stand aside to allow the political system to operate. Take, for example, the Massachusetts litigation. In 1993, the court struck down the commonwealth's school finance system and the legislature responded with a robust set of reforms, including "large infusions of money into property-poor districts along with the introduction of rigorous standards, graduation exams, and overall accountability." This policy reform resulted in achievement gains, particularly among Hispanic students. In 2005, when the court was again asked to review the constitutionality of the finance system, it cited the achievement gains, and refused to intervene. One interpretation of this is that the court found its proper role in educational-policy reform.

4. THE JUDICIAL INEFFECTIVENESS OBJECTION

Twenty years into the adequacy movement and some forty years into school-finance-reform litigation generally, it is fair to ask whether judicial involvement works. Here the authors diverge not only on their presentation and interpretation of evidence, but also on the standard for success.

Following in the tradition of "judicial impact" research in school finance, Hanushek and Lindseth analyze observable educational outcomes — primarily fourth grade reading and math and eighth grade math achievement on the National Assessment of Educational Progress ("NAEP") — in four states that were subject to judicial decisions striking down the states' respective school-finance systems sufficiently long ago such that any results would have taken hold. In three of those four states — Kentucky, Wyoming, and New Jersey — they show that, from 1992 to 2007, achievement did not grow any faster (and, in some places, grew slower) than the nation as a whole. In Massachusetts, the fourth state, they acknowledge the quicker pace of growth among white and Hispanic students, while pointing out the mixed success of African American students. While one could quibble with the methodological choices they made, Hanushek and Lindseth are very clear about their definition of "success" (raised achievement), while applying reasonable methods to available data to determine the extent of success. Their reliance on student achievement as an outcome measure is also based on the compelling case they make in Chapters One and Two for the link between achievement and various important life outcomes for individuals and the well-being of the nation generally. Even so, demonstrating that judicial intervention in three states did not unequivocally improve NAEP scores in fourth grade reading and math and eighth grade math cannot be dispositive on the question of court efficacy. Nor does it address the question whether litigation or threatened litigation has catalyzed reform in literally dozens of states — reform that has enhanced and may further enhance educational outcomes.

Rebell, however, in his second chapter "Defining Success in Sound Basic Education Litigations" — does not specifically identify how success should be measured, but rather opts for a process orientation toward defining success. There he first rehashes the treadworn arguments over whether money matters. (It does, if well spent.) He then criticizes the sole reliance on test scores as a measure of success. (Agreed.) Then, as the suspense builds, he stops short of providing a specific definition of success:

> [U]ltimately the measure of success for constitutional purposes — and indeed for all purposes — must be whether the state has succeeded in establishing and maintaining an educational system that provides meaningful educational opportunities to all students and graduates students who have the knowledge and skills needed to function as capable citizens and productive workers. And in the end, whether the state has provided its students with such a sound basic education is a judgment question that must be based not only on the available, but inherently limited, indicators of student outcomes but also on an assessment of the appropriateness and effective use of the standards, resources, and other inputs into the system and whether the systems in place are likely to prepare students to function productively in a modern, diverse society.

(Who could argue with that proposition, stated so vaguely?) Rather than providing specifics as to the measures of success, Rebell instead makes the case for a process orientation to these questions in which the judiciary serves as the body that makes specific determinations regarding the legislature's pursuit of the abstract outcomes he identifies. (Perhaps this is why he uses the gerund "Defining" in the title of the chapter, which suggests an ongoing process.) No doubt this is a productive proposal for approaching the process of remedying educational failure and a process orientation is quite comfortable territory for courts, but it does little to advance the specifics of how we gauge success.

This round cannot be called. Depending upon one's views of the judiciary's role, its capacity to develop and implement remedial measures, and the evidence of judicial efficacy, the authors present compelling cases to support either side. What is most telling, however, is that neither book rejects judicial involvement wholesale. Rather, common ground might be found in defining a narrow and effective role for courts to play.

B. The Role of Science in Decision Making

What level of scientific certainty is necessary for remedial educational-policy decision making? The answer to this question appears to drive much of Hanushek and Lindseth's concern that courts and their typical remedies of no-strings-attached additional funding or specific programmatic mandates are not up to the task of fixing failing schools. *Schoolhouses, Courthouses, and State-houses* provides a thoroughgoing critique of the state of educational research and, more specifically, the so-called "costing out" or "cost" studies that frequently are introduced in or ordered by school-finance-reform litigations. Put simply, Hanushek and Lindseth forcefully argue that "[w]hile science is potentially a source of reliable, objective information about programs and their expense, applying scientific methods to complex educational and funding decisions is fraught with problems." As a result, they are concerned that judges (and legislators!) presented with studies based on suspect methodologies, limited data, and biased authors will make bad policy decisions.

Hanushek and Lindseth aim most of their punches at cost studies. Those studies are frequently relied upon in crafting remedies in school-finance cases and are designed to systematically analyze the costs of the resources that are needed to ensure the provision of an adequate education or implement state standards effectively. Although Hanushek and Lindseth identify four distinct methodologies employed in cost studies, the basic divide is between professional-judgment models and those that employ statistical methodologies to estimate the costs of an adequate education. "Professional judgment" studies convene panels comprised of educators, administrators, and other experts to develop a basket of educational resources that would be necessary for a school or district to provide students with an adequate education and then place a price tag on those resources. Hanushek and Lindseth's primary objection to these studies is that they do not consider the source of the revenues for their model schools and therefore result in inefficiently high cost estimates. Put simply, "[w]ith no incentive to be mindful of costs in coming up with their model school, panel members tend to go on a shopping spree and order everything their hearts desire." A variant, or sometimes add-on, to the professional judgment approach is the evidence-based approach in which expert consultants identify specific research-based programs and services for the model school that are necessary to achieve adequacy. But that method similarly leads to inefficient cost estimates.

The second broad type of cost study—composed of the successful schools and cost function approaches—uses actual student achievement data and educational expenditure data to estimate the costs of achieving proficiency on state standards, while adjusting for the additional costs of educating children who either live in poverty or have language or special education needs. While somewhat warmer toward these methods, Hanushek and Lindseth argue that they too fail because of the inability to correlate spending with outcomes and because the "black box" nature of the statistical analyses do not identify any set of policies, personnel decisions, or the like, that contribute to success.

Beyond their critique of studies seeking to put a price tag on adequacy, Hanushek and Lindseth argue that it is inappropriate to base policy decisions that would mandate the use of particular educational programs or strategies on limited or unreliable research. Here they go after two of the sacred cows of educational-reform advocates—class size reduction and preschool. While they do not argue that these policies and programs are not helpful or essential, they do argue that the limited research into their efficacy and the failure to have implemented these strategies in an appropriate manner have created inefficiencies and even adverse, unintended consequences. Again, Hanushek and Lindseth caution against the misuse of available scientific evidence in the policymaking process.

Rebell, on the other hand, would not hold policymakers hostage to the scientific certainty that Hanushek and Lindseth would demand. While acknowledging the imperfections of cost studies, he nonetheless argues that courts and legislatures should look to those studies because they are better than the alternative of doing nothing and maintaining the status quo of failure. Moreover, Rebell touts the transparency of the cost studies' methodologies (a debatable proposition given the opacity of the cost-function and successful schools approaches) and argues that the courtroom crucible helps to ensure the integrity of these methods. With that latter point, Hanushek and Lindseth would disagree, arguing that the legislative and judicial processes lack scientific checks and balances. They would prefer that cost studies and other policy research be subjected to "the continuing dialog within disciplines, the scientific peer review system, and the mores of science work."

This dispute may be an irresolvable culture clash over the appropriate choice of institutions. Rebell, a courtroom lawyer and advocate, is clearly more comfortable with the hurly burly of the courtroom and the legislative chamber and the outcomes of those processes. Indeed, his faith in the adversarial justice system makes him favor the policy "truth" that comes from that process over others. Hanushek (and I say only Hanushek here, as Lindseth is a lawyer) is a social scientist and is more comfortable with decision making based on the certainty that science demands. But even Hanushek is pragmatic in the end. He recognizes that policymaking will be paralyzed if programmatic and funding decisions must await the final judgment of the peer review process. Instead, he proposes a performance-based funding model that would reward good policy and programs and weed out the poor performers and bad ideas. . . .

NOTES AND QUESTIONS

1. Koski's article and the books it reviews lay out many of the objections to and defenses of school finance litigation. Which do you find persuasive? Is evaluating complex school funding schemes or the necessary elements of an adequate education an appropriate task for judges? Why or why not?
2. What do you think of the "equity" versus "adequacy" debate? Is it more important to try to equalize resources or to ensure a minimum quantum of education for all students? Are equity and adequacy goals incompatible, or is one more advantageous as a strategic matter?

D. THE FEDERAL ROLE IN EDUCATION

Despite the Supreme Court's *Rodriguez* decision and the subsequent concentration of education litigation in state courts, the federal government still plays an important role in education policy and funding. Although federal education funding amounts to only about 10 percent of all education funding in the United States, federal policy has played a significant role in shaping state education programs. The next excerpt describes the origins and contours of current federal education policy, whose latest chapter is the controversial No Child Left Behind Act of 2001. This section also shifts our focus away from litigation and toward legislation aimed at improving the nation's lowest-performing schools and aiding its neediest children.

MICHAEL A. REBELL, *THE RIGHT TO COMPREHENSIVE EDUCATIONAL OPPORTUNITY*

47 Harv. C.R.-C.L. L. Rev. 47 (2012)

... In the wake of *Brown* and the civil rights movement, in 1965, the federal government committed itself to extending America's historical commitment to equal educational opportunity to racial minorities and low-income students with the passage of the Elementary and Secondary Education Act of 1965. Given the entrenched resistance of most southern states to implementing *Brown*'s mandate and the limited efforts being made by many other states to provide meaningful educational opportunities to Black, Latino, and other minority students, to low-income students, and, in many cases, to girls and women, a proactive stance on these issues by the federal government was of critical importance.

... The centerpiece of the ESEA was Title I, which distributed nearly $1 billion to school districts throughout the country to provide extra services to students from low-income families. It "established a federal priority in education, to improve education for children from poor families.... [It was] an expression of the old American idea ... that public schools could be the 'balance wheel of the social machinery,' righting wrongs that the economy and society imposed on children."

Historically, federal involvement in educational matters had been relatively minor. Despite the founders' strong belief in the importance of education, throughout most of the nation's history schooling was left largely to states and localities, consistent with the basic federalist structure of the U.S. Constitution. [President Lyndon] Johnson was able to change this legacy and promote a key role for the federal government in promoting equal educational opportunity by taking advantage of the public goodwill that followed the assassination of President John F. Kennedy, a large Democratic congressional majority, and his own deft political skills. Significantly, he was able to overcome the historical opposition to federal aid to education precisely because Title I did not provide general aid to education, but, consistent with the tenets of the American dream, only categorical aid targeted to assist needy students.

With the passage of the ESEA, federal spending on education rose to 10% of total education funding by 1968 and has remained at about that level ever since. To gain passage of the Act, however, Johnson had to agree to a number of political compromises that inhibited the development of strong evaluation and accountability requirements and that blunted its potential as a vehicle for meeting the educational needs of low-income children.... States and localities would control how the money would be spent and that was the one political price of passage for the 1965 ESEA.

Over the next three decades, as evaluation reports began to document waste and abuse in local Title I programs and disappointing educational results despite the expenditure of billions of federal dollars, Congress increasingly began to focus on tighter controls and accountability mechanisms. Major new initiatives were included in the revisions to the law in the 1990s that emphasized performance-based accountability systems which required states to test students to assess their academic progress, issue school report cards, and provide assistance to low-performing schools.

The emphasis on performance-based accountability intensified after reports in the 1980s, such as A Nation at Risk, raised alarms about the quality of the education American students were receiving and about their ability to compete effectively in the global economy. Responding to these concerns, both Presidents George H.W. Bush and Bill Clinton pressed Congress to incorporate goals, standards, and outcome assessments into Title I. In doing so, they sought to increase substantially the federal role in educational policy and to induce the states to move in coherent and consistent ways to improve equity and excellence in the nation's schools.

The original national goals and standards that both presidents had contemplated were quite robust. . . . In his State of the Union address in 1990, President Bush announced the goals, which included achieving a 90% high school graduation rate, being first in the world in math and science, and providing every graduate the knowledge and skills necessary to compete in the global marketplace. These performance targets were accompanied by a clear recognition that, to achieve these ends, substantial efforts would be required to prepare economically disadvantaged students to learn at higher levels. . . .

The original drafters of [the Goals 2000: Educate America Act of 1994] assumed that the statute that would emerge from their deliberations would also ensure that the resources necessary to provide all students the opportunity inputs for which they were advocating would be an integral part of the statutory scheme. A federal task force established to propose mechanisms for implementing Goals 2000 explained why "opportunity to learn" standards must be considered a necessary part of the standards-based reform approach:

> [I]f not accompanied by measures to ensure equal opportunity to learn, national content and performance standards could help widen the achievement gap between the advantaged and the disadvantaged in our society. If national content and performance standards and assessment are not accompanied by clear school delivery standards and policy measures designed to afford all students an equal opportunity to learn, the concerns about diminished equity could easily be realized. Standards and assessments must be accompanied by policies that provide access for all students to high quality resources, including appropriate instructional materials and well-prepared teachers.

The Clinton Administration's original Goals 2000 legislative proposal responded to this recommendation by including provisions for national "opportunity to learn" standards that would be developed by a National Education and Standards Council. Strong opposition to federal oversight of state spending, however, led to a substantial watering down of this concept in the final Goals 2000 legislation enacted in 1994; that statute called for only "voluntary" national school delivery standards that states could choose to adopt or state "opportunity to learn" standards that states could voluntarily develop. Even these minimal, voluntary "opportunity to learn" standards were revoked after the Republicans took control of Congress later that year. Given these realities, the administration did not push to include any of the specific school readiness concepts that the drafting committees had proposed.

Although Congress has not adopted the strong approach to national goals and standards that the first Bush and Clinton Administrations had contemplated, in its reauthorization processes since 1990, Congress did steadily enhance many other evaluation and accountability provisions of the Act, and the net effect has been a substantial increase in the federal government's oversight role. The culmination of these efforts was the No Child Left Behind Act of 2001, supported by President George W. Bush and strong bipartisan majorities in Congress. NCLB accepted and expanded the performance-based accountability provisions that had been introduced in the 1994 Improving America's Schools Act, but added more stringent requirements and sanctions to compel the states to take these responsibilities seriously. The law also substantially increased federal funding and expanded the civil rights aims and mandates of the ESEA, including a specific requirement that achievement gaps be substantially eliminated by 2014 by requiring that all students be proficient according to challenging state standards. In essence, therefore, NCLB might be said to implicitly support students' rights to meaningful educational opportunity — but without ensuring that the resources and mechanisms necessary to achieve these challenging mandates were in place. . . .

* * *

A good summary of the major provisions of the 600-page NCLB statute is contained in a 2010 Sixth Circuit decision rejecting a school district's challenge to the testing provisions, from which the following excerpt is drawn.

SCH. DIST. OF PONTIAC v. SEC'Y OF EDUC.

584 F.3d 253 (6th Cir. 2009), *cert. denied,* **130 S. Ct. 3385 (2010)**

A. THE NO CHILD LEFT BEHIND ACT

On January 8, 2002, then-President George W. Bush signed NCLB into law. The Act — "a comprehensive educational reform" — amended the Elementary and Secondary Education Act of 1965 [ESEA]. The ESEA targeted funding to students in low-income schools, and its purposes included overcoming "any effects of past racial discrimination." The ESEA was periodically reauthorized and amended over the next few decades. In contrast to prior ESEA iterations, NCLB "provides increased flexibility of funds, accountability for student achievement and more options for parents." 147 Cong. Rec. S13365, 13366 (2001) (statement of Sen. Bunning). The Act focuses federal funding more narrowly on the poorest students and demands accountability from schools, with serious consequences for schools that fail to meet academic-achievement requirements. States may choose not to participate in NCLB and forgo the federal funds available under the Act, but if they do accept such funds, they must comply with NCLB requirements. *See, e.g.,* 20 U.S.C. § 6311 ("For any State *desiring* to receive a grant under this part, the State educational agency shall submit to the Secretary a plan. . . .") (emphasis added); *see also* [Connecticut v.] Spellings, 453 F. Supp. 2d 459, 469 [(D.Conn. 2006)] ("In return for federal educational funds under the Act, Congress imposed on states a comprehensive regime of educational assessments and accountability measures."). In addition, with enumerated exceptions, under NCLB "the Secretary may waive any statutory or regulatory requirement . . . for a State educational agency, local educational agency, Indian tribe, or school through a local educational agency, that . . . receives funds under a program authorized by this Act."

Title I, Part A, of NCLB, titled "Improving Basic Programs Operated by Local Educational Agencies," continues to pursue the objectives of the ESEA and imposes extensive educational requirements on participating States and school districts, and, likewise, provides the largest amount of federal appropriations to participating States. For example, in fiscal year 2006, NCLB authorized $22.75 billion in appropriations for Title I, Part A, compared to $14.1 billion for the remaining twenty-six parts of NCLB combined. Title I, Part A's stated purposes include meeting "the educational needs of low-achieving children in our Nation's highest-poverty schools, limited English proficient children, migratory children, children with disabilities, Indian children, neglected or delinquent children, and young children in need of reading assistance."

In addition to Title I, Part A, NCLB establishes numerous other programs, including a literacy initiative for young children and poor families, special services for the education of children of migrant workers, requirements that all teachers be "highly qualified," and instruction in English for children with limited English ability. . . .

To qualify for federal funding under Title I, Part A, States must first submit to the Secretary a "State plan," developed by the State's department of education in consultation with school districts, parents, teachers, and other administrators. A State plan must "demonstrate that the State has adopted challenging academic content standards and challenging student academic achievement standards" against which to measure the academic achievement of the State's students. The standards in the State plan must be uniformly applicable to students in all of the State's public schools, and must cover at least reading or language arts; math; and, by the fourth grade, science skills. States also must develop, and school districts must administer, assessments to determine students' levels of achievement under plan standards. These assessments must show the percentage of students achieving "proficiency" among "economically disadvantaged students," "students from major racial and ethnic groups," "students with disabilities," and "students with limited English proficiency." Schools and districts are responsible for making "adequate yearly progress" ("AYP") on these assessments, meaning that a minimum percentage of students, both overall and in each subgroup, must attain proficiency.

A school's failure to achieve AYP triggers other requirements of Title I, Part A. If a school fails to make AYP for two consecutive years, it must be identified by the local educational agency for school improvement. Among other things, a school in improvement status must inform all of its students, including those who have been assessed as proficient, that they are permitted to transfer to any school within the district that has not been identified for school improvement. The school also must develop a two-year plan setting forth extensive measures to improve student performance, including further education for teachers and possible before- or after-school instruction or summer instruction.

If a school does not achieve AYP after two years of improvement status, it is "identif[ied] . . . for corrective action." Corrective action involves significant changes, such as replacing teachers who are "relevant to the failure to make [AYP]," or instituting an entirely new curriculum. If, after a year of corrective action, a school still has not reached AYP, the district must restructure the school entirely; options for restructuring include "[r]eopening the school as a public charter school," replacing the majority of the staff, or allowing the State's department of education to run the school directly. . . .

* * *

NCLB's standards, testing, and accountability provisions have all been subjected to significant and bipartisan criticism since the law's implementation, particularly as the 2014 deadline for all students to achieve proficiency approaches. The following excerpt from education expert Richard D. Kahlenberg summarizes many of the issues.

RICHARD D. KAHLENBERG, CENTURY FOUND., *FIXING NO CHILD LEFT BEHIND* (2008)

The No Child Left Behind Act (NCLB) was passed in 2001 with broad bipartisan support, but in the years since its enactment it has come under sharp attack from many quarters. The controversial legislation, which requires states receiving federal funding to test students in reading and math in grades 3 through 8 and to hold schools accountable for making adequate yearly progress in raising student achievement, is now widely acknowledged to need a major overhaul when it is reauthorized.

The sound idea of standards-based education reform — that states should establish clear content standards that define what students should know and be able to do at each grade level; that students should take rigorous and sophisticated tests to see whether they have mastered the material; and that students, teachers, and school administrators should be held accountable for results — is now threatened by major flaws in the way that NCLB embodies such reform. NCLB is being criticized not only by those on the far left and far right who never liked standards-based reform in the first place, but also by moderates who find several elements of NCLB untenable. In particular, critics rightly object to three central features of the act: the underfunding of NCLB; the flawed implementation of the standards, testing, and accountability provisions; and major difficulties with the provisions that are designed to allow students to transfer out of failing public schools. . . .

THE ORIGINAL IDEA OF STANDARDS-BASED REFORM

Standards-based reform, as envisioned by leading educators such as Albert Shanker, Marshall "Mike" Smith, Diane Ravitch, Lauren Resnick, and Chester Finn, as well as governors and business leaders from outside of education, would provide a sound way of promoting higher educational achievement and greater equality of educational opportunity. These educators believed that there was a big hole at the center of American education: a lack of agreement on what skills and knowledge students should master. Teachers had textbooks, but no real guidance on what to prioritize, so they were, essentially, asked to create their own curricula. Teachers ended up choosing very different topics to pursue, based on personal interests, which created confusion and incoherence.

There was also little outside pressure for anyone in the system to work very hard. . . . For the small number of students applying to selective colleges, doing well academically mattered a great deal, but not so for the vast majority of students going on to non-selective colleges or going straight into the workforce, where employers rarely looked at grades achieved.

In an influential paper, Smith and his coauthor Jennifer O'Day suggested an alternative to this chaos: standards-based reform. They outlined a systemic reform in which all horses—standards, curriculum, textbooks, tests, teacher training, and teacher development—pulled the cart in the same direction. States would establish clear content standards, which would direct the curriculum, teacher training, and assessments. Looking abroad at what successful competitors did, some, like Shanker, argued for national standards to provide even greater coherence. . . .

Likewise, standards-based reform also envisioned consequences for students and for teachers and principals whose students failed their assessments. Other countries had systems of accountability in place, and standards-based reform advocates saw this feature as critical. The key insight was that achievement is fueled by effort, as well as innate ability, and new ways were needed to create greater efforts by both students and teachers.

Early advocates of standards-based reform recognized that they were asking schools to do what had never been done before—educate all students to high levels. In the past, under a manufacturing economy, it was acceptable to hold a small group of students to high standards and let the majority slip by. But in the new, knowledge-based economy, educators needed genuinely to educate far more students, and advocates realized that in order to reach new performance standards, more funding would be required. The essential bargain, then, was more funding for greater accountability.

A final piece of the larger standards-based reform scheme was providing a mechanism so that children stuck in failing schools had the opportunity to transfer to better-performing public schools. This provision was a part of the accountability structure, to the extent that poor-performing schools would be "punished" by losing students, with the ultimate threat of being closed down. Providing the ability to transfer was also an acknowledgment that standards-based reform was a long-term strategy and that, even as schools slowly improved, families whose children were trapped in bad schools deserved a form of immediate relief.

. . . Not surprisingly, most researchers have found that NCLB has failed to live up to its goal of substantially increasing academic achievement and closing the achievement gap between racial, ethnic, and income groups. While there have been some achievement gains since the beginning of the standards-based reform movement, most of those gains occurred prior to the enactment of NCLB. A widely cited June 2007 study by the Center on Education Policy found gains in state test scores under NCLB, but a July 2007 study by Bruce Fuller at the University of California at Berkeley and others found that, on the more reliable National Assessment of Educational Progress, in twelve states studied, test score gains actually slowed with the enactment of NCLB. . . .

II. Flaws in NCLB's Funding

NCLB's grand bargain—greater federal funding in exchange for stricter accountability for results—has broken down in two respects. The first problem is the obvious mismatch between authorization and appropriation. The legislation authorized substantial increases in federal funding of K-12 education, but actual appropriations have fallen many billions of dollars below the authorized levels.

In FY 2002, the Congress authorized $26.4 billion but appropriated only $22.2 billion, a $4.2 billion shortfall. Over time, in general the shortfall grew progressively worse: from $5.4 billion in FY 2003 to $7.6 billion in FY 2004, $9.8 billion in FY 2005, $13.4 billion in FY 2006, $15.8 billion in FY 2007 and $14.8 billion in FY 2008. Between FY 2002 and FY 2008, the accumulated gap between authorization and appropriations was $70.9 billion. Taking into account the FY 2009 Bush administration budget request, the total gap rises to $85.7 billion.

In fact, however, the shortfall goes even deeper than that in a second respect, according to a new study of how much it would cost actually to reach some of the goals of No Child Left Behind. In [*Dollars Without Sense: The Mismatch Between the NCLB Accountability System and Title I Funding*, researchers from Syracuse University and the University of Nevada–Las Vegas] find that federal funding would have to multiply many times over to help districts succeed in meeting even the intermediate goals of NCLB (short of the act's ultimate goal of 100 percent student proficiency)....

III. Flaws in NCLB's System of Standards, Testing, and Accountability Standards

Most fundamentally, NCLB has failed to spur states to develop clear content standards, the lynch-pin necessary to inform teacher development, the curriculum, assessments, and the ultimate system for accountability. Content standards, which are supposed to drive the rest of the system, are often ill-defined, so teachers have to intuit the standards from previous tests. "In many places," Lauren Resnick of the University of Pittsburgh notes, we have seen "the virtual hijacking of standards and education by narrow tests." The existence of fifty different state standards also introduces chaos and confusion. As Shanker asked, "Should children in Alabama learn a different kind of math or science from children in New York?"

NCLB not only fails to encourage states to set rich and consistent content standards, it also allows them to set wildly different performance standards for what constitutes "proficiency." According to a 2007 study by Northwest Evaluation Associates and the Thomas B. Fordham Institute, passing scores vary from the sixth to the seventy-seventh percentile. Worse, by requiring 100 percent proficiency, NCLB actually provides a perverse incentive for states to lower performance standards of proficiency in order to avoid districts being sanctioned.

TESTING

As the standards are poorly constructed, so too are the tests. In part, perhaps, because of the large number of tests required (tests in math and reading for grades 3 to 8 as well as one grade in high school), states have adopted inexpensive, low-quality tests that rely on students answering multiple-choice questions by filling in bubbles. The low quality of the assessment is critical because under any system in which teachers are judged based on test scores they will inevitably "teach to the test." As Albert Shanker noted, "Teaching to the test is something positive when you have really good tests." But when the tests are poor quality, teaching to the test devolves into rote memorization and mastery of test-taking techniques rather than rich learning.

The assessments not only tend to be of low quality, their timing also tends to make them fairly unhelpful in diagnosing problems of individual students. Tests generally are given at the end of the year, and results do not come back until after the students have moved on to another grade. The timing and nature of the tests robs them of their diagnostic function . . . and reduces their value to teachers and students alike.

ACCOUNTABILITY

The third prong of the standards-based system of reform, accountability, is equally problematic under NCLB. . . .

NCLB requires states to set a single cut-point for proficiency and mandates that 100 percent of students meet the performance standard in math and reading by 2014. Most serious educators believe this goal to be a fantasy because it denies the reality of human variability. No society throughout history has ever achieved 100 percent proficiency in education. To suggest that all students, including those who are severely disabled, will reach a meaningful standard of proficiency is a nice political slogan, but it is absurd to punish schools, principals, and teachers — and ultimately, students and their families — for failing to reach an impossible goal. Moreover, . . . a single performance standard that is impossibly high for certain special education students to meet may at the same time be too low for the vast majority of students who will not be challenged sufficiently. The problem, therefore, is not that the performance standard is set too high or too low — it is that a single standard will be both. Finally, a single performance standard necessarily will lead to an emphasis on helping children who are on the cusp of being proficient. Teachers will "concentrate on the students who are almost proficient and ignore those judged to be well above the proficiency mark, and those who are so far below it that there is little chance of helping them to reach the mark in time for the test."

NCLB does not separate out the effects of family and the effects of school on student achievement, thereby holding teachers in high-poverty schools responsible for factors outside their control. Research going back four decades has found that the socioeconomic status of the family is the most important predictor of student achievement, yet NCLB requires all schools to reach the same exact standard, irrespective of the number of low-income students being educated. . . .

NCLB holds teachers and principals accountable, but not students. NCLB contains no sanctions for students who fail to achieve proficiency on standardized tests. Some states have adopted, on their own, incentives for students to work hard (to be promoted to the next grade or to receive a graduation diploma), but NCLB itself does not contain such sanctions. Most European nations have a system of incentives and outcomes for their students recognizing that academic performance represents a combination of good teaching and hard work by students. "Imagine saying we should shut down a hospital and fire its staff," Shanker wrote, "because not all its patients became healthy—but never demanding that the patients also look out for themselves by eating properly, exercising, and laying off cigarettes, alcohol, and drugs."

NCLB lacks what former Educational Testing Service researcher Paul Barton calls a "rule of reason," lumping all those schools which barely miss making adequate yearly progress (AYP) with a single subgroup of students together with schools that fail by a wide margin with all groups. NCLB's provision requiring that schools make AYP with all subgroups of students—disaggregated by race, income, education status, and so on—is generally thought to be a good provision because it does not allow schools to hide the failure of various subgroups of students behind generally good average achievement scores. But the law does not distinguish between a school that fails to make adequate progress with one group and a school that is generally failing with all of its students; either way, the school publicly is branded as a failure....

IV. FLAWS IN NCLB'S STUDENT TRANSFER PROVISIONS

NCLB provides that when Title I (high poverty) schools fail to make AYP for two years in a row, the school district must allow students to transfer to better-performing public schools within the district. The provision is meant to accomplish three goals: to serve as a sanction and form of accountability for low-performing schools, hopefully pressuring them to improve; to provide immediate relief for students stuck in failing schools; and (in the minds of some progressive reformers) to provide an opportunity for low-income students to escape high-poverty schools, thereby reducing concentrations of school poverty.

In practice, however, the student transfer provisions have been one of the most disappointing features of NCLB. Various studies and surveys have found that about 1 percent of students eligible to transfer actually do so. Some argue that the minute number of transfers suggest parents simply like neighborhood schools and do not want to get out of failing schools, or that districts are not providing enough information to parents about transfer options, and there is probably some truth to both of those. But there is another likely cause: many parents may not even apply to have their children transfer because there are so few good options within many urban school districts. Lacking the chance to send their children to demonstrably better schools in the suburbs, many urban parents may fail to see much comparative advantage to transferring from a failing segregated school to an almost-failing segregated school. In some school districts, such as Providence, Rhode Island, there have been literally no non-failing schools to transfer into at particular grade levels. It is not surprising, then, that the U.S. Department of Education found that, in a survey of nine urban districts, participation in Title I school choice was about 0.5 percent, even lower than the national average of 1 percent. While NCLB encourages urban and suburban districts to set up "cooperative agreements" to allow student transfers, virtually none of the country's suburban districts has voluntarily agreed to do this.

It is little wonder why suburban middle-class schools do not welcome low-income transfer students: all the incentives align against their doing so. As the University of Virginia's James Ryan notes, a receiving school that takes in low-income students faces a double risk. Because low-income students, on average, score lower than middle-class children, an influx of low-income transfer students initially is likely to depress aggregate school scores, increasing the chances that the receiving school will itself fail to make AYP. The other risk stems from a laudable feature of the legislation: the requirement that schools do a good job of raising proficiency in general, but also of raising the scores of groups of students, disaggregated by race and income. Homogenous schools with few poor or minority students are exempt from this requirement, because a critical mass of students is required to make disaggregation valid statistically. But an influx of poor and/or minority students might push a school over the threshold number triggering disaggregation, thus increasing the number of targets the school has to hit to make AYP and thereby increasing the risk of failing. This proves, says Ryan, "an incentive to minimize the number of African-American or poor students in a school or district."

These disincentives to cross-district transfers are problematic not only because they undercut the accountability rationale of NCLB and fail to provide immediate relief to students trapped in failing schools, but more importantly because they undermine NCLB's potential to break down economic segregation in our schools.

A wide body of research has found that concentrations of poverty create enormous difficulties for schools. On average, low-income fourth-grade American students given a chance to attend more affluent schools scored almost two years ahead of low-income students stuck in high-poverty schools on the National Assessment of Educational Progress (NAEP) in math. Indeed, low-income students in middle-class schools performed better, on average, than middle-class students attending high-poverty schools. Likewise, data from the 2006 Program for International Student Assessment (PISA) for fifteen-year-olds in science showed a "clear advantage in attending a school whose students are, on average, from more advantaged socio-economic backgrounds." The report continued, "Regardless of their own socio-economic background, students attending schools in which the average socio-economic background is high tend to perform better than when they are enrolled in a school with a below-average socio-economic intake." Middle-class schools provide not only more financial resources on average, but also a more positive peer environment, better teachers, and more actively involved parents.

More than forty school districts across the country now use socioeconomic status of student families as a factor in student assignment. In Wake County (Raleigh), North Carolina, for example, in 2000, the school board adopted a policy goal that no school should have more than 40 percent of students eligible for free and reduced price lunch or more than 25 percent performing below grade level. The program has been successful: low-income and minority students are performing better than comparable students in other large North Carolina districts, and middle-class students are excelling as well.

The Wake County socioeconomic school integration plan works well in part because the school district encompasses both the city of Raleigh and its surrounding suburbs. In much of the country, however, urban and suburban areas are cut into separate school districts, so it is imperative that creative efforts be made to provide meaningful choice extending across school district lines. . . .

NOTES AND QUESTIONS

1. Many school districts and some states have protested the perceived under-
    funding of the NCLB requirements. Some have sued for a declaration that
    they are not required to comply with NCLB's mandates in the absence of full
    funding, but the courts have generally been inhospitable to such suits. *See,
    e.g.*, Sch. Dist. of Pontiac v. Sec'y of Educ., 584 F.3d 253 (6th Cir. 2009), *cert.
    denied*, 130 S. Ct. 3385 (2010); Connecticut v. Duncan, 612 F.3d 107 (2d Cir.
    2010), *cert. denied*, 131 S. Ct. 1471 (2011). The Supreme Court held in 2009
    that NCLB does not create a private right of action for parents to enforce
    its provisions regarding transfers or supplemental educational services.
    Horne v. Flowers, 557 U.S. 433 (2009). An overview of many of the lawsuits,
    along with issues facing Congress in NCLB reauthorization, can be found at
    Regina R. Umpstead & Elizabeth Kirby, *Reauthorization Revisited: Framing the
    Recommendations for the Elementary and Secondary Education Act's Reauthorization
    in Light of No Child Left Behind's Implementation Challenges*, 276 Educ. Law
    Reporter 1 (2012).
2. In May 2012, the nonprofit Center on Education Policy, which has been
    tracking school progress on NCLB's "Adequate Yearly Progress" (AYP)
    measure, released figures for the 2010-2011 year. The report found that:

    > [A]n estimated 48% of the nation's public schools did not make AYP in 2011,
    > an increase from 39% in 2010 and the highest percentage since NCLB took
    > effect. In 24 states and the District of Columbia, at least half of the public
    > schools did not make AYP in 2011. In a majority of the states (43 and D.C.), at
    > least one-fourth of the schools did not make AYP. The percentage of public
    > schools not making AYP in 2011 varied greatly by state, from about 11% in
    > Wisconsin to about 89% in Florida.

    Alexandra Usher, Ctr. on Educ. Policy, *AYP Results for 2010-11* (2012).
3. Criticism of NCLB has been widespread and bipartisan, especially of the
    provision requiring all students to be proficient in math and English by
    2014. Education historian Diane Ravitch summed up the criticism of the
    100 percent proficiency requirement in a pithy blog post in 2012: "It's
    comparable to Congress mandating that every city, town, and village in
    the nation must be crime-free by 2014 . . . or their police departments
    would be severely punished." Diane Ravitch, *Obama Grants Waivers to
    NCLB and Makes a Bad Situation Worse*, The Daily Beast (Feb. 10, 2012,
    12:00 A.M.), http://www.thedailybeast.com/articles/2012/02/10/obama-
    grants-waivers-to-nclb-and-makes-a-bad-situation-worse.html; *see also* James
    E. Ryan, *The Perverse Incentives of the No Child Left Behind Act*, 79 N.Y.U. L.
    Rev. 932 (2004). As noted education expert Linda Darling-Hammond noted
    in 2008,

    > [s]ince the start of the 2003-04 school year, at least twenty states and a number
    > of school districts have officially protested the NCLB Act, voting to withdraw
    > from participation, to withhold local funding for implementation, or to resist
    > specific provisions. Members of the Congressional Black Caucus, among other
    > federal legislators, have introduced bills to amend the law by placing a mor-
    > atorium on high-stakes standardized testing, a key element of NCLB; withhold-
    > ing school sanctions until the bill is fully funded; and requiring progress
    > toward adequate and equitable educational opportunities for students in

public schools. The Harvard Civil Rights Project, along with other advocacy groups, has warned that the law threatens to increase the growing dropout and pushout rates for students of color, ultimately reducing access to education for these students, rather than enhancing it. As the evidence of NCLB's unintended consequences emerges, it seems increasingly clear that, despite its good intentions and admirable goals, NCLB as currently implemented is more likely to harm than to help most of the students who are the targets of its aspirations, and it is more likely to undermine — some would say even destroy — the nation's public school system than to improve it.

Linda Darling Hammond, *From "Separate but Equal" to "No Child Left Behind": The Collision of New Standards and Old Inequities*, in *Many Children Left Behind: How the No Child Left Behind Act Is Damaging Our Children and Our Schools* (Deborah Meier & George Wood eds., 2004).

* * *

NCLB has also had a significant effect on the lawsuits over educational adequacy currently pending in many states, as the following excerpt explains.

MICHAEL HEISE, *THE UNINTENDED LEGAL AND POLICY CONSEQUENCES OF THE NO CHILD LEFT BEHIND ACT*
86 Neb. L. Rev. 119 (2007)

. . . The passage and implementation of NCLB helped solidify the interaction between adequacy litigation and the standards and assessments movement. Under NCLB, those states that had not already done so were required to establish school accountability systems that annually assess student proficiency in math and reading. A sliding scale of NCLB-specific consequences befalls any school that does not achieve adequate yearly progress. Thus, a school's failure to achieve sufficient student achievement and progress now generates liability under federal law. The full contour of NCLB liability was not fully appreciated, however, until school finance activists, in school finance litigation, began to advance inadequate yearly progress under NCLB as legal proof of inadequate education.

. . . Modern school finance litigation contends not that all students are entitled to the same resources, but rather that all students should receive the funds necessary to finance an adequate education. Indicia of school adequacy are critical to the success of adequacy-based lawsuits.

NCLB data and annual yearly progress (AYP) determinations directly speak to assessments of school adequacy. Specifically, NCLB and AYP data supplement the evidentiary foundation for school finance adequacy lawsuits. At the individual student level, the more poorly students perform on academic assessments the better it is from a litigation standpoint. Similarly, at the school level, a determination that a school failed to achieve AYP under NCLB greatly assists litigants seeking to establish that such a school is "inadequate" in a school finance adequacy lawsuit. That states set their own student performance thresholds make such determinations even more powerful. To the extent that school finance litigants seek to transform failure in the classroom into success in the courtroom, NCLB can provide invaluable evidentiary support. . . .

Recent adequacy litigation in Kansas illustrates how school finance adequacy litigants leveraged state standards and NCLB consequences into a successful legal claim for greater resources. The Kansas Constitution, as amended in 1966, requires the legislature to "make suitable provision for finance of the educational interests of the state." To fulfill [this] constitutional duty, in 1992, Kansas lawmakers passed the School District Finance and Quality Performance Act ("SDFQPA"). The SDFQPA created a statewide property tax and a statewide system for collecting and distributing property tax revenues. Although the SDFQPA begins from a presumption of equal per pupil spending, the presumption is modified by district-specific weighting factors. In addition, the SDFQPA established a guaranteed state per pupil floor along with an accountability system tied to state minimum student performance standards in specific subjects. Despite a guaranteed per pupil spending floor, a school finance lawsuit challenging SDFQPA succeeded in 2003.

NCLB data played a role in the court's conclusion that SDFQPA violated the Kansas Constitution. Specifically, part of the court's rationale for striking down the Kansas school finance system pivoted on student academic performance. In assessing whether student academic performance evidenced "adequacy" from a school finance perspective, the Kansas trial court assessed performance data generated by NCLB. . . .

E.   ALTERNATIVES TO TRADITIONAL PUBLIC SCHOOLS: CHARTER SCHOOLS

Advocates, parents, and others have sought alternatives to traditional public schools for decades. Education historian Diane Ravitch describes two principal roots of the modern school choice movement: the Southern resistance to integration following Brown v. Board of Education, and an influential 1955 essay by economist Milton Friedman (*The Role of Government in Education*), which argued that the government should not provide education at all, but instead issue a voucher that parents could use to purchase schooling of their choice from any school, including parochial schools, for-profit schools, and nonprofit schools. Diane Ravitch, *The Death and Life of the Great American School System* (2010).

The framework of today's charter schools is explained in Professor James Ryan's 2008 essay.

JAMES E. RYAN, *CHARTER SCHOOLS AND PUBLIC EDUCATION*
4 Stan. J. C.R. & C.L. 393 (2008)

Charter schools are public schools that are exempt from some rules and regulations that govern traditional public schools. The first charter school opened in Minnesota in 1992. A little more than 15 years later, roughly four thousand charter schools exist in forty states and the District of Columbia. The schools are not evenly distributed across the country but are instead concentrated in a handful of states, including California, Arizona, and Texas as well as in Washington, D.C., where a startling 25% of all students attend charter schools. Charter schools educate a little more than one million students. This number, while large, only represents about two percent of the total public school enrollment. Nonetheless, charter schools — like voucher programs, which involve even fewer students — have garnered a great deal of attention over the last decade or so.

The basic idea behind charter schools is simple: these schools are given freedom from some public regulations in exchange for greater accountability. They are publicly funded, tuition-free, and non-sectarian. Although state laws vary in detail, in general charter schools can be created by private individuals, such as a group of parents or teachers, by non-profit organizations, and, in some states, by for-profit companies. Charter schools can be created from scratch or by "converting" a traditional public school. Groups interested in creating a school apply for a charter to the entity designated by state law as the authorizing agency. Depending on the state, that agency might be a local school district, the state department of education, an independent organization tasked specifically with authorizing charter schools, or a college or university. The relevant authorizing agency reviews the application and, if satisfied, grants a charter to the group to create a school.

The charter is supposed to set out the goals for the school and to act as a contract. Charters are not granted in perpetuity but instead for a definite time period, usually five years. If the goals identified in the charter are not met in that time period, the charter is supposed to be rescinded. If the goals are met, the charter is updated and renewed.

Charter schools are exempt from some of the rules and regulations that govern traditional public schools, including those regarding teacher certification, mandatory bargaining with teachers' unions, the school calendar, and the curriculum. The scope of regulatory exemptions varies from state to state; some states grant quite a few exemptions while others keep charters on a fairly short leash. Most states have a cap on the total number of charter schools that can either open in a given year or operate at all. In all states, by virtue of the federal No Child Left Behind Act (NCLB), charter schools are expected to administer the same standardized tests that are administered in traditional public schools, and they are subject to the same accountability provisions as traditional public schools.

The initial hope was that, by granting charter schools greater flexibility, innovative educational methods — if not goals — would be encouraged. Charter schools would also offer parents and students more choices among schools and might even encourage some healthy competition. In a sense, charter schools began as and remain a halfway station between traditional public schools and a voucher program. The schools themselves stand somewhere between regular public schools and traditional private ones; they are freed from some regulations but remain publicly funded, non-sectarian, subject to the state standardized testing regime, and have limited control over admissions. . . .

NOTES AND QUESTIONS

1. The evidence on whether students in charter schools do better academically than students in traditional public schools is decidedly mixed. In 2009, the Center for Research on Education Outcomes at Stanford University released the first national assessment of charter school impacts on educational achievement. While documenting wide variation in charter school effect

on student performance, the study concluded that overall, 17 percent of charter schools outperformed their traditional school counterparts (based on student test scores), while nearly half had no difference in result and 37 percent deliver "learning results that are significantly worse" than the charter students would have experienced in traditional public school. While Black and Hispanic students had significantly worse learning gains than their counterparts in traditional public schools, two subgroups of students, English-language learners and students in poverty, "outperformed their [traditional public school] counterparts in both reading and math." Ctr. for Research on Educ. Outcomes, *Multiple Choice: Charter School Performance in 16 States* (2009).

2. In an increasing number of jurisdictions around the country, charter schools have experienced scandals ranging from financial mismanagement to teacher or administrator involvement in cheating or altering test scores. A 2010 *New York Times* article describes scandals in Texas, Georgia, Indiana, Massachusetts, Nevada, and Virginia. Trip Gabriel, *Under Pressure, Teachers Tamper with Tests*, N.Y. Times (June 11, 2010), at A1. *See also* Howard Blume, *Charter School Group's Chief Blamed for 2010 Cheating Scandal*, L.A. Times (Aug. 17, 2012) (describing cheating scandal at several campuses of Southern California's Crescendo Charter Schools); David L. Kirp, *Failing the Test: Why Cheating Scandals and Parent Rebellions Are Erupting in Schools in New York, Washington, D.C., and Atlanta*, Slate (May 7, 2013, 2:49 P.M.), http://www.slate.com/articles/news_and_politics/science/2013/05/cheating _scandals_and_parent_rebellions_high_stakes_school_testing_is_doomed.html.

3. A growing body of evidence suggests that charter schools may be more racially segregated than traditional public schools. In 2010, the UCLA Civil Rights Project released a report analyzing charter schools across the nation, which found that:

> [C]harter schools are more racially isolated than traditional public schools in virtually every state and large metropolitan area in the nation. While examples of truly diverse charter schools exist, our data show that these schools are not reflective of broader charter trends. . . . [B]lack students in charter schools are far more likely than their traditional public school counterparts to be educated in intensely segregated settings. At the national level, seventy percent of black charter school students attend intensely segregated minority charter schools (which enroll 90-100% of students from under-represented minority backgrounds), or twice as many as the share of intensely segregated black students in traditional public schools.

The study also noted the difficulty of determining whether charter schools are serving all students:

> [M]ajor gaps in multiple federal data sources make it difficult to answer basic, fundamental questions about the extent to which charter schools enroll and concentrate low-income students and English Language Learners (ELLs). Charter schools receive public funding and therefore should be equally available to all students regardless of background. Approximately one in four charter schools does not report data on low-income students. Since eligibility for receiving free lunch is proof that families cannot afford to provide it, the lack of a free lunch program at school would impose a severe economic barrier to attending a charter school. There is a similar lack of information on ELLs.

Federal data on charter schools in California, arguably the country's most significant gateway for immigrants, describe just seven ELL students attending its state charter programs. In general, state charter school legislation is less likely to contain requirements for enrolling ELL students than for racial balance or diversity standards. The glaring lack of data on each of these traditionally underserved groups makes it difficult to assess charter schools as an educational reform, or monitor their compliance with basic civil rights regulations and state charter school legislation.

Erika Frankenberg et al., UCLA Civil Rights Project, *Choice Without Equity: Charter School Segregation and the Need for Civil Rights Standards* (2010).

F. EMERGING TOPIC: SCHOOL-TO-PRISON PIPELINE

In recent years, education advocates have focused attention on the phenomenon that has come to be known as the "school-to-prison pipeline," which encompasses zero-tolerance policies and other measures that increasingly steer youth with school disciplinary infractions out of school and into the criminal justice system. Much research shows that such policies have a disproportionate effect on poor children and youth of color.

The following excerpts explain the issue and describe some strategies to address it.

DEBORAH N. ARCHER, *CHALLENGING THE SCHOOL-TO-PRISON PIPELINE*
54 N.Y.L. Sch. L. Rev. 867 (2010)

Despite clear evidence that violence and crime in our schools is decreasing, the often misguided approaches of our criminal justice system, with its focus on punishment rather than rehabilitation, are bleeding into our schools. This has led many school districts to "crack down" on our children, focusing on punishment and criminalization rather than education. Today, children are far more likely to be arrested at school than they were a generation ago. The number of students suspended from school each year has nearly doubled from 1.7 million in 1974 to 3.1 million in 2000. And, in 2006, one in every fourteen students was suspended at least once during the year.

This disturbing phenomenon is called the school-to-prison pipeline. The school-to-prison pipeline is the collection of education and public safety policies and practices that push our nation's schoolchildren out of the classroom and into the streets, the juvenile justice system, or the criminal justice system.

There are both direct and indirect avenues through the pipeline. Directly, schools put students into the pipeline through excessive police involvement in imposing discipline and zero-tolerance policies that often end in arrest or referral to the juvenile justice system. . . . Across the country, an alarming number of students, and a disproportionate number of students of color, are being removed from mainstream educational environments for nonviolent violations of school policy, which many would consider to be typical childhood behavior.

Schoolchildren who are removed from mainstream education environments, even for short periods of time, are far more likely to become involved with the criminal justice system, use drugs, or drop out of school. . . .

Indirectly, schools put children on a path that far too often ends with incarceration through suspensions, expulsions, high-stakes testing, push-outs, and the removal of students from mainstream educational environments and into disciplinary alternative schools. Our under-resourced public education system is often linked to behavioral problems and violence in schools. Therefore, it is not surprising that the impact of school-to-prison pipeline policies are most severely felt by students in high-minority and high-poverty schools, where overcrowding, unqualified teachers, and fewer resources collide with these misguided policies.

The school-to-prison pipeline is also one of the most urgent civil rights challenges we face. Minority students are disproportionately impacted by the pipeline and are among those most severely disciplined in school. Studies have shown that African American students are disproportionately suspended, expelled, or arrested for conduct similar to that of their white classmates. And although African American students represented only 17% of public school enrollment nationwide, they accounted for 34% of school suspensions in 2000. . . .

* * *

Legal strategies for dealing with the school-to-prison pipeline can be elusive, however. The following excerpt describes some of the research on differential discipline rates and analyzes the difficulty of using federal constitutional tools to attack them.

RUSSELL J. SKIBA ET AL., *AFRICAN AMERICAN DISPROPORTIONALITY IN SCHOOL DISCIPLINE: THE DIVIDE BETWEEN BEST EVIDENCE AND LEGAL REMEDY*

54 N.Y.L. Sch. L. Rev. 1071 (2010)

. . . While it would seem that inconsistent application of disciplinary measures would prove fertile ground for student lawsuits, students have often been unsuccessful when challenging school disciplinary decisions. One explanation for this lack of success is that the courts have recognized that it is necessary for school officials to have discretion in disciplinary matters. Therefore, courts tend to defer to school officials when it comes to disciplinary matters. Kevin Brady reports that because courts "have been extremely reluctant to overturn school disciplinary decisions, particularly long-term suspensions and expulsions, on substantive due process grounds," school districts maintain great control over student disciplinary matters. So long as a disciplinary decision is "justified by a legitimate educational interest," the courts tend to side with school officials in many discipline-related disputes.

State law and school district policies generally document the grounds for suspension and expulsion as well as the required procedures for employing these measures. These policies must align with the Due Process Clause of the Fourteenth Amendment. . . . Thus, when disciplining students, school officials must demonstrate that their policies and actions are related to a legitimate state interest. Here, the interest is in creating a safe environment in which students can learn. In the context of school discipline, then, punishment does not implicate substantive due process unless the action is "arbitrary, capricious, or wholly unrelated to the legitimate state goal of maintaining an atmosphere conducive to learning." Finally, school administrators must put procedures in place, such as notices and hearings, which allow the student to respond to the allegations made against him or her. Generally, if discipline procedures satisfy due process requirements of the Fourteenth Amendment, courts uphold the actions of educators as long as they are reasonable. . . .

Goss v. Lopez [419 U.S. 565 (1975)] set the standard for the minimal constitutional requirements when a student is suspended for ten days or less. The Court stated that students must be given oral or written notice of the charges; then, if the student denies the charges, school officials must present an explanation of the evidence and offer the student an opportunity to present his or her side of the story. Therefore, while students who are expelled or suspended are entitled to some form of procedural due process, school officials merely need to employ fair procedures in order to fulfill the constitutional requirement. . . .

STATUS OF RESEARCH AND CASE LAW WITH RESPECT TO RACIAL DISPROPORTIONALITY IN DISCIPLINE

Studies have demonstrated that a disproportionate number of students who are expelled from school are from low-income families or are students of color. For example, Donald Stone reported that black students were either suspended or expelled at a rate 250% higher than the rate at which white students are expelled. In this empirical study, Stone surveyed thirty-five school divisions representing a population of 1,382,562 students about information relating to school suspensions. Within this population, 46% of the student body was white, 44% was black, and 10% was made up of other races. Even though the black and white population was almost equal, the study found that when examining suspension rates, 71.5% of the suspended students were black and 28.5% were white. The study did not note if the offenses were different or more severe between the different racial groups, but it did indicate that the most common offenses included fighting, cursing, weapons on campus, and skipping class. Similarly, Wu found that when socioeconomic indicators are held constant, black students were still disciplined at higher rates than white students. Students of color are also disproportionately represented in discipline related to off-campus crimes. . . .

A.   SCIENTIFIC RESEARCH ON RACIAL/ETHNIC DISPROPORTIONALITY IN SCHOOL DISCIPLINE

For over thirty years, in national, state, district, and building level data, the documentation of disciplinary overrepresentation for African American students has been highly consistent. Recent analyses have found rates of out-of-school suspensions between two to three times greater for African American elementary school students than white students, although findings of Latino disparities have been somewhat less consistent. . . .

1. *Socioeconomic Status*

Race and socioeconomic status ("SES") are unfortunately highly connected in American society. This connection suggests that apparent racial disproportionality in school discipline could be simply a by-product of disproportionality associated with SES. Statistical analyses have indeed found low SES to be a risk factor for school suspension. Yet multivariate statistical models have also shown that nonwhite students still report and experience significantly higher suspension rates than white students, even after statistically controlling for poverty. Thus, although economic disadvantage may contribute to disproportionate rates of discipline for students of color, it cannot completely explain racial and ethnic disparities in school suspension and expulsion.

2. *Disparate Rates of Disruption*

Implicit in the poverty hypothesis is the assumption that African American students may engage in higher rates of disruptive behavior than other students. Yet investigations of student behavior, race, and discipline have yielded no evidence that African American over-representation in school suspension is due to higher rates of misbehavior, regardless of whether the data are self-reported, or based on analysis of disciplinary records. If anything, studies have shown that African American students are punished more severely for less serious or more subjective infractions. Ann McFadden and her colleagues reported that black pupils in a Florida school district were more likely than white students to receive severe punishments (e.g., corporal punishment, school suspension) and less likely to receive milder consequences (e.g., in-school suspension). . . .

B.   CASE LAW REGARDING RACIAL/ETHNIC DISPARITIES IN DISCIPLINE

The courts have become involved in school cases concerning racially disproportionate discipline actions in a few instances. . . .

One avenue for students of color who assert such claims is the Equal Protection Clause of the Fourteenth Amendment. The Equal Protection Clause states that "No State shall . . . deny to any person within its jurisdiction the equal protection of the laws." Under this Clause, courts apply different tests depending on school officials' motivation for taking action. If school officials are motivated by legitimate educational considerations, then the court will apply a rational basis test, asking whether the school officials' actions are reasonably related to these legitimate educational reasons. This test is generally considered deferential to school administrators. It is born out of a notion that government officials are the experts in how best to conduct their business. Therefore, courts should not seek to impose their own judgments on the decisions of governmental actors, as long as there is a reasonable basis for the decision. If, however, school officials are motivated by racial animus, then courts will apply strict scrutiny. Under this test, school officials must supply a compelling justification for their actions and those actions must be narrowly tailored to advancing the compelling justifications. This heightened scrutiny, however, does not apply, for example, if non-racially motivated actions produce a disparate impact on the educational opportunities of black students. If black students are disciplined at much higher rates than white students, but these disparities are shown to be based on racially neutral decision making by school officials, then the disparity is not considered unconstitutional racial discrimination. Instead, it is simply the unfortunate result of the application of legitimate decision making by educational officials.

Another claim that students assert in school disciplinary cases involving racial discrimination comes under Title VI of the Civil Rights Act of 1964. Title VI prohibits discrimination on the basis of "race, color, or national origin . . . under any programs or activity receiving Federal financial assistance." When plaintiffs use Title VI they may assert that school disciplinary practices result in disparate treatment of students of color. Disparate treatment requires the student to demonstrate that school officials acted intentionally in creating the inequitable environment. The Supreme Court has held that disparate treatment under Title VI is, therefore, similar to racial discrimination recognized under the Equal Protection Clause in that the student must demonstrate that the school officials acted with discriminatory intent. In order to prove intent, the plaintiff must demonstrate that a "challenged action was motivated by an intent to discriminate," and plaintiffs may present evidence of intent that is direct or circumstantial. As a result of the intent requirement, it is difficult for students to bring successful Title VI actions. The Harvard Civil Rights Project and the Advancement Project contend that Title VI has been "ineffective and [is] rarely enforced" in discipline cases.

In the past, the Title VI regulations provided some assistance to students alleging racial discrimination in school discipline cases under a disparate impact claim. Disparate impact occurs when students demonstrate that a facially neutral policy has a negative impact on a protected class of students. Specifically, while a successful argument under Title VI requires intentional discrimination, its accompanying regulations permitted a broader interpretation of the law, allowing plaintiffs to argue disparate impact. In earlier cases, the U.S. Supreme Court also found that these regulations may prohibit discrimination that has a disparate impact on protected groups — even if there was no evidence of intentional discrimination. . . . [H]owever, private rights of actions under Title VI regulations were foreclosed by the 2001 U.S. Supreme Court case Alexander v. Sandoval [532 U.S. 275 (2001)].

Other students claiming that school disciplinary actions are racially discriminatory have relied on section 1981 of the Civil Rights Act of 1866. In the past, students have also included a section 1983 claim in discipline cases involving discrimination. Both section 1981 and section 1983 were passed following the Civil War in order to eliminate racial discriminatory policies. Enacted as part of the Civil Rights Act of 1866, section 1981 prohibits discrimination on the basis of race in both the right to engage in certain legal action and the right to contract. Additionally, it enables the person experiencing the discrimination to sue both public and private parties and it provides that people within the United States' jurisdiction are accountable to all laws and regulations. Only five years later, in the Civil Rights Act of 1871, Congress passed section 1983, which provided civil remedies, including the collection of monetary damages, for civil rights violations. Section 1983 is now used to collect money damages when a government actor violates a statutory or constitutional provision, including, but not limited to, Equal Protection, the First Amendment, and the Due Process Clause.

The cases below illustrate how these four claims have played out in courts across the nation. In most cases, the courts have given great discretion to school officials in matters of discipline. Additionally, statistical evidence of disproportionate discipline of minority students has rarely been sufficient in and of itself to result in findings in favor of the plaintiffs. It is important to note that several of the earlier cases presented below would have been decided differently if heard today, due to the impact of the Washington v. Davis and Alexander v. Sandoval decisions, discussed below. . . .

STATISTICAL EVIDENCE AS PROOF OF INTENTION TO DISCRIMINATE

Although the U.S. Supreme Court decision in Washington v. Davis[426 U.S. 229, 242 (1976), discussed in Chapter 3], does not involve a school disciplinary matter, it is sometimes cited in school discipline cases, as it highlights the difficulty of demonstrating school officials' intention to discriminate. In [*Washington*], the plaintiffs used statistical evidence to document the racial disparities that existed in a job-related test used for prospective police recruits. . . . The Court did not find the test in practice to violate the law because the test was not motivated by a discriminatory purpose, explaining that a test is not unconstitutional merely because it produces a disproportionately adverse effect on a racial group. . . . Although, as a result of *Washington*, some courts have required that students use statistical data when trying to prove that school officials intended to discriminate, this decision and others demonstrate that statistical evidence showing that black students are disciplined more harshly or frequently than white students does not necessarily result in a verdict for the plaintiffs.

STATISTICAL EVIDENCE AS INSUFFICIENT PROOF OF DISCRIMINATION

One early application of the Washington v. Davis decision occurred in a 1981 discipline case. In Tasby v. Estes [643 F.2d 1103 (5th Cir. 1981)], parents of black students sought injunctive relief from the school district's discipline practices, arguing that black students were punished more harshly than white students. The plaintiffs relied on the experts' testimony that black students were disciplined more frequently than white and Mexican American students, statistical evidence demonstrating that black students received the most extreme forms of punishment as compared to other student populations in the school, and data linking such disciplinary disparity with an imbalance between the race of school personnel and the race of the students.

The district court dismissed the case because the parents did not present evidence that such statistical disparities constituted racial discrimination. On appeal, the Fifth Circuit Court of Appeals affirmed, holding that the parents failed to demonstrate that school officials were motivated by a discriminatory purpose when they disciplined the black students. . . . [T]he court did not find that the statistically disproportionate punishment was a result of the requisite discriminatory intent. . . .

The *Tasby* case thus demonstrates the need for plaintiffs to offer more specific and measurable evidence to support the claim that students of color are being treated differently than white students. In other cases, courts have found in favor of school districts even though there was evidence that the black students received harsher treatment because the student could not demonstrate that the school district's actions were based on racially discriminatory motives. . . .

Conclusion

Review of the case law reveals that in order to successfully challenge racial/ethnic disparities in discipline policies and practices of schools under existing federal law, students must generally prove that school officials were motivated by discriminatory intent when they adopted or implemented them. Under the Equal Protection Clause, heightened scrutiny only applies to governmental actions motivated by intentional racial decision making. Thus, disparate impact alone in a public school's disciplinary practices is insufficient to generate strict scrutiny. Federal courts generally determine the constitutionality of racially neutral policies and practices that generate a disparate impact by the deferential rational basis test. The determination of illegal race/ethnic discrimination under Title VI mirrors the Equal Protection Clause. As a result, to demonstrate race discrimination by a public school's disciplinary policies and practices under Title VI also requires that challengers prove that the adoption and implementation of the polices were motivated by racial animus. The implementing regulations under Title VI, as opposed to Title VI [itself], do allow for the establishment of racial/ethnic discrimination by proving disparate impact, even in the absence of discriminatory intent. However, the Supreme Court has noted that the disparate impact regulations under Title VI are in considerable tension with Title VI. In addition, the Supreme Court in its 2001 decision in *Sandoval* concluded that private rights of action to enforce the implementing regulations of Title VI do not exist. As a result, the federal government is the only entity that can enforce the disparate impact regulations of Title VI. It also appears that private entities and individuals cannot enforce the disparate impact regulations of Title VI through 1983 actions. Finally, when challenging a public or private school's disciplinary practices under section 1981, students must also demonstrate intentional discrimination. . . .

For the foreseeable future, the most fruitful remedies for those seeking to challenge racial/ethnic discrimination in school discipline may well be extra-judicial. One approach that could be used to address the lack of legal remedies in this area would be for advocacy groups interested in disciplinary reform to lobby Congress to pass previously proposed amendments to Title VI. In addition, the continued dissemination of evidence-based practices in school discipline and school violence prevention, especially to school administrators, is important in order to increase understanding of the impact of expulsion and suspension, especially on students of color.

It is somewhat startling to realize that, fifty years after Brown v. Board of Education, there exists no sure legal remedy that would allow African American students to challenge even those practices that create the most disparate negative outcomes. The unanimous *Brown* decision led to a relatively brief period of activism and optimism that viewed the law as an affirmative tool to address the effects of historical and current discrimination. Yet since the mid-1970s, the courts have increasingly retreated into a narrow interpretation of discrimination that is at variance with both logic and evidence, effectively closing off challenges to the racial impact of educational practices. On May 17, 1954, African Americans were finally granted the right to send their children to a public school of their choosing. It remains to be seen when children of color will be guaranteed the right to be treated equally once they arrive at school.

NOTES AND QUESTIONS

1. Do you agree with Professor Skiba that the federal courts are unlikely to offer much relief to those seeking to challenge school-to-prison pipeline policies? What strategies might be more successful than federal court litigation?

2. Several national civil rights groups, including the ACLU and the NAACP, have formally begun school-to-prison pipeline advocacy projects, several of which do include litigation. One case filed in 2008 and settled in 2009 successfully targeted the searching of students without reasonable suspicion, among other practices. Documents from the case are available at http://www.aclu.org/racial-justice/harris-et-al-v-atlanta-independent-school-system. Legislative advocacy on disproportionate and discriminatory discipline is also increasing. *See, e.g., School to Prison Pipeline*, NAACP Legal Def. & Educ. Fund, http://www.naacpldf.org/case/school-prison-pipeline. The National Economic & Social Rights Initiative uses a human rights framework to attack what it terms "the school pushout." *See Human Right to Education Program*, Nat'l Econ. & Soc. Rights Initiative, http://www.nesri.org/programs/education.

3. A 2010 book includes a comprehensive look at the school-to-prison pipeline phenomenon, with chapters on the right to education, students with disabilities, legal strategies to challenge suspensions and expulsions, the rise of "disciplinary alternative schools" where children expelled from traditional schools are often sent, and the criminalization of school misconduct. *See* Catherine Y. Kim et al., *The School-to-Prison Pipeline* (2010).

CHAPTER
9

Criminalization

INTRODUCTION

As discussed in Chapters 2 and 4, social welfare policy has frequently played a disciplining function with respect to the labor market and social mores. Until now, we have primarily focused on these issues in the civil justice system. While this book does not cover the criminal justice system per se, this chapter explores some of the ways in which criminal law intersects with the lives of the poor. For many people, "criminalization of poverty" conjures up images of homeless people being cited, arrested, or jailed for doing things in public—sometimes as basic as sitting or sleeping—that would be legal in the privacy of their own homes. But there are many other ways in which low-income people, especially those receiving public assistance, are subject to criminal or quasi-criminal laws and policies that do not apply in practice to the non-poor.

Since the 1960s, poverty and crime have become increasingly linked in both the public imagination and public policy. As we will examine below, public housing tenants can be denied shelter or evicted for the alleged criminal acts of others, and housing voucher holders face legal and extralegal discrimination in the private rental market. Welfare recipients in some jurisdictions are fingerprinted, drug tested, and/or subjected to home searches as a condition of receiving aid. To some, these sanctions are reasonable mechanisms to prevent fraud, discourage abuse, and protect the public fisc. To others, such sanctions regulate, punish, and stigmatize the poor in a manner that would never be tolerated by middle- or upper-income Americans.

Further, after several decades of the "wars" on crime and drugs, the United States leads the world in incarcerating its citizens. Low-income people and people of color—including undocumented immigrants—are disproportionately likely to be arrested, prosecuted, and convicted of crimes. Beyond the direct and immediate impact on individuals, families, and communities, mass incarceration has created an entire class of quasi-citizens who suffer social, economic, and political consequences long after their release from prison. That is, not only are the poor more likely to be treated as criminals, but people with criminal records face barriers that make it much harder to escape poverty.

Section A of this chapter considers the relationship between poverty and criminalization, with a special focus on public housing and welfare. Section B examines the relationship between a criminal record and poverty, including the deepening intersection between immigration law and criminal law.

A. POVERTY AND CRIMINALIZATION

As you know from earlier chapters, housing and welfare are core government antipoverty programs. As needs-based programs, they are the site of some of the more restrictive regulations in the social welfare system. In this section, we will explore the relationship between publicly subsidized housing and criminalization, including obstacles to securing and remaining in public housing. We will then consider cash transfer programs and criminalization, including the increasingly stringent measures being taken to police welfare rolls.

Before turning to housing and welfare, we begin with an introduction to the topic through the experience of a working-class family during the Great Recession and a description of historical and contemporary treatment of homeless people.

BARBARA EHRENREICH, *HOW AMERICA TURNED POVERTY INTO A CRIME*
Salon (Aug. 9, 2011)

Take the case of Kristen and Joe Parente, Delaware residents who had always imagined that people turned to the government for help only if "they didn't want to work." Their troubles began well before the recession, when Joe, a fourth-generation pipe-fitter, sustained a back injury that left him unfit for even light lifting. He fell into a profound depression for several months, then rallied to ace a state-sponsored retraining course in computer repairs — only to find that those skills are no longer in demand. The obvious fallback was disability benefits, but — catch-22 — when Joe applied he was told he could not qualify without presenting a recent MRI scan. This would cost $800 to $900, which the Parentes do not have; nor has Joe, unlike the rest of the family, been able to qualify for Medicaid.

When they married as teenagers, the plan had been for Kristen to stay home with the children. But with Joe out of action and three children to support by the middle of this decade, Kristen went out and got waitressing jobs, ending up, in 2008, in a "pretty fancy place on the water." Then the recession struck and she was laid off.

Kristen is bright, pretty, and to judge from her command of her own small kitchen, probably capable of holding down a dozen tables with precision and grace. In the past she'd always been able to land a new job within days; now there was nothing. Like 44 percent of laid-off people at the time, she failed to meet the fiendishly complex and sometimes arbitrary eligibility requirements for unemployment benefits. Their car started falling apart.

So the Parentes turned to what remains of welfare — TANF, or Temporary Assistance to Needy Families. TANF does not offer straightforward cash support like Aid to Families with Dependent Children, which it replaced in 1996. It's an income supplementation program for working parents, and it was based on the sunny assumption that there would always be plenty of jobs for those enterprising enough to get them.

After Kristen applied, nothing happened for six weeks — no money, no phone calls returned. At school, the Parentes' seven-year-old's class was asked to write out what wish they would present to a genie, should a genie appear. Brianna's wish was for her mother to find a job because there was nothing to eat in the house, an aspiration that her teacher deemed too disturbing to be posted on the wall with the other children's requests.

When the Parentes finally got into "the system" and began receiving food stamps and some cash assistance, they discovered why some recipients have taken to calling TANF "Torture and Abuse of Needy Families." From the start, the TANF experience was "humiliating," Kristen says. The caseworkers "treat you like a bum. They act like every dollar you get is coming out of their own paychecks."

The Parentes discovered that they were each expected to apply for 40 jobs a week, although their car was on its last legs and no money was offered for gas, tolls, or babysitting. In addition, Kristen had to drive 35 miles a day to attend "job readiness" classes offered by a private company called Arbor, which, she says, were "frankly a joke."

Nationally, according to Kaaryn Gustafson of the University of Connecticut Law School, "applying for welfare is a lot like being booked by the police." There may be a mug shot, fingerprinting, and lengthy interrogations as to one's children's true paternity. The ostensible goal is to prevent welfare fraud, but the psychological impact is to turn poverty itself into a kind of crime.

How the Safety Net Became a Dragnet

The most shocking thing I learned from my research on the fate of the working poor in the recession was the extent to which poverty has indeed been criminalized in America.

Perhaps the constant suspicions of drug use and theft that I encountered in low-wage workplaces should have alerted me to the fact that, when you leave the relative safety of the middle class, you might as well have given up your citizenship and taken residence in a hostile nation.

Most cities, for example, have ordinances designed to drive the destitute off the streets by outlawing such necessary activities of daily life as sitting, loitering, sleeping, or lying down. Urban officials boast that there is nothing discriminatory about such laws: "If you're lying on a sidewalk, whether you're homeless or a millionaire, you're in violation of the ordinance," a St. Petersburg, Florida, city attorney stated in June 2009, echoing Anatole France's immortal observation that "the law, in its majestic equality, forbids the rich as well as the poor to sleep under bridges. . . ."

In defiance of all reason and compassion, the criminalization of poverty has actually intensified as the weakened economy generates ever more poverty. So concludes a recent study from the National Law Center on Poverty and Homelessness, which finds that the number of ordinances against the publicly poor has been rising since 2006, along with the harassment of the poor for more "neutral" infractions like jaywalking, littering, or carrying an open container.

The report lists America's ten "meanest" cities — the largest of which include Los Angeles, Atlanta, and Orlando — but new contestants are springing up every day. In Colorado, Grand Junction's city council is considering a ban on begging; Tempe, Arizona, carried out a four-day crackdown on the indigent at the end of June. And how do you know when someone is indigent? As a Las Vegas statute puts it, "an indigent person is a person whom a reasonable ordinary person would believe to be entitled to apply for or receive" public assistance.

That could be me before the blow-drying and eyeliner, and it's definitely Al Szekeley at any time of day. A grizzled 62-year-old, he inhabits a wheelchair and is often found on G Street in Washington, D.C. — the city that is ultimately responsible for the bullet he took in the spine in Phu Bai, Vietnam, in 1972.

He had been enjoying the luxury of an indoor bed until December 2008, when the police swept through the shelter in the middle of the night looking for men with outstanding warrants. It turned out that Szekeley, who is an ordained minister and does not drink, do drugs, or cuss in front of ladies, did indeed have one — for "criminal trespassing," as sleeping on the streets is sometimes defined by the law. So he was dragged out of the shelter and put in jail.

"Can you imagine?" asked Eric Sheptock, the homeless advocate (himself a shelter resident) who introduced me to Szekeley. "They arrested a homeless man *in a shelter* for being homeless?"

1. Homelessness

Vagrancy laws historically criminalized the status of being homeless. Imported to the American colonies from England, the extent and enforcement of such laws have ebbed and flowed in response to local conditions. The following excerpt recounts this history from colonial times through the early 1990s.

HARRY SIMON, *TOWNS WITHOUT PITY: A CONSTITUTIONAL AND HISTORICAL ANALYSIS OF OFFICIAL EFFORTS TO DRIVE HOMELESS PERSONS FROM AMERICAN CITIES*

66 Tul. L. Rev. 621 (1992)

Vagrancy legislation in America started in colonial times and closely followed English models. American vagrancy laws, like their English counterparts, punished a wide variety of individuals who were considered potential criminals or otherwise vaguely undesirable. Both English and American vagrancy laws provided few procedural protections to those charged with vagrancy. American statutes, like the English laws, empowered local authorities to oust the newly arrived poor against their will and to remove them to their last places of residence. In addition, both American and English laws conditioned receipt of public assistance on lengthy periods of residence.

During the eighteenth and nineteenth centuries, the federal government officially sanctioned the hostility to the poor manifested by these statutes. The Articles of Confederation specifically excluded paupers from the right of free ingress to and egress from any state and from the privileges and immunities guaranteed to all other citizens. In Mayor of New York v. Miln, [36 U.S. 102 (1837)] the United States Supreme Court approved the efforts of the State of New York to exclude paupers arriving by ship, noting that it is "as competent and as necessary for a state to provide precautionary measures against the moral pestilence of paupers, vagabonds, and possibly convicts; as it is to guard against the physical pestilence, which may arise from unsound and infectious articles."

Under the authority of such decisions, every state in the Union enforced vagrancy laws against the unemployed poor. Vagrancy laws were justified as a legitimate exercise of the states' police powers, directed at the prevention of crime thought to flow from poverty. Vagrancy legislation varied from state to state but contained one common element: vagrancy laws punished idle persons without visible means of support who, although able to work, failed to do so. Unlike most criminal statutes, vagrancy laws punished status rather than conduct. Thus, an illegal act was unnecessary—vagrancy alone was a sufficient reason to arrest.

During the twentieth century, the legal structure supporting government efforts to regulate and punish the displaced poor collapsed. The Great Depression brought the first successful challenges to official efforts to exclude the itinerant poor. During the Depression, states continued to enforce removal laws, ousting the newly arrived poor and sending them to their last places of residence. Some states, however, went further, attempting to enforce laws that criminalized the knowing importation of paupers into their jurisdictions.

In Edwards v. California [314 U.S. 160 (1941)], the United States Supreme Court struck down a California law that prohibited the importation of paupers into that state. The Court concluded that California's efforts to isolate itself from the effects of the depression in other states violated the Commerce Clause. In response to California's suggestion that its prohibition on the importation of indigent migrants enjoyed a firm basis in English and American history, the Court stated that "the theory of the Elizabethan poor laws no longer fits the facts." In a concurring opinion, Justice Jackson questioned the legality of California's statute under the Privileges and Immunities Clause, encouraging the Court to "say now, and in no uncertain terms, that a man's mere property status, without more, cannot be used by a state to test, qualify, or limit his rights as a citizen of the United States."

Official efforts to exclude the displaced poor suffered another defeat in Shapiro v. Thompson [394 U.S. 618 (1969)]. In *Shapiro*, the Court invalidated various state statutes conditioning the receipt of welfare benefits on the satisfaction of durational residence requirements. The Court reasoned that such residence requirements violated indigents' constitutionally protected right to travel interstate. In reaching this decision, the Court held that if a state statute's purpose was to inhibit the migration by needy persons into the state, it was constitutionally impermissible.

Following World War II, vagrancy and loitering laws also became the object of criticism. During the 1960s and early 1970s, numerous state and federal decisions struck down loitering and vagrancy laws on various constitutional grounds. Courts overturned vagrancy laws as invidious discrimination against the poor. The hostility that animated the enforcement of these laws was readily apparent to reviewing courts. For example, in reviewing New York's vagrancy ordinance, the New York Court of Appeals recognized that the statute targeted individuals "whose main offense usually consists in their leaving the environs of skid row and disturbing *by their presence* the sensibilities of residents of the nicer parts of the community."

Courts also overturned vagrancy laws on the grounds that they punished status or condition, which amounted to cruel and unusual punishment. Chief Justice Thompson of the Nevada Supreme Court eloquently stated the rationale for this holding in Parker v. Municipal Judge [83 Nev. 214 (1967)]:

It simply is not a crime to be unemployed, without funds, and in a public place.
To punish the unfortunate for this circumstance debases society. The comment of
Justice Douglas is relevant: "How can we hold our heads high and still confuse with
crime the need for welfare or the need for work?"

Lower courts also overturned both vagrancy and loitering laws as impermissible restrictions on the right to travel. In addition, many courts held that these
laws impermissibly punished essentially innocent conduct.

Finally, in Papachristou v. City of Jacksonville [405 U.S. 156 (1972)], the
United States Supreme Court overturned Jacksonville's vagrancy ordinance
on due process grounds. Writing for a unanimous Court, Justice Douglas stated
that the ordinance was void for vagueness in that it failed to give fair notice of
prohibited conduct and, further, that its indefiniteness encouraged arbitrary
arrests and convictions. In reaching this conclusion, the Court made a number
of observations. Recounting the history of vagrancy laws, the Court condemned
them as "archaic classifications." It also noted that Jacksonville's ordinance
criminalized activities which, by modern standards, are entirely innocent. The
Court further objected to the criminalization of wandering and strolling —
activities that it suggested enjoy constitutional protection. In addition, the
Supreme Court rejected the justification that vagrancy laws prevented future
criminality as inconsistent with Fourth Amendment guarantees of arrest upon
probable cause. In conclusion, the Court warned that these laws, aimed as they
were against the poor and other so-called undesirables, "teach that the scales of
justice are so tipped that even-handed administration of the law is not possible.
The rule of law, evenly applied to minorities as well as majorities, to the poor as
well as the rich, is the great mucilage that holds society together."

Following the *Papachristou* decision, police officers continued to arrest "sus-
picious" individuals under the guise of loitering laws. State courts continued to
uphold loitering laws that provided for the arrest of individuals who failed to
"account for themselves" to the satisfaction of the police on the ground that the
police needed such laws to prevent crime. However, in Kolender v. Lawson [461
U.S. 352 (1983)], the United States Supreme Court struck down a California
loitering statute that punished failure by any person wandering the streets to
produce credible identification when requested by a police officer to do so. The
Supreme Court held that this statute, like the vagrancy law invalidated in *Papachristou*, was too vague to satisfy the requirements of due process.

With the Supreme Court's decisions in *Papachristou* and *Kolender*, loitering and
vagrancy laws ceased to be effective tools to punish and control the displaced
poor. While judicial attitudes on vagrancy and loitering laws had changed, local
officials perceived the invalidation of these laws as a dangerous assault on their
authority to enforce social order.

In the 1980s, academic commentators defended police use of "street justice"
to keep the homeless and other "disorderly persons" in line. In one highly
influential article, Professors James Wilson and George Kelling compared
vagrants to broken windows in a building. When a piece of property is left
untended it "becomes fair game for people out for fun or plunder." By analogy,
the authors argued that while the arrest of "a single drunk or a single vagrant
who has harmed no identifiable person seems unjust . . . [f]ailing to do anything
about a score of drunks or a hundred vagrants may destroy an entire community." In the eyes of some officials, the use of such arguments by academic
theorists legitimized their efforts to maintain order within American cities
through punishment of the displaced poor. With the growth of a new, highly

visible class of homeless persons, local officials soon began to search for new ways to achieve these ends.

During the 1980s, the number of homeless individuals living in American cities skyrocketed. According to official estimates, the homeless population of New York City increased approximately 350% in the eight years between 1981 and 1989. The National Coalition for the Homeless has estimated that three million homeless individuals live on the streets of American cities. [In the early 1990s], the homeless problem has worsened. In the last year, American cities have seen substantial increases in demands for emergency shelter and in the average length of time that most homeless individuals remain without permanent housing. Homelessness has become a seemingly intractable problem. At the same time, public attitudes towards the homeless have become increasingly hostile. . . .

To alleviate the problem of homelessness, cities have also increasingly attempted to expel their homeless populations. With the invalidation of vagrancy and loitering laws, cities have adopted two new methods to communicate the message that the homeless poor are not welcome in their communities. First, local authorities have conducted homeless arrest sweeps and arrest campaigns, usually on charges of camping on public land or sleeping in public. Second, cities have engaged in property sweeps to seize and destroy the possessions of the homeless. . . .

* * *

In the wake of deinstitutionalization of people with mental illness beginning in the 1970s (see Chapter 6, p. 350), large social service cuts during the 1980s, and the recession in the early 1990s, local officials began looking for new ways to address the sharp rise in homelessness. In 1993, Seattle passed one of the first ordinances banning people from sitting or lying on commercial sidewalks. The Seattle law was challenged on the grounds that it violated the First and Fourteenth Amendments to the U.S. Constitution, but was eventually upheld as facially valid by the U.S. Court of Appeals for the Ninth Circuit. Roulette v. City of Seattle, 97 F.3d 300 (9th Cir. 1996).

During the 1960s, some cities had passed sweeping ordinances to keep "hippies" off the streets and out of parks. One such ordinance was adopted in 1968 in Los Angeles, California. Though it had lain relatively dormant during the 1980s and 1990s—as city attorney and later mayor, James Hahn refused to enforce it against homeless people unless the city could offer sufficient shelter—Los Angeles began enforcing the ordinance in the early 2000s against homeless people. A group of homeless people challenged the ordinance in the following case.

JONES v. CITY OF LOS ANGELES
444 F.3d 1118 (9th Cir. 2006)

Appellants are six of the more than 80,000 homeless individuals in Los Angeles County on any given night. . . . Los Angeles's Skid Row has the highest concentration of homeless individuals in the United States. According to the declaration of Michael Alvidrez, a manager of single-room-occupancy ("SRO") hotels in Skid Row owned by the Skid Row Housing Trust, since the mid-1970s Los Angeles has chosen to centralize homeless services in Skid Row. The area is now largely comprised of SRO hotels (multi-unit housing for very low income persons typically consisting of a single room with shared bathroom), shelters, and other facilities for the homeless.

Skid Row is a place of desperate poverty, drug use, and crime, where Porta-Potties serve as sleeping quarters and houses of prostitution. Recently, it has been reported that local hospitals and law enforcement agencies from nearby suburban areas have been caught "dumping" homeless individuals in Skid Row upon their release. . . .

For the approximately 11,000-12,000 homeless individuals in Skid Row, space is available in SRO hotels, shelters, and other temporary or transitional housing for only 9000 to 10,000, leaving more than 1000 people unable to find shelter each night. In the County as a whole, there are almost 50,000 more homeless people than available beds. In 1999, the fair market rent for an SRO room in Los Angeles was $379 per month. Yet the monthly welfare stipend for single adults in Los Angeles County is only $221. Wait-lists for public housing and for housing assistance vouchers in Los Angeles are three- to ten-years long. . . . Thus, for many in Skid Row without the resources or luck to obtain shelter, sidewalks are the only place to be.

As will be discussed below, Appellants' declarations demonstrate that they are not on the streets of Skid Row by informed choice. In addition, the Institute for the Study of Homelessness and Poverty reports that homelessness results from mental illness, substance abuse, domestic violence, low-paying jobs, and, most significantly, the chronic lack of affordable housing. It also reports that between 33% and 50% of the homeless in Los Angeles are mentally ill, and 76% percent of homeless adults in 1990 had been employed for some or all of the two years prior to becoming homeless.

Against this background, the City asserts the constitutionality of enforcing Los Angeles Municipal Code section 41.18(d) against those involuntarily on the streets during nighttime hours, such as Appellants. It provides:

> No person shall sit, lie or sleep in or upon any street, sidewalk or other public way.
>
> The provisions of this subsection shall not apply to persons sitting on the curb portion of any sidewalk or street while attending or viewing any parade permitted under the provisions of Section 103.111 of Article 2, Chapter X of this Code; nor shall the provisions of this subsection supply [sic] to persons sitting upon benches or other seating facilities provided for such purpose by municipal authority by this Code. A violation of section 41.18(d) is punishable by a fine of up to $1000 and/or imprisonment of up to six months.

Section 41.18(d) is one of the most restrictive municipal laws regulating public spaces in the United States. The City can secure a conviction under the ordinance against anyone who merely sits, lies, or sleeps in a public way at any time of day. Other cities' ordinances similarly directed at the homeless provide ways to avoid criminalizing the status of homelessness by making an element of the crime some conduct in combination with sitting, lying, or sleeping in a state of homelessness. . . .

The record before us includes declarations and supporting documentation from nearly four dozen other homeless individuals living in Skid Row who have been searched, ordered to move, cited, arrested, and/or prosecuted for, and in some cases convicted of, violating section 41.18(d). Many of these declarants lost much or all of their personal property when they were arrested.

[Appellants] seek a permanent injunction against the City of Los Angeles and L.A.P.D. Chief William Bratton and Captain Charles Beck (in their official capacities), barring them from enforcing section 41.18(d) in Skid Row between the hours of 9:00 p.m. and 6:30 a.m. Appellants allege that by enforcing section 41.18(d) twenty-four hours a day against persons with nowhere else to sit, lie, or sleep, other than on public streets and sidewalks, the City is criminalizing the status of homelessness in violation of the Eighth and Fourteenth Amendments to the U.S. Constitution [and several state claims.] . . . Relying heavily on Joyce v. City and County of San Francisco, 846 F.Supp. 843 (N.D.Cal.1994), the district court held that enforcement of the ordinance does not violate the Eighth Amendment because it penalizes conduct, not status. This appeal timely followed. . . .

Our analysis begins with *Robinson* [*v. California*, 370 U.S. 660 (1962)], which announced limits on what the state can criminalize consistent with the Eighth Amendment. In *Robinson*, the Supreme Court considered whether a state may convict an individual for violating a statute making it a criminal offense to "be addicted to the use of narcotics." . . . At a minimum, *Robinson* establishes that the state may not criminalize "being"; that is, the state may not punish a person for who he is, independent of anything he has done. However, as five Justices would later make clear in *Powell*, *Robinson* also supports the principle that the state cannot punish a person for certain conditions, either arising from his own acts or contracted involuntarily, or acts that he is powerless to avoid.

Six years after its decision in *Robinson*, the Supreme Court considered the case of Leroy Powell, who had been charged with violating a Texas statute making it a crime to "get drunk or be found in a state of intoxication in any public place." [*Powell v. Texas*, 392 U.S. 514 (1968)] The trial court found that Powell suffered from the disease of chronic alcoholism, which "destroys the afflicted person's will" to resist drinking and leads him to appear drunk in public involuntarily. Nevertheless, the trial court summarily rejected Powell's constitutional defense and found him guilty. On appeal to the United States Supreme Court, Powell argued that the Eighth Amendment prohibited "punish[ing] an ill person for conduct over which he has no control."

In a 4-1-4 decision, the Court affirmed Powell's conviction. The four Justices joining the plurality opinion interpreted *Robinson* to prohibit only the criminalization of pure status and not to limit the criminalization of conduct. The plurality then declined to extend the Cruel and Unusual Punishment Clause's protections to any involuntary conduct, citing slippery slope concerns, and considerations of federalism and personal accountability. Because Powell was convicted not for his status as a chronic alcoholic, but rather for his acts of becoming intoxicated and appearing in public, the *Powell* plurality concluded that the Clause as interpreted by *Robinson* did not protect him. . . .

Following *Robinson*'s holding that the state cannot criminalize pure status, and the agreement of five Justices in *Powell* that the state cannot criminalize certain involuntary conduct, there are two considerations relevant to defining the Cruel and Unusual Punishment Clause's limits on the state's power to criminalize. The first is the distinction between pure status—the state of being—and pure conduct—the act of doing. The second is the distinction between an involuntary act or condition and a voluntary one. Accordingly, in determining whether the state may punish a particular involuntary act or condition, we are guided by Justice White's admonition that "[t]he proper subject of inquiry is whether volitional acts brought about the 'condition' and whether those acts are sufficiently proximate to the 'condition' for it to be permissible to impose penal sanctions on the 'condition.'"

The *Robinson* and *Powell* decisions, read together, compel us to conclude that enforcement of section 41.18(d) at all times and in all places against homeless individuals who are sitting, lying, or sleeping in Los Angeles's Skid Row because they cannot obtain shelter violates the Cruel and Unusual Punishment Clause. As homeless individuals, Appellants are in a chronic state that may have been acquired "innocently or involuntarily." Whether sitting, lying, and sleeping are defined as acts or conditions, they are universal and unavoidable consequences of being human. It is undisputed that, for homeless individuals in Skid Row who have no access to private spaces, these acts can only be done in public. In contrast to Leroy Powell, Appellants have made a substantial showing that they are "unable to stay off the streets on the night[s] in question."

In disputing our holding, the dissent veers off track by attempting to isolate the supposed "criminal conduct" from the status of being involuntarily homeless at night on the streets of Skid Row. Unlike the cases the dissent relies on, which involve failure to carry immigration documents, illegal reentry, and drug dealing, the conduct at issue here is involuntary and inseparable from status — they are one and the same, given that human beings are biologically compelled to rest, whether by sitting, lying, or sleeping. The cases the dissent cites do not control our reading of *Robinson* and *Powell* where, as here, an Eighth Amendment challenge concerns the involuntariness of a criminalized act or condition inseparable from status. The City and the dissent apparently believe that Appellants can avoid sitting, lying, and sleeping for days, weeks, or months at a time to comply with the City's ordinance, as if human beings could remain in perpetual motion. That being an impossibility, by criminalizing sitting, lying, and sleeping, the City is in fact criminalizing Appellants' status as homeless individuals.

. . . [T]he state may not make it an offense to be idle, indigent, or homeless in public places. Nor may the state criminalize conduct that is an unavoidable consequence of being homeless — namely sitting, lying, or sleeping on the streets of Los Angeles's Skid Row. As Justice White stated in *Powell*, "[p]unishing an addict for using drugs convicts for addiction under a different name."

Homelessness is not an innate or immutable characteristic, nor is it a disease, such as drug addiction or alcoholism. But generally one cannot become a drug addict or alcoholic, as those terms are commonly used, without engaging in at least some voluntary acts (taking drugs, drinking alcohol). Similarly, an individual may become homeless based on factors both within and beyond his immediate control, especially in consideration of the composition of the homeless as a group: the mentally ill, addicts, victims of domestic violence, the unemployed, and the unemployable. That Appellants may obtain shelter on some nights and may eventually escape from homelessness does not render their status at the time of arrest any less worthy of protection than a drug addict's or an alcoholic's.

Undisputed evidence in the record establishes that at the time they were cited or arrested, Appellants had no choice other than to be on the streets. Even if Appellants' past volitional acts contributed to their current need to sit, lie, and sleep on public sidewalks at night, those acts are not sufficiently proximate to the conduct at issue here for the imposition of penal sanctions to be permissible. In contrast, we find no Eighth Amendment protection for conduct that a person makes unavoidable based on their own immediately proximate voluntary acts, for example, driving while drunk, harassing others, or camping or building shelters that interfere with pedestrian or automobile traffic.

Our holding is a limited one. We do not hold that the Eighth Amendment includes a mens rea requirement, or that it prevents the state from criminalizing conduct that is not an unavoidable consequence of being homeless, such as panhandling or obstructing public thoroughfares. We are not confronted here with a facial challenge to a statute. And we are not called upon to decide the constitutionality of punishment when there are beds available for the homeless in shelters.

We hold only that, just as the Eighth Amendment prohibits the infliction of criminal punishment on an individual for being a drug addict, or for involuntary public drunkenness that is an unavoidable consequence of being a chronic alcoholic without a home; the Eighth Amendment prohibits the City from punishing involuntary sitting, lying, or sleeping on public sidewalks that is an unavoidable consequence of being human and homeless without shelter in the City of Los Angeles.

. . . By our decision, we in no way dictate to the City that it must provide sufficient shelter for the homeless, or allow anyone who wishes to sit, lie, or sleep on the streets of Los Angeles at any time and at any place within the City. All we hold is that, so long as there is a greater number of homeless individuals in Los Angeles than the number of available beds, the City may not enforce section 41.18(d) at all times and places throughout the City against homeless individuals for involuntarily sitting, lying, and sleeping in public.

* * *

In the last two decades, dozens of cities across the country have enacted "sit-lie" laws similar to Seattle's, and most have been more narrowly tailored than the Los Angeles ordinance at issue in *Jones*. Homelessness has risen again during the economic recession that began in 2007, and cities have more vigorously enforced a variety of ordinances against homeless people. The next excerpt describes the many forms of restrictions, types of activities targeted, and recent trends in criminalization measures.

NAT'L LAW CTR. ON HOMELESSNESS & POVERTY, *CRIMINALIZING CRISIS: THE CRIMINALIZATION OF HOMELESSNESS IN U.S. CITIES* (2011)

. . . The criminalization of the homeless takes many forms, including:

- Enactment and enforcement of laws that make it illegal to sleep, sit, or store personal belongings in public spaces in cities without sufficient shelter or affordable housing.
- Selective enforcement against homeless persons of seemingly neutral laws, such as loitering, jaywalking, or open container ordinances.
- Sweeps of city areas in which homeless persons live to drive them out of those areas, frequently resulting in the destruction of individuals' personal property such as important personal documents and medication.
- Enactment and enforcement of laws that punish people for begging or panhandling in order to move poor or homeless persons out of a city or downtown area.

- Enactment and enforcement of laws that restrict groups sharing food with homeless persons in public spaces.
- Enforcement of "quality of life" ordinances related to public activities and hygiene (e.g., public urination) when no public facilities are available to people without housing.

. . . The Law Center surveyed 154 service providers, advocates, and people experiencing homelessness from 26 different states. The results of the survey indicate that the criminalization of homelessness continues to be a pervasive and persistent problem in communities across the country.

Respondents reported arrests, citations, or both for the following activities in their cities:

- Public urination/defecation: 73 percent of respondents;
- Camping/sleeping in public: 55 percent of respondents;
- Loitering: 55 percent of respondents;
- Panhandling: 53 percent of respondents;
- Public storage of belongings: 20 percent of respondents; and
- Sidewalk-sitting: 19 percent of respondents.

At the same time, more than 80 percent of respondents who reported restrictions on public camping/sleeping, urination/defecation, and/or storage of belongings indicated that their cities lack sufficient shelter beds, public bathrooms, and/or free-to-low cost storage options for the personal belongings of homeless persons.

City ordinances are frequently tools for criminalizing homelessness. Of the 234 cities surveyed . . . :

- 40 percent prohibit "camping" in particular public places in the city, while 16 percent prohibit "camping" citywide;
- 33 percent prohibit sitting/lying in certain public places;
- 56 percent prohibit loitering in particular public places, while 22 percent prohibit loitering citywide; and
- 53 percent prohibit begging in particular public places while 53 percent prohibit "aggressive" panhandling and 24 percent prohibit begging citywide.

The trend of criminalizing homelessness continues to grow. Among the 188 cities reviewed for the prohibited conduct chart . . . , we identified the following increases in criminalization measures:

- 7 percent increase in prohibitions on begging or panhandling;
- 7 percent increase in prohibitions on camping in particular public places; and
- 10 percent increase in prohibitions on loitering in particular public places.

NOTES AND QUESTIONS

1. The *Jones* case was later vacated by settlement. *See* Jones v. City of Los Angeles, 505 F.3d 1006 (9th Cir. 2007), *vacating*, 444 F.3d 1118 (9th Cir. 2006).

In exchange for the plaintiffs dismissing the lawsuit, the city agreed to suspend enforcement of the sit-lie ordinance between the hours of 9:00 P.M. and 6:00 A.M. until it constructed 1,250 units of permanent supportive housing for chronically homeless people, half of which were located in Skid Row and/or downtown Los Angeles. According to statistics cited by the court at the time, more than 80,000 people were homeless in Los Angeles, including 11,000-12,000 homeless individuals on Skid Row. Why do you think advocates settled the case for a number of housing units they knew would be insufficient to house all but a small percentage of homeless people in Los Angeles?

2. As in *Jones*, a Florida district court held that Miami's practice of arresting homeless people for activities such as sleeping and eating in public places constituted cruel and unusual punishment in violation of the Eighth Amendment. Pottinger v. City of Miami, 810 F. Supp. 1551 (S.D. Fla. 1992), *remanded for limited purposes*, 40 F.3d 1155 (11th Cir. 1994), *directed to undertake settlement discussions*, 76 F.3d 1154 (11th Cir. 1996). Yet the U.S. Court of Appeals for the Eleventh Circuit upheld an Orlando anticamping ordinance enforced against homeless people because "[they] are not a suspect class, nor is sleeping out-of-doors a fundamental right." Joel v. City of Orlando, 232 F.3d 1353 (11th Cir. 2000), *cert. denied*, 532 U.S. 978 (2001). In *Joel*, the court relied in part on evidence that the city had sufficient shelter beds to deny the Eighth Amendment claim. In what ways are homeless people like or different from other politically vulnerable groups subjected to laws and practices you have learned about in this course?

3. In June 2009, a state court struck down Portland's sit-lie ordinance for prohibiting conduct permitted by state law and thereby violating the Oregon Constitution. The city, however, quickly adopted a new "sidewalk management plan" to move homeless people from public places. According to Professor Susan Schweik:

> Publicity for the new Sidewalk Management Plan emphasized its novel approach: for the first time, a city's policing of its sidewalks would be "based on the federal American with Disabilities Act [ADA] . . . which includes specific design guidelines that disabled citizens need for unobstructed passage on public sidewalks. In this pedestrian use zone, persons must be on foot to be able to move immediately to accommodate people with disabilities as well as other sidewalk users."

Susan Schweik, *Kicked to the Curb: Ugly Law Then and Now*, 46 Harv. C.R.-C.L. L. Rev. Amicus 1 (2011).

Professor Schweik and others have decried pitting the rights of disabled people and homeless people against each other, especially since homeless people were integrally involved in the movement that led to passage of the ADA: "[T]he plan's invocation of the Americans with Disabilities Act as its grounding legal framework reveals itself as hypocritical, a cynical manipulation of the principle of disability access as a weapon against homeless people in the city's 'arsenal of exclusion.'" How would you balance the various interests at stake in devising and enforcing local efforts to maintain accessible public space for everyone?

4. The nonpartisan U.S. Conference of Mayors conducts an annual survey and reports on recent trends in hunger and homelessness. In its December 2012

report, the mayors found increased homelessness in 60-70 percent of the cities, including a 7 percent rise in homeless individuals and an 8 percent rise in homeless families:

> City officials cited the lack of affordable housing as the leading cause of home-lessness among families with children. This was followed by poverty, unem-ployment, eviction, and domestic violence. Lack of affordable housing also led the list of causes of homelessness among unaccompanied individuals, fol-lowed by unemployment, poverty, mental illness and the lack of needed ser-vices, and substance abuse and the lack of needed services. The survey cities reported that on average, 30 percent of homeless adults were severely mentally ill, 18 percent were physically disabled, 17 percent were employed, 16 percent were victims of domestic violence, 13 percent were veterans, and four percent were HIV Positive.

The report said that most cities expected continued increases over the next year. How should cities address rising homelessness that accompanies eco-nomic downturns, especially when public resources typically decline at the same time?

2. Housing

As we discussed in Chapter 6, the U.S. Department of Housing and Urban Development (HUD) provides shelter assistance to some low-income people at fixed sites and through vouchers that can be used in the private market. Eligibility for public housing is governed by admission criteria, including grounds for mandatory, presumptive, and permissive denial based on criminal background and activity. Project residents and voucher holders can also lose their housing for lease violations.

More than 3,000 local Public Housing Authorities (PHAs) manage the proj-ect-based and voucher programs, and can institute policies that are more restrictive than the federal law and regulations. For example, PHAs have the authority to bar eligibility for a reasonable period of time after any criminal activity. PHAs and voucher landlords can terminate or evict residents for any new criminal activity, and they can require the exclusion of an offending household member as a condition of admission or continued benefits.

a. Public Housing Projects

According to HUD, approximately 1.2 million low-income households live in public housing units. More than 50 percent of the residents in these "projects" are elderly and disabled. Most projects are located in areas with low or moderate poverty rates (20 percent are in high-poverty neighborhoods).

In his January 1996 State of the Union address, President Bill Clinton said, "I challenge local housing authorities and tenant associations: Criminal gang members and drug dealers are destroying the lives of decent tenants. From now on, the rule for residents who commit crime and peddle drugs should be one strike and you're out." Two months later, President Clinton signed into law the Housing Opportunity Program Extension Act of 1996, and announced a "One Strike and You're Out" policy for public housing residents.

The one-strike policy provided PHAs with additional authority to screen and evict tenants as part of an antidrug and anticrime campaign in public housing. In HUD v. Rucker, excerpted and discussed in Chapter 6, a unanimous Supreme Court held that by statute PHAs have "the discretion to evict tenants for the drug-related activity of household members and guests whether or not the tenant knew, or should have known, about the activity." As set out in the following excerpts, conservatives lauded the opinion for helping make public housing safe for law-abiding tenants, while liberal critics raised due process and other concerns about the impact on low-income families targeted by the policy.

WASHINGTON LEGAL FOUND., *COURT PERMITS EVICTION OF DRUG DEALERS FROM PUBLIC HOUSING* (2002)

The U.S. Supreme Court ruled unanimously today that public housing authorities are authorized to evict tenants from public housing if the tenant, a household member, or a guest engages in drug-related criminal activity.

The decision was a victory for the Washington Legal Foundation (WLF), which had filed a brief in the case, HUD v. Rucker, in support of the housing authorities. The Court agreed with WLF that such evictions are permissible even if the tenant himself has no knowledge of, or control over, the criminal activity.

WLF had argued that unless housing authorities are permitted to take strong steps to rid public housing of the criminal element, law-abiding tenants of such housing will continue to be denied safe housing that is not ravaged by the effects of drug dealing. "Those who suffer the most from the drug trade and associated violence are those, such as occupants of government-subsidized housing, who cannot afford to move to areas away from the center of the drug trade," said WLF Chief Counsel Richard Samp after the Court's decision. "The Court was correct that when an apartment is turned into a crack house, housing authorities should not be required to delay eviction until they can absolutely prove that the tenant on the lease knows what other members of his household are up to," Samp said.

This case arose in connection with efforts by the Oakland Housing Authority (OHA) to evict four of its public-housing tenants whose household members had been discovered to have engaged in illegal drug activity. The tenants thereafter filed suit in federal court against OHA and the U.S. Department of Housing and Urban Development (HUD), alleging that the attempted evictions violated federal housing law. The lower courts agreed and enjoined OHA from evicting any tenant for illegal drug activity in the absence of evidence that the tenant knew of the activity and had failed to take appropriate steps to eliminate it. The lower courts also struck down a HUD regulation which had interpreted federal housing law as permitting such evictions. The Supreme Court overturned those lower court decisions.

The Court agreed with WLF's argument that the lower courts had wholly misinterpreted federal housing law. The Court held that Congress, when it adopted the Anti-Drug Abuse Act of 1988, explicitly required that public housing leases include a clause permitting eviction whenever a household member engages in illegal drug activity, and that the mandated clause permits eviction regardless of the tenant's knowledge of that activity. The Court noted that the mandated clause does not *require* eviction in every case in which illegal drug activity is detected, but held that Congress gave housing authorities the flexibility to decide which instances of illegal drug activity warrant eviction in order to preserve public safety, and which do not.

The Supreme Court also rejected the lower court's position that eviction of tenants who lack knowledge of the household members' illegal activities is irrational and thus unconstitutional. WLF had argued that it can be extremely difficult for housing authorities to prove a tenant's knowledge of her household members' illegal activities and thus that imposing a "knowledge" requirement would place huge obstacles in the way of efforts to rid public housing of drug activity, even when the tenant does, in fact, have such knowledge. Accordingly, WLF argued, the HUD rule is a wholly rational tool to assist in the effort to clean up public housing. WLF also argued that it is eminently reasonable for HUD to assume that public housing will be safer if housing authorities evict tenants whose household members and guests have been engaging in drug activity, regardless how "innocent" of wrongdoing those tenants may be. . . .

CATERINA GOUVIS ROMAN & JEREMY TRAVIS, THE URBAN INST., *TAKING STOCK: HOUSING, HOMELESSNESS, AND PRISONER REENTRY* (2004)

The scarcity of federally subsidized housing creates barriers for all individuals seeking affordable housing. It has been estimated that only one-third of all individuals and families eligible for subsidized housing actually gain access to federally subsidized housing. During the last decade the number of available public housing units has decreased. The HOPE VI public housing redevelopment program [providing federal funds to housing authorities to demolish distressed housing projects and replace them with scattered site housing] has contributed to the reduction in the nation's supply of public housing. Estimates suggest that tens of thousands of families nationally have been displaced by HOPE VI activities.

Some community leaders have suggested that given an individual's criminal history, it may not be feasible to expect that returning prisoners access this housing resource when thousands of law-abiding individuals are awaiting housing. In addition, some communities have voiced concerns about concentrating individuals with criminal histories into disadvantaged communities.

With regard to regulations, current HUD policy provides public housing authorities (PHAs) power to deny admission or to terminate the lease of individuals with a history of use or abuse of drugs or alcohol, or of criminal behavior. The PHA property manager has discretion to determine admission policies. The same One Strike policy, upheld by the U.S. Supreme Court (Department of Housing and Urban Development v. Rucker), encourages housing authorities to include in leases a provision that a tenant in public housing can be evicted if the tenant, any member of the tenant's household, or any guest engages in drug-related criminal activity on or off the premises. A 1997 HUD survey shows that housing authorities are using the regulations to deny admission or evict individuals with criminal histories from public housing. That year, the One-Strike regulation was used to deny 19,405 individuals admission, out of a total 45,079 individuals denied admission for various reasons.

Looking at individual cities, *The View From the Ground*, an occasional online publication produced by representatives of the Stateway Gardens public housing development on Chicago's South Side, reports that Chicago Housing Authority (CHA) statistics show that of One-Strike cases initiated between August, 2000, and April, 2002, 717 One-Strike cases involving families were concluded. The dispositions of these cases were as follows: 26 percent of all judgments were in favor of the CHA; 37 percent ended in "agreed orders" (negotiated settlements where offending party is taken off lease, barred from unit, or put on probation); and 20 percent resulted in move-outs (tenants move out on their own after receiving an eviction notice). Only 1 percent of the judgments were for the tenant.

NOTES AND QUESTIONS

1. With respect to no-fault (one-strike) evictions, the *Rucker* Court said that "[s]trict liability maximizes deterrence and eases enforcement difficulties." The Washington Legal Foundation says that "when an apartment is turned into a crack house," authorities need to be able to evict the offending tenants quickly and regardless of whether the leaseholder knows of the activity. In *Rucker*, however, two of the four plaintiffs were evicted because their grandsons "were caught in the apartment complex parking lot smoking marijuana." What are the pros and cons of a zero tolerance drug use policy in public housing?

2. As noted above, public housing tenants can contest evictions through a pre-termination hearing process. In fact, one commentator observed that the one-strike policy "does seem to conform to the standards set forth in Goldberg v. Kelly. In *Rucker*, the Court notes the applicability of the Due Process Clause and points out that there has been no indication that tenants would be evicted without notice and an opportunity to be heard." Jim Moye, *Can't Stop the Hustle: The Department of Housing and Urban Development's "One-Strike" Eviction Policy Fails to Get Drugs Out of America's Projects*, 23 B.C. Third World L.J. 275 (2003). On the other hand, Roman and Travis suggest that a very small percentage of tenants prevail in such hearings. How would you balance the due process rights of public housing tenants accused of violating the one-strike policy with the quiet enjoyment rights of public housing residents more generally?

b. The Housing Choice Voucher Program

In addition to public housing project tenants, more than 5 million low-income Americans receive housing vouchers ("Section 8") to rent apartments on the private market. The voucher program is administered by local PHAs, who verify tenant and landlord eligibility (see Chapter 6, pp. 353-364, for a more detailed description of the Section 8 program). Just under half of all Section 8 tenants are elderly and disabled, and — because of voucher mobility — are more likely than project-based tenants to live in lower-poverty neighborhoods. Compared to low-income tenants without vouchers, voucher holders live in higher-quality housing with lower rent burdens.

Such tenants nevertheless face many challenges in finding landlords willing to accept Section 8 vouchers. With the exception of a handful of jurisdictions nationally, landlords in most rental markets can legally refuse to rent to Section 8 tenants. According to HUD statistics, in some jurisdictions, over 50 percent of voucher holders are unable to find housing.

Even though rent is essentially guaranteed through the program, many landlords associate Section 8 with administrative burdens. For some landlords, vouchers are a proxy for race and criminality. As the following excerpt suggests, even when landlords are willing to rent to voucher holders, public officials and other residents may object to the presence of Section 8 tenants in their communities.

PRISCILLA OCEN, *THE NEW RACIALLY RESTRICTIVE COVENANT: RACE, WELFARE, AND THE POLICING OF BLACK WOMEN IN SUBSIDIZED HOUSING*

59 UCLA L. Rev. 1540 (2012)

In 1974, the federal government enacted legislation that "signaled a significant shift in the federal housing strategy from locally owned public housing to privately owned rental housing." The Housing and Community Development Act of 1974 privatized housing and moved away from large-scale public housing projects, which critics charged concentrated poverty. Instead, the Act authorized the creation of the Section 8 Housing Choice Voucher Program, a federally funded housing program designed to "aid lower income families in finding a decent and safe place to live in an economically mixed community." Indeed, Section 8 housing vouchers were envisioned as a way to break up poor enclaves in urban centers by "dispers[ing] families throughout the community" and to allow more people to move to economically integrated communities, where they could potentially get better jobs and send their children to better schools.

To qualify for participation in the Section 8 program, an applicant household must earn below 50 percent of the median income for the relevant jurisdiction. Voucher holders pay up to 30 percent of the rent and a local housing authority pays the remainder directly to the landlord. Those who successfully obtain a Section 8 voucher can utilize the voucher in a neighborhood of their choosing. Individuals, however, are not eligible for the Section 8 voucher if they have been convicted of certain types of criminal offenses. Moreover, families that have successfully obtained a Section 8 voucher may have them terminated if they fail to report income, fail to disclose additional residents who are not listed on the lease agreement filed with the local housing authority, or otherwise violate the terms of their Section 8 lease.

As the name suggests, housing choice is an important element of the Section 8 program. According to the Department of Housing and Urban Development (HUD), Section 8 vouchers allow for both "a choice of housing and anonymity." To function, both the privatization and decentralization of public housing depend on private landlords' willingness to accept Section 8 vouchers. The program, however, operates on a terrain of racialized community boundaries and in the context of a pervasive history of housing segregation. Consequently, Section 8 recipients often have a very difficult time obtaining housing in the predominately white, high-opportunity neighborhoods that the program was designed to integrate.

Despite the intentions of the Section 8 program, recipients are often subject to racial discrimination that prevents them from moving into economically and racially segregated communities. Because the program relies on the private market to provide the rental properties, many Section 8 recipients confront land-lords who are unwilling to rent to them. Moreover, Black and Latino recipients confront a higher level of discrimination when seeking housing. A Chicago study estimated that recipients are "denied access to approximately 70% of the market rate units that are supposedly available to them." Consequently, "[m]any recipi-ents end up using their subsidies to pay for their current low-income housing units or move within their own segregated neighborhoods."

After 2005, however, the economic downturn opened up opportunities for Section 8 recipients to obtain housing in a number of predominately white communities that were formerly unavailable to them. Cities like Antioch, Lan-caster, and Palmdale [in northern and southern California] had expanded at a rapid pace and were devastated by the foreclosure crisis. Faced with the prospect of going into foreclosure or renting to low-income Section 8 recipients, many landlords chose the latter. Landlords advertised acceptance of Section 8 vouchers, and Section 8 recipients responded, seeking better opportunities for themselves and their families. . . .

. . . [And yet, racially restrictive] dynamics operate in Antioch, Lancaster, and Palmdale, albeit through the use of police and politicians rather than the Court. In Antioch, city council members and law enforcement collaborated with com-munity groups (such as [United Citizens for Better Neighborhoods]) to gener-ate complaints regarding Section 8 tenants for submission to police or to the housing authority for further investigation. Officers solicited neighbor com-plaints by placing door hangers on the homes of suspected Section 8 recipients and their neighbors. The door hangers invited neighbors to call police regard-ing so-called quality-of-life issues in their community. The complaints usually specified whether tenants used Section 8 vouchers. If this information was not provided, officers would often follow up with residents to determine whether the subject of the complaint was a Section 8 recipient.

Similarly, in Lancaster and Palmdale, white individuals and neighborhood associations who objected to the presence of Black female-headed Section 8 households in their communities used the coercive power of the law to enforce and effectuate their exclusion. For example, individuals and groups prevailed upon legislative bodies to pass nuisance ordinances and to impose a require-ment that landlords obtain licenses prior to renting to Section 8 households. Politicians, for their part, were more than willing to align themselves with the rhetoric and demands of residents.

In Lancaster, the mayor asserted that Section 8 was "crushing the commu-nity" and that it was "time to go to war." The response to the moral panic regarding Section 8 drew upon longstanding notions of recipients as presumed criminal and morally deviant. Such a framing of recipients invited a response governed by principles of crime and punishment. Thus, the coercive power of the law functioned most significantly through the deployment of police units dedicated to regulating and policing Section 8 households.

The cities of Antioch, Lancaster, and Palmdale formed police units specifi-cally to address so-called quality-of-life issues and issues related to rental prop-erties in various neighborhoods. In reality, however, the police units focused on surveilling, regulating, and intimidating Black Section 8 voucher holders. Non-Black section 8 voucher holders were largely ignored by these units. Rather, in an effort to push Black Section 8 households out of their communities, police engaged in broad surveillance of these households (more often than not for noncriminal activities), engaged in warrantless searches of these homes, and investigated the intimate lives of Black women on Section 8, including seeking information about their children and sexual partners.

In Lancaster and Palmdale, for example, the specialized police and administrative units obtained lists of all Section 8 properties. Law enforcement agents engaged in multiagency compliance checks of these properties, bringing together sheriff's deputies with welfare fraud investigators, often with as many as fifteen armed agents entering into homes of Section 8 residents. Some sweeps of Section 8 homes "involved not only the Sheriff's deputies, but also the Department of Children and Family Services, the Probation Department and Code Enforcement officials."

When officers did not have the right to enter Section 8 properties under the auspices of an administrative compliance check, city ordinances permitted officers to investigate neighbor complaints against Section 8 households. Officers were alleged to have unnecessarily used handcuffs or weapons during searches. Families often felt threatened with arrest or termination of their housing vouchers if they did not consent to searches of their homes. As part of their investigations of Section 8 households, police routinely obtained school and other records of minor children. In Antioch, members of the specialized unit engaged in searches of homes without consent and monitored Section 8 households by parking squad cars on blocks where voucher holders were known to live.

Instead of investigating crimes against Black women on Section 8, the specialized police units used at least two calls for such crimes as opportunities to investigate potential violations of lease terms. For example, in Antioch, a Black woman phoned police to seek assistance with a domestic violence situation. When police arrived, she alleged that they did not vigorously investigate her complaint but instead asked her about her Section 8 status and whether her alleged assailant was living with her. In another case, police came to the home of another Black woman in response to a break-in, and instead of investigating that claim, the police searched her home. Out of fear of inviting additional harassment, some Black women stopped calling the police when they needed assistance.

Officers also targeted landlords that rented to Section 8 recipients. Landlords were threatened with criminal and civil penalties for any nuisance activity occurring on their property. The cities implemented programs to regulate landlords who rented to individuals with Section 8 vouchers. The City of Lancaster, for example, passed an ordinance that required landlords to obtain licenses to rent units in multi-and single-family buildings. As part of the application, landlords had to indicate whether they accepted Section 8 tenants. To obtain the license, the ordinance required that the city inspect all units and allowed for additional inspections to take place if complaints were lodged against tenants. In Lancaster, the city could fine landlords under the nuisance ordinance. Similar types of harassment occurred in Antioch. In one woman's case, officers sent letters and repeatedly called her Antioch landlord regarding her tenancy. Antioch police followed up with in-person visits to the landlord. During one of the calls an officer allegedly told the landlord that he should be careful when renting to African Americans. As a result of the letters and calls, the landlord forced the woman to move out of her home.

After surveilling and searching the homes of Section 8 tenants, law enforcement agents petitioned local housing authorities to terminate Section 8 vouchers. During investigations of Black women on Section 8, police often focused their resources on identifying misbehaving children and men who were claimed to be "unauthorized tenants." These alleged "unauthorized tenants" were often the children or intimate partners of voucher holders. The aggressive and targeted tactics of law enforcement resulted in four times more termination recommendations by law enforcement in Lancaster than in the remainder of Los Angeles County. These petitions, however, were largely unsuccessful. Nevertheless, many women lost their homes or their vouchers as a result of police actions. Others decided to leave the communities as a result of the pervasive harassment by police and private citizens. Consequently, the collaboration between law enforcement and private citizens has accomplished many of the same exclusionary outcomes as did the regime of judicial enforcement of racially restrictive covenants. . . .

Like the racially restrictive covenant of the early twentieth century, the disproportionate burden of the public and private surveillance and harassment of Section 8 tenants fell on African American households, most of which were headed by women. In Antioch, for example, African Americans composed only 20 percent of the population yet constituted two-thirds of the people investigated by CAT officers [from Antioch's specialized police unit called the Community Action Team]. For example, they were four times as likely as whites to be searched based on noncriminal complaints.

The pervasive racial marginalization of Section 8 tenants led to rampant racial hostilities toward individual Black women and their families. In a suit filed against the City of Lancaster, a Black woman, identified as Jane Roe, noted that after she had been subject to police searches of her home and publicly identified as a Section 8 recipient, she began to receive racist threats and taunts. Another Black woman was identified as a Section 8 recipient when information about her home was posted on the internet. Shortly thereafter, community members began to threaten her and her family—even threatening to burn her house down. Racial epithets were hurled at her children as they walked down the street. Her children were called "dirty Section 8 niggers." On one occasion, a substance that appeared to be urine was thrown at her children as they played outside of her home. Ultimately, her lease was terminated by her landlord after police contacted him regarding her tenancy. Following the termination of her lease, she was unable to find a landlord willing to accept her Section 8 voucher. She felt that her inability to find a rental was based on the fact that "landlords . . . appeared to accept the . . . message that most Section 8 tenants were criminals and should not be welcomed."

As I noted previously, within the public outcry over Section 8, the rhetoric from politicians conflated race, criminality, and participation in the Section 8 program. The chief of police in Antioch suggested that Section 8 recipients were committing fraud by living in nice homes that were subsidized with public funds, despite the fact that public subsidy for the cost of housing was precisely the intent of the program. The mayor of Lancaster suggested that Blacks were committing fraud simply because they were overrepresented in the class of Section 8 recipients in the city. Residents also suggested that recipients were improperly housing formerly incarcerated individuals or were themselves formerly incarcerated and that the city would be "inundated" with criminals.

While ostensibly race-neutral, these rationales from the public and the resulting investigatory practices by police rely on longstanding ideological constructs of Black women. Black women have been derided in their identities as mothers and cast as propagators of their own criminal activity and that of their children. They have been held up as fraudulent recipients of government aid and deployed as tools to generate support for welfare reform. Black women have been constructed as sexually promiscuous and lacking in moral standards. Taken together, these racialized, gendered stereotypes "provide[] the rationale for society's restrictions on black female" autonomy. This rationale provides the basis for intrusive public and private monitoring of even the most intimate aspects of Black women's lives and legitimizes the use of police force to remove Black women from historically white communities.

These dynamics — and the central role of Black women's identities — come together in a form that is analogous to the racially restrictive covenant. Through implicit associations between race, criminality, and subsidy reliance, white collective action to resist the inclusion of poor Section 8 voucher holders from white spaces, and police enforcement of the racialized resistance to Section 8, the basic framework of the racially restrictive covenant is preserved. Just as it was used to outlaw judicial enforcement of the racially restrictive covenant, however, the Supreme Court's rationale in *Shelley* — that public enforcement of private discrimination is constitutionally impermissible — can be leveraged by poor Black women and their advocates to combat their exclusion from white-identified spaces and to achieve the goals of integration and opportunity that are represented by programs such as Section 8.

NOTES AND QUESTIONS

1. Public interest and pro bono lawyers filed a lawsuit against the city of Antioch in 2008, and against the cities of Lancaster and Palmdale in 2011, to end the discrimination against African-American and Latino Section 8 voucher holders. The cases against all three cities were resolved separately in 2012, which ended the most egregious practices described above.

2. Recall what you learned in Chapter 6 about the *Gautreaux* case in Chicago and other similar efforts to deconcentrate poverty. Is it ever legitimate for a city or neighborhood to object to the siting of public housing or the presence of publically subsidized tenants? Does it matter whether it is inner-city residents or suburban communities who object?

3. As noted above, a handful of jurisdictions have banned discrimination against tenants based upon their source of income in general and against Section 8 voucher holders in particular. Landlords have challenged the latter statutes, arguing that they interfere with their freedom of contract and are incompatible with the voluntary nature of Section 8 participation under federal law. Most state courts, and the only federal court to consider the issue, have rejected these challenges, holding that federal law is a "uniform federal floor below which protections for tenants could not drop, not a ceiling above which they could not rise." Barrientos v. 1801-1825 Morton LLC., 583 F.3d 1197 (9th Cir. 2009). Is banning discrimination

against voucher holders the same thing as requiring landlords to rent to Section 8 tenants? To combat housing discrimination, should landlords be *required* to rent to voucher holders, regardless of the administrative or other burdens involved?

4. Professor Ocen refers to specialized police units assigned to monitor section 8 voucher holders and landlords. Some housing authorities have their own internal investigative units tasked with policing participants' compliance with program rules. Among the grounds for denial or termination from Section 8 is the family's failure to comply with "obligations under the program," such as providing the housing authority with required information, including changes in household composition. 24 C.F.R. § 982.552. Many legal aid offices represent tenants in Section 8 termination proceedings, which function much like the pre-termination welfare hearings required by Goldberg v. Kelly, discussed in Chapter 3. Recalling the prior era of "man in the house" rules for welfare recipients, these hearings often include inquiries about "unauthorized occupants" and testimony from housing authority investigators about men's clothing and belongings visible in a "consent" search. We turn to welfare next.

3. *Welfare*

As described in earlier chapters, welfare has long been a site of policy contest. Certain categories of people are prohibited from receiving important safety net benefits. For example, as a result of 1996 welfare reform, federal law imposes a lifetime ban on anyone with a drug-related felony conviction from receiving TANF or SNAP (food stamps). States can opt out of or modify the ban, and as of 2013, only about a dozen states maintained the absolute lifetime bans for one or both programs.

Even people otherwise eligible for welfare face increased scrutiny in the application and renewal processes. In recent years, states have imposed criminal-like procedures on welfare applicants and recipients. In this section, we will review the history of the intersection between welfare and criminal law, including cases related to home visits and drug testing.

KAARYN GUSTAFSON, *THE CRIMINALIZATION OF POVERTY*

99 J. Crim. L. & Criminology 643 (2009)

FROM 1935 THROUGH THE 1960s: CHANGES IN WELFARE DEMOGRAPHICS AND THE RISE OF MIDNIGHT SEARCHES

The criminalization of welfare recipients entails a long historical process of public discourse and welfare policies infused with race, class, and gender bias. State and federal government aid programs developed in the first half of the twentieth century supported white, male workers and the white women and children dependent upon their wages while they excluded a huge segment of poor women of color and their children. The Social Security Act created Aid to

Dependent Children (ADC), a program specifically designed for poor mothers and their children and originally intended to support the widows of working men. After World War II, the ADC rolls grew—from about 900,000 individuals in 1945 to approximately three million in 1960. The proportion of families headed by divorced or unmarried mothers grew, while the proportion of families headed by widows declined. In addition, the number of African-American families receiving welfare rose, especially as poor African-American families, seeking economic opportunity, migrated from southern agricultural areas to the industrial hubs of the North.

Welfare offices in many states and locales adopted "suitable home" and "substitute parent" rules, which were essentially morality standards, and which were arbitrarily and discriminatorily applied, and commonly excluded women of color from the welfare rolls, especially in the South. Notwithstanding a 1961 rule issued by the Secretary of Health, Education and Welfare barring the arbitrary application of suitable home requirements, many welfare offices continued to engage in midnight raids on the homes of ADC recipients in order to police "man in the house" rules. The stated reason for surprise visits was to catch men sleeping in the homes of women receiving welfare. Unmarried women with men in their beds were deemed morally unfit and their households therefore unsuitable for assistance. In addition, the men discovered in the homes were considered household breadwinners who had hidden their income support from the aid office. The unstated but underlying goals of the rules were to police and punish the sexuality of single mothers, to close off the indirect access to government support of able-bodied men, to winnow the welfare rolls, and to reinforce the idea that families receiving aid were entitled to no more than near-desperate living standards.

Midnight raids on welfare recipients continued for most of the 1960s. During that time, a number of publicized cases of welfare fraud charges resulted from the raids. In many of those cases, though, the men, not the women, were charged with fraud. Men found residing with women receiving welfare aid were treated as the welfare cheats. The prosecutions of men, rather than women, suggest that the welfare and law enforcement officials considered women to be easily manipulated by the men, but ultimately blameless in the cheating. This view of the innocence of women, however, changed over time.

By the mid-1960s, low-income women of color were being blamed for all sorts of social problems. An oft-cited 1965 report by Daniel Patrick Moynihan promoted the idea that the problems of inner cities—poverty, joblessness, and crime—could be traced to a "tangle of pathology" perpetuated by unmarried black mothers. The Moynihan Report identified family disorganization and disintegration among poor African Americans as a source of social, moral, and economic instability in the United States. The report stated that "[a]s a direct result of this high rate of divorce, separation, and desertion, a very large percent of Negro families are headed by females. While the percentage of such families among whites has been dropping since 1940, it has been rising among Negroes." Even worse, according to the report, many of the children in female-headed households received Aid to Families with Dependent Children (AFDC, formerly ADC), a program originally designed for widows and orphans. In Moynihan's popular portrayal, low-income African-American mothers were a social threat because they gave birth to and raised sons who became the criminal, urban underclass. [Ed. note: See Chapter 2, p. 81, for more information on the Moynihan Report.]

In 1968, the Supreme Court handed down a decision that halted the "substitute father" rule, which had stipulated that any man cohabiting with a mother should be considered a substitute father and should be held responsible for supporting the entire family. [Ed. note: This decision, King v. Smith, 392 U.S. 309 (1968), is excerpted in Chapter 2.] While the decision lifted the stigma of welfare cheating from fathers and boyfriends, it also intensified the stigma on mothers. . . .

THE 1970S: GROWING CONCERNS ABOUT GOVERNMENT WASTE AND ABOUT CRIME

Beginning in the 1970s, it became more difficult for welfare recipients to live on their welfare grants. Throughout the 1970s, '80s, and '90s, the value of the welfare grant, adjusted for inflation, declined dramatically. The weighted average maximum benefit per three-person family was $854 in 1969 (in 2001 dollars), but plummeted to $456 by 2001. It became increasingly hard for welfare recipients to cover their most basic expenses — food, clothing, and rent — with their welfare grants. Unable to survive on welfare checks and facing barriers to employment, many welfare recipients turned to other sources of income, whether help from kin or participation in underground labor markets, and attempted to hide those sources from the welfare office for fear of losing the small checks they received.

Also in the 1970s, as a part of welfare reforms under President Richard Nixon, the AFDC system became more bureaucratic. The practice of social workers visiting the homes of welfare recipients and verifying financial need ended. Office caseworkers, hired to replace the social workers, processed the routine paperwork that welfare recipients regularly submitted to the office to document their continuing financial need. In a process known as "churning," the federal government increased the amount of information and paperwork required to determine welfare eligibility, and denied benefits to low-income families who failed to keep up with the paperwork. Income-eligible families were removed from the aid rolls for their failures to provide verification documents in a timely manner. Home visits by welfare caseworkers, particularly unannounced visits, virtually stopped during the 1970s. During that period, welfare recipients gained greater expectations of privacy in their own homes. . . .

Welfare cheating had always been an issue in poverty politics. Senator Robert Byrd made a highly publicized investigation of welfare fraud in Washington, D.C. in 1962. In 1972, when President Richard Nixon was considering an overhaul of the welfare system, Senator Russell Long of Louisiana declared that "the welfare system, as we know it today, is being manipulated and abused by malingerers, cheats and outright frauds." While distrust of those low-income adults unattached to the wage labor market had always existed in the United States, it appeared to grow throughout the 1970s. Concerns about welfare cheats, in particular, began to rise. Beginning in 1977, those who applied for food stamps had to disclose their Social Security numbers to receive benefits. This marked the first use of an extensive data exchange using Social Security numbers among government agencies, and the beginning of computer data tracking of the poor.

That is not to say that there were not individuals who defrauded the welfare system. In the late 1970s and early 1980s, there were a few particularly notable cases of welfare fraud in large U.S. cities. It was not happenstance that a number of welfare fraud cases involving double-dipping crooks were uncovered in the late 1970s, as it was then that the AFDC system was computerized and that identifying and documenting cases of fraud became much easier for welfare officials. What may have appeared to the public and to policymakers to be a spike in cases of welfare fraud was actually a sudden improvement in the ability of officials to root out fraud effectively. And while this transformation — the computerization of the system — might have been heralded as a means of both providing aid more efficiently and policing fraud more effectively, the transformation marked instead a period of zealous attacks on welfare recipients and a public perception that welfare cheating was on the rise.

The 1980s: The Rise of the Welfare Queen

The election of Ronald Reagan as President in 1980 marked a significant transition in public opinions towards the poor and in government services for the poor. From the first moment of his bid for presidential election, Ronald Reagan used anecdotes about welfare queens to exemplify everything he believed was wrong with government programs — excessive spending on domestic programs and misuse of government money. Reagan apparently merged the identities of two well-known women convicted of welfare fraud — Linda Taylor, the Chicago "welfare queen," and Barbara Jean Williams, the Cadillac-driving "Queen of Welfare" from Compton — into a single persona who starred in an often-used anecdote. Reagan regularly exaggerated the number of aliases used by these women so that his welfare queen had 100 of them. The welfare queen played a prominent role in Reagan's presidential campaign.

Programs providing assistance to the poor changed after Reagan took office. Whereas Nixon, during his 1973 State of the Union Address, proudly stated that federal spending on food assistance programs had tripled during his presidency, Reagan regarded those same programs as government waste. Under Reagan's direction, the federal government cut funding for food stamps in 1981. The federal government also tightened the eligibility requirements for the federal school lunch program, eliminating 2.6 million children from the program. . . .

Where the welfare queen stereotype was accurate was in its characterization of poverty and welfare as women's issues. Indeed, in 1984, two-thirds of the adults living below the poverty line were women, and households headed by single mothers were five times more likely to live in poverty than two-parent families. Moreover, with rising divorce rates and an increasing number of non-marital births in the United States, the disproportionate representation of women and their children would become a growing trend.

The 1990s: Welfare Reform and the Convergence of the Welfare System and the Criminal Justice System

Vilifying the low-income mothers receiving welfare became a bi-partisan project in the 1990s. Survey research revealed that Americans associated welfare with African Americans and viewed the welfare system as a program that rewarded laziness among African Americans. "Welfare dependency" became a keyword associated not only with economic risk and social disorder, but also with crime.

In the 1990s, states began to attack welfare recipients through aggressive welfare fraud investigations and criminal prosecutions. California again became a leader in these new punitive approaches to welfare reform. By 1993, twenty-six other states had joined California in establishing pre-eligibility fraud investigation units, which conducted investigations of individuals applying for cash aid. The pre-eligibility fraud investigation units checked on welfare applicants' assets, sources of property, household composition, and address. Investigators conducted their investigations by interviewing relatives, friends, neighbors, employers, and landlords of welfare applicants; visiting and conducting surveillance of applicants' homes; investigating financial resources through database searches; and interviewing the welfare applicants themselves. In 1995, all of the states that had established welfare fraud investigation units housed them separately from the eligibility workers in order to avoid conflicts of interest between government employees trying to provide for the poor and those focused on deterring and capturing welfare fraud. . . .

In 1996, California legislators stiffened the penalties for welfare fraud. Legislators passed bills that would permanently disqualify individuals convicted of welfare fraud from ever receiving welfare again. At the same time, they voted to reduce welfare benefits. California also began shifting the investigation and punishment of welfare cheating from the welfare office to district attorneys. Beginning in July 1996, district attorneys rather than staff from public social services agencies assumed the role of conducting welfare overpayment investigations. Functionally, California — like many other states — made it increasingly difficult for welfare recipients to survive on their welfare grants alone, and shifted state money from aiding low-income women to policing and punishing them through the criminal justice system when they sought unreported income.

Then came an overhaul of the welfare system at the federal level. In the debates leading up to the votes on the welfare legislation, federal lawmakers employed dehumanizing rhetoric to describe welfare recipients. In a particularly vivid example of the dehumanization of welfare recipients, John Mica, a Republican Congressional Representative from Florida, held up a sign during a congressional debate that read, "Don't feed the alligators." On the House floor, Mica argued that providing aid to poor women would do nothing but spur them to reproduce, entice them to return for more free handouts, and threaten the general public safety.

Congress passed the Personal Responsibility and Work Opportunity Reconciliation Act in 1996. The legislation eliminated the broad, federally-governed AFDC program and ended cash aid as a federal entitlement to all income-qualified families. Replacing AFDC entitlements, the federal government distributed state block grants through a federal program known as Temporary Assistance for Needy Families (TANF). The new welfare policies threatened that those who failed to play by the rules — by meeting mandatory work requirements, by abiding by behavior reforms, and by reporting all details of income and household composition — would be harshly punished with new penalties. In addition, states were allowed to place their own conditions upon receipt of welfare and could establish time limits even shorter than the federal ones. Those welfare recipients who failed to meet their obligations under the new system would be excluded from benefits and have the safety net pulled out from under them — in some cases permanently. . . .

THE CRIMINALIZATION OF POVERTY TODAY

Welfare reform not only produced punitive policies, but also established a system that blurred the boundaries between the welfare system and the criminal justice system. Until the 1990s, the welfare system was relatively simple and self-contained. The rules of AFDC and Food Stamps were handed down by the federal government, and eligibility rules and violations of welfare rules were consistent from state to state. If families were found ineligible for aid, they were given notice and their benefits ended. If they were found cheating—for example, underreporting their income or failing to report a change of household composition—but were still income-eligible for aid, then the penalties were civil: their welfare benefits would typically be reduced by a certain percentage each month until any overpayments were recouped by the state.

As a result of the reforms, the federal government and the states instituted policies and practices that burdened welfare receipt with criminality; policed the everyday lives of poor families; and wove the criminal justice system into the welfare system, often entangling poor families in the process. David Garland notes that the "themes that dominate crime policy—rational choice and the structures of control, deterrents, and disincentives, the normality of crime, the responsibilization of individuals, the threatening underclass, the failing, overly lenient system—have come to organize the politics of poverty as well." The welfare reform policies were designed to punish the poor; to stigmatize poverty, particularly poverty that leads to welfare receipt; and to create a system of deterrence aimed at the middle class.

a. Home Visits

As Professor Gustafson notes, welfare recipients were frequently subjected to home visits, especially as the rolls grew after World War II and African Americans began to make up a larger percentage of the caseloads. Professor Charles Reich described the constitutional concerns about such visits more than a half a century ago:

> It is most unfortunate that the Social Security Act should have become a means, however, indirect, for depriving some persons of the privacy guaranteed by the fourth amendment. . . . To insist that welfare officials obey the fourth amendment is no more than to insist that the high aim of the Social Security Act not be forgotten in the day-to-day difficulties of carrying it out; and to make certain that the Act remains what it was, above all, intended to be—a guardian and insurer of the dignity of man.

Charles Reich, *Midnight Welfare Searches and the Social Security Act*, 72 Yale L.J. 1347 (1963).

A few years after the U.S. Supreme Court struck down Alabama's man-in-the-house rule in King v. Smith (excerpted in Chapter 2), the Court considered the constitutionality of a New York state law conditioning receipt of welfare benefits on a caseworker home visit in Wyman v. James (1971). In Sanchez v. County of San Diego (2006), the U.S. Court of Appeals for the Ninth Circuit revisited *Wyman*'s reasoning in reviewing a California program that conditioned welfare benefits on unannounced home visits by investigators from the District Attorney's office. We consider *Wyman* and *Sanchez* next.

WYMAN v. JAMES
400 U.S. 309 (1971)

Mr. Justice BLACKMUN delivered the opinion of the Court.

This appeal presents the issue whether a beneficiary of the [AFDC] program may refuse a home visit by the caseworker without risking the termination of benefits. . . .

Plaintiff Barbara James is the mother of a son, Maurice, who was born in May 1967. They reside in New York City. Mrs. James first applied for AFDC assistance shortly before Maurice's birth. A caseworker made a visit to her apartment at that time without objection. The assistance was authorized.

Two years later, on May 8, 1969, a caseworker wrote Mrs. James that she would visit her home on May 14. Upon receipt of this advice, Mrs. James telephoned the worker that, although she was willing to supply information "reasonable and relevant" to her need for public assistance, any discussion was not to take place at her home. The worker told Mrs. James that she was required by law to visit in her home and that refusal to permit the visit would result in the termination of assistance. Permission was still denied.

On May 13 the City Department of Social Services sent Mrs. James a notice of intent to discontinue assistance because of the visitation refusal. The notice advised the beneficiary of her right to a hearing before a review officer. The hearing was requested and was held on May 27. Mrs. James appeared with an attorney at that hearing. They continued to refuse permission for a worker to visit the James home, but again expressed willingness to cooperate and to permit visits elsewhere. The review officer ruled that the refusal was a proper ground for the termination of assistance. His written decision stated:

> The home visit which Mrs. James refuses to permit is for the purpose of determining if there are any changes in her situation that might affect her eligibility to continue to receive Public Assistance, or that might affect the amount of such assistance, and to see if there are any social services which the Department of Social Services can provide to the family.

A notice of termination issued on June 2.

Thereupon, without seeking a hearing at the state level, Mrs. James, individually and on behalf of Maurice, and purporting to act on behalf of all other persons similarly situated, instituted the present civil rights suit under 42 U. S. C. § 1983. She alleged the denial of rights guaranteed to her under the First, Third, Fourth, Fifth, Sixth, Ninth, Tenth, and Fourteenth Amendments, and under Subchapters IV and XVI of the Social Security Act and regulations issued thereunder. . . .

When a case involves a home and some type of official intrusion into that home, as this case appears to do, an immediate and natural reaction is one of concern about Fourth Amendment rights and the protection which that Amendment is intended to afford. Its emphasis indeed is upon one of the most precious aspects of personal security in the home: "The right of the people to be secure in their persons, houses, papers, and effects. . . ." This Court has characterized that right as "basic to a free society." And over the years the Court consistently has been most protective of the privacy of the dwelling. . . .

This natural and quite proper protective attitude, however, is not a factor in this case, for the seemingly obvious and simple reason that we are not concerned here with any search by the New York social service agency in the Fourth Amendment meaning of that term. It is true that the governing statute and regulations appear to make mandatory the initial home visit and the subsequent periodic "contacts" (which may include home visits) for the inception and continuance of aid. It is also true that the caseworker's posture in the home visit is perhaps, in a sense, both rehabilitative and investigative. But this latter aspect, we think, is given too broad a character and far more emphasis than it deserves if it is equated with a search in the traditional criminal law context. We note, too, that the visitation in itself is not forced or compelled, and that the beneficiary's denial of permission is not a criminal act. If consent to the visitation is withheld, no visitation takes place. The aid then never begins or merely ceases, as the case may be. There is no entry of the home and there is no search.

If however, we were to assume that a caseworker's home visit, before or subsequent to the beneficiary's initial qualification for benefits, somehow (perhaps because the average beneficiary might feel she is in no position to refuse consent to the visit), and despite its interview nature, does possess some of the characteristics of a search in the traditional sense, we nevertheless conclude that the visit does not fall within the Fourth Amendment's proscription. This is because it does not descend to the level of unreasonableness. It is unreasonableness which is the Fourth Amendment's standard. . . .

There are a number of factors that compel us to conclude that the home visit proposed for Mrs. James is not unreasonable:

1. The public's interest in this particular segment of the area of assistance to the unfortunate is protection and aid for the dependent child whose family requires such aid for that child. The focus is on the *child* and, further, it is on the child who is *dependent*. There is no more worthy object of the public's concern. The dependent child's needs are paramount, and only with hesitancy would we relegate those needs, in the scale of comparative values, to a position secondary to what the mother claims as her rights.

2. The agency, with tax funds provided from federal as well as from state sources, is fulfilling a public trust. The State, working through its qualified welfare agency, has appropriate and paramount interest and concern in seeing and assuring that the intended and proper objects of that tax-produced assistance are the ones who benefit from the aid it dispenses. Surely it is not unreasonable, in the Fourth Amendment sense or in any other sense of that term, that the State have at its command a gentle means, of limited extent and of practical and considerate application, of achieving that assurance.

3. One who dispenses purely private charity naturally has an interest in and expects to know how his charitable funds are utilized and put to work. The public, when it is the provider, rightly expects the same. It might well expect more, because of the trust aspect of public funds, and the recipient, as well as the caseworker, has not only an interest but an obligation.

4. The emphasis of the New York statutes and regulations is upon the home, upon "close contact" with the beneficiary, upon restoring the aid recipient "to a condition of self-support," and upon the relief of his distress. The federal emphasis is no different. It is upon "assistance and rehabilitation," upon maintaining and strengthening family life, and upon "maximum self-support and personal independence consistent with the maintenance of continuing parental care and protection. . . ." It requires cooperation from the state agency upon specified standards and in specified ways. And it is concerned about any possible exploitation of the child.

5. The home visit, it is true, is not required by federal statute or regulation. But it has been noted that the visit is "the heart of welfare administration"; that it affords "a personal, rehabilitative orientation, unlike that of most federal programs"; and that the "more pronounced service orientation" effected by Congress with the 1956 amendments to the Social Security Act "gave redoubled importance to the practice of home visiting."

6. The means employed by the New York agency are significant. Mrs. James received written notice several days in advance of the intended home visit. The date was specified. Privacy is emphasized. The applicant-recipient is made the primary source of information as to eligibility. Outside informational sources, other than public records, are to be consulted only with the beneficiary's consent. Forcible entry or entry under false pretenses or visitation outside working hours or snooping in the home are forbidden. All this minimizes any "burden" upon the homeowner's right against unreasonable intrusion.

7. Mrs. James, in fact, on this record presents no specific complaint of any unreasonable intrusion of her home and nothing that supports an inference that the desired home visit had as its purpose the obtaining of information as to criminal activity. She complains of no proposed visitation at an awkward or retirement hour. She suggests no forcible entry. She refers to no snooping. She describes no impolite or reprehensible conduct of any kind. She alleges only, in general and nonspecific terms, that on previous visits and, on information and belief, on visitation at the home of other aid recipients, "questions concerning personal relationships, beliefs and behavior are raised and pressed which are unnecessary for a determination of continuing eligibility." Paradoxically, this same complaint could be made of a conference held elsewhere than in the home, and yet this is what is sought by Mrs. James. The same complaint could be made of the census taker's questions. What Mrs. James appears to want from the agency that provides her and her infant son with the necessities for life is the right to receive those necessities upon her own informational terms, to utilize the Fourth Amendment as a wedge for imposing those terms, and to avoid questions of any kind. [Ed. note: In a footnote, the court suggests that Mrs. James is demanding, uncooperative, evasive and occasionally belligerent, and "[t]here are indications that all was not always well with the infant Maurice (skull fracture, a dent in the head, a possible rat bite). The picture is a sad and unhappy one."]

8. We are not persuaded, as Mrs. James would have us be, that all information pertinent to the issue of eligibility can be obtained by the agency through an interview at a place other than the home, or, as the District Court majority suggested, by examining a lease or a birth certificate, or by periodic medical examinations, or by interviews with school personnel. Although these secondary sources might be helpful, they would not always assure verification of actual residence or of actual physical presence in the home, which are requisites for AFDC benefits, or of impending medical needs. And, of course, little children, such as Maurice James, are not yet registered in school.

9. The visit is not one by police or uniformed authority. It is made by a caseworker of some training whose primary objective is, or should be, the welfare, not the prosecution, of the aid recipient for whom the worker has profound responsibility. As has already been stressed, the program concerns dependent children and the needy families of those children. It does not deal with crime or with the actual or suspected perpetrators of crime. The caseworker is not a sleuth but rather, we trust, is a friend to one in need.

10. The home visit is not a criminal investigation, does not equate with a criminal investigation, and despite the announced fears of Mrs. James and those who would join her, is not in aid of any criminal proceeding. If the visitation serves to discourage misrepresentation or fraud, such a byproduct of that visit does not impress upon the visit itself a dominant criminal investigative aspect. And if the visit should, by chance, lead to the discovery of fraud and a criminal prosecution should follow, then, even assuming that the evidence discovered upon the home visitation is admissible, an issue upon which we express no opinion, that is a routine and expected fact of life and a consequence no greater than that which necessarily ensues upon any other discovery by a citizen of criminal conduct. . . .

It seems to us that the situation is akin to that where an Internal Revenue Service agent, in making a routine civil audit of a taxpayer's income tax return, asks that the taxpayer produce for the agent's review some proof of a deduction the taxpayer has asserted to his benefit in the computation of his tax. If the taxpayer refuses, there is, absent fraud, only a disallowance of the claimed deduction and a consequent additional tax. The taxpayer is fully within his "rights" in refusing to produce the proof, but in maintaining and asserting those rights a tax detriment results and it is a detriment of the taxpayer's own making. So here Mrs. James has the "right" to refuse the home visit, but a consequence in the form of cessation of aid, similar to the taxpayer's resultant additional tax, flows from that refusal. The choice is entirely hers, and nothing of constitutional magnitude is involved. . . .

Our holding today does not mean, of course, that a termination of benefits upon refusal of a home visit is to be upheld against constitutional challenge under all conceivable circumstances. The early morning mass raid upon homes of welfare recipients is not unknown. But that is not this case. Facts of that kind present another case for another day.

We therefore conclude that the home visitation as structured by the New York statutes and regulations is a reasonable administrative tool; that it serves a valid and proper administrative purpose for the dispensation of the AFDC program; that it is not an unwarranted invasion of personal privacy; and that it violates no right guaranteed by the Fourth Amendment.

Reversed and remanded with directions to enter a judgment of dismissal. . . .

Mr. Justice DOUGLAS, dissenting.

We are living in a society where one of the most important forms of property is government largesse which some call the "new property." [Charles Reich, *The New Property*, 73 Yale L.J. 733 (1964).] The payrolls of government are but one aspect of that "new property." Defense contracts, highway contracts, and the other multifarious forms of contracts are another part. So are subsidies to air, rail, and other carriers. So are disbursements by government for scientific research. So are TV and radio licenses to use the air space which of course is part of the public domain. Our concern here is not with those subsidies but with grants that directly or indirectly implicate the *home life* of the recipients. . . .

Yet almost every beneficiary whether rich or poor, rural or urban, has a "house" — one of the places protected by the Fourth Amendment against "unreasonable searches and seizures." The question in this case is whether receipt of largesse from the government makes the *home* of the beneficiary subject to access by an inspector of the agency of oversight, even though the beneficiary objects to the intrusion and even though the Fourth Amendment's procedure for access to one's *house* or *home* is not followed. The penalty here is not, of course, invasion of the privacy of Barbara James, only her loss of federal or state largesse. That, however, is merely rephrasing the problem. Whatever the semantics, the central question is whether the government by force of its largesse has the power to "buy up" rights guaranteed by the Constitution. But for the assertion of her constitutional right, Barbara James in this case would have received the welfare benefit. . . .

Is a search of her home without a warrant made "reasonable" merely because she is dependent on government largesse?

Judge Skelly Wright has stated the problem succinctly:

> Welfare has long been considered the equivalent of charity and its recipients have been subjected to all kinds of dehumanizing experiences in the government's effort to police its welfare payments. In fact, over half a billion dollars are expended annually for administration and policing in connection with the Aid to Families with Dependent Children program. Why such large sums are necessary for administration and policing has never been adequately explained. No such sums are spent policing the government subsidies granted to farmers, airlines, steamship companies, and junk mail dealers, to name but a few. The truth is that in this subsidy area society has simply adopted a double standard, one for aid to business and the farmer and a different one for welfare.

If the welfare recipient was not Barbara James but a prominent, affluent cotton or wheat farmer receiving benefit payments for not growing crops, would not the approach be different? Welfare in aid of dependent children, like social security and unemployment benefits, has an aura of suspicion. There doubtless are frauds in every sector of public welfare whether the recipient be a Barbara James or someone who is prominent or influential. But constitutional rights — here the privacy of the *home* — are obviously not dependent on the poverty or on the affluence of the beneficiary. It is the precincts of the *home* that the Fourth Amendment protects; and their privacy is as important to the lowly as to the mighty. . . .

It may be that in some tenements one baby will do service to several women and call each one "mom." It may be that other frauds, less obvious, will be perpetrated. But if inspectors want to enter the precincts of the home against the wishes of the lady of the house, they must get a warrant. The need for exigent action as in cases of "hot pursuit" is not present, for the lady will not disappear; nor will the baby.

I would place the same restrictions on inspectors entering the *homes* of welfare beneficiaries as are on inspectors entering the *homes* of those on the payroll of government, or the *homes* of those who contract with the government, or the *homes* of those who work for those having government contracts. The values of the *home* protected by the Fourth Amendment are not peculiar to capitalism as we have known it; they are equally relevant to the new form of socialism which we are entering. Moreover, as the numbers of functionaries and inspectors multiply, the need for protection of the individual becomes indeed more essential if the values of a free society are to remain. . . .

Mr. Justice MARSHALL, whom Mr. Justice BRENNAN joins, dissenting.

Although I substantially agree with its initial statement of the issue in this case, the Court's opinion goes on to imply that the appellee has refused to provide information germane to a determination of her eligibility for AFDC benefits. The record plainly shows, however, that Mrs. James offered to furnish any information that the appellants desired and to be interviewed at any place other than her home. Appellants rejected her offers and terminated her benefits solely on the ground that she refused to permit a home visit. In addition, appellants make no contention that any sort of probable cause exists to suspect appellee of welfare fraud or child abuse.

Simply stated, the issue in this case is whether a state welfare agency can require all recipients of AFDC benefits to submit to warrantless "visitations" of their homes. In answering that question, the majority dodges between constitutional issues to reach a result clearly inconsistent with the decisions of this Court. We are told that there is no search involved in this case; that even if there were a search, it would not be unreasonable; and that even if this were an unreasonable search, a welfare recipient waives her right to object by accepting benefits. I emphatically disagree with all three conclusions. Furthermore, I believe that binding regulations of the Department of Health, Education, and Welfare prohibit appellants from requiring the home visit.

The Court's assertion that this case concerns no search "in the Fourth Amendment meaning of that term" is neither "obvious" nor "simple." . . .

Even if the Fourth Amendment does not apply to each and every governmental entry into the home, the welfare visit is not some sort of purely benevolent inspection. No one questions the motives of the dedicated welfare caseworker. Of course, caseworkers seek to be friends, but the point is that they are also required to be sleuths. The majority concedes that the "visitation" is partially investigative, but claims that this investigative aspect has been given too much emphasis. Emphasis has indeed been given. Time and again, in briefs and at oral argument, appellants emphasized the need to enter AFDC homes to guard against welfare fraud and child abuse, both of which are felonies. The New York statutes provide emphasis by requiring all caseworkers to report any evidence of fraud that a home visit uncovers. And appellants have strenuously emphasized the importance of the visit to provide evidence leading to civil forfeitures including elimination of benefits and loss of child custody. . . .

Conceding for the sake of argument that someone might view the "visitation" as a search, the majority nonetheless concludes that such a search is not unreasonable. However, its mode of reaching that conclusion departs from the entire history of Fourth Amendment case law. Of course, the Fourth Amendment test is reasonableness, but in determining whether a search is reasonable, this Court is not free merely to balance, in a totally ad hoc fashion, any number of subjective factors. An unbroken line of cases holds that, subject to a few narrowly drawn exceptions, any search without a warrant is constitutionally unreasonable. In this case, no suggestion that evidence will disappear, that a criminal will escape, or that an officer will be injured, justifies the failure to obtain a warrant. Instead, the majority asserts what amounts to three state interests that allegedly render this search reasonable. None of these interests is sufficient to carve out a new exception to the warrant requirement.

First, it is argued that the home visit is justified to protect dependent children from "abuse" and "exploitation." These are heinous crimes, but they are not confined to indigent households. Would the majority sanction, in the absence of probable cause, compulsory visits to all American homes for the purpose of discovering child abuse? Or is this Court prepared to hold as a matter of constitutional law that a mother, merely because she is poor, is substantially more likely to injure or exploit her children? Such a categorical approach to an entire class of citizens would be dangerously at odds with the tenets of our democracy.

Second, the Court contends that caseworkers must enter the homes of AFDC beneficiaries to determine eligibility. Interestingly, federal regulations do not require the home visit. In fact, the regulations specify the recipient himself as the primary source of eligibility information thereby rendering an inspection of the home only one of several alternative secondary sources. The majority's implication that a biannual home visit somehow assures the verification of actual residence or actual physical presence in the home strains credulity in the context of urban poverty. Despite the caseworker's responsibility for dependent children, he is not even required to see the children as a part of the home visit. Appellants offer scant explanation for their refusal even to attempt to utilize public records, expenditure receipts, documents such as leases, non-home interviews, personal financial records, sworn declarations, etc. — all sources that governmental agencies regularly accept as adequate to establish eligibility for other public benefits. In this setting, it ill behooves appellants to refuse to utilize informational sources less drastic than an invasion of the privacy of the home.

We are told that the plight of Mrs. James is no different from that of a taxpayer who is required to document his right to a tax deduction, but this analogy is seriously flawed. The record shows that Mrs. James has offered to be interviewed anywhere other than her home, to answer any questions, and to provide any documentation that the welfare agency desires. The agency curtly refused all these offers and insisted on its "right" to pry into appellee's home. Tax exemptions are also governmental "bounty." A true analogy would be an Internal Revenue Service requirement that in order to claim a dependency exemption, a taxpayer *must* allow a specially trained IRS agent to invade the home for the purpose of questioning the occupants and looking for evidence that the exemption is being properly utilized for the benefit of the dependent. If such a system were even proposed, the cries of constitutional outrage would be unanimous.

Appellants offer a third state interest that the Court seems to accept as partial justification for this search. We are told that the visit is designed to rehabilitate, to provide aid. This is strange doctrine indeed. A paternalistic notion that a complaining citizen's constitutional rights can be violated so long as the State is somehow helping him is alien to our Nation's philosophy. More than 40 years ago, Mr. Justice Brandeis warned: "Experience should teach us to be most on our guard to protect liberty when the Government's purposes are beneficent."

Throughout its opinion, the majority alternates between two views of the State's interest in requiring the home visit. First we are told that the State's purpose is benevolent so that no search is involved. Next we are told that the State's need to prevent child abuse and to avoid the misappropriation of welfare funds justifies dispensing with the warrant requirement. But when all the State's purposes are considered at one time, I can only conclude that the home visit is a search and that, absent a warrant, that search is unreasonable.

Although the Court does not agree with my conclusion that the home visit is an unreasonable search, its opinion suggests that even if the visit were unreasonable, appellee has somehow waived her right to object. Surely the majority cannot believe that valid Fourth Amendment consent can be given under the threat of the loss of one's sole means of support. Nor has Mrs. James waived her rights. Had the Court squarely faced the question of whether the State can condition welfare payments on the waiver of clear constitutional rights, the answer would be plain. The decisions of this Court do not support the notion that a State can use welfare benefits as a wedge to coerce "waiver" of Fourth Amendment rights. . . .

In deciding that the homes of AFDC recipients are not entitled to protection from warrantless searches by welfare caseworkers, the Court declines to follow prior case law and employs a rationale that, if applied to the claims of all citizens, would threaten the vitality of the Fourth Amendment. This Court has occasionally pushed beyond established constitutional contours to protect the vulnerable and to further basic human values. I find no little irony in the fact that the burden of today's departure from principled adjudication is placed upon the lowly poor. Perhaps the majority has explained why a commercial warehouse deserves more protection than does this poor woman's home. I am not convinced; and, therefore, I must respectfully dissent.

SANCHEZ v. CITY OF SAN DIEGO

464 F.3d 916 (9th Cir. 2006)

TASHIMA, Circuit Judge.

[San Diego County welfare recipients] contend that the district court erred in concluding that [San Diego] County's welfare eligibility program ("Project 100%"), which requires all welfare applicants to consent to a warrantless home visit as a condition of eligibility, does not violate their rights under the United States Constitution, the California Constitution, or California welfare regulations prohibiting mass and indiscriminate home visits. . . .

In 1997, the San Diego County District Attorney ("D.A.") initiated a program whereby all San Diego County residents who submit welfare applications under California's welfare program ("CalWORKS"), and are not suspected of fraud or ineligibility, are automatically enrolled in Project 100%. The parties are essentially in agreement as to the structure and operation of Project 100%. Under Project 100%, all applicants receive a home visit from an investigator employed by the D.A.'s office. The visit includes a "walk through" to gather eligibility information that is then turned over to eligibility technicians who compare that information with information supplied by the applicant. Specifically, the investigator views items confirming that: (1) the applicant has the amount of assets claimed; (2) the applicant has an eligible dependent child; (3) the applicant lives in California; and (4) an "absent" parent does not live in the residence.

When applicants submit an application for welfare benefits, they are informed that they will be subject to a mandatory home visit in order to verify their eligibility. Applicants are also informed that the home visit must be completed prior to aid being granted, but are not given notice of the exact date and time the visit will occur. The visits are generally made within 10 days of receipt of the application and during regular business hours, unless a different time is required to accommodate an applicant's schedule. The home visits are conducted by investigators from the Public Assistance Fraud Division of the D.A.'s office, who are sworn peace officers with badges and photo identification. The investigators wear plain clothes and do not carry weapons.

The actual home visit consists of two parts: an interview with the applicant regarding information submitted during the intake process, and a "walk through" of the home. The visit takes anywhere from 15 minutes to an hour, with five to 10 minutes generally allocated to the "walk through." If the applicant refuses to allow a home visit, the investigator immediately terminates the visit and reports that the applicant failed to cooperate. This generally results in the denial of benefits. The denial of welfare aid is the only consequence of refusing to allow the home visit; no criminal or other sanctions are imposed for refusing consent.

The "walk through" portion of the home visit is also conducted with the applicant's consent. The applicant is asked to lead the "walk through" and the investigator is trained to look for items in plain view. The investigator will also ask the applicant to view the interior of closets and cabinets, but will only do so with the applicant's express permission. While the investigators are required to report evidence of potential criminal wrongdoing for further investigation and prosecution, there is no evidence that any criminal prosecutions for welfare fraud have stemmed from inconsistencies uncovered during a Project 100% home visit.

Appellants challenge the lawfulness of Project 100% [under numerous federal and state constitutional theories and on state regulatory grounds]. . . .

I. Fourth Amendment Claim

. . . Appellants argue that the warrantless home visits conducted under Project 100% violate the Fourth Amendment's protection against unreasonable searches as it applies to the State of California via the Fourteenth Amendment.

A. The Home Visits Are Not Searches Under the Fourth Amendment

We must first decide the threshold question of whether the home visits qualify as searches within the meaning of the Fourth Amendment. Appellants contend that the home visits are searches because they are highly intrusive and their purpose is to discover evidence of welfare fraud. The Supreme Court, however, has held that home visits for welfare verification purposes are not searches under the Fourth Amendment. . . .

Wyman directly controls the instant case. Here, as in *Wyman*, all prospective welfare beneficiaries are subject to mandatory home visits for the purpose of verifying eligibility, and not as part of a criminal investigation. The investigators conduct an in-home interview and "walk through," looking for inconsistencies between the prospective beneficiary's application and her actual living conditions. As in *Wyman*, the home visits are conducted with the applicant's consent, and if consent is denied, the visit will not occur. Also as in *Wyman*, there is no penalty for refusing to consent to the home visit, other than denial of benefits. The fact that the D.A. investigators who make the Project 100% home visits are sworn peace officers does not cause the home visits to rise to the level of a "search in the traditional criminal law context" because the visits' underlying purpose remains the determination of welfare eligibility.

Therefore, because we are bound by *Wyman*, we conclude that the Project 100% home visits do not qualify as searches within the meaning of the Fourth Amendment.

B. EVEN IF THE HOME VISITS ARE SEARCHES, THEY ARE REASONABLE

"[W]hether a particular search meets the reasonableness standard is judged by balancing its intrusion on the individual's Fourth Amendment interests against its promotion of legitimate governmental interests." The district court found that the Project 100% home visits, even if considered searches, were reasonable under *Wyman*. Although we need not reach the question to decide Appellants' Fourth Amendment challenge, because the home visits do not constitute searches under *Wyman*, we agree with the district court that even if the home visits are searches under the Fourth Amendment, they are reasonable.

1. *Wyman v. James*

In *Wyman*, the Court concluded that the home visits, even if considered a search, were valid under the Fourth Amendment "because [they] did not descend to the level of unreasonableness . . . which is the Fourth Amendment's standard." The Court weighed several factors in balancing the governmental interest in conducting home visits against the intrusion into the welfare applicant's privacy. Relevant to this analysis were: (1) the public's strong interest in the protection of dependent children and ensuring that aid provided from tax revenue reaches its intended and proper recipients; (2) the statute's focus on assistance and rehabilitation; (3) that the home visit was not a criminal investigation and did not involve police or uniformed authority; (4) the visits' procedural safeguards, including providing advanced written notice and prohibiting forced entry or "snooping" within the home; and (5) the serious administrative difficulties posed by a warrant requirement in the welfare context.

Here, as in *Wyman*, the home visits serve the important governmental interests of verifying an applicant's eligibility for welfare benefits and preventing fraud. As the Court acknowledged in *Wyman*, the public has a strong interest in ensuring that aid provided from tax dollars reaches its proper and intended recipients. While the visits in this case differ from those in *Wyman* in that they are conducted by peace officers, this distinction does not transform a Project 100% visit into a "search in the traditional criminal law context." The investigators are not uniformed officers and will only enter the applicant's home with consent. Although the investigators will report any evidence of criminal activity for potential prosecution, this is not the underlying purpose of the visit, and no criminal prosecutions for welfare fraud have stemmed from inconsistencies uncovered during a Project 100% home visit since the program's inception in 1997 [citing *Wyman* for the proposition that "[i]f the visitation serves to discourage misrepresentation or fraud, such a byproduct of that visit does not impress upon the visit itself a dominant criminal investigative aspect. And if the visit should, by chance, lead to the discovery of fraud and a criminal prosecution should follow, . . . that is a routine and expected fact of life and a consequence no greater than that which necessarily ensues upon any other discovery by a citizen of criminal conduct."].

The Project 100% home visits also have many of the same procedural safe-guards that the *Wyman* Court found significant. Applicants are given notice that they will be subject to a mandatory home visit and visits generally occur only during normal business hours. When the investigators arrive to conduct the visit, they must ask for consent to enter the home. If the applicant does not consent to the visit, or withdraws consent at anytime during the visit, the visit will not begin or will immediately be terminated, as the case may be. . . .

[B]ecause the Project 100% visits serve an important governmental interest, are not criminal investigations, occur with advance notice and the applicant's consent, and alleviate the serious administrative difficulties associated with wel-fare eligibility verification, we hold that the home visits are reasonable under the Supreme Court's decision in *Wyman*.

FISHER, Circuit Judge, dissenting.

I cannot agree with the majority's conclusion that Wyman v. James "directly controls" our resolution of this case. . . .

I find the majority's analysis troubling in several respects. To begin, the majority admittedly draws a "fine line" between searches to determine eligibility and those aimed at investigating fraud. In practice, the distinction is one without a difference. In verifying eligibility, fraud investigators — as their job title suggests — necessarily are investigating potential fraud through their enforce-ment of welfare laws and regulations. Indeed, unlike in *Wyman*, the investigators testified that as peace officers they have a duty to — and do — look for and report evidence of crimes. Thus, we do not, as the majority suggests, deal here with a visitation that "serves to discourage misrepresentation or fraud" as a mere "*byproduct* of that visit," as was the case in *Wyman*.

At the same time, the majority overlooks a key distinction between the New York home visits and those carried out by the County of San Diego, namely, that the Project 100% home visits have only a minimal, if any, rehabilitative function. The record reveals that the program is operated *exclusively* by the District Attorney's Public Assistance Fraud Division, which is the County's Special Investigative Unit (SIU), as an "early fraud prevention *and detection* program;" the County's welfare agency does not exercise any supervisory responsibility over the program. Thus, whereas in *Wyman* the home visits were conducted by social workers who had "profound responsibility" for the aid recipient, here the visits are conducted by agents of the district attorney charged only with verifying welfare eligibility and detecting fraud using investi-gative techniques. . . .

Finally, it is far from clear that Project 100% forbids "snooping," as was the case in *Wyman*. When walking through the welfare applicant's home, a fraud investigator may request to look at the contents of bedrooms, closets, kitchens, bathrooms, medicine cabinets and drawers in search of evidence of ineligibility or fraud. The majority reasons that because consent is required, the investigator's activity "cannot fairly be characterized as 'snooping.'" But obtaining consent to snoop cannot change the nature of the ensuing conduct — *snooping* — any more than obtaining consent to search changes the nature of the *search* that follows. The question is whether looking in medicine cabinets, laundry baskets, closets and drawers for evidence of welfare fraud — even with consent — constitutes snooping. I doubt my colleagues in the majority would disagree that an IRS auditor's asking to look in such places within their own homes to verify the number of dependents living at home would constitute snooping.

Far from having "direct application," *Wyman* is factually distinguishable from the case at bar, and does not preclude our holding that the home visits carried out by the County of San Diego are unreasonable searches under the Fourth Amendment. . . .

In the context of welfare benefits, where government aid is an important means of providing food, shelter and clothing to a family, the coercive nature of the home visit renders the notion of consent effectively meaningless. Although *Wyman* stated that "nothing of constitutional magnitude is involved" when a welfare aid recipient's benefits are terminated as a consequence of the plaintiff's refusal to undergo a home visit, the Court there was not faced with a situation in which coercion may have played a role. Indeed, *Wyman*'s statement that the plaintiff's "choice is entirely hers" suggests that the Court did not believe coercion was an issue at all. Yet the Court has made clear since *Wyman* that the Fourth Amendment requires that consensual searches be voluntary and uncoerced. Under the circumstances of this case, one cannot reasonably expect an individual who has made the difficult—and often desperate—decision to apply for welfare aid to then deny consent to a mandatory home visit when the consequence is denial of the application. Where such coercion is present, the option to refuse the home visit or the walk-through cannot reduce the intrusion on the applicant's privacy any more than it can reduce the applicant's privacy expectation in the home. . . .

NOTES AND QUESTIONS

1. *Wyman* was viewed at the time by supporters and detractors alike as a major setback for welfare rights. Since *Wyman*, the Supreme Court has held repeatedly that fraud investigations outside the welfare context constitute searches for Fourth Amendment purposes, yet the *Sanchez* majority says "a person's relationship with the state can reduce that person's expectation of privacy even within the sanctity of the home." One leading scholar has described this as "reverse scrutiny when those affected are poor by refusing to apply the normal heightened scrutiny otherwise associated with various existing constitutional protections." Julie A. Nice, *No Scrutiny Whatsoever: Deconstitutionalization of Poverty Law, Dual Rules of Law, and Dialogic Default*, 35 Fordham Urb. L.J. 629 (2008). The majority in *Sanchez* stresses that an applicant's consent is required before and during the home visit. The dissent questions whether consent can truly be given under such circumstances. Do you think that welfare recipients are in a position to refuse mandatory home visits, regardless of their purpose?

2. The *Sanchez* court also rejected state constitutional and statutory claims raised by welfare recipients. In considering the applicability of a 1967 California Supreme Court case—which struck down as unconstitutional Alameda County's "Operation Bedcheck," a series of "suspicionless, unannounced early-morning raids of the homes of the county's welfare recipients in order to detect the presence of unauthorized males" (Parrish v. Civil Serv. Comm'n, 66 Cal. 2d 260 (1967))—the court distinguished the public

nature of those mass raids with Project 100%'s "orderly daytime administrative searches conducted to verify welfare eligibility and prevent fraud." The court similarly dismissed the plaintiff's argument that the home visits violated a state welfare regulation prohibiting "[m]ass or indiscriminate home visits" on the ground that such visits are only prohibited when they are based on a suspicion of fraud as opposed to an eligibility determination. What are the policy arguments for and against these distinctions?

3. The *Sanchez* dissent asks whether the majority thinks an IRS auditor conducting a home visit to verify the number of dependents would constitute snooping. Should the IRS condition receipt of the dependent tax exemption (deduction) on a home visit? What about receipt of Social Security or Veterans' benefits? Farm subsidies? Your student loans? Does your answer depend on the distinction between public assistance and tax breaks or whether the recipient has "earned" the welfare or subsidy?

4. Commentators defended San Diego's Project 100% on efficiency grounds — it gets benefits to needy people quickly and "eliminates waste, fraud and abuse." Charles "Cully" Stimson, *San Diego Prosecutors Devise Welfare Fraud Strategy*, Heritage Found. (Jan. 4, 2008). Scholars made similar arguments prior to *Sanchez*. Asserting that "welfare fraud is an epidemic," Professor Eric Luna argued that home visits balance "the public's right to prevent fraud and the [welfare] recipient's constitutional right to be free from unreasonable searches and seizures." Erik G. Luna, *Welfare Fraud and the Fourth Amendment*, 24 Pepp. L. Rev. 1235 (1997). Luna contends that reducing fraud helps worthy recipients by preserving program resources, increasing program integrity, and broadening public support. How would you balance program integrity and public support with values such as individual privacy?

b. Fingerprinting and Drug Testing

As a result of the 1996 welfare reform bill, states were required — or given broad latitude — to implement additional fraud prevention programs. Many states began mandating fingerprinting and other biometric imaging measures of TANF and food stamp recipients. Under welfare reform, states were also permitted to test and sanction welfare recipients for drug use. Several states piloted such programs, including Michigan. A federal district court enjoined the Michigan welfare agency "from conducting suspicionless drug testing of . . . applicants or recipients, such a practice being an unconstitutional infringement of Plaintiffs' Fourth Amendment rights." Marchwinski v. Howard, 113 F. Supp. 2d 1134 (E.D. Mich. 2000).

The district court's injunction was initially overturned by a three-judge panel of the U.S. Court of Appeals for the Sixth Circuit, which — citing a Supreme Court case upholding random drug testing of employees in safety-sensitive positions — observed that "welfare assistance is a very heavily regulated area of public life with a correspondingly diminished expectation of privacy." Some lauded the decision as good for children. Jason Turner, *States and Advocates for Children Should Hail Sixth Circuit Court Decision Allowing Drug Testing of Welfare Recipients*, Heritage Found. (Feb. 19, 2003). The district court's injunction, however, was reinstated when an en banc panel of the U.S. Court of Appeals for the Sixth Circuit evenly split on the issue. *Marchwinkski*, 113 F. Supp. 2d 1134, *rev'd*, 309 F.3d 330 (6th Cir. 2002), *aff'd by an equally divided court*, 60 F. App'x 601 (6th Cir. 2003) (en banc).

Since 2011, legislators in several dozen states have introduced laws to drug-test recipients of public assistance, including TANF, SNAP, Medicaid, unemployment insurance, and other local benefits. As of 2013, nine states had enacted laws requiring drug testing of TANF recipients, and two—Florida and Georgia—imposed drug testing as an application requirement. In February 2013, the U.S. Court of Appeals for the Eleventh Circuit ruled on a challenge to Florida's drug-testing program in the case excerpted next.

LEBRON v. FLA. DEP'T OF CHILDREN & FAMILIES
710 F.3d 1202 (11th Cir. 2013)

BARKETT, Circuit Judge.

The Secretary of the Florida Department of Children and Families ("State") appeals from the district court's order enjoining the State of Florida from requiring Luis W. Lebron to submit to a suspicionless drug test pursuant to Section 414.0652 of the Florida Statutes, as a condition for receipt of government-provided monetary assistance for which he was otherwise qualified.

Lebron is an honorably discharged veteran of the United States Navy, college student, single unmarried father and sole caretaker of his young child. Lebron resides with and also cares for his disabled mother, who subsists on Social Security Disability benefits. In July 2011, Lebron applied for financial assistance benefits for himself and his son through Florida's Temporary Assistance for Needy Families program ("TANF"), which, if he were eligible, would have provided him with a maximum of $241 per month to assist in the support of himself and his child. . . .

Florida's mandatory drug-testing requirement for all TANF applicants was enacted in May 2011. Under the statute, when an individual applies, he is notified that he will be required to submit to and pay for drug testing as a condition of receiving TANF benefits. If the applicant submits to the drug testing and tests negative, the cost of the test will be reimbursed to the applicant through a one-time increase in his TANF benefits. If the applicant tests positive for controlled substances, he is ineligible to receive TANF benefits for one year, but can reapply in six months if he completes a substance abuse treatment program and passes another drug test, both at his own expense.

Although an adult applicant who fails the drug test is ineligible for TANF benefits, the applicant's dependent child may still receive TANF benefits so long as the adult designates an appropriate protective payee to receive the child's benefits. However, the individual who wishes to serve as the protective payee must also submit to and pass mandatory drug testing to receive benefits for the child, even though he is not requesting any TANF benefits for himself.

In addition to the mandatory drug test, applicants are required to sign a release acknowledging their consent to be tested. At the time Lebron applied for TANF benefits, he was notified of Florida's mandatory drug testing requirement and that he was required to sign the release before DCF would allow him to proceed with the application process. Lebron signed the release, completed the application process and was found eligible for TANF benefits. However, he did not submit to the drug test, but instead filed this lawsuit seeking to enjoin the enforcement of Florida's mandatory suspicionless drug testing as a violation of his and all other TANF applicants' Fourth Amendment right to be free from unreasonable searches and seizures.

The district court granted a preliminary injunction against the enforcement of the drug testing statute against Lebron and the State agreed to discontinue its drug testing regime as to all TANF applicants until this litigation is fully resolved. . . .

I. Standard of Review

. . . Here, the State challenges only the district court's conclusion that Lebron has shown a "substantial likelihood of success on the merits" of his claim that Florida's mandatory suspicionless drug testing of TANF applicants violates his Fourth Amendment right against unreasonable searches. Accordingly, in reviewing the district court's grant of the preliminary injunction, we do not resolve the merits of the constitutional claim, but instead address whether the district court abused its discretion in concluding that Lebron is substantially likely to succeed in establishing that Florida's drug testing regime for TANF applicants violates his Fourth Amendment rights.

II. Discussion

. . . [T]he State argues that there is a "special need" to test TANF applicants because TANF funds should not be used for drugs as drug use undermines the program's goals of moving applicants into employment and promoting child welfare and family stability. But this argument, which assumes drug use, begs the question. The question is not whether drug use is detrimental to the goals of the TANF program, which it might be. Instead, the only pertinent inquiry is whether there is a substantial special need for mandatory, suspicionless drug testing of TANF recipients when there is no immediate or direct threat to public safety, when those being searched are not directly involved in the frontlines of drug interdiction, when there is no public school setting where the government has a responsibility for the care and tutelage of its young students, or when there are no dire consequences or grave risk of imminent physical harm as a result of waiting to obtain a warrant if a TANF recipient, or anyone else for that matter, is suspected of violating the law. We conclude that, on this record, the answer to that question of whether there is a substantial special need for mandatory suspicionless drug testing is "no."

As the district court found, the State failed to offer any factual support or to present any empirical evidence of a "concrete danger" of illegal drug use within Florida's TANF population. The evidence in this record does not suggest that the population of TANF recipients engages in illegal drug use or that they misappropriate government funds for drugs at the expense of their own and their children's basic subsistence. The State has presented no evidence that simply because an applicant for TANF benefits is having financial problems, he is also drug addicted or prone to fraudulent and neglectful behavior [noting the burden is on the state to provide such evidence and citing research and data "suggesting that TANF applicants are no more likely than any other recipient of government benefits to misuse funds for drug use or expose their children to drugs."] . . .

There is nothing so special or immediate about the government's interest in ensuring that TANF recipients are drug free so as to warrant suspension of the Fourth Amendment. The only known and shared characteristic of the individuals who would be subjected to Florida's mandatory drug testing program is that they are financially needy families with children. Yet, there is nothing inherent to the condition of being impoverished that supports the conclusion that there is a "concrete danger" that impoverished individuals are prone to drug use or that should drug use occur, that the lives of TANF recipients are "fraught with such risks of injury to others that even a momentary lapse of attention can have disastrous consequences." Thus, the State's argument that it has a special need to ensure that the goals of the TANF program are not jeopardized by the effects of drug use seems to rest on the presumption of unlawful drug use. But the Supreme Court has required that a state must present adequate factual support that there exists a "concrete danger," not simply conjecture that there is a substantial "special need" that cannot be met by ordinary law enforcement methods warranting the drastic action of abrogating an individual's constitutional right to be free from unreasonable government searches.

Moreover none of the State's asserted concerns will be ameliorated by drug testing. While we recognize that Florida has a significant interest in promoting child welfare, the State has presented no evidence that the general welfare of the children in the TANF program is at greater risk absent its drug testing. Nor has the State shown that Florida's children will be better protected because of mandatory drug testing of TANF applicants. As the district court noted, even if a parent tests positive for drugs and is precluded from receiving TANF funds, the TANF program has no impact on the familial and custodial relationships of its would-be participants. . . .

In short, we cannot say that the district court erred in determining that the State failed to meet its burden of showing a substantial special need permitting the suspension of the Fourth Amendment's protections. The simple fact of seeking public assistance does not deprive a TANF applicant of the same constitutional protection from unreasonable searches that all other citizens enjoy. Because we agree with the district court that the State failed to meet its burden in establishing a special need for its mandatory, suspicionless drug testing of TANF applicants, that ends our inquiry into the testing regime's validity for Fourth Amendment purposes, and thus, we need not weigh any competing individual and governmental interests.

We turn then to the State's alternative argument that even if we find no substantial special need supporting Florida's mandatory drug testing of TANF recipients, the drug testing program is still constitutionally valid because it is based on consent. As noted, under Florida's program, an applicant is required to sign an acknowledgment that he or she consents to drug testing. Accordingly, the State argues that because the drug test is administered only to those persons who have consented to the test and because a consented-to search is deemed reasonable, Florida's mandatory drug testing program does not run afoul of the Fourth Amendment.

We cannot say that the district court abused its discretion in concluding that the "State's exaction of consent" failed to render the otherwise unconstitutional drug testing valid for Fourth Amendment purposes. We disagree with the State that the mandatory "consent," which Florida's drug-testing statute makes a condition to the receipt of benefits, is of any constitutional significance. Although a "search conducted pursuant to a valid consent is constitutionally permissible," a valid consent means one which is "in fact, freely and voluntarily given." The State's assertion that the "consent" that is provided by TANF applicants renders the drug testing reasonable for Fourth Amendment purposes is belied by Supreme Court precedent, which has invalidated searches premised on consent where it has been shown that consent "was granted in submission to authority rather than as an understanding and intentional waiver of a constitutional right."

By informing TANF applicants that the drug test is one of many conditions to receiving this government-issued benefit and that the applicant's refusal to give consent means that he is ineligible to receive TANF assistance, the State conveys a message that it has the unfettered lawful authority to require such drug testing — period. But it does not and can only do so upon a showing of individualized suspicion or a special need beyond the need for normal law enforcement, both of which are absent in Florida's drug testing program. Accordingly, a TANF applicant's "consent" to the testing by signing a form waiving his constitutional rights amounts to nothing more than "submission to authority rather than . . . an understanding and intentional waiver of a constitutional right."

We note that even though each of the drug testing regimes in [earlier cases] required the affected employees, students or political office candidates to "consent" to the drug testing in order to maintain employment, participate in school activities or gain access to the ballot, the Supreme Court has never held that such drug testing regimes were constitutionally reasonable because of consent. Instead, every time that the Supreme Court has been asked to address the validity of a government mandated drug testing policy, it has applied the same special needs analysis and reasonableness balancing, whether upholding or rejecting those policies. Simply put, we have no reason to conclude that the constitutional validity of a mandated drug testing regime is satisfied by the fact that a state requires the affected population to "consent" to the testing in order to gain access or retain a desired benefit.

The State's reliance on Wyman v. James to support its contention that the mandatory consent here renders the drug testing reasonable for Fourth Amendment purposes is misplaced. [. . . In *Wyman*], the Court went on to hold that the state welfare worker's home visit was not a search, and thus the Fourth Amendment or any of its requirements or protections did not matter. . . .

In this case, however, the fact that government-mandated drug testing is a search has been well-settled and beyond any debate since the Court's decision in *Skinner* [v. Railway Lab. Execs. Ass'n, 489 U.S. 602 (1989)]. This fundamental difference between the state welfare worker's home visit (which is not a search) and the drug testing at issue here (which is a search) renders *Wyman* inapplicable to the constitutionally significant question of whether the mandated consent that is part of Florida's drug testing regime makes the search reasonable. . . . [B]ecause there was no search, the Court had no reason to decide whether the AFDC recipient's "consent" would have rendered the home visit constitutionally reasonable for purposes of the Fourth Amendment. . . .

Moreover, the mandated "consent" the State relies on here, which is not freely and voluntarily given, runs afoul of the Supreme Court's long-standing admonition that the government "may not deny a benefit to a person on a basis that infringes his constitutionally protected interests." The Court reiterated in a subsequent case that "[u]nder the well-settled doctrine of 'unconstitutional conditions,' the government may not require a person to give up a constitutional right . . . in exchange for a discretionary benefit conferred by the government where the benefit sought has little or no relationship to [the right]." . . .

Here, because the state of Florida cannot drug test TANF applicants absent individualized suspicion or a showing of a governmental substantial special need that outweighs the applicant's privacy rights, it cannot do so indirectly by conditioning the receipt of this government benefit on the applicant's forced waiver of his Fourth Amendment right. . . . The State cannot mandate "consent" to drug testing, which essentially requires a TANF applicant to choose between exercising his Fourth Amendment right against unreasonable searches at the expense of life-sustaining financial assistance for his family or, on the other hand, abandoning his right against unreasonable government searches in order to access desperately needed financial assistance, without unconstitutionally burdening a TANF applicant's Fourth Amendment right to be free from unreasonable searches. Accordingly, we cannot say that the district court abused its discretion in rejecting the State's "consent" argument as a violation of the unconstitutional conditions doctrine. . . .

JORDAN, Circuit Judge, concurring.

. . . I am skeptical about the state's insistence at oral argument that the Fourth Amendment permits the warrantless and suspicionless drug testing of all TANF applicants even if the evidence shows, conclusively and beyond any doubt, that there is 0% drug use in the TANF population. The state's rationale — that such drug testing is permissible because the TANF program seeks to "move people from welfare to work" — proves too much. Every expenditure of state dollars, taxpayers hope, is for the purpose of achieving a desirable social goal. But that does not mean that a state is entitled to require warrantless and suspicionless drug testing of all recipients of state funds (e.g., college students receiving Bright Futures scholarships) to ensure that those funds are not being misused and that policy goals (e.g., the graduation of such students) are being achieved. Constitutionally speaking, the state's position is simply a bridge too far.

NOTES AND QUESTIONS

1. The Eleventh Circuit panel in *Lebron* rejected Florida's analogy of suspicionless drug testing to New York's home visits in *Wyman* because the Supreme Court deemed such visits not to constitute a search for Fourth Amendment purposes. Without mentioning the case, the panel also rejected the Ninth Circuit's reasoning in *Sanchez*, which held that even if San Diego's suspicionless welfare home visits constituted a search, they fell under the "special needs" exception to Fourth Amendment warrant requirements. Why do you think San Diego's home visits represent a special government need but Florida's drug testing does not?

2. Professor Gustafson and others argue that the costs of antifraud efforts outweigh the direct savings. A 2012 study found that Florida's program — in the four months before being enjoined by the federal district court in

Lebron—cost the state more than the benefits it would have paid out to people who failed the test (and the most common reason for failure was marijuana use). Lizette Alvarez, *No Savings Are Found from Welfare Drug Tests* (N.Y. Times, Apr. 18, 2012), at A14. Policymakers who favor drug testing argue that they aim primarily to deter fraud rather than detect it, but statistics suggest that measures such as fingerprinting also deter eligible families from applying. Should antifraud programs be required to pay for themselves through direct savings or are other public values at stake? Is it reasonable for some of the savings to come from discouraging eligible families from applying for benefits?

3. By 2011, only California, Arizona, and New York City still required fingerprinting for SNAP. Effective January 1, 2012, California repealed the requirement, and in his 2012 State of the State speech, New York Governor Andrew Cuomo said:

> For all of our progress, there are still basic wrongs to right. There is never an excuse for letting any child in New York go to bed hungry. Statewide, 1 in 6 children live in homes without enough food on the table. Yet 30 percent of new Yorkers eligible for food stamps—over 1.4 million people—do not receive them, leaving over $1 billion in federal funds unclaimed every year. We must increase participation in the food stamp program, remove barriers to participation, and eliminate the stigma associated with this program. And we must stop fingerprinting for food.

Governor Cuomo's administration ended the practice in New York City by issuing new regulations effective November 1, 2012. What in his message suggests why many states continue to fingerprint for TANF, which reaches fewer than 5 million people, but not for SNAP, which reaches 47 million people?

B.   CRIMINALIZATION AND POVERTY

As discussed above, people living in poverty face disproportionate exposure to criminal or quasi-criminal sanction through homelessness or participation in public housing and welfare programs. In this section, we will consider the long shadow cast by the criminal justice system in low-income communities and communities of color, including significant limitations on access to social and economic goods beyond public benefits.

Mass incarceration has put millions of Americans behind bars, but the vast majority of state and federal inmates are released back into their communities. People with criminal records—even after paying their debt to society—face legal and extralegal barriers to employment, housing, education, and civic participation. In her book *The New Jim Crow* (2010), scholar Michelle Alexander notes:

> [M]ore African American adults are under correctional control today—in prison or jail, on probation or parole—than were enslaved in 1850, a decade before the Civil War began. . . . More are disenfranchised today than in 1870, the year the

Fifteenth Amendment was ratified prohibiting laws that explicitly deny the right to vote on the basis of race.

Alexander goes on to compare the collateral consequences of mass incarceration to the post–Civil War South: "Young black men today may be just as likely to suffer discrimination in employment, housing, public benefits, and jury service as a black man in the Jim Crow era—discrimination that is perfectly legal, because it is based on one's criminal record." Further, the criminal justice system has increasingly been used to enforce the nation's immigration laws, resulting in the detention and deportation of hundreds of thousands of undocumented immigrants each year. This section explores mass incarceration, the collateral consequences of criminalization, and the growing intersection between criminal law and immigration policy.

1. Mass Incarceration

The number of adults under correctional supervision in the United States—including in jails and prisons and on parole or probation—skyrocketed from 1.8 million (about 1.1 percent of the population) in 1980 to 7.2 million (about 3.1 percent of the population) in 2009. In particular, Black men disproportionately suffer under the phenomenon of mass incarceration. According to criminologist Jonathan Simon, "[t]he odds of an African American man going to prison today are higher than the odds he will go to college, get married, or go into the military." Jonathan Simon, *Governing Through Crime: How the War on Crime Transformed American Democracy and Created a Culture of Fear* (2007).

At the same time, there is increasing recognition by policymakers that mass incarceration has come at too high a cost in human and economic terms. As we will see next, all three branches of government and both political parties have begun to look for ways to reverse the worst excesses of several decades of tough-on-crime rhetoric and practice.

MICHELLE ALEXANDER, *THE NEW JIM CROW* (2010)

This, in brief, is how the system works: The War on Drugs is the vehicle through which extraordinary numbers of black men are forced into the cage. The entrapment occurs in three distinct phases. . . . The first stage is the roundup. Vast numbers of people are swept into the criminal justice system by the police, who conduct drug operations primarily in poor communities of color. They are rewarded in cash—through drug forfeiture laws and federal grant programs—for rounding up as many people as possible, and they operate unconstrained by constitutional rules of procedure that once were considered inviolate. Police can stop, interrogate, and search anyone they choose for drug investigations, provided they get "consent." Because there is no meaningful check on the exercise of police discretion, racial biases are granted free rein. In fact, police are allowed to rely on race as a factor in selecting whom to stop and search (even though people of color are no more likely to be guilty of drug crimes than whites)—effectively guaranteeing that those who are swept into the system are primarily black and brown.

The conviction marks the beginning of the second phase: the period of formal control. Once arrested, defendants are generally denied meaningful legal representation and pressured to plead guilty whether they are or not. Prosecutors are free to "load up" defendants with extra charges, and their decisions cannot be challenged for racial bias. Once convicted, due to the drug war's harsh sentencing laws, drug offenders in the United States spend more time under the criminal justice system's formal control—in jail or prison, on probation or parole—than drug offenders anywhere else in the world. While under formal control, virtually every aspect of one's life is regulated and monitored by the system, and any form of resistance or disobedience is subject to swift sanction. This period of control may last a lifetime, even for those convicted of extremely minor, nonviolent offenses, but the vast majority of those swept into the system are eventually released. They are transferred from their prison cells to a much larger, invisible cage.

The final stage has been dubbed by some advocates as the period of invisible punishment. This term, first coined by Jeremy Travis, is meant to describe the unique set of criminal sanctions that are imposed on individuals after they step outside the prison gates, a form of punishment that operates largely outside of public view and takes effect outside the traditional sentencing framework. These sanctions are imposed by operation of law rather than decisions of a sentencing judge, yet they often have a greater impact on one's life course than the months or years one actually spends behind bars. These laws operate collectively to ensure that the vast majority of convicted offenders will never integrate into mainstream, white society. They will be discriminated against, legally, for the rest of their lives—denied employment, housing, education, and public benefits. Unable to surmount these obstacles, most will eventually return to prison and then be released again, caught in a closed circuit of perpetual marginality.

In recent years, advocates and politicians have called for greater resources devoted to the problem of "prisoner re-entry," in view of the unprecedented numbers of people who are released from prison and returned to their communities every year. While the terminology is well-intentioned, it utterly fails to convey the gravity of the situation facing prisoners upon their release. People who have been convicted of felonies almost never truly re-enter the society they inhabited prior to their conviction. Instead, they enter a separate society, a world hidden from public view, governed by a set of oppressive and discriminatory rules and laws that do not apply to everyone else. They become members of an undercaste—an enormous population of predominantly black and brown people who, because of the drug war, are denied basic rights and privileges of American citizenship and are permanently relegated to an inferior status. This is the final phase, and there is no going back.

***

In 2011, a sharply divided U.S. Supreme Court held that California's prison system was unconstitutionally overcrowded and upheld a lower court–ordered inmate reduction in the nation's single-largest prison system. Brown v. Plata, 131 S. Ct. 1910 (2011). A commentator considers the implications of *Plata* for the future of mass incarceration.

MARIE GOTTSCHALK, *PRISON OVERCROWDING AND BROWN v. PLATA*

The New Republic (June 8, 2011)

Today the United States is the world's warden, incarcerating more people than any other country. With just 5 percent of the world's population, it has 25 percent of its prisoners. Since the 1970s, the United States has built the largest penal system in the world to accommodate a sixfold increase in its inmate population. But what happens behind its prison walls generally remains far removed from public consciousness. In this context, the Supreme Court's landmark decision in Brown v. Plata last month, which declared that the degrading and inhumane conditions in California's grossly overcrowded prisons are unconstitutional, was an exceptional moment when the prison wall was briefly breached.

Of course, Brown v. Plata does not mark the beginning of the end of mass incarceration in the United States, nor of the abusive conditions that proliferate in U.S. prisons and jails. Unlike the landmark prisoners' rights cases of the 1960s and 1970s, this decision is unlikely to spur many successful copycat lawsuits to impose prison population caps and revitalize the courts as a major forum to challenge abusive prison conditions. The Prison Litigation Reform Act (PLRA), enacted by Congress in 1996 to greatly constrict prisoners' access to the courts and to reduce the judiciary's role in monitoring the penal system, continues to present formidable obstacles for inmates seeking to challenge their conditions of confinement. For those few cases that successfully navigate the PLRA and make it into the courts, the legal process is long and protracted. Remarkably, the U.S. prison and jail population has more than doubled since 1990, the year that one of the two lawsuits eventually consolidated in Brown v. Plata was initially filed.

Moreover, Brown v. Plata is not even likely to spur major reductions in California's inmate population any time soon. This is because the Supreme Court conceded great latitude to the Golden State in how to reduce overcrowding in its prisons and by when. State officials could choose to release some prisoners early. But they could also address the population cap affirmed by the Supreme Court by sending more prisoners to out-of state penal facilities or to county jails in California. Or California could simply build more prisons.

So why, then, is this a landmark decision with enormous implications for the future course of penal policy reform in the United States? More so than many other Supreme Court decisions, Brown v. Plata was as much a political statement as a legal one. It did not render the PLRA restrictions on challenging the conditions of confinement through the courts any less arduous. But it did pry open some important political space that could help incubate political solutions to the problem of mass incarceration in the United States.

The first way in which the Court opened up some political space for prison reform was by making the abhorrent conditions in California's prisons strikingly visible. In the nineteenth century, prisons opened their doors to the public and were popular destinations for gawking domestic and foreign tourists. In the 1960s and early 1970s, prison memoirs and accounts of life behind bars regularly turned up on best-seller lists. Today, however, the U.S. penal system is distinctive not only because of its huge size, but also because of its relative invisibility — leaving aside television shows like Oz, which contribute to a grossly distorted view of what is at stake in mass incarceration. The hundreds of prisons and jails that dot rural America and the desolate outskirts of cities, the 2.4 million men and women currently locked up, the 750,000 former offenders released from prison each year with stunted life chances, and the struggles of the millions of children with an incarcerated mother or father tend to leave little trace on the wider public consciousness.

Justice Anthony M. Kennedy, writing for the majority in this acrimonious 5-4 decision, graphically catalogued the appalling conditions in California's penal system, which operates at about 200 percent of capacity: as many as 50 sick inmates at a time held in 12 by 20 foot cages for up to five hours as they await medical treatment; as many as 54 prisoners sharing a single toilet; year-long waits for mental health treatment; a suicide rate nearly twice the national average for prisoners; a needless death every six to seven days because of delayed or inadequate medical care; and the "dry cages," where suicidal prisoners are kept in telephone booth-sized enclosures without toilets. In case words were not enough, Kennedy appended to his decision photos of the "dry cages" and of a gymnasium-style room crammed with dozens of prisoners and their bunk beds. This was a rare instance where the Court turned to visual evidence to bolster a decision.

The second way in which the Court's decision may prove important is its assiduous efforts to bring wider perceptions of the public safety effects of incarceration into better alignment with the latest social science research. In the decades-long prison build-up, penal expertise has been sidelined for the most part in public debates over crime and punishment. In an important departure, Kennedy showcased key findings of leading experts on crime and punishment about the association between mass incarceration and public safety. Kennedy noted that several states have successfully cut their prison populations without seeing their crime rates escalate. He also highlighted other important research findings, including that prisons might actually be criminogenic. As many experts on crime have noted, mass incarceration may actually increase the crime rate because imprisonment severs inmates' ties to their jobs, families, and communities, expands opportunities for criminal networking, and subjects inmates to overcrowded and abusive conditions.

But if Brown v. Plata gives politicians in California some political cover to begin charting a new course for penal reform in the Golden State, what is still lacking in California and elsewhere is a political movement that can transcend the current political climate, which remains deeply and reflexively punitive. As Kennedy made clear in his decision, absent a political push for reform neither this ruling nor others by the courts are likely to be the major catalyst to reverse the prison boom or ameliorate abusive prison conditions. The "constitutional violations in conditions of confinement are rarely susceptible of simple or straightforward solutions," Kennedy explained. "In addition to overcrowding the failure of California's prisons to provide adequate medical and mental health care may be ascribed to chronic and worsening budget short-falls, a lack of political will in favor of reform, inadequate facilities, and systemic administrative failures," he continued.

As of yet, no factor, including the current fiscal crises in the states, has provided sufficient political impetus for comprehensive penal reform to slash the inmate population. California, for instance, has been teetering on the brink of fiscal and social disaster for several years. Yet the state has been unable or unwilling to pursue sensible and proven penal reforms to reduce its prison population in ways that do not seriously jeopardize public safety. Indeed, over the past three decades, the Golden State has gone from spending five dollars on higher education for every dollar spent on corrections to almost a dead-heat on spending. And yet California still holds fast to the toughest three-strikes law in the nation. [In November 2012, California voters approved Proposition 36, which tempered the state's three strikes law by requiring that a third felony conviction be of a more serious or violent nature.]

Moreover, recent attempts at reform have fallen flat. California voters soundly rejected a ballot initiative in 2008 that would have expanded alternative sentences for nonviolent drug offenders and saved billions of dollars. Governor Arnold Schwarzenegger and four former governors opposed this measure, including Jerry Brown, who was then attorney general and is now once again governor. And a legislative proposal in 2009 to release some nonviolent offenders in response to the federal lawsuit ultimately decided by Brown v. Plata created a political firestorm. A significantly weaker bill eventually passed the state assembly without a vote to spare. One assemblyman opposed to the measure warned: "We might as well set off a nuclear bomb in California with what we are doing with this bill."

Brown v. Plata has unleashed comparable over-the-top law-and-order rhetoric, beginning with the Supreme Court justices who dissented from this decision. They were dismissive of leading social science evidence that prison populations could be lowered without adversely affecting public safety. Justice Samuel A. Alito denounced what he misleadingly characterized as "the premature release of approximately *46,000 criminals — the equivalent of three Army divisions*." (Yes, the italics are his.) He charged that the Court was "gambling with the safety of the people of California" and that the result would likely be "a grim roster of victims."

Mass incarceration in the United States is the result of a complex set of political, institutional, and economic developments. No single factor explains the unprecedented rise in the U.S. incarceration rate, and no single factor will reverse the prison boom. What is needed is a broad-based political movement that focuses not just on the economic burden of the penal system, but also on how the massive carceral state rests on stark racial and other inequities and is itself a threat to public safety. Without such a movement, it will not be possible to make deep and sustainable cuts in the incarcerated population and to address the needs of the individuals, families, and communities decimated by the decades-long build-up of the carceral state. One can only hope that Brown v. Plata proves an important first step.

NOTES AND QUESTIONS

1. Professor Alexander's invocation of Jim Crow to explain current conditions for African Americans has been the subject of much debate. Professor James Forman has suggested that:

    [while Professor Alexander and others] have effectively drawn attention to the injustices created by a facially race-neutral system that severely ostracizes offenders and stigmatizes young, poor black men as criminals . . . , the Jim Crow analogy leads to a distorted view of mass incarceration. The analogy presents an incomplete account of mass incarceration's historical origins, fails to consider black attitudes toward crime and punishment, ignores violent crimes while focusing almost exclusively on drug crimes, obscures class distinctions within the African American community, and overlooks the effects of mass incarceration on other racial groups. Finally, the Jim Crow analogy diminishes our collective memory of the Old Jim Crow's particular harms.

> James Forman, *Racial Critiques of Mass Incarceration: Beyond the New Jim Crow*, 87 N.Y.U. L. Rev. 21 (2012).

2. As *Plata* worked its way through the courts, California undertook "realignment" to shift inmates convicted of lower-level, nonviolent, non-sex crimes from state prison to county custody and supervision. The process is ongoing, but some observers have raised concerns about how—with fewer inmates centralized in state prisons—advocates will monitor jail conditions in the state's 58 counties. *See* Margo Schlanger, Plata v. Brown *and Realignment: Jails, Prisons, Courts, and Politics*, 48 Harv. C.R.-C.L. L. Rev. 165 (2013).

3. The dissent in *Plata* warned of "the inevitable murders, robberies, and rapes to be committed by the released inmates." While it is too early to assess the impact of realignment on crime rates, others have criticized the longstanding mismatch between local policing, prosecution, and sentencing decisions on the one hand and state incarceration costs on the other. W. David Ball, *Tough on Crime (on the State's Dime): How Violent Crime Does Not Drive California Counties' Incarceration Rates—And Why It Should*, 28 Ga. St. U. L. Rev. 987 (2012). Professor Ball identifies large disparities in county practices that have a direct impact on the state prison population and costs. Do you think incarceration rates would decrease if local jurisdictions could no longer pass along most or all of the costs to the state?

2. Collateral Consequences of a Criminal Record

Mass incarceration has done more than put millions of Americans behind bars. Once released from prisons and jails, people with criminal records face significant and persistent barriers to employment, housing, education, and civic participation. Even when incarceration is not involved—for example, for misdemeanor and other less serious offenses—the mere fact of a criminal record can have persistent consequences.

The negative impact of criminal records has increased with their pervasiveness. Security concerns post-9/11 have heightened the use of criminal background checks by government, employers, landlords, and others. Advances in technology have permitted the unprecedented production, aggregation, and sharing of criminal records. And "tough on crime" policies at the state and federal level have expanded the legal bases for discriminating against people with criminal records.

We consider next the relationship between criminal records and inequality.

BRUCE WESTERN & BECKY PETTIT, *INCARCERATION AND SOCIAL INEQUALITY*

139 Daedalus 8 (2010)

The influence of the penal system on social and economic disadvantage can be seen in the economic and family lives of the formerly incarcerated. The social inequality produced by mass incarceration is sizable and enduring for three main reasons: it is invisible, it is cumulative, and it is intergenerational. The inequality is invisible in the sense that institutionalized populations commonly lie outside our official accounts of economic well-being. Prisoners, though drawn from the lowest rungs in society, appear in no measures of poverty or unemployment. As a result, the full extent of the disadvantage of groups with high incarceration rates is underestimated. The inequality is cumulative because the social and economic penalties that flow from incarceration are accrued by those who already have the weakest economic opportunities. Mass incarceration thus deepens disadvantage and forecloses mobility for the most marginal in society. Finally, carceral inequalities are intergenerational, affecting not just those who go to prison and jail but their families and children, too. . . .

Class inequalities in incarceration are reflected in the very low educational levels of those in prison and jail. The legitimate labor market opportunities for men with no more than a high school education have deteriorated as the prison population has grown, and prisoners themselves are drawn overwhelmingly from the least educated. State prisoners average just a tenth grade education, and about 70 percent have no high school diploma.

Disparities of race, class, gender, and age have produced extraordinary rates of incarceration among young African-American men with little schooling. . . . These incarceration rates provide only a snapshot of a point in time. We can also examine the lifetime chance of incarceration — that is, the chance that someone will go to prison at some point in his or her life. This cumulative risk of incarceration is important if serving time in prison confers an enduring status that affects life chances after returning to free society. The lifetime risk of imprisonment describes how many people are at risk of these diminished life chances.

The ubiquity of penal confinement in the lives of young African American men with little schooling is historically novel, emerging only in the last decade. However, this new reality is only half the story of understanding the significance of mass incarceration in America. The other half of the story concerns the effects of incarceration on social and economic inequality. The inequalities produced by contemporary patterns of incarceration have three characteristics: the inequalities associated with incarceration invisible to our usual accounting of the economic well-being of the population; the inequality is cumulative, deepening the disadvantage of the most marginalized men in society; and finally, the inequality is intergenerational, transmitting the penalties of a prison record from one generation to the next. Because the characteristic inequalities produced by the American prison boom are invisible, cumulative, and intergenerational, they are extremely enduring, sustained over life times and passed through families.

Invisible Inequality. The inequality created by incarceration is often invisible to the mainstream of society because incarceration is concentrated and segregative. We have seen that steep racial and class disparities in incarceration have produced a generation of social outliers whose collective experience is wholly different from the rest of American society. The extreme concentration of incarceration rates is compounded by the obviously segregative function of the penal system, which often relocates people to far-flung facilities distant from their communities and families. As a result, people in prison and jail are disconnected from the basic institutions — households and the labor market — that dominate our common understanding and measurement of the population. The

Table 1

Cumulative Risk of Imprisonment by Age Thirty to Thirty-Four for Men Born from 1945 to 1949 and 1975 to 1979, by Educational Attainment and Race/Ethnicity

	All	*High school dropouts*	*High school/GED**	*College*
1945-1949 cohort				
White	1.4	3.8	1.5	0.4
Black	10.4	14.7	11.0	5.3
Latino	2.8	4.1	2.9	1.1
1975-1979 cohort				
White	5.4	28.0	6.2	1.2
Black	26.8	68.0	21.4	6.6
Latino	12.2	19.6	9.2	3.4

*Denotes completed high school or equivalency.

Source: Becky Pettit, Bryan Sykes & Bruce Western, *Technical Report on Revised Population Estimates and NLSY79 Analysis Tables for the Pew Public Safety and Mobility Project* (Harvard University, 2009).

segregation and social concentration of incarceration thus help conceal its effects. This fact is particularly important for public policy because in assessing the social and economic well-being of the population, the incarcerated fraction is frequently overlooked, and inequality is underestimated as a result.

The idea of invisible inequality is illustrated by considering employment rates as they are conventionally measured by the Current Population Survey, the large monthly labor force survey conducted by the Census Bureau.

The negative effects of incarceration, even among men with very poor economic opportunities to begin with, are related to the strong negative perceptions employers have of job seekers with criminal records. Devah Pager's experimental research has studied these employer perceptions by sending pairs of fake job seekers to apply for real jobs. In each pair, one of the job applicants was randomly assigned a resume indicating a criminal record (a parole officer is listed as a reference), and the "criminal" applicant was instructed to check the box on the job application indicating he had a criminal record. A criminal record was found to reduce callbacks from prospective employers by around 50 percent, an effect that was larger for African Americans than for whites.

Incarceration may reduce economic opportunities in several ways. The conditions of imprisonment may promote habits and behaviors that are poorly suited to the routines of regular work. Time in prison means time out of the labor force, depleting the work experience of the incarcerated compared to their non-incarcerated counterparts. The stigma of a criminal conviction may also repel employers who prefer job applicants with clean records. Pager's audit study offers clear evidence for the negative effects of criminal stigma. Employers, fearing legal liability or even just unreliability, are extremely reluctant to hire workers with criminal convictions.

A simple picture of the poor economic opportunities of the formerly incarcerated is given by the earnings mobility of men going to prison compared to other disadvantaged groups.

Intergenerational Inequality. Finally, the effects of the prison boom extend also to the families of those who are incarcerated. Through the prism of research on

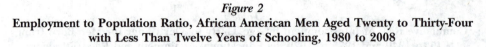

Figure 2
**Employment to Population Ratio, African American Men Aged Twenty to Thirty-Four
with Less Than Twelve Years of Schooling, 1980 to 2008**

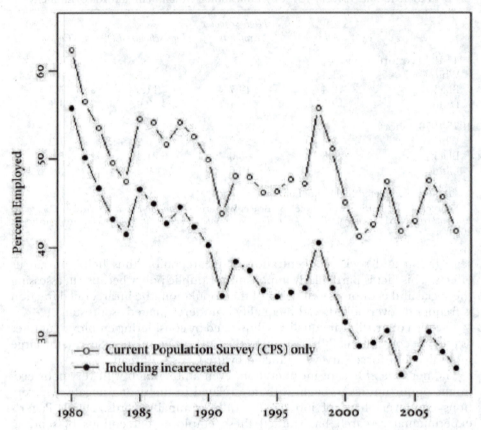

poverty, scholars find that the family life of the disadvantaged has become dramatically more complex and unstable of the last few decades. Divorce and non-
marital births have contributed significantly to rising rates of single parenthood,
and these changes in American family structure are concentrated among low-
income mothers. As a consequence, poor children regularly grow up, at least for
a time, with a single mother, and at different times, with a variety of adult males
in their households.

High rates of parental incarceration likely add to the instability of family life
among poor children. Over half of all prisoners have children under the age of
eighteen, and about 45 percent of those parents were living with their children
at the time they were sent to prison. . . .

Partly because of the burdens of incarceration on women who are left to raise
families in free society, incarceration is strongly associated with divorce and
separation. In addition to the forced separation of incarceration, the post-
release effects on economic opportunities leave formerly incarcerated parents
less equipped to provide financially for their children. New research also shows
that the children of incarcerated parents, particularly the boys, are at greater risk
of developmental delays and behavioral problems. . . .

Figure 3
**Twenty-Year Earnings Mobility Among Men in the Bottom Quintile of Earnings
Distribution in 1986, National Longitudinal Survey of Youth (NLSY) Men**

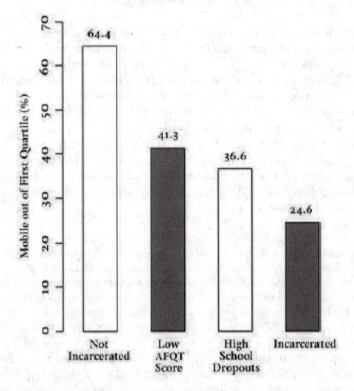

Much of the political debate about crime policy ignores the contemporary scale of criminal punishment, is unequal distribution, and its negative social and economic effects. Our analysis of the penal system as an institution of social stratification, rather than crime control, highlights all these neglected outcomes and leaves us pessimistic that widespread incarceration can sustainably reduce crime. The current system is expensive, and it exacerbates the social problems it is charged with controlling. Our perspective, focused on the social and economic inequalities of American life, suggests that social policy improving opportunity and employment, for young men in particular, holds special promise as an instrument for public safety.

Our perspective on inequality points to a broader view of public safety that is not produced by punishment alone. Robust public safety grows when people have order and predictability in their daily lives. Crime is just one danger, joining unemployment, poor health, and family instability along a spectrum of threats to an orderly life. Public safety is built as much on the everyday routines of work and family as it is on police and prisons. Any retrenchment of the penal system therefor must recognize how deeply the prison boom is embedded in the structure of American social inequality. Ameliorating these inequalities will be necessary to set us on a path away from mass incarceration and toward a robust, socially integrative public safety.

GABRIEL J. CHIN, *THE NEW CIVIL DEATH: RETHINKING PUNISHMENT IN THE ERA OF MASS CONVICTION*

160 U. Pa. L. Rev. 1789 (2012)

. . . [A] new civil death is meted out to persons convicted of crimes in the form of a substantial and permanent change in legal status, operationalized by a network of collateral consequences. A person convicted of a crime, whether misdemeanor or felony, may be subject to disenfranchisement (or deportation if a noncitizen), criminal registration and community notification requirements, and the ineligibility to live, work, or be present in a particular location. Some are not allowed to live outside of civil confinement at all. In addition, the person may be subject to occupational debarment or ineligibility to establish or maintain family relations. While the entire array of collateral consequences may not apply to any given person, the State is always able to add new disabilities or to extend existing limitations. As a practical matter, every criminal sentence contains the following unwritten term:

> The law regards you as having a "shattered character." Therefore, in addition to any incarceration or fine, you are subject to legal restrictions and limitations on your civil rights, conduct, employment, residence, and relationships. For the rest of your life, the United States and any State or locality where you travel or reside may impose, at any time, additional restrictions and limitations they deem warranted. Their power to do so is limited only by their reasonable discretion. They may also require you to pay the expense of these restrictions and limitations.

For many people convicted of crimes, the most severe and long-lasting effect of conviction is not imprisonment or fine. Rather, it is being subjected to collateral consequences involving the actual or potential loss of civil rights, parental rights, public benefits, and employment opportunities.

The magnitude of the problem is greater than ever. The commonly used term "mass incarceration" implies that the most typical tool of the criminal justice system is imprisonment. Indeed, there are two million people in American prisons and jails, a huge number, but one which is dwarfed by the six-and-a-half million or so on probation or parole and the tens of millions in free society with criminal records. The vast majority of people who have been convicted of crimes are not currently in prison. However, because of their criminal records, they remain subject to governmental regulation of various aspects of their lives and concomitant imposition of benefits and burdens. People convicted of crimes are not subject to just one collateral consequence, or even a handful. Instead, hundreds and sometimes thousands of such consequences apply under federal and state constitutional provisions, statutes, administrative regulations, and ordinances. As one Ohio court recognized in 1848, "[D]isabilities . . . imposed upon the convict" are "part of the punishment, and in many cases the most important part."

As practically important as collateral consequences are, in a line of cases examining individual restrictions, the Court has held they are subject to extremely limited constitutional regulation. Because collateral consequences are deemed to be something other than criminal sanctions, they can generally be applied without notice from the court or defense counsel at the time of a guilty plea. Moreover, new ones can be imposed retroactively after plea bargains have been made and sentences fully satisfied.

There is a little-noticed but significant countertradition. In Weems v. United States [217 U.S. 349 (1910)] and Trop v. Dulles [356 U.S. 86 (1958)], the Supreme Court found punishments cruel and unusual under the Eighth Amendment in part because of burdensome and systematic collateral consequences. In addition, alongside cases holding that particular collateral consequences were not punishment, other Supreme Court decisions have shaped the right to jury trial, right to counsel, and other aspects of criminal procedure in light of the fact that collateral consequences are at stake in criminal judgments.

The Court's cases, then, simultaneously suggest that individual collateral consequences are not punishment, but that systematic loss of legal status in the form of actual or potential subjection to an interlocking system of collateral consequences is punishment. This paradox can be reconciled by understanding the degradation of a convict's legal status to be a unitary punishment, the new civil death. . . .

Every conviction implies a permanent change, because these disabilities will "carry through life." For citizens, a prominent collateral consequence is the loss of civil rights: "A convicted criminal may be disenfranchised, lose the right to hold federal or state office, be barred from entering certain professions, be subject to impeachment when testifying as a witness, be disqualified from serving as a juror, and may be subject to divorce." To this ever-increasing list may be added the loss of the right to keep and bear arms. For noncitizens, conviction may result in deportation.

The effects of the loss of status are particularly profound given the many areas of life now subject to governmental regulation. Conviction potentially affects many aspects of family relations, including, for example, the ability to adopt, be a foster parent, or retain custody of one's own children. Conviction can make one ineligible for public employment, such as in the military and law enforcement. It can preclude private employment, including working in regulated industries, with government contractors, or in fields requiring a security clearance.

Conviction can also restrict one's ability to hold a government contract, to obtain government licenses and permits, or to collect a vested public pension. Those convicted of certain crimes may lose the right to drive a car. Persons convicted of sex offenses usually have to register, may be excluded from living in particular areas, and are even subject to post-incarceration civil confinement. . . .

The modern law of collateral consequences seems to have begun with Hawker v. New York [170 U.S. 189 (1898)]. Hawker, a physician, was convicted of performing an abortion, a felony at the time. The New York legislature later passed a law prohibiting those convicted of a felony from being licensed to practice medicine. The Supreme Court upheld the prohibition by a vote of six to three, with Justice Harlan writing for the dissenting Justices.

The majority concluded that the disqualification was not truly based on the conviction; the conviction was mere evidence. The disability was instead based on violating the law, which made Hawker ineligible because he had a bad moral character. The law was not ex post facto, because the disability was based on the illegal conduct of which the conviction is mere evidence. Anyone proved to have performed abortions would be similarly ineligible. . . .

Because collateral consequences are not, strictly speaking, punishment, existing limitations may be imposed retroactively on people not subject to them at the time of conviction. In addition, states are free to create new restrictions in previously unregulated areas. Thus, if rational basis review is taken seriously, then it appears that a truly unfortunate and spectacular range of potential discriminations may be visited long after the fact on those convicted of crime.

It would seem that virtually all denials of public benefits or services are rational because such benefits direct scarce resources to the most deserving. The federal government could, apparently, deny applications for Social Security, Medicare, and Medicaid from some or all people with felony convictions—because "conservation of funds constitutes a rational basis on which to deny assistance to convicted felons and sex offenders." In the absence of some positive federal law to the contrary, states apparently could deny people with convictions access to public hospitals, higher education, and state benefit programs for the same reason.

Courts could find virtually all employment and licensing restrictions rational, as long as the job or occupation is one for which honesty, integrity, and moral character are relevant, for "[i]t is not open to doubt that the commission of crime—the violation of the penal laws of a state—has some relation to the question of character." It is hard to imagine a job so insignificant and inconsequential that it could be done as well by a person of bad character as by someone who was hard working and honest. Because public employment is both a public benefit and a public trust, perhaps all restrictions in that area are rational. . . .

Models promulgated by the Uniform Law Commission and the American Bar Association require broad notice of collateral consequences. The Uniform Collateral Consequences of Conviction Act contains a general warning which offers plain language covering much of the territory:

NOTICE OF ADDITIONAL LEGAL CONSEQUENCES

If you plead guilty or are convicted of an offense you may suffer additional legal consequences beyond jail or prison, [probation] [insert jurisdiction's alternative term for probation], periods of [insert term for post-incarceration supervision], and fines. These consequences may include:

- being unable to get or keep some licenses, permits, or jobs;
- being unable to get or keep benefits such as public housing or education;
- receiving a harsher sentence if you are convicted of another offense in the future;
- having the government take your property; and
- being unable to vote or possess a firearm.

If you are not a United States citizen, a guilty plea or conviction may also result in your deportation, removal, exclusion from admission to the United States, or denial of citizenship.

The law may provide ways to obtain some relief from these consequences.

The Act also provides that "[b]efore the court accepts a plea of guilty or nolo contendre from an individual, the court shall confirm that the individual received and understands the notice required by subsection (a) and had an opportunity to discuss the notice with counsel."

NOTES AND QUESTIONS

1. In recognition of the obstacles facing people released from prisons and jails, President George W. Bush signed into law the Second Chance Act of 2007:

Community Safety Through Recidivism Prevention. The act provides grants to government and nonprofit agencies to facilitate reentry and reduce recidivism by assisting people with mental health and substance use services, housing, education, and employment.

2. As Professor Chin notes, collateral consequences flow even from misdemeanor convictions. The American Bar Association has inventoried thousands of local, state, and federal consequences of convictions. For a comprehensive treatment of "collateral consequences, attorney's duties regarding consequences, constitutional challenges to consequences, access to and the use of criminal records, regulation of employment and occupational licensing, and restoration of rights after a conviction," see Margaret Colgate-Love et al., *Collateral Consequences of Criminal Convictions: Law, Policy and Practice* (2013).

3. At the same time, states provide various remedial schemes such as pardons, record sealing, expungements, and certificates of rehabilitation for those who qualify. Most state laws typically only cover less serious crimes, and often do not permanently remove convictions from so-called RAP ("record of arrests and prosecutions") sheets. To help people with criminal records avail themselves of state remedies, an increasing number of public defender offices, law school clinics, and legal services programs have begun providing reentry legal assistance. Such efforts take a variety of forms, but generally involve helping people with criminal records to overcome collateral consequences of their convictions and reintegrate in their communities. Are you aware of reentry or "clean slate" legal services in your community?

3. "Right on Crime"

Conservative criminal justice reform—including the "Right on Crime" movement—seeks to reduce government spending on the criminal justice system by lowering prison populations and increasing efficacy and transparency in the corrections system. It also stresses victim's rights, public safety, better incentives within the criminal justice system, and the involvement of community organizations. Consider the following, coauthored by the former Republican attorney general for the Commonwealth of Virginia, Mark L. Earley.

MARK L. EARLEY & KATHRYN WILEY, *THE NEW FRONTIER OF PUBLIC SAFETY*

22 Stan. L. & Pol'y Rev. 343 (2011)

The increase in incarceration and stubborn recidivism rates result in a huge cost to the taxpayers: over $68 billion was spent on corrections in 2010. Second only to Medicaid, spending on corrections has become the fastest growing general fund expenditure in the nation. State spending on corrections has increased over $40 billion in the last 20 years, up over 30% in the past 10 years alone. The current approach to incarceration is breaking the bank. If for no other reason, the stress on state budgets—in no small part due to burgeoning correctional system budgets—has finally captured the attention of policymakers and focused their efforts on the poor return they are getting for their dollars.

. . . Indeed, if the billions spent nationwide ensured that prisoners would return to our neighborhoods in greater numbers as peaceful, productive, and law-abiding citizens, we might argue that it was money well spent. But according to the Bureau of Justice Statistics, of the hundreds of thousands of inmates that leave prisons and return home, two-thirds will be rearrested and almost one-half re-incarcerated within three years. Is it too much to suggest that prisons resemble graduate schools of crime more than places of correction and rehabilitation? With a 50% recidivism rate after three years, public safety is corroded on the back end of the criminal justice system.

"What happens inside jails and prisons does not stay inside jails and prisons. It comes home with prisoners after they are released. . . ." Indeed, all too often inmates return home more criminally savvy and prepared to fail at real life than before they went in. No other enterprise could remain in business with such a dismal performance and return on investment. Yet, prisons seem to expand by failing.

To ensure public safety, save taxpayers' dollars, and reverse the trend toward mass incarceration, we must start by seeking the transformation of individuals in prison to get them ready to come home. Departments of Corrections and Rehabilitation should be living up to their names.

. . . [W]hen it comes to rehabilitation of prisoners, the state, by its very nature, will not and cannot do the job. Having served in the Virginia Senate for ten years and as Virginia's Attorney General for four, I know only too well that in times of fiscal stress, correctional budgets are the first to be cut. Within those budgets, rehabilitation and educational programs tend to be the first and proportionally the deepest cuts to be made. That is not likely to change in the real-world competition for dollars. Even when state treasuries are bulging, these programs historically receive relatively low priority because of demand in other "high profile" areas such as education and transportation. But even if these realities changed overnight and prisoner rehabilitation and reentry became the number one priority of state governments, government agencies are by nature woefully incapable of rehabilitation that transforms.

State employees cannot primarily deliver prisoner rehabilitation and reentry efforts. For starters, it is anything but a nine to five job. Instead, such efforts must be delivered through properly trained volunteers in the community through loving relationships that are patient, nurturing, sacrificial, holistic, tough, and able to sustain a genuine long-term commitment to the welfare of prisoners and ex-prisoners. These efforts must be administered by those who believe that darkness can be overcome by light, evil by good, fear by faith, despair by hope, and addiction by freedom. They must be delivered by men and women who believe that transformed prisoners and ex-prisoners, in spite of and precisely because of their past, are uniquely situated to contribute to society because they have experienced brokenness, forgiveness, and restoration. Rehabilitation must be rooted in transformation of the heart, disposition, and character. It must equip prisoners with the knowledge and skills for productive work. It must be characterized not by a systems approach, but by a relational (mentoring) approach. It must begin in prison and continue for up to two years after release from prison — a critical transitional stage. And since it will not and cannot be provided primarily by the state, it must be provided by community-based nonprofits and volunteers.

To focus on the importance of rehabilitation is not "soft on crime," nor does it compromise public safety. Indeed, the State has a duty to protect the public, restore the victim, guard the treasury, and ensure the safety of inmates in prison. A commitment to rehabilitation is consistent with each of these goals.

4. *"Crimmigration"*

The criminalization of immigrants — and the immigration consequences of a criminal conviction — have given rise to a field that some have called "crimmigration." Juliet Stumpf, *The Crimmigration Crisis: Immigrants, Crime, and Sovereign Power*, 56 Am. U. L. Rev. 367 (2006). Until recently, immigration policy was largely distinct from criminal law. As one prominent criminal law scholar has noted:

> Criminal justice and immigration enforcement used to be separated in four critical respects: immigration violations were not prosecuted as crimes; criminal activity was not punished by deportation; immigration proceedings were administrative rather than criminal in character; and local police officers did not enforce immigration laws. None of these propositions remain true today; that is why the line between criminal justice and immigration enforcement has all but disappeared.

David Alan Sklansky, *Crime, Immigration, and Ad Hoc Instrumentalism*, 15 New Crim. L. Rev. 157 (2012).

The blurring of these lines and the use of the criminal justice system to manage migration — including by states and localities — mirrors developments described above with respect to the intersection of the traditionally civil and administrative matters of housing and welfare with the punitive enforcement mechanisms of the criminal justice system. As you read the following excerpt, consider in its particulars how the criminalization of undocumented immigrants — "illegals" in the parlance of some — is like and different from the criminalization of people living in poverty more generally.

JENNIFER M. CHACÓN, *MANAGING MIGRATION THROUGH CRIME*
109 Colum. L. Rev. Sidebar 135 (2009)

The regulation of migration has long taken place primarily in the civil sphere. In recent years, however, the U.S. government has increasingly handled migration control through the criminal justice system. . . .

Since the 1980s, Congress has passed legislation subjecting more and more acts associated with migration to criminal penalties, or increasing the severity of criminal sanctions imposed for the commission of those acts. Criminal offenses newly created in the 1980s included the hiring of unauthorized noncitizen workers, reliance on false documents to evade employer sanctions laws, and marriage fraud. In the late 1980s and the 1990s, illegal reentry provisions were added and strengthened, as were various fraud provisions relating to the processes of seeking immigration benefits and citizenship. And in 2000, penalties were raised for various offenses relating to trafficking in persons.

Although the criminalization of migration-related offenses used to be entirely federal in nature, in recent years, states and localities have added a host of anti-loitering laws and other similar ordinances that are clearly intended to—and have been used to—facilitate the criminal prosecution of unauthorized migrants at the state and local level. One example is Arizona's version of the identity theft law. The crime—entitled "Taking identity of another person or entity"—creates criminal culpability for the use of an alternate identity whether or not the defendant knows that he is using the identity of an actual person and whether or not another person with such an identity actually exists. This offense, which does not require theft of an actual identity, can be deployed as a means of prosecuting noncitizens who have used false identities to obtain employment in cases where there is no loss to anyone as a result of the use of that identity. Several other states have also enacted provisions that mirror federal prohibitions on immigration crimes like smuggling and harboring of unauthorized migrants and false proof of citizenship or immigration status. These statutes take advantage of federally created immigration categories to create a space for local enforcement.

Related to, but even more striking than the steady increase in migration-related criminal offenses is the rising tidal wave of immigration-related criminal prosecutions of the past decade. After remaining relatively flat in the period from 1986 to 1996, the number of immigration prosecutions almost quadrupled over the next ten years. The prosecution of migration-related offenses exploded in the wake of September 11, 2001. In 2004, U.S. magistrates convicted 15,662 noncitizens of immigration crimes, and U.S. district court judges convicted another 15,546. The numbers continued to climb thereafter. Since 2004, immigration prosecutions have topped the list of federal criminal prosecutions, outstripping federal drug and weapons prosecutions, and dwarfing many other forms of federal criminal prosecutions.

This trend has continued even with the change in presidential administrations. And, as previously noted, states and localities—long thought to be excluded from the enforcement of immigration law—have found ways to use their own criminal laws to supplement these federal prosecutions. . . .

The well-known constitutional maxim that deportation (now "removal") is not punishment provides longstanding precedent for important legal distinctions between civil immigration proceedings and criminal proceedings. Noncitizens in removal proceedings are not entitled to counsel at the government's expense. Evidence obtained in violation of a noncitizen's constitutional rights generally is not subject to suppression in civil removal proceedings. And immigration detention—which is also not legal "punishment"—is not subject to the same constitutional constraints as criminal detention. These distinctions have frequently caused immigration attorneys to yearn for the constitutional protections of criminal proceedings, even while acknowledging the inadequacies of those protections.

Unfortunately, recent developments suggest that the lower standards of procedural protections that apply in removal proceedings have made ultra vires incursions into the criminal realm. . . .

The ongoing erosion of the procedural rights of these criminal defendants thus far has been effectively normalized. Such procedural moves can be framed as nothing more than an extension of long-standing limitations on the due process rights of noncitizens in immigration proceedings. However, it is important not to lose sight of the legal distinctions that separate the criminal from the civil realm. The prosecution of these offenses should not be allowed to reshape the criminal sphere to look more like the less rights-protective civil system where immigration enforcement has typically been centered. Unfortunately, at the moment, this is exactly what is happening.

NOTES AND QUESTIONS

1. Since the publication of Professor Chacón's article, immigration detentions have accelerated, topping 400,000 annually. Not only are immigration cases the largest single category of federal prosecutions, they now represent more than half of *all* such prosecutions. This explosion in detentions and prosecutions cannot be explained by high crime rates among immigrants. In fact, evidence suggests that crime rates are lower among foreign-born residents than native-born Americans. Why do you think — under Republican and Democratic administrations alike — we have seen this dramatic change in recent decades?

2. Does the "Right on Crime" focus on reducing government spending change the way you understand the intersection of criminal law with poverty and immigration? Can you think of specific ways to align conservative fiscal principles with liberal social welfare values when it comes to fighting both crime and poverty?

CHAPTER
10

Access to Justice

INTRODUCTION

"Access to justice" is a concept used to analyze and evaluate whether people, especially but not exclusively the poor, can effectively use the courts and other fora to resolve disputes or protect rights. The Supreme Court has held that "the right of access to courts for redress of wrongs is an aspect of the First Amendment right to petition the government. . . ." Sure-Tan, Inc. v. NLRB, 467 U.S. 883, 896-897 (1984). The United Nations defined access to justice as a fundamental human right in 1948, in Article 8 of the Universal Declaration of Human Rights: "Everyone has the right to an effective remedy by the competent national tribunals for acts violating the fundamental rights granted him by the constitution or by law." Many state constitutions guarantee that courts shall remain open to adjudicate grievances.

Because "mere access to the courthouse doors does not by itself assure a proper functioning of the adversary process . . . ," Ake v. Oklahoma, 470 U.S. 68, 77 (1985), an access to justice framework is a way of analyzing whether the "equal justice under law" so often promised on the facade of courthouses (including the U.S. Supreme Court) is a reality for the indigent, those with disabilities, non-English speakers, and other vulnerable groups. Barriers to access include filing and other fees imposed by the courts, high cost or lack of legal assistance, and lack of translation or interpretation services, all of which make using the courts difficult or impossible for certain litigants. In recent years, attention to these barriers has increased along with the number of indigent and unrepresented litigants. Likewise, awareness of access problems in nonjudicial settings such as administrative tribunals and transactional work is also growing.

This chapter includes in Section A a survey of barriers to equal justice that particularly affect the poor, and the work that lawyers, judges, and others are doing to address them through litigation, legislation, expansion of self-help tools and strategies, and other measures. In Section B, we discuss the need for legal assistance and the system of providing legal services to the poor. Section C describes restrictions on and criticisms of that legal services system, while Section D discusses private sector efforts including pro bono and "low bono" work. Delving in somewhat more detail into issues first introduced in Chapter 3, Section E includes the Supreme Court's principal cases on whether and when due process or equal protection require fee waivers or appointed counsel for indigents. Section F covers the revitalized "civil *Gideon*" movement, or quest for a right to counsel in civil cases akin to that available under Gideon v. Wainwright in criminal cases, and includes materials questioning whether that goal is a wise one. Finally, Section G discusses the growing movement to assist unrepresented litigants.

A.   THE COSTS OF JUSTICE: FILING FEES

Poor people have civil legal problems common to many Americans, such as divorce and child custody; credit or collection problems; eviction or foreclosure; and employment issues, including unpaid wages, wrongful termination, and discrimination. They also have legal problems particular to their poverty, such as difficulty accessing or retaining public benefits, or the need to raise a habitability defense to an action for unpaid rent.

Seeking the court's help with legal issues, however, is not free. In federal court, Congress has set the fee for filing a complaint at $350 (28 U.S.C. § 1914), and the "District Court Miscellaneous Fee Schedule" requires an additional $50 administrative fee (the fee schedule can be accessed at http://www.uscourts.gov/FormsAndFees/Fees/DistrictCourtMiscellaneousFeeSchedule.aspx). Many state courts charge similar fees, and 12 states even charge a defendant to file an answer, according to the National Center for State Courts. Fees for filing motions, settlement agreements, and postjudgment documents are common.

Beginning in the 1950s, a series of cases came before the Supreme Court challenging various types of fees required in civil and criminal litigation. As noted in Chapter 3, the Court held in Griffin v. Illinois, 351 U.S. 12 (1956), that indigent criminal defendants could not be denied a certified copy of the trial record necessary for appeal, and in Boddie v. Connecticut, 401 U.S. 371 (1971), that due process required waiver of the filing fee for an indigent seeking a divorce. It appeared (not least to the dissenters in these cases) that all filing fees would soon be vulnerable to such due process or equal protection challenges. However, the Court abruptly changed direction in 1973, in United States v. Kras, which follows.

UNITED STATES v. KRAS
409 U.S. 434 (1973)

Mr. Justice BLACKMUN delivered the opinion of the Court.

The Bankruptcy Act . . . impose[s] fees and make[s] the payment of those fees a condition to a discharge in voluntary bankruptcy. Appellee Kras, an indigent petitioner in bankruptcy, challenged the fees on Fifth Amendment grounds. . . .

[The uncontested facts establish that] Kras has been unemployed since May 1969 except for odd jobs producing about $300 in 1969 and a like amount in 1970. His last steady job was as an insurance agent with Metropolitan Life Insurance Company. He was discharged by Metropolitan in 1969 when premiums he had collected were stolen from his home and he was unable to make up the amount to his employer. Metropolitan's claim against him has increased to over $1,000 and is one of the debts listed in his bankruptcy petition. He has diligently sought steady employment in New York City, but, because of unfavorable references from Metropolitan, he has been unsuccessful. Mrs. Kras was employed until March 1970, when she was forced to stop because of pregnancy. All her attention now will be devoted to caring for the younger child who is coming out of the hospital soon.

The Kras household subsists entirely on $210 per month public assistance received for Kras' own family and $156 per month public assistance received for his mother and her daughter. These benefits are all expended for rent and day-to-day necessities. The rent is $102 per month. Kras owns no automobile and no asset that is non-exempt under the bankruptcy law. He receives no unemployment or disability benefit. His sole assets are wearing apparel and $50 worth of essential household goods. . . .

Kras contends that his case falls squarely within Boddie [v. Connecticut, *supra* Chapter 3]. The Government, on the other hand, stresses the differences between divorce (with which *Boddie* was concerned) and bankruptcy, and claims that *Boddie* is not controlling and that the fee requirements constitute a reasonable exercise of Congress' plenary power over bankruptcy.

Boddie was a challenge by welfare recipients to certain Connecticut procedures, including the payment of court fees and costs, that allegedly restricted their access to the courts for divorce. The plaintiffs, simply by reason of their indigency, were unable to bring their actions. . . .

We agree with the Government that our decision in *Boddie* does not control the disposition of this case and that the District Court's reliance upon *Boddie* is misplaced. *Boddie* was based on the notion that a State cannot deny access, simply because of one's poverty, to a "judicial proceeding (that is) the only effective means of resolving the dispute at hand." . . .

. . . The *Boddie* appellants' inability to dissolve their marriages seriously impaired their freedom to pursue other protected associational activities. Kras' alleged interest in the elimination of his debt burden, and in obtaining his desired new start in life, although important and so recognized by the enactment of the Bankruptcy Act, does not rise to the same constitutional level. See Dandridge v. Williams. . . . If Kras is not discharged in bankruptcy, his position will not be materially altered in any constitutional sense. Gaining or not gaining a discharge will effect no change with respect to basic necessities. We see no fundamental interest that is gained or lost depending on the availability of a discharge in bankruptcy.

Nor is the Government's control over the establishment, enforcement, or dissolution of debts nearly so exclusive as Connecticut's control over the marriage relationship in *Boddie.* In contrast with divorce, bankruptcy is not the only method available to a debtor for the adjustment of his legal relationship with his creditors. The utter exclusiveness of court access and court remedy, as has been noted, was a potent factor in *Boddie.* But "(w)ithout a prior judicial imprimatur, individuals may freely enter into and rescind commercial contracts. . . ."

However unrealistic the remedy may be in a particular situation, a debtor, in theory, and often in actuality, may adjust his debts by negotiated agreement with his creditors. At times the happy passage of the applicable limitation period, or other acceptable creditor arrangement, will provide the answer. Government's role with respect to the private commercial relationship is qualitatively and quantitatively different from its role in the establishment, enforcement, and dissolution of marriage. . . .

We are also of the opinion that the filing fee requirement does not deny Kras the equal protection of the laws. Bankruptcy is hardly akin to free speech or marriage or to those other rights, so many of which are imbedded in the First Amendment, that the Court has come to regard as fundamental and that demand the lofty requirement of a compelling governmental interest before they may be significantly regulated. Neither does it touch upon what have been said to be the suspect criteria of race, nationality, or alienage. Instead, bankruptcy legislation is in the area of economics and social welfare. *See Dandridge.* . . . There is no constitutional right to obtain a discharge of one's debts in bankruptcy. The Constitution, Art. I, s 8, cl. 4, merely authorizes the Congress to "establish . . . uniform Laws on the subject of Bankruptcies throughout the United States." . . .

The rational basis for the fee requirement is readily apparent. Congressional power over bankruptcy, of course, is plenary and exclusive. It sought to make the system self-sustaining and paid for by those who use it rather than by tax revenues drawn from the public at large. . . . If the $50 filing fees are paid in installments over six months as General Order No. 35(4) permits on a proper showing, the required average weekly payment is $1.92. If the payment period is extended for the additional three months as the Order permits, the average weekly payment is lowered to $1.28. This is a sum . . . less than the price of a movie and little more than the cost of a pack or two of cigarettes. . . . [T]his much available revenue should be within [Kras'] able-bodied reach when the adjudication in bankruptcy has stayed collection and has brought to a halt whatever harassment, if any, he may have sustained from creditors. . . .

We decline to extend the principle of *Boddie* to the no-asset bankruptcy proceeding. That relief, if it is to be forthcoming, should originate with Congress.

Reversed.

Mr. Justice STEWART, with whom Mr. Justice DOUGLAS, Mr. Justice BRENNAN, and Mr. Justice MARSHALL join, dissenting.

In my view, this case, like Boddie, does not require us to decide "that access for all individuals to the courts is a right that is, in all circumstances, guaranteed by the Due Process Clause . . . so that its exercise may not be placed beyond the reach of any individual. . . ." It is sufficient to hold, as Boddie did, that "a State may not, consistent with the obligations imposed on it by the Due Process Clause . . . , pre-empt the right to dissolve this legal relationship without affording all citizens access to the means it has prescribed for doing so."

The Court today holds that Congress may say that some of the poor are too poor even to go bankrupt. I cannot agree.

Mr. Justice MARSHALL, dissenting.

The majority notes that the minimum amount that appellee Kras must pay each week if he is permitted to pay the filing fees in installments is only $1.28. It says that "this much available revenue should be within his able-bodied reach."

Appellee submitted an affidavit in which he claimed that he was "unable to pay or promise to pay the filing fees, even in small installments." This claim was supported by detailed statements of his financial condition. . . . The majority seems to believe that it is not restrained by the traditional notion that judges must accept unchallenged, credible affidavits as true, for it disregards the factual allegations and the inferences that necessarily follow from them. . . .

. . . I cannot agree with the majority that it is so easy for the desperately poor to save $1.92 each week over the course of six months. The 1970 Census found that over 800,000 families in the Nation had annual incomes of less than $1,000 or $19.23 a week. I see no reason to require that families in such straits sacrifice over 5% of their annual income as a prerequisite to getting a discharge in bankruptcy.

It may be easy for some people to think that weekly savings of less than $2 are no burden. But no one who has had close contact with poor people can fail to understand how close to the margin of survival many of them are. A sudden illness, for example, may destroy whatever savings they may have accumulated. . . . A pack or two of cigarettes may be, for them, not a routine purchase but a luxury indulged in only rarely. The desperately poor almost never go to see a movie, which the majority seems to believe is an almost weekly activity. They have more important things to do with what little money they have — like attempting to provide some comforts for a gravely ill child, as Kras must do.

It is perfectly proper for judges to disagree about what the Constitution requires. But it is disgraceful for an interpretation of the Constitution to be premised upon unfounded assumptions about how people live.

. . . I view the case as involving the right of access to the courts, the opportunity to be heard when one claims a legal right, and not just the right to a discharge in bankruptcy. When a person raises a claim of right or entitlement under the laws, the only forum in our legal system empowered to determine that claim is a court. Kras, for example, claims that he has a right under the Bankruptcy Act to be free of any duty to pay his creditors. There is no way to determine whether he has such a right except by adjudicating his claim. Failure to do so denies him access to the courts. . . .

NOTES AND QUESTIONS

1. What is the relationship between the Court's determination that bankruptcy is not a fundamental right and its ultimate holding that no waiver of the filing fee is constitutionally required? Can the Court's rationale in *Kras* be squared with that of Griffin v. Illinois (Chapter 3), which held that convicted indigents must be provided a free transcript necessary for appeal, even though there is no underlying constitutional right to an appeal of a criminal conviction?

2. What do you make of Justice Marshall's accusation that the majority relies upon "unfounded assumptions about how people live"? What role do (or should) the facts of an individual plaintiff's circumstances play in a constitutional challenge? How are such facts gathered and presented to the Court?

3. As noted in Chapter 3, the Court was careful in *Boddie* and MLB v. SLJ to note that it did not hold that states must "adjust all tolls to account for 'disparity in material circumstances.'" How does the Court determine when due process or equal protection demands that "tolls" be adjusted?

4. Despite the Court's cases holding that the Constitution rarely requires that court fees be waived, Congress has done so for general civil cases in federal court through the indigent litigant statute, 28 U.S.C. § 1915(a)(1), which

states that "any court of the United States may authorize the commence-ment, prosecution or defense of any suit, action or proceeding, civil or criminal, or appeal therein, without prepayment of fees or security there-fore, by a person who submits an affidavit" of indigence. In 1993, Congress effectively overruled *Kras* by amending the Bankruptcy Act to allow for the filing of bankruptcy petitions under §1915(a). The federal affidavit forms required to obtain a fee waiver are found at http://www.uscourts.gov/uscourts/FormsAndFees/Forms/AO239.pdf and require applicants to sub-mit detailed information about employment, income, savings, assets, public assistance, expenses, household members, and debts.

The states also provide for fee waivers for indigents in most or all civil cases in state court. However, as the next excerpt describes, even where statutes require fee waivers and set forth the process for obtaining them, problems of implementation often persist.

LAURA ERNDE, *FEE WAIVERS DENIED FOR THE POOR*
L.A. Daily J. (Sept. 14, 2011)

When indigent litigant Nylonda "Jazz" Sharnese brought her fraud case to Los Angeles County Superior Court last year, she was blindsided by a judge grilling her about whether she needed to have her court fees waived due to financial hardship.

"Do you have proof of your food stamps?" Superior Court Judge Michael Latin asked her after remarking that she was represented by private counsel.

Sharnese, whose attorney was working pro bono, told him she had proof, but the judge revoked her fee waiver anyway. When Sharnese wasn't able to pay the fees, her case against American Intercontinental University Inc. and Higher One Inc. was dismissed.

As financial troubles plague both litigants and the courts who serve them, public interest lawyers said more indigent clients are being improperly denied fee waivers. They say Latin made multiple errors in his handling of Sharnese's matter and they're hoping to use her case — which is pending at the 2nd District Court of Appeal — to remind judges about the rules regarding fee waivers. Sharnese v. American Intercontinental University, B227344.

"These seem to be really flagrant violations by the court of the fee waiver statutes," said David S. Ettinger, of Horvitz and Levy, who is handling Sharnese's appeal pro bono. "We're in a period where the judiciary has really been savaged by budget cuts, but it's very important that those budget cuts not disadvantage indigent litigants and bar them from the courts."

Fees vary in each case and from county to county, but even an initial filing fee typically runs several hundreds of dollars. Sharnese had taken law school classes so she knew that the judge wasn't supposed to withdraw her fee waiver without a proper hearing. Also, she knew that any discussion of her finances should have taken place in chambers.

"I was so humiliated and shocked," said Sharnese who was relying on public assistance while studying for a master's degree in business. Latin, who recently retired and joined ADR Services, declined to comment, saying it wouldn't be appropriate to talk about a pending case.

Sharnese took her case to the appellate self-help clinic at the 2nd District, where Lisa Jaskol of Public Counsel had been on the lookout for exactly this kind of situation to fix a larger problem. "We need the courts of appeal to step in and remind the superior courts of how these rules work and of the importance of these rules to ensure litigants have access to justice when they need it in these important cases," Jaskol said. Jaskol contacted Ettinger, her former colleague at Horvitz and Levy LLP, and he immediately agreed to take the case.

Litigants requesting a fee waiver must fill out a form declaring under penalty of perjury that they fall into one of three categories of eligibility: they are receiving public assistance, their income falls below 125 percent of the poverty level, or paying fees would leave them unable to afford "the common necessaries of life."

Clerks may grant fee waiver requests, but only judges have the power to deny them, said Tai E. Glenn, pro bono director at Legal Aid of Los Angeles, who is assisting Ettinger in the appeal. Also, a fee waiver cannot be denied or revoked without a hearing that the litigant has 10 days to prepare for, she said.

Even though her case was dismissed, Sharnese said she was able to obtain a confidential settlement of her claims, in which she accused the defendants of failing to follow through with promised job placement and forcing her to pay fees to access her student loan funds.

The settlement makes the case technically moot, but it doesn't prevent the 2nd District from weighing in on the larger issue, Ettinger and Glenn said. The court has scheduled oral argument for Oct. 18. No one has filed papers in opposition since the defendants don't have a stake in the outcome.

"It's always been a misunderstood law that people haven't been trained on," Glenn said, adding that she's been hearing more examples lately of fee waivers being improperly denied. She said she suspects that some judges and clerks throughout the state, whether unconsciously or not, may be unnecessarily scrutinizing fee waivers due to the financial pressure on the courts. "It's a difficult position for everyone to be in," she said. "The courts have a financial problem and our clients have a financial problem."

Glenn was involved in an earlier Court of Appeal case that largely helped determine the ground rules in use today. In 2004, the 2nd District ruled that judges couldn't deny litigants a fee waiver without a hearing. While the courts have improved their handling of fee waivers since that decision, the problem remains, Glenn said.

In another example of a fee waiver denied, a judge in Los Angeles refused to hold a hearing on a Skid Row tenant's complaint that he was illegally locked out of his unit until the client showed proof of his benefits, which is not required under the law, she said. In that case, Legal Aid paid the fee so the time-sensitive case could be heard earlier. But other litigants who don't have counsel might not be so lucky, she said. Officials in one small northern county have been scheduling financial review hearings for litigants who have previously obtained fee waivers, she said. If the litigant fails to appear, even if the case has been disposed of, the court is retroactively denying the fee waiver and ordering payment.

In other cases, Glenn said she's heard of judges scrutinizing fee waivers of those who ask for interpreters or jury trials, which are huge expenses for the court. Once a fee waiver has been granted, a judge must have a valid reason for questioning eligibility, she said. "What we're seeing is the people we represent and can stand up for," she said. "What about people who walk up to the window and are turned away?"

B.   THE NEED FOR LEGAL ASSISTANCE

Even those who can pay filing fees or qualify for a waiver often find that their problems accessing justice are far from over. While most people who can afford it would not dream of pursuing or defending a lawsuit without an attorney, millions of Americans do so every year, because they cannot afford counsel. It comes as a surprise to many Americans, and even to many law students, that American law recognizes no general right to a lawyer for persons with non-criminal legal problems, no matter how important the problem or how poor the litigant. The familiar phrases "You have a right to a lawyer. If you cannot afford a lawyer, one will be appointed for you," though well known to the millions who watch television police dramas, have no application in most civil settings, even where the interests at stake are as weighty as the right to maintain a legal relationship with one's children, to contest eviction proceedings, to secure or retain a job, health care or subsistence income, or to gain legal protection from domestic violence.

While surveys by bar associations and others have frequently found that many Americans believe that a person sued in a civil case has a right to a publicly funded lawyer, in reality there is no such right in most circumstances, and the availability of lawyers to handle the problems of low-income Americans is extremely limited.

1.   Who Provides Legal Services to the Poor?

DEBORAH L. RHODE, *ACCESS TO JUSTICE* (2004)

"Equal justice under law" is one of America's most proudly proclaimed and widely violated legal principles. It embellishes courthouse entrances, ceremonial occasions, and constitutional decisions. But it comes nowhere close to describing the legal system in practice. Millions of Americans lack any access to justice, let alone equal access. According to most estimates, about four-fifths of the civil legal needs of the poor, and two- to three-fifths of the needs of middle-income individuals, remain unmet. Government legal aid and criminal defense budgets are capped at ludicrous levels, which make effective assistance of counsel a statistical impossibility for most low-income litigants. We tolerate a system in which money often matters more than merit, and equal protection principles are routinely subverted in practice. . . .

CIVIL LEGAL SERVICES FOR THE (DESERVING) POOR

Until the late nineteenth century, the limited legal services available to the poor were provided by individual lawyers on an ad hoc basis. Efforts to create a more stable and systematic structure of assistance evolved in three phases. The first organizations were private charities for particular groups. Many of these organizations then expanded to provide routine assistance to all "deserving poor." In their most recent form, legal aid programs generally receive public support and focus on law reform as well as individual services. But in none of these phases has civil legal assistance been considered a basic individual right, and the aid programs have never been able to meet more than a small fraction of the needs of low-income communities.

LEGAL AID AS PRIVATE CHARITY

The nation's first legal aid organization began in 1876 as part of an effort by New York German-American merchants to assist German immigrants. As initially conceived, the mission of what became the New York Legal Aid Society was to "render legal aid and assistance, gratuitously, to those of German birth, who may appear worthy thereof, but who from poverty are unable to procure it." Fifteen years later, the Society dropped the restriction of German nationality, authorized charging its clients small fees, and broadened its base of charitable sponsors. Around the same time, two other legal aid organizations formed in Chicago. One was the Protective Agency for Women and Children. It was launched by the Chicago Women's Club to address sexual exploitation of innocent immigrants lured into sin by false promises of legitimate employment. This agency also outgrew its initial mission and soon began providing legal services of all sorts to women and children. A second organization, the Bureau of Justice, was sponsored by Chicago's Ethical Culture Society to assist needy individuals regardless of sex, race, or nationality. Shortly after the turn of the twentieth century, these organizations merged, and similar legal aid societies had formed in a half dozen major cities. By 1917, there were forty-one such societies across the nation, but with only sixty-two full-time attorneys and a combined budget of under $200,000.

The founders of these organizations had mixed motives that were typical of other progressive reformers throughout this period. Early supporters of legal aid were primarily concerned about the working poor, whose inability to assert basic rights made them vulnerable to exploitation. But most of these supporters had a profoundly conservative view of the mission of legal assistance. Their objective was not to reform the law but to enhance its credibility and ensure its acceptance in the eyes of the lower classes, who might otherwise be led astray by "social agitators." In *Justice and the Poor* (1919), [Reginald Heber] Smith confidently asserted that "the substantive law, as a whole, is remarkably free from any taint of partiality. The legal disabilities of the poor in nearly every instance result from defects in the machinery of the law," not in its substance. But, Smith warned, the machinery had to be fixed: "Injustice leads directly to contempt for law, [and] disloyalty to the government, and plants the seeds of anarchy." Arthur Von Breisen, the first Director of the New York Legal Aid Society, sounded similar themes. Legal Assistance "keeps the poor satisfied because it establishes and protects their rights; it produces better working men . . . and better house servants; it antagonizes the tendency toward communism. . . ." Speakers at the twenty-fifth anniversary of the Legal Aid Society delivered the same message. Legal assistance, as Theodore Roosevelt put it, was a bulwark against "violent revolution." Other proponents stressed professional as well as societal interests. Aid to the deserving poor could serve as an ideal "vehicle for public relations"; it could renew popular "faith in the integrity of the bar and relieve the professions of [its] legal and ethical burden" to provide such services free.

The Role of the Bar

Yet most lawyers remained unconvinced or unconcerned. As Smith noted with frustration, "the majority of our judges and lawyers view the situation with indifference. They fail to see behind the denial of justice the suffering and the tragedy which it causes." The American Bar Association did make some efforts to address the situation. In 1917, it passed a resolution urging state and local bars to "foster the formation and efficient administration of Legal Aid societies . . . for the worthy poor," and appointed its own legal aid committee in 1920. But the response among the rank and file was less than enthusiastic. Smith's 1919 study found that fewer than 10 percent of the lawyers in any surveyed city contributed support, and in some metropolitan areas, the proportion was only 2 or 3 percent. A representative Chicago campaign in 1913 found only twenty firms willing to donate at least $150 for legal services; the New York Legal Aid Society's 1934 effort yielded support from only 339 of the city's some 17,000 attorneys. In other metropolitan areas, after much debate and dispute, bar associations contributed only token amounts, on the order of $100. As late as 1950, only about 9 percent of legal aid funding came from the profession. The majority was from local charities, supplemented by private contributions. The "unhappy truth," reported a comprehensive 1951 bar survey, was that "no substantial progress" in expanding services had occurred since Smith's study in 1919.

Not only were most lawyers unprepared to contribute their own funds to legal aid programs, they were unwilling to support public subsidies. Summarizing widespread views, the ABA's president warned in 1950 that the "entry of the government into the field of legal services is too dangerous to be permitted to come about in our free America." Among elite lawyers, the primary concern was "socialization" of the profession and the threat to an independent bar. Among small and solo practitioners, an additional concern was loss of income from prospective clients who might be poached by government-supported legal services offices.

The Scope of Assistance

To allay such concerns and retain support from conservative donors, legal aid offices throughout the first part of the twentieth century generally steered clear of public funding and took only the most unremunerative and uncontroversial cases. Clients had to be "worthy," and claims had to be meritorious, but not financially rewarding enough to attract any private practitioners. The policy of the New York Legal Aid Society was typical. According to its director, Von Breisen, "Whoever receives our attention must show that he has done some work and that he is entitled to a corresponding consideration." Yet financial eligibility standards were set so low that they often excluded not only the working poor, but even families officially below the poverty line. Some offices also charged modest retainer fees to encourage "self-respect" and a "responsible" attitude toward legal aid bureaus. Almost all offices required clients to subsidize court costs. Such policies helped to reduce caseloads and to discourage time-consuming legal proceedings, but at the cost of foreclosing assistance to many who needed it most.

Legal aid agencies also operated with highly moralistic and frequently condescending policies in selecting among the "deserving" poor. Some societies excluded bankruptcies entirely or imposed restrictions, such as requirements that the claimant have a "reputation for honesty." Part of the reason was to avoid antagonizing creditors whose good will was necessary in negotiating settlements for other clients. But some bar members of legal aid boards were reluctant to sanction "technical" defenses to merchants' claims. Similar policies governed consumer debt cases, and aid was often denied in matters involving "luxury goods," such as automobiles or television sets. Divorce was also excluded unless there were special circumstances demonstrating a "social need," such as a defendant who was in a mental institution or in prison for a "heinous" crime, or who was engaging in "actual physical violence," or "continuing molestation." A client's "desire to remarry" was not enough. The class bias underlying such policies was occasionally explicit. As one attorney put it, most members of the local bar "feel that the poor don't need divorce in quite the same way middle-income people do." As late as 1966, fewer than 15 percent of legal aid offices had unrestrictive policies concerning divorce.

Lack of resources also severely limited the number of clients legal aid programs could reach and the quality of assistance they could provide. In 1963, only about 400 lawyers were available to serve some 50 million eligible clients, which worked out to about one attorney for every 120,000 poor persons. Some estimates suggested that legal aid reached fewer than 1 percent of those in need. Less than two-tenths of 1 percent of the nation's total legal expenditures went to provide representation of the quarter of the population unable to afford it. Despite a high frequency of legal problems, two-thirds of low-income Americans had never consulted a lawyer. Many programs refused to take appeals, appear in court or administrative proceedings, or handle "complicated" matters. Some agencies followed policies of seeking "reasonable compromise," regardless of the client's preferences. On average, assistance consisted of one meeting with an attorney. Legal aid attorneys did not pursue class actions or law reform, and seldom undertook community education or outreach for fear of antagonizing the local bar and creating demands that they could not satisfy. Prior to 1965, no legal aid case ever reached the Supreme Court. The low pay, routine work, and crushing caseloads made it difficult to recruit and retain qualified lawyers. Persevering advocates who attempted to challenge settled doctrine or procedures often met with resistance from trial judges, whose crowded dockets made any novel claims and pretrial motions unwelcome. In one telling example, a Chicago judge wadded up a motion and threw it at the offending legal aid attorney with the advice that if he wanted the matter decided, he should "take it to the Supreme Court."

LEGAL AID AS A PUBLIC RESPONSIBILITY

The social activism of the 1960s brought new resources, new priorities, and new disciples to legal aid work. The transformation began with a series of foundation grants to law reform projects as part of multiservice programs for low-income communities. Then, in the mid-1960s, in a burst of rhetorical exuberance, the nation declared war on poverty. Lawyers were among the first recruits. A newly created Office of Economic Opportunity launched a legal services program inspired by the foundation-sponsored projects. Although the American Bar

Association had traditionally opposed government funding and had not been consulted about the OEO's initiative, ABA leaders saw a need to become partners, not opponents, in the venture. This change in position reflected multiple considerations. One was the long-standing inability of privately funded programs to generate anywhere near the resources necessary to provide adequate service. A more effective approach could respond to growing societal concern about access to justice and enhance the profession's image. Bar leaders were also aware of the public relations disaster that had resulted from the American Medical Association's opposition to Medicare. The prudent course was for the organized bar to help shape program design and for local lawyers to maintain control of government boards of federally funded programs.

Many of the rank and file were initially unconvinced. Some local bar groups brought legal challenges or filed ethical grievances against the new programs. Other lawyers sought OEO funding themselves, as part of Judicare programs that would reimburse private attorneys who took legal aid cases. Some board members resisted the OEO's insistence on law reform as a guiding priority. One representative case history of local bar responses to the new national program reported substantial turf battles among attorneys, including "fisticuffs" in the hallways of an open meeting.

By the close of the 1960s, however, much of the opposition had been overcome, partly because it was apparent that expanded legal services programs were not reducing the client base of private lawyers. To the contrary, subsidized advocacy for the poor created new opportunities for paid work on behalf of their opponents, such as landlords, creditors, and employers. A consensus also developed among bar leaders and OEO officials that Judicare was not a desirable model. Such approaches would not create the kind of efficiency, expertise, and law reform capacity that staffed offices provided and might unleash an unseemly scramble for business among marginal practitioners. With powerful backing from the legal profession, federal funding grew at a healthy clip. Annual expenditures for legal aid increased from $4 million in 1963 to $72 million in 1971. Law schools, often with the support of private foundations, also dramatically increased their support of legal clinics serving low-income communities. This exposure to poverty law, together with the greater status and challenge associated with reform-oriented work, helped recruit a new corps of highly qualified practitioners.

The heightened emphasis on law reform was also supported by national backup centers with expertise in the specific needs of low-income clients. Results were quickly apparent, as offices scored major victories on welfare, housing, education, tenant, consumer, and related issues. Between 1967 and 1972, legal aid lawyers brought over 200 cases before the Supreme Court and won most of the decisions that reached the merits. But these legal achievements also brought a political backlash. Suits against state, local, and national governmental entities provoked the greatest resistance, as many politicians began questioning whether taxpayers should be financing both sides of a lawsuit. During the early 1970s, Congress came close to passing an amendment that would have barred such suits, and the Nixon Administration succeeded in curtailing program activities and budgets.

To provide greater political insulation for poverty law offices, Congress in 1974 established the Legal Services Corporation, with board members appointed by the President and confirmed by the Senate. In exchange for support from conservative critics, the authorizing legislation prohibited

Corporation-funded attorneys from engaging in lobbying, political organization, and representation in controversial areas such as school desegregation, abortion, and military service. Under the new Corporation charter, the earlier OEO rhetoric of "law reform" and "social change" was also absent. Emphasis shifted to the more neutral goal of enhancing "access to justice." Although financial support initially remained strong, another round of restrictions soon followed. The Reagan Administration initially recommended dissolving the Legal Services Corporation, and subsequently secured legislation that reduced its budget by about a third and limited permissible activities. Congress imposed further restrictions in the 1990s. Recipients of government funds could not, for example, represent aliens, pursue cases involving homosexual rights, or initiate class actions.

This history underscores both the capacities and constraints of American approaches to civil legal assistance. The evolution from private charity to public responsibility has brought vastly expanded resources and a new reformist ethic to poverty lawyering. Support from the organized bar has also helped to preserve some measure of independence through a separate Legal Services Corporation, decentralized priority-setting by individual offices, and ethical rules safeguarding lawyer-client relationships. But restrictions on the cases and strategies that publicly funded programs can pursue have deprived attorneys of their most effective methods of law reform and have prevented legal representation of unpopular clients who need it most.

The reliance on a small group of poverty law practitioners to provide assistance to a relatively narrow band of the population has also been a mixed blessing. This approach provides the most efficient services to those at the bottom of the socio-economic scale. But it lacks the widespread political support that some countries have achieved by at least partially subsidizing private practitioners to represent a broader group of individuals. . . . [T]oo few lawyers and clients have a stake in the American system to provide the political base necessary for adequate coverage. And despite impressive efforts, the contributions of privately subsidized pro bono and public interest attorneys have failed to fill the gap. . . .

2. How Much Does the United States Spend on Legal Services for the Poor?

EARL JOHNSON, JR., *JUSTICE FOR AMERICA'S POOR IN THE YEAR 2020: SOME POSSIBILITIES BASED ON EXPERIENCES HERE AND ABROAD*

58 DePaul L. Rev. 393 (2009)

. . . Until 1965, the federal and state governments failed to accept any obligation to provide legal representation for the poor in civil cases, thus leaving legal aid entirely dependent on private charity. As a result, the combined budgets of all legal aid societies in the country totaled less than $5.4 million in that year (about thirty million dollars in 2008 dollars).

The next year, 1966, ushered in the Office of Economic Opportunity (OEO) Legal Services Program, a creation of the nation's short-lived "War on Poverty" — a "war" that turned out to be a mere "skirmish." Yet, in the next three years that program managed to raise the nation's annual investment in civil legal aid to more than forty-five million dollars (over $200 million in 2008 dollars). In 1975, the Legal Services Corporation (LSC) supplanted the OEO program and in its first five years increased the federal investment another five fold, to $321 million. While in the next three decades the LSC budget was jolted twice by huge reductions and has never approached its early peak in real, inflation-adjusted dollars, many state governments and other public funding sources — principally Interest on Lawyers Trust Accounts (IOLTA)[6] — have stepped in to help fill the gap, as has the private sector in some jurisdictions. Thus, by 2008, federal, state, and local governments supplemented by IOLTA are devoting a combined total of over $750 million to civil legal aid with private foundations, charitable donors, and court-awarded fees adding another nearly $250 million. This sounds like a significant sum, but how does it stack up in comparison to need and other relevant measures?

To provide a frame of reference, first consider the size of the population unable to afford to hire counsel. It is not a small number: about fifty million Americans are considered financially eligible for services from lawyers funded by the federal LSC under its very tough standard — 125% of the poverty level, roughly $25,000 annual income for a family of four. That is one in every six Americans. But in some states, programs supported with non-federal funds find the federal standard unrealistic and consider those up to 200% of poverty as financially eligible. Applying that more generous and probably more realistic test of who cannot afford counsel in most cases in most courts, ninety million Americans — almost a third of the nation's population — are in need of government-funded legal counsel.

For those fifty or ninety million people, there are approximately 6500 civil legal aid lawyers in the entire country — funded by a combination of federal and state governments, IOLTA, private foundations, and charitable donations (mainly from lawyers). That is only one lawyer for every 6861 eligible people, or one for every 13,000, depending on where the line is drawn. In contrast, there is approximately one lawyer for every 525 people in the rest of the population.

Those 6500 civil legal aid lawyers represent less than .65% of the nation's lawyers. Yet they are expected to serve as much as one third of the nation's population. Moreover, the combined budgets of all the programs employing these lawyers is less than one half of a percent of what the country spends on lawyers.[17] Indeed, there are two corporate law firms — Skadden, Arps, Slate, Meagher & Flom LLP and Latham & Watkins LLP — each of which received

---

6. These programs make use of the interest earned on trust accounts maintained by lawyers for client funds that are too small or held for such a short period of time that the interest cannot be economically allocated to the individual clients. In the past, the banks paid no interest on such pooled accounts and had free use of those funds. IOLTA programs require the banks to pay interest on the accounts and to send the interest payments to a central fund for the use of legal services for the poor, and in some states also for other improvements in the justice system. . . . At this point, all fifty states and the District of Columbia have some form of IOLTA. . . . [Ed. note: The constitutionality of IOLTA programs has twice come before the Supreme Court, which held that although the payment of interest on funds held in trust could be a taking of property under the Just Compensation Clause of the Fifth Amendment, the amount of compensation that was due was zero, since by definition the IOLTA programs take only interest generated by the pooling of deposits, which would individually be too small to generate interest that exceeded the bookkeeping and banking fees required to maintain individual accounts. Brown v. Legal Fdn. of Wash., 538 U.S. 216 (2003).]

17. In 2005, $221.6 billion was spent on the services of lawyers in the United States. . . . Thus, the roughly one billion dollars currently spent on civil legal aid is roughly .5% of the total amount American society spends on lawyers.

over two billion dollars in legal fees during 2007 from its comparative handful of wealthy clients. This is twice as much as all the legal aid programs in the country presently receive from all sources to purportedly meet the legal needs of fifty million, or as many as ninety million, people.

To see how things could have been better, turn back to 1981, the high point for the LSC's appropriation from Congress. That year LSC had a budget of $321 million — in 1981 dollars, of course. If that budget had merely stayed even with inflation, today the LSC would have an appropriation of over $730 million instead of its current $340 million. To put it another way, in 1981 dollars, the LSC budget has retreated from $321 million in 1981 to $121 million in 2008. And, if the LSC budget had kept pace with the overall federal budget — that is, if it were the same percentage of the government's 2008 budget as it was of the 1981 budget — its appropriation would be over $1.45 billion.

But perhaps most significantly, if the LSC budget today were as large a percentage of the nation's legal resources as it was in 1981, this year's LSC appropriation would be in the range of $2.8 billion. In 1981, the LSC budget was nearly 1.4% of the nation's total expenditures on lawyers — then twenty-three billion dollars — while in 2008, the LSC budget is barely .16% of the over $200 billion spent on lawyers in 2005. Only because in recent years the LSC funding has been augmented by IOLTA, state government funding, and foundation and charitable donations does the combined funding reach even .5% of the nation's expenditure on legal services. LSC funding remains woefully inadequate, but the total is better than if federal funding remained the sole source of support of civil legal aid in this nation. Yet given this tiny share of the nation's legal resources, it is small wonder that so few lower income people can get a lawyer when they need one.

But wait, one might say. Maybe it is just inevitable. Poor people simply are never destined to get a decent share of any nation's legal resources. The rest of the population and its elected representatives simply will refuse to devote significant public funds to supply lawyers for those unable to afford their own. Perhaps an examination of the experience in some other countries can tell us whether this reluctance to pay the price for equal justice is indeed inevitable. What we find is that most other common law countries spend from three to ten times as much of their gross national product on civil legal aid as we do in the United States. England, with a population slightly more than one-sixth that of the United States, actually spends more on civil legal aid out of its national budget than the United States does from all public and private sources. If the United States was as generous as England, our nation's civil legal aid budget would be over nine billion dollars.

There are several European nations willing to devote a much larger percentage of their GDP to civil legal aid than the United States. As reflected by the chart [below], Germany, Finland, and Ireland each provide over three times as much in public funding for civil legal aid as the United States, Canada about four times as much, New Zealand five times as much, Scotland seven times as much, the Netherlands about ten times as much, and England twelve times as much. Six thousand miles east, Hong Kong devotes over six times as much of its GDP to civil legal aid as does the United States. Hong Kong, now a part of communist China, is willing to spend six times more on securing equal justice for its lower income residents than the United States, whose citizens think of it as the home of "justice for all." Based on the experience in these comparable industrial nations, it is difficult to assume America's current reluctance to adequately

fund civil legal aid somehow represents an inevitable or inherent political limit
on funding for this purpose. . . .

Comparison of National Investment in Legal Aid

Nation	Public Civil Legal Aid Investment	Public Civil Legal Aid Investment Per $10k GDP	U.S. Public Civil Legal Aid Investment Required to Match This Nation's Investment Per $10k GDP
U.S.A.	$800 million	$0.65	$800 million
Germany	$520 million	$2.25	$2.85 billion
Ireland	$26.9 million	$2.35	$2.9 billion
Finland	$35.6 million	$2.35	$2.9 billion
Canada	$287 million	$2.80	$3.4 billion
New Zealand	$30 million	$3.25	$4.0 billion
Hong Kong	$67 million	$4.07	$5.1 billion
Scotland	$33.5 million	$4.90	$6.0 billion
Netherlands	$300 million	$6.90	$8.5 billion
N. Ireland	$27 million	$7.00	$8.56 billion
England	$1.24 billion	$7.90	$9.6 billion
10-Nation Average	—	$4.38	$5.36 billion

3. The "Justice Gap": How Much Legal Services Funding Is Enough?

The Johnson article above notes the disparity in spending between the United
States and its peer nations, as well as the decline in U.S. legal services spending
over the last few decades. But these numbers cannot reveal whether a particular
level of spending is enough to meet the needs of the poor or those unable to
afford representation on the private market. Over the years, the LSC has
attempted to measure the "justice gap," a term intended to capture the
difference between the demand or need for legal services and the availability
of those services. In 2005, and again in 2009, LSC released major reports detailing its findings about what percentage of the legal needs of the poor were able to
be met by legal services programs. The 2009 report, *Documenting the Justice Gap in
America: The Current Unmet Civil Legal Needs of Low-Income Americans — An Updated
Report of the Legal Services Corporation* (available at http://www.lsc.gov/sites/
default/files/LSC/pdfs/documenting_the_justice_gap_in_america_2009.pdf)
concluded that for every client served by an LSC-funded program, another
was turned away for lack of program resources, and that fewer than 20 percent
of the legal needs of the poor were addressed by a pro bono, paid, or legal
services lawyer. Many states have conducted similar studies, with similar results.
For example, a 2007 report from Maine's Justice Action Group, available
at http://mbf.org/sites/default/files/JAGReportExecutiveSummary12-17-07
.pdf, concluded that of those able to receive some help from legal aid programs,
85 percent received only brief service or consultation. At one Maine legal services provider, 83 percent of low-income individuals seeking assistance were
turned away. The New Jersey Poverty Research Institute reported in 2009,
based on a random survey of 2,846 households in the state, that approximately

one-third of the respondents with incomes below 200 percent of the federal poverty level, or $33,200 for a household of three at the time of the survey, experienced a legal problem during the course of a year. Only one in five of those secured the assistance of a lawyer. Legal Services of N.J. Poverty Research Inst., *Unequal Access to Justice: Many Legal Needs, Too Little Legal Assistance: The Continuing Civil Justice Gap for Lower-Income New Jerseyans* (2009), available at http://www.lsnj.org/PDFs/PovertyResearchInstitute/LegalNeeds2009.pdf.

NOTES AND QUESTIONS

1. Is a comparison between the number of lawyers serving the poor and the number available in general in America a meaningful one? Likewise, is it meaningful to compare the dollars spent on lawyers in America generally to those spent on legal services? What criticisms could be brought against such comparisons?

2. Earl Johnson, Jr., the author of the previous excerpt, is one of the fathers of the legal services movement in the United States and a longtime proponent of equal access to justice. After serving as a legal aid lawyer and early director of the national legal services program, he became a law professor and then an appellate justice in California, where he continued to write and advocate for more and better legal services for the poor. As his article notes, most European nations spend far more on civil legal services for the indigent (and middle class) than does the United States. In England, the right to legal assistance (and fee waivers) for indigent plaintiffs dates to the Statute of Henry VII in 1495, while most of Europe passed such statutes in the mid-to-late nineteenth century. What accounts for the greater willingness of other nations to recognize the need for legal assistance and to spend much larger sums than the United States?

3. Federally funded legal services dollars, while still the largest single source of funds for legal assistance to low-income Americans, are now a minority of all funds spent on legal aid in the United States, totaling 43.6 percent of all legal aid program funds in 2010. Legal Servs. Corp., *Fact Book 2010* 7 (2011), *available at* http://www.lsc.gov/sites/default/files/LSC/pdfs/LSC_2010_ Fact_Book.pdf. In order of size, other funding sources include state and local grants (17.8 percent of all funds), other non-LSC funds (12.9 percent), other federal grants (9 percent), IOLTA grants, described in note 6 of the Johnson article above (7.1 percent), private grants (4.9 percent), and filing fees (4.7 percent).

4. The history of America's legal services movement is also recounted in a new, three-volume work. *See* Earl Johnson, Jr., *To Establish Justice for All: The Past and Future of Civil Legal Aid in the United States* (2014); *see also* Alan W. Houseman & Linda E. Perle, Ctr. for Law & Soc. Policy, *Securing Equal Justice for All: A Brief History of Civil Legal Assistance in the United States* (2007), *available at* http://www.clasp.org/admin/site/publications/files/0158.pdf (documenting this history in less exhaustive form). An excellent history of the origins of the private charitable programs that preceded publicly funded legal services is included in Martha F. Davis, *Brutal Need: Lawyers and the Welfare Rights Movement* (1993).

C. RESTRICTIONS ON FEDERAL LEGAL SERVICES FUNDING AND ACTIVITIES

When Bill Clinton was elected President in 1992, initially with Democratic majorities in both houses of Congress, many advocates expected an increase in legal services funding. First Lady Hillary Clinton's prior service on the LSC board seemed to bode well for the fortunes of the LSC. However, the 1994 congressional elections brought new Republican majorities to both the House and Senate, including many who had signed on to House Speaker Newt Gingrich's "Contract with America," which included the elimination of the LSC as one of its goals.

The new Congress imposed stringent restrictions on recipients of LSC funding. In addition to the longstanding prohibitions against cases involving abortion, redistricting, or voting rights, grant recipients were prohibited from, *inter alia*, accepting attorneys' fees under fee-shifting statutes (long a means of leverage in litigation as well as an important source of income for some programs), participating in class action litigation, representing incarcerated persons even on matters unconnected to their incarceration, representing persons charged with drug offenses in evictions from public housing, and participating in efforts to amend or otherwise challenge the validity of welfare laws. All federal funding for the national and state backup centers (sources of much impact litigation and some of the landmark constitutional cases such as Goldberg v. Kelly) was eliminated. Congress also prohibited LSC-funded programs from using other funds to conduct activities that federal money could not cover, effectively preventing LSC grantees from engaging in these activities at all. The legal services restrictions, together with political attacks in state legislatures on law school clinics and Supreme Court interpretations rendering statutory attorneys' fees more difficult to obtain, were the focus of the following powerful critique by law professor David Luban.

DAVID LUBAN, *TAKING OUT THE ADVERSARY: THE ASSAULT ON PROGRESSIVE PUBLIC-INTEREST LAWYERS*

91 Cal. L. Rev. 209 (2003)

This Essay concerns laws and doctrines, some very recent, that undermine the capacity of progressive public-interest lawyers to bring cases. It asks a simple-sounding question: how just is the adversary system if one side is not adequately represented in it? And it defends a simple-sounding answer: It is not just at all. As we shall see, however, neither the question nor the answer is quite as simple as it sounds.

Like most issues implicating distributive justice, the question of who has access to lawyers and who does not has become a political football. Political partisans do not care about impartial justice. They care about rewarding their friends and defeating their enemies, and that means ensuring that their enemies receive as little money as possible, including money to pay for legal advocacy. Advocacy, after all, might be used to turn the tables. In the last few years, a disturbing pattern of legal attacks on public-interest lawyers has emerged, targeting every one of the principal sources of support for progressive public-interest law: the Legal Services Corporation ("LSC"), state Interest on Lawyers Trust Account ("IOLTA") programs, law school clinics, and civil rights attorney's fees. The attacks seek to win political disputes not by offering better arguments, but by defunding or otherwise hobbling the advocates who make the arguments for the other side. . . .

Audi Alteram Partem and the Adversary System

In his recent book *Justice Is Conflict*, the distinguished philosopher Stuart Hampshire . . . offers a principle of bare-minimum procedural justice, "the single prescription *audi alteram partem* ('hear the other side')." Hampshire titles this maxim the "principle of adversary argument," and the label is an apt one. The common-law maxim *audi alteram partem* has long been recognized as a fundamental principle of adversary adjudication, reflecting the common lawyer's deep suspicion of ex parte decision making. . . .

Properly understood, the principle of adversary argument requires more than merely letting the other side say its piece before a closed-minded tribunal that has already prejudged the matter. Even show trials do that. *Audi alteram partem* requires actually listening to the other side in good faith, even when the chance of changing the decision maker's mind is virtually nil. Hearing the other side in good faith requires setting one's prejudices aside, and that makes it a powerful, hard-to-live-up-to moral requirement, even though it is "merely" procedural.

. . . [A]n adversary system with only one adversary is an adversary system in name alone, and in that case, all justifications are simply beside the point. When judges and legislatures create doctrines that enable well-funded parties to take out the other side's lawyer, they undermine basic fairness and turn the adversary system into a system of procedural injustice.

Silencing Doctrines

My specific topic, then, is the deliberate attempt to keep progressive voices out of the legal system by taking away their lawyers. . . . [I]t is unsurprising that opposing parties will take away their adversaries' lawyers if they can. The adversary system provides them powerful incentives to do so. Their effort cannot succeed, however, without legal weapons. These I call "silencing doctrines." Silencing doctrines include statutes, rules, and judicial decisions that allow opponents to attack the funding or restrict the activity of their adversaries' advocates.

In recent years, a pattern of silencing doctrines has begun to emerge challenging — to greater or lesser extent — virtually every principal source of support for low-income public-interest lawyering: the LSC, state IOLTA programs, law school clinics, and fee awards in civil rights cases. . . .

A. THE 1996 LEGAL SERVICES CORPORATION RESTRICTIONS

The single biggest source of funding for poor people's lawyers is the Legal Services Corporation. . . . In 1998, this budget funded 3,590 attorneys at an average salary of just under $40,000, along with 4,637 paralegals. The pathetic numbers — one underpaid legal-services lawyer per 10,000 poor people — have not prevented decades of political assaults on the program, including the outright lie that poor people have no trouble finding a free lawyer.

Restrictions on the use of LSC funding have always existed. . . .

In 1996, however, Congress enacted restrictions on legal-services lawyers that went much further. Not only do they prohibit LSC recipients from taking on certain issues, but they also forbid them from representing entire classes of clients. These include whole classes of aliens, many of whom are legal. The new regulations likewise prohibit the representation of all incarcerated people, including those not convicted of a crime, and those whose cases have nothing to do with why they are in jail, as, for example, in parental-rights lawsuits. The restrictions also prevent LSC attorneys from using specific procedural devices or arguments. They cannot attempt to influence rulemaking or lawmaking, participate in class actions, request attorney's fees under applicable statutes,[21] challenge any welfare reform, or defend anyone charged with a drug offense in a public-housing eviction proceeding. Furthermore, LSC grant recipients must file statements revealing the identity of their clients and stating the facts of the case, and these statements must be made available "to any Federal department or agency that is auditing or monitoring the activities of the Corporation or of the recipient."

Perhaps the most devastating regulation, however, is Congress's prohibition on LSC recipients using their nonfederal funds for these prohibited activities. This requirement had a drastic effect. A legal-aid office could no longer accept an LSC grant if it did any prohibited legal work. This provision forced legal-services providers to split into separate organizations with separate offices, one receiving federal funds and abiding by the restrictions, the other maintaining its freedom of action at the cost of its LSC grant. LSC enacted "program integrity" regulations to implement this restriction by ensuring that the two offspring organizations maintained physical and financial separation. The result was bifurcated organizations substantially weaker than the initial organization. Some organizations had to purchase duplicate computer systems and hire duplicate staff. . . .

Do these restrictions compel legal-services lawyers to practice law unethically? The American Bar Association ("ABA") Model Rules of Professional Conduct forbid lawyers from letting a nonclient who pays them interfere with their professional judgment on the client's behalf. Suppose a legal-aid lawyer wants to go after a revolving-credit scam that has bilked 1,000 poor people out of $20 each. She cannot very well litigate 1,000 individual cases, and her best professional judgment screams "class action!" But the restrictions forbid class actions. . . . Are such lawyers then violating the Model Rules by abiding by the regulations? The answer is no, because attorneys have an obvious recourse: they can simply decline to accept cases that are best pursued through forbidden means. Nothing prevents the legal-services lawyer from turning down the revolving-credit case that needs a class action, and to comply with both the congressional restrictions and the Model Rules, she may well turn down the case. The perverse result: the more poor people a legal problem affects, the less likely they are to find a lawyer to represent them. . . .

. . . [T]hese results are deeply problematic from an ethical standpoint. Viewed in the most favorable light, the 1996 restrictions represent Congress's legitimate

21. [Ed. note: The attorneys' fees ban was lifted by Congress in 2010.]

attempt to ensure that legal-services lawyers accept only cases that carry no tincture of political advocacy or social engineering. . . . However, those poor enough to meet legal-aid eligibility criteria are extremely unlikely to have the money to hire a lawyer, and non-LSC-funded public-interest lawyers are rare. Thus, the overwhelming presumption must be that the vast majority of cases that legal-services lawyers turn down will never be brought by anyone. It follows, then, that the restrictions ensure that entire subgroups of low-income people will never be heard in the legal system, including many aliens, all prisoners (including those in jail for only a brief time and those whose incarceration has nothing to do with their legal-services case), public-housing residents accused (perhaps falsely) of drug offenses and facing eviction, and clients for whom a class action is the most effective means of representation. . . .

Disappointingly, neither the Bar nor the legal-services establishment offered any organized protest when the 1996 restrictions were enacted — unlike a similar assault in 1981, when law school deans and the organized bar united in protest against efforts to abolish the LSC. The reason was pure fear that Congress, in the heady days of Newt Gingrich's revolution and the Contract With America, would simply abolish the LSC. Even attempts to challenge the restrictions in court were discouraged by many people in the legal-services community. The ABA Ethics Committee's response was entirely typical: instead of writing a formal opinion insisting that the restrictions violate the ideals of the legal profession, it chose instead to write an opinion insisting that a legal-services grant recipient could practice law ethically by abandoning clients to keep its funding intact. The advice is undoubtedly accurate: declining cases is a sure-fire way to stay out of trouble. Nevertheless, the LSC restrictions undercut the legal profession's ideals because they instruct legal-services lawyers not to represent certain classes of clients, regardless of whether they have meritorious or important claims. . . .

Lawsuits eventually were brought challenging the LSC restrictions, although the results to date have been discouraging. An unconstitutional-conditions challenge to the restrictions failed in the Ninth Circuit, as did an equal-protection challenge. A due process and First Amendment challenge in the Second Circuit also failed, except for one portion of it, directed against the ban on legal arguments against the validity of welfare laws. The 1996 restrictions prohibited LSC lawyers from arguing that welfare laws are invalid but not from arguing that they are valid. The Second Circuit held — and the U.S. Supreme Court agreed — that this remarkable restriction on what legal-services lawyers may say in court was not viewpoint-neutral, and thus it violated the First Amendment. Although the objection seems decisive, the victory affects only a small part of the regulation. The statute remains intact to silence legal-services lawyers in the other ways we have examined. Hear the other side — except when the other side is an indigent who is also a prisoner or alien, a member of a class, someone who objects to a rulemaking process, or someone who would be adversely affected by a lawyer who abides by the restrictions. In that case, defund his lawyer. . . .

D. THE CIVIL RIGHTS FEE CASES

In more than half a dozen decisions over the past fifteen years, the U.S. Supreme Court has cut back on statutorily authorized attorneys' fees given to prevailing parties in civil rights and environmental cases. Because they create weapons that adversaries can use to attack the funding of civil rights and environmental lawyers, at least two of these decisions create silencing doctrines.

The first is the Court's 1986 decision Evans v. Jeff D., 475 U.S. 717 (1986). Here, a civil rights defendant offered a settlement granting the plaintiff full relief, provided that the plaintiff waived statutory attorneys' fees. Legal-aid lawyers represented the plaintiff. Counsel concluded that they had no ethical alternative to accepting the offer, but later moved to have the fee-waiver set aside because the defendant had exploited their ethical obligation and undercut Congress's intention in enacting the fee-award statute. The Court, through Justice Stevens, disagreed. The Court admitted that a "sacrifice offer" (that is, "tell your client that we will give her everything she wants provided that you do not get paid") creates an instant tension between attorney and client; the client wins only if the attorney loses. However the Court denied that this raises any genuine problem of legal ethics, because plaintiff's counsel can always fulfill their ethical obligations by sacrificing their statutorily authorized fees. The Court acknowledged but dismissed the possibility that the widespread practice of skillfully targeted sacrifice offers could put a public-interest firm out of business.

In practice, private civil rights lawyers have avoided the problem of sacrifice offers by writing retainer agreements that make clients responsible for the attorney's fees if they accept a sacrifice offer. But as Justice Brennan noted in his dissent in Jeff D., public-interest lawyers who write such retainer agreements risk their tax-exempt status. Additionally, even private practitioners report that the Court's Jeff D. decision has cut back their ability to negotiate good settlements for their clients by requiring them to negotiate the merits and the fees separately. . . . In addition to Jeff D., the Court recently decided Buckhannon v. West Virginia Department of Health and Human Services, 532 U.S. 598 (2001).The Buckhannon Court held, in a five-to-four decision, that if a defendant gives a plaintiff the sought-after relief before there has been a judicial decision or a judicially approved settlement, then the plaintiff does not count as a prevailing party and receives no statutory attorneys' fees. This eliminates a so-called catalyst theory used by many courts, according to which plaintiffs were awarded attorneys' fees if it was determined that their litigation efforts were the catalyst bringing about the relief or settlement, so that they deserve the fees that go to prevailing parties. After Buckhannon, a vindictive defendant can throw in the towel on the eve of judgment to stop the onset of fee shifting, after the plaintiff and plaintiff's counsel have accrued years of expenses. Buckhannon thus creates another silencing doctrine by discouraging plaintiffs' lawyers from litigating expensive suits that previously held the allure of recouping costs through fee shifting. . . .

CONCLUSION

Silencing doctrines raise the prospect of an adversary system in which one set of adversaries, the progressive public-interest lawyers and the clients they represent, is relentlessly squeezed by political opponents who would rather muzzle them than argue against them. Those who value procedural justice should find silencing doctrines deeply offensive.

The argument of this Essay is not that lack of lawyers is the greatest evil a low-income person can face, nor do I suggest that legal injustice is worse than injustice in other forms and forums. . . . America's thirty million poor people have long lists of needs, and legal representation may be far down the list. But that misses the point. Even if silencing doctrines are not among life's gravest injustices, they represent an outrageous violation of what the legal system should be.

NOTES AND QUESTIONS

1. Do you agree with Professor Luban that restrictions on the types of work that can be done with LSC funding are ethically troubling or improper? Why or why not? What about restricting the work that federal grantees can do with funds from other sources?
2. Over a vigorous dissent by Justice Scalia, the Supreme Court adopted a version of Luban's "*audi alteram partem*" theory in its decision striking down the legal services restrictions on welfare advocacy, Legal Servs. Corp. v. Velazquez, 531 U.S. 533 (2001). The Court held that the restrictions violated the First Amendment and "threaten[] severe impairment of the judicial function" by limiting the arguments and theories that can be presented to the court. *Id.* at 534.

1. Criticism of Publicly Funded Legal Services: From the Right

Support for the LSC and for public funding for lawyers for the poor remains far from a given. From the right, critics frequently charge that legal services programs pursue not client-driven assistance to the poor but the particular social or political agenda of the attorneys running or working in the programs. During the 1980s, political conflict over the continued existence of the federal legal services program intensified when President Reagan used recess appointments to name to the LSC board several new members who were publicly committed to dismantling the program. LSC staff members lobbied Congress to reduce or eliminate LSC appropriations, and the board hired a consultant to write a legal opinion concluding that LSC itself was unconstitutional. Typical of the criticisms of LSC are the allegations leveled in an article by Kenneth F. Boehm, a Reagan-era former chairman of the board of directors of the LSC.

KENNETH F. BOEHM, *THE LEGAL SERVICES PROGRAM: UNACCOUNTABLE, POLITICAL, ANTI-POOR, BEYOND REFORM, AND UNNECESSARY*

17 St. Louis U. Pub. L. Rev. 321 (1998)

Imagine designing a federal program to promote poverty. Imagine you had over $5 billion in federal funds to spend over several decades. You also had a national network of thousands of lawyers largely free to decide which cases they would take and what causes they would support with litigation and lobbying. Keeping

in mind that the goal of this imaginary exercise is to design a program to maximize poverty, consider the following approaches to achieve such a dubious goal:

- Promote welfare dependency by litigating to expand the number of poor
  people dependent on welfare programs.
- Encourage drug and alcohol abuse by subsidizing addiction through [dis-
  ability] checks. If drug and alcohol abusers beat their addiction, they lose
  their check.
- Use legal action to thwart drug-related evictions from public housing. Litigate against public housing authorities which try to screen out drug criminals from getting public housing units.
- Promote unemployment among farm workers by filing numerous abusive
  lawsuits against farmers, forcing them to mechanize to avoid going out of
  business.
- Encourage broken homes by stressing the welfare benefits of divorce, discouraging mediation and providing more than a million free divorces to
  poor clients.

The above approaches to increasing poverty do work. Increasing welfare
dependency, subsidizing substance abuse, promoting unemployment, breaking
up families and thwarting drug-related evictions all contribute to the perpetu-
ation of poverty. Unfortunately, the federal program which funds these debilitating actions is not imaginary. The program just described is the Legal Services
Corporation (LSC), funded entirely with federal tax dollars since its founding in
1974. . . .

* * *

Mr. Boehm, now Chairman of the National Legal and Policy Center, which
"promotes ethics in public life through research, investigation, education and
legal action" and champions smaller government, continues to urge the
defunding of the Legal Services Corporation, including in testimony to Congress in March 2012. *See* National Legal and Policy Center Staff, *What the Legal
Services Corporation Doesn't Want You to Know*, http://nlpc.org/stories/2012/03/
22/what-legal-services-corporation-doesn%E2%80%99t-want-congress-know.

2.   Criticism of Legal Services: From the Left

Legal services as currently structured also has critics on the left, even among its
supporters. Gary Bellow, one of the pioneering public interest lawyers of the
1960s and 1970s, and a founder of Harvard Law School's clinical programs, was
an early leader of the "loyal opposition." In an influential article, *Turning Solutions into Problems: The Legal Aid Experience*, 34 NLADA Briefcase 106 (1977),
Bellow chastised legal services programs for their routinization of cases, low
client autonomy, narrow definitions of client concerns, and inadequate outcomes, arguing that in many cases inadequately trained and supervised lawyers
were failing in their professional responsibilities to their clients. Bellow placed
responsibility for these failures upon the enormous caseloads of legal services
agencies, which generated tremendous pressure to "process" and settle cases
even when a more labor-intensive or aggressive alternative might be in the
client's best interest. He urged that programs be more selective in their

acceptance of cases, engage lawyers at all levels in more detailed supervision and review, engage clients more in the choice and handling of problems, and participate more actively in institutional reform work. Other classic criticisms from legal services supporters include Anthony V. Alfieri, *Reconstructive Poverty Law Practice: Learning Lessons of Client Narrative*, 100 Yale L.J. 2107 (1997); Jeanne Kettleson, *Caseload Control*, 34 NLADA Briefcase 111 (1977); and Raymond H. Brescia et al., *Who's in Charge, Anyway? A Proposal for Community-Based Legal Services*, 25 Fordham Urb. L.J. 831 (1998).

Another strand of early criticism of legal services is articulated in the well-known article below by Stephen Wexler, now a law professor but once a staff attorney for the National Welfare Rights Organization. Wexler argues that merely delivering legal services to poor people was at best inadequate and at worst damaging to the political and community organizing necessary to address poverty.

STEPHEN WEXLER, *PRACTICING LAW FOR POOR PEOPLE*
79 Yale L.J. 1049 (1970)

Poverty will not be stopped by people who are not poor. If poverty is stopped, it will be stopped by poor people. And poor people can stop poverty only if they work at it together. The lawyer who wants to serve poor people must put his skills to the task of helping poor people organize themselves. This is not the traditional use of a lawyer's skills; in many ways it violates some of the basic tenets of the profession. Nevertheless, a realistic analysis of the structure of poverty, and a fair assessment of the legal needs of the poor and the legal talent available to meet them, lead a lawyer to this role.

If all the lawyers in the country worked full time, they could not deal with even the articulated legal problems of the poor. And even if somehow lawyers could deal with those articulated problems, they would not change very much the tangle of unarticulated legal troubles in which poor people live. In fact, only a very few lawyers will concern themselves with poor people, and those who do so will probably be at it for only a while. In this setting the object of practicing poverty law must be to organize poor people rather than to solve their legal problems. The proper job for a poor people's lawyer is helping poor people to organize themselves to change things so that either no one is poor or (less radically) so that poverty does not entail misery.

Two major touchstones of traditional legal practice — the solving of legal problems and the one-to-one relationship between attorney and client — are either not relevant to poor people or harmful to them. Traditional practice hurts poor people by isolating them from each other, and fails to meet their need for a lawyer by completely misunderstanding that need. Poor people have few individual legal problems in the traditional sense; their problems are the product of poverty and are common to all poor people. The lawyer for poor individuals is likely, whether he wins cases or not, to leave his clients precisely where he found them, except that they will have developed a dependency on his skills to smooth out the toughest spots in their lives. . . .

* * *

A more recent article, from the director of one of the nation's largest legal services program, picks up some of the same themes as these early critics and connects them to a critique of the concept of access to justice itself.

GARY F. SMITH, *POVERTY WARRIORS: A HISTORICAL PERSPECTIVE ON THE MISSION OF LEGAL SERVICES*

45 Clearinghouse Rev. 34 (2011)

"I do believe we can end poverty in America." (R. Sargent Shriver, 1965).

The recent passing of Robert Sargent Shriver, a true American hero of the 20th Century, is an opportunity to reexamine the original mission of one of his signature anti-poverty programs — the first national Legal Services for the Poor program. The legal services community should contemplate, in particular, (1) how that mission became so diluted over the next half-century, in contrast to its initial vibrant vision, and (2) whether that mission remains viable for the current generation of legal services advocates. The original, undisputed objective of Legal Services for the Poor — to use the law to challenge and remedy the causes and effects of poverty — remains within the grasp of those legal aid programs and lawyers who are inspired to pursue it.

Every so often within the national legal services community an article circulates to remind us — perhaps painfully — of our undeniable roots as anti-poverty lawyers, whose mission, so hopefully launched by that first Legal Services for the Poor program within the Office of Economic Opportunity in 1965, was to use the law to help poor and disadvantaged communities, long excluded from participation in the mainstream American political process, to attack and overcome the social and economic effects of poverty. Typically such articles describe an ongoing "debate" within our community between two conflicting legal services missions, each struggling for prioritization, a dialectic once characterized as "law reform v. individual service," and, more recently, as "alleviation of poverty v. equal access to justice." This "debate" over the appropriate focus of our work is widely assumed to reflect some primordial tension that arose simultaneously with the very creation of Legal Services for the Poor in 1965.

On the contrary, there should be no lingering ambiguity over the true goals and intent of the original federal legal services program. As Director of the first OEO, Sargent Shriver oversaw the creation of Legal Services for the Poor, alongside the other OEO anti-poverty programs — Head Start, Job Corps, Neighborhood Health Services, Community Action Agencies, and more — with an express mission to fund lawyers who would give entire poor *communities* a legal voice. That voice was intended to sound not only in the courts, but also in the various corridors of power where decisions were made that affected the poor. There was no "debate" over the proper mission of Legal Services for the Poor: it was an antipoverty agency that shared the same single goal as its many sister programs within the constellation of Lyndon Johnson's "Great Society," a goal that Sargent Shriver repeatedly articulated with his characteristic boundless optimism: "I do believe we can end poverty in America."

Thus there was no dispute among the principal architects of that first federally funded legal services program for the poor — Sargent Shriver, Earl Johnson, Clint Bamberger, Edward Sparer, Edgar and Jean Cahn, and so many more — over the proper "mission" of that program. Legal Services for the Poor was conceived and constructed — explicitly and unashamedly — as a critical weapon in the "war on poverty." No less a public figure than the attorney general of the United States, speaking forcefully in support of the new program in 1964, praised its potential for creating "a new breed of lawyers . . . dedicated to using the law as an instrument of orderly and constructive social change."

A year later, Sparer described the "new legal aid lawyer's central role" in terms of "helping to articulate and promote the hopes, the dreams, and the real possibility for the impoverished to make the social changes that they feel are needed, through whatever lawful methods are available," and he understood that role to be "defined by the broadest reaches of advocacy, just [like] the role of the corporation lawyer and the labor lawyer and the real estate lawyer."

Most astonishingly, the broad anti-poverty mission of the "new legal aid lawyers" was expressly endorsed by a sitting Justice of the United States Supreme Court:

> [T]he lawyer in America is uniquely situated to play a creative role in American social progress. Indeed I would make bold to suggest that the success with which he responds to the challenges of what is plainly a new era of crisis and promise in the life of our nation may prove decisive in determining the outcome of the social experiments on which we are embarked. . . .

William J. Brennan Jr., The Responsibilities of the Legal Profession, 54 ABA Journal 121-22 (1968).

Indeed, Justice Brennan echoed Atty. Gen. Nicholas de B. Katzenbach's understanding that the successful pursuit of an aggressive antipoverty mission would require a "new breed" of legal aid lawyers: "What we need are not narrow-minded, single track poverty lawyers," but rather lawyers equipped with "the background and breadth of understanding to recognize the scope of the poverty problem."

To be sure, some of the leaders of that first generation of poverty warriors differed over the most effective strategies to implement Legal Services for the Poor's anti-poverty objectives. However, they were united in the goal to achieve social and economic *justice* for the poor, in the moral sense, with all the stirring reverberations of the parallel civil rights movement giving full meaning to that term. The mission was to provide justice itself, not merely "access" to it.

THE "ACCESS TO JUSTICE" MODEL

The term "equal *access* to justice" is a modern formulation, unknown in the 1960s, that describes piecemeal assistance to handle the personal legal problems of disconnected individual clients who cannot afford lawyers, without necessary reference to the critical needs of the larger poor community. The resolution of these individual demands for personal service, either singly or in the aggregate, has no necessary correlation whatsoever to the causes or conditions of poverty. To Shriver and his contemporaries, a model in which the poverty of the client mattered only to the extent it rendered the client unable to pay for a lawyer (to tend to some personal "legal problem") would have made no sense; for them, the poverty of the client was *itself* the "legal problem" in need of redress.

Of course, in the decades that followed, the political and social winds in America changed direction, bringing an end to that shining moment in our history when the collective social consciousness briefly supported a national consensus around the need, in Lyndon Johnson's words, "to free forty million Americans from the prison of poverty." The years passed, and optimism waned for the potential for achieving broad social improvements for disadvantaged groups in America through government intervention waned. In particular, the affirmative use of the law to provide, in the words of Justice Brennan, "justice, equal and practical, . . . to all . . . who do not partake of the abundance of American life," fell into political disfavor. So did the poor themselves. The same clients for whom Legal Services for the Poor attorneys fought to establish "welfare rights" in the 1960s were, by the 1980s, derided by prominent public figures as "welfare queens." The Legal Services Corporation (LSC), which succeeded Legal Services for the Poor in 1974, responded to decades of political attacks by discouraging the second and third generations of legal aid lawyers from engaging in antipoverty advocacy in an effort to deflect the relentless critique of their work as "social activism" (a characterization that Sargent Shriver would have warmly embraced).

By the first decade of this century, LSC had been reduced to a battered and tarnished keeper of the old Legal Services for the Poor's anti-poverty flame. Grateful for having survived political extinction in 1996, at the price of accepting humiliating and intentionally burdensome restrictions upon its grantees' advocacy, LSC withdrew from the lofty aspirations of its original mission, and formally downgraded its institutional focus from "justice" to "access."

Various social and cultural changes since the 1960s had by then conveniently produced vast numbers of people who perfectly fit the new client paradigm for legal services: individuals who had personal legal problems, not necessarily related to their poverty, and who needed to process those problems through the court system, and who were unable to afford private attorneys to help them do so. In the early 1960s, the practice of "family law" was a relatively obscure specialty; the divorce rate was negligible, and the stigmatization attached to children born of unmarried parents made such births rare. But by the 1990s the cultural forces unleashed in the 1960s had wrought wholesale societal changes in attitudes towards marriage, divorce, gender roles, and family relations, creating millions of new clients—rich and poor—requiring a court's intervention to bring resolution to personal relationship disputes involving spouses, partners, and children. The sheer number of such clients, and the expense of their full representation, overwhelmed the ability and inclination of the private bar to assist them.[13]

Eventually this flood of unrepresented, often low-income litigants created an efficiency crisis for the family law courts, which turned, for the first time, to the legal services community for "collaboration."[14] Over the past ten years, the bar and the courts have effectively redefined the primary mission of legal services, at least from their institutional perspectives, in terms of the provision of individual assistance to unrepresented litigants in family court.[15] Today, many of the legal services organizations that, like LSC, now pursue a mission of legal *access* for the

13. The California Commission on Access to Justice has estimated that over 70% of all divorces begin without an attorney, and over 80% end without an attorney. The California Judicial Council estimated in 2007 that over 4.3 million litigants in California's court system are unrepresented, and that the average percentage of unrepresented plaintiffs in family court matters exceeds 75%.

14. The courts also discovered that, under the rubric of "access to justice" they could help alleviate their efficiency problems in family court dockets by accessing streams of "legal aid" type revenue, funding in-house legal staff to try and bring some order (but not legal representation) to the family law chaos.

15. With only a few exceptions, neither the courts nor the bar have perceived any similar crisis in the eviction dockets, even though 90% of the defendant-tenants are unrepresented, because the fact that the vast majority of the plaintiff-landlords are represented ensures that those courts operate very "efficiently."

poor find no shortage of work in this great multitude of unrepresented family court litigants. . . .

THE MYTH OF LSC'S ROLE IN THE DECLINE OF ANTI-POVERTY ADVOCACY

The major cause of the discontinuance of antipoverty work by many legal aid lawyers is widely assumed in our national community, and especially among the community of legal services programs funded by LSC, to have been the relentless, decades-long pressure from LSC to abandon "impact" advocacy for the poor, culminating in the regime of restrictions imposed by Congress in 1996. I think that this assumption is wrong. By the late 1980s and early 1990s, most LSC-funded programs already had abandoned their original anti-poverty missions, mostly by default rather than by design or compulsion. From my observation, however, there is one *primary* reason for that abandonment: most of the second (and now third) generation of leaders and advocates of the legal services community simply lacked the desire or the creativity or both to pursue such a mission under vastly different and challenging legal, socioeconomic, and cultural circumstances.

The 1996 LSC restrictions did pose some frustrating and irritating impediments to traditional legal services "impact advocacy," but they were not fatal impediments. For too long, our community has wrongly blamed LSC for our collective loss of interest and initiative in using the law to challenge the causes and effects of poverty. Proof of this hypothesis is easily found: First, a small but still significant number of LSC-funded programs have continued to engage in very inspired and very effective anti-poverty advocacy, all in full compliance with LSC's rules. Second, although most of the legal services organizations today are *not* subject to LSC regulation, relatively few of *those* organizations aggressively pursue an anti-poverty agenda, even though they are unconstrained in their ability to do so.

The LSC restrictions have been around for fifteen years; the national legal services community no longer should hide behind them to excuse its own collective disinterest in going to war against poverty. Indeed, to its credit, LSC itself took a significant step towards redemption with the 2007 publication of its "performance criteria," which actually *encourage* programs to engage in advocacy which will achieve systemic benefits and create broad legal remedies, not only for individual clients, but for similarly-situated low-income persons and indeed the poor community as a whole. . . .

CONCLUSION

Creating and supporting an anti-poverty mission in a legal services program is not easy. . . . Certainly programs may legitimately choose *not* to pursue such a mission. Organizational missions are value-neutral; one legal aid mission is not "better" or "worse" than another so long as both are carefully considered, thoughtfully articulated, and faithfully implemented. A mission of "access to the courts for the poor" is a vital and noble mission; indeed, it is a fundamental governmental obligation of a democratic society.

But it was not Sargent Shriver's mission, nor was it the mission of the first federal legal services program. The good news is that the continued pursuit of that original mission also remains possible, a half-century later, for those legal aid lawyers and programs who want to pursue it.

NOTES AND QUESTIONS

1. Should taxpayer dollars be spent to pay for lawyers to attack legislative enactments such as welfare laws or public housing requirements? What is your response to Boehm's view that helping clients access public benefits promotes undesirable dependency? Who should decide the priorities of legal services programs — clients (how?), the public, Congress, the bar, or the programs themselves? Is "law reform" an appropriate goal for publicly funded legal services? Why or why not?

2. Do you agree with Gary Smith's definition of access to justice? Do you agree with him that an access to justice focus can undermine efforts to reduce poverty? Are Smith's and Stephen Wexler's calls for action consistent with each other?

3. Legal services for the poor is one measure now reaching greater prominence in the work of antipoverty advocates in developing countries. In contrast to traditional rule of law initiatives that aim to build or improve government or judicial systems that might one day indirectly benefit the poor, the umbrella term "legal empowerment" refers to the process of using law to increase the control of the poor over their lives. It typically includes articulation and recognition of property rights, labor rights, access to justice, and legal identity, with a focus specifically on how legal changes affect the poor directly. *See* International Development Law Organization, *What Is Legal Empowerment? An Introduction* (2010), http://www.idlo.int/Publications/Golub_Introduction.pdf. The United Nations, through the Committee on the Elimination of Racial Discrimination (CERD) and the Office of the High Commissioner for Human Rights, has also turned attention in recent years to the importance of access to justice and the impacts of racially disproportionate access. International frameworks to address poverty are discussed in Chapter 12.

4. Dollars spent on legal services tell only part of the story of what clients receive when they need free legal help. LSC reports that of the nearly one million cases closed by all LSC-funded legal services programs in 2010, only 2.9 percent, or 26,668 cases, involved what LSC terms "extensive services," defined as cases in which the program "undertook extensive research, preparation of complex legal documents, extensive interaction with third parties on behalf of an eligible client, or extensive ongoing assistance to clients who are proceeding pro se." Legal Servs. Corp., *Fact Book 2010* (2011), *available at* http://www.lsc.gov/sites/default/files/LSC/pdfs/LSC_2010_Fact_Book.pdf. Over half of all clients (573,881) received "counsel and advice," while approximately 150,000 received "limited action" such as "communications by letter, telephone or other means to a third party [or] preparation of a simple legal document such as a routine will or power of attorney." Does the fact that only a tiny percentage of LSC clients actually receive legal representation support any of the critics' points?

D.   IS THERE A ROLE FOR THE PRIVATE SECTOR IN PROVIDING ACCESS TO JUSTICE?

1.   Pro Bono Work

Private lawyers perform hundreds of thousands of hours of pro bono work in America, in an enormous variety of settings, including volunteering hours at legal services agencies or other nonprofits, providing "one-shot" advice at clinics, and co-counseling "impact litigation" cases that may last for years. (Lawyers also provide thousands of hours of pro bono services to non-poverty-related clients or causes, such as cultural institutions, schools, and environmental and civil rights causes.) Unquestionably, pro bono hours are critical to the success of most legal services agencies in serving large numbers of clients. In part because of this success, questions periodically arise as to whether pro bono work should be mandatory for lawyers. The following excerpt summarizes many of the arguments commonly heard in the debate.

DOUGLAS W. SALVESEN, *THE MANDATORY PRO BONO SERVICE DILEMMA: A WAY OUT OF THE THICKET*

82 Mass. L. Rev. 197 (1997)

The debate over mandatory pro bono service has been ongoing for more than 20 years[1] and probably will not be resolved anytime soon. The factions on each side of the debate are well-entrenched and there appears to be little movement towards a rapprochement. Those in favor of mandatory pro bono service point out that the poor have little real access to the courts and the provision of legal services for free or at reduced rates, while not a complete solution, is a necessary and practical way to provide access. Those opposed to mandatory pro bono service generally agree that access is a serious problem but believe that imposing a form of involuntary servitude on lawyers is an impractical and ineffective method for solving the problem. The recent experiences of Florida, Nevada, Texas, Maryland, and other states show how divisive the issue of mandatory pro bono service can be. . . .

THE PROS AND CONS OF MANDATORY PRO BONO SERVICE

Its proponents believe that mandatory pro bono service is necessary because the other steps taken to date, including increases in state appropriations for legal service programs, the provision of IOLTA funds and the surcharges in the filing fee that fund such service programs, and the appeals to lawyers by judicial officers and bar leaders to increase their voluntary pro bono service, have been insufficient to meet the extensive legal needs of the poor. The arguments made in favor of establishing a mandatory obligation to perform pro bono service include the following:

---

1. The issue of mandatory pro bono service first arose in 1972 when the American Bar Foundation proposed drafting or socializing a percentage of a lawyer's time for public interest work.

- Lawyers have a moral and ethical obligation to ensure that the legal needs of the disadvantaged are being met. The widespread unavailability of legal assistance to the poor undermines ideals we all take seriously such as equal justice under the law, access to the legal system, and the rule of law.
- As officers of the court, attorneys have a mandatory duty to assist in the administration of justice which requires them to represent those who cannot afford to pay for legal services.
- As members of the legal profession, attorneys owe a duty of public service which embraces the provision of equal access to justice.
- Requiring attorneys to provide pro bono services is fair where they have been granted the exclusive privilege of practicing law. The legal profession cannot insist that only those admitted to the bar be permitted to practice law without undertaking a complementary obligation to ensure that legal assistance is available for all persons.
- To a certain degree, lawyers have a collective responsibility for the high cost of access to the formal system of civil justice which is beyond the reach of low income persons unless there is mandatory pro bono service.
- Mandatory pro bono services need not unfairly impact sole practitioners, members of small law firms, and nonlitigators whose legal expertise is not required by the poor. These lawyers can have the option of fulfilling their pro bono requirement by making a contribution to a fund that will be used to purchase legal services for the poor.

Those opposed to mandatory pro bono service generally agree that there is a shortage of legal services to the poor. Instead, their opposition, listed below, centers on the problems arising from enforcing a requirement that pro bono service be mandatory.

- As a practical matter, the courts cannot, and should not, mandate acts of charity. An attorney's altruism should not be the subject of an ethical violation. Making the provision of legal services to the poor compulsory is offensive because it tarnishes the contribution of those attorneys who voluntarily provide their services as a matter of professional responsibility, and rankles those who are coerced into making such a contribution.
- The shortage of legal services for the poor is a broad social problem. It is undemocratic to attempt to resolve this problem solely by relying on the legal profession. Society as a whole has an obligation to ensure its members access and should seek political solutions.
- Mandatory pro bono services alone will not significantly increase the poor's access to the civil justice system. Moreover, though the poor need legal services, their need for decent housing, meaningful education, a sufficient supply of food, adequate clothing and appropriate medical attention is greater. Resources devoted to the poor should include access to legal services.
- By requiring that an attorney provide pro bono services to the poor, the courts will reduce the amount of time that lawyers devote to other public organizations, such as church, school, and community groups.
- A mandatory pro bono requirement would mean that some attorneys would be forced to represent clients in areas where they have no expertise. A system that forces such representation is, as Justice Sandra Day O'Connor observed, a "recipe for malpractice," and systemic inefficiency.

- Mandatory pro bono service violates constitutional guarantees of freedom of association and belief (First Amendment), freedom from uncompensated takings (Fifth Amendment), and freedom from involuntary servitude (Thirteenth Amendment).
- A requirement of mandatory pro bono service discriminates against the sole practitioner and small law firms who, in a fiercely competitive legal market, are not financially able to devote a significant amount of time to non-income generating work.
- The coordination required to make mandatory pro bono service a success, including the development and operation of a statewide client referral system, the implementation of a reporting system, and a structure to monitor and ensure compliance, would be an administrative behemoth.
- Mandatory pro bono representation will result in an increased burden on an already overloaded court system. Without a corresponding increase in the number of judges, clerks, and administrative staff to handle the new filings and judicial proceedings, mandatory pro bono will fail.

The various arguments noted above generally fall into one of three categories: the obligation to perform pro bono services, the mechanisms for delivering those services, and the methods used to enforce pro bono obligations. Each of these three facets of the mandatory pro bono issue is discussed below.

OBLIGATION TO PERFORM PRO BONO

Although there will undoubtedly be those who doubt the poor's need for increased legal services, the Report of the Commission on Equal Justice and virtually every other study confirms that there is an overwhelming need and that additional action is required. Those opposed to mandatory service point out that the issue of the poor's access to the courts is a social problem which the provision of mandatory pro bono services will not solve. This is undoubtedly true and efforts to encourage the federal and state legislatures to increase funding for legal service programs should continue, but this does not conclude the issue of the bar's obligations. While the imposition of pro bono service on moral or ethical grounds probably cannot be justified, most of us would agree that lawyers at least have a professional obligation to contribute to the improvement of the legal system and to increase access to the courts. Of course, the fact that there may be an obligation does not necessarily lead to the conclusion that the obligation ought to be compelled by the state. In fact, while there are very few lawyers who are unwilling to perform voluntarily some pro bono service, it appears that there would be some whose sensibilities would be offended if that service were to be compelled. Yet, where there is such a desperate need for pro bono services, it is difficult to believe that this is a deeply held objection. For instance, most attorneys would never think of revealing a client confidence or appropriating a client's funds, yet no lawyer objects to the "mandatory" rules precluding such conduct. . . .

DELIVERY OF LEGAL SERVICES

One of the most common objections to mandatory pro bono service is that it would compel attorneys to perform services in legal areas in which they have little or no training. This concern can be addressed by broadly defining pro bono service to include an array of legal services to disadvantaged groups, charitable corporations or other organizations that address the needs of such persons, as well as participation in activities intended to improve the law, the legal system, or the legal profession. Within this description, most lawyers should be able to discover some service that they could provide; given the exceptional need for pro bono services and the significant number of legal service organizations . . . that are always seeking lawyers to represent their pro bono clients, it should not be difficult for any lawyer to find pro bono work. In addition to broadly defining pro bono service, lawyers could also be given the option of fulfilling a pro bono obligation by making a monetary contribution to a legal service fund.

The other objection is that providing more attorneys to represent the poor will actually result in an increased burden on the trial courts. While this may be true in a small number of cases, the increased representation generally would be welcomed by most judges since the involvement of lawyers in court proceedings streamlines those proceedings. Where both parties are represented, the relevant issues are more aptly identified and presented for judicial action. Consequently, judges do not have to spend their valuable time drawing out the factual background of the case or ensuring that the pro se litigants understand the proceedings.

ENFORCEMENT OF PRO BONO OBLIGATIONS

The most serious objections to mandatory pro bono service, and the objections that I believe keep most lawyers from embracing a mandatory requirement, concern how those obligations would be mandated. The infrastructure required to ensure that the 58,000 Massachusetts lawyers meet their pro bono service obligations is impractical. The resources needed to verify that the services reported were actually performed are enormous. Even if only a very small percentage of lawyers fail to meet their commitments, the time required of the Board of Bar Overseers to prosecute such matters would be substantial. Moreover, a system that checks up on lawyers to ensure that they discharge their pro bono services is unseemly. It is largely for this reason that those objecting to a mandatory requirement suggest that an aspirational goal is preferable.

A PROPOSAL FOR PASSIVE ENFORCEMENT

A choice between a toothless aspirational statement that we should perform pro bono services and an unworkable requirement that we must do so is not much of a choice. Nevertheless, I believe there is a possibility of mediating between these two alternatives by establishing a passive enforcement mechanism that respects a lawyer's autonomy. Such an enforcement process would operate only after a[n] investigation confirms independent ethical violations against an attorney. This will eliminate the need for an administrative monitoring system. However, if allegations of ethical violations are proved against the attorney, the [bar] will be authorized to take into account the attorney's pro bono services or absence of such services in determining an appropriate sanction. The pro bono service requirement thus has some teeth, while at the same time it permits the vast majority of lawyers to fulfill their obligation without burdensome administrative requirements. . . .

NOTES AND QUESTIONS

1. Is mandatory pro bono a politically, ethically, or economically viable solution or partial solution to the legal problems of the poor? Many law schools require mandatory pro bono hours by students. Do the arguments for law student pro bono requirements differ from those pertaining to attorneys?

2. No state currently requires attorneys to perform pro bono work, though most have adopted a version of the ABA's Model Rule 6.1, which says "a lawyer should aspire to render at least 50 hours of pro bono publico legal services per year." Seven states require attorneys to report the number of pro bono hours they perform, and several of these treat failure to report as a disciplinary offense. A due process, equal protection, and takings clause challenge to Florida's reporting requirement was rejected in Schwartz v. Kogan, 132 F.3d 187 (11th Cir. 1998), in which the court noted that the provision of pro bono services has long been an "essential component" of the practice of law and that even if the plaintiff were correct that the reporting requirement "coerced" attorneys into performing pro bono work, such a result would further the legitimate state purpose of increasing the amount of pro bono services rendered. In the rule's first ten years, reported pro bono hours in Florida increased from just over 25 to over 48 hours per attorney. Standing Comm. on Pro Bono Legal Serv., *Report to the Supreme Court of Florida, the Florida Bar, and the Florida Bar Foundation on the Voluntary Pro Bono Attorney Plan* (2006). Does Florida's experience suggest that Salvesen's "passive enforcement" is a potentially valuable solution?

3. Beginning January 1, 2015, New York will require applicants for bar membership to have completed 50 hours of pro bono work before applying for admission. Chief Justice Jonathan Lippman, a leader in the national access to justice movement, stated that the new requirement had two purposes: to address the huge unmet need for lawyers to represent the poor and to inculcate in new lawyers a duty to serve the public. "If pro bono is a core value of our profession, and it is—and if we aspire for all practicing attorneys to devote a meaningful portion of their time to public service, and they should—these ideals ought to be instilled from the start, when one first aspires to be a member of the profession," Lippman said in announcing the requirement. Details can be found at http://www.nycourts.gov/attorneys/probono/baradmissionreqs.shtml.

4. As announced, New York's requirement will apply only to lawyers entering the state's bar after the effective date of the requirement and not to the 160,000 lawyers already holding New York licenses. Is this fair? Is it wise as a policy matter?

2.   *"Low Bono," Unbundling, and "Judicare"*

Many thoughtful advocates and policymakers worry not only about the indigent, but also about the plight of the middle class and near poor, who are not generally eligible for free legal services but can rarely afford to pay lawyers market rates. One potential solution is "unbundling" legal services, sometimes referred to as "limited legal representation" or "discrete task representation." The idea is that clients who cannot afford to pay for the full range of services expected in traditional representation can pay for an attorney to perform only certain discrete functions, such as preparing an answer, appearing in court, or negotiating a settlement agreement. Many states have amended their ethical rules in recent years to permit lawyers to offer unbundled services without running afoul of prohibitions on client abandonment, and a growing body of scholarship examines the concept. So far, little empirical information is available to test the effectiveness or dangers of unbundling, although the findings of one admittedly imperfect study of a small number of housing cases in one California court cast some doubt on the viability of unbundled services for tenants. Jessica Steinberg, *In Pursuit of Justice? Case Outcomes and the Delivery of Unbundled Legal Services*, 18 Geo. J. on Poverty L. & Pol'y 453 (2011); *see also* Molly M. Jennings, *The Evolution of Unbundling in Litigation Matters: Three Case Studies and a Literature Review*, 89 Denv. U. L. Rev. 825 (2012).

In addition to unbundling, some attorneys are experimenting with "low bono" practice. As Professor Luz Herrera explains,

> ... "Low bono" takes into account that clients should have lawyer alternatives other than market rates and free. "Low bono" is the most popular term used to describe discounted-rate arrangements between attorneys and clients, particularly those clients who are underrepresented. "Low bono" arrangements consider the financial constraints of those who seek representation and the attorneys who must charge fees to sustain their own livelihood. Individuals who are unable to obtain free legal services but who cannot pay market rates, and attorneys who depend on paying clients for their livelihood both benefit from such arrangements. Although "low bono" work is not new, it has gained more recognition in the last ten to fifteen years due in large part to law school initiatives primarily led by the City University of New York (CUNY) School of Law and the University of Maryland School of Law.
>
>   CUNY ... and the University of Maryland ... along with two other schools, were funded by the Open Society Institute in 1997 to provide training, mentoring, and support to solo and small-firm lawyers to develop economically viable law practices while serving low- and moderate-income communities. The group of law schools formed the Law School Consortium Project (LSCP) in 1997 to expand law schools' professionalism missions beyond graduation to train, mentor, and provide other support to community solo and small-firm lawyers. By supporting small-firm lawyers that provided "low bono" work, LSCP sought to increase the availability of quality legal services to low- and moderate-income individuals and communities. ... "Low bono" advocates approach the problem of access to legal services with reduced-fee programs that provide alternatives for the poor and the non-poor.

Luz E. Herrera, *Rethinking Private Attorney Involvement Through a Low-Bono Lens*, 43 Loy. L.A. L. Rev. 1 (2009); *see also* http://www.lowbono.org.

Finally, there continues to be sporadic interest in exploring arrangements under which private lawyers would handle certain kinds of legal services clients or certain kinds of problems, in exchange for a publicly funded capitated rate or a per-case fee. As the Rhode excerpt at the beginning of this chapter notes, the United States relies primarily on specialized poverty law practitioners rather than a broader swath of all lawyers to provide services to the poor.

The alternative of compensating private attorneys for providing services is sometimes called "judicare" in America, in reference to the Medicare program, in which the government reimburses private doctors for treating patients. Judicare is much more widely used in some other countries with more robust legal services funding. What are the advantages and disadvantages of judicare? Should judicare be more widely used in the United States? A 2007 article urges consideration of the question. Michael Millemann, *Diversifying the Delivery of Legal Services to the Poor by Adding a Reduced Fee Private Attorney Component to the Predominantly Staff Model, Including Through a Judicare Program*, 7 U. Md. L.J. Race, Religion, Gender & Class 227 (2007); *see also* Jeanne Charn, *Foreword, Toward a Civil* Gideon: *The Future of American Legal Service*, 7 Harv. L. & Pol'y Rev. 1, 3 (2013) (discussing widespread use of judicare in other countries and comparing predominance of staff model in America).

E.   DOES THE CONSTITUTION REQUIRE LAWYERS FOR THOSE WHO CANNOT AFFORD THEM?

The Supreme Court held in Gideon v. Wainwright, 372 U.S. 335 (1963), that the federal Constitution's Sixth Amendment right to counsel (binding on states by way of the Fourteenth Amendment) includes the right to state-funded counsel for indigent felony defendants facing incarceration. In ringing language, the Court noted that not only its precedents but "also reason and reflection require us to recognize that in our adversary system of criminal justice, any person haled into court, who is too poor to hire a lawyer, cannot be assured a fair trial unless counsel is provided for him. This seems to us to be an obvious truth." Quoting from Powell v. Alabama, 287 U.S. 45 (1932), the Court went on:

> The right to be heard would be, in many cases, of little avail if it did not comprehend the right to be heard by counsel. Even the intelligent and educated layman has small and sometimes no skill in the science of law. If charged with crime, he is incapable, generally, of determining for himself whether the indictment is good or bad. He is unfamiliar with the rules of evidence. Left without the aid of counsel he may be put on trial without a proper charge, and convicted upon incompetent evidence, or evidence irrelevant to the issue or otherwise inadmissible. He lacks both the skill and knowledge adequately to prepare his defense, even though he have a perfect one. He requires the guiding hand of counsel at every step in the proceedings against him. Without it, though he be not guilty, he faces the danger of conviction because he does not know how to establish his innocence.

Following *Gideon* and the line of cases discussed in Chapter 3 mandating waiver of fees necessary for indigent litigants to appeal criminal convictions, many advocates hoped that the Court would hold that due process also required the appointment of counsel for civil litigants, or at least for those whose cases involved interests the Court categorized as fundamental under the Constitution. In 1981, however, the Court issued a decision that seemed emphatically to slam shut the federal constitutional door to a categorical right to counsel for civil litigants, at least in most cases.

LASSITER v. DEP'T OF SOC. SERVS. OF DURHAM CNTY.
452 U.S. 18 (1981)

Justice STEWART delivered the opinion of the Court.

[In 1975, after a hearing which Abby Lassiter did not attend, a North Carolina trial court transferred custody of her youngest son to the county, after finding him to be a neglected child, based on evidence that she had not provided him with proper medical care. In 1976, Ms. Lassiter was convicted of second-degree murder and began a 25-40 year sentence.[1] In 1978 the Department petitioned the court to terminate Ms. Lassiter's parental rights, alleging she had had no contact with him in several years.]

Ms. Lassiter was served with the petition [to terminate her rights] and with notice that a hearing on it would be held. Although her mother had retained counsel for her in connection with an effort to invalidate the murder conviction, Ms. Lassiter never mentioned the forthcoming hearing to him (or, for that matter, to any other person except, she said, to "someone" in the prison). At the behest of the Department of Social Services' attorney, she was brought from prison to the hearing, which was held August 31, 1978. Ms. Lassiter did not aver that she was indigent, and the court did not appoint counsel for her.

A social worker from the respondent Department was the first witness. . . . Ms. Lassiter conducted a cross-examination of the social worker. . . . The judge explained several times, with varying degrees of clarity, that Ms. Lassiter should only ask questions at this stage; many of her questions were disallowed because they were not really questions, but arguments.

Ms. Lassiter herself then testified, under the judge's questioning, that she had properly cared for William. Under cross-examination, she said that she had seen William more than five or six times after he had been taken from her custody and that, if William could not be with her, she wanted him to be with her mother since "He knows us. Children know they family. . . . I got four more other children . . . they know they little brother when they see him. . . ."

On appeal, Ms. Lassiter argued only that, because she was indigent, the Due Process Clause of the Fourteenth Amendment entitled her to the assistance of counsel, and that the trial court had therefore erred in not requiring the State to provide counsel for her. . . .

For all its consequence, "due process" has never been, and perhaps can never be, precisely defined. "[U]nlike some legal rules," this Court has said, due process "is not a technical conception with a fixed content unrelated to time, place and circumstances." Rather, the phrase expresses the requirement of "fundamental fairness," a requirement whose meaning can be as opaque as its importance is lofty. Applying the Due Process Clause is therefore an uncertain enterprise which must discover what "fundamental fairness" consists of in a particular situation by first considering any relevant precedents and then by assessing the several interests that are at stake.

---

1. The Court of Appeals . . . indicated that the murder occurred during an altercation between Ms. Lassiter, her mother, and the deceased: "Defendant's mother told [the deceased] to 'come on.' They began to struggle and deceased fell or was knocked to the floor. Defendant's mother was beating deceased with a broom. While deceased was still on the floor and being beaten with the broom, defendant entered the apartment. She went into the kitchen and got a butcher knife. She took the knife and began stabbing the deceased who was still prostrate. The body of deceased had seven stab wounds."

The pre-eminent generalization that emerges from this Court's precedents on an indigent's right to appointed counsel is that such a right has been recognized to exist only where the litigant may lose his physical liberty if he loses the litigation.... It is against this presumption that all the other elements in the due process decision must be measured....

The case of Mathews v. Eldridge propounds three elements to be evaluated in deciding what due process requires, viz., the private interests at stake, the government's interest, and the risk that the procedures used will lead to erroneous decisions. We must balance these elements against each other, and then set their net weight in the scales against the presumption that there is a right to appointed counsel only where the indigent, if he is unsuccessful, may lose his personal freedom.

This Court's decisions have by now made plain beyond the need for multiple citation that a parent's desire for and right to "the companionship, care, custody and management of his or her children" is an important interest that "undeniably warrants deference and, absent a powerful countervailing interest, protection." Here the State has sought not simply to infringe upon that interest but to end it. If the State prevails, it will have worked a unique kind of deprivation. A parent's interest in the accuracy and injustice of the decision to terminate his or her parental status is, therefore a commanding one.

Since the State has an urgent interest in the welfare of the child, it shares the parent's interest in an accurate and just decision. For this reason, the State may share the indigent parent's interest in the availability of appointed counsel. If, as our adversary system presupposes, accurate and just results are most likely to be obtained through the equal contest of opposed interests, the State's interest in the child's welfare may perhaps best be served by a hearing in which both the parent and the State acting for the child are represented by counsel, without whom the contest of interests may become unwholesomely unequal....

The State's interests, however, clearly diverge from the parent's insofar as the State wishes the termination decision to be made as economically as possible.... But though the State's pecuniary interest is legitimate, it is hardly significant enough to overcome private interests as important as those here....

Finally, consideration must be given to the risk that a parent will be erroneously deprived of his or her child because the parent is not represented by counsel....

The respondent argues that the subject of a termination hearing — the parent's relationship with her child ... is one as to which the parent must be uniquely well informed and to which the parent must have given prolonged thought. The respondent also contends that a termination hearing is not likely to produce difficult points of evidentiary law, or even of substantive law, since the evidentiary problems peculiar to criminal trials are not present and since the standards for termination are not complicated.... [T]he North Carolina Departments of Social Services are themselves sometimes represented at termination hearings by social workers instead of by lawyers.

Yet the ultimate issues with which a termination hearing deals are not always simple, however commonplace they may be. Expert medical and psychiatric testimony ... is sometimes presented. The parents are likely to be people with little education, who have had uncommon difficulty in dealing with life, and who are, at the hearing, thrust into a distressing and disorienting situation. That these factors may combine to overwhelm an uncounseled parent is evident from the findings some courts have made. Thus, courts have generally held that the State must appoint counsel for indigent parents at termination proceedings. . . .

The dispositive question . . . is whether the three *Eldridge* factors, when weighed against the presumption that there is no right to appointed counsel in the absence of at least a potential deprivation of physical liberty, suffice to rebut that presumption. . . . To summarize the above discussion, . . . the parent's interest is an extremely important one (and may be supplemented by the dangers of criminal liability inherent in some termination proceedings); the State shares with the parent an interest in a correct decision, has a relatively weak pecuniary interest, and, in some but not all cases, has a possibly stronger interest in informal procedures; and the complexity of the proceeding and the incapacity of the uncounseled parent could be, but would not always be, great enough to make the risk of an erroneous deprivation of the parent's rights insupportably high.

If, in a given case, the parent's interests were at their strongest, the State's interests were at their weakest, and the risks of error were at their peak, it could not be said that the *Eldridge* factors did not overcome the presumption against the right to appointed counsel, and that due process did not therefore require the appointment of counsel. But since the *Eldridge* factors will not always be so distributed, and since "due process is not so rigid as to require that the significant interests in informality, flexibility and economy must always be sacrificed," neither can we say that the Constitution requires the appointment of counsel in every parental termination proceeding. We therefore . . . leave the decision whether due process calls for the appointment of counsel for indigent parents in termination proceedings to be answered in the first instance by the trial court, subject, of course, to appellate review.

[The Court then turned to a determination of whether Ms. Lassiter's circumstances required the appointment of counsel under its case-by-case standard.]

. . . The Department . . . was represented at the hearing by counsel, but no expert witnesses testified and the case presented no specially troublesome points of law, either procedural or substantive. While hearsay evidence was no doubt admitted, and while Ms. Lassiter no doubt left incomplete her defense that the Department had not adequately assisted her in rekindling her interest in her son, the weight of the evidence that she had few sparks of such interest was sufficiently great that the presence of counsel for Ms. Lassiter could not have made a determinative difference. True, a lawyer might have done more with the argument that William should live with Ms. Lassiter's mother — but that argument was quite explicitly made by both Lassiters, and the evidence that the elder Ms. Lassiter had said she could not handle another child . . . and that the grandmother had displayed scant interest in the child . . . was, though controverted, sufficiently substantial that the absence of counsel's guidance on this point did not render the proceedings fundamentally unfair.

Finally, a court deciding whether due process requires the appointment of counsel need not ignore a parent's plain demonstration that she is not interested in attending a hearing. Here, the trial court had previously found that Ms. Lassiter had expressly declined to appear at the 1975 child custody hearing. . . . In view of all these circumstances, we hold that the trial court did not err in failing to appoint counsel for Ms. Lassiter.

For the reasons stated in this opinion, the judgment is affirmed.

It is so ordered.

Justice BLACKMUN, with whom Justice BRENNAN and Justice MARSHALL join, dissenting.

The Court today denies an indigent mother the representation of counsel in a judicial proceeding initiated by the State to terminate her parental rights with respect to her youngest child. The Court most appropriately recognizes that the mother's interest is a "commanding one," and it finds no countervailing state interest of even remotely comparable significance. Nonetheless, the Court avoids what seems to me the obvious conclusion that due process requires the presence of counsel for a parent threatened with judicial termination of parental rights, and, instead, revives an ad hoc approach thoroughly discredited nearly 20 years ago in Gideon v. Wainwright. . . .

Outside the criminal context, . . . the Court has relied on the flexible nature of the due process guarantee whenever it has decided that counsel is not constitutionally required. The special purposes of probation revocation determinations, and the informal nature of those administrative proceedings, including the absence of counsel for the State, led the Court to conclude that due process does not require counsel for probationers. In the case of school disciplinary proceedings, which are brief, informal, and intended in part to be educative, the Court also found no requirement for legal counsel. Most recently, the Court declined to intrude the presence of counsel for a minor facing voluntary civil commitment by his parent, because of the parent's substantial role in that decision and because of the decision's essentially medical and informal nature.

In each of these instances, the Court has recognized that what process is due varies in relation to the interests at stake and the nature of the governmental proceedings. Where the individual's liberty interest is of diminished or less than fundamental stature, or where the prescribed procedure involves informal decisionmaking without the trappings of an adversarial trial-type proceeding, counsel has not been a requisite of due process. Implicit in this analysis is the fact that the contrary conclusion sometimes may be warranted. Where an individual's liberty interest assumes sufficiently weighty constitutional significance, and the State by a formal and adversarial proceeding seeks to curtail that interest, the right to counsel may be necessary to ensure fundamental fairness. . . .

. . . North Carolina law requires notice and a trial-type hearing before the State on its own initiative may sever the bonds of parenthood. The decisionmaker is a judge, the rules of evidence are in force, and the State is represented by counsel. The question, then, is whether proceedings in this mold, that relate to a subject so vital, can comport with fundamental fairness when the defendant parent remains unrepresented by counsel. . . .

In this case, the State's aim is not simply to influence the parent-child relationship but to *extinguish* it. A termination of parental rights is both total and irrevocable. Unlike other custody proceedings, it leaves the parent with no right to visit or communicate with the child, to participate in, or even to know about, any important decision affecting the child's religious, educational, emotional, or physical development. It is hardly surprising that this forced dissolution of the parent-child relationship has been recognized as a punitive sanction by courts, Congress, and commentators. The Court candidly notes, as it must, that termination of parental rights by the State is a "unique kind of deprivation."

The magnitude of this deprivation is of critical significance in the due process calculus, for the process to which an individual is entitled is in part determined "by the extent to which he may be 'condemned to suffer grievous loss.'" Surely there can be few losses more grievous than the abrogation of parental rights. Yet the Court today asserts that this deprivation somehow is less serious than threatened losses deemed to require appointed counsel, because in this instance the parent's own "personal liberty" is not at stake.

I do not believe that our cases support the "presumption" that physical confinement is the only loss of liberty grievous enough to trigger a right to appointed counsel under the Due Process Clause. Indeed, incarceration has been found to be neither a necessary nor a sufficient condition for requiring counsel on behalf of an indigent defendant. . . .

Moreover, the Court's recourse to a "pre-eminent generalization," misrepresents the importance of our flexible approach to due process. That approach consistently has emphasized attentiveness to the particular context. Once an individual interest is deemed sufficiently substantial or fundamental, determining the constitutional necessity of a requested procedural protection requires that we examine the nature of the proceeding—both the risk of error if the protection is not provided and the burdens created by its imposition. . . .

In [virtually every] respect[], the procedure devised by the State vastly differs from the informal and rehabilitative probation revocation decision in *Scarpelli*, the brief, educative school disciplinary procedure in *Goss*, and the essentially medical decision in *Parham*. Indeed, the State here has prescribed virtually all the attributes of a formal trial as befits the severity of the loss at stake in the termination decision—every attribute, that is, except counsel for the defendant parent. The provision of counsel for the parent would not alter the character of the proceeding, which is already adversarial, formal, and quintessentially legal. It, however, would diminish the prospect of an erroneous termination, a prospect that is inherently substantial, given the gross disparity in power and resources between the State and the uncounseled indigent parent.

The legal issues posed by the State's petition are neither simple nor easily defined. The standard is imprecise and open to the subjective values of the judge. A parent seeking to prevail against the State must be prepared to adduce evidence about his or her personal abilities and lack of fault, as well as proof of progress and foresight as a parent that the State would deem adequate and improved over the situation underlying a previous adverse judgment of child neglect. The parent cannot possibly succeed without being able to identify material issues, develop defenses, gather and present sufficient supporting nonhearsay evidence, and conduct cross-examination of adverse witnesses. . . .

The Court, of course, acknowledges that these tasks "may combine to overwhelm an uncounseled parent." I submit that that is a profound understatement. . . . [T]he defendant parent plainly is outstripped if he or she is without the assistance of "the guiding hand of counsel." When the parent is indigent, lacking in education, and easily intimidated by figures of authority, the imbalance may well become insuperable.

The risk of error thus is severalfold. The parent who actually has achieved the improvement or quality of parenting the State would require may be unable to establish this fact. The parent who has failed in these regards may be unable to demonstrate cause, absence of willfulness, or lack of agency diligence as justification. And errors of fact or law in the State's case may go unchallenged and uncorrected. Given the weight of the interests at stake, this risk of error assumes extraordinary proportions. By intimidation, inarticulateness, or confusion, a parent can lose forever all contact and involvement with his or her offspring.

The final factor to be considered, the interests claimed for the State, do not tip the scale against providing appointed counsel in this context. The State hardly is in a position to assert here that it seeks the informality of a rehabilitative or educative proceeding into which counsel for the parent would inject an unwelcome adversarial edge. . . .

. . . The State's financial concern indeed is a limited one, for the right to appointed counsel may well be restricted to those termination proceedings that are instituted by the State. The instant due process analysis takes full account of the fundamental nature of the parental interest, the permanency of the threatened deprivation, the gross imbalance between the resources employed by the prosecuting State and those available to the indigent parent, and the relatively insubstantial cost of furnishing counsel. An absence of any one of these factors might yield a different result. But where, as here, the threatened loss of liberty is severe and absolute, the State's role is so clearly adversarial and punitive, and the cost involved is relatively slight, [counsel should be required].

The Court's analysis is markedly similar to mine; it, too, analyzes the three factors listed in Mathews v. Eldridge, and it, too, finds the private interest weighty, the procedure devised by the State fraught with risks of error, and the countervailing governmental interest insubstantial. Yet, rather than follow this balancing process to its logical conclusion, the Court abruptly pulls back and announces that a defendant parent must await a case-by-case determination of his or her need for counsel. Because the three factors "will not *always* be so distributed," reasons the Court, the Constitution should not be read to "requir[e] the appointment of counsel in *every* parental termination proceeding." This conclusion is not only illogical, but it also marks a sharp departure from the due process analysis consistently applied heretofore. The flexibility of due process, the Court has held, requires case-by-case consideration of different decisionmaking *contexts*, not of different *litigants* within a given context. . . .

The Court's own precedents make this clear. In Goldberg v. Kelly, the Court found that the desperate economic conditions experienced by welfare recipients *as a class* distinguished them from other recipients of governmental benefits. In Mathews v. Eldridge, the Court concluded that the needs of Social Security disability recipients were *not* of comparable urgency, and, moreover, that existing pretermination procedures, based largely on written medical assessments, were likely to be more objective and even-handed than typical welfare entitlement decisions. . . . A showing that a particular welfare recipient had access to additional income, or that a disability recipient's eligibility turned on testimony rather than written medical reports, would not result in an exception from the required procedural norms. . . .

Moreover, the case-by-case approach advanced by the Court itself entails serious dangers for the interests at stake and the general administration of justice. The Court assumes that a review of the record will establish whether a defendant, proceeding without counsel, has suffered an unfair disadvantage. But in the ordinary case, this simply is not so. . . . Determining the difference legal representation would have made becomes possible only through imagination, investigation, and legal research focused on the particular case. Even if the reviewing court can embark on such an enterprise in each case, it might be hard pressed to discern the significance of failures to challenge the State's evidence or to develop a satisfactory defense. Such failures, however, often cut to the essence of the fairness of the trial, and a court's inability to compensate for them effectively eviscerates the presumption of innocence. . . .

The problem of inadequate representation is painfully apparent in the present case. Petitioner, Abby Gail Lassiter, is the mother of five children. The State moved to remove the fifth child, William, from petitioner's care on the grounds of parental neglect. . . .[S]he did not appear at the hearing and was not represented. . . . At some point, petitioner evidently arranged for the other four children to reside with and be cared for by her mother, Mrs. Lucille Lassiter. They remain under their grandmother's care at the present time.

As the Court notes, petitioner did not visit William after July 1976. She was unable to do so, for she was imprisoned. . . . [Immediately upon being informed of the petition to terminate her rights], Petitioner . . . expressed strong opposition to that plan and indicated a desire to place the child with his grandmother. . . . [P]etitioner informed her prison guards about the legal proceeding. They took no steps to assist her in obtaining legal representation. . . . Under these circumstances, it scarcely would be appropriate, or fair, to find that petitioner had knowingly and intelligently waived a right to counsel.

At the termination hearing, the State's sole witness was the county worker who had met petitioner on . . . one occasion. . . . This worker had been assigned to William's case in August 1977, yet much of her testimony concerned events prior to that date; she represented these events as contained in the agency record. Petitioner failed to uncover this weakness in the worker's testimony. That is hardly surprising, for there is no indication that an agency record was introduced into evidence or was present in court, or that petitioner or the grandmother ever had an opportunity to review any such record. The social worker also testified about her conversations with members of the community. In this hearsay testimony, the witness reported the opinion of others that the grandmother could not handle the additional responsibility of caring for the fifth child. There is no indication that these community members were unavailable to testify, and the County Attorney did not justify the admission of the hearsay. Petitioner made no objection to its admission.

. . . An experienced attorney might have translated petitioner's reaction and emotion into several substantive legal arguments. The State charged petitioner with failing to arrange a "constructive plan" for her child's future or to demonstrate a "positive response" to the Department's intervention. A defense would have been that petitioner had arranged for the child to be cared for properly by his grandmother, and evidence might have been adduced to demonstrate the adequacy of the grandmother's care of the other children. . . .

Petitioner plainly has not led the life of the exemplary citizen or model parent. It may well be that if she were accorded competent legal representation, the ultimate result in this particular case would be the same. But the issue before the Court is not petitioner's character; it is whether she was given a meaningful opportunity to be heard when the State moved to terminate absolutely her parental rights. . . . [I]n light of the unpursued avenues of defense, and of the experience petitioner underwent at the hearing, I find virtually incredible the Court's conclusion today that her termination proceeding was fundamentally fair. . . .

NOTES AND QUESTIONS

1. Note the Court's description of Ms. Lassiter's criminal case in footnote 1. Is this necessary to the disposition of the case? What does it suggest about the Court's attitude toward this particular litigant, or toward parents in termination of parental rights proceedings? Does it cast doubt upon any of the choices made in the litigation by plaintiff's lawyers? Do you agree with the majority that the presence of counsel "could not have made a determinative difference" in the outcome of this case? Should that matter?

2. Does the majority respond to Justice Blackmun's concern in dissent that a case-by-case inquiry on appeal as to whether counsel should have been appointed can never rationally be done, because it will be based on a record made without counsel that will therefore inevitably be incomplete? How might the record in this case have been different with counsel? The story of *Lassiter*, including much detail about the procedural aspects of the case, is recounted in detail in Elizabeth G. Thornburg, *The Story of* Lassiter*: The Importance of Counsel in an Adversary System*, in *Civil Procedure Stories* (Kevin M. Clermont ed., 2d ed. 2008).

3. In *Lassiter*, the Court announces a "presumption" that a right to appointed counsel exists "only where the litigant may lose his physical liberty if he loses the litigation. . . ." Does the Constitution require this prioritizing of physical liberty over virtually all other interests? Does the presumption correspond with your ideas about the personal interests most worthy of legal protection?

* * *

Although the Court in *Lassiter* held that federal due process did not require the provision of counsel at state expense to all indigents facing termination of parental rights, it did suggest that counsel *sometimes* would be required in such circumstances. Two advocates set out in 2006 to determine how often counsel was appointed or appeals from the denial of counsel were undertaken. One's analysis follows.

CLARE PASTORE, *A CIVIL RIGHT TO COUNSEL: CLOSER TO REALITY?*

42 Loy. L.A. L. Rev. 1065 (2009)

Advocates and scholars typically, and rightly, view the Supreme Court's 1981 decision in *Lassiter* as a terrible blow to the effort to achieve a broad right to counsel in civil cases under a federal due process framework. In *Lassiter*, applying the familiar three-part test for due process enunciated in Mathews v. Eldridge, the Court held that the Constitution does not require appointment of counsel as a matter of right in state-initiated proceedings to terminate parental rights. Worse, the Court announced a "presumption that an indigent litigant has a right to appointed counsel only when, if he loses, he may be deprived of his physical liberty."

Notably, however, the Court did not hold in *Lassiter* that due process never requires the appointment of counsel when parental rights may be terminated. Instead, it held that due process does not always require it. The Court noted that "the complexity of the proceeding and the incapacity of the uncounseled parent could be, but would not always be, great enough to make the risk of an erroneous deprivation of the parent's rights insupportably high." Thus, the Justices specifically declined to "formulate a precise and detailed set of guide-lines to be followed in determining when the providing of counsel is necessary to meet the applicable due process requirements," and instead left the appropri-ateness of appointment in any individual case "to be answered in the first instance by the trial court, subject, of course, to appellate review."

It is remarkable that almost no published decisions show lower courts actually taking up that challenge. In 2006, Paul Marvy of the Northwest Justice Project and I read every one of the approximately 500 published state court decisions citing Lassiter and dealing with requests for counsel. Strikingly, only in Tennes-see do the courts seem to have taken seriously Lassiter's invitation to determine on a case-by-case basis the need for counsel. After discussing the Mathews fac-tors, the Tennessee Court of Appeals held in 1990 that in termination of paren-tal rights ("TPR") cases, "the chance that the failure to appoint counsel will result in an erroneous decision becomes the main consideration." The court listed seven factors that bear on the question of whether counsel is necessary in any individual TPR case: (1) whether expert medical and/or psychiatric testi-mony is presented at the hearing; (2) whether the parents have had uncommon difficulty in dealing with life and life situations; (3) whether the parents are thrust into a distressing and disorienting situation at the hearing; (4) the diffi-culty and complexity of the issues and procedures; (5) the possibility of criminal self-incrimination; (6) the educational background of the parents; and (7) the permanency of potential deprivation of the child in question.

Rigorous application of these factors would certainly seem to suggest that counsel should be granted in many if not all TPR cases, and indeed, several Tennessee appellate courts have reversed or remanded TPR decisions where there is no record of the trial court's consideration of these factors, or where the trial court did not advise indigent parents of their right to request counsel, even while describing facts that make the termination of rights seem a foregone conclusion.

There is no apparent reason why advocates elsewhere cannot secure the same serious application of the Lassiter requirements as Tennessee courts have required.[71] A strategy, perhaps implemented by special appear-ances of counsel arguing only the appointment issue, could aim at actually forcing courts to hold hearings, develop a list of factors to consider, and make determinations of whether Lassiter requires counsel in any given individual case. While it would not establish a categorical right to counsel (and for this reason is controversial among right to counsel advocates), this strategy could secure counsel for many litigants who are currently unrepresented, would likely create a body of cases documenting the difficulties that pro se litigants face which could be useful both for litigation and legislation, and might enlighten judges and the public as to the quality of justice to be expected by unrepresented litigants. Moreover, if advocates explored a strategy of enter-ing limited appearances for the sole purpose of seeking appointment of counsel, courts of appeals might one day face the "innumerable post verdict challenges to the fairness of particular trials" that helped persuade the Court

---

71. Texas advocates recently tried just such a strategy, seeking certiorari at the U.S. Supreme Court for a case alleging that due process was violated by, inter alia, a Texas state court's failure to conduct a Lassiter inquiry into the need for appointment of counsel in one parental rights termi-nation case. The petition for certiorari was denied. Rhine v. Deaton, 130 S. Ct. 1281 (2010).

to overturn Betts v. Brady's case-by-case approach to the need for counsel in criminal cases in favor of Gideon v. Wainwright's categorical approach. . . .

* * *

The Supreme Court returned to the *Lassiter* presumption in 2011 in a case in which a South Carolina father convicted of civil contempt for failure to pay child support argued that his incarceration was unconstitutional because he had not been appointed an attorney.

<h3 style="text-align:center">TURNER v. ROGERS</h3>
131 S. Ct. 2507 (2011)

Justice BREYER delivered the opinion of the Court.

South Carolina's Family Court enforces its child support orders by threatening with incarceration for civil contempt those who are (1) subject to a child support order, (2) able to comply with that order, but (3) fail to do so. We must decide whether the Fourteenth Amendment's Due Process Clause requires the State to provide counsel (at a civil contempt hearing) to an *indigent* person potentially faced with such incarceration. . . .

. . . Each month the family court clerk reviews outstanding child support orders, identifies those in which the supporting parent has fallen more than five days behind, and sends that parent an order to "show cause" why he should not be held in contempt. At the [subsequent] hearing that parent may demonstrate that he is not in contempt, say, by showing that he is not able to make the required payments. If he fails to make the required showing, the court may hold him in civil contempt. And it may require that he be imprisoned unless and until he purges himself of contempt by making the required child support payments (but not for more than one year regardless).

In June 2003 a South Carolina family court entered an order, which . . . required petitioner, Michael Turner, to pay $51.73 per week to respondent, Rebecca Rogers, to help support their child. Over the next three years, Turner repeatedly failed to pay the amount due and was held in contempt on five occasions. The first four times he was sentenced to 90 days' imprisonment, but he ultimately paid the amount due (twice without being jailed, twice after spending two or three days in custody). The fifth time he did not pay but completed a 6-month sentence.

After his release in 2006 Turner remained in arrears. On March 27, 2006, the clerk issued a new "show cause" order. And after an initial postponement due to Turner's failure to appear, Turner's civil contempt hearing took place on January 3, 2008. Turner and Rogers were present, each without representation by counsel.

The hearing was brief. The court clerk said that Turner was $5,728.76 behind in his payments. The judge asked Turner if there was "anything you want to say." Turner replied,

"Well, when I first got out, I got back on dope. I done meth, smoked pot and everything else, and I paid a little bit here and there. And, when I finally did get to working, I broke my back, back in September. I filed for disability and SSI. And, I didn't get straightened out off the dope until I broke my back and laid up for two months. And, now I'm off the dope and everything. I just hope that you give me a chance. I don't know what else to say. I mean, I know I done wrong, and I should have been paying and helping her, and I'm sorry. I mean, dope had a hold to me."

[The court found Turner in willful contempt and sentenced him to twelve months in county jail, noting that Turner could purge the contempt by paying the arrearage at any time.]

The court made no express finding concerning Turner's ability to pay his arrearage (though Turner's wife had voluntarily submitted a copy of Turner's application for disability benefits). Nor did the judge ask any followup questions or otherwise address the ability-to-pay issue. . . .

We must decide whether the Due Process Clause grants an indigent defendant, such as Turner, a right to state-appointed counsel at a civil contempt proceeding, which may lead to his incarceration. This Court's precedents provide no definitive answer to that question. This Court has long held that the Sixth Amendment grants an indigent defendant the right to state-appointed counsel in a *criminal* case. And we have held that this same rule applies to *criminal contempt* proceedings (other than summary proceedings).

But the Sixth Amendment does not govern civil cases. Civil contempt differs from criminal contempt in that it seeks only to "coerc[e] the defendant to do" what a court had previously ordered him to do. A court may not impose punishment "in a civil contempt proceeding when it is clearly established that the alleged contemnor is unable to comply with the terms of the order." And once a civil contemnor complies with the underlying order, he is purged of the contempt and is free.

Consequently, the Court has made clear . . . that, where civil contempt is at issue, the Due Process Clause allows a State to provide fewer procedural protections than in a criminal case.

This Court has decided only a handful of cases that more directly concern a right to counsel in civil matters. And the application of those decisions to the present case is not clear. On the one hand, the Court has held that the Fourteenth Amendment requires the State to pay for representation by counsel in a civil "juvenile delinquency" proceeding (which could lead to incarceration). Further, in *Lassiter v. Department of Social Servs.*, the Court wrote that the "preeminent generalization that emerges from this Court's precedents on an indigent's right to appointed counsel is that such a right has been recognized to exist only where the litigant may lose his physical liberty if he loses the litigation." . . . [T]he Court then drew from these precedents "the presumption that an indigent litigant has a right to appointed counsel only when, if he loses, he may be deprived of his physical liberty."

. . . We believe those statements are best read as pointing out that the Court previously had found a right to counsel "*only*" in cases involving incarceration, not that a right to counsel exists in *all* such cases.

Civil contempt proceedings in child support cases constitute one part of a highly complex system designed to assure a noncustodial parent's regular payment of funds typically necessary for the support of his children. Often the family receives welfare support from a state-administered federal program, and the State then seeks reimbursement from the noncustodial parent. Other times the custodial parent (often the mother, but sometimes the father, a grandparent, or another person with custody) does not receive government benefits and is entitled to receive the support payments herself. . . .

We here consider an indigent's right to paid counsel at such a contempt proceeding. It is a civil proceeding. And we consequently determine the "specific dictates of due process" by examining the "distinct factors" that this Court has previously found useful in deciding what specific safeguards the Constitution's Due Process Clause requires in order to make a civil proceeding fundamentally fair. *Mathews v. Eldridge.* As relevant here those factors include (1) the nature of "the private interest that will be affected," (2) the comparative "risk" of an "erroneous deprivation" of that interest with and without "additional or substitute procedural safeguards," and (3) the nature and magnitude of any countervailing interest in not providing "additional or substitute procedural requirement[s]."

The "private interest that will be affected" argues strongly for the right to counsel that Turner advocates. That interest consists of an indigent defendant's loss of personal liberty through imprisonment. . . .

Given the importance of the interest at stake, it is obviously important to assure accurate decisionmaking in respect to the key "ability to pay" question. Moreover, the fact that ability to comply marks a dividing line between civil and criminal contempt reinforces the need for accuracy. That is because an incorrect decision (wrongly classifying the contempt proceeding as civil) can increase the risk of wrongful incarceration by depriving the defendant of the procedural protections (including counsel) that the Constitution would demand in a criminal proceeding. And since 70% of child support arrears nationwide are owed by parents with either no reported income or income of $10,000 per year or less, the issue of ability to pay may arise fairly often.

On the other hand, the Due Process Clause does not always require the provision of counsel in civil proceedings where incarceration is threatened. And in determining whether the Clause requires a right to counsel here, we must take account of opposing interests, as well as consider the probable value of "additional or substitute procedural safeguards." Doing so, we find three related considerations that, when taken together, argue strongly against the Due Process Clause requiring the State to provide indigents with counsel in every proceeding of the kind before us.

First, the critical question likely at issue in these cases concerns, as we have said, the defendant's ability to pay. That question is often closely related to the question of the defendant's indigence. But when the right procedures are in place, indigence can be a question that in many — but not all — cases is sufficiently straightforward to warrant determination *prior* to providing a defendant with counsel, even in a criminal case.

Second, sometimes, as here, the person opposing the defendant at the hearing is not the government represented by counsel but the custodial parent *un*represented by counsel. The custodial parent, perhaps a woman with custody of one or more children, may be relatively poor, unemployed, and unable to afford counsel. Yet she may have encouraged the court to enforce its order through contempt. She may be able to provide the court with significant information. And the proceeding is ultimately for her benefit.

A requirement that the State provide counsel to the noncustodial parent in these cases could create an asymmetry of representation that would "alter significantly the nature of the proceeding." Doing so could mean a degree of formality or delay that would unduly slow payment to those immediately in need. And, perhaps more important for present purposes, doing so could make the proceedings *less* fair overall, increasing the risk of a decision that would erroneously deprive a family of the support it is entitled to receive. The needs of such families play an important role in our analysis.

Third, as the Solicitor General points out, there is available a set of "substitute procedural safeguards," which, if employed together, can significantly reduce the risk of an erroneous deprivation of liberty. They can do so, moreover, without incurring some of the drawbacks inherent in recognizing an automatic right to counsel. Those safeguards include (1) notice to the defendant that his "ability to pay" is a critical issue in the contempt proceeding; (2) the use of a form (or the equivalent) to elicit relevant financial information; (3) an opportunity at the hearing for the defendant to respond to statements and questions about his financial status, (*e.g.*, those triggered by his responses on the form); and (4) an express finding by the court that the defendant has the ability to pay.

. . . In our view, a categorical right to counsel in proceedings of the kind before us would carry with it disadvantages (in the form of unfairness and delay) that, in terms of ultimate fairness, would deprive it of significant superiority over the alternatives that we have mentioned. We consequently hold that the Due Process Clause does not *automatically* require the provision of counsel at civil contempt proceedings to an indigent individual who is subject to a child support order, even if that individual faces incarceration (for up to a year). In particular, that Clause does not require the provision of counsel where the opposing parent or other custodian (to whom support funds are owed) is not represented by counsel and the State provides alternative procedural safeguards equivalent to those we have mentioned (adequate notice of the importance of ability to pay, fair opportunity to present, and to dispute, relevant information, and court findings).

We do not address civil contempt proceedings where the underlying child support payment is owed to the State, for example, for reimbursement of welfare funds paid to the parent with custody. Neither do we address what due process requires in an unusually complex case where a defendant "can fairly be represented only by a trained advocate. . . ."

We vacate the judgment of the South Carolina Supreme Court and remand the case for further proceedings not inconsistent with this opinion.

It is so ordered.

NOTES AND QUESTIONS

1. *Turner* marked a departure from the Court's sharply divided holdings in many prior cases seeking a right to counsel, in that no Justice would have found a categorical right in the civil contempt circumstances presented, and none dissented from the Court's reaffirmation of the *Lassiter* presumption against counsel where physical liberty is not at stake. (Justice Thomas dissented in *Turner*, but only because he would not have required the "substitute procedural safeguards" the Court held to be a sufficient alternative to counsel satisfying due process.)

2. Does *Turner* represent, as some have argued, the final nail in the coffin of a federal right to counsel in most civil cases? If so, is that a bad thing? Section G in this chapter addresses the growing self-help and pro se court reform movement and the debate over whether court simplification is a wiser goal than a broad right to counsel. Section F discusses advocacy in state courts and other fora.

3. While many commentators and right to counsel advocates deplored the *Turner* decision, some see it as an opportunity. *See, e.g.,* Laura Abel, *Turner v. Rogers and the Right of Meaningful Access to the Courts,* 89 Denv. U. L. Rev. 805 (2012) (arguing that *Turner* can be read as a reinvigoration of the doctrine of meaningful access announced by the Supreme Court in Bounds v. Smith, 430 U.S. 817 (1977), but severely limited by later cases); *see also* Russell Engler, *Turner v. Rogers and the Essential Role of the Courts in Delivering Access to Justice,* 7 Harv. L. & Pol'y Rev. 31 (2013) (detailing how the procedural safeguards embraced by the *Turner* court fit in with a comprehensive access to justice strategy and vision). The law blog Concurring Opinions held an online symposium shortly after the *Turner* decision was issued, with vigorous debate about the case and its implications. The posts are available at http://www.concurringopinions.com/archives/2011/06/a-final-post-from-your-co-hosts-richard-zorza-david-udell.html.

F. THE REVITALIZED QUEST FOR A CIVIL RIGHT TO COUNSEL

Lassiter made clear that the U.S. Supreme Court was highly unlikely to expand its jurisprudence to recognize a right to counsel in civil matters under the federal Constitution. It did not end the quest for a broader right to counsel in important civil matters, however. This goal is sometimes referred to as a "civil *Gideon,*" a term coined by U.S. District Judge Robert Sweet in 1997, referring to the need for a civil equivalent to the Supreme Court's 1963 Gideon v. Wainwright decision mandating counsel for felony defendants facing incarceration.[1] Since the early 2000s, advocates and scholars have turned to other federal law (such as the Americans with Disabilities Act or Rehabilitation Act), state constitutions, state courts, and state legislatures to seek a right to counsel regardless of whether the federal Constitution requires it. Scholarship on the issue has proliferated, with at least seven law reviews devoting symposium issues to civil right to counsel since 2005. The National Coalition for a Civil Right to Counsel, founded in 2004, now includes over 200 advocates in 35 states and a website, http://www.civilrighttocounsel.org, with an expansive collection of articles, pleadings, decisions, research memoranda, statutes, and other materials. Some state laws expanding access to counsel have been passed, and pilot programs testing the effect of expanding access to counsel are underway in California and Texas, recently concluded in Massachusetts, and under consideration elsewhere. Many states' access to justice commissions and bar associations established task forces or subcommittees to study or recommend measures related to the expansion of counsel as of right in civil matters.

Most advocates view state constitutions as more fertile ground than the federal for several reasons. First, many state constitutions contain provisions not found

---

1. Many advocates resist the "civil *Gideon*" label, in part to avoid embracing some of the failures of the post-*Gideon* criminal defense system, and in part to make clear that these advocates support the focusing of representation to where it is most likely to make a difference, as discussed in Section F.2 below, rather than a call for lawyers in all situations, regardless of merit, representation of opponent, or importance of a matter. For a discussion of the terminology question and the connection between *Gideon* and a right to counsel in civil cases, see John Pollock, *It's All About Justice: How* Gideon *Relates to the Right to Counsel in Civil Cases,* 39 ABA Human Rights No. 4 (2013).

in the U.S. Constitution, such as an "open courts" clause, or an express right to access the courts. Second, while many state constitutions contain due process or equal protection clauses similar or identical to their federal counterparts, some state high courts have nonetheless held that interpretations of the federal Constitution are not binding on state judges in evaluating their own similar or even identical measures. Third, many advocates view the U.S. Supreme Court's "fundamental rights" jurisprudence as profoundly inconsistent with sensible notions of which interests are most in need of legal protection. That is, because the Court has found that housing, public benefits, education, health care, etc., are not fundamental rights, measures curtailing or denying such interests are subject only to rational basis review and not often successfully challenged, as we saw in Chapter 3, regardless of how large they loom in the lives of the individuals affected. Douglas Besharov pinpointed an absurd aspect of the Court's disparate treatment of criminal and civil interests in his often-quoted statement that "*Lassiter*, for all practical purposes, stands for the proposition that a drunken driver's night in the cooler is a greater deprivation of liberty than a parent's permanent loss of rights in a child." Douglas Besharov, *Terminating Parental Rights: The Indigent Parent's Right to Counsel After* Lassiter v. North Carolina, 15 Fam. L.Q. 205, 219 (1981).

The disconnect between the Supreme Court's fundamental rights jurisprudence and the concerns of antipoverty law was implicitly recognized by the American Bar Association in 2006, when it unanimously passed a resolution urging "federal, state, and territorial governments to provide legal counsel as a matter of right at public expense to low income persons in those categories of adversarial proceedings where *basic human needs* are at stake, such as those involving shelter, sustenance, safety, health or child custody, as determined by each jurisdiction." ABA House of Delegates Resolution 112A (Aug. 7, 2006) (emphasis added). The "basic human needs" framework of the resolution sidesteps the limited definition of fundamental rights the federal courts have recognized, and instead enumerates shelter, sustenance, safety, health, and child custody as cardinal interests. Numerous state and local bar associations have endorsed the ABA resolution, and the needs it prioritizes have also been prioritized in at least one statute, enacting the California pilot program, as described below.

State courts have indeed recognized rights to counsel where federal courts have not, including in paternity, termination of parental rights (the context of *Lassiter*), adoption, and other areas. For example, as the ABA Report accompanying Resolution 112A notes:

> [T]he Maine and Oregon Supreme Courts declared the constitutional right to due process required that their state governments provide free counsel to parents in dependency/neglect cases. The Alaska Supreme Court ruled that counsel must be appointed at public expense to an indigent party in a child custody proceeding if the other party was provided free representation. The California Supreme Court found a due process right to counsel for defendants in paternity cases and an equal protection right for prisoners involved in civil litigation. The New York Court of Appeal fell only one vote short of declaring a constitutional right to free counsel for poor people in divorce cases.

Report Accompanying ABA Resolution 112A (Aug. 7, 2006). Recent test cases have not fared so well. In Washington, a claim that a right to counsel in child custody matters was required under the state constitution failed (King v. King, 174 P.3d 659 (Wash. 2007)), and test cases in both Maryland (Frase v. Barnhart, 840 A.2d 114 (Md. 2003)) and Alaska (Office of Pub. Advocacy v. Alaska Court Sys., No. S-12999) ended inconclusively in their states' high courts without establishing such a right. However, recent cases have drawn *amicus* support from judges, a new and unusual development. In the *Office of Public Advocacy* litigation in Alaska, ten retired Alaska judges (identified in the brief as having "more than 90 collective years of distinguished service on the bench") filed a brief supporting the appointment of counsel and describing, from the vantage point of the bench, the unfavorable outcomes for the litigants, the difficulties faced by judges presiding over such cases, the costs in time and efficiency to the judicial system, and the deleterious effects on public confidence in the integrity of the system when indigents with important cases have no counsel. (The brief is available at http://www.civilrighttocounsel.org/pdfs/Alaska%20Retired%20Judges %20Amicus%20Brief.PDF). In this, the retired judges echoed to some extent the comments of the concurring justice in the Maryland *Frase* litigation, who dissented from his colleagues' refusal to reach the issue of whether indigent litigants were entitled to counsel: "[I]t is my belief that there is no judge on this Court that believes in his or her heart or mind, that justice is equal between the poor and the rich. . . . Each of us knows, I believe, that an unrepresented parent . . . when opposed by competent counsel . . . is normally not afforded the equal protection of the laws." *Frase*, 840 A.2d at 134.

In some states, the right to counsel has been expanded legislatively. Laura Abel's article *Keeping Families Together, Saving Money, and Other Motivations Behind New Civil Right to Counsel Laws*, 42 Loy. L.A. L. Rev. 1087 (2009), describes new measures in seven states expanding statutory rights to counsel in termination of parental rights, juvenile immigration, custody, and abuse/neglect cases. In California, despite times of fiscal austerity, a 2009 law allocated approximately $11 million per year (in funds derived from postjudgment court fees) to a three-year pilot program (renewable for a second three years) funding court innovations and more lawyers for low-income people in selected counties in housing, custody, domestic violence, guardianship, and conservatorship matters, closely echoing the "basic human needs" framework of the ABA Resolution. The legislative findings of the pilot statute explicitly tied the lack of counsel to the courts' inability to deliver justice:

> The adversarial system of justice relied upon in the United States inevitably allocates to the parties the primary responsibility for discovering the relevant evidence, finding the relevant legal principles, and presenting them to a neutral judge or jury. Discharging these responsibilities generally requires the knowledge and skills of a legally trained professional. The absence of representation not only disadvantages parties, it has a negative effect on the functioning of the judicial system. When parties lack legal counsel, courts must cope with the need to provide guidance and assistance to ensure that the matter is properly administered and the parties receive a fair trial or hearing. Those efforts, however, deplete scarce court resources and negatively affect the court's ability to function as intended, including causing erroneous and incomplete pleadings, inaccurate information, unproductive court appearances, improper defaults, unnecessary continuances, delays in proceedings for all court users, and other problems that can ultimately subvert the administration of justice.

2009 Cal. Legis. Serv. 457 (A.B. 590) (West).

Two important pilot projects have also recently taken place in Massachusetts. After a 2008 Boston Bar Association report urging a pilot to study how a civil right to counsel in the areas of housing, family, juvenile, and immigration law could be implemented, private foundation funding was obtained for two pilots involving eviction cases in two different courts in Massachusetts.

The results are discussed in the next subsection.

1. Do Lawyers Make a Difference?

Right to counsel advocates are focusing new energy on attempting to determine when representation is most needed, or when it makes the most difference in outcomes. Professor Russell Engler concludes in *Connecting Self-Representation to Civil* Gideon: *What Existing Data Reveal About When Counsel Is Most Needed*, 37 Fordham Urb. L.J. 37 (2010) that:

> [n]otwithstanding methodological differences, reports consistently show that rep-resentation is a significant variable affecting a claimant's chances for success in eviction, custody, and debt collection cases. That finding also applies to adminis-trative proceedings. Rebecca Sandefur's meta-analysis of studies of the effects of representation reports that parties represented by lawyers are between 17% and 1380% more likely to receive favorable outcomes in adjudication than are parties appearing pro se.

Professor Engler goes on to suggest two conclusions about when and what kind of representation makes an important difference to outcome:

> The first is the importance of power. The greater the power opposing a litigant, and the more that litigant lacks power, the greater will be the need for representation. . . . The second theme is the importance of having not just any advocate, but of having a skilled advocate with knowledge and expertise relevant to the proceeding.

Id.; *see also* Rebecca Sandefur, *The Impact of Counsel: An Analysis of Empirical Evidence*, 9 Seattle J. Soc. Just. 51 (2010); Laura Abel & Susan Vignola, *Economic and Other Benefits Associated with the Provision of Civil Legal Aid*, 9 Seattle J. Soc. Just. 139 (2010).

Rigorous empirical study of the effects of representation has been, with few exceptions, almost entirely absent until recently. Virtually none of the studies mentioned in the Engler and Sandefur works used random assignment of sub-jects or control groups. Many simply compared outcomes for represented and unrepresented clients, without accounting for the possibility of selection bias (that is, the possibility that represented clients may have been able to secure representation because they had stronger cases) or other factors. However, more recently, the Massachusetts housing pilots mentioned above were studied in detail by both the Boston Bar Association, which produced one report, and three Harvard professors, who collaborated on two other reports. *See* Bos. Bar Ass'n Task Force on the Civil Right to Counsel, *The Importance of Representation in Eviction Cases and Homelessness Prevention* (2012); D. James Greiner et al., *How Effective Are Limited Legal Assistance Programs? A Randomized Experiment in a*

Massachusetts   Housing   Court   (2011),   *available   at*   http://ssrn.com/
abstract=1880078; D. James Greiner et al., *The Limits of Unbundled Legal Assistance: A Randomized Study in a Massachusetts District Court and Prospects for the
Future*, 126 Harv. L. Rev. 901 (2013).

One pilot took place in the Quincy District Court and the other in the Northeast Housing Court. Both reports examining the Quincy pilot concluded that
the pilot, in which tenants facing eviction were randomly assigned to receive
either limited assistance in filling out forms and an instructional session, or full
representation, established that the offer of full representation greatly affected
the tenant's chance of retaining possession of the housing unit and that represented tenants received significantly greater rent forbearance or payments. The
authors of the studies differed on the import of the Northeast pilot, however,
which compared the effect of full representation to that of referral to a "lawyer
for the day" program. While both studies agreed that the pilot's results showed
no measurable difference in outcomes between the treatment and control
groups in Northeast, the Bar Association's report noted that the existing lawyer
for a day program was unusually robust and that "possession rates for both the
treated and control groups of tenants are well above the state average for possession rates for tenants generally, confirming the importance of representation
in Northeast as well as Quincy."

A recent article discusses and compares the studies in detail, and also analyzes
a smaller, nonrandomized study of representation in housing cases in one
California county. *See* John Pollock, *Recent Studies Compare Full Representation to
Limited Assistance in Eviction Cases*, 42 Housing L. Bull. 72 (2012).

Empirical evidence regarding the need for and effectiveness of counsel is
likely to become more sought after in the wake of Turner v. Rogers, because
of the Court's holding that while counsel was not required in all civil contempt
cases, it could be constitutionally required in some cases where the "substitute
procedural safeguards" the Court endorsed were not adequate. *See* 131 S. Ct. at
2518. Indeed, at the oral argument in *Turner*, several Justices asked whether
there were data regarding how often counsel appears in child support cases,
whether the relative costs of appointing counsel and incarcerating contemnors
had been calculated, and other empirical questions. *See* Jeffrey Selbin et al.,
*Service Delivery, Resource Allocation, and Access to Justice: Greiner and Pattanayak
and the Research Imperative* (2012), *available at* http://papers.ssrn.com/sol3/
papers.cfm?abstract_id=2003960 (discussing increased need for empirical
evidence after *Turner*); Steven Eppler-Epstein, *Passion, Caution, and Evolution:
The Legal Aid Movement and Empirical Studies of Legal Assistance*, 216 Harv. L. Rev.
102 (2013).

2.   Is Access to Justice an Antipoverty Strategy?

The "civil *Gideon*" or right to counsel movement is not uncontroversial even
among poverty lawyers and those unquestionably committed to advocacy for the
poor. The excerpt that follows is from the article included earlier in this
chapter by Gary Smith, long-time executive director of one of the country's
largest legal services programs, in which Smith casts a critical eye on what he
sees as the distinctions between "civil *Gideon*" and antipoverty work.

GARY F. SMITH, *POVERTY WARRIORS: A HISTORICAL PERSPECTIVE ON THE MISSION OF LEGAL SERVICES*

45 Clearinghouse Rev. 34 (2011)

. . . In the national legal services community the new enthusiasm accompanying the quest for a so-called "Civil Gideon" model ultimately may serve to erode any resemblance between today's legal services "advocacy," and the antipoverty mission envisioned by the founders of the original legal services program. Civil Gideon is simply the logical — perhaps the ultimate — extension of the "access to justice" model; indeed, Civil Gideon is essentially "access to justice" on steroids.

The Civil Gideon "movement" was fueled initially by the efforts of various legal academics and civil rights/public interest lawyers to establish, through a "test-case" litigation approach, an entitlement to counsel in civil cases as a matter of state constitutional interpretation. The movement has since spurred the drafting of model "right-to-counsel" statutes. California has also enacted a pilot project to fund partnerships between courts and legal aid programs to represent poor litigants in certain kinds of cases.

For the most part, the Civil Gideon model seems even more narrowly focused than the "access to justice" model upon a single forum — the courts — and seems primarily concerned with providing assistance to unrepresented *defendants* in court. . . . Some thoughtful leaders within the Civil Gideon movement have acknowledged that a comprehensive right-to-counsel model should include "representation in administrative forums, non-lawyer assistance, advice and counsel, and self-help assistance." The overall focus, however, remains centered upon assisting unrepresented litigants (primarily defendants) in court, and, as in the "access to justice" model, the poverty of the litigant is primarily relevant only to the extent it renders the litigant unable to afford an attorney.

The Civil Gideon movement has gained momentum over the last decade in large part because of support from prominent members of the judiciary. Although these individual judges no doubt are genuinely concerned over the plight of low-income *pro per* litigants, the judiciary's growing *institutional* support for a Civil Gideon model not surprisingly coincides with the undeniable efficiency crisis in the courts, precipitated by the ever-increasing flood of *pro per* filings, particularly in the family courts. Indeed, no Civil Gideon model could successfully be implemented, let alone funded, without the strong support of a state's judiciary. Because the courts simply have no institutional interest in supporting any right-to-counsel model that does not directly and positively impact their caseloads, a model that does not specifically target those concerns will not succeed.

Notwithstanding the Civil Gideon momentum, the continuing national discussion around this effort is mostly silent on how such a model might cause a massive paradigm shift in how existing legal services programs understand their missions. More specifically, there is little discussion of a Civil Gideon regime's impact on the advocacy of those remaining legal aid programs that (1) prioritize the use of the law to challenge the causes and effects of poverty; and (2) consider their primary "client" to be the entire poor *community* they serve.

* * *

Two civil right to counsel advocates responded to Smith's criticisms in 2011, disputing (among other things) his prediction of the likely displacement of legal services funds and priorities.

DEBRA GARDNER & JOHN POLLOCK, *CIVIL RIGHT TO COUNSEL'S RELATIONSHIP TO ANTIPOVERTY ADVOCACY: FURTHER REFLECTIONS*
45 Clearinghouse Rev. 150 (2011)

... [D]espite Smith's legitimate concern, we are not aware of situations where new rights to counsel have displaced or interfered with legal services systemic advocacy efforts, and the legal services programs that have led efforts for new rights to counsel seem to have come to terms with that concern. For example, the recent legislative success in Massachusetts in establishing a right to counsel in guardianship proceedings was the result of legal services advocacy, and similar legal services organizations have driven and supported legislation for a right to counsel for seniors in eviction and foreclosure proceedings in New York City. These legal services communities grappled with the very concerns we discuss here and determined how to move through them.

Far from detracting from systemic work, a civil right to counsel can enhance antipoverty efforts. For instance, a new right to counsel can lead to the creation of new organizations with new funding streams to handle the right, freeing up legal services organizations to do the impact antipoverty work we see as critical for our client communities. In fact, some of the systemic advocacy that Smith describes (such as extending the notice period statewide for evictions) could have diminished value if tenants did not have attorneys to enforce such new rights. And some efforts arising from the momentum to achieve a civil right to counsel, such as California's Sargent Shriver Civil Counsel Act (A.B. 590), have infused new funding into legal services organizations.

... The civil right to counsel can ... be an antipoverty strategy in its own right. For instance, tenants are unrepresented 90 percent to 99 percent of the time, depending on the jurisdiction, while landlords are represented at least 90 percent of the time. Landlords are aware of this imbalance, and landlord-tenant courts are chronically underfunded, resulting in ... rampant abuse of the rights of low-income tenants. . . . Beyond the impact on each client's life, the mere presence of a guaranteed attorney in indigent tenants' cases and landlords' awareness of that presence should cause a seismic shift in the treatment of tenants even prior to any litigation. . . .

The right to counsel dramatically increases the prospects for law reform through appellate advocacy that could set statewide precedents on a breathtaking range of key issues affecting poor people. Litigation of mass numbers of cases would also offer greater ability to identify and tackle systemic issues and trends.

Given that the right-to-counsel movement focuses exclusively on basic human-needs cases such as shelter, sustenance, and health — needs that are undeniably caused or exacerbated by poverty — providing counsel for people who face legal harm in these arenas clearly will itself help counter the causes and effects of poverty. Countless studies show the economic consequences to both individuals and communities when indigent people lose their homes, their medical care, and their life-sustaining benefits, and an equal number of studies show how lawyers help avoid these outcomes more often than not. We are not, however, simply resting on prior studies but rather are attempting the difficult work of measuring the actual economic and societal costs and benefits associated with providing counsel in basic human-needs cases. Such is the purpose of pilot programs operating in California, Massachusetts, and Texas. . . .

G. THE SELF-HELP MOVEMENT

In recent years, as legal services veteran and expert Jeanne Charn has explained:

> [A] revolution is underway in state trial courts dealing with housing, consumer, family, and similar everyday problems of low- and middle-income households. These courts have huge volumes of unrepresented litigants. Prior practice was to urge unrepresented parties to 'get a lawyer.' In the past decade, however, lower trial courts in state after state have fundamentally altered their processes, staffing, and self-conceptions to facilitate and, in many instances, welcome litigants without lawyers.

Jeanne Charn, *Legal Services for All: Is the Profession Ready?*, 42 Loy. L.A. L. Rev. 1021, 1039 (2009).

Some commentators argue that accepting the reality of large numbers of unrepresented litigants and simplifying court procedures are wiser policy goals than seeking a broader right to counsel in civil cases. One of the most emphatic voices in this camp is that of Professor Benjamin Barton, as exemplified by the following excerpt.

BENJAMIN BARTON, *AGAINST CIVIL* GIDEON
(AND FOR PRO SE COURT REFORM)
62 Fla. L. Rev. 1227 (2010)

"Civil *Gideon*" is a short-hand name for a concept that has been the white whale of American poverty law for the last forty years — a constitutional civil guarantee to a lawyer to match the criminal guarantee from Gideon v. Wainwright. This Article argues that the pursuit of civil *Gideon* is an error logistically and jurisprudentially and advocates an alternate route for ameliorating the execrable state of pro se litigation for the poor in this country: pro se court reform.

This Article and the civil *Gideon* advocates agree on one key point. The current treatment of persons too poor to afford counsel in America's civil courts is an embarrassment and is a serious and growing problem. Despite this common ground, three key difficulties led to this Article. First, *Gideon* itself has largely proven a disappointment. Between overworked and underfunded lawyers and a loose standard for ineffective assistance of counsel, there is little in indigent criminal defense that makes one think that a guarantee of civil counsel will work very well. Second, focusing our attention on pro se court reform is a much, much more promising and likely palliative to the legal problems of the poor. Lastly, and most importantly, civil *Gideon* is a deeply conservative and backward looking solution to this problem, while pro se court reform has the potential to do more than just help the poor. It has the potential to radically reshape our justice system in ways that assist everyone. At the end of this Article, I describe a science fiction thought experiment: imagine a world where the courts that deal with the poor are so simple, efficient, transparent, and pleasant that for once the justice system of the poor was the envy of the rich. Pro se court reform actually offers this possibility.

If civil *Gideon* were merely a mildly bad idea, the division among poverty lawyers and community advocates on this issue would be of limited import. The fact that civil *Gideon* is a bad idea and saps energy and resources from a better, more workable solution, however, necessitates an effort to convince others to join the pro se court reform movement.

Nevertheless, bar associations, academics, and poverty lawyers are working harder on civil *Gideon* than ever. In 2006, the ABA House of Delegates unanimously approved a report calling for a national civil *Gideon* to "provide legal counsel as a matter of right at public expense to low income persons in those categories of adversarial proceedings where basic human needs are at stake, such as those involving shelter, sustenance, safety, health or child custody." There has likewise been an uptick of favorable scholarly attention, including at least three recent law review symposia pushing for civil *Gideon*. Public interest lawyers have filed recent cases and formed civil *Gideon* working groups.

There are three caveats before the argument begins in earnest. First, while this Article is quite critical of civil *Gideon*, no disrespect whatsoever is meant to its many proponents. As a general rule, any focus on the problems of the poor is welcome, and the civil *Gideon* supporters have their hearts in the right place. Second, part of the argument is a comparison between the lofty rhetoric and great promise of *Gideon* and the sad reality of our current system of indigent defense. This Article does not argue that *Gideon* itself is wrong or should be overturned; rather the focus is on its deeply flawed implementation, not *Gideon* itself. Last, this Article includes some rather distressing facts, figures, and anecdotes concerning public defenders and appointed counsel for the indigent. There are many, many excellent criminal defense lawyers working and representing the poor all over the country, and I have had the pleasure of meeting and working with some of them over my career. So, nothing stated herein should be seen as an indictment of all criminal defense lawyers or public defenders.

It is fair to indict the system as a whole, however. System-wide, the view is beyond disturbing. It is bad enough that any civil *Gideon* advocate should think twice before importing a broken criminal system into our civil courts. As written, *Gideon* is an iconic case that makes an important statement about the nature of the criminal process in the United States. Yet as applied, *Gideon* has hardly guaranteed equal access to the courts for the poor. To the contrary, two factors have made *Gideon*'s promise illusory indeed: the reticence of courts to set funding levels or limit caseloads for *Gideon*'s guaranteed counsel and the galling laxity of the Court's definition of the ineffective assistance of counsel.

In fact, there is an argument to be made that *Gideon* has worked out great for everyone in the system except criminal defendants. The legal profession won because a massive new source of guaranteed business emerged. Judges won because lawyers, in comparison to pro se litigants, make every judge's job easier. Society wins because everyone gets to feel better about guaranteeing defendants a lawyer. The psychological value of *Gideon*—that everyone can rest easy knowing that lawyers are theoretically ensuring that the system works for rich and poor alike—should not be underestimated. The double bonus is that system-wide the lawyers are so underpaid and overburdened that in most jurisdictions they are unable to put up much of a fight, so society gets the appearance of fairness without a high rate of acquittals or actual trials.

Moreover, Strickland v. Washington [466 U.S. 668 (1984)] sets the standards for ineffective assistance of counsel so low that sleeping lawyers have been found effective. So while *Gideon* guarantees a robust right to counsel, Strickland and its progeny have powerfully diluted the content of that guarantee.

If civil *Gideon* became a reality, it is extremely unlikely that civil lawyers would be better supported. Courts would likely not require limits on caseloads or increased expenditures on a guaranteed right to civil counsel. Nor would civil plaintiffs be guaranteed a competent lawyer with time to investigate, research, and try their cases. To the contrary, if the absolutely critical rights theoretically protected by *Gideon* can be so watered down, a civil *Gideon* would likely fare much worse. The government's long-term treatment (read: starvation) of civil legal aid societies also does not make civil *Gideon* look particularly promising.

Civil *Gideon* is also very unlikely to occur. The Supreme Court chose not to extend *Gideon* to termination of parental rights cases in Lassiter v. Department of Social Services. This was a brutal defeat for civil *Gideon* because a termination of parental rights case presents the closest possible civil analogy to *Gideon* that does not involve imprisonment, but rather a liberty interest (the right to keep one's children) that the Court has repeatedly credited as powerful, as well as coercive, state action; the State of North Carolina itself sought to take the mother's children. No state or federal court since has recognized a broad civil right to counsel since the loss in *Lassiter*. Moreover, the current fiscal situation makes this an awkward time to ask a court to guarantee an expensive new constitutional right. . . .

Nonetheless, *Gideon* is a little bit like Brown v. Board of Education. It may not have been consistent with the original understanding of the Constitution, but it is hard to argue in retrospect that it was not absolutely the right decision. *Gideon* certainly struck a chord when it held that "reason and reflection require us to recognize that in our adversary system of criminal justice, any person haled into court, who is too poor to hire a lawyer, cannot be assured a fair trial unless counsel is provided for him. This seems to us to be an obvious truth." Nevertheless, every new extension of *Gideon* takes it a step beyond the point where it is "an obvious truth" that constitutional fairness requires a new guarantee of counsel and runs the risk of replacing legislative funding priorities with those of judges. Thus, extending the right to counsel too far could threaten the legitimacy of *Gideon* itself. In fact, some recent commentators have argued that the best way to protect and enforce *Gideon* is to roll back its extension to misdemeanor cases in Argersinger v. Hamlin. The broadening of *Gideon* to include misdemeanors, juvenile cases, and other, less serious types of offenses alone may have led to *Gideon*'s destruction. Courts may have defended a right limited to felonies more zealously or at least recognized that more work was necessary on those cases than was being provided.

There are also particular reasons to be concerned in an area where judges require the appointment of lawyers. One might question whether the problems of the poor are really best solved by more lawyers or more due process. Stated flatly, there are many reasons for advocates for the poor to worry when courts or bar associations announce an intention to assist the poor. The implementation of *Gideon* alone should offer a hint as to how these things work out in the long run. In *Gideon*, and other due process cases, the Court has often followed up high-minded rhetoric with a shameful lack of substance. At a certain point, courts are no longer to blame, and advocates for the poor must take some responsibility. Like Charlie Brown trying to kick Lucy's football, it may be time to try a different game.

Lastly, there is a cheaper, less constitutionally troubling, and more likely solution: an overhaul of the courts that handle the bulk of the nation's pro se matters would go a long way towards reaching the aims of civil *Gideon*. As it stands now, most courts are not set up to cope with a substantial pro se docket. Clerks are instructed not to give "legal advice" to pro se litigants. In many courts, no one explains to pro se litigants what papers need to be filed, what needs to be argued in court, or even how the process is supposed to operate. In many courts, judges do not consider it their responsibility to ameliorate any of this. Often, very little effort has been made to streamline or simplify either the law or the procedure in the courts where much unrepresented poverty work occurs.

If a systematic effort were made to simplify the law and procedure in courts with large pro se dockets, it could improve outcomes in those courts and do more for the poor than a guarantee of counsel, all at less cost. Too often, access to justice only means access to lawyers. Rather than seeing the plight of the poor as an opportunity to fund more lawyers, we should see it as an opportunity to make American law simpler, fairer, and more affordable. If courts with substantial pro se dockets were actually able to reform, the justice system for the poor would, for once, be the envy of the rich. . . .

* * *

Richard Zorza, a leader in the self-help movement, has written extensively about the changes to courts in response to the surge in the number of unrepresented litigants. The next excerpt describes many of the most significant innovations.

RICHARD ZORZA, *SELF-REPRESENTED LITIGANTS AND THE ACCESS TO JUSTICE REVOLUTION IN THE STATE COURTS: CROSS-POLLINATING PERSPECTIVES TOWARD A DIALOGUE FOR INNOVATION IN THE COURTS AND THE ADMINISTRATIVE LAW SYSTEM*

29 J. Nat'l Ass'n Admin. L. Judiciary 63 (2009)

In the last ten to fifteen years, state courts have responded to a tidal wave of self-represented litigants with a wide range of innovations that are fundamentally transforming the courts. These innovations impact the whole system and range from new ways of accepting cases into the system to innovative courtroom procedures and management practices, and from a more proactive process of managing the flow of cases to innovations that help make sure that the parties comply with the court's orders. Indeed, the Self-Represented Litigation Network, a national network of groups working for access to justice for the self-represented, has identified a total of forty-two such "Best Practices" based on these innovations.

Most importantly, state courts are transforming themselves from being just "case deciding" institutions to institutions with a broader access-to-justice mission. They are moving from a focus on the number of decisions and the quality of those individual decisions in the context of the information placed before them, to a focus on the extent to which, as institutions, they are accessible to those seeking justice. Thus, state courts are focusing more on the quality of decisions relative to the underlying facts of the case, rather than just the papers that might in the past have been presented to the forum. . . .

B.   Innovations in Detail

1.   Self-Help Centers

Many courts across the country have established self-help centers. These programs use court staff to provide neutral information of the kind described above to litigants about the underlying processes and procedures, as well as provide appropriate forms. The Self-Represented Litigation Network has identified over 130 such centers, varying from those serving one court and dealing with only one topic, to those providing technology-assisted services statewide on a variety of topics. There are also a wide range of actual services provided, including: drop-in counter information; detailed clinics; assistance completing forms; referrals to brief attorney-client consultation; and mediation and other alternative dispute resolutions options, many of which can assist in preparing the litigant for hearing, even if they do not result in an agreement. The centers represent the hub of services, and are becoming the focal point for needs assessment. An extension of these services is the provision of caseflow management services in which the process of the case is monitored, and additional information is provided to litigants (often by bringing them in to the courthouse) if needed to keep the case moving.

These programs have very high consumer satisfaction levels (often well into the 90s) and are generally agreed to have a significant impact on the overall operations of the court. In part, this is because the directors of the programs become informal ombudsmen, and they are able to deal directly with judges and court administrators on matters of general concern.

2.   Forms Innovations

These centers have found the obvious — the self-represented have almost no access to the system unless forms are available for litigants to use to present their cases. Centers have found the need for a comprehensive statewide forms program covering the main types of cases and the most frequent procedural situations in these cases. That is consistent with the experience of administrative agencies, which also often have staff complete the forms for the applicant. It is critical that, whenever possible, the forms be accepted statewide. Any other system is highly expensive to maintain and makes it much harder to deliver services to a broad area.

There have been two important additional sets of innovations building on this foundation in the courts. The first is the movement to so called "plain English" in which the forms are redesigned for comprehensibility and ease of use. The Self-Represented Litigation Network, in cooperation with the LSC, has conducted a training aimed at improving the comprehensibility and forms design skills of court and legal aid staff responsible for forms. There is now a whole body of knowledge on how to make forms easy to use, and on what process a court should go through to achieve this goal. The process of simplifying forms is as much common sense as it is technical, and the skills can be shared with relative ease. While some judges and lawyers may fear that simplification will result in "dumbing down," as a practical matter this fear can be avoided by careful attention to the substance of what needs to be communicated. The set of skills to develop such forms should transfer easily into the administrative agency context.

In addition, using one of a variety of available technologies, the State Justice Institute (SJI) and LSC have cooperated to create and support a national capacity for online automated forms. When a court or legal aid program takes their forms and programs them using this capacity, litigants can then go online, answer questions about the case, and obtain completed forms that meet the appropriate court's requirement. These forms are much easier and more efficient for the courts to process, as well as more effective at telling the litigant's complete story to the court. The use of branching logic in the questions saves time for the litigants and focuses them on the relevant issues; thus, it also saves time in the courtroom. Furthermore, this technology could be applied with great ease in the administrative law context.

3.   TECHNOLOGY FOR ACCESS

Additional access technologies include webpages carefully built to provide maximum information about the law, the courts, and the procedural steps litigants need to take to protect their rights. In addition to what might be called "traditional" webpages, courts and legal aid programs have taken the lead in such technologies as document assembly; user-friendly electronic filing; online chat, in which volunteers or staff help users find the information they need; video conferencing, which allows self-help center staff to provide services to remote locations; and online video segments explaining law and procedure. These innovations require significant investment, but then provide services at very low per user marginal cost. They also facilitate access for those who live in rural areas, or for those who for other reasons are unable to come to court easily. They must, however, be deployed with care and with sufficient human support.

4.   STAFF TRAINING ON ACCESS

One of the greatest impacts on the court experience of the self-represented has come from the adoption of guidelines and rules in many states on what court staff can and cannot do to help litigants. While administrative agency staff are often less reluctant than court staff to provide the information that litigants need, the experiences of courts in clarifying what is appropriate can be of great use in introducing similar improvements into the administrative agency system.

In particular, the emphasis of these guidelines, and the staff training based on them, is to clarify the appropriateness of the "information-providing role" described in more detail below. Staff find these guidelines and programs empowering, since without them they have often been frustrated by their perceived inability to provide information that is so clearly needed by the people in crisis in front of them.

The programs allow information about the options available to a litigant, information about the range of choices available to a court under the law, and information about what forms should be filed. The programs, however, do not allow advice about the choices the litigant should make, predictions about what a judge might actually do, and they cannot tell them the specifics of what to say in the forms.

As courts have gained experience with these programs, they have found that a greater level of fact-based engagement with the litigants is appropriate without putting the court on the side of the litigant. It is appropriate, for example, for staff to pull a file, explain the procedural situation, and discuss what is needed to get the case moving.

5. DISCRETE TASK REPRESENTATION (UNBUNDLING)

An important innovation that can improve the entire process is the establishment of Discrete Task Representation, also known as "unbundling" programs. In "unbundling programs" the litigant and the lawyer agree that the lawyer will handle a part of the case, such as perhaps the hearing or all tasks related to a particular issue, such as child custody, while the litigant will self-represent on the remaining matters.

Such programs sometimes are established by the private bar, and at other times are set up by the courts to facilitate pro bono participation. Some state courts have played a major role by setting up rules to authorize the practice, by regulating such matters as making sure that the attorney is not forced by the judge to stay in the case after the end of the task for which attorney participation has been agreed, and by dealing with issues such as service and communication. . . .

The second major area of innovation concerns the processes of the courtroom itself. As a result of research conducted into courtrooms with self-represented litigants, we now have a much deeper understanding of what hearing processes are most effective in helping litigants get their story out, and in making sure that judges get the information that they need to make the best decisions. The research supports and is consistent with modifications to the ABA Model Code of Judicial Conduct. Best practices that reflect these insights can improve the efficiency of the courtroom and save time for litigants and judges, and even for lawyers who are waiting for their cases to be called. . . .

[The article goes on to describe in detail ten "best practices" for hearings, including setting the stage; explaining the process that will be followed; using varied techniques such as questioning from the bench or breaking the hearing into sub-topics, probing for detail, and so on; involving the litigants in the decision making to the extent possible; articulating the order or decision from the bench; explaining and summarizing the decision; identifying and resolving barriers to compliance; providing a written order or decision; preparing the parties for the next steps and outcomes; and using non-verbal behaviors to control who is speaking, show attention, etc.]

NOTES AND QUESTIONS

1. Is self-help or self-representation a viable strategy for low-income litigants? Do the measures advocated by Richard Zorza and others in the self-help community offer a realistic hope of reforming courts to such a degree that

the need for representation at public expense can be reduced or eliminated?

2. Little or no empirical evidence about the efficacy of self-help measures exists. Should advocates or policymakers urge the expansion of self-help strategies in the absence of such evidence?

3. Do you agree with Professor Barton that "civil *Gideon*" is neither an achievable nor a worthy goal? Why or why not? Is an expanded right to counsel in civil cases analogous to the right at stake in *Gideon*? Are there arguments for providing lawyers only in some civil cases or only to some civil litigants even though the criminal right is a categorical one?

4. Are self-help and "civil *Gideon*" mutually exclusive goals? If not, how should advocates, judges, or policymakers determine which is more appropriate in a given setting? *See* Richard Zorza, *Access to Justice: the Emerging Consensus and Some Questions and Implications*, 94 Judicature 156 (2011) (arguing that a consensus is now forming in the courts and the profession around the need for court simplification, continued legal aid, and an effective triage system for determining which cases require counsel and which can be handled by a self-represented litigant with proper support).

5. Professor Russell Engler has written extensively about the modern right to counsel movement and its embrace of an incremental, line-drawing approach, which explicitly declines to endorse a goal of publicly funded lawyers for all civil litigants in all circumstances. *See, e.g.*, Russell Engler, *Reflections on a Civil Right to Counsel and Drawing Lines: When Does Access to Justice Mean Full Representation by Counsel, and When Might Less Assistance Suffice?*, 9 Seattle J. Soc. Just. 97, 113 (2010) (arguing that access to justice requires "expansion of the roles of the court system's key players," including judges, mediators, and clerks to better assist unrepresented litigants, increased evaluation and use of self-help measures, and a civil right to counsel "where the expansion of the roles of the key players and assistance programs do not provide the necessary help to vulnerable litigants"). This approach was taken in the ABA resolution mentioned in Section G above, which endorsed a right to counsel only in cases involving "basic human needs," and in the Sargent Shriver Civil Counsel Act now in effect in California, which has provided a six-year funding stream for pilot programs in several counties to increase the availability of counsel and the adoption of court innovations to better serve unrepresented litigants in certain targeted areas of the law, but only where it is determined that measures short of counsel cannot suffice to deliver justice. *See* Sargent Shriver Civil Counsel Act, Cal. Civ. Code §§ 68650 *et seq.* (2010); *see also* Clare Pastore, *California's Sargent Shriver Civil Counsel Act Tests Impact of More Assistance for Low-Income Litigants*, 47 Clearinghouse Rev. 97 (2013).

CHAPTER
11

Markets

INTRODUCTION

Market responses to poverty play an increasingly significant role in how poverty is addressed both in the United States and internationally. A conservative turn against the notion of welfare rights in the United States, by the Supreme Court and by the elected branches, has narrowed the opportunities for state-centric responses to domestic poverty. And, for developing countries, small national budgets create a substantial gap between what government antipoverty efforts can accomplish and the enormity of the needs related to widely shared poverty. Although not fitting neatly into any one category, market efforts to reduce poverty are worthy of attention not only because the political limits on traditional state-centered approaches suggest the need for creativity on the part of antipoverty advocates, but also because market solutions may offer new ways of thinking about how to support poor communities.

Poverty in the United States is closely connected with the country's capitalist economic system. Poverty law might be thought of as the way society responds to the inequality and deprivations that some people and groups of people experience in connection with this system. Accordingly, most of the chapters in this textbook focus on obligations that the state does or does not have to lessen the harmful effects of poverty or to guarantee that the poor have access to particular resources. As we have seen, antipoverty efforts are often politically unpopular, and rights-based arguments similarly often fail before the courts. The popular notions that capitalism is good, that the market is inherently different from the state, and, as much as possible, that the state should limit its role in the market all fall under the banner of *laissez-faire* capitalism. Although there is no such thing as "the market" given the many forms that capitalism takes around the world and even within the United States, market institutions and ideas have played a defining role in the country's economic structure and pattern of development since independence.

This chapter's exploration of "market" antipoverty work highlights the challenges of any attempt to present nongovernmental or postgovernmental responses to poverty and the expansive reach of any such effort. The chapter is divided into three primary sections: Access to Credit and Financial Services (focusing on the Community Reinvestment Act and microcredit), Place-Based Strategies (focusing on community economic development and enterprise/empowerment zones), and Charity (focusing on individual giving and the role of religious organizations). The goal of the chapter is not to canvas all the ways in which the market could have and has responded to poverty, but to use a few case studies to highlight the possibilities and challenges of market efforts — broadly understood to include state-market linkages and corrective private charity. But before moving to specific issues, it is worth considering the nature of capitalism and the role markets play in reducing poverty.

1.   What Is Capitalism?

Markets are so ubiquitous in our lives that it is easy not to consider the under-lying structure that supports and defines them. Although economists tend to think about markets in terms of demand and supply, the rules and norms — in other words, the law — surrounding particular markets shape those markets and help establish market winners and losers. As Professor Justin Desautels-Stein highlights in a recent article, "Competitive markets are legal constructs, both constituted and managed by legal rules, top to bottom. Consequently, it's just plain wrong to think of the legal system as only responding to the market — the legal system creates the market as well." *The Market as a Legal Concept*, 60 Buff. L. Rev. 387, 393 (2012). There are multiple markets and markets change with time. For example, the market for gasoline is not uniform across the entire United States; simply crossing a state line can change how much is paid at the pump. Similarly, the market for recent law school graduates reflects both changes in demand (as can be seen in the significant decline in hiring during the Great Recession starting in 2008) and in legal requirements to become a lawyer (such as the requirement in most states that lawyers be law school graduates). Despite their many forms, markets tend to have certain characteristics — most notably, a reliance on markets for economic transactions tied to individual ownership and the profit motive — that in some circumstances may make market responses to poverty effective.

Perhaps surprisingly, one of the best descriptions of the power of markets and capitalism comes from the *Communist Manifesto*. Karl Marx and Friedrich Engels predicted that the structural weaknesses and instability of capitalism would lead to its own downfall. This prediction has not been realized, at least not yet, but Marx and Engels correctly identified the dynamic productive capacity of capi-talism and the centrality of what we now call creative destruction. The excerpt that follows is one of the most influential (and controversial) descriptions of capitalism in history.

KARL MARX & FRIEDRICH ENGELS, *MANIFESTO OF THE COMMUNIST PARTY* (SAMUEL MOORE TRANS., 1888)

The history of all hitherto existing societies is the history of class struggles.

Freeman and slave, patrician and plebeian, lord and serf, guild-master and journeyman, in a word, oppressor and oppressed, stood in constant opposition to one another, carried on an uninterrupted, now hidden, now open fight, a fight that each time ended, either in a revolutionary re-constitution of society at large, or in the common ruin of the contending classes.

... The modern bourgeois society that has sprouted from the ruins of feudal society has not done away with class antagonisms. It has but established new classes, new conditions of oppression, new forms of struggle in place of the old ones. Our epoch, the epoch of the bourgeoisie, possesses, however, this distinctive feature: it has simplified the class antagonisms. Society as a whole is more and more splitting up into two great hostile camps, into two great classes, directly facing each other: Bourgeoisie and Proletariat.

The discovery of America, the rounding of the Cape, opened up fresh ground for the rising bourgeoisie. The East-Indian and Chinese markets, the colonisation of America, trade with the colonies, the increase in the means of exchange and in commodities generally, gave to commerce, to navigation, to industry, an impulse never before known, and thereby, to the revolutionary element in the tottering feudal society, a rapid development.

... Modern industry has established the world-market, for which the discovery of America paved the way. This market has given an immense development to commerce, to navigation, to communication by land.

... Each step in the development of the bourgeoisie was accompanied by a corresponding political advance of that class.

... The bourgeoisie, wherever it has got the upper hand, has put an end to all feudal, patriarchal, idyllic relations. It has pitilessly torn asunder the motley feudal ties that bound man to his "natural superiors," and has left remaining no other nexus between man and man than naked self-interest, than callous "cash payment." ... It has resolved personal worth into exchange value, and in place of the numberless and indefeasible chartered freedoms, has set up that single, unconscionable freedom—Free Trade. In one word, for exploitation, veiled by religious and political illusions, naked, shameless, direct, brutal exploitation.

... The need of a constantly expanding market for its products chases the bourgeoisie over the whole surface of the globe. It must nestle everywhere, settle everywhere, establish connexions everywhere.

... In place of the old wants, satisfied by the productions of the country, we find new wants, requiring for their satisfaction the products of distant lands and climes. In place of the old local and national seclusion and self-sufficiency, we have intercourse in every direction, universal inter-dependence of nations. ...

The bourgeoisie, by the rapid improvement of all instruments of production, by the immensely facilitated means of communication, draws all, even the most barbarian, nations into civilisation. The cheap prices of its commodities are the heavy artillery with which it batters down all Chinese walls, with which it forces the barbarians' intensely obstinate hatred of foreigners to capitulate. It compels all nations, on pain of extinction, to adopt the bourgeois mode of production; it compels them to introduce what it calls civilisation into their midst, i.e., to become bourgeois themselves. In one word, it creates a world after its own image.

... In proportion as the bourgeoisie, i.e., capital, is developed, in the same proportion is the proletariat, the modern working class, developed—a class of labourers, who live only so long as they find work, and who find work only so long as their labour increases capital. These labourers, who must sell themselves piece-meal, are a commodity, like every other article of commerce, and are consequently exposed to all the vicissitudes of competition, to all the fluctuations of the market.

Owing to the extensive use of machinery and to division of labour, the work of the proletarians has lost all individual character, and consequently, all charm for the workman. He becomes an appendage of the machine, and it is only the most simple, most monotonous, and most easily acquired knack, that is required of him. . . .

Modern industry has converted the little workshop of the patriarchal master into the great factory of the industrial capitalist. Masses of labourers, crowded into the factory, are organised like soldiers. As privates of the industrial army they are placed under the command of a perfect hierarchy of officers and sergeants. Not only are they slaves of the bourgeois class, and of the bourgeois State; they are daily and hourly enslaved by the machine, by the over-looker, and, above all, by the individual bourgeois manufacturer himself. The more openly this despotism proclaims gain to be its end and aim, the more petty, the more hateful and the more embittering it is.

. . . [T]he theory of the Communists may be summed up in the single sentence: Abolition of private property.

We Communists have been reproached with the desire of abolishing the right of personally acquiring property as the fruit of a man's own labour, which property is alleged to be the groundwork of all personal freedom, activity and independence.

. . . You are horrified at our intending to do away with private property. But in your existing society, private property is already done away with for nine-tenths of the population; its existence for the few is solely due to its non-existence in the hands of those nine-tenths. You reproach us, therefore, with intending to do away with a form of property, the necessary condition for whose existence is the non-existence of any property for the immense majority of society.

In one word, you reproach us with intending to do away with your property. Precisely so; that is just what we intend.

. . . Working Men of All Countries, Unite!

NOTES AND QUESTIONS

1. Though Marx and Engel believed there was a natural progression of economic systems, with capitalism falling in between feudalism and communism, many societies did not attempt communism. In the United States, concern that communism would overtake the country and the world led to the Red Scare, McCarthyism, and military engagement in Southeast Asia and Central America. With the fall of the Berlin Wall in 1989, the West enjoyed a moment of triumph and a seeming affirmation of the democratic-capitalist system. Recently, however, the record of economic growth among the Asian Tiger economies (Hong Kong, Singapore, South Korea, Taiwan) and especially the phenomenal, and unequaled, growth of China's economy present a challenge to the free market model. Depending on one's perspective, the sustained rise of China's GDP represents either (a) the pent-up potential of an economy slowly switching from socialism to capitalism, or (b) the advantages of state-led growth.

2. A common observation, traceable to Adam Smith, is that capitalism unleashes both creativity and destruction. *See* Adam Smith, *The Wealth of Nations* (1776). To understand creative destruction, imagine that Company X produces popular widgets. The company flourishes, making a good profit and employing

many people until a competitor, Company Y, starts producing a widget that is better in some way (it is cheaper or of better quality). The rise of Company Y may be coupled with a related decline of Company X: just as Company Y makes more profit and hires more employees, Company X sees profits decline and has to fire employees. Although the above is framed in terms of individual companies, the same basic story can be told about entire industries and countries (for example, U.S. car manufacturing declined as Japanese car manufacturers offered strong competition on price and quality). This dynamic attribute of capitalism has many positive societal consequences, but can also have a lasting negative impact on individuals or whole communities who see their jobs and economic base disappear. In addition to some forms of social support such as unemployment benefits and various forms of welfare, should communities have a say in corporate decisionmaking? *See, e.g.*, Fran Ansley, *Standing Rusty and Rolling Empty: Law, Poverty, and America's Eroding Industrial Base*, 81 Geo. L.J. 1757 (1993) (arguing against profit maximization and for stakeholder participation in plant-closing decisions).

3. Marx and Engels argued that the property enjoyed by the top 10 percent is made possible by the lack of property enjoyed by the other 90 percent. Do you agree or disagree with this argument?

* * *

Although Marx and Engels see capitalism in terms of despotism and the enslavement of the working class, for others, capitalism has been perhaps the most important antipoverty mechanism in history. In the excerpt that follows, Jeffrey Sachs, one of the leading economists of the last two decades, argues that capitalism is the best path to development and has been the driver of reductions in global poverty.

JEFFREY D. SACHS, *TWENTIETH-CENTURY POLITICAL ECONOMY: A BRIEF HISTORY OF GLOBAL CAPITALISM*

15 Oxford Rev. Econ. Pol'y 90 (1999)

INTRODUCTION

When communism collapsed in Eastern Europe in 1989, the running quip was that socialism was simply the longest road from capitalism to capitalism. The socialist detour, which carried along roughly one-third of humanity as of the mid-1980s, has nearly vanished by the end of the twentieth century, the result of de-communization in Eastern Europe, the collapse of the Soviet Union in 1991, and China's adoption of market reforms after 1978 (even if under one-party rule). Though the post-communist societies face enormous economic, social, and political challenges, not one has the announced goal of restoring central planning or comprehensive state ownership. The governments of the world have embraced Adam Smith as never before, at least on the rhetorical level.

It is not just the post-communist economies that are going through deep institutional change at the century's end. Virtually the entire developing world has been abandoning key assumptions of state-led development adopted in the wake of national independence by state-builders such as Nasser, Sukarno, Ataturk, and Nehru. Even the long-independent states of Latin America came to view themselves as semi-colonial or 'dependent' economies in the wake of the Great Depression, and they too adopted statist models of development similar to those of the post-colonial nations. Those statist models are now being abandoned, though heated debates continue about the appropriate role of the state in the economy.

By the end of the twentieth century, almost all of the world nations — even the very poorest countries — have adopted the basic framework of modern capitalism, though few societies have done so without deep and continuing controversy. The twenty-first century opens with a recognizable international system that can be fairly characterized as global capitalism, though it is a system fraught with social conflict and political contestation at the national and international levels. As has been true for much of the past two centuries, capitalism continues to be viewed in much of the world, especially the poorer countries, as a system of exploitation rather than as a reliable path to economic prosperity. Many governments are turning to capitalist institutions out of the exhaustion of alternative models, or in order to curry favour with powerful nations, rather than out of any particular conviction that market reforms will solve long-standing problems of economic backwardness.

Though 1989 was hailed everywhere as the collapse of Marxism, in one sense it represented the fulfilment of one of Marx's most famous predictions. Writing in *The Communist Manifesto* in 1848, Marx and Engels portrayed the newly emergent capitalist system of western Europe as historically unprecedented in its dynamism and productivity, so dynamic and productive in fact, that the whole world would become capitalist, forced to change in response to the awesome capacity of Western economies. . . .

In this light, 1989 can be seen as a watershed predicted by Marx, though one that arrived perhaps a century later than Marx might have expected.

Let's be clear, however. The rest of Marx's predictions, about the demise of capitalism following the immiserization of the masses, turned out to be wildly off base. These errors in forecast can be traced to Marx's reliance on a very crude labour theory of value, according to which Marx claimed that the income of capitalists resulted from the exploitation of labour. Marx fundamentally misunderstood that economic value is created not only by labour, but also by entrepreneurship, saving, and technological progress. Marx's most deadly legacy, indeed, was the interpretation that gaps in income between rich and poor are caused by exploitation rather than differences in productivity. This Marxist attack on wealth as ill-gotten exploitation fuelled most anti-capitalist ideologies of the twentieth century. . . .

THE CHALLENGE OF EUROPEAN CAPITALISM

. . . By the opening year of the twentieth century, the European imperial powers (now joined by an imperial United States, owner of Puerto Rico and the Philippines following the Spanish-American War) had indeed created a world in their image. Five-sixths of the world's inhabited land area was effectively under political control of Europeans (counting Russia, the Americas, and Oceania). This world was linked together by global trade, financed heavily by British banks and capital markets, and with gold and silver monetary standards that were nearly universal, and that provided the monetary framework for the rapidly growing international commerce. This global system, centered on western

Europe, was elegantly described by John Maynard Keynes in the opening pages of *The Economic Consequences of the Peace.*

> What an extraordinary episode in the economic progress of man that age was which came to an end in August 1914! . . . The inhabitant of London could order by telephone, sipping his morning tea in bed, the various products of the whole earth, in such quantity as he might see fit, and reasonably expect their early delivery upon his doorstep; he could at the same moment and by the same means adventure his wealth in the natural resources and new enterprises of any quarter of the world, and share, without exertion or even trouble, in their prospective fruits and advantages; or he could decide to couple the security of his fortunes with the good faith of the townspeople of any substantial municipality in any continent that fancy or information might recommend. He could secure forthwith, if he wished it, cheap and comfortable means of transit to any country or climate without passport or other formality, could despatch his servant to the neighbouring office of a bank for such supply of the precious metals as might seem convenient, and could then proceed abroad to foreign quarters, without knowledge of their religion, language, or customs, bearing coined wealth upon his person, and would consider himself greatly aggrieved and much surprised at the least interference. But, most important of all, he regarded this state of affairs as normal, certain, and permanent, except in the direction of further improvement, and any deviation from it as aberrant, scandalous, and avoidable.

THE LONGEST ROAD FROM CAPITALISM TO CAPITALISM

. . . By the start of 1929 one might have had some justifiable confidence that pre-First-World-War normalcy was indeed being re-established, except with the anomaly of Bolshevik Russia. Even Germany seemed to be making some recovery after two emergency loans and partial restructuring of reparations obligations. But then the Great Depression erupted, ushering in the most fateful collapse of capitalist economies during the 200 years from the start of the Industrial Revolution till today. The causes of the Great Depression continue to be debated. Some see the decade of depression as a confirmation of Keynes's 1919 warnings about the instability that would follow a Carthaginian peace in Central Europe. Others see it as the result of clinging too long to *laissez-faire* doctrines in a world of large-scale industry. Still others see a concatenation of errors by the major central banks of the day. . . .

THE AGE OF GLOBAL CAPITALISM

Much of the world arrived at capitalist institutions the hard way, having passed through decades of colonial rule, only to be followed by misguided adventures of socialism or state-led industrialization. Even countries that had maintained their independence, such as China, Turkey, and Russia, rejected the models of capitalism on offer from the rich countries of western Europe. Capitalism seemed too dangerous, or too tough a path to follow, starting from so far behind in the process of industrialization.

By the 1980s, however, these alternative models had failed, typically leading to profound macroeconomic instability and state insolvency. In Latin America, the turn towards market reforms began in Chile in 1973, in the aftermath of a brutal coup that overturned a left-wing government intent on establishing socialism.

Other countries began to follow suit in the 1980s, following the onset of the debt crisis. In Eastern Europe, the debt crisis would also have been the spur to rapid change, but change was crushed in the region until the late 1980s. India began very gradual market reforms in the 1980s, and these picked up speed in 1991, when India too came to the edge of the financial abyss. In the impoverished countries of Sub-Saharan Africa, market reforms came in the context of the IMF-World Bank structural adjustment programmes of the 1980s and 1990s.

. . . By the 1990s, then, almost the entire world had adopted the fundamental elements of a market economy, including private ownership at the core of the economy, a currency convertible for international trade, shared standards for commercial transactions (for example as codified in the agreements of more than 120 country members of the World Trade Organization), and market-based transactions for the bulk of the productive sectors of the economy.

LESSONS OF INSTITUTIONAL CHANGE

. . . Since the rise of Britain as an industrial power, capitalism has demonstrated its ability to "deliver the goods". Capitalism fuelled the rise of continental western Europe in the first half of the nineteenth century. It similarly fuelled the rise of the United States. It powered Japan to industrialization after the Meiji Restoration of 1868. One would have thought that capitalism would have been an alluring model for the world, and that the adoption of capitalist institutions would have come much more rapidly and readily than it did.

This article has hinted at some of the reasons for the long and twisted course of the diffusion of capitalist institutions. The first obstacle to diffusion was conceptual. Since Marx, if not before, the gains of the capitalist economies (and of the rich within those societies), have been viewed as ill-gotten exploitation. This was an easy interpretation. After all, the rich countries did indeed grossly exploit the rest of the world, via slavery, colonial rule, military pressures, and the like. Yet the causality was mostly the other way around: exploitation was made possible by superior power and wealth, and was not the cause of that superior power and wealth. Still, the exploitation theory of development was convenient: it allowed the laggard states to see themselves as victims needing to sever relations with the rich countries, rather than as societies in need of reform. The image of victimization in anti-capitalist ideologies has remained strong for two centuries.

The second obstacle was the period of colonial rule itself. The capitalist institutions hardly practised what they preached in their imperial possessions. Who but the Europeans introduced statism, coercion of labour, and other pervasive non-market mechanisms into much of Africa? The colonial inheritance in many cases (though not all) was not conducive to a market-based rule of law. Moreover, as already noted, the post-colonial elites in the Third World viewed open trade and investment as a veritable threat to hard-won national independence.

The third obstacle was the revolutionary nature of capitalism itself, in comparison with the stratification of traditional societies. In the late twentieth century, capitalism was often viewed as a conservative's doctrine, the preserve of the rich over the poor. But in actual history, capitalism has challenged traditional authority, of the landed nobility, upper castes, religious authorities, or foreign conquerors who ruled over indigenous populations. The elites of such highly stratified societies often opted for bastardized capitalism, or rejected capitalism altogether, in order to avoid the social and economic mobility that would be unleashed by market forces, and that could therefore endanger their dominant social and economic positions.

The fourth obstacle was that capitalism itself failed to deliver at a crucial historical juncture: the Great Depression. The importance of the Great Depression in international economic history is probably on par with the importance of the First World War in political history. The Great Depression taught many lessons, most of them wrong. Keynes, the greatest political economist of the century, made a grave mistake when he titled his text *The General Theory of Employment, Interest, and Money*. He left the impression that the Great Depression was a 'general' situation of market economies, not a one-time fluke of grotesque proportions. He failed to make clear that it occurred because of the international gold standard, a monetary arrangement that Keynes had heatedly attacked and abhorred, but strangely under-emphasized in *The General Theory*. In any event, the Great Depression left the world deeply skeptical about self-organizing market systems. It took decades more to revive robust confidence in market economies.

NOTES AND QUESTIONS

1. Do you agree with Sachs that the Great Depression was "a one-time fluke of grotesque proportions," or do you see the global capitalist structure as inherently unstable? Though not of the same scale as the Great Depression, the Great Recession that started in 2008 has led some economists to question the idea that the tools are now in place to prevent such economic turmoil. *See* Paul Krugman, *How Did Economists Get It So Wrong?*, N.Y. Times Mag. (Sept. 2, 2009).

2. Western institutions and economists have played a particularly important role in advising developing countries how to structure their economies. When following such advice was made a condition for receipt of emergency loans from the Bretton Woods institutions, the IMF, and the World Bank, advice took the form of a requirement. In 1989, economist John Williamson laid out the ten requirements that were standard to these imposed reform packages. The "Washington Consensus," as it became known, embodied the economic prescription of neoliberalism: support of free markets, free trade, and a set of institutions that mirror the institutional framework of the United States. But some economists, notably members of the New Institutional Economics school of thought, argue that for institutions to work, they have to be appropriate for the particular society being considered, and that there is no single set of best institutions. *See* Douglas C. North, *Institutions, Institutional Change and Economic Performance* (1990).

3. Notice Keynes's description of the 1914 global market. What has changed and what has not changed since then?

4. Although Sachs presents capitalism in the singular, a range of alternative frameworks can fall within the large category of market-based economies. For example, many Latin-American economies were advised by U.S. economists from the 1950s to the 1980s to use trade protectionism and local subsidies to develop an internal market to replace the importation of finished goods. Unfortunately for Latin America, import substitution industrialization, or ISI, proved to be far less of an economic engine than the export-led growth that was championed by many Asian countries.

2.   Businesses and Social Obligations

A recurring question, asked by politicians, academics, and business leaders, is: What obligations do for-profit companies have to society? Although the way it is raised varies according to the politics of the moment — Should companies be able to replace striking workers at will? Is it wrong for companies to switch from U.S. production to offshore suppliers? and so on — questions about the role that business plays or should play in responding to social problems, including poverty, resurface constantly. In an oft-cited article, *The Social Responsibility of Business Is to Increase Its Profits,* published by the *New York Times Magazine* on September 13, 1970, Milton Friedman argued that it was the responsibility of corporate managers to focus on the best interests of shareholders and not on social responsibility. After giving examples in which a corporate executive wrongly pursued social values over profit, such as reducing pollution even where not legally required to do so and hiring "hardcore" unemployed with a poverty-reduction goal in mind even where more qualified people could be hired, Friedman argued that "[i]n each of these cases, the corporate executive would be spending someone else's money for a general social interest." Specifically, through such actions, an executive harms shareholders, customers, and/or employees. Friedman's conclusion was that "there is one and only one social responsibility of business — to use its resources and engage in activities designed to increase its profits so long as it stays within the rules of the game, which is to say, engages in open and free competition without deception or fraud."

Friedman's argument finds ready support in the law and economics literature as well as in U.S. corporate law. According to a leading treatise, for example, "the primary function of corporations is to create wealth by pursuing profits." Robert Cooter & Thomas Ulen, *Law and Economics* (4th ed. 2004). Indeed, should the managers of a publicly traded corporation engage in socially minded activities to the detriment of the business, investors may demand a change in leadership or outsiders may see the opportunity for a hostile takeover made possible in part by the weakened position of the company. Judge Richard Posner explains:

> . . . [T]he basic point is that in competitive markets, a sustained commitment to any goal other than profitability will result in the firm's shrinking, quite possibly to nothing. The firm that channels profits into pollution control will not be able to recoup its losses by charging higher prices to its consumers. Consumers do not benefit as consumers from such expenditures; more precisely, they benefit just as much from those expenditures if they purchase the lower-priced product of a competing firm that does not incur them.

Richard Posner, *Economic Analysis of Law* (7th ed. 2007). U.S. corporate law further supports this perspective by imposing a fiduciary relationship between managers and owners (shareholders) that requires managers to prioritize profitability and shareholder value. *But see* Einer Elhauge, *Sacrificing Corporate Profits in the Public Interest,* 80 N.Y.U. L. Rev. 733 (2005) (arguing that there is legal space for managers to act differently). In contrast, corporate law in many European nations, most notably Germany, explicitly provides for involvement of multiple stakeholders in corporate governance in a way that may further corporate social responsibility.

One response to attacks on corporate social responsibility (CSR) involves showing the many ways that companies can benefit from being more socially responsible, including actions that benefit the poor. For example, a better record on CSR may lower the cost of capital for firms. *See* Beiting Cheng et al., *Corporate Social Responsibility and Access to Finance*, 10 Strategic Mgmt. J. 2131 (2013). In some sectors of the economy, the business model itself may depend on CSR. The expanding market for fair trade products—everything from coffee and chocolate to t-shirts and handicrafts—shows that some consumers place a value on how goods are produced and are willing to pay a premium to companies that engage in good practices. *See generally* Ezra Rosser, *Offsetting and the Consumption of Social Responsibility*, 89 Wash. U. L. Rev. 27 (2011).

Similarly, corporate social responsibility may take the form of expanding into markets or communities that have been underserved. For example, Bill Gates, Jr., the founder of Microsoft, has argued that many companies have figured out how they "can do good and do well at the same time." Gates laid out his vision for "creative capitalism" to help the world's poor in an article published in 2008:

> Capitalism has improved the lives of billions of people—something that's easy to forget at a time of great economic uncertainty. But it has left out billions more. They have great needs, but they can't express those needs in ways that matter to markets. So they are stuck in poverty, suffer from preventable diseases and never have a chance to make the most of their lives. Governments and nonprofit groups have an irreplaceable role in helping them, but it will take too long if they try to do it alone. It is mainly corporations that have the skills to make technological innovations work for the poor. To make the most of those skills, we need a more creative capitalism: an attempt to stretch the reach of market forces so that more companies can benefit from doing work that makes more people better off. We need new ways to bring far more people into the system—capitalism—that has done so much good in the world. . . .
>
> Naturally, if companies are going to get more involved, they need to earn some kind of return. This is the heart of creative capitalism. It's not just about doing more corporate philanthropy or asking companies to be more virtuous. It's about giving them a real incentive to apply their expertise in new ways, making it possible to earn a return while serving the people who have been left out. This can happen in two ways: companies can find these opportunities on their own, or governments and nonprofits can help create such opportunities where they presently don't exist.

Bill Gates, *Making Capitalism More Creative*, Time Mag. (July 31, 2008). Not surprisingly, Gates focuses part of his article on how technology can help companies reach poor people. But the idea that there are market opportunities even in poor communities that can benefit companies and the poor alike in myriad ways is not a novel one. Both Earvin "Magic" Johnson and President Clinton got considerable attention for opening businesses and offices in Harlem, New York. Indeed, as the next section will discuss, getting mainstream businesses to locate in distressed communities is one of the standard hopes of community economic development work. CSR brings into relief a number of large questions about the relationship between capitalism and poverty. For example, has capitalism overall been a force for good and has lifted billions out of poverty, or, building off the writing of Marx, is capitalist economic organization primarily a tool of oppression? Additionally, even though poverty law traditionally has focused on the programs that assist the "losers" in the market system or the need to protect the vulnerable from the harshness of laissez-faire capitalism, to the extent that markets can help individual workers and entrepreneurs escape poverty, should more attention be paid to the larger capitalist structure instead of just the system's insurance-equivalent programs?

A. COMMUNITY ECONOMIC DEVELOPMENT

A market or economic approach to poverty provides the foundation for one of the most significant antipoverty efforts of the past 20 years: community economic development (CED). Although CED has a longer lineage than just the past two decades, it came into vogue in the 1990s during the Clinton years. CED involves the work of organizers, lawyers, and community members who share a commitment to grounding antipoverty and economic growth efforts in local communities. This focus can be controversial insofar as it deemphasizes external influences on communities and broad-based mobilization, often relying instead on market development as the best way to help select communities. CED is practiced across the country by everyone from lawyers working for community development corporations (CDCs) to faculty and students in law clinics. Though it is supported by numerous organizations and programs, CED defies precise and concise definitions. Even though CED work varies by location and by the needs of the relevant communities, the following excerpt describes the characteristics of the CED in general terms.

WILLIAM H. SIMON, *THE COMMUNITY ECONOMIC DEVELOPMENT MOVEMENT*

2002 Wis. L. Rev. 377

Within a five-minute walk of the Stony Brook subway stop in the Jamaica Plain section of Boston, you can encounter the following:

- A renovated industrial site of about five acres and sixteen buildings that serves as a business incubator for small firms that receive technical assistance from the Jamaica Plain Neighborhood Development Corporation (JPNDC), a nonprofit community development corporation, which is also housed there. Known as the Brewery after its former proprietor, a beer-maker, the complex is owned by a nonprofit subsidiary of JPNDC.
- A 44,000-foot "Stop & Shop" supermarket. The market opened in 1991 after years in which the community had been without a major grocery store. It lies next to a recently renovated Community Health Center and a large high-rise public housing project. The land on which the market and health center sit was developed and is owned by a limited partnership that includes, in addition to a commercial investor, JPNDC and the Tenant Management Corporation of the housing project. Some of the income from the market and health center leases goes into a Community Benefits Trust Fund that supports job training and business development activities.
- A cluster of small, attractive multi-unit residential buildings containing a total of forty-one homes. These units were built with support from the

Federal Low Income Housing Tax Credit, and they are occupied by low and moderate income families at rents limited to thirty percent of family income. The buildings are owned by a limited partnership in which the general partners are a subsidiary of JPNDC and a resident cooperative; the limited partners include five conventional business corporations and a nonprofit corporation with a board composed of prominent government and business figures that promotes housing development throughout the state.

- Two recently renovated apartment buildings — one with eleven units and one with forty-five units — designed with common areas and facilities for medical support for elderly residents. The project benefits from large federal grants. It is owned by JPNDC; the units are rented to the tenants at rents that cannot exceed thirty percent of their income.

- A wood-frame building containing three apartments recently renovated by JPNDC with support from various public programs. JPNDC then sold it at a price well below market value to an individual, who, as a condition of ownership set out in the deed, must live in one of the units and rent the others only to people who meet specified income eligibility conditions at specified rents.

These institutions are products of the Community Economic Development (CED) Movement. Although it is unusual to find so many concentrated in such a small area — there are still others there that I have not mentioned — such projects can be found in most cities; their numbers have increased substantially in recent years, and there will be many more of them if current programs succeed. Such projects figure prominently in the most optimistic and innovative approaches to urban poverty on both the left and the right. They exemplify a kind of social entrepreneurialism that is flourishing across the country. As support for traditional welfare and public housing programs has waned, there has been a corresponding (though far from proportionate) increase in support for CED. The Movement has been fueled by trends toward decentralizing public administration on the one hand and channeling the development of local markets along socially desirable paths on the other. It has also been encouraged by changes in the contours of urban politics, especially new strategies by neighborhood activists.

Though there are many variations, the core definition of CED embraces: (1) efforts to develop housing, jobs, or business opportunities for low income people, (2) in which a leading role is played by nonprofit, nongovernmental organizations and (3) that are accountable to residentially defined communities. . . .

CED practitioners think of the Movement as a grassroots affair. To begin an account of CED by reviewing national, regional, and state support structures might strike them as looking through the wrong end of the telescope. Yet, no one denies that grassroots CED activities depend on an elaborate network of larger-scale efforts. Moreover, the increasing salience of CED in political and policy discourse can be most readily seen in the recent growth of national, regional, and state programs designed to encourage and sustain it. . . .

Looming over the current CED Movement are memories of two earlier experiments in community development, "urban renewal" or Redevelopment (a word I capitalize to indicate that it is a term of art referring to a special legal process), and the Community Action Program. Both are widely regarded as discredited, and to some extent, the current Movement has been shaped in reaction to their failures. However, in some respects, current efforts might also seem to be a continuation and vindication of the earlier movements. . . .

. . . In 1968, the Equal Opportunity Act was amended to provide for grants to "Community Development Corporations," which were defined as locally-initiated nonprofits focused on the problems of low income areas. At least half of the seats on the organization's governing body were required to be held by residents of the relevant geographical area. . . .

Moreover, the federal urban grant programs that succeeded the Community Action Program, most importantly the Community Development Block Grant (CDBG) program, continued to mandate "public participation," though more ambiguously and less ostentatiously than in the past. . . .

Despite the lowered profile of federal support for community-based organizations in the 1970s and 1980s, this period saw an explosion in neighborhood activism that has been described as a "backyard revolution," a "rebirth of urban democracy," and a "rise of sublocal structures in urban governance." Community groups formed to demand more and better services from city governments. They formed to influence land use and investment decisions, protesting proposed uses with negative externalities (dumping facilities, high-density public housing projects, freeways) and pushing for uses likely to enhance the community (parks, schools). Many of these groups were reacting to decades of municipal policies that appeared to lavish investment on downtown areas at the expense of outlying neighborhoods. . . .

With the advent of the Clinton Administration, the federal government re-embraced the combination of developmental and participatory themes associated with the War on Poverty in the Empowerment Zone/Enterprise Community program. Announced at the beginning of the Clinton Administration with great fanfare, the program offered an extraordinary package of federal benefits over a ten-year period to a small number of competitively selected "Empowerment Zones" and a smaller package to a larger number of "Enterprise Communities." After an initial application period, HUD designated nine Empowerment Zones in 1994. Impressed by initial reports, Congress then authorized funding for an additional twenty in 1997. Ninety-five "Enterprise Communities" received the smaller set of benefits in 1994.

Empowerment Zone benefits include increased grants for social services and economic development, regulatory waivers, use of tax-exempt bonding authority, and tax benefits for employers including a credit for wage payments to employees who reside in the Zone. Communities with "pervasive poverty" compete for selection by producing "strategic plans" of coordinated public and private efforts at housing, business, and job development. Congress mandated that the affected community was to be a full partner in the development of the plans. An important criterion in evaluating the plans is the extent to which the affected community and its community-based organizations have participated in the plan's development and their commitment to implementing it. Regulations require that applicants identify the community groups participating in the development of the plan, explain how they were chosen to participate, describe their history, show that they are collectively representative of the full range of the community, and "describe the role of the participants in the creation, development and future implementation of the plan."

CED institutions have three salient functional characteristics. The first is relational density and synergy. CED efforts are designed to multiply the contexts and roles in which people confront each other. As the political process links political activity to residence, so CED links economic development to residence. By striving to internalize control over economic processes within the community, CED increases the number of linked roles that residents potentially play. People who might otherwise encounter each other only as neighbors now meet as employers and employees, sellers and consumers, property owners and property occupiers, planners and citizens, administrators and service recipients.

The second is geographic focus. At the most mundane level, the physical community is a focal point, a convenient space to bring people together for multiple, varied encounters. More ambitiously, a residential community can give physical expression to a sense of distinctive common culture. The new social policy now emphasizes the call of modern urbanism with space for "detail, identity, and a sense of place," as opposed to, for example, "the anonymity of much public housing that is divorced from its surroundings."

The third characteristic is face-to-face encounters. CED efforts tend to replace remote impersonal relations, for example, between absentee owners and tenants or customers, or distant bureaucrats and their charges, with face-to-face relations. In doing so, they extend to economic development generally a basic principle of land use planning — the physical structure of the urban environment should be configured so that there will be more face-to-face interactions among neighbors. . . .

There is no single dominant theory of CED. Rather, these programs rest on a variety of convergent rationales. They can be grouped in three clusters: economic, social, and political.

A.   ECONOMIC

CED programs arise in part from dissatisfaction with bureaucracy. The principal economic complaint about bureaucracy is that bureaucrats have poor incentives and poor information. Because they do not have strong personal stakes in their decisions, their motivation to perform well is weak. Because power tends to reside at the top, while critical information is dispersed at the bottom, the key decision-makers tend to be poorly informed.

The economist's stock alternative to bureaucracy is the market. But economists acknowledge that markets have incentive and information problems too, and they are more likely than bureaucratic organizations to be thwarted by difficulties that can be called coordination problems. Market limitations with respect to incentives, information, and coordination seem especially important in the principal areas of CED activity — housing, job training, and job and business development in low income communities. So the turn to CED also reflects a sense of the limits of conventionally understood markets. . . .

B.   SOCIAL

The sociologist's complaint about bureaucracy and markets is that they engender alienation — a sense of disconnection and ineffectuality. The remedy for alienation is "empowerment," a pervasive term in CED rhetoric. The ideal of "community" associated with "empowerment" is significantly different from the Romantic conception that influenced the 1960s left. The Romantic conception connotes intimate, indiscriminate altruism. But the "community" of the

CED Movement has more sober and restrained connotations. The most important of these connotations are captured in the sociological themes of Social Capital and the Protestant Ethic. . . .

. . . CED strategies tend to increase the expectation of consistent repeat dealings among people whose encounters would otherwise be sporadic. . . .

CED strategies . . . assume that one will be more scrupulous in fulfilling duties that are associated with face-to-face relations and they try to induce such relations. . . .

C. POLITICAL

The political intuitions that underpin the CED Movement can be distinguished in terms of an interest group perspective and a republican perspective.

1. The Interest Group Perspective

From the interest group perspective, CED looks like a strategy by poor communities to increase the resources they extract from outside institutions. The importance of multistranded relations, geographic focus, and face-to-face encounters is that they facilitate more cohesive and assertive organizations that can subsequently exert greater pressure, especially against municipal government. . . .

2. The Republican Perspective

Republican political thought offers another perspective on the CED Movement. Republicanism has its origins in antiquity; it received its canonical modern formulations in the Renaissance and the seventeenth century, and was strongly influential in eighteenth and nineteenth century American thought. . . .

Republicanism is an exceptionally strong form of democracy, one with a preference for small, geographically-based political units. It exalts qualities of civic virtue and deliberation that have some resemblance to the sociological notion of social capital. Like economics, it also has an interest in material incentives, though it is primarily concerned with incentives for political rather than economic activity. . . .

From a more general perspective, Republicanism gives a political cast to the three defining themes of CED. By insisting on linking political and economic roles, Republicanism prescribes a form of relational density as a vindication of democracy. By taking ownership of real property as the critical economic underpinning of local democracy, Republicanism also adopts a geographical focus. And by insisting on the importance of direct participation, it gives priority in political terms to face-to-face relations.

Specific CED practices also resonate with the Republican program. CED is an effort to subject economic forces to democratic control. Economic self-sufficiency is an important background value in much CED discourse. Its emphasis on security of tenure and, sometimes, home ownership, can be seen as a form of propertied "independence." Its characteristic business programs provide credit and technical support to small, locally-controlled businesses in the manner of late nineteenth-century Republicanism. The Republican's favorite business form, the cooperative, makes a frequent appearance on the CED landscape.

Moreover, the charitable corporation, especially in the form of the CDC, manifests many Republican themes.

... Much of CED can be seen as an effort to translate political into economic power, and in circumstances where disadvantaged groups have more of the former than the latter, this may be a plausible strategy.

III.   CONCLUSION: THE MURAL TEST

A mural that covers the side of a building on Dudley Street depicts some of the major figures in the Dudley Street Neighborhood Initiative's remarkable efforts to revitalize that community. The impressive new construction in the neighborhood sits amid many older, still deteriorated buildings that have a good deal of graffiti on them. Although the mural sits on one of the old, unrenovated buildings, ... there has not been a mark of graffiti on it in the several years since it was painted.

Here is a vivid illustration of all three logics of collective action. The mural's pristine condition reflects at once informal coordination that enhances the value of an economic investment, social capital, and collective discipline that enhances bargaining power with outsiders. A community group that can credibly promise this type of support can thereby induce significant investments both by its own members and outsiders.

NOTES AND QUESTIONS

1. As Professor Simon's excerpt highlights, numerous federal and state programs—including enterprise and empowerment zones—support CED and related place-based economic development. Enterprise and empowerment zones enjoyed broad bipartisan support when they were introduced, in part because they seemed to promise that communities could escape poverty through deregulation and support. *See* Audrey McFarlane, *Race, Space, and Place: The Geography of Economic Development*, 36 San Diego L. Rev. 295 (1999) (describing the enterprise/empowerment zone concept and then critiquing the background assumption that all that poor communities need is business subsidies and deregulation).

* * *

In the influential article that follows, Professor Scott Cummings notes the prominent place CED has assumed in antipoverty work, identifies CED's central characteristics, and critiques the market-based approach of CED.

SCOTT L. CUMMINGS, *COMMUNITY ECONOMIC DEVELOPMENT AS PROGRESSIVE POLITICS: TOWARD A GRASSROOTS MOVEMENT FOR ECONOMIC JUSTICE*

54 Stan. L. Rev. 399 (2001)

INTRODUCTION

During the unprecedented surge of 1990s prosperity, community economic development (CED) emerged as the dominant approach to poverty alleviation, touted by politicians as a market-based alternative to outdated welfare policies and championed by civil rights leaders as a critical link to economic equality. At a time of dizzying wealth accumulation, declining welfare rolls, and burgeoning budget surpluses, a consensus formed around the idea that market-based CED programs were necessary to revitalize the lingering pockets of poverty that blotted an otherwise vibrant economic landscape. Espoused by advocates of different ideological stripes, the simple logic of market-based CED — that increasing for-profit initiatives in geographically discrete low-income neighborhoods could produce economic transformation and community empowerment — became an antipoverty axiom.

Over the past decade, the ascendance of market-based CED has fundamentally shaped the development of social policy, community-based practice, and legal advocacy. At the national policy level, a private sector approach has defined the federal government's response to poverty issues, as support programs have yielded to market-based antipoverty initiatives, such as the Empowerment Zone Program and the New Markets Tax Credit. This federal agenda has been augmented by state and local efforts to adopt market-based programs to stimulate investment and business activity in low-income neighborhoods.

Against this policy backdrop, CED professionals working to implement revitalization programs on the ground have also embraced a private sector model, reconfiguring low-income communities as underutilized markets with rich economic opportunities for businesses. According to this model, effective CED involves identifying the competitive advantages of conducting business in inner city areas and structuring the proper incentives to lure reluctant enterprises into neglected markets. Advocates of this approach have therefore suggested that distressed communities revalue and promote indigenous assets such as public transportation and proximity to existing commercial centers. Once these assets are identified and properly packaged for outside investors, private sector capital can be channeled to poor neighborhoods through innovative financial tools, bringing with it stable jobs and needed services.

In response to this privatization of social policy and community action, poverty lawyers have increasingly incorporated market techniques into their antipoverty arsenals, altering the terrain of legal services delivery. In an effort to improve the physical infrastructure and strengthen the economic fabric of distressed communities, practitioners have provided transactional legal assistance in the areas of real estate, tax, and corporate law to community-based organizations engaged in neighborhood revitalization initiatives. CED legal programs have created jobs for the poor through microenterprise and commercial development, increased the stock of affordable housing units through tax credit syndication, and expanded access to capital through the development of community-based financial institutions. As a measure of its appeal, CED legal practice has attracted financial support from government agencies and private foundations, resulting in the development of a significant number of CED legal services programs.

. . . Market-based CED, which appealed both to conservative proponents of free market politics and progressive advocates of local empowerment, emerged at the forefront of social change efforts. . . .

Beginning in the 1980s, Presidents Ronald Reagan and George Bush initiated a retrenchment of government-sponsored antipoverty programs. This occurred as a part of a strong backlash against the very entitlement programs that economic justice activists had sought to expand a decade before. . . .

In this political and economic environment, activists began to focus greater attention on market-based strategies to address issues of urban poverty. CDCs emerged during this period as the critical institutional apparatus for implementing the market approach. Analysts have suggested that the prominence of the CDC model during the 1980s was the result of community-based organizations assimilating the dominant market ideology into their advocacy strategies. The rise of CDCs was also a matter of necessity: In a time of resource scarcity, CDCs were one of the few politically viable antipoverty approaches, embracing the value of self-help and promoting private-public partnerships. Further, CDCs were considered effective vehicles for dealing with localized poverty, since they were physically situated in neighborhoods suffering from disinvestment and joblessness. Thus, in addition to curtailed social programs and heightened economic insecurity for the poor, one of the main legacies of the Reagan-Bush years was the increasing importance of market-oriented CDCs in local revitalization efforts.

. . . Under Clinton, the goal of poverty alleviation programs became market expansion, while the idea of income maintenance policies was largely discredited. Market-based CED replaced welfare as the touchstone of national antipoverty policy.

Clinton's emphasis on market-driven revitalization efforts was most apparent in his Empowerment Zone Program, created in 1993 in an effort to expand business activities in geographically identified low-income neighborhoods by offering tax benefits to employers that located within the zones. In addition, as part of a broader market-based CED policy initiative, Congress passed Clinton's New Markets Tax Credit, which was designed to spur private sector equity investments in low-income community businesses. These programs underscored Clinton's effort to align antipoverty policies with his neoliberal economic agenda and marked the culmination of a two-decade-long ideological shift in favor of market-based antipoverty strategies.

. . . By the mid-1990s, a strong consensus had formed around market-based CED precisely because of its broad ideological appeal — resonating both with conservative proponents of free market principles and progressive advocates of localized empowerment strategies. The model of market-based CED that has emerged reflects its diverse ideological lineage, integrating the principles of market expansion, localism, and community empowerment into a conceptual framework for redressing poverty.

1. The Role of the Market

The current CED paradigm is defined by an adherence to market principles and a belief in the efficacy of market-based antipoverty remedies. It rests on the premise that the market does not function properly in low-income communities and that creative efforts to build market capacity are necessary to stimulate flagging local economies. The main programmatic goal, advanced primarily by CDCs, has been to restructure market incentives to leverage private investment for the development of community-based businesses, affordable housing, and financial institutions.

A central component of market-based CED strategies has been the promotion of local business development as a vehicle for creating jobs for low-income workers. Toward this end, community organizations have acted as financing intermediaries for neighborhood businesses, provided technical assistance to community entrepreneurs, and developed local real estate projects such as shopping centers, supermarkets, and industrial business parks. A significant portion of the funding for these efforts has come through federal, state, and local economic development agencies, supplemented by foundation grants, private investments, and commercial loans. Community groups have also made efforts to stimulate economic growth through microenterprise and nonprofit business ventures. Thus, many organizations have provided technical assistance and microloans to very small businesses owned by low-income community residents. In addition, some nonprofit groups have sought to employ low-income people directly by starting their own business ventures, often termed social enterprises. CED lawyers have played a variety of roles in these business development projects, establishing appropriate legal structures, reviewing contracts and financial instruments, evaluating the tax consequences of development projects, and handling real estate matters.

Affordable housing development constitutes another important programmatic element of the market-based CED model. The Low-Income Housing Tax Credit (LIHTC) has, perhaps more than any other program, exemplified the market-based approach to CED. . . .

Consistent with the goal of market expansion, CED has also focused on increasing access to financial institutions in low-income communities to augment the flow of capital resources to areas that have suffered disinvestment. One of the main efforts in this regard has been to develop banking alternatives in economically distressed neighborhoods. Most prominently, the Community Development Financial Institutions Act (CDFI Act) of 1994 created a fund to invest in community development financial institutions (CDFIs), which are community-based organizations dedicated to investing, lending, and providing basic banking services in support of community development efforts. . . .

2. The Ideal of Localism

Market-based CED is also rooted in the ideal of localism. The postmodern emphasis on the microcosm of local community action has given credence to the idea — quite prevalent in the CED literature — that the struggle against injustice must be waged at the local level. Against this backdrop, CED proponents have generally accepted the local community as the appropriate locus of targeted economic revitalization activities, while portraying CED as a strategy uniquely capable of redressing local poverty.

Different justifications have been offered in support of localized CED efforts. Some have argued that the local focus is a strategic necessity — an effort to maximize the impact of advocacy undertaken with limited financial resources. Others have suggested that there is a stronger imperative for localism, one rooted in a model of "bottom-up" social change that relies on the active participation of community residents to produce meaningful, long-term results. In either case, there has been a powerful tendency to treat the local neighborhood as a discrete economic unit in need of rebuilding. Commentators have generally presumed the fixity of local neighborhood boundaries, suggesting that the primary objective of CED should be the creation of new investment, jobs, and development projects within defined geographic spheres. CED has therefore evolved as a "place-based" strategy that attempts to enlist the support of community residents to effect changes in their immediate surroundings. . . .

3. Community Empowerment

Since the establishment of community action agencies in the 1960s to facilitate the participation of neighborhood residents in the implementation of antipoverty programs, the idea of community empowerment has been a defining goal of CED efforts. . . . Thus, one of the most frequently cited justifications for CED as a social change strategy is its capacity to "empower poor people to work for their own economic and social betterment."

The concept of community empowerment is linked to the idea of local control. CED scholars have suggested that if neighborhood residents are incorporated as active participants in the reconstruction of their local economies, they will be empowered through the process. In particular, CED proponents have argued that communities build power by exerting ongoing influence over local decision-making structures in a way that ensures that development efforts are responsive to community needs. CED work has therefore been focused on establishing mechanisms for ensuring that ultimate control of neighborhood-based initiatives resides in low-income community members. . . .

In the legal scholarship, CED lawyers have been portrayed as particularly effective in fostering community empowerment. For instance, it has been argued that CED lawyers can empower their clients both by demystifying the law and by ensuring that the development process is successfully implemented. . . .

II.   A Critique of Market-Based CED

The emergent consensus in favor of market-based CED, while profoundly influencing the direction of antipoverty advocacy, has also galvanized an indigenous critique of social change practice. At the grassroots level, dissatisfaction with the current orientation of CED work has begun to percolate, as the market consensus has shown signs of fissure. Many community activists have recoiled from CED's lack of political engagement and have started to register their dissent from the chorus of market-based CED boosterism, which has promoted the value of market integration without questioning the fairness of existing institutional arrangements. Progressive scholars have initiated a critical exchange over the efficacy of place-based CED strategies focusing on market expansion. . . .

A.   MARKET-BASED CED DOES NOT ADEQUATELY REDRESS POVERTY

The argument in favor of market-based CED has been premised on the assumption that local economic growth, by itself, diminishes poverty. However, the literature analyzing the efficacy of market-based CED efforts suggests that this simple equation does not accurately capture the relationship of market strategies to poverty alleviation. . . .

Overall, the tenuous evidence of poverty reduction that emerges from studies of market-based CED techniques points to the need for a more targeted CED approach that provides stronger mechanisms for channeling the benefits of economic growth to the poor.

B. MARKET-BASED CED DEPOLITICIZES ANTIPOVERTY ADVOCACY

A second limitation of market-based CED is that it does not address the crucial political dimension of poverty. The market-based model has conceptualized poverty alleviation as primarily a matter of structuring the appropriate economic incentives to spur capital inflow and business expansion in distressed neighborhoods. Within this framework, the notion of building political power among the poor to challenge institutional arrangements is viewed as inimical to the goal of packaging low-income communities as attractive business environments. However, rather than fostering community renewal, the depoliticization of CED work has instead circumscribed antipoverty efforts and hindered progressive movement building.

. . . [A] market-based CED approach that emphasizes economic expansion and ignores the complementary need for political mobilization is insufficient to redress poverty. Without community-based efforts to demand greater access to public resources—in the form of education, job training, child care, and other services—low-income communities continue to lack the infrastructure necessary to build economic growth.

By privileging market-based housing and business development strategies, CDCs have distanced themselves from the type of political engagement necessary to redress the problems of concentrated poverty, joblessness, and income stratification. . . . Others have argued that market-oriented strategies have undermined the struggle for economic justice by diverting scarce resources away from grassroots political mobilization and providing a justification for the withdrawal of government programs from distressed communities. It is true that many CDCs have made the strategic decision to adopt market-based approaches not out of a conscious rejection of political action, but rather out of financial necessity. . . . [T]he structural constraints imposed by funding sources on CDC activities have led to a drift away from political confrontation and have reinforced the dominance of market-based strategies.

The failure to confront the politics of poverty has limited the effectiveness of CED efforts. It has also enervated progressive political energies by focusing resources on creating efficient market actors rather than building political power. To the extent that CED has become aligned with the neoliberal tenets of privatization and economic growth, it has reinforced the perceived immutability of existing market arrangements. Although not responsible for the rise of what Pierre Bourdieu has termed the "tyranny of the market," the current approach to CED nevertheless has supported the market order by placing the weight of progressive advocacy behind a program of business expansion. Offering a market-friendly, depoliticized, version of social change practice, CED has been readily assimilated into the discourse of free market orthodoxy. This orthodoxy, in turn, has been translated into a programmatic agenda inimical to social welfare policies and labor protections that interfere with market efficiency. Therefore, despite its sensitivity to community needs, the market orientation of CED advocacy has prevented it from mobilizing the type of grassroots political resources necessary to advance a redistributive, worker-centered agenda.

C.   MARKET-BASED CED PRIVILEGES LOCAL INCREMENTALISM OVER BROAD STRUCTURAL REFORM

A further limitation of market-based CED is its emphasis on local economic reform. CED's focus on localism does nothing to seriously challenge the structural determinants of poverty and diminishes the importance of large-scale, coordinated social change strategies.

. . . [S]cholars have questioned whether postmodern micropolitics, which privileges local empowerment over broad-based structural change, can provide a viable foundation for a progressive response to the increasing concentration of political and economic decision-making power. . . .

The limitations of localism identified in these analyses underscore the need for a revised conception of CED practice that links "inner-city residents to a larger scope of economic and social opportunity." Rather than concentrating exclusively on neighborhood development as a poverty reduction strategy, practitioners must begin to look beyond community boundaries to a more comprehensive antipoverty approach that acknowledges the significance of regional and transnational networks in the process of economic reform.

D.   MARKET-BASED CED IMPEDES THE FORMATION OF CROSS-RACIAL ALLIANCES

By employing a geographically targeted approach that seeks to create economically self-sufficient neighborhoods, market-based CED programs largely accept the existing spatial framework of urban geographies, often imposing official designations—such as Empowerment Zones, redevelopment project areas, CDC service areas—on enclaves of economic distress. This reinscription of community boundaries is central to the logic of the market approach: It is necessary to define economically disadvantaged urban space in order to effectively structure tax incentives, favorable loan packages, and other financial benefits that would induce increased commercial and real estate investment. Thus, the CED model works within the existing spatial distribution of poverty and does not address the nexus between poverty concentration and residential segregation—leaving unchallenged the racial cleavages that dissect urban geographies. . . .

Focusing on relative economic disadvantage, market-based CED minimizes the racial dimensions of poverty. By accepting existing neighborhood configurations, the market approach tends to reinforce racialized community borders and maintain existing patterns of racial segregation. This place-based focus impedes efforts to forge a cross-racial coalition to advance a political agenda sensitive to the needs of low-income workers. As CED advocates target resources to specific underdeveloped neighborhoods, they neglect to foster inter-community collaboration around issues of common concern to poor city residents. Instead, they work with outside elites to leverage financial capital to increase neighborhood wealth without challenging the institutional discrimination and governmental policies that perpetuate racial and economic stratification. In order to respond adequately to the racialized nature of poverty, particularly in light of the increasing diversity of American cities, a new CED agenda is required—one that promotes inter-racial solidarity and coordinates diverse groups into an effort to rebuild the economic justice movement.

III. Reclaiming CED as Progressive Political Action

. . . In order to promote politically engaged CED, scholar-activists have urged greater collaboration between the organizing and CED communities, highlighting how an integrated approach can more effectively advance shared goals of community building and economic redistribution. . . .

The second key attribute of this new model is that it seeks to situate CED advocacy within the context of a broader progressive movement on behalf of marginalized communities. This has been most evident in the increasing formation of strategic alliances between CED practitioners and other grassroots actors — such as community organizers, labor representatives, and clergy — who have the mass-based constituencies necessary to leverage structural change. . . .

As this analysis suggests, the new approach to CED is not a repudiation of market-centered practices; rather, it represents an effort to democratize the market by redirecting economic benefits to low-income community members. . . .

CED lawyers have begun to play increasingly important roles in promoting the expansion of living wage protections.

. . . [L]awyers working at the grassroots level are shifting their attention away from the traditional emphasis on commercial projects and small business programs, and are focusing greater resources on the development of worker cooperative businesses.

. . . [A]s CED advocates increasingly turn away from this market approach, they are employing an organizing-based model of job creation that enlists the public sector in redistributing the benefits of business growth to low-income constituencies. . . . This emerging approach has focused on exacting greater community benefits from locally subsidized development projects, structuring job creation and retention plans under the auspices of federal laws, and establishing employment training programs upon the foundation of federal workforce development mandates.

Conclusion

. . . Market-based CED as a vehicle for local economic empowerment emerged as the ideal form of antipoverty advocacy for the 1990s, one that did not challenge the fundamental tenets of a system that was fueling unprecedented stock market gains and creating a record number of paper-billionaires. This model of CED accepted wealth creation as a bedrock principle and suggested that the tools used by the rich to bolster their portfolios should also be applied to redressing the problems of the poor.

. . . The market consensus, however, was always an unstable one. The product of a volatile mix of black power ideology, supply-side economics, and empowerment theory, market-based CED maintained its strong appeal so long as the economic upswing continued to create media-friendly examples of urban renaissance. As the 1990s waned, evidence of market failure disrupted the tenuous bonds of this consensus. Against the garish glow of dot-com consumption, at the height of the New Economy boom, poverty persisted — growing more extreme in many urban areas — while income inequality grew more pronounced. Despite the well-publicized success of the wealthy few, the portrait of fin-de-siecle America that emerged was one of intransigent class divisions, a growing low-wage workforce, and deep economic cleavages along racial lines.

For all its fanfare, the doctrine of business development that was the hallmark of market-based CED had not significantly altered the geography of urban poverty. Moreover, the market version of CED generated a political passivity among progressive advocates for low-income constituencies.

NOTES AND QUESTIONS

1. Reflecting some of the same concerns as Professor Cummings—that CED amounts to an uncritical embrace of the market and economic growth—the East Bay Community Law Center of the University of California, Berkeley, chose to shift their work from CED to community economic justice. *See* Angela Harris et al., *From "The Art of War" to "Being Peace": Mindfulness and Community Lawyering in a Neoliberal Age*, 95 Cal. L. Rev. 2073 (2007).

2. Part of the challenge of CED is that it takes so many forms. To better understand the nature of CED, consider the example given by Professor Simon of work involving a community bank:

> CED programs do not respond to [market and government problems] by abandoning markets or reverting to conventional bureaucracies. They create structures that combine and rearrange a variety of organizational attributes. However, at the center are usually community-based organizations characterized by multistranded relations, geographical focus, and face-to-face relations. These characteristics have some capacity to mitigate the problems of incentives, information, and coordination. They do so by facilitating informal negotiation and collective action. The geographical focus means that the membership will include people with tangible stakes in each other's activities and investments. Multistranded relations create economies of scope in the development of information; information generated through one strand can often be used in another strand. Face-to-face dealings enhance possibilities for both gaining information and for negotiating coordination.
>
> As an example of a CED institution that seems especially responsive to these economic problems, consider the South Shore Bank, founded in 1972 in what was then a seriously distressed neighborhood of Chicago. A group of social activists was able to raise $ 3.2 million in philanthropic support to buy an existing commercial bank. They then proceeded to re-orient the bank's practices to support a CED strategy.
>
> The South Shore Bank is owned by a nonprofit holding company that controls several for-profit subsidiaries and nonprofit affiliates: The City Lands Corporation is a for-profit that develops residential real estate projects; the Neighborhood Institute is a nonprofit that operates training and social services programs. The Institute has a subsidiary of its own—TNI Development Corporation—which also conducts affordable housing development. The Neighborhood Fund, a for-profit, is a minority-enterprise small business investment corporation licensed and supported by the Small Business Administration. Shorebank Advisory Services, a for-profit, provides consulting on development banking issues.
>
> The bank's lending strategy has four especially interesting features. First, in "concentrated lending," the bank focuses its commercial real estate lending on a specific community, and within the community on specific areas targeted for development. Second, in "leverage," the bank tries to focus commercial lending in a way that complements its affiliates' subsidized housing development. It makes commercial loans to private, preferably small and local

developers to build or rehabilitate housing near the subsidized projects its affiliates are developing. Development activities occur in mutually reinforcing "concentric rings" of private and NGO-led effort.

Third, in addition to being geographically targeted, some of the bank's private lending is conditional. The bank initially limited its purchase-money lending for rental properties to borrowers planning to live on the premises. It eventually relaxed this requirement, but it has continued to insist that the borrower commit to rehabilitate the property. It will not lend to landlords who simply want to hold the property for speculative purposes or to "milk" it to maximize short-term return while permitting it to deteriorate.

Finally, the bank's affiliates provide technical assistance to its local landlord borrowers on such matters as construction, maintenance, regulatory compliance, and accounting. Many of these borrowers are new landlords entering their first business venture. Experience in the training programs has developed face-to-face, mutually supportive relations among them. Two ethnically-based networks of small landlords—one African-American, the other recent Croatian immigrants—have developed; they maintain and continue to invest in small-scale, moderate-rental property. The bank's founder insists that these people could not have been identified through conventional business methods: "Had we conducted a market survey in 1973 to get a sense of how many potential entrepreneurs we had in the community . . . the answer would have been 'none'. . . . [These people were] invisible, and now they're an industry—the core of the South Shore's recovery."

Here we have an institutional structure designed to facilitate coordination among private investments with public investments, and of real estate investment with training opportunities. It also strives to canalize for-profit activity in ways most likely to produce positive externalities. Moreover, it generates the kind of multistranded relations that create economies of scope in information.

William H. Simon, *The Community Economic Development Movement*, 2002 Wis. L. Rev. 377.

B. ACCESS TO CREDIT AND FINANCIAL SERVICES

Being poor often is associated with an inability to access and benefit from the formal banking and finance system. The most recent FDIC study, FDIC National Survey of Unbanked and Underbanked Households (2009), reports that 7.7 percent of households in the United States are unbanked. Among households making less than $30,000 annually, nearly one in five do not have a bank account. Globally, one-half of all adults, most of them in the developing world, do not have a bank account. Asli Demirguc-Kunt & Leora Klapper, *Measuring Financial Inclusion: The Global Findex Database* (World Bank, Working Paper No. 6025, 2012). Though taken for granted by the non-poor, the services and products offered by banks play a significant role in daily life. Credit and debit cards facilitate payments, especially with types of consumption that do not allow for cash purchases, such as purchases over the Internet. Additionally, for workers who do not have a bank account, just getting paid can be expensive, given the need to rely upon check-cashing businesses that often charge high fees for their services. Improving access holds the promise not only of lowering the transaction costs, but also of removing some of the credit barriers that raise the borrowing costs faced by poor people. Part of the challenge of making credit available to poor people is that they do not fit nicely into traditional lending models because attributes of their poverty — low incomes and few assets that can serve as collateral — make lending risky and administratively burdensome. This section focuses on two efforts to lower these hurdles and to improve poor people's access to credit and to the banking system: the Community Reinvestment Act and microcredit.

1. The Community Reinvestment Act

The Community Reinvestment Act (CRA) is the primary piece of legislation specifically aimed at improving access to financial services and credit for under-served groups and communities. In the excerpt that follows, Ben Bernanke, currently the Chairman of the Federal Reserve, explains the origin and evolution of the Act.

BEN S. BERNANKE, CHAIRMAN, FED. RESERVE, ADDRESS AT THE COMMUNITY AFFAIRS RESEARCH CONFERENCE (MAR. 30, 2007)

. . . Enacted in 1977, the CRA affirmed the obligation of federally insured depository institutions to help meet the credit needs of communities in which they are chartered, consistent with safe and sound operations. The act also charged the federal bank regulatory agencies, including the Federal Reserve, with implementing the CRA through regulations and with examining banks and thrifts to determine whether they meet their CRA obligations. . . .

Public and congressional concerns about the deteriorating condition of America's cities, particularly lower-income and minority neighborhoods, led to the enactment of the Community Reinvestment Act. In the view of many, urban decay was partly a consequence of limited credit availability, which encouraged urban flight and inhibited the rehabilitation of declining neighborhoods. Some critics pinned the blame for the lack of credit availability on mainstream financial institutions, which they characterized as willing to accept deposits from households and small businesses in lower-income neighborhoods but unwilling to lend or invest in those same neighborhoods despite the presence of creditworthy borrowers.

Several social and economic factors help explain why credit to lower-income neighborhoods was limited at that time. First, racial discrimination in lending undoubtedly adversely affected local communities. Discriminatory lending practices had deep historical roots. . . .

Besides discrimination a variety of economic and institutional factors help to explain the relative unavailability of credit in lower-income neighborhoods. . . .

Taken together, these social, economic, and regulatory factors contributed to the perception that banking institutions were failing to adequately serve the credit needs of some residents of their communities, a concern that led the Congress to enact the CRA. The CRA reaffirmed the long-standing principle that financial institutions must serve "the convenience and needs," including credit needs, of the communities in which they are chartered. The obligation of financial institutions to serve their communities was seen as a quid pro quo for privileges such as the protection afforded by federal deposit insurance and access to the Federal Reserve's discount window.

The CRA was only one of a series of laws passed during the 1970s intended to reduce credit-related discrimination, expand access to credit, and shed light on lending patterns. The CRA itself focused on the provision of credit to low- and moderate-income communities rather than on discrimination by race, sex, or other personal characteristics. . . . From an economic perspective, the CRA can be interpreted as an attempt to rectify market failures — for example, by inducing banks to invest in building the knowledge and expertise necessary to lend profitably in lower-income neighborhoods. Similarly, to the extent that the CRA encouraged coordinated or simultaneous efforts by banks to lend in underserved areas, it had the potential to reduce the first-mover problem.

The debate surrounding the passage of the CRA was contentious, with critics charging that the law would distort credit markets, create unnecessary regulatory burden, and lead to unsound lending. Partly in response to these concerns, the Congress included little prescriptive detail in the law. Instead, the CRA simply directs the banking regulatory agencies to ensure that banks serve the credit needs of their local communities in a safe and sound manner. In effect, the agencies were left with considerable discretion and flexibility to modify the rules in light of changes in the economy and in financial markets. At times, this discretion has been the source of some uncertainty on the part of regulated institutions concerned with compliance. However, the flexibility has proved valuable in allowing the CRA to remain relevant despite rapid economic and financial change and widely differing economic circumstances among neighborhoods. . . .

For more than a decade after its enactment, the CRA was a rather low-profile banking regulation, one that set minimal compliance requirements for depository institutions and attracted limited supervisory attention from the bank regulatory agencies. By the late 1980s, however, the issues surrounding access to credit were attracting renewed interest. . . .

Further attention to CRA was generated by the surge in bank merger and acquisition activities that followed the enactment of the Riegle-Neal Interstate Banking and Branching Efficiency Act of 1994. As public scrutiny of bank merger and acquisition activity escalated, advocacy groups increasingly used the public comment process to protest bank applications on CRA grounds. In instances of highly contested applications, the Federal Reserve Board and other agencies held public meetings to allow the public and the applicants to comment on the lending records of the banks in question. In response to these new pressures, banks began to devote more resources to their CRA programs. Many institutions established separate business units and subsidiary community development corporations to facilitate lending that would be given favorable consideration in CRA examinations. Local and regional public-private partnerships and multibank loan consortia also gained more prominence as banks developed strategies for expanding and managing CRA-related activities. . . .

Bankers were also gaining experience in underwriting and managing the risk of lending in lower-income communities. After years of experimentation, the managers of financial institutions found that these loan portfolios, if properly underwritten and managed, could be profitable. In fact, a Federal Reserve study found that, generally, CRA-related lending activity was at least somewhat profitable and usually did not involve disproportionately higher levels of default.

Moreover, community groups and nonprofit organizations began to take a more businesslike, market-oriented approach to local economic development, leading them to establish more-formalized and more-productive partnerships with banks. Community groups provided information to financial institutions on the needs of lower-income communities for credit and services, offered financial education and counseling services to community members, and referred "bankable" customers to partner banks. Specialized community development banks and financial institutions with the mission of providing financial services and credit to lower-income communities and families emerged and grew. . . .

Even as CRA-related lending became more extensive and more market-based, concerns were expressed about the implementation of the law. Financial institutions complained about compliance costs. Both bankers and community groups criticized the CRA examination procedures as emphasizing process over results, arguing that the examination criteria were too subjective and that a more-quantitative system for evaluating institutions' CRA performance should be developed.

The CRA regulations adopted in 1995 established for large institutions a three-pronged test based on performance in the areas of lending, investments, and services. While the regulations placed the greatest emphasis on lending, they encouraged innovative approaches to addressing community development credit needs. Several provisions were included to reduce compliance costs, among them a new rule that allowed small banks to meet their requirements by means of a streamlined examination focused on lending activities. . . .

a.   Critiquing the CRA

Is the CRA necessary? Does it work? Are its benefits worth its costs? Such questions surround the CRA. In an influential article, professors Jonathan Macey and Geoffrey Miller argue that the CRA not only weakens the banking sector but also paradoxically hurts the very communities the Act was intended to help.

JONATHAN R. MACEY & GEOFFREY P. MILLER, *THE COMMUNITY REINVESTMENT ACT: AN ECONOMIC ANALYSIS*

79 Va. L. Rev. 291 (1993)

The Community Reinvestment Act ("CRA") provides, innocuously enough, that federal bank supervisors must assess how a depository institution (a bank or savings association) serves the credit needs of its "entire community, including low- and moderate-income neighborhoods," consistent with safe and sound operation. The supervisors must "take such record into account" in evaluating applications to acquire deposit facilities.

For many years after its adoption in 1977, the CRA was little more than a vague statement of principle without much real-world effect. In 1989, however, Congress greatly enhanced the CRA's impact as part of the comprehensive banking legislation of that year. Consequently, CRA-based challenges to bank mergers and other transactions subject to CRA scrutiny are now routine, even when the institution in question has received high marks for CRA compliance in recent examinations. Some deals are actually derailed by the statute, and the costs of consummating a transaction in the face of a CRA challenge can be substantial.

The CRA is now controversial. Many bankers object that the statute imposes burdensome requirements and unfairly disadvantages depository institutions as compared with their nonbank competitors. Community activists argue that the CRA is only beginning to address problems of access to credit in low-income communities. . . .

The CRA impairs the safety and soundness of an already overstrained banking industry: it promotes the concentration of assets in geographically nondiversified locations, encourages banks to make unprofitable and risky investment and product-line decisions, and penalizes banks that seek to reduce costs by consolidating services or closing or relocating branches. The statute, moreover, imposes a significant tax on bank mergers and deters transactions that would otherwise improve the efficiency and solvency of the nation's banking system. . . .

Tragically, the CRA poorly furthers the purposes for which it was designed. It penalizes institutions that actually serve low-income and moderate-income neighborhoods, while rewarding those that do not. It drives capital away from poor neighborhoods by imposing a tax on those depository institutions foolhardy enough to do business in such communities. It discourages innovation in the provision of financial services to low-income and moderate-income neighborhoods. It might even impair the market position of existing institutions that serve local community needs. . . .

Depository institutions are not automatically sanctioned for failing to satisfy their CRA obligations. Rather, because most significant forms of bank expansion require applications subject to CRA scrutiny, the Act represents a meaningful threat that the responsible federal agency will deny a bank's application to expand. Thus, any bank that contemplates establishing new branches, acquiring other banks, or merging into or being acquired by another bank must consider the possibility that its business plan will be stymied by an adverse CRA finding. . . .

The basic principle of localism, as the Supreme Court once observed, is that "both as a matter of history and as a matter of present commercial reality, banking and related financial activities are of profound local concern." Underlying the principle of localism are several related propositions, each of which was stressed in one form or another in the congressional debates on the act. Although these propositions may have had some validity earlier in our history, and may even have retained some force at the time the CRA was enacted, they bear little relationship to contemporary banking realities. Localism has a nostalgic ring in American folklore, but it no longer characterizes the American banking industry — especially not the larger firms that have been the principal targets of CRA scrutiny. The underlying propositions are these: (1) banking is a local industry, (2) banks drain credit out of local communities, and (3) banks owe special duties to their local communities. . . .

A particularly troubling effect of the Act is its discrimination against depository institutions serving poor neighborhoods. Because a bank's CRA rating is based on its lending practices in the area contiguous to its offices, the CRA imposes greater costs on banks in poor areas than those in wealthy areas to the extent that it causes banks to lend funds locally. Banks located in wealthy areas can elect not to make loans in poor areas without risking serious CRA challenge. Banks located in poor areas, on the other hand, are effectively forced to devote a substantial proportion of their loan portfolios to their local communities. Because of these additional regulatory requirements and costs, banks seeking to expand will be less likely to establish new branches or offices in poor areas than they were prior to the promulgation of the CRA. . . .

It is quite evident that, despite the occasional profitable CRA loan, the general effect of the CRA is to reduce depository institution safety and soundness. . . .

The CRA might seem to impose relatively minor costs of compliance on depository institutions and their regulators. The institution must come up with a CRA plan, file a notice, maintain a file for public inspection, and stand ready to answer queries of federal bank examiners about CRA policies and procedures. The examiner must evaluate the institution's record of meeting community credit needs in connection with on-site examinations. The burden seems, though not minimal, at least bearable.

This view of the CRA, however, greatly understates the actual compliance costs. Bankers today regard the CRA as the single most costly regulation facing them, a statement that carries weight in light of the manifold, complex, and arcane regulations governing depository institutions today. That bankers should single out the CRA among this parade of red tape is a powerful testament to the actual costs of compliance. . . .

Perhaps the most problematic feature of the CRA is its impact on the communities it was principally designed to serve — low-income, deteriorating urban communities. As noted above, it requires little imagination to see that a depository institution not presently serving such a community would be cautious about entering that market, even if it believed that there might be opportunities for profit in performing depository services there. Serving such communities means including the area in the institution's community, and therefore being subject to the CRA's requirement of making loans within the neighborhood that might be significantly more extensive than the institution would want to make as a matter of its own business judgment. As a result, the CRA probably harms the very areas that it was ostensibly designed to serve by actually reducing the amount of credit that would be available in those areas as compared with what would be the situation in the absence of the CRA. . . .

Thus, the political science of the CRA seems to reduce to this: Supporting the statute is a broad coalition of powerful groups including activist community groups, small businesses, small farms, and the bank regulators themselves; opposing it is only a banking industry that has been relatively politically impotent. Others harmed by the statute — the general public, and, arguably, the residents of the deteriorating urban neighborhoods whom the Act was ostensibly designed to serve — are not politically organized and play no part in the calculus. . . .

NOTES AND QUESTIONS

1.   Macey and Miller argue that the CRA, even though it is designed to help poor communities, will hurt the supposed beneficiaries by interfering with the market. Similar arguments against antipoverty programs abound. Some have argued, for example, that rent control and the implied warranty of habitability lessen the incentive to construct rental housing, which ends up meaning there is less housing for poor people. Similarly, generous welfare programs are critiqued as hurting welfare recipients by disincentivizing

work and family. What do you think explains the prevalence of arguments that market distortions will hurt the poor?

b. Defending the CRA

Partly in response to Macey and Miller's 1993 article, Professor Michael Barr argues that the CRA has helped low- and moderate-income areas get access to credit and to financial services. As Barr notes, the goals of the CRA are important because "[a]ccess to an appropriate bank account for most low-income 'unbanked' individuals could mean the opportunity for lower transaction costs, greater consumer protection, more access to loans, and increased savings as a cushion against financial emergency and as a predicate for borrowing." Michael S. Barr, *Credit Where It Counts: The Community Reinvestment Act and Its Critics*, 80 N.Y.U. L. Rev. 513 (2005). Regulatory oversight of whether banks are meeting their CRA responsibilities is done according to a standard, not a bright line rule. According to Barr, the use of a standard in this case is preferable because it allows for banks (and regulators) to take into account local needs and preserves the possibility of flexible responses and programs. Barr notes that "recent evidence shows that CRA provides important benefits to low-income communities . . . careful studies have found support for a statistically significant and economically important role for CRA." *Id.* Barr concludes that such "studies cast serious doubt on the contention of CRA's critics that CRA provides little benefit to low-income communities and borrowers." *Id.*

Reaching a similar conclusion, Professor Richard Marsico explains how the CRA benefits low- and moderate-income communities:

> One of the CRA's unique contributions has been to "democratize capital." It has done so in two ways. The first may be analogized to voting. The CRA has democratized decisions about the distribution of capital by extending at least part of the decisionmaking "franchise" to previously "disenfranchised" people, in particular low-income and minority persons. Second, the CRA has played a role in distributing loans to people — particularly low-income and minority individuals — who previously did not receive loans, thus including them in the economic mainstream and giving them the same economic opportunity as others. The CRA has done this by influencing banks to make loans to low-income and minority individuals to purchase, refinance, or improve a home; to open or expand a small business; or to support a small farm.
>
> By democratizing capital, the CRA has made great progress in eliminating redlining and promoting reinvestment in redlined neighborhoods. Despite the federal banking agencies' record of weak CRA enforcement, there is substantial evidence that supports the conclusion that the CRA has encouraged banks to lend more money to LMI [low- and moderate-income individuals] and minority persons and neighborhoods than they would have without the CRA. The opportunity for disenfranchised members of redlined neighborhoods to comment on a bank's CRA record when it files an expansion application has given them a powerful voice in decisions about the distribution of loans. Banks, which are generally sensitive to bad publicity and risk-averse in their expansion applications, are anxious to have good CRA records both as good public relations and to ensure approval of their expansion applications. Public comments, and the delay and risk they cause to bank expansion plans, have brought banks to the bargaining table with

community groups resulting in bank pledges to lend more than one trillion dollars to LMI and predominantly minority neighborhoods nationwide. Even if banks do not have expansion plans in the immediate future, their desire for good public relations, their discovery that CRA-related lending can be profitable, and their desire to prevent comments opposing future expansion applications have motivated banks to change their lending practices, introduce new loan products, and partner with community groups to make lending to LMI and minority persons and neighborhoods part of their business strategies.

Richard D. Marsico, *Democratizing Capital: The History, Law, and Reform of the Community Reinvestment Act*, 49 N.Y.L. Sch. L. Rev. 217 (2004).

NOTES AND QUESTIONS

1. Is expanding access to credit for low- and moderate-income communities always a good thing? In a *Wall Street Journal* op-ed, Professor Russell Roberts argues that the CRA was partly to blame for the massive expansion in sub-prime loans that led, in part, to the 2008 housing crisis. *See* Russell Roberts, *How Government Stoked the Mania*, Wall St. J. (Oct. 3, 2008). The view that the CRA is to blame, however, has been challenged. Professor Raymond Brescia argues:

    The Community Reinvestment Act of 1977 (CRA) has been called many things. For some, it represents a lifeline, as community reinvestment advocates, working in conjunction with banks, have generated trillions of dollars in desperately needed capital investment in communities that historically have been excluded from mainstream banking and community development activities. For others, it is a burden, reflecting misguided judgments about the proper role of regulatory oversight in capital allocation. Still others believe it is an abomination, one that spurred the mortgage crisis and the financial fallout that has followed. . . .

    As the subprime mortgage meltdown has spurred the wider financial crisis, some commentators have blamed the CRA, passed in 1977, for the events that began to unfold twenty-five years later. According to the theory, the CRA forced banks to engage in risky loans to risky borrowers in risky neighborhoods — predominantly in low-income and minority communities. If it were not for this decades-old law and aggressive efforts by community advocates promoting compliance with it, commentators posit that events in the earlier part of this decade, where questionable loans were extended on unfavorable terms to borrowers that could not afford them, might have turned out differently. Were it not for this law and the power of community-based groups that championed it, the argument goes, long-standing underwriting principles would not have given way to exotic loans made to borrowers who had no business owning a home. While this theory might offer cold comfort to those who believe that banks, left to their own devices, will act with prudence, the theory cannot stand up to any sober assessment of the subprime mortgage meltdown and the financial crisis that has followed. . . .

    . . . Several facts expose the true role of the CRA in the subprime mortgage crisis, however. For example, the CRA was not too strong, but rather too weak. The CRA's limitations gave banks and their regulators broad discretion to carry out the CRA's goals. This fact, coupled with the approach of federal bank regulators towards subprime lending generally and the failure of the courts to serve as a check on administrative neglect under the CRA, meant that instead of causing the subprime mortgage crisis, the CRA simply failed to prevent the crisis. The CRA was not strong enough, and it allowed banks and regulators free rein to ignore the central premise of the Act: that banks must meet the needs of the communities they serve consistent with safe and sound banking practices.

It is within this phrase, the key statutory directive under the CRA—"to encourage [banks] to help meet the credit needs of the local communities . . . consistent with the safe and sound" banking practices, which is the articulated letter and spirit of the law—that we recognize the seeds of the subprime debacle that has swept the globe. First, at the height of the housing bubble that saw the explosive growth of subprime lending, banks covered by the CRA rarely made subprime loans in such a way that would give them CRA credit; instead, in the overwhelming majority of cases, institutions not covered by the CRA issued the subprime loans. Second, the geographic location of the "communities" the banks served could easily be manipulated, so when traditional banks did engage in subprime lending, it was typically outside of the communities they served for the purposes of the CRA. Third, risky lending all too often carried out in low- and moderate-income communities and communities of color by nonbank lenders—precisely because borrowers in such communities tended to be unsophisticated and unwary—could hardly be considered "consistent with the safe and sound" banking practices. Yet, regulators regularly turned a blind eye to this conduct, considering it beyond the scope of the CRA and even stepping in to prevent regulatory efforts to rein it in at the state level.

Tragically, the CRA's structure itself created gaping loopholes in coverage, which made it possible for subprime lenders to operate freely—beyond the scope of the federal oversight contemplated by the Act, and inconsistent with the Act's letter and spirit.

Raymond H. Brescia, *Part of the Disease or Part of the Cure: The Financial Crisis and the Community Reinvestment Act*, 60 S.C. L. Rev. 617 (2009). Nevertheless, as Ben Bernanke notes in the speech excerpted above, "recent problems in mortgage markets illustrate that an underlying assumption of the CRA— that *more* lending equals *better* outcomes for local communities—may not always hold."

2. Why should regulators care if banks associate local deposits with local lending? One of the drivers of the economic growth of the Sunbelt (the South and Southwest) has been the ability of banks to take deposits from wealthier parts of the country—particularly the Northeast—and redirect such funds to the Sunbelt in the form of interstate lending. Given the advantages to banks and to communities with opportunities but insufficient capital, why should banks have special obligations to the communities within their area?

3. The CRA was enacted in 1977, yet a sizable percentage of lower-income households continue to rely on payday lending, tax-preparation loans, check-cashing businesses, and money order companies. For more on the check-cashing industry and the cost of being unbanked, see Peggy Delinois Hamilton, *Why the Check Cashers Win: Regulatory Barriers to Banking the Unbanked*, 30 W. New Eng. L. Rev. 119 (2007). What should the government or community organizations be doing to bring more people into the formal banking sector?

2. *Microcredit*

Having a bank account alone does not mean a poor person can get a loan. Indeed, because being poor often means having few assets and a low income, bank loans are often not available for poor people. Banks traditionally limit the risk of default on loans they originate and maximize their return by relying heavily on credit ratings, high incomes, and assets that can serve as collateral to screen loan applicants. Consequently, even with the aid of laws such as the CRA, the poor often do not qualify for traditional loans. The administrative cost of smaller loans — for which banks still have to originate and track payments — serves as an additional barrier, even in cases where the poor person may have been able to qualify for a small loan.

Filling the formal credit gap are a range of products and services that enable people of many social classes to obtain credit for everything from emergency needs to basic consumption. Credit cards are perhaps the most ubiquitous, but to the list can be added payday lending, pawn shops, rent-to-own stores, tax-preparation lenders, loan sharks, and friends and family. With the possible exception of friends and family, common denominators of such nonbank borrowing are high fees and high interest rates. The related enforcement risks involved in such credit arraignments can be seen in Williams v. Walker-Thomas Furniture Co., 350 F.2d 445 (D.C. Cir. 1965), a case included in many 1L Contracts textbooks, in which J. Skelly Wright ruled that an installment contract that allowed the seller to repossess all goods that had been sold on credit was unconscionable. For more on legal regulation of the rent-to-own market, see Jim Hawkins, *Renting the Good Life*, 49 Wm. & Mary L. Rev. 2041 (2008).

Microcredit initiatives stand as one possible response to these challenges. Microcredit refers to small personal loans, often not tied to traditional forms of collateral. Borrowers frequently use these small loans to invest or purchase goods for small, sometimes formal but often informal, businesses. This section starts with the leading microcredit institution in the world, the Grameen Bank, whose success helped raise the profile of microcredit around the world. It then covers the ways that microcredit in the United States borrows, and deviates, from the Grameen Bank model.

a. Rise of the Microcredit Model Internationally

Microcredit's biggest champion has been Muhammad Yunus, who founded the Grameen Bank and subsequently earned, with the Bank, the Nobel Peace Prize in 2006 for "their efforts to create economic and social development from below." In the two selections that follow, Yunus explains the origins of the Grameen Bank and the nature of its lending practices.

MUHAMMAD YUNUS, NOBEL LECTURE (DEC. 10, 2006)

I became involved in the poverty issue not as a policymaker or a researcher. I became involved because poverty was all around me, and I could not turn away from it. In 1974, I found it difficult to teach elegant theories of economics in the university classroom, in the backdrop of a terrible famine in Bangladesh.

Suddenly, I felt the emptiness of those theories in the face of crushing hunger and poverty. I wanted to do something immediate to help people around me, even if it was just one human being, to get through another day with a little more ease. That brought me face to face with poor people's struggle to find the tiniest amounts of money to support their efforts to eke out a living. I was shocked to discover a woman in the village, borrowing less than a dollar from the money-lender, on the condition that he would have the exclusive right to buy all she produces at the price he decides. This, to me, was a way of recruiting slave labor.

I decided to make a list of the victims of this money-lending "business" in the village next door to our campus.

When my list was done, it had the names of 42 victims who borrowed a total amount of US $27. I offered US $27 from my own pocket to get these victims out of the clutches of those money-lenders. The excitement that was created among the people by this small action got me further involved in it. If I could make so many people so happy with such a tiny amount of money, why not do more of it?

That is what I have been trying to do ever since. The first thing I did was to try to persuade the bank located in the campus to lend money to the poor. But that did not work. The bank said that the poor were not creditworthy. After all my efforts, over several months, failed I offered to become a guarantor for the loans to the poor. I was stunned by the result. The poor paid back their loans, on time, every time! But still I kept confronting difficulties in expanding the program through the existing banks. That was when I decided to create a separate bank for the poor, and in 1983, I finally succeeded in doing that. I named it Grameen Bank or Village bank.

MUHAMMAD YUNUS, *HOW LEGAL STEPS CAN HELP TO PAVE THE WAY TO ENDING POVERTY*

35 ABA Human Rights (2008)

HOW THE TRUST-BASED GRAMEEN BANK WORKS

The Grameen Bank issues loans using very simple trust-based financial arrangements; no legal documents are involved because, in part, Grameen's borrowers are poor and have no collateral. So, Grameen relies on trust and the positive incentives of continued access to credit and other support to ensure repayments—and Grameen's repayment rates have averaged better than 98 percent. Because Grameen's loans are based on trust and positive incentives and no legal documents, Grameen has never used lawyers or courts to collect any of its loans. Grameen has about 7.5 million borrowers in Bangladesh, and has loaned approximately $7 billion since its inception, with an average loan size of about $150.

When a potential borrower wants a loan, she has to form a group of five or join such a group of borrowers from her neighborhood and agree to meet with that group once a week. Each loan is made to an individual in the group and is the responsibility of that one individual, but others in the group cannot get their next loans if any member of the group is late in her payments.

Grameen's borrowers are also required to maintain a regular savings plan, and today its borrowers and their nonborrowing neighbors as a group have $150 in savings for every $100 in loans outstanding. Today, the Grameen Bank is funded by the savings deposits of the poor. It has been profitable for all but three of the last twenty-five years.

...All loans are intended for income-producing activities, housing, or education, not for consumption. The basic interest rate for most business loans is 20 percent. In addition, Grameen has issued more than 600,000 housing loans at 8 percent and about 20,000 educational loans at 5 percent.

Grameen also has arranged loans for about 100,000 beggars, whom it calls "struggling members." These loans are interest-free and offered without time limits. The goal is to encourage these members to cease begging and to become regular savers and borrowers. To date, 10 percent of these borrowers have left begging behind completely.

The Grameen bank is 96 percent owned by the borrowers, 97 percent of whom are women. Nine of its twelve directors are women.

Its bankers, using bicycles or motorcycles, go to a borrower's neighborhood for the weekly meetings. Typically, ten or so groups of five borrowers (sixty individual borrowers total) meet every week for about an hour to pay back existing loans, to receive new loans, and to exchange ideas in an open and transparent way in front of the whole group of fellow borrowers. The approach is practical also because Grameen's borrowers typically cannot read financial statements. . . .

We must all believe in people and their ability to change their own lives. All people, including the poor, have enormous capacity to help themselves. Despite appearances, deep inside every human being exists a precious treasure of initiative and creativity waiting to be discovered, to be unleashed, to change life for the better. If we look at each and every poor person from this perspective, we will find enormous possibilities for this world.

NOTES AND QUESTIONS

1. The *New York Times* reports that microcredit "reach[ed] more than 91 million customers, most of them women, with loans totaling more than $70 billion by the end of 2009." Half of all borrowers were from either India or Bangladesh. Vikas Bajaj, *15 Years In, Microcredit Has Suffered a Black Eye*, N.Y. Times (Jan. 6, 2011).

b.   Bringing Microcredit and Microfinance to the United States

Although at various points it has been supported by a host of powerful interests—principally banks and the federal government—microcredit has not taken off in the United States in the same way as it has in other parts of the world. Efforts to bring the Grameen model to the United States have not fared particularly well:

> Well known as "the land of opportunity," the U.S. would seem like the perfect fit for an entrepreneurial means of ending poverty. Many of the same reasons credit is unavailable to low-income persons in Asia and throughout the Third World apply equally to low-income Americans. . . . Nevertheless, microcredit in the U.S. has faced a rocky start, and not all organizations have survived. Microcredit has been available in the U.S. since the 1980s and has been present in all fifty states since the 1990s, but less than one percent of micro-entrepreneurs in the U.S. have

received microloans. In the late 1980s, Grameen Bank failed in its first attempt at transferring the Grameencredit model. In conjunction with Southern Bancorp Bank and the Good Faith Fund in Arkansas, Grameen Bank attempted to mimic the social ties and group-lending strategies of Grameencredit by establishing a mandatory six-week training program for individuals and then creating groups from among the training program's participants. However, even after a minimum of six weeks of familiarity and the prospect of a continued group relationship over the life of the loan, the groups lacked the social cohesion to enforce payments above a 70 percent repayment rate.

Courtney L. Gould, *Grameencredit: One Solution for Poverty, but Maybe Not in Every Country*, 28 UCLA Pac. Basin L.J. 1, 10 (2010). Differences in the U.S. market and the needs of borrowers have meant that domestic microcredit differs in structure and scale from many of the models found in the developing world, as is described in the two excerpts below. The first excerpt puts a human face on microcredit, showing the impact such credit can have on particular individuals before describing the rise of microlending. The second excerpt describes some of the challenges confronting domestic microcredit activities.

OLIVIA L. WALKER, *THE FUTURE OF MICROLENDING IN THE UNITED STATES: A SHIFT FROM CHARITY TO PROFITS?*

6 Entrepreneurial Bus. L.J. 383 (2011)

When the economy tanked in 2008, Kimberly Frye of Ramona, California knew what she needed to do in order to save her auto repair shop. She needed to hire more employees so that she could stay open longer and add services for low-income individuals in order to broaden her clientele. However, the banks she approached were not willing to lend to her. Thankfully for Frye, the Small Business Administration's ("SBA") microloan program saw the potential in her business plan and loaned her the program maximum of $35,000. Because of this loan she was able to keep her shop open on Saturdays and maintain a cash cushion that allowed her to accept state vouchers for smog repairs — decisions that saved her business. She now has enough business to support four mechanics, up from two, and she is especially proud of being the only repair shop in the area that is able to participate in the state's program that provides vouchers to low-income clients. Frye says, "It was the best decision that I could have ever made. Being a single woman, a single mom in business, they saved me."

Two brothers in their twenties, Dan and Joe Gram, had a dream to turn their years of experience in fitness, gymnastics and coaching into their own business. They stumbled upon the opportunity to purchase an elite gymnastics-training center. After raising $15,000 on their own, they needed an additional $30,000 to take over the business and its ten employees. They visited at least six banks with no success. An SBA microloan allowed them to realize their dream, and now Joe says, "So far, so good. We're pretty much break-even, moving toward profitability. We're learning a lot as we go, being young entrepreneurs."

Brent Baker founded an innovative company in the Bronx that converts used cooking oil from restaurants around New York City into fuel that it then sells. In 2009, the company was in dire need of an equipment upgrade, but three major commercial banks that had financed the company in the past were suddenly no longer lending. Baker was able to receive a $50,000 loan from Boc

Capital, a lender that received $750,000 in federal stimulus funds to help small businesses. Baker said, "The loan increased our profitability and put us in a position where we could expand." He was able to hire ten additional workers with the loan. He added, "It shows how a relatively small amount of credit can be such a huge advantage, and we really did create jobs."

Each of these individual anecdotes is just one example of the thousands of success stories of American microlending. In the United States, a microloan is usually classified as a short-term loan of $35,000 or less, and the SBA defines a microenterprise as a business with five or fewer employees. Microlending abroad has become a hotly recognized and discussed topic in recent years, mainly through the successes of Nobel Prize laureate Muhammad Yunus and his international Grameen Bank. Microlending is at an all-time high in the United States and has the potential to have a real impact on the business culture and climate of the United States. However, to many Americans, the term "microlending" still has the connotation of a tiny loan given as charity to those in dire poverty in exotic locales.

Abroad, two major microlending organizations have transitioned from traditional non-profits to for-profit corporations being traded on the public market. Today in the United States, the time is right for microlending to have a big impact on American business. The growing disparity of income distribution, the loss of blue-collar jobs, the shift from relatively well-paying manufacturing jobs to minimum wage service-sector jobs, corporate downsizing, outsourcing, and unemployment all contribute to a greater opportunity for self-employment that could be helped by microloans. Additionally, more women in the workplace, as well as an increasing number of single and "stay at home" fathers, are seeking self-employment as a way to balance work and family, the aging population is choosing self-employment, and self-employment is being seen as a way to remain in rural communities. . . .

. . . The foundation for microlending in the United States was laid in 1977 through the passage of the Community Reinvestment Act ("CRA"), which first started the process of banks being rated by regulators based in part on their participation of funneling resources directly or indirectly (through nonprofit organizations) into low-income communities. It was not until 1991 that the SBA first recognized microenterprise as a separate category of business and established the Microloan Demonstration Project. Also in 1991, a trade organization for microlenders, the Association for Enterprise Organization ("AEO"), was founded. By 1992, only a year after this official recognition, there were already 108 separate organizations working in American microfinance. Even with this sudden surge of interest, by 1995 no microlender in the United States had come anywhere close to breaking even — each individual microlender was functioning strictly as a charity, unable to make a sustainable difference. In 1999, federal funding for microlending programs increased through the passing of the Program for Investment in Microentrepreneurs ("PRIME") Act; however, during the Bush administration era from 2001 to 2005, federal funding for microfinance was cut drastically. By 2002, there were 650 separate organizations in microfinance. . . .

Virtually all microlenders in America are organized as non-profit organizations and serve as local intermediaries for federal funds. The SBA dominates the American microloan market; with loans averaging around $13,000, the federal funds are first lent to specially designated nonprofit, community-based organizations that then deal directly with the borrowers. There are also a few non-profit organizations in the private sector that issue smaller loans without this federal backing. The American Recovery and Reinvestment Act ("ARRA"), signed into law in February 2009, included $50 million in federal funds designated as microloans for small businesses. . . .

The current major players in American microlending fall into two categories: non-profit organizations that act as distributors of federal funds, and non-profit organizations that operate independently from the government. The biggest and most established network of microlenders in the United States is Accion USA. Accion serves as an intermediary for SBA funds, and is responsible for more than two-thirds of all the domestic microlending completed in the past twenty years. Accion's interest rates are set between 8.99% and 15.99%. Grameen America, founded by Yunus and following his microloan model that was first applied internationally, was started in 2008. Interest rates hover around fifteen percent. Yunus is very optimistic about the future of Grameen America and hopes it will be self-sustaining by 2013 — he believes that "there has been no financial crisis in microlending." In addition to the major non-profits, commercial banks such as Citibank are also beginning to see microcredit as a core business opportunity.

ZAHIR VIRANI, *AMERICAN MICROFINANCE: OPPORTUNITIES AND CHALLENGES*
27 Rev. Banking & Fin. L. 370 (2008)

Microfinance is most simply defined in economic terms as the supply of loans, savings, and other basic financial services to the poor. . . . The funds and services of microfinance [in the United States] are used to develop microenterprises, which are defined as businesses with five or fewer employees that require $35,000 or less in start-up capital, and which do not have ready access to the commercial banking sector. According to ACCION USA, of the more than 13.1 million microentrepreneurs in the United States, the overwhelming majority did not receive and were unlikely to apply for commercial bank loans. Domestically, certain microenterprise development organizations offer peer group loans in amounts ranging from $500 to $35,000.

Although the primary social and economic goals of microfinance are the same throughout the world, domestic micro-entrepreneurs require greater management skills to successfully compete in U.S. markets than would be required to compete in the markets of developing countries. As a result, domestic microfinance programs distinguish themselves from foreign programs by offering new entrepreneurs a far more diverse program of services beyond simply providing credit. Such additional services include upfront business training, specialized technical assistance, mentoring programs, sector-specific advice and support, networking opportunities, coordinated sales and marketing programs, and the development of formal links with banks, local community colleges, and other institutions. Moreover, the diversified services offered improve the survival rate of the start-up businesses and reduce the lender's credit risks. . . .

Domestic microlenders replicated some of the successes of the Grameen Bank's solidarity group structure, most notably the Women's Self-Employment Project. The project further demonstrated benefits to the microlenders, as the solidarity groups proved effective mechanisms for self-monitoring. Moreover, the group collected deposits for each member's savings account, which contributed to a collective emergency fund to provide group insurance, emergency loans to a group member, or additional working capital for member businesses. Such activities greatly reduced the likelihood of default and thus lowered significant costs and risks to the lender.

Despite the successes of some peer lending experiments, overall, the peer lending model has had very limited domestic success, with only a small number of domestic microfinance institutions currently offering loans to peer groups. As a result, microfinance in the US has tended to be more expensive than elsewhere, and has had to find other alternative strategies for cost reduction. One of the main avenues that microlenders in the US have explored in finding alternative strategies to reduce costs are developing cooperative efforts with commercial banks and financial institutions to meet the needs of American microentrepreneurs.

Despite their number, microentrepreneurs have largely been ignored by commercial banks because microentrepreneur needs are often too small for the banks to profitably address. However, commercial banks have taken an interest in the activities of microfinance lenders as a possible way to improve Community Reinvestment Act requirements. As a result, commercial banks have stepped in as an important source of financial support for major microfinance organizations like ACCION USA. Large financial institutions such as Citigroup have started charitable funds to help wealthy clients donate money to microfinance institutions. Moreover, microlenders and commercial banks have created channels to refer microentrepreneurs who wouldn't normally qualify for a bank loan and wouldn't know about the services of microlenders, thus furthering the exposure of domestic microlenders. The financial support provided by commercial banks has included collaborative lending. In addition to financial support, commercial banks have stepped in to provide training programs, technology and infrastructure, market data, and governance support. Such financial and strategic support greatly benefits the efficiency of microlenders, and directly strengthens the sustainability of microlender operations.

NOTES AND QUESTIONS

1. If domestic microcredit providers need charitable donations from commercial banks and from individuals, should they be considered self-sustaining?
2. Like the Grameen Bank, the Women's Self-Employment Project also focuses on women borrowers and has been relatively successful. Is there something about lending to women that is likely to make microcredit lending more successful when women are the primary beneficiaries? What do you see as the positive and negative aspects of using a gendered framework for expanding access to the poor?
3. A recent noteworthy innovation in microcredit systems is the peer-to-peer lending facilitated by Kiva, http://www.kiva.org. Much like traditional microfinance entities, Kiva takes deposited money and through its field workers administers microloans. What makes Kiva different is that the deposits come from individual lenders who as a matter of charity select a recipient and then, 99 percent of the time, are repaid. The deposited money is a form of charity because they do not earn any interest on their loan. The

donor then can decide if he or she wants to withdraw the amount originally loaned or recycle the loan to other recipients. The Kiva website allows those seeking a loan to post information about how the money will be used and lenders to search through such postings for individuals, projects, or businesses that appeal to them. For more on Kiva and Globalgiving, another online microcredit philanthropy website, see Raj. M. Desai & Homi Kharas, *Democratizing Foreign Aid: Online Philanthropy and International Development Assistance*, 42 N.Y.U. J. Int'l L. & Pol. 1111 (2010).

4. Can microcredit solve the problem of poverty? Microcredit can be thought of as a tool to allow poor people access to economic opportunities and to allow them to make use of their own entrepreneurial ideas and drive. But is microcredit being oversold? Professor Rashmi Dyal-Chand argues that the transformative potential of microcredit is limited and that its reliance on solidarity circles as the basis for lending may be ill-suited for poor people in the United States. Rashmi Dyal-Chand, *Reflection in a Distant Mirror: Why the West Has Misperceived the Grameen Bank's Vision of Microcredit*, 41 Stan. J. Int'l L. 217 (2005).

5. Perhaps the most radical idea for helping the poor have better access to credit that has gained traction internationally is the proposal that countries convert informal title held by the poor into formal title. Championed by Peruvian economist Hernando de Soto, land titling programs have been adopted across the developing world and been applauded by politicians of all stripes and by the major international development institutions. The basic idea is that in many parts of the world the poor occupy space — live in houses, farm plots of land, operate businesses — but do not have formal title to such land. Lack of formal title does not mean their holdings are necessarily insecure; even if the land formally belongs to a different private landowner or to the state, the right of the poor to the land is socially recognized. The analogy de Soto uses is that of barking dogs: even though the poor do not have formal title, if you walk through a neighborhood the dogs bark in ways that show where one property line ends and another begins. According to de Soto, the state simply needs to listen to the barking dogs. Land titling converts the social understanding — an understanding that is often accompanied by documents attesting to ownership even though the property is held informally by the poor — into formal title. Once the poor have formal title, they can use their land (now that it is recognized officially by the state as theirs) as collateral for bank loans. *See generally* Hernando de Soto, *The Mystery of Capital: Why Capitalism Triumphs in the West and Fails Everywhere Else* (2000).

   Land titling is not without controversy; scholars have questioned its efficacy at reducing poverty and, especially, the downside risks to the poor that they might lose their property through foreclosure after they mortgage their now formally recognized title. The domestic implications of land titling have been the subject of considerable academic commentary. *See, e.g., Hernando de Soto and Property in a Market Economy* (D. Benjamin Barros ed., 2010). At first glance, the land titling does not seem that relevant to the United States. Very few properties are successfully acquired through adverse possession, in part because private and public property owners are diligent about policing the use of their property and can rely on effective government enforcement of their exclusionary rights. On the other hand, much of the country was settled through programs that arguably are fairly analogous to land titling. The federal government, through homesteading and similar practices, distributed land to Americans willing to settle the Midwest and West through heavily subsidized sales. Doing so helped create an agrarian middle class, but was also associated with the loss of considerable amounts of land by the original inhabitants and owners of those lands, namely American Indians. More recently, the prospect of a foreclosure wave in the wake of the 2008 housing crisis raised the question, dormant since the 1980s, of whether urban squatters should be able to occupy and assert ownership over abandoned properties.

C.   CHARITY

In contrast to publicly funded welfare programs, private charity does not depend on the coercive power of the state to redistribute resources. Instead, charity is understood as more of an unqualified good. Accordingly, recipients of charitable donations, whether the recipient is a nonprofit or an individual, often are expected to and do show gratitude toward the donor. Through the charitable tax deduction—which amounts to a tax expenditure—the federal government, in effect, participates in the charitable act.

Before turning to the specific connection between charity and poverty, it is worth taking a glimpse at charitable giving generally. According to the Giving USA 2012 report, total charitable contributions in 2011 came to nearly $300 billion, with individuals contributing 73 percent of that total, foundations 14 percent, bequests 8 percent, and corporations 5 percent. The table below shows the percentage of this total received by different types of organizations:

Religion	32	Public-Society Benefit	7
Education	13	Arts, Culture, and Humanities	4
Human Services	12	Environment/Animals	3
Foundations	9	Unallocated*	3
Health	8	To Individuals	1
International Affairs	8		

*Includes foundations.

Giving USA 2012 reports that total charitable giving has fluctuated between a low of 1.7 percent and a high of 2.3 percent as a percentage of GDP since 1971. But such figures are only part of the story. According to the National Center for Charitable Statistics at the Urban Institute's Nonprofit Almanac 2011, among public charities, private contributions amounted to only 13.6 percent of their revenue in 2009. More than half, 52.4 percent, of revenue came from fees for services and goods from private sources; similar fees from the government explain another 23.2 percent; 8.9 percent came from government grants; and the final 2.1 percent of revenue came from other sources. Notably, when combined, the health and education sectors account for more than 70 percent of both revenue and assets among public charities. What does all this mean? Among other things, it means that only a small fraction of charitable donations directly support antipoverty efforts. Below are the results of a study that focused specifically on this issue:

> The Center on Philanthropy at Indiana University and Google partnered in early 2007 to estimate how much of the charitable giving by households in the U.S. focuses on the needs of the poor. This analysis finds that less than one-third of the money individuals gave to nonprofits in 2005 was focused on the needs of the economically disadvantaged. Of the $250 billion in donations, less than $78 billion explicitly targeted those in need.
>
> Only 8 percent of households' donated dollars were reported as contributions to help meet basic needs — providing food, shelter, or other necessities. An estimated additional 23 percent of total private philanthropy (including donations from foundations, corporations, and estates) went to programs specifically intended to help people of low income — either providing other direct benefits (such as medical treatment and scholarships) or through initiatives creating opportunity and empowerment (such as literacy and job training programs).

Ctr. on Philanthropy at Indiana Univ., *Patterns of Household Charitable Giving by Income Groups, 2005* (2007).

1. Individual Charitable Giving

The role of individual charitable giving in fighting poverty is intimately tied to the level of both societal inequality and government spending on social problems. In the first of this section's two excerpts, Andrew Carnegie presents his "gospel of wealth." A self-made man, in the late nineteenth century Carnegie helped build what would become U.S. Steel, but is perhaps best known today for his philanthropy. Besides Carnegie Hall, Carnegie Mellon University, and other similar institutions bearing his name, Carnegie funded the creation of more than 2,500 public libraries. Written in 1889 during the Gilded Age, Carnegie's gospel of wealth has been one of the most influential statements regarding the responsibilities of the wealthy to the poor.

ANDREW CARNEGIE, *WEALTH*
148 N. Am. Rev. 653 (June 1889)

This then is held to be the duty of the man of wealth. First: to set an example of modest, unostentatious living, shunning display; to provide moderately for the legitimate wants of those dependent upon him, and after doing so, to consider all surplus revenues which come to him simply as trust funds, which he is strictly bound as a matter of duty, to administer in the manner which in his judgment is best calculated to produce the most beneficial results for the community.

The man of wealth must become a trustee and agent for his poorer brethren, bringing to their service his superior wisdom, experience, and ability to administer. Those who would administer wisely must indeed be wise. For one of the serious obstacles to the improvement of our race is indiscriminate charity. It were better for mankind that the millions of the rich were thrown into the sea than so spent as to encourage the slothful, the drunken, the unworthy.

In bestowing charity, the main consideration should be to help those who help themselves. It provides part of the means by which those who desire to improve may do so; to give to those who desire to rise the aids by which they may rise; to assist but rarely or never to do all.

He is the only true reformer who is careful and as anxious not to lead the unworthy as he is to lead the worthy, and perhaps even more so, for in alms giving, more injury may be done by promoting vice than by relieving virtue. Thus, is the problem of the rich and poor to be solved.

The laws of accumulation should be left free; the laws of distribution free. Individualism will continue. But the millionaire will be but a trustee for the poor; entrusted for a season with a part of the increased wealth of the community, but administering it for the community far better than it did, or would have done, of itself. The best in minds will thus have reached a stage in the development of the race in which it is clearly seen that there is no mode of disposing of surplus wealth creditable to thoughtful and earnest men into whose hands it flows save by using it year-by-year for the general good. This day already dawns.

Men may die without incurring the pity of their fellows, sharers in great business enterprises from which their capital cannot be, or has not been withdrawn, upon which is left entirely a trust for public uses.

Yet the day is not far distant when the man who dies, leaving behind him millions of available wealth, which was free for him to administer during life, will pass away "unwept, unhonored, and unsung," no matter to what use he leaves the dross which he cannot take with him. Of such as these, the public verdict will then be: the man who dies thus rich, dies disgraced. Such in my opinion is the true gospel concerning wealth, obedience to which is destined someday to solve the problems of the rich and the poor, to hasten the coming brotherhood of man, and at last to make our earth a heaven.

* * *

In an op-ed published in 2007, Professor (and Carnegie biographer) David Nasaw questions the reliance on charitable contributions applauded by Andrew Carnegie and the idea that charity can or should displace the state.

DAVID NASAW, *WE CAN'T RELY ON THE KINDNESS OF BILLIONAIRES*

Wash. Post (Sept. 23, 2007)

Giving, Bill Clinton's folksy first-person tour of worthy causes and the good people who support them, is so relentlessly upbeat that only the most churlish professor would say a discouraging word about the book. But the former president is so intent on celebrating 21st-century philanthropy — and highlighting his and Hillary's role in promoting "the explosion of private citizens doing public good" — that he blithely ignores a hard reality: Philanthropy and democracy don't get along nearly as seamlessly as *Giving* would have us believe.

Private giving is not the panacea for all that ails us. Clinton concedes early on that many problems "cannot be adequately addressed without more enlightened government policies," but he then devotes only 19 of his 211 pages to government's role in advancing the common welfare. In urging us to do good privately, he tacitly reinforces a lack of faith in the capacity of democratic governance to cure our social ills.

As Clinton remarks, without comment or regret, today's startling expansion of the philanthropic sector is being fueled by a "vast pool of new wealth." According to a recent study by two economists, "the share of gross personal income of the top 1 percent of American earners rose to 17.4 percent in 2005, from 8.2 percent in 1980." Some of this new wealth is being given away, but not nearly as much as we might wish. "The rich when alive give away a smaller share of their income than the rest of us," Fortune magazine noted. "And when it comes time to die, the rich leave their money mostly to their children." About 9 percent goes to charitable causes. Pets get about 2 percent.

The recent philanthropic surge has been fueled by a few highly publicized mega-gifts. In 2006, 21 individuals each gave $100 million or more to philanthropy. The largest donation was Warren Buffett's pledge of $31 billion to the Bill and Melinda Gates Foundation, which focuses on global health and education. In 2005, the largest benefaction was Cordelia Scaife May's gift of most of her $400 million estate to the Colcom Foundation of Pittsburgh, which, while also funding conservation efforts and cultural institutions in the Pittsburgh area and giving $1.3 million for a bronze statue of Mr. Rogers, directs the greatest part of its funding toward "efforts to significantly reduce immigration levels in the U.S."

The largest gift given this year will most likely be one from Helen Walton, wife of Wal-Mart founder Sam Walton. She died in April, and her $16 billion estate is widely expected to go to the Walton Family Foundation, making it the second largest in the United States. The Waltons' foundations contribute millions each year to charter schools, charter-school advocacy groups and think tanks such as the American Enterprise Institute and the Heritage Foundation, whose "top policy analysts," the New York Times reported in 2005, have defended Wal-Mart against its critics in op-eds, interviews and testimony before government committees. Such foundations can pretty much do as they please with their grants, as long as they spend at least 5 percent of their assets every year and don't blatantly enrich their directors or donors.

In 1915, during the first great wave of giving, the Commission on Industrial Relations—created by Congress—undertook what its chairman called "a sweeping investigation of the country's greatest benevolent organizations . . . to ascertain if they were a menace to the Republic's future." Missouri lawyer Frank P. Walsh, the chairman, feared that self-perpetuating, tax-exempt foundations would expand the power of the rich so far that democratic decision-making would be threatened. He suggested that the federal government "take over such accumulations of wealth" as held by the Rockefeller, Carnegie and Russell Sage foundations "by taxation similar to the income tax" and use the money for widely agreed-upon public projects. The commission urged Congress to spend more on education and social services to counter the foundations' influence, investigate all endowed institutions and force foundations to accept federal regulation.

A year ago, while applauding Buffett's commitment to give billions to the Gates foundation, I raised questions similar to those the commission asked in 1915: Is society well-served by letting so few accumulate so much? What becomes of a society that relies on "gifts" from a handful of socially conscious billionaires to save schools, cure disease and alleviate poverty? The conservative journalist Bill O'Reilly suggested, somewhat longingly, that 50 years earlier, such questions would have resulted in my "invitation to appear before the House Committee on Un-American Activities."

My remarks may have upset O'Reilly because they questioned powerful assumptions about the relationship among capitalism, philanthropy and democracy so famously articulated by Andrew Carnegie, the founder of modern American philanthropy. Philanthropy, as Carnegie understood full well, was not a democratic institution.

Carnegie's advice on the "best methods" for giving away money was fiercely autocratic. He urged his fellow millionaires to donate to causes that appealed to them, so long as they did not encourage dependence. Neither the people nor their elected officials were to be consulted. In 1895, at the dedication of his new library in Pittsburgh, Carnegie acknowledged that the thousands of men working in his steel mills would have preferred that he give his money to them to spend as they saw fit. He refused because he believed he knew better than they did what they "required." Had his money gone directly to the people in the form of bigger paychecks, it would have been "frittered away, nine times out of 10, in things which pertain to the body and not to the spirit; upon richer food and drink, better clothing, more extravagant living, which are beneficial neither to rich nor poor." Instead, he gave them a multimillion-dollar complex with a museum, an art gallery and a concert hall to minister "to the higher, the divine, part of man."

Many of today's millionaires are following Carnegie's lead: setting up their own foundations and choosing their own causes. "New age donors are hands-on," the Hudson Institute reported in its 2007 Index of Global Philanthropy. "They want to participate directly in the design, operation and measurement of their endeavors."

He who pays the piper calls the tune. Researchers in New York have discovered, to no one's surprise, that parks in the city's wealthier neighborhoods receive more private money and are cleaner, safer and better maintained than those in poorer areas. The same process is at work in other public institutions that have begun to rely on private funding. Wealthy donors are more likely to give to the schools, colleges and cultural institutions that they or their families use.

These inequities get worse when we factor in the effects of charitable deductions allowed by the tax code. For every $3 the wealthy give away, the federal government adds the fourth that would have been collected in taxes had charitable deductions not been permitted. In effect, Washington is contributing $40 billion to institutions and causes selected for funding by foundations and individuals who earn enough to justify itemizing their deductions.

Former labor secretary Robert Reich estimates that only 10 percent of the contributions that qualified for charitable deductions in 2006 were "directed at the poor." The percentage of philanthropic giving that went toward disaster relief, services for the disadvantaged and alleviating poverty has dropped about 12 percent from 2005 to 2006, after the surge prompted by Hurricane Katrina and the 2004 tsunami in Southeast Asia, according to the Giving USA Foundation.

While we should applaud donors' goodwill, as Clinton does, those who write about giving must also ask some difficult questions. What becomes of a society that relies on the benevolence of a wealthy few to address its most pressing social problems? Is success in the marketplace, as measured in dollars, proof positive (as Carnegie believed) that the wealthy and their advisers are better suited than the rest of us, including elected representatives, to solve our problems?

My greatest fear is that the growth of private philanthropy may be both symptom and cause of our weakening faith in democratic government. In "Giving," Clinton recounts the failures of the federal government to confront global warming, then segues into praise for the private individuals, foundations and companies that are tackling the problem. But the fact that governments have failed in the past should not lead us to flee the public sphere for the private, as Clinton appears to be doing. There is nothing intrinsically wrong with trying to raise private money for public purposes, but we cannot let such efforts distract us from pressuring government to do its best to save the environment, adequately fund our public parks, schools and universities, and provide medical care and support for the weakest among us.

* * *

Charitable donations qualify for a tax deduction, which means that the state can be thought of as a partial contributor to any gift that results in lower taxes for the individual donor. Such deductions only make sense for individuals whose combination of income and expenses, including other deductions such as the mortgage deduction, make them exceed the standard deduction. Although this is not a tax law textbook, it is worth considering whether the charitable deduction makes sense in light of the limited amount of giving that is directly aiding the poor. The excerpt that follows highlights the ways in which politicians use the rhetoric of poverty to shore up the deduction even though most charitable donations go to other causes.

PAUL VALENTINE, *A LAY WORD FOR A LEGAL TERM: HOW THE POPULAR DEFINITION OF CHARITY HAS MUDDLED THE PERCEPTION OF THE CHARITABLE DEDUCTION*

89 Neb. L. Rev. 997 (2011)

In the United States there is a deeply held conviction "that taxpayers who donate to charity should generally not be subject to the same income tax liability as similarly situated taxpayers." This innate sense about the Internal Revenue Code's § 170, otherwise known as the charitable deduction, resonates with Americans' sense of fairness and creates strong barriers to curtailing its function.

This same sense of fairness is tied to the perceived effects of the charitable deduction. Yet, how "charitable" is the charitable deduction, and how charitable do we expect it to be? This Article argues that the discrepancy between the popular meaning of the word "charitable" and the legal meaning has distorted both the perception of, and the political justifications for, the provision.

The charitable deduction's definitional discrepancy is perhaps not immediately apparent, because often the legal and layperson's definitions of the word are the same. However, on occasion, the legal and popular definitions vary. One such example is the difference between the Tax Code's and layperson's definition of the word "charitable." The laypersons' definition is simple; the Merriam-Webster dictionary defines charity as "generosity and helpfulness especially toward the needy or suffering." The legal definition is not quite as succinct. The Treasury regulations define charitable as:

> relief of poor and distressed or of the underprivileged; advancement of religion;
> advancement of education or science, erection or maintenance of public

buildings, monuments, or works; lessening of the burdens of Governments; and promotion of social welfare by organizations designed to accomplish any of the above purposes, or (i) to lessen neighborhood tensions; (ii) to eliminate prejudice and discrimination; (iii) to defend human and civil rights secured by law; or (iv) to combat community deterioration and juvenile delinquency.

Thus, although the legal definition does cover direct relief of the poor, it also has a much wider mandate, including advancing religion, science and education, constructing public buildings, lessening neighborhood tensions, and other public benefit purposes. These types of causes may provide a service to society, but they are neither charitable under the popular meaning of the word nor would most individuals consider organizations that provide such services a charity.

This broad legal definition of "charitable" has created a misperception in the American psyche of where the benefits of the charitable deduction are allocated. The very use of the word "charitable" in the statutory language creates a powerful association in most non-lawyers that ties the deduction to churches and poverty relief organizations, when in reality this is only a small portion of the tax subsidy. Further, the emotive rhetoric used by politicians when attacking proposed amendments curtailing the charitable deduction is grossly out of sync with the primary beneficiaries of the provision. . . .

Public Justifications — The Misguiding Rhetoric in Defense of the Charitable Deduction

President Barack Obama's 2010 budget contains a proposed reduction of the charitable deduction for the highest income-level taxpayers. The proposal plans to reduce the deduction value of high income-level taxpayers from the current 35% rate to 28%. Regardless of the merits and flaws of such tax policy, the critics of the amendment all sang from the same hymnbook — the President should not penalize churches and welfare organizations because they aid those who need it most. For example, Rep. Ted Poe, of Texas, stated:

> Thus, charities . . . such as churches, the YMCA and groups that that [sic] feed the hungry and help in disasters, take care of crime victims and help the homeless, will be struggling for funds.

Similarly, Rep. Joe Pitts, of Pennsylvania, quoted one of his constituents in the disapproval of the proposed legislation:

> We donate a very large percentage of our income to the hungry, homeless, orphaned and widowed. We are in the top tax bracket. Any increase in our taxes or decrease in our charitable deductions will not hurt our standard of living, it will indeed, hurt the very people that the government is trying to help.

Along the same lines, Rep. Gus Bilirakis, of Florida, said:

> Every year, Americans give hundreds of billions of dollars to charity. In turn, they provide funding to shelters, food banks, health care clinics and a host of other charitable programs which benefit the needy. During this recession, their services are needed more than ever.

Opposition to this provision in the Senate used similar rhetoric in their critique of the bill. For instance, Sen. John Ensign stated:

> Most Americans believe that the private sector can deal with problems in our communities person to person through charitable giving. . . . We have some amazing charities that give compassionate care to those who truly need it.

Sen. Mitch McConnell reiterated:

> At a time of economic distress, when more people than ever depend on these organizations, the administration's budget reduces the incentive for people to donate to them.

Each of the Congressmen quoted above focused on the role of charities that help the neediest members of society, and these statements represent a sample of the typical arguments against the proposed modifications of § 170. The author acknowledges that members of Congress also mentioned health and educational organizations. However, the most prevalent and impassioned rhetoric was reserved to explain how the charitable deduction helps those who need it most and that any change to this provision would cripple these organizations. Accepting that these Congressmen were simply using the best rhetorical tools available — one of which was pulling on the heartstrings of the American public — if the Congressional justification for not amending the charitable deduction is that the deduction helps the neediest, then the data should show a significant correlation between the articulated justification and § 170's primary beneficiaries. . . . [T]he actual percentage of the charitable deduction used to benefit "those who really need it" is nowhere close to the attention it received in Congress.

. . . [A]pproximately 8% of the charitable deduction is apportioned to direct poverty relief organizations. . . .

TAXPAYERS' DONATIVE PREFERENCES RELATE TO TAXPAYERS' LEVELS OF INCOME

Individuals' donative preferences correlate with income levels. One study conducted in 2007 by the Center on Philanthropy at Indiana University (the Indiana Study) measured individual taxpayers' charitable donations in 2005 and broke down the donations according to income level and charitable purpose. It found that very wealthy donors primarily gave contributions to educational institutions (25.2%), health organizations (25.3%), and to a lesser extent the arts (15.4%). Wealthy and very wealthy donors gave a much smaller proportion of their charitable contributions to organizations that address basic human needs, such as shelter, food, and medical care for the indigent — 3.4% of individuals with income over $1 million and 5.8% of individuals with income between $200,000 and $1 million gave to these causes.

The Indiana Study also showed that low- and middle-income taxpayers primarily supported religious organizations. Low- and middle-income households gave just under $9.5 billion, or about 49% of total giving, to direct assistance of poverty charities. . . .

... [T]he word "charitable" dupes many Americans into believing the deduction is spent on a certain traditional set of charitable causes. By changing the name of § 170 to the "qualified donation deduction" this misunderstanding will be reduced. Further, it allows Congress to debate the merits of the provision, including each of its individual components, and to determine whether each subsection should continue to receive the benefits of a subsidy without fear of political backlash. ...

CONCLUSION

A former chief economist at the U.S. Department of Labor stated that if any proposed amendments curtailing the charitable deduction passed, "the government would gain billions in tax revenue, but charities and others would lose. That would lessen the ability of charities to help the neediest. ...." It is these types of misleading assertions that this Article hopes to address. The neediest receive only 8% in direct assistance from the charitable deduction. High-income individuals contribute less as a percentage of their total giving to direct assistance of poverty organizations than their middle- and-low-income counterparts. To continue justifying the 35% deduction for high-income individuals under the assumption that it protects the neediest is a fallacy, and to continue advertising it as such constitutes fraud.

* * *

But should the tax code be changed, with the full deduction available only to gifts that benefit the poor? The two excerpts that follow give alternative answers to this question. The first, written by Robert Reich, who served as Secretary of Labor under President Clinton and wrote *The New Property*, excerpted in Chapter 3, argues for limiting the full deduction to antipoverty institutions. The second, written by John Colombo, a tax law professor, argues against such a narrowing of the deduction. Though focused on the tax implications of donations, the excerpts raise the definitional issues that surround labeling something charity or deciding something should not count as charity.

ROBERT B. REICH, *IS HARVARD REALLY A CHARITY?*
L.A. Times (Oct. 1, 2007)

This year's charitable donations are expected to total more than $200 billion, a record. But a big portion of this impressive sum — especially from the wealthy, who have the most to donate — is going to culture palaces: to the operas, art museums, symphonies and theaters where the wealthy spend much of their leisure time. It's also being donated to the universities they attended and expect their children to attend, perhaps with the added inducement of knowing that these schools often practice a kind of affirmative action for "legacies."

I'm all in favor of supporting the arts and our universities, but let's face it: These aren't really charitable contributions. They're often investments in the lifestyles the wealthy already enjoy and want their children to have too. They're also investments in prestige — especially if they result in the family name being engraved on the new wing of an art museum or symphony hall.

It's their business how they donate their money, of course. But not entirely. Charitable donations to just about any not-for-profit are deductible from income taxes. This year, for instance, the U.S. Treasury will be receiving about $40 billion less than it would if the tax code didn't allow for charitable deductions. (That's about the same amount the government now spends on Temporary Assistance for Needy Families, which is what remains of welfare.) Like all tax deductions, this gap has to be filled by other tax revenues or by spending cuts, or else it just adds to the deficit.

I see why a contribution to, say, the Salvation Army should be eligible for a charitable deduction. It helps the poor. But why, exactly, should a contribution to the already extraordinarily wealthy Guggenheim Museum or to Harvard University (which already has an endowment of more than $30 billion)?

Awhile ago, New York's Lincoln Center had a gala supported by the charitable contributions of hedge-fund industry leaders, some of whom take home $1 billion a year. I may be missing something, but this doesn't strike me as charity. Poor New Yorkers rarely attend concerts at Lincoln Center.

It turns out that only an estimated 10% of all charitable deductions are directed at the poor. So here's a modest proposal. At a time when the number of needy continues to rise, when government doesn't have the money to do what's necessary for them and when America's very rich are richer than ever, we should revise the tax code: Focus the charitable deduction on real charities.

If the donation goes to an institution or agency set up to help the poor, the donor gets a full deduction. If the donation goes somewhere else — to an art palace, a university, a symphony or any other nonprofit — the donor gets to deduct only half of the contribution.

JOHN D. COLOMBO, NAT'L CTR. ON PHILANTHROPY & THE LAW, *THE ROLE OF REDISTRIBUTION TO THE POOR IN FEDERAL TAX EXEMPTION FOR CHARITIES* (2009)

In an opinion piece published by the L.A. Times in October, 2007, Robert B. Reich opined that tax law should differentially treat contributions to a charity based upon whether the charity's purpose was to help the poor. "If the donation goes to an institution or agency set up to help the poor, the donor gets a full deduction. If the donation goes somewhere else — to an art palace, a university, a symphony or any other nonprofit — the donor gets to deduct only half of the contribution." . . .

This is hardly the first time an observer has suggested that tax law ought to distinguish among various charitable activities. . . . Many of the policy proposals that have been floated recently, however, either explicitly or implicitly tie tax benefits to a specific view of charity as being primarily concerned with helping the poor — or in other words, a conception of charity as a tool for wealth redistribution. . . .

HISTORY: THE IRS REDISTRIBUTIVE VIEW OF CHARITY PRIOR TO 1959

Though it may seem hard to believe from the vantage point of the early 21st century, at one time IRS seemed to view relief of the poor as the only rationale for exemption for organizations that fell outside those specifically enumerated (e.g., religious and educational) in what is now Code Section 501(c)(3). In 2923, the IRS ruled that a civic association whose purpose was to promote "a higher civic and social life" through camps, clubs and classes was not exempt because the word "charitable" as used in the existing exemption provision was limited to "relief of the poor" and not the broader charitable trust definition which encompassed virtually any benefit to a broad charitable class. Though the Service recognized the broader meaning of "charitable" in the common law, it concluded that because Congress specifically listed certain charitable organizations (e.g., religious, educational) that would have been included in a broad reading of the word "charitable," Congress must have meant to limit "charitable" in the statue to its more "common" meaning of relief of the poor. Regulations from 1943 issued under the 1939 Code reaffirmed the view that "charitable" in the exemption statutes was limited to relief of the poor: "Corporations organized and operated exclusively for charitable purposes comprise, in general, organizations for the relief of the poor."

It was not until 1959 that the IRS officially reversed course and adopted new regulations under 501(c)(3) that embraced the broad common law view of charity. In this new regulation, the IRS stated that "charitable" in the statute was used in its "generally accepted legal sense," and included:

> Relief of the poor and distressed or of the underprivileged; advancement of religion; advancement of education or science; erection or maintenance of public buildings, monuments, or works; lessening of the burdens of Government; and promotion of social welfare by organizations designed to accomplish any of the above purposes, or (i) to lessen neighborhood tensions; (ii) to eliminate prejudice and discrimination; (iii) to defend human and civil rights secured by law; or (iv) to combat community deterioration and juvenile delinquency. . . .

THE REDISTRIBUTION BENT, HISTORICAL PERSPECTIVES, AND THEORY

Whatever the explanation may be, the current fascination by some commentators with defining charity as almost exclusively associated with helping the poor is contrary to the historical definitions of charity and conflicts with all the theories on the table for explaining charitable tax exemption. In addition, proposals to align charitable tax incentives with redistribution to the poor in effect represent a choice of one view of distributive justice as the prevailing rationale for exemption without much in the way of critical examination of what that choice means for the charitable sector generally, or other views of distributive justice (or economic efficiency) that also might define the scope of the charitable sector.

On the historical front, while relief of the poor certainly has been a major part of the definition of charity for centuries, it has never been the only part. Indeed, tax-exemption for charitable organizations originally had nothing at all to do with redistribution to the poor. Rather, the practice can be traced to the simple proposition that human beings shouldn't try to tax God: churches were the original tax-exempt entities. Exemption for educational institutions was simply an extension of the religious exemption, since virtually all schools prior to the Reformation were church-affiliated. The 1601 Elizabethan Statute of Charitable Uses certainly highlighted the relief of the poor as a charitable purpose (and was passed as part of the "poor laws" enacted at that time), but also included "schools of learning, free schools and scholars in universities," as well as "repair of bridges, ports, havens, causeways, churches, sea-banks and highways . . . maintenance for houses of correction, . . . help of young tradesmen" and so forth. . . .

CONCLUSION

A conception of charity for federal tax exemption purposes that is limited to poor relief is contrary to history, to the IRS's own regulations, and to every theory set forth so far to explain exemption. Such a view also unwittingly adopts a particular formulation of distributive justice without thoroughly examining competing views of distributive justice or even competing theoretical concerns such as economic efficiency.

. . . "Helping the poor" is such a long-standing part of the core conception of charity that one can hardly blame policy makers for gravitating toward it as the bright line in question. The bulk of tax theory on exemption and legal philosophy, however, does not support such a narrow view of charity. . . .

NOTES AND QUESTIONS

1. Major national events such as 9/11 can generate an outpouring of donations, big and small, but the hopes among antipoverty advocates that Hurricane Katrina would have a lasting impact on the nature of charitable giving have not panned out. *See* Stephanie Strom, *What Is Charity?*, N.Y. Times (Nov. 14, 2005).
2. Should the government stop subsidizing charitable contributions? Or is this a tax expenditure that should be expanded to be available to all tax filers by, for example, allowing the charitable deduction to supplement the standard deduction?

2.   Faith-Based

As the figures at the start of this section on charity highlight, religious organizations receive a significant portion, nearly one-third, of all money given to charity. Religiously affiliated organizations provide services that benefit poor people and low-income communities through major organizations — Habitat for Humanity, the Salvation Army, Catholic Charities — and through formal and informal support programs (such as emergency relief, child care, drug-treatment facilities) that can play important roles in many people's lives. During the George W. Bush administration, issues involving religion and charity became more prominent because of the President's efforts to facilitate government support for faith-based organizations. In the first excerpt that follows, President Bush explains his support; the second excerpt questions some of the claims made by the President.

PRESIDENT GEORGE W. BUSH, *FOREWORD,*
IN *RALLYING THE ARMIES OF COMPASSION* (2001)

America is rich materially, but there remains too much poverty and despair amidst abundance. Government can rally a military, but it cannot put hope in our hearts or a sense of purpose in our lives.

Government has a solemn responsibility to help meet the needs of poor Americans and distressed neighborhoods, but it does not have a monopoly on compassion. America is richly blessed by the diversity and vigor of neighborhood healers: civic, social, charitable, and religious groups. These quiet heroes lift people's lives in ways that are beyond government's know-how, usually on shoestring budgets, and they heal our nation's ills one heart and one act of kindness at a time.

The indispensable and transforming work of faith-based and other charitable service groups must be encouraged. Government cannot be replaced by charities, but it can and should welcome them as partners. We must heed the growing consensus across America that successful government social programs work in fruitful partnership with community-serving and faith-based organizations — whether run by Methodists, Muslims, Mormons, or good people of no faith at all.

The paramount goal must be compassionate results, not compassionate intentions. Federal policy should reject the failed formula of towering, distant bureaucracies that too often prize process over performance. We must be outcome-based, insisting on success and steering resources to the effective and to the inspired. Also, we must always value the bedrock principles of pluralism, nondiscrimination, evenhandedness and neutrality. Private and charitable groups, including religious ones, should have the fullest opportunity permitted by law to compete on a level playing field, so long as they achieve valid public purposes, like curbing crime, conquering addiction, strengthening families, and overcoming poverty.

[M]y agenda [is] to enlist, equip, enable, empower and expand the heroic works of faith-based and community groups across America. The building blocks are two Executive Orders, signed yesterday, that call for the creation of a high-level White House Office of Faith-Based and Community Initiatives, and instruct five Cabinet departments to establish Centers for Faith-Based and Community Initiatives.

As President, I will lead the federal government to take bold steps to rally America's armies of compassion. I look forward to working with Congress on these issues and am open to additional ideas to meet our shared goals. I invite all Americans to join this effort to unleash the best of America.

AMY SULLIVAN, *FAITH WITHOUT WORKS: AFTER FOUR YEARS,*
THE PRESIDENT'S FAITH-BASED POLICIES HAVE PROVEN
TO BE NEITHER COMPASSIONATE NOR CONSERVATIVE

Wash. Monthly (Oct. 2004)

When George W. Bush first hit the national political scene in the crowded field for the 2000 Republican nomination, what made him different, what made even liberal Americans take a second look, was his declaration that he was a "compassionate conservative." Unlike the flinty old conservatives of the past, Bush explained, a compassionate conservative would not be afraid to harness the power of government to minister to the unfortunate. But unlike traditional liberal Democrats, who relied on fumbling government bureaucracies, a compassionate conservative would empower and fund the charitable sector, particularly religious groups, to help those in need.

This breakthrough political slogan was embodied by a "faith-based initiative" that Bush talked about incessantly on the campaign trail and rolled out within the first month of taking over the White House. And Bush's image as a different kind of Republican was only reinforced by the tableau of black pastors, conservative evangelical leaders, and liberal crusaders for social justice who gathered around him as he introduced his faith-based domestic policy. The first part of the initiative sought to make it easier for religious organizations to get government grants to provide social services. Trumpeting the success of faith-based groups in Texas that ran drug rehabilitation and prison counseling programs, Bush argued that religious organizations could outperform their secular equivalents and so should be allowed to compete for the same government funds. The policy's second aspect was a proposed tax break to make it worthwhile for individuals to contribute more of their money to charities. By allowing non-itemizers (70 percent of taxpayers) to deduct their charitable contributions, the proposal could infuse as much as $80 billion into the charitable sector. Together, the two ideas embraced classic conservative principles: honoring the unique ability of religious organizations to help those in need, and empowering individuals in the civil sector instead of government. . . .

BLIND FAITH

From the very beginning, Bush has argued that faith-based groups should be judged on their results, and he insists that they do work better. The difference, he contends, is that they do more than simply minister to physical needs. On the campaign trail in the summer of 2000, Bush told audiences that religious organizations succeed where others fail "because they change hearts, they convince a person to turn their life over to Christ." Whenever "my administration sees a responsibility to help people," he promised, "we will look first to faith-based organizations that have shown their ability to save and change lives." Bush had little empirical evidence to back up the claim that religious organizations were more effective. But he relentlessly talked of two seemingly-promising programs that the Texas state government had supported while he was governor. One was Teen Challenge, a drug rehabilitation program that claimed an astonishing 86 percent success rate. The other was InnerChange, a counseling program for prisoners that boasted impressively low levels of recidivism among its graduates. Certain critics raised questions about the reliability of the studies that produced these figures. But Bush kept repeating the claims, and most of the press corps passed them along uncritically. . . .

Critics worried that faith-based groups would be unduly privileged in the newly expanded grant-making world. For them, Bush had one word: results, results, results. In an interview with the religious Web site Beliefnet, he was asked whether he would support government money going to a Muslim group that taught prisoners the Koran. "The question I'd be asking," Bush replied, "is what are the recidivism rates? Is it working? I wouldn't object at all if the program worked." Four more times in the interview, Bush mentioned "results," noting that instead of promoting religion, "I'm promoting lower recidivism rates, and we will measure to make sure that's the case."

This rhetoric matched the administration's focus in other policy areas — like education — on accountability. Conservatives traditionally criticize government programs for throwing good money after bad, rewarding those who have not proven themselves effective with hard numbers like higher test scores, lower poverty rates, or reduced recidivism. Mel Martinez, Secretary of Housing and Urban Development, echoed the results-oriented sentiment in December 2002, telling an audience that "faith-based organizations should be judged on one central question: Do they work?" Conservatives thought they already knew the answer. "The fact is, we don't just suspect that faith-based programs work best," said Tucker Carlson on "Crossfire," "we know it."

Actually, we knew no such thing. But now we've had four years to measure results and reach a conclusion. Unfortunately, in the midst of all of the instructions included in the various executive orders, it turns out that the Bush administration forgot to require evaluation of organizations that receive government grants. . . . The accountability president has chosen not to direct any money toward figuring out whether faith-based approaches really work.

So, it's a good thing that some academics and private organizations have picked up the slack. In the last few years, a few studies have looked at both faith-based and secular social service providers, and they have particularly tried to replicate the incredible results boasted by the model Texas programs. The verdict? There is no evidence that faith-based organizations work better than their secular counterparts; and, in some cases, they are actually less effective. . . .

THE CHOSEN ONES

The fact that there is no proof that faith-based programs are more effective has not stopped the president from claiming that they are. . . . Bush simply shifts his emphasis when one argument begins to lose luster. These days, he is most likely to promote the faith-based initiative by contending that religious groups have been discriminated against and merely deserve the same chances that everyone else has. . . .

And, in fact, federal policy has not always been blind to religious character. This is often for good reason — the Constitution prohibits government promotion of religion — but it sometimes seems arbitrary. . . .

Yet despite some unfair kinks in federal contracting procedures, the truth is that the playing field isn't all that slanted against faith-based groups. Organizations like Catholic Charities and Lutheran Social Services have been mainstay providers of social services and have received government funding for decades. Instead of acknowledging this fact, the administration indulges in rhetoric that is almost a parody of left-wing identity politics — including making false accusations of discrimination. For example, the Department of Housing and Urban Development's audit of its dealings with religious groups reports that no faith-based organizations received funding under the department's $20 million Self-Help Homeownership Opportunity Program. HUD apparently forgot that Habitat for Humanity — which has received over half of that program's total funding in recent years — is a faith-based organization. . . .

NOTES AND QUESTIONS

1. Before President Bush's Faith-Based Initiative, in order for a faith-based
    organization (for example, a church) to receive public funding to provide
    services, it had to create a separate 501(c)(3) organization. Is this an overly
    burdensome requirement?
2. At various points in history, religious organizations have played an active role
    in the fight against poverty and subordination. Rev. Martin Luther King, Jr.'s
    civil rights efforts were supported by the Southern Christian Leadership
    Conference, which he helped found and led. Latin-American Catholic
    priests similarly advocated a "preferential option for the poor" in the
    1970s-1990s as part of liberation theology. *See* Russell Powell, *Theology in
    Public Reason and Legal Discourse: A Case for the Preferential Option for the
    Poor*, 15 Wash. & Lee J. Civ. Rts. & Soc. Just. 327 (2009). For more on similar
    religious traditions of supporting the needy, see Joseph William Singer, *The
    Edges of the Field: Lessons on the Obligations of Ownership* (2000).

CHAPTER
12

Human Rights

INTRODUCTION

More than forty years after lawyers first began their aggressive efforts to address economic inequality through law, poverty persists. Four decades of poverty law courses and poverty lawyers have not succeeded in eradicating it. The human rights paradigm, by expanding the dialogue to a more global context, and by embracing interdisciplinary approaches, promises to at least give law students a more nuanced understanding of the force of economic inequality and at best, to give them additional tools and leverage to make gains against poverty domestically as well as internationally.

Martha F. Davis, *The Pendulum Swings Back: Poverty Law in the Old and New Curriculum*, 34 Fordham Urb. L.J. 1391 (2007).

Poverty law, policy, and practice take place in an increasingly interdependent world. On the global stage, international human rights law is a significant source of antipoverty rhetoric and activity. Some countries have incorporated human rights — including economic, social, and cultural rights — into their modern constitutions. As the above excerpt suggests, advocates believe that human rights can both enhance our understanding of inequality and serve as an important antipoverty tool.

Federal courts in the United States have been reluctant to incorporate international human rights law in their jurisprudence. Nevertheless, lawyers have begun to seize opportunities to deploy human rights in state courts and other settings to advance domestic antipoverty efforts. In addition to domesticating international norms, human rights approaches to poverty can also internationalize local problems. This chapter explores the potential, limits, and desirability of applying human rights instruments and norms to combat poverty in the United States.

Section A offers a definition of human rights, which are generally viewed as universal and immutable — "indivisible, interdependent, and integrated," in the language of the United Nations — and are meant to obligate states to provide citizens and others residing within their borders *access to* certain goods and *protection from* certain harms. Section B sets out the international human rights law framework and enforcement mechanisms. Section C describes the key role the United States played in shaping this regime. Section D considers the relationship between human rights and the multifaceted deprivations of poverty.

Section E explores the application of human rights to domestic antipoverty efforts, and it concludes with a case study of one such effort.

A. WHAT ARE HUMAN RIGHTS?

The international human rights framework has generated controversy and debate about the meaning, categorization, and extent of such rights. The first excerpt is a definition of human rights from the late Lou Henkin, a leading human rights scholar and practitioner.

LOUIS HENKIN, *THE AGE OF RIGHTS* (1990)

The contemporary idea of human rights was formulated and given content during the Second World War and its aftermath. During the War, the Allied powers had proclaimed that assuring respect for human rights was their war aim. In 1945, at Nuremberg, the Allies included crimes against humanity among the charges on which Nazi leaders were tried. The United Nations Charter declared that promoting respect for human rights was the principal purpose of the United Nations Organization. The human rights idea found its contemporary expression in the Universal Declaration of Human Rights adopted by the United Nations General Assembly in 1948, and in the numerous covenants and conventions derived from it.

"Rights" have figured prominently in moral, legal, and political theory. The idea of rights is related to theories of "the good," of "the right," of "justice," and to conceptions of "the good society." . . .

The idea of human rights that has received currency and universal (if nominal) acceptance in our day owes much to these antecedents but it is discrete and different from them. The contemporary version does not ground or justify itself in natural law, in social contract, or in any other political theory. In international instruments, representatives of states declare and recognize human rights, define their content, and ordain their consequences within political societies and in their system of nation-states. The justification of human rights is rhetorical, not philosophical. Human rights are self-evident, implied in other ideas that are commonly intuited and accepted. Human rights are derived from accepted principles, or are required by accepted ends — societal ends such as peace and justice; individual ends such as human dignity, happiness, fulfillment. . . .

Human rights are the rights of individuals in society. Every human being has, or is entitled to have, "rights" — legitimate, valid, justified claims — upon his or her society; claims to various "goods" and benefits. Human rights are not some abstract, inchoate "good"; they are defined, particular claims listed in international instruments such as the Universal Declaration of Human Rights and the major covenants and conventions. They are those benefits deemed essential for individual well-being, dignity, and fulfillment, and that reflect a common sense of justice, fairness and decency. In the constitutional jurisprudence of the United States, as we shall see, individual rights have long been thought of as consisting only of "immunities," as limitations on what government might do *to* the individual. Human rights, on the other hand, include not only these negative "immunity claims" but also positive "resource claims," claims to what society is deemed required to do *for* the individual. They include liberties—freedom *from* (for example, detention, torture), and freedom *to* (speak, assemble); they include also the right to food, housing, and other basic human needs.

Human rights are universal; they belong to every human being in every human society. They do not differ with geography or history, culture or ideology, political or economic system, or stage of societal development. To call them "human" implies that all human beings have them, regardless of sex, race, and age; regardless of high or low "birth," social class, national origin, ethnic or tribal affiliation; regardless of wealth or poverty, occupation, talent, merit, religion, ideology, or other commitment. Implied in one's humanity, human rights are inalienable and imprescriptible: they cannot be transferred, forfeited or waived; they cannot be lost by having them usurped, or by one's failure to exercise or assert them.

Human rights are *rights*; they are not merely aspirations, or assertions of the good. To call them rights is not to assert, merely, that the benefits indicated are desirable or necessary; or merely, that it is "right" that the individual shall enjoy these goods; or even, merely, that it is the duty of society to respect the immunity or provide the benefits. To call them "rights" implies that they are claims "as of right," not by appeal to grace or charity, or brotherhood, or love; they need not be earned or deserved. The idea of rights implies entitlement on the part of the holder in some order under some applicable norm; the idea of human rights implies entitlement in a moral order under a moral law, to be translated into and confirmed as legal entitlement in the legal order of a political society. When a society recognizes that a person has a right, it affirms, legitimates, and justifies that entitlement, and incorporates and establishes it in the society's system of values, giving it important weight in competition with other societal values. . . .

Human rights are claims upon society. These claims may derive from moral principles governing relations between persons, but it is society that bears the obligation to satisfy the claims. Of course, the official representatives of society must themselves respect individual freedoms and immunities; political society must also act to protect the individual's rights against private invasion. As regards claims to economic and social benefits, society must act as an insurer to provide them if individuals cannot provide them for themselves. Thus, government must protect me from assault by my neighbor, or from wolves, and must ensure that I have bread or hospitalization; in human rights terms, my rights are against the state, not against the neighbor or the wolves, the baker, or the hospital. The state may arrange to satisfy my claims by maintaining domestic laws and institutions that give me, say, rights and remedies in tort against my neighbor, or administrative remedies against a corrupt, misguided, or inefficient bureaucrat, or access to public schools or health services. Those legal rights and remedies against individuals or agencies within society give effect to my human rights claims upon society.

The idea of human rights has implications for the relation of the individual's rights to other public goods. It is commonly said that human rights are "fundamental." That means that they are important, that life, dignity, and other important human values depend on them; it does not mean that they are "absolute," that they may never be abridged for any purpose in any circumstances. Human rights enjoy a prima facie, presumptive inviolability, and will often "trump" other public goods. Government may not do some things, and must do others, even though the authorities are persuaded that it is in society's interest (and perhaps even the individual's own interest) to do otherwise; individual human rights cannot be lightly sacrificed even for the good of the greatest number, even for the general good of all. But if human rights do not bow lightly to public concerns, they may be sacrificed if countervailing societal interests are important enough, in particular circumstances, for limited times and purposes, to the extent strictly necessary. The Universal Declaration recognizes that rights are subject to limitations determined by law "for the purpose of securing due recognition and respect for the rights and freedoms of others and of meeting the just requirement of morality, public order, and the general welfare in a democratic society."

The idea of rights accepts that some limitations on rights are permissible but the limitations are themselves strictly limited. Public emergency, national security, and public order are weighty terms, bespeaking important societal interests, but they are not to be lightly or loosely invoked, and the conception of national security or public order cannot be so large as to swallow the right. Derogations are permitted only in time of a public emergency that threatens the life of the nation, not as a response to fears (warranted or paranoid) for other values, or for the security of a particular regime. Even in an authentic emergency, a society may derogate from rights only to the extent strictly required by the exigencies of the situation, and even such necessary derogations must not involve invidious inequalities, and may not derogate from basic rights: they must not invade the right to life, or involve torture or cruel, inhuman punishment, slavery or servitude, conviction of crime under ex post facto laws, denial of rights as a person before the law, or violate freedom of thought, conscience, or religion. Moreover, considerations of public emergency permitting derogations, or of national security or public order permitting limitations on certain rights, refer to a universal standard, monitored by external scrutiny and judgment.

In sum, the idea of human rights is that the individual counts—independent of and in addition to his or her part in the common good. Autonomy and liberty must be respected, and the individual's basic economic-social needs realized, as a matter of entitlement, not of grace or discretion (even by wise and benevolent authority, or even by "the people"). The individual has obligations to others and to the community, and society may ask all individuals to give up some of their rights for the rights of others and for the common good, but there is a core of individuality that cannot be invaded or sacrificed. And all individuals count equally. An individual's right can be sacrificed to another's right only when choice is inevitable, and only according to some principle of choice reflecting the comparative value of each right. No particular individual can be singled out for particular sacrifice, except at random or by some other "neutral principle," consistent with the spirit of equal protection of the laws. . . .

NOTES AND QUESTIONS

1. How does Professor Henkin's definition of human rights relate to the various issues you have studied this semester, like housing, income, health, and education?

2. Do you think access to these goods should be a "right" in the sense he describes, especially the idea that minimum access to such goods should not be a matter of grace or charity and does not need to be earned or deserved?

B. THE INTERNATIONAL HUMAN RIGHTS LAW FRAMEWORK

On December 10, 1948, the U.N. General Assembly unanimously adopted the Universal Declaration of Human Rights (UDHR). While not a binding treaty, parts of the UDHR are considered customary law and binding on member states. The UDHR together with the International Covenant on Civil and Political Rights (ICCPR) and the International Covenant on Economic, Social and Cultural Rights (ICESCR) — both adopted in 1966 and entered into force in 1976 — constitute what is known as the International Bill of Rights.

The first excerpt in this section is from a glossary published by the U.N. Office of the High Commissioner on Human Rights. The second excerpt was written with a domestic poverty law audience in mind and describes the U.N.'s human rights law framework. Relevant portions of the UDHR and the ICESCR are reproduced next.

U.N. OFFICE OF THE HIGH COMM'R FOR HUMAN RIGHTS, *HUMAN RIGHTS TREATY BODIES: GLOSSARY OF TREATY BODY TERMINOLOGY* (2013)

This glossary is intended to explain some of the important elements of the treaty body system and highlight some of the most significant differences in terminology.

Consent to Be Bound

In order to become a party to a multilateral treaty, a State must demonstrate, through a concrete act, its willingness to undertake the legal rights and obligations contained in the treaty. In other words, it must express its consent to be bound by the treaty. A State can express its consent to be bound in several ways, in accordance with the final clauses of the relevant treaty. The most common ways are: definitive signature; ratification; acceptance or approval; and accession. The act by which a State expresses its consent to be bound by a treaty is distinct from the treaty's entry into force. Consent to be bound is the act whereby a State demonstrates its willingness to undertake the legal rights and obligations under a treaty through definitive signature or the deposit of an instrument of ratification, acceptance, approval or accession. Entry into force of a treaty with regard to a State is the moment the treaty becomes legally binding for the State that is party to the treaty. Each treaty contains provisions dealing with both aspects.

Entry into Force

Entry into force of a treaty is the moment in time when a treaty becomes legally binding on the parties to the treaty. The provisions of the treaty determine the moment of its entry into force. This may be a date specified in the treaty or a date on which a specified number of ratifications, approvals, acceptances or accessions have been deposited with the depositary. The date when a treaty deposited with the Secretary-General enters into force is determined in accordance with the treaty provisions.

General Comment

A treaty body's [see below] interpretation of the content of human rights provisions, on thematic issues or its methods of work. General comments often seek to clarify the reporting duties of State parties with respect to certain provisions and suggest approaches to implementing treaty provisions. Also called "general recommendation."

Ratification, Acceptance or Approval

Ratification, acceptance and approval all refer to the act undertaken on the international plane, whereby a State establishes its consent to be bound by a treaty. [Under Article II, Section 2 of the U.S. Constitution, the President has the power to make treaties "provided two thirds of the Senators present concur."] Most multilateral treaties expressly provide for States to express their consent to be bound by signature subject to ratification, acceptance or approval. Providing for signature subject to ratification allows States time to seek approval for the treaty at the domestic level and to enact any legislation necessary to implement the treaty domestically, prior to undertaking the legal obligations under the treaty at the international level. Once a State has ratified a treaty at the international level, it must give effect to the treaty domestically. This is the responsibility of the State. Generally, there is no time limit within which a State is requested to ratify a treaty which it has signed. Upon ratification, the State becomes legally bound under the treaty. Ratification at the international level, which indicates to the international community a State's commitment to undertake the obligations under a treaty, should not be confused with ratification at the national level, which a State may be required to undertake in accordance with its own constitutional provisions before it expresses consent to be bound internationally. Ratification at the national level is inadequate to establish a State's intention to be legally bound at the international level. The required actions at the international level shall also be undertaken.

Reservation

A reservation is a statement made by a State by which it purports to exclude or alter the legal effect of certain provisions of a treaty in their application to that State. A reservation may enable a State to participate in a multilateral treaty that it would otherwise be unable or unwilling to participate in. States can make reservations to a treaty when they sign, ratify, accept, approve or accede to it. When a State makes a reservation upon signing, it must confirm the reservation upon ratification, acceptance or approval.

Reservations cannot be contrary to the object and purpose of the treaty, which means that a State may, when signing, ratifying, accepting, approving or acceding to a treaty, make a reservation unless:

(a) The reservation is prohibited by the treaty;
(b) The treaty provides that only specified reservations, which do not include the reservation in question, may be made.

Signature

Multilateral treaties usually provide for signature subject to ratification, acceptance or approval — also called simple signature. In such cases, a signing State does not undertake positive legal obligations under the treaty upon signature. However, signature does indicate the State's intention to take steps to express its consent to be bound by the treaty at a later date. In other words, signature is a preparatory step on the way to ratification of the treaty by the State. Signature also creates an obligation, in the period between signature and ratification, acceptance or approval, to refrain in good faith from acts that would defeat the object and purpose of the treaty.

State Party

A State party to a treaty is a State that has expressed its consent to be bound by that treaty by an act of ratification, acceptance, approval or accession, etc., where that treaty has entered into force for that particular State. This means that the State is bound by the treaty under international law. Some treaties are only open to States whereas others are also open to other entities with treaty-making capacity.

Treaty Body

A committee of independent experts appointed to monitor the implementation by States parties of the core international human rights treaties. They are called "treaty bodies" because each is created in accordance with the provisions of the treaty which it oversees. In many important respects, they are independent of the United Nations system, although they receive support from the United Nations Secretariat and report of the General Assembly. Also referred to as the "committee" or "treaty-monitoring body".

RISA E. KAUFMAN & JOANN KAMUF WARD, *USING HUMAN RIGHTS MECHANISMS OF THE UNITED NATIONS TO ADVANCE ECONOMIC JUSTICE*

45 Clearinghouse Rev. 259 (2011)

I. The Mechanics of the U.N. Human Rights System

The U.N. Charter, which established the United Nations in 1945, committed the institution and its members to promote and protect human rights and fundamental freedoms. The charter was soon followed by the Universal Declaration of Human Rights, adopted by the U.N. General Assembly in 1948. The Universal Declaration of Human Rights, though not a legally enforceable document, articulates a specific and comprehensive set of rights—social, economic, cultural, civil and political rights—which all U.N. members pledge to uphold. Following the Universal Declaration of Human Rights, U.N. member countries drafted, negotiated, and adopted a series of agreements, or treaties, articulating these rights in greater detail. Two types of U.N. mechanisms emerged to promote and monitor countries' compliance with human rights: U.N. treaty-based mechanisms and U.N Charter-based mechanisms.

Table 1
Core U.N. Treaties

Treaty	Description	Signed by President?	Ratified by Senate?
International Covenant on Economic, Social and Cultural Rights	Principal human rights treaty on economic and social rights. Protects rights to housing, work, social security, highest attainable standard of health, and continuous improvement of living conditions. Prohibits all forms of discrimination in enjoyment of these rights	Yes	No
International Covenant on Civil and Political Rights	Protects broad range of civil and political rights (e.g., right to life, freedom of association, right to be free from torture and slavery, nondiscrimination, and certain fair trial rights). Nondiscrimination provisions may be invoked to protect economic and social rights	Yes	Yes
International Convention on the Elimination of All Forms of Racial Discrimination	Principal human rights treaty on racial discrimination. Prohibits discrimination in education, health, housing, property, social security and employment, among others	Yes	Yes
Convention on the Elimination of All Forms of Discrimination Against Women	Principal human rights treaty on sex discrimination. Provides for women's equal access to—and equal opportunities in—private, political, and public life	Yes	No

Treaty	Description	Signed by President?	Ratified by Senate?
Convention on the Rights of the Child	Principal human rights treaty on rights of children. Has extensive economic and social rights provisions. Most widely ratified treaty in international human rights system (United States is one of only two U.N. member states not to have ratified it)	Yes	United States has not ratified Convention on the Rights of the Child but has ratified two optional protocols to the Convention, one on Sale of Children and the other on Children in Armed Conflict
Convention Against Torture and Other Cruel, Inhuman, or Degrading Treatment or Punishment	Requires states to take measures to prevent and punish torture under any circumstances (even wartime). Forbids states from sending individuals to other countries if there is reason to believe they will be tortured. Prohibits acts of cruel, inhuman, or degrading treatment by public officials	Yes	Yes
Convention on the Rights of Persons with Disabilities	Promotes disabled persons' rights to equal protection, equal participation, and accessibility. Provides special protection for women and children with disabilities	Yes	No
International Convention on the Protection of the Rights of All Migrant Workers and Members of Their Families	Stresses Fundamental Rights of both documented and undocumented migrants	No	No
International Convention for the Protection of All Persons from Enforced Disappearances	Most recent U.N. human rights treaty. Protects against forced disappearance	No	No

A. U.N. HUMAN RIGHTS TREATIES AND TREATY-BASED MECHANISMS

A handful of international human rights treaties (along with regional human rights agreements) make up the core of human rights law. The Universal Declaration of Human Rights takes up the full panoply of rights; however, economic, social, and cultural rights and civil and political rights were grouped into separate core treaties for political and historical reasons related to Cold War politics and America's legacy of racial injustice. Thus, along with the Universal Declaration of Human Rights, two key treaties form the International Bill of Rights: the International Covenant on Civil and Political Rights and the International Covenant on Economic, Social, and Cultural Rights. Nine core U.N. treaties are in force to protect and promote human rights (see Table 1).

The United States has ratified the International Covenant on Civil and Political Rights and has signed but not ratified the International Covenant on Economic, Social, and Cultural Rights. Indeed, as Table 1 reflects, the United States has ratified several core U.N. human rights treaties and signed but not ratified several others. Treaties that the United States has ratified are binding under the supremacy clause [U.S. Const. art. VI, § 2].

Although the United States has signed but not ratified the core treaties directly referring to economic and social rights, it has international obligations with respect to those treaties. A country that has signed a treaty has a specific obligation "to refrain from acts which would defeat the object and purpose of a treaty" until the country expresses its intention not to become a party. The treaties that the United States has ratified, in particular the International Covenant on Civil and Political Rights and the International Convention on the Elimination of All Forms of Racial Discrimination, contain antidiscrimination provisions that can be invoked to protect economic and social rights in such areas as health, education, housing, employment, and social security. These nondiscrimination provisions have been interpreted more broadly than federal constitutional prohibitions on discrimination, such that policies that have disparate impact but not discriminatory intent may violate norms of nondiscrimination under these treaties. Note that, because the United States ratifies most human rights treaties with a statement that they are "non-self-executing," ratified treaties are generally not directly enforceable in domestic courts. The U.S. Supreme Court's recent decision in *Medellin v. Texas* [552 U.S. 491 (2008)] underscores this point. Nevertheless, the United States has international legal obligations to adhere to the standards that the treaties set forth and to report on American compliance periodically.

One of the obligations that the United States accepts when it ratifies a human rights treaty is periodic reporting to a committee of independent experts. Monitoring countries' treaty compliance, these committees (also known as treaty bodies) serve certain functions.

First, by conducting periodic reviews, they establish an accountability mechanism, if an imperfect one. As part of the review, countries must submit reports on how they are meeting their treaty commitments; this offers opportunities for advocates to engage with both their governments and the U.N. system on issues of domestic importance. In examining a country report, a treaty body may prepare a list of issues and questions for the country to answer as a supplement to and clarification of its report. The review itself is a public session, intended to serve as a productive dialogue between treaty experts and the government to identify human rights concerns and potential solutions. At the end of a review, treaty bodies issue concluding observations highlighting specific areas of concern. All treaty bodies issue general interpretations of treaty provisions; known as General Comments or General Recommendations, the interpretations have become influential in defining the scope of treaty obligations. Although the findings and recommendations of the treaty bodies generally are not binding, advocates may offer them as persuasive authority in U.S. courts and leverage them in domestic non-litigation advocacy efforts.

A number of the treaty bodies can accept individual complaints or petitions. However, because the United States has not made the necessary declarations or ratified the relevant optional protocols, treaty bodies generally are not authorized to accept individual complaints or petitions directly involving U.S. practice.

Table 2 outlines the most prominent international human rights treaty bodies and U.S. obligations with regard to each.

B.   U.N. CHARTER-BASED MECHANISMS

Besides the treaty-specific monitoring bodies described above, the United Nations human rights system has bodies created by the U.N. Charter. In particular, the Human Rights Council is an intergovernmental body comprising forty-seven countries charged with promoting and protecting human rights around the world. It was created in 2006 to replace the U.N. Commission on Human Rights. Among the council's monitoring and review mechanisms are the Universal Periodic Review and the appointing of "Special Procedures."

U.N. Charter-based mechanisms may be of particular use to legal aid attorneys advocating a range of social and economic rights for their clients. Unlike treaty bodies, they monitor countries' compliance with the full range of rights in the Universal Declaration of Human Rights. Thus U.N. Charter-based mechanisms offer a way to measure the United States' compliance with economic, social, and cultural rights, notwithstanding its failure to ratify treaties focusing specifically on those rights.

1. Universal Periodic Review

The Universal Periodic Review is a mechanism by which the Human Rights Council reviews the human rights records of all U.N. member states every four years.

Created in 2006 as an opportunity for each country to discuss actions it has taken to fulfill its human rights obligations, the Universal Periodic Review offers civil society a unique platform to advocate greater human rights protections. The United States' first Universal Periodic Review occurred in November 2010 with unprecedented civil society engagement.

2. Special Procedures

Special Procedures are the mechanisms established by the United Nations to serve as its "eyes and ears" in evaluating and dealing with human rights concerns in specific countries or pertaining to particular thematic issues. Special

Table 2
International Human Rights Treaty Bodies and U.S. Obligations

Treaty Body	Relevant Treaty	U.S. Obligation
Human Rights Committee	International Covenant on Civil and Political Rights	Reporting every four years (but committee often varies requirement)
Committee on the Elimination of Racial Discrimination	International Convention on the Elimination of All Forms of Racial Discrimination	Reporting every two years (often every four years as two combined periodic reports)
Committee on Economic, Social, and Cultural Rights	International Covenant on Economic, Social, and Cultural Rights	No obligation (not a party)
Committee on the Elimination of All Forms of Discrimination Against Women	Convention on the Elimination of All Forms of Discrimination Against Women	No obligation (not a party)
Committee Against Torture	Convention Against Torture and Other Cruel, Inhuman, or Degrading Treatment or Punishment	Reporting every four years (but committee often varies requirement)
Committee on the Rights of the Child	Convention on the Rights of the Child	Reporting every five years on U.S. compliance with two optional protocols that the United States has ratified
Committee on Migrant Workers	International Convention on the Protection of the Rights of All Migrant Workers and Members of Their Families	No obligation (not a party)
Committee on the Rights of Persons with Disabilities	Convention on the Rights of Persons with Disabilities	No obligation (not a party)
Committee on Enforced Disappearances	International Convention for the Protection of All Persons from Enforced Disappearances	No obligation (not a party)

Procedures are either an individual (usually called a special rapporteur, special representative, or independent expert) or a working group with deep subject-matter expertise. They serve independently of governments, in their personal capacities and on a voluntary basis. Each Special Procedure has its own mandate, defined by the resolution that created it. Current mandates are for thirty-three thematic and eight country-specific Special Procedures. Thematic mandates cover a broad range of issues — adequate housing, education, extreme poverty, and health among them. There is no Special Procedure with a mandate specific to the United States.

Special Procedures base their evaluations on standards drawn from the Universal Declaration of Human Rights and internationally recognized human rights standards relevant to their mandates. Special Procedures are not limited by a country's failure to ratify a certain treaty — a fact particularly useful to legal services attorneys working on economic and social rights. Special Procedures' core functions are receiving information about specific human rights abuses and sending urgent appeals to governments seeking clarification of the allegations. Country visits are also conducted to investigate human rights concerns on the ground. . . .

UNIVERSAL DECLARATION OF HUMAN RIGHTS

G.A. Res. 217 (III) A, U.N. Doc.
A/RES/217(III) (Dec. 10, 1948)

Preamble

Whereas recognition of the inherent dignity and of the equal and inalienable rights of all members of the human family is the foundation of freedom, justice and peace in the world,

Whereas disregard and contempt for human rights have resulted in barbarous acts which have outraged the conscience of mankind, and the advent of a world in which human beings shall enjoy freedom of speech and belief and freedom from fear and want has been proclaimed as the highest aspiration of the common people,

Whereas it is essential, if man is not to be compelled to have recourse, as a last resort, to rebellion against tyranny and oppression, that human rights should be protected by the rule of law,

Whereas it is essential to promote the development of friendly relations between nations,

Whereas the peoples of the United Nations have in the Charter reaffirmed their faith in fundamental human rights, in the dignity and worth of the human person and in the equal rights of men and women and have determined to promote social progress and better standards of life in larger freedom,

Whereas Member States have pledged themselves to achieve, in cooperation with the United Nations, the promotion of universal respect for and observance of human rights and fundamental freedoms,

Whereas a common understanding of these rights and freedoms is of the greatest importance for the full realization of this pledge,

Now, Therefore THE GENERAL ASSEMBLY proclaims THIS UNIVERSAL DECLARATION OF HUMAN RIGHTS as a common standard of achievement for all peoples and all nations, to the end that every individual and every organ of society, keeping this Declaration constantly in mind, shall strive by teaching and education to promote respect for these rights and freedoms and by progressive measures, national and international, to secure their universal and effective recognition and observance, both among the peoples of Member States themselves and among the peoples of territories under their jurisdiction. . . .

ARTICLE 1 [FREEDOM AND EQUALITY]

All human beings are born free and equal in dignity and rights. They are endowed with reason and conscience and should act towards one another in a spirit of brotherhood.

ARTICLE 2 [ANTI-DISCRIMINATION]

Everyone is entitled to all the rights and freedoms set forth in this Declaration, without distinction of any kind, such as race, colour, sex, language, religion, political or other opinion, national or social origin, property, birth or other status. Furthermore, no distinction shall be made on the basis of the political, jurisdictional or international status of the country or territory to which a person belongs, whether it be independent, trust, non-self-governing or under any other limitation of sovereignty. . . .

ARTICLE 22 [SOCIAL SECURITY]

Everyone, as a member of society, has the right to social security and is entitled to realization, through national effort and international cooperation and in accordance with the organization and resources of each State, of the economic, social and cultural rights indispensable for his dignity and the free development of his personality.

ARTICLE 23 [WORK AND TRADE UNIONS]

1. Everyone has the right to work, to free choice of employment, to just and favourable conditions of work and to protection against unemployment.
2. Everyone, without any discrimination, has the right to equal pay for equal work.
3. Everyone who works has the right to just and favourable remuneration ensuring for himself and his family an existence worthy of human dignity, and supplemented, if necessary, by other means of social protection.
4. Everyone has the right to form and to join trade unions for the protection of his interests.

ARTICLE 24 [REST AND LEISURE]

Everyone has the right to rest and leisure, including reasonable limitation of working hours and periodic holidays with pay.

ARTICLE 25 [STANDARD OF LIVING]

1. Everyone has the right to a standard of living adequate for the health and well-being of himself and of his family, including food, clothing, housing and medical care and necessary social services, and the right to security in

the event of unemployment, sickness, disability, widowhood, old age or other lack of livelihood in circumstances beyond his control.

2. Motherhood and childhood are entitled to special care and assistance. All children, whether born in or out of wedlock, shall enjoy the same social protection.

ARTICLE 26 [EDUCATION]

1. Everyone has the right to education. Education shall be free, at least in the elementary and fundamental stages. Elementary education shall be compulsory. Technical and professional education shall be made generally available and higher education shall be equally accessible to all on the basis of merit.
2. Education shall be directed to the full development of the human personality and to the strengthening of respect for human rights and fundamental freedoms. It shall promote understanding, tolerance and friendship among all nations, racial or religious groups, and shall further the activities of the United Nations for the maintenance of peace.
3. Parents have a prior right to choose the kind of education that shall be given to their children. . . .

ARTICLE 30

Nothing in this Declaration may be interpreted as implying for any State, group or person any right to engage in any activity or to perform any act aimed at the destruction of any of the rights and freedoms set forth herein.

INTERNATIONAL COVENANT ON ECONOMIC, SOCIAL, AND CULTURAL RIGHTS, DEC. 16, 1966

993 U.N.T.S. 3, *entered into force* Jan. 3, 1976

PREAMBLE

The States Parties [countries] to the present Covenant,

Considering that, in accordance with the principles proclaimed in the Charter of the United Nations, recognition of the inherent dignity and of the equal and inalienable rights of all the members of the human family is the foundation of freedom, justice and peace in world,

Recognizing that these rights derive from the inherent dignity of the human person,

Recognizing that, in accordance with the Universal Declaration of Human Rights, the ideal of free human beings enjoying freedom from fear and want can only be achieved if conditions are created whereby everyone my enjoy his economic, social and cultural rights, as well as his civil and political rights and freedom,

Realizing that the individual, having duties to other individuals and to the community to which he belongs, is under a responsibility to strive for the promotion and observance of the rights recognized in the present Covenant,

Agree upon the following articles:

ARTICLE 1 [SELF-DETERMINATION]

All peoples have the right of self-determination. By virtue of that right they freely determine their political status and freely pursue their economic, social and cultural development.

All peoples may, for their own ends, freely dispose of their natural wealth and resources without prejudice to any obligations arising out of international economic co-operation, based upon the principle of mutual benefit, and international law. In no case may a people be deprived of its own means of subsistence. . . .

ARTICLE 2 [PROGRESSIVE REALIZATION AND NON-DISCRIMINATION]

Each State Party to the present Covenant undertakes to take steps, individually and through international assistance and co-operation, especially economic and technical, to the maximum of its available resources, with a view to achieving progressively the full realization of the rights recognized in the present Covenant by all appropriate means, including particularly the adoption of legislative measures.

The States Parties to present Covenant undertake to guarantee that the rights enunciated in the present Covenant will be exercised without discrimination of any kind as to race, colour, sex, language, religion, political or other opinion, national or social origin, property, birth or other status. . . .

ARTICLE 3 [EQUAL RIGHTS]

The States Parties to the present Covenant undertake to ensure the equal right of men and women to the enjoyment of all economic, social and cultural rights set forth in the present Covenant.

ARTICLE 4 [GENERAL WELFARE]

The States Parties to the present Covenant recognize that, in the enjoyment of those rights provided by the State in conformity with the present Covenant, the State may subject such rights only to such limitations as are determined by law only in so far as this may be compatible with the nature of these rights and solely for the purpose of promoting the general welfare in a democratic society. . . .

ARTICLE 6 [WORK]

The States Parties to the present Covenant recognize the right to work, which includes the right of everyone to the opportunity to gain his living by work which he freely chooses or accepts, and will take appropriate steps to safeguard this right.

The Steps to be taken by a State Party to the present Covenant to achieve the full realization of this right shall include technical and vocational guidance and training programmes, policies and techniques to achieve steady economic, social and cultural development and full and productive employment under conditions safeguarding fundamental political and economic freedoms to the individual.

ARTICLE 7 [WORK CONDITIONS]

The States to the present Covenant recognize the right of everyone to the enjoyment of just and favourable conditions of work which ensure, in particular:

(a) Remuneration which provides all workers, as a minimum, with:

(i) Fair wages and equal remuneration for work of equal value without distinction of any kind, in particular women being guaranteed conditions of work not inferior to those enjoyed by men, with equal pay for equal work;

(ii) A decent living for themselves and their families in accordance with the provisions of the present Covenant;

(b) Safe and healthy working conditions;

(c) Equal opportunity for everyone to be promoted in his employment to an appropriate higher level, subject to no considerations other than those of seniority and competence;

(d) Rest, leisure and reasonable limitation of working hours and periodic holidays with pay, as well as remuneration for public holidays.

ARTICLE 8 [TRADE UNIONS]

The States Parties to the present Covenant undertake to ensure:

(a) The right of everyone to form trade unions and join the trade union of his choice, subject only to the rules of the organization concerned, for the promotion and protection of his economic and social interests. No restrictions may be placed on the exercise of this right other than those prescribed by law and which are necessary in a democratic society in the interests of national security or public order or for the protection of the rights and freedoms of others. . . .

ARTICLE 9 [SOCIAL SECURITY]

The States Parties to the present Covenant recognize the right of everyone to social security, including social insurance.

ARTICLE 10 [FAMILY, MOTHERS AND CHILDREN]

The States Parties to the present Covenant recognize that:

The widest possible protection and assistance should be accorded to the family, which is the natural and fundamental group unit of society, particularly for its establishment and while it is responsible for the care and education of dependent children. Marriage must be entered into with the free consent of the intending spouses.

Special protection should be accorded to mothers during a reasonable period before and after childbirth. During such period working mothers should be accorded paid leave or leave with adequate social security benefits.

Special measures of protection and assistance should be taken on behalf of all children and young persons without any discrimination for reasons of parentage or other conditions. Children and young persons should be protected from economic and social exploitation. Their employment in work harmful to their morals or health or dangerous to life or likely to hamper their normal development should be punishable by law. States should also set age limits below which the paid employment of child labour should be prohibited and punishable by law.

ARTICLE 11 [FOOD, CLOTHING AND HOUSING]

The States Parties to present Covenant recognize the right of everyone to an adequate standard of living for himself and his family, including adequate food, clothing and housing, and to the continuous improvement of living conditions. The States Parties will take appropriate steps to ensure the international co-operation based on free consent. . . .

ARTICLE 12 [HEALTH]

The States Parties to the present Covenant recognize the right of everyone to the enjoyment of the highest attainable standard of physical and mental health. . . .

ARTICLE 13 [EDUCATION]

The States Parties to the present Covenant recognize the right of everyone to education. They agree that education shall be directed to the full development of the human personality and the sense of its dignity, and shall strengthen the respect for human rights and fundamental freedoms. They further agree that education shall enable all persons to participate effectively in a free society, promote understanding, tolerance and friendship among all nations and all racial, ethnic or religious groups, and further the activities of the United Nations for the maintenance of peace. . . .

ARTICLE 16 [REPORTING]

The States Parties to the present Covenant undertake to submit in conformity with this part of the Covenant reports on the measures which they have adopted and the progress made in achieving the observance of the rights recognized herein.

All reports shall be submitted to Secretary-General of the United Nations, who shall transmit copies to the Economic and Social Council for consideration in accordance with the provisions of the present Covenant;

The Secretary-General of the United Nations shall also transmit to the specialized agencies copies of the reports, or any relevant parts therefrom, from States Parties to the present Covenant which are also members of these specialized agencies in so far as these reports, or parts therefrom, relate to any matters which fall within the responsibilities of the said agencies in accordance with their constitutional instruments. . . .

ARTICLE 28 [EXTENSION TO ALL PARTS OF FEDERAL STATES]

The provisions of the present Covenant shall extend to all parts of federal States without any limitations or exceptions. . . .

NOTES AND QUESTIONS

1. Most people in the United States are not familiar with these human rights treaties and mechanisms. What about them was new or surprising to you? Why do you think the U.S. has ratified some treaties and not others? In particular, what do you think explains the different U.S. positions on the ICCPR (signed and ratified) and the ICESCR (signed but not ratified)?

2. In 1990, the U.N. Office of the High Commission for Human Rights issued "General Comment 3" to the ICESCR setting forth general legal obligations of member states (countries) that are party to the agreement. "General Comment 3" elaborates on the obligations imposed by Article 2 of the ICESCR, which calls on parties "to take steps, individually and through international assistance and co-operation, especially economic and technical, to the maximum of its available resources, with a view to achieving progressively the full realization of the rights recognized in the present Covenant by all appropriate means, including particularly the adoption of legislative measures." "General Comment 3" notes distinctions and similarities with the analogous Article 2 in the ICCPR. The ICCPR and the ICESCR are products of the post–World War II era—and the Cold War in particular—which you should consider as you read the following descriptions of the key U.S. role in shaping international human rights.

C. THE U.S. ROLE IN SHAPING INTERNATIONAL HUMAN RIGHTS LAW

In the future days, which we seek to make secure, we look forward to a world founded upon four essential human freedoms:

The first is freedom of speech and expression everywhere in the world.

The second is freedom of every person to worship God in his own way everywhere in the world.

The third is freedom from want, which, translated into universal terms, means economic understandings which will secure to every nation a healthy peacetime life for its inhabitants everywhere in the world.

The fourth is freedom from fear, which, translated into world terms, means a world-wide reduction of armaments to such a point and in such a thorough fashion that no nation will be in a position to commit an act of physical aggression against any neighbor anywhere in the world.

President Franklin Delano Roosevelt, *Annual Message to the Congress* (Jan. 6, 1941).

Roosevelt's articulation of a *freedom from want*—a part of his "Four Freedoms" speech—laid the groundwork for what would come to be called *social, economic, and cultural rights.* In a subsequent address, Roosevelt elaborated on this concept and called for a "second Bill of Rights." The following excerpt traces the treatment of such rights by ensuing U.S. administrations.

PHILLIP ALSTON, *PUTTING ECONOMIC, SOCIAL AND CULTURAL RIGHTS BACK ON THE AGENDA IN THE UNITED STATES*, IN *THE FUTURE OF HUMAN RIGHTS: U.S. POLICY FOR A NEW ERA* (WILLIAM F. SCHULZ ED., 2008)

The internationally recognized catalogue of human rights consists of two broad categories. First and, in the view of most, foremost, are the more traditional civil and political rights. Because their ancestry is most readily traceable to two eighteenth-century landmarks—the United States Bill of Rights and the French Declaration of the Rights of Man and the Citizen—their importance is almost never challenged in the United States. Second and, according to the United Nations, of equal importance, are the economic, social, and cultural rights that the sociologist T. H. Marshall famously referred to as the major contribution of the twentieth century to the evolution of human rights. Because most of these have no counterpart in the U.S. Bill of Rights, they are inevitably considered more exotic within the United States.

Despite the UN's insistence that all human rights are "indivisible and interdependent and interrelated," the reality is that civil and political rights (CPR) have dominated the international agenda while economic, social, and cultural rights (ESCR) have been accorded second-class status. This is not to say that ESCR have not been the subjects of long and noisy rhetorical campaigns championed in particular by developing countries, or that the UN and other actors have not mounted a significant number of initiatives designed to promote and enhance the status of these rights. The bottom line remains, however, that ESCR continue to enjoy an inferior status and that endeavors to enhance that status have often been blocked. . . .

It is a fact, albeit an uncomfortable one for many non-American observers and proponents of international human rights law, that the United States has been the single most important force in shaping the international human rights regime. This is by no means the same as arguing that it has been the most positive or constructive force; only that its influence has made a very big difference for better or worse in relation to many of the more important initiatives.

This impact is important to note in the present context because the United States has played a central role in discouraging and sometimes blocking the development of the concept of ESCR. This opposition has not, however, followed a single unchanging course. . . .

ECONOMIC, SOCIAL, AND CULTURAL RIGHTS BEFORE BUSH

President Franklin Delano Roosevelt is often credited with having first launched the specific proposals that led to the inclusion of ESCR in the Universal

Declaration of Human Rights. In developing the notion of freedom from want into a proposed "second Bill of Rights" for the United States, Roosevelt urged the recognition of "the right of every family to a decent home; the right to adequate medical care and the opportunity to achieve and enjoy good health; the right to adequate protection from the economic fears of old age, sickness, accident, and unemployment; [and] the right to a good education."

President Harry Truman supported including ESCR in the Universal Declaration and it was under his auspices that Eleanor Roosevelt participated in the early and crucial phases of the drafting of the International Covenant on Economic, Social, and Cultural Rights (ICESCR). President Dwight Eisenhower, under the impetus of the debates surrounding the Bricker amendment [a series of proposed constitutional amendments introduced in the 1950s that would have limited the treaty power of the U.S. government], repudiated both the draft covenant and the draft of the International Covenant on Civil and Political Rights (ICCPR), but neither he nor other opponents of the UN's human rights aspirations expressed special animus toward the covenant that dealt with ESCR.

The administration of President Lyndon Johnson not only participated in the resumed drafting of the ICESCR but also voted in favor of its adoption in 1966 by the UN General Assembly. And the same administration supported the inclusion of economic and social rights provisions in the International Convention on the Elimination of All Forms of Racial Discrimination.

In 1975, President Gerald Ford signed the Helsinki Accords, which proclaimed that the participating states would "promote and encourage the effective exercise of civil, political, economic, social, cultural and other rights and freedoms all of which derive from the inherent dignity of the human person and are essential for his free and full development." By agreeing to a follow-up declaration, adopted in Vienna in January 1989 by the Conference on Security and Cooperation in Europe, the United States joined other countries in recognizing that the promotion of ESCR "is of paramount importance for human dignity and for the attainment of the legitimate aspirations of every individual." Accordingly the United States said it would guarantee the "effective exercise" of economic, social, and cultural rights and to consider acceding to the ICESCR.

The administration of President Jimmy Carter embraced ESCR as a central part of its human rights policy; Carter signed the ICESCR in 1978 and transmitted to the Senate for its advice and consent. Although hearings were held which included coverage of the ICESCR, the Senate took no action in relation to it.

One of the first acts of President Ronald Reagan's administration in the human rights field was to signal a clear and straightforward policy of opposition to economic and social rights. The earliest and best known statement of policy was included in the introduction written in 1982 by the new assistant secretary of state for human rights and humanitarian affairs, Elliott Abrams, and published in the State Department's annual review of human rights practices around the world. This report explicitly removed the treatment of economic and social rights, which had previously been included in the reports. Abrams subsequently offered several justifications for the policy change. The most significant was that the inclusion of these rights blurred "the vital core of human rights." The distinction he drew was between economic and social rights, which he portrayed as "goods [which] the government ought to encourage over the long term," and civil and political rights, which are "rights [that] the government has an absolute duty to respect at any time." The second reason given was that economic and social rights are easily exploited for propaganda purposes by unscrupulous governments whose real aim is to avoid respect for civil and political rights. Because such abuses have occurred, the more prudent path was seen to be to deny the very existence of economic and social rights.

The administration of George H. W. Bush was considerably less ideologically engaged, at least overtly, in its opposition to these rights but, when it advanced (and achieved) the ratification of the Covenant on Civil and Political Rights in 1992, no thought was given to advocating concurrent action on the "other" covenant.

The administration of President Bill Clinton initially proclaimed an inclusive approach that included a commitment to support ESCR in international fora and to promote U.S. ratification of the covenant. As a result, one of its first major international acts was to participate in the consensus emerging from the 1993 Vienna World Conference on Human Rights, which proclaimed that "all human rights are universal, indivisible and interdependent and interrelated. The international community must treat human rights globally in a fair and equal manner, on the same footing, and with the same emphasis." Fairly soon thereafter, however, the Clinton administration began to distance itself from its original embrace of ESCR and adopted a number of policies effectively designed to marginalize them.

It reluctantly signed on to the Convention on the Rights of the Child (CRC) but the fact that this treaty contained a number of provisions giving effect to ESCR was often cited as a reason for not proceeding with ratification. This was rather ironic since most of the relevant formulations had in fact been significantly watered down at the insistence of the Reagan administration during the process of drafting the CRC in the 1980s. At the end of the day, the Clinton policy was an uneasy combination of affirming its general support, at least in principle, for ESCR while creating considerable difficulties in relation to most efforts undertaken in UN fora to make progress in relation to specific rights. It also made no attempt to promote ratification of the ICESCR, insisting only that its priority was to achieve ratification of the Convention on the Elimination of All Forms of Discrimination against Women.

The Bush Administration and Economic and Social Rights

The administration of President George W. Bush has not diverged fundamentally from the policies towards ESCR that its predecessors had developed since 1982. "Goods" such as food, housing, education, and water are acknowledged to be desirable components of an adequate standard of living but they do not constitute "human rights" in the full sense of the term. Thus there can be no claim to their realization as a matter of right on the part of those who are being denied those "goods" even if the denial threatens the individuals' survival. Despite this, the United States regularly invokes the Universal Declaration (with its clear recognition of ESCR) in relation to other states.

Because the administration has not adopted any comprehensive policy statements relating to economic and social rights, its views must be discerned from the various speeches and interventions made by U.S. officials in the context of debates and votes within the relevant international forums. The most important of these has been the UN Commission on Human Rights up until 2006, and subsequently the Human Rights Council. Close inspection reveals that the Bush administration has varied its attitude toward economic and social rights significantly in the course of its first seven years.

At least four separate concerns relating to economic, social, and cultural rights motivate the United States position, although they are usually expressed together as though they were part of a seamless whole. They are: 1) a belief in the chronological priority of civil and political rights; 2) an objection to the terminological equivalence of the different sets of rights; 3) a concern over what might be termed the "internationalization of responsibility" for failures to meet economic and social rights; and 4) a concern about the justiciability of [meaning the ability of courts to adjudicate] economic and social rights. . . .

* * *

In 2010, U.S. Department of State Legal Adviser Harold Koh issued the following memorandum to state governments regarding U.S. human rights treaty obligations.

MEMORANDUM FROM HAROLD HONGJU KOH, LEGAL ADVISER, U.S. DEP'T OF STATE, TO STATE GOVERNORS, RE: U.S. HUMAN RIGHTS TREATY REPORTS (2010)

This electronic communication contains information on several human rights treaties to which the United States is party, and which are implemented through existing laws at all levels of government (federal, state, insular and local). To promote knowledge of these treaties in the United States, we would appreciate your forwarding this communication to your Attorney General's office, and to the departments and offices that deal with human rights, civil rights, housing, employment and related issues in your administration.

Specifically, this memorandum provides background information on five human rights treaties to which the United States is a party and on which the United States has filed reports with the United Nations from 2005-2008: the Convention Against Torture and other Cruel, Inhuman or Degrading Treatment or Punishment (CAT); the International Covenant on Civil and Political Rights (ICCPR); the International Convention on the Elimination of All Forms of Racial Discrimination (CERD); and two optional protocols to the Convention on the Rights of the Child—the Optional Protocol on the Involvement of Children in Armed Conflict and the Optional Protocol on the Sale of Children, Child Prostitution, and Child Pornography (CRC Optional Protocols). The United States is party to each of these treaties and, pursuant to obligations under each of these treaties, is obliged to submit reports to treaty monitoring bodies on the implementation of U.S. obligations thereunder. Because U.S. treaty obligations may apply to all levels of government throughout the territory of the United States and because of the important issues of U.S. law and practice addressed in our reports, we wish to make you and the appropriate members of your staff aware of these reports.

United States obligations under the ICCPR, CERD and the CRC Optional Protocols are implemented under existing law; in other words, prior to becoming a party to each of these treaties, the U.S. State Department, coordinating with other relevant agencies, reviewed the treaties and relevant provisions of U.S. law and determined that existing laws in the United States were sufficient to implement the treaty obligations, as understood or modified by reservations, understandings or declarations made by the United States at the time of ratification in order to ensure congruence between treaty obligations and existing U.S. laws. With regard to the CAT, Congress passed specific implementing legislation. Although these treaties do not give rise directly to individually enforceable rights in U.S. courts, the United States is bound under international law to implement all of its obligations under these treaties and takes these obligations very seriously.

As noted above, among these obligations are requirements to submit to the United Nations periodic reports of the actions the United States has taken in implementation of these treaties. Subsequent to submission of the reports, representatives of the United States (and in some cases representatives of the states) met with the relevant United Nations committees involved to present these reports, answer questions, and provide further information. In the context of these reports and meetings, the United Nations committees have expressed interest in confirming that the existence and substance of these treaties is made known throughout the territory of the United States. For example, one of these committees expressly urged the United States to "make government officials, the judiciary, federal and state law enforcement officials, teachers, social workers and the public in general aware about the responsibilities of the State party under the Convention." Because implementation of these treaties may be carried out by officials at all levels of government (federal, state, insular, and local) under existing laws applicable in their jurisdictions, we want to make sure that the substance of these treaties and their relevance to the United States is known to appropriate governmental officials and to members of the public. . . .

* * *

Legal Adviser Koh's memo does not mention the ICESCR because the United States is not a party to the treaty, having signed but not ratified it. Nevertheless, as noted in the following 2011 speech by Michael Posner, Assistant Secretary of State for Democracy, Human Rights, and Labor, "[w]hile the United States is not a party to the Covenant, as a signatory, we are committed to not defeating the object and purpose of the treaty."

MICHAEL H. POSNER, U.S. ASSISTANT SEC'Y OF STATE FOR DEMOCRACY, HUMAN RIGHTS, AND LABOR, *THE FOUR FREEDOMS TURN 70* (ADDRESS TO THE AMERICAN SOC'Y OF INT'L LAW, MAR. 24, 2011)

Seventy years ago, President Franklin Delano Roosevelt delivered his famous Four Freedoms speech as he was steeling the United States for war. Three years later he elaborated further on his vision of human rights and security in a State of the Union address delivered at a moment when the democratic way of life was under assault around the world.

Roosevelt framed the war aims broadly in terms of core American values. And he warned that "enduring peace cannot be bought at the cost of other people's freedom."

Roosevelt's premise was that our liberty rested on Four Freedoms: freedom of speech and expression, freedom to worship, freedom from fear, and freedom from want. He identified freedom of speech and freedom to worship as core civil and political rights, just as we do now. He defined "freedom from fear" as a reduction in arms, so as to diminish our collective destructive capabilities — and that's a component of the U.S. National Security Strategy to this day. And with the indelible phrase — "freedom from want" — Roosevelt linked the liberty of our people with their basic economic and social wellbeing. . . .

Roosevelt concluded with words that still guide us today: "Freedom means the supremacy of human rights everywhere."

There are many ways to think about what should or should not count as a human right. Perhaps the simplest and most compelling is that human rights reflect what a person needs in order to live a meaningful and dignified existence. It is the core belief in the supreme value of human dignity that leads us, as Americans, to embrace the idea that people should not be tortured, discriminated against, deprived of the right to choose their government, silenced, or barred from observing the religion of their choosing. As President Obama has made clear, it is this same belief in human dignity that underlies our concern for the health, education, and wellbeing of our people.

Human dignity has a political component and an economic component — and these are inexorably linked. Participation, transparency and accountability are valuable not just because they contribute to the dignity of the governed, but because they enhance the responsiveness of those who govern.

Amartya Sen . . . has spotlighted the connection between freedom of speech, democracy and good governance. He said elections, uncensored news reporting and unfettered public criticism prompt governments to address hunger. Freedom to criticize and make demands "promote the political incentive for governments to be responsive, caring and prompt." . . .

It was recognition of the importance of human dignity that guided Eleanor Roosevelt as she led the effort to persuade the United Nations to adopt the Universal Declaration of Human Rights in 1948. She used FDR's words as moral cornerstones for the international legal and institutional regimes that would later arise — regimes that address economic social and cultural rights, as well as civil and political rights. . . .

Although the freedom from want is not explicitly contained in the U.S. Constitution, concern about the economic wellbeing of the American populace is deeply embedded in our nation's history and culture.

After all, in the Preamble to the Constitution, the Framers aimed to "promote the general welfare." From our earliest days, state laws and constitutions sought to promote our people's economic security. And the American Dream is predicated on the belief that allowing individuals to flourish is the best way for our nation to flourish. . . .

The United States has taken steps to provide for economic, social and cultural rights but we understand them in our own way and, at any given time, we meet them according to our domestic laws — laws that emerge from a political system based on representative democracy, free speech and free assembly.

But since the founding of the U.N., some Americans have worried that the international movement to recognize economic, social and cultural rights would obligate us to provide foreign assistance commitments that went beyond what was decided by the U.S. This has never been true. Human rights law doesn't create an obligation to any particular level of foreign assistance.

The U.S. is a leading contributor to global efforts to alleviate poverty and promote development—not because we have an obligation to but because it is in our interest. We do this through our bilateral aid programs, through our multilateral contributions, and through the American people—who annually contribute financially and through voluntary service to development and humanitarian activities around the world. . . .

Some have also been concerned that using the language of human rights could create new domestic legal obligations that would be enforceable though the courts and tie the hands of Congress and the states. But we have been careful to ensure that any international agreements we endorse protect the prerogatives of the federal government, as well as those of our states and localities.

Under the U.S. federal system, states take the lead on many economic, social and cultural policies. For example, all 50 states are committed through their constitutions to providing education for all children. But our federal Constitution makes no mention of rights to education, health care, or social security.

Nevertheless, as my late friend and mentor Professor Louis Henkin wrote, once economic and social rights are granted by law, they cannot be taken away without due process. And these rights also fall under the general requirement that government act rationally and afford equal protection under the law.

Our government's commitment to provide for the basic social and economic needs of our people is clear, and it reflects the will of the American people. . . .

Some of our suspicion of the international focus on economic, social and cultural rights springs from the misuse of these demands in earlier times. For decades, the Soviet states and the Non-Aligned Movement critiqued the United States for a perceived failure to embrace economic and social rights. They used the rhetoric of economic, social and cultural rights to distract from their human rights abuses. They claimed economic rights trumped political rights, while in fact failing to provide either. We have prioritized political and civil rights because governments that are transparent and respect free speech are stable, secure and sustainable—and do the most for their people. . . .

Therefore, we will work constructively with like-minded delegations to adopt fair and well-reasoned resolutions at the U.N. that speak to the issues of economic, social and cultural rights and are consistent with our own laws and policies.

We will do this understanding that these goals must be achieved progressively, given the resources available to each government. But we will also stress that nothing justifies a government's indifference to its own people. And nothing justifies human oppression—not even spectacular economic growth.

When negotiating language on these resolutions and in our explanations of position, we will be guided by the following five considerations:

First, economic, social and cultural rights addressed in U.N. resolutions should be expressly set forth, or reasonably derived from, the Universal Declaration and the International Covenant on Economic, Social and Cultural Rights. While the United States is not a party to the Covenant, as a signatory, we are committed to not defeating the object and purpose of the treaty.

Second, we will only endorse language that reaffirms the "progressive realization" of these rights and prohibits discrimination.

Third, language about enforcement must be compatible with our domestic and constitutional framework.

Fourth, we will highlight the U.S. policy of providing food, housing, medicine and other basic requirements to people in need.

And fifth, we will emphasize the interdependence of all rights and recognize the need for accountability and transparency in their implementation, through the democratic participation of the people.

At the same time, the U.S. will not hesitate to reject resolutions that are disingenuous, at odds with our laws, or contravene our policy interests. Just because a resolution is titled "a right to food" doesn't mean it is really about the right to food. Resolutions are not labeling exercises. Rather, they are about substance. . . .

HOPE LEWIS, *NEW HUMAN RIGHTS? U.S. AMBIVALENCE TOWARD THE INTERNATIONAL ECONOMIC AND SOCIAL RIGHTS FRAMEWORK*, IN *BRINGING HUMAN RIGHTS HOME: A HISTORY OF HUMAN RIGHTS IN THE UNITED STATES* (CYNTHIA SOOHOO ET AL. EDS., 2009)

Why were and are the rights outlined in instruments like the ICESCR so controversial within the U.S. official and civil society circles? They seem so clearly to codify the Four Freedoms and the "second bill of rights" envisioned in the 1940s by President Roosevelt. Clues can be found in Mrs. Roosevelt's statements in support of bifurcating the ICCPR from the ICESCR. Although at least rhetorically acknowledging that civil and political rights should have the same normative status as economic, social, and cultural rights, she accepted the view that the two categories of rights were different in nature and required different mechanisms of implementation. The Commission on Human Rights had failed to attach the kind of implementation machinery to economic and social rights that were included for civil and political rights provisions in a draft Covenant on Human Rights. . . .

. . . Mrs. Roosevelt was not alone in the view that socioeconomic rights were to be treated differently in the international human rights legal regime. But the differences were sometimes exaggerated or misunderstood in order to protect the international or domestic balance of power. Both West and East feared the implications of strong economic, social, and cultural rights enforcement. The test of the ICESCR reflected such concerns, but it also reflected strong pressure from the peoples of the world to hold their governments and the international community accountable for poverty and social injustice.

NOTES AND QUESTIONS

1. The distinctions between civil and political rights, on the one hand, and economic, social, and cultural rights, on the other, are typically characterized as follows:

Civil and Political Rights, or "Liberty Rights"	*Economic, Social, and Cultural Rights, or "Welfare Rights"*
a. Absolute and immediate	a. Program goals, "progressive realization"
b. Justiciable (role for the courts)	b. Nonjusticiable (no role for courts)
c. Free (negative obligations)	c. Expensive (positive obligations)
d. States willing to recognize rights	d. States reluctant to recognize entitlements

There is considerable, ongoing debate about these characterizations, but how do such distinctions in the international human rights framework resonate in the context of domestic antipoverty debates about the right to housing, health care, income, and education? More specifically, do you recall cases in earlier chapters when courts said that these issues were not "justiciable," that is, that courts were not institutionally competent to adjudicate certain rights?

2. Like his predecessor, Elliott Abrams, some three decades earlier ("economic and social rights are easily exploited for propaganda purposes by unscrupulous governments whose real aim is to avoid respect for civil and political rights"), Assistant Secretary Posner also cautions, "[T]he U.S. will not hesitate to reject resolutions that are disingenuous, at odds with our laws, or contravene our policy interests." Does this position represent U.S. exceptionalism? Should the disregard of treaties and covenants by other signatory states reduce U.S. obligations to implement human rights?

D.   WHAT DO HUMAN RIGHTS HAVE
TO DO WITH POVERTY?

> I am often asked: "[W]hat do you think is the worst human rights problem in our world today?" I reply "extreme poverty." Extreme poverty means a denial of the exercise of all human rights and undermines the dignity and worth of the individual.

Mary Robinson, U.N. High Comm'r for Human Rights, *Poverty and Racism: Challenges for Human Rights and Development in Africa* (Address Before the U.N. Econ. Comm'n for Africa, Dec. 10, 2001).

Extreme poverty—defined as living on less than $1.25 per day—is experienced by more than a billion people globally. Three billion people live on $2.50 per day or less. High Commissioner Robinson was not likely thinking of the United States when she made the statement above. As we will see next, however, poverty and associated deprivations can be considered human rights violations.

U.N. OFFICE OF THE HIGH COMM'R FOR HUMAN RIGHTS,
*PRINCIPLES AND GUIDELINES FOR A HUMAN RIGHTS
APPROACH TO POVERTY REDUCTIONS STRATEGIES* (2006)

The human rights approach underlines the multidimensional nature of poverty, describing poverty in terms of a range of interrelated and mutually reinforcing deprivations, and drawing attention to the stigma, discrimination, insecurity and social exclusion associated with poverty. The deprivation and indignity of poverty stem from various sources, such as the lack of an adequate standard of living, including food, clothing and housing, and the fact that poor people tend to be marginalized and socially excluded. The commitment to ensure respect for human rights will act as a force against all these forms of deprivation.

The essential idea underlying the adoption of a human rights approach to poverty reduction is that policies and institutions for poverty reduction should be based explicitly on the norms and values set out in international human rights law. Whether explicit or implicit, norms and values shape policies and institutions. The human rights approach offers an explicit normative framework — that of international human rights. Underpinned by universally recognized moral values and reinforced by legal obligations, international human rights provide a compelling normative framework for the formulation of national and international policies, including poverty reduction strategies.

The application of human rights to poverty reduction reinforces some of the existing features of antipoverty strategies. For example, antipoverty strategies that demand transparent budgetary and other governmental processes are congruent with the right to information, while the insistence that strategies are "country-owned" corresponds to the right of peoples to self-determination. The value added by the human rights approach to poverty reduction consists both in the manner in which it departs from existing strategies and in the manner in which it reinforces them.

One reason why the human rights framework is compelling in the context of poverty reduction is that it has the potential to empower the poor. As is now widely recognized, effective poverty reduction is not possible without the empowerment of the poor. The human rights approach to poverty reduction is essentially about such empowerment.

The most fundamental way in which empowerment occurs is through the introduction of the concept of rights itself. Once this concept is introduced into the context of policymaking, the rationale of poverty reduction no longer derives merely from the fact that the people living in poverty have needs but also from the fact that they have rights — entitlements that give rise to legal obligations on the part of others. Thus, the human rights perspective adds legitimacy to the demand for making poverty reduction the primary goal of policymaking. The human rights perspective draws attention to the fact that poverty signifies the non-realization of human rights, so that the adoption of a poverty reduction strategy is not just desirable but obligatory for States which have ratified international human rights instruments.

Most of the salient features of the human rights normative framework can contribute to the empowerment of the poor in one way or another. These features include the principles of universality, non-discrimination and equality, the principle of participatory decision-making, the notion of accountability, and the recognition of the interdependence of rights.

The twin principles of equality and non-discrimination are among the most fundamental elements of international human rights law. Recognition of these principles helps to highlight the fact that a great deal of poverty originates from discriminatory practices — both overt and covert. This recognition calls for the reorientation of poverty reduction strategies from a tendency to focus on narrow economic issues towards a broader strategy that also addresses the socio-cultural and political-legal institutions which sustain the structures of discrimination. Thus, the human rights approach to poverty reduction requires that the laws and institutions which foster discrimination against specific individuals and groups be eliminated and that more resources be devoted to the areas of activity with the greatest potential to benefit the poor.

While the human rights approach imposes an obligation on duty-bearers to work towards poverty reduction, it recognizes that, due to resource constraints, some human rights may have to be realized over a period of time. Making trade-offs among alternative goals in the light of social priorities and resource constraints is an integral part of any approach to policymaking. The human rights approach, however, imposes certain conditions on the act of prioritization which protect the poor against certain trade-offs that may be harmful to them. In particular, it cautions against any trade-off that leads to the retrogression of a human right from its existing level of realization and rules out the non-achievement of certain minimum levels of realization.

Unlike earlier approaches to poverty reduction, the human rights approach attaches as much importance to the processes which enable developmental goals to be achieved as to the goals themselves. In particular, it emphasizes the importance of ensuring the active and informed participation by the poor in the formulation, implementation and monitoring of poverty reduction strategies. It draws attention to the fact that participation is valuable not just as a means to other ends, but also as a fundamental human right that should be realized for its own sake. Effective participation by the poor requires specific mechanisms and arrangements at different levels of decision-making in order to overcome the impediments that people living in poverty, and marginalized groups in general, face in their efforts to play an effective part in the life of the community.

The human rights approach to poverty reduction emphasizes the accountability of policymakers and others whose actions have an impact on the rights of people. Rights imply duties, and duties demand accountability. It is therefore an intrinsic feature of the human rights approach that institutions and legal/administrative arrangements for ensuring accountability are built into any poverty reduction strategy. While duty-bearers must determine for themselves which mechanisms of accountability are most appropriate in their particular case, all mechanisms must be accessible, transparent and effective.

In many countries, poverty reduction strategies are bedeviled by corruption. However, corruption is unlikely to flourish where there is access to information, freedom of expression, participation and accountability—all key human rights features. Therefore, a human rights approach has the power to protect a poverty reduction strategy from being undermined by the corroding effects of corruption.

Yet another feature of the human rights approach is that poverty reduction becomes a shared responsibility. While a State is primarily responsible for realizing the human rights of the people living within its jurisdiction, other States and non-State actors also have a responsibility to contribute to, or at the very least not to violate, human rights.

The international human rights framework also broadens the scope of poverty reduction strategies by recognizing the interdependence of rights. Although poverty may seem to concern mainly economic, social and cultural rights, the human rights framework highlights the fact that the enjoyment of these rights may be crucially dependent on the enjoyment of civil and political rights. The human rights approach thus dispels the misconception that civil and political rights and freedoms are luxuries relevant only to relatively affluent societies, and that economic, social and cultural rights are merely aspirations and not binding obligations. Accordingly, it demands that civil and political as well as economic, social and cultural rights are integral components of poverty reduction strategies. . . .

NOTES AND QUESTIONS

1. The U.N. Office of the High Commissioner on Human Rights' approach to poverty reduction suggests that the distinction between civil and political rights and ESCR is not so clear. Human rights scholars have made similar arguments about the relationship between so-called *positive rights* and *negative rights*:

> All human rights require a combination of negative and positive conduct from states and various levels of resources. For instance, an individual's political right to participate in the political life of her state by exercising her right to vote cannot be ensured without the state providing that elections are held at regular intervals. Furthermore, it is clear that social and economic rights do not merely impose positive obligations. Where someone enjoys a social and economic right, the state is prohibited from acting in a way that would interfere with or impair the individual's enjoyment of that right.

> Aoife Nolan et al., *The Justiciability of Social and Economic Rights: An Updated Appraisal* 7 (Ctr. on Human Rights & Global Justice, Working Paper No. 15, 2007).

2. What is the difference in practice between positive (economic, social, and cultural) and negative (civil and political) rights? Is one set of rights a precondition for the others? Keep these questions in mind as you next consider how advocates have attempted to incorporate human rights into domestic antipoverty efforts.

E.   HOW DO INTERNATIONAL HUMAN RIGHTS TRANSLATE INTO THE DOMESTIC CONTEXT?

International human rights have begun making their way into domestic adjudication across the globe. Even "nonjusticiable" ESCR are being invoked in court cases, either through their inextricable link to civil and political rights, or on their own terms. In this section, we'll consider the application of human rights generally, and economic and social rights in particular, in both foreign and domestic courts.

1. ESCR Outside the United States

Economic, social, and cultural rights are being adjudicated by courts in countries around the world. Courts in South Africa, India, Colombia, and elsewhere have begun to give shape and content to such rights. As Shivani Verma of the U.N. Office of the High Commissioner for Human Rights has noted:

> [The] expanding ESCR jurisprudence has manifested itself in two ways. First, civil and political rights have been shown to possess socio-economic dimensions. These more traditional rights have been employed in a fashion to extend the right to non-discrimination and equality into the socio-economic arena (e.g., prevention of forced evictions, exclusion of minorities from social programs or education). . . .

In other cases, ESCRs themselves have been directly derived from civil and political rights (e.g., the right to life implies the right to water and food). . . .

Secondly, a more noticeable ESCR jurisprudence has emerged as central to constitutions that emerged in the wave of democratization in the 1980s and 90s, particularly Latin America and South Africa. Many of these constitutions grant ESCRs a fully justiciable status.

Shivani Verma, U.N. Office of the High Comm'r for Human Rights, *Justiciability of Economic, Social and Cultural Rights: Relevant Case Law, The International Council on Human Rights Policy* (2005).

The following case decided by South Africa's Constitutional Court (the equivalent of our Supreme Court) is widely regarded as a leading example of the justiciability of ESCR. As you read the case, consider some similarities and differences with U.S. law and context: first, like the United States, South Africa has signed but has not ratified the ICESCR; and second, unlike the United States, South Africa's post-apartheid constitution directly enshrined ESCR, and it requires consideration of international law as a means of interpreting its own Bill of Rights.

GOV'T OF REP. OF S. AFR. v. GROOTBOOM

2001 (1) SA 46 (CC)

Judge YACOOB delivered the unanimous decision of the court:

. . . Mrs. Irene Grootboom and the other respondents were rendered homeless as a result of their eviction from their informal homes situated on private land earmarked for formal low-cost housing. They applied to the Cape of Good Hope High Court (the High Court) for an order requiring government to provide them with adequate basic shelter or housing until they obtained permanent accommodation and were granted certain relief. The appellants were ordered to provide the respondents who were children and their parents with shelter. The judgment provisionally concluded that "tents, portable latrines and a regular supply of water (albeit transported) would constitute the bare minimum." The appellants who represent all spheres of government responsible for housing challenge the correctness of that order. . . .

The cause of the acute housing shortage lies in apartheid. A central feature of that policy was a system of influx control that sought to limit African occupation of urban areas. . . . Despite the harsh application of influx control in the Western Cape, African people continued to move to the area in search of jobs. . . . The legacy of influx control in the Western Cape is the acute housing shortage that exists there now. . . .

Mrs. Grootboom and most of the other respondents previously lived in an informal squatter settlement called Wallacedene. . . . The conditions under which most of the residents of Wallacedene lived were lamentable. A quarter of the households of Wallacedene had no income at all, and more than two thirds earned less than R500 per month. About half the population were children; all lived in shacks. They had no water, sewage or refuse removal services and only 5% of the shacks had electricity. . . .

Many had applied for subsidised low-cost housing from the municipality and had been on the waiting list for as long as seven years. Despite numerous enquiries from the municipality no definite answer was given. Clearly it was going to be a long wait. Faced with the prospect of remaining in intolerable conditions indefinitely, the respondents began to move out. . . . They put up their shacks and shelters on vacant land that was privately owned and had been earmarked for low-cost housing. They called the land "New Rust."

They did not have the consent of the owner and . . . he obtained an eject-ment order against them in the magistrates' court. The order was served on the occupants but they remained in occupation beyond the date by which they had been ordered to vacate. Mrs. Grootboom says they had nowhere else to go. . . . Negotiations resulted in the grant of an order requiring the occu-pants to vacate New Rust and authorising the sheriff to evict them and to dismantle and remove any of their structures remaining on the land. . . . The magistrate also directed that the parties and the municipality mediate to identify alternative land for the permanent or temporary occupation of the New Rust residents.

. . . [A]t the beginning of the cold, windy and rainy Cape winter, the respon-dents were forcibly evicted at the municipality's expense. This was done prematurely and inhumanely: reminiscent of apartheid-style evictions. The respondents' homes were bulldozed and burnt and their possessions destroyed. Many of the residents who were not there could not even salvage their personal belongings. . . .

D.   THE RELEVANT CONSTITUTIONAL PROVISIONS AND THEIR JUSTICIABILITY

The key constitutional provisions at issue in this case are section 26[, which] provides:

(1) Everyone has the right to have access to adequate housing.
(2) The state must take reasonable legislative and other measures, within its available resources, to achieve the progressive realisation of this right.
(3) No one may be evicted from their home, or have their home demolished, without an order of court made after considering all the relevant circum-stances. No legislation may permit arbitrary evictions. . . .

These rights need to be considered in the context of the cluster of socio-economic rights enshrined in the Constitution. They entrench the right of access to land, to adequate housing and to health care, food, water and social security. . . .

While the justiciability of socio-economic rights has been the subject of considerable jurisprudential and political debate, the issue of whether socio-economic rights are justiciable at all in South Africa has been put beyond question by the text of our Constitution as construed in the Certification judg-ment [when] . . . this Court held:

[T]hese rights are, at least to some extent, justiciable. As we have stated in the previous paragraph, many of the civil and political rights entrenched in the [constitutional text before this Court for certification in that case] will give rise to similar budgetary implications without compromising their justiciability. The fact that socio-economic rights will almost inevitably give rise to such implications does not seem to us to be a bar to their justiciability. At the very minimum, socio-economic rights can be negatively protected from improper invasion.

Socio-economic rights are expressly included in the Bill of Rights; they cannot be said to exist on paper only. Section 7(2) of the Constitution requires the state "to respect, protect, promote and fulfil the rights in the Bill of Rights" and the courts are constitutionally bound to ensure that they are protected and fulfilled. The question is therefore not whether socio-economic rights are justiciable under our Constitution, but how to enforce them in a given case. . . .

E.   OBLIGATIONS IMPOSED UPON THE STATE BY SECTION 26

I)   APPROACH TO INTERPRETATION

Like all the other rights in Chapter 2 of the Constitution (which contains the Bill of Rights), section 26 must be construed in its context. The section has been carefully crafted. It contains three subsections. The first confers a general right of access to adequate housing. The second establishes and delimits the scope of the positive obligation imposed upon the state to promote access to adequate housing and has three key elements. The state is obliged: (a) to take reasonable legislative and other measures; (b) within its available resources; (c) to achieve the progressive realisation of this right. . . . The third subsection provides protection against arbitrary evictions.

Our Constitution entrenches both civil and political rights and social and economic rights. All the rights in our Bill of Rights are inter-related and mutually supporting. There can be no doubt that human dignity, freedom and equality, the foundational values of our society, are denied those who have no food, clothing or shelter. Affording socio-economic rights to all people therefore enables them to enjoy the other rights enshrined in Chapter 2. The realisation of these rights is also key to the advancement of race and gender equality and the evolution of a society in which men and women are equally able to achieve their full potential.

The right of access to adequate housing cannot be seen in isolation. There is a close relationship between it and the other socio-economic rights. Socio-economic rights must all be read together in the setting of the Constitution as a whole. The state is obliged to take positive action to meet the needs of those living in extreme conditions of poverty, homelessness or intolerable housing. Their interconnectedness needs to be taken into account in interpreting the socio-economic rights, and, in particular, in determining whether the state has met its obligations in terms of them.

Rights also need to be interpreted and understood in their social and historical context. The right to be free from unfair discrimination, for example, must be understood against our legacy of deep social inequality. . . .

II)   THE RELEVANT INTERNATIONAL LAW AND ITS IMPACT

During argument, considerable weight was attached to the value of international law in interpreting section 26 of our Constitution. Section 39 of the Constitution obliges a court to consider international law as a tool to interpretation of the Bill of Rights. . . . The relevant international law can be a guide to interpretation but the weight to be attached to any particular principle or rule of international law will vary. However, where the relevant principle of international law binds South Africa, it may be directly applicable.

The amici submitted that the International Covenant on Economic, Social and Cultural Rights (the Covenant) is of significance in understanding the positive obligations created by the socio-economic rights in the Constitution. Article 11.1 of the Covenant provides:

> The States Parties to the present Covenant recognize the right of everyone to an adequate standard of living for himself and his family, including adequate food, clothing and housing, and to the continuous improvement of living conditions. The States Parties will take appropriate steps to ensure the realization of this right, recognizing to this effect the essential importance of international co-operation based on free consent.

This Article must be read with Article 2.1 which provides:

> Each State Party to the present Covenant undertakes to take steps, individually and through international assistance and co-operation, especially economic and technical, to the maximum of its available resources, with a view to achieving progressively the full realization of the rights recognized in the present Covenant by all appropriate means, including particularly the adoption of legislative measures.

The differences between the relevant provisions of the Covenant and our Constitution are significant in determining the extent to which the provisions of the Covenant may be a guide to an interpretation of section 26. These differences, in so far as they relate to housing, are:

(a) The Covenant provides for a right to adequate housing while section 26 provides for the right of access to adequate housing.
(b) The Covenant obliges states parties to take appropriate steps which must include legislation while the Constitution obliges the South African state to take reasonable legislative and other measures.

The obligations undertaken by states parties to the Covenant are monitored by the United Nations Committee on Economic, Social and Cultural Rights (the committee). The amici relied on the relevant general comments issued by the committee concerning the interpretation and application of the Covenant, and argued that these general comments constitute a significant guide to the interpretation of section 26. In particular they argued that in interpreting this section, we should adopt an approach similar to that taken by the committee in paragraph 10 of general comment 3 issued in 1990, in which the committee found that socio-economic rights contain a minimum core. . . .

It is clear . . . that the committee considers that every state party is bound to fulfil a minimum core obligation by ensuring the satisfaction of a minimum essential level of the socio-economic rights, including the right to adequate housing. Accordingly, a state in which a significant number of individuals is deprived of basic shelter and housing is regarded as prima facie in breach of its obligations under the Covenant. A state party must demonstrate that every effort has been made to use all the resources at its disposal to satisfy the minimum core of the right. However, it is to be noted that the general comment does not specify precisely what that minimum core is. . . .

The determination of a minimum core in the context of "the right to have access to adequate housing" presents difficult questions. This is so because the needs in the context of access to adequate housing are diverse: there are those who need land; others need both land and houses; yet others need financial assistance. There are difficult questions relating to the definition of minimum core in the context of a right to have access to adequate housing, in particular whether the minimum core obligation should be defined generally or with regard to specific groups of people. As will appear from the discussion below, the real question in terms of our Constitution is whether the measures taken by the state to realise the right afforded by section 26 are reasonable.

III)   ANALYSIS OF SECTION 26

I consider the meaning and scope of section 26 in its context. Its provisions are repeated for convenience:

(1) Everyone has the right to have access to adequate housing.
(2) The state must take reasonable legislative and other measures, within its available resources, to achieve the progressive realisation of this right.
(3) No one may be evicted from their home, or have their home demolished, without an order of court made after considering all the relevant circumstances. No legislation may permit arbitrary evictions.

Subsections (1) and (2) are related and must be read together. Subsection (1) aims at delineating the scope of the right. It is a right of everyone including children. Although the subsection does not expressly say so, there is, at the very least, a negative obligation placed upon the state and all other entities and persons to desist from preventing or impairing the right of access to adequate housing. The negative right is further spelt out in subsection (3) which prohibits arbitrary evictions. Access to housing could also be promoted if steps are taken to make the rural areas of our country more viable so as to limit the inexorable migration of people from rural to urban areas in search of jobs.

The right delineated in section 26(1) is a right of "access to adequate housing" as distinct from the right to adequate housing encapsulated in the Covenant. This difference is significant. It recognises that housing entails more than bricks and mortar. It requires available land, appropriate services such as the provision of water and the removal of sewage and the financing of all of these, including the building of the house itself. For a person to have access to adequate housing all of these conditions need to be met: there must be land, there must be services, there must be a dwelling. Access to land for the purpose of housing is therefore included in the right of access to adequate housing in section 26. . . .

Subsection (2) speaks to the positive obligation imposed upon the state. It requires the state to devise a comprehensive and workable plan to meet its obligations in terms of the subsection. However subsection (2) also makes it clear that the obligation imposed upon the state is not an absolute or unqualified one. The extent of the state's obligation is defined by three key elements that are considered separately: (a) the obligation to "take reasonable legislative and other measures"; (b) "to achieve the progressive realisation" of the right; and (c) "within available resources."

Reasonable Legislative and Other Measures

What constitutes reasonable legislative and other measures must . . . clearly allocate responsibilities and tasks to the different spheres of government and ensure that the appropriate financial and human resources are available.

Thus, a coordinated state housing programme must be a comprehensive one determined by all three spheres of government in consultation with each other. . . .

The measures must establish a coherent public housing programme directed towards the progressive realisation of the right of access to adequate housing within the state's available means. . . . In any challenge based on section 26 in which it is argued that the state has failed to meet the positive obligations imposed upon it by section 26(2), the question will be whether the legislative and other measures taken by the state are reasonable. A court considering reasonableness will not enquire whether other more desirable or favourable measures could have been adopted, or whether public money could have been better spent. The question would be whether the measures that have been adopted are reasonable. It is necessary to recognise that a wide range of possible measures could be adopted by the state to meet its obligations. . . .

The state is required to take reasonable legislative and other measures. Legislative measures by themselves are not likely to constitute constitutional compliance. Mere legislation is not enough. The state is obliged to act to achieve the intended result, and the legislative measures will invariably have to be supported by appropriate, well-directed policies and programmes implemented by the executive. These policies and programmes must be reasonable both in their conception and their implementation. . . .

In determining whether a set of measures is reasonable, it will be necessary to consider housing problems in their social, economic and historical context and to consider the capacity of institutions responsible for implementing the programme. The programme must be balanced and flexible and make appropriate provision for attention to housing crises and to short, medium and long term needs. A programme that excludes a significant segment of society cannot be said to be reasonable. Conditions do not remain static and therefore the programme will require continuous review.

Reasonableness must also be understood in the context of the Bill of Rights as a whole. The right of access to adequate housing is entrenched because we value human beings and want to ensure that they are afforded their basic human needs. A society must seek to ensure that the basic necessities of life are provided to all if it is to be a society based on human dignity, freedom and equality. To be reasonable, measures cannot leave out of account the degree and extent of the denial of the right they endeavour to realise. Those whose needs are the most urgent and whose ability to enjoy all rights therefore is most in peril, must not be ignored by the measures aimed at achieving realisation of the right. It may not be sufficient to meet the test of reasonableness to show that the measures are capable of achieving a statistical advance in the realisation of the right. Furthermore, the Constitution requires that everyone must be treated with care and concern. If the measures, though statistically successful, fail to respond to the needs of those most desperate, they may not pass the test.

Progressive Realisation of the Right

The extent and content of the obligation consist in what must be achieved, that is, "the progressive realisation of this right." It links subsections (1) and (2) by making it quite clear that the right referred to is the right of access to adequate housing. The term "progressive realisation" shows that it was contemplated that the right could not be realised immediately. But the goal of the Constitution is that the basic needs of all in our society be effectively met and the requirement of progressive realisation means that the state must take steps to achieve this goal. It means that accessibility should be progressively facilitated: legal, administrative, operational and financial hurdles should be examined and, where possible, lowered over time. Housing must be made more accessible not only to a larger number of people but to a wider range of people as time progresses. The phrase is taken from international law and Article 2.1 of the Covenant in particular. . . .

Although the committee's analysis is intended to explain the scope of states parties' obligations under the Covenant, it is also helpful in plumbing the meaning of "progressive realisation" in the context of our Constitution. The meaning ascribed to the phrase is in harmony with the context in which the phrase is used in our Constitution and there is no reason not to accept that it bears the same meaning in the Constitution as in the document from which it was so clearly derived.

Within Available Resources

The third defining aspect of the obligation to take the requisite measures is that the obligation does not require the state to do more than its available resources permit. This means that both the content of the obligation in relation to the rate at which it is achieved as well as the reasonableness of the measures employed to achieve the result are governed by the availability of resources. Section 26 does not expect more of the state than is achievable within its available resources. . . . There is a balance between goal and means. The measures must be calculated to attain the goal expeditiously and effectively but the availability of resources is an important factor in determining what is reasonable. . . .

F.   DESCRIPTION AND EVALUATION OF THE STATE HOUSING PROGRAMME

. . . The national government bears the overall responsibility for ensuring that the state complies with the obligations imposed upon it by section 26. The nationwide housing programme falls short of obligations imposed upon national government to the extent that it fails to recognise that the state must provide for relief for those in desperate need. They are not to be ignored in the interests of an overall programme focused on medium and long-term objectives. It is essential that a reasonable part of the national housing budget be devoted to this, but the precise allocation is for national government to decide in the first instance.

. . . This programme, on the face of it, meets the obligation which the state has towards people in the position of the respondents[, h]owever, [w]hat remains is the implementation of the programme by taking all reasonable steps that are necessary to initiate and sustain it. And it must be implemented with due regard to the urgency of the situations it is intended to address.

Effective implementation requires at least adequate budgetary support by national government. This, in turn, requires recognition of the obligation to meet immediate needs in the nationwide housing programme. Recognition of such needs in the nationwide housing programme requires it to plan, budget and monitor the fulfilment of immediate needs and the management of crises. This must ensure that a significant number of desperate people in need are afforded relief, though not all of them need receive it immediately. Such planning too will require proper co-operation between the different spheres of government.

In conclusion it has been established in this case that as of the date of the launch of this application, the state was not meeting the obligation imposed upon it by section 26(2) of the Constitution. . . . In particular, the programmes adopted by the state fell short of the requirements of section 26(2) in that no provision was made for relief to the categories of people in desperate need identified earlier. . . .

H.   EVALUATION OF THE CONDUCT OF THE APPELLANTS TOWARDS THE RESPONDENTS

. . . But section 26 is not the only provision relevant to a decision as to whether state action at any particular level of government is reasonable and consistent with the Constitution. The proposition that rights are interrelated and are all equally important is not merely a theoretical postulate. The concept has immense human and practical significance in a society founded on human dignity, equality and freedom. It is fundamental to an evaluation of the reasonableness of state action that account be taken of the inherent dignity of human beings. The Constitution will be worth infinitely less than its paper if the reasonableness of state action concerned with housing is determined without regard to the fundamental constitutional value of human dignity. Section 26, read in the context of the Bill of Rights as a whole, must mean that the respondents have a right to reasonable action by the state in all circumstances and with particular regard to human dignity. In short, I emphasise that human beings are required to be treated as human beings. . . .

I.   SUMMARY AND CONCLUSION

This case shows the desperation of hundreds of thousands of people living in deplorable conditions throughout the country. The Constitution obliges the state to act positively to ameliorate these conditions. The obligation is to provide access to housing, health-care, sufficient food and water, and social security to those unable to support themselves and their dependants. The state must also foster conditions to enable citizens to gain access to land on an equitable basis. Those in need have a corresponding right to demand that this be done.

I am conscious that it is an extremely difficult task for the state to meet these obligations in the conditions that prevail in our country. This is recognised by the Constitution which expressly provides that the state is not obliged to go beyond available resources or to realise these rights immediately. I stress however, that despite all these qualifications, these are rights, and the Constitution obliges the state to give effect to them. This is an obligation that courts can, and in appropriate circumstances, must enforce.

Neither section 26 nor section 28 entitles the respondents to claim shelter or housing immediately upon demand. The High Court order ought therefore not to have been made. However, section 26 does oblige the state to devise and implement a coherent, coordinated programme designed to meet its section 26 obligations. The programme that has been adopted and was in force in the Cape Metro at the time that this application was brought, fell short of the obligations imposed upon the state by section 26(2) in that it failed to provide for any form of relief to those desperately in need of access to housing.

In the light of the conclusions I have reached, it is necessary and appropriate to make a declaratory order. The order requires the state to act to meet the obligation imposed upon it by section 26(2) of the Constitution. This includes the obligation to devise, fund, implement and supervise measures to provide relief to those in desperate need. . . .

NOTES AND QUESTIONS

1. According to Geoff Budlender, Director of the Constitutional Litigation Unit at the Legal Resources Centre and Visiting Professor of Law at the University of the Witwatersrand:

    The impact of the [*Grootboom*] judgment has been varied. Government has started shifting its housing programme to have regard to the needs of people in intolerable conditions, or threatened with eviction—a process which has recently been accelerated by a highly publicized land invasion. When local councils seek to evict homeless people, they no longer obtain a court order for the asking—courts increasingly ask the councils what they have done, and what they are going to do, to meet their *Grootboom* obligations in respect of the people concerned. But the Grootboom community are still living under highly unsatisfactory circumstances. Further litigation may result. Many other people continue to live in desperate circumstances. The picture is generally uneven, but I think there is no doubt that we have taken a major step forward.

    Geoff Budlender, *Justiciability of the Right to Housing* 14, *available at* http://www.escr-net.org/sites/default/files/budlender_housing_ms.pdf.

2. The Court held that under the South African Constitution, the state has a "positive obligation" to ameliorate the desperate housing needs of the poor even while acknowledging the challenges entailed and not insisting on a judicially prescribed remedy. The Court also assessed the "reasonableness" of government intervention by whether it is sufficient to meet the needs of the most desperate members of society, but also said that remedial measures need not be undertaken immediately.

    Cass Sunstein has described the *Grootboom* Court's "middle course" as "promoting a certain kind of deliberation, not by preempting it, as a result of directing political attention to interests that would otherwise be disregarded in ordinary political life." Cass R. Sunstein, *Designing Democracy: What Constitutions Do* (2001). Sunstein and others suggest that, in this way, *Grootboom* deftly navigates the twin problems of institutional competence and democratic legitimacy in court-enforced economic and social rights. Does this "weak form review," as Mark Tushnet has described *Grootboom*'s holding, seem like a promising balance between the courts and legislatures? Mark V. Tushnet, *State Action, Social Welfare Rights, and the Judicial Role: Some*

Comparative Observations, 3 Chi. J. Int'l L. 435 (2002). Or put another way, is such strong rhetoric, in which courts tell the political branches what to do — but not how to do it — a viable path forward for enforcing social and economic rights?

3. As a practical matter, the Court is concerned that recognizing such rights might encourage people to "queue-jump." That is, people might squat on land in horrid conditions to coerce the government to provide them housing on a preferential basis over people who are already on waiting lists for housing. Does this strike you as a reasonable concern? If so, is this kind of unintended consequence a good reason for courts to stay out of mandating or enforcing social welfare policy?

4. Other countries with modern constitutions that have incorporated ESCR have grappled with many of these questions, including the Supreme Court of India with respect to the rights of slum dwellers (Olga Tellis v. Bombay Mun. Corp., A.I.R. 1986 S.C. 180 (India)), and the Constitutional Court of Colombia in the case of internally displaced people (Corte Constitucional [C.C.] [Constitutional Court], enero 22, 2004, Sentecia T-024/04 (Colom.), http://www.corteconstitucional.gov.co/relatoria/2004/t-024-04.htm). We turn next to the question of whether such rights can be invoked in U.S. federal courts in the absence of constitutional provisions like those in South Africa and elsewhere.

2.   *International Law in U.S. Federal Courts*

The place of international law in the United States legal framework has been described as a deep puzzle. Oona Hathaway et al., *International Law at Home: Enforcing Treaties in U.S. Courts*, 37 Yale J. Int'l L. 51 (2012). While international treaties signed by the United States are legally binding, these treaties are not easily enforceable in domestic courts. In federal courts, judges occasionally cite to international law, though not without controversy. In *Roper*, excerpted next, the majority and dissenting opinions expressed strongly divergent views about the proper place of international law in domestic jurisprudence.

ROPER v. SIMMONS
543 U.S. 551 (2005)

Justice KENNEDY delivered the opinion of the Court.

This case requires us to address, for the second time in a decade and a half, whether it is permissible under the Eighth and Fourteenth Amendments to the Constitution of the United States to execute a juvenile offender who was older than 15 but younger than 18 when he committed a capital crime. In *Stanford v. Kentucky*, 492 U.S. 361 (1989), a divided Court rejected the proposition that the Constitution bars capital punishment for juvenile offenders in this age group. We reconsider the question.

. . . Our determination that the death penalty is disproportionate punishment for offenders under 18 finds confirmation in the stark reality that the United States is the only country in the world that continues to give official sanction to the juvenile death penalty. This reality does not become controlling, for the task of interpreting the Eighth Amendment remains our responsibility. Yet at least from the time of the Court's decision in *Trop*, the Court has referred to the laws of other countries and to international authorities as instructive for its interpretation of the Eighth Amendment's prohibition of "cruel and unusual punishments."

As respondent and a number of *amici* emphasize, Article 37 of the United Nations Convention on the Rights of the Child, which every country in the world has ratified save for the United States and Somalia, contains an express prohibition on capital punishment for crimes committed by juveniles under 18. No ratifying country has entered a reservation to the provision prohibiting the execution of juvenile offenders. Parallel prohibitions are contained in other significant international covenants. . . .

Respondent and his *amici* have submitted, and petitioner does not contest, that only seven countries other than the United States have executed juvenile offenders since 1990: Iran, Pakistan, Saudi Arabia, Yemen, Nigeria, the Democratic Republic of Congo, and China. Since then each of these countries has either abolished capital punishment for juveniles or made public disavowal of the practice. In sum, it is fair to say that the United States now stands alone in a world that has turned its face against the juvenile death penalty. . . .

It is proper that we acknowledge the overwhelming weight of international opinion against the juvenile death penalty, resting in large part on the understanding that the instability and emotional imbalance of young people may often be a factor in the crime. The opinion of the world community, while not controlling our outcome, does provide respected and significant confirmation for our own conclusions.

Over time, from one generation to the next, the Constitution has come to earn the high respect and even, as Madison dared to hope, the veneration of the American people. The document sets forth, and rests upon, innovative principles original to the American experience, such as federalism; a proven balance in political mechanisms through separation of powers; specific guarantees for the accused in criminal cases; and broad provisions to secure individual freedom and preserve human dignity. These doctrines and guarantees are central to the American experience and remain essential to our present-day self-definition and national identity. Not the least of the reasons we honor the Constitution, then, is because we know it to be our own. It does not lessen our fidelity to the Constitution or our pride in its origins to acknowledge that the express affirmation of certain fundamental rights by other nations and peoples simply underscores the centrality of those same rights within our own heritage of freedom.

The Eighth and Fourteenth Amendments forbid imposition of the death penalty on offenders who were under the age of 18 when their crimes were committed. The judgment of the Missouri Supreme Court setting aside the sentence of death imposed upon Christopher Simmons is affirmed.

Justice SCALIA, with whom THE CHIEF JUSTICE and Justice THOMAS join, dissenting.
. . . Because I do not believe that the meaning of our Eighth Amendment, any more than the meaning of other provisions of our Constitution, should be determined by the subjective views of five Members of this Court and like-minded foreigners, I dissent. . . .

Though the views of our own citizens are essentially irrelevant to the Court's decision today, the views of other countries and the so-called international community take center stage.

The Court begins by noting that "Article 37 of the United Nations Convention on the Rights of the Child, which every country in the world has ratified *save for the United States* and Somalia, contains an express prohibition on capital punishment for crimes committed by juveniles under 18." *Ante*, at 22 (emphasis added). The Court also discusses the International Covenant on Civil and Political Rights, which the Senate ratified only subject to a reservation that reads:

> The United States reserves the right, subject to its Constitutional restraints, to impose capital punishment on any person (other than a pregnant woman) duly convicted under existing or future laws permitting the imposition of capital punishment, including such punishment for crime committed by persons below eighteen years of age.

Unless the Court has added to its arsenal the power to join and ratify treaties on behalf of the United States, I cannot see how this evidence favors, rather than refutes, its position. That the Senate and the President — those actors our Constitution empowers to enter into treaties, see Art. II, § 2 — have declined to join and ratify treaties prohibiting execution of under-18 offenders can only suggest that *our country* has either not reached a national consensus on the question, or has reached a consensus contrary to what the Court announces. That the reservation to the ICCPR was made in 1992 does not suggest otherwise, since the reservation still remains in place today. It is also worth noting that, in addition to barring the execution of under-18 offenders, the United Nations Convention on the Rights of the Child prohibits punishing them with life in prison without the possibility of release. If we are truly going to get in line with the international community, then the Court's reassurance that the death penalty is really not needed, since "the punishment of life imprisonment without the possibility of parole is itself a severe sanction," *ante*, at 18, gives little comfort.

It is interesting that whereas the Court is not content to accept what the States of our Federal Union *say*, but insists on inquiring into what they *do* (specifically, whether they in fact *apply* the juvenile death penalty that their laws allow), the Court is quite willing to believe that every foreign nation — of whatever tyrannical political makeup and with however subservient or incompetent a court system — in fact *adheres* to a rule of no death penalty for offenders under 18. Nor does the Court inquire into how many of the countries that have the death penalty, but have forsworn (on paper at least) imposing that penalty on offenders under 18, have what no State of this country can constitutionally have: a *mandatory* death penalty for certain crimes, with no possibility of mitigation by the sentencing authority, for youth or any other reason. I suspect it is most of them. To forbid the death penalty for juveniles under such a system may be a good idea, but it says nothing about our system, in which the sentencing authority, typically a jury, always can, and almost always does, withhold the death penalty from an under-18 offender except, after considering all the circumstances, in the rare cases where it is warranted. The foreign authorities, in other words, do not even speak to the issue before us here.

More fundamentally, however, the basic premise of the Court's argument — that American law should conform to the laws of the rest of the world — ought to be rejected out of hand. In fact the Court itself does not believe it. In many

significant respects the laws of most other countries differ from our law—
including not only such explicit provisions of our Constitution as the right to
jury trial and grand jury indictment, but even many interpretations of the Constitution prescribed by this Court itself. The Court-pronounced exclusionary
rule, for example, is distinctively American. When we adopted that rule in
Mapp v. Ohio, 367 U.S. 643, 655 (1961), it was "unique to American Jurisprudence." Since then a categorical exclusionary rule has been "universally
rejected" by other countries, including those with rules prohibiting illegal
searches and police misconduct, despite the fact that none of these countries
"appears to have any alternative form of discipline for police that is effective in
preventing search violations." England, for example, rarely excludes evidence
found during an illegal search or seizure and has only recently begun excluding
evidence from illegally obtained confessions. Canada rarely excludes evidence
and will only do so if admission will "bring the administration of justice into
disrepute." The European Court of Human Rights has held that introduction of
illegally seized evidence does not violate the "fair trial" requirement in Article 6,
§ 1, of the European Convention on Human Rights.

The Court has been oblivious to the views of other countries when deciding
how to interpret our Constitution's requirement that "Congress shall make no
law respecting an establishment of religion." . . . Most other countries—
including those committed to religious neutrality—do not insist on the degree
of separation between church and state that this Court requires. For example,
whereas "we have recognized special Establishment Clause dangers where the
government makes direct money payments to sectarian institutions." . . . Even
in France, which is considered "America's only rival in strictness of church-state
separation," "[t]he practice of contracting for educational services provided by
Catholic schools is very widespread."

And let us not forget the Court's abortion jurisprudence, which makes us one
of only six countries that allow abortion on demand until the point of viability.
Though the Government and *amici* in cases following *Roe v. Wade*, 410 U.S. 113
(1973), urged the Court to follow the international community's lead, these
arguments fell on deaf ears. . . .

The Court should either profess its willingness to reconsider all these matters
in light of the views of foreigners, or else it should cease putting forth foreigners'
views as part of the *reasoned basis* of its decisions. To invoke alien law when it
agrees with one's own thinking, and ignore it otherwise, is not reasoned decisionmaking, but sophistry.

The Court responds that "[i]t does not lessen our fidelity to the Constitution
or our pride in its origins to acknowledge that the express affirmation of certain
fundamental rights by other nations and peoples simply underscores the centrality of those same rights within our own heritage of freedom." To begin with, I
do not believe that approval by "other nations and peoples" should buttress our
commitment to American principles any more than (what should logically
follow) disapproval by "other nations and peoples" should weaken that commitment. More importantly, however, the Court's statement flatly misdescribes
what is going on here. Foreign sources are cited today, *not* to underscore our
"fidelity" to the Constitution, our "pride in its origins," and "our own
[American] heritage." To the contrary, they are cited *to set aside* the centuries-old American practice—a practice still engaged in by a large majority of
the relevant States—of letting a jury of 12 citizens decide whether, in the
particular case, youth should be the basis for withholding the death penalty.

What these foreign sources "affirm," rather than repudiate, is the Justices' own notion of how the world ought to be, and their diktat that it shall be so henceforth in America. The Court's parting attempt to downplay the significance of its extensive discussion of foreign law is unconvincing. "Acknowledgment" of foreign approval has no place in the legal opinion of this Court *unless it is part of the basis for the Court's judgment*—which is surely what it parades as today.

NOTES AND QUESTIONS

1.   The majority in *Roper* invokes international law by reference both to foreign practice (executing minors) and to treaties, including one to which the United States is a signatory, but has not ratified (the Convention on the Rights of the Child), and another that the United States has ratified, but entered a reservation on the issue at hand (the ICCPR). While the majority makes clear that these judicially acknowledged facts are not controlling in U.S. courts, are they nevertheless persuasive arguments? Or should they have "no place in the legal opinion of this Court unless it is part of the basis for the Court's judgment," as the dissent argues?

2.   Since ESCR are not found explicitly in the U.S. Constitution and invocation of international law outside of express treaty obligations is hotly contested and uncertain, the following subsections consider state court and other legal sources and venues for enforcing human rights law and norms domestically.

3.   Human Rights Law in U.S. State Courts

Outside of federal courts, state courts increasingly offer a venue for antipoverty advocates to advance international human rights arguments. The next three excerpts identify the potential to invoke and enforce human rights in state constitutional and common law claims.

HELEN HERSHKOFF, *"JUST WORDS": COMMON LAW AND THE ENFORCEMENT OF STATE CONSTITUTIONAL SOCIAL AND ECONOMIC RIGHTS*

62 Stan. L. Rev. 1521 (2010)

Commentators generally do not associate American constitutionalism with positive rights. Social and economic rights such as those to education or to health care do not appear in the Federal Constitution, and the Supreme Court has refused to locate in the text's penumbra any "affirmative right to government aid, even where such aid may be necessary to secure life, liberty, or property interests of which the government itself may not deprive the individual." [DeShaney v. Winnebago Cnty. Dep't of Soc. Servs., 489 U.S. 189, 196 (1989)]. Limiting the constitution to "negative rights" confines federal courts to the important goal of protecting the individual against government power, but leaves the individual relatively unprotected from private domination in social and economic relationships.

By now it is well acknowledged that contemporary constitutions, at least those post-dating World War II, reflect greater attention to the "social dimension" of rights, in the sense of affording protection against nongovernment power — what Ulrich Scheuner has referred to as "the menace to individual liberty [that] comes . . . from the side of social power assembled in the hands of mighty economic units and of professional or social organizations which try to prescribe a certain behaviour and to limit individual independence." Socio-economic rights thus are justified as serving as an important bulwark against power, whatever its source, and their absence from the Federal Constitution often is attributed simply to the document's eighteenth-century origins.

By contrast to the Federal Constitution, every state constitution in the U.S. includes some textual commitment to a social or economic right; in addition, more than a dozen state constitutions in their eighteenth-century versions included provisions concerning important public goods such as free public schooling or public hospitals for the indigent. Some state constitutions currently embrace guarantees to decent work and opportunities for livelihood that commentators associate with social citizenship; some states go even further and authorize or guarantee the provision of a safety net during times of financial distress, emergency housing, and protection of the environment as a way to vouchsafe a communal future.

Among the earliest social and economic clauses contained in state constitutions relate to the provision of free public schooling. The 1776 Pennsylvania Constitution, for example, mandated that the legislature establish and fund common schools for all of the children in the state: "A school or schools shall be established in each county by the legislature, for the convenient instruction of youth, with such salaries to the masters paid by the public, as may enable them to instruct youth at low prices." The Northwest Ordinance of 1785 required the setting aside of land for public schools in each town within the Northwest Territory; in addition, provision for free common schools in a state constitution was mandated for the most recent sixteen states as a condition of their admission to the union, and state constitution education clauses increasingly have clarified the legislature's duty to establish and fund public schools.

Almost two dozen state constitutions likewise currently authorize provision of some kind of financial assistance to those who are in economic need. One commentator writes, "Twenty three state constitutions recognize that someone or something in the individual states will provide for those in need. No two constitutional provisions are exactly the same. The duty of providing welfare — or mere recognition of the need for it — is unique in each state." These clauses reflect diverse origins. Pennsylvania, in 1790, amended its constitution to include protection of debtors, and newly admitted Western states later adopted similar provisions. State constitutions providing financial assistance to the poor began to appear in Reconstruction constitutions in 1868, and other states adopted welfare assistance clauses during the Great Depression. Moreover, over the years, state constitutions have been amended to meet different forms of socio-economic distress. The Ohio Constitution of 1802, for example, made explicit that even a pauper's children could attend the public schools; the state amended its constitution in 1990 to authorize the legislature to provide subsidized housing for low-income individuals. Since the nineteenth century, some state constitutions have been amended to include clauses that regulate private workplaces. The Declaration of Rights of the Wyoming Constitution was amended in 1889 to provide: "The rights of labor shall have just protection through laws calculated to secure to the laborer proper rewards for his service and to promote the industrial welfare of the state." More typical are constitutional provisions that treat specific aspects of the workplace relation, such as workplace safety, compensation for occupational injuries, regulation of children's labor, restrictions on the length of the working day, minimum wage levels, the right to join a union, and the right not to join a union. In 1876, Colorado amended its state constitution to include child labor restrictions, maximum-hours protections, and employer liability for workplace injuries. State constitutions in the late nineteenth century also were amended to protect a worker's right to unionize, followed by amendments in the twentieth century protecting the right to bargain collectively. Later in the twentieth century, some state constitutions were amended to protect a worker from being denied or terminated from employment for refusal to join a union.

A number of state constitutions include "dignity" and "safety and happiness" clauses. The New Hampshire happiness clause dates to the eighteenth century: "All men have certain natural, essential, and inherent rights—among which are, the enjoying and defending life and liberty; acquiring, possessing, and protecting, property; and, in a word, of seeking and obtaining happiness." The Puerto Rico and Montana constitutions, amended in the twentieth century, incorporate a concept of dignity that draws from international and foreign law. The Louisiana "individual dignity" clause, which functions as that state's equal protection provision, traces to different sources. A happiness and safety clause appears in the constitutions of Ohio, New Jersey, and about a dozen other states, and some courts and commentators have treated these provisions as support for social and economic claims. . . .

MARTHA DAVIS, *PUBLIC RIGHTS, GLOBAL PERSPECTIVES, AND COMMON LAW*

36 Fordham Urb. L.J. 653 (2008)

[D]omestic common law adjudication has long encompassed international and comparative law. In recent decades, however, that global consciousness has often been casual and sporadic, rather than deliberate and focused. A return to a more intentional global perspective in common law adjudication will pose challenges for both judges and advocates. Three challenges are particularly acute and frequently raised during judicial and practitioner training that touches on this material.

First, how can judges and lawyers gain facility with relevant international and comparative material? This challenge might once have seemed insurmountable, but today, international and foreign legal materials are readily available to everyone who has computer access. . . .

Just having access to the materials is not enough, however, if the litigator or judge does not have enough background information to use them properly. . . .

It is worth noting that in the longer term, these basic questions of education and training may fall by the wayside. Across the country, law school curricula are being reshaped to take account of the growth in globalization, with international and comparative law increasingly incorporated into first year courses. In the upper level curriculum, international and comparative offerings are also growing, and international human rights clinics are increasingly becoming a law school staple. The next generation of law graduates will likely be quite familiar with these materials and adept at using them for advocacy or as a resource for adjudication.

Second, once judges find pertinent resource material, how can they and lawyers ascertain which judicial decisions or other sources of law are most pertinent to their task, and which should be given the most decisional weight? This question has been raised with regularity in the context of the debate concerning constitutional adjudication and international/foreign law, and it is also pertinent in the context of common law adjudication. The answer to this question builds directly on the role of analogy and precedent in common law reasoning: one should start by examining cases from legal systems that share historical, jurisprudential, or constitutional roots with the United States. It is these cases that, as Daniel Farber cogently and simply states, "are most likely to be relevant." Farber cites the opinions of the Canadian Supreme Court, the European Court of Human Rights, the European Court of Justice, the German Constitutional Court, and the Israeli Supreme Court as deserving consideration. Depending on the issue pending before the domestic adjudicator, many might add the South African Constitutional Court or the Colombian Constitutional Court to this list, given their leadership in adjudication involving human rights norms.

Within this sturdy analytical framework, however, it is ultimately a matter of judicial discretion, aided by the good faith briefing of counsel, to ascertain what weight these materials should be given. Those who are mistrustful of judicial integrity or who object to any hint of judicial lawmaking as a political matter may cry that this power will be abused. There is absolutely no evidence anywhere, however, that any U.S. judge has made the legal error of treating a foreign decision as binding precedent. As for international law, there is a legitimate debate as to when some aspects of the law of nations, such as customary international law, may be directly binding on local judges. Yet very few, if any, judges have issued rulings that rely on international law to justify a move to abandon or ignore domestic precedent. Rather, judges routinely examine these materials for their persuasive value and cite them to bolster conclusions that are well-supported by domestic law. Further, if a judge were to make an error, the result would be no different than what happens when the judge errs in her interpretation of domestic law — the parties may move for reargument, appeal, or seek redress through other means such as legislative relief.

For those judges and litigators who are sincerely grappling with the weight to be given to various types of foreign cases and international materials, . . . the Opportunity Agenda has compiled an extensive state-by-state guide to decisions that cite international and comparative material, and that can provide models for how that material has been treated by domestic courts. . . .

A third challenge to using transnational law in domestic common law advocacy is one that confronts advocates who are interested in the long-term progressive development of both domestic and international law. In particular, to the extent that advocacy invokes international human rights norms, advocates may be concerned about diluting the moral power of human rights claims, squandering its force on issues that are not critical human needs. . . .

This critique may be particularly salient in developed countries like the United States, where some argue that human rights are simply irrelevant — that these are concepts really meant to be applied to the practices of developing countries somewhere far away. . . . Advocates must always make individual strategic decisions as they pursue litigation in these areas, and may choose to save relevant human rights arguments for more dramatic fact situations in order to introduce human rights principles to domestic courts in the most strategically favorable setting. But a blanket rule that reserves human rights arguments only for the most outrageous, dire, and life-threatening injustices simply serves to make human rights irrelevant to most of those in the developed world and significantly limits the scope of such rights. Far from diluting human rights, it may actually undermine the general value and reach of these norms.

. . . [C]ommon law adjudication involving such claims as contractual breaches, wrongful termination, and tort can be, and often are, public rights litigation. Many common law decisions have significant impacts in the community, and — because of the nature of precedent — become quickly embedded in the law where they contribute to the outcomes of future cases as well. Common law cases are a particularly important aspect of public rights litigation because of the paucity of constitutional protections for economic and social rights. In the absence of constitutional protections for such rights, rigorous enforcement of common law claims addressing housing, work, and marketplace transactions can go at least part way to filling that gap. Further, as federal courts cut back on the scope of available statutory remedies, common law litigation may continue to offer relief to litigants. . . .

From the judicial perspective, inquiry into global context has historically contributed to judges' ability to reach sound conclusions in cases where domestic precedent does not provide for the resolution of the matter. In such cases, international and comparative materials do not substitute for binding precedent, they do not dictate results, but they provide additional relevant materials, examples and perspectives for thoughtful judges who are called on to consider open questions in the common law tradition.

From the perspective of public interest litigators working in the common law, references to global context may be useful for many of the same reasons. A soundly-reasoned opinion from a peer foreign court that has grappled with the same issues may provide important confirmation of the workability of an otherwise "novel" approach urged by counsel. Similarly, references to international law may help open a domestic court's eyes to the global significance of a seemingly private, domestic issue, and its relationship to larger issues of human rights and human dignity.

Such inquiries into relevant foreign and international law are part of our common law heritage. The recent tempest concerning citation of international and comparative law in domestic constitutional cases should not obscure the continued relevance and utility of such global perspectives in the wide variety of common law contexts that affect so many areas of our day-to-day lives.

THE OPPORTUNITY AGENDA, *HUMAN RIGHTS IN STATE COURTS: AN OVERVIEW AND RECOMMENDATIONS FOR LEGAL ADVOCACY*

45 Clearinghouse Rev. 233 (2011)

Human rights are a crucial part of the United States' legal and cultural foundation. We are, the founders of our country declared, all created equal and endowed with certain inalienable rights. The notion of human rights has been central to our nation's struggles to achieve equality and justice for all.

The United States helped craft the Universal Declaration of Human Rights and the international human rights system in response to World War II and the horrors of the Holocaust. Yet, despite that legacy, international human rights laws have not played a major role in legal efforts to pursue fundamental rights, justice, and equality in the United States. That trend has begun to change over the last decade as more and more legal advocates have begun to incorporate human rights arguments into their work and as the U.S. Supreme Court, in particular, has increasingly cited human rights law as persuasive authority for constitutional decisions.

The federal courts, however, are in flux in the consideration of individual rights in general and human rights in particular. Federal constitutional and legislative protections tend not to include economic, social, and cultural rights that are part of the international human rights system. State courts, by contrast, more often consider such protections and, in interpreting state law, have the independence to recognize a broader panoply of rights. State courts have authority to interpret international treaties. . . .

HUMAN RIGHTS ARGUMENTS IN STATE COURTS

State courts can draw upon a number of arguments to support their use of international human rights principles in their decision making. Under Article VI, Section 2, of the U.S. Constitution, treaties are the "supreme Law of the Land," binding on the "Judges in every State." The United States has signed and ratified the International Covenant on Civil and Political Rights, the International Convention on the Elimination of All Forms of Racial Discrimination, and the Convention against Torture and Other Cruel, Inhuman, or Degrading Treatment or Punishment and is therefore bound by these treaties.

Implementation of these treaties and their principles is the responsibility of state, as well as federal, government. Under the federal system, states are responsible for regulating areas of substantive law, including criminal, family, and social welfare law. The U.S. Senate's reservations when it ratified the treaties make clear that states are responsible for implementing international human rights law in these areas. Although the treaties are "non-self-executing"— meaning that they cannot be directly enforced in U.S. courts—they impose concrete obligations on states.

Ratified treaties "have a legal status equivalent to enacted federal statutes." Once ratified, treaties prevail over previously enacted conflicting federal statutes and inconsistent state law. However, in ratifying the International Covenant on Civil and Political Rights, the Senate mandated that its protections go no further than corresponding protections in domestic law. Advocates and scholars have argued that such a reservation frustrates the purpose of the treaty and may be invalid under international law. Nevertheless, state courts routinely invoke Senate reservations to deny individuals' claims under treaties.

Courts can look to international human rights treaties for interpretive guidance, whether or not the treaties are signed, ratified, or considered customary international law. Specifically courts can turn to international human rights law to help clarify the meaning of vague or unsettled domestic law. Even if human rights principles are not directly binding, they can influence courts as they define and explain statutory provisions, and as they give meaning to domestic constitutional rights. Courts have looked to unratified as well as ratified treaties for this purpose.

. . . A number of decisions have used international law as persuasive authority for the interpretation of state constitutions, statutes, and common law. These are some highlights of state-court decisions that draw upon international human rights law:

- A Florida court used international human rights law to analyze sentencing juvenile offenders to life in prison without the possibility of parole. Although the decision referred to both international treaties and "international pressure to change our existing legal system" as the defendant's strongest argument, the court declined to create a per se ban on the punishment for juveniles.
- Courts have used human rights law, in particular the Hague Convention on Civil Aspects of International Child Abduction, to analyze both procedural and substantive rights in the family law context.
- California courts have cited the Universal Declaration of Human Rights to support their interpretation of the right to practice one's trade, the right to privacy, the meaning of "physical handicap," the right to freedom of movement, and the scope of welfare provisions.
- The Maryland Supreme Court relied heavily on the Nuremberg Code to find a greater duty toward subjects for researchers conducting nontherapeutic programs.
- The Missouri Supreme Court cited the International Convention on the Rights of the Child in striking down the juvenile death penalty.
- New York courts invoked the Universal Declaration of Human Rights in cases involving the rights to work and to strike, a transnational discovery dispute, and the act of state doctrine.
- The Oregon Supreme Court looked to the Universal Declaration of Human Rights, the International Convention on Civil and Political Rights, and the European Convention to interpret the meaning of the state constitution's provision on the treatment of prisoners.
- The West Virginia Supreme Court invoked the Universal Declaration of Human Rights to review the financing scheme for public schools and to define the right to education.
- A Montana Supreme Court concurring opinion in support of a ruling that a state university's denial of health coverage to same-sex partners was not rationally related to a legitimate government interest recognized that the state's constitution was steeped in a history of human rights.
- [In a concurring opinion, the chief justice of the Connecticut Supreme Court invoked the Universal Declaration of Human Rights and the International Covenant on Economic, Social and Cultural Rights to recognize a limited state constitutional right to governmental assistance for low-income citizens.]

RECOMMENDATIONS FOR A STATE-COURT HUMAN RIGHTS STRATEGY

The survey of state-court cases reveals that courts have most frequently addressed international human rights in death penalty cases, when defendants argue that the International Convention on Civil and Political Rights or customary international law prohibits capital punishment. Other than in the juvenile context, these arguments have proven largely unsuccessful. Courts either have accepted U.S. Senate reservations to human rights treaties uncritically or, in some instances, have simply refused to adjudicate human rights defenses. A more promising area for the development of international human rights jurisprudence is in civil lawsuits. As the survey shows, some state courts have started to look to human rights principles to help define state constitutional or statutory guarantees, and there are openings for further development of the law in this manner.

As one scholar noted, while courts have proven "reluctant to view themselves as bound directly by international human rights principles on substantive issues, they are much more willing to invoke such principles — whether embodied in treaties or in other manifestations of customary international law — to guide the interpretation of domestic legal norms." Scholars have repeatedly argued, "This 'indirect incorporation' of international human rights law continues to be a promising approach warranting greater attention and increased use by human rights advocates."

When strategically possible, state-court litigators should therefore consider using international human rights standards as interpretive guides for state constitutional and statutory rights. Invoking international human rights law as an interpretive guide, while relying on state law for the rule of decision, has several advantages. Reliance on state law insulates decisions from review by the U.S. Supreme Court and makes them more resistant to removal to federal court. State courts can thus safely develop their own jurisprudence of international human rights without the possibility that federal courts will intervene and frustrate the project altogether. An "indirect incorporation" approach also allows state courts to circumnavigate the self-execution doctrine and reservations to treaties that otherwise may limit treaties' impact. These limitations are less relevant when state courts are not asked to apply treaties as governing law.

Moreover, the development of a jurisprudence in which human rights law plays a subsidiary but interpretive role may encourage state courts, which have limited familiarity with such law, to examine international sources of obligation more frequently. As state courts become more familiar with international human rights law, they may prove more willing to adjudicate a violation of international human rights law standing alone, without having to rely on analogous standards in state law for the rules of decision. And over time, as international human rights principles become more integrated into state law, courts will define rights more broadly and will hold government accountable for enforcing those rights, thereby expanding opportunity for all Americans.

4. Other U.S. Human Rights Strategies

As described in the Kaufman and Ward excerpt that follows, U.N. treaty and Charter-based mechanisms can be invoked on behalf of domestic clients on a wide range of issues and in multiple settings. This chapter concludes with a case study of one such effort on behalf of homeless clients in Sacramento, California, during the Great Recession.

RISA E. KAUFMAN & JOANN KAMUF WARD, *USING HUMAN RIGHTS MECHANISMS OF THE UNITED NATIONS TO ADVANCE ECONOMIC JUSTICE*

45 Clearinghouse Rev. 259 (2011)

II.   OPPORTUNITIES FOR ENGAGEMENT

Taken together, U.N. treaty bodies and Charter-based mechanisms offer a range of opportunities for advocates to publicize their clients' concerns within their clients' communities, with government officials, and in the international arena.

A.   TREATY REVIEW

Treaty review is an opportunity for advocates to document human rights concerns by submitting "shadow reports" to treaty-monitoring bodies to supplement or clarify information from governments' official reports. The review is also an opportunity for direct government engagement. For example, the U.S. government often holds civil society consultations before drafting its official report for review by a treaty body. At these consultations, advocates can draw attention to and urge action on specific issues. After the review, advocates can request that local officials hold hearings to consider the concluding observations in light of local policy and practice, submit the treaty bodies' observations as support for domestic administration and litigation advocacy, and, through media and other outreach, raise general public awareness on issues raised during the review.

U.S. advocacy to establish the right to counsel in civil cases illustrates how advocates can engage with treaty bodies. This so-called Civil Gideon movement is attempting to secure the right to counsel for individuals in civil cases where basic human needs are at stake. Although the U.S. Supreme Court established the right to counsel for criminal defendants in Gideon v. Wainwright [372 U.S. 335 (1963)], the Court held that there was no general federally protected right to counsel in civil proceedings. Some state and municipal legislatures nevertheless have provided indigent parties with the right to counsel in certain categories of civil cases, such as those involving child custody or a person's liberty. Yet these policies are not consistent, and, funding for legal aid programs being inadequate, many low- and moderate-income people lack necessary legal assistance in protecting or vindicating their rights in civil matters.

The absence of a right to counsel in civil cases concerning basic needs is both out of step with practices in many European and commonwealth countries and an abdication of the United States' responsibilities under at least two ratified treaties: the International Convention on the Elimination of All Forms of Racial Discrimination and the International Covenant on Civil and Political Rights. Advocates of Civil Gideon have engaged U.N. treaty bodies to apply international pressure to U.S. policymakers.

In 2007, during the last International Convention on the Elimination of All Forms of Racial Discrimination review, Northeastern University School of Law's Program for Human Rights in the Global Economy spearheaded the drafting of a shadow report highlighting the disproportionate impact of the absence of a right to civil counsel on racial minorities in the United States. At the formal review of the United States in Geneva, Switzerland, in 2008, representatives from the program and other advocates spoke directly with International Convention on the Elimination of All Forms of Racial Discrimination delegates and urged the U.N. Committee on the Elimination of Racial Discrimination to take up the United States' failure to meet its obligations. As a direct result, the committee admonished the United States for failing to provide civil counsel to low-income individuals. The committee noted "with concern the disproportionate impact [of existing practice] on indigent persons belonging to racial, ethnic and national minorities" and urged the United States to "allocate sufficient resources to ensure legal representation of [these persons] in civil proceedings, [particularly] where basic human needs, such as housing, health care, or child custody, are at stake." . . .

Legal services lawyers and other advocates can raise awareness, both internationally and domestically, about these and other issues by detailing their continuing concerns in shadow reports and governmental consultations. And advocates can work creatively to parlay success from the international arena into domestic efforts — for example, by citing U.N. committee recommendations in litigation and other advocacy and bringing recommendations to the attention of local policymakers, state and local human rights and human relations commissions, and the public at large.

B. COUNTRY VISITS BY SPECIAL RAPPORTEURS

Fact-finding missions by U.N. Special Rapporteurs and independent experts present opportunities for domestic advocates to increase the visibility of domestic causes, garner media coverage, raise awareness of human rights violations, meet with government officials, and build networks. The recent U.S. visits by the U.N. Special Rapporteur on Violence Against Women, Its Causes and Consequences, Rashida Manjoo (discussed below), and by the U.N. Independent Expert on the Human Right to Water and Sanitation are paradigmatic.

Since at least 1993, when the U.N. General Assembly adopted the Declaration on the Elimination of Violence Against Women, the United Nations has recognized violence against women as a human rights concern. Manjoo's 2011 visit was not the first time that U.N. mechanisms have focused on this issue in the United States; the Committee on the Elimination of Racial Discrimination has also drawn attention to violence against women, and in 1999, focusing on violence in prisons, the first Special Rapporteur on Violence Against Women visited the United States. This international scrutiny can be attributed to several factors, such as the persistently high rates of violence against women in the United States. Domestic legal developments, such as the critical gaps in the protections afforded by the federal Violence Against Women Act, have contributed to the international attention. The U.S. Supreme Court rejected an attempt to establish a civil remedy for victims of gender-based violence, and the Court held that a domestic violence victim whose husband violated an order of protection had no constitutional right to police enforcement of that order.

In this context, Manjoo's visit created opportunities for engagement. In a two-week fact-finding mission, Manjoo met across the country with government officials and civil society, members, domestic violence survivors among them. She visited local communities, detention centers, and women's shelters to document and evaluate the causes and consequences of various forms of violence against women; she probed the role of discrimination in perpetuating these human rights abuses.

In anticipation of the visit, advocates organized a roundtable with Manjoo on the domestic legal framework and gaps in protection for women in the United States. Several participants agreed to draft reports on particular issues — gun violence, women in detention, women in the military, and U.S. compliance with the international legal obligations to "exercise due diligence to prevent, investigate and . . . punish acts of violence against women." From the roundtable and briefing papers Manjoo gained a more nuanced understanding of the facts on the ground.

Local, national, and international organizations ensured that Manjoo heard the perspectives of multiple stakeholders, from affected individuals to policy-oriented organizations and academics. In Cherokee, North Carolina, for example, Manjoo learned about the prevalence of violence against Native American women (one out of three of whom will be raped during her lifetime) and the lack of adequate legal protections to deter this violence. These firsthand accounts underscored the need for a more comprehensive approach to violence against women in the United States. Manjoo also met with federal, state, and local government officials to learn about replicable local practices in confronting some types of violence and strengthening domestic protections.

At the conclusion of her visit, Manjoo noted some recent positive steps by the U.S. government but stated that further protections were needed, calling for the creation and full implementation of laws and policies preventing acts of violence and calling for resources and improved services. In their litigation and advocacy efforts, advocates can draw upon Manjoo's final report's comprehensive overview of the human rights violations occurring across the country.

U.N. human rights mechanisms are platforms for legal services lawyers to raise their clients' concerns nationally and internationally and leverage international attention to advance advocacy at home. Treaty reviews and visits by U.N. Special Rapporteurs are opportunities to build alliances among advocates, empower local communities to voice their experiences, engage government officials in conversations on human rights practices and the need for change, and advance change on critical issues by using international standards. For legal services and poverty lawyers, U.N. human rights mechanisms are another avenue to advance rights-based protections and fight systemic human rights abuses.

* * *

In the following case study, legal services advocates filed a confidential complaint with the U.N. Special Rapporteur on the Human Right to Safe Drinking Water and Sanitation asserting multiple human rights violations on behalf of homeless people living in California's state capital. Named in the complaint were the United States, the State of California, and the City and County of Sacramento. The complaint sought immediate relief "to ensure that all residents of the Riverview region, including those people who are homeless, are provided with adequate access to sanitation services and clean water for drinking and bathing." In a postscript following the case study, one of the lead lawyers in the case considers the longer-term limits and possibilities of such advocacy.

MONA TAWATAO & COLIN BAILEY, *TOWARD A HUMAN RIGHTS FRAMEWORK IN HOMELESSNESS ADVOCACY: BRINGING CLIENTS FACE-TO-FACE WITH THE UNITED NATIONS*

45 Clearinghouse Rev. 169 (2011)

I haul between 130 and 230 pounds of human waste from SafeGround each week. My record is four bags. I bicycle about one and a half to two miles, bring it to the men's room, wait for a big john to be available and dispatch it on its way and then pack all those bags with the residue that is left over, put them all in one bag, tie it all in one bag, put it in the rubbish, after which I wash my hands, scrub them and lemonize them. . . . The first few times it was horrible. It's a difficult job but some-one's got to do it and is it worthwhile, absolutely. The men can rough it if they have to, but women . . . gees whiz, if my ma was out there, I would want her to have it. The women really appreciate it. We all do because it makes us feel rehumanized, because we're not just thrown aside.

Tim Buckley, SafeGround Elder and Self-Described "Sanitation Technician," Testimony Submitted to the United Nations Independent Expert on the Human Right to Water and Sanitation, February 28, 2011.

The modern human rights framework seeks to ensure that all people are treated with dignity and that their most basic human needs are met. In Sacramento, California, homeless people are forced to live in tent camps along the American River Parkway. Despite the demands and protestations of the homeless community and their supporters, however, the city has failed to provide access to clean water and adequate sanitation facilities. It has also obstructed homeless persons' access to existing infrastructure and forbidden private charities from providing additional infrastructure to the camps in the form of portable toilets and potable water tanks.

As part of a broader campaign for a safe ground for people transitioning from homelessness, Legal Services of Northern California submitted to the United Nations a complaint in June 2011 against human rights abuses on behalf of our homeless clients whose access to clean water and sanitation is blocked by both government action and inaction. This effort is greatly aided by the U.N. General Assembly's adoption on July 28, 2010, of a resolution recognizing access to clean water and sanitation as a human right and the Legal Services of Northern California's recent success in facilitating a face-to-face meeting with our homeless clients and the U.N. Special Rapporteur on access to water and sanitation.

Human rights advocates in the United States have fought for many decades to enforce human rights norms in this country or to at least leverage such norms' moral force to create positive change in our communities. As a nationwide network that serves this nation's most vulnerable individuals, legal services attorneys are a necessary part of the struggle to make human rights real in America and part of multi-forum legal services advocacy strategy to fight poverty and homelessness.

What follows is the story of how the human rights abuses suffered by our homeless clients were laid bare before the community of nations and how we aim to use this exposure to empower our clients to achieve dignity in their daily lives and lasting improvements in their access to water and sanitation and other basic human needs.

THE BIRTH OF SAFEGROUND: ADVOCATING HUMAN RIGHTS FOR HOMELESS PEOPLE

The homeless situation in Sacramento is typical of many medium-sized cities in the western United States. However, Sacramento's homeless population is unique in at least one way. Immediately adjacent to downtown Sacramento sits the American River Parkway, a largely undeveloped stretch of oak and cottonwood forest, which extends over fifty miles and thousands of acres and is connected by some parks and narrow bike and pedestrian trails. A significant and growing percentage of Sacramento's homeless population has been forced to live along the river's banks in tent camps, a phenomenon that sparked a national debate just two years ago.

. . . Several leaders, homeless and housed, emerged from the tent city struggle to change local policies on homelessness. The name of the organization these leaders formed is called Safe Ground Sacramento, or SafeGround, which is eponymous with the group's primary goal to create a "safe ground" area in Sacramento. The area envisioned will be a transitional housing community of sixty sleeping cabins and a community facilities building, all of which are free of drugs, alcohol, and violence. The area will assist residents in getting permanent housing and link residents to jobs and health care. Here, unsheltered homeless persons would be able to live safely, in peace and with dignity, without disturbance from law enforcement.

SafeGround advocates share the belief of other homeless and housing advocates and many public officials that the best response to homelessness is to create, as quickly as possible, enough decent affordable homes as needed to house homeless people and those at risk of becoming homeless. SafeGround also acknowledges that emergency and temporary shelters can play a limited role in meeting the Sacramento area's vast unmet housing need. In this vein SafeGround promotes a safe ground area as part of a continuum that alleviates, rather than criminalizes, homelessness. Consistent with human rights principles, SafeGround calls for a moratorium on the enforcement of Sacramento's anti-camping laws and other laws that treat homeless people as criminals on the basis of their homeless status. . . .

In the days and months surrounding the dismantling of tent city, Legal Services of Northern California and others worked as SafeGround's general counsel to build a litigation strategy to enjoin on constitutional or other or both grounds the city and other entities from enforcing local anti-camping laws. . . .

With input from Legal Services of Northern California and SafeGround representatives, the National Law Center on Homelessness and Poverty also issued a statement in support of SafeGround's goals. The statement, read by a homeless rights advocate at a rally organized by SafeGround at the California State Capitol, linked human rights standards to the homeless groups' goals:

> Housing is a basic element of survival, and therefore a basic human right. . . . [T]he U.S. ratified the International Covenant on Civil and Political Rights, which has been interpreted as requiring the government to take basic measures to protect homeless persons from exposure to the elements to uphold their right to life. . . . [A]t the end of March [2009] the [Sacramento] City Council agreed with over three quarters of the American population when they declared, "housing is a basic human right." . . . Ignoring the plight of over 1,200 unsheltered individuals and enforcing laws that criminalize homelessness is a direct violation of the legal obligations tied to the human right to housing. . . . In a similar situation, the

Supreme Court of British Columbia in Canada . . . found that prohibiting homeless individuals from sleeping in public places when the number of available
shelter beds was insufficient was a violation of their right to life.

The National Law Center on Homelessness and Poverty called upon authorities to designate a safe ground area and "plac[e] a moratorium on police
enforcement of laws that criminalize homelessness at least until adequate
shelter and housing is available to all homeless individuals in the
community." . . .

SACRAMENTO'S HOMELESSNESS STORY IN FILM TO THE UNITED NATIONS

Through their newly established relationship, the National Law Center on
Homelessness and Poverty informed Legal Services of Northern California
that the United Nations Special Rapporteur on Housing, Rachel Rolnik, was
coming to the United States in November 2009 to gather public testimony about
the state of housing and homelessness in America. The National Law Center on
Homelessness and Poverty invited Legal Services of Northern California and
SafeGround to testify about homelessness and their advocacy at a meeting
with the Special Rapporteur in Washington, D.C.
    At the time SafeGround members were focused on advancing the strategy of
camping on civil rights attorney Mark Merin's private property to push Sacramento to change its criminalization policies and establish a safe ground. These
members determined that sending even one member to Washington, D.C., was
time- and cost-prohibitive. SafeGround, however, recognized the opportunity to
tell its story in its own words and submitted testimony, in a film, to the Special
Rapporteur.
    . . . The film appears to have had an impact because her final report recom-
mended that "[t]he [U.S.] Interagency Council on Homelessness should
develop constructive alternatives to the criminalization of homelessness in
full consultation with members of civil society. When shelter is not available
in the locality, homeless persons should be allowed to shelter themselves in
public areas."

THE UNITED NATIONS IN SACRAMENTO

. . . Against this backdrop, the National Law Center on Homelessness and Poverty facilitated another opportunity for SafeGround and Legal Services of
Northern California to bring Sacramento's homeless issue to light by connecting them with Catarina de Albuquerque, the United Nations' Special Rapporteur on Access to Water and Sanitation. De Albuquerque was slated to spend part
of her U.S. fact-finding mission in Northern California in late February 2011 and
to take testimony at the California state capitol from groups who lacked adequate access to water and sanitation. The initial plan was for SafeGround members to travel to the capitol to give a few minutes of testimony, but the leaders
decided that inviting de Albuquerque to meet directly and privately with them
would have more impact. SafeGround enlisted Legal Services of Northern
California to help implement its plan. De Albuquerque accepted SafeGround's
invitation enthusiastically.

In preparation for de Albuquerque's visit, Legal Services of Northern California interviewed SafeGround members and other homeless people and compiled the information in a report to de Albuquerque. The stories were compelling. Homeless people described their constant thirst and belief that the public officials cut off water spigots near their campsites along the American River deliberately to keep homeless people from using them. Women described being fearful about having to find a place distant from camp to relieve themselves in the middle of the night. Others with diabetes and other illnesses that caused frequent urination said they often felt panicked and trapped because they had no access to restroom facilities. One SafeGround member testified that a law enforcement officer threatened to charge him with indecent exposure, which is a sex offense under California law, when he was urinating near an alley dumpster after being turned away from or locked out of all other nearby facilities. De Albuquerque heard these stories in a two-hour interview session and dialogue held with the SafeGround members on February 28, 2011.

Perhaps most moving was the testimony of Tim Buckley, the self-described SafeGround "sanitation technician," who created the SafeGround privy and made it his job to haul away its contents every day for his fellow campers. De Albuquerque remarked on Buckley's and everyone's generosity and industriousness (SafeGround members systematically kept their campsites as clean as possible) but reminded them all that the conditions under which they were being forced to live were unsanitary and unacceptable under human rights norms. The empowering effect of this validation from a human rights monitor who had investigated water and sanitation conditions in Africa, India, and other parts of the developing world was palpable.

At the close of the meeting, de Albuquerque expressed support for SafeGround's demands for local officials to install temporary or permanent toilet and hand-washing facilities close to the present campsites and for SafeGround's ultimate goal to establish a safe and sanitary self-governing transitional housing community. De Albuquerque's preliminary findings describe the water and sanitation conditions in Sacramento as "unacceptable, an affront to human dignity, and a violation of human rights that may amount to cruel, inhuman or degrading treatment." She concludes that, while more permanent solutions are sought, "[a]n immediate, interim solution is to ensure [that homeless persons have] access to restrooms facilities in public places, including during the night." Her final report will be released soon.

Submitting a Formal Human Rights Complaint

Encouraged by de Albuquerque's findings, Legal Services of Northern California submitted a formal human rights complaint to the United Nations on behalf of SafeGround about Sacramento's barring access to proper water and sanitation facilities for homeless persons. The thrust of the complaint is that until sufficient permanent and transitional housing is there for all people in Sacramento as well as a safe ground area, as a matter of human rights and basic decency, local officials must ensure that all people in the area have access to proper toilet facilities and potable water.

The complaint relies on a human rights normative framework that begins with the premise of the 1948 Universal Declaration of Human Rights that "[a]ll human beings are born free and equal in dignity and rights." The complaint also relies on the United States' present acknowledgment, as a member of the United Nations' Human Rights Council, that the right to water derives from the right to an adequate standard of living. The complaint cites various international instruments and resolutions establishing the human right to water and sanitation for populations, such as women and people with disabilities, that the United Nations identifies as having special needs for access to water and proper sanitation. The complaint asserts that the United States is bound by the obligations contained in the foregoing international human rights authorities because President Bill Clinton signed, in 1998, Executive Order 13107 confirming that the United States would adhere to the norms set forth in international human rights treaties and conventions, whether or not Congress ratified those treaties.

SafeGround's hope is that the complaint will result in human rights abuse findings directed to local officials in Sacramento and move these officials to make good on their promised support for a safe ground community.

Observations and Lessons: A Long Hill to Climb but Worth It

With the help of dedicated SafeGround members and supporters, the National Law Center on Homelessness and Poverty, and others throughout the ongoing struggle toward establishing a safe ground community, Legal Services of Northern California has seen the benefits of using a human rights framework in homeless advocacy. This has been particularly true with respect to the empowering and validating nature of such a framework as, by definition and operation, it enables our homeless clients to feel that there are others, people in power among them, who share their vision of a world in which everyone, regardless of housing or other status, is treated with dignity and basic human decency.

In all candor, concerning the direct impact and effectiveness of a human rights approach to homeless advocacy, there seems still much work to be done. Can a human rights abuse finding by the United Nations persuade municipalities and law enforcement agencies to stop criminalizing homelessness? If international human rights conventions and norms can be used successfully to challenge the constitutionality of permitting the imposition of the death penalty on juveniles, can they also be used to challenge the continual rousting of homeless campers who have nowhere else to live and sleep or might using international human rights conventions and norms even spur a community to establish a safe ground area?

COLIN BAILEY, *SAFEGROUND HUMAN RIGHTS ADVOCACY POSTSCRIPT* (2012)

In her August 2, 2011 report to the General Assembly's Human Rights Council, de Albuquerque described what she witnessed firsthand in Sacramento as a "failure by the State to meet its responsibilities to ensure the provision of the most fundamental of services." SafeGround and Legal Services of Northern California attempted to leverage the prominence of this statement to engage the City in discussions around its policy and practice of frustrating, if not denying, homeless people's access to water and sanitation along the American River

Parkway. However, the report received scant media attention and, consequently, SafeGround's invitation to dialog received a cool reception from City Hall. Undeterred and understanding the campaign to be long-term, Legal Services of Northern California maintained contact with de Albuquerque and provided updates on the City's response or lack thereof to SafeGround's entreaty.

When, in January 2012, it looked as though one sympathetic City Council-member would be successful in fostering discussion by the full City Council on the subject of its policies and practices towards the homeless population, Safe-Ground and Legal Services of Northern California geared up to provide public testimony, demanding the provision of adequate water and sanitation facilities for the homeless and citing to international human rights law and de Albuquerque's earlier report for support. While the City Council's hearing on homelessness was subsequently postponed, in anticipation of that hearing, something extraordinary and unprecedented happened.

While Legal Services of Northern California had discussed the possibility of further action by de Albuquerque, unbeknownst to Legal Services of Northern California, de Albuquerque had actually sought and been granted special permission by the U.S. State Department to deviate from longstanding international protocol requiring that communiques from the United Nations not issue directly to local municipalities, but rather to the formal diplomatic channels of the relevant nation state, in this instance, the United States' permanent mission in Geneva, Switzerland. On January 23, 2012, without any forewarning to Legal Services of Northern California or SafeGround, de Albuquerque sent a forcefully-worded letter directly to Sacramento City Mayor Kevin Johnson, citing international legal authority for the right to water and sanitation, recounting her observations of the restricted access of homeless encampments to water and sanitation in Sacramento, circumstances which her letter called "unacceptable," and "call[ing] on your government to make the right decision to ensure the realization of the human rights to water and sanitation of the homeless people living in the city of Sacramento, thereby ensuring their life in dignity."

Understanding that de Albuquerque's letter was then known only to the Mayor's office, Legal Services of Northern California, SafeGround, and the National Law Center on Homelessness and Poverty, advocates leveraged the implied threat of embarrassing publicity around the letter to seek a meeting with the Mayor, which they hoped would result in a formal initiative to establish safe ground and provide access to water and sanitation. After several days without a response from the Mayor, SafeGround, Legal Services of Northern California, and the National Center on Homelessness and Poverty issued a joint press release condemning the City's role in failing to provide homeless residents of Sacramento adequate access to water and sanitation, complete with the full text of de Albuquerque's letter. The media response was tremendous.

In the words of the Sacramento Bee reporter, whose front page article on the matter called SafeGround's publication of de Albuquerque's letter "an international coup," the story was "going viral." Spurred by outreach to various media outlets and a march, demonstration, and press conference on the steps of City Hall orchestrated by SafeGround, local, state and national news coverage of de Albuquerque's letter lasted for more than a week. SafeGround and its advocates and allies suddenly had a prominent platform and a newfound legitimacy in advancing its human rights frame.

Immediately following the flurry of press coverage, there was a sense that the local conversation about homelessness — with the new emphasis on human rights and backed by the moral authority of the United Nations — had shifted. The Mayor's office, previously silent on the matter, felt obligated to make a public statement professing broad support for the provision of services to the homeless and an openness to the establishment of a safe ground with the City.

At the same time, months after the Mayor's pronouncement, stakeholder meetings regarding the creation of a safe ground are infrequent, ad hoc, and show modest signs of progress, at best. The City has yet to uncap drinking fountains or make public restrooms available after hours along the American River Parkway, and reports from homeless campers along the American River parkway suggest that City police officers and County park rangers have actually stepped up both the frequency and viciousness of their raids of homeless encampments.

On the other hand, in part as a result of the publicity and interest de Albuquerque's letter generated for SafeGround's mission and message, SafeGround and a prominent, local architect are collaborating to design a functional and stylish, 300-square-foot modular shelter, which they intend to put on public display and develop into a public demonstration project about the possibilities for addressing the crisis.

Additionally, a local, faith-based organizing group whose membership includes several parishes that minister to the homeless has taken interest in bringing a community organizing approach to the human rights and homelessness advocacy. The first of the meetings between the existing advocacy team and the community organizers will take place in late summer 2012.

SafeGround and its legal advocates maintain a close relationship with de Albuquerque and her staff, who have expressed interest in exploring how they might continue to support the human rights of homeless residents in Sacramento, possibly with another in-person visit and press conference. At the same time, SafeGround's legal advocates are exploring creative, albeit untested, legal strategies to combine international human rights law with possible enforcement actions based on state and local laws designed to protect the public health, including the health of homeless people who are suffering through a shelter crisis.

While the ultimate impact of the human rights approach to homeless advocacy in Sacramento is yet to be seen, it is clear that the human rights component of this broader campaign has validated and emboldened SafeGround and its supporters. It has garnered considerable public support and interest in the plight of Sacramento's homeless residents, and brought much-needed attention to the issues. From what we can tell, this approach also seems to have increased the general public's compassion for those lacking adequate access to water and sanitation, while inspiring creative and ongoing efforts by new community partners to contribute their skills and resources to the realization of the human rights to water and sanitation, health, housing, and dignity. The movement to realize human rights for homeless residents of Sacramento and the power it represents continue to grow. It is anyone's guess what the end result will be, but it is clear that the campaign to achieve safe ground in Sacramento has benefitted from engaging the human rights framework, which continues to serve as a source of publicity, a rallying point for evermore community allies, and an inspiration to those who fight on.

NOTES AND QUESTIONS

1. The case study and postscript are replete with exciting developments and uncertain outcomes. Importantly, after all of the progress made at the international level, the conditions on the ground for homeless people do not appear to have changed materially (in terms of access to water and sanitation). On the other hand, the human rights framework and rhetoric appear to have yielded other benefits, whose long-term impacts remain to be seen. What does this case study suggest about the potential for using non-court-based human rights advocacy in local communities?

2. More broadly, think of a problem in a low-income community that has a human rights dimension. Of the various international human rights tools and mechanisms described in this chapter, are there any that might be brought to bear to address the problem?

TABLE OF CASES

Principal cases are indicated by italics.

INDEX